Foreign Relations of the
United States, 1964–1968

Volume XIX

Arab-Israeli Crisis and War, 1967

Editor   Harriet Dashiell Schwar

General Editor   Edward C. Keefer

United States Government Printing Office
Washington
2004

DEPARTMENT OF STATE PUBLICATION 11043

OFFICE OF THE HISTORIAN

BUREAU OF PUBLIC AFFAIRS

For sale by the Superintendent of Documents, U.S. Government Printing Office
Internet: bookstore.gpo.gov   Phone: Toll Free (866) 512-1800;   DC area (202) 512-1800
Fax: (202) 512-2250 Mail: Stop SSOP, Washington, DC 20402-0001

ISBN 0-16-051513-0

The Office of the Historian is confident, on the basis of the research conducted in preparing this volume and as a result of the declassification review process described above, that the documentation and editorial notes presented here provide an accurate account of U.S. policy toward the Middle East immediately before, during, and after the 1967 Arab-Israeli war.

Acknowledgements

The editor wishes to acknowledge the assistance of officials at the Lyndon B. Johnson Library of the National Archives and Records Administration, especially Regina Greenwell and Charlaine Burgess, who provided key research assistance. The editor also wishes to acknowledge the assistance of historians at the Central Intelligence Agency, especially Scott Koch, and the assistance of historians at the National Security Agency and the Naval Security Group.

Harriet Dashiell Schwar collected documentation, selected, and edited the volume, under the general supervision of former General Editor David S. Patterson. Gabrielle Mallon prepared the lists of names, sources, and abbreviations. Vicki E. Futscher and Rita M. Baker did the copy and technical editing and Susan C. Weetman coordinated the final declassification review. Do Mi Stauber prepared the index.

Marc J. Susser
The Historian
Bureau of Public Affairs

January 2004

Johnson Administration Volumes

Following is a list of the volumes in the *Foreign Relations* series for the administration of President Lyndon B. Johnson. The year of publication is in parentheses.

I	Vietnam, 1964 (1992)
II	Vietnam, January–June 1965 (1996)
III	Vietnam, July–December 1965 (1996)
IV	Vietnam, 1966 (1998)
V	Vietnam, 1967 (2002)
VI	Vietnam, January–August, 1968 (2002)
VII	Vietnam, September 1968–January 1969 (2003)
VIII	International Monetary and Trade Policy (1998)
IX	International Development and Economic Defense Policy; Commodities (1997)
X	National Security Policy (2002)
XI	Arms Control and Disarmament (1997)
XII	Western Europe (2001)
XIII	Western Europe Region (1995)
XIV	Soviet Union (2001)
XV	Germany and Berlin (1999)
XVI	Cyprus; Greece; Turkey (2002)
XVII	Eastern Europe; Austria; Finland (1996)
XVIII	Arab-Israeli Dispute, 1964–1967 (2000)
XIX	Arab-Israeli Crisis and War, 1967 (2003)
XX	Arab-Israeli Dispute, 1967–1968 (2001)
XXI	Near East Region; Arab Peninsula (2000)
XXII	Iran (1999)
XXIII	Congo
XXIV	Africa (1999)
XXV	South Asia (2000)
XXVI	Indonesia; Malaysia-Singapore; Philippines (2001)
XXVII	Mainland Southeast Asia; Regional Affairs (2000)
XXVIII	Laos (1998)
XXIX	Part 1, Korea (2000)
XXIX	Part 2, Japan
XXX	China (1998)
XXXI	South and Central America; Mexico
XXXII	Dominican Crisis; Cuba; Caribbean
XXXIII	Organization and Management of Foreign Policy; United Nations
XXXIV	Scientific and Humanitarian Affairs (1999)

Preface

The *Foreign Relations of the United States* series presents the official documentary historical record of major foreign policy decisions and significant diplomatic activity of the United States Government. The Historian of the Department of State is charged with the responsibility for the preparation of the *Foreign Relations* series. The staff of the Office of the Historian, Bureau of Public Affairs, under the direction of the General Editor, plans, researches, compiles, and edits the volumes in the series. This documentary editing proceeds in full accord with the generally accepted standards of historical scholarship. Official regulations codifying specific standards for the selection and editing of documents for the series were first promulgated by Secretary of State Frank B. Kellogg on March 26, 1925. These regulations, with minor modifications, guided the series through 1991.

A new statutory charter for the preparation of the series was established by Public Law 102–138, the Foreign Relations Authorization Act, Fiscal Years 1992 and 1993, which was signed by President George Bush on October 28, 1991. Section 198 of P.L. 102–138 added a new Title IV to the Department of State's Basic Authorities Act of 1956 (22 USC 4351, *et seq.*).

The statute requires that the *Foreign Relations* series be a thorough, accurate, and reliable record of major United States foreign policy decisions and significant United States diplomatic activity. The volumes of the series should include all records needed to provide comprehensive documentation of major foreign policy decisions and actions of the United States Government. The statute also confirms the editing principles established by Secretary Kellogg: the *Foreign Relations* series is guided by the principles of historical objectivity and accuracy; records should not be altered or deletions made without indicating in the published text that a deletion has been made; the published record should omit no facts that were of major importance in reaching a decision; and nothing should be omitted for the purposes of concealing a defect in policy. The statute also requires that the *Foreign Relations* series be published not more than 30 years after the events recorded. The editors are convinced that this volume, which was compiled in 1997–1998, meets all regulatory, statutory, and scholarly standards of selection and editing.

Structure and Scope of the Foreign Relations Series

This volume is part of a subseries of volumes of the *Foreign Relations* series that documents the most important issues in the foreign policy of the 5 years (1964–1968) of the administration of Lyndon B. Johnson. The subseries presents in 34 volumes a documentary record of major foreign policy decisions and actions of President Johnson's administration. This volume documents U.S. policy immediately before, during and after the June 1967 Arab-Israeli war.

Focus of Research and Principles of Selection for Foreign Relations, 1964–1968, Volume XIX

The editor of the volume sought to include documentation illuminating the foreign policymaking process of the U.S. Government, with emphasis on the highest level at which policy on a particular subject was determined. The documents include memoranda and records of discussions that set forth policy issues and show decisions or actions taken. The emphasis is on the development of U.S. policy and on major aspects and repercussions of its execution rather than on the details of policy execution.

Major topics covered in this volume include: 1) the U.S. search for a peaceful solution to the crisis that erupted in the Middle East in May 1967, including efforts to persuade both sides to avoid military action, and attempts after Egypt's closure of the Strait of Tiran to obtain international action to guarantee the right of passage by ships of all nations through the Gulf of Aqaba; 2) the U.S. desire to avoid involvement in the war that broke out on June 5 and to see it end swiftly, including the halting of military shipments to both sides, U.S. support for UN Security Council resolutions calling for a cease-fire, and U.S. efforts to persuade Israel to comply with the resolutions; 3) the U.S. response to the decision by Egypt and some other Arab states to break off relations with the United States and to Egyptian charges of U.S. involvement in Israel's air strikes against Egypt; 4) U.S. concern with the possibility of Soviet involvement in the war and the exchange of hot-line messages between President Johnson and Soviet Premier Alexei Kosygin in which Johnson assured Kosygin of the U.S. desire for a swift end to the conflict and requested that the Soviet Union urge restraint on Egypt and Syria; 5) the U.S. response to the June 8 Israeli attack on the USS *Liberty* in international waters; 6) U.S. support for a comprehensive peace settlement in which Israel would exchange the territories it had conquered for recognition and secure borders, including U.S. attempts to persuade Israel against taking steps that might tend toward making its occupation of the occupied territories permanent; 7) the concern of Johnson administration officials with massive Soviet aid to Arab countries after the war and its effect on the military balance in the Middle East; 8) U.S. efforts to bring about a compromise UN Security Council resolution linking withdrawal of Israeli forces with mutual recognition and an end to belligerence, leading to the passage of UN Security Council Resolution 242 on November 22, 1967.

Lyndon Johnson made the major foreign policy decisions during his presidency, and the editor sought to document his role as far as possible. Although the foreign policy record of the Johnson administration is voluminous, not all internal discussions between Johnson and his advisers were documented. The record of Johnson's involvement as well as that of Secretary of State Rusk in the policy process often had to be pieced together from a variety of sources.

Editorial Methodology

The documents are presented chronologically according to Washington time or, in the case of conferences, in the order of individual meetings. Memoranda of conversation are placed according to the time and date of the conversation, rather than the date the memorandum was drafted.

Editorial treatment of the documents published in the *Foreign Relations* series follows Office style guidelines, supplemented by guidance from the General Editor and the chief technical editor. The source text is reproduced as exactly as possible, including marginalia or other notations, which are described in the footnotes. Texts are transcribed and printed according to accepted conventions for the publication of historical documents in the limitations of modern typography. A heading has been supplied by the editors for each document included in the volume. Spelling, capitalization, and punctuation are retained as found in the source text, except that obvious typographical errors are silently corrected. Other mistakes and omissions in the source text are corrected by bracketed insertions: a correction is set in italic type; an addition in roman type. Words or phrases underlined in the source text are printed in italics. Abbreviations and contractions are preserved as found in the source text, and a list of abbreviations is included in the front matter of each volume.

Bracketed insertions are also used to indicate omitted text that deals with an unrelated subject (in roman type) or that remains classified after declassification review (in italic type). The amount of material not declassified has been noted by indicating the number of lines or pages of source text that were omitted. Entire documents withheld for declassification purposes have been accounted for and are listed by headings, source notes, and number of pages not declassified in their chronological place. The amount of material omitted from this volume because it was unrelated to the subject of the volume, however, has not been delineated. All brackets that appear in the source text are so identified by footnotes.

The first footnote to each document indicates the document's source, original classification, distribution, and drafting information.

This note also provides the background of important documents and policies and indicates whether the President or his major policy advisers read the document. Every effort has been made to determine if a document has been previously published, and, if so, this information has been included in the source footnote.

Editorial notes and additional annotation summarize pertinent material not printed in the volume, indicate the location of additional documentary sources, provide references to important related documents printed in other volumes, describe key events, and provide summaries of and citations to public statements that supplement and elucidate the printed documents. Information derived from memoirs and other first-hand accounts has been used when appropriate to supplement or explicate the official record.

Advisory Committee on Historical Diplomatic Documentation

The Advisory Committee on Historical Diplomatic Documentation, established under the *Foreign Relations* statute, reviews records, advises, and makes recommendations concerning the *Foreign Relations* series. The Advisory Committee monitors the overall compilation and editorial process of the series and advises on all aspects of the preparation and declassification of the series. Although the Advisory Committee does not attempt to review the contents of individual volumes in the series, it does monitor the overall process and makes recommendations on particular problems that come to its attention.

The Advisory Committee has not reviewed this volume.

Declassification Review

The Information Response Branch of the Office of Information Resources Management Programs and Services, Bureau of Administration, Department of State, conducted the declassification review of the documents published in this volume. The review was conducted in accordance with the standards set forth in Executive Order 12958 on Classified National Security Information and applicable laws.

The principle guiding declassification review is to release all information, subject only to the current requirements of national security as embodied in law and regulation. Declassification decisions entailed concurrence of the appropriate geographic and functional bureaus in the Department of State, other concerned agencies of the U.S. Government, and the appropriate foreign governments regarding specific documents of those governments. The final declassification review of this volume, which began in 1999 and was completed in 2003, resulted in the decision to withhold 12 documents in full, excise a paragraph or more in 12 documents, and make minor excisions of less than a paragraph in 15 documents.

Contents

Sources

Sources for the Foreign Relations Series

The editors of the *Foreign Relations* series have complete access to all the retired records and papers of the Department of State: the central files of the Department; the special decentralized files ("lot files") of the Department at the bureau, office, and division levels; the files of the Department's Executive Secretariat, which contain the records of international conferences and high-level official visits, correspondence with foreign leaders by the President and Secretary of State, and memoranda of conversations between the President and Secretary of State and foreign officials; and the files of overseas diplomatic posts. All of the Department's indexed central files for 1964–1968 have been permanently transferred to the National Archives and Records Administration (Archives II) at College Park, Maryland. Almost all the Department's decentralized office (or lot) files covering this period, which the National Archives deems worthy of permanent retention, have been transferred or are in the process of being transferred from the Department's custody to Archives II.

The editors of the *Foreign Relations* series also have full access to the papers of President Johnson and other White House foreign policy records. Presidential papers maintained and preserved at the Presidential libraries include some of the most significant foreign affairs-related documentation from the Department of State and other Federal agencies including the National Security Council, the Central Intelligence Agency, the Department of Defense, and the Joint Chiefs of Staff.

Department of State historians also have full access to records of the Department of Defense, particularly the records of the Joint Chiefs of Staff and the Secretaries of Defense and their major assistants. The Central Intelligence Agency provided full access to its files.

Sources for Foreign Relations, 1964–1968, Volume XIX

In preparing this volume, the editor made extensive use of Presidential papers and other White House records at the Lyndon B. Johnson Library, which proved the best source of documentation on President Johnson's role in the Middle East. Within the National Security File, the Country Files, including the Middle East Crisis File, the Head of State Correspondence Files, the file of Memos to the President, the files of the Special Committee of the National Security

Council, the National Security Council Meetings Files, and the files of Walt Rostow and Harold Saunders were particularly valuable. The National Security Council history of the Middle East Crisis at the Johnson Library also provided some important documents.

Thanks to the Johnson Library, Department of State historians have full access to the audiotapes of President Johnson's telephone conversations, including conversations between President Johnson and Secretary of State Rusk, Secretary of Defense McNamara, Special Assistant to the President Rostow, and key members of Congress. The editor of this volume, however, found almost no tapes dealing with the 1967 Middle East conflict. One taped conversation has been used as the basis for an editorial note dealing with the beginning of the war.

Second in importance to the records at the Johnson Library were the records of the Department of State. The Department's central files contain the cable traffic recording U.S. diplomatic relations with the countries of the Middle East, memoranda of diplomatic conversations, and memoranda proposing action or providing information. Some important documents are found only in the Department's lot files. The Conference Files maintained by the Executive Secretariat contain briefing materials as well as records of conversations. Documentation on initiatives that were not approved is often found only in desk or bureau files. The Rusk Files contain records of Secretary Rusk's telephone conversations.

The Central Intelligence Agency provides access to Department of State historians to high-level intelligence documents from those records in the custody of that Agency and at the Presidential libraries. This access is arranged and facilitated by the History Staff of the Center for the Study of Intelligence, Central Intelligence Agency, pursuant to a May 2002 memorandum of understanding.

Among the intelligence records reviewed for the volume were files of the Directors of Central Intelligence, the CIA Registry of National Intelligence Estimates and Special National Intelligence Estimates, DCI Executive Registry Files, DDI Files, Directorate of Operations Near East Division files on the 1967 Middle East crisis, and files including material concerning the attack on the USS *Liberty* at the Central Intelligence Agency, and the Department of State's Bureau of Intelligence and Research Historical Files. The editor of this volume also had access to NSA records at the National Security Agency Archives, including crisis files and files dealing with the USS *Liberty* incident.

Almost all of this documentation has been made available for use in the *Foreign Relations* series thanks to the consent of the agencies mentioned, the assistance of their staffs, and especially the cooperation and support of the National Archives and Records Administration.

The following list identifies the particular files and collections used in the preparation of this volume. The declassification and transfer to the National Archives of these records is in process. Most of the records are already available for public review at the National Archives.

Unpublished Sources

Department of State

Central Files. See National Archives and Records Administration below.

Lot Files. For other lot files already transferred to the National Archives and Records Administration at College Park, Maryland, Record Group 59, see National Archives and Records Administration below.

INR/IL Historical Files:
> Files of the Office of Intelligence Coordination, containing records from the 1940s through the 1970s, maintained by the Office of Intelligence Liaison, Bureau of Intelligence and Research, Department of State

National Archives and Records Administration College Park, Maryland

Record Group 59, Department of State Records

Subject-Numeric Central Files. The subject-numeric system is divided into broad categories: Administration, Consular, Culture and Information, Economic, Political and Defense, Science, and Social. Within each of these divisions are subject subcategories. For example, Political and Defense contains four subtopics: POL (Politics), DEF (Defense), CSM (Communism), and INT (Intelligence). Numerical subdivisions further define the subtopics. The following are the principal files consulted for this volume:

DEF 12 ISR: armaments, equipment, supplies, Israel
DEF 12–5 ISR: procurement and sale of armaments, Israel
DEF 12–5 JORDAN: procurement and sale of armaments, Jordan
DEF 12 NEAR E: armaments, equipment, supplies, Near East
DEF 12 US: armaments, U.S.
DEF 19–8 US–ISR: defense equipment and supplies, U.S.–Israel
DEF 19–8 US–JORDAN: defense equipment and supplies, U.S.–Jordan
DEF 19–8 US NEAR E: defense equipment and supplies, U.S.–Near East
DEF 19–8 US–USSR: defense equipment and supplies, U.S.–U.S.S.R.
NATO 3 LUX (LU): North Atlantic Treaty Organization meetings, Luxembourg
ORG 7 S: travel by the Secretary of State
POL ARAB–ISR: Arab-Israeli political affairs and relations
POL ARAB–ISR/UN: Arab-Israeli political issues at the United Nations
POL ISR–US: political affairs and relations, Israel–U.S.
POL JORDAN–US: political affairs and relations, Jordan–U.S.
POL MOR–US: political affairs and relations, Morocco–U.S.
POL UAR–US: political affairs and relations, United Arab Republic–U.S.
POL UK–US: political affairs and relations, United Kingdom–U.S.
POL US–USSR: political affairs and relations, U.S.–U.S.S.R.
POL 7 SUDAN: Arab summit meeting in Khartoum
POL 7 UAR: visits, meetings with leaders of the U.A.R.
POL 7 UK: visits, meetings with British leaders

POL 7 US/ANDERSON: visits, meetings of Robert Anderson
POL 15 UAR: U.A.R. Government
POL 15–1 ISR: head of state, Israel
POL 15–1 JORDAN: head of state, Jordan
POL 15–1 UAR: head of state, United Arab Republic
POL 15–1 US/JOHNSON: President Johnson's meetings and correspondence with
    heads of state
POL 17 ISR–US: diplomatic and consular representation, Israel–U.S.
POL 17 UAR–US: diplomatic and consular representation, U.A.R.–U.S.
POL 23–9 UAR: rebellion, coups, U.A.R.
POL 27 ARAB–ISR: Arab-Israeli military operations
POL 27 ARAB–ISR/UN: Arab-Israeli conflict issues at the United Nations
POL 27 YEMEN: military operations, Yemen
POL 27–2 ARAB–ISR: Arab-Israeli military operations, blockade
POL 27–4 PAL/UN: United Nations Emergency Force in the Middle East
POL 27–4 UN: United Nations Emergency Force in the Middle East
POL 27–14 ARAB–ISR: Arab-Israeli cease-fire or peace settlement
POL 27–14 ARAB–ISR/SANDSTORM: Jordan–Israel talks concerning a peace settlement
POL 27–14 ARAB–ISR/UN: Arab-Israeli peace settlement issues at the United Nations
POL 29 UAR: political prisoners, U.A.R.
POL 32–1 ISR–JORDAN: territory and boundary disputes, Israel–Jordan
POL 32–1 ISR–SYR: territory and boundary disputes, Israel–Syria
POL 32–1 ISR–SYR/UN: territory and boundary disputes, Israel–Syria–UN
PS 8–4 US–ISR: protection of property, seizure, damage, U.S.–Israel
REF ARAB: Arab refugees
TRV ANDERSON: travel by Robert Anderson

Lot Files.

Conference Files: Lot 66 D 110, Entry 3051B
    Records of official visits by heads of government and foreign ministers to the United
    States and international conferences attended by the President, the Secretary of State,
    and other U.S. officials, 1966–1972, maintained by the Executive Secretariat.

Executive Secretariat, Middle East Crisis Files, 1967, Entry 5190
    Files on the 1967 Middle East crisis, including telegrams and records of the Control
    Group, maintained by the Executive Secretariat.

Kohler Files: Lot 71 D 460
    Files of Ambassador Foy Kohler for 1967 and 1968 including Kohler/Dobrynin and
    Rusk/Gromyko Memoranda of Conversation, maintained by the Executive
    Secretariat, Department of State.

NEA Files: Lot 71 D 79
    Files of the Assistant Secretary of State for Near Eastern and South Asian Affairs,
    1967–1969.

NEA/IAI Files: Lot 70 D 304
    Files on Arab-Israel affairs for 1953–1954; 1963–1966; 1967, maintained by the Office
    of Near Eastern Affairs (later, the Office of Israel and Arab-Israel Affairs) of the
    Department of State.

Rusk Files: Lot 72 D 192, Entries 5376–5381
    Files of Secretary of State Dean Rusk, 1961–1969, including texts of speeches and pub-
    lic statements, miscellaneous correspondence files, White House correspondence,
    chronological files, and memoranda of telephone conversations.

Central Intelligence Agency, Langley, Virginia

DCI Files, Job 80–B01285A
Files of Directors of Central Intelligence John A. McCone (1961–1965), William F. Raborn (1965–1966), and Richard M. Helms (1966–1973).

DCI Executive Registry Files, Job 80–R01580

DDI Files, Job 80–R01447R

ODDI Registry of National Intelligence Estimates and Special National Intelligence Estimates, Job 79–R01012A

DDO/NE Files, Job 68–S–626
Directorate of Operations Near East Division files on the 1967 Middle East crisis.

DDO/NE Files, Job 85–01007R
Directorate of Operations Near East Division files, including material concerning the attack on the USS *Liberty*.

Lyndon B. Johnson Library, Austin, Texas

Papers of President Lyndon B. Johnson

National Security File
Country File: Canada, Israel, Jordan, Lebanon, Middle East Crisis, Saudi Arabia, United Arab Republic, USSR
Head of State Correspondence File
Special Head of State Correspondence File
Agency File, United Nations
Name File, Saunders Memos, Califano Memos
Memos to the President, Walt W. Rostow
National Security Council Meetings File
Files of the Special Committee of the National Security Council
NSC Histories, Middle East Crisis
Files of Walt W. Rostow
Files of Harold H. Saunders

Special Files
Meeting Notes File
Office of the President File
President's Daily Diary
Tapes and Transcripts of Telephone Conversations and Meetings

White House Central Files

Other Personal Papers
Rusk Appointment Book
Tom Johnson's Notes of Meetings

National Security Agency

Center for Cryptologic History Historical Collection
Series VIII, Crisis Files

NSA Archives, Accession No. 33824, Special Cryptologic Collection, U.S.S. *Liberty* Incident

NSA Archives, Accession No. 45981, U.S.S. *Liberty* Correspondence and Messages

Naval Historical Center

Operational Archives Branch, Immediate Office Files of the Chief of Naval Operations, 1969 Files, *Liberty* Incident

Operational Archives Branch, U.S.S. *Liberty* Incident, Message File

Naval Security Group

Naval Security Group Files, CNSG Pre-76 Inactive Files, Box 702
Naval Security Group File on U.S.S. *Liberty.*

Naval Security Group Files, Box 896, Pre-76 Inactive Files
U.S.S. *Liberty*

Washington National Records Center, Suitland, Maryland

Records Group 330, Records of the Office of the Secretary of Defense

OASD/ISA Files: FRC 71 A 4919
Top Secret files of the Office of the Assistant Secretary of Defense for International Security Affairs for 1967.

OASD/ISA Files: FRC 76–140
Secret files of the Office of the Assistant Secretary of Defense for International Security Affairs for 1967–1968.

OSD Files: FRC 72 A 2467
Top Secret files of the Office of the Secretary of Defense, the Deputy Secretary, and their Special Assistants for 1967.

OSD Files: FRC 72 A 2468
Files of the Secretary of Defense, Deputy Assistant Secretary of Defense, and their Special Assistants for 1967.

OSD Files: FRC 73 A 1250
Files of the Secretary of Defense, Deputy Assistant Secretary of Defense, and their Special Assistants for 1968.

OSD Files: FRC 77–0075
Top Secret files maintained in Secretary McNamara's office, 1961–1968, including records relating to Vietnam, draft presidential memoranda, and memoranda of conversations.

Published Sources

Documentary Collections

Central Intelligence Agency, *Corona: America's First Satellite Program*. Washington: 1995.

Israeli Ministry for Foreign Affairs, *Israeli Foreign Relations: Selected Documents, 1947–1974*. Jerusalem: 1976.

United Nations, *Public Papers of the Secretaries-General of the United Nations, Vols. III and IV, Dag Hammarskjöld, 1956–1957*.

_____, *Public Papers of the Secretaries-General of the United Nations, Vol. VII, U Thant, 1965–1967*.

_____, *Yearbook of the United Nations, 1947–1949*.

U.S. Congress. Senate. *U.S. Commitments to Foreign Powers*, Hearings Before the Senate Committee on Foreign Relations, Ninetieth Congress, First Session. Washington: 1967.

U.S. Department of Defense, *Review of Department of Defense Worldwide Communications, Phase I:* Report of the Armed Services Investigating Subcommittee of the Committee on Armed Services, House of Representatives, Ninety-Second Congress, First Session, May 10, 1971. Washington: 1971.

U.S. Department of State *Bulletin, 1951–1981*. Washington: U.S. Government Printing Office, 1951–1981.

_____, *A Decade of American Foreign Policy: Basic Documents, 1941–1949*. Washington: U.S. Government Printing Office, 1985.

_____, *American Foreign Policy: Current Documents, 1957–1967*. Washington: U.S. Government Printing Office, 1961–1969.

U.S. National Archives and Records Administration, *Public Papers of the Presidents of the United States, Dwight D. Eisenhower, 1957*. Washington: U.S. Government Printing Office, 1961.

_____, *Public Papers of the Presidents of the United States, John F. Kennedy, 1963*. Washington: U.S. Government Printing Office, 1964.

_____, *Public Papers of the Presidents of the United States, Lyndon B. Johnson, 1966–1967*. Washington: U.S. Government Printing Office, 1968.

Memoirs

Michael Brecher, with Benjamin Geist. *Decisions in Crisis: Israel, 1967 and 1973*. Berkeley: University of California Press, 1980.

Eban, Abba. *An Autobiography*. New York: Random House, 1977.

_____. *Personal Witness: Israel Through My Eyes*. New York: G.P. Putnam's Sons, 1992.

Johnson, Lyndon B. *The Vantage Point: Perspectives of the Presidency, 1963–1969*. New York: Holt, Rinehart and Winston, 1971.

McPherson, Harry. *A Political Education*. Boston: Little Brown and Company, 1972.

Parker, Richard B., ed. *The Six-Day War: A Retrospective*. Gainesville, Florida: University Press of Florida, 1996.

Rafael, Gideon. *Destination Peace: Three Decades of Israeli Foreign Policy: A Personal Memoir*. New York: Stein and Day, 1981.

Rikhye, Maj.-Gen. Indar Jit. *The Sinai Blunder: Withdrawal of the United Nations Emergency Force Leading to the Six-Day War of June 1967*. London and Totowa, N.J.: Frank Cass and Company Limited, 1980.

Rusk, Dean (as told to Richard Rusk). *As I Saw It*, Daniel S. Papp, ed. New York: Penguin Books, 1990.

Wilson, Harold. *The Chariot of Israel: Britain, America, and the State of Israel*. Weidenfeld and Nicolson and Michael Joseph, 1981.

Abbreviations

ACFT, aircraft
AD, Assistant Director (CIA)
AF, Air Force
AIG, address indicating group
ALUSNA, American Legation U.S. Naval Attaché at (place)
AMB, Ambassador
AMEMB, American Embassy
APC, armored personnel carrier
ARAMCO, Arabian-American Oil Company
ASAP, as soon as possible
ASW, anti-submarine warfare
ATAF, Allied Tactical Air Force
AUC, American University Cairo

CANE, distribution indicator for telegrams pertaining to a proposed Middle
    East arms limitation initiative
CARE, Cooperatives for American Relief Everywhere, Inc.
CDR, Commander
CIA, Central Intelligence Agency
CINCEUR, Commander in Chief, European Command
CINCLANT, Commander in Chief, Armed Forces, Atlantic
CINCMEAFSA, Commander in Chief, Middle East/South Asia and Africa
    South of the Sahara
CINCSTRIKE, Commander in Chief, Strike Command
CINCUSAREUR, Commander in Chief, U.S. Armed Forces, Europe
CINCUSNAVEUR, Commander in Chief, U.S. Naval Forces, Europe
CLG, guided missile light cruiser
CNO, Chief of Naval Operations
CO, Commanding Officer
COB, close of business
COMAC, Commanding Officer, Mixed Armistice Commission
COMIDEASTFOR, Commander, Middle East Forces
COMSERVLANT, Commander, Service Forces, Atlantic Fleet
COMSIXTHFLT, Commander, Sixth Fleet
CONGEN, Consulate General
CONUS, Continental United States
COS, Chief of Station (CIA); Chief of Staff (military)
CTF, Commander, Task Force (U.S. Navy)
CTG, Commander, Task Group (U.S. Navy)
CVA, aircraft carrier, attack
CW, chemical weapons

DAO, Defense Attaché Office
DATT, Defense Attaché

DCI, Director of Central Intelligence
DCM, Deputy Chief of Mission
DD, destroyer
DDP, Directorate for Plans (CIA)
DEFATT(S), Defense Attaché(s)
DEG, degree
DEL(S), delegation(s)
Deptel, Department of State telegram
Deptoff, Department of State officer
DG, Director General
DIA, Defense Intelligence Agency
DMZ, DZ, Demilitarized Zone
DOD, Department of Defense
DOD/ISA, Department of Defense, International Security Affairs
DTG, date-time-group

E, Bureau of European Affairs, Department of State
ECM, electronic countermeasures
EDT, Eastern Daylight Time
EIMAC, Egypt–Israel Mixed Armistice Commission
ELINT, electronic intelligence
EMB, Embassy
EmbOff, Embassy officer
ENDC, Eighteen Nation Disarmament Commission
EP, East Pakistan
ESSGA, Emergency Special Session of the General Assembly, United Nations
ETA, estimated time of arrival
EUCOM, European Command (Army)
EURATOM, European Atomic Energy Community
Exdis, Exclusive Distribution
EXIM, Export-Import Bank

FAO, Food and Agriculture Organization, United Nations
FLO, Foreign Liaison Office (Israeli Defense Ministry)
FonMin, Foreign Minister
FonOff, Foreign Office
FORAC, for action
FRG, Federal Republic of Germany
FYI, for your information

G, Office of the Deputy Under Secretary of State for Political Affairs
GA, General Assembly (UN)
GAA, General Armistice Agreement
GMT, Greenwich Meridian Time
GOF, Government of France
GOI, Government of Israel
GOJ, Government of Jordan
GOK, Government of Kuwait
GOL, Government of Lebanon

GOM, Government of Morocco
GOP, Government of Pakistan
GUAR, Government of the United Arab Republic

HHH, Hubert H. Humphrey
HMG, Her Majesty's Government
HQ, headquarters

IAEA, International Atomic Energy Agency
IAI, Office of Israel and Arab-Israel Affairs, Department of State; Israel
    Aircraft Industries
IAW, in accordance with
ICJ, International Court of Justice
ICRC, International Committee of the Red Cross
IDF, Israel Defense Forces
IIS, Israeli Intelligence Service
IMAC, Israel Mixed Armistice Commission
IMF, International Monetary Fund
INR, Bureau of Intelligence and Research, Department of State
IO/UNP, Office of United Nations Political Affairs, Bureau of International
    Organization Affairs, Department of State
IPC, Iraq Petroleum Company
ISA, Office of the Assistant Secretary of Defense for International Security
    Affairs
ISMAC, Israel–Syria Mixed Armistice Commission

JAA, Jordan Arab Army
JCS, Joint Chiefs of Staff
JRC, Joint ATAF/Army Group Reconnaissance Center (JCS)

L, Office of the Legal Adviser, Department of State
LA(s), Latin American(s)
LBJ, initials of President Lyndon B. Johnson
Limdis, Limited distribution

M, Office of the Under Secretary of State for Political Affairs
MAC, Mixed Armistice Commission
MADEC, Maritime Declaration
MAP, Military Assistance Program
ME, Middle East
MEDICO, Medical International Cooperation
memcon, memorandum of conversation
MFA, Ministry of Foreign Affairs
MIG, A.I. Mikoyan i M.I. Gurevich (Soviet fighter aircraft named for design-
    ers Mikoyan and Gurevich)
mil, military
MinDef, Minister of Defense
MisOff, Mission Office
MOD, Minister of Defense
Molink, Special teletype circuit linking Moscow and Washington

msg, message
MTB, motor torpedo boat
mtg, meeting

NATO, North Atlantic Treaty Organization
NE, Near East
NEA, Bureau of Near Eastern and South Asian Affairs, Department of State
NEA/ARN, Office of Lebanon, Jordan, Syrian Arab Republic, and Iraq Affairs, Bureau of Near Eastern and South Asian Affairs, Department of State
NEA/ARP, Office of Saudi Arabia, Kuwait, Yemen, and Aden Affairs, Bureau of Near Eastern and South Asian Affairs, Department of State
NEA/IAI, Office of Israel and Arab-Israel Affairs, Bureau of Near Eastern and South Asian Affairs, Department of State
NEA/UAR, Office of United Arab Republic Affairs, Bureau of Near Eastern and South Asian Affairs, Department of State
NIPE, National Intelligence Programs Evaluation (CIA)
NMCC, National Military Command Center
Nodis, No distribution (other than to persons indicated)
Noforn, No foreign dissemination
Notal, not received by all addressees
NPT, Nuclear Non-proliferation Treaty
NSA, National Security Agency
NSC, National Security Council
NYT, *New York Times*

OCAM, Organisation Commune Africaine et Malagache (Common Afro-Malagasy and Mauritian Organization)
OC/T, Communications Center, Department of State
OECD, Organization for Economic Cooperation and Development, Paris
OSA, Office of the Secretary of the Army (U.S.)
OSD, Office of the Secretary of Defense

PCC, Palestine Conciliation Commission, United Nations
PERMREP, Permanent Representative, United Nations
PLA, Palestine Liberation Army
PLO, Palestine Liberation Organization
POL, petroleum, oil, lubricants; political
POLAD, Political Adviser
posit, position
PriMin, Prime Minister

R&D, Research and Development
RAFI, Israel Workers List (Israel political party)
reftel, reference telegram
res, resolution
RG, Record Group
RJAF, Royal Jordanian Air Force
rpt, repeat

S, Office of the Secretary of State
SAG, Saudi Arabian Government

SARG, Syrian Arab Republic Government
SC, Security Council (UN)
septel, separate telegram
SFRC, Senate Foreign Relations Committee
SITREP, Situation Report
Sit Room, Situation Room
SNIE, Special National Intelligence Estimate
Sov, Soviet
SSM, surface-to-surface missiles
STBD, starboard
SYG, Secretary-General of the United Nations

TAPLINE, Trans-Arabian Pipeline
TASS, official Soviet news agency
TDCS, Timely Dissemination of a Clandestine Service Message
TF, Task Force
Tosec, series indicator for telegrams from the Department to the Secretary of State (or his delegation) in connection with international conferences

U, Office of the Under Secretary of State
UAR, United Arab Republic
UARG, United Arab Republic Government
UK, United Kingdom
UKUN, United Kingdom Mission at the United Nations
UN, United Nations
UNEF, United Nations Emergency Force
UNGA, United Nations General Assembly
UNHCR, United Nations High Commissioner for Refugees
UNICEF, United Nations International Children's Emergency Fund
UNMO, United Nations Military Observer
UNMOGIP, United Nations Military Observer Group for India and Pakistan
UNRWA, United Nations Relief and Works Agency
UNSC, United Nations Security Council
UNSYG, United Nations Secretary-General
UNTSO, United Nations Truce Supervision Organization (Palestine)
UPI, United Press International
USAF, United States Air Force
USAFE, United States Air Force, Europe
USDAO, U.S. Defense Attaché Office
USG, United States Government
USIA, United States Information Agency
USIB, United States Intelligence Board
USIS, United States Information Service (overseas branches of USIA)
USN, United States Navy
USRO, United States Mission to European Regional Organization, Paris
USS, United States Ship
USSR, Union of Soviet Socialist Republics
USUN, United States Mission at the United Nations

WHO, World Health Organization

Persons

Alphand, Hervé, Secretary-General of the French Foreign Office
Amer, Field Marshal Abdel Hakim, Vice President and Deputy Supreme Commander of the Armed Forces of the United Arab Republic until June 1967
Amit, Major General Meir, Chief of Israeli Intelligence
Anderson, Robert B., former Secretary of the Treasury; special Presidential envoy to the United Arab Republic
Atassi, Noureddine El-, President of Syria
Atherton, Alfred L., Jr., Country Director for Israel and Arab-Israel Affairs, Bureau of Near Eastern and South Asian Affairs, Department of State, from January 1967

Ball, George W., former Under Secretary of State
Barbour, Walworth, Ambassador to Israel
Battle, Lucius D., Assistant Secretary of State for Near Eastern and South Asian Affairs from April 1967
Bergus, Donald C., Country Director for United Arab Republic Affairs, Bureau of Near Eastern and South Asian Affairs, Department of State, until July 1967; thereafter, Principal Officer of the U.S. Interests Section of the Spanish Embassy in the United Arab Republic
Brewer, William D., Country Director for Saudi Arabia, Kuwait, Yemen, and Aden, Bureau of Near Eastern and South Asian Affairs, Department of State
Brown, George, British Secretary of State for Foreign Affairs
Buffum, William B., Deputy Representative to the United Nations
Bull, Lieutenant General Odd, Chief of Staff of the United Nations Truce Supervision Organization in Palestine
Bunche, Ralph J., Under-Secretary of the United Nations for Special Political Affairs
Bundy, McGeorge, Executive Secretary of the Special Committee of the National Security Council, June 7–August 24, 1967; also Special Consultant to the President from June 7, 1967
Burns, Findley, Jr., Ambassador to Jordan until November 1967

Caradon, Lord (Hugh Mackintosh Foot), British Permanent Representative to the United Nations
Chernyakov, Yuri N., Minister-Counselor of the Soviet Embassy in the United States
Christian, George, White House Press Secretary
Church, Frank, Democratic Senator from Idaho
Clifford, Clark M., Chairman of the President's Foreign Intelligence Board
Cottam, Howard R., Ambassador to Kuwait
Couve de Murville, Maurice, French Foreign Minister

Davies, Rodger P., Deputy Assistant Secretary of State for Near Eastern and South Asian Affairs

Davis, Nathaniel, member of the National Security Council staff

Dayan, Moshe, Israeli Defense Minister from June 1967

Dean, Sir Patrick, British Ambassador to the United States

De Gaulle, Charles, President of France

Dobrynin, Anatoliy F., Soviet Ambassador to the United States

Eban, Abba, Foreign Minister of Israel

Eilts, Hermann F., Ambassador to Saudi Arabia

Eshkol, Levi, Prime Minister of Israel; concurrently, Defense Minister until May 30, 1967

Evron, Ephraim, Minister of the Israeli Embassy in the United States

Fawzi, Mahmoud, Deputy Prime Minister for Foreign Affairs of the United Arab Republic until June 1967; thereafter, President's Counselor for Foreign Affairs

Fawzi, General Mohammed, Chief of Staff, United Arab Republic armed forces until June 1967; thereafter, Commander in Chief of Joint UAR Forces

Fedorenko, Nikolai Trofimovich, Soviet Permanent Representative to the United Nations

Feinberg, Abraham, Chairman of the Executive Committee of the American Bank and Trust Company, New York City

Feki, Ahmed Hassan el-, Under-Secretary of State, United Arab Republic Ministry of Foreign Affairs, until December 1967; thereafter, Ambassador to the United Kingdom

Fulbright, J. William, Democratic Senator from Arkansas; Chairman of the Senate Foreign Relations Committee

Geva, Brigadier General Joseph, Defense and Armed Forces Attaché, Embassy of Israel

Goldberg, Arthur J., Permanent Representative to the United Nations

Gromyko, Andrei A., Soviet Foreign Minister

Handley, William J., Deputy Assistant Secretary of State for Near Easter and South Asian Affairs

Harman, Avraham, Israeli Ambassador to the United States

Harriman, W. Averell, Ambassador at Large

Helms, Richard M., Director of Central Intelligence

Hoopes, Townsend W., Deputy Assistant Secretary of Defense for International Security Affairs

Houghton, Robert B., Country Director for Lebanon, Jordan, Syrian Arab Republic, and Iraq, Bureau of Near Eastern and South Asian Affairs, Department of State, from January 1967

Hughes, Thomas L., Director, Bureau of Intelligence and Research, Department of State

Humphrey, Hubert H., Vice President of the United States

Hussein I, ibn Talal, King of Jordan

Jessup, Peter, member of the National Security Council staff
Johnson, Lyndon B., President of the United States
Johnson, W. Thomas (Tom), White House Deputy Press Secretary
Jones, Jim R., Assistant to the President under Special Assistant Marvin
    Watson until January 1968; Deputy Special Assistant to the President
    January–May 1968; thereafter Special Assistant
Jordan, Colonel Amos A., Jr., Regional Director, Near East and South Asia,
    Office of the Assistant Secretary of Defense for International Security
    Affairs, Department of Defense
Juma, Saad, Prime Minister of Jordan April–October 1967

Kamel, Mustafa, Ambassador of the United Arab Republic to the United
    States until June 1967
Katzenbach, Nicholas deB., Under Secretary of State
Khammash, General Amer, Chief of Staff, Jordanian Arab Army
Khouli, Hassan Sabri El-, top adviser to U.A.R. President Nasser
Kitchen, Jeffrey C., Deputy Assistant Secretary of State for Politico-Military
    Affairs until August 1967
Kohler, Foy D., Deputy Under Secretary of State for Political Affairs
Kony, Mohammed Awad El, Permanent Representative of the United Arab
    Republic to the United Nations
Kosygin, Alexei N., Chairman of the Council of Ministers of the U.S.S.R.
Kuznetsov, Vasili Vasilievich, Deputy Foreign Minister of the USSR; First
    Deputy Chairman of the Presidium of the Supreme Soviet of the USSR;
    Representative to the UN Security Council in 1967

Leddy, John M., Assistant Secretary of State for European Affairs
Lemnitzer, General Lyman L., USA, Commander in Chief, European
    Command
Lucet, Charles, French Ambassador to the United States

Macomber, William B., Jr., Assistant Secretary of State for Congressional
    Relations
Makhous, Ibrahim, Deputy Premier and Foreign Minister of Syria
Martin, Vice Admiral William I., USN, Commander, Sixth Fleet, from April
    1967
McCain, Admiral John S., Jr., USN, Commander in Chief, Naval Forces,
    Europe
McCloskey, Robert J., Deputy Assistant Secretary of State for Public Affairs
    and Director of Office of News
McDonald, Admiral David L., USN, Chief of Naval Operations until August
    1967
McNamara, Robert S., Secretary of Defense
McPherson, Harry C., Jr., Special Counsel to the President
Meeker, Leonard C., Legal Adviser, Department of State
Meir, Golda, Secretary-General of Mapai (Israeli political party)
Mohieddin, Zakaria, Vice President of the United Arab Republic until June
    1967; thereafter, Deputy President and Vice Prime Minister
Morgan, Thomas E. (D–Pennsylvania), Chairman of the House Foreign
    Relations Committee

Nasir, Salah, Director of Egyptian Intelligence
Nasser, Gamal Abdel, President of the United Arab Republic
Nitze, Paul H., Secretary of the Navy until June 1967; Deputy Secretary of
  Defense from July 1967
Nolte, Richard H., Ambassador to the United Arab Republic until June 1967

Pachachi, Adnan al, Iraqi Permanent Representative to the United Nations
Parker, Richard B., Political Counselor at the Embassy in Cairo until June
  1967; Country Director for United Arab Republic Affairs, Bureau of Near
  Eastern and South Asian Affairs, Department of State, from August 1967
Pearson, Lester B., Prime Minister of Canada
Pedersen, Richard F., Deputy Representative in the UN Security Council
Popper, David H., Deputy Assistant Secretary of State for International
  Organization Affairs
Porter, Dwight J., Ambassador to Lebanon

Rabin, Lieutenant General Yitzhak, Chief of Staff of the Israel Defense Forces
Rafael, Gideon, Israeli Permanent Representative at the United Nations
  May–December 1967
Read, Benjamin H., Special Assistant to the Secretary of State, and Executive
  Secretary of the Department of State
Riad, Mahmoud, Foreign Minister of the United Arab Republic; head of the
  UAR delegation to the 22nd Session of the UN General Assembly,
  September–December 1967
Riad, Mohamed, Counselor, UAR Foreign Ministry; member of the UAR dele-
  gation to the Fifth Emergency Special Session of the UN General
  Assembly, June–September 1967, and the 22nd Session of the UN General
  Assembly, September–December 1967
Rifai, Abdul Monem, Jordanian representative to the United Nations
Rifai, Zaid, Secretary-General of the Royal Court of Jordan; King Hussein's
  private secretary
Rikhye, Major General Indar Jit, Commander of the United Nations
  Emergency Force in the Middle East
Rostow, Eugene V., Under Secretary of State for Political Affairs
Rostow, Walt W., Special Assistant to the President
Rusk, Dean, Secretary of State

Saqqaf, Sayyid Omar, Deputy Foreign Minister of Saudi Arabia; Personal
  Representative of King Faisal on diplomatic missions
Saunders, Harold H., member of the National Security Council staff
Schubeilat, Farhan, Jordanian Ambassador to the United States until August
  1967
Schwartz, Harry H., Deputy Assistant Secretary of Defense for International
  Security Affairs
Seydoux, Roger, French Permanent Representative to the United Nations
Sharaf, Abdul Hamid, Jordanian Ambassador to the United States from
  August 1967
Sisco, Joseph J., Assistant Secretary of State for International Organization
  Affairs
Smith, Bromley K., Executive Secretary of the National Security Council

Smythe, Hugh H., Ambassador to Syria until June 1967
Sober, Sidney, Director, Office of Regional Affairs, Bureau of Near Eastern and South Asian Affairs, Department of State
Solomon, Anthony M., Assistant Secretary of State for Economic Affairs
Sowayel, Ibrahim Abdallah Al-, Saudi Arabian Ambassador to the United States
Sterner, Michael, Office of Israel and Arab-Israel Affairs, Bureau of Near Eastern and South Asian Affairs, Department of State
Stoessel, Walter J., Deputy Assistant Secretary of State for European Affairs until July 1968; thereafter, Ambassador to Poland
Symmes, Harrison M., Ambassador to Jordan from November 1967

Tabor, Hans R., Danish Permanent Representative to the United Nations
Tasca, Henry J., Ambassador to Morocco
Taylor, Vice Admiral Rufus L., USN, Deputy Director of Central Intelligence
Tcherniakov, Yuri N., Minister-Counselor of the Soviet Embassy
Thant, U, Secretary-General of the United Nations
Thompson, Llewellyn E., Jr., Ambassador to the Soviet Union
Thomson, George, British Minister of State for Foreign Affairs
Tomeh, George J., Syrian Permanent Representative to the United Nations
Touqan, Ahmed, Jordanian Foreign Minister until October 1967; thereafter, Vice-Prime Minister

Vance, Cyrus R., Deputy Secretary of Defense until June 1967; thereafter, Special Representative of the President on Cyprus

Walsh, John C., Deputy Executive Secretary, Department of State
Warnke, Paul C., General Counsel, Department of Defense, until August 1967; thereafter, Assistant Secretary of Defense for International Security Affairs
Wehmeyer, Donald A., Assistant Legal Adviser for Near Eastern and South Asian Affairs, Department of State
Weizman, Brigadier General Ezer, Chief of Operations of the Israel Defense Forces
Wheeler, General Earle G., USA, Chairman of the Joint Chiefs of Staff
Wilson, Harold, British Prime Minister
Woods, George D., President, International Bank for Reconstruction and Development (World Bank); Coordinator, Israeli Desalting Project
Wriggins, W. Howard, member of the National Security Council staff

Yamani, Ahmed Zaki, Saudi Minister of Petroleum and Mineral Resources
Yost, Charles W., former Ambassador to Laos, Syria, and Morocco; former Deputy Representative to the United Nations; member, Council on Foreign Relations

Arab-Israeli Crisis and War, 1967

Prewar Crisis, May 15–June 4, 1967

1. President's Daily Brief

Washington, May 15, 1967.

[Source: Johnson Library, National Security File, NSC Histories, Middle East Crisis, Vol. 6, Appendix A. Top Secret; [*codeword not declassified*]. 1 page of source text not declassified.]

---

2. Telegram From the Embassy in Israel to the Department of State[1]

Tel Aviv, May 15, 1967, 1920Z.

3604. Ref: Cairo 7494.[2]

1. Bitan (Fon Off) advises Battle saw Harman this morning and expressed concern at reports Egyptian troop concentration in Canal area which blocked to normal traffic and interpreted development as Egyptian demonstration solidarity with Syrians who apprehensive possible Israeli intentions.[3]

---

[1] Source: National Archives and Records Administration, RG 59, Central Files 1967–69, POL 32–1 ISR–SYR. Confidential; Immediate. Repeated Priority to Amman and to Baghdad, Damascus, Jidda, Beirut, Kuwait, Dhahran, London, USUN, CINCSTRIKE, CINCMEAFSA, Jerusalem, Aden, and Sanaa. Received at 5:14 p.m. Passed to the White House and USIA at 5:40 p.m.

[2] Telegram 7494 from Cairo, May 15, reported that UAR military forces had been placed on alert and that extensive movement of troops and matériel was in process. (Ibid.)

[3] No memorandum of this conversation between Battle and Ambassador Harman has been found. Secretary Rusk told Battle that morning that "we should have a very frank talk with the Israelis" and that "it was very important for the Israelis to sit tight." (Notes of telephone conversation at 9:46 a.m. on May 15, prepared by Rusk's personal assistant Carolyn J. Proctor; ibid., Rusk Files: Lot 72 D 192, Telephone Calls) Telegram 194189 to Tel Aviv, May 15, instructed the Embassy to approach the Israeli Government at the highest level and express the U.S. hope that the Israelis would "maintain steady nerves in interest avoiding serious deterioration area situation." (Ibid., Central Files 1967–69, POL ARAB–ISR)

2. Bitan said that following talks with PM Eshkol and FM Eban he authorized give following GOI reaction this representation.

A. There no Israeli troop concentration Syrian, Egyptian or other frontier. (This corresponds with US Attachés reconnaissance to this hour.)

B. GOI hopes infiltration and sabotage will stop.

C. If there no further sabotage there no reason anyone to worry.

D. GOI interpretation Egyptian demonstration troop activities is that Syrians trying involve Egypt in Syrian-Israeli issue and if Egyptian concentration true Syrians could represent this as support.

3. GOI has no objection foregoing being transmitted to Cairo.

4. Situation with Syria is obviously precarious and, if additional serious sabotage incidents such as attacks on settlements, main roads etc. continue it impossible predict GOI will sit idly by without reacting. However, I believe GOI aware risks escalation, disposed make minimum effective response, and exercise what to them would seem maximum patience. I doubt that they will be very impressed in any event with Nasser's foot shuffling one way or the other.

Barbour

---

3.   **Circular Telegram From the Department of State to Certain Posts**[1]

Washington, May 15, 1967, 9:04 p.m.

194945. 1. Under Secretary Rostow called in British and French Ambassadors jointly May 15 for exchange of views on current Syro-Egyptian-Israeli situation, emphasizing in particular following points:

---

[1] Source: National Archives and Records Administration, RG 59, Central Files 1967–69, POL 32–1 ISR–SYR. Confidential; Priority. Drafted by Atherton, cleared in draft by Davies, and approved by Under Secretary of State for Political Affairs Eugene V. Rostow. Sent Priority to Tel Aviv, Cairo, Amman, Baghdad, Damascus, Jidda, Beirut, Kuwait, Dhahran, London, USUN, Paris, Jerusalem, CINCSTRIKE/CINCMEAFSA, and Moscow.

A. In view state of alarm in Damascus and reports of UAR troop movements, USG had today taken initiative to urge restraint on GOI, SARG[2] and UARG.[3]

B. In New York, Ambassador Goldberg had issued statement supporting SYG's efforts maintain area peace.[4] In addition Goldberg, UK and French Ambassadors to UN had agreed make joint approach to SYG to explore whether situation warranted convening Security Council.

C. Latest reports from Israel (Tel Aviv 3604)[5] were reassuring, but it still not clear what UAR up to and fact remained that another terrorist incident could spark outbreak hostilities.

D. By diplomatic approaches Damascus and Cairo, we hope reassure GOI and relieve pressure on Israelis to take unilateral action in response recent terrorist attacks whose increased sophistication makes them particularly serious.

E. USG hoped UK and French Governments would also use their influence in Cairo and Damascus. Such diplomatic pressures were useful and consistent with Tripartite Declaration[6] which had never been rescinded.

2. French Ambassador Lucet commented that Tripartite Declaration remains basis for French policy. While agreeing on usefulness of diplomatic approach, Lucet expressed reservations re Security Council meeting. UK Ambassador Dean concurred, stating situation did not appear serious enough convene Security Council particularly in view latest information from Tel Aviv.

3. Rostow raised question as to whether it might possibly be useful to approach USSR in view strong Soviet position in Syria, noting indi-

---

[2] Assistant Secretary of State Lucius D. Battle met with Syrian Chargé Galeb Kayali on May 15. Battle said that guerrilla incursions into Israeli territory were exacerbating Arab-Israeli tensions and urged all parties to exercise restraint. (Memorandum of conversation; ibid.)

[3] Telegram 7496 from Cairo, May 15, reported that Chargé David Nes had raised the subject of the Israel-Syrian crisis with UAR Foreign Minister Mahmoud Riad that morning. Riad said that his government viewed the events of the last few days "most seriously," that "all necessary military precautions" were being taken, and that "any move by Israel would be met by immediate UAR response." (Ibid.)

[4] Telegram 5299 from USUN, May 15, conveyed the text of a press release issued by U.S. Representative to the United Nations Arther Goldberg that day. (Ibid., POL ARAB–ISR)

[5] Document 2.

[6] Reference is to a statement issued on May 25, 1950, by the U.S., British, and French Governments expressing their interest in the maintenance of peace and stability between the Arab states and Israel, their opposition to an arms race in the area, and their opposition to the use of force or threat of force between any of the states in that area. It stated that if the three governments were to find that any of the states in the area was preparing to violate frontiers or armistice lines, they "would, consistently with their obligations as members of the United Nations, immediately take action, both within and outside the United Nations, to prevent such violation." For text, see *Foreign Relations, 1950,* vol. V, pp. 167–168.

cations that Soviets have in past attempted exercise restraining influence on Damascus.

4. British and French Ambassadors said they had no reports of initiatives by their Governments in present situation but would report Rostow's presentation including his question as to whether it might be useful to approach the Soviets.[7]

---

[7] Printed from an unsigned copy.

---

4. Memorandum From the President's Special Assistant (Rostow) to President Johnson[1]

Washington, May 15, 1967, 7:15 p.m.

SUBJECT

Your meeting with Messrs. Feinberg and Ginsburgh[2]

I am attaching two memos on the Israeli aid package[3] for your reference. The first (Tab A)[4] is the full description of the package. The second (Tab B)[5] is a note describing the disadvantages of urging the Israelis to buy the Italian-made version of our APC.

You will know how far you want to go in discussing this package with them. Ambassador Harman has simply been told that the package "will substantially meet their requests."[6]

---

[1] Source: Johnson Library, National Security File, Country File, Israel, Vol. VI. Confidential.

[2] The President's Daily Diary indicates that he met from 11:30 a.m. to 12:10 p.m. on May 16 with New York banker Abraham Feinberg and Washington attorney David Ginsburg, who were to report on their trips to Israel. (Johnson Library) No record of the meeting has been found.

[3] A package of military and economic assistance to Israel had been under discussion for several weeks; see Foreign Relations, 1964–1968, vol. XVIII, Documents 414 and 416.

[4] Tab A was not found attached.

[5] Tab B was a brief memorandum of May 12 from Harold Saunders of the NSC Staff to Rostow, with an attached memorandum dated May 1 from Deputy Assistant Secretary of Defense for International Affairs Townsend Hoopes to Rostow and another dated April 17 from Secretary of Defense McNamara to the President. For text of the McNamara memorandum, see Foreign Relations, 1964–1968, vol. XVIII, Document 405.

[6] A note attached to a May 15 memorandum from Saunders to Rostow on the Israel–Syria–UAR tension states that Battle said this to Harman at their meeting that morning, making clear that the decision had been made before the border tension. (Johnson Library, National Security File, Country File, Middle East Crisis, Vol. 1)

I have put to Gene[7] the question of sending the Vice President to Israel and Egypt.[8] Luke Battle thinks it's a good idea, but Secretary Rusk may not agree. However, we cannot decide until the Egyptians come through on their promise to get our AID fellows out of jail in Yemen[9] and until the threat of war between Israel and Syria lessens.

In hearing their report on their trip to Israel, you may want to ask whether they have any feeling for Eshkol's intention to attack Syria. Border tension mounted sharply over the weekend after Eshkol and the Israeli Chief of Staff threatened an attack if terrorist raids from Syria into Israel continue. The UAR has ostentatiously put its forces on alert.

We sympathize with Eshkol's need to stop these raids and reluctantly admit that a limited attack may be his only answer. However, without preaching, you would be justified in letting these gentlemen know that a miscalculation causing a Mid-East blow-up right now would make life awfully hard for you. We want to make Eshkol think twice without giving him cause to blame us for holding him back if events later prove that a limited attack now would have been the best answer.

Walt

---

[7] Under Secretary of State for Political Affairs Eugene V. Rostow.

[8] A May 15 memorandum from Saunders to Rostow commented on a possible vice-presidential visit to the Middle East, arguing that if the situation cooled off, a high-level meeting with UAR President Nasser might clear the air in U.S.–UAR relations. (Johnson Library, National Security File, Name File, Saunders Memos)

[9] Two Americans at the AID mission in Yemen had been jailed in April on charges of attempting to destroy the city of Taiz; they were released on May 17. For information concerning this episode, see the Yemen compilation in *Foreign Relations, 1964–1968,* volume XXI; see also ibid., vol. XVIII, Document 417.

5. Telegram From the Embassy in the United Arab Republic to the Department of State[1]

Cairo, May 16, 1967, 0834Z.

7544. Ref. State 194188.[2]

1. I have seen El Feki regarding the mounting tensions in the Near East and in particular on the Israeli-Syrian border.

2. Referring to my talk with FonMin Riad of yesterday I reiterated USG concern with situation and said that we had urged restraint in the strongest terms and at the highest level of the Israeli Government. I said that based on info avail to us in Israel we were not aware of any major changes in the disposition of Israeli forces or of any "mobilization" measures. I then provided verbatim the Israeli response to our expressions of concern per State 194639.[3] From USUN 5302[4] I also quoted to El Feki the two points which Israel had asked the Secretary General to convey to the Egyptian and Syrian Govts.

3. El Feki followed all of this most carefully and with genuine interest. He said that he was particularly struck by the fact that whereas the Israelis denied any build up on the Syrian border, no mention was made of Jordanian border. He also read from one of his intelligence reports which highlighted fact that yesterday's Jerusalem parade did not include any significant heavy equipment, thus revealing that such equipment had been kept with units.

---

[1] Source: National Archives and Records Administration, RG 59, Central Files 1967–69, POL 32–1 ISR–SYR. Confidential; Priority. Repeated Immediate to Amman and to USUN, CINCSTRIKE/CINCMEAFSA, Damascus, and Tel Aviv.

[2] Telegram 194188 to Cairo, May 15, instructed Nes to meet again with Foreign Minister Riad, express U.S. concern at the increase in tension, tell him the United States had urged restraint on the Israelis and was unaware of any major changes in disposition of Israeli forces, tell him the United States was also urging restraint on the Syrians, and suggest that the UAR could play a useful role in urging the Syrians to put an end to the terrorist incidents that were inflaming the border situation. (Ibid.)

[3] Telegram 194639 to Cairo, May 15, conveyed the points made by Bitan to Barbour. (Ibid.) See Document 2.

[4] Telegram 5302 from USUN, May 16, reported conversations at the United Nations, including an Israeli request that the Secretary-General convey two points to the UAR and Syrian representatives: the Israeli Government was not making any military dispositions on the borders with Syria and the UAR, and it was planning no military action unless action was taken against Israel. (National Archives and Records Administration, RG 59, Central Files 1967–69, POL 32–1 ISR–SYR/UN)

4. We then discussed over-all Israeli-Arab confrontation in general terms and I read from President Kennedy's statement of May 9, 1963,[5] saying that in my view my govt would never tolerate unprovoked aggression by Israel against its Arab neighbors. We had intervened against the tripartite aggression of 1956 and in my view we would do so again. The UARG should place due credence with respect to its security in our statements regarding our position in the event of aggression and in the United Nations.

5. El Feki said that the position of his govt was likewise very clear and had been stated repeatedly. The UAR will never take the initiative in attacking Israel. However, in the event of any large scale Israeli attack against its neighbors the UARG cannot await UN intervention or even that of the great powers but would have to come to the assistance of victim of aggression without delay.

6. El Feki seemed genuinely eager to be in touch with us regarding present Near Eastern tensions and I think we should maintain a continuing dialogue here, in Washington and in New York with the Egyptians with a view to reassuring them and calming their fears. I am certain that they are now merely reacting to those fears and have no aggressive intent.

Nes

---

[5] President Kennedy stated during a press conference on May 8, 1963, "We support the security of both Israel and her neighbors." He also stated, "This Government has been and remains strongly opposed to the use of force or the threat of force in the Near East. In the event of aggression or preparation for aggression, whether direct or indirect, we would support appropriate measures in the United Nations, adopt other courses of action on our own to prevent or to put a stop to such aggression, which, of course, has been the policy which the United States has followed for some time." For text, see *Public Papers of the Presidents of the United States: John F. Kennedy, 1963*, p. 373.

---

6.   Editorial Note

At 10 p.m. Gaza time on May 16, 1967, United Arab Republic Brigadier Eiz-El-Din Mokhtar gave Major-General Indar Jit Rikhye, the commander of the United Nations Emergency Force in the Middle East, a letter from Lieutenant General Mohammed Fawzi, Chief of Staff of the UAR armed forces, stating that in accordance with his instructions to the UAR armed forces to be ready for action against Israel in case of any aggressive Israeli action against any Arab country, UAR troops were concentrated in Sinai on the UAR eastern borders. He requested that

Rikhye withdraw all the UNEF troops in the observation posts along those borders. Rikhye replied that he would report the request to UN Secretary-General U Thant. The Secretary-General replied at 6:45 p.m. on May 16 through the UAR permanent representative at the United Nations asking for a clarification of the request. His reply stated in part:

"If it was the intention of the government of the United Arab Republic to withdraw the consent which it gave in 1956 for the stationing of UNEF on the territory of the United Arab Republic and Gaza it was, of course, entitled to do so. Since, however, the basis for the presence of UNEF was an agreement made directly between President Nasser and Dag Hammarskjöld as Secretary-General of the United Nations, any request for the withdrawal of UNEF must come directly to the Secretary-General from the government of the United Arab Republic. On receipt of such a request, the Secretary-General would order the withdrawal of all UNEF troops from Gaza and Sinai, simultaneously informing the General Assembly of what he was doing and why."

The Secretary-General's message is quoted in a report which he submitted to the UN General Assembly on May 18. For text of the report, see *Public Papers of the Secretaries-General of the United Nations,* Volume VII, U Thant, 1965–1967, pages 424–433. Concerning the establishment of UNEF, see Secretary-General Hammarskjöld's report to the General Assembly on November 20, 1956, with an annexed aide-mémoire on the basis for the UNEF presence in Egypt; ibid., Volume III, Dag Hammarskjöld, 1956–1957, pages 373–376. An aide-mémoire of August 5, 1957, in which Hammarskjöld described his November 1956 exchanges with the Egyptian Government over the conditions that should govern UNEF's withdrawal, is ibid., pages 377–382. General Rikhye recorded his recollections of the UAR demand and subsequent events in *The Sinai Blunder: Withdrawal of the United Nations Emergency Force Leading to the Six-Day War of June 1967* (London and Totowa, N.J.: Frank Cass and Company Limited 1980). Documentation relating to UNEF is in the National Archives and Records Administration, RG 59, Central Files 1967–1969, POL 27–4 UN, although most of the documentation pertaining to UNEF withdrawal is ibid., POL ARAB–ISR.

7.   **Memorandum From the President's Special Assistant (Rostow) to President Johnson**[1]

Washington, May 17, 1967.

SUBJECT

Urgent Message to Eshkol

We had hoped yesterday that tension in the Israel–Syria–UAR triangle was dropping after an ostentatious Egyptian show of putting its forces around Cairo on alert. Last night, however, we and the Israelis learned that the Egyptians have moved forces into the Sinai. Now they have moved forces in front of the UN Emergency Force on the Israel–UAR border and all but ordered it to withdraw.

The UAR's brinksmanship stems from two causes: (1) The Syrians are feeding Cairo erroneous reports of Israeli mobilization to strike Syria. Regrettably, some pretty militant public threats from Israel by Eshkol and others have lent credibility to the Syrian reports. (2) Nasser probably feels his prestige would suffer irreparably if he failed a third time to come to the aid of an Arab nation attacked by Israel. Moderates like Hussein have raked him over the coals for not coming to Jordan's aid in November or to Syria's when Israel shot down 6 of its MIG's last month.

In this highly charged atmosphere, it's probably impossible for Israel to get away with a limited retaliatory strike for the next terrorist attack from Syria. But the Syrians may try harder than ever by turning loose the terrorists either to force Israel to eat crow by taking further sabotage attacks without reacting or to drag them and the UAR into a fight. Eshkol may even decide that Egypt's move to the border pushes him too far.

Secretary Rusk personally recommends the attached message[2] to Eshkol urging him not to put a match to this fuse. A week ago, I would have counseled closing our eyes if Eshkol had decided to lash back at the Syrians. We just don't have an alternative way to handle these terrorist raids that are becoming more and more sophisticated. Unfortunately, however, his own public threats seem to have deprived him of the flexibility to make a limited attack today.

---

[1] Source: Johnson Library, National Security File, Country File, Middle East Crisis, Vol. I. Secret.

[2] The draft message as approved by the President, with an attached note directing that it should be sent LDX to Ben Read, is ibid.

I have worked with State to make this message as sympathetic as possible while trying still to strengthen Eshkol's hand against his hawks. Arthur Goldberg is aware of the Secretary's proposal and approves. We will follow events closely to be sure the message isn't overtaken by events before delivery.

Approve[3]
See me

Walt

---

[3] Neither option is checked. On the memorandum "Call me. L." appears in Johnson's handwriting next to the two options. A note in Rostow's handwriting at the top of the page states that the President approved by telephone at 6 p.m.

---

8. Telegram From the Department of State to the Embassy in Israel[1]

Washington, May 17, 1967, 7 p.m.

196541. Please deliver following personal message from President to Prime Minister Eshkol:

"Dear Mr. Prime Minister:

I am following very closely the tense situation in the Near East and am deeply concerned about the maintenance of peace in that area. We have made known our concern in Damascus and Cairo and are working closely with other countries in the United Nations. Our efforts will continue.

I know that you and your people are having your patience tried to the limits by continuing incidents along your border. In this situation, I would like to emphasize in the strongest terms the need to avoid any action on your side which would add further to the violence and tension in your area. I urge the closest consultation between you and your principal friends. I am sure that you will understand that I cannot accept any responsibilities on behalf of the

---

[1] Source: National Archives and Records Administration RG 59, Central Files 1967–69, POL ARAB–ISR. Secret; Immediate. Drafted and approved by Rusk; cleared by Battle; and cleared with changes by Walt Rostow.

United States for situations which arise as the result of actions on which we are not consulted.

With personal regards.

Sincerely,

Lyndon B. Johnson"

Rusk

---

9. President's Daily Brief

Washington, May 18, 1967.

[Source: Johnson Library, National Security File, NSC Histories, Middle East Crisis, Vol. 6, Appendix A. Top Secret; [*codeword not declassified*]. 1 page of source text not declassified.]

---

10. Information Memorandum From the Deputy Assistant Secretary of State for International Organization Affairs (Popper) to Secretary of State Rusk[1]

Washington, May 17, 1967.

SUBJECT

The UAR and UNEF

As you know, the Arab-Israeli situation has changed considerably during the day, and as of 7:00 p.m. (yesterday)[2] we still do not know exactly how matters stand. It is clear that the UAR has requested that UNEF Forces withdraw from certain observation posts along the UAR-

---

[1] Source: National Archives and Records Administration, RG 59, Central Files 1967–69, POL ARAB–ISR. Confidential. Drafted by Popper on May 17. The memorandum was evidently sent to Rusk on May 18.

[2] "Yesterday" is a handwritten addition on the memorandum.

Israeli frontier (presumably this does not include the Gaza Strip). The UN Secretariat has told us that at some points the Egyptian forces are now standing between the UNEF Force and the border, thus facing Israeli territory. The Secretariat also says that the UAR has requested within 48 hours the evacuation of the UNEF observation post at Sharm al-Shaikh, strategically situated on the Gulf of Aqaba. The deadline for this movement would be tonight[3] our time.

During the day (yesterday),[4] the Secretary General announced that he was urgently seeking clarification from the UAR as to its intentions with respect to the continued presence of UNEF in the area. The UN spokesman's announcement said:

"The UNEF went into Gaza and Sinai over ten years ago with the consent of the government of the UAR and has continued there on that basis. As a peacekeeping force it could not remain if that consent were withdrawn or if the conditions under which it operates were so qualified that the force was unable to function effectively. The Secretary General regards the situation as being potentially very grave. On the basis of reports thus far received from the Chief of Staff of UNTSO, the Secretary General knows of no troop movements or concentrations along any of the lines which should give rise to undue concern."

This statement obviously impairs our ability to keep the Force in place over UAR opposition. The general principle has been that UN peacekeeping forces are emplaced with the consent of the government on whose territory they are stationed. What is not clear—and there is no precedent—is whether, that consent being removed, the UN Force is required to depart.

On this issue, in a report of the Secretary General on a study of the experience with UNEF (Document A/3943, 9 October 1958)[5] Secretary General Hammarskjold stated:

"The consequence of such a bilateral declaration is that, were either side to act unilaterally in refusing continued presence or deciding on withdrawal, and were the other side to find that such action was contrary to a good-faith interpretation of the purposes of the operation, an exchange of views would be called for towards harmonizing the positions. This does not imply any infringement of the sovereign right of the host Government, nor any restriction of the right of the United Nations

---

[3] "Tomorrow night" was changed by hand to "tonight" on the memorandum.

[4] "Yesterday" is a handwritten addition on the memorandum.

[5] Secretary-General Hammarskjöld's report of October 9, 1958, on the experience with UNEF is printed in *Public Papers of the Secretaries-General of the United Nations*, Vol. III, Dag Hammarskjöld, 1956–1957, pp. 230–292.

to decide on the termination of its own operation whenever it might see fit to do so. But it does mean a mutual recognition of the fact that the operation, being based on collaboration between the host Government and the United Nations, should be carried on in forms natural to such collaboration, and especially so with regard to the questions of presence and maintenance."

Our first reports of the Secretary General's discussion today with the countries contributing forces to UNEF indicate that he is playing for time. He appears to have said that any request for withdrawal of UNEF Forces should be sent to him and not to General Rikhye, the UNEF Commander. The UAR representative in New York has not as yet received instructions to approach the Secretary General on this subject. The Secretary General has given the UAR representative an 8-page Aide-Mémoire[6] recalling the circumstances under which the Force was established and apparently appealing for a delay. However, it is our estimate that neither the Secretary General nor the troop-contributing nations would be eager for a test of will on this issue.

USUN agrees that every effort should be made to delay any UNEF withdrawal by all appropriate means. The personal message which U Thant is sending to Nasser today may help. There will be Big Four consultations today[7] (US, UK, France, USSR) with or without the participation of the Secretary General. If the situation has not eased, Ambassador Goldberg will be asking you for authority to move urgently toward a Security Council meeting. Other UN representatives have suggested that the General Assembly, which is in session, might also take up the matter.

---

[6] The aide-mémoire is quoted in Secretary-General Thant's May 18 report to the UN General Assembly. (Ibid., Vol. VII, U Thant, 1965–1967, pp. 424–433)

[7] "Tomorrow" was changed by hand to "today" on the memorandum.

11. Telegram From the Mission to the United Nations to the Department of State[1]

New York, May 19, 1967, 0149Z.

5357. UNEF. I called on SYG and Bunche this morning accompanied by Pedersen to survey present status of UNEF and to urge strongly SYG not take decision to withdraw UNEF without fullest consultation with perm members SC and with GA.

SYG said he had not yet received official request for withdrawal, although El Kony (UAR) was scheduled to see him right after I did (at which time he did present the request).

I urged SYG to consult with Fedorenko (USSR) in interest of peaceful situation in Middle East, saying I intended to do same myself. Noted today was key day. SYG indicated he understood importance of Sovs but did not make clear commitment to contact them. I told SYG we had consulted background of statements made by Hammarskjold at time of UNEF's establishment.[2] These indicated that while basic principle obviously was that UNEF was on territory with consent of UAR, there was the "good faith" agreement specifically reached with them and many other indications that response to request to withdraw need not be automatic but result in consultations. Bunche said Secretariat had been looking into matter carefully and had sent UAR two messages yesterday, one the eight page memo he had previously told us about. While he was not specific about its contents I had impression memo had covered these points but probably concluded that if UAR seriously requested withdrawal SYG would do so. Bunche said their legal examination indicated decision on withdrawal was something SYG could make and did not require any UN political action.

I also suggested SYG's first response to request for withdrawal might be appeal to Nasser, which we had previously been told he was considering. SYG said he had this morning been "advised seriously and confidentially" not to make such appeal. (He did not say who this came from.)

I told SYG we suspected there was a great deal of face and political maneuvering in current situation and that with careful handling we might yet preserve situation and UNEF role. Canadians had told us that

---

[1] Source: National Archives and Records Administration, RG 59, Central Files 1967–69, POL 27–4 PAL/UN. Confidential. Repeated to Amman, Beirut, Damascus, Jerusalem, Tel Aviv, Cairo, Moscow, London, and Paris. Received on May 18 at 10:43 p.m.

[2] See Document 6.

in Riad's approach to them in Cairo he had said they were not prepared to discuss principle of withdrawal but were prepared to discuss modalities. Perhaps this was something that could be worked on. Perhaps an appeal from him or a request by him for SC meeting under Article 99 would provide means to restore situation.

SYG said he would make report to GA and to SC but he was resistant to idea of using Article 99. Bunche also expressed view UAR was quite serious, noting he had just received report from Rikhye that UAR troops in Sinai had gone right up to borderline, so that now they were directly opposite Israeli battalions.

Bunche also emphasized practical difficulty of supplying and maintaining force if UAR wanted to harass it and said that in any case most countries supplying contingents would withdraw them immediately if UAR so demanded.

In concluding session I again urged that SYG not take responsibility upon himself. I noted this was matter of great political consequence and I urged he consult widely with members, especially perm members of SC and defer any commitment in response to UAR request until he had done so.

SYG said I should know that Syrians had alleged to him there was wide-spread conspiracy to attack Syria involving Saudi Arabia, Jordan and Israel and in which US and UK were implicated. I told him categorically this was not true and that US policy continued be opposed to use of force and violence in Middle East and to favor maintenance of peace and security in area. Told him we had conveyed these views to all govts in area, including Israel. Read him some of the things we had said. Told him charges were ridiculous and pointed to statement I had ready and intended to use with press after meeting, in which I denied it.[3]

Goldberg

---

[3] Telegram 5360 from USUN, May 19, conveyed the text of the statement. (National Archives and Records Administration, RG 59, Central Files 1967–69, POL ARAB–ISR)

12. Telegram From the Embassy in Jordan to the Department of State[1]

Amman, May 18, 1967, 1505Z.

3612. Ref: Amman's 3596.[2] Subject: Conversation with Hussein re Present Situation in Middle East.

1. In discussing the present situation in the Middle East, Hussein observed that the apparent target for possible Israeli attack is Syria. If the UAR does not react militarily to an Israeli attack on Syria, Jordan will stand still. If, as is more probable, Nasser must and does react, if only nominally, Jordan will have to take sufficient action to keep from being a conspicuous scapegoat, but this would not entail a direct armed clash with Israel so long as an Israeli attack on Syria were of limited duration.

2. The King feels that the Middle East is in for an extended period of serious trouble. He views the factors and issues involved as much more complicated than they appear on the surface. He considers, for example, that infiltration is only symptomatic of the underlying situation. He believes it is important that all concerned will keep the entire picture in the broadest possible focus to insure that all of the factors involved, both short and long range, are properly and accurately calculated. In this context he noted that while Syria might logically be the next target of attack, Jordan is just as likely a target in the short run and, in his opinion, an inevitable one in the long run. In support of this he said that he is not at all convinced that the Israelis have accepted the status quo as a permanent solution. Israel has certain long range military and economic requirements and certain traditional religious and historic aspirations which in his opinion they have not yet satisfied or realized. The only way in which these goals can be achieved, he said, is by an alteration of the status of the West Bank of Jordan. Thus in the King's view it is quite natural for the Israelis to take advantage of any opportunity and force any situation which would move them closer to this goal. His concern is that current area conditions provide them with just such opportunities—terrorism, infiltration and disunity among the Arabs being the most obvious. The present state of tension in the

---

[1] Source: National Archives and Records Administration, RG 59, Central Files 1967–69, POL 32–1 ISR–JORDAN. Secret; Priority; Limdis. Repeated to Baghdad, Cairo, Jerusalem, USUN, CINCSTRIKE, Jidda, Beirut, Damascus, London, and Tel Aviv. Received at 3:23 p.m.

[2] Telegram 3596 from Amman, May 17, reported that Ambassador Burns had met that afternoon with King Hussein, who said he viewed the situation in the Middle East as the most critical since 1956. (Ibid.)

Middle East provides a cover, so to speak, for an Israeli attack on anyone of their choosing. Hussein pointed out that in 1956 Israel was
threatening Jordan but in fact attacked Egypt; in November 1966 it was
the Syrians with whom Israel's relations were at a nadir yet it was
Jordan who was attacked. Admittedly, said Hussein, there would have
to be a casus belli for an Israeli attack against Jordan, such as a terrorist
incident in Israel across from the Jordanian border. In such event Israel
might attack Jordan alone, or Jordan and Syria together. The Jordanians
are making the maximum effort to interdict terrorists, but, he observed,
there always exists the possibility a terrorist would get through who
would do serious damage. Or, he added, an incident could be manu-
factured if the risks and gains appeared worth it.

3. I challenged Hussein's thesis and in addition pointed out to him
there was no evidence Israel was planning to attack Jordan and that all
factors and indicators argued against the Israelis doing so. Hussein
remained unconvinced, arguing that neither he nor we could afford to
rule such a possibility out of our overall considerations. He conceded
that Israel could not successfully annex the West Bank in one action, but
any move which would tend to neutralize the West Bank or weaken
Arab control over it would put Israel a step closer to a goal which was in
her long-term strategic interest. The temporary seizure and occupation
of a piece of Jordanian territory would place Israel in a position to extract
a price for withdrawal, such as, possibly, demilitarization of the West
Bank or some form of UN control over the West Bank. Israel could make
as much of a case for such action on grounds of security against infiltration and sabotage as she did in Suez. His regime could not pay a price
for Israeli withdrawal and still survive. Hussein said that if Israel
launched another Samu-scale attack against Jordan[3] he would have no
alternative but to retaliate or face an internal revolt. If Jordan retaliates,
asked Hussein, would not this give Israel a pretext to occupy and hold
Jordanian territory? Or, said Hussein, Israel might instead of a hit-and-
run type attack simply occupy and hold territory in the first instance. He
said he could not exclude these possibilities from his calculations and
urged us not to do so even if we felt them considerably less than likely.

4. In any event, asked Hussein, what would the US do if his hypothesis proved correct? He had been assured on countless occasions by US
officials that the US would not permit the Israelis to alter the status quo.
He had been told when last in Washington, he said, that Jordan did not
need additional armament because the Sixth Fleet would protect him.

---

[3] Israel attacked the Jordanian village of Samu on November 13, 1966, in a large-scale
raid in retaliation for recent terrorist incidents. Documentation relating to the incident is
in *Foreign Relations, 1964–1968*, vol. XVIII, Document 332 ff.

5. I replied that the US stood by its declarations (Tripartite Declaration, Eisenhower reaffirmation of November 9, 1955, Eisenhower Doctrine and Kennedy statement of May 8, 1963) that the US would not acquiesce in changes of the border by force. Just what form US action would take would have to be decided at the time in the light of circumstances then existing.

6. Hussein replied: "Yes, I know those declarations. In such a contingency as I have described there would be need for immediate US assistance to force Israeli withdrawal. The other Arab states would not help Jordan, and it would take too long for the US to act. I predict that if the Israelis remain in Jordan for any extended length of time, the present regime here would fall. The same thing would happen if the Israelis succeeded in extracting significant concessions as the price for withdrawal. As you know, I no longer believe the Israelis have a stake in my regime, so that its demise would not deter them from such action. In my opinion, the chances of the contingency we have talked about arising would be practically eliminated if the Israelis were clearly on notice you would forcibly intervene."

7. *Comment:* Whatever Hussein's beliefs he does not want to tangle with Israel and will be guided by prudence. If, however, a serious terrorist incident should occur in Israel across from the Jordanian border, I defer to judgment of Embassy Tel Aviv but I would imagine that, given the present tense atmosphere and the precedent of Samu, no one could rule out the possibility that Israel might hit Jordan. There is little doubt the Jordanians would in such event counterattack. The King realizes a counterattack would court escalation, but he is convinced that not to counterattack would mean the end of his regime through internal upheaval. I would guess the counterattack would follow swiftly upon the attack, and be of lesser scale than the original attack.

8. I plan to see the King again in a few days to review the situation with him. I will continue to encourage him in his present course of prudence. Would appreciate any views or reassurances the Department would wish transmitted to Hussein.[4]

Burns

---

[4] Telegram 198899 to Amman, May 20, approved the line Burns had taken with the King as reported in telegram 3612. It instructed him to reiterate to the King the assurances contained in the President's letter of November 23 (see ibid., Document 346) and to inform him that the U.S. Government still stood by President Kennedy's statement of May 8, 1963, and that the U.S. estimate of Israeli intentions toward the Jordanian regime had not changed. (National Archives and Records Administration, RG 59, Central Files 1967–69, POL 32–1 ISR–JORDAN)

13.   Telegram From the Embassy in Israel to the Department of State[1]

Tel Aviv, May 18, 1967, 1630Z.

3648. Ref: State 196541[2] and Tel Aviv 3640.[3]

1. FonMin Eban gave me at 1700 hrs reply to President's message from Prime Minister Eshkol. Eban added series amplifying comments on PriMin's behalf contained my immediately following telegram.[4]

2. Text Eshkol reply as follows:

"Jerusalem, May 18, 1967

Dear Mr. President,

I have received your personal message of May 18, 1967.

I agree with you that the situation is tense and I welcome your readiness for close and continuous consultation. Foreign Minister Eban gave detailed information to Ambassador Barbour today[5] and our representatives are exchanging ideas with yours in Washington and at United Nations headquarters.

I should like to summarize my main conclusions:

First: The primary link in the chain of tension is the Syrian policy of terrorist infiltration and sabotage. From Under Secretary Rostow's conversation with Ambassador Harman,[6] I am glad to learn that your government and mine are agreed on this. You are correct, Mr. President, in

---

[1]   Source: National Archives and Records Administration, RG 59, Central Files 1967–69, POL ARAB–ISR. Secret; Nodis. Received at 4:30 p.m. Walt Rostow sent a copy to the President with a May 19 8:30 a.m. covering memorandum. Johnson wrote on the memorandum: "Get meeting set up." (Johnson Library, National Security File, Country File, Middle East Crisis, Vol. VII)

[2]   Document 8.

[3]   Telegram 3640 from Tel Aviv, May 18, reported that Ambassador Barbour had delivered the message conveyed in telegram 196541 (Document 8) to Foreign Minister Eban, since he already had a meeting scheduled with Eban at the latter's request. (National Archives and Records Administration, RG 59, Central Files 1967–69, POL ARAB–ISR)

[4]   Document 14.

[5]   Barbour reported his conversation with Eban in telegram 3639, May 18. Eban stated the Israeli view that if the UAR were to order UNEF off its soil, it would be necessary to reconvene the UN General Assembly. He warned that if the UAR military buildup were to continue, there would be a buildup on the Israeli side as well and urged U.S. efforts to convince the Soviets that it was in their interest to diffuse the tension. (National Archives and Records Administration, RG 59, Central Files 1967–69, POL ARAB–ISR)

[6]   Circular telegram 196738, May 17, summarized Rostow's conversation with Harman that afternoon. Harman stated that the nub of the problem was Syrian support of terrorism and urged public reiteration of U.S. opposition to terrorism. Rostow stressed the importance of Israel's taking no military action without consultation with the U.S. Government, "since such action would involve us all." (Ibid.)

stating that we are having our patience tried to the limits. There have been 15 attempts at murder and sabotage in the past six weeks. We have not reacted. This in itself proves that there is no lack of temperance and responsibility on our part. On the other hand, the problem is not solved indefinitely by inaction. We cannot always rely on the stroke of fortune which has so far prevented the terrorist acts from taking the toll of life and injury intended by the perpetrators. Although many acts have been committed from Lebanon and Jordan, our present conviction is that Syria is responsible and is attempting to embroil other Arab states. We are alive to this stratagem and shall not cooperate with it.

My first conclusion, therefore, is that every effort should be made to emphasize, proclaim and condemn Syrian responsibility for these terrorist acts, in order to deter their continuation.

Second: The Egyptian build-up of armour and infantry in Sinai, to the extent so far of approximately four divisions including 600 tanks, is greater than ever before, and has no objective justification. Egypt knows that there is no foundation for reports of troop concentration against Syria. Yet even after receiving information on this subject from UN and other sources, the UAR has increased its troop concentration. This naturally forces me to undertake precautionary reinforcement in the south. One of the dangers that we face is that the Egyptian troop concentration may encourage Syria to resume terroristic acts under the false impression of immunity.

The only way of avoiding the effects of an escalating reciprocal build-up is for Egypt to return to the previous posture in Sinai. This would immediately affect our own decisions and arrangements.

I urge the full application of international influence to secure the end of abnormal troop concentrations.

Third: It would be very unfortunate if the UN authorities were to give an impression of irresolution in connection with the presence of the UNEF in Sinai. It is not the function of the United Nations to move out of the way in order to facilitate warlike acts. I hope that the Secretary General will insist that he cannot affect the status quo concerning the UN force in Sinai without a mandate from the General Assembly. There is ample legal basis for this.

I must point out that Israel was a party to the arrangement which led in March 1957 to the stationing of the UNEF. At United States initiative, we took far-reaching measures in exchange for the UNEF arrangement.[7]

---

[7] Extensive documentation on the negotiations leading to the creation of UNEF under General Assembly resolution 1000(ES–I), November 5, 1956, and the replacement of Israeli troops by UNEF troops in Sinai and Gaza, completed March 8, 1957, is in *Foreign Relations*, 1955–1957, volumes XVI and XVII.

Fourth: There may be an impression in Cairo and Damascus that Soviet support for Egypt and Syria is assured, and that therefore they have no need of restraint. This factor would be an emphatic clarification by the United States to the Soviet Union of the American commitment to Israel's independence and integrity and the American will and capacity to defend stability in the Middle East. I can hardly exaggerate the importance and urgency of such an approach to the USSR. It is one of the central keys to the improvement of the situation.

Five: In this connection, Mr. President, I am solemnly bound to refer to the specific American commitment so often reiterated to us between May 1961 and August 1966. I especially remember our own conversations in June 1964.[8] Your note of May 18 does not explicitly refer to the commitment by the United States to act both inside and outside the UN in support of Israel's integrity and independence. I understand that you do not wish to be committed without consultation. But with a massive build-up on our southern frontier linked with a terrorist campaign from the north and Soviet support of the governments responsible for the tension, there is surely an urgent need to reaffirm the American commitment to Israel's security with a view to its implementation should the need arise.

In view of the magnitude of the issues involved, I have felt at liberty to speak with frankness on five problems in all of which I believe that the United States is in a position to make a vital contribution to the avoidance of dangers and the reinforcement of peace.

Signed Levi Eshkol."

Barbour

---

[8] Concerning the conversations between Johnson and Eshkol, June 1–2, see ibid., 1964–1968, vol. XVIII, Documents 65 and 66.

14.   Telegram From the Embassy in Israel to the Department of State[1]

Tel Aviv, May 18, 1967, 1720Z.

3650. Ref: Tel Aviv 3648.[2]

1. Following are amplifying comments re Eshkol message made by Foreign Minister Eban referred to in my immediately preceding telegram.

2. First, GOI wished to point up fact of Syrian responsibility. One had only to look at what Syria had achieved in Middle East: it had involved itself in troubles with Israel; it had embroiled the UAR in crisis that short time ago UAR had no intentions get embroiled in; and it was trying similarly to embroil Jordan and Lebanon. Syrian responsibility had to be brought to light and emphasized in most explicit way. GOI realized what Syria trying to do re Lebanon and Jordan, and not prepared to be taken in. Focus GOI interest remained Syria.

3. GOI appreciated advice and exhortations contained in President's letter but it had to ask what could be the President's advice if there were another terrorist incident, and another. The logic of advising patience in the current context was understandable but GOI had to ask at what point did the US think that a maximum accumulation of this kind of incidents would be reached when further patience could no longer be warranted.

4. Second, GOI wished to point up false premise on which the Egyptian troop concentrations rested. Egypt has been informed by those who should know including the US that there were no Israeli concentrations opposite Syria. If this escalation continues, soon there will be large armies facing each other across a short distance. The international community had a legitimate interest in trying to bring this situation back to normal. Israel did not know by what means this might be achieved, through diplomatic channels or otherwise. It was not for Israel to say, but in Eban's opinion if present UNSYG's predecessor were still in that position "he would have been out here three times already."

5. Third point related to the UN is thought that UNSYG has thus far shown too little resistance to UAR's UNEF demands. Already at one UNEF post within view Israeli positions UNEF personnel had moved out. There were reports out of UAR today that UAR wanted UNEF out

[1] Source: National Archives and Records Administration, RG 59, Central Files 1967–69, POL 27 ARAB–ISR/UN. Secret; Immediate; Nodis.
[2] Document 13.

of UAR and Gaza, though there no confirmation of these reports yet. In Israel's view any changes in status UNEF was not unilateral act but matter involving several parties. It resulted from agreement with UN signed by UAR. As Eban recalled understanding voiced by US representative UN at time was UAR had agreed force to remain until its removal would no longer result in military confrontation in ME. To yield to Egyptian demands would be against spirit these arrangements. Israel had accepted the establishment of UNEF on its southern borders under certain conditions and so Israel is party to this arrangement. Eban recalled US–Israel discussions in which US took responsibility suggesting March 1957 arrangement by which Israeli troops were withdrawn from Gaza. Thus this was not a matter for SYG to decide "at drop of a hat." Changes UAR was suggesting re UNEF would involve intricate structure of Middle East stability. Israel regarded this as a major development and hoped SYG would not yield without serious and earnest discussion in GA or Security Council acting as GA's agent.

6. Fourth was the question of the USSR. This was aspect of problem in which only the US could exercise its unique influence. GOI must observe that Soviet commitment to Syria was being articulated more loudly than US position of support of Israel and more generally of status quo in area. GOI would not suggest form in which US might reiterate its support but it felt that unless it was done there would be no restoration of equilibrium in area. GOI knew that USG did not want to reiterate its commitments unnecessarily but if there was ever a time for such a reiteration it was now, with terrorism in the north, mobilization in the south and the Soviets hovering over it all. It did not matter how the Soviets got the message, publicly or privately, just so they got it.

Barbour

15.   Circular Telegram From the Department of State to Certain Posts[1]

Washington, May 18, 1967, 10:01 p.m.

197665. 1. During call by Israeli Ambassador Harman on Under Secretary Rostow and Assistant Secretary Battle afternoon May 18, Rostow reported he had just called in Soviet Chargé (a) to apprise him of rumors being spread by Syria in Middle East that Syria had unlimited Soviet political and military support and (b) to state we "assumed" and "hoped" this not true. Soviet Chargé indicated he doubted rumors were true.[2]

2. Re reports SYG would order UNEF withdrawal, Harman suggested every effort should be made to play for time by (a) stressing logistical problems involved and (b) raising legal questions—e.g. need to consult members UNEF Advisory Commission per earlier Hammarskjold position.

3. Rostow agreed delaying tactics desirable; problem was that, despite valid question whether SYG has authority withdraw UNEF, he might simply announce decision to do so. Hopeful sign was that SYG reportedly anxious go to Middle East and now awaiting Cairo reaction this proposal.

4. Harman summarized Israeli intelligence re UAR buildup in Sinai along lines Tel Aviv's 3639,[3] adding that there had also been reinforcement UAR air power in Sinai. Harman indicated GOI now revising earlier estimate that UAR military moves were only for show; such concentration of troops near Israeli borders required GOI take precautionary measures. In summary Harman said key elements in situation were (a) need to preserve UNEF and exert pressure on Cairo to withdraw UAR forces, (b) effect of UAR buildup on Syrians and (c) Soviet role, which he considered most important of all. Expressing apprecia-

---

[1] Source: National Archives and Records Administration, RG 59, Central Files 1967–69, POL ARAB–ISR. Secret; Priority; Limdis. Drafted by Atherton and cleared by Eugene Rostow. Sent to Tel Aviv, Cairo, Amman, Baghdad, Damascus, Jidda, Beirut, Kuwait, Dhahran, London, USUN, Paris, Jerusalem, Moscow, and CINCSTRIKE/CINCMEAFSA.

[2] Telegram 197661 to Moscow, May 18, informed the Embassy of Rostow's conversation with Soviet Chargé Tcherniakov and suggested "making same point in low key in Moscow." (Ibid., POL 27 ARAB–ISR) Ambassador Thompson reported in telegram 5016 from Moscow, May 19, that he told Soviet Ambassador Dobrynin during a brief luncheon discussion that day that the United States was using its influence to calm the situation and hoped the Soviets were exercising as much pressure in Syria as the United States was in Israel. Dobrynin replied, "I think we can match you." (Ibid., POL ARAB–ISR)

[3] See footnote 5, Document 13.

tion for USG approach to Soviets, Harman urged we continue pressing USSR.

5. Rostow said he hoped report was not true that UAR had moved troops to Sharm el-Shaikh. Even if this was the case, however, it would be mistake to initiate any action against such deployment of Egyptian troops on Egyptian soil. Rostow emphasized USG would not wish to see Gulf of Aqaba closed but nothing should be done until and unless this was attempted. (Rostow made it clear in previous discussions that no action should be taken without prior consultation.)

6. In subsequent conversation with Battle, Harman stated there had been USG-GOI agreement, at time Gulf opened to Israel, with respect to grave consequences of any future interference with Israeli shipping.[4] Battle emphasized that important thing was not to assume interference would occur as result presence UAR troops at Sharm el-Shaikh; these two aspects of problem should be kept separate.

Rusk

---

[4] See Document 36.

---

16.   Circular Telegram From the Department of State to Certain Posts[1]

Washington, May 18, 1967, 9:39 p.m.

197664. 1. Action addressees unless overriding objection perceived should approach Governments at appropriately high level along following lines:

A. In current dangerous situation in Middle East, USG has been urging restraint on Israel and considers it important that Arab states do like-

---

[1] Source: National Archives and Records Administration, RG 59, Central Files 1967–69, POL 32–1 ISR–SYR. Secret; Priority. Drafted by Atherton; cleared in draft by Popper, in substance by Director of the Office of Inter-African Affairs Fred Hadsel, and by Under Secretary Rostow; and approved by Davies. Sent to Amman, Baghdad, Beirut, Jidda, Kuwait, Algiers, Khartoum, Rabat, Tripoli, and Tunis and repeated to Tel Aviv, Jerusalem, Damascus, London, Paris, and Moscow.

wise in Damascus and Cairo. We consider UNEF important instrument for stability and urge other governments to convey to UAR the hope that UNEF can continue play useful role it has fulfilled for over a decade.

B. Main thrust of our policy is to work through and support United Nations efforts to preserve peace in Middle East. We are giving urgent consideration to steps that might be required in support of UN role.

C. Since Soviet position will be important factor in present crisis, we are encouraged by report we have of statement by one Soviet representative to high official of another government that, while Soviets have supported Arabs against Israel on numerous occasions, they would not wish Arabs to force confrontation with Israel which could escalate into open hostilities. This position was supported by statement Soviet Chargé Washington to Under Secretary Rostow on 18th that although Soviet sympathies on side of countries representing "National Liberation movements" Soviets desire area remain calm and rumors heard by USG that Syrian Government had been promised unlimited military as well as political support from the Soviet Union were unlikely.

2. *For Jidda and Amman:* We are concerned by reports that UAR forces occupying Sharm el-Shaikh. While recognizing sensitivity this issue for GOJ and SAG, we must convey to those governments sense of extreme importance we attach to maintaining free passage for all shipping in Gulf of Aqaba.

3. *For Amman:* Suggest for obvious reasons you omit para C above from your presentation.

Rusk

---

17. President's Daily Brief

Washington, May 19, 1967.

[Source: Johnson Library, National Security File, NSC Histories, Middle East Crisis, Vol. 6, Appendix A. Top Secret; [*codeword not declassified*]. 1 page of source text not declassified.]

18.   Telegram From the Embassy in Israel to the Department of State[1]

Tel Aviv, May 19, 1967, 1430Z.

3679. Ref: Tel Aviv 3648 and 3650.[2]

1. Eshkol and Eban are taking announcement of General Rikhye that as of 1600 hours UNEF no longer operating very hard. Coupled with reassessment UAR dispositions now as of offensive character (my 3654)[3] and reports UAR troops moving into Sharm-el-Sheikh, level their apprehensions has risen markedly. Response my determined probing they claim GOI has not as I suggested "pushed the panic button," and they only taking minimum defensive precautionary measures. However, they describing U Thant's capitulation in such terms as "unheard of destruction important defensive mechanism operating for eleven years." My argument that, unfortunate as it is, it does not affect fundamental military situation which depends on Nasser's intentions and there every reason for Nasser not embark on attack on Israel, seemed me fall on deaf ears.

2. Specifically, they ask whether they will receive answer Eshkol's reply to President, which they hope, and urge that in altered circumstances they would regard it appropriate that US assurances to Israel re support in event aggression be reiterated publicly.

3. I have put to them in strong terms importance they keep their nerve and not do anything in their anxiety to heat up the situation further. I have gone so far as to say that their professed frustration at this development and apparent fright of UAR force now facing them, which although large is obviously not of invasion magnitude, is giving me qualms as to their own strictly defensive intentions. Naturally they protest vigorously, and as of now I think truthfully. However, the potentialities are such and Israel's concerns with Nasser as principal opponent in Arab world so deep seated and long enduring that I find it con-

---

[1] Source: National Archives and Records Administration, RG 59, Central Files 1967–69, POL 27 ARAB–ISR/UN. Secret; Immediate; Nodis. Received at 2:23 p.m.

[2] Documents 13 and 14.

[3] In telegram 3654 from Tel Aviv, May 19, Barbour reported that the Israelis considered UAR troop dispositions to be assuming a posture more capable of offensive action than they had previously thought, and that consequently the Israelis had increased their counter measures somewhat. Barbour had urged that Israel take only the barest minimum dispositions and avoid measures on a scale that would increase the danger in the situation. (National Archives and Records Administration, RG 59, Central Files 1967–69, POL ARAB–ISR)

ceivable at least that counsels of opportunity could sway them into major adventure next few days.

4. I consequently recommend that we consider what we can do to calm them down. Anything the President could say in reply Eshkol that would strengthen latter's resolve continue limit his objective to restoration status quo would be helpful. This connection, particular reference to Sharm-el-Sheikh obviously especially telling.

Barbour

---

19.   **Information Memorandum From the Deputy Assistant Secretary of State for International Organization Affairs (Popper) to Secretary of State Rusk**[1]

Washington, May 19, 1967.

SUBJECT

Latest on the Middle East

At John Walsh's suggestion, I am summarizing what we know about the Arab-Israeli crisis as of mid-afternoon today.

1. The Secretary General today released his report to the UN General Assembly on the withdrawal of UNEF.[2] The report indicates that from the first U Thant took the line that if the UAR wanted UNEF to leave, he had no alternative but to order it to leave—which he did. He makes it clear that he did so with great misgivings as to the consequences in the area. He also indicates quite clearly that the UAR has provoked the present crisis.

2. The report describes the way in which the UAR penetrated the UNEF area of observation, moved past the observation posts toward the frontier, and issued ultimata to the UNEF troops to withdraw, even going to the length of firing two artillery ranging shots. This is counterbalanced by a comment on the Israeli "buzzing" of General Rikhye's aircraft.

---

[1]   Source: National Archives and Records Administration, RG 59, Central Files 1967–69, POL ARAB–ISR. Confidential. Drafted by Popper.

[2]   A copy is attached to the memorandum. The text is printed in *Public Papers of the Secretaries-General of the United Nations*, Vol. VII, U Thant, 1965–1967, pp. 433–438.

3. The Canadians were instructed to call a Security Council meeting today, but have delayed in response to the Secretary General's plea to give him at least 24 hours more.

4. Exdis—The Secretary General's plea for delay is based on his assumption that he will be able to announce tomorrow his trip to the Middle East. This information is very closely held.[3] End Exdis.

5. Ambassador Goldberg saw Fedorenko this noon.[4] Fedorenko said the Russians wanted no trouble, appeared to recognize that the Soviets had some responsibilities here, but refused to meet in a 4-Power group, preferring to talk to us alone.

6. Ambassador Goldberg also saw El Kony (UAR) and Tomeh (Syria).[5] He told both that allegations of a "U.S. conspiracy" were ridiculous and asked El Kony to have the UAR use its influence to restrain the Syrians.

7. The Israelis have conveyed an urgent message from their Foreign Minister to the Secretary General protesting the "breathless speed" of his withdrawal of UNEF and claiming that the UN should have had the right and duty to ponder the matter.[6] Orally, the Israelis said that:

(a) Any interference with free passage through the waters off Sharm al-Shaikh would have "grievous and grave consequences";

(b) Any aggressive move by UAR forces, directly or through encouragement of infiltration, would have grave consequences;

(c) Any resumption of the Syrian campaign against Israel would have grave consequences no matter which border it crossed (no doubt a reference to Syrian terrorists coming from Jordan or Lebanon).

8. A mechanically transmitted copy of the Secretary General's report is attached, with apologies for the poor legibility.

---

[3] Goldberg reported in telegram 5375 from USUN, May 19, that UN Under-Secretary for Special Political Affairs Ralph J. Bunche had told him Secretary-General Thant would be leaving for Cairo on May 22 to try to establish a basis for a continuing UN presence in the area. (National Archives and Records Administration, RG 59, Central Files 1967–69 POL ARAB–ISR)

[4] Goldberg's conversation with Fedorenko was reported in telegram 5370 from USUN, May 19. (Ibid.)

[5] Goldberg's conversation with El Kony was reported in telegram 5364 from USUN, May 19. (Ibid.)

[6] Telegram 5374 from USUN, May 19, transmitted the text of the message that Israeli representative Gideon Rafael had given to Richard F. Pederson of the U.S. delegation. (Ibid.)

20. Memorandum From the President's Special Assistant (Rostow) to President Johnson[1]

Washington, May 19, 1967.

SUBJECT

Our Commitments to Israel

Attached is a rundown of our major official statements.[2] It does not, of course, include anything that might have been said privately by you to Eshkol or others.

In essence, our commitment is (a) to prevent Israel from being destroyed and (b) to stop aggression—either through the UN or on our own.

The immediate questions before us, which you will want to discuss this afternoon, are (a) whether we should reiterate this position publicly and (b) if so, what we are prepared to do to back up that statement.

We understand that U Thant is prepared to go to the Middle East to try to defuse this situation. On the negative side, he appears ready to withdraw the UN Emergency Force on the UAR–Israel border.

Our first effort must be to keep him out in front and stiffen his spine.

Next, we must learn from Secretary McNamara what we could do militarily if we had to move.

Only then should we decide whether to restate our commitment. Personally, I would prefer to keep a public statement until last but to consider first another private approach to the USSR and private assurances to Eshkol.

This is the broader framework for our discussion this afternoon.[3] I will follow up later with any further material that appears useful.

W. W. Rostow[4]

---

[1] Source: Johnson Library, National Security File, Country File, Israel, Israeli Aid. Secret.

[2] The attachment, titled "The US Commitment to Israel," is not printed.

[3] See Document 22.

[4] Printed from a copy that bears this typed signature.

21.	Memorandum From the President's Special Assistant
	(Rostow) to President Johnson[1]

Washington, May 19, 1967.

SUBJECT

Other Israeli Items

In talking with Luke Battle yesterday, Ambassador Harman made the two following points:

1. Prime Minister Eshkol would like to make an official visit to the US. Early October would be particularly convenient because he could stop here in conjunction with a visit to Argentina. He would simply like to discuss future trends in the Middle East. Ambassador Harman noted that this request pre-dates the current crisis. Luke acknowledged the request and said he assumed that the Israelis would not expect an immediate response.

2. He asked whether there were any further progress on the aid package. Luke said we would not have any final answers yet and suggested that now might not be the time for us to go before the world with a large aid commitment to Israel. Harman said that, of course, it could be kept quiet for as long as we wished.

We have had other quiet suggestions from the Israeli Embassy that an answer on the aid package now would be a big boost for morale in Jerusalem. I think, if you want, we could give them answers on everything but the APCs without much harm, provided we asked them to keep it quiet for the moment. They do want to get on with their PL 480 and long range military spares buying.

One new note has been injected into the problem of APCs. The Israelis announced quietly right before their Independence Day Parade that they would be buying some armored cars from France. They probably still want the APCs from us but these French cars are ideal for patrolling, so it looks as if they want the APCs for other purposes. This might provide an added reason for our separating APCs from the rest of the aid package. We could give them the rest of our answers and ask them to explain where these French cars fit into the picture before talking about APCs further.

Rostow

Go ahead with economic parts of the package and military credit

Ask about French armored cars too[2]

Don't do anything

---

[1]	Source: Johnson Library, National Security File, Country File, Middle East Crisis, Vol. I. Secret.

[2]	The last two options are checked.

22. Editorial Note

President Johnson met from 5:38 to 6:59 p.m. on May 19, 1967, with Secretary of State Rusk, Secretary of Defense McNamara, Special Assistant to the President Walt Rostow, and White House Press Secretary George Christian. (Johnson Library, President's Daily Diary) According to Rostow's notes of the meeting, they agreed that Ambassador to France Charles E. Bohlen and Ambassador to the United Kingdom David K.E. Bruce should ask the French and British Governments what they were prepared to do concerning the Middle East situation, with a view to reviving "as much of the tripartite as we can." Rostow's notes continue: "President wants to make sure Arabs know what our declarations are." The agenda for the meeting had listed U.S. contingency plans among the items for discussion under "Middle East," but Rostow's notes state, "Wasn't much discussion about contingency plan." The bulk of the discussion concerned Vietnam. (Notes of meeting with the President, May 19, and agenda for meeting; ibid., National Security File, Rostow Files, Meetings with the President, January–June, 1967) A May 1966 paper entitled "Politico-Military Contingency Planning for the Arab-Israeli Dispute" was sent to Rostow on May 19 with a covering memorandum from Art McCafferty. The paper stated that it was unlikely that U.S. forces would be committed to combat participation in Arab-Israeli hostilities but that they might have essential roles to fill defending U.S. interests, protecting U.S. nationals, discouraging Soviet intervention, and possibly providing logistics support for UN military operations. (Ibid., Country File, Middle East Crisis, Vol. I)

23.   Memorandum From the Deputy Assistant Secretary of
       Defense for International Security Affairs (Hoopes) to
       Secretary of Defense McNamara[1]

I–6576/67   Washington, May 19, 1967.

SUBJECT

   Possible Redeployment of 6th Fleet

Mr. McNaughton and I have just returned from a meeting in the State Department which was devoted to an assessment of the fluid situation in the Middle East. One action to emerge from the meeting was the decision to reconvene immediately the Contingency Coordinating Group[2] to reexamine the major issues and options in light of the developing Arab-Israeli situation. There was also discussion of Sixth Fleet deployments.

Mr. McNaughton and I are aware that this latter subject may have been discussed and perhaps decided at your White House meeting later this afternoon. In any event, we recommend that the major fleet elements (the two carrier task forces and the Marine Battalion) which are currently off the west and southern coasts of Italy be ordered to move now toward the Eastern Mediterranean.[3] We believe this can be done quietly and without publicity and will have the effect of reducing the reaction time should its presence be desired in the vicinity of Israel.

---

[1] Source: Washington National Records Center, OSD Files: FRC 330 72 A 2468, Middle East 092. Confidential. A copy was sent to Department of Defense General Counsel Paul C. Warnke on June 9.

[2] Three papers prepared by the Contingency Coordinating Committee over the weekend to update the contingency paper of May 1966 (see Document 22) were sent to the White House from the Department of State on May 22. They are filed with a covering memorandum of May 22 from Art McCafferty to Walt Rostow. (Johnson Library, National Security File, Country File, Middle East Crisis)

[3] A note in McNamara's handwriting connected to this sentence reads: "5/19. I will talk to Gen. Wheeler. RMcN." In a telephone conversation that evening, McNamara and Rusk agreed that the Sixth Fleet should steam at normal speed until it reached a position approximately 1 day's distance from the Eastern end of the Mediterranean. (Notes of telephone conversation at 7:20 p.m. on May 19 prepared by Rusk's Special Assistant C. Arthur Borg; National Archives and Records Administration, RG 59, Rusk Files: Lot 72 D 192, Telephone Calls) JCS telegram 5893 to USCINCEUR, May 20, confirmed telephone instructions that elements of the Sixth Fleet should be moved to the Eastern Mediterranean, with the center of gravity of the area of operations within 2 days' steaming of the Eastern shore, and the Eastern edge no more than 1 day's time. (Johnson Library, National Security File, NSC Histories, Middle East Crisis, Vol. 7, Appendix H)

Attached is a summary of present dispositions of the major fleet elements.[4]

Townsend Hoopes

---

[4] The attachment, entitled "Sixth Fleet—Position of Major Units, 19 May 1967" lists CTG 61.7 (Com PhibRon 6), with 1,431 Marines on the USS *Cambria*, in Naples; CTG 60.1, USS *America* and 3 DDs, with approximately 120 Marines on board, in Livorno and CTG 60.2, USS *Saratoga* and 6 DDs and 1 CLG, with approximately 100 Marines on board, en route to Palermo.

---

24. President's Daily Brief

Washington, May 20, 1967.

[Source: Johnson Library, National Security File, NSC Histories, Middle East Crisis, Vol. 6, Appendix A. Top Secret; [*codeword not declassified*]. 1 page of source text not declassified.]

---

25. Telegram From the Department of State to the Embassy in Israel[1]

Washington, May 20, 1967, 7:17 p.m.

198916. Ambassador Harman called urgently on Under Secretary Rostow morning May 20.

1. Harman said GOI pleased to note reaffirmation 1957 agreement re status Gulf of Aqaba.[2] GOI considers this most solid agreement between governments within framework U.S. commitment to Israel's security. GOI has also noted U.S. injunction Israel not move unless Egyptians take

---

[1] Source: National Archives and Records Administration, RG 59, Central Files 1967–69, POL ARAB–ISR. Secret; Priority; Nodis. Drafted by Davies, cleared by Popper, and approved by Under Secretary Rostow. Also sent priority to Cairo, Moscow, and USUN.

[2] Reference is apparently to Harman's May 18 conversations with Rostow and Battle; see Document 15.

action to close straits. Under Secretary replied there is no disagreement on gravity of situation. 1957 understanding valid but should be read in context President's letter re consultation. Should Egyptians block passage of Israeli shipping, we should consult as to measures to be taken.

2. Ambassador Harman reported "disturbing conversation" between FonMin Eban and Soviet Ambassador. Latter asserted terror incidents on Syrian border work of CIA, adding "We have warned you. You are responsible. You are responding to provocation by CIA." Harman said this raised possibility we may be getting double talk from Soviets. Supporting this, he noted Syrian press and radio trumpeting Soviet Novostny Agency statement that Soviets stood behind Syria and would support if Israel attacked. Ambassador thought it important to get to the Soviets since they and the Syrians now were "pointing the finger." Situation raised possibility of Soviet-Syrian-Egyptian collusion. He also stressed great importance of prompt public and diplomatic reaffirmation USG support of Israel against aggression. Under Secretary replied that request will be at forefront our considerations.

3. Under Secretary asked whether Israel knew French view on the validity of the Tripartite Declaration. Harman replied the French were taking serious view of situation and intervening in Cairo. Under Secretary said it would be useful if Israel could clarify French position for if situation becomes bad, Tripartite planning would be useful. Ambassador Harman indicated that while Israel had liaison with French military, there had been no joint planning.

4. Ambassador Harman reverted to importance Israel ascribed to right of passage through Gulf of Aqaba, noting that the British, French, and Canadians had been involved with us in 1957 assurances. Stressed importance U.S. policy remaining diplomatically apparent.

5. Harman said U.S. DefAtts briefed yesterday in Israel on danger posed Israel by UAR deployments which now clearly taking form offensive posture. This had required precautionary measures on Israel's part.

6. Ambassador Harman said Ambassador Barbour had been asked to see whether U.S. destroyer which had departed Gulf of Aqaba after visit Jordan could not reenter and visit Eilat. Davies (NEA) who present said ship was unarmed flagship COMIDEASTFOR and now in Yenbo. Department believed that given furor raised by PriMin Eshkol's remarks re role Sixth Fleet, unscheduled appearance U.S. naval unit might well aggravate situation.[3]

---

[3] Telegram 198809 to Tel Aviv, May 20, states that the Department had given careful consideration to Bitan's request for a U.S. destroyer visit to Eilat but had concluded that it would not contribute to a lessening of tension. (National Archives and Records Administration, RG 59, Central Files 1967–69, POL ARAB–ISR)

7. Ambassador noted Israeli intelligence reports UAR forces had gas and troops equipped with gas masks. Asked for urgent response Israel's request purchase 20,000 masks.[4] He noted that when gas first used Yemen, Golda Meir remarked that if Nasser gets to point of using gas on Arab brothers, we must expect the worst.

Rusk

---

[4] A May 19 memorandum from NSC Executive Secretary Bromley K. Smith to Walt Rostow states that Eugene Rostow had called to report that he had given Department of State approval to the shipment of 20,000 gas masks; the shipment was to be processed over the weekend. (Johnson Library, National Security File, Country File, Middle East Crisis, Vol. I)

---

26. Telegram From the Mission to the United Nations to the Department of State[1]

New York, May 20, 1967, 2149Z.

5388. Middle East Crisis.

1. I called on SYG and Bunche this noon right after release of announcement of his trip to Cairo. Told him I was pleased he was making trip and that I would say so publicly after meeting. On basis telecon with Under Secy Rostow, told him that while Israelis were playing situation cool, they were reappraising situation and now believe UAR had offensive intentions. Told him troop movements and dispositions of UAR forces indicated to them operations of offensive character. Bunche then said UN reports today were that there were heavy Syrian concentrations in Galilee area.

2. I told SYG we had a second concern which was UAR use of poison gas in Yemen. Said evidence included canisters with Cyrillic markings. Said we had grave apprehensions lest this gas also be employed in present circumstances, consequences of which would be grave. My own impression was that he would express apprehensions in Cairo on this point.

---

[1] Source: National Archives and Records Administration, RG 59, Central Files 1967–69, POL ARAB–ISR. Confidential; Priority; Exdis. Repeated to Cairo and Tel Aviv. Received at 7:33 p.m.

3. I also told him our current reports from AmEmb Cairo were alarming about mood now prevailing there. Told him I had spoken yesterday to El Kony (UAR), Tomeh (Syria), Fedorenko (USSR), all troop contributing countries, all members of SC except Keita (Mali), as well as reps of other Arab countries in area. Told him I had given El Kony and Tomeh solemn assurances that US was not involved in any steps in area in spite of anything Syrians were saying. Told SYG this applied to CIA as well as to other agencies of USG. There no CIA operation going on. There was nothing to it. Matter had been carefully reviewed with Director of CIA. Allegations were complete nonsense. Told him UAR line, elaborated in *Al Ahram* this morning, was alleging great plot, in which culmination would be establishment of UNEF on Syrian frontier after battle between Israel and Arabs.

4. Told SYG we were receiving confusing signals from Sovs. Noted I had obtained nothing really from Fedorenko except his statement USSR did not want war and that he would report to his govt. Also noted Ukrainian and Byelorussian reps yesterday had expressed satisfaction over current situation and noted UN ought to get out of peace-keeping business and that Fedorenko had said this demonstrated undesirability of UN force under SYG control. Noted for his private information only that in Moscow after Thompson had said US was using its influence against any kind of use of force no matter what the provocation was, Dobrynin said USSR would do no less. Added however that since that time Sovs appeared to be supporting stories of US involvement and even to have initiated them. (I also told SYG our approaches urging restraint upon Israel had been at highest levels.)

5. SYG said he going to area with some trepidation. He may or may not have any success. He had some ideas which he had discussed with Martin (Canada) which Martin fully shared. His basic idea was to enlarge the effect of UNTSO in area as well as on other frontiers. This would have to include enlarging of the units. He said first step already under way. He then read telegram from General Bull reporting from EIMAC Chairman that Egyptians had suggested EIMAC occupy three platoon camps in Gaza as observation posts. SYG said he had sent instructions to accept this immediately and he expected eleven UNMOs, transferred from other posts, to be there within two days.

6. SYG said that for 17 years Secretariat had exercised its initiative to augment or diminish observers, who had once totaled over 750. More recently Sovs had for first time questioned SYG's authority to do this with respect to UNMOGIP in Oct 1965. In private Fedorenko had complained mainly about national composition of the observers, but in Feb he had also had confidential note from Fedorenko taking position he

could not increase UNTSO without SC action. Thought it highly likely Sovs would raise this matter if he took any current steps and suggested that perhaps SC meeting would be wisest course in present circumstances. I replied that of course there was current opposition to SC meeting on the part of some members and that both Israel and UAR were against it. I said this could not be controlling. I noted that SC could not, for example, stand aside if fighting broke out. With respect to enlargement of TSO I said I thought current situation might be distinguishable from normal augmentation.

7. I asked him whether in request for UNMOs UAR had included Sharm el Sheikh. He said no but that he proposed to raise matter of Sharm el Sheikh in major effort in Cairo. (He did not elaborate on the context in which he would raise it, but he is clearly fully conscious of implications that would flow from stopping shipping.) Bunche said UAR and UN were currently in joint occupation of Sharm el Sheikh and that so far UAR forces had not sought to interfere with shipping which is going through the straits.

8. I noted that if UNTSO and IMAC operations were to be recommenced Israeli cooperation would be required. Told him I had already advised Rafael this morning of my personal view that Israel should reexamine its position on this matter and I had subsequently had confirmation this was Washington's viewpoint as well.

9. I also suggested that inasmuch as Israeli cooperation would be required he should also consider extending his visit to include Jerusalem and Damascus. SYG replied he thought not now and that inclusion of Israel might jeopardize efforts. On basis of how matters developed in Cairo, however, visit to Israel would not be precluded. He said he planned to be gone about 2-1/2 days, returning to NY next Friday. I stressed again importance of having Israel on board in whatever his plans were. Urged him to tell Israelis in advance about UNMOs going into Gaza and desirability of refraining from any more public comment than necessary until matters worked out with all concerned. SYG said there were three stops on his plane trip to Cairo but he would not see press at any of them. I again offered to provide a jet if he needed it, painted with UN markings if he wished, but he said he thought his present arrangements for commercial travel would be satisfactory. We both agreed to touch base on Monday[2] before his departure. I read him my proposed statement dealing with his report of this morning to the SC and he expressed approval of our statement.

Goldberg

---

[2] May 22.

27.   Telegram From the Embassy in Syria to the Department of State[1]

Damascus, May 20, 1967, 1330Z.

1156. Subject: Arab-Israel Crisis. Ref: Damascus 1151[2] (Notal).

1. In hour and half session with FonMin Makhus (reftel) early afternoon May 20, whom Ambassador met without usual accompaniment DCM or Pol Chief at FonMin request, Makhus discussed points raised by Ambassador in friendly but inflexible manner.

2. In response Ambassador's caution at explosive potential recent arms buildup, Makhus replied US aware of threats Israeli leaders have made against Syria which left SARG and UARG no choice but believe Israeli aggressive intents. Said also SARG investigations showed Israeli troops in DMZ. SARG and UARG thus mobilized and made mutual defense treaty operative. Said although Israel created tense situation, measures SARG and UARG have taken are welcomed by all Arabs. Palestine issue is "sacred cause" and will never die, never be extinguished. Citing Crusaders, Makhus said "occupation of another's territory can never be eternal." Reiterating all Arabs ready, Makhus wanted USG understand any Israeli attack will be answered by war, regardless of consequences.

3. As for guerrillas, which Ambassador noted could trigger war no one wants, Makhus emphasized Palestinians are single people, wherever scattered, and no one has right rule them. They need not ask anyone's permission fight for usurped homeland. Having waited 18 years for UN carry out resolutions which Israel refuses honor, Palestinians have right self-determination and right fight for freedoms guaranteed by UN Charter, UN resolutions, and internal law. SARG refuses "for once and for all" take any responsibility for actions Palestinians in their fight for rights and for despoiled homeland, since Palestinians not under command Syria. "Israel took their land; Israel must deal with Palestinian people." As for infiltrators, "all might US armed forces

---

[1] Source: National Archives and Records Administration, RG 59, Central Files 1967–69, POL ARAB–ISR. Confidential; Priority. Repeated Priority to Amman and to Baghdad, Beirut, Cairo, Jerusalem, London, Jidda, Moscow, Paris, Tel Aviv, CINCSTRIKE, DIA, and Aleppo. Received at 12:56 p.m. Advance copies were sent to the White House, USIA, CIA, DOD, and NSA at 1:45 p.m.

[2] In telegram 1151 from Damascus, May 20, Ambassador Smythe reported that he was seeking an appointment with Syrian Foreign Minister Makhus to urge Syrian restraint, restate U.S. policy on aggression in the area, support UN peacekeeping instruments and measures, caution that a guerrilla incident could spark a conflagration, and inform Makhus that the United States was counselling restraint at the highest levels of the Israeli Government. (Ibid.)

Vietnam unable contain guerrillas there." SARG refuses be threatened by others every time Palestinian takes action as infiltrator, such accusations being but excuse for aggression against Syria. Re UN peacekeeping, said SARG and all other Arabs had welcomed UNEF, but defended UARG right to request departure.

4. As for Kennedy statement endorsed by President Johnson,[3] Makhus called Syria victim of aggression. Mere presence Israel is aggression against Arab nation which USG should oppose. Not to US advantage support such aggression or equate acts of Israeli aggression with Arab actions in fight for freedom, independence, and to regain lost territory. Neither US nor any other country has right serve as deterrent those fighting for rights or stop fight between independent states when one side struggling regain its heritage. Makhus concluded SARG thus does not accept Kennedy statement as operative in preventing Arabs from fighting for own rights.

5. In reply Ambassador's emphatic denial that USG or any agency seeking overthrow SARG or plot against it, Makhus said he pleased have USG deny such role and hoped sincerely US will prove it speaks truth and show this in practical manner. Said he hoped fog between our countries and people would be dispersed, and that American people and "Embassy staff in Syria" will work to see no conspiracy against SARG occurs.

Smythe

---

[3] Concerning President Kennedy's statement of May 8, 1963, see footnote 5, Document 5. President Johnson endorsed Kennedy's statement in a toast at a dinner for Israeli President Zalman Shazar, August 2, 1966. For text, see *Public Papers of the Presidents of the United States: Lyndon B. Johnson, 1966,* Book II, pp. 796–797.

28.   Telegram From the Embassy in the United Arab Republic to
        the Department of State[1]

Cairo, May 21, 1967, 0900Z.

7760. Middle East Crisis. Ref: Cairo 7754.[2]

1. Last night Parker took up with Zakaria Muhieddin's secretary
Mustafa Abdul Aziz latter's remarks as reported Miles Copeland (para
2 reftel).[3] Abdul Aziz said: (a) regular UAR units as opposed PLA occupying all front line positions and under strict order not to start anything. If Israelis began anything however, Egyptians, who had largest
concentration troops and heavy equipment ever seen in Sinai, would
react immediately and would crush Israelis with brute force. He hoped
Israelis started something. This time Egyptians would win. (b) Altho he
personally reluctant believe stories of US-Israeli plot, series US actions,
beginning with our forcing Germans to supply arms to Israel and culminating recent spate pro-Israeli and anti-UAR statements by public
figures in US, including McNamara, Javits, Robert Kennedy and
McCloskey, who said we wanted strengthen UNEF, meaning stationing
it on Syrian border, created strong presumption story of plot was true.

2. When Parker pointed out that statements by US Senators not
statements official US policy and that we had been endeavoring restrain
Israelis as well as Arabs, Abdul Aziz asked why there had been no statement by responsible American allocating responsibility fairly. Israelis
had threatened attack Syria and had massed troops near border for that
purpose. USG had said nothing. As soon as UAR took defensive measures however USG had gone into orbit. It clear we prepared protect
Israel but didn't care about Egypt or Syria.

3. When told Egyptians committing major mistake in basing their
estimates of situation on what Soviets and Syrians telling them about

---

[1] Source: National Archives and Records Administration, RG 59, Central Files
1967–69, POL ARAB–ISR. Secret; Priority. Repeated to Amman, Baghdad, Beirut, London,
Tel Aviv, and USUN. Received at 6:18 a.m. Passed to the White House, DOD, CIA, USIA,
and NSA at 6:45 a.m.

[2] In telegram 7754 from Cairo, May 20, Chargé Nes declared that the UAR
Government regarded the situation as serious and was "not play acting" and reported
indications of UAR officials' state of mind. (Ibid.)

[3] In paragraph 2 of telegram 7754, Nes reported that Aziz had told Miles Copeland
that UAR forces had been given orders to "hit Israelis with everything they have" if anything erupted along the border and that Palestine Liberation Organization leader Ahmed
Shukairy had moved his headquarters to Gaza, PLA units were in the front lines, feda-
yeen raids would occur, and if the Israelis retaliated, the Egyptians would strike back.
Aziz had also said that Nasser "believes what he says about CIA plots and this is major
factor contributing to present crisis." Copeland, a former CIA officer, was in Cairo on private business. Nes commented that his account might not be accurate.

our intentions, Abdul Aziz said Egyptians not relying on either of those powers for its assessment but had reached their conclusions all by themselves. Those conclusions based essentially on public record USG statements and actions, including its failure deny Eshkol remarks that we had urged Israelis rely on Sixth Fleet for their protection.[4] He produced sheaf of carefully arranged Arabic translations news reports and public statements from US. Seemed particularly incensed by Robert Kennedy warning to Arabs not to attack Israel.

4. *Comment:* It clear to us UARG had talked itself into believing story of US-Israeli plot to create incident which would result in stationing UNEF along Israel-Syrian border. It also seems clear that Nasser has resolved to deal with this imagined threat thru massive power play which, if successful, will be his biggest political victory since Suez, even if no shot is fired. If Syrians continue Fedayiin incursions and Israelis retaliate, there will be serious hostilities and Arabs apparently confident they can win in long run. If Israelis do not retaliate, Nasser will have forced them to back down and will have won first Arab victory over Israelis, and incidentally will have won another victory over US in Arab eyes. By his present posture Nasser has abandoned his traditional position of not wishing to start fight except at time and place of his own choosing because timing of hostilities now in hands Fatah-Asifa and Israelis. Do not believe Nasser would have done so unless he fairly confident of victory. He is playing for keeps and we should make no mistake this regard. We hope visit of UNSYG will lead to at least temporary deescalation of war atmosphere now prevailing.

Nes

---

[4] Reference is to a statement made by Eshkol in an April 1967 interview. Asked whether he would expect help from the United States if Israel were attacked in force by its neighbors, he stated that Israel would rely primarily on its own army but that he would expect help, "especially if I take into consideration all the solemn promises that have been made to Israel. We get these promises when we ask the United States for arms and are told: 'Don't spend your money. We are here. The Sixth Fleet is here.' My reply to this advice is that the Sixth Fleet might not be available fast enough for one reason or another, so Israel must be strong on its own." (*U.S. News and World Report*, April 17, 1967, p. 76)

29. Telegram From the Department of State to the Embassy in the United Kingdom[1]

Washington, May 21, 1967, 9:49 p.m.

198959. Middle East Crisis.

Ambassador Dean (UK) called on Under Secretary Rostow this afternoon and made following points:

1. He invited comments on draft of letter George Brown is planning to send to U Thant before Thant's trip to Cairo, assuring him of UK support for a peaceful solution through the UN, urging Thant to seek to persuade UAR to allow UNEF to remain in Gaza area and pressing strongly for a continuing UN presence in area either in form of expanded UNTSO or some new UN body. Brown stresses continuation of UN presence in Sharm-el-Sheikh and emphasizes importance UK attaches to rights of free navigation in international waterways and seriousness with which UK would view any interference with free passage in Gulf of Aqaba. Brown also urges U Thant to visit Tel Aviv and to hold an immediate meeting of Security Council after his return from area.

2. Dean said London agreed that US–UK assessments of situation are similar and wants to keep in close touch. UK had no objection to bringing others into these consultations from time to time but would object to joint daily meetings with French.[2] UK view was that information passed in meetings with French would leak and would also lead to queries about the present status of the Tripartite Declaration which the UK regarded as out of date. Rostow indicated US position was that the principles of the Tripartite Declaration still apply. Dean indicated that in UK view Tripartite Declaration had been superseded by the

---

[1] Source: National Archives and Records Administration, RG 59, Central Files 1967–69, POL ARAB–ISR. Secret; Exdis. Drafted by Eugene Rostow and his Staff Assistant Robert T. Grey, Jr., and approved by Eugene Rostow. Also sent to Paris and repeated to USUN, Tel Aviv, Cairo, and Damascus.

[2] Telegram 198944 to London and Paris, May 21, reported that regular meetings had been held concerning the Middle East crisis with British and French representatives in Washington and at the United Nations, and summarized the discussion at a meeting held in Washington that day. The statements by Ambassador Dean recorded in paragraphs 3 and 4 of telegram 198959 were in response to questions raised by U.S. representatives at that meeting. (Ibid.) French Ambassador Lucet told Under Secretary Rostow on May 23 that while the French wished to continue regular U.S.-French exchanges on Middle East questions, they would prefer not to continue on a tripartite basis, since regular daily meetings on such a basis might become conspicuous and create false ideas in public opinion. (Ibid., POL 27 ARAB–ISR)

Kennedy–Macmillan statements of 1963.[3] Dean noted that in Macmillan's statement UK had laid great stress on UN role in any Middle East dispute and that UK view was that object of Kennedy–Macmillan declarations was to move away from earlier Tripartite Declaration. Macmillan had made his statement on that basis. Rostow indicated that there were several reasons why it would be advantageous now to breathe new life into Tripartite Declaration if at all possible. US takes the view that Tripartite Declaration is right policy for three governments. Dean indicated that he would seek further clarification of UK position from London.

3. Dean stated that while UK wished to have close continuing political consultations with US HMG did not wish to become involved in military contingency planning at this time, especially contingency planning which involved possible military action outside of the UN. Rostow indicated that primary US objective was to use all political means to prevent the outbreak of hostilities but that the possibility of a flare-up could not be excluded and it was unlikely we could obtain Security Council action if hostilities did break out. Therefore we cannot ignore risk of being required to honor previous commitments.

4. Dean indicated UK felt it would heighten tension now to advise British tourists to leave or stay away from the area and that it was not necessary to do so at this time. They were taking line their Missions should inform inquirers that there were obvious dangers in the area.

5. Rostow indicated USG was considering presenting a written paper to all the governments in area reiterating US position. Such a paper could be presented jointly by US, UK and French, or separately by the three governments, as well as by Canada, with respect especially to Gulf of Aqaba. We would have draft for his consideration tomorrow.

6. Dean passed copies of exchange of letters between Wilson and Eshkol. Eshkol's letter follows line taken with President Johnson. Wilson letter states UK has made strong representations to Syrians regarding need to stop infiltration of terrorists and UK misgivings about dangers involved in forceful reprisals. Wilson also asked Eshkol to reconsider GOI's own policy of not permitting UNEF to operate on Israeli territory and stressed UK support through UN to secure free passage through the Gulf of Aqaba. Wilson also stated that George Brown will urge USSR to counsel restraint during his trip to Moscow.

---

[3] In a statement in the House of Commons, May 14, 1963, Prime Minister Harold Macmillan endorsed President Kennedy's statement of May 8, 1963 (see footnote 5, Document 5). The text of Macmillan's statement is in *Hansard*, vol. 677, col. 142.)

Rostow subsequently called Dean and brought following statement made in Commons by Wilson on April 13, 1965 to his attention:

"The tripartite declaration of 1950 was intended to express the policy of Britain, France and the United States at that time. It has not been retracted. I expressed the government's deep concern for the peace and stability of the Middle East when, in the course of the foreign affairs debate on 16 December, 1964, I endorsed Mr. Macmillan's statement of 14 May 1963."

For London and Paris: In the light of the ambiguities revealed in this conversation, you should now urgently request authoritative confirmation from HMG and GOF that Trilateral Declaration of 1950 remains the policy of those two Governments, as it is of ours.

In this period of stress among allies on so many issues it is of particular importance that our unity on fundamentals be reaffirmed. The implications of failure in our strenuous efforts to prevent hostilities from breaking out in the Middle East are far-reaching. A war in the Middle East would gravely and fundamentally affect the security of all three countries, of Europe, and of the West. We believe a strong clear stand now is indispensable to deter those who might be tempted to take advantage of such a situation.

FYI for Paris: You may have copy as we do of Confidential French letter to GOI which was never made public. End FYI.

Rusk

30.   **Telegram From the Department of State to the Embassy in Israel**[1]

Washington, May 21, 1967, 9:02 p.m.

198955. Please deliver following reply from President to Prime Minister Eshkol's May 18 letter (Tel Aviv 3648).[2]

Dear Mr. Prime Minister:

Thank you for your prompt and detailed reply to my message of May 18.

Ambassador Barbour has informed me of your assurances, conveyed through Mr. Bitan yesterday, that the measures your Government is taking are precautionary in nature and that you will continue to do all you can to avoid further deterioration of the present grave situation on your borders.[3] By continuing to display steady nerves you can, I am convinced make a major contribution to the avoidance of hostilities.

I fully agree that, for tranquillity to return, there is an urgent need for the cessation of terrorism and the reversal of military movements of the type we have witnessed during the past week. We and our friends have done all we can to make this amply clear in both Cairo and Damascus.

As you know, we have also been in touch with the Soviet Government and are somewhat encouraged by the tone of their reaction to our approaches. I am confident they are under no illusions about the firmness of our commitment to support appropriate measures in the United Nations, or outside,[4] to counter aggression or the threat of

---

[1] Source: National Archives and Records Administration, RG 59, Central Files 1967–69, POL ARAB–ISR. Secret; Priority; Nodis. Drafted by Atherton; cleared by Battle, Eugene Rostow, and Walt Rostow; and approved by Eugene Rostow for Rusk with revisions. The President's handwritten revisions appear on a draft copy sent to him with a May 21 memorandum from Walt Rostow noting that it had been cleared with Rusk. (Johnson Library, National Security File, Country File, Middle East Crisis, Vol. I)

[2] Document 13. Telegram 198954 to Tel Aviv, May 21, instructed Barbour in delivering the letter to stress the need to do everything possible to restore and maintain the effectiveness of the United Nations in the area. The purpose of this, it noted, was to help moderate Israeli opposition to any UN observation or peacekeeping activity on Israel's side of the Armstice Line. (National Archives and Records Administration, RG 59, Central Files 1967–69, POL ISR–US)

[3] Barbour reported the conversation in telegram 3681 from Tel Aviv, May 19. (Ibid., POL ARAB–ISR)

[4] Johnson substituted the words "or outside" for "or to take other action on our own".

aggression in the Middle East. As you so well know, that commitment was made publicly by Presidents Truman, Eisenhower, and Kennedy as well as myself, and by the British, French and United States governments in their Tripartite Declaration in 1950. I can assure you that I hope all parties concerned will act firmly and in unison to meet any challenges to the peace.[5] We have suggested to your Ambassador that you consult, as we are doing, with the other two governments with respect to these assurances.

So far as a United Nations presence on the boundary between Israel and the United Arab Republic is concerned, we strongly objected, as you know, to the Secretary General's decision with regard to the status of the UNEF in Sinai. We continue to regard a United Nations presence in the area as important and desirable.

I have been giving serious thought to the question of what further steps we might take to ease the situation and am giving most urgent consideration to your suggestion to Ambassador Barbour that a public statement by me would have a calming effect. In making this decision, I am weighing the possible bearing of such a statement now on Secretary General Thant's visit to Cairo. I am sure you will agree that nothing should be said or done at this time which might complicate or distract attention from the efforts of the Secretary General. In the meantime the problems discussed in your letter to me are occupying the attention of the highest officials of this government and will continue to do so until they are resolved.

With personal regards,

Sincerely,

Lyndon B. Johnson[6]

Rusk

---

[5] Before Johnson's revisions, the previous two sentences read: "As you know, that commitment, which has been made publicly by Presidents Truman, Eisenhower, and Kennedy as well as myself, and by the British, French and United States governments in their Tripartite Declaration in 1950, definitely includes Israel. I can assure you that it remains firm so far as we are concerned."

[6] Barbour reported in telegram 3712 from Tel Aviv, May 22, that he had delivered the message to Bitan that day. He had stated that the United States felt it necessary to do everything possible to restore and maintain UN effectiveness in the area and had taken issue with Israeli opposition to a UN presence on the Israeli side of the border. (National Archives and Records Administration, RG 59, Central Files 1967–69, POL ARAB–ISR) Foreign Minister Eban's reaction had been "strongly negative" when Barbour raised this possibility on May 21. (Telegram 3692 from Tel Aviv, May 21; ibid.) Eugene Rostow and Battle both pressed Harman on this point in a May 22 meeting. (Telegram 198964 to Tel Aviv, May 21; ibid.)

31. Telegram From the Embassy in the United Kingdom to the Department of State[1]

London, May 22, 1967, 1800Z.

9732. For Secretary from McGeorge Bundy.

1. I had an hour with George Brown this morning and he spent most of it on the Middle East. I pointed out, of course, that I was here as a private citizen. But George is an old friend, and there was no holding him.

2. Embassy tells me Brown's comments on the Middle East diverged somewhat from those of his civil servants. He is not at all sure that Nasser will stop with ousting the UNEF force from the Egyptian-Israeli border and in particular is worried that Nasser may move to interdict shipping into the Gulf of Aqaba. While Brown, like his civil servants, is immediately focused on trying to get U Thant to play a more effective role, he was quite strong in saying that if access to the Gulf is impeded and thus becomes a freedom-of-the-seas issue and if the UN then fails to provide an effective means to deal with this problem, the British will probably feel able to find some other direct way of doing so, though they would hope to be able to enlist the help of other maritime nations. Brown strongly implied that in view of their military and naval forces presently East of Suez, this is probably the piece of the Egypt–Israel problem the British could and would be most disposed to take a direct hand in themselves. The freedom-of-the-seas context would in Brown's view reduce the risk of hostile reactions from other Arabs.

3. With respect to the Tripartite Declaration, Brown pointed out that the Labor government is clearly on record in support of Macmillan's 1963 statement. They construe this essentially as relieving the British of their commitments under the Tripartite Declaration. I think the chance of reversing this view is zero. However, when I suggested that it would be both unnecessary and undesirable to underline this position at this time Brown seemed to agree. He is to make a television statement on the Middle East tonight and I am hopeful he will avoid comment on the status of the Tripartite Declaration. David Bruce has phoned him to reiterate the desirability of avoiding a statement and so keeping the situation flexible.

[1] Source: National Archives and Records Administration, RG 59, Central Files 1967–69, POL ARAB–ISR. Secret; Immediate; Nodis. Received at 2:18 p.m.

4. On Viet Nam, I found Brown understanding of American problems and quite staunch in support. He was also modest and realistic in appraising how much the British (and he personally) can do with the Russians in helping promote negotiations. My impression is that he is less interested in this role than his boss.

Bruce

---

32. **Telegram From the Mission to the United Nations to the Department of State**[1]

New York, May 22, 1967, 2111Z.

5399. Subj: Middle East Crisis.

May 22, 1967

Dear Mr. Secretary General:

As you depart for your highly significant trip to the Middle East I wish to convey to you the best wishes of the United States Government and our support for your efforts to preserve the peace and maintain an effective United Nations presence in the area.

We share your view that the situation in the Middle East is more menacing than at any time since 1956. We are especially concerned that, whatever intentions may have been when the current crisis began, miscalculation or uncontrolled provocation may now slide the area into direct conflict. Every effort must be made to avoid this and to preserve for the future, at a minimum, the relative calm that has prevailed in the Middle East for the past ten years. The United Nations and its effective presence on the ground is in our view the most likely means through which this might be accomplished.

I have already expressed to you the profound regret of the United States Government about the decision to withdraw UNEF from the area. While we are not unaware of the physical and factual problems which confronted you, nevertheless it was and is our view that a decision of this magnitude required as a minimum adequate consultation

---

[1] Source: National Archives and Records Administration, RG 59, Central Files 1967–69, POL ARAB–ISR. Confidential; Priority; Exdis. Repeated Priority to Cairo, and to Tel Aviv. Received at 7:33 p.m.

with all appropriately concerned governments, including our own. The first official information the United States received of the initial exchange in which the basic decision was taken was over 16 hours after it had taken place.

I have also indicated to you that it was and remains the view of the United States that while non-enforcement peacekeeping operations require consent of the governments concerned, nevertheless in this instance the consent to the establishment of the force carried with it understandings regarding the circumstances of its withdrawal, and that in any event the final decision could only be appropriately taken after consideration by the General Assembly. The record to us is compelling. The manner and circumstances under which withdrawal of UNEF would be decided was thoroughly examined at the time of its establishment with a view to averting precipitate incidents of the sort we have just faced, and in fact the departure of the force to the United Arab Republic was delayed over this area.

The then Secretary General on November 13, 1956 completed a series of exchanges with the Foreign Minister of Egypt leading to the despatch of the force, stating that "withdrawal of consent leading to the withdrawal of forces before the task was completed, although within the rights of the Egyptian Government, would go against its acceptance of the basic resolution of the General Assembly" and that "the question of withdrawal would be a matter for discussion to the extent that different views were held as to whether the task established by the General Assembly was fulfilled or not".[2] The Secretary General made it clear to us, as to others, that the question of whether the task assigned to the force was completed would have to be submitted to the General Assembly. This was explicitly also his view with respect to the aide-mémoire concluded with Egypt and noted with approval by the General Assembly in Resolution 1121 (XI)[3] which followed shortly thereafter.

This corresponded to the views and understandings of other governments involved in the establishment of UNEF, including the United States. Our view on this was officially stated at various times. A memorandum to this effect delivered to the then Secretary General on March 15, 1957, on the occasion of a visit by him to Cairo, is attached.[4]

---

[2] For information concerning the exchanges under reference, see *Public Papers of the Secretaries-General of the United Nations*, Vol. III, Dag Hammarskjöld, 1956–1957, p. 369.

[3] The aide-mémoire on the basis for the UNEF presence in Egypt, annexed to Secretary-General Hammarskjöld's report to the General Assembly of November 20, 1956, is printed ibid., pp. 375–376. It was noted with approval by the General Assembly in resolution 1121 (XI), November 24, 1956; see ibid., pp. 396–397.

[4] The text of the memorandum given to Secretary-General Hammarskjöld on March 15, 1957, prior to his visit to Cairo is printed in *Foreign Relations, 1955–1957*, vol. XVII, pp. 422–423.

I do not seek to document fully in this letter the history of this issue, other aspects of which I referred to in our conversation of May 17 in which I urged you to consult with the General Assembly before any decision was taken.[5] But I do wish to say that the United States, having itself brought the 1956 crisis to the Security Council against the wishes of its closest allies and having been one of the most firm supporters of UNEF throughout its history also had and continues to have a special concern in the matter.

We have refrained from commenting publicly on these matters other than to express our regret at the decision because of the extreme delicacy and gravity of the situation and because we do not believe such comment would be helpful to the United Nations in circumstances where it is already suffering in both general and informed opinion as a result of last week's developments. We are expressing ourselves in candor on this subject because of its overriding importance for the future and not out of any desire to second guess your actions, which we recognize were taken under difficult circumstances and obviously out of the best of motives.

I am sure we share the common view that the imperative task now is to make all possible efforts to turn aside the rising state of tension and the military buildup in the Middle East and re-establish conditions under which the prohibition of the use of force in any form, is fully respected. I have previously advised you that the United States Government is using its fullest diplomatic influence with all governments in the area, as with others, to this effect. I have also previously told you that any allegations that the United States Government or any of its agencies are engaged in a conspiracy in the Middle East are totally unfounded. These allegations have been mischievously and deliberately spread. You are authorized to convey our firm denial of them and our reaffirmation that the United States is opposed to any aggression or violence in the Middle East regardless of the direction from which it comes and whether it is direct or indirect.

As you go to Cairo you will be speaking on behalf of an organization which has repeatedly—both through the Security Council and through the General Assembly—called for the maintenance of peace in the Middle East. You will be speaking against the background of constructive exercise of United Nations authority in the area for twenty years. Nowhere in the world has the United Nations exercised such decisive influence in the interests of peace, and we know that your objective will be to revitalize that contribution to the maximum.

---

[5] Reference is apparently to the May 18 conversation reported in Document 11.

In particular, the United States urges that in your discussions in the area your primary specific objective, in the pursuit of restoring peaceful conditions, be to retain the maximum possible degree of effective United Nations presence on the ground along the frontiers and points of sensitivity between the United Arab Republic and Israel. We fully share your view as expressed in your report to the Security Council that the Gaza Strip and the Sharm-el-Sheikh are particularly sensitive areas, involving as they do a large number of refugees and the Palestine Liberation Organization and the international character of the Straits of Tiran and Gulf of Aqaba.

In this connection, you are no doubt aware of the policy of the United States Government with respect to the Straits of Tiran and the Gulf of Aqaba as stated by Ambassador Lodge in the General Assembly on March 1, 1957, a policy which remains that of the United States Government today:

"The United States believes that the Gulf comprehends international waters and that no nation has the right to prevent free and innocent passage in the Gulf and through the Straits giving access thereto. We have in mind not only commercial usage, but the passage of pilgrims on religious missions, which should be fully respected.

"The United States recalls that on January 28, 1950, the Egyptian Ministry of Foreign Affairs informed the United States that the Egyptian occupation of the two islands of Tiran and Senafir at the entrance of the Gulf of Aqaba was only to protect the islands themselves against possible damage or violation and that 'this occupation being in no way conceived in a sprit of obstructing in any way innocent passage through the stretch of water separating these two islands from the Egyptian coast of Sinai, it follows that this passage, the only practicable one, will remain free as in the past, in conformity with international practices and recognized principles of the law of nations.'

"In the absence of some overriding decision to the contrary, as by the International Court of Justice, the United States, on behalf of vessels of United States registry, is prepared to exercise the right of free and innocent passage and to join with others to secure general recognition of this right."[6]

The right of free and innocent passage through these waters is a vital interest of the international community and a vital interest, as you know, of the State of Israel in particular. I hope you will convey to the

---

[6] For the complete text of Lodge's statement before the General Assembly on March 1, 1957, see Department of State *Bulletin*, March 18, 1957, pp. 431–434. The quoted paragraphs are from the published version of an aide-mémoire that Secretary of State John Foster Dulles gave Israeli Ambassador Abba Eban on February 11, 1957, which was made public in slightly revised form on February 17, 1957. For text of the published version of the aide-mémoire, see ibid., March 11, 1957, pp. 392–393. The text of the aide-mémoire as given to Eban on February 11, 1957, is printed in *Foreign Relations, 1955–1957*, vol. XVII, pp. 132–134.

UAR the conviction that any interference whatever with these international rights could have the gravest international consequences.

What the details of a continued effective United Nations presence on the ground would be we do not seek at this point to define, as this necessarily must be explored in the first instance in negotiations with the parties concerned. But we do believe that you should not yield on the principle of an effective United Nations presence on the ground, the experience of so many years having demonstrated the decisive contribution it can make.

While the situation between the United Arab Republic and Israel is currently acute because of the movements of troops and ships and extensive mobilization involved, we trust also that you will give close attention to the problems on other frontiers, especially that between Syria and Israel. The record of Security Council action in the past two years demonstrates that recent tensions have most often arisen in that area, and the current critical situation clearly arises from those troubles. Questions of the degree to which the armistice agreement is really being carried out and of the capability of United Nations machinery are both involved. We concur in your statement that El Fatah activities are a major factor and that some recent incidents indicate a new level of organization and training as well as your statement opposing resort to force by any party and appeal to all parties to observe the armistice agreements.[7] We would accordingly urge that you appropriately consult the governments concerned about these problems as well.

From all parties concerned we suggest that a first objective should be to obtain immediate assurance of peaceful intent and a commitment to remove troops from direct juxtaposition with each other. While this may be easiest to achieve with regular forces it will be equally if not more important that irregular groups such as the Palestine Liberation Army and the El Fatah organization be promptly restrained.

You might also wish to consider other steps you might take with the parties at the outset, such as a special message to their heads of state urging them to exercise the greatest reserve and to make no adverse changes in the status quo while your consultations are proceeding.

Whatever agreements you work out for a continuing effective United Nations presence should, of course, be generally acceptable, as presumably others than the United Arab Republic will also be involved. Consequently I would renew my suggestion that you seriously contemplate proceeding after Cairo to Damascus and to Tel Aviv before finalizing any arrangements.

---

[7] Secretary-General Thant made these statements in response to a question at a luncheon of the United Nations Correspondents Association on May 11; for text, see *Public Papers of the Secretaries-General of the United Nations*, Vol. VII, U Thant, 1965–1967, p. 414.

We will of course be carefully watching the situation ourselves as a member of the Security Council while you are on your important mission.

The United States, of course, would not wish to initiate any steps which would interfere with the Secretary General's efforts to pacify the situation in the Middle East. Nevertheless, conscious of the primary responsibility of the Security Council for maintenance of international peace, we shall continue to give the closest attention to developments and will be consulting further with other Council members to review what other constructive steps may be required in the interest of maintaining peace.

We wish you Godspeed and you carry with you our hopes that you will return with positive and constructive proposals to report to the Security Council, the organ with primary responsibility for the maintenance of international peace and security. Should you not make satisfactory progress, we believe that the present state of tension in the area would make it imperative for you to call a meeting of the Security Council in accordance with Article 99 of the Charter.

With best wishes for a successful mission in the interest of peace.

Sincerely yours,

Arthur J. Goldberg

[Omitted here is the text of the memorandum cited in footnote 4.]

Goldberg

---

33. Telegram From the Mission to the United Nations to the Department of State[1]

New York, May 22, 1967, 2350Z.

5405. Re: Middle East Crisis.

I called on SYG and Bunche this afternoon accompanied by Pedersen to convey our letter prior to his departure (USUN 5399),[2] to

---

[1] Source: National Archives and Records Administration, RG 59, Central Files 1967–69, POL ARAB–ISR. Confidential; Immediate; Exdis. Repeated Priority to Cairo, and to Tel Aviv. Received at 9:41 p.m. and passed to the White House on May 23 at 12:20 a.m.

[2] Document 32.

discuss his mission and to wish Godspeed. SYG said he was scheduled to arrive back in NY at 3:30 p.m. on Friday and would want to consult on Saturday with perm members of SC, UNEF Advisory Comite, and troop contribution countries. Said he would be cancelling his appearance at Pacem in Terris tomorrow or Wed.

I told SYG we had letter to deliver to him expressing views of USG which I would give to him at end of meeting and substance of which I would discuss. In addition I had one statement of very grave importance to make. In light of tensions in area US had been called upon to reaffirm commitments four of our Preses had made with respect to protecting any countries in ME against aggression. Noted original expression was contained in Tripartite Declaration 1950 and that Preses Truman, Eisenhower, Kennedy and Johnson had independently reaffirmed and restated US commitment. Our basic commitment was to support appropriate measures in UN or outside to counter aggression or threat of aggression in ME.

I told him I wished to say what we had not said publicly, so that he would know as he went to Cairo, that the US would keep that commitment. I observed that this carried with it grave implications and added that we were of course tremendously concerned that efforts should be made within UN context. We therefore completely supported him and all he could do to pacify situation in the area. We were committed to prevent aggression in the interest of the political independence and territorial integrity of states in the ME. This we had said on various occasions, including statements I had made in SC last year.

I told him we may or not not yet have to say publicly what I had just told him. But I thought there should be no misunderstanding and that ambiguity might lead to great misunderstandings.

Bunche observed that Nasser would assert that UAR actions were reaction to Israeli invasion threat against Syria. He wondered whether SYG would be authorized to say that our commitment applied to Syria as well as to Israel. I replied that our policy applied to all govts in ME. It applied to the political independence and territorial integrity of all. He could therefore say that US position on this was very clear and that it was against any form of aggression in ME from any country whether overt or clandestine. Our aim was to seek solution to these problems within UN as there were too many confrontations in world already.

I added that our letter explicitly said there was no US design on Syria or conspiracy to overthrow other govts. Allegations to the contrary were nonsense. Our commitments extended to the whole area, and the letter contained explicit language which he was authorized to convey.

I then told him our letter contained a number of comments about the termination of UNEF, which had been a matter of grave concern in Wash. We had hoped for consultation. US had particularly been involved in the establishment of UNEF and we wanted to recall to him past record on questions of consent and withdrawal and US views with respect to them, in particular for his use with Nasser. US had broken with its allies at time of Suez in the interest of the law of the Charter and rights of Egypt. We had therefore taken different view than SYG re withdrawal. We had been instrumental in great measure in helping stop the attack on Egypt. If we had not acted when we did Nasser probably would not even be there now. There was a specific history on matter of consent and withdrawal and we believe Nasser was under obligation not to disturb situation and insist on withdrawal under circumstances such as prevailed.

Bunche asked if we planned to release letter. I said no and reiterated that in spite of domestic pressures and criticisms we had not made public our divergence of views on this issue, as others had, because we did not think it was in interest of UN. I reiterated that we respected motives of SYG on this and the practical problems with which he was concerned. Letter was for him but we had no objections to his talking to Nasser about these points because we thought Nasser, having done what he had done, now has some obligations to SYG and UN.

Future, however, was the important thing and a main purpose of presenting our views was to give him in writing our thoughts about necessity of preserving an effective UN presence in area.

I said this could not be done just on Nasser's own terms. From our contacts here it appeared that UAR line would be that they have now gotten rid of UNEF; if Israel would only be willing to revert to EIMAC and support it everything would be fine. I said this would not resolve the issue because it would require still further concessions to UAR position beyond what it has already gained. It would be necessary to bring all concerned on board and some way must be found to accommodate viewpoints of both parties.

I observed that Israel was involved too. We had told Israelis we want them to cooperate with SYG, but it would be necessary to obtain their views as well. I referred to my recommendation that he extend his visit to include Damascus and Tel Aviv, saying I understood why he did not wish to say anything about such visits now but I thought they would be highly desirable.

Referring to Sharm el-Sheikh I said this was one of most critical points. (Bunche interjected, "the most".) Bunche observed ships were still going through but commented critically on Jordanian broadcasts criticizing UAR for this. I told him we had intervened on this and believed they had stopped. I noted many maritime countries would be concerned with passage through straits, including, French, Scands, Israelis and ourselves, and read him section of letter in which we restated our position on transit. Told him consequences could not be predicted if transit through straits was interfered with. Told him he could use passage on our policy on straits with Nasser if he wished to.

I commented also that situation of refugees and PLO in Gaza Strip made that a danger point also. Bunche said they were aware of this. Added that info PLO had taken over UNEF post was not correct according to info from Rikhye. Added that El Auya would be another difficult point, as Nasser would raise fact that Israelis had occupied this area in 1955. SYG noted Israel still appeared be negative on EIMAC and TSOs on UAR border. I suggested that he might want to consider creating new instrument. Perhaps something with new initials would be acceptable to both sides where old one might not be.

I then said we thought early disengagement of forces would be especially helpful. Bunche interjected "yes" and SYG nodded. I said it was especially important that PLO be kept away from frontier. Noted that value of UNEF had been that it had controlled Sharm el-Sheik and had been shield against Liberation Army and refugee problems, as well as against retaliatory raids.

I noted also that origins of present problem came from Syrian frontier and said our letter re-enforced statements I [he] had made about hits on May 11 and 13.[3] We thought GAA should be respected and operate fully on that frontier and efforts needed to be made by him on this border as well as on UAR border.

Finally I called attention to our suggestion for his consideration that he might send messages to heads of states in area, either publicly or privately, calling for restraint and no adverse changes in status quo while he was consulting. He said he would give thought to this.

When I told him I thought he ought to report to SC when he returned and call meeting under Art 99 if necessary, he said he was clear he would have to make report to SC when he came back.

I also told him we had in various ways communicated with Sovs about the situation, the essence of our approaches being to appeal for cooperation with SYG in preserving peace in area.

SYG expressed his appreciation for our good wishes and indicated he well understood difficulties of mission he was undertaking and said he would study our views carefully.

Goldberg

---

[3] Thant's May 11 statement is cited in footnote 7, Document 32; his May 13 statement is not printed.

34.   Telegram From the Department of State to the Embassy in the United Arab Republic[1]

Washington, May 22, 1967, 8:49 p.m.

199704. Deliver following through quickest means to President Nasser from President Johnson:

"May 22, 1967

Dear President Nasser:

I have spent much of these past days thinking of the Middle East, of the problems you face, and the problems we face in that area.

Various of our common friends, including Ambassador Battle, have told me of your concern that the United States may have indicated an unfriendliness toward the UAR. This, I would wish you to know directly, is far from the truth.

I have watched from a distance your efforts to develop and modernize your country. I understand, I think, the pride and the aspirations of your people—their insistence that they enter as soon as possible the modern world and take their full part in it. I hope that we can find public as well as private ways to work more closely together.

I also understand the political forces at work in your region, the ambitions and tensions, the memories and the hopes.

Right now, of course, your task and mine is not to look back, but to rescue the Middle East—and the whole human community—from a war I believe no one wants. I do not know what steps Secretary General U Thant will be proposing to you; but I do urge you to set as your first duty to your own people, to your region, and to the world community this transcendent objective: the avoidance of hostilities.

The great conflicts of our time are not going to be solved by the illegal crossings of frontiers with arms and men—neither in Asia, the

---

[1] Source: National Archives and Records Administration, RG 59, Central Files 1967–69, POL ARAB–ISR. Secret; Flash; Nodis. Drafted and approved by Eugene Rostow and cleared by Walt Rostow. Repeated to USUN Eyes Only for Ambassador Goldberg. Walt Rostow sent a copy to the President at 4:30 p.m. with a covering note stating that he had dictated it and sent it to Eugene Rostow's Middle East task force that afternoon. Rostow added: "From previous experience I know Nasser is vulnerable to direct communication from the President of the United States." (Johnson Library, National Security File, Country File, Middle East Crisis, Vol. I) Another memorandum from Walt Rostow to Johnson that evening states that Eugene Rostow and Battle recommended sending messages to Prime Minister Eshkol and Syrian Prime Minister Atasi in case Nasser should release the President's message to him. (Ibid.) Messages from Johnson to Atasi and Eshkol urging restraint were transmitted in telegrams 199728 to Damascus and 199729 to Tel Aviv, both dated May 22. (National Archives and Records Administration, RG 59, Central Files 1967–69, POL ARAB–ISR)

Middle East, Africa, or Latin America. But that kind of action has already led to war in Asia, and it threatens the peace elsewhere.

I had expected that I might ask our Vice President to go to the Middle East to talk with you and other Arab leaders, as well as with the leaders of Israel. If we come through these days without hostilities, I would still hope that visit by my most trusted friend could result immediately.

Each of us who has the responsibility for leading a nation faces different problems shaped by history, geography, and the deepest feelings of our peoples. Whatever differences there may be in the outlook and interests of your country and mine, we do share an interest in the independence and progress of the UAR and the peace of the Middle East.

I address you at this critical moment in the hope that you share that assessment and will find it possible to act on it in the hours and days ahead.

Sincerely, Lyndon B. Johnson"

Rusk

35. Telegram From the Department of State to the Embassy in the United Arab Republic[1]

Washington, May 22, 1967, 9:38 p.m.

197710. *For Damascus, Tel Aviv, Amman, Beirut, Jidda, Algiers:* The following telegram is being sent to Cairo. You should make appropriate substitutions and deliver identical note to your government.

For London, Rome, Paris, Ottawa, Ankara, Moscow, Tehran: You should inform your host government of our action, and request that we remain in closest contact in light of reports of UAR decision to close Strait of Tiran.[2]

---

[1] Source: National Archives and Records Administration, RG 59, Central Files 1967–69, POL ARAB–ISR. Confidential; Immediate. Drafted by Bergus and Sterner, cleared by Atherton and Davies, and approved by Eugene Rostow. Repeated to London, Paris, Tel Aviv, Damascus, Amman, Beirut, Jerusalem, Ottawa, USUN, Moscow, Ankara, Tehran, Rome, Algiers, and Jidda.

[2] Telegram 199773 to Baghdad, Kuwait, and Sanaa, May 23, sent similar instructions to those Embassies. (Ibid.)

For Cairo:

1. You should request urgent meeting with Foreign Minister Riad to convey following note verbale:

2. In recent days, tension has again risen along armistice lines between Israel and Arab States. We agree with view of Secretary General of United Nations that situation there is matter of concern to international community as whole. It is our earnest wish to support efforts in which he is taking lead to reduce tensions, and to restore conditions of stability and trust.

3. We have no reason to believe, in present situation, that any of parties to Armistice Agreements between Arab States and Israel has intention of committing aggression. Danger, and it is grave danger, lies in misadventure and miscalculation. There is risk that those in authority in area may misapprehend or misinterpret intentions and actions of others.

4. Three aspects of situation cause us particular concern. First is continuing terrorism being carried out against Israel with Syrian approval, and at least in some cases, from Syrian territory. This is directly contrary to the General Armistice Agreements which call on signing governments to assure that no warlike act or act of hostility shall be conducted from territory of one against other party or against civilians or territory under control of that party. We believe General Armistice Agreements remain best basis for maintenance of peaceful conditions along borders. We hope that UAR will join us as well as other governments in urging all parties to Agreements to observe scrupulously their provisions.

5. Secondly, we are concerned that a precipitate withdrawal of the United Nations Emergency Force may make the problem of maintaining peace along the UAR-Israeli border more difficult. In our opinion, the presence of UNEF has been an important aid in preserving basic security along this border. USG supports Secretary General Thant's mission to Cairo and earnestly trusts that the UARG will explore fully with him possibilities for continued UN peacekeeping presence in some form along UAR-Israel border.

6. Third, USG considers it particularly important that the present cycle of troop build-up on both sides be arrested and reversed. We have noted statements of United Arab Republic and Israel indicating that their military movements are defensive in purpose and we would hope that both parties, as well as other states in the area which have taken military precautions, will return their forces to their normal dispositions. In doing so, they could perform an important service toward relieving the present tense situation.

7. We would also take this opportunity to reaffirm our continued adherence to principle of free access to Gulf of Aqaba for ships of all

nations. The right of free and innocent passage of these waters is a vital interest of the international community. We are convinced that any interference whatever with these international rights could have the gravest international consequences.[3]

8. In present situation UARG, as well as other Arab governments can rely on certainty that USG maintains firm opposition to aggression in the area in any form—overt or clandestine, carried out by regular military forces or irregular groups. This has been policy of this government under four successive administrations. Record of our actions over the past two decades, within and outside the United Nations is clear on this point.

9. In conclusion USG expresses its sincere hope that UAR will join it as well as numerous other nations in their efforts, both within UN and outside of that body, to bring about a lessening of tension and restoration of area stability.

Rusk

---

[3] Telegram 199681 to Cairo, May 22, sent at 7:58 p.m., requested confirmation of an Agence France Press report that Nasser had announced that the UAR had closed the Gulf of Aqaba to Israeli ships. It instructed the Embassy to convey to the UAR Government "our gravest concern" if this was true. (Ibid.) Nasser made the announcement in a May 22 speech to UAR air force officers, broadcast at 0400 Greenwich time on May 23. (FBIS Daily Report, May 23; Johnson Library, National Security File, NSC Histories, Middle East Crisis, Vol. I)

36.   Letter From the Under Secretary of State for Political Affairs
        (Rostow) to the Israeli Ambassador (Harman)[1]

Washington, May 22, 1967.

Dear Mr. Ambassador:

This will acknowledge your letter to me, delivered on May 20.[2] I
think it useful to review our conversation of May 18 in light of our several discussions over the last few days and President Johnson's messages to Prime Minister Eshkol of May 18, 1967,[3] and May 21, 1967,[4]
well as the United States Memorandum of February 11, 1957.[5]

In our view, as I said to you in our talks on the subject, the problem
of the Gulf of Aqaba, like other aspects of the situation, is governed by
the policy set forth in the President's letters to Prime Minister Eshkol.

The United States' position is that the present grave problem
should be handled in a peaceful manner, preferably through the United
Nations. We understand and appreciate the calm and deliberate way in
which your government is reacting to this latest crisis.

We share your concern about reports that United Arab Republic
troops have taken up positions at Sharm-el-Sheikh. You will recall that

---

[1] Source: National Archives and Records Administration, RG 59, Central Files
1967–69, POL 27–2 ARAB–ISR. Secret; Nodis. Drafted by Eugene Rostow, Meeker, and
Rostow's Staff Assistant Robert T. Grey, and cleared by Rusk, Walt Rostow, Goldberg,
Battle, Meeker, and Popper. A May 20 letter from Eugene Rostow was sent to Walt Rostow
on May 21 with a covering memorandum from Department of State Deputy Executive
Secretary John P. Walsh requesting that it be brought to the attention of the President. Walt
Rostow sent it to the President for his approval with a covering memorandum of May 21.
(Johnson Library, National Security File, Country File, Middle East Crisis, Vol. I) The let-
ter printed here is a revised version of the May 20 letter, which was not sent. The text of
the letter printed here was transmitted to the Embassy in Tel Aviv in telegram 199930,
May 23. (National Archives and Records Administration, RG 59, Middle East Crisis Files,
E. 5190, Box 6, Arab-Israeli Crisis, Chron, Tel Aviv)

[2] Harman's undated letter to Rostow stated that in their May 18 conversation (see
Document 15), Rostow had informed Harman that the U.S. Government was fully aware
of the "nature of the agreements between our two Governments in 1957 relating to Sharm-
el-Sheikh and the straits", was still "motivated by these commitments", and regarded the
straits as an international waterway. He stated that Foreign Minister Eban and Prime
Minister Eshkol welcomed Rostow's "assurances" regarding the "reaffirmation of the
agreement between our two countries", and that he was therefore instructed to inform
Rostow that Israel would not move against the Egyptian forces in Sharm-el-Sheikh unless
and until the Egyptians took action to close the straits. (National Archives and Records
Administration, RG 59, Central Files 1967–69, POL 27–2 ARAB–ISR)

[3] For text of Johnson's message of May 17, delivered on May 18, see Document 8.

[4] For text of Johnson's message of May 21, see Document 30.

[5] See Document 32 and footnote 6 thereto.

I pointed out that the presence of United Arab Republic troops on United Arab Republic territory is not in itself illegal.

The United States' position on the international status of the Gulf of Aqaba and the Strait of Tiran is set forth in this government's memorandum of February 11, 1957, made public on February 17, and quoted in Ambassador Lodge's statement in the General Assembly on March 1. 1957. I am enclosing a copy of this memorandum for your convenience.[6]

Should there be any attempt to interfere with free and innocent passage through the Strait or in the Gulf, the United States Government would wish to consult immediately with the Government of Israel, and with the other governments which took the same view in 1957, about steps to keep the Gulf open. We would expect the Government of Israel to work together with those governments to bring this matter to the immediate attention of the United Nations Security Council.

My Government is proceeding in this matter, as the President made clear in his letter to Prime Minister Eshkol of May 18, on the basis that Israel will take no unilateral military action at any time. Military operations at this time, in our view, may well lead to general hostilities in the area. We are convinced that the issue of the Strait of Tiran must be handled as an international matter.[7]

Yours sincerely,

Eugene V. Rostow[8]

---

[6] The attachment is headed "Memorandum of February 11, 1957." The text consists of the portion of the published version of the aide-mémoire quoted in Document 32.

[7] The last three sentences in the May 20 version of Rostow's letter read as follows: "My Government will expect Israel to take no unilateral military action to open the Straits until all peaceful means have been fully utilized. It further believes that since military activities at this particular point would be very likely to open up general hostilities in the area, the issue of the Strait of Tiran should be handled as an international matter. In this effort, Israel will have the full support of the United States."

[8] Printed from a copy that indicates Rostow signed the original.

37. Memorandum From the Deputy Assistant Secretary of Defense for International Security Affairs (Hoopes) to Secretary of Defense McNamara[1]

Washington, May 22, 1967.

SUBJECT

Gas Masks for Israel

Israel asked on 19 May to buy for cash[2] on an urgent basis 20,000 US Army M–17 gas masks to be air shipped to Israel for immediate distribution. The US Army can make 20,000 masks available immediately from its stocks. These are being prepared for shipment and could be dispatched as quickly as the GOI can arrange air charter.

The Egyptians have used chemical agents, including nerve gas, in the Yemen recently. Israeli intelligence reports that Egypt has brought gas shells or bombs forward to the Sinai in its recent deployments. Although we believe it highly unlikely that Egypt would use gas against Israel, this possibility cannot be altogether discounted.

Secretary Rusk is aware of and supports the Israeli request to purchase American masks, even though all concerned (including the Israelis) recognize that the number of masks involved is too small to do much good and that by themselves could not assure adequate protection against the type of gas which may be used. This would be essentially a psychological gesture.

Under the circumstances I recommend we respond affirmatively to Israel, on the condition that it not publicize this action as evidence of US support for the GOI in the current crisis.[3] We do not believe however that a public disclosure stating (without linkage to the US) that Israeli troops were being equipped with gas masks would, on balance, be detrimental. On the contrary, it might force the Egyptians into a denial of any intention to use gas. Under Secretary Rostow is concurrently examining measures at the UN also designed to force an Egyptian denial of intent.[4]

Townsend Hoopes

---

[1] Source: Washington National Records Center, Records of the Office of the Secretary of Defense, OSD Files: FRC 330 72 A 2468, Israel 400.137. Secret.

[2] The words "for cash" are a handwritten addition on the memorandum.

[3] Neither the "approved" nor "disapproved" option was checked.

[4] Rostow discussed this in a May 20 memorandum to Rusk. He stated that according to an Israeli intelligence report, Egyptian troops in the Sinai were equipped with gas masks, and canisters of gas had been seen. Whether or not this was true, he continued, "we know that the Egyptians have used several kinds of poison gas in their aerial bombing of the Yemen, and that some of the gas at least is extremely lethal, and of Soviet origin and manufacture." He suggested several possible actions, including the possibility of briefing the Secretary-General before his trip to Cairo. (National Archives and Records Administration, RG 59, Middle East Crisis Files, E. 5190, Box 19, NE Situation, May–June 1967, Folder 1)

38.   Telegram From the Department of State to the Embassy in
        the Soviet Union[1]

Washington, May 23, 1967, 2:45 a.m.

199746. Within past few hours, situation in Middle East has seriously worsened. Nasser has announced that Gulf of Aqaba will be
closed to Israeli flagships, and while we have Israeli commitment to
consult with us before attempting to run the blockade, we cannot hope
to restrain Israeli action much beyond next 24 hours. Obviously, Nasser
must be restrained from further hostile action if we are to avoid serious
flare-up.

We are concerned lest Soviets may not be fully aware of recent
Nasser moves and the dangers they hold for peace in the area.
Accordingly we believe it would be useful for you to see Gromyko
soonest to express our grave concern at deterioration of situation, cata-
loging for his information following recent moves giving rise to this
concern:

1. Egyptians have mounted massive military buildup in Sinai
despite fact Israelis at that time had taken no action on their side of frontier that would justify this move.
2. This buildup has increased Egyptian military strength in area
from normal level of 30,000 to 50,000.
3. Egyptians have demanded withdrawal of UNEF and SYG has
complied.
4. Egyptians have moved naval units south into Red Sea toward
entrance to Gulf of Aqaba.
5. Nasser has just announced Gulf would be closed to Israeli flagships, adding that if "Israelis want war, we welcome it."

You should inform Gromyko that Sovs themselves have said war in
Middle East is in interest of no one. We are doing what we can to avoid
flare-up. Purpose of this démarche is to share with Soviets evidence
available to us that gives rise to concern. We assume Soviets as anxious
as we to avoid further worsening of situation, and that they are aware
of our repeated public commitments to support the territorial integrity
and political independence for all countries in the Near East, and our
opposition to aggression and the use of force and the threat of force
against any country.

Rusk

---

[1] Source: National Archives and Records Administration, RG 59, Central Files
1967–69, POL 27 ARAB–ISR. Secret; Immediate; Exdis. Drafted by Toon; cleared by
Stoessel, Leddy, and Davies; and approved by Eugene Rostow. Repeated Immediate to
USUN.

39. President's Daily Brief

Washington, May 23, 1967.

[Source: Johnson Library, National Security File, NSC Histories, Middle East Crisis, Vol. 6, Appendix A. Top Secret; [*codeword not declassified*]. 1 page of source text not declassified.]

40. Telegram From the Embassy in the United Arab Republic to the Department of State[1]

Cairo, May 23, 1967, 1140Z.

7868. Ref: State 199710.[2]

1. Accompanied by DCM I have just spent hour and 45 minutes with FonMin Riad in frank, cordial sometimes forceful discussion current crisis.[3]

2. Will convey here key points and follow with more detailed summary.

3. In response Riad's request for my views on situation after conclusion initial pleasantries incident my presentation copies letters credence and recall,[4] I said that recent events have persuaded me of extreme seriousness of developments and I hoped it was not improper on this occasion to set forth frankly my govt's views.

4. Giving Riad copy of note verbale reftel, I waited his reading of it and then said that four U.S. Presidents had been committed to act in support of measures to counter aggression overt or clandestine in Near

---

[1] Source: National Archives and Records Administration, RG 59, Central Files 1967–69, POL ARAB–ISR. Secret; Immediate; Exdis. Received at 9:48 a.m. and passed to the White House at 10:10 a.m.

[2] Document 35.

[3] Nolte reported in telegram 7864 from Cairo, May 23, that he had given the President's letter to Foreign Minister Riad and asked him to deliver it to President Nasser. (National Archives and Records Administration, RG 59, Central Files 1967–69, POL ARAB–ISR)

[4] Nolte, a newly appointed ambassador, arrived in Cairo on May 21 and had not yet presented his credentials to Nasser.

East and to support territorial integrity and independence of all countries in the area. I hoped FonMin and his govt were fully aware of these
commitments. Referring to Rostow's talk with Amb Kamel last night
(State 199731),[5] I stressed UARG should fully understand USG would
make every effort avoid war or stop one if started and that we were urging restraint with Israel. However, issue of freedom of passage through
Gulf of Aqaba was issue of far-reaching importance and any violation
of this freedom would, in US view, constitute aggression. Requested
clarification UAR intent re Aqaba.

5. FonMin said UAR would stop Israeli ships and confiscate strategic cargoes all other vessels. UAR would not commit aggression but
would resolutely defend itself against attack. We conclude US is thus in
direct confrontation with UAR.

6. Very little flexibility in UAR position as stated by Riad. Only possible opening was his extensive references to MAC as device which
might have worked had Israel supported it. Will report this in full separately.[6]

7. FonMin cordial, candid, resolute, position well thought out.
Strong impression Egypt would carry through as advertised.

Nolte

---

[5] Telegram 199731 to Cairo, May 22, summarized a conversation that evening
between Ambassador Kamel and Under Secretary Rostow. (National Archives and
Records Administration, RG 59, Central Files 1967–69, POL ARAB–ISR)

[6] Nolte reported the conversation in detail in telegram 7873 from Cairo, May 23.
(Ibid.)

41.   Telegram From the Embassy in the Soviet Union to the Department of State[1]

Moscow, May 23, 1967, 1310Z

5078. Refs: State 199710, 199746.[2]

1. I saw Gromyko at 2:30 today and after informing him of note verbale (State 199710) sent to Israel and Arab states, I carried out instructions contained in State 199746.

2. In reply Gromyko noted that President Johnson's message to Kosygin[3] had referred to the Middle East problem and said that this message was under consideration by the Soviet Govt. With reference to the statement I had just made, he said the Soviet Union considers war in this area was not needed by anyone. It would cause damage to the countries in that area and increase tension in the world as a whole. This was not needed by the United States or any other country. The Soviet Union's position was in accordance with its general political line which was that peace should reign in that part of the world. All powers, and particularly the big ones, should prevent the development of a situation leading toward war. The Soviet Union had reached the conclusion that the reason for the current tension was the policy of Israel, and certain circles or groups in Israel which had determined this policy.

It was difficult to say what reasons they had. Possibly these groups were counting on success in their ventures. All statements that Israel was allegedly threatened and that other countries, and particularly Syria, were following policies to the detriment of Israel, were groundless. From the first days of its existence, Israel had followed an unfriendly policy toward the Arab states. Circles in Israel claimed that there was subversive activity against Israel and that they would counter this by their own actions. Such charges were groundless, and the

---

[1] Source: National Archives and Records Administration, RG 59, Central Files 1967–69, POL 27 ARAB–ISR. Secret; Immediate; Exdis. Received at 10:53 a.m. and passed to the White House at 11:20 a.m.

[2] Documents 35 and 38.

[3] The portion of Johnson's May 22 message to Kosygin concerning the Middle East reads as follows:

"The increasing harassment of Israel by elements based in Syria, with attendant reactions within Israel and within the Arab world, has brought the area close to major violence. Your and our ties to nations of the area could bring us into difficulties which I am confident neither of us seeks. It would appear a time for each of us to use our influence to the full in the cause of moderation, including our influence over action by the United Nations."

This message was transmitted in telegram 198583 to Moscow, May 19; for text, see *Foreign Relations, 1964–1968*, vol. XIV, Document 215.

Soviets did not believe them. This was nonsense. There was a certain analogy between these charges and those that were traditionally made about Soviet activities against the West. The Soviet Union considered these charges as a pretext for Israeli actions. The Soviets had good relations with Syria and the Syrians categorically rejected the Israeli charges and said they were only a pretext. The Soviet Union thought that certain nations including the US could exert a restraining influence in greater degree than it had up to now. We had special relations with Israel and would best know how to go about this. It was not up to the Soviet Union to tell us what to do. We were aware of the démarche which the Soviet Govt had made to the Israeli Govt. Gromyko said that of course his remarks today did not predetermine the answer which might be made to the President's message to Kosygin.

3. I said he was doubtless aware of the fact that the Soviet Chargé in Washington had been informed of rumors which were apparently put out by the Syrians to the effect that they had the full backing of the Soviet Union. I said I thought it would be pointless at this time for us to argue the general question of Israeli-Arab relations and would only refer to the fact that at the time of the Suez crisis, we had shown our good faith. I thought the important thing was to address ourselves to the immediate problem that was made particularly acute by the Egyptian action with respect to shipping in the Gulf of Aqaba. I pointed out that Nasser's actions had been taken after the statement of the Israeli Govt that it could not tolerate a blockade of the Gulf and a few hours after the statement of the US Govt that it considered these to be international waters.

4. I was struck by the fact that Gromyko did not pursue either of these statements further. He said many cables were coming in on this subject, and [I] concluded the conversation by thanking him for receiving me promptly.

5. Would appreciate knowing if anything is to be said to the press.

Thompson

42. Memorandum From the President's Special Assistant (Rostow) to President Johnson[1]

Washington, May 23, 1967, 12:45 p.m.

Mr. President:

As instructed, I talked this morning with Bob Anderson.[2] He reports as follows.

1. He is going to Beirut on Thursday on business. (The Panamanian Eleta is going on the same day to Spain to see his daughter graduate from school.)

2. From Beirut he goes to Amman in Jordan to see King Hussein. He is going because he has been asked to arrange the lease of the Jordanian Airlines to a U.S. firm, and to help develop potash and phosphates in Jordan.

3. He talked yesterday with Secretary Rusk,[3] who told him to send word to Nasser that he was in Beirut. If Nasser communicates, well and good. He will make no move beyond letting Nasser know he is there, unless instructed.

4. I asked him for any observations on the present scene. He says he doesn't believe the Arab nations want war. Nasser, however, faces a "terrible internal problem." His people are very close to starvation. A month ago when a food ship came into harbor, shopkeepers were instructed to put a sack of flour in front of their shops to prevent food riots. He believes we made a serious mistake in cutting off Nasser without food as we did. He said that he found no obstacle in his conversations in the Senate. When I said that the problem appeared to be in the House, he said: "No one asked me to talk to anyone in the House."

5. Moreover, Nasser feels cut off from the United States. He is an informal rather than formal man, and State Department communica-

---

[1] Source: Johnson Library, National Security File, Country File, Middle East Crisis, Vol. I. Secret. Received at 1:05 p.m., according to a handwritten note on the memorandum. A handwritten note on another copy states that Rostow took a copy to the Tuesday lunch. (Ibid., Middle East Crisis, Anderson Cables) The President had lunch at 1:18 p.m. with Rusk, McNamara, Walt Rostow, George Christian, and Helms. (Johnson Library, President's Daily Diary) No other record of the discussion has been found. The Middle East was at the top of the agenda. (Ibid., National Security File, Rostow Files, Tuesday Luncheon Suggested Agenda)

[2] Former Secretary of the Treasury Robert B. Anderson.

[3] Anderson called Rusk the morning of May 23 and told him he was going to Beirut and to Jordan and asked if there was anything he could do. Rusk mentioned a possible message to Nasser and said he might want someone to talk to Anderson when he was in Beirut. (Notes of telephone conversation at 9:35 a.m. on May 23, prepared by Carolyn J. Proctor; National Archives and Records Administration, RG 59, Rusk Files: Lot 72 D 192, Telephone Calls)

tions are, for him, no substitute for informal, high-level communications—Presidential letters and emissaries.

6. Nasser's present action, in Anderson's view, is a reflection of his internal tribulations. They have been made worse by some ill-advised Israeli statements, and Nasser's knowledge that the only thing that can congeal the split Arab world is uniting against Israel.

7. He then made two concrete suggestions:

—He believes it would be wise to have Marshal Amir,[4] Nasser's #2, come over to the U.S.—perhaps to the UN. He believes if you could talk with Amir, this would go a long way to settle down the problem. He will arrange this if you wish it.

—If you wished him to proceed beyond Amman to Cairo, assuming that Nasser did receive him—he is willing to do that. But he will make no move without your instruction.[5]

Walt

---

[4] Field Marshal Abdel Hakim Amer, Vice President and Deputy Supreme Commander of the UAR Armed Forces.

[5] Rusk called Anderson later that day and said he had had a further talk with the President. He asked if it was possible for Anderson to go to Cairo and Anderson expressed willingness and said the Egyptian Ambassador had encouraged him to go. Rusk suggested he tell the Ambassador he would be glad to come. Anderson asked if Rusk had talked to the President about his earlier suggestion that someone come to Washington to see the President. Rusk said they had not discussed it but suggested that Anderson tell the Ambassador that if a high Egyptian official were to come to New York for a Security Council meeting, it could be arranged for him to make a quiet visit to Washington and see the President. (Notes of telephone conversation at 7 p.m. on May 23, prepared by Carolyn J. Proctor; National Archives and Records Administration, RG 59, Rusk Files: Lot 72 D 192, Telephone Calls)

43.   Memorandum From the President's Special Assistant (Rostow) to President Johnson[1]

Washington, May 23, 1967.

SUBJECT

Israeli Aid Package

Attached is Secretary Rusk's brief recommendation to approve the Israeli aid package.[2] We've known from Jerusalem and from Ambassador Harman that our continued delay in responding is becoming an increasing irritant in our relationship. At a time when we are trying to put ourselves on as close a working relationship with the Israelis as we can without losing the Arabs, this is an obvious move. The Israelis are good about keeping this sort of thing secret.

However, one major point is unclear—the APC's. There was a time when I felt you might want to split these off from the rest of the package. This would disturb the Israelis now but the long range reasons for doing so have not changed. Gene in drafting the attached recommendation for the Secretary intended to include the APC's. However, we want to be clear on this with you because this may get us into delivering hardware either in the middle of a conflict or shortly after. It could be a promise that would be hard to live up to.

The alternative is to give them answers on all but the APC's and say we'd like to talk about them.

For your reference, the whole package is described on the attached chart.[3]

Walt

---

[1] Source: Johnson Library, National Security File, Country File, Israel, Israeli Aid, 5/67. Secret. A handwritten "L" on the memorandum indicates that it was seen by the President.

[2] Rusk's memorandum of May 22, attached, recommended approval of the aid package for Israel on a secret basis. It commented that the $16 million credit for military spare parts was of particular importance. Concerning the package of military and economic assistance to Israel that was under discussion prior to the outbreak of the crisis, see *Foreign Relations, 1964–1968*, volume XVIII.

[3] The attached chart, headed "Israeli Aid Package," dated May 8, listed the various elements of the package in three columns, headed "Israeli Request," "Katzenbach–McNamara–Goldberg Proposal," and "Your Decision."

Approve all but APC's[4]
Approve whole package in middle column on chart
See me

---

[4] None of the options is checked. A list of the President's decisions is attached to a May 23 memorandum from Rostow to the President that states this was what he had decided at lunch about the Israeli aid package. It records Johnson's approval of a cash sale of 100 APC's for $3.7 million, preferably the sale of 100 Italian APC's with U.S. license, with a direct U.S. sale only if that arrangement was not workable, a $2 million cash sale of tank spare parts, $14 million military credit at 5 percent interest for Hawk and tank spare parts, sale of $27.5 million in food at 2-1/2 percent interest, $20 million in Ex-Im loans, $5 million for special Africa assistance, agreement to establishment of facilities for Hawk missile maintenance, and agreement to offshore procurement for U.S. aid programs. A handwritten note on Rostow's memorandum reads: "Feinberg–Krim: Pres has agreed to this, but nothing can be announced." (Johnson Library, National Security File, Country File, Israel, Israeli Aid, 5/67) Telegram 200673 to Tel Aviv, May 23, states that Eugene Rostow had informed Harman of the decisions with the understanding that there should be no publicity until mutually agreed upon. (National Archives and Records Administration, RG 59, Central Files 1967–69, DEF 19–8 US–ISR)

---

44. Memorandum Prepared in the Central Intelligence Agency[1]

Washington, May 23, 1967.

SUBJECT

Overall Arab and Israeli Military Capabilities

1. The judgment of the intelligence community is that Israeli *ground forces* "can maintain internal security, defend successfully against simultaneous Arab attacks on all fronts, launch limited attacks simultaneously on all fronts, or hold on any three fronts while mounting successfully a major offensive on the fourth." *In the air,* the judgment is less clear: the Israelis "probably could defeat the Egyptian air force if Israel's air facilities were not damaged beyond repair."

2. Those judgments rest essentially on the proposition that the quality of Israel's military leadership, its ability to organize operations and maintain its equipment in a high state of readiness, and the high morale

---

[1] Source: Johnson Library, National Security File, Memos to the President, Walt W. Rostow, Vol. 28. Secret; No Foreign Dissem. The memorandum is unsigned, and bears no drafting information. It was sent to the President with a brief covering memorandum from Walt Rostow stating that two memoranda from Helms, which the President had requested that morning, were attached. The second memorandum has not been identified.

and intelligence of the individual Israeli ground soldier will make up for Israel's quantitative inferiority in men and equipment. The Israelis have consistently stressed intensive training, with emphasis on armor, standardization of weapons, rapid and reliable communications, and a very strong tactical intelligence effort. Egyptian capabilities in these areas appear to be inferior.

3. Moreover, in the air, the Israelis have been acutely conscious of the difficulty of defending their air facilities, and have made strenuous efforts to overcome the fact that their bases are very short warning time from the Arab borders. They have "hardened" their fields with dispersed pens, for example. Israeli pilots and tactics are considered superior, and, in terms of *operationally assigned* fighter aircraft rather than total inventory, Israel has a slight edge—256 to 222.

4. Israeli planning is based on a short war, conducted by ground forces with air cover. If this assumption should prove wrong, Israel might well be in trouble, since the Arabs' quantitative superiority would come into play. At M+48 hours, for example, Israel would have 280,000 men vs. the Arabs' 117,000 deployed in the vicinity of the Israeli borders. But the *total* strength of the Arab armies is nearly 500,000, vs. the same 280,000 on the Israeli side.

5. This is not to say that the rout of the Egyptians in 1956 will be repeated. The Egyptian forces have improved substantially in the past eleven years, and they have acquired considerable operational know-how by rotating combat units in Yemen. Nevertheless, we consider that the Israeli forces have retained an over-all superiority.

---

45.   Briefing Notes for Director of Central Intelligence Helms for Use at a White House Meeting[1]

Washington, May 23, 1967.

[Omitted here are pages 1–10 unrelated to the Middle East.]

---

[1] Source: Central Intelligence Agency, DCI Executive Registry Files: Job 80–R01580, Box 10, Folder 210, President's Foreign Intelligence Advisory Board. Top Secret; [*codeword not declassified*]. Helms used the notes for a briefing at a White House meeting on May 23; see footnote 1, Document 42.

THE MIDDLE EAST

I. The situation in the Middle East took a very serious turn last night, although there is no evidence that either Israel or the Arab nations really want a war.

A. The trouble is that—except for the smaller nations like Jordan and Lebanon—neither do they want peace very badly.

B. Now Nasir has announced that he is closing the Gulf of Aqaba to Israeli shipping, and he must know that to the Israelis, this ranks as a casus belli.

1. [*1 line of source text not declassified*] an Egyptian coast artillery unit has been sent to take over positions being given up by the United Nations Emergency Force at the mouth of the Gulf, where the shipping channel lies within easy artillery range.

2. [*1-1/2 lines of source text not declassified*]

II. The crisis has arisen from the persistent raids by Palestinian terrorists, supported by Jordan, into Israel.

A. The Israelis trounced the Syrians in an air battle on April 7. There have been 14 terrorist incidents since then. The Israelis, concerned because the raids are showing growing capabilities, have renewed their standard warnings of retaliation.

1. [*4-1/2 lines of source text not declassified*]

B. The Syrians, chronic believers in an aggressive U.S.-Zionist conspiracy, [*less than 1 line of source text not declassified*]. The Egyptians, embarrassed because they had not helped the Syrians in April, then made a big show of marching into Sinai, partly to show good faith, partly in hopes of deterring the Israelis.

C. Egyptian intentions are not yet clear. [*4-1/2 lines of source text not declassified*]

1. Our knowledge of the movements of non-bloc shipping is incomplete. [*1-1/2 lines of source text not declassified*]

2. At least one British and one Panamanian ship are on their way in, but we think they are bound for Aqaba, in Jordan.

3. There is also one Soviet ship due to leave Aqaba. Another, now in the Mediterranean, is also bound there. We doubt that the Egyptians will bother them.

4. Most important, we believe that one or more tankers must be en route from the Persian Gulf ports to Eilat because this is how petroleum reaches Israel. We have not yet identified any such tankers yet, however.

III. Now the Egyptians have about 50,000 men, 71 aircraft, and 500 tanks in Sinai on or near the Israeli border. This falls short of figures claimed [*less than 1 line of source text not declassified*] but it is still twice as many tanks, three times the air strength, and 20,000 more men than Egypt has normally had there.

IV. The Israelis in turn are convinced that they are facing a new situation, with UAR forces beefed up and the UNEF safety mechanism withdrawn. They have carried out at least 40 to 50 percent mobilization as a protective measure, and are re-assessing their security requirements. Today, Levi Eshkol called an emergency meeting of the national security panel.

A. As I remarked earlier, we have considered that the Israelis probably rate any attempt to interfere with shipping to their southern port of Eilat as a cause for war.

B. They have also been quite firm in the warning that any new terrorism involving Israeli loss of life will bring some form of retaliation against the Arabs.

C. We believe Tel Aviv will *not* accept any attempt to impose a U.N. presence or controls on Israel.

IV. The Soviet attitude is of the utmost importance to the Arabs at present, [1 *line of source text not declassified*].

A. [2 *lines of source text not declassified*] The Arabs, [1-1/2 *lines of source text not declassified*] they must maintain the line in their propaganda that the Soviets will somehow come to their aid.

B. The Soviets face real difficulties; they don't want a full-blown war, particularly one which could well bring U.S. commitments into play, [1-1/2 *lines of source text not declassified*] than come down unequivocally on the side of peace. Unrest and tension are and have been exceptionally useful to the Soviets in their attempt to erode Western influence in the Middle East.

C. The private Soviet line was probably given to Ambassador Thompson in Moscow last Friday when Thompson told Dobrynin he hoped that the Soviets were exerting as much pressure in Syria as we were in Israel. Dobrynin answered: "I think we can match you."

V. Even with restraining Soviet pressures, the danger lies in the fact that the leaders on each side are being moved by the chain of events, rather than controlling those events at this point.

A. The Israelis, for example, feel that they *must* now patrol by land and air into Sinai, and there is a hint of fatalism in the Arab moves which is clearly expressed in Nasir's aggressive announcement about the Gulf of Aqaba.

B. Under the circumstances, war can now come from accident, incident, or miscalculation.

46.   Telegram From the Director of the National Security Agency
       (Carter) to the Joint Chiefs of Staff/Joint Reconnaissance
       Center[1]

Washington, May 23, 1967, 1729Z.

ADP/224–67. Subj: Diversion of USS *Liberty*.

Due to present Middle East crisis request USS *Liberty* be directed to
depart Abidjan immediately and proceed at best poss SOA to Rota
Spain to pick up tech support material/personnel, thence proceed to
OP area off Port Said.[2] Tasking and specific areas will be fwd ASAP.

---

[1] Source: National Security Agency, NSA Archives, Accession No. 45981, U.S.S.
Liberty Correspondence and Messages, 1965–1968. Secret. Repeated to CNO, CINCLANT,
CINCLANTFLT, COMSERVLANT, COMSERVRON 8, DIRNAVSECGRU, DIRNAVSEC-
GRULANT, NSA REP LANT, ASSTDIRNAVSECGRU, DIRNAVSECGRUEUR, HQ
NSAEUR. The following note appears on the telegram:

"M/R: The present situation in the Middle East has resulted in NSA declaring a SIG-
INT readiness Bravo. In order to augment coverage in the area, the diversion of the USS
Liberty (USN 855) is considered a necessary course of action in view of the *Liberty*'s excellent collection, processing and reporting capabilities and her ability to remain on station
for extended periods. USNS *Valdez* will be directed to leave all available ME tech support
at Rota, Spain [*less than 1 line of source text not declassified*] when she makes a scheduled call
o/a 24/25 May.

"The diversion of the *Liberty* will result in the loss [*less than 1 line of source text not
declassified*] for the remainder of the presently scheduled cruise due to terminate 25 Aug
67. However, in view of the potential US involvement in the ME, this must be considered
an acceptable loss."

[2] After approval by the JCS/JRC, the Deputy Secretary of Defense, and the 303
Committee, the JCS/JRC directed movement of the *Liberty* to the Eastern Mediterranean
by way of Rota, Spain, through a message from COMSERVRON 8, 240020Z May 67.
("Report of the JCS Fact Finding Team: USS *Liberty* Incident, 8 June 1967"; JCS Files,
898/392)

47.   Telegram From the Embassy in France to the Department of State[1]

Paris, May 23, 1967, 1747Z.

18864. I called on Alphand this afternoon to discuss Middle East situation. While I was there telegram (State 199710)[2] was delivered to me and I read him contents and at his request will send him written copy.

Alphand at this juncture considers situation extremely serious and said that Egypt's decision to close Gulf of Aqaba put an entirely new light on the situation, particularly in view of the various declarations Israel, British and French had made in the UN at the time of withdrawal of Israeli troops from Sinai in early 1957. He offered his opinion that there was a high degree of possibility that Israel would attack if Egypt actually stopped a ship.

In reply to my question as to the validity or not of the Tripartite Declaration, Alphand said French Government was not taking any position in principle on this but felt it would be a mistake to invoke this declaration; the French were all in favor of informal consultation taking place but he felt that a formal reference to the Tripartite Declaration would not have a positive effect in the Arab world. Therefore the French preferred to consult without mentioning the declaration.

At this point a telegram was brought in to Alphand from Seydoux reporting that the "not-aligned members" as he phrased it of the Security Council would request a meeting of the four this afternoon in New York at 2:00 p.m. New York time to consider the situation between Israel and the Arab states and to decide what actions the Security Council should take.

In reply to my question Alphand said he did not know whether the French would be prepared to attend this meeting since, in his words, it depended a great deal on the attitude of the Russians. Alphand said if three powers were to meet formally without Russia it would give the appearance of a "cold war". I told Alphand this was all very well but that refraining from "cold war" would have to work both ways, with which he agreed.

---

[1] Source: National Archives and Records Administration, RG 59, Central Files 1967–69, POL ARAB–ISR. Secret; Immediate. Repeated to Amman, Baghdad, Beirut, Cairo, CINCSTRIKE/MEAFSA, Damascus, DOD, Jerusalem, Jidda, London, Moscow, Tel Aviv, and USUN. Received at 3:37 p.m. and passed to the White House and USIA at 4:20 p.m.

[2] Document 35.

Alphand had told me earlier that the French had already made a démarche in Cairo and admitted that their approach to the Soviets two days ago had yielded very little satisfaction.

Comment: It seems to me the French are playing a very careful game with considerable eye to their relations with the Soviet Union, and are not prepared to act in a tripartite fashion. I think they are uncertain as to the Soviet attitude but until this becomes clear I do not think they will be disposed to take many very active steps on their own for counseling moderation and restraint.

Bohlen

48.   Memorandum by the Executive Secretary of the Department of State (Read)[1]

Washington, May 23, 1967, 4:30 p.m.

Results of 4:30 Meeting with Secretary Rusk, Messrs. Rostow, Kohler, Popper and Read

1. The Secretary decided against holding a backgrounder tonight in view of the President's reconsideration and decision to go on television this evening with a statement of his own.

2. It was decided that evacuation from Tel Aviv and Damascus should occur simultaneously but that all posts would be given discretionary authority to proceed with evacuation of USG dependents.

3. It was the consensus that the Soviets probably do not want a blow-up in the Middle East based on our knowledge here of Soviet intent.

4. On Congressional matters the Secretary indicated that the President considers it vital that we have Congress with us on each important move. Ambassador Battle is scheduled to brief the Hill further on the House and Senate sides tomorrow. The White House has been strongly advised by members of Congress that we obtain a joint resolution of support for USG actions if there is going to be actual fighting.

---

[1]   Source: National Archives and Records Administration, RG 59, Central Files 1967–69, POL 27 ARAB–ISR. Secret. Drafted by Read.

5. The UK, Canada and Denmark have already agreed to join us in a letter requesting Security Council action. Brazil has raised certain problems. When signed, the letter would become public. The Secretary General has sent word that he does not want to stand in the way of Security Council action if that is the wish of the members, but if there is a division of opinion he hopes such action will await the SYG's return on Friday. The Secretary General's first meeting with a UAR official, Foreign Minister Riad, is at 3:00 a.m. EDT Wednesday.

6. George Thomson arrives in Washington at 8:30 a.m. on Wednesday and will see Under Secretary Rostow at 10:30 and the Secretary at 11:00. The Secretary wants the control group to initiate urgent consideration of what the Maritime powers might say and do. He thinks that Maritime action may proceed concurrent with Security Council action or before or after the latter, but he emphasized that Maritime actions must be approved at the highest level and have strong Congressional support.

7. Noted.

8. Not resolved.

---

49.   Editorial Note

At 6:10 p.m. on May 23, 1967, President Johnson made a statement for radio and television on rising tensions in the Near East. He stated that the United States was particularly concerned with three potentially explosive aspects of the situation: the "warlike acts" from the territory of one state against another, the "hurried withdrawal" of the United Nations Emergency Force from Gaza and Sinai, and the recent buildup of military forces. He stated that the purported closing of the Gulf of Aqaba to Israeli shipping had brought a new and grave dimension to the crisis and that the United States considered the gulf to be an "international waterway" and felt that a blockade of Israeli shipping was "illegal and potentially disastrous to the cause of peace." He declared that the right of free, innocent passage of the international waterway was a "vital interest of the international community," and said the United States was "firmly committed to the support of the political independence and territorial integrity of all the nations of the area" and "strongly opposes aggression by anyone in this area, in any form, overt or clandestine." He stated that he had been in close contact with

Ambassador Goldberg at the United Nations and hoped the Security Council could act effectively. The text of the statement is in *Public Papers of the Presidents of the United States: Lyndon B. Johnson, 1967,* Book I, pages 561–563. The initial draft of the statement, prepared in the Department of State, was sent to the President with a May 22 memorandum from Rusk. (Johnson Library, National Security File, NSC Histories, Middle East Crisis, Vol. I) Additional drafts, along with related material, are filed ibid. and ibid., Country File, Middle East Crisis.

---

50.   Telegram From the Embassy in Israel to the Department of State[1]

Tel Aviv, May 23, 1967, 2145Z.

3746. Ref: State 199836.[2] For Under Secretary Rostow from Ambassador.

1. Cabinet meeting just concluded has decided to despatch Foreign Minister Eban to Washington, London and Paris leaving here 0300 hours Wednesday, May 24. Public announcement will state trip for purpose participation UN deliberations.

2. This decision follows strong representations I made in accordance your reftel in which I drew fully upon your conversation with Ambassador Dal (State's 199747).[3] Aside from emphasizing gravity of situation from our standpoint and our determination implement and abide by our obligations by action within and without the UN, I particularly reiterated Israeli commitment to US which we regarded as firm that they consult before embarking on unilateral action. Main purpose Eban's visit is to continue such consultation and he hopes highest levels US Government will be available to him.

---

[1] Source: National Archives and Records Administration, RG 59, Central Files 1967–69, POL ARAB–ISR. Secret; Immediate; Nodis. Received at 6:37 p.m.

[2] Telegram 199836 to Tel Aviv, May 23, conveyed instructions from Eugene Rostow to Barbour to explain that U.S. views on the gravity of the situation had been fully and forcefully set forth in Cairo and Moscow. It stated that the Department expected the problem to be handled along the lines of the President's letter to Eshkol (Document 30) and Rostow's letter to Harman (Document 36). (National Archives and Records Administration, RG 59, Office of the Executive Secretariat, Middle East Crisis Files, 1967, Entry 5190, Box 10, Arab/Israeli Crisis, By Post)

[3] Not found.

3. I believe that our conveying strong sense of US recognition its involvement in Israel's problem at this time has had major effect in buying time. Whether unilateral Israeli action was imminent in matter of hours I suppose only history will reveal but my impression is that it was and that it has now been postponed for several days, although I am aware of possibility postponement is wishful thinking my part. In any case it has been made clear to me that further decisions as to Israeli action will depend on outcome Eban's talks primarily Washington, but also London and to lesser extent Paris, and he has been told to be back in Israel by end of week.

Barbour

51.   Telegram From the Mission to the United Nations to the Department of State[1]

New York, May 24, 1967, 0318Z.

5426. Subject: ME Crisis.

1. Although he had studiously avoided contact with other SC members during the day seeking to discuss ME crisis, Sov Rep Fedorenko saw Goldberg at his request on short notice at 7:30 p.m. May 23. Atmosphere was cordial despite obvious differences of approach.

2. Goldberg, who accompanied by Buffum, explained we had from beginning of this crisis sought to include Sovs in consultation including suggestion to SYG that he consult Sovs since we consider both of us have major responsibilities for preventing war in ME. He said our understanding, based on various talks with Sov officials including Gromyko, was that Sovs shared our view that war in this area was undesirable and it was in our joint interests to try and prevent it. Fedorenko agreed this was so.

3. Goldberg then explained reasons why we support convening May 23 SC to discuss issue and outlined approach we planned to take in Council mtg as follows:

---

[1] Source: National Archives and Records Administration, RG 59, Central Files 1967–69, POL ARAB–ISR. Confidential; Priority; Limdis. Repeated Priority to Moscow, and to Cairo and Tel Aviv. Received at 12:32 a.m. and passed to the White House, DOD, CIA, USIA, NSA, and CINCSTRIKE at 12:50 a.m.

A. Although SYG is in Cairo, we share Sov view that SC has primary responsibility for keeping the peace and believe it should not shirk this responsibility.

B. As result Nasser statement on closing Gulf of Aqaba and Eshkol's announcement this wld constitute act of aggression, we are convinced current situation extremely fragile and cld erupt into hostilities momentarily.

C. Under circumstances while we wld not advocate giving SYG blank check, we think SC cld contribute to his efforts pacify situation by calling on parties to exercise maximum restraint and cooperate with U Thant's efforts.

D. Another facet of current situation involving both Sovs and US, indeed all maritime powers, was Nasser's decision not only to close entrance to Gulf of Aqaba to Israeli shipping but also to prevent shipment of "strategic materials" through gulf. Over thirty countries involved in shipping via this route who, like ourselves, would be unwilling to submit to interception and inspection by UAR. We assumed USSR, as proud country, wld also be unwilling accept similar limitations. Goldberg said that if Dardanelles closed to Sov Union, for example, we cld imagine this cld create intolerable situation for them.

E. US approach in SC mtg wld be calm and unprovocative seeking maximum degree of agreement of Council members designed to facilitate U Thant's efforts and not to impede them. We believe the maximum support of appeal for restraint by Council cld have salutary effect particularly if supported by both Sovs and US.

4. Fedorenko heard out Goldberg's presentation in more serious vein than usual but demurred on several points. In particular, he argued that SC mtg not necessary now; various govts concerned, including our own, have just made statement on this issue which should suffice. Implying—but not saying—that Sovs had made bilateral approaches to Arabs, he said that what our govts do directly in a matter of this kind is much more important than what is done at UN. He professed view that SC likely inflame situation further, said he sees no need for SC to move so rapidly and expressed preference mtg be delayed until SYG ready to report. He acknowledges, however, right of members to request mtg under present circumstances and intimated that while he was opposed to holding mtg this evening as we had originally suggested, he wld acquiesce in mtg tomorrow (Goldberg assented re timing).

5. Fedorenko also recalled that Sov position in earlier days (1957) had held that entrance to Gulf of Aqaba was in Egyptian territorial waters and therefore under UAR control. He seemed unprepared to respond to Goldberg's observation that past eleven years' practice of free passage had proved, if anything necessary to do so, that Gulf of Aqaba is international passage. He also did not appear to have recognized that not only Israel but large number of maritime countries were directly involved by terms of Nasser's closure of gulf.

6. He seemed to take at face value US assurance that our purpose in Council wld be to avoid polemics and seek non-contentious outcome designed to strengthen peace in ME and was remarkably mild in his protestations that SC mtg not necessary for this purpose.

7. At conclusion of mtg Fedorenko suggested we review situation tomorrow once more to ascertain real need of SC pursuing matter to conclusion now. Goldberg readily agreed, emphasizing once more that peace extremely precarious and that while we have urged Israel that confrontation shld be avoided, we had no assurance this was possible. Our one concern was to leave no channel unexplored for maintaining peace.

8. Interesting sidelight was Fedorenko's almost open contempt for GA as reflected in his comments on lack of judgment and utility in convening special session on SWA; he has made similar disparaging remarks concerning GA in past.

9. He also seemed most susceptible to Goldberg's argument that in crisis situation of this kind, if SC is to retain any respect and authority, it must not abdicate its responsibilities. He also appeared take some comfort in statement that US did not believe SYG shld get blank check and that SC had its own responsibilities apart from U Thant's.

Goldberg

---

52. Memorandum From the President's Special Assistant (Rostow) to President Johnson[1]

Washington, May 24, 1967, 8:45 a.m.

Mr. President:

[4 paragraphs (8 lines of source text) not declassified]

As Tommy Thompson points out in the third attachment,[2] "the key question is which of the two aspects of the Soviet public statement they are emphasizing in private." If private counsel from Moscow remains moderate, there is scope for diplomacy here.

Walt

---

[1] Source: Johnson Library, National Security File, Country File, Middle East Crisis, Vol. I. Top Secret; [codeword not declassified]. A handwritten "L" on the memorandum indicates the President saw it.

[2] Not printed.

53.   Memorandum of Conversation[1]

Washington, May 24, 1967, 11–11:40 a.m.

SUBJECT

The Near East Crisis

PARTICIPANTS

United States
Secretary of State
Eugene Rostow, Under Secretary for Political Affairs
Foy D. Kohler, Deputy Under Secretary for Political Affairs
William J. Handley, Deputy Assistant Secretary for Near Eastern and South Asian Affairs
John P. Walsh, Deputy Executive Secretary

United Kingdom
George Thomson, Minister of State for Foreign Affairs
Sir Patrick Dean, UK Ambassador to the US
Rear Admiral Bartosik
Christopher H. D. Everett, First Secretary of Embassy

Following welcoming remarks by the Secretary, Minister Thomson said he would like to describe to the Secretary the decisions of last night's Cabinet meeting. He said the meeting was called in a crisis atmosphere. Intelligence information indicated that there was an immediate threat by the UAR to close the Strait of Aqaba and that, unless action were taken, the Israelis might well be involved in a pre-emptive strike. The Cabinet recognized that there were obvious risks in any action that was undertaken by HMG; however, a failure to act might well contribute to an outbreak of fighting between the Israelis and the Arabs which could escalate into an East-West confrontation. Under these circumstances, the Cabinet had decided to authorize steps to assure the right of innocent passage through the Straits with a thought in mind that this could be a deterrent to Israeli action. It was agreed that Prime Minister Wilson would issue a statement tonight reaffirming the UK statements on this subject in 1957. In addition, George Brown was sent East to Moscow to discuss this subject with the Soviets and he had been sent West to Washington to do like-

---

[1] Source: National Archives and Records Administration, RG 59, Office of the Executive Secretariat, Middle East Crisis Files, 1967, Entry 5190, Box 3, Other. Secret; Nodis. No drafting information appears on the memorandum. Filed with a memorandum of a conversation between Eugene Rostow and Thomson that began prior to the conversation with Rusk and resumed following it, and a memorandum of a U.S.-British plenary session held that afternoon. The time of the meeting is from Rusk's Appointment Book. (Johnson Library)

wise. He had been instructed to discuss this matter in depth with the USG and to bring back a practical scheme of action which would include the nuts and bolts of a maritime agreement. An instruction had been sent by HMG to the British Embassies in main maritime countries advocating a declaration of principle on the right of peaceful passage and indicating a willingness to explore the possibilities of international action. With crossed fingers HMG felt that procedures of this nature might deter the Israelis and the UAR and take some of the heat out of the crisis. He wanted to share the thinking of his government on this subject with us and to try to work out a practical, reasonable and workable scheme of action. It was hoped that we could, in cooperation with as many other countries as possible, mount an operation to deter the UAR. This would have two legs in naval terms: (1) a probing escort operation in the region of the Strait of Tiran; and (2) this operation would be momentarily exposed and therefore must be backed up by a credible military operation in the Eastern Mediterranean which would show adequate forces to the UAR. The essential attributes of the proposal would be (a) based firmly on US/UK cooperation and (b) should be international in nature including countries other than UK and US. The British Government also felt that some type of political proposal should be developed to provide a face-saving device for Israel and the Arabs.

The Secretary responded by stating that we welcome the visit of the Minister and the British activities in this matter. The current situation confronts us with certain problems which he would wish to call to the attention of the Minister. We need, he said, before any shooting starts to make sure that Congress was with us. This would involve some delay. We will have to explore carefully the British proposal and discuss it with Congress. The Secretary said that he had had a long session with the SFRC yesterday. There had been a general recognition that we can not stay out of the problems of the NE and that the Arabs cannot be permitted to drive the Israelis into the sea. On the other hand, it was the consensus that any decisions taken must involve multilateral action and the UN must be utilized to the maximum degree in this situation. Any declaration that might be developed should be supported by as many countries as possible. In this situation, he said the "more" truly the "merrier".

The Secretary urged that on an ad referendum basis our two staffs should try to work out a feasible plan which would involve as many countries as possible. We should carefully box the compass in respect to these proposals and should endeavor to persuade the French, Italians, Scandinavians and as many others as possible to join.

The general problem of UN involvement in this issue was then explored. It was noted that paragraph 4 of Article 16 of the Geneva Law of the Sea Convention of 1958[2] might provide a valuable formulation. The Secretary requested that the legislative history of this paragraph be reviewed to see whether it directly involved the Strait of Aqaba [*Tiran*]. It was also agreed to review the implications and applications of the Armistice Agreements of 1949[3] and 1956.[4]

---

[2] Reference is to the Convention on the Territorial Sea and the Contiguous Zone signed at Geneva, April 29, 1958; for text, see UST 15 1606.

[3] Egypt–Israel General Armistice Agreement, signed at Rhodes on February 24, 1949; for text, see UN doc. S/1264/Corr. 1 and Add. 1. A copy is in the National Archives and Records Administration, RG 59, Office of the Executive Secretariat, Middle East Crisis Files, 1967, Entry 5190, Box 16, Israel and Egypt Armistice Agreement.

[4] Documentation pertaining to the cease-fire arranged under United Nations auspices on November 6, 1956, is in *Foreign Relations, 1955–1957,* volume XVI.

---

54.   Memorandum for the Record[1]

Washington, May 24, 1967, 12:35–1:25 p.m.

SUBJECT

Record of National Security Council Meeting held on May 24, 1967 at 12 noon—
Discussion of Middle East Crisis[2]

THOSE PRESENT

The President
The Vice President
Secretary Rusk
Secretary McNamara
Secretary Fowler

---

[1] Source: Johnson Library, National Security File, NSC Files, NSC Meetings, Vol. 4, Tab 52. Top Secret. No drafting information appears on the memorandum but according to a May 25 memorandum from Saunders to Bromley Smith, it was drafted by Saunders. (Ibid.) The time of the meeting is from the President's Daily Diary. (Ibid.)

[2] The meeting had been scheduled for a discussion of South Arabia, but Walt Rostow recommended in a May 23 memorandum to the President that he use the meeting for discussion of the Middle East crisis. (Ibid., Meeting Notes File, Briefing Papers for NSC Meeting, May 24, 1967) A May 23 briefing memorandum from Rostow to the President prepared for discussion of South Arabia reads in part as follows: "The main issue in the Middle East today is whether Nasser, the radical states and their Soviet backers are going to dominate the area. A related issue is whether the US is going to stand up for its friends, the moderates, or back down as a major power in the Near East." For text, see *Foreign Relations, 1964–1968,* vol. XXI, Document 96.

General Wheeler
Mr. Leonard Marks
Under Secretary Eugene Rostow
Assistant Secretary Lucius Battle
Mr. Walt W. Rostow
Mr. Farris Bryant
Mr. George Christian
Mr. Bromley Smith
Mr. Francis Bator
Mr. Harold Saunders

Secretary Rusk opened the meeting with a report on the current Arab-Israeli situation. He described it as serious but not yet desperate:

—*The U. N.* Security Council is meeting, and it is important to have it in session on this issue. We do not yet have a full report from U Thant's talks in Cairo, but Bunche reports that the Egyptians have suggested a return to the General Armistice Agreements as they stood before the 1956 fighting. That might relieve the pressure in the Straits of Tiran, but the Israelis might not be in the mood to make that kind of concession.

—We are in touch with *the USSR.* Privately we find the Russians playing a generally moderate game, but publicly they have taken a harsh view of the facts and have laid responsibility at Israel's door—and by inference at ours. Syria and Cairo say publicly they have Soviet support; but our general impression is that this is somewhat less than complete.

—*Israeli* Foreign Minister Eban will be here on May 25. We have insisted on consultation, and he is here to consult. The borders have been reasonably quiet, but the Straits to the Gulf of Aqaba are the main issue, both for Israel and for the major maritime nations. We are consulting with the British about this today.

—In a "thoughtful discussion" with the *Senate Foreign Relations Committee* on May 23, he found unanimity that we should not act unilaterally, and that we should work through the UN and multilaterally.

In summary, he could not promise that this crisis would be over in 24 hours; but he had the impression that no government wants war.

Secretary Fowler asked to what extent we were looking into economic sanctions and to what extent we should be trying to influence the IMF and World Bank to operate in this situation. He had in mind economic sanctions that might be in the nature of a counter-blockade. We might hold the Israelis off if we could convince them we are hurting the UAR more than the blockade is hurting them. Secretary Rusk said that from the Fund's viewpoint, any agreement with the UAR consummated today would be reckless.

The President suggested that Eugene Rostow and Secretary Fowler look at all the cards we have had to play in this field. Secretary Fowler indicated that he was seeing Mr. Schweitzer of the IMF and private bankers from New York in the next couple of days, and we could begin laying any ground work necessary.

The President then said he would like to hear views on what we do if all these other measures fail. We should play out the UN and other multilateral efforts until they are exhausted. "I want to play every card in the UN, but I've never relied on it to save me when I'm going down for the third time. I want to see Wilson and De Gaulle out there with their ships all lined up too." But all of these things have a way of falling apart. He mentioned, for instance, early Congressional support for his actions in Vietnam. Therefore, we have to figure out what we can do if all these other courses fail.

In a parenthetical exchange, the President alluded to statements by Senators Symington and Fulbright to the effect that the U. S. could not manage two crises at once. They see it as a choice between Israel and Vietnam and believe we ought to withdraw from Vietnam. He told Secretary Rusk to let Senator Mansfield know that this kind of music in the Senate is just what Kosygin wants to hear.

Secretary Rusk before leaving the meeting commented that we were witnessing an interesting reversal of roles—doves have become hawks, and vice versa.

The President then turned to Secretary McNamara for a military appraisal of the situation. The Secretary said in general that there is no substance to the Fulbright/Symington notion that the U. S. cannot manage both Vietnam and the Middle East crises at the same time. He then turned to General Wheeler for a detailed run down of our military posture in the Mediterranean and the current disposition of Arab and Israeli forces.

In addition to those facts widely current in our intelligence estimates today, General Wheeler indicated that it would be harder to open the Gulf of Aqaba than we had at first thought. Because of the two Egyptian submarines in the Red Sea, we would need an ASW unit, the nearest of which is now in Singapore—two weeks away.

General Wheeler suggested that if Israel does try to open the Gulf, it will attack first by air, striking initially the UAR's naval forces in the Red Sea and the air bases in the Sinai. Only after establishing air superiority would the Israelis try to take out the battery at Sharm al-Sheikh. Therefore if the Israelis move, it might not be possible to localize a strike designed simply to open the Straits.

A brief discussion of possible presence of unconventional weapons followed. General Wheeler pointed out that the Egyptians have used three kinds of gas in Yemen. However, Mr. Helms was quite positive in stating there were no nuclear weapons in the area. General Wheeler said he was less well informed "but more skeptical."

In summary, General Wheeler noted that we have a powerful naval force in the Mediterranean; that our land forces are few, limited to about 1400 Marines now ashore at Naples, three days away; that our nearest ASW unit is two weeks away, since we cannot send one through the Suez Canal; that the UAR coastal battery and naval and air forces in the Red Sea will be the units employed to blockade the Gulf of Aqaba; that we will have trouble with overflight and staging rights in Turkey, Libya and Spain if we have to introduce our own ground forces; and that the Israelis can hold their own.

On the last point, the President asked for a new reading on Israeli capability. He said Ambassador Goldberg is less certain about Israeli superiority. Mr. Helms noted that he had sent a recent assessment to Ambassador Goldberg but had had no response yet. Both Mr. Helms and General Wheeler promised to review this estimate.

The President came back to his initial question: "Suppose Gene doesn't deliver in the UN and suppose Bob is not as persuasive with Healey[3] as he is with us, and suppose we have to have somebody carry a message to Garcia. What do we do?"

General Wheeler responded by saying that our first approach should be to give Israel military aid and all the support it needs for long-term military operations. If we are convinced that the Israelis can hold the Arabs, then we should back them down the line and rely on Arab inefficiency and lack of homogeneity to weaken the Arab cause. We should start immediately discussions with Israelis on their stock-piles and our replenishment capability. Our current understanding is that they are stocked for about 30 days.

The President then turned to Soviet motives and asked General Wheeler whether or not the Soviets had staged this Middle East crisis, the trouble in Hong Kong, and other such diversions simultaneously to force us to turn our attention from Vietnam. Neither General Wheeler nor Mr. Helms saw any sign of Soviet calculation behind these crises, though of course both admitted that the Soviets would view them as a godsend.

The President returned to the question of what we would do after relying on Israeli forces. General Wheeler noted that a long war would hurt the Israeli economy. At that point we would have to decide whether we were going to send in forces and confront Nasser directly.

---

[3] British Defence Minister Denis W. Healey.

The President asked whether, if we intervened, the USSR could avoid doing likewise. General Wheeler said he thought the USSR might just cut its losses and back out.

Secretary McNamara saw the whole situation evolving somewhat differently. He thought the initial exchange would be a fierce air battle for air superiority which would deplete aircraft inventories on both sides. Then both the U.S. and the USSR would be faced with requests for air support. He felt that the USSR might supply Soviet-piloted aircraft.

The President returned to Soviet motives. Mr. Helms said that he felt the USSR likes the situation as it is now but is not ready to rush in. The Soviets would like to bring off a propaganda victory as in the 1950's with them as the peacemakers and saviors of the Arabs, while we end up fully blackballed in the Arab world as Israel's supporter.

Mr. Helms said he was not as bearish as Secretary McNamara on Israeli air capability. He said the Israelis had taken the MIG that defected from Iraq last year through all kinds of maneuvers in Israel and had demonstrated in the 7 April air battle with Syria that they had learned their lessons well.

The President asked what is in Nasser's mind. Mr. Helms thought he had achieved his objective now. Secretary Fowler asked whether he might be looking for someone to hold him back. Mr. Eugene Rostow noted that he was looking for someone to hold the Israelis back.

The President asked about British Minister of State George Thomson and Israeli Foreign Minister Eban, and whether he should see either of them. Eugene Rostow said that Thomson had not raised the subject, but that Eban will definitely want to see the President. When the President asked whether this would be desirable, Mr. Rostow replied that he felt we had held the Israelis back from a strike yesterday and that the President would undoubtedly have to see Eban.

In conclusion, the President asked Mr. Battle for an assessment of what is in Nasser's mind. Mr. Battle said that, until Nasser threatened to blockade the Gulf of Aqaba, he would have agreed with Mr. Helms that all Nasser wanted was a limited propaganda victory. Now that he has gone as far as he has, Battle said he cannot help but wonder whether Nasser either has more Soviet support than we know about, or had gone slightly insane. He noted that it is most uncharacteristic for Nasser not to leave a door open behind him, and that is exactly what he appears to have done in this case.

Battle sketched Nasser's problems and motives on the broader front to include internal economic trouble and a tightening food supply, his drive to regain leadership in the Arab world, and his need to recoup his position on the world stage.

55. Telegram From the Department of State to the Embassy in the United Arab Republic[1]

Washington, May 25, 1967, 10:37 a.m.

201638. Following based on uncleared memcon, is FYI, Noforn and subject to revision upon review:

Egyptian Ambassador accompanied by Chief of Protocol and Battle made farewell call President May 24.[2] Ambassador made warm statements friendship US, reviewed his efforts strengthen friendship between US and UAR, and said he left with sad heart. Then followed his standard line of stating importance US leverage Cairo and hoped that after current crisis over (and he did not think situation yet out of hand) US would again make effort reestablish good relations UAR. Hoped US would be able cooperate with UAR, ignoring superficial matters such as speeches and protect basic American interests in area. To fail to do so would leave vacuum for communists and that vacuum would be filled. Urged President keep door open and look at long-range need for US influence UAR which must be viewed in its historic perspective.

President referred to grave situation facing Middle East, pointing out he had in recent letter to Nasser and in communications over the past always indicated willingness find road to friendship. Former Secretary Bob Anderson, a trusted friend of President's since latter's days with NYA, would soon be in Beirut and available consultation Egyptians if they so desired. If Egyptians would listen to Secretary Anderson, President Johnson would listen to him and believed Anderson's mission clearly offered opportunity for contact with trusted friend of President's.

Comment: Battle has talked with Secretary Anderson who said Ambassador Kamel called him immediately following White House appointment. Anderson has told Ambassador Kamel he will be Beirut Hotel Vendome for day or two and if Egyptians wish, he will be happy come over meet with Nasser but only if Egyptians want him to do so and consider trip useful. Anderson intends primarily to listen and will make no effort mediate current crisis.

---

[1] Source: National Archives and Records Administration, RG 59, Central Files 1967–69, POL 17 UAR–US. Secret; Priority. Drafted by Battle, cleared by Bromley Smith, and approved by Department of State Deputy Executive Secretary Herbert B. Thompson.

[2] UAR Ambassador Mustafa Kamel made a farewell call on the President from 2:32 to 3 p.m. (Johnson Library, President's Daily Diary)

In view Department, Anderson's presence will offer special opportunity to Egyptians to pass word through special channel if they wish re current crisis. If Anderson comes, he will be in touch with Ambassador Nolte and will undoubtedly want briefing current Arab-Israeli confrontation.

Anderson, if he visits Cairo, will state he is on one his frequent trips to discuss phosphate reserves along Red Sea. Visit should in every respect be handled in very routine fashion.[3]

---

[3] Printed from an unsigned copy.

---

56. Memorandum for the Record[1]

Washington, May 24, 1967.

SUBJECT

Conversation with ARAMCO Representative

ARAMCO's Washington representative, John Pendleton, called me this afternoon to read a telegram which he had received from ARAMCO's Vice President Brougham, who is currently visiting Beirut.

Brougham reports a conversation with Saudi Arabian Petroleum Minister Yamani at Beirut airport on 23 May. Yamani is convinced there will be war between the Arabs and Israel. Syria is pushing Nasser toward war, and Russia must not resist the Syrians too sharply because Moscow fears Syria is leaning toward Peiping.

Yamani recommends that the US keep hands off this crisis, work through the UN and not try to be a policeman. He disagrees flatly with our position on the Gulf of Aqaba[2] and says that if the US directly supports Israel, ARAMCO can anticipate being nationalized "if not today, then tomorrow." If the US does not stay out of this conflict, the US is finished in the Middle East.

---

[1] Source: Johnson Library, National Security File, Country File, Middle East Crisis, Vol. I. Secret. An attached note indicates a copy was sent to Read.

[2] Telegram 4848 from Jidda, May 24, reported that when Ambassador Herman Eilts gave Saudi Deputy Foreign Minister Sayyid Omar Saqqaf a copy of the note verbale contained in Document 35, Saqqaf stated that the Saudi Government did not agree that the Gulf of Aqaba was an international waterway; in the Saudi view, it represented Arab waters, and the Arabs had the right to close it. (National Archives and Records Administration, RG 59, Central Files 1967–69, POL ARAB–ISR)

When Brougham asked Yamani why Saudi Arabia would object to our standing up to Nasser, Yamani replied, "We are all Arabs. Your government would be foolish if it does not keep out."[3]

H.H.S.

---

[3] Telegram 206646 to Jidda, June 1, states that on May 25 Eugene Rostow sent an informal message via Aramco to Yamani assuring him that the U.S. Government was doing all possible to restrain the Israelis, reiterating U.S. dedication to the principle of free passage in the Gulf of Aqaba, and expressing the hope that the Saudi Government would realize that it too had a stake in this principle. Yamani later told Aramco he had conveyed this message to the King. Yamani commented that in his opinion, the UAR and Syria could handle Israel and therefore efforts at restraint were not important, and that even if Saudi Arabia had an interest in keeping the Gulf of Aqaba open, it could not say so. (Ibid.)

---

57. **Telegram From the Department of State to the Mission to the United Nations**[1]

Washington, May 24, 1967, 11:13 p.m.

201585. Subj: Four-Power Meeting on Middle East.

1. Lucet came in to see Undersecretary Rostow this afternoon to propose a quadripartite meeting of Ambassadors to the UN. Paris is making similar approaches in Moscow and London.

2. Lucet's instruction said that situation has sharply aggravated in the past few days, particularly following Egypt's announcement to close straits. Whatever the different points of view, it read, question now is to preserve peace and to make sure that no party is contemplating any action which might endanger it. Nothing can be attained unless four great powers agree on necessity of maintaining peace. Therefore they should meet together to examine what to propose and undertake and particularly to be sure that none of the parties concerned engages in any operation of force. Subsequently the four powers can take up discussions of various modus vivendi. In the immediate future, the four Ambassadors to the UN should meet in New York. Very fact of their meeting should have a calming effect.

---

[1] Source: National Archives and Records Administration, RG 59, Central Files 1967–69, POL ARAB–ISR. Secret; Priority. Drafted by Eugene Rostow's Special Assistant Thomas O. Enders and approved by Rostow. Also sent Priority to London, Moscow, and Paris, and to Cairo, Tel Aviv, Damascus, and Amman.

3. Rostow replied that the US has been trying to arrange such a meeting but Soviets have been unwilling. Goldberg on instruction again expressed this afternoon hope that the four meet.[2]

4. Real problem, Rostow said, is not whether you meet but whether you can agree. French statement says in effect that no one should make the situation worse. Does that mean that the Israelis should refrain from challenging blockade or that Arabs should desist from their claim? US has taken very grave responsibility of asking Israel to refrain from sending a ship down from Gulf of Aqaba. But that is not a position that can be held indefinitely. Israelis might well have moved to strike yesterday had it not been for US intervention. They will not hold off for long unless Cairo gives assurance it will not exercise their claim. Any number of formulas can be found but basic point is that there is no way to compromise on free passage through straits.

5. Rostow outlined British proposal for declaration by maritime powers and said we thought well of it. Lucet had no reaction from Paris to our earlier queries.

6. Rostow also raised report we have had that Egyptians are trying to buy wheat in France and urged French to delay. This is no time, he said, to slacken pressure on Nasser.

7. Rostow asked about resupply position for French equipment in Israeli armed forces should war break out. Lucet said he would look into the question.

Rusk

---

[2] Goldberg said this at the conclusion of a statement to the UN Security Council on May 24; for text, see Department of State *Bulletin*, June 12, 1967, pp. 871–873.

58.   Memorandum of Conversation[1]

Washington, May 25, 1967, 11:15 a.m.

SUBJECT

Middle East Situation

PARTICIPANTS

George Thomson, Minister of State for Foreign Affairs
Sir Patrick Dean, British Ambassador
Christopher Everett, First Secretary, British Embassy

The Secretary
Thomas M. Judd, EUR/BMI

The Secretary asked Mr. Thomson if he had any further news about George Brown's talks in Moscow. Mr. Thomson replied that Mr. Brown had talked for over an hour with Kosygin. They had also had a private talk. In the main talk, Kosygin took a hard line, merely repeating the official announcement the Soviets had issued. When chided by Brown, Kosygin had heatedly denied that the Soviets were standing by doing nothing. Brown got the impression that an argument was going on in the Soviet Government as to what their policy should be. He also got the impression that the Russians were greatly worried about the situation and that they were working on the Arabs. Mr. Brown did not think this necessarily meant that the Russians would be willing to work with us constructively in the Security Council or on the Gulf of Aqaba problem.

Mr. Thomson mentioned that Prime Minister Wilson had sent a message to Kosygin endorsing the idea of a four power meeting. George Brown was not sure the Soviets would be willing to do anything about this proposal. Brown had mentioned it to Gromyko, who had not responded.

Mr. Thomson went on to say that the British Cabinet had met that morning (May 25). There had been little substantive discussion in the meeting. It had consisted mainly of a briefing by the Prime Minister on the talks which Brown had in Moscow and those he (Thomson) had in Washington. The Cabinet endorsed the idea of a four power meeting, preferably under UN auspices. It had also decided to send Fred Mulley, Minister of State at the Foreign Office, to Paris to sound out the French as to precisely what they in mind.

---

[1] Source: National Archives and Records Administration, RG 59, Central Files 1967–69, POL 27 ARAB–ISR. Secret; Exdis. Drafted by Thomas M. Judd (EUR/BMI). The meeting took place in the Secretary's office.

The Secretary said we were not happy with the idea of a four power meeting outside the UN. Mr. Thomson replied that he had discussed this matter with the Prime Minister the previous night. The British Government now thought that a meeting under UN auspices would be best.

Mr. Thomson asked the Secretary what he thought of US-UK planning to date. The Secretary said he hoped we could get something together today to show to the President. The Secretary said we were worried about the time element. We didn't know how long the situation could be held.

Mr. Thomson asked how long we thought the Israelis could be held. The Secretary replied he did not know. We were making it clear to the Israelis they shouldn't count on our support if they moved on their own. They were probably most worried about the Straits of Tiran. They remembered that in 1956 they had been promised that their ships could go through the Suez Canal but nothing had been done to implement the promise.

Mr. Thomson said that agreement had been reached in the Anglo-American talks the preceding day on the main outlines. A draft declaration by the maritime powers had been prepared. It had been agreed which countries should be asked to sign. It also had been agreed that approaches should be made to capitals. There was a problem as to how to marry this with the UN procedures.

Mr. Thomson said there were some difficulties on the military side in regard to the plan to organize a naval force in the Red Sea. The British thought this should be a limited force. If we acted with determination, it should be sufficient. If Nasser should react, we had adequate retaliatory force available in the Eastern Mediterranean. Mr. Thomson said the Americans wished to put a strong force into the Red Sea. The British felt that a carrier in the Red Sea would be a sitting duck if Nasser got nasty.

Continuing, Mr. Thomson said that there would be many formidable obstacles to overcome in organizing the task force. The UK thought the task force should at least nominally be more than Anglo-American. The Dutch and Italians might be possibilities. It might even be possible to put one of their admirals in command of the Red Sea force. The overall commander would have to be American.

There was another problem, Mr. Thomson said. The vital traffic to Eilat was tankers carrying POL for Israel. They all flew the Liberian flag. It would be embarrassing if these Liberian ships were not willing to accept our protection and escort. A prior approach to the Liberian Government would be necessary. Mr. Thomson thought this could be best made by the American Government.

The Secretary said that Mike Pearson, a number of years ago during the Suez incident, had suggested that the smaller countries might do a job like this. He doubted that there would be any volunteers this time. The Secretary asked if the British had any information as to the Norwegian attitude.

Mr. Thomson said they had heard nothing. This was disturbing inasmuch as they had several times asked the Norwegians about their attitude.

Mr. Thomson said we might wish to explore the possibility of a floating UNEF. This would have the advantage of being something new. It would not involve Nasser having to retreat from his present position. There might even be Egyptian participation in such a fleet which would probably consist of a few small patrol craft, and possibly a helicopter. Such a course might be sufficiently reassuring to the Israelis.

The Secretary said one of his colleagues had mentioned that morning that under the UNEF Resolution the Secretary General of the UN had the authority to organize a naval force for the Gulf of Aqaba. The Secretary said he doubted very much if the Secretary General would be willing to touch this one.

---

59.   Telegram From the Embassy in the Soviet Union to the Department of State[1]

Moscow, May 25, 1967, 1415Z.

5125. 1. From the way the Soviets are handing the Middle East crisis, I conclude that they were well aware of Egyptian plans and probably not averse to the Egyptian action in stirring up this affair. I have considerable doubts however that this included the closing of the Gulf of Aqaba. The omission of reference to this action in the official Soviet statement, the fact that a high Foreign Office official alleged that he did not know of it at 11:00 a.m. on Tuesday, and the fact that that this would

[1] Source: National Archives and Records Administration, RG 59, Central Files 1967–69, POL ARAB–ISR. Secret; Priority. Repeated to USUN, Tel Aviv, Cairo, and Paris. Received at 1:18 p.m. A copy was sent to the President on May 26 at 11:30 a.m. with a memorandum from Walt Rostow noting that it was Ambassador Thompson's assessment of the Middle East crisis. (Johnson Library, National Security File, Country File, Middle East Crisis)

not fit in with what I would conceive to be Soviet strategy, lead to this conclusion. I am convinced that the Soviets would not want to become militarily physically involved in a Middle East war. If we and the British and perhaps others force the opening of the Gulf, the consequent damage to Nasser's prestige, as well as the demonstration of Soviet impotence to render other than moral support, make this a stupid move from the Soviet point of view unless, of course, they are convinced that Nasser can get away with it. On the other hand, I do not think that if war had started without this move the Soviets would have been too concerned about their ability to stay clear and yet make appropriate noises which they could exploit whenever a settlement was reached. Even if the Israelis should clobber their Arab neighbors, the Soviets might calculate that the hatred this would engender for the West would enable them to reestablish their position in the Arab world.

2. Unless Nasser is hell bent upon having a fight, it seems natural to suppose that he has some demand which he hopes to achieve in return for a retreat on the Gulf, and in this connection the thesis put forward by the Moroccan Ambassador (USUN 5422)[2] would seem to be most plausible. With UN troops on the Israeli-Syrian border, Nasser would achieve some protection for Syria which is in his and Soviet interests, but also would reduce the possibility of the Syrians stirring up a crisis at a time which might be inconvenient to him.

Thompson

---

[2] Telegram 5422 from USUN, May 24. (National Archives and Records Administration, RG 59, Central Files 1967–69, POL ARAB–ISR)

60. Draft Memorandum by the Ambassador to Canada (Butterworth)[1]

Lake Harrington, Canada, May 25, 1967.

SUBJECT

Conversations of the President on May 25, 1967, with External Affairs Minister Martin and Prime Minister Pearson

I do not believe that any significant exchanges of views took place between the President and the Minister for External Affairs until after the President met with the Prime Minister and Martin at Lake Harrington. [Omitted here is a description of the trip to Lake Harrington.]

The discussions at Harrington Lake can be divided into three unequal parts, the longest of which took place between the President and the Prime Minister and Martin after lunch within hearing of all the United States and Canadian advisers.[2] Careful notes were taken by the former. In point of time the subject of Vietnam bulked largest, but what was said about the Near Eastern crisis constituted the essence of the attitudes enunciated by the President on the one hand and the Prime Minister and Martin on the other at the luncheon.[3] This second exchange was stimulated by the arrival of the telegram from Prime Minister Wilson to Prime Minister Pearson which, as intended by the former, was read in whole or in part by the Prime Minister to the President and those assembled.[4]

---

[1] Source: Johnson Library, National Security File, Country File, Canada, Vol. V. Secret. Drafted on May 26. The President met with Prime Minister Pearson and External Affairs Minister Martin at the Prime Minister's summer residence at Lake Harrington, Quebec, following a visit to the Canadian Universal and International Exhibition (EXPO '67) in Montreal. According to Johnson's Daily Diary, he was at Lake Harrington from 1:25 to 3:45 p.m. (Ibid.)

[2] The conversation after lunch is recorded in a May 25 memorandum of conversation drafted by Davies and Country Director for Canada Rufus Z. Smith, except for a private conversation between the President and Prime Minister, which according to Prime Minister Pearson, concerned Vietnam. (Ibid., National Security File, Country File, Canada, Vol. V)

[3] According to the memorandum of conversation cited in footnote 2 above, Pearson said he thought the best course was to seek quadripartite agreement in the Security Council but if necessary, they should accept quadripartite talks outside the United Nations. Johnson responded that he would consider quadripartite talks only in the framework of the United Nations.

[4] According to the memorandum of conversation cited in footnote 2, it contained the following points: George Brown reported that the Soviet attitude on the Near East was not particularly encouraging; Eban had told the British that the Israelis would not strike until he returned from his talks in Washington but if nothing had been worked out by then, Israel would have to strike first; and the British supported De Gaulle's proposal for quadripartite talks even if it meant talks outside the United Nations.

The second division of the discussions occurred at the luncheon table at which were present the President, the Prime Minister, the Minister for External Affairs, Special Assistant Rostow, Canadian Ambassador Ritchie and myself. The only matter of consequence that was discussed was the Near Eastern crisis and, as mentioned above, the basic position the President took in these discussions and that by the Prime Minister and Martin were repeated in the general discussion held later in the living room. Other aspects were as follows: (a) Martin, backed by Pearson, was at pains to make clear that the report was false that the Secretary General of the United Nations had disapproved of the Canadian-Danish initiative in the Security Council. Martin said that he had been able to reach U Thant in Cairo by telephone and had been assured by him that the report was untrue. (b) Correspondingly the President made clear that the U.S. had not accepted the French proposal, that he had only authorized Ambassador Goldberg to talk bilaterally with representatives of any government and that Goldberg had been misunderstood.[5] (c) The Prime Minister indicated that there were still some 800 peace-keeping Canadians in the UAR, that the Canadian force was being run down more slowly than the others because Canada was responsible for those logistics. (d) At one point in the conversation there was a discussion about the extent of the respective commitments of the U.S. and Canada to Israel, particularly with regard to the Gulf of Aqaba. As I recall it, it arose out of a remark of Rostow's that Israel had paid for its right of free passage into the Gulf with its blood and it had obtained guaranteed recognition from the international community of this right. Mention was made of the Tripartite Declaration, of the fact that Great Britain had virtually withdrawn from its commitment and of a letter of commitment which former Secretary of State Dulles had written. The Prime Minister was obviously anxious to make the point that whereas Canada had recognized the right of Israel to have access to the Gulf of Aqaba, it had not done what he regarded the U.S. as having done, namely, made any commitment towards guaranteeing that right. (e) Rostow once or twice expressed views which were along the lines of paragraph 1 B of Department's ExDis Circular 202592, May 26.[6] (f) He also brought out the fact that according to the information supplied by

---

[5] Reference is to Goldberg's May 24 statement before the UN Security Council; see footnote 2, Document 57. A memorandum concerning the background of Goldberg's statement is attached to a June 1 memorandum from Read to Rusk. (National Archives and Records Administration, RG 59, Central Files 1967–69, POL 27–14 ARAB–ISR)

[6] Circular telegram 202592, May 26, stated the options open to the U.S. Government seemed to be twofold: to limit its actions to UN and diplomatic channels, which would "almost certainly" lead to an Israeli strike against the UAR and perhaps hostilities with Syria, or to give firm assurances to the Israelis that the Strait of Tiran would remain open and take all necessary measures either alone or with the British to enforce them. Paragraph 1(B) was the second option. (Ibid., POL ARAB–ISR)

Lloyds a tanker of Liberian registry was loading and was due to reach the mouth of the Gulf of Aqaba on May 29 and drew the inference that this interval was available to formulate an effective decision. (g) There also occurred an exchange of information about the stated determination of the Government of Israel to go to war rather than to submit to the closure of the Gulf of Aqaba and Pearson and Martin quoted statements made to them by the President of Israel, who was just completing his visit to Canada, and from the Government of Israel received through diplomatic channels. (h) There was also some discussion of whether U Thant had obtained any assurances of value from President Nasser and Pearson seemed to harbor a faint hope that this could mean a willingness to withdraw the blockade of the mouth of the Gulf in exchange for Israel accepting what it had previously refused, namely, a peace-keeping contingent on its side of the border as well as on the UAR side. Incidentally there was no note taking at the table and the atmosphere of the conversation was friendly and casual rather than intense and precise; views were exchanged with no attempt to concert.

The third phase of the conversations occurred after lunch when the President and the Prime Minister decided as all rose from the table that they would like to remain and have a talk à deux. This lasted for some time during the course of which, having checked with Rostow, I went into the dining room to hand the President the original of ExDis telegram 201714 of May 25[7] from the Department, which an officer had just brought from the Embassy for delivery to the President.[8]

[Omitted here is a summary of the conversation, on unrelated matter, en route to the airport.]

W.W. Butterworth

---

[7] Telegram 201794 to Ottawa, May 25, conveyed briefing points for the President's discussion of the Middle East situation with Pearson. (Ibid., POL 27 ARAB–ISR)

[8] According to the President's Daily Diary, on the helicopter from Andrews Air Force Base to the White House, Johnson and Rostow talked briefly about the meeting with Pearson, "summarizing by saying that 'Canadians and Europeans will still not accept responsibility . . . they say it's not their trouble, and why should they get in the Middle East now, too.'" (Johnson Library)

61.   **Memorandum From the President's Special Assistant (Rostow) to President Johnson**[1]

Washington, May 25, 1967, 6 p.m.

[*1 paragraph (4 lines of source text) not declassified*]

Also attached is a CIA appraisal of this estimate which throws a great deal of cold water on the Israeli estimate.[2]

Walt

P.S. The two estimates—Israeli and CIA—both show how explosive are:

—Israeli anxieties;
—Nasser's hopes of picking up prestige;
—USSR desires for gaining prestige, short of a war.

W.[3]

---

[1] Source: Johnson Library, National Security File, Country File, Middle East Crisis, Vol. II. No classification marking. A handwritten "L" on the memorandum indicates the President saw it.

[2] Richard Helms described and quoted from the CIA appraisal at a conference on the Six-Day War, held June 3–5, 1992. He stated that Johnson met with him and some of his other advisers after his return from Canada and asked Helms and JCS Chairman General Earle Wheeler to "have this scrubbed down," that is, to re-examine the situation and produce a new paper. (Parker, Richard B., ed., *The Six-Day War: A Retrospective* (Gainesville, Florida: University Press of Florida, 1996), pp. 216–217) Johnson met with Rusk, Deputy Secretary of Defense Cyrus Vance, Helms, Eugene Rostow, General Wheeler, Battle, and Walt Rostow from 7:02 to 8 p.m. on May 25. Vice President Humphrey joined them at 7:25 p.m. (Johnson Library, President's Daily Diary) No record of their discussion has been found.

[3] The postscript is written in Rostow's handwriting on the memorandum.

Attachment

MEMORANDUM FOR

Mr. Bromley Smith, White House
Mr. Rusk, State
Mr. Eugene Rostow, State
Mr. Hughes, State
Mr. McNamara, Defense
General Carroll, Defense

SUBJECT

Appraisal of an estimate of the Arab-Israeli Crisis by the Israeli Intelligence Service

1. The Director has asked that an appraisal be made of the "Israeli Intelligence Estimate of the Israeli-Arab Crisis," dated 25 May 1967, a copy of which has already been sent to you.[4] The appraisal follows.

2. We do not believe that the Israeli appreciation presented [*less than 1 line of source text not declassified*] was a serious estimate of the sort they would submit to their own high officials. We think it is probably a gambit intended to influence the US to do one or more of the following: (a) provide military supplies, (b) make more public commitments to Israel, (c) approve Israeli military initiatives, and (d) put more pressure on Nasser. The bases for our disagreement with the Israeli view follow.

3. Not all the statements in paragraph 2 are confirmed by what we now know. According to our information:

Only the 3rd Brigade of the Fourth Armored Division is in Sinai

A. The Fifteenth Armored Brigade has been ordered to leave Yemen.
B. We have no information on the formation of a Second Army Group.
C. We are unaware of any message from the Iraqi Ambassador in Cairo informing Baghdad of the UAR's military aims.
D. We know of no UAR naval vessels which have left the Red Sea and entered the Mediterranean.
E. The UAR Defense Minister did go to Moscow, but we know nothing of his plans.

In our view, UAR military dispositions in Sinai are defensive in character.

---

[4] Not printed, this estimate is an unsigned memorandum of May 25, headed "Israeli Intelligence Estimate of the Israeli-Arab Crisis," [*text not declassified*]. The latter, citing various pieces of information, stated their conclusion that the UAR was now actively seeking war. The memorandum notes that the Israelis believed that holding the initiative was the key to the situation and that the opportunity to take the initiative would soon be gone. It notes that they strongly urged that the issue at stake was not Israel but whether the Middle East would fall under Soviet control.

4. Nasser has already had significant success in exploiting the crisis to restore his influence and acceptance at home and abroad as leader of all the Arabs. He probably realizes that these gains would be quickly reversed if he were humiliated or suffered military defeat. He probably calculates, however, that his interests would be satisfied by any resolution of the crisis other than humiliation or defeat. He may not regard military victory over Israel as essential to his ends.

5. We believe that the UAR is acting in this crisis essentially to put pressure on Israel short of attack on Israeli soil. Whereas the UAR armed forces have improved in capability during the past decade, Nasser still probably estimates that he does not have—even with the support of the other Arabs—the capability to destroy Israel by a military attack. On the other hand, Nasser shows increasing willingness to pursue a policy of high risk in challenging Israeli interests, such as free access to the port of Elath. Nasser may be convinced that his armed forces are sufficiently strong to be able successfully to hold off an Israeli attack at least for long enough to get great power intervention. Nasser evidently estimates that his ability to inflict damage through bombing on Israeli cities would discourage an Israeli attack.

6. The steps taken thus far by Arab armies do not prove that the Arabs intend an all-out attack on Israel. The Iraqis have long been obliged to send troops to assist Israel's Arab neighbors in case of conflict. The Iraqis simply lack the ability to send meaningful amounts of troops to fight against Israel. They are not prepared to supply and maintain sizeable units in a conflict. Lebanon's military capability is insignificant and the Lebanese are likely to participate in a conflict only to the minimum extent consistent with maintaining relations with the other Arab world. There have been no coordinated maneuvers by the various Arab states and it would be difficult if not impossible for the various Arab units cited in paragraph 3 of the Israeli estimate to be used in concert. In sum we believe these are merely gestures which all Arab states feel compelled to make in the interests of the fiction of Arab unity, but have little military utility in a conflict with Israel.

7. As for the report that the Egyptians are preparing to use chemical warfare in the Sinai, the use of gas in this terrain and in mobile engagement would be difficult if not entirely counterproductive for the UAR. And given Israeli air defense, we do not believe that the UAR has the capability to make effective use of gas against urban concentrations.

8. We believe the Soviet aim is still to avoid military involvement and to give the US a black eye among the Arabs by identifying it with Israel. Once this is accomplished—and this is happening fast—we think that the Soviets will not wish to increase the crisis further. They probably fear an Israeli victory over the Arabs and that it would damage their image as defender of the Arabs. They probably could not openly help the Arabs because of lack of capability, and probably would not for fear of confrontation with the US.

62.   Message From Prime Minister Wilson to President Johnson[1]

London, May 25, 1967.

I have not been in touch with you direct so far about the Middle East situation because our people have been in such close and continuous touch and particularly because George Thomson has himself been in Washington discussing all this with Dean Rusk. But we have taken stock today in the cabinet in the light of what we have heard from George Brown in Moscow (which I am bound to say, is not so far particularly encouraging on this front: of George Thomson's report: of my own talk yesterday with Eban (you will have had an account of this via George Thomson): and, finally, in the light of de Gaulle's proposal that this should be handled, at least initially, on a four power basis.

The French have told us—and no doubt yourselves—that they are thinking in the first instance of a meeting of the four permanent representatives in New York. Their approach rests as you know on the basic proposition that, if any good is to come out of the Security Council, it can only result from some four power understanding. It is not at all clear to me how far de Gaulle has thought through this proposition. His political purposes are, of course, fairly transparent in terms of French influence and of seeking to avoid French involvement in any exclusively Western approach. (Eban told me that de Gaulle advised him strongly not to get too closely involved in any exclusively Western tie-up.)

But the fact that this approach may be designed to enhance French standing and, perhaps, to cut down to size some of the General's Western allies, need not, in my view, prevent our recognizing its intrinsic merits. It seems to us to have two potential advantages. First, if we can get the Russians into a four power discussion—and as far as I am concerned I would be glad for this to happen either at ambassadorial level in New York as at present suggested by the French, or eventually at a much higher level somewhere else (summit

---

[1] Source: Johnson Library, National Security File, Country File, Middle East Crisis, Vol. II. Secret. The transmission time on the message is 2313Z, which is apparently in error, since Rostow sent it to the President at 6:45 p.m. with a memorandum noting that it was more detailed than the indirect report the President had received that afternoon in Canada. He also noted that Rusk was reading it. For Wilson's account of British policy during the crisis, the war, and its immediate aftermath, see Harold Wilson, *The Chariot of Israel: Britain, America and the State of Israel,* pp. 329–361.

if necessary in view of the terrible dangers involved)—this could mean that they are clear-headed enough to see the immense dangers of a major confrontation with the West in a part of the world where neither side can confidently expect to control the passions or reactions of the local participants. In that situation, there might be a prospect of reaching agreement with them. Secondly, if the French initiative peters out because the Russians will have nothing to do with it, the French can hardly then just fold their hands and play no further part. The prospect of drawing them into a wider Western operation should be somewhat enhanced. Either way, the prospects for peace should be a little brighter.

These are the reasons why we decided today to announce our support for the French proposal—and I dare say that in authorizing Arthur Goldberg's statement of support for the idea, which I saw last night, your government had the same kind of considerations in mind.

Meanwhile, we have, as you will have heard, agreed that George Thomson should continue to work out with Dean Rusk the terms of any eventual approach to the other maritime powers and of the draft declaration for which we might canvass their support. When the cabinet discussed this this morning, it was clear to us, from the reports already received from our ambassadors in a number of key maritime countries, that we should not get the kind of support that is required for any such declaration until all efforts to get something constructive out of the Security Council have demonstrably failed. In these circumstances, and given the intrinsic value of the French proposal anyway, we felt that before we could finally decide on the terms and method of proposing the joint approach to the maritime powers, we must give the French four power approach a chance to prove itself.

As I write this, I learn that by the time it reaches you, you will probably have talked with Mike Pearson. I need not say how much I welcome this meeting. Canada has a key role to play in all this and we shall of course be keeping in the closest touch with them too. This is indeed a further reason why I am very glad that I shall be able next week to see both Mike and yourself. Clearly we shall have to give a good deal of time to the Middle East situation. I hope things there will be a bit clearer by the time we meet—and I hope even more that there will not have been a major explosion there—but I am sure you share my own desire that, overshadowed as events may be for the time being by the Arab–Israel crisis, we shall be able to have a good talk about the other important issues on our agenda.

If, meanwhile, you can let me know how you see things, especially in the light of your talk with Mike, I shall welcome this.

63. Telegram From the Embassy in Israel to the Department of State[1]

Tel Aviv, May 25, 1967, 2240Z.

3785. 1. FonOf Director General Levavi accompanied by Argov of American Department came to NA House 2300 hours this evening. Levavi said they called at moment of grave peril for Israel. Instructions had been sent to Harman for Eban, who should be consulting with highest U.S. levels within hours, to say that attack by Egypt and Syria appeared imminent and that it essential for U.S. to declare its intention to abide by its commitments and to implement declaration by appropriate movement U.S. forces to Israel's support.

2. Information on which this conclusion of Egyptian and Syrian intentions based is: (1) Egypt has held establishment of second army group in Sinai to reinforce divisions already there and has ordered armored brigade from Yemen to join such group. It has increased tanks in Sinai to total of 800. It has reversed naval forces proceeding to Aqaba and ordered them returned to Mediterranean. It has sent cabinet minister to Moscow to coordinate operations between Egyptian and Soviet Governments. (2) Syria is to receive Iraqi troops by airlift and has increased offensive posture its forces already on frontier. (3) Jordanians have announced willingness accept Iraqi and Saudi Arabian troops.

3. In addition to foregoing Egypt has started fabricating incidents with Israelis such as alleged clash with border patrol.

4. All this indicates that Egyptians and Syrians no longer concerned with Aqaba but prepared launch full scale attack against Israeli existence.

5. I noted there appeared doubt that in fact Jordanians anticipate any Iraqi or Saudi troops there to which Levavi responded Jordanians

---

[1] Source: Johnson Library, National Security File, Country File, Middle East Crisis, Vol. II. Top Secret; Nodis; Flash. Received at 8:05 p.m. Walt Rostow sent this telegram to the President at 10:14 p.m. with an attached note: "Herewith the same message Eban transmitted to Secretary Rusk as it was received and evaluated by Ambassador Barbour." Telegram 202239 to Cairo, May 25, states that at 5 p.m. Eban advised Rusk of a flash message from Eshkol that the Israeli Government was convinced a UAR-Syrian attack was imminent. (National Archives and Records Administration, RG 59, Central Files 1967–69, POL ARAB–ISR) No memorandum of this conversation between Rusk and Eban has been found. In a telephone conversation with Goldberg, Rusk referred to a message from Israel and stated that the Israelis "are calling on us for an immediate statement that an attack on them is an attack on us." (Notes of telephone conversation prepared in S, May 25, 8:15 p.m.; ibid., Rusk Files: Lot 72 D 192, Telephone Calls) Eban described the message and his conversation with Rusk in *An Autobiography* (New York: Random House, 1977), pp. 348–350, and in more detail in *Personal Witness: Israel Through My Eyes* (New York: G.P. Putnam's Sons, 1992), pp. 382–383.

not important. The seriousness of the situation is Egypt and Syria and he reiterated that these developments most perilous for Israel.

6. While it obvious this further attempt strengthen Foreign Minister Dan's hand in discussions in Washington, I am confident that Israeli apprehensions are to them most genuine. As indicated in more detail in report forwarded by another channel earlier today information repeated to me tonight as to Egyptian moves is in large part result hard intelligence and there every collateral indication Egyptian belligerence unabated.

7. I told Levavi that since Eban had departed for Washington I did not have further information in addition to that I had passed on on Tuesday but that it my impression there had been no change in U.S. determination as I had expressed it to them at that time.

Barbour

64.   Memorandum of Conversation[1]

Washington, May 25, 1967, 8:30 p.m.

PARTICIPANTS

United States	*Israel*
The Secretary	Foreign Minister Abba Eban
C. Arthur Borg (notetaker)	Ambassador Avraham Harman

The Secretary said that the President wanted him to make a number of points: 1) The information available to us does not really support the belief that an attack by the UAR and Syria is imminent. We have looked into the examples cited by the Chief of Israeli Intelligence very carefully throughout the course of the day including the reports of armored brigade movements from Yemen, movement of UAR naval vessels, and the nature of military dispositions in Sinai. With regard to the latter they appear defensive to us (Eban interjected to point out that a defensive alignment in one area may mask an offensive preparation in another). 2) We wish to make available to the Israeli Government, through our Embassy all the information we obtain; it is important that

---

[1] Source: Johnson Library, National Security File, Country File, Middle East Crisis, Vol. II. Secret; Exdis. Drafted by Rusk's Special Assistant C. Arthur Borg. Sent to the President at 11 a.m. on May 26 with a covering note from Walt Rostow.

there be a prompt sharing of all information available to each of us in order to permit the fullest possible analysis of the situation. 3) At this juncture we need to know the Secretary General's impressions from his trip to the Middle East. We believe that a UAR attack will be irrational before his report is submitted to the Security Council. Such an attack would impose "enormous political burdens on Nasser." 4) The President particularly wanted Eban to understand that our government did not have the authority to give an assurance along the lines of "an attack on you is an attack on us" without full Congressional association with such an undertaking. Such NATO-type treaty language would be unfortunate because of the tremendous debate it would raise regarding war-making power under the Constitution. (The Secretary commented at this point on the curious reversal of the dove and hawk roles induced by the Middle East situation and noted the unfortunate inference that the United States might be forced to make a choice between the Middle East and Southeast Asia. Eban replied that everyone has his own "favorite part of the world." Eban stressed in a more serious vein, however, that Prime Minister Eshkol should not be held to specific language with regard to his request of the President. The important point was that there must be an effective expression of "warning and deterrent".) 5) We wish to make a maximum effort multilaterally. The United Nations should have a chance to find an answer before we consider other initiatives. At the same time the UK initiative regarding a declaration by Maritime countries is a good one and we are working urgently on this. The more countries that could be associated with the British proposal the better. We consider the situation in the Tiran Strait a grave matter: for Israel, for us and because of principles that have a worldwide effect. 6) The President asked that it be particularly emphasized that preemptive action by Israel would cause extreme difficulty for the United States. In our position of world leadership, the American people would do what has to be done if "the fault is on the other side and there is no other alternative". Therefore, the question of responsibility for the initiation of hostilities is a major problem for us. Of course if we had information that the other side was moving this would be a matter of great concern.

In response to the Secretary's query, Eban confirmed that Eshkol had sent messages to the British and the French similar to the message to the President. With regard to the question of possible preemptive action he wished to comment that during the past two weeks "the reality has been consistently worse than the projections". The Secretary interjected that this was behind our desire for more intensive mutual consultation. We wish to keep very urgently in close touch on all aspects of the situation. It is essential that we share our information in order that we can evaluate it together.

The Secretary stated that the President was not taking Prime Minister Eshkol's message or the Middle East situation lightly. Eban then said that he wished to discuss the Strait situation although he would talk in greater detail at the working dinner.[2] He described the attitude in Israel as "apocalyptic" and that Israel could not take much more if it were a question of surrender or action. He said that when he returned to Tel Aviv it was important that he be able to state that something concrete was being done about the Strait situation. If there was nothing concrete to say Israel would feel alone. If on the other hand, international action were instituted, Israel would "harmonize" its effort with the others. The Secretary replied that we are urgently ascertaining what can be said before the Foreign Minister leaves. There is the problem of the time factor but we hope to isolate the Strait problem and keep it localized. Eban responded that the United States commitment to Israel is the most localized specific commitment we have and that it seems to him important that the United States meets this "easy commitment" in the light of its over-all position. The Secretary observed that we must take our Constitutional problem into account and that the President and the Congress must move with solidarity in dealing with the problem. The Secretary commented for Eban's private information that Prime Minister Pearson had told the President he could probably furnish a couple of ships to a multilateral effort in the Strait.

The Secretary asked what the key element was in Israel's withdrawing from the general armistice arrangements. Eban stated that two elements are vital: an effective cease-fire and frontiers which are respected. The machinery utilized is not the essence and UNEF was effective from 1956 to 1967 because the two vital elements were present. Ambassador Harman also noted that the Suez blockade against Israeli ships was not compatible with the armistice agreement.

With regard to the Secretary's query about the Israeli attitude toward foreign forces on its territory, Eban replied that the key question is one of function. UNEF, for example, has been tied to a specific geographical situation; if UN forces were moved from Gaza to Israel they would lose their deterrence.

---

[2] Eban, Harman, Rafael, Evron, and Israeli Attaché Brigadier General Joseph Geva met with Eugene Rostow, Deputy Under Secretary of State for Political Affairs Foy D. Kohler, Battle, Sisco, Legal Adviser Leonard C. Meeker, and Walsh for a working dinner after Eban's meeting with Rusk. A memorandum of the conversation is in the National Archives and Records Administration, RG 59, Central Files 1967–69, POL ISR–US. After the dinner Eban met privately with Eugene Rostow. A memorandum of that conversation, which Walt Rostow sent to the President along with the memorandum of the conversation with Rusk, is in the Johnson Library, National Security File, Country File, Middle East Crisis, Vol. II.

Eban emphasized that his government was interested in any possible action related to the Strait problem. It would be most useful, for example, if the President were to send Prime Minister Eshkol a message commencing with the statement that "we are going to open the Straits" and then proceeding with discussion of detail. The Secretary replied that it was important to find out what the various alternatives can yield. He noted, for example, that the President had decided that we should complain to the non-permanent members of the Security Council (except Bulgaria) about their "soggy attitude" on the Middle East situation. This was in line with our view that members are entitled to act in support of the United Nations Charter despite the possibility of a veto. With regard to action in the Security Council Eban replied that Israel wants a verdict for something it is already entitled to do. He cited Secretary Dulles as thinking that the onus should be put on others. It was therefore important to take effective action with regard to the Strait and then let others come to the Council with a complaint if they wished.

The Secretary returned to the vital importance of more intensive mutual consultation and stated that we would start this tonight. He commented that our Embassy in Tel Aviv had been worried about "an arm's length attitude" on the part of the host government and we hoped this could be corrected.

---

65. Telegram From the Department of State to the Embassy in the United Arab Republic[1]

Washington, May 26, 1967, 12:43 a.m.

202587. On instructions Undersecretary Rostow called in UAR Ambassador at 10 p.m. to transmit the following message: "Your adversaries believe that a surprise attack by UAR from Egypt and Syria is imminent from moment to moment. We know this is unthinkable. We cannot believe the government of the UAR would be so reckless. Such

---

[1] Source: National Archives and Records Administration, RG 59, Central Files 1967–69, POL ARAB–ISR. Secret; Flash; Exdis. Drafted and approved by Eugene Rostow. Cleared by Lucien L. Kinsolving for the NEA crisis task force. Also sent Flash to London, Tel Aviv, Moscow, and USUN. A copy was sent to the President on May 26 with a memorandum from Walt Rostow stating, "You may wish to see how the message to the UAR Ambassador was handled last night." (Johnson Library, National Security File, Country File, Middle East Crisis, Vol. II)

a course would obviously have the most serious possible consequences. Therefore we are continuing to advise restraint on the part of GOI." We do not wish you to follow this up directly, but you must know about the message if the issue is raised.

Rostow explained that we were transmitting this rumor, which we believed and hoped was not true, as a friendly act.

Ambassador replied that he too believed the rumor to be untrue, but would transmit it immediately as a precautionary measure. He thought our announcement about withdrawing dependents[2] was probably interpreted in the Middle East as a signal that war was coming, and might well be the source of the rumor. He knew that for us such steps were routine in troubled times. But it was probably interpreted otherwise in Cairo.

FYI: The basis of this warning is an urgent report transmitted this afternoon by FonMin Eban to the Secretary. The answer to the Israelis is being considered. President will see him tomorrow. Meanwhile, we felt it indispensable to transmit this warning. End FYI.

Rusk

---

[2] Telegram 202576 to all American diplomatic missions, sent at 10:26 p.m. on May 25, stated that the embassies in Cairo, Tel Aviv, and Amman had decided on evacuation of official dependents. (National Archives and Records Administration, RG 59, Central Files 1967–69, POL ARAB–ISR)

---

66.   Message From President Johnson to Prime Minister Wilson[1]

Washington, May 25, 1967.

CAP 67447. From the President to the Prime Minister.

I had a good talk today with Mike Pearson. He can, evidently, talk for himself. But it is my impression that he wishes us all to stay together in this Middle East crisis: First, to see if anything useful can be accomplished in the UN; and then to work out something along the lines that you have suggested and about which George Thomson has been talk-

---

[1] Source: Johnson Library, National Security File, Head of State Correspondence File, United Kingdom, Vol. 6, Prime Minister Wilson Correspondence File, 12/31/66–12/31/67. Secret. The message was transmitted May 26 at 0453Z. Filed with a draft that Rostow sent to the President on May 25 with a memorandum indicating that it had been amended by Rusk. Johnson initialed the memorandum, "OK. L."

ing with our people in Washington. I have the impression that—if it comes to the point—the Canadians will join the party.

We had hoped—and still hope—that this track will keep the Israelis steady; but I should report to you that Eban came in this afternoon to Dean Rusk, on a very urgent basis, with the following.

He reported that a message from his Prime Minister indicates they fear an early general attack on Israel by the UAR and Syria. What they have asked for in this situation is immediate application of the U.S. commitment, backed up by a public declaration as well as practical actions. They would like a statement by us that an attack on Israel is equivalent to an attack on the U.S. They also want this announcement accompanied by an instruction to U.S. forces in the area to coordinate action with the Israeli Defense Force against any possible attack.

Our own intelligence estimate does not back up their statement, and we are not inclined to be as alarmed as they appear to be. We are taking the line with them here that our own knowledge does not coincide with their estimates. We are also pointing out that as far as the U.S. is concerned, the President and the Congress must proceed together in dealing with this problem, and on a multilateral basis.

We are also urging upon Eban the real danger of any pre-emptive action by the Israelis which would create an impossible situation in the Middle East as well as in the U.S. It would, we fear, create real difficulty in getting the support of other countries, to say nothing of Congressional support in the U.S.

I will see Eban tomorrow, as I feel I must. I plan to follow the same line with him Dean Rusk is taking tonight.

I would be interested to know whether your intelligence people share our judgment that the Israeli assessment is overdrawn; and, indeed, what your estimate of Nasser's intentions is.

I should also like you to know directly my own view about the notion of four-power meetings outside the United Nations. I am against them, for reasons we can discuss when we meet on June 2. I am, of course, quite content to have the permanent representatives of the members of the Security Council meet in New York; but I do believe it would be unwise now to encourage quadripartitism outside that framework.

I must say that the initiative you have showed in this crisis thus far has been greatly appreciated here where our capacity to act hinges so greatly on some of us at least being able to move together.

67.   Telegram From the Embassy in the United Arab Republic to the Department of State[1]

Cairo, May 26, 1967, 1000Z.

8003. Ref: Amman's 3775[2] and Cairo's 7956.[3]

1. DCM, Parker and I impressed by cogency of King Hussein's message to US reftel (Amman's 3775).

2. We agree that our efforts should be directed toward dissociation from appearances of support for Israel versus Arabs and strictly toward UAR–Israel confrontation. We should remain neutral in this confrontation stepping in only if hostilities erupt and then as peacemaker.

3. Otherwise, we foresee heavy cost to US in terms political, economic and other relationships in Arab world, and in terms cold war balance of power. Equally, see little chance viable future for Israel save as armed beachhead, guaranteed by US (Cairo 7956).

Department pass Amman, Beirut, Damascus, Jidda, Tel Aviv.

Nolte

---

[1] Source: National Archives and Records Administration, RG 59, Central Files 1967–69, POL ARAB–ISR. Secret; Priority; Exdis; Noforn. Received at 7:32 a.m. and passed to the White House at 7:50 a.m. A copy was sent to the President with a May 26 memorandum from Walt Rostow stating, "You may wish to get the flavor of the perspective of our Embassy in Cairo." (Johnson Library, National Security File, Country File, Middle East Crisis, Vol. I)

[2] Telegram 3775 from Amman, May 26, transmitted an oral message from King Hussein to the highest U.S. authorities stating that the United States was risking the hostility of the entire Arab world and complete loss of influence in the area for the indefinite future by the appearance it was giving of identifying itself with Israel over the Tiran Strait and related issues. (National Archives and Records Administration, RG 59, Central Files 1967–69, POL ARAB–ISR)

[3] In telegram 7956 from Cairo, May 25, Nolte suggested a possible package deal in which Israel would give refugees a choice between peaceful repatriation or full compensation, international status for Jerusalem and the question of frontiers under the original partition arrangements would be subject to negotiation, Israel's existence would "in effect" be recognized by the Arabs, and Israel would gain freedom of passage through the Gulf of Aqaba and an end to the Arab boycott. (Ibid.)

68.   Paper Prepared in the Department of State[1]

Washington, May 26, 1967.

UK–US TALKS ON THE NEAR EAST

At the request of the UK, intensive US–UK talks occurred on Wednesday and Thursday[2] on the Near East Crisis. The British delegation was headed by George Thomson, Minister of State for Foreign Affairs, and the U.S. delegation by Under Secretary Rostow.

Thomson reported that the Cabinet: feared that the imminent closure of the Gulf of Aqaba would inspire a counterstrike by the Israelis. This, in turn, might lead to a bloodier war than occurred in 1956, possibly involving the major powers. In view of these dangerous possibilities, the Cabinet authorized discussions in Washington and Moscow, a public statement by the Prime Minister reaffirming the right of free and innocent passage in the Gulf of Aqaba, a cautionary warning to the Israeli Government, and approaches to the maritime powers proposing a multilateral Declaration of the rights of innocent passage.

The U.S. side shared the British assessment of the seriousness of the Near East Crisis.

The ensuing discussions resulted in tentative agreement on a staffing and ad referendum basis along the following lines:

1. Press for effective action through the United Nations, and in particular at the current meeting of the Security Council, to guarantee freedom of passage through the Straits of Tiran and the Gulf of Aqaba. We should seek to ensure that any resolution included an endorsement of the principle of freedom of passage. If the Soviet Government abstained, the principle would have received U.N. approval. In the event of a Soviet veto, action by the maritime powers would nevertheless be seen to have received wide international support.

2. U.S. and U.K. diplomatic approaches in the capitals of maritime states to canvass support for a multilateral declaration (text attached)[3] to assert freedom of passage through the Straits of Tiran. This diplomatic action would take place at the same time as action in the United Nations. The countries to be approached might include Denmark,

---

[1] Source: National Archives and Records Administration, RG 59, Central Files 1967–69, POL UK–US. Secret; Nodis. No drafting information indicated. The date is handwritten on the paper with a query but is evidently correct. The text, except the last paragraph, was sent to London in telegram 203642, May 26. (Ibid., POL ARAB–ISR)

[2] May 24 and 25

[3] The draft declaration, dated May 24, is attached but not printed.

Norway, Sweden, the Netherlands, Belgium, Italy, Greece, France, Panama, Liberia, Japan, Canada, Australia, New Zealand, Portugal, Turkey, Honduras, Argentina, Brazil, Philippines, Ethiopia, Kenya and Malagasy Republic.

3. U.S. and British military advisers were to explore the possibilities and modalities of military actions deemed necessary to assert freedom of passage through the Straits of Tiran and the Gulf of Aqaba. Discussions commenced on the basis of a tentative British plan involving (a) a small UK–US probing force to escort merchant vessels in the Straits of Tiran; (b) a covering force consisting of the British carrier *Hermes* and its escorts; and (c) a deterrent force in the Eastern Mediterranean consisting of the 6th Fleet, the British attack carrier *Victorious* and the British bombing force on Cyprus. The British contemplated these forces to be under U.S. command.

The JCS prefer that the force be designed as a protective presence—not for escort duty—and be capable of defending itself. There is as yet no meeting of the minds between the military on the design of the force, which will have to be taken up by the two Governments.

Minister Thomson flew back to London last night and will report to the Cabinet today. An attached report from Ambassador Bruce[4] indicates that the Cabinet is taking a cautious approach to the Near East Crisis and will only reluctantly assume a leading role.

---

[4] The report from Bruce is not attached.

69.   Memorandum of Conversation[1]

I–35592/67   Washington, May 26, 1967, 10:30 a.m.

SUBJECT

Dangers of Arab-Israeli War

PARTICIPANTS

Israeli Side
Foreign Minister Abba Eban
Ambassador Avraham Harman
Brigadier General Joseph Geva, Defense Attaché

United States Side
Secretary of Defense—Robert S. McNamara
Deputy Secretary of Defense—Cyrus Vance
Chairman, Joint Chiefs of Staff—General Earle G. Wheeler
Deputy Assistant Secretary of State (NEA)—Rodger Davies
Director, Near East and South Asia Region, OASD/ISA—Col. Amos Jordan

Mr. Eban said there were three key elements in the situation as it has developed over the past week or so. First, the Syrian terrorist attacks, second, the Egyptian troop concentration in the Sinai and the precipitate withdrawal of the UNEF and third, the blockade of the Gulf of Aqaba. Mr. Eban said, as an aside, that the withdrawal of UNEF would prove a historic tragic blunder. The immediate danger now is the Gulf of Aqaba situation which fundamentally alters the geo-political dimensions of the Arab-Israeli dispute and threatens the very existence of Israel. It is far more serious than terrorist attacks or troop deployments, for its consequences would be to cut Israel off from one-half of the world and leave it crippled.

Mr. Eban felt this was the strongest possible issue to draw a line on, since the Israeli position was not only juridically sound but had been "consecrated" by thousands of sailings under dozens of flags over a period of ten years. Nasser had tried to cancel this right in one brief speech. Closure of the Gulf is cause for war; it is as if the U.S. were to continue its Pacific maritime activities but to have all its Atlantic ports and trade closed off.

Mr. Eban said the Israeli Cabinet had met just before his trip and the decision was made to fight rather than to surrender to a blockade in

---

[1] Source: Washington National Records Center, OSD Files: FRC 330 77–0075, Memoranda of Conversations between Secretary of Defense McNamara and Heads of State (other than NATO). Top Secret. Drafted by Jordan and approved on June 5 by Deputy Assistant Secretary of Defense for International Security Affairs Townsend Hoopes. The meeting was held in McNamara's office at the Pentagon.

Aqaba; Israel would not try to live on one lung. It had delayed thus far in striking because of President Johnson's urgings and because Ambassador Barbour had spoken of another alternative to surrender or war, namely, that the maritime nations would keep the Straits open. His (Eban's) mission to the U.S. was to find out if this was a real alternative and what steps the U.S., the UK, and others were prepared to take regarding it. Israel believed that the U.S. could open the Straits easily and with virtually no risk. It would only take a few U.S. escort vessels.

Mr. Eban turned to the theme of American commitments to Israel and read from a document which he called an "Agreed Minute" of February 26, 1957[2] (it was brought to him in the middle of the meeting). He said that he and Secretary Dulles had worked it out together, as they had Mrs. Meir's speech to the UN on the same topic on 1 March.[3] In effect the document stated that the U.S. asserted the right to free passage of the Gulf and that it would act to defend this right. Mr. Eban said this was probably the least ambiguous and the easiest executed commitment the U.S. had.

Secretary McNamara asked how long Israel envisaged that the U.S. would have to escort merchant ships through the Gulf if it adopted Israel's plan. Minister Eban did not answer directly but said that

---

[2] Ambassador Harman delivered a copy of this document, unsigned and untitled, dated February 26, 1957, to Eugene Rostow with a covering letter of May 26. It states that at a meeting on February 24, 1957, the Israeli Ambassador sought clarification on U.S. attitudes and intent on matters discussed in the U.S. memorandum of February 11, 1957. It continues with side-by-side summaries of questions asked by Ambassador Eban and replies given by Secretary Dulles. (National Archives and Records Administration, RG 59, Central Files 1967–69, POL 27–2 ARAB–ISR) The U.S. record of the meeting on February 24, 1957, between Dulles and Eban is in *Foreign Relations, 1955–1957*, vol. XVII, pp. 254–267. The next day Reuven Shiloah, Minister of the Israeli Embassy, gave Assistant Secretary of State for Near Eastern, South Asian, and African Affairs William M. Rountree an Israeli working paper, unsigned and undated, summarizing Eban's queries and Dulles' comments. According to the U.S. memorandum of the conversation, Shiloah emphasized that the paper had no status as a document. (Ibid., pp. 270–271) No record has been found in Department of State records showing U.S. acceptance of the Israeli paper as an agreed minute.

[3] A second document delivered to Rostow by Harman on May 26, headed "Summary of Conversation, Secretary Dulles' Residence, Washington, D.C., 24 February 1957," quotes paragraph 13 of a speech given by Israeli Foreign Minister Golda Meir before the UN General Assembly on March 1, 1957. It states that the quoted passage was drafted by Eban and Dulles and that Eban had in his possession in Jerusalem a draft with the words "by armed force" added in Dulles' handwriting. (National Archives and Records Administration, RG 59, Central Files 1967–69, POL 27–2 ARAB–ISR) An extract of the paragraph is quoted in footnote 2, Document 131. Dulles and Eban discussed the statement to be made by Meir in two meetings on February 28, 1957. Memoranda of the conversations are in *Foreign Relations, 1955–1957*, vol. XVII, pp. 311–313 and 325–326. The text of the Israeli draft declaration, as revised after Dulles' meeting with Eban, is ibid., pp. 313–317. The complete text of Meir's statement is in UN document A/PV.666; also printed in *American Foreign Policy: Current Documents, 1957*, pp. 936–940.

it was important for the U.S. to begin escorting immediately and not to let the present situation jell as had occurred with respect to the Suez Canal. In time Egypt would find its interests served by a removal of whatever US–UK naval presence would be necessary in the area for escort duty and therefore would relieve the blockade. Egypt would find it too humiliating to have indefinitely to "submit to force."

Mr. McNamara questioned whether the situation would move in this way inasmuch as Egypt really would not be submitting to force and the continuance of its posture would cost it nothing. Mr. Eban's response was only that we were all faced with an immediate problem and he could not see very far into the future in this matter. He then went on to say he thought the "balloon would go up" next week unless he could take back with him definite American assurances of ultimate action to keep the Straits open. Such assurances should not be conditional on others joining; if the U.S. left it conditional, others would not join. On the other hand, if the U.S. made clear its determination to support free passage, unilaterally if necessary, then other nations would join. He said he needed to take back to the Prime Minister a clear idea of the "logistics" of necessary action to assemble forces and to push ships through the Gulf.

Again reverting to the scope and firmness of prior U.S. commitments he said Aqaba would be a test of whether the U.S. keeps its commitments. Mr. McNamara replied that there should be no question in anybody's mind about the U.S. willingness to honor its commitments; we had demonstrated that in many ways. Mr. Eban suggested that there was question in some minds about whether the U.S. could both carry on in Vietnam and honor its commitments in the Middle East. Mr. McNamara said he hoped there was no doubt in Minister Eban's mind for there certainly was no question of our military capabilities.

Mr. McNamara went on then to say, however, that Israel should realize that an Israeli attack under present circumstances would have most serious consequences. We cannot undertake to support Israel if Israel launches an attack. He said that the U.S. agreed with the Israeli view that Israel would prevail in a conflict, even if hostilities were initiated by Egypt, and that the issue before us should not be a preemptive attack by Israel but how to prevent hostilities. He read the pertinent passage from the President's speech of May 24 and said that he thought this made clear our continuing commitments. We must, however, exhaust the UN route and secure Congressional and public support for necessary measures.

Mr. Eban observed that action through the UN could not amount to anything in view of Russian intransigence. He said that Mr. deGaulle had tried fruitlessly with his 4-power approach and Foreign Minister Brown had been equally unsuccessful in Moscow. The UN phase of the action should be very short for that route is a cul-de-sac.

Mr. McNamara asked how General deGaulle saw the situation. Mr. Eban responded that he had seen Mr. deGaulle early on in the crisis when he still had his fixation about the 4-power approach. Now that that approach had foundered Mr. deGaulle should be approached again since in 1957 the French had been the strongest supporter of Israel's rights in the Gulf.

At this point in the meeting Ambassador Harman was called to the telephone urgently and he reappeared in a couple of minutes with a note which said that a recheck of Israel's intelligence had confirmed Prime Minister Eshkol's flash warning of yesterday that a UAR-Syrian attack was imminent. Mr. Eban said this is not just an evaluation of intelligence but is "information", a word he later changed to "knowledge." Mr. McNamara said that our intelligence differed on some of the facts Prime Minister Eshkol had relied upon; but, more importantly, our appraisal of the facts was different. We thought the Egyptian deployments were defensive in character and anticipatory of a possible Israeli attack.

General Wheeler asked if Minister Eban's reference to the reaffirmed intelligence of an imminent attack as "knowledge" meant that Israel knew with certainty the Egyptians' intent, for example through an agent, as well as their troop dispositions. Mr. Eban reaffirmed the statement that this was knowledge.

General Wheeler restated the American view of Israel's military superiority and said that, although we recognize that casualties would be greater than in 1948 and 1956, Israel would prevail. He went on to observe that as far as the ground situation was concerned, if the Egyptians came out of their prepared positions to attack they would be at a further disadvantage. He added that an attack against Israel would also importantly change the political picture.

Mr. Eban's rejoinder was that Israel believed its forces would win and he agreed that the balance of power had not been shifted by deployment of the last few days. He added that he assumed the American commitment to Israel was not, however, restricted only to the circumstances in which Israel was losing. Under the best of circumstances casualties would be great and Israel's urban areas were open to devastation. Shouldn't there now be a plan for joint action if hostilities break out? Surely the U.S. does not intend to stand by and merely watch. The Foreign Minister said that if Prime Minister Eshkol's suggested formula for an American statement (in essence, "An attack on Israel is an attack on the U.S.") was not a feasible way to proceed, surely another way could be found. The Prime Minister wants to know what the U.S. is prepared to say and do.

Mr. McNamara said that the President would respond on these points. He felt that there had been inadequate exchanges of intelligence and supply information between us and he hoped that we could improve these. He said that he now understood the Israelis' problem better and that he felt the conversation had been very useful to him.

70.   **Memorandum From the President's Special Assistant (Rostow) to President Johnson**[1]

Washington, May 26, 1967, 11:10 a.m.

Mr. President:

Herewith our Military Attachés in Tel Aviv state their belief that "Israel is approaching a decision in favor of a preemptive attack"; and they explain why.[2]

[2-1/2 *lines of source text not declassified*][3]

One underlying problem is, of course, that the Israelis feel that the longer a confrontation over Aqaba is avoided—and the issue is kicked around in the UN—the more their rights in the Straits will become eroded.

Walt

---

[1] Source: Johnson Library, National Security File, Country File, Middle East Crisis, Vol. II. Top Secret; [*codeword not declassified*].

[2] The attachment conveying this assessment was telegram STRIKE 4553 from CINC-STRIKE, May 26, 0801Z.

[3] [*text not declassified*]

71.   Memorandum From Secretary of State Rusk to President
       Johnson[1]

Washington, May 26, 1967.

SUBJECT

Your Conversation with the Israeli Foreign Minister

As you know, the Israelis have told us their intelligence indicates that an Egyptian and Syrian attack is imminent. They have therefore requested a U.S. public statement of assurance and support to Israel against such aggression. Our intelligence does not confirm this Israeli estimate. Foreign Minister Eban, in his conversation with me last evening, indicated that he would not press this Israeli view and request. He said the telegram would not have been written as it was had he been there. He seems satisfied on this point with the precautionary message we gave the Egyptian Ambassador. He also agreed that improved cooperative arrangements with our intelligence were urgently needed.

In our conversations with Eban last night, he made clear that Ambassador Barbour's intervention on May 23 held off a preemptive strike. Barbour was authorized to float the British idea of a maritime group, which could effectively protect maritime rights in the Gulf of Aqaba if UN action failed. That idea gave the Israelis hope for the first time that there might be a third choice for them, apart from surrender or war. Eban is here to find out whether this alternative is feasible. Their Ambassador describes the visit as "a fateful mission".

You have two basic options now:

(1) to let the Israelis decide how best to protect their own national interests, in the light of the advice we have given them: i.e., to "unleash" them. We recommend strongly against this option.

(2) To take a positive position, but not a final commitment, on the British proposal. The British Cabinet meets on the plan tomorrow.

We recommend this policy, as our best hope of preventing a war which could gravely damage many American national interests.

Leaving aside detail, the essence of the plan that we have in mind following our talks with George Thomson is this:

---

[1] Source: Johnson Library, National Security File, Country File, Israel, Vol. XII, 1965–1968. Secret. No drafting information appears on the memorandum. Walt Rostow forwarded it to the President at 12:07 p.m. with a covering memorandum commenting: "It follows the lines you suggested to me earlier but lacks an answer to the questions: Who would join the British party; What would be consequences of this approach in Arab world and elsewhere." (Ibid., NSC Histories, Middle East Crisis, Vol. 2)

(a) a short, energetic effort in the Security Council;

(b) a public declaration by the maritime powers, which would be made as soon as possible, preferably while the Security Council was in session; and

(c) a contingency plan for an international naval presence in the area of the Gulf. That plan is now being drafted by British and American experts. If the governments reached agreement on the program as a whole, the naval force would be assembled as soon as the scheme was approved. It would not become operational for a time. And hopefully, its presence would itself deter UAR from an attack on shipping.

(d) at the same time, we should prepare the way to propose in the U.N. that a U.N. presence between Israel and Egypt take a position along both sides of the Israeli-UAR frontier. If Egypt refuses, we can ask Israel to accept. Such a force could prevent hostilities along that frontier, if both sides pulled back, as Eshkol has proposed.

Eban's preliminary reaction to the British idea is hopeful, provided we can be positive enough about our commitment to it to justify Israel in not going to war at once. He now thoroughly and I think sympathetically understands your political and constitutional problem. What he wants is as specific and definite a statement as you can make under the circumstances that we are seriously considering joining with other maritime nations at the end of the U.N. road in the plan for an international naval presence.

We put the case against preemptive strikes to Eban very hard last night, both from the military and the political points of view. I pointed out to him that we have lived with this issue a long time in connection with the Soviet Union, and come down definitively against the idea.

Despite this, Eban still believes, I think, that in the context of Israel's problem, surrounded by menacing concentrations (armed among other things, with nerve gas), he needs something pretty solid to hold the line against his hawks.

They have absolutely no faith in the possibility of anything useful coming out of the U.N.

Continuing informal consultations with Congress indicate support for an international approach and caution regarding U.S. unilateral commitments and action. We will have a draft joint resolution for your consideration by the end of the day.

We would suggest that you make the following principal points to Foreign Minister Eban:

1. We do not disagree with the Israeli assessment of the unlikelihood that the Security Council will be able to adopt a resolution which would be effective in assuring free and innocent passage through the Straits and the Gulf. However, we do believe that an attempt must be

made even if only to demonstrate that the United Nations is unable to act in this situation. The proposals which are presently being discussed in New York are: a resolution assuring the free and innocent passage of vessels in the Straits and the Gulf; the resumption of full implementation of the Egyptian-Israeli Armistice Agreement; and a possible UN naval patrol comprised of such middle powers as Canada, the Scandinavian countries and others. Moreover, the Secretary General is apt to come up with some other ideas, but his report is not expected before Saturday of this week. These matters being discussed in New York will have to be dealt with even though it is unlikely that formal Security Council action will result.

2. We believe that the UK proposal for a declaration on the part of the principal maritime powers in support of freedom of passage in the Gulf of Aqaba should move forward, after appropriate consultations with Congress and concurrently with the UN consideration. We would then be prepared to encourage maritime powers to join in such a Declaration which would be presented to the Security Council, not for formal approval, but for inclusion in the record of proceedings. Several governments have already made or have under consideration statements to this effect.

3. Our intention is to see to it that the Straits and Gulf remain open to free and innocent passage of vessels of all nations.[2] We cannot, at this time, see all the steps that would be required to achieve this objective. To this end, we are examining thoroughly and carefully the UK proposal calling for the creation of an international naval force to escort merchant vessels safely through the Strait of Tiran. We assure the Israeli Government of our positive interest in this proposal.

4. We will consult with the Israeli Government at every step of the way, and we expect the Israelis to reciprocate. We know and appreciate that in light of the difficulties which have developed as a result of Nasser's unilateral steps, it is difficult for Israel to be patient and pru-

---

[2] A memorandum Rostow sent to Johnson at 12:35 p.m. summarizes Goldberg's comments, conveyed through Sisco, on Rusk's recommendations. It states that Goldberg thought this sentence went too far; he preferred: "Our intention is to pursue appropriate measures that the Straits and Gulf remain open." (Ibid., Country File, Middle East Crisis, Vol. II) A message from Goldberg to the President, conveyed by telephone at 2 p.m. that day, suggested a "face-saving solution" involving recognition of UAR sovereign rights over the Straits of Tiran, recognition of the right of international innocent passage through the Straits for non-strategic cargoes, and a confidential "gentleman's agreement" that the UAR would not intercept non-Israeli flag ships for inspection and that Israel would neither send Israeli flag ships through the Straits nor send strategic goods through the Straits on flag ships of other nations. He suggested that such a proposal might be floated through a third party. (Message from Goldberg to the President, received by telephone May 26; ibid.)

dent in circumstances where its vital interests could be adversely affected. Nevertheless we can proceed only on the assumption that Israel will make no military move that would precipitate hostilities in the area. Preemptive action by Israel would cause extreme difficulty for the United States. In our position of world leadership, the American people would do what has to be done if "the fault is on the other side and there is no other alternative". Therefore, the question of responsibility for the initiation of hostilities is a major problem for us. Of course if we had information that the other side was moving this would be a matter of great concern.

5. The fundamental guiding principles of the U.S. are the preservation of international peace and security and the preservation of the political independence and territorial integrity of states of the Near East. We have opposed aggression from any source in the past and will continue to do so.

6. We recognize the stresses and the economic cost to which the current situation is subjecting Israel. Bearing this in mind, the United States is prepared to discuss with Israel means of relieving the economic impact of current special burdens on the Israeli economy. We will continue to review the military supply requirements in light of the changing situation.

Dean Rusk

72.   Memorandum for the Record[1]

Washington, May 26, 1967, 1:30 p.m.

SUBJECT

Meeting on the Arab-Israeli Crisis, May 26, 1:30 p.m.

THOSE PRESENT

The President	Clark Clifford
The Vice President	Justice Fortas
Secretary Rusk	General Wheeler
Secretary McNamara	Richard Helms
Undersecretary Vance	Joseph Sisco
Lucius Battle	Walt Rostow
Eugene Rostow	George Christian
George Ball	Harold Saunders

The President began the meeting by asking General Wheeler to summarize the military picture.

General Wheeler described Israeli and UAR forces as follows:

Israeli forces are 55–65% mobilized with 160,000 now in the ground forces. Israel has not yet called to duty the support forces that would be necessary for a long campaign. The Air Force and Navy are fully mobilized. The UAR has moved some 50,000 troops into Sinai and established them along two defensive lines, one behind the other. They have moved a number of fighter aircraft into the Sinai. In addition, they have established a small Naval force and 12 MIGs at Hurghada, across the Red Sea from Sharm al-Sheikh where there are a 3000-man parachute battalion and 4 coastal defense guns.

He described the military situation as of the moment as basically static. Although there have been two overflight incidents, neither side looks as if it is readying for attack. The UAR's dispositions are defensive and do not look as if they are preparatory to an invasion of Israel. The UAR has gained some military advantage by moving into Sharm al-Sheikh and by advancing its forces into the Sinai. He concluded, however, that Israel should be able to resist or undertake aggression and that in the long term Israel would prevail.

---

[1] Source: Johnson Library, National Security File, Country File, Middle East Crisis, Miscellaneous Material. Top Secret. Drafted on May 27. Filed with a covering memorandum from Saunders to George Christian stating that he had dictated this draft from his notes and Christian could make additions or revisions before putting it in the President's records. A few handwritten corrections by Saunders appear on the source text and on a copy that Saunders sent to Walt Rostow. (Ibid., Vol. II) No copy with further revisions has been found. The agenda for the meeting, prepared by Rostow, is ibid. The meeting, held in the Cabinet Room, began at 1:33 p.m. The President left the meeting at 3:10 p.m. and returned at 3:51 p.m.; the meeting ended at 4:05 p.m. (Ibid., President's Daily Diary)

In response to the President's question, he believed that Israel could maintain the present level of mobilization for two months without causing serious economic trouble. Full mobilization, however, would cut into the economy. We believe Israel's full war stocks are designed to carry three or four weeks. To continue beyond that would require resupply. He thought the UAR could continue for at least a month.

The President asked General Wheeler to confirm whether anything indicates that either side will attack. General Wheeler answered that there were no indications that the Egyptians would attack. If the UAR moved, it would give up its defensive positions in the Sinai for little advantage.

He believed that the Israelis would win air superiority. The UAR would lose a lot of aircraft. Israel's military philosophy is to gain tactical surprise by striking airfields first but he believes this is not absolutely essential to Israel's gaining air supremacy.

He concluded by noting that on the Israeli side the greatest danger is the state of mind. The Israelis believed that if the situation jells, it jells in favor of the Arabs.

The President asked whether there was any military reason why we should make any declaration or any military moves now. General Wheeler said he saw none.

In response to the President's request, Secretary Rusk summarized the situation. Israeli Foreign Minister Eban had come in the previous afternoon with a flash message from Eshkol that the Israeli government expected an Arab attack imminently. Eshkol requested that we put our Mediterranean forces in touch with the Israeli Defense Force to coordinate action in the event of such an attack.

Secretary Rusk had told Eban that our intelligence does not support the view that Israel is threatened with imminent attack. He noted that U Thant said that everything he had heard in Cairo tends to exclude that likelihood also. He explained to Eban the President's problems with Congress and strong Congressional feeling that the US must not act unilaterally. He cautioned against a preemptive Israeli attack and said that we could not be responsible if Israel goes off on its own.

Secretary Rusk felt that Eban the following morning had pulled away somewhat from the message of Thursday evening. He indicated to the Secretary on the phone that he would not have sent that message had he been in Jerusalem. However, he did cite the "apocalyptic" mood in Israel and the heavy pressure for a strike. Eban expected to return to Jerusalem for a Sunday Cabinet meeting which might be "the most important to be held in the history of Israel."

Secretary McNamara had reported that he had met with Eban from 10:30 to 11:20 a.m. He said Eban was back on the tack of the night before—that a surprise Arab attack was imminent. Eban said Israel by itself had two alternatives—surrender or a preemptive strike. He had come to explore a third—what the US might do to open the Gulf of Aqaba. He stressed US commitments and expressed concern that so far he had had no indication that the US was ready to use force. During the meeting Eban received a message stating that the prediction of attack was no longer just an appraisal but was solid information. However, he was vague on the source of this information.

Secretary McNamara had said that the Israelis would stand alone if they initiated an attack. He cited the importance of our gaining Congressional support and working through the UN. Eban had questioned the efficacy of the UN. He predicted nothing would happen there and asked why Israel should not act now.

Eban cited a 27 February 1957 agreed Minute between Secretary Dulles and himself,[2] then Israel's Ambassador in Washington. The substance of that understanding was that Israel would withdraw from Sharm al-Sheikh if passage through the Straits of Tiran was assured. Eban interpreted our statement at that time (we believe the Straits comprehend international waters)[3] as a US commitment to use force to keep the Straits open.

Secretary McNamara said that, after reviewing the documents of that 1957 exchange, he had learned that Eban was ignoring a 19 February 1957 statement by Secretary Dulles at a news conference. In effect, Secretary Dulles said he would not think the US had the right to use force to protect vessels of other flags. That would require Congressional action.[4]

Secretary Rusk stated that Eban and Secretary Dulles had jointly drafted the paragraphs that Israeli Foreign Minister Golda Meir had agreed [included?] in her statement to the UN on 1 March 1957.[5] This in effect said that interference of shipping by armed force would constitute

---

[2] See Document 69 and footnote 2 thereto.

[3] The aide-mémoire of February 11, 1957, as made public on February 17, 1957, and Lodge's statement before the General Assembly on March 1, 1957, stated that the United States believed that the Gulf of Aqaba comprehended international waters. See footnote 6, Document 36, and footnote 6, Document 32. President Eisenhower reiterated this position in an address of February 20, 1957. (*Public Papers of the Presidents of the United States: Dwight D. Eisenhower, 1957*, pp. 147–156)

[4] At his news conference on February 19, 1957, Dulles said, "The President has inherent power to use the forces of the United States to protect American ships and their rights all over the world. But he has no power, in my opinion, to use the forces of the United States on behalf of the vessels of another flag unless he is given that authority by some congressional resolution or by a treaty." (Department of State *Bulletin*, March 11, 1957, p. 404) The complete record of the news conference is ibid., pp. 400–406.

[5] See footnote 3, Document 69.

an imposition on Israeli rights that would justify exercise of the right of self-defense under Article 51 of the UN Charter.

Mr. Eugene Rostow interjected that it was important to settle in our own minds the doctrine of "first strike." It was important to decide whether the UAR by proclaiming a blockade of the Straits, had already made a first strike.

The President then asked Mr. Battle to describe the Arab situation and Mr. Sisco to describe the Israeli position.

Mr. Battle noted a vigorous Soviet effort to turn this crisis into a US-Arab confrontation. He suggested that Syria had been ahead of Nasser for a while but would now follow his lead. He suggested that Saudi Arabia, Jordan and Lebanon will probably be weakened in the current crisis. The closer we get to Israel, the more difficult it will be for the moderate Arabs to stay at arms length from Nasser. He was sure Hussein and Faisal must be having nightmares over being drawn into this conflict, but they could not stay out of a holy war against Israel. The rest of the Arab world would not be important, except that Kuwait will probably be pressed to bail the UAR out financially and Libya may be under pressure to abrogate our base rights at Wheelus.

Mr. Battle summarized by saying: (1) whatever we do we are in trouble. If we fail to stand by Israel, the radical Arabs will paint us as a paper tiger. If we stand by Israel, we will damage ourselves seriously with all the Arabs. (2) We must remember that the Arabs never stick together for long. We know that eventually strains will reappear.

Mr. Sisco described access to the Gulf of Aqaba as the "gut issue" for Israel. Backing down would amount to surrender and maybe even the beginnings of dissolution of the State of Israel. On the economic side, Israel depends on this route for most of its oil imports and for many exports to the markets of Africa and Asia it is trying to develop. Legally, Israel has the same interest as we do in keeping the Straits open as a matter of principle. Israel has made it clear that if the choice is surrender or action on any of these fronts, it will choose action. Mr. Sisco pointed out that Israel has no faith in the UN. The UN Security Council proved itself unable to deal with the problem of cross border terrorism after the Syrian incidents last October. Nor does Israel have faith in the ability of UN Truce Supervisory Organization to in any way limit these incidents. It has no faith in the General Assembly as now constituted. The composition of the General Assembly of today is quite different from the Assembly which after Suez established the UNEF. Mr. Sisco predicted that any General Assembly action today would be anti-Israeli. To top off their lack of faith in the UN, they feel U Thant is biased against them. He rushed to pull out the UNEF, and his slowness in getting out his report played into the UAR's hands. Then he went to Cairo and not to Tel Aviv. They feel he will not come up with anything more than some "gimmick proposals" to rationalize the status quo.

In summary, the Israelis are deeply concerned that with the passage of time and with the double standard in New York, they can hope for little more than gradual quiet acquiescence in the status quo. The Israelis believe that they have a special relationship with us. They are willing to exhaust the UN avenue if it does not take too much time, but they want assurance that at the end of that road the Straits will remain open. Mr. Sisco thought that cooperation among the maritime states perhaps with the support of a Naval escort to keep the Straits open would be the kind of concrete proposal the Israelis might be willing to accept.

The President asked what kind of force might be available. Mr. Sisco believed it would be impossible for the UN to approve any such UN force. However, we are working on a force involving at first the US–UK and maybe Canada—and then the Dutch, other Commonwealth nations, the Japanese and maybe the Argentines.

The President interjected that the Canadians had not promised anything but he felt from his conversation with Prime Minister Pearson that they would probably go along.

Secretary McNamara questioned whether the UK proposal brought here by Minister of State George Thomson had full UK military approval. This is something we will have to work out. In any case, we would not want to launch any Naval probe of the Straits until the UN has played itself out and until Congress has endorsed our proposal.

In response to the President's further question, General Wheeler described briefly the Naval forces now in the vicinity of the Red Sea—two U.S. destroyers (the *Fisk* and the *Kennedy*) and the flagship of COMIDEASTFOR (the *Valcour*). The UK has several frigates and minesweepers in the immediate area and the *Hermes*, a commando carrier, is somewhere not far from Aden. In the Mediterranean there is a substantial US force, and we hope we might persuade the Italians and even the Greeks to join. However, what is in the Mediterranean may not be useful in the Red Sea.

Mr. Eugene Rostow briefly described Eban's purpose in coming to Washington. He stated his belief that on Tuesday, May 23, we had held the Israelis off from striking. At that time he had authorized Ambassador Barbour to describe to the Israelis the proposal that George Thomson had brought to Washington. Eban now described that as Israel's first ray of hope and said that he had come to Washington to find out how serious that proposal was. Israel would regard the closing of the Straits as justifying self-defense under Article 51, but Eban is disposed to recommend that his government go along with us in an effort to unite the maritime nations behind a plan to keep the Straits open by collective action. He felt that if there were some hope that an international group would keep the Straits open, this would be sufficient to stay Israel's hand. Eban had said he also was disposed to go along with this plan if the President were behind it. Mr. Rostow said that this was the specific question the President could expect Eban to put to him when they met.

Secretary Rusk added that Eban needs to take home something that he and his government can use to contain the "apocalyptic pressures" they face. He said he recognized that that was the Israeli government's problem. He assured the President that Eban understands the nature of our public relations problems.

The President then asked what he should tell Eban.

Secretary Rusk noted that U Thant had categorical assurances from Nasser that the UAR would not make a preemptive attack.[6] The UAR wants to reestablish the General Armistice Agreements. He recommended that we try to concentrate on the problem of the Straits and get Israeli minds off the fear of an imminent Arab attack. He noted that the UAR Embassy had held a press conference that morning trying to calm the atmosphere. He pointed out that it is still unclear what ground rules the UAR plans to apply in controlling shipping through the Straits. The UAR keeps referring to the Battle Act[7] as a possible criterion, and the Battle Act does not include oil.

Secretary Rusk pointed out that the sensitive issue is whether Israel will insist on the right of passage for Israeli flag vessels. As a practical matter, the UAR might allow the continued passage of non-Israeli ships, but Israel may not be willing to settle for that. In any case though we should concentrate on the Straits, we won't get too far until U Thant reports.

Secretary McNamara said he saw no "perishability" in the situation as it stands except for the fact that Israel probably can not sustain its mobilization for too long without economic cost. He asked the President whether getting support for a probe would be politically harder two to three weeks from now. The President asked whether a probe could actually be made.

Secretary Rusk said he had told Eban what he had said to Gromyko in the Berlin crisis of 1961–62. He had said then that the USSR could

---

[6] The Secretary-General so stated in his report to the Security Council on May 26. For the text, see *Public Papers of the Secretaries-General of the United Nations*, Vol. VII, U Thant, 1965–1967, pp. 438–443.

[7] The Mutual Defense Assistance Control Act of 1951 (P.L. 213), approved October 26, 1951, provided for the suspension of economic aid to nations supplying strategic commodities to Communist countries. (65 Stat. 644)

have war in five minutes but a peaceful answer would take more time to work out. The Secretary said he had told Eban that Israel has a tremendous stake in the world's view of its actions, particularly who is responsible for a shooting war if one starts. He had told Eban that Israel would not be alone unless it chose to go alone. He had emphasized that the US can not be drawn into war by the unilateral action of others. Because of US public opinion and the views of Congress we must exhaust all other avenues first. The Israelis must give our efforts a chance.

The President asked General Wheeler to comment on the efficacy of an effort by the maritime powers to keep the Straits open. He suggested that he could tell Eban that we would work through the UN even though we have our doubts what that course will produce. Then we could put our eggs in a multilateral basket by the maritime powers provided the military situation does not deteriorate in the meantime.

General Wheeler said that if the President decides to force the Straits the best way is by a series of steps. First, we might send a non-Israeli flag cargo vessel into the Straits. Then a cargo vessel with military escort (he noted apparent UAR instructions not to accost any vessel with a military escort). If these vessels were attacked, the least we could do would be to strike the air and naval bases from which the attack was launched. This would be a more limited operation than what the Israelis would have to mount. They would probably have to destroy all the Sinai airfields as part of any air attack on Sharm al-Sheikh or Hurghada.

In summary, General Wheeler expressed the view that the UAR would back down if the maritime powers were able to muster an impressive enough force. He felt that this would be the most precise military response we could mount; a show of force by the Sixth Fleet near the UAR's coast line might encourage the Israelis to attack or trigger an attack by Nasser as a last desperate act.

The President asked whether the UK has enough interest to "stand up with us like men." General Wheeler cited the UK's substantial oil interests and opined that the UK could not tolerate Nasser as the dominant force in the Middle East. The President asked, "If you were in Eban's place and we told you we were relying on the UN and a group of maritime powers, would that be enough to satisfy you?" General Wheeler answered that he would drive a harder bargain. He would agree to go along provided that the US guarantee to back Israel if these efforts failed. He said he might gamble that the US would have to back Israel anyway but would try to get some more formal assurance. The President turned to the rest of the group around the table and asked two questions: (1) Are there other elements of the situation we have overlooked? (2) What do you recommend? "Dean has to fly off to Iowa for a speech; the Vice President has a birthday party; and along about sundown I have to bell this cat. I need to know what I am going to say."

The Vice President summarized his view by focusing on the Gulf of Aqaba as the central issue and expressed his doubt that the UAR would attack. He felt the UAR would understand that we have a great stake in the freedom of the seas. He noted that this is a matter of life or death for Israel and we could not expect Israel to trust Nasser's word.

The Vice President then asked what about the UAR's capability to endure a high degree of mobilization over any period given its economic weakness. He wondered whether Nasser wasn't trying to blackmail us. He felt the UN would not do much. At the end of the road, we have a large stake in keeping the Straits open. Unless Israel thinks we are going to back them, it will attack.

The Vice President suggested that the President tell Eban that we have a stake in the freedom of the seas but that we also have a stake in peace in the Middle East. The Israelis have to have faith and we will use everything we can to achieve our ends.

The President asked whether he could go that far, and Secretary McNamara said he didn't think so.

Mr. Clifford pointed out that all we are acting from at the moment is a UAR announcement that it would close the Straits. As far as we know—since the UAR had been talking about our Battle Act—the UAR might allow even oil tankers to go through the Straits.

The President asked whether we expected a test soon and Mr. Vance and Mr. Eugene Rostow noted that there are conflicting reports. The Israelis say that one tanker has already been stopped in the Red Sea but we have no confirmation.

Mr. Walt Rostow pointed out that in the language which Secretary Dulles and Foreign Minister Meir had worked out in 1957,[8] the Secretary's addition of the words "by armed force" acted as a limitation on the circumstances which would permit the Israelis to exercise their right of self defense—not as an expansion of our obligation.

Mr. Clifford went on to say that regardless of the legal points involved, in world opinion the UAR has not yet moved. So far we have had only an oral threat. He felt it exceedingly important that Israel not take the first overt step. If it does, we will bear the brunt of the world's reaction.

---

[8] Reference is to the language agreed upon by Secretary Dulles and Ambassador Eban on February 28, 1957; for Foreign Minister Meir's statement the next day, see footnote 3, Document 69.

Nevertheless, Mr. Clifford felt that Israel's life was indeed at stake and that we must assure access to the Gulf. If Nasser succeeds in closing the Gulf, he will have won a major victory.

He felt that we have an excellent issue in the freedom of the seas and that we must call Nasser's bluff. We must put him in a position where he either takes an overt act against free shipping or backs down. Mr. Clifford made a major point of the fact that our ultimate objective is to put an Israeli ship through the Straits and on into its port.

He concluded that there is no obligation to say all of this to Eban later in the day. He felt it would be enough to say that we sympathize, that we are studying this but have no commitment to make yet. The President asked whether Eban would not misjudge this as a cold shoulder and go home to advise his Cabinet that it could not count on the US. Mr. Clifford felt that our expression of sympathy would be enough. Secretary Rusk asked whether this would not sound as if we are diluting our commitment. Mr. Clifford said we need not volunteer any statement on what we would do in the Straits, but the President laughingly said he was sure he would have a chance to discuss that subject.

The President asked whether this would be enough for Eban to take home to keep the Israeli Cabinet from deciding to strike. Secretary McNamara said he thought a little more was necessary. He said that in his conversation with Eban that morning Eban had in a sense asked whether we were not walking away from the commitments of our predecessors. Secretary McNamara would stop short of endorsing all previously made commitments because "there is some pretty bad language in them." He suggested writing a new statement of our position.

Mr. Ball suggested that two problems should be separated: (1) the principle of free passage in international waterways has been covered in the 1958 Convention of the Seas; (2) the question of belligerent rights is a separate one.

Mr. Ball indicated on the basis of his conversation with Mr. Shoaib of the World Bank that Muslim world opinion is coalescing against Israel. Shoaib felt that even the Iranians would have to line up against Israel eventually. Therefore, the Israelis would be "out of their minds" to attack. Their rights will be as clear two weeks from now as now. We should live up to past commitments but we should not underestimate the possibility of a grave oil crisis if we end up on the Israeli side of a fight. US companies would be under serious attack and would probably be nationalized.

Mr. Fortas described the problem as how to keep the Israelis from striking. We will open the Straits over the long run but the critical time is Israel's Cabinet Meeting Sunday. Mr. Fortas did not feel that Mr.

Clifford's suggestion went far enough. He felt we would have to assure Eban that one of these days we will assure that an Israeli flagship will get into the Gulf. Mr. Fortas felt that Eban understands our problems but needs a package he can sell to the Cabinet in Jerusalem.

The President asked whether Mr. Fortas meant we would enforce the passage of an Israeli vessel with our men and ships. Mr. Fortas answered that we would use whatever force necessary. The President said he did not believe he was in a position now to say that.

The President indicated that Eban would not get all he wants. The big question was whether we will regret on Monday not having given him more. Nevertheless, we have the unanimous pressure of the Congress to try the UN and multilateral machinery.

The Vice President reiterated his point that we should tell Eban we have as big a stake in freedom of the seas as Israel does and that Israel should have faith that we will do what we can to protect that principle.

The President left the meeting at this point and suggested that the other participants might want to stay on and draft a statement for him to use with Eban later.

In the subsequent conversation, Secretary McNamara suggested four elements as part of what the President might tell Eban: If Israel initiates an attack, it will stand alone. If the UN fails and subject to Congressional approval, the President would work with other nations to insure keeping the Gulf open.

Mr. Fortas warned that we would not have a realistic choice between participating and not participating even if Israel provokes hostilities. He did not feel we could say that Israel will be alone.

Secretary Rusk stated that if Israel strikes first, it would have to forget the U.S. The Vice President countered that hostilities would face the President with the most serious politics imaginable. We will not be able to play with legalisms.

Secretary Rusk then tabled for the group's consideration a possible statement for the President to use in talking with Eban. That draft and a copy of the statement as the President amended it and finally used it are attached.[9] The President rejoined the meeting long enough to make those changes.

Meeting adjourned.

H.S.

---

[9] Not attached but see Document 74.

73.   Special Report of the Watch Committee[1]

No. 874A   Washington, May 26, 1967, 2 p.m.

The Watch Committee met in special session at 1400 on 26 May to review the possibility of hostilities in the Middle East, [1-1/2 lines of source text not declassified].

The Watch Committee findings are as follows:

1. On the basis of our review of all available intelligence, we do not believe the Israeli claim that Egypt is preparing to launch an attack against Israel [2-1/2 lines of source text not declassified].

2. Concern of the Israelis that their strategic position is deteriorating could lead to a decision to attack or retaliate for reasons other than a blockade of the Gulf or Israeli deaths resulting from Arab terrorist acts. A test of the more limited issue of the Strait of Tiran may not come in the immediate future since the tanker Nora, previously scheduled for Eilat, has been diverted.

---

[1] Source: Johnson Library, National Security File, Country File, Middle East Crisis, Situation Reports. Top Secret; [codeword not declassified]. The cover sheet indicates the report was sent to Bromley Smith and seen by Walt Rostow.

---

74.   Draft Statement[1]

Washington, May 26, 1967.

The United States has its own constitutional processes which are basic to its action on matters involving war and peace. The Secretary General has not yet reported to the UN Security Council and the Council has not yet demonstrated what it may or may not be able or

---

[1] Source: Johnson Library, National Security File, Country File, Middle East Crisis, Vol. II. Secret. The statement, headed "Draft," is unsigned. It is filed as an attachment to Rostow's May 26 memorandum conveying Goldberg's views on Rusk's recommendations for the President's meeting with Eban. (See footnote 2, Document 71.) Rusk's handwritten draft of the statement is in the Johnson Library, National Security File, NSC Histories, Middle East Crisis, Vol. 2. A copy with the President's handwritten revisions is ibid., Appointment File, June 1967.

willing to do although the United States will press for prompt action in the UN.

I have already publicly stated this week our views on the safety of Israel and on the Strait of Tiran. Regarding the Strait, we plan to pursue vigorously the measures which can be taken by maritime nations to assure that the Strait and Gulf remain open to free and innocent passage of the vessels of all nations.

I must emphasize the necessity for Israel not to make itself responsible for the initiation of hostilities. Israel will not be alone unless it decides to go alone. We cannot imagine that it will make this decision.

---

75. Memorandum

Washington, undated.

[Source: Johnson Library, National Security File, Country File, Middle East Crisis, Filed by the Johnson Library. Top Secret; [*codeword not declassified*]. 2 pages of source text not declassified.]

---

76. Intelligence Memorandum Prepared in the Central Intelligence Agency[1]

[*document number not declassified*]   Washington, May 26, 1967.

MILITARY CAPABILITIES OF ISRAEL AND THE ARAB STATES

Summary

Israel could almost certainly attain air superiority over the Sinai Peninsula in 24 hours after taking the initiative or in two or three days

---

[1] Source: Johnson Library, National Security File, Country File, Middle East Crisis, CIA Intelligence Memoranda, 5/67–7/67. Top Secret; [*codeword not declassified*]. Prepared in the Central Intelligence Agency's Directorate of Intelligence. An attached note from Helms to the President states, "This is our response to your request of two days ago that we review again the military capabilities of Israel versus the Arab States."

if the UAR struck first. In the latter case, Israel might lose up to half of its air force. We estimate that armored striking forces could breach the UAR's double defense line in the Sinai within several days. Regrouping and resupplying would be required before the Israelis could initiate further attacks aimed at driving to the Suez Canal. Israel could contain any attacks by Syria or Jordan during this period.

Discussion

I. General Assessment

1. The Israel Defense Forces (IDF) are at a numerical disadvantage to the combined strength of Israel's Arab neighbors in terms of aircraft, armor, artillery, naval vessels, and manpower. Nonetheless, the IDF maintain qualitative superiority over the Arab armed forces in almost all aspects of combat operations. The high quality of training and maintenance, the degree of operational proficiency, and the important, but intangible, morale factor give the advantage to the IDF, which operates through a single command structure and over interior lines of communication.

2. In contrast, the Arab states are hampered by a lack of cohesiveness and by friction among Arab leaders. The United Arab Command (UAC), even at the present state of alert, is ineffective either as a command or a coordinating structure. Only the UAR, Syria, and Iraq are coordinating military activity to any extent. Jordan, with limited offensive strength, is reluctant to become heavily engaged. Iraqi participation is limited by distance and internal security needs. Lebanon has no offensive capability. The principal Arab military strength lies with the UAR, which has now mobilized and has deployed the equivalent of about five divisions for a strength of over 50,000 in the Sinai Peninsula. Though field experience acquired by Egyptian forces in Yemen has improved their over-all military capabilities, the presence of some 35,000 UAR troops in Yemen and limited reserves at home restrict the additional forces available for use against Israel.

[Omitted here is more detailed discussion.]

77. Memorandum of Conversation[1]

Washington, May 26, 1967, 7:15–8:40 p.m.

PARTICIPANTS

The President
Secretary Robert S. McNamara
Mr. Eugene Rostow
Mr. Walt W. Rostow
Mr. George Christian
Mr. Joseph J. Sisco

Foreign Minister Eban
Ambassador Harman
Minister Evron

Eban opened the discussion by saying the Cabinet meeting on Sunday[2] was very important; there has never been a moment like this in Israeli history; and the country is on the footing of expectancy. If Israel is denied access to the Gulf of Aqaba, its primary line to East Africa and Asia—half of the world—would be cut off. From a legal point of view, the Law of the Sea Conference in 1958 clearly supported the principle of freedom of the seas as applied to Gulf of Aqaba and Strait of Tiran. Nasser has committed an act of aggression and his objective is the strangulation of Israel. Israel is confronted with two alternatives: either to surrender or to stand, and we are confident if we stand we will win.

We had raised the possibility of a third alternative: an international solution.

He had come to explore that possibility. Eban referred to possible action by 17 maritime powers in the Suez crisis who came out strongly for freedom of passage and freedom of the seas.

He reviewed for the President his conversation with DeGaulle, characterizing DeGaulle's attitude as "everything having to be talked

---

[1] Source: Johnson Library, President's Appointment File, May 26, 1967. Secret; Nodis. The date and time of the meeting are from the President's Daily Diary. (Ibid.) No drafting information appears on the memorandum, but it was apparently drafted by Sisco, whose handwritten notes are in Department of State, Sisco Files: Lot 70 D 237, Middle East. Earlier, from 6:11 to 6:45 p.m., the President met with Israeli Minister Evron and Walt Rostow. (Johnson Library, President's Daily Diary) No U.S. record of the meeting with Evron has been found. According to Evron's report of the meeting, printed in Michael Brecher, with Benjamin Geist, *Decisions in Crisis: Israel, 1967 and 1973* (Berkeley: University of California Press, 1980), pp. 136–137, the substance of the President's comments was similar to his statements to Eban. Johnson described his meeting with Eban in *The Vantage Point: Perspectives of the Presidency, 1963–1969* (New York: Holt, Rinehart and Winston, 1971), pp. 293–294. Eban described it in *An Autobiography*, pp. 354–359, and in *Personal Witness*, pp. 386–391.

[2] May 28.

out between France and the Soviet Union". Eban did not have great expectations regarding French support, although he said that the French in the last few days, have been helping them with assistance for the Israeli armed forces. France has "opened its armories" to Israel. Regarding his conversation with Wilson, he was pleased that the UK is willing to play an active role in this matter on an international basis, but only if the US was part of the whole effort.

First question raised by Eban was what can and will the US do to carry out its commitments to keep the Straits and the Gulf open? Eban, referring to the President's statement of a few days ago, said the policy is there but the question is what are you willing to do to enforce it. He characterized the Straits and Gulf issue as the crux of the matter, since the Israeli position in Africa and Asia is dependent on this link.

Second question related to UAR intentions. Eban said he has been receiving numerous cables from home that UAR preparing overall attack on Israel. He said the US is skeptical, but his Prime Minister has told him the Israeli assessment is based on facts. What if this Israeli assessment is true? Should there not be a US warning? He stressed that Israel has to take this matter seriously since Nasser, in his speeches and otherwise, has made it clear that the UAR objective is destruction of Israel. He then suggested that it was desirable for Israeli and American military to get together and to plan what should be done if the Israeli assessment proves true.

President Johnson said he had made the US view absolutely clear in his public statement a few days ago. He thought it was wise for him to make that statement when he did, and he continued to believe this today. It may not have had the effect it should have, (he said he saw tonight on television a parade in Cairo against the US) but we feel strongly on this matter and therefore I decided to make this statement to the American people and to the world.

What to do and when to do it in order to assure free access to the Straits and the Gulf is another question. President Johnson said he is of no value to Israel if he does not have the support of his Congress, the Cabinet and the people. Going ahead without this support would not be helpful to Israel. We have a vital interest in maintaining free access to the Gulf and Strait, and we have made it clear that the closing of the Straits by Nasser would be illegal. As to the Israeli Cabinet meeting on Sunday, this is a decision for the Israeli Government to take without direction from us. However, the Cabinet should know that our best efforts and our best influence will be used to keep the Strait and the Gulf open to Israeli ships. We must now await the Secretary General's report. If we move precipitously, it would only result in strengthening

Nasser. Moreover, we must do everything we can through the UN, we must see where it leads, even though we do not have great hopes.

The President continued that when we have the Secretary General's report, we intend to pursue the UN track vigorously. How satisfactory the result would be he did not know. He said he was not confident, and he cited the inability of the UN to do something about Viet-Nam. He said nevertheless the UN course must be pursued in the first instance. The President then went on to say that when it becomes apparent that UN is ineffective, Israel and its friends, including the United States, who are willing to stand up and be counted can give specific indication of what they can do. He referred to a public declaration by the maritime powers and an international naval force in the Straits area. We are making our best effort, the President said, and Israel ought promptly to get some judgment as to what other maritime powers are willing to do, what the French and British are willing to do. We would like to try to formulate an effective plan. Maybe other countries such as Italy, Canada, Argentina, Japan and the Netherlands might join with us. Eban interjected perhaps the Scandinavians would join.

The President then stressed that he did not want any of this information to get out of this room, but he said to Eban very confidentially that he thought Canada would be willing to provide a couple of ships if necessary. The President thought that it ought to be possible with Israeli, US and UK leadership to evolve an effective plan. How effective a plan could be would depend on many factors that we cannot now see. We do not know what the Secretary General will report. We do not know what the Security Council will do or not do. We did not know what our Congress would do. We are fully aware of what three past Presidents have said but this is not worth five cents if the people and the Congress did not support the President. After the Secretary General's report and the Security Council has considered the matter, we can see where we go from here. He said it would be well for the Israeli Cabinet to focus promptly on how to get the seventeen maritime countries to take steps to keep the Straits open. We want to keep the waterway open for Israeli ships as well as for the vessels of other countries. We will have to face up to this at some point.

The President said candidly that he did not find appealing Prime Minister Eshkol's ideas which were conveyed to him yesterday. We are not retreating, we are not backing off or forgetting what we have said publicly, but if he were to respond affirmatively to Prime Minister Eshkol's request of yesterday, this wouldn't be worth ten cents and Israel could get no help from the US. The US assessment does not agree with that of the Israelis: our best judgment is that no military attack on Israel is imminent, and, moreover, if Israel is attacked, our judgment is that the Israelis would lick them. Time would not work against Israel, it would not lose by waiting for the Secretary General's report and Security Council consideration. During this period there would not be any deterioration in the Israeli military position. We know it is costly economically, but it is less costly than it would be if Israel acted precipitously and if the onus for initiation of hostilities rested on Israel rather than on Nasser.

The President continued that the US, its people, its friends hold similar views to those of the Israelis regarding the waterway, and we are determined to find a resolution of this problem. The President expressed doubt that a number of other maritime powers would be willing to take steps unless UN processes had been exhausted. We must mobilize international support for our effort. He realized that the world had been brought to a new and grave situation, that the Gulf is an international waterway, and that the blockade is illegal and dangerous. But Eban should also tell his Cabinet about our problems.

The President, drawing from the notes drafted earlier in the day in his meeting with high-level advisers,[3] said the following with great deliberation. We have Constitutional processes which are basic to any action the US takes in this matter. The Secretary General has not yet reported to the Security Council and the Council has not shown what it can or cannot do. You can assure the Cabinet, the President said, we will pursue vigorously any and all possible measures to keep the Strait open. If the Israelis had a better plan than that suggested by the UK, he was willing to consider it. He had stated our views publicly last week on the Strait of Tiran.

At the same time, Israel must not make itself responsible for initiating hostilities. With emphasis and solemnity, the President repeated twice, Israel will not be alone unless it decides to go it alone. The President added he did not know much about the Israeli Cabinet but he could not imagine that they could make such a decision. The President stressed that he had been spending most of his time on this problem and he intends to continue to do so in order to bring about a satisfactory resolution. At the same time he stressed that this must be done on a step-by-step basis, and that he would do everything that he is permitted to do. When we make a decision on what we will do, we will and must have reasonable expectation of support at home and internationally for the action that we intend to take. We are Israel's friend. The Straits must be kept open. We cannot bring about a solution the day before yesterday. If he were to take a precipitous decision tonight he could not be effective in helping Israel. Eban knew his

---

[3] Document 74.

Cabinet, the President knew his Congress after 30 years of experience. He said that he would try to get Congressional support; that is what he has been doing over the past days, having called a number of Congressmen. It is going reasonably well. He had also asked Bohlen and Bruce for suggestions that they might have or the Governments to which they are accredited might have to bring about a satisfactory solution.

At this point the President put a paper he was holding in his hands in front of Harman and told him he could take whatever notes he wished from it (attached).[4] The President said again the Constitutional processes are basic to actions on matters involving war and peace. We are trying to bring Congress along. He said: "What I can do, I do". He stressed also that he would pursue every conceivable road he could find and take measures in concert with other maritime nations to assure that the Gulf and the Straits remain free and open to the vessels of all nations. His views are in his May 23 statement. He stressed again that while this process was going on, Israel should not make itself the guilty party by starting a war, and that it was inconceivable the Cabinet would take such a fateful decision.

Eban said the President had said many impressive and sympathetic things. If the United States puts together a maritime group, Eban said Israel should be part of that group. Going to the UN is not enough, since the Soviet veto would prevent any action. Eban added with emotion that Israel was full of indignation at the Secretary General, whose precipitous decision to pull out UNEF had done greater harm to Israel than any other single act that he could recall. The Secretary General took this step without consulting Israel as his predecessor, Hammarskjold, had indicated would be done. Eban said Thant owes Israel a great deal for his blunder. The UN was a useful diplomatic conference, but it is not today an organ of security upon which Israel or any other state can rely. Referring to the possible restoration of the Armistice Agreement, Eban said this had two holes in it: the Egyptian blockade of the Gulf and of the Suez Canal. Eban hoped the UN exercise could be gone through quickly and as innocuously as possible. In response to the President's query, Eban said he was hopeful the Netherlands, Sweden, Japan and a number of others would respond favorably to join in a naval escort plan. These had responded favorably in support of the principle, but there would have to be US encouragement in order to get them to take concrete steps.

---

[4] The paper is not attached, but is quoted in Document 139. The slightly different text quoted by Eban in *Personal Witness*, p. 390, is presumably based on Harman's notes.

The discussion turned briefly as to when action is taken to transit the Straits and Gulf, and Eban said the test did not have to be with an Israeli ship. The President interjected we are not going to say it's all right if the rest go through, but Israel's ships cannot.

Then Eban spoke slowly and precisely, and said the question he posed was is there a disposition on the part of the US to take action? Time is important. I intend to respond to the Cabinet that there is such a disposition on the part of the US to act. He was confident that when Nasser saw a US-UK flag on an escort ship, he would think twice about violating the rights of nations in international waters, especially if the vessels are escorted. Eban inquired whether he could show the Cabinet a systematic plan to act, this would help him a great deal.

In response to Secretary McNamara's query, Eban ticked off Uganda, Malaysia, Ethiopia, Kenya, Japan, Netherlands as other possibilities if a naval escort team is formed. But he stressed that each one of these countries has asked or will ask, is the US with us? He thought they would join in international effort, but these countries would not want to take the first leap, and that the US role was key. He also thought the Scandinavians might participate, particularly in view of the fact that Sweden, on behalf of the Nordics, had made a statement in support of freedom of shipping in international waterways. The President, at this point, urged Eban to step up their efforts in the capitals in this regard.

Once again, choosing his words carefully, Eban said "I would not be wrong if I told the Prime Minister that your disposition is to make every possible effort to assure that the Strait and the Gulf will remain open to free and innocent passage?" The President responded, "yes".

Eban then returned to the question of the possible imminent attack of the UAR on Israel, stressing that they had information which led them to this conclusion. He didn't understand why the US didn't believe this, and stressed the need to put our intelligence people together to evaluate the situation. Under Secretary Rostow raised the question of improved military and other liaison with the Israelis, suggesting that our intelligence people should get together and compare evaluations.

Secretary McNamara, in some detail, explained to Eban that three separate intelligence groups had looked into the matter in the last twenty-four hours and that our judgment was that Egyptian deployments made were defensive. Secretary McNamara said that, if attacked, Israel would deal the UAR a set-back. Under Secretary Rostow reminded Eban we had conveyed to the Egyptians this concern of the Israelis. Eban stressed Israel wants contact at the military level, the military people want some link. The President stressed that all of our intelligence people are unanimous regarding the assessment; that an attack is not imminent; and that if the UAR attacks "you will whip hell out of them".

Eban referred to the apocalyptic atmosphere which existed in Israel. Harman said he hoped they were wrong and their assessment was incorrect, but nevertheless if Israel was attacked it would not have any telephone number to call, no military group to plan with, and he, too, stressed the need for planning. Under Secretary Rostow recalled that we had given the UAR an additional warning on the hypothesis that our intelligence estimate might be incorrect.

President Johnson, while saying we do not want to establish any joint staff which would become known all over the Middle East and the world, told Secretary McNamara to get together with the Israelis and to look into this problem. Secretary McNamara said we feel we are not getting the information we should from the Israelis and that an exchange of information would be useful. It was agreed some liaison arrangements would be made.

---

78.   Memorandum From the President's Special Assistant (Rostow) to President Johnson[1]

Washington, May 26, 1967.

Mr. President:

I have a memorandum of conversation, October 12, 1966, between Nasser and Mr. James E. Birdsall of New York,[2] a lawyer and friend of Arthur Krim's.

Also he called on me and reported directly his impression that Nasser desperately needed a food loan and that we should comply.[3] You will recall this was a view conveyed to us by a number of transient businessmen late last year. At that time Mr. Birdsall's contact with Nasser came through a Mr. Siddiqui, of ALCO Products, Inc., and Ali Hafiz, member of the Egyptian National Assembly.

---

[1] Source: Johnson Library, National Security File, Country File, Middle East Crisis, Vol. II. Confidential. A note on the memorandum in Johnson's handwriting reads: "Walt, What do you suggest—L." A copy was sent to Rusk with a handwritten note: "Sir: This is the roundabout message from Nasser mentioned by Walt Rostow." (National Archives and Records Administration, RG 59, Central Files 1967–69, POL UAR–US)

[2] Not found, but see Foreign Relations, 1964–1968, vol. XVIII, Document 341.

[3] No other record of this conversation has been found.

Against this background, I report the following:

At 4:10 p.m. today, Friday, May 26, 1967, Mr. James E. Birdsall telephoned the following message:

"I have this message, conveyed from Nasser. I don't vouch for it. I am just the conduit.

"Earlier Siddiqui visited Cairo and had a visit with Nasser. Nasser told him he would still like to be friendly with the U.S. and would like to see Siddiqui again after May 20. On May 20 Siddiqui cabled Ali Hafiz in Cairo and inquired whether visit still desired. Less than 24 hours had reply that emphatically Nasser wanted to see him. On May 24 he visited Nasser.

"This is the message from Nasser: 'Now is the time when all Arab people are waiting to see an act of friendship on the part of the USA. His urgent request is that the U.S. undertake no direct military action in the form of landings, shifting of naval fleet, or otherwise. Nasser assured Siddiqui that the UAR had no intention of fighting. What they are doing is returning to the 1956 frontier. He assured Siddiqui that this matter would soon be terminated without any fighting. He informed Siddiqui that his current actions were intended only to prove to the Arab world that Saudi Arabia and Jordan are false friends. And the Arabs should follow Nasser who is their friend. He also wishes to prove that President Johnson is impartial as between the Arabs and Israel and that he will not take any sides in the present war of nerves. If President Johnson can grant Nasser's request, he can be assured that Nasser will place his entire services at President Johnson's disposal.'

"If, after President Johnson's consideration, there is any good news to convey to Cairo, Nasser requests that he (Birdsall said he assumed it would be from him (Birdsall) to Siddiqui to Ali Hafiz to Nasser) cable to arrange another meeting at an early date."

Mr. Birdsall ended by saying he would like a telephone call as to whether message given to President Johnson, so he can notify Nasser.

Walt

79. Memorandum From the Central Intelligence Agency's Board of National Estimates to Director of Central Intelligence Helms[1]

Washington, May 26, 1967.

SUBJECT

The Middle Eastern Crisis

1. The first thing that calls for explanation in the present crisis is why Nasser chose at this moment to abandon his long-standing reluctance to risk military confrontation with Israel.

a. At the immediate moment Nasser was probably prompted to initiate these maneuvers by Israeli threats against Syria. He probably felt that he had to identify himself with Arab nationalist interests and that some action on his part would refurbish his image in the Arab world. These views, however, are probably insufficient to explain all the events that have occurred.

b. He probably had decided (though he stated the contrary not long ago) that his armed forces were improved to the point where they could successfully stand off an Israeli offensive, even though they might be unable to defeat Israel decisively. Accordingly, he may have felt that if he could get his army properly deployed in the Sinai Peninsula and elsewhere, the chances of war would be acceptable.

c. It is possible that the Soviets encouraged him in these views. We do not believe that the whole operation is a Soviet plan, or even that the Soviets urged him to his present course of action, but their attitude must have been sufficiently permissive so that he knew he could count on political and logistic support from them in the course of the crisis. The interests of the Soviet Union itself would obviously be served by successes for Nasser at the expense of Israel and the US.

d. The US preoccupation with Vietnam and the bad blood occasioned thereby between the US and the USSR, probably had some important influence on the nature of Nasser's decision as well as its timing.

e. There may have been some element of desperation in Nasser's attitude, arising from the parlous condition of the Egyptian economy, the worsening of relations with the US, a belief that some sort of US-Israeli plot against him existed, and perhaps a fatalistic conclusion that

---

[1] Source: Johnson Library, National Security File, Country File, Middle East Crisis, Vol. II. Secret.

a showdown with Israel must come sooner or later, and might best be provoked before Israel acquired nuclear weapons.

f. He may also have concluded, from a tactical point of view, that he could gamble on US influence and perhaps some Israeli indecisiveness to prevent an Israeli offensive at the early and most vulnerable stages of his deployments.

2. The movement of UAR troops seems to have gone smoothly and expertly. Yet there must have been in this as in other crises a large element of accident in the actual course of events. For example, Nasser probably did not expect such a speedy departure of UN forces from Sharm el Sheikh, giving him opportunity for a quick seizure of the position and an announced closing of the Strait. He has thus far managed the crisis, from his point of view, with great skill and success.

3. Clearly Nasser has won the first round. It is possible that he may seek a military show-down with Israel, designed to settle the whole problem once and for all. This seems to us highly unlikely. We still do not believe that Nasser considers his forces (together with those of other Arab states) capable of carrying such a campaign to a successful conclusion. And in our opinion they are not so capable. Moreover we believe that the Soviets would almost certainly advise Nasser against a military effort of this magnitude, perhaps with strong insistence.

4. The most likely course seems to be for Nasser to hold to his present winnings as long as he can, and in as full measure as he can. As of the moment he has vastly enhanced his own prestige in Egypt and throughout the Arab world, diminished the standing of Israel and, at least for the moment, administered a serious setback to the US. Moreover, by simply standing where he is he places the Israelis in an extremely difficult position. He keeps the crisis at high pitch, and as long as this continues the Israelis must remain mobilized. This they cannot do for long without adverse effects upon their economy.

5. The Israelis face dismaying choices. Surprised and shaken by Nasser's action, they failed to take the instant military counteraction which might have been most effective. If they attack now they will face far more formidable opposition than in the rapid campaign of 1956. We believe that they would still be able to drive the Egyptians away from the entrance to the Strait of Tiran, but it would certainly cost them heavy losses of men and matériel. We are not sure that they have sufficient stockpiles of ammunition and equipment for a war lasting more than three or four weeks, and it is possible that they would not embark upon a major campaign without prior assurances from the US of adequate resupply.

6. But the alternative for the Israelis is perilous. To acquiesce in the permanent closing of the Strait of Tiran would constitute an economic

and political setback from which no early recovery would be foreseeable. The Israelis would expect, correctly we believe, that the Arabs over the long run would be encouraged to undertake new and still more dangerous harassments. We are inclined to believe that unless the US and other major powers take whatever steps are necessary to reopen the Strait, the Israelis will feel compelled to go to war.

7. In this event they might choose to begin hostilities by attacking Syria and wait for the Egyptians to respond. If the Egyptians did not, Nasser would lose much of what he has gained. If they did, they would lose the advantage of their defensive positions.

8. The Soviets are unlikely to take vigorous steps to calm down the crisis so long as it continues to produce deleterious effects upon Israel (and the US) and advantages for Nasser. Nevertheless they may be apprehensive about the future course of events. They may not have known in advance about the closing of the Strait. We do not believe that they desire a Middle Eastern war or that they have planned with Nasser the destruction of Israel at this juncture. They will probably oppose by diplomatic and propagandistic means any efforts by the US and the Western Powers to open the Strait. But, if we assume an attempt by the Western Powers to open the Strait by military force, we do not think that the Soviets would use their own armed forces in opposition.

9. One almost certain objective of the Soviets is to see the US more firmly and publicly identified with Israel. This would have the obvious effect of making the entire Arab world—including in an ambivalent way even the more conservative states—convinced that the US is irrevocably committed to their common enemy. It would further weaken the US position in the area, threaten US oil interests, and strengthen the Soviet position as friend and protector of all Arabs against their imperialist foes. This Soviet aim has already been realized in considerable degree. Moreover the Soviets must be glad to see US attention diverted from Vietnam, but it does not seem likely that they think the Middle Eastern crisis will appreciably affect US military capabilities or intentions in Southeast Asia.

10. One important question is what the Soviets would do if the Israelis attacked the UAR and waged a successful campaign. Such an event would be a grave setback for Nasser and, by extension, for the USSR itself. Nevertheless we do not believe that the Soviets would intervene in the conflict with their own combat forces. They could, of course, use their bomber and missile forces against Israel, but they would be very unlikely to do so, though they might threaten it. They do not have the capability of introducing lesser kinds of forces (ground troops, or volunteers) in this area with sufficient speed to be decisive, and we do not think they would try to do so. They would be cautious about the risk of armed confrontation with US forces. And they would probably count

upon the political intervention of great powers, including themselves, to stop the fighting before Nasser had suffered too much damage.

11. The position of other Arab countries than the UAR is, at this stage of crisis, ancillary and comparatively unimportant. Conceivably Syria might touch off larger hostilities by attacking Israel in force, but we believe that both Nasser and the USSR would be opposed to such action. If war broke out Syrian forces would engage, other Arab states would send help, but it would not matter very much. The crisis in its present acute intensity is essentially one between Israel and the UAR, the US and the UAR, and (to a more moderate degree) between the US and the USSR. The course of events will depend upon the action and reactions of these powers.

For the Board of National Estimates:

Sherman Kent
Chairman

---

80.   **Telegram From the Department of State to the Embassy in the United Kingdom**[1]

Washington, May 27, 1967, 1:42 a.m.

203800. Memcon Between Ambassador Dean and Under Secretary Rostow.

At his request Ambassador Dean called on Under Secretary Rostow, 10:30 p.m., May 26, to inquire about the results of the Eban visit.

1. Mr. Rostow opened the conversation by saying that USG was still not sure whether the basic strategy was going to work but we would know very soon. Our evaluation, which was confirmed by Eban, was that we had held the Israelis from making a strike by raising the possibility of a third solution between surrender or war. When we floated the British suggestion of a maritime force Eban had come over to determine whether this third option was in fact assured.

---

[1] Source: National Archives and Records Administration, RG 59, Central Files 1967–69, POL ARAB–ISR. Secret; Priority; Nodis. Drafted by Eugene Rostow and his staff assistant Robert T. Grey, Jr., and approved by Rostow. Repeated Priority to Cairo, Tel Aviv, Paris, and USUN.

2. The Government's policy was explained to him along these lines: a) Exhaustion of UN proceedings; b) A public declaration by the maritime powers as soon as possible; c) Determination to pursue vigorously and urgently the question of a maritime presence to insure passage through the Gulf of Aqaba for all nations specifically including Israel.

3. We had two days of intensive discussions with Eban to make this third alternative as specific as possible under the circumstances, taking into account our Constitutional procedures and the necessity for making any maritime force an international effort.

4. We do not know if this will hold the Israelis but we emphasized to Eban over and over again the grave imprudence of Israel striking the first blow. We did not thoroughly examine the question whether the announcement of intention to close the Gulf as distinguished from an actual closing would justify retaliatory action by the Israelis under Article 51.

5. The purport of our statements was explicit, that Israel should not act alone and not take on the onus of acting alone.

6. Our intelligence has been reviewed by three different groups and we are convinced that the UAR is in a defensive rather than an offensive posture. Nasser has Sharm-el-Shaikh and seems to be holding on all other fronts. The Israelis have come back over and over again checking and rechecking their own military estimates. We expected that they would tell us they were going to strike but instead they merely requested clarification regarding the proposed maritime plan.

7. Everett, UK, said that UK assessment was that there was a continuing steady military buildup in the UAR and that the UAR could now assume an offensive posture. Rostow reported that USG had some disquieting intelligence which indicated that the Soviets had been egging the UAR on. This was not solid but it was worth taking a look at.

8. Dean asked how Rostow had found Eban. Rostow replied that Eban was not agitated and appeared serious and moderate. He gave a sober rather than a passionate presentation. Eban had indicated that he thought the maritime plan was a starter if he got solid assurances from the President. We have no direct evidence as yet of Eban's conclusions, and what he will recommend. Rostow thought in the light of his talk last night and his impressions today that Eban's recommendation would be positive.

9. Dean said UK reports indicated that Israeli Cabinet was in joint consultation and that Ben Gurion was back. UK felt that there would be a crucial Cabinet meeting either Sunday morning or Saturday evening. Their word is that it will be a "peace or war Cabinet."

10. On the question of using a neutral tanker to test the Straits, Rostow indicated that while we were inclined yesterday to let a test come, USG would consider the Prime Minister's advice very carefully and would take no steps on the matter without further consultation.

11. Rostow indicated that Israel had not discussed the modalities of the proposed maritime force but that Eban did ask that Israel be allowed to participate in it. USG had urged them to mount a diplomatic effort in making the enterprise a success.

12. Rostow asked Ambassador Dean what news he had about Cabinet meeting. Dean indicated that the *Hermes* had been turned around and was now sailing west toward Aden and that the Cabinet did not like the idea of a test probe in the Gulf. The Cabinet was, however, most anxious to learn about the results of the Eban visit.

13. Dean said that his own view was that any UN action would be exceedingly slow and that we would be lucky if we got an SC meeting by next Wednesday.

14. Rostow noted that the Russians had been reticent on the status of the Gulf as an international waterway and cited article in the Soviet press which was guarded. He also indicated that USG was considering what tactics we propose to take in the UN and that we would want to remain in close touch with the UK on this in New York. In any event USG felt that maritime planning should move ahead.

15. Rostow suggested that US and UK should move on the maritime declaration at the same time we move on the SC. The question with the maritime declaration was how clear you could make the implied commitment to use force if necessary to protect freedom of the sea and still induce governments to sign on.

Rusk

81. Telegram From the Mission to the United Nations to the Department of State[1]

New York, May 27, 1967, 0809Z.

5493. Goldberg–Eban Conversation May 26. Reference: State 203796;[2] USUN 5492.[3] Fol is uncleared summary main points from Goldberg conversation with Israeli FonMin Eban late May 26:

1. Eban had received encouragement from talk with President, noting goodwill toward Israel shown by President.

2. He stressed GOI desire avoid war

3. He said that if GOI had commitment to timetable or scenario on establishing innocent passage of Straits of Tiran within a few weeks, it could live with it. Main problem was that precise agreed sequence events lacking.

4. Eban observed that Israeli military not spoiling for fight.

5. He stressed that principle of free passage could not be abandoned since this would be surrender. While he recognized difference between proposal SYG believed to have made in Cairo and proposal he made today (USUN 5492)[4] for two week moratorium on GOI flagship move and UAR moratorium on stopping other ships, he said GOI could not explicitly accept conditions on right innocent passage its ships. Noted that Liberian tanker headed for Elath now near Straits but no Israeli flagship due for some time.

6. Expressed gratification for undertakings in last para ref Deptel.[5]

7. In response Eban questions, Goldberg refrained from interpreting key passage President's statement[6] (ref Deptel) which he said spoke for itself.

---

[1] Source: National Archives and Records Administration, RG 59, Central Files 1967–69, POL ARAB–ISR. Secret; Immediate; Nodis. Repeated to Tel Aviv Immediate, and to London and the White House. Received at 4:08 a.m.

[2] Telegram 203796 to Tel Aviv, repeated to USUN, May 27, summarized the meetings with Eban, including his meeting with the President. (Ibid.)

[3] Telegram 5492 from USUN, May 27, transmitted the text of a memorandum from Eban on the 1957 U.S. "commitment on free passage in the Straits of Tiran." (Ibid.)

[4] The citation is incorrect. Telegram 5494 from USUN, May 27, transmitted the portion of the text of the Secretary General's May 26 report to the Security Council that concerned his talks in Cairo, assessment of the situation, and possible courses of action. The report is cited in footnote 6, Document 72.

[5] The last paragraph of telegram 203796 to Tel Aviv reads: "Israelis agreed to cooperate in improving intelligence cooperation, and we undertook to look into possible liaison arrangements through DOD."

[6] Telegram 203796 quotes a slightly revised version of Document 74, with one sentence added at the end of the first paragraph: "It is our considered judgment, based upon information from many sources, that an imminent surprise attack is not indicated."

8. While Eban could not predict GOI reaction to it, Goldberg strongly reminded him of necessity further consultation before any die cast and Eban recognized such necessity.

9. Eban observed DeGaulle had only pronounced lofty phrases signifying nothing about what French would do about Straits. French however giving GOI for first time all military equipment they asked for and were not pressing on money aspect. Goldberg informed Eban about Seydoux statement that France would not support SC res on innocent passage because wished avoid any commitment take action to uphold it.

Goldberg

82. Telegram From the Embassy in Israel to the Department of State[1]

Tel Aviv, May 27, 1967, 1150Z.

3808. Ref: State 203796[2] and 203752.[3]

1. Eshkol in continuous session with colleagues and military. FonOff rep called me in great urgency 1100 hours to ask if I had report Eban conversation with President. No report received by GOI. In view obvious agitation of caller I judged situation critical and called at Defense Ministry at once where I conveyed to Levavi (Director General FonOff) who immediately informed Eshkol substance reftels re conversations with President and UnSec Rostow.

2. Believe this helpful. However, Israelis took occasion embark on emotional, evidently sincere, exposition their thesis that evidence available to them conclusive that Nasser has "crossed his Rubicon" and surprise aerial attack expected any moment. My remonstrances that our most careful and equally authoritative assessment is to contrary were

---

[1] Source: Johnson Library, National Security File, Country File, Middle East Crisis, Vol. II. Top Secret; Flash; Nodis. Received at 8:23 a.m.

[2] See footnotes 2, 5, and 6, Document 81.

[3] Telegram 203752 to Tel Aviv, May 26, summarized Eugene Rostow's May 25 conversation with Eban after the latter's meeting with Rusk. (National Archives and Records Administration, RG 59, Central Files 1967–69, POL ARAB–ISR) See footnote 2, Document 64.

met by argument we behind times and essential intelligence this regard had been received in last few hours. They talked in terms of surprise air strike knocking out Israeli airfields and rendering their response ineffective. They said they had intercepts of Egyptian messages to confirm situation as they see it. Also frightened by fact four MIGs overflew Israel yesterday and Israeli Airforce not able intercept.

3. Levavi also read translation note received last evening from Soviet Ambassador advising caution and saying Soviets not want war Middle East. But, Israelis added, this not what Egyptian War Minister Moscow telling Cairo. Note seemed to me mild in tone and sound in content. I asked if Soviet Ambassador indicated similar message sent Nasser and they said he had said he did not know. I said I would think similar message probably has been sent Nasser.

4. Clearly, Israeli military pressing very hard for authority to take preemptive action and probably threatening Eshkol with dire military consequences for Israel if he does not do so. I emphasized again and again in strongest terms I could muster President's statement to Eban that "they would not be alone unless they decide to go alone." Also said essential at minimum they await Eban's arrival with full report before taking any action. They gave impression Eshkol will do so.

5. Broadest impact this session with me is that GOI cannot be convinced Nasser will not strike first. If he does, Israelis have no secondary response capability and they think they likely be lost. Crunch in government decision is what specifically we prepared do in event they eschew initiative and rely on our intervention if Egyptian attack occurs.

6. Levavi said in most earnest voice that, in his view, immediate despatch covertly of U.S. military officer to talk in terms U.S. estimates and capabilities directly with Israeli military might succeed in lessening IDF apprehensions to acceptable degree. In circumstances, if at all possible, I urge that we send such an officer. Eban may be able provide voice of reason on his arrival but I am convinced GOI situation so closely balanced as of moment that this additional exercise worth the effort.

Barbour

83.   Telegram From the Department of State to the Embassy in Jordan[1]

Washington, May 27, 1967, 9:57 p.m.

203947. 1. Following based on uncleared memcon,[2] is FYI, Noforn and subject to change on review.

2. On behalf all Arab Ambassadors, Lebanese, Kuwaiti and Libyan Ambassadors called on the Secretary May 27 on instructions their governments to express concern of Arab countries about present Arab-Israeli crisis. Lebanese, who was principal spokesman, explained that in interest US-Arab relations, he wished to express to the Secretary deep feelings of the Arabs in the current crisis. Following represents main points of presentation.

3. Present situation had deep roots in Palestine problem beginning with creation of Israel. Although Arabs had many differences among themselves, they were all united on Palestine problem and against Israel.

4. Arabs were concerned about Zionist pressure in US. Prior receiving copy President's recent statement on crisis,[3] Ambassadors had received distorted impression from US radio, press and TV of statement and feared return to 1956 situation. When Lebanese Ambassador received full text of statement (said he was talking personally, but other two Ambassadors did not question his remarks), he found balanced and accurate assessment of problem. Nonetheless, Arabs were still worried that Zionist pressure would change spirit or objective of policy. Their fears heightened by recent visit to Washington of Foreign Minister Eban.

5. Present situation was very dangerous one. President, in emphasis in his statement on having problem handled by UN had taken wise course. This was best way of avoiding irritations caused by Suez crisis, which had same roots in basic Palestine problem. Was sure wise leadership of US would facilitate solution in UN, but to do so and not lose support Arabs, US must remain impartial in UN deliberations.

6. Ambassadors emphasized that no Arab state wanted to start war and no one wanted unfriendly relations with US.

---

[1] Source: National Archives and Records Administration, RG 59, Central Files 1967–69, POL ARAB–ISR. Confidential. Drafted by Houghton, and approved by Pierre Shostal in S/S. Also sent to Baghdad, Beirut, Cairo, Damascus, Jidda, London, Kuwait, Tel Aviv, Tripoli, Jerusalem, and USUN.

[2] Not found.

[3] See Document 49.

7. The Secretary welcomed opportunity to hear their views. Although he could understand deep roots of feelings in that part of world, US had nonetheless been working for closer relations with our Arab friends. He noted that some of problems stemmed not from Israel but from differences among the Arab states themselves.

8. The Secretary noted two elements in current situation. The first was possibility of an outbreak of hostilities. He was pleased to note that Ambassadors felt no Arab state wanted war. In existing tension, this was important if present situation was not to degenerate into hostilities. On our part, we had made strong efforts with all parties concerned to urge calm and restraint. He hoped there would be no military initiatives. We did believe UN should be in forefront in finding solution.

9. The second element was problem of Straits of Tiran. This was not just an Israeli problem, but one for all maritime states. If solution could be found to this problem, he thought tensions would perhaps subside.

10. He was not sure about the Fatah or the Palestine Liberation Force. If they continued activities, there would be trouble. He could not understand why Nasser announced his blockade of the Gulf of Aqaba at the very time that the Secretary General of the United Nations was on his way to Cairo. Nasser should surely have known from the President's statement of the deep concern over this problem. He assured the Ambassadors that we would be making maximum efforts during next few days here and in the Security Council to find a solution to the problem. We did not think any country wanted war, but that did not produce a solution.

11. A discussion then ensued on the problem of the Straits of Tiran. The Arab Ambassadors pointed out that no Israeli ships had passed through the Straits during the period 1947 through 1956. Consequently, the Straits could not be of vital importance to the Israelis. The Straits had been opened to the Israelis as a result of the aggression of 1956. Nasser, by his action, had restored the position pertaining prior to that aggression. The Ambassadors hoped the United States could use its good offices to persuade Israelis not to begin war over Straits issue.

12. The Secretary emphasized again the seriousness of the problem and the importance of the right of innocent passage through the Straits being maintained.

Rusk

84. Letter From Premier Kosygin to President Johnson[1]

Moscow, May 27, 1967.

Dear Mr. President:

According to information being received by the Soviet Government the State of Israel is actively engaged in military preparations and evidently intends to carry out armed aggression against neighboring Arab States. Under conditions of extreme tension at the borders of Israel with the UAR and Syria, Israeli militant circles are attempting to impose upon their Government, their country and their people an "adventurist" action for the purpose of resolving all problems by military means. There is a danger that these circles may cause an armed conflict, which would be fraught with important consequences for the cause of peace and international security.

We understand that in the situation now taking shape much depends upon the United States and upon you personally, Mr. President, as to whether Israel will undertake such a reckless act. In this respect there cannot be any other view. If there will be no encouragement on the part of the US, then Israel will not dare step over the line.

In your letter of May 22[2] you called upon us to exercise our influence along with yours in the direction of restraint. We are for restraint. We are convinced that no matter how complex the situation in the area along the borders of Israel, Syria and the United Arab Republic may be, measures must be found to prevent this conflict from becoming a military one. The situation is such that, in our opinion, this can be done. A new hotbed of war must not be permitted to develop in the world.

That's why we are in favor of a restraining influence, but, of course, not to the detriment of the lawful interests of the Arab States. Their actions are of a defensive nature. Moreover, it is precisely restraint that

---

[1] Source: Johnson Library, National Security File, Special Head of State Correspondence File, U.S.S.R.—Presidential Correspondence. Secret; Nodis. The source text, a translation transcribed in the Division of Language Services of the Department of State, was sent to Walt Rostow, along with the original letter in Russian, with a covering memorandum of May 31 from Read. The classification appears on the translation but not on the original letter. Soviet Chargé Yuri N. Chernyakov gave the letter to Secretary Rusk at 3 p.m. on May 27. After Soviet Country Director Malcolm Toon translated the letter, Rusk told Chernyakov he would transmit it to the President immediately. He told Chernyakov he could inform his government that Rusk regarded the letter as highly important, especially its last paragraph, and that the U.S. Government was making a maximum effort to restrain all governments in the crisis area, including Israel. (Ibid., Country File, Middle East Crisis)

[2] See footnote 3, Document 41.

they are exercising and, as we know, they do not want a military conflict.

Of course, if the "adventurist" line should prevail and if arms should be used, this could be the beginning of far-reaching events. Should Israel commit aggression and military operations begin, then we will render aid to those countries that are subjected to aggression.

Neither we, nor you, nor the Arab countries, nor the people of Israel are interested in a conflict. We appeal to you to take all necessary measures to prevent an armed conflict. We, for our part, will also undertake measures in that direction.

Respectfully,

A. Kosygin
Chairman of the Council of Ministers
of the USSR

---

85. Telegram From the Department of State to the Embassy in Israel[1]

Washington, May 28, 1967, 2:05 a.m.

203966. Memcon Between Ambassador Harman and Under Secretary Rostow.

At his request Ambassador Harman called on Under Secretary Rostow, 6:30 p.m., May 27.

1. Mr. Rostow opened the conversation by saying that we had many rumors, some good some bad. The news from the Dutch was good and the British were standing firm on their proposal. Harman asked about the French. Mr. Rostow said that we had pushed the French very hard on the UK proposal. We had pushed the Indian Ambassador very hard as well.

2. Ambassador Harman indicated that he had talked to Mr. Sisco about the UN situation and that he had heard that USG was working out solution putting the finger on belligerency. Mr. Rostow replied yes and that in our view positions taken in the UN tended to become per-

---

[1] Source: National Archives and Records Administration, RG 59, Central Files 1967–69, POL ARAB–ISR. Secret; Immediate; Nodis. Drafted by Grey and approved by Grey for Eugene Rostow.

manent. He noted that Harman had heard what highest authority had said on question of passage for Israeli flag ships through Gulf of Aqaba. The USG was not opposed to a two or three week even-handed moratorium which would enable a high-level representative of the Secretary General to visit the area and study the situation. The key issue in any proposed moratorium was whether or not the UAR would agree not to blockade the Strait of Tiran.

3. Ambassador Harman asked if USG was firm on the question of allowing Israeli flag shipping into the Strait of Tiran. Rostow replied that Ambassador had heard what US officials had said on this question during Eban visit.

4. Ambassador Harman asked what other nations were taking same line. Rostow replied that to date we had affirmative responses from the UK, Dutch and Canada. Rostow also said that USG was working out a tentative scenario over the weekend. Harman emphasized that it was important for him to be in every step of the way as GOI expected to sign maritime declaration. Rostow said USG expected that GOI would sign declaration and that it was possible that GOI could have ship in escort squadron as well.

5. Rostow asked that GOI give us report on the actual number of Israeli flag vessels in the last five years which had actually passed through Strait of Tiran. Harman agreed to provide this information but said it was academic in view USG position.

6. Harman asked when USG thought that tentative scenario would jell. Rostow said probably this weekend.

7. Rostow noted that escort force was merely to show flag and that the ultimate guarantee for safety of this force was US 6th Fleet and vessels from other maritime powers stationed in Mediterranean. Our general thought was to get the maritime declaration out soon and continue planning to assemble naval presence but not to surface it until SC action reached certain point probably in two or three weeks. Rostow also noted that USG would have to consult with Congress and mobilize public support for its position. Harman said that two or three weeks' delay disturbed him as actions were beginning to take place on the ground. This was part of over-all situation and it was time for quick action. The tactics taken in the SC were of crucial importance.

8. Rostow noted that when Foreign Minister Eban had asked if it was USG position to pursue UK initiative vigorously he received an affirmative answer. Harman said that he had been asked for a detailed appraisal of US position and wanted to use the word determination. Rostow said words that had been used were fealty to prior commitments and determination but that problems of US Constitutional process and necessity of gaining public support had been clearly explained.

9. Harman asked about question of liaison between Israeli and US military. Rostow replied that in fact the place to start was with intelligence and that we should inform Ambassador tomorrow as to first steps.

10. At 9:15 p.m., May 27, Ambassador Harman was called in by Rostow who explained the USG had just received important message from Soviets which was phrased not as threat but as an appeal. The Soviets claim to have information that an Israeli attack was imminent. They had appealed to the US to use its offices to prevent the Israeli attack. Rostow also indicated that Soviet message had indicated a desire to use Soviet influence to restrain Arabs. We had forwarded an urgent message to GOI stressing importance of GOI not making first military move.

Rusk

---

86.   **Telegram From the Department of State to the Embassy in Israel**[1]

Washington, May 27, 1967, 9:09 p.m.

203943. You are instructed to proceed at once whatever the hour or the circumstances to deliver the following message from the President to the Prime Minister[2] even if the Cabinet is sitting.[3]

---

[1] Source: National Archives and Records Administration, RG 59, Central Files 1967–69, POL ARAB–ISR. Top Secret; Flash; Nodis; Literally Eyes Only for Ambassadors. Drafted by Eugene Rostow, cleared by Walt Rostow, and approved by Secretary Rusk. Repeated to London and USUN.

[2] Walt Rostow sent the draft message to the President at the LBJ Ranch in CAP 67455, May 27, noting that it had been cleared by Rusk and McNamara. Johnson's revisions are indicated in an attached note by Assistant to the President Jim Jones, who informed Walt Rostow. (Johnson Library, National Security File, Country File, Middle East Crisis, Vol. II) Rostow relayed them to Rusk by telephone. (Notes of telephone conversation, May 27, 7:40 p.m.; National Archives and Records Administration, RG 59, Rusk Files: Lot 72 D 192, Telephone Calls)

[3] Barbour reported in telegram 3822 from Tel Aviv, May 28, that he had delivered the message at 6 a.m. He also reported that the atmosphere prevailing the day before, that a decision on a military initiative was only hours away, had been dispelled. (Johnson Library, National Security File, Country File, Middle East Crisis, Vol. II)

"Dear Mr. Prime Minister:

I have just this afternoon received a most important and private message from the Soviet Union. I am sharing its contents with you on a personal and intimate basis. It should under no circumstances become public.

The Soviets tell me that they have information that you are preparing to take military action against your Arab neighbors, and provoke a conflict which would be fraught with great consequences. They emphasize their commitment to restraint on all sides and the Soviet view that solutions must be found without a military conflict. They tell us that they know the Arabs do not wish a military conflict. The message adds, however, that if Israel begins military action, the Soviets will give aid to the countries attacked. This message also makes clear the Soviet view that the Soviet Union, the Arab peoples and the people of Israel are not interested in a conflict.[4] The Soviet Union appeals to us to take all measures to insure that there be no military conflict. They state that they will undertake measures in the same direction.

Mr. Eban will be reporting to you fully on my talk with him, and on our interest in the safety and vital concerns of Israel.

As your friend, I repeat even more strongly what I said yesterday to Mr. Eban. Israel just must not take any preemptive military action[5] and thereby make itself responsible for the initiation of hostilities.[6]

In my reply to the Soviets I shall of course take up your and our common views about the international character of the Gulf of Aqaba and the Strait of Tiran.

Yours faithfully,

Lyndon B. Johnson"

If any explanation is necessary, you should add that the British and we are proceeding urgently to prepare the military aspects of the international naval escort plan, and that other nations are responding vigorously to the idea. The Dutch and Canadians have already joined, even before a text was presented to them. With that assurance of international determination to make every effort to keep the straits open to the

---

[4] This is a slightly revised version of a sentence added by the President.

[5] In the draft, the first part of this sentence read: "It is essential that Israel not take any preemptive military action".

[6] The President eliminated a sentence at this point in the draft that read: "Preemptive actions by Israel would make it impossible for the friends of Israel to stand at your side." Jim Jones' note states that if Walt Rostow and Rusk felt something like this was necessary, the President suggested, "Without exception our Congressional leaders have made it clear that preemptive actions would find no support here." Jones stated that if something like that was used, the President wanted to talk about it first.

flags of all nations, unilateral action on the part of Israel would be irresponsible and catastrophic.

Rusk

---

87.   Telegram From the President's Special Assistant (Rostow) to President Johnson in Texas[1]

Washington, May 28, 1967, 0152Z.

CAP 67462.

Mr. President,

Herewith Prime Minster Wilson weighed in on the Middle East with an acceptable proposal and a phrase nice to read: Countries, "with the guts to stand-up and be counted." Let's hold him to it.

Signed

WWR

Many thanks for your message. I'm grateful too for the very full account we have had of Eban's talks with yourself and others in Washington. I warmly welcome the insistence with which you urged caution on the Israelis. But I am addressing you now because I fear that, despite all your efforts and ours, there must be a serious likelihood that, after the Israeli Cabinet has met tomorrow (correction—today) to consider Eban's report, you and we will find ourselves confronted with what could amount to an Israeli ultimatum—that, if we do not give them even more categorical assurances than both of us have given so far about the right of passage through the Straits of Tiran, they will feel obliged to assert those rights by force, in whatever manner and at whatever time seem most appropriate to them. This is the vital issue. Closure of the Straits is what Nasser has gained. It affects a vital Israeli interest.

George Thomson and your people made good progress this week and now the military are following this up urgently. It is clear that we

---

[1] Source: Johnson Library, National Security File, Country File, Middle East Crisis, Vol. II. Secret. Received at the LBJ Ranch at 9:53 p.m. An attached typed note, dated May 27, 11 p.m., quotes Johnson's comment to Jim Jones: "I don't see where he says, 'let's stand up and be counted.'"

shall soon have a workable schema, though I know you agree with me that it is vitally important that we should plan to develop this through the United Nations, if possible, and in any case on the widest possible basis of international co-operation (even if you and we are going to have to do most of the donkey work). But I am gravely concerned at the time factor. An Israeli ultimatum (or something like it) on the lines I have suggested would open up a dramatic prospect of great power confrontation in an area where, as I said to you the other day, none of us can hope to control the local combatants, except perhaps by such direct military involvements on one side or the other as to constitute an unavoidable challenge to the other side. The potential dangers of that happening are such as to make it essential that everything is done to avoid it. I have in mind particularly the need to avoid a situation in which it could seem to the world—and, even more important, the Soviet Union would be enabled to claim—that the United States and Britain were taking sides militarily in the Arab–Israel conflict. In fact we have made it clear that our commitment is addressed to the principle of freedom of passage through the Straits as an international waterway: and, given a workable scheme, this is what we should do with you and any others we can persuade to join us. But, as I said in my earlier message, we can be under no illusion that we shall easily get them to do so unless we have demonstrably exhausted the United Nations possibilities. And part of this effort at the United Nations must, I am convinced, turn around an attempt to get the Russians involved on a four-power basis. We are going into this with our eyes open, knowing full well that French and Soviet estimates of the possibilities are likely to be different from our own. But we believe that we must exploit the intrinsic merits in the four-power approach, which is to get the Russians to face up to their responsibilities to prevent a really dangerous confrontation. We may not succeed: Probably we shall not. But our public opinion will not, I believe, understand or support what we may have to do hereafter if we cannot show convincingly that we have tried.

Accordingly, I want you to know that I have tonight sent a personal message to Kosygin urging on him the dangers of this situation and inviting him to get Fedorenko to join with Goldberg, Seydoux and Caradon, in the context of the present meeting of the Security Council, to see whether it really is impossible for them to hammer out something which could make sense in this crazy Middle Eastern situation. One of the main reasons I have done this was because George Brown had come back from Moscow convinced that the Russians are beginning to realize the gravity of the situation for which they themselves are so largely responsible and are really concerned to avoid an escalation into a major confrontation. I am not so naive as to believe that this means that they will cooperate with us at New York. But I believe it is our duty to try. If we fail and if the Security Council likewise fails then I believe that there are enough countries in the world with the sense to realize that world peace is more important even than trying to go on working through an impotent United Nations, and with the guts to stand up and be counted. In those circumstances, we should I believe get the broad basis of support that we want for our declaration and for any eventual enforcement action—who knows, perhaps even France might agree?

I need not say that in addressing Kosygin I have had much in mind your own reservations about four-power action outside the United Nations framework: and I have said nothing to him about any four-power activity anywhere else or at any level.

I am of course informing De Gaulle as well. We have heard today from the French that they still have no reply from the Russians. And they seem content simply to sit tight and wait for it to turn up, as if delay were what they really wanted. But the French clearly can have no objection to my urging Kosygin to support a French initiative.

Since I wrote this, we have heard from Pat Dean of the Russian approach to you. I note that you will be sending a message to Eshkol. I do not think I need send him any further message since our Ambassador in Israel was instructed this afternoon (in the light of a somewhat ominous remark to George Thomson by the Israeli Ambassador here) to make a further urgent approach to the Israeli Government urging them to maintain their present policy of restraint while international efforts to find a solution continue.

I think this latest news adds force to the approach I have made to Kosygin as described in this message.

88.   Telegram From the Department of State to the Embassy in
        the Soviet Union[1]

Washington, May 28, 1967, 1:31 a.m.

203963. Following is text of letter from President to Kosygin handed Soviet Chargé tonight. Deliver text to Gromyko soonest possible
Sunday, informing him we have used both channels because of importance of message.

Begin Text.

"Dear Mr. Chairman:

I am replying immediately to your letter of today about the critical
situation in the Near East. Since receiving your message, I have sent a
further communication to Prime Minister Eshkol.

I can assure you that I have been making a maximum effort to
counsel moderation on Israel and its neighboring Arab States. I agree
that you and we both must do everything we can to prevent the outbreak of hostilities. We welcome your assurances as to your efforts in
this direction.

The Israeli Government and people are in a state of high tension. They
have heard the announcement as to the closing of the Strait of Tiran, they
have seen the withdrawal of UN forces along their border and that of the
United Arab Republic and they hear daily calls for a 'holy war' on the part
of the Arabs to destroy Israel. It is important for both of us to do everything we can to reduce the further inflammation of the situation.

It seems to us of vital importance that a prompt solution be found
to the issue of the Strait of Tiran. You and we, as important maritime
powers, have a large interest in international passage through narrow
waters connecting international seas. We urge you to counsel the United
Arab Republic to refrain from interfering with the passage of vessels
through the Strait. We hope that the Secretary General or the Security
Council can find an early answer but I do not wish to underestimate the
gravity of this particular problem. If this issue can be resolved, I should
think that the prospects for reducing tension and restoring stability in
the area would be greatly improved.

---

[1] Source: Johnson Library, National Security File, Head of State Correspondence File,
USSR, Kosygin Correspondence, Vol. I. Top Secret; Immediate; Nodis; Literally Eyes Only
for Ambassador. Drafted and approved by Rusk. Walt Rostow sent the draft message to
the President at the LBJ Ranch in CAP 67457, May 27, noting that it had been cleared by
Rusk and McNamara. An attached typewritten note, dated May 27, 9:30 p.m., contains the
President's comment: "That's okay with me." It indicates that Jim Jones relayed this to
Walt Rostow. (Ibid., Country File, Middle East Crisis, Vol. II)

I do hope that your and our parallel efforts to avoid hostilities in this situation will succeed.

Yours faithfully,

Lyndon B. Johnson" *End Text*.

Rusk

---

89.   **Telegram From the President's Special Assistant (Rostow) to President Johnson in Texas**[1]

Washington, May 28, 1967, 1653Z.

CAP 67467. This Flash has just come in. It looks as though they have decided not to go to war at this time.[2]

1. Cabinet meeting which began at 1500 hours local has recessed subject to call if necessary. Foreign Affairs and Security Committee of Knesset now in session. PM Eshkol will address Knesset tomorrow probably in afternoon or early evening.

2. Bitan of FonOff has just responded my inquiry with above info and has added that, while "problem not yet solved, of course" decisions have been taken "along your line."[3]

3. He busy drafting documents confirming this position which he hopes be able hand me for transmission to Washington in next three hours or so.[4]

Barbour

---

[1] Source: Johnson Library, National Security File, Country File, Middle East Crisis, Vol. II. Secret. Received at the LBJ Ranch at 12:14 p.m. A handwritten "L" on the telegram indicates that it was seen by the President.

[2] The remainder of the telegram quotes the text of telegram 3832 from Tel Aviv, May 28. (National Archives and Records Administration, RG 59, Central Files 1967–69, POL 15–1 ISR)

[3] Barbour reported in telegram 3834 from Tel Aviv, May 28, that the Cabinet decision was "to postpone military action for few weeks in favor of continuing effort to ascertain whether diplomatic activity can solve crisis." (Ibid., Office of the Executive Secretariat, Middle East Crisis Files, 1967, Entry 5190, Box 6, Arab-Israeli Crisis, Chron, Tel Aviv)

[4] In telegram 3835 from Tel Aviv, May 28, Barbour transmitted the text of draft paragraphs that Prime Minister Eshkol intended to include in his speech to the Knesset. (Ibid., Central Files 1967–69, POL ARAB–ISR) Telegram 204024 to Tel Aviv, May 28, conveyed suggested changes, primarily to eliminate any suggestion of the content of Eban's conversation with Johnson. (Ibid.) The text of Eshkol's statement before the Knesset on May 29 is printed in *Israel's Foreign Relations: Selected Documents, 1947–1974* (Jerusalem: Ministry for Foreign Affairs, 1976), pp. 774–777.

90.   Telegram From the Department of State to the Embassy in
        the Soviet Union[1]

Washington, May 28, 1967, 11:30 p.m.

204027. Please transmit the following message from the Secretary to
the Foreign Minister.

Dear Mr. Gromyko,

Following the exchange of letters yesterday between Chairman
Kosygin and President Johnson,[2] and our further communication with
Prime Minister Eshkol, I am encouraged to believe that there is no basis
for your report that Israel will soon initiate hostilities.

You will already have seen the press statement of Prime Minister
Eshkol[3] which indicates that our vigorous representations in Israel have
indeed had the effect we both hoped for. On the other hand, we have
been dismayed by the almost simultaneous press conference of
President Nasser[4] committing himself again to the closing of the Strait
of Tiran. This is the central point and it is about this that I wish to write
you as a supplement to the President's letter to Chairman Kosygin of
last night.

I should like to add some thoughts to the President's letter of yesterday, in further response to Mr. Kosygin's welcome appeal for cooperation in preventing an outbreak of military conflict in the Middle East.

Your Chairman states that you are convinced that "however complicated the situation may be in the region of the boundaries of Israel,
Syria, and the United Arab Republic, means must be found to liquidate
this conflict as a military one". We completely agree.

We are concerned that your and our separate appeals for restraint
will be to no avail unless we act during the next few days to liquidate
what we regard as the primary point of danger in the situation,
President Nasser's announced policy of blockade against Israeli shipping and what the government of the United Arab Republic considers

---

[1] Source: National Archives and Records Administration, RG 59, Central Files
1967–69, POL ARAB–ISR. Secret; Immediate; Nodis. Drafted by Eugene Rostow, cleared
by Walt Rostow, and approved by Rusk. Repeated to London, USUN, Paris, and Tel Aviv.

[2] Documents 84 and 88.

[3] Reference is apparently to a May 28 radio broadcast by Eshkol; for text, see *Israel's
Foreign Relations: Selected Documents, 1947–1974*, pp. 773–774.

[4] A situation report sent to President Johnson at the LBJ Ranch in CAP 67472, May
28, stated that Nasser's press conference that day showed Nasser "still supremely confident on a possible military outcome, and unyielding on transit of the Strait of Tiran."
(Johnson Library, National Security File, NSC Histories, Middle East Crisis) The text of the
press conference was sent to Johnson in WH 70283, May 28. (Ibid.)

"strategic" cargoes bound for Israel through the Strait of Tiran. All other aspects of the controversy should be soluble by the usual procedures of negotiation. On this one point, we think it is indispensable that you and we reach an understanding as soon as possible.

As you know, we take the view that the Gulf of Aqaba comprehends international waters, and that no nation has the right to prevent passage in the Gulf or through the Strait. And we agree with earlier statements by the Secretary General of the United Nations and others that belligerent rights cannot be considered to exist between Israel and the United Arab Republic.

As a maritime nation, we and you both regard the preservation of the principles of international law regarding freedom of navigation on international waterways as a vital interest of the international community. Beyond that, we are persuaded that Israel considers its right of transit through the Strait of Tiran so fundamental to her national interest that she can be forced to take action to preserve it. Israel has made it clear to us that she would consider any interference by armed force with Israeli vessels or with Israel-bound cargo an act of aggression justifying action on her part as a matter of self-defense. We do not believe that Israel will back down on this point, nor that she should be asked to do so.

I have noted that the government of the United Arab Republic has not yet taken armed action to carry out its policy of closing the Strait.

Our governments should favor through a Security Council Resolution or in some other appropriate manner a moratorium for at least two weeks on the execution of the United Arab Republic's policy of closing the Strait. Such a moratorium would preserve the position as it was before President Nasser announced his policy, and give us and others a chance to mediate in this situation. I earnestly appeal to you to support this position, which in my judgment offers us both the best basis on which to achieve the goal we both seek in the Middle East—the avoidance of hostilities, and the resolution of its complex problems by peaceful means.

I would welcome your thoughts on the points raised in this letter, and above all on how the issue of the Straits can be dealt with consistently with its character as an international waterway. I should be happy to accept any procedure you deem wise for the further examination of these points by our two governments through consultations here, in Moscow, or through our permanent representatives to the UN.

Sincerely yours,

Dean Rusk

Rusk

91.   Memorandum From the Acting Assistant Secretary of
      Defense for International Security Affairs (Hoopes) to
      Secretary of Defense McNamara[1]

Washington, May 28, 1967.

SUBJECT

JCS Paper on US Military Actions Regarding the Strait of Tiran[2]—Preliminary ISA
Comments

Attached is the subject JCS paper which was received in ISA at 9
p.m. Saturday[3] evening. Time has not permitted a comprehensive
review of the document. The following comments represent first
impressions of Colonel Jordan and myself:

1. The JCS paper responds to a request which assumed a very narrow time frame for US military reaction to the announced blockade of
the Strait of Tiran—i.e., when the request was made, we were operating
on the assumption that a probe would probably be required before 1
June, if we were to hold Israel from pre-emptive military action. The
paper accordingly concentrates on courses of action based on forces
immediately on the scene, and makes only passing reference to possible
augmentation. It states that augmentation is not feasible before 20 June,
but confines definition of such augmentation to "a balanced task force".

2. Even within the limits defined by the assumed time frame, the
paper seems unduly pessimistic with respect to the chances of success
and the attendant risks. It believes there is a "high probability" that the
probe force would come under attack by the UAR, and it lays emphasis
on the vulnerability of the probe force. In this regard, it makes the surprising statement that US destroyers cannot "out-gun" the UAR shore

---

[1] Source: Washington National Records Center, OSD Files: FRC 330 72 A 2468, Middle
East, 381.3. Secret. A stamped notation of June 14 on the memorandum indicates that
McNamara saw it. McNamara's handwritten comments read as follows: "Possible Arab
reactions: Nationalization of oil firms, Closing of Suez Canal, Denial of com & mil over-
flts, Banning of U.S. ships in Arab ports, Closing of Wheelus AB."

[2] A JCS memorandum for McNamara on "U.S. Military Actions Regarding UAR
Blockade of the Straits of Tiran," JCSM–301–67, May 27, states that McNamara's office had
requested JCS examination of early U.S.-British military actions that might be taken to test
UAR intentions with respect to free passage through the Strait of Tiran and the Gulf of
Aqaba. The paper discusses four possible courses of action involving probes of the Strait
of Tiran by U.S. forces or U.S. and British forces, either using forces east of Suez or aug-
menting them with Mediterranean forces. It concluded that all the courses of action considered entailed serious risks and could easily escalate the current situation into a full-
scale Arab-Israeli conflict or U.S.–UAR confrontation, and that U.S. action should not be
undertaken unless the U.S. Government was prepared "to respond appropriately." (Ibid.)

[3] May 27.

batteries; and it seems to discount the possibility of supporting the force with long-range ASW aircraft based on Cyprus and with tactical air cover from Sixth Fleet carriers in the Eastern Mediterranean (ISA understands that carrier aircraft have the range to reach the Strait of Tiran area and remain on station for 30–40 minutes. It would be possible to avoid UAR airspace by overflying Israel and the Gulf of Aqaba).

3. The paper (in paragraph 4d. of the covering memorandum) probably underestimates the US ability to restrain an Israeli attack on the UAR, in the context of a US–UK probing action; similarly, it appears to exaggerate the likelihood of a UAR attack on Israel as a consequence of such a US–UK probe.

4. On the other hand, the paper seems quite correct in stating that the immediately available probe force in the Red Sea area is weak and that action dependent primarily on it would carry heavier risks of both (a) UAR defiance and (b) damage to force, than if a larger, stronger, and more balanced force could be assembled.

The situation remains fluid and fast moving. But in view of the new prospect that the US may have succeeded in restraining an Israeli attack for at least the time required to consult Congress, pursue possibilities at the UN, and develop adherents to a maritime declaration, I recommend that you consult with General Wheeler, Mr. Vance and others with respect to

1. more detailed plans for the formation and deployment of an "augmented" force that could be in position in 2–3 weeks;

2. the prospects for strengthening the immediately available probe force by providing airborne ASW, carrier-based air cover from the Sixth Fleet, and land-based air cover from CONUS;

3. a more precise scenario for the activation of a probe of the Strait of Tiran—e.g., whose merchant ship? escorted or unescorted? US reaction to a UAR attempt to prevent passage by military attack? by lesser means? the role of Israeli military forces, if any? etc.; and

4. the timing and modalities of joint military planning with the UK and others. Should the Israelis be included at some point?

Townsend Hoopes

92.　　Telegram From the President's Special Assistant (Rostow) to President Johnson in Texas[1]

Washington, May 29, 1967, 1528Z.

CAP 67478. At a meeting early this morning with Secretaries Rusk and McNamara they agreed to recommend to you that we dispatch the carrier *Intrepid* through the Suez Canal.

As you know, it is slated to take up a position off Viet Nam.

Bob McNamara would feel more comfortable if it were on the other side of the Canal if needed in connection with a crisis at the Gulf of Aqaba. Both Secretaries believe it would be useful to test the Egyptians on the transit of a U.S. warship very soon. They do not expect Nasser to refuse transit.

Whether the *Intrepid* stayed in the Red Sea (or Indian Ocean) or proceeded to Viet Nam could be decided after it had transited to Canal and in the light of the situation at that time.

Dispatch *Intrepid* through Canal[2]
Hold in Mediterranean
Discuss before decision

---

[1] Source: Johnson Library, National Security File, Country File, Middle East Crisis, Vol. II. Secret. Received at the LBJ Ranch at 11:04 a.m.

[2] None of the options is checked. A handwritten note of May 29 on the telegram in Jim Jones' handwriting reads: "If everybody agreeable—go on with it. Pres. told Walt." JCS telegram 6600, May 29, instructed USCINCEUR to direct the *Intrepid* to proceed to Southeast Asia via the Suez Canal. (Ibid., NSC Histories, Middle East Crisis)

93.   Memorandum From Nathaniel Davis of the National
       Security Council Staff to the President's Special Assistant
       (Rostow)[1]

Washington, May 29, 1967.

SUBJECT

Security Council Resolution on the Near East

You asked me to check that our tactics and resolution in New York are consistent with the Secretary's message to Gromyko. The Secretary told Gromyko we should favor a Security Council resolution whose effect would be to call a moratorium for at least two weeks on closing the Straits and preserve the position before Nasser announced his policy.

I called Joe Sisco. His reaction was that we are supporting the Danish resolution[2] and this furthers the line the Secretary took with Gromyko. I also checked informally with New York and the situation is as follows: The Danish resolution supports paragraph 14 of the Secretary General's report—calling for a breathing spell, urging all parties to exercise special restraint, to forego belligerence and to avoid all other actions which could increase tension, to allow the Council to seek solutions.

In Ambassador Goldberg's speech today[3] he plans to interpret the resolution as supporting innocent passage and calling on the UAR not to interrupt shipping. We are trying to get other delegates to make the same interpretation. We plan no mention of any time limit such as two weeks.

The issue may hinge on the interpretation more than the resolution itself. Nigeria, Ethiopia, Argentina, Brazil and Japan have all indicated support for the resolution, so the prospects for at least nine votes are good. Whether we can make our interpretation stick is not so sure.

ND

---

[1] Source: Johnson Library, National Security File, Country File, Middle East Crisis, Vol. II. No classification marking. A copy was sent to Saunders. Davis noted at the bottom of the page: "If you think these tactics should be changed, we would have to move fast!"

[2] Telegram 5500 from USUN, May 27, reported on the proposed Danish draft resolution. (National Archives and Records Administration, RG 59, Central Files 1967–69, POL ARAB–ISR/UN) The resolution was never introduced.

[3] Goldberg urged the Security Council on May 29 to support the Secretary-General's call for a breathing spell and his appeal for all the parties concerned to exercise restraint and forego belligerence. Goldberg argued that "foregoing belligerence" must mean foregoing any blockade of the Gulf of Aqaba during the breathing spell. For text of his statement, see Department of State *Bulletin,* June 19, 1967, pp. 920–924.

94.   Telegram From the Department of State to the Embassies in Lebanon and the United Arab Republic[1]

Washington, May 29, 1967, 1:18 p.m.

204116. For Ambassadors from Battle.

Anderson[2] proceeding Cairo May 30 MEA 306 arrive 1530. Depart Cairo June 1 1000. Based on earlier understanding here no specific instructions would be provided Anderson whose primary effort would be listen and feel out situation Nasser. Suggest however Ambassador Nolte with participation Ambassador Yost, who has just been Washington and talked with us, provide full briefing current situation.[3]

Not sure whether hotel reservations made. Leave to your discretion whether EmbOff meets but suggest visit be handled most routine fashion to avoid attracting any more attention than necessary.

Rusk

---

[1] Source: National Archives and Records Administration, RG 59, Central Files 1967–69, POL 7 US/ANDERSON. Secret; Nodis. Drafted and approved by Battle and cleared in substance by Walt Rostow and Saunders.

[2] Robert B. Anderson; see Document 42.

[3] Telegram 203978 to Beirut, May 28, asked Ambassador Porter to get in touch with Anderson and tell him the White House hoped he would remain in the Beirut area for a few more days. It stated: "We have no indication of Egyptian interest but are trying to prod them in hope contact might be forthcoming." (National Archives and Records Administration, RG 59, Central Files 1967–69, POL 7 US/ANDERSON) Telegram 10970 from Beirut, May 29, reported that the UAR Ambassador had called Anderson immediately after his arrival in Beirut and told him the UAR wished to know the flight and time of his arrival in Cairo. (Ibid.) Regarding Yost's role, see footnote 2, Document 100.

---

95.   Telegram From the President's Special Assistant (Rostow) to President Johnson in Texas[1]

Washington, May 29, 1967, 2248Z.

CAP 67486. Gene Black came in today to present his impressions and recommendations after being thoroughly briefed by Luke Battle and his people.

---

[1] Source: Johnson Library, National Security File, NSC Histories, Middle East Crisis, 5/12–6/19/67, Vol. 2. Secret. Received at the LBJ Ranch at 6:37 p.m. A handwritten "L" on the telegram indicates that it was seen by the President.

1. If we do nothing about Aqaba there will certainly be a war. The Israelis will fight if Nasser seizes their ships. Therefore, he sees no alternative to the kind of plan we are organizing.

2. It is important that we get the declaration of the maritime powers out as soon as possible. Nasser must realize the strength and universality of the principle that is being applied to Aqaba and of the opinion that supports that principle.

3. He talked with U Thant, who was pessimistic about anything helpful happening in the UN. It might buy us two or three weeks; but we can't wait that long for the declaration. It must be agreed by as many maritime countries as possible.

4. The declaration must, of course, be backed by naval and military power. It would be foolish to try to enforce this universal principle by ourselves. We would have trouble with both Congress and the country. On the other hand, he thinks that the Congressional leadership would support us if we were with others.

5. He agrees that a Congressional resolution will probably be required at some stage. It must be strong—but not too strong—against the background of the Tonkin Gulf.

6. U Thant reports that Nasser says he will take any ship in Aqaba except a "tanker or one flying an Israeli flag." Black thinks this will be wholly unacceptable to Israel.

7. Ultimately—down the road—is this question: How do we get Nasser to go back on his word? What will he do? Is there any way for him to save face? If not, we shall have to face issues like the canceling of oil contracts; the closing of the Suez Canal; etc.

8. Incidentally, Nasser told U Thant he would "never take" any American wheat.

9. Black also reports U Thant's view that the crisis must be solved, in the end, "through Moscow."

10. Black will keep in touch with the situation and let us have any further thoughts.

FYI. A draft of the proposed declaration will be in your hands tomorrow. If and when you approve it, State has cranked up with the British to seek support fast. It is their hope that more than 20 powers will accept it. The number putting in ships, if required, will, of course, be less.

96. Telegram From the Department of State to the Embassy in the United Kingdom[1]

Washington, May 29, 1967, 7:30 p.m.

204573. Subject: Middle East.

1. Under Secretary Rostow today briefed British Ambassador on current status our consideration Middle East crisis. He said Secretaries Rusk and McNamara had drawn up our "marching orders" for next two weeks. We were prepared to proceed with next steps to resolve crisis now that Israelis had reached decision not to attack. Plans would be presented to President for his approval and accordingly were not firm at this time. President would want to consult with Congressional leaders, because of possibility force might be needed at end of road. But we hoped to have Presidential answer on "marching orders" and declaration very soon. All our planning is ad referendum the President.

2. Re joint planning for naval force in Red Sea, discussions still going on in Pentagon as to size of force. McNamara thinking now in terms of a staged escalation, with a larger force positioned in the Red Sea, so that our capability doesn't in the first instance depend so much on Sixth Fleet. Decision probably reached in next few days. McNamara would then suggest time for meeting of naval groups and locus of meeting later this week.

3. We have learned Israeli owned ship flying Panamanian flag carrying cargo of hides in vicinity. Might be useful for this ship to go through Strait, forcing Nasser to clarify his stand. Israelis tell us that if ship stopped, they will protest but will not open fire.

4. In UN, we aiming for moratorium on Nasser's threat to close the Straits, with transit available to all flags, in the situation as it was.

5. Re declaration of maritime nations, we will try to get as many signers as possible. Declaration would not mention threat of force but would not exclude this possibility.

6. At same time we plan approaches to a smaller group of countries concerning naval escort plan. We would wish in first instance to establish who should approach whom. For instance, British and Dutch might go to Nordics.

---

[1] Source: National Archives and Records Administration, RG 59, Central Files 1967–69, POL ARAB–ISR. Secret; Immediate; Nodis. Drafted by Eugene Rostow's Special Assistant Alan R. Novak and Thomas M. Judd (EUR/BMI), and approved by Rostow. Repeated to Tel Aviv, Cairo, Bonn, The Hague, and Paris.

7. Ambassador Dean asked how many countries were on smaller list. Under Secretary Rostow replied this not final. We are thinking of France and Italy among others. Ambassador Bohlen will receive instructions to weigh in with the French. We might even wish to use Djibouti for naval escort force.

8. On precise details of escort plan, there are various possible scenarios. The choice will depend on events as they develop.

9. Rostow said he had noticed Bonn not on list of countries to be approached to sign declaration of maritime powers. He thought British should approach Germans. In view fact declaration referred to signers' membership in UN, probably necessary for Bonn to issue a separate but parallel statement.

Rusk

---

97. Telegram From the Department of State to the Embassy in Israel[1]

Washington, May 29, 1967, 9:08 p.m.

204800. 1. At Israeli request, Amb Harman accompanied by Evron called afternoon May 29 on Under Secretary Rostow. Harman said he had feeling he did not know precisely what going on within USG and was not in position report to his Government. Rostow explained weekend had been consumed in meetings and drafting messages to set out scenario agreed with FonMin Eban. Rostow said we hope have necessary messages ready for Secretary's signature this evening and get them to President.

2. In reply Harman's question, Rostow assured him we will be in touch with Israelis re form of maritime declaration. Under Sec said declaration will not contain threat of force since we wish secure participation largest number states possible. However, this aspect will be discussed with main partners in declaration. Harman raised question coordination and expressed hope we could move rapidly into joint Israeli-

---

[1] Source: National Archives and Records Administration, RG 59, Central Files 1967–69, POL ARAB–ISR. Secret; Immediate; Limdis. Drafted by David Korn (NEA/ARP); cleared by Atherton, Davies, and Grey; and approved by Eugene Rostow. Repeated Priority to USUN, Cairo, and London.

US planning. He requested intelligence exchange take place primarily in Washington so as to make it more effective.[2]

3. Harman said preliminary report sent him of May 28 Israeli Cabinet meeting made clear GOI decision had been extremely difficult one. It had been touch and go. Harman said GOI decision had been taken on basis Israeli reliance on President and with emphasis on time factor. In response Under Sec's question re his estimate of time GOI can wait, Harman stressed Nasser's moves amount to declaration of intention to destroy Israel. Harman said ten to fifteen day period would seem to be "on the long side." Under Sec said we see signs UAR forces beginning to hurt from lack food and water in their desert deployment.

4. Under Sec noted we watching very closely movement Panamanian flag freighter *Fenice* toward straits Tiran. DeptOff said we believe Egyptians aware vessel is of Israeli ownership. DeptOff said we would appreciate it if Ambassador could find out intentions owner. Noted we understand cargo is non-strategic.

5. Under Sec said he had instructions begin contingency planning for new US aid to Israel taking account of burdens occasioned by Israeli mobilization. Under Sec assured Harman USG proceeding as rapidly as possible carry through with scenario. We hope have President's final approval proposed steps by May 30 or 31. Congressional consultations scheduled begin May 31. Under Sec said we have taken steps to put financial pressure on UAR, and suggested Israelis also take what measures they can this direction. Pointed out we very conscious of time element but believe UAR likely suffer more from long mobilization than Israel.

6. Following meeting DeptOff informed Harman and Evron all USG officials under strictest instructions not to talk to press on trends policy thinking and diplomatic exchanges. DeptOff expressed concern re recent reports apparently originating with Israeli sources. Harman and Evron assured DeptOff that Israeli Emb and GOI not responsible for any leaks and will continue observe strictest press silence.

Rusk

---

[2] According to the minutes of the May 28 meeting of the Control Group, Under Secretary Rostow stated that "We should deepen our intelligence exchanges with the Israelis. Liaison should at this time be limited to intelligence matters." Rostow stated that he would speak to Helms about this and would inform Ambassador Harman. (Ibid., Office of the Executive Secretariat, Middle East Crisis Files, 1967, Entry 5190, Box 12, Minutes/Decisions of the Control Group, Folder 1)

98.   Telegram From the Embassy in Israel to the Department of State[1]

Tel Aviv, May 30, 1967, 0900Z.

3857. 1. In hour long meeting at his request Eban reviewed to me developments to date and Israelis' current concerns and ideas as to next steps.

2. He said Cabinet decision on May 28 not to go it alone had been taken decisively in closely balanced situation largely on basis message received by Prime Minister that morning and on his (Eban's) report his conversation Washington. Cabinet fully persuaded by his report of wisdom playing out diplomatic hand including the Security Council on understanding that effective enforcement capabilities to assure assertion of right to free and innocent passage through the Straits would be marshalled during same period. The relatively few additional politicians such as the Security and Foreign Affairs Committee to which he had also been able to make his classified exposition had also welcomed US position. However, Eban sensed that the widespread uninformed public here is becoming increasingly uneasy as to just where Israel stands in the diplomatic arena. Consequently, while he does not advocate any public revelation results his Washington conversations he would appreciate it if anything could be done in the background, perhaps off the record with the press in the United States, to re-emphasize determination displayed by President in latter's May 23 statement.

3. Turning to the Security Council, Eban said he could not urge too strongly that we avoid any resolution on the legal rights of free and innocent passage through the Straits. He said he had discussed this with Ambassador Goldberg on his way back to Israel. In Eban's view, any effort discuss such a resolution would inevitably give opponents opportunity to becloud and weaken essential impression of world support such legal rights. He strongly urged that instead we follow 1957 General Assembly procedure of tabling a declaration by those powers willing to agree on legal validity of rights. He added a general resolution by the Security Council in favor of peace and tranquility would be acceptable provided its negotiation did not unduly protract Security Council deliberations. He emphasized that situation still so delicate that time is very limited. Eban said he considering going to New York for Security Council meeting. He would like to put Israeli case personally. However, he had not yet made up his mind. He feels such trip might be

¹ Source: Johnson Library, National Security File, Country File, Middle East Crisis, Vol. II. Top Secret; Priority; Nodis. Received at 7:05 a.m.

misinterpreted here publicly as suggesting too much Israeli reliance on UN which in present circumstance would weaken government's control of internal situation. In this connection, in line with request made to him in Washington that GOI use its efforts to enlist support of others, Ambassador Comay, formerly Israeli rep to United Nations, is embarking on visit several countries this morning. However, since GOI not fully informed as to exact state of play of consultations between US, UK and other governments and does not wish to cross any wires they are instructing Ambassador Harman to ascertain in Washington our ideas as to where and how Comay could make most useful contribution. Meanwhile, he is proceeding to the Netherlands since the Netherlands have already been in direct touch with GOI.

4. GOI does not of course anticipate that Security Council will be able to do anything effective to open Straits. It is relying on US–UK plan for international force to provide decisive capability.

5. Eban then remarked that crucial as the Straits issue is, even perhaps a more dangerous situation exists as a result of the confrontation of large Israeli and Egyptian forces in the Sinai. Incidents there so far have been minor but a major clash could set off a conflagration at any time. In view of GOI best hope avoiding conflict that front is Soviets if they could persuade Nasser of necessity diminish tension by thinning out his concentrations. GOI would be more than happy to make parallel pullback. Eban hopes US going to bat with Sovs to this end.

6. Finally, Eban noted, while US and GOI intelligence estimates still considerably at variance but nevertheless Israelis prepared accept our conclusion that Egyptian attack not imminent, it impossible to rule out completely continued danger of full scale surprise attack by Nasser. It consequently essential everything possible be done to assure optimum US-Israeli posture in such an event. US had agreed to increase liaison in intelligence field, which being done. He had also discussed in Washington desirability of direct military liaison for contingency planning purposes and he wished reiterate importance GOI attaches to this matter.

7. Eban presented foregoing in measured non-emotional terms. It was remarked to me later by official also present that obviously Prime Minister and Eban have staked everything on assurances of support he obtained in Washington and there is considerable apprehension here that they may be optimistic in believing Nasser will give us time to follow scenario on which we have embarked. Same official also commented however that despite personal misgivings Chief of Staff Rabin is displaying firmest determination hold the hawks in line and strictly subject to political, that is Prime Minister's, orders.

Barbour

99. Memorandum of Conversation[1]

I–23434/67   Washington, May 30, 1967, 10 a.m.

SUBJECT

US Support of Israel

PARTICIPANTS

Israel
Brigadier General Joseph Geva, Israeli Defense Attaché
Lt Col Moshe Amir, Assistant Israeli Defense Attaché

United States
Colonel Amos A. Jordan, Jr., Director, Near East South Asia Region[2]
Philip E. Barringer, Deputy Director, NESA
Delavan P. Evans Assistant for Middle East Affairs, NESA

At his request, General Geva called to discuss US support of Israel in the present crisis. In essence, General Geva asked for a policy decision that the US would set aside previous policies and procedures and agree to far-reaching military cooperation and support of Israel in the light of the present crisis.

General Geva introduced the discussion by stating that Israel has accepted US advice about restraint, but when he left Mr. McNamara's office after the 26 May discussion with Foreign Minister Eban[3] he was very worried. He focused on General Wheeler's statement that even after an initial UAR attack on Israeli airfields, Israel would win any war. General Geva agreed with that assessment but said Israel would pay a heavy penalty. General Geva was much concerned that in making its estimate the US was assuming that Israel had equipment and capabilities it does not have. General Geva further stated that four Presidents of the United States have made commitments to Israel. Israel does not expect US forces to intervene but wants to know whether it will be able to obtain "special assistance" from the US. General Geva also referred to President Johnson's statement to Foreign Minister Eban during a preceding trip to the effect that Israel was so strong that the Arabs would never attack, and to Mr. Hoopes' statements that the deterrent strength of the Israeli Defense Forces is a factor for peace in the area.

General Geva insisted that both Israel and the US have accepted a grave responsibility by restraint. He emphasized that Israel had nothing

---

[1] Source: Washington National Records Center, OASD Files: FRC 330 71 A 4919, 333, Israel. Secret; Sensitive. Drafted on June 2. The meeting was held at the Pentagon. A typed notation on the memorandum indicates Hoopes saw it.

[2] In the Office of the Assistant Secretary of Defense for International Security Affairs.

[3] See Document 69.

to gain by war. General Geva went on to indicate his concern with events in Jordan and stated that while he did not think the Soviet Union would interfere physically in the conflict it was supporting the Arab States diplomatically and with equipment.

General Geva stated it was his understanding that a "special relationship" between the US and Israel now exists. Under these circumstances he could not understand why Mr. McNamara had refused to loan Israel 150 to 200 thousand gas masks. Colonel Jordan explained that a loan might not be legal but that the US would supply the gas masks as soon as we could work out the necessary arrangements.

General Geva indicated that he foresaw problems with respect to military hardware. As examples, he mentioned the following:

(1) Israel is in the process of converting M–48A1 tanks to diesel-powered M–48A3's. This conversion process will take a year and a half, during which time these tanks are not available for operational use. Israel is now exploring the question of whether to request additional US tanks because of this difficulty.

(2) Israel had requested certain ECM equipment which had previously been refused. He asked whether it was necessary in this case to follow previous procedures (i.e., policies). Given the present "special relationship", he could not understand why the US seemed unwilling to release this equipment. (On at least one previous occasion Israel was refused ECM equipment on both policy and security grounds; the Senior Control Group recently decided to take no action on this ECM request for the time being since the time required to deliver and put this equipment in operation would be so long that it would not be useful in the present crisis.)

(3) Israel had asked that the USAF ship gas masks to Israel in Air Force C–130 aircraft but had been refused. General Geva felt that the "new approach" to Israel's problems should result in positive decisions on this kind of request. He foresaw that Israel would have serious financial and operational difficulties in transporting equipment to Israel in time to be useful during the present crisis.

Colonel Jordan indicated that he recognized the Israeli concern, but the issues General Geva was raising went far beyond the responsibilities of his Directorate. He would, however, take up these matters with Mr. Hoopes and Mr. McNamara. Colonel Jordan pointed out that the US has many interests in this crisis, one of which is to attempt to defuse the crisis. In his personal opinion it might make matters worse if the USAF were to deliver equipment in C–130 aircraft since such action might send the wrong signal to the other side. It was important for the US to maintain its ability to take the heat out of the situation by diplomacy and to stave off a conflict.

General Geva then took up the problem of US support of Israel's position with respect to the Gulf of Aqaba and possible US military support of Israel. He stated that in the present crisis the US is surely not neutral. President Eisenhower and Secretary Dulles had given commitments with respect to freedom of passage through the Gulf of Aqaba. He referred to written assurances by Secretary Dulles and statements by Ambassador Lodge in early 1957. He also stated that Nasser seems to consider that Israel is isolated and is therefore playing all of his cards. It is important that Nasser understand that Israel is not isolated, and that the US in effect is supporting Israel's position.

An informal discussion of the US position and problems ensued. In general, DoD spokesmen pressed the ideas that we have interests in other countries in the area such as Saudi Arabia and Jordan; that the US is in a very difficult position which requires that it maintain flexibility. Maintaining flexibility may preclude overt, massive aid. If we can carry through with some influence in the Arab world, we may be able to achieve a settlement which will protect not only US interests throughout the area but also the long-range interests of Israel.

General Geva raised the question of combined contingency planning. He foresaw a situation in which Hussein might be overthrown or for some other reason the US would consider it necessary to intervene with military forces. He pressed the thought that combined planning after a decision had been made to undertake joint action would not work. Would it not be better therefore to undertake discussions and possibly combined planning at an early date?

General Geva indicated that despite the President's commitments to closer cooperation with Israel in defense and intelligence fields, the Israelis were finding that these commitments were being construed narrowly by those given the responsibility for carrying them out. Colonel Jordan indicated that he understood the point General Geva was making but that these matters were far beyond the responsibility of his Directorate. However, General Geva's views would be made known to the proper authorities. Colonel Jordan went on to reemphasize the fact that the US is involved in a very delicate situation. People at all levels including Secretaries McNamara and Rusk are wrestling with these problems and are making plans. These also involve the UK and other maritime countries. The President also wished to have consultations with Congress, which will take time. Colonel Jordan expressed the opinion that when these matters have reached an appropriate point he felt sure that discussions with Israel would be undertaken. At the moment we are most concerned that these efforts, which were of interest both to Israel and the US, not be jeopardized by hostilities.

100.   Telegram From the Embassy in the United Arab Republic to the Department of State[1]

Cairo, May 30, 1967, 1528Z.

8218. Department for Battle from Yost.[2]

1. I find Ambassador and other two senior officers this Embassy are all firmly convinced (1) that Nasser had publicly committed himself to course in this crisis from which he cannot and will not retreat, (2) that his commitment includes application of Aqaba blockade to oil, (3) that Nasser would not be deterred by threats except clear and credible intent to apply overwhelming force, from which he would expect to harvest major political victory, and (4) he would probably welcome, but not seek, military showdown with Israel. Substantially same appraisal has been made to me by General Rikhye and AUC President Bartlett.

2. I have been here too short a time myself to make personal assessment of UAR intentions, particularly whether there may be some flexibility as to scope of blockade and exactly how they would react to action by some maritime powers to break it. I am however impressed by quasi-unanimity with which area posts, in commenting on Department's circular 202592,[3] have expressed view consequences our following course B[4] would gravely undermine, if not destroy, US position throughout Arab world. If this view is correct, and from my experience in area I believe it is, principal profit of our following this course would accrue to Soviets, and over longer run position of Israel would be weakened rather than reenforced.

Nolte

---

[1]   Source: National Archives and Records Administration, RG 59, Central Files 1967–69, POL ARAB–ISR. Secret; Immediate; Exdis. Repeated to USUN for Goldberg. Received at 12:58 p.m. and passed to the White House at 1:09 p.m. Walt Rostow transmitted the text to the President at the LBJ Ranch in CAP 67501, May 30. (Johnson Library, National Security File, NSC Histories, Middle East Crisis, 5/12–6/19/67, Vol. 2)

[2]   Retired Ambassador Charles Yost. Telegram 203930 to Cairo, May 27, informed Nolte that the Department was sending Yost, then serving as consultant to the Department of State, to Cairo to talk to Nolte and members of the Embassy staff and to bring back to Washington a first-hand impression of the situation and the possibility of finding solutions. (National Archives and Records Administration, RG 59, Central Files 1967–69, POL ARAB–ISR)

[3]   See footnote 6, Document 60.

[4]   Course B was the second option: to give firm assurances to the Israelis that the Strait of Tiran would remain open and take all necessary measures either alone or with the British to enforce them.

101. Telegram From the President's Special Assistant (Rostow) to President Johnson in Texas[1]

Washington, May 30, 1967, 2038Z.

CAP 67504. Evron came in to see me at 3:00 p.m. with these points.

1. A message from Eshkol to you will probably come in tomorrow.

2. The Finney story[2] was deeply upsetting in Israel. The government was forced to say: we know of no such proposal; we are against any such proposal.

3. He said you made extremely clear to Eban your political problems and the implications of those problems for timing. From letters that came in the Israeli pouch today, it is clear that they also have acute problems of timing. I asked how long they could sit still before there is show down on the Aqaba issue. He said about 10 days.

4. As for tests in the Gulf as to which kind of ships Nasser would turn back. He felt them extremely dangerous unless we were prepared to back our play promptly. It would be politically and psychologically most disheartening to a have a series of tests in which the ships were turned back by the Egyptians. It would also commit Nasser more deeply each time. Therefore, he was against tests until we had mounted the force to make innocent passage stick as a principle.

5. He said that Prime Minister Eshkol was likely to express to you his "disappointment" that we had not picked up the suggestion of Eban for some sort of military liaison. He said the Israeli record of security in matters of this kind was excellent—citing a secret visit of the Chief of Staff of the Israeli Army to the Sixth Fleet. Such liaison need not be permanent but merely for the duration of this particular crisis. Without such liaison, we might get into a situation of conflict without even knowing the aircraft signals on both sides which could produce a first-class disaster.

---

[1] Source: Johnson Library, National Security File, Country File, Middle East Crisis, Vol. II. Secret. Received at the LBJ Ranch at 4:28 p.m. A handwritten "L" on an attached note by Jim Jones, May 30, 7:35 p.m., indicates the President saw it. Another attached note indicates that Rostow sent copies to Rusk and McNamara.

[2] An article in the May 30 *New York Times* by John W. Finney, attributed to Congressional sources, reported that the Johnson administration was considering a possible compromise solution to the Middle East crisis under which the Gulf of Aqaba would be open to all non-Israeli ships, including those carrying cargoes to Israel, until an international convention on the Strait of Tiran could be negotiated. The note by Jim Jones cited in footnote 1 states: "Rostow says both he and Rusk have talked to Finney and Tom Wicker about the injustice and inaccuracy of the story today. Walt does not know what the *NY Times* will do about it however. Jim." It continues: "George Christian talked to Max Frankel who agreed that the story should not have been printed."

6. I asked him if he thought Nasser was interested in fighting Israel or only in picking up political capital in the Middle East at the expense of Hussein and Feisal. He said for the first time in his life he believes that Nasser on balance wants to fight Israel.

---

102.   Diplomatic Note From the Israeli Ambassador (Harman) to Secretary of State Rusk[1]

Washington, May 30, 1967.

The Ambassador of Israel presents his compliments to the Honorable the Secretary of State and has the honor to convey the following message from His Excellency Levi Eshkol, Prime Minster of Israel, to His Excellency Lyndon Baines Johnson, President of the United States of America.

"Dear Mr. President,

"On May 28 I received your message through Ambassador Barbour and his verbal message on behalf of Secretary Rusk.[2] Foreign Minister Eban had also reported fully to me and to the Cabinet on your long and frank conversation with him.

"Your message and your remarks and assurances to Mr. Eban had an important influence on our decision to await developments for a further limited period before taking measures of our own to meet the challenge of the illegal blockade, the aggressive build-up of Egyptian forces on our southern frontier and the continuation of terrorist incursions into Israel territory. These provocations are further heightened by President Nasser's proclaimed intention to strike at Israel at the first opportunity with a view to bringing about her destruction.

The accumulation of hostile acts and pressures is extraordinarily intense. In the light of these pressures and of the possibility of a concerted Arab assault, a point is being approached at which counsels to Israel will lack any moral or logical basis. I feel I must make it clear in

---

[1] Source: Johnson Library, National Security File, Country File, Middle East Crisis, Vol. II. Secret; Nodis. Sent to the President with a covering note from Walt Rostow: "Mr. President: Herewith a somber letter from Prime Minister Eshkol, foreshadowed this afternoon by Evron."

[2] See Document 86.

all candour that the continuation of this position for any considerable time is out of the question.

"The sympathy and understanding which you have expressed towards my country encourages me to summarize the steps which need to be taken in order to restore a minimal stability:

"(a) *The Straits of Tiran:* I welcome the assurance that the United States will take any and all measures to open the Straits of Tiran to international shipping, and that the United States and Britain are proceeding urgently to prepare the military aspects of the international naval escort plan, thus underlining the international determination to make every effort to keep the straits open to the flags of all nations, including Israel. It is crucial that the international naval escort should move through the straits within a week or two. With every further delay, President Nasser will consolidate his illegal policy of a fait accompli. Any hope of getting effective United Nations action for opening the straits is doomed to failure. I rely on your own friendship, your principles of international legality and on your assurances that the United States, if necessary, will open the straits on its own. Without freedom of passage through the Gulf, Israel's vital interests, her national and regional status, her relations with Africa and Asia and her international trade will be gravely undermined. We shall in no circumstances accept such a situation. We reserve our right of self-defense as was agreed with the United States Government in February 1957. Recent history shows that the appeasement of an aggressive dictator in one matter leads to a further escalation of extortionist demands.

"(b) *The United Nations:* We have conveyed to Secretary General of the United Nations U Thant our view that in the light of the United Nations failure, the very least he can do is to insist that the blockade and troop concentrations be cancelled. There can be no reward for unprovoked aggression, and the idea of President Nasser putting conditions to Secretary General U Thant is unacceptable. We cannot entertain any discussion based on conditions prescribed by President Nasser.

"(c) *American-Israel Consultations:* On the best intelligence estimates available to me, I am convinced that there continues to hover over my country the danger of an Egyptian-Syrian attack. President Nasser's speeches of May 26, 28 and 29 cannot be ignored. In these circumstances, we have no alternative but to keep our armed forces in a state of the highest alertness and fully mobilized. In the message Foreign Minister Eban conveyed to you on May 26,[3] I asked urgently for a statement of American solidarity with Israel in case of attack. I also asked that, in addition to the intelligence coordination to which you have agreed, immediate coordination be established between the United

---

[3] See Document 77 and footnote 1, Document 63.

States forces in the Middle East and the Israel Defense Forces in order to examine how the United States can help to prevent or halt aggression. Without such concrete measures the American commitment to Israel's security will remain less credible and effective than it should. You may recall that I raised the point with you in 1964.[4] I was moved by what you told Mr. Eban about your fealty to all American commitments to Israel. I have never doubted this. Surely the present situation demands that the commitment should be given its full deterrent effect, both by reaffirmation and by entering a planning stage.

"One of the difficulties that I face is that I must call on my people to meet sacrifices and dangers without being able fully to reveal certain compensating factors, such as the United States commitment and the full scope of your determination on the matter of the Straits of Tiran. You may have seen in my public utterances an effort to meet this dilemma. Our nation is passing through some of the heaviest days in its history. It has every legal and moral justification and, indeed, it is in the supreme national interest to resist the aggression of an adversary who has committed one act of war and proclaims his intention to commit others. Such resistance would encounter, we believe, broad international understanding, and would encourage those forces in the Middle East which you and we regard as basically peace-loving and dedicated to stability. If present trends continue unchecked, there will be further erosion of the Western position in the Middle East. President Nasser's rising prestige has already had serious effects in Jordan, as proved by the agreement between President Nasser and King Hussein in Cairo.[5] The time is ripe for confronting Nasser with a more intense and effective policy of resistance. The people of Israel is the remnant of a nation which suffered tragic blows in the Hitler era. It is determined to defend its rights and its integrity with the utmost resolution. In this hour of destiny I appeal to you, Mr. President, to give effective response to what I have here written.

Respectfully yours,

Levi Eshkol

Prime Minister"

The Ambassador of Israel avails himself of this opportunity to convey to the Honorable the Secretary of State the renewed assurances of his highest consideration.

---

[4] For documentation concerning Eshkol's visit to Washington in June 1964, see *Foreign Relations, 1964–1968*, vol. XVIII, Documents 65–67.

[5] On May 30 King Hussein and President Nasser signed a mutual defense agreement providing that an attack on either party would be considered an attack on both and that any joint operations would be under the command of the chief of staff of the UAR armed forces. The text is printed in *The New York Times*, May 30, 1967. Iraq adhered to the agreement on June 4.

103. Memorandum From Secretary of State Rusk and Secretary of Defense McNamara to President Johnson[1]

Washington, May 30, 1967.

SUBJECT

Arab-Israel Crisis

1. Middle East Scenario

As you know, our scenario on the Middle East situation envisages three steps:

a. Action in and outside the United Nations to head off the imminent threat of Arab-Israeli hostilities and to seek a political settlement of the Gulf of Aqaba question;

b. Formal and public affirmation by the largest possible number of maritime nations of their support for the principle that the Strait of Tiran and the Gulf of Aqaba are international waterways; and

c. Contingency planning for testing UAR interference with the right of free passage for ships of all nations through the Strait and the Gulf, and contingency planning for the use of force, as necessary, to support that right. Implementing action would be undertaken only after measures in the United Nations had been exhausted and after Congressional approval had been obtained.

2. Handling of Declaration

The debate in the Security Council will probably be long and drawn out; the May 29 session indicated little disposition to agree on any specific resolution at this stage. During Council discussion, there will be substantial opportunity to launch various private negotiations, involving the President of the Council (Denmark, in June); the Secretary General; the British, French and Russians; and the protagonists themselves. These are a part of the UN process which may be of greatest importance in the end. At the proper time, the text of the Joint Declaration should be circulated in the Security Council for the information of UN Members.

---

[1] Source: Johnson Library, National Security File, Country File, Middle East Crisis, Vol. II. Secret; Exclusive Distribution. No drafting information appears on the memorandum. It was sent to the President with a covering note from Walt Rostow, dated May 30, 6:30 p.m., stating that it was the basic background paper on the Middle East, for discussion and decision at lunch on May 31. A May 30 memorandum from Read to Rostow, which accompanied the memorandum when it was sent to the White House, states that it had been approved by Rusk and McNamara. (Ibid., Vol. III)

a. Preliminary Soundings

The British have already made soundings on the proposed Declaration (without providing a text) with the Italians, Norwegians, Danes, Dutch, Belgians, Greeks, Panamanians, Liberians, and Japanese. We believe they have also discussed the idea of an international naval task force in the Red Sea with these nations.

We have made informal soundings on the Declaration (also without providing a text) and on the possible use of force, with the French, Belgians, Canadians, Dutch, Indians, Italians, and Norwegians.

b. Reactions to Soundings

The reactions to the soundings have varied. Most nations are prepared to support the principle regarding international waterways, but shy away from considering the use of force to secure adherence to that principle. Apart from the British and the Dutch, only the Canadians have so far indicated a possible willingness to participate in a naval task force; the extent to which the Dutch and particularly the Canadians would be prepared to join with us in the use of force is not yet clear.

c. Need to Move on the Declaration

Subject to Congressional consultations, we believe we should move promptly to present the proposed Declaration to the maritime nations, in order that our over-all scenario may move forward. Instructions to our posts on the Declaration (Enclosure 1)[2] indicate the division of responsibility between the British and ourselves for making approaches in selected capitals. The text of the Declaration is at Enclosure 2.

The purpose of these approaches would be to obtain signatures to a Declaration, which reaffirms the principles you set forth in your statement of May 23, but which does not commit the signatories to participate in the use of force. The British and we would inform the Israelis when these approaches are made, and suggest that they back them strongly in certain capitals. We would also at the same time determine whether certain nations would join with us in the use of force, if necessary. These nations should include: Italy, France, Argentina, Brazil, and Japan in the first instance. We have suggested that the British and Dutch approach the Nordic countries.

3. Possible Early Movement of Ships Through the Strait to Eilat

Decisions are desirable on the movement of merchant vessels through the Strait to the Israeli port of Eilat. We have discouraged such tests of UAR intentions thus far, although some ships have gone through to Aqaba, the Jordanian port. All such ships have acknowl-

---

[2] The enclosures are not printed, but see Documents 111 and 112.

edged the UAR controls, although none has been stopped, so far as we know. Armed force has not been used.

As part of our contingency planning, we are considering the possibility of tailoring the traffic pattern of ships entering the Strait during the next 10 days, in order to clarify the limits of the UAR policy of blockade—e.g., whether they intend to bar Israeli-owned as well as Israeli flag ships, and how they propose to define "strategic goods." We might for example encourage the attempted passage of an Israeli-owned (but non-Israeli-flag) ship carrying clearly nonstrategic cargo to Eilat; and if that passed without interference, we might attempt passage with a more "strategic" cargo (e.g., oil). Within this period, such tests would involve no armed escort and no counteraction in the event passage was refused. The purpose would be to clarify the limits of UAR policy and to build a public case for support of free passage.

A serious program of this kind would require consultation with Congressional leaders and an Israeli promise to accept the possibility of rebuff without retaliation. Tel Aviv may not be able to give such a promise, and the scheme may prove infeasible for other reasons—e.g., our inability to stage-manage the ownership, flag, and cargo of the shipping headed for Eilat. On the other hand, limited tests appear feasible within the next few days, and we propose to go forward with these where the risks appear acceptable. A Panamanian ship (Israeli-owned) loaded with hides is now heading for the Strait, bound for Eilat. We plan to do nothing to discourage its passage through the Strait.

4. A Military Plan to Deal With the Straits of Tiran Question

A military task force may be required to support, with force, the right of innocent passage, on behalf of the international community, through the Gulf of Aqaba in view of the UAR's announced blockade. The essence of this concept is that an international force could keep the Strait open for all flags, thereby obviating an Arab-Israeli war. Such a task force should be composed of as many maritime nations as are prepared to join it in a reasonable time. In practice, only the US, the UK and possibly the Dutch and Canadians are likely to participate.

Conceptually, the task force would consist of two parts. First, a *protective force* in the northern Red Sea which would provide a protective presence for merchantmen testing the Straits, and an escort if the UAR, should turn back or fire on unescorted ships; second, a *reinforcing force* in the Eastern Mediterranean which would be available for reinforcing support if the UAR fired on merchantmen and their escort.

A limited protective force of four destroyers (two US and two UK), a tactical command ship (US), and a light aircraft carrier (UK) could be assembled in the northern Red Sea in about a week. If the carrier *Intrepid*, now in the Mediterranean, transits the Suez Canal in the next few days, together with her appropriate escorts, these could be added to the force. Application for transit of the Canal has been filed. Even with these additions, however, such a force would be devoid of adequate self-contained air cover and ASW protection and thus subject to attack and damage by UAR sea and air forces in the area (the reinforcing force could provide some air cover over the Tiran area, but the distances from the Eastern Mediterranean would limit operational effectiveness). A stronger, better balanced protective force—augmented primarily by US naval units from CONUS—could be assembled in 25–30 days.

US and UK forces already in the Mediterranean provide a powerful reinforcing force (consisting of 3 US carriers, 1 UK carrier, and numerous other vessels). British air forces in Cyprus may also be available. If the UAR fired on merchantmen and their escorts, aircraft from these Mediterranean forces could, and might have to, intervene in the Tiran area or strike at major air bases and installations in the UAR.

The risks involved in testing the blockade with a limited or even an augmented protective force are not negligible. If Nasser is not deterred, the possibility would exist of wider conflict. This possibility is being urgently studied, both politically and militarily.

5. Congressional Consultation

Much of the Congress is away until Wednesday and some, including Senator Fulbright, will be away longer. We recommend immediate Congressional consultations on the Hill on the Declaration with the leadership, the key Committees (Foreign Relations, Foreign Affairs and Commerce), and with senior members of the Armed Services and Appropriations Committees. This meeting would be for the purpose of: (1) providing an up-to-date briefing on the current situation, and (2) reviewing our general strategy, with specific reference to the proposed Maritime Declaration. We recommend that the formal approaches to other nations regarding the text of the Declaration not be undertaken until after your discussions with the Congressional leaders.

Additionally, we plan to continue our daily efforts to brief other members of the Congress. As in the past few days, however, these briefings will continue to concentrate on current developments, and to avoid speculation about future developments.

In this situation, we believe that a Joint Congressional resolution would be politically necessary before US military forces are used in any way. The timing of a formal request to the Congress for such a resolution should, however, be carefully considered. While it is true that many Congressional doves may be in the process of conversion to hawks, the problem of "Tonkin Gulfitis" remains serious. Thus an effort to get a meaningful resolution from the Congress runs the risk of becoming bogged down in acrimonious debate. We recommend therefore that a formal request for such a resolution be delayed until (1) it has become clear to the Congress that we have exhausted other diplomatic remedies in and outside of the United Nations, and (2) our soundings indicate that such a request will receive prompt and strong support. The text of an appropriate resolution is Enclosure 3.

6. Timing

We hope to complete actions on the Declaration toward the end of this week. We would seek to have the military contingency planning, with the UK at least, well under way by the end of the week of June 5.

7. Recommendations[3]

1. That you approve the draft Declaration of the Maritime nations, at Enclosure 2.

2. That following Congressional consultations on Wednesday you authorize us to send a telegram substantially in the form of the text at Enclosure 1, instructing our Ambassadors in selected countries to seek commitments from the Governments to which they are accredited to adhere to the Declaration.

3. That following Congressional consultations, you authorize us to proceed at once to sound out France, Italy, Argentina, Brazil and Japan on an informal basis about the possibility of their participating with us in the use of force if necessary to secure effective observance of the right of free passage for all nations.

4. That you authorize us to add the Dutch, the Canadians, and other prospective members of the action party at a later point to form an international planning group which would be built around the British-American naval consultations.

5. That you approve the enclosed draft Joint Resolution for preliminary discussion late this week, or early next week, with Congressional leaders.

Dean Rusk[4]
Robert S. McNamara

---

[3] No indication of the President's decisions on the recommendations appears on the memorandum. Walt Rostow told Rusk in a telephone conversation the next morning that the President wanted "some inventive thinking done on plans for dealing with this thing" and "did not want us to get too locked in to the maritime idea if in fact it turns into bilateral action." In addition, Rostow said, the President wanted the Israelis and the British "out in front in organizing the party." (Notes of telephone conversation prepared by Carolyn J. Proctor, May 31, 11:32 a.m.; National Archives and Records Administration, RG 59, Rusk Files: Lot 72 D 192, Telephone Calls)

[4] Printed from a copy that bears these typed signatures.

104. Telegram From the Department of State to the Embassy in France[1]

Washington, May 30, 1967, 11:59 p.m.

204948. For the Ambassador.

1. We are seeking tomorrow to obtain at least nine votes in SC for resolution supporting para 14 of SYG's report to SC, calling on all parties to refrain from acts of belligerence or other acts that might exacerbate tensions.

2. Crucial goal of our strategy in seeking to avoid general war in M.E. is to restore status quo ante, so far as shipping to Eilat is concerned. A predicate to that strategy is a vote backed by at least nine members of SC supporting SYG's suggestion of a moratorium which would include UAR's not carrying out its threat to close the Strait to Israeli shipping and the shipping of what it regards as strategic cargoes to Israel.

3. The vote of France is crucial to this plan. Please see Couve if possible or Alphand if he is not available to request instruction for Seydoux urgently permitting him to join us and others in achieving a moratorium period within which negotiations could go forward.[2]

Unless such a suspension of UAR plans can be achieved, our considered judgment is that force will almost surely be involved, either by Israel under Article 51 of the Charter or by international maritime group to open the Strait, or by both.

Please stress that this note does not prejudice position GOF may decide to take later on basic issue of international law as applied to Strait of Tiran, should the issue arise in S.C. We are seeking now no more than a pause for diplomacy, which otherwise would have very few days to avert a clash whose implications are nearly impossible to foresee. We find it almost inconceivable that GOF would not support this moratorium plan.

Rusk

---

[1] Source: National Archives and Records Administration, RG 59, Central Files 1967–69, POL ARAB–ISR. Secret; Priority; Exdis. Repeated Priority to London and USUN. Drafted by Eugene Rostow and approved in substance by Rusk.

[2] Bohlen reported in telegram 19549 from Paris, May 31, that he had seen Alphand, had given him "the current French line," that putting forward a resolution that would not receive Soviet support would only sharpen the issue, harden positions, and make negotiations more difficult. Alphand had agreed, however, to telephone Couve de Murville in Venice to get his decision on instructions to the French representative at the United Nations. (Ibid., POL 27 ARAB–ISR)

105. President's Daily Brief

Washington, May 31, 1967.

[Source: Johnson Library, National Security File, NSC Histories, Middle East Crisis, Vol. 6, Appendix A. Top Secret; [*codeword not declassified*]. 1 page of source text not declassified.]

106. Editorial Note

On May 31, 1967, from 1:15 to 2:30 p.m., President Johnson held a luncheon meeting with Secretaries Rusk and McNamara, Vice President Humphrey, George Christian, and Walt Rostow. The latter's agenda for the meeting indicates that next steps in the Near East crisis headed the agenda, with the focus on the Rusk–McNamara recommendations in Document 103. A briefing memorandum prepared for Secretary Rusk similarly indicates that the Rusk–McNamara recommendations would be discussed and lists three additional points under the topic Middle East Crisis. The first item, "Use of U–2," is not further explained. An attached "G memo" (presumably a memorandum from Kohler) is not attached to the briefing memorandum. The second item states that the President wanted Rusk or Eugene Rostow to call in Harman and "indicate to him formally where the Eshkol letter exceeded the statement of our commitment." The third item states that Sisco, Battle, and Meeker were forming a Task Force to consider urgently possible solutions other than the US/UK Maritime Plan, and that the President had told Walt Rostow that morning that he "wanted urgent work done on this." (National Archives and Records Administration, RG 59, President's Luncheon Memoranda: Lot 70 D 164)

107.   Telegram From the Embassy in Jordan to the Department of State[1]

Amman, May 31, 1967, 1825Z.

3932. Ref. Amman's 3929.[2]

1. During meeting with Ambassador reported reftel, King said with great earnestness that he wished to propose to the President that he authorize issuance of public statement by a White House spokesman clarifying US policy towards the current crisis which would include the following points:

A. The USG seeks to be neutral between the parties to this dispute.
B. The main objective of the USG is to preserve peace and it is willing to use its good offices to this end.
C. The USG will not be responsible for hostilities in Middle East and will not be party to them.
D. USG will oppose any party who starts a war.

2. King said that he was making this suggestion as an old friend of the US. He felt such a statement would be a contribution to peace and consistent with what the Arabs knew were the moral principles of US.

3. Without such clarification, and however the crisis turned out, said the King, he was concerned that the US could suffer irretrievable loss among the Arabs.

Burns

---

[1] Source: National Archives and Records Administration, RG 59, Central Files 1967–69, POL ARAB–ISR. Secret; Priority; Exdis. Rostow sent a typed copy of the telegram to the President on June 1, with an attached note that reads: "Mr. President: Herewith King Hussein asks for your neutrality. Our Arab friends really find it difficult to remember what President Eisenhower had to do to get the Israeli troops out of Sinai. Walt." (Johnson Library, National Security File, Country File, Middle East Crisis, Vol. III)

[2] Telegram 3929 from Amman, May 31, reported a meeting between Burns and King Hussein. The King told Burns that after his trip to Cairo, he was convinced Nasser would not back down on the Strait of Tiran issue. He said Nasser believed the United States had the power to prevent Israel from going to war. Burns replied that if Israel concluded its survival was at stake, no amount of U.S. pressure would help. Hussein said Nasser and all the Arabs fervently hoped that in the event of hostilities, the United States would take no action against the Arabs. Nasser also told the King that in case of U.S. intervention against the UAR, he was prepared to ask for Soviet assistance. King Hussein said Nasser seemed confident that if the U.S. Government took "aggressive action" against the UAR the Soviets would give him "the required support." (Ibid.)

108. Telegram From the Department of State to the Embassy in Israel[1]

Washington, June 1, 1967, 11:08 p.m.

206657. Memcon Between Ambassador Harman and Under Secretary Rostow.

At his request Ambassador Harman called on Under Secretary Rostow afternoon May 31.

1. Mr. Rostow opened the conversation by showing Ambassador Harman a copy of the joint maritime declaration[2] and asking for his comments. After reviewing the draft, Ambassador Harman said he did not like the reference to the SC because it could conceivably stall the whole problem in the SC indefinitely. Mr. Rostow reminded the Ambassador of the US purpose in first seeking to resolve this problem through the UN. Ambassador Harman also asked why there was no reference to the 1958 convention on the Law of the Sea. Mr. Rostow explained that we had considered including a specific reference to the convention but had decided not to as many states had not signed. He thought the last paragraph of declaration putting the issue in the context of 1957, was more important.

2. Ambassador Harman inquired about the French position on this question. His own feeling was that signing a declaration was one thing but that he doubted whether the French would participate in the naval exercise.

3. Ambassador Harman then pressed the Under Secretary what US next step would be, asking specifically how long we would drag out the action in the SC. Mr. Rostow replied that Ambassador Goldberg was pressing hard for the disposition of his motion and that the US was standing firm on paragraph 14 of the SG report which raised the question of belligerency.

4. Mr. Rostow said that in his opinion Nasser would be inclined to hold on to what he has and not take any more risks, concentrating on the moderate Arab States rather than Israel, if he could hold to his victory at Sharm al-Sheikh. The issue of how to test the announced blockade was crucial in getting back to the status quo ante.

---

[1] Source: National Archives and Records Administration, RG 59, Central Files 1967–69, POL ARAB–ISR. Secret; Immediate; Nodis. Drafted by Grey and Eugene Rostow and approved by Eugene Rostow. Also sent to Cairo and USUN.

[2] See Document 112.

5. Ambassador Harman then asked when and what test would we use to force the Strait. Mr. Rostow replied that we were discussing two sets of plans: (1) possibility of sending unescorted ship through the Strait and (2) question of sending escorted ship through the Strait. He indicated that the question of force was a difficult one. Who uses force first and in what way would it be used could determine many aspects of the outcome. We were studying this one very carefully. In all our planning, however, the doctrine of the measured response applies. He reiterated to the Ambassador that our policy still ad referendum was to have the international community take on the question of the Gulf of Aqaba and hence separate it from the Arab-Israeli conflict. He reiterated the advice that GOI should not strike first.

6. Mr. Rostow said that we were joining HMG in proposing the maritime declaration overnight and moving ahead on Congressional consultations.

7. After a brief discussion of the situation in Jordan, Ambassador Harman pointed out that it was his Government's understanding that the planes USG had recently provided to Jordan were for training and defense against Syria and would not be used against Israel. Under the present circumstances the Israeli Government would expect that these planes be withdrawn.

8. Ambassador Harman then made a presentation of the problems his Government was facing. While it was rational to suppose that Nasser might refrain from attacking Israel, and concentrate on oil and the moderate Arab States, no one should underestimate the wave of irrational passion sweeping through the Arab world. From the Israeli point of view the military situation was worsening every day. Referring to the Gulf of Aqaba, Ambassador said that from May 22 USG had been asking the Israeli Government to refrain from unilateral action whereas it would have been logical from their point of view to have tested the blockade quickly and then exercised their right of self-defense. Now the Israelis had given the USG ten days and only today had he been informed that a final decision on the draft declaration had been made. Meantime, Israel faces a mounting array of force and there is no indication that Nasser intends to stay where he is. Nasser started off by referring to the status quo ante prior to 1956 and to Israel this means two things, the resumption of terrorist attacks and a blockade. To Israel a blockade was an act of belligerence. More alarming, however, was the fact that after a few days Nasser began to refer to the status quo ante prior to 1948. Nasser has made a military pact with Jordan. Iraqis are moving into Jordan and are being airlifted to Egypt. All this has strategic significance. Ambassador said that frankly his Government was not reassured by USG view of the situation which was taken from many

thousands of miles away. Nobody can be sure what Nasser would do. Mr. Rostow reminded the Ambassador that the USG had assured Eban three times that if Israel did not act alone it would not be alone.[3] The real question was what Nasser was doing and there is no sign yet that he was bent on enforcing his announced blockade. Harman said there was a simple explanation for that. No ships had come through the Gulf to Eilat since May 23. Rostow asked him to check this statement. Our information was that at least two ships had passed through for Eilat recently.

9. Ambassador then raised the question of liaison between USG and GOI military. If Nasser decided to strike it would be a quick strike, perhaps only 5 or 6 minutes flying time separated the opposing air forces. He said USG must appreciate that with this buildup continuing every day GOI was becoming more and more nervous. He reminded the Under Secretary that the US was still talking about an ad referendum scenario whereas Israel could be attacked at any moment. His Government had clear indications that Nasser had been disappointed when Israel did not strike first last week. They had no telephone number to call, no code for plane recognition, no way of getting in touch with the Sixth Fleet.

10. On instructions Harman again asked for a military liaison arrangement with the USG. This arrangement could be kept secret and this is what the Prime Minister was talking about in his recent letter to the President. Harman said he must convey his Government's real sense of urgency. Mr. Rostow replied that USG was conscious of its responsibilities and that he would raise question of military liaison with appropriate USG officials.[4]

11. Ambassador Harman then informed the Department that he would make three immediate requests: (a) One Hawk battery and 100 missiles to be flown to Israel immediately; (b) 140 M60 tanks. (The 140 M–48A1's previously purchased were being upgraded and this work would not be finished for another year.); (c) 24 A–4E Skyhawks for immediate delivery with ground equipment, armaments and operating parts for 5,000 flying hours. GOI also needed 10 chief petty officers to assist them in establishing a crash program to train 10F to use these planes. Mr. Rostow said he would inform DOD immediately. The requests would of course be presented in detail in the normal way to the DOD.

Rusk

---

[3] Reference is to the President's statement to Eban; see Document 77.

[4] The minutes of the June 3 meeting of the Control Group state that the group discussed this request and agreed that it would be kept under daily review. (National Archives and Records Administration, RG 59, Office of the Executive Secretariat, Middle East Crisis Files, 1967, Entry 5190, Box 17, Minutes/Decisions of the Control Group, Folder 1)

109.   Memorandum From the President's Special Assistant
(Rostow) to President Johnson[1]

Washington, May 31, 1967, 6:45 p.m.

Mr. President:

As instructed, I had Evron in this afternoon at 5:30. I explained to
him your concern at the language used with respect to the U.S. commitment in Prime Minister Eshkol's message of yesterday. I went over
again your talking paper which, I reminded him, was your formal communication to which the rest of what you said was an elaboration. He
said he understood what I had told him; but he was deeply concerned.

The reason was this. He went up to New York to meet Minister
Sapir, who has just arrived in the U.S. to raise money for Israel. Sapir
told him that after Eban reported, the Cabinet voted on war or delay,
and split 9 to 9.

The Prime Minister then cabled Harman and asked Harman his
and Evron's personal assessment of the President's intentions.

Harman and Evron then said that it was their personal assessment
that President Johnson intended to see this through even if, in the end,
the United States was the only nation standing beside Israel. They did
not for one moment imply that this is what you told Eban. They merely took on their shoulders the "heavy burden" of giving to their
Government their assessment of the feelings and intentions of the
President of the United States.

Evron added that for some reason he—Evron—is regarded in Israel
as a hawk. Sapir told him that it was this personal assessment which
tipped the balance.

Evron wanted me to be extremely clear that:

—he in no way attributed his judgment to what the President told
Eban;
—he and Harman held themselves alone responsible for making
this assessment of President Johnson.

He said he told me this story to understand what the effects might
be of a message from Washington which appeared to be a "backing
away" from what the President told Eban.

---

[1] Source: Johnson Library, President's Appointment File, June 1967, Middle East
Crisis. Secret. Rostow sent a copy to McNamara with a note saying that the President
wanted him to have it. (Washington National Records Center, OSD Files: FRC 330 72 A
2468, Israel 091.112) He also sent a copy to Rusk. (National Archives and Records
Administration, RG 59, Central Files 1967–69, POL ISR–US)

He then asked me: "Has the President's attitude changed since he saw Eban?" I said I did not believe that the President's attitude had changed since that time. What the President was reacting to was language in a communication between Chiefs of Government which was inexact. The President felt that it was extremely important for the Government of Israel fully to understand the constitutional setting in which the President had to make his dispositions. The whole context of the talk with Eban was the limitations which the President had to face in implementing his policy stated on May 23.

He then said, "Am I wrong in assessing the President's personal determination as I did?" I said that, as a government servant, it would be wrong for me to communicate that kind of judgment. I said, "You have known President Johnson for a long time and have a right to make your own assessment."

With tears in his eyes, he said: "So much hinges on that man."

I told him that our reaction to Prime Minister Eshkol's formulation would be conveyed more formally; but that I wished him to understand the kind of difficulty it posed for the President.

He then went on to make three observations:

—the first soundings taken by their ambassadors in Scandinavia, Canada, etc., were not hopeful, although this may not be the last word;

—in their contacts with the Congress they believe support is building for a strong stand by the United States not confined to former doves. He said that in this matter Nasser was doing their work for them;

—finally, he said that Israel expects war. They do not expect to attack, but to be attacked. They are grateful for the swiftness with which the Pentagon is now dealing with the pipeline; but Harman will be in to see the Secretary of State with requests for an additional Hawk battalion for air defense and some other urgent military assistance. He hopes that we shall be able to respond.

Walt

110.   Memorandum of Telephone Conversation Between the
President's Special Assistant (Rostow) and Secretary of State
Rusk[1]

Washington, May 31, 1967, 8:05 p.m.

Telephone Call From Mr. Walt Rostow

R said that was the quickest sale he had ever made; Pres said he
wanted Sec to get cable out to Bob Anderson and tell him to tell Nasser
that if he lays off and puts Israeli flag [issue?] into the Court of Justice
it might create an atmosphere in which we could be helpful in his other
problems;[2] Pres wanted Sec to get word to Bob Anderson and then we
could get some Swiss out there to tidy it up.

R said second point was Pres wants Sec and Bob and R and
Goldberg to figure out some move we can make militarily to show we
are not scared of these Russian ships; R will put Bob working on that.[3]

---

[1] Source: National Archives and Records Administration, RG 59, Rusk Files: Lot 72
D 192, Telephone Calls. No classification marking. A handwritten notation indicates there
was no distribution. Prepared by Carolyn J. Proctor.

[2] No such message has been found. Telegram 205677 to Cairo, May 31, sent at 9:17
p.m., asked whether Anderson was still in Cairo and whether he could remain one more
day. (Ibid., Central Files 1967–69, POL 7 US/ANDERSON) Telegram 8296 from Cairo,
June 1, received at 1:33 a.m., replied that Anderson was leaving at 9 a.m. and that it was
not possible to alter the arrangements. (Ibid.)

[3] Deputy Secretary of Defense Cyrus Vance called Rusk at 9:25 p.m. to say that
Rostow had called to ask what Rusk, McNamara, Vance, and Eugene Rostow wanted to
do about the Soviet ships in the Mediterranean. Vance said he and McNamara thought
that if the President wanted to do something, they should announce the next day, after the
Intrepid went through the Suez Canal, that they were holding it and two or three destroyers in the Red Sea pending events. Rusk said he thought this would be more inflammatory than Sixth Fleet action, and would "look like a doublecross." He was inclined to say
more about movements from the East Coast or the North Atlantic. Vance said they could
look at this again the next day. (Notes of telephone conversation prepared by Proctor, May
31, 9:25 p.m.; ibid., Rusk Files: Lot 72 D 192, Telephone Calls)

111. Circular Telegram From the Department of State to All Posts[1]

Washington, May 31, 1967, 10:46 p.m.

205690. Subj: Maritime Declaration.

1. To provide helpful support for UN and other efforts resolve current NE crisis, we have been examining with British desirability of issuing joint declaration by maritime nations. Draft text being sent you septel.[2] The Netherlands is prepared to and we believe Canada is disposed to support the proposed course of action and the Government of Israel is to back up with a strong diplomatic effort. All addressees should coordinate with British to ensure most effective mutual support. British have already authorized their Ambassador in Paris, Ottawa, The Hague, and Rome to make approach after concerting with you. We have proposed broader initial approach and expect London will issue further instructions soonest.

2. After coordination with British following action addressees should deliver draft declaration urgently to host Governments, making points set out below and soliciting their prompt support: Athens, Panama, Monrovia, Tokyo, Ankara, Tehran, Buenos Aires, Rio de Janeiro, Dublin, Manila, Addis Ababa, Abidjan, Mexico City, Caracas, Lisbon, Tananarive, Reykjavik. Since FRG is not UN member, approach in Bonn should seek separate FRG statement conforming as closely as possible to draft declaration.

3. British will make initial approach in following capitals, with U.S. following up, Copenhagen, Oslo, Helsinki, The Hague, Paris, Brussels, Stockholm, Rome, Ottawa, Canberra, Wellington, Accra, Nairobi.

4. This message sent other recipients for info only.

5. In presenting declaration, you should stress following:

a. Current Near East crisis is worst since 1956. Withdrawal UNEF at UAR request has removed essential buffer between UAR and Israel and

---

[1] Source: National Archives and Records Administration, RG 59, Central Files 1967–69, POL ARAB–ISR. Secret; Priority; Limdis. Drafted by Battle, William D. Brewer, and Director of the Office of OECD, European Community, and Atlantic Political-Economic Affairs Deane R. Hinton; cleared by Eugene Rostow and Walt Rostow; and approved by Secretary Rusk. Walsh initialed for Rusk. Davies cleared the list of addressees with Counselor Nigel C. Trench at the British Embassy. Also sent to Dhahran, Jerusalem, U.S. Mission Geneva, Hong Kong, Paris, USRO Paris, CINCSTRIKE for POLAD, MAC for POLAD, and CINCEUR for POLAD. Rostow sent a draft to the President at 4 p.m. on May 31, with a covering memorandum stating that it would serve as a talking paper when the Declaration of Maritime Nations was presented, and that he thought the President should personally clear it. The "Cleared" option on Rostow's memorandum is checked.

[2] Document 112.

their two armies now confront each other. Accident or miscalculation could be calamitous.

b. Situation has been made even more acute by announced UAR intention close Gulf of Aqaba both to Israel-flag vessels and to vessels of all other flags carrying "strategic cargoes" to Israel. UAR has thus put forward claim to control Israel's sole seaward access from south. Israel regards such access as essential and considers any interference with it as a threat to Israel's very existence. Gravest questions of war and peace accordingly arise. In judgment USG joint action by maritime nations is the only alternative to an almost certain war.

c. It is the view of the USG that Straits of Tiran and Gulf of Aqaba constitute international waterway both by test customary usage (innocent passage for all Israeli-bound vessels has been normal for decade) and by general provisions international law which are reflected in 1958 Geneva Convention on Territorial Sea to which 33 states, including USSR, are parties. (FYI of Aqaba riparians, only Israel is a party. End FYI.) The UAR action clearly poses a test to these recognized rights of navigation through international waterways.

d. Through the efforts of the UNSYG and the current consideration of the problem by the UN Security Council it is hoped that processes can be brought to bear leading to a satisfactory solution of the present critical problem. As part of this general effort, the USG believes it is important for the world's major maritime states clearly and with solidarity to reiterate their views regarding both the general principles involved in this situation and their specific application to the Aqaba case.

e. Issuance of a declaration with such broad support would be most useful at this juncture in supporting current UN efforts and the rule of law with respect to maritime traffic. The USG hopes that host government will be willing join with other like-minded states who also being approached in issuing declaration in very near future. The declaration reaffirms position taken by maritime powers in 1957 which was subsequently reflected in the 1958 Geneva Convention.

6. In response to queries you may take following line:

a. If asked re our basic intention, you should respond our aim is to remove present danger to peace and resolve current problem by means of international action through the United Nations.

b. If asked what our intention would be should efforts through the United Nations fail, you should state that we would address questions which would then arise at that time, but we would not now exclude the possibility of protecting maritime rights outside the UN.

c. If asked how far association with joint declaration would commit host governments to further joint action as opposed to consultations, you should give assurance that participation in issuance declaration constitutes a commitment only to the statement of principles contained therein.

d. If asked whether changes can be made in the text you should say that we will of course consider most carefully any suggestions but that many nations are being approached and that the mechanics of substantial redrafting would obviously be difficult.

7. FYI. A number of maritime states publicly supported principle freedom of transit through Gulf of Aqaba in United Nations debates in early 1957 as part general international effort secure Israeli withdrawal from Sinai Peninsula. These included: UK, France, Italy, Canada, Sweden, Belgium, New Zealand and several others. If addressees able ascertain host government took such clear position at that time, point should of course be stressed that what is needed now is merely reaffirmation host government's longstanding position.

8. It is expected that Israeli Ambassador will be in touch with you and will strongly support your efforts and those your British colleagues.

9. *For Tel Aviv*—Under Secretary Rostow gave text declaration this afternoon to Ambassador Harman.

10. *For Bonn*—Septel of instructions follows. End FYI.

11. Report reactions priority.

Rusk

---

112.   **Circular Telegram From the Department of State to All Posts**[1]

Washington, May 31, 1967, 10:47 p.m.

205691. There follows draft declaration of maritime nations sent you either for action in accordance septel or for info:

---

[1]   Source: National Archives and Records Administration, RG 59, Central Files 1967–69, POL ARAB–ISR. Secret; Priority; Limdis. Drafted by Legal Adviser Leonard C. Meeker and Hinton; cleared by Battle, Eugene Rostow, and Walt Rostow; and approved by Rusk. Walsh initialed for Rusk. Also sent to Dhahran, Jerusalem, U.S. Mission Geneva, Hong Kong, Paris, USRO Paris, CINCSTRIKE for POLAD, MAC for POLAD, and CINCEUR for POLAD.

The Governments of maritime nations subscribing to this Declaration express their grave concern at recent developments in the Middle East which are currently under consideration in the United Nations Security Council. Our countries, as Members of the United Nations committed to the Purposes and Principles set forth in the Charter, are convinced that scrupulous respect for the principles of international law regarding freedom of navigation on international waterways is indispensable.

In regard to shipping through the waterways that serve ports on the Gulf of Aqaba, our Governments reaffirm the view that the Gulf is an international waterway into and through which the vessels of all nations have a right of passage. Our Governments will assert this right on behalf of all shipping sailing under their flags, and our Governments are prepared to cooperate among themselves and to join with others in seeking general recognition of this right.

The views we express in this Declaration formed the basis on which a settlement of the Near East conflict was achieved in early 1957—a settlement that has governed the actions of nations for more than ten years.

These views will guide our policies and action in seeking to assure peace and security in the Near East.

Rusk

---

113.   Memorandum From the President's Special Assistant (Rostow) to President Johnson[1]

Washington, May 31, 1967.

SUBJECT

Today's Security Council Meeting

We presented our interim resolution—calling for Security Council endorsement of Thant's appeal to forego belligerence and for further diplomatic and UN efforts to resolve the crisis.[2] In his speech, Justice Goldberg called on the members of the Security Council to have the

---

[1] Source: Johnson Library, National Security File, Country File, Middle East Crisis, Vol. III. Confidential. A handwritten "L" on the memorandum indicates the President saw it.

[2] UN document S/7916.

courage to exercise their responsibilities and to harmonize their actions to save the world from the scourge of war.

The UAR subsequently presented a resolution essentially calling for a reversion to the situation before 1956.[3] The UAR Representative attacked the 1951 Security Council Resolution (which said that neither side was entitled to belligerent rights). His basis was that some of the states voting for the resolution should have abstained as parties to the dispute and that the resolution was based on the "permanent character" of the Armistice which had been shattered by the 1956 attack.

Fedorenko maintained a running, sarcastic challenge to Goldberg to explain our naval blockade of Cuba in 1962 in light of our present championing of maritime rights.

Various Arab countries continued their attacks on Israel. Japan supported Thant; India supported the UAR Resolution; Ethiopia made a temporizing down-the-middle statement; and France called for—and got—an adjournment until 10:30 a.m. Friday[4] in order to study both resolutions (and, obviously, to get further instructions).

Walt

---

[3] UN document S/7919.

[4] June 2.

---

114.   **Memorandum by Harold Saunders of the National Security Council Staff to the President's Special Assistant (Rostow)**[1]

Washington, May 31, 1967.

WWR:

Just to keep thoughts flowing to you, attached are two papers which add up to a debate:

First are some hasty reflections on where we are and the proposition that circumstances may create a situation where we would want to

---

[1] Source: Johnson Library, National Security File, Country File, Middle East Crisis, Vol. II. Secret. Saunders sent the memorandum and its attachment to Walt Rostow with another memorandum, which states that Saunders wanted to ensure that "we consider a quite different alternative than you were discussing this morning." It also notes that "we may face a situation where no one will come in with us on the regatta" and in that case, Saunders hoped they would "at least stop and reconsider."

modify our course. These are irresponsible thoughts, but they badly need stating, especially when you read the parade of horribles in the Task Force's economic paper.[2]

Second is a memo on my luncheon conversation today with one of King Faisal's sons.[3] In effect, he suggests an umbrella under which we might preserve a chance to split the moderates—along the lines we were discussing this morning.

The first is an argument for letting Israel go. The second is an argument for avoiding Israeli involvement at all costs.

Hal

Attachment 1

ARAB-ISRAEL: WHERE WE ARE AND WHERE WE'RE GOING

What has happened. In the two weeks since Nasser mobilized we have reversed the policy of 20 years. Instead of staking our bets on an evenhanded relationship with the Arabs—moderate and radical alike—and the Israelis, we are now committed to a course that will more likely than not lead us into a head-on clash with a temporarily united Arab world. Whereas we relied on Israel to hold its own militarily and built our influence with Arab moderates to Israel's benefit, today we are acting as if we can only protect Israel by confronting the Arab world and surrendering our influence with the moderates to Nasser.

What else we could have done. By not stopping an Israeli strike as early as 21 May when Egyptian positions were still fluid, we would probably have witnessed a limited Arab defeat and then had to move the international machinery in to restore peace. Israel's reputation would have suffered and long-range prospects for reconciliation would have been set back. But assuming she held her own, we would not have been linked with Israel and she would have brought to bear the only counter that the US or anyone else has yet found to the war of national liberation—force. Nasser as a dominating force would have been physically weakened, and the moderate governments might have been freed to ignore him and concentrate on their own development in association with us.

---

[2] Reference is apparently to Document 115.

[3] This memorandum recorded a conversation with Saudi Prince Mohammed and another Saudi visitor, both of whom urged that any U.S. action to open the Strait of Tiran must be based on international law rather than on the basis of helping Israel, or no Arab moderate could support it.

Why we held Israel back. As a humane government, we are naturally inclined to choose peace over the unknowns of war. Though we have ourselves chosen force to stop aggression in Vietnam, we argued strongly against pre-emptive war on the basis of our own decision not to use this device against the USSR and because world opinion would not permit us to come to the aid of an aggressor.

The price we have paid. It seems that the UAR has won all the chips to date, but Israel may really be the big winner. For twenty years Israel has sought a special relationship—even a private security guarantee—with us. We have steadfastly refused in order to preserve our other interests in the Middle East. We argued that our policy worked to Israel's best interest too. Now we are committed to side with Israel and, in opening the Straits of Tiran, even to wage war on the Arabs. In short, we have chosen sides—not with the constructive Arabs *and* Israel but with Israel alone against all the Arabs.

Whoever is the bigger winner, we are the sure loser. If we follow our present course, we stand to lose economically (see the Task Force's rundown of the "economic vulnerabilities") and to suffer substantial Soviet gains. If we back away from Israel, we're a paper tiger. In building a new Middle East along the regional lines in your vision, the closer we get to Israel, the longer we delay our constructive contribution to make that vision a reality.

Need we pay that price. When we committed ourselves last week to open the Straits for Israel, we did so believing that Nasser might back down or, at least, would not tangle with militarily escorted vessels. Instead, in his Sunday press conference and other conversations, he has made it clear he is not trying to open any doors behind him. To the contrary, he made clearer than ever his determination to close the Straits to Israeli flag vessels and oil tankers headed for Eilat. Ambassador Yost warns vividly that we can no longer count on Nasser to back down.

While Nasser may not shoot at a destroyer escort, he is lining up the other Arab countries to retaliate against all blockade runners by closing off oil supply, nationalizing property, closing bases, boycotting commerce, closing ports to shipping, etc. If we follow our present course, it is hard to see how we can make good our commitment without paying a tremendous price in the Arab world—unless Nasser backs off, and he shows no sign of doing that.

The other choice. Events may show that other maritime powers are not willing to join the regatta. Congress at that point may not support our opening the Straits alone. Or a major terrorist incident may open the whole situation up again by shifting attention from the Straits to a new front. If any of these happen, I would enter the strongest plea to stop and think about whether we shouldn't put the brakes on a little.

The other choice is still to let the Israelis do this job themselves. Eshkol himself says he'll have to go this route within a week or two if we can't produce. He's correct that we don't have any right to hold him back longer while his enemy gets stronger unless we're willing to take on the Arabs ourselves. Pretty soon we'll have Soviet warships in the Red Sea. We ought to consider admitting that we have failed and allow fighting to ensue.

I know this may fly in the face of the President's own feelings about Israel. But the question is whether we can help Israel more in the long run by alienating ourselves from the Arab world or by backing off just enough to keep our hand in there.

Hal

---

115.   Report of the Working Group on Economic Vulnerabilities[1]

Washington, May 31, 1967.

GULF OF AQABA: THE ECONOMIC VULNERABILITIES

The papers attached[2] outline a first look at the probable economic consequences of a US/UK decision to hold open the Gulf of Aqaba to Israeli-bound shipping, if necessary by force. We find that:

(i) *We have little economic leverage on the Arab countries, almost none on Egypt.* We have run down our aid programs close to the vanishing

---

[1] Source: Johnson Library, National Security File, Country File, Middle East Crisis, Vol. II. Secret. Read sent the report to Walt Rostow with a May 31 covering memorandum. A May 31 memorandum from Battle to Rusk, also attached, states that it was the first report of the Working Group on Economic Vulnerabilities, comprised of representatives of the Departments of State, Defense, Treasury, and the Joint Chiefs of Staff, and the White House staff. The group was a subcommittee of the Middle East Task Force. A May 31 memorandum by Eugene Rostow formally established the Task Force and a Control Group, chaired by Rostow and including Walt Rostow, Vance, Kohler, and Battle. Battle chaired the Task Force, which included Hoopes, Popper, Country Director for Soviet Affairs Malcolm Toon, Assistant Legal Adviser for Near Eastern and South Asian Affairs Donald A. Wehmeyer, Assistant Secretary of State for Economic Affairs Anthony M. Solomon, and Saunders. (Ibid., Vol. III) The Task Force suspended its formal meetings on June 15. (Memorandum from Eugene Rostow to the Control Group and Task Force, June 15; ibid., Vol. VI)

[2] The attachments, titled "Vulnerabilities of Arab Countries to US Economic Actions," "Oil," "Financial Aspects," and "Airline Traffic Rights," are not printed.

point, except to Jordan—where a cut-off would almost certainly bring down Hussein's moderate regime. The food import needs of Egypt and other Arab countries are less this year than normally; the USSR can supply them—at least through the summer—without difficulty. Our exports are largely standard items easily available elsewhere; denial would hurt the Arabs only in the implausible event of a worldwide embargo. We could deny them use of their deposits—more than $2 billion in London, $700 million in New York. But this is more a gun at our head than at theirs.

(ii) *The Arab countries together have powerful economic weapons to use against the Atlantic nations, particularly Britain.*

(iii) *Egypt and Syria alone cannot inflict serious damage.* Their direct power is limited to closure of the Canal and pipelines; we could manage the effects of both of these acts.

(iv) *The costs become very high when the oil-producing states—Saudi Arabia, Kuwait, Iraq, and the Gulf Shaikhdoms—find it necessary to move against Anglo-American oil interests.*

(v) *At worst the oil producers could expropriate our holdings and deny petroleum exports to the Atlantic countries.* This would mean:

—Loss of up to $500 million in net US foreign exchange earnings from oil holdings per year;
—Loss of net *non-oil* trade earnings of up to an additional $500 million;
—Loss of billions of dollars in US capital assets;
—UK loss of up to $1 billion in foreign exchange earnings;
—A crisis in sterling and in the international monetary system.

(vi) *There is a high risk that the oil producers would do their worst in the event of a military engagement—or perhaps even escort action—in the Gulf of Aqaba.*

(vii) *Short of a military confrontation, we would have to expect the oil-producing countries to take some action against us, ranging from scattered sabotage to sequestration of oil holdings and selective prohibition of exports.* These costs would be more manageable, but the effects might at least in part be irreversible.

(viii) *Our ability to minimize these costs depends on:*

—Holding the Europeans to a common front by presenting a credible prospect that we can face Nasser down quickly enough to avoid major disruption in oil supplies (most of them have stocks for 50 days).
—Making it clear to the Europeans and Japanese that we stand ready to bear our share of the physical and money costs of disruption in oil flows, including eventual rationing.
—Giving the producing countries the best possible excuse for moderation by presenting a plausible image of evenhandedness towards Arab and Israeli, along with a prospect of Nasser's failure.

(ix) *If it appears that there will be a major and continuing interruption in oil flows,* the Europeans and Japanese will be seriously tempted to make side deals with the producers—including takeover of US and UK operations.

(x) *Even if the Arabs do their worst, we believe we can maintain the flow of aviation and other fuels to Viet-Nam—now supplied almost entirely from Saudi Arabia and Bahrain—from domestic sources.* This would require protection controls and product allocation procedures in the US.

---

116.   President's Daily Brief

Washington, June 1, 1967.

[Source: Johnson Library, National Security File, NSC Histories, Middle East Crisis, Vol. 6, Appendix A. Top Secret; [*codeword not declassified*]. 2 pages of source text not declassified.]

117.   Telegram From the Embassy in Syria to the Department of State[1]

Damascus, June 1, 1967, 1346Z.

1224. Ref: State 204952.[2] Arab Israel Crisis.

1. After careful review reftel, I can only concur with dismay in Cairo's assertion (Cairo 8093)[3] that shape US policy taking in present crisis sharply divergent from views reported area posts. Appears field assessments have played no role in policy formulation. Our appreciation situation contained Damascus 1200.[4] I fully endorse views Beirut, Baghdad, Amman, Jidda, Cairo, Kuwait, Algiers and others. Not necessary at this point to repeat eloquent and consistent argumentation of latter for, in effect, "hands off" policy in current Arab-Israel confrontation.

2. There appears to be consensus best minds, most knowledgeable area experts that outline US policy to date directly opposed short and especially long term US national interests in area. Policy charts collision course with monolithic Nasser-led Arab nation. Deterioration US position has been so rapid that I believe we faced with few alternatives beside mounting salvage mission. Plan "isolate UAR from our ME

---

[1]   Source: National Archives and Records Administration, RG 59, Central Files 1967–69, POL ARAB–ISR. Secret; Priority; Exdis. Repeated to Aleppo, Algiers, Amman, Baghdad, Beirut, Cairo, Jerusalem, Jidda, Kuwait, USUN, Tel Aviv, London, Paris, and Moscow. Received at 11:43 a.m. and passed to the White House at 12:15 p.m. Walt Rostow sent a copy to the President, at 2:10 p.m., with a memorandum calling it the "full flavor and feeling of one of our Arabist Ambassadors." Rostow also attached a copy of telegram 8313 from Cairo, June 1, which reported the Belgian Ambassador's view that Nasser "would not budge an inch on Aqaba" and that Israeli military action would be preferable to action by the Western powers. Rostow's memorandum states he wanted the President to have before him as wide a range of perspectives as possible. (Johnson Library, National Security File, Country File, Middle East Crisis, Vol. III)

[2]   Circular telegram 204952, May 31, sent to all U.S. missions, stated in part, "we are inclined to believe that unless a war between Israel and UAR breaks out, the political goals of the UAR and the Soviet Union are Nasser's ascendancy in the Arab world, and Soviet control of oil and other interests vital to the security of the United States, Europe and the free world generally." It outlined the steps underway to obtain action in the UN Security Council and signature of a Declaration of Maritime Nations, and it stated that contingency planning was underway for testing the UAR blockade and establishment of an international task force to support free passage for ships of all nations through the Strait and Gulf. (National Archives and Records Administration, RG 59, Central Files 1967–69, POL ARAB–ISR)

[3]   Telegram 8093 from Cairo, May 28. (Ibid.)

[4]   Smythe argued in telegram 1200 from Damascus, May 29, that the only U.S. commitment to the area was to oppose aggression from any source and that this should include an "aggressive act reopen Straits of Tiran." (Ibid.) He cited telegram 8046 from Cairo, May 27, in which Nolte argued that Israel had used force to acquire passage rights in the Gulf of Aqaba in 1956 and was now faced with the same situation in reverse with the UAR's reestablishment of the status quo ante 1956. (Ibid.)

friends" feeble if not ridiculous hope, particularly in light Husayn's dramatic trip to Cairo and solidarity views all Arab leaders well-disposed to US vs. our present policy stance.

3. US firm determination keep Tiran Straits open either through UN mechanism or by joint operation major maritime powers seems foredoomed. Cards already stacked against any effective UN action this sort in view indications substantial support UAR stance, and ambivalence SC members, others not fully committed support UAR, Arabs. Action by maritime powers would be thinly veiled direct US, UK intervention which destined produce perilous confrontation.

4. US "evenhanded" ME policy is viewed by Arabs as fraud, and US actions during current crisis have confirmed this belief. Our Arab friends have pleaded that we simply take our "even-hand" off. Nebulous commitments we have re Tiran Straits must be weighed in view area consequences if we honor them. Consensus informed opinion indicates disaster for us if it pushes Tiran claim either in multilateral guise or unilaterally

5. My view of situation, perhaps oversimplified, is that US reaping full harvest 20 year area policy which has regarded Israel as fulcrum, highest priority interest. This has rankled Arabs who now feel strong enough to challenge US, hoping jar it into full realization its total position now in jeopardy unless it revises its priorities in light overall US national interest. Failing this, Arabs determined smash US influence in area (in which they expect USSR backing). On scales we have Israel, an unviable client state whose ties, value to US primarily emotional, balanced with full range vital strategic, political, commercial/economic interests represented by Arab states. The folly of US pursing present policy obvious without further elaboration.

Smythe

118.   Telegram From the Joint Chiefs of Staff to the Commander in Chief, European Command (Lemnitzer)[1]

Washington, June 1, 1967, 1545Z.

6724. Subj: USS *Liberty* Sked (U). Ref: DIRNSA G/104/311906Z May 67 (Notal-BOM).[2]

1. (S) When RFS request sail *Liberty* IAW following sked:

a. 2 Jun. Depart Rota.

b. 2–8 Jun. En route via Gibraltar Strait CPA as safe nav permits. Then via northern Africa coastal route to posit 32–00N 33–00E. CPA Morocco, Malta 3 NM: claimed list 3 NM. CPA Spain, Tunisia, Sardinia, Sicily, Crete 7 NM; claimed dist 6 NM. CPA Algeria, Libya, UAR 13 NM; claimed dist 12 NM.

c. 9–30 Jun. Conduct ops south of 32–00N and between 33–00E and 34–00E.[3] While conducting ops CPA UAR 12.5 NM, CPA Israel 6.5 NM.

2. (U) Request JCS (JRC), CNO, CINCLANT (JRC), CINCLANTFLT be included as info addees on all Movereps, Daily Sitreps, and Incident Reports.

3. (U) En route tech tasking IAW ref.

4. (U) Procedures for developing July sked follow.

---

[1] Source: Johnson Library, National Security File, NSC Histories, Middle East Crisis, Vol. 7, Appendix H. Secret. Repeated to CNO, CINCLANT, CINCLANTFLT, CINCUS-NAVEUR, COMSIXTHFLT, CTF 64, USS *LIBERTY*, DIRNSA, NSAEUR, DIRNAVSEC-GRU, ADIRNAVSECGRU, DIRNAVSECGRULANT, DIRNAVSECGRUEUR.

[2] DIRNSA G/104, 311960Z May 67, not printed.

[3] DIRNSA ADP/242–67, 292013Z May 67, had requested that the *Liberty* operate in this area, which was proposed operational area 3 of five proposed operational areas. It stated that the actual operating area should be adjusted as necessary for operational and safety reasons. (National Security Agency, Center for Cryptologic History Historical Collection, Series VII, Crisis Files, Box 16e, COMSIXTHFLT Messages re *Liberty*)

119.   Telegram From the Embassy in the United Arab Republic to
        the Department of State[1]

Cairo, June 1, 1967, 1435Z.

8333. For Battle from Yost. Ref: State 205157.[2]

1. Agree that Arab unity is fragile affair and present display will not last indefinitely. However, there is agreement among those I have consulted that it has been extremely well orchestrated and has acquired sufficient momentum to carry it for some time, certainly several weeks.

2. While popular enthusiasm is helpful, and can be turned on and off with relative ease, it is not essential, at least in UAR, to maintaining firm military and political posture. This depends almost wholly on leaders and armed forces. There is little likelihood of "battle fatigue" among either of these in near future.

3. There is little question that passage of time without serious challenge to UAR or Arab positions would create more flexible situation and less heated atmosphere. However, continued public challenge to UAR position on Aqaba and reports of maritime powers preparing to break blockade by force constitute built-in issue on which to keep tempers at high pitch and maintain Arab unity at current or higher level.

4. I recognize problem Department faces in endeavoring to restrain Israelis from military action by assuring them of alternative means of breaking blockade. However, as long as prospect either of Israeli attack or Western use of force in straits seems imminent, Arab excitement and unity will probably mount rather than decline.

5. Crisis could probably be defused if way could be found to put Aqaba issue on ice for few weeks. However, this would presumably require either UAR temporarily permitting oil to pass or Israel temporarily acquiescing in oil being excluded. We doubt Nasser could tolerate former without unacceptable loss of face.

6. If crisis could be defused in this respect, we believe, barring accidents or provocations, modus vivendi governing other elements of

---

[1] Source: National Archives and Records Administration, RG 59, Central Files 1967–69, POL ARAB–ISR. Secret; Priority; Exdis. Repeated Priority to USUN. Received and passed to the White House at 11:58 a.m. A copy was sent to the President by Walt Rostow at 4:05 p.m. with a note describing it as "an evenhanded view" from Yost. (Johnson Library, National Security File, Country File, Middle East Crisis, Vol. III)

[2] In telegram 205157 to Cairo, May 31, Battle responded to Yost's views in Document 100. He stated that past experience had shown that "bursts of Arab determination and 'unity' were of relatively short duration," and he asked, "Are we right in assuming that passage of time without direct Israel challenge to UAR or Arab positions would make more flexible situation in which to work?" (National Archives and Records Administration, RG 59, Central Files 1967–69, POL ARAB–ISR)

problem, such as UN observers along UAR-Israeli frontier, could probably be worked out. Under these circumstance passions would cool off and traditional Arab diversity be likely to reassert itself.

7. This estimate is based on assumption, which I am inclined to believe is correct but cannot vouch for, that Nasser will be satisfied at this juncture with substantial restoration status quo ante 1956 and will not exploit or be swept along by present Arab euphoria to claim further gains at Israeli expense. Of course, longer crisis continues at current temperature greater is danger bids might be raised on both sides.

Nolte

---

120.   Telegram From the Mission to the United Nations to the Department of State[1]

New York, June 1, 1967, 2246Z.

5561. USUN 5555;[2] USUN 5559.[3] ME Crisis: Talk with Israeli PermRep.

I talked to Israeli PermRep Rafael shortly after noon June 1 and told him that on a personal and confidential basis I had probed with both Iraqi FonMin Pachachi and Yugo PermRep Lekic possibility of exercising influence on Nasser to back down sufficiently in order to achieve a breathing spell during which crude oil shipments would continue to pass through the Straits of Tiran to Elath. Rafael did not demur nor approve. He did comment in a negative sense on the prospect of prolonging present UN debate. I told him we not prepared for showdown vote on our draft res June 2 and that he should anticipate probability delay action on res until June 5.

Goldberg

---

[1] Source: National Archives and Records Administration, RG 59, Central Files 1967–69, POL ARAB–ISR. Secret; Immediate; Nodis. Received at 7:46 p.m.

[2] Telegram 5555 from USUN, June 1, reported a conversation at breakfast that day between Goldberg and Iraqi Foreign Minister Adnan Pachachi. (Ibid.)

[3] Telegram 5559 from USUN, June 1, reported a conversation that morning between Goldberg and Yugoslav representative Danilo Lekic. (Ibid.)

121.   Memorandum From the President's Special Assistant
        (Rostow) to President Johnson[1]

Washington, June 1, 1967, 1 p.m.

Mr. President:

As instructed, I called on Congressman Celler[2] and Congressman Morgan[3] at noon in the Rayburn Building.

Congressman Celler explained that he and Morgan were working closely together in providing leadership in the House with respect to the Mid East crisis.

They wish me to convey to you the following:

1. The clear majority sentiment in the House of Representatives is pro-Israel. They feel Israel is being "pushed around" by Nasser.

2. They are worried about the effect of the passage of time on Israel with respect to the build-up of Egyptian forces in Sinai and the debilitating consequences for the Israeli economy.

3. They feel we shall, in the end, have to "do something" to open the blockade at Aqaba—multilaterally or otherwise.

4. They do not believe that the Soviet Union will directly confront us if we so act. They will react indirectly.

5. They wanted it clearly understood that they are "Administration men"; they fully support the President; they fully support your statement of May 23; and they wish to do nothing that you would not regard as helpful.

6. Celler then asked, "Would the President regard it as helpful if we generated a strong statement of support for his position on Aqaba?" He said that without even trying, they got over 100 signatures last week.

I replied that I could not speak for the President. It was my impression that the President might need their support in the days ahead, and it might be wise to await the President's direct guidance. But I could be wrong; and if the President wished them to generate a statement of support, I would let them know.

---

[1] Source: Johnson Library, National Security File, Country File, Middle East Crisis, Vol. III. No classification marking. A handwritten notation on the memorandum indicates that it was received at 1:25 p.m.

[2] Representative Emmanuel Celler of New York.

[3] Representative Thomas E. Morgan of Pennsylvania, Chairman of the House Foreign Affairs Committee.

Celler did most of the speaking; but, at each point, he asked Morgan for confirmation that this was also his view. Morgan explicitly stated his agreement at each point and at the end when I summarized their message to you.

Walt

No Congressional statement wanted now[4]

Tell Celler and Morgan to do the following

See me

---

[4] This option is checked.

---

122. Memorandum From Harold H. Saunders of the National Security Council Staff to the President's Special Assistant (Rostow)[1]

Washington, June 1, 1967.

SUBJECT

Arab-Israeli Control Group Meeting, 4:30 p.m.[2]

Now that State has reorganized with the Task Force under Luke Battle funnelling recommendations to the top level Control Group,[3] I will try to feed to you before the Control Group meetings the main issues that I see that need special attention. This will give you a chance either to weigh in when you go to the meeting or on the phone with Gene beforehand. Today, under the main agenda items, there are the following:

1. Tim Hoopes' subcommittee[4] organized a scenario for a test probe in the Straits of Tiran that projects 15 to 18 days to mobilize the necessary charter vessels to test the blockade. Since the Israelis may well be assembling their own group to move sooner, I wonder if we have this much time and whether we don't need something sooner. Eshkol doesn't sound as if he can sit still this long.

---

[1] Source: Johnson Library, National Security File, Country File, Middle East Crisis, Vol. III. Secret.

[2] The agenda for the meeting is ibid.

[3] See footnote 1, Document 115.

[4] Hoopes chaired the Task Force subcommittee on contingency military planning.

2. In responding to Israeli economic and military aid requests,[5] the best avenues seem to be further military credit or EXIM bank. I have no quarrel with this but we will want to be sensitive to conspicuously moving heavy equipment in at this point.

3. Dave Popper does not see 9 votes for our resolution in the UN Security Council. They are now inclined to let the debate fall over until Monday.[6] Secretary Rusk has sent notes to the Brazilian and Argentine Foreign Ministers. We badly need to make sure we are doing everything possible on this front. Nat Davis undoubtedly has a more precise reading but for purposes of this meeting, I think you merely need to ask questions to underscore urgency.

4. The British Foreign Office opposes active Israeli support for the Maritime Declaration. The present draft of the President's reply to Eshkol[7] urges active Israeli support. The British and a lot of our people fear this would scotch the declaration. Perhaps this sentence should be taken out of the President's reply.

5. Prime Minister Wilson is scheduled to hold a press conference at the British Embassy late tomorrow afternoon. We want to nail down what he is going to say so that he will not take us any farther than we want to be taken.

Hal Saunders[8]

---

[5] See Document 108. Walt Rostow's handwritten notes on the memorandum summarize the requests: "1 Hawk battery, 25 A 4 E's, 140 tanks, M–60" with the note, "No extras." Harman made the requests formally in a June 1 note to Rusk. A June 2 memorandum from Battle to Rusk states that the Department of Defense was still examining the requests but had indicated already that neither A4s nor Hawks were available; concerning the M–60 tanks, "our production line is tight but we are studying availabilities." (Harman's note is filed as an attachment to Battle's memorandum; National Archives and Records Administration, RG 59, Central Files 1967–69, DEF 19–8 US–ISR)

[6] June 5.

[7] The draft has not been found, but see Document 139.

[8] Printed from a copy that bears this typed signature.

123.   Telegram From the Embassy in Portugal to the Department of State[1]

Lisbon, June 1, 1967, 1700Z.

1514. Dept pass President and SecState only from Robert Anderson.

1. I spent more than two hours Wednesday night[2] with President Nasser. There was no opportunity to send message from there or to brief Embassy Cairo on conversation. I plan to return New York Saturday or Sunday. Please advise me whether you would like for me to dictate and send a full review of my conversation with President Nasser or wait until I return.

2. I discussed with him possibility Marshal Amer or Zakaria Mohieddin coming to United Nations for routine visit and then going secretly with me to Washington to see President and SecState. Nasser replied that he could not send Amer because of crisis, but would very much like to send Zakaria Mohieddin and would have him there Sunday or Monday if he received a message from me confirming that Zakaria Mohieddin could secretly visit with President and explain all of Nasser's points of view. He asked me if any exploration of this subject had been made before I left and I replied affirmatively. However, before Zakaria Mohieddin should come, I would want to confirm that President would see him under these circumstances. I earnestly recommend that Zakaria Mohieddin be received and have an opportunity of visiting with President and SecState. I have arranged to send message from here through Embassy Cairo which will be understood by Nasser and Zakaria Mohieddin will leave immediately if your rely to me is affirmative.

3. In all my years of visiting Middle East I believe that this is the most tense time I have ever observed and Arab unity is almost unanimous. Nasser is supremely confident, but I think earnestly desires friendship of US. He took great pains to explain his feelings and to express the hope Zakaria Mohieddin could visit with President. I will appreciate your advising me soonest in order that I may send cable to

---

[1] Source: National Archives and Records Administration, RG 59, Central Files 1967–69, POL 7 US/ANDERSON. Top Secret; Immediate; Exdis; Handled as Nodis. Received at 4:34 p.m. and passed to the White House at 5 p.m.
[2] May 31.

Nasser and know whether or not to send full text of my meeting with Nasser from here or to wait until my return.[3]

Wellman

---

[3] Telegram 206060 to Lisbon, June 1, asked Anderson for a detailed summary of his report as soon as possible. In telegram 206614 to Lisbon, June 1, Rusk told Anderson that the President would like to see a cable report on the most significant points made by Nasser as soon as possible after his return. It further stated that the President would be glad to receive Mohieddin privately if he came to the United Nations. (National Archives and Records Administration, RG 59, Central Files 1967–69, POL 7 US/ANDERSON)

---

124.   Memorandum for the Record[1]

Washington, June 1, 1967.

SUBJECT

Conversation between Major General Meir Amit and Secretary McNamara—late afternoon, 1 June 1967[2]

1. In response to a question from Secretary McNamara regarding Russian knowledge of the blockade of the Straits of Tiran, Gen. Amit stated that he doubted if the Russians knew of this in advance but were not reluctant to seize the opportunity to take advantage of it. Gen. Amit

---

[1] Source: Washington National Records Center, OSD Files: FRC 330 77–0075, Memoranda of Conversations Between Secretary McNamara and Heads of State (Other than NATO). Top Secret; Personal and Eyes Only for the Secretary of Defense and the Director of Central Intelligence. Prepared on June 2. A copy was sent to the Director of Central Intelligence and a stamped notation on the memorandum indicates McNamara saw it on June 2.

[2] Amit visited Washington May 31–June 2. At a conference on the Six-Day War held June 3–5, 1992, he stated that he had three objectives in this mission: first, to compare notes on the situation, second, to find out whether any action was being planned to reopen the Strait of Tiran, and third, "to tell the Americans, I, Meir Amit, am going to recommend that our government strike, and I wanted to sense what would be their response, their attitude toward that." (Parker, Richard B., ed., *The Six-Day War: A Retrospective,* (Gainesville, Florida: University Press of Florida, 1996), p. 139)

Amit said that he met with McNamara for 40 minutes and told him three things: first, a short description of the military situation, second, the impact of the Israeli mobilization on Israel's economy and the fact that it could not be sustained for a long period, and third, "I told him that I'm personally going to recommend that we take action, because there's no way out, and please don't react. He told me it was all right, the president knows that you are here and I have a direct line to the president." He said McNamara asked only two questions: how long a war would last, to which Amit replied, "Seven days," and how many casualties Israel would sustain. Amit said, "Here I became a diplomat. I said less than in 1948, when we had 6,000." (Ibid., p. 140)

then went on to describe the situation as he sees it which is to the effect that the blockade of Tiran is window dressing. He believes a grand design, which he termed the "Domino Effect," has now developed. That is, that the UAR, with Russian backing, hopes to roll up the whole of the Middle East all the way to the borders of Russia, to include Iran, under Arab domination. While this whole matter is close to and vital for Israel, the long range effect would be deeply inimical to U.S. interests. Gen. Amit would not go so far as to say he believed that this grand design lay behind the original move of the UAR but he feels strongly that it now exists as an opportunity being seized by the Russians, whatever the origin of the present confrontation. He indicated his view that the U.S. is already damned in the eyes of the Arabs no matter what we do.

2. Gen. Amit expressed the view that the U.S. could demonstrate its commitment to its interests in the Middle East very cheaply by doing the following:

a. Providing the necessary weapons and economic support over the long term to Israel. (In this connection he stressed that it is too late now for any additional weapons to have any immediate effect on the crisis.)
b. U.S. clearly demonstrate its political backing of Israel.
c. U.S. isolate the area from Russian intervention.

3. Gen. Amit stressed that time is very much against Israel. 10 days ago Israel could have contained the situation but as time goes on and the Arabs get more deeply entrenched, the problem becomes increasingly difficult for Israel. He stated Israel has now mobilized 100,000 people and this hurts the economy. He pointed out that it is impossible to keep the entire nation mobilized for long and still maintain its economic viability.

4. Gen. Amit indicated that one of the great worries of Israel is the possibility of a pre-emptive air attack by the UAR which would cripple the Israeli Air Force and result in loss of air superiority which would be vital to Israeli success if hostilities break out.

5. Returning to the issue of the Straits of Tiran, Gen. Amit said that while they are not crucial, loss of free passage has become a political symbol and that therefore we must go through the motions of solving that problem.

6. Gen. Amit, returning to his main theme, stressed his opinion that it is a U.S. problem as much as an Israeli problem, and maybe even more so, and that he feels extreme measures are needed quickly. He stressed that his remarks were entirely informal, off the record and should not be regarded as an official representation or request of the Israeli Government. He was simply taking advantage of the opportunity to insure that the highest American authorities understand the picture as the Israelis see it.

7. He informed the Secretary that there were no differences between the U.S. and the Israelis on the military intelligence picture or its interpretation. He added that the Russian story of a planned attack against Syria was a sheer fabrication.

8. Gen. Amit asked the Secretary whether naval action in the Straits of Tiran is contemplated soon. The Secretary responded by saying that this was just one of a number of possibilities which are under consideration by the U.S. Mr. McNamara asked Gen. Amit how many casualties he thought he would incur in an attack in the Sinai. Gen. Amit indicated that this was a tough question to answer, stating that it would depend a great deal on who hit first. He said that such a fight would be much more severe and difficult than the last one because the Egyptians have a well balanced defense of 6 Divisions in 3 lines, the most interior line to Egypt being held by the 4th Armored Division. Amit indicated that without air superiority this would be a tough defense to crack but that with it he thought the Israelis could do the job with somewhere in the neighborhood of 4,000 casualties. He stated in connection with the matter of air superiority that the loss of Israeli air fields would inevitably involve the U.S. physically in the conflict if Israel were to have any chance.

9. In closing the meeting Mr. McNamara thanked Gen. Amit for his candid discussion and indicated that he, the Secretary, would be seeing the President shortly and would convey Amit's views to him. Amit stressed that he did not want this conversation to become wide-spread knowledge and took notice of the fact that the undersigned had been taking notes throughout. Mr. McNamara assured Gen. Amit that the information would not go beyond him and the top senior officials of the government who needed to know. On the way back to the hotel I showed Gen. Amit my notes, indicated they would be incorporated in a Memorandum for Record and that he need have no fear of wide dissemination. He expressed satisfaction with the entire interview and wondered aloud if he shouldn't have tried to see the President also. I told him such a move would be entirely out of the question, totally inappropriate, and that the President was quite well aware of Amit's visit and would receive from the Secretary all of the information Amit had conveyed. He then wondered whether he should stay around town a little longer to see what happens even though the Secretary of Defense had previously indicated this would serve no purpose. I urged him to get a night's sleep and go back to Israel as soon as possible because he would be needed more there than here.

Rufus Taylor
Vice Admiral, U.S. Navy
Deputy Director of Central Intelligence

125. Telegram From the Department of State to the Embassy in Syria[1]

Washington, June 1, 1967, 5:49 p.m.

206179. 1. In dealing with special problems of protecting American interests and assuring firm awareness of United States position in the countries to which you are accredited, please convey the following thoughts urgently to the Foreign Minister at least or to higher authority, as you deem most effective. You may of course draw on Circular 204952,[2] and other recent telegrams in your discretion.

2. Our position in the Middle East crisis rests on two principles which are applicable across the board and not solely in relation to Israel and the UAR.

3. The first is that we support the territorial integrity and political independence of all the countries of the Middle East. This principle has been affirmed by four American Presidents and was clearly invoked to protect Egypt against Israel in 1956. American policy has given strong support to other Arab states as they have passed through difficult periods. FYI. Libya in 1956 against UAR subversion, Lebanon 1958, recognition of Kuwait 1961 at expense our Embassy in Baghdad, generous economic aid, etc. End FYI.

4. We wish all the friendly Arab governments thoroughly to understand this fact, and recall that the principle has been invoked in their behalf.

5. The second is our defense of the basic interest of the world community in upholding freedom of the seas, and the right of free and innocent passage through straits of an international character. Our position on the application of this principle to the Strait of Tiran goes back to 1957. President Eisenhower then said:

"With reference to the passage into and through the Gulf of Aqaba, we expressed the conviction that the Gulf constitutes international waters, and that no nation has the right to prevent free and innocent passage in the Gulf. We announced that the United States was prepared to exercise this right itself and to join with others to secure general recognition of this right."

---

[1] Source: National Archives and Records Administration, RG 59, Central Files 1967–69, POL ARAB–ISR. Secret; Exdis. Drafted on May 31 and June 1 by Eugene Rostow, cleared by Popper and Davies, and approved by Rostow. Also sent to Beirut, Baghdad, Cairo, Amman, Jidda, Kuwait, Tripoli, Kuala Lumpur, Algiers, Rabat, Addis Ababa, Tehran, Rawalpindi, Djakarta, and New Delhi and repeated to Tel Aviv.

[2] See footnote 2, Document 117.

6. The context of this statement should be clearly understood. President Eisenhower persuaded the Israelis to evacuate Sharm al-Sheikh, and allow United Nations forces to be stationed there as observers, in exchange for this assurance, among others. At the same time, the Ambassador of Israel stated in the United Nations that Israel would regard any violation of this principle by armed force as a hostile act justifying retaliation under Article 51 of the United Nations Charter. Our Ambassador "took note" of this statement. The Government of Israel has recently reaffirmed the view that it regards its rights of passage through the Strait, as they have been exercised for ten years, as a vital national interest.

7. Accordingly, we are seriously concerned with the decision of the UAR to terminate the regime in the Strait which has been in effect for over ten years and which has been sanctioned by international law and the Geneva Convention on the Law of the Sea.

8. We wish finally to reaffirm our desire to live on friendly terms with all the Arab States, and to express our concern over the course of developments which not only threaten these relations we value so highly, but also the very integrity and well being of some of the states involved. Because of the devastation and destruction that would ensue in the event of conflict, we have thus far successfully urged restraint. Our capabilities, however, are limited. It is to avert conflict that we have strongly supported the Secretary General of the UN in his efforts to obtain a breathing spell and made clear our support for the right of free and innocent passage through the Strait of Tiran. Our main objectives are to preserve peace, maintain relations based on mutual respect with all the states of the area, and to honor our responsibilities. We seek understanding of our policies and support for all efforts to ease tensions and ensure a peaceful solution to potentially explosive situation.

Rusk

126. Memorandum From the Board of National Estimates to Director of Central Intelligence Helms[1]

Washington, June 1, 1967.

IMPLICATIONS IN THE MOSLEM WORLD OF FORCING THE STRAIT OF TIRAN

Problem: To estimate the reactions of the Arab and other major Moslem states to keeping open the Strait of Tiran by naval escort forces of the US in association with other countries.

1. The course of the present Arab-Israeli crisis has already done considerable damage to the US position in the Arab world. Most Arabs believe the US is the staunch ally of Israel and can in effect control its actions. The US cannot expect to receive sympathy if it employs force in the Strait, but it will also not get any gratitude if it fails to do so. This is so even though many of Nasser's Arab adversaries hardly welcome the kind of sweeping political and psychological victory he would enjoy if he brings off his move with impunity. Even King Hussein in Jordan and King Feisal in Saudi Arabia feel increasingly compelled to move into camp with Nasser and to reassess their ties with the US.

2. Nasser himself, whether or not he resists the forcing of the Straits, will take advantage of the opportunities provided to discredit the US and reduce its influence and presence in the area. He may at the same time find in the US action a release from the danger of Israeli attack and a way out of his present dilemma which would leave him with most of his gains.

3. Reactions in non-Arab Moslem states would be much less intense than in the Arab Middle East. US military and intelligence facilities in non-Arab Moslem states (Turkey, Iran, and Pakistan) probably would not be significantly affected, though the Turks would be unlikely to permit their soil to be used for staging military operations against any Arab state. Over the longer term, however, if this action set in motion a permanent trend toward increased Russian and Egyptian influence in the Middle East at US expense, Iran, Pakistan, and even Turkey might feel it necessary to adjust their policies to these trends.

4. The Arabs would consider any such multilateral force, no matter how constituted, to be an instrument of US policy. The climate of pop-

---

[1] Source: Johnson Library, National Security File, Country File, Middle East Crisis, Vol. III. Secret. Sent to the President on June 1 with an attached memorandum from Helms stating, "This is the Agency estimate which I indicated to you yesterday would be in your hands today."

ular opinion toward the US would become more hostile and emotional, and popular anti-US demonstrations would almost certainly occur, possibly including violence. The seriousness of such outbreaks would be greater if US action in the Strait involved shooting.

5. All Arab governments would feel compelled to demonstrate solidarity by making anti-US gestures or taking more serious anti-American actions. The UAR would probably close the Suez Canal to US naval ships and at least during the height of the crisis might refuse passage to other American flag vessels, particularly oil tankers. Jordan, the only eastern Arab state receiving any significant amount of US economic aid, would feel compelled to minimize its US ties. Hussein would then become politically at the mercy of the UAR and economically dependent on the other Arab states. King Feisal would probably feel it necessary to make a public accommodation with Nasser, though he would try to avoid breaking relations with the US. The Libyan Government might feel compelled to terminate the US base at Wheelus. Throughout the area US communications facilities, air traffic rights, etc., might be withdrawn or subjected to strikes and harassments.

6. The main target of attack against the US in the Arab world would be the oil industry. Unquestionably all US oil operations would be subjected to harassments. In all Arab countries sabotage incidents would be likely against American oil facilities. Strikes of oil workers with accompanying rioting are likely to tie up oil production and might threaten loss of American life. IPC and Aramco pipelines across Syria might be cut. The effects in the Persian Gulf sheikdoms would be less. Iran could of course increase production to offset in some measure a slowing in Arab output. There is, however, some question about Iran's willingness to do so. Algerian oil is produced mainly by French companies and would probably continue to flow.

7. Saudi Arabia, Kuwait, and Libya will be under very heavy pressure to retaliate against American companies, but will be concerned with the effects on their own revenues of any retaliatory measures. They might halt oil production by US firms only temporarily. Libya might attempt to institute a selective boycott against those countries which contributed ships to the effort to force the blockade. Initially, at least, outright nationalization seems unlikely even in the UAR.

8. Once the situation in the Strait of Tiran was settled in one way or another, and assuming no major hostilities in the area occurred, many of the anti-US activities would tend to slacken off. The chief producing countries are almost certainly hoping for some outcome which will not upset the highly profitable flow of oil. The Egyptians themselves are heavily dependent upon the West for the processing and marketing of petroleum. Even if nationalization occurred in some places, it might prove more a token than a definitive change.

9. The judgments above would not give a balanced picture unless some mention is made of the consequences of failure to end the blockade of the Tiran Straits. Unless the issue can be resolved in some manner tolerable to the Israelis, the odds are at least even that sooner or later they will feel impelled to take some form of military action. The Israeli Government is already under severe domestic attack for having failed to take prompt counteraction against Nasser's move a week ago, and Israeli military leaders are almost certainly pressing hard for a military move against Nasser. In their view, acquiescence in this kind of a victory for Nasser would spell more and more trouble for Israel as time went by, and we believe these fears are well grounded. Hence, their temptation will be great to fight back while their forces are mobilized and their supporters are rallied—even if the costs and risks are comparatively high. They probably would not prove able to pull off the kind of smashing defeat of Egyptian forces they accomplished in 1956, but we believe the alternative—of impotent acquiescence in a formidable political and psychological victory by Nasser—would incline them to accept the risks.

For the Board of National Estimates:
Sherman Kent
Chairman

---

127.   President's Daily Brief

Washington, June 2, 1967.

[Source: Johnson Library, National Security File, NSC Histories, Middle East Crisis, Vol. 6, Appendix A. Top Secret; [*codeword not declassified*]. 1 page of source text not declassified.]

128.   Telegram From the Embassy in the United Arab Republic to
        the Department of State[1]

Cairo, June 2, 1967, 1038Z.

8362. SecState for Battle from Yost.

1. There is unanimity among observers I have seen here that UARG at this point cannot and will not relax position on closure Tiran Straits except as result overwhelming application of military force. Opinion in other Arab countries seems practically unanimous in backing UAR on this issue.

2. While this may appear in US as "aggression", it is seen here as entirely legitimate restoration 1956 status quo which was upset by Israeli aggression. In light UAR "belligerency", moreover, legal case is at least open to doubt.

3. As consequence I have reluctantly come to conclusion that there is no prospect for success our present tactic of mobilizing maritime powers to reopen Straits, except by exercise military force which would be out of proportion to real US interests at stake and would have most damaging repercussions on US position throughout Arab world. If we pursue this tactic much further, I am afraid we may find ourselves in same dead end as British and French in 1956.

4. Proposed declaration by maritime powers would have no effect on UAR stand nor would show of naval strength in neighborhood, though latter would increase Arab agitation, reinforce Arab unity and provoke anti-US demonstrations. Actual use of sufficient military force could presumably open Straits but force would have to be maintained there indefinitely and political consequences would be as indicated above.

5. While I realize very great importance Israel attaches to keeping Straits open, I cannot believe this is vital to Israel's existence, especially recalling that Straits were closed prior to 1957.[2] Gain to Nasser's prestige resulting from this victory will be unfortunate and troublesome but

---

[1] Source: National Archives and Records Administration, RG 59, Central Files 1967–69, POL ARAB–ISR. Secret; Immediate; Exdis. Repeated to USUN for Goldberg. Received at 7:45 a.m. and passed to the White House at 9:17 a.m.

[2] Riad said this to Yost during a conversation the previous evening, which Yost reported in telegram 8349 from Cairo, June 2. Riad told Yost that the UAR had no alternative but to fight anyone who tried to force passage of the Strait of Tiran, but that if oil was kept away from the strait, there would be no problem. Yost said he had heard apprehension expressed that the UAR would not only insist on closing the strait but would proceed to other demands also unacceptable to Israel. Riad replied that the refugee problem was the underlying cause of difficulty but that the UAR had no other demands. (Ibid.)

post facto attempts by either great powers or Israel to reverse it are more likely to prolong than to curtail his currently resurrected leadership of Arab world.

6. I would have thought more productive tactic would be henceforth to concentrate on limiting damage, primarily by finding means acceptable to both parties of strengthening UNTSO machinery all along Israeli frontiers but particularly on Israel–UAR line. If some action on Tiran necessary, complaint could be presented to ICJ and interim arrangements made to supply Israel with oil through other ports. I would presume Israel would expect and should receive renewed assurances of US support in case its existence or integrity is threatened.

7. If stability is to be preserved in area over long run, it will also be important that US endeavor within reasonable limits to maintain contact and some measure cooperation with UAR. Pressure tactics, such as fleet movements or blocking IMF action and bank credits, will have precisely contrary effect, throw UAR even more into Soviet arms and make future aggressive action vis-à-vis Israel more likely.

8. There can be no assurance that Arab appetites, whetted by unexpected and intoxicating show of unity, will not soon demand further satisfaction, despite Riad statement to me UAR has no such present intention. However, I am convinced we would have much better prospect obtaining world and perhaps even some Arab support against more obvious and brutal threat to Israeli security than closure Straits is generally conceived to be. Either overt or covert sanctions are at this time more likely to provoke than to discourage more aggressive Arab policy.

9. Believe I have felt pulse here as fully as may be feasible or useful in near future and that, unless Department wished me to undertake some negotiation, I might plan to return to Washington to report in two or three days.[3] I should probably see Riad once more before leaving but Ambassador Nolte now has easy access to him and will be fully capable henceforth of carrying on.[4]

Nolte

---

[3] Battle authorized Yost's return in telegram 207517 to Cairo, June 2. He commented that while Riad's apparent desire to prevent further deterioration of U.S.-UAR relations was reassuring, "he gives us little room in which to work", since there were issues at stake involving long-held U.S. policies. (Ibid.)

[4] During Yost's June 1 meeting with Riad (see footnote 2 above), he expressed the hope that Nolte might have an early opportunity to present his credentials. Riad replied that Nasser was extremely busy, but he asked Yost to tell Nolte that he should carry on business as if he had already presented credentials and should feel free to call on Riad at any time.

129.   Telegram From the Embassy in Portugal to the Department
         of State[1]

Lisbon, June 2, 1967, 1030Z.

1517. Eyes Only for President and SecState from Robert Anderson.

1. There follows a summary of my talk with President Nasser. Unless otherwise indicated, I will be trying to express his point of view to me.

2. After exchange of pleasantries, Nasser said he became worried and afraid of Israeli attack because of speeches and his own intelligence of mobilization by Israel and the intelligence shared with Syrian Govt. As an example, he stated that 13 brigades were mobilized near Syria.

3. Nasser explained that he did not want repetition of 1956 affair when he was reluctant to believe that an attack had begun and was slow in moving troops to Sinai only to be caught between the Israelis in the north and the British at Port Said. He said he felt he had no choice but to mobilize and send troops to Sinai, which he did, and request the removal of UN forces. While he did not say so, I believe he was surprised at the rapidity of the removal of UN troops because he said they were only a token force and would have created no real obstacle.

4. He was asked specifically if he intended to begin any conflict and he said to please explain to my govt that he would not begin any fight but would wait until the Israelis had moved. This was qualified by saying that he did not know what the Syrians would do and had worried all day (Wednesday)[2] for fear the Syrians might start something out of anger because of the pact which he had made with Hussein. He also stated, that, contrary to most public opinion, he did not have control over the radical elements of refugee organizations who were interested only in starting a conflict because they had no real responsibility for the conduct of military affairs. He was asked if this conflict occurred, for example, if Syria should attack against his desires, whether he would

---

[1] Source: National Archives and Records Administration, RG 59, Central Files 1967–69, POL ARAB–ISR. Top Secret; Immediate; Nodis. Received at 8:29 a.m. Walt Rostow sent a copy to the President at 12:40 p.m. with a memorandum stating, "It is urgent that we decide whether we should inform the Israelis of this visit. My guess is their intelligence will pick it up. We would be wise to have Sec. Rusk tell Harman." He also added, "In the light of this picture of Nasser's mind, we must work out most carefully the scenario for talks with Mohieddin." (Johnson Library, National Security File, Country File, Middle East Crisis, Anderson Cables)

[2] May 31.

respond and he answered affirmatively, saying that any conflict begun, whether in Jordan or Syria, would necessarily bring response from him.

5. It was pointed out that if Israel felt she was virtually alone she might be motivated to strike first in order to secure a strategic advantage and that so long as she felt she had friends she might be restrained. Nasser replied that this was a risk which he would have to accept and that he thought first Israeli target and main thrust of Israeli offensive would be against Egypt and Cairo. He said that elaborate plans had been made for instant retaliation, and that he was confident of the outcome of a conflict between Arabs and Israelis.

6. Nasser said that Hussein requested a meeting with him and that he agreed on the basis that it would be secret unless an agreement was reached between them. Nasser then consulted with the govts of Morocco, Algeria, Iraq and Syria. All of these agreed that some agreement with Hussein was desirable except Syria who was opposed to any agreement with Jordan. He was asked if he had consulted directly or indirectly [with] the Saudi Arabs and he replied that he had no contact, direct or indirect, with the Saudi Arabs or Faisal. However, Nasser felt that Faisal was in a difficult position and could not avoid participation if fighting began.

7. With reference to Gulf of Aqaba, Nasser stated that for eight years after 1948 the Straits had been closed to Israeli shipping and was open only by the illegal act of Israel, France and England, and he proposed merely to return to the status of 1956 which had been at least tolerated by all the nations for eight years. He explained that even we had deplored and opposed the act of the Israelis, British and French which changed the status quo in 1956. He stated that the Straits of Tiran were navigable only in a width of three miles which was clearly territorial waters and that he intended to maintain this position. He was asked specifically what commerce he would allow through the Straits under his concept and he replied by saying that the exclusions would be 1) Israeli ships, 2) oil or any refined products, and 3) arms for Israel. Here he stated that all countries claimed territorial waters to a greater distance offshore than he was asserting and further that he was at war with Israel and had been since 1948 with nothing existing between them except an armistice, and that under these circumstances he was entitled to assert jurisdiction.

8. He was asked if he would consider referring this matter of the Straits to either the United Nations or the World Court, in view of the fact that four countries had borders on the Gulf. He replied that he would not submit the question to the UN because the Israelis normally treated resolutions of the UN not favorable to them as "pieces of paper." He said that he did not have sufficient knowledge of the World Court to

answer specifically about referring the matter to the World Court for decision but would consult his legal advisers. This was qualified by saying that he did not want to undertake any course of action that would take "years" to decide.

9. He also stated that even if he agreed on some other course of action, any other course of action would be strongly opposed by all Arab countries who were now his allies. On this point he seemed on the one hand adamant about the position he had taken in the Straits and yet he did not rule out completely possibility of a World Court review if it could be done speedily. For the time being I think he will remain firm.

10. He was asked if he was not prepared to accept Israel as a matter of fact, even though he might have emotional and legal feelings concerning the establishment of the country in Palestine. Nasser replied by saying that he did not believe stable and lasting peace could be achieved without disposing of the refugee problem. He was asked if this could be done by compensation as well as some limited return of refugees. He replied that he thought practically all refugees would return if permitted and that even if compensation were paid they would not be satisfied but would continue to agitate for return to Palestine. He went into long discourse on Arab mentality as it affects their feelings toward the place where they were born and reared.

11. Nasser stated that he had been prepared to sign an agreement with the Monetary Fund but had just received a letter saying that the Fund wished to review their relationships with Egypt further. He then stated he was glad he had not signed the agreement with the Fund because they were unreasonable and left him no flexibility. He emphasized that he did not want to be subject to economic pressure. It was explained to him that neither the Fund nor local American banks were in fact exerting pressure when they did not comply with national requests since they were all governed by strict rules that limited their own flexibility in making loans to countries that did not comply with all regulations.

12. Nasser expressed keen desire to have friendship of American people and American Govt explaining that under no circumstances was he a Communist. On other hand, he felt that US policy was motivated largely by the large Jewish vote in US and that American Govt would be reluctant to oppose this voting strength. He then called attention to the fact that Eisenhower had taken a strong position in 1956 against Israeli invasion and this had not hurt him politically.

13. He seemed anxious to have Zakaria Mohieddin explain his position directly to US Govt and said he hoped we would take the long view because the Arab countries stretched from Morocco on the west to Pakistan on the east and that now he even had the support of Pakistan

and India. He did not see how a minority in the US could influence US policy to oppose what such a vast region and such large numbers of people believed proper. It was explained to him that the US Govt was not motivated by political considerations but was concerned essentially in maintaining peace and the integrity of countries.

14. At this time Nasser said that if the policy was for Arabs and Israelis to live together harmoniously and Israel should allow a million refugees to come back to Palestine, which would solve the refugee problem and still the Israelis would have two million of their own citizens in the same country, this, he said, would be true "living together."

15. He made it clear that he felt US was taking the lead in peace efforts but that these efforts were oriented toward Israel and not toward the Arab point of view. He kept reassuring me that he was not going to start a war but that he was not responsible for all groups and that he would intervene in any actual conflict begun. He stated that under present circumstances Jordanian troops, insofar as the Israeli problem was concerned, were under UAR command. This of course is applicable to other troops such as Iraqis and Algerians who were reporting for duty.

16. This I think summarizes the basic points of our conversation on which I will elaborate further on my return.

17. For your general information I spent three days in Beirut before going to Cairo. During this visit I saw Saudi Arabs, Kuwaitis and Iraqis, as well as Lebanese. They are people who are generally moderate and have a tendency to oppose Nasser. At this time they were all applauding Nasser's action, insisting on the closing of the Gulf of Aqaba and taking a position that the US was supporting a minority for political purposes. I am impressed more because of the quality of the people who made these assertions than the fact that they were made. Under the circumstances it would seem desirable that whatever international arrangements are thought proper it would be helpful if the initiative could be taken by some country other than US and that US be in a position of support of international efforts to secure peace rather than leadership which seems to be construed as favoring Israeli cause.

17. [*sic*] During our conversation Nasser was relaxed, in sport clothes, and seemed confident both of his intelligence and of his military capability. We had no discussion re Soviets except his assertion that he was not and would not be Communist. I believe he would regard any effort to open the Straits of Tiran as hostile and any act of aggression, whether originating from Israel or resulting from actions in Syria by the terrorist groups, would bring response. He stated that his target system was prepared and that this time he would be ready.

18. I am proceeding to send message to Cairo through US Embassy to Nasser which will result in Zakaria Mohieddin arriving in New York presumably Sunday or early in week. I will return to New York Saturday[3] afternoon and will be available to come to Washington Sunday or thereafter. I can be reached through Embassy here today and tomorrow morning, if desired.

19. Upon rereading this text I want to make clear as I understand it UAR has military command over its own troops, the Jordanian troops as related to any Israeli problem, the troops committed by Iraq, Algeria or any country sending troops, but does not include command over Syrian troops. It is because of this latter situation which I think bothers Nasser as to whether or not the Syrians might undertake unilateral action designed to force a confrontation. It was because of his concern on this subject that he was asked if he would intervene even if the Syrians acted against UAR desires and the reply was affirmative.

Wellman

---

[3] June 3.

---

130. Memorandum of Conversation[1]

Washington, June 2, 1967, 11:30 a.m.–1:15 p.m.

SUBJECT

Middle East

PARTICIPANTS

Americans present
Secretary of State
Secretary of the Treasury (part time)

---

[1] Source: National Archives and Records Administration, RG 59, Central Files 1967–69, POL 27 ARAB–ISR. Secret. Drafted by Assistant Secretary of State for European Affairs Leddy and approved by the White House and S on June 14. The memorandum is part I of IV. The meeting took place in the Cabinet Room of the White House. At the same time (11:35 a.m. to 1:30 p.m.), President Johnson and Prime Minister Wilson met privately in the Oval Office. (Johnson Library, President's Daily Diary) No record of their meeting has been found.

Secretary of Defense
Ambassador Bruce
Mr. Walt Rostow (part time)
EUR—Mr. John M. Leddy
Mr. Francis Bator (part time)
S/CPR—Mr. James W. Symington

British present:
Sir Burke Trend, Secretary of the Cabinet
Sir Patrick Dean, Ambassador
Admiral Sir Nigel Henderson, Head, British Defense Staff
Sir Solly Zuckerman, Chief Scientific Advisor
T. T. Brenchley, Assistant Secretary Foreign Office
Donald Murray, Head, South East Asian Department, Foreign Office
A. N. Halls, Principal Private Secretary to Prime Minister
A. M. Palliser, Private Secretary to Prime Minister
T. D. Floyd-Huges, Press Secretary to Prime Minister

This conversation ranged over various aspects of the Arab-Israeli confrontation in the Middle East and lasted about an hour and a half. The following brings together the main substantive points brought out in the discussion.

Security Council Action

There are now two resolutions on this subject in the Security Council: the American resolution and the Egyptian resolution. Possibly two more resolutions will be submitted, including one from India. The Secretary felt that there was virtually no chance for any resolution to be agreed upon and that the inability of the Council to act would probably become clear next Tuesday[2] or Wednesday. However, even if the Council was unable to adopt a resolution, it was important to have the Council remain seized of the problem. It was just possible that as events develop certain prestige elements can be thrown into the Council machinery as happened in the case of the Cuban missile crisis.

Limits on Israeli Restraint

The Secretary observed that we have a breathing spell for the moment, but unless there is some change in Nasser's intentions regarding the Straits of Tiran this will not last long and it will be impossible to hold the Israelis. We had a great deal of difficulty with them last Sunday[3] when the decision in the Israeli Cabinet to hold back for the time being was very close (9 to 9). The new Cabinet was meeting again this coming Sunday or Monday and we may face a crisis. The appointment of Moshe Dayan as Defense Minister was hardly favorable to

---

[2] June 6.
[3] May 28.

restraint. Secretary McNamara thought that the one thing which might deter the Israelis would be their fear that the Soviets might enter a war on the side of the Arabs.

Israeli/Arab Military Capabilities

Secretary McNamara said that the Israelis feel that they could start hostilities now or a week from now and prevail. They believe their capabilities are perishable as time goes on, but Secretary McNamara thought they could delay from 2–4 weeks and still accomplish their military objective. They would try to destroy the Egyptian airforce first and thus gain ability for a tank strike to take Sinai and the Straits.

Secretary McNamara said the Israelis think they can win in 3–4 days; but he thinks it would be longer—7 to 10 days.

Secretary McNamara said that the Israelis felt that they could not keep up their mobilization for more than a week or two. He believed that they could sustain it for a longer time economically (it is costing them about $1 million a day); but the real problem is political and because of this they probably would have to act within two weeks. The economic strain of mobilization was much greater on the Israelis in their tight manpower situation than on the Arabs with their large unemployment.

Sir Burke Trend, in response to a question from Secretary McNamara, said that the UK military analysis of the Israeli capabilities was close to that of the US but perhaps a bit more conservative and rested on the assumption that the Israelis would not let things go too long. Both sides agreed that an Israeli military success would take more than a few days and possibly a week plus. Certainly it would take longer than it took in 1956 and it would be bloodier.

Sir Burke Trend inquired what effect an Arab-Israeli war would have on Egypt's ability to maintain its forces in Yemen. Secretary McNamara said he did not have a firm opinion. His best guess is that they could contain the military—it was a very small force—but that it would be politically difficult for Nasser to do so at the moment when he is faced with an all-out Israeli attack.

The Secretary thought that the worst problem that would face the US would be if the Israelis were defeated and were about to be driven into the sea. Secretary McNamara doubted that the Israelis would lose; and that we would have a real problem if the Soviets came in to save Egypt.

Sir Burke Trend thought that Nasser may have his eye on the next step—beyond the Straits problem. The Secretary thought that Nasser was riding a tiger. He had been preaching Jihad or Holy War. If it doesn't occur, or if the Straits don't remain closed, he may find it impossible to restrain popular passions.

Situation in the Straits

The Secretary said that although there had earlier been some confusion on the point it was now clear that the Egyptian blockade covered oil—in other words it is the Battle Act list plus oil. It was not yet clear however what the Egyptians would do if a non-Israeli flagship carrying oil for Eilat should attempt passage.

The Secretary observed that there were two passages into the Gulf of Aqaba other than the Straits of Tiran; one of these—the Enterprise Passage—appeared to be navigable and was some four miles from the Egyptian coast. The navigability of the third passage was in some doubt. Both of these possibilities should be looked into. Secretary McNamara said it was highly unlikely that these have been mined.

It was brought out in the discussion that no ship so far had transited to Eilat; all have gone into Aqaba in Jordan.

The Secretary observed that Israeli access to Eilat is not really vital in an economic sense. The question is rather political. The Israelis consider that they have had a firm international commitment for guaranteed access since 1957 and the legitimacy of their territorial position in Eilat is not really in doubt.

The Soviet Attitude

Both sides felt that the Soviets probably had not been informed by Nasser of his intended action regarding the Straits of Tiran. In their public statements the Soviets have carefully skirted the question of the Straits, simply supporting the Egyptian claim to territorial waters which is beside the point. We have nothing back ourselves from the Soviets on the Straits question.

The Secretary thought that if the Israelis attack and are winning that the Soviets would do "something;" they would "help;" but we do not really know what kind of help this would be. He observed that apparently both the Arabs and the Soviets think the US is capable of commanding Israel.

Anderson Report

The Secretary paraphrased a cable which had just been received reporting on Robert Anderson's conversation with Nasser.[4] (The Secretary made it clear that Anderson was in Egypt in an entirely private capacity.) The Secretary wondered about the reference in Anderson's report to Nasser's apparent willingness to envisage World

---

[4] See Document 129.

Court consideration provided that the Court would act in a hurry. This made no sense unless Nasser anticipated maintaining freedom of passage pending the Court's decision.

Economic and Financial Aspects

Sir Burke Trend wondered what economic pressures might be brought to bear against the Arabs. Secretary Fowler pointed out that more economic and financial pressure could be exercised from the other side than from ours—cutting off of oil exports, expropriation, monetary measures damaging to sterling, etc. The Egyptians can depend on the Soviets for wheat and on the Kuwaitis for money. He observed that the recent failure of the IMF to extend a $30 million loan to the UAR was not really so disadvantageous to the Egyptians since the main purpose of the credit was to enable them to make good on their default to private banks and reestablish their credit position.

The Secretary thought that with respect to the Israelis other countries could help. He would not be surprised if the Israelis didn't get as much as $100 million from the American Jewish community.

Commenting on the British financial situation, Secretary Fowler felt that outstanding swaps, including those with the Continent, provided a healthy cushion. It would be undesirable to try to improve the situation in advance of hostilities since it would cause speculation. It was agreed on both sides that for the time being at least the market was in fairly good shape.

The Secretary pointed out that if the Arabs should do anything to cut off the flow of oil Europe would face a serious shortfall even with maximum supplies from the Western Hemisphere.

Proposed Maritime Declaration

Responding to Sir Burke Trend, Secretary McNamara said that the circular instruction on the Maritime Declaration[5] had just gone out last night and it was too early to have had a response. Mr. Leddy expressed the opinion that it would not be too bad a result if we could get as many as twelve countries lined up behind us. No doubt there would be questions as to whether this Declaration implied the use of force. When it was made clear that it did not it would make things somewhat easier. Later in the day the Secretary said perhaps we could get as many as 20 or 30.

Sir Burke Trend suggested that perhaps after the Maritime Declaration had been issued the powers supporting the Declaration might propose a specific convention dealing with the Strait of Tiran and

---

[5] Document 111.

the Gulf of Aqaba. The Secretary thought that perhaps the Arabs might come to a conference on this subject if called by the Secretary General of the UN. However, he recalled that the Aqaba clause in the Convention in 1958 had been adopted 31–30 with 10 abstentions. The Arabs would no doubt use the "belligerent" argument and assert that the 1956 resolution had been imposed by aggression. He observed that the Montreux Convention on the Bosporus[6] provided a precedent for the Trend proposal.

The Declaration speaks of "asserting rights" to innocent passage in the Straits. Sir Burke Trend inquired what was meant by asserting rights other than through the use of force. The Secretary replied that this could cover various actions such as public statements, appeals to the World Court, proposed UN resolutions, economic reprisals, etc. He suggested that at some point it might be useful to introduce the Declaration into the UN machinery in order to keep the talk going. For example, the Danish Chairman of the Security Council might possibly use this in talking with the Arabs.

Possible Naval Task Force

Secretaries Rusk and McNamara made it very clear that any participation by the US in the use of force would have to be supported by Congressional action. We have consulted intensively with the Congressional leaders in the last ten days. It is clear that there is a passionate aversion on the Hill to any unilateral action by the US. We would have to have UN action or at least broad multilateral participation. If we were to ask for Congressional support at this moment we could not get it. We will first have to continue our efforts in the UN and achieve multilateral support for the Maritime Declaration. Secretary McNamara recalled that Secretary Dulles in 1956–57 had made it very clear that Congressional action would be required for the use of force in the Middle East.

In a further discussion of this point it was agreed on both sides that there would be no US-UK joint planning in the military field at this stage. The danger of leaks was too great. The British side indicated that it, too, was hesitant to move too fast in the military area.

Possible Appointment of Mediator

There was some discussion of the possible naming of a mediator. Perhaps someone like Gus Lindt, Swiss Ambassador to Moscow.

---

[6] The Montreux Convention, signed June 20, 1936, by Britain, Bulgaria, France, Japan, Rumania, the Soviet Union, and Turkey; for text, see League of Nations Treaty Series, Vol. CLXXIII, p. 213.

Sir Burke Trend inquired what a mediator might conceivably do in terms of speculation. The Secretary replied that one thing he might do would be to try to persuade each side of the consequence of a war and from a realization of this perhaps build toward a way out. He observed that this was the way the Berlin crisis had been handled.

Position of Prime Minister Pearson

Secretary McNamara asked about Pearson's position on the use of force. Sir Burke Trend said that Pearson was not yet ready to answer.

The Secretary inquired whether Pearson might not play a mediating role as he had in the past. The British side said he felt that he would be regarded by the Arabs as being too biased.

U Thant

Both sides agreed that SYG U Thant had acted precipitately in removing the UNEF. The Secretary pointed out that he had gone beyond what Nasser requested and had moved faster than Nasser expected. Moreover, the Secretary understood that during U Thant's trip to Cairo he had proposed to the Egyptians a strategic embargo including oil but that the Israelis had turned this down. The question was why did U Thant feel that he had the right to make an offer of this kind?

Egypt's Use of Gas in Yemen

The British asked why the US has not made public the Egyptian use of gas in Yemen. The Secretary replied that this information would have greater impact internationally if it came from the Red Cross rather than from the US. Mr. Rostow said that we had just released a report to the four governments concerned and planned to publish text he thought about June 5 or 6. (Reference to the report appeared in *The New York Times* on June 3.)

Future Joint Planning

Ambassador Dean raised the question of further planning. He said that there were four separate areas: political; military; oil; and finance. He thought that we should keep these four areas under some kind of overall control and also to give consideration to making them multilateral at some stage.

It was again pointed out by Secretaries Rusk and McNamara that it was too early for military planning (for example, it would have been disastrous if we had been caught in military planning last week) and that we will just have to see how things develop. Secretary Fowler emphasized the importance of immediate planning in both the financial and oil fields. We would be derelict if we did not plan for these.

The following appeared to be generally agreed:

1. There would be a small group on overall matters on the US side to keep in touch with a similar group on the UK side.
2. Military planning was out for the time being.
3. The British are ready to come to Washington to talk about oil next week.
4. Monetary and financial discussions should be developed between the US and the UK through established official channels including the two Treasuries, the Bank of England and the New York Fed. There should be no approaches to the private sector at this stage because of the dangers of speculation.

---

131. Memorandum From the President's Special Assistant (Rostow) to President Johnson[1]

Washington, June 2, 1967, 12:45 p.m.

Mr. President:

Evron came in today at 11:00 a.m. with the following extremely important statement. It is not (repeat not) a communication from the Government of Israel. Moreover, he underlined several times the need for it to be held within our government in the narrowest possible circle.

Nevertheless, Evron does not talk irresponsibly.

Here is his statement.

1. Time is working rapidly against Israel.

Nasser's forces are being built up and digging in. The Arab military forces are being unified and consolidated. The economic costs for Israel are rising. The political and psychological pressures for a prompt solution are increasing.

---

[1] Source: Johnson Library, National Security File, Country File, Middle East Crisis, Vol. III. Secret; Eyes Only. A handwritten "L" on the memorandum indicates the President saw it. Saunders sent a copy to John Walsh with a memorandum of December 10, 1968, commenting that the memorandum was the clearest statement "on whether we had a 'commitment' from Eshkol to wait two weeks." He added, however, "but even there there's a possibility of our overreading. I was there and sat through Walt's dictation of the memo and believed at the time it reflected accurately what Eppie said. But by that time, even Eppie may have been overtaken by thinking in Jerusalem." Saunders indicated that Walsh should particularly note Evron's reply to Rostow's first question in paragraph 6. (National Archives and Records Administration, RG 59, Central Files 1967–69, POL ISR–US)

2. They took our advice to wait as a cold, responsible calculus. Nevertheless, it is now clear that the military cost to them of a war with Egypt is rising every day.

3. He then asked what our reaction would be to the following scenario:

The probe at the Gulf of Aqaba would not be made under the protection of an international armada. It would be made by an Israeli ship. The first shot would be fired by the UAR. Acting on the principle asserted by Golda Meir in the attached UN statement of 1 March 1957[2] (to which Lodge assented),[3] Israel would attack the installations at Sharm al-Sheikh covering the straits of Aqaba. The next move would be Nasser's. The Israelis believe he would attack Israel on a wide front and probably other Arab nations would join in the attack.

4. His questions then were:

—Would the United States stand by its political commitment in 1957 that Israel under these circumstances was asserting a legitimate right of self-defense?

—Would the United States stand off any Soviet intervention in that kind of war?

5. I immediately replied that this was not a question to which I could give a responsible answer. I said that the scenario he outlined was not the one raised by Foreign Minister Eban with the President; but, obviously, it was an alternative which might be considered. I said I would report it to the President.

6. I then asked some questions on a wholly personal basis:

First: How much time did they think they had?

He replied that they had made a commitment to hold steady for about two weeks. He would measure that from the Cabinet meeting last Sunday. Therefore, he was talking about things that might happen in the week after next; that is, the week beginning Sunday, June 11—although he indicated that there was nothing ironclad about the time period being exactly two weeks.

---

[2] Reference is to a copy of the second document that Harman gave to Eugene Rostow on May 26; see footnote 3, Document 69. It quotes paragraph 13 of Foreign Minister Golda Meir's speech of March 1, 1957, before the UN General Assembly, which reads in part: "Interference, by armed force, with ships of Israel flag exercising free and innocent passage in the Gulf of Aqaba and through the Straits of Tiran, will be regarded by Israel as an attack entitling it to exercise its inherent right of self-defence under Article 51 of the United Nations Charter and to take all such measures as are necessary to ensure the free and innocent passage of its ships in the Gulf and in the Straits."

[3] The attachment also quotes Lodge's statement before the UN General Assembly on March 1, 1957, taking note of the declarations in Meir's statement and indicating that its expectations were "not unreasonable."

Second, I asked him what about the stories of the Israelis buying and organizing ships to run the blockade on a national basis?

He said they were taking action of this kind; but they would not move to run the blockade without there being a clear political decision in Israel, of which we would be made aware.

7. Two other points emerged in the final stage of our conversation. First, he appeared to suggest that it might be better for us in our relations with both the Arab world and the Soviet Union if we were not the ones to force the issue. He also referred to intelligence which we share that Nasser's response to a U.S.-escorted probe would be not to fire. Therefore, the issue of Israeli access to the Gulf of Aqaba might be left hanging indecisively.

8. Second—and fundamental to his whole presentation—was the question: Do we still stand by Lodge's assent (and Foster Dulles') to Golda Meir's statement in General Assembly? The track discussed between Eban and the President—on which we have hitherto been moving—is consistent with the commitments made in 1957 that we would ourselves assert the right of innocent passage; that we would assert that right on behalf of others; but that we would have to engage through our constitutional processes if we were to use force to assert that right with force on behalf of others. What is involved in the track he is suggesting is reaffirmation of the other branch of our 1957 commitment incorporated in the Golda Meir statement and Lodge's assent.

WWR comment: Although it cannot be emphasized too strongly that Evron was not making a formal communication from his Government, I believe we should most urgently consider the track he suggests. It has always been an alternative. It has its attractions, as one measures up the consequences for our relations with the Arab world and the Soviet Union, as compared to that which was agreed with Eban. It also carries the risk of a terrible blood bath. There is also the possibility of a combined scenario—in which the Israelis assume responsibility for responding to attack on their flag ship, but against the background of a naval force standing by to shepherd through other flagships. But this—like the Eban scenario—would require a prior Congressional Resolution.

Walt

132.   Memorandum of Conversation[1]

Washington, June 2, 1967, 3:47–4:45 p.m.

SUBJECT

Near East Crisis

PARTICIPANTS

H. E. Avraham Harman, Ambassador of Israel
Mr. Ephraim Evron, Minister of Israel

The Secretary
M—Mr. Eugene V. Rostow
NEA—Rodger P. Davies

Ambassador Harman, departing for consultation in Israel within a few hours, had asked to see the Secretary to learn what he could tell his government concerning U.S. assurances of support. The Secretary responded that at this juncture nothing could be added to what the President had already communicated to Prime Minister Eshkol.

In answer to Ambassador Harman's question on the Maritime Declaration, the Secretary said we hoped to get at least 14 adherents. Both the Dutch and the Belgians seemed to be aboard and, since Costa Rica supported the principle in 1957, we hoped to get support from this country and other Latin American states. The reaction in Bonn had been encouraging, but it might be well if Israel could work on the French and Canadians who seemed to be lagging.

Ambassador Harman said reports of Portuguese support for the Declaration were embarrassing since the Africans would be extremely sensitive to anything supported by Portugal. The important thing to Israel is the timetable. We should assure the closing off of Security Council action soon; the longer it runs on, the more difficulties there will be. Already the "breathing spell" was giving rise to rumors and reports of "deals".

The Secretary said that apparently there had been a complete misrepresentation of the U.S. Government's position on the Declaration stemming from briefings that had been given in the Congress. It might ease matters if the Declaration could be made public, but we could not move in this direction until other governments had a chance to discuss it. We hope it can be released when it is clear that the Security Council can do nothing on the problem.

---

[1] Source: National Archives and Records Administration, RG 59, Central Files 1967–69, POL ISR–US. Top Secret; Nodis. Drafted by Davies. The time is from Rusk's Appointment Book. (Johnson Library)

In answer to the Ambassador's question, the Secretary said that the key issue was return to the status quo ante on use of the Gulf of Aqaba. Nasser, however, was firm on his present stand. Whether he can be moved is anybody's question. The Secretary indicated that the Maritime Declaration might provide a "handle" for the Secretary General to take further action and indicated that we have not had anything back from the Soviets on their attitude toward the question of the Strait.

The Ambassador asked whether he could faithfully report that the USG position is that there must be a return to the status quo ante, that there would be no "deal".

The Secretary said this was what we were seeking to bring about. In the Security Council it is apparent that the Soviets would veto anything calling for the parties to forego belligerency. We believe we have eight votes in support of our draft resolution and are somewhat hopeful that we may be able to line up nine.

The Secretary said that in his talks with Iraqi Foreign Minister Pachachi[2] he did not find any "give" in the Arab position on the Gulf. Mr. Rostow said that he detected a little more flexibility in the course of his talks, although whether Pachachi had, in fact, any authority to negotiate was questionable.

The Ambassador repeated that the timetable on the Naval Task Force and next steps was of supreme importance to Israel.

The Secretary said we are going ahead on all contingencies, looking at all factors. Joint consultations would be started shortly. At present we have not developed a multilateral context, and from the Congressional angle this was of great importance. We believe the Dutch would join with us but are not sure now of the Canadians. It is important that we be joined by a half dozen or so before we can move ahead on timing. There have been no final decisions. On these, the President and the Prime Minister must be in touch.

The Ambassador said he would come to the crux of Israel's concern. The military situation is deteriorating rapidly.

Hussein's accord with Nasser, Arab military coordination, the dispatch of Iraqi troops to the UAR and Jordan, the move of Saudi troops to the Aqaba Gulf area, the big build-up of Syrian forces, the caving in of Lebanon with respect to Palestine Liberation Army (PLA) activities, and the stationing of PLA units on all frontiers are causing heightened

---

[2] Rusk and Eugene Rostow met separately with Iraqi Foreign Minister Pachachi on June 1. Telegram 206672 to Baghdad, June 2, which summarized their conversations, is printed in *Foreign Relations, 1964–1968*, vol. XXI, Document 193. After meeting with Rusk and Rostow, Pachachi met with the President. No record of that conversation has been found.

concern in Israel. The time has come for effective resistance to Nasser. Nasser's declaration that the situation had been returned to that of 1956 was now followed by threats that it would be returned to that of 1948. Israel has mobilized 100,000 reservists in addition to its regular forces. In these circumstances Israel must know the modalities of the U.S. commitment. In addition to the direct threat to Israel of the coalescence of the Arabs around Nasser, there were ripples which must certainly concern the West, not only in connection with its position vis-à-vis the Soviets but also with the implications for Turkey and Iran. If there is a rapid show of strength in Tiran, this could affect the entire situation. Everyday the situation was allowed to continue however heightened pressures and danger. The question he would be asked in Jerusalem was: What is the attitude of the U.S. toward the question of the Strait and toward the general situation? What action would the U.S. take if hostilities began in either connection?

The Secretary said on such matters the President and the Prime Minister should be in touch. However, the question of who initiates military activities is important. The Soviets will support the Arabs if they are attacked. An Arab onslaught on Israel would create a different situation from that of an Israeli attack on the Arabs. This is a most important consideration for the Congress. Israel should weigh heavily any decision to attack.

Ambassador Harman said that those responsible for the destiny of Israel will not be prepared for any deal or a "Munich". Israel is prepared to face the present danger and would prefer to face it than to have its security slowly eroded. Israel understands the importance of who fires the first shot, but does Israel have to accept 10,000 casualties before the U.S. will agree that aggression has occurred? Aggression exists in the build-up of forces on all of Israel's borders, the blockade of the Strait of Tiran, and the belligerent statements threatening the extinction of Israel. In the context of President Kennedy's statement of May 8, 1963, the aggression is already mounted.

The Secretary said that there is some difference between what is said and what is actually done.

The Secretary said that no one can say what the Soviets will do in the event of hostilities. However, if a Jihad mentality is evoked by the Arabs and the Arabs don't attack, how long can this state be maintained. A stalemate could work against Nasser.

Mr. Evron replied that a military build-up sets in motion a chain of events that probably will lead to military action.

The Secretary said we have been told categorically that Egypt will not attack. If we had these assurance from the Soviets in connection with our own security, the U.S. would not rush into a confrontation.

Ambassador Harman said the Soviets were a different people from the Arabs. The Soviets played a rational form of brinkmanship. In answer to the Secretary's question as to how much influence the Soviets actually wielded in Cairo, Ambassador Harman said that this was a weakness on the Soviet side through which their restraint could be neutralized. Nasser's momentum is such that Israel's assumption is that he must be in deadly earnest.

Had Israel acted on May 23 against the advice received from the U.S., Israel would be facing a different political and military situation from that faced today. Israel was at a disadvantage.

The Secretary said that Nasser was sending former Prime Minister and Vice President Zakariyah Muhi ad-Din to Washington this week end. If he should say anything significant, we would let Israel know.

Ambassador Harman said Soviet moves now seemed directed toward gaining time and confirming the new status quo. Israel had a strong feeling that the Soviets would not seek a confrontation with the U.S. in the Middle East. The gut question in Israel is what would the U.S. do to help Israel?

The Secretary said this depends in part on who initiates hostilities. Ambassador Harman questioned what this meant. What does Israel have to take in a situation where she is threatened not with aggression but with genocide? Egypt's action in closing the Strait is a clear act of aggression. Israel was convinced that an attack was inevitable. Nasser has cast himself in a certain role, and now there is no room for any other course of action. If he is challenged quickly and strongly, this might prevent inflation of the conflict. Since May 16, Nasser has shown how he can make rapid moves. Israel operates from five airfields. This question is foremost in Israel's mind. Air power is decisive. If Israel loses initially, Israel has had it. There will be little to salvage. This situation can arise any time. Israel did not agree with the estimate given by Mr. McNamara and General Wheeler that it could absorb a first strike. Israel is not seeking hostilities, but Nasser seems to be playing "for broke". The situation calls for speedy action. The farce in the Security Council must be broken up.

The Secretary said that there were some advantages to Security Council considerations. The fact that the Cuban problem was in the Security Council didn't affect the settlement, but it did allow some prestige to be salvaged which weighed in the settlement.

Ambassador Harman said the test of the Strait must be made in the course of next week. Secretary Rusk replied that the test would take place seven to nine days after a decision was reached.

Ambassador Harman said that any testing must include an Israeli flagship. They had one, the *Dolphin* (ex–*Arion*)[3] in Massawa ready to go.

The Secretary said that John Finney and Chalmers Roberts do not speak for the USG. What the Prime Minister and the President say to each other is the important factor. Ambassador Harman said the public in Israel lives on the *New York Times* and the *Washington Post*.

The Ambassador said he expected to return by Sunday[4] evening.

---

[3] According to a telegraphic summary of the conversation, the *Dolphin* was formerly the Greek-owned *Arion*. (Telegram 207977 to Tel Aviv, June 3; National Archives and Records Administration, RG 59, Central Files 1967–69, POL ARAB–ISR)

[4] June 4.

---

133. Telegram From the Embassy in France to the Department of State[1]

Paris, June 2, 1967, 1910Z.

19777. Ref: State 206658.[2] I saw Couve de Murville this afternoon at 5:00 o'clock for about half an hour.

1. Couve was in complete agreement with our assumption that war in the Middle East would be disastrous. He also agreed that the Israelis consider the blockade of the Gulf of Aqaba a matter of the highest national importance. He also agreed that the Soviets' behavior is far from clear and did not question my statement that they had not shown any inclination to act responsibly in the present crisis. He said that when the Soviets gave their refusal to French suggestion of a four power get together last Sunday[3] night it had been couched in very courteous way but did not appear to be categoric in its refusal. He said it was impossible to determine exactly what had started this crisis and did not completely exclude an element of Soviet responsibility, but said that this had been bypassed by events. He agreed however that the ultimate

---

[1] Source: National Archives and Records Administration, RG 59, Central Files 1967–69, POL ARAB–ISR. Secret; Immediate; Nodis. Received at 4:46 p.m.

[2] In telegram 206658 to Paris, June 1, Rusk asked Bohlen to see Couve de Murville as soon as possible to review the British proposal for a Maritime Declaration and to urge French cooperation. (Ibid.)

[3] May 28.

Soviet objective was to reduce Western influence in the Middle East and substitute therefor Soviet influence.

2. Couve then said that he would give me what he had just said this afternoon to the Israeli Ambassador, which he thought fully reflected present French attitude toward the situation [in] the Middle East. It follows:

Soviet attitude still uncertain although there had been some indications in New York from Fedorenko of his desire to maintain contact individually with Western powers and that Fedorenko showed no desire to poison the atmosphere. He said he had told Eytan that there were essentially only two solutions to the present state of affairs in the Middle East. One was to go to war, which he impressed on Eytan would be folly since even if Israel scored a military victory it would certainly not lay any groundwork for the future which must in some form or other and at some time or other include accommodation between the Arab states and Israel. If war is excluded, the only other way was negotiation, which would include not only the question of the Gulf of Aqaba but also other questions of a military nature dealing with terrorism, etc., in the area. He told Eytan if the status of the Gulf of Aqaba is discussed neither side will get one hundred percent of what they want and compromise would probably be necessary and to the French Government this should include the normal passage of civilian goods. Couve admitted that the question of the Egyptian attitude towards POL as to whether or not it is a strategic cargo remains unclear and would obviously be a subject of discussion. Eytan asked how could any negotiations take place, to which Couve had replied that it was obviously not possible at the present juncture to have direct Arab/Israeli discussions but there were many other intermediaries, including the great powers. He said he had taken the liberty of mentioning to Eytan that he was convinced of the good will of the U.S. but some indication of a comparable attitude was needed from the USSR. Couve said Eytan had made no comment but Couve had emphasized very strongly the point with him that apart from war the only way out was negotiation. Couve then told me that in regard to the Security Council it was quite clear that neither the U.S. resolution nor the Indian (of course Egyptian inspired) had any chance of obtaining the votes of all members of the Security Council. Therefore, Seydoux had been instructed to point this out to the Council and to suggest the drafting of a resolution which would merely urge calm on the countries directly involved, which conceivably might obtain the support of all members. Couve however admitted that there was as yet no sign that the Russians were willing to meet in a group of four.

I asked Couve (although State 206752[4] arrived afterwards) what was meant by the statement following the cabinet meeting that the country that fired the first shot would receive no support and no arms from France, and asked him if this meant that stoppage of a ship going into the Gulf of Aqaba would fall within this category. Couve said that if the Egyptians fired on a ship that this would undoubtedly fall within the terms of the declaration but was not clear at all as to whether or not a forceable stoppage of a ship by the Egyptians would be so considered. In fact, he said that in his view it was the height of prudence to avoid the passage of any ships through the Straits of Tiran for the immediate future.

3. Couve said the statement issued after the cabinet meeting this morning set forth France's opinion towards the Maritime Declaration. He said France did not consider this a good idea at the present time and was therefore not "a partisan" thereof. In reply to my question he said it was not an absolute flat refusal but a disinclination to go along with it at present.

Comment: Couve's general attitude showed that French position had not really changed since the beginning of this crisis; that they still are hopeful that the Soviets will change their negative attitude and be willing to join in some form of negotiations and that through these negotiations there might be some arrangement made which would cover the passage of cargo of a non-strategic value, particularly POL through the Straits. He showed no willingness at all to consider the issuance of a Maritime Declaration and certainly none to even contemplate the action in the event it was rejected.

Bohlen

---

[4] Telegram 206752 to Paris, June 2, noted that news reports were quoting a comment by French President De Gaulle concerning the Middle East to the effect that whoever shot first would not have French support and asked the Embassy to check on the accuracy of the statement and its meaning. (National Archives and Records Administration, RG 59, Central Files 1967–69, POL ARAB–ISR)

134. Telegram From the Embassy in the United Arab Republic to the Department of State[1]

Cairo, June 2, 1967, 2029Z.

8397. 1. Following is text UAR Foreign Office "unofficial translation" of letter to President Johnson from President Gamal Abdul Nasser. With reference penultimate paragraph, was explicitly assured by Foreign Minister Riad that it was up to President Johnson to decide whether to send Vice President Humphrey here or invite Vice President Mohieddin to go to Washington, with no expression of UARG preference.[2] While waiting for typing to be completed, enjoyed long pleasant conversation Foreign Minister Riad on non-political matters. Will pouch original letter in Arabic and Foreign Office translation. Text follows:

2. Cairo, June 2, 1967. Dear President,

3. I welcome your initiative in writing to me on the current situation in the Arab homeland. For however distant the point of agreement between us seems from the scope of our outlook at the present stage, I am convinced that any joint endeavor on our part to establish communication of thought, might at least contribute to dissipate part of the artificial clouds intended to depict the exercise of right as a sin and the right of defense as aggression.

4. It would be useful in the assessment of current events, to view them in their chronological and logical entity, to avoid misunderstanding and make a sound, reasonable, and fair evaluation of the facts we face.

5. Hence, I shall try to set forth a number of facts which I would term as preliminary:

6. First: It is essential that we go back to the few days which preceded the measures which the United Arab Republic took of late, and to

---

[1] Source: National Archives and Records Administration, Central Files 1967–69, POL ARAB–ISR. Secret; Immediate; Nodis. Received at 6:20 p.m. A copy was sent to the President on June 3 with a note from Walt Rostow calling Nasser's response "quite uncompromising," noting that Nasser was willing to receive Vice President Humphrey or to send Vice President Mohieddin to Washington, and stating that he and Rusk agreed that "we should proceed to get Mohieddin here." (Johnson Library, National Security File, Country File, Middle East Crisis)

[2] Telegram 207861 to Cairo, June 3, states that the President would welcome a visit from Mohieddin and that in view of the urgency of the situation, "we hope it will be possible for him to come without delay." It states that, if asked, Nolte could say that a corresponding visit to Cairo by a "very senior representative of the President" would be sympathetically considered if both Presidents decided such a step could be useful. It states that Harman had been informed about the possibility of the visit. (National Archives and Records Administration, RG 59, Central Files 1967–69, POL ARAB–ISR)

recall the dangerously aggressive situation created by the Israeli authorities vis-à-vis the Syrian Arab Republic, the hostile threats proclaimed by a number of Israeli leaders, and the accompanying mass troop concentrations on the Syrian border in preparation for an imminent aggression on Syria. It was only natural then, that the United Arab Republic should assume her responsibilities and take all measures necessary for defense and to deter the planned aggression against our countries.

7. Second: Defense measures taken by the United Arab Republic made it imperative that our armed forces move to their advanced positions on the border to be able to cope with developments and through their very presence foil Israel's premeditated invasion. Urged by our concern for the United Nations Emergency Forces, we found it imperative that they should withdraw: such has become our final position on the matter.

8. Third: Following the withdrawal of the UNEF, it was only logical that the United Arab Republic armed forces should occupy their positions, among which was the area of Sharm el Sheikh overlooking the Straits of Tiran. It was equally logical that we exercise our established sovereign rights on the Straits and on our territorial waters in the Gulf.

9. Here again, I wish to take you a few years back to the tripartite aggression on Egypt: We still recall with appreciation, the fair position adopted by your country with regard to that aggression.

10. Prior to the aggression, the United Arab Republic exercised its established legal rights with regard to Israeli shipping in the Straits and the Gulf. These rights are indisputable. Following the departure of the United Nations Emergency Forces and their replacement by our armed forces in the area, it was unthinkable that Israeli shipping or strategic materials destined for Israel be allowed passage. Our position thereon, in addition to Ily being legitimately established, it indeed aims at removing the last vestige of the tripartite aggression, in consonance with the moral principle which rules that no aggressor be rewarded for his aggression.

11. In all the measures we have adopted in defense of our land and our rights, we have underlined two points:

12. First: That we shall defend ourselves against any aggression, with all our means and potentialities

13. Second: That we shall continue to allow innocent passage of foreign shipping in our territorial waters.

14. These are facts relevant to the direct position proclaimed by the United Arab Republic, and which we feel afford no ground for some to create a climate of crisis or to launch that psychological campaign against us.

15. While this campaign takes on new dimensions and forms we notice complete and regrettable overlooking of a number of other facts which I wish to term as basic. These are the very facts which carry full weight on current events and will continue to have their bearing on the future until all appreciate fully and assess their dimensions and roots. Here I shall refer to two facts:

16. First: The rights of the Arab people of Palestine. In our view, this is the most important fact that should be recognized. An aggressive armed force was able to oust that people from their country and reduce them to refugees on the borders of their homeland.

17. Today the forces of aggression impede the Arab people's established right of return and life in their homeland, despite the UN resolutions, the last of which was adopted last year.

18. The second fact is related to Israel's position towards the Armistice Agreements: a position represented not merely by the constant violation of those agreements, but which has gone as far as to deny their presence and refuse to adhere to them. It has even gone as far as to occupy the demilitarized zones, oust the UN observers and insult the international organization and its flag.

19. Those are two basic facts which should be considered in the assessment of today's events and developments.

20. In your message you referred to two points:

21. First: you urge that we put the past aside and endeavor to rescue the Middle East or rather the whole human community through the avoidance of hostilities. Here, allow me to refer to the policy of the United Arab Republic which does not restrict herself to placing world peace as an objective, but goes beyond that and assumes a positive role on which I do not wish to elaborate lest I should border on the area of self-glorification. As for endeavors to avoid military operations, I have but to emphasize what I have already declared that the measures we have adopted were imposed by the forces of aggression and their conceit as well as by their belief that they have reached the stage where they could impose their aggressive policy. Yet, our forces have not initiated any aggressive act, but no doubt, we shall resist with all our potentialities any aggression launched against us or against any Arab state.

22. Second: Your observation that the conflicts of our time cannot be solved by the crossings of frontiers with arms and men. Here, I share your view. Yet, we have to see how this principle is applied to every case. If you are referring to the crossing of the demarcation lines by some individuals of the Palestinian people I would urge the importance of considering this aspect in the general perspective of the question of Palestine. Here also, I may ask how far any government is able to control the feelings of more than one million Palestinians who, for twenty

years, the international community—whose responsibility herein is inescapable—has failed to secure their return to their homeland. The UN General Assembly merely confirms that right at every session. The crossing of the demarcation lines by some Palestinian individual is, in point of fact, merely a manifestation of anger by which those people are naturally possessed as they meet with the full denial of their rights by the international community, and by the powers which side with Israel and assist it materially and morally.

23. Whatever our attempts to divide the aspects of the problem, it is imperative in the end that we return to its origin and fundamentals, namely the right of Palestinian people to return to their homeland, and the responsibility of the international community in securing them the exercise of this right.

24. My letter may seem rather long in a way: Yet, it was my wish to explain briefly some of the basic features of the situation we now face in the Arab region.

25. Finally, I wish to assure you that we would welcome listening to Mr. Hubert Humphrey, the United States Vice President, at anytime he may choose to visit the UAR. We shall provide him with a picture of the situation as we conceive it amidst the fundamental events faced by the Arab nation today. I am ready to send Vice President Zakareya Mohieddin, to Washington immediately to meet with you and expound our viewpoint.

26. Please accept my regards and considerations.

27. (Sgd) (Gamal Abdel Nasser) President of the United Arab Republic.

Nolte

---

135.   **Memorandum From Director of Central Intelligence Helms to President Johnson**

Washington, June 2, 1967.

[Source: Johnson Library, National Security File, Country File, Middle East Crisis, Vol. III. Secret; Sensitive. 5 pages of source text not declassified.]

136. **Memorandum From Nathaniel Davis of the National Security Council Staff to the President's Special Assistant (Rostow)[1]**

Washington, June 2, 1967.

SUBJECT

A Scenario of the Soviet Role

From the bits and pieces of Intelligence we have been receiving on the Soviet role in this crisis, it might be useful to set down the following "scenario." It's a guess, but I think it is about as probable as any other hypothesis.

The understandings reached during Gromyko's trip in late March were probably general in nature, and not an "attack plan."

In early May, it is probable that Soviet agents actually picked up intelligence reports of a planned Israeli raid into Syria. I would not be surprised if the reports were at least partly true. The Israeli have made such raids before; they have been under heavy provocation; and they maintain pretty good security (so we might well not know about a planned raid).

Intelligence being an uncertain business, the Soviet agents may not have known the scale of the raid and may have exaggerated its scope and purpose.

Apparently the Soviets warned the Syrians. Whether they deliberately magnified the threat is hard to say. They bear neither the Israeli nor ourselves any great love, and there may well have been some element of deliberate exaggeration. However, this was *not* necessarily a calculated incitement to conflict—made out of whole cloth and responsive to a global design. The Soviets did accompany their warnings of Israeli action with advice toward restraint.

The Syrians and the UAR were also quite ready to exaggerate what the Soviets said and feed on their own fears and ambitions.

There is still no evidence that Nasser consulted with the Soviets or got their agreement to close the straits. In fact, the Soviets have still taken no position on the straits issue.

Like everybody else, the Soviets know that Nasser is two strikes ahead—with the withdrawal of UNEF and the strait now effectively closed for almost two weeks. They are in a position where it is extremely difficult to back out of a position of supporting their friends across

---

[1] Source: Johnson Library, National Security File, Country File, Middle East Crisis, Vol. III. Top Secret; Nodis.

the board. Whatever the situation before, they have the strongest interest in maintaining the status quo and consolidating the victory. About the only negative influence from the point of view of their self-interest is the danger that things will really get out of hand. However, they increasingly realize how close to out-of-hand things are. We understand from New York that Fedorenko now is taking things more seriously.

I doubt that the Soviets are much more confident than we are in their ability to call the shots and control their friends. That's not very confident.

N.D.

---

137. **Memorandum From the Deputy Assistant Secretary of Defense for International Security Affairs (Hoopes) to Secretary of Defense McNamara**[1]

I–23411/67   Washington, June 2, 1967.

SUBJECT

Middle East Situation

Attached is the paper on the question of tailoring the traffic pattern in the Strait of Tiran.[2] This was addressed by the Control Group (Rostow, Vance, Kohler) yesterday evening. I sent you a copy earlier yesterday, but I feel it is now important (following our telephone conversation of this morning) to re-emphasize several significant points in it.

As indicated on page 2, the basic difficulty in organizing a controlled series of probes is the general unavailability of appropriate shipping. Only tankers present a test case, but these will be hard to come by unless the US takes positive action (through charter or other means) to

---

[1] Source: Washington National Records Center, OSD Files: FRC 330 72 A 2468, Middle East, 381.3. Secret; No Release. A stamped notation on the memorandum, dated June 14, indicates that McNamara saw it.

[2] The attachment, a June 1 memorandum from Hoopes to the Middle East Control Group, recorded a May 31 meeting of the Military Contingency Working Group that considered the feasibility of testing the UAR blockade by unescorted ships. The working group also decided to continue military supply shipments to Near East countries under existing commitments, but to make no new commitments. A copy of Hoopes' memorandum is in the National Archives and Records Administration, RG 59, Office of the Executive Secretariat, Middle East Crisis Files, 1967, Entry 5190, Box 18, Control Group Data, Vol. I, Folder 1.

arrange for a group of ships of appropriate registries. The options have been further narrowed by the Israeli position that it cannot permit even the peaceful refusal of an Israeli-owned ship at the Strait without having immediate recourse to military retaliation. Moreover, increasing doubt is being expressed by people like Walter Levy, the reputable oil consultant to the State Department, that the Shah of Iran will be able politically to go on supplying oil to Israel. Levy strongly recommended at the Control Group meeting yesterday evening that we should avoid pressing the Shah to include his oil in a test tanker, but should try to find oil from another source—e.g., Indonesia. This judgment was challenged, and attempts to have Iran stand firm will be quickly made, through Ambassador Meyer in Teheran and through Mr. Harriman (who will see the Shah in Europe over this weekend).[3] But if Levy is reflecting the political reality in Iran, this would further circumscribe and delay even an unescorted test probe.

I refer you also to page 5 (paragraph 4) and the judgment that even the successful passage of an unescorted US flag tanker would set in motion Cairo's propaganda media, denouncing us as the enemy of the Arabs and as Israel's protector. The CIA judgment (expressed on page 6),[4] which is addressed to the political consequences of a passage by a ship under US naval escort, is also highly relevant. If true, Nasser could severely damage the United States and West Europe, politically and economically, without firing a shot.

I attach particular importance to the conclusion reached by the Working Group (on page 6) that, given the present atmosphere in the Arab world and the effectiveness of Arab and Soviet propaganda, it would not be possible to present a Western blockade running (particularly if armed escort were involved) as simply an assertion of a recognized international right. Those propaganda media would almost cer-

---

[3] For Harriman's conversations with the Shah, see telegrams 19869 and 19914 from Paris, June 5 and 6 in *Foreign Relations, 1964–1968*, vol. XXII, Documents 207 and 208.

[4] The reference is to a quotation in Hoopes' memorandum from a May 31 CIA report (not found). It estimates that if a U.S. ship were escorted through the Strait of Tiran by a U.S. naval vessel, ignoring all challenges, UAR forces would let them through under protest. It continues: "We do not believe that Cairo wishes to make any direct encounter with US military power. Indeed the UAR may see a US naval challenge of the blockade as serving their interests, as the political consequences of such a move would be far-reaching. The UAR would formally accuse the US of acting as Israel's military ally to commit aggression against the Arabs. It would expand and intensify its propaganda and diplomatic efforts against special US positions throughout the Arab world. In particular it would seek to harass US oil operations and urge the nationalization of US oil properties in Saudi Arabia, Iraq, Kuwait, and Libya. During the present super-heated and emotional climate prevailing in the Arab world, US interests in the area would almost certainly suffer considerably."

tainly succeed in branding the US as the ally and protector of Israel against the Arabs. On this judgment, we could not avoid a damaging political polarization in the event that we organize and attempt to use a naval task force (whether US or multilateral).

One reason why I am pessimistic about the number and quality of likely adherents to a maritime declaration is that many of the potentials are now beginning to believe that even such a declaration on their part would lead to serious discrimination against their Middle Eastern interests by Nasser-directed Arab actions. Their judgment in this respect acknowledges Nasser's political power. As you know, the French are extremely cool to both the declaration and the naval escort, the Canadians have made quite clear that they will not participate in a naval force and that even their adherence to a declaration depends on the adherence of several others and on a "balanced program" designed to resolve the crisis without violence. The British Cabinet gives increasing evidence of softening its position, as it contemplates the UK's severe economic vulnerabilities in the Middle East (oil revenues, passage through Suez, and the fact that Saudi and Kuwaiti deposits in London represent two-thirds of the UK's sterling balance).

It is increasingly my conviction (as I believe it is Mr. Vance's) that we must put our major efforts into seeking a political settlement based on compromise, and should be extremely cautious about pinning our hopes on a broadly supported maritime declaration and especially about getting publicly committed to a naval escort force. It is possible that the indication in yesterday's Cairo press that oil may not be a "strategic" commodity in the UAR view is an important ingredient of such a political compromise.

A further significant development yesterday was King Hussein's request for the removal of the US training detachment in Jordan, followed almost immediately by his request for the removal of the five F–104 aircraft.[5] Last evening he also made known his decision to withdraw the Jordanian aviation cadets from the pilot training programs in the US. The full implications of these acts are not yet clear, but it does seem evident that Nasser has required him at least to delimit sharply

---

[5] In a meeting with Ambassador Burns on May 31, King Hussein requested withdrawal of a small USAF detachment stationed in Jordan to provide training on F–104 aircraft to Jordanian pilots. Burns reported the meeting in telegram 3929 from Amman (cited in footnote 2, Document 107). Circular telegram 206650, June 1, states that the Jordanian Government had requested withdrawal of the USAF aircraft as well. (National Archives and Records Administration, RG 59, Central Files 1967–69, POL ARAB–ISR) The USAF personnel and aircraft were in Jordan to provide training to Jordanian pilots for 18 F–104 aircraft Jordan was purchasing, which were scheduled to begin arriving in July 1967. See *Foreign Relations, 1964–1968*, vol. XVIII, Document 373, footnote 3.

his politico-military relations with the US as a condition of their new defense pact. UAR–Jordan amity remains, however, very fragile.

Townsend Hoopes

---

138.   **President's Daily Brief**

Washington, June 3, 1967.

[Source: Johnson Library, National Security File, NSC Histories, Middle East Crisis, Vol. 6, Appendix A. Top Secret; [*codeword not declassified*]. 1 page of source text not declassified.]

---

139.   **Letter From President Johnson to Prime Minister Eshkol**[1]

Washington, June 3, 1967.

Dear Mr. Prime Minister:

I am grateful for your letter of May 30.[2] I appreciate particularly the steadfastness with which the Government and people of Israel have maintained a posture of resolution and calm in a situation of grave ten-

---

[1] Source: Johnson Library, National Security File, Country File, Middle East Crisis, Vol. III. Secret. Rostow sent a draft letter, drafted by Battle and Sisco, with his handwritten revisions to the President at 7:25 p.m. on June 2. Johnson marked his approval on Rostow's covering memorandum. (Ibid.) Rostow sent him the letter for signature with a covering memorandum on June 3 at 2:50 p.m., noting that he understood Johnson wanted to read it again before it was sent and adding, "It may be urgent that we put this letter on record soon." (Ibid.) The final letter includes additional revisions, which, according to a handwritten note by Harold H. Saunders, were given to him by the President on the telephone on the afternoon of June 3. (Ibid., NSC Histories, Middle East Crisis) A copy of the draft with Saunders' handwritten revisions is filed ibid., Memos to the President, Walt Rostow, Vol. 30. A handwritten note on the letter states that it was sent to the Department of State at 4:30 p.m.

[2] See Document 102.

sion. All of us understand how fateful the steps we take may be. I hope we can continue to move firmly and calmly toward a satisfactory solution.

Our position in this crisis rests on two principles which are vital national interests of the United States. The first is that we support the territorial integrity and political independence of all of the countries of the Middle East. This principle has now been affirmed by four American Presidents. The second is our defense of the basic interest of the entire world community in the freedom of the seas. As a leading maritime nation, we have a vital interest in upholding freedom of the seas, and the right of passage through straits of an international character.

As you know, the United States considers the Gulf of Aqaba to be an international waterway and believes that the entire international maritime community has a substantial interest in assuring that the right of passage through the Strait of Tiran and Gulf is maintained.

I am sure Foreign Minister Eban has reported to you the written statement which I had prepared and from which Ambassador Harman made notes during our meeting of May 26.[3] The full text of that statement is as follows:

"The United States has its own constitutional processes which are basic to its action on matters involving war and peace. The Secretary General has not yet reported to the UN Security Council and the Council has not yet demonstrated what it may or may not be able or willing to do although the United States will press for prompt action in the UN.

"I have already publicly stated this week our views on the safety of Israel and on the Strait of Tiran. Regarding the Strait, we plan to pursue vigorously the measures which can be taken by maritime nations to assure that the Strait and Gulf remain open to free and innocent passage of the vessels of all nations.

"I must emphasize the necessity for Israel not to make itself responsible for the initiation of hostilities. Israel will not be alone unless it decides to go alone. We cannot imagine that it will make this decision."

I explained to Mr. Eban, I want to protect the territorial integrity of Israel and other nations in that area of the world and will provide as effective American support as possible to preserve the peace and freedom of your nation and of the area.[4] I stressed too the need to act in concert with other nations, particularly those with strong maritime interests. As you will understand and as I explained to Mr. Eban, it would be

---

[3] See Document 77.

[4] Before Saunders added Johnson's revisions, the first two sentences of this paragraph read: I told Mr. Eban I could not foresee then, and I cannot now foresee, the specific steps which may prove desirable and necessary. I explained that I want to do everything I can to provide Israel with effective American support."

unwise as well as most unproductive for me to act without the full consultation and backing of Congress. We are now in the process of urgently consulting the leaders of our Congress and counseling with its membership.[5]

We are now engaged in doing everything we can through the United Nations. We recognize the difficulties of securing constructive action in the Security Council, but we are convinced that the world organization, which for the past decade has played a major role in the Middle East, must make a real effort to discharge its responsibilities for the maintenance of peace.

We are moving ahead in our diplomatic efforts, in concert with the United Kingdom and with your diplomatic representatives, to secure a declaration by the principal maritime powers asserting the right of passage through the Strait and Gulf. A copy of this declaration has been given to your Ambassador. Such a declaration could be an important step both in relation to the proceedings in the Security Council and also in the event those proceedings do not lead to a successful outcome.

We are also exploring on an urgent basis the British suggestion for the establishment of an international naval presence in the area of the Strait of Tiran. As I said to Mr. Eban, there is doubt that a number of other maritime powers would be willing to take steps of this nature unless and until United Nations processes have been exhausted. We must continue our efforts to mobilize international support for this effort. Our leadership is unanimous that the United States should not move in isolation.[6]

On the matter of liaison and communication, I believe our relations can be improved. We have completely and fully exchanged views with General Amit.

We will remain in continuing communication with Ambassador Harman and Minister Evron here in Washington and value greatly the exchanges we are able to have through them with the Government of Israel, as well as through Ambassador Barbour in Tel Aviv.

Sincerely,

Lyndon B. Johnson

---

[5] Before Saunders added Johnson's revisions, the last two sentences of this paragraph read: "And, as you will understand, I cannot act at all without full backing of Congress. I am now in the process of urgently consulting the leaders of our Congress."

[6] Before Saunders added Johnson's revisions, the last sentence of this paragraph read: "I would not wish the United States to move in isolation."

140.   Telegram From the Department of State to the Embassy in
        Israel[1]

Washington, June 4, 1967, 2:03 p.m.

208004. 1. Secretary called in Israeli Chargé to present President
Johnson's reply Prime Minister's letter (sent separately).[2] Noted letter
did not attempt repeat everything that had been said previously but
was designed summarize where we are at moment. He reviewed current efforts within Security Council and discussions re Maritime
Declaration. Then stated U.S. had nothing further on Russian position
on important aspects current issues. He asked Eshkol [Evron] whether
GOI had info this matter. Eshkol [Evron] replied in negative, indicating,
however, he had Eshkol's letter to Kosygin which he would provide us
after translation. There were in opinion GOI indications USSR prod-
ding Egyptians but still no reflection their attitude on Straits. It was
agreed U.S. and GOI would keep in close touch regarding Russian
intentions.

2. Secretary briefed Chargé in general terms talks Prime Minister
Wilson in which Middle East problems had figured prominently. Clear
from these discussions that U.S. and U.K. were mobilizing support on
Declaration and considering carefully contingencies that might follow.
In addition, U.S. and U.K. looking carefully into economic, financial,
and other aspects problem. Clear that U.K. regards matter as serious
issue to which it is giving most urgent attention. From U.S. point of
view, important question was how involve as many governments as
possible in plans for future. Secretary assumed GOI talking to France
and Canada. French position at present unsatisfactory which was perhaps not too surprising. One key question was what France would do if
merchant vessel transited Straits and UAR fired first shot. De Gaulle
statement not precise on point.

3. Evron pressed Secretary re time factors current plans to which
Secretary replied U.S. working very hard several tracks. Should know
by about Monday what Security Council can do. We are trying speed up
consideration Declaration with target for mid-week to know how much
support we have. Moreover, Department spending much time with

---

[1] Source: National Archives and Records Administration, RG 59, Central Files
1967–69, POL ARAB–ISR. Secret; Exdis. Drafted by Battle on June 3 and approved by
Rusk.

[2] Document 139; the text was transmitted in telegram 207955 to Tel Aviv, June 3,
which states that Rusk gave the letter to Evron that afternoon. (National Archives and
Records Administration, RG 59, Central Files 1967–69, POL ARAB–ISR) Rusk met with
Evron from 5:15 to 5:40 p.m. (Johnson Library, Rusk Appointment Book)

Congressional groups to inform them of situation. So far response in Congress constructive and encouraging but indicates strong feeling U.S. should deal with problem multilaterally.

4. Evron agreed transmit letter Prime Minister soonest.

Rusk

---

141.   Circular Telegram From the Department of State to Arab Capitals[1]

Washington, June 3, 1967, 7:17 p.m.

207956. Eyes Only for Ambassador from Secretary.

I wish to express my personal appreciation to our Ambassadors in Arab Capitals for their full and timely reporting and for frank expressions of views on the present situation in the Near East. The considerations which you have advanced are being taken fully into account in a situation which is as complex and as dangerous as any we have faced. I should like to put before you some additional considerations and ask you to put your minds to possible solutions which can prevent war.

1. You should not assume that the United States can order Israel not to fight for what it considers to be its most vital interests. We have used the utmost restraint and, thus far, have been able to hold Israel back. But the "Holy War" psychology of the Arab world is matched by an apocalyptic psychology within Israel. Israel may make a decision that it must resort to force to protect its vital interests. In dealing with the issues involved, therefore, we must keep in mind the necessity for finding a solution with which Israel can be restrained.

2. Each side appears to look with relative equanimity upon the prospect of major hostilities and each side apparently is confident of success. Which estimate is correct cannot be fully known unless tested by the event but someone is making a major miscalculation. It does not help that Israel believes that time is working against them because of

---

[1] Source: National Archives and Records Administration, RG 59, Central Files 1967–69, POL ARAB–ISR. Secret. Drafted and approved by Rusk. Sent to Algiers, Amman, Baghdad, Baida, Beirut, Cairo, Jidda, Kuwait, Rabat, Sanaa, Tel Aviv, and Tunis.

the continuing Arab build-up and deployment of forces. If anything could be done in the direction of reversing the mobilization on both sides, this would, of course, be a great advantage.

3. You should bear in mind the background of the application of the statement of four American Presidents that (to quote from President Johnson's statement of May 23) "The United States is firmly committed to the support of the political independence and territorial integrity of all the nations of that area." You will recall the actions taken by the Eisenhower Administration when Egypt was attacked by Israel, Britain and France and when Lebanon was seriously threatened by Syria. You will recall our steady and substantial support to Jordan to reinforce its position over and against Egypt. You will recall that President Kennedy sent a squadron of U.S. fighters to Saudi Arabia as a demonstration of support when Saudi Arabia was being threatened by Egypt. Most of you may know that we used a major diplomatic effort in Cairo to cool off subversive and propaganda assaults upon Libya. We supported Algeria's demand for independence and have tried to steady the nerves of Tunisia and Morocco when they felt threatened by Algeria. When Israel has been attacked by terrorist groups we have supported Israel; when Israel resorted to disproportionate actions of retaliation against Samu in Jordan, we publicly and privately censored Israel in the strongest terms. I suggest we have a strong case for the idea that we have been even-handed with respect to the political independence and territorial integrity of Near Eastern countries.

A major issue for us in this present crisis involves the commitments we made at the time of the wind-up of the Suez affair. At that time we were acting on behalf of Egypt. As a part of the settlement which obtained the withdrawal of Israeli forces from the Sinai, including Sharm el Sheikh, we assured Israel that we would support an international right of passage through the Strait of Tiran. We endorsed Israel's statement in the General Assembly (in fact it was drafted in consultation with Secretary Dulles) that Israel would have the right under Article 51 of the Charter to protect its flagships transiting that Strait if fired upon. Egypt was aware of these positions and, although it did not endorse them at the time, it was the beneficiary of the arrangements made.

4. The central principle of international law involved in the Strait of Tiran was encompassed in the Conventions on the law of the sea of 1958. This principle is of vital importance to us all over the world where there are many such narrow passages connecting bodies of international waters. In any event, the United States has given some pledges on the matter and we must give the most sober attention to all the implications of such pledges and any failure on our part to insist upon them.

5. There may be some flexibility in what Cairo would be willing to do before major hostilities. The Strait of Tiran is a key issue. The free passage of crude oil is a major part of that issue. We shall not know details until further explorations of the problem with Cairo or intermediaries. We cannot abandon, in principle, the right of Israeli flagships to transit the Strait. There might be some possibility of a breathing space if in fact passage were permitted for genuinely peaceful traffic, including crude oil. This is not a proposal on our side but an indication of a possible de facto standstill pending further diplomatic effort.

6. I have presented these considerations in order to enlist the best thought of our Ambassadors in Arab Capitals as to profitable approaches to the problem. It will do no good to ask Israel simply to accept the present status quo in the Strait because Israel will fight and we could not restrain her. We cannot throw up our hands and say that, in that event, let them fight while we try to remain neutral. I should be glad to have any further suggestions any of you might have on this situation.

Rusk

---

142.   Memorandum From Robert N. Ginsburgh of the National Security Council Staff to the President's Special Assistant (Rostow)[1]

Washington, June 3, 1967.

SUBJECT

Who Would Win a War? Israel or the UAR

1. The attached document[2]—prepared a week ago—is the best I have seen on comparing the military capabilities of Israel and the UAR. I suggest you read all of it.

2. It concludes:

—Israel could get air supremacy over the Sinai in one to three days—depending on who struck first.

---

[1] Source: Johnson Library, National Security File, Country File, Middle East Crisis, Situation Reports. Top Secret; [codeword not declassified].

[2] The attachment is apparently a draft of Document 76.

—Israel would lose a third to half of its air force. (This estimate may be high; one-fourth to one-third losses might be closer to the mark.)

—Israel would drive the Egyptians west of the Suez Canal in seven to nine days.

—Israel could contain any attacks by Syria or Jordan during this period.

3. Since this was written, the UAR has gained a number of military benefits:

—The UAR has consolidated positions in Sinai.
—The UAR has manned the Straits of Aqaba.
—The UAR has mined certain areas.
—Arab command, control, and planning has probably improved.
—The threat to Israel posed by Jordan has increased.
—UAR logistics in the Sinai have probably improved.

4. By a delay of one week—28 May to 4 June—the Arabs have made a net military gain if war should now occur. The ultimate outcome—according to "my experts"—would be unchanged. Israel would still win, but

—It *might* take 8–10 days to drive to the Suez.
—Israel *might* suffer 5–10% more casualties.

5. If war outbreak were delayed one more week—to 11 June, the Israeli military position would probably deteriorate further—but at a slower rate. "My experts" judge that:

Israel would still win, but

—It *might* take as much as 9 days to two weeks.
—Israelis *might* suffer an additional 5% casualties.

6. After 11 June, the military balance would not change until the economic effects of mobilization began to affect military posture.

7. Some of my experts think that the above underrates Israel. I suspect that if I were a responsible Israeli commander, I might be less sanguine even though I had no doubt about the ultimate military outcome. The only other nagging doubt is that sometimes in the past professional military opinion has been awfully wrong, but I can find no objective basis to challenge the present estimate.

8. Thus, I conclude that Israeli concern about delaying a war which they fear is inevitable is based primarily on their concern about a deterioration in their political and diplomatic position rather than on military factors.

G

143.   Intelligence Memorandum Prepared in the Central
         Intelligence Agency[1]

[*document number not declassified*]   Washington, June 3, 1967.

THE CURRENT FOCUS OF THE NEAR EAST CRISIS

Summary

Reporting during the past few days has focused on two primary aspects of the Near East crisis. One is the rapidly growing belief in Israel that time is running out, and that if Israel is not to suffer an ultimately fatal defeat it must very soon either strike or obtain absolutely iron-clad security assurances from the West. The second aspect is the rise of a euphoric, band-wagon spirit among the Arab States, leading even moderate Arabs to believe that the time may in fact have come when the Arabs can close in on Israel with some hope of success. There are in addition a number of reports indicating that anti-US actions are being planned, to be put in motion if the US moves to frustrate what the Arabs now tend to see as a "victory."

1. All reporting from Israel shows mounting pressure for a "decision." The popular applause greeting General Moshe Dayan's appointment as defense minister—"go, go Moshe"—indicates that the mood is strongly "action." Dayan's appointment should assure that the "hawks" accept decisions of the coalition government more readily than they otherwise would, but it also indicates that Prime Minister Eshkol has suffered a setback and must adapt his policy to the views of the tough-minded military whom Dayan represents.

2. The Israeli military, [*1 line of source text not declassified*], have already shown apprehension over the consequences of extended delay. The Egyptians have been permitted to make an orderly build-up of ground forces in Sinai, moving aircraft to advanced fields and setting up at least the rudiments of an air defense system there. The Israeli strategy calls for gaining control of the air as the first essential step in the campaign. Although all reports indicate that the Israelis are still confident of victory, they are increasingly nervous about the cost, and, even more important, about the possibility that the Egyptians may somehow get in an initial air strike on Israeli cities or air fields. The Israeli "hawks" may fear that such a strike would do significant psychological

---

[1] Source: Johnson Library, National Security File, Country File, Middle East Crisis, CIA Intelligence Memoranda, 5/67–7/67. Top Secret; [*codeword not declassified*]. Prepared in the Central Intelligence Agency's Directorate of Intelligence.

damage to the affluent Israeli society, even if it did not have much material effect.

3. The Arabs are sniffing blood. So fast and far does Nasir's bandwagon seem to be rolling that even the Iranian government, long friendly to Israel and bitterly hostile to Nasir, has been compelled to issue a statement mouthing phrases about Muslim solidarity. Tunisian President Bourguiba, the only "Arab" leader in recent years to suggest publicly some modus vivendi with Israel, has also had his government say that it stands behind, though evidently not with, Nasir.

4. The Arabs evidently expect that the US and the UK will come to Israel's rescue, and are doing some planning for this eventuality. Their view of US and British policy is being fed by a stream of "intelligence" reports—e.g., that US airborne brigades in West Germany are on alert; "confirmed" information that Wheelus Field is being used to ship US arms to Israel; that British, French, and US airmen have arrived in Israel; that Israeli rockets have been stationed at Eilat under US instructions.

5. The range of Arab reaction in the event of US and UK intervention, or indeed before such a development, is indicated not only by public threats to close up the Suez Canal, to destroy Western oil assets, etc., but also by some specific preparations. [4 lines of source text not declassified] Terrorist bombing against US offices in Saudi Arabia was resumed on 2 June. Meanwhile, the US Embassy in Kuwait has reported that it assesses the possibility of an oil shutdown there as more real than it had been earlier in the crisis. In Libya, the present mood is that the US base at Wheelus would be closed.

6. Although the tenor of many of the anti-US pronouncements suggests that they are being issued more to head off pro-Nasir pressures than to express actual intentions, there seems to be a real danger in the cumulative effect of the threats. In countries where there are obvious and available targets other than oil or military installations—e.g., the American University of Beirut, US or UK airline and branch bank offices—these might be subjected to direct attack even before Arab governments moved in on oil or base installations where their own interests are more heavily engaged.

7. In less tangible terms, the damage to the US position in the area already appears serious. During the past twenty years, a generation of Arab youth have grown to maturity under bombardment of the idea that Israel would not exist if the US had not created it. This conviction is hardening, and is reflected in the new, rude frankness with which Arab leaders talk to our representatives, as well as in such out-of-the-way items as a Sudanese editorial calling for local enforcement of the Arab boycott against Ford and Coca Cola. These things are not serious

in themselves—and some of the editorials and demonstrations are no doubt paid for by the Egyptians or Soviets—but they are pointers of the way in which minds are moving as the crisis deepens.

8. Nor are hardening attitudes toward the US limited to the Arabs. In Israel, particularly among the hawks, there is a rising chorus of sentiment which sees Washington as holding Israel back and thereby selling the Israelis out. This is the other side of the general belief in Israel that only the Israelis really know how to deal with the Arabs and could do so successfully were it not for US pressures.

---

144.   Memorandum From the President's Special Assistant (Rostow) to President Johnson[1]

Washington, June 4, 1967, 11:30 a.m.

Mr. President:

The purpose of this memorandum is to lay out a course of action for the coming week (or two weeks) which will maximize the chance that we can: (1) achieve our objectives in the Middle East without an Arab-Israeli war; and (2) should such an Arab-Israeli war come about, produce minimum damage to the U.S. position in the world and to our position in our own country, including continued support for the war in Viet Nam.

I. The Situation.

It is now increasingly clear that the Israelis will wait only about a week to take on themselves the forcing of the blockade at the Gulf of Aqaba. They clearly envisage forcing Nasser to fire the first shot; they will respond on a limited basis in Sinai but be prepared to fight a war against all the Arab forces arrayed against them without external assistance in manpower or other direct application of foreign military force.

The plan for an international regatta to force, say, an oil ship through the Straits is unlikely to get operational support except for four countries: the U.S., the U.K., Australia, and Netherlands.

---

[1] Source: Johnson Library, National Security File, Country File, Middle East Crisis, Vol. III. Secret. Rostow sent copies to Rusk and McNamara.

The moderate Arabs—and, in fact, virtually all Arabs who fear the rise of Nasser as a result of this crisis—would prefer to have him cut down by the Israelis rather than by external forces.

Beyond these factors the situation in the Middle East is that the radical nationalism represented by Nasser, while powerful at the moment in the wake of his breakthrough against U Thant, is waning: Arab socialism and other such doctrines have not proved successful; the moderates of the region (Turkey, Iran, Jordan, Saudi Arabia, Lebanon) have done better than Egypt, Syria, and Iraq; Nasser's plans for external expansion have not gone well; in short, we are dealing with Nasser not on a rising trend but in somewhat the same as Khrushchev in the Cuba missile crisis; Nasser is trying to achieve a quick fix against an underlying waning position.

Just beneath the surface is the potentiality for a new phase in the Middle East of moderation; a focusing on economic development; regional collaboration; and an acceptance of Israel as part of the Middle East if a solution to the refugee problem can be found. But all this depends on Nasser's being cut down to size.

The problem before us is whether this crisis can be surmounted in ways which lead on to that historical transition and which avoid: the destruction of Israel, on the one hand, or the crystallization of a bloc unified only by a hostility to Israel, which would require us to maintain Israel as a kind of Hong Kong enclave in the region.

II. The Israeli Case for Unilateral Action.

The Israelis believe that their long-run future in the area—including the Arab mentality—requires that they solve the problem before them on their own. They wish in the end to be part of the Middle East. They feel that dealing with this situation on their own is necessary to achieve not merely self-respect but respect in the region.

They believe taking on the blockade themselves will make it easier for the United States to support them in other ways, short of troops. They believe it easier for the U.S. to honor its commitment of 1957 to recognize the legitimacy of their forcing the blockade than to mobilize on an international basis an effective U.S. and international commitment to use force to break the blockade. Their own diplomatic soundings, like ours, make clear how small the party would be prepared to use force to assert the international interests in the Gulf of Aqaba, including Israeli interests.

They perceive that the USSR is less likely to intervene with military force if they take on Nasser than for U.S. and a few friends to take on Nasser on the Aqaba issue; and they judge it would be better for U. S.-Arab relations in the long run, but also in terms of Western interests in Middle Eastern oil.

III. The Moderate Arab View.

Although there is some conflict of judgment, the bulk of the evidence before us indicates that the moderate Arab view—as well as the view among our Ambassadors to the Arab world—is that it would be wiser for the Israelis to deal with the present situation than it would be for us.

IV. The U.S. Interest and Our Task.

—To open the Gulf of Aqaba to at least oil for Israel—which has become the test of who wins this trial of will and nerve—without war if possible.

—To do so in ways which maximize the chance of long-run peace in the area, including movement towards acceptance of Israel as part of the Middle East.

—In any case, to honor all commitments made in 1957—even, if, in the end, an Arab-Israeli war comes about; that is, our commitment to put through a U.S. flagship; to assert the right of free passage for others; and to regard Israeli counteraction to a UAR attempt to close Aqaba by armed force as involving for Israel legitimate rights of self-defense under the UN Charter.

—To act, in general, in such a way as to unify the political base in the U.S. around our Middle East policy so that we do not weaken the political foundations for our further conduct of the war in Viet Nam.

V. A Possible Scenario.

Here are the main elements in a scenario and their sequence—required to achieve these objectives.

—First, we must urgently make it clear to Nasser—which has not yet been made clear—that we intend to honor our 1957 commitments. His letter to you completely ignores what happened in 1957. He must be reminded that we undertook our commitments in order to get the Israelis off his neck; and it is a matter of honor and continuity of the American word that these commitments be honored. (In this context, a statement by General Eisenhower, and perhaps even a special visit to Cairo by Cabot Lodge—who was personally and directly involved in those events—may be important, as well as our conversations with Mohieddin and your reply to Nasser's letter.)[2]

In making this point clear, we must also present to him a willingness to move forward with other critical issues in the area where progress is required, if, indeed, the region is to settle down and move towards peace and stability, including: the placement of UN observers on both sides of the borders; Arab refugees; regional economic devel-

---

[2] See footnote 2, Document 148.

opment; water; and the damping down of the arms race. There is considerable legitimate argument as to whether Nasser is now postured as a Hitler, determined at all costs to exploit temporary Arab unity to crush Israel once and for all, or whether he is a shrewd operator, working off a weak base, willing to settle for as much as he can get from this crisis. If the latter is the case, a package deal of this kind is the best way to smoke him out. If he wants war, the Israelis and we will be in much better shape if we have laid the deal before the world.

—In any case, so far as U.S. public opinion is concerned, opinion in the Middle East, and opinion in the world, we must quickly produce a posture in which the hard-core issue of oil through Aqaba is diluted by the evocation of a larger, more attractive, and more basic objective; namely, to begin to transform the Middle East from its present dangerous, unstable situation into one in which there is the possibility, at least, of movement forwards toward cooperation, development and acceptance of Israel as part of the region.

—By the time we have transmitted this offer to Nasser, we would also have been able to take stock of the response to the declaration of innocent passage through Aqaba and have some feel for how many countries are willing to escort vessels going through the Gulf to Eilat. The stage would then be set for going to Congress and asking for a resolution. (About, say, Thursday of the coming week.)

—The resolution for which we would ask in this scenario would have these characteristics: It would recall and state the three 1957 commitments; it would empower us to use force, if necessary, to support the transit of Aqaba by U.S. flagships and those of other nations, except Israel; it would recognize the government of Israel's expressed desire that it handle the question of its own flagships with its own force; but it would recognize that if the transit of such ships was met by armed force, the Israelis had the right of self-defense. The resolution would call for all parties to permit transit of the Gulf on the basis of the situation between 1957 and the present crisis; and it would appeal for movement forward with respect to peace in the area, including action on UN observers, refugees, development, the regional arms race, etc.

—Behind the scene we would be working for an Aqaba formula in which the oil flow would continue to Eilat; the Israelis would maintain their claim to put flagships through, but not exercise it; the UAR would ignore the fishing trawlers that go in and out of the Gulf; the International Court of Justice would take over the legal controversy involved; the forces in Sinai would demobilize; and, in this interval, we would try to get the Middle East and the world community to go to work on UN observers; refugees; development; etc. (With that kind of resolution and an explicit understanding that we would recognize Israeli rights of self-defense if their vessels were stopped by armed force, it might be possible to hold the Israelis for another week; that is, from Sunday, June 11 (roughly their present D-day) to the 18th of June. In that interval we would have to do two things: bring maximum pressure to bear to get a diplomatic settlement, including maximum pressure on Moscow; and organize a forcing of the blockade in terms of something like the following sequence, designed to fulfill the three U.S. commitments.

—A U.S. vessel goes through with escort, bearing a civilian non-strategic cargo; although it might contain oil. On present evidence, that vessel would not be fired on, although if it contained oil it might be contested.

—A non-U.S. flagship (either Israeli-owned or not) would go through with a civil cargo, backed by whomever the naval powers turn out to be;

—Then, finally, an Israeli vessel would go through and the issue would be put squarely to Nasser to whether he would fire upon it, our having made it clear that we regard Israeli rights of self-defense as legitimate, if armed force were used to stop it; but the background to such Israelis forcing action would be a known formula that if oil were permitted to flow to Eilat, the Israelis were willing to have the whole matter put to the International Court of Justice.

VI. There are several gut questions unresolved in this proposed scenario, among them these:

—*Timing and the Israeli tactical military situation.* As we now know, they would prefer to go directly to the test of the Israeli flag, and, in effect, have us stand down on our other commitments, except, of course, our commitment to regard their case as legitimate. Another reason they may wish this to have some element of control over the time which Nasser faces this showdown. If the objective of the exercise is a situation where we achieve oil to Eilat without a war, marching down quite openly to the sequence described above, is a superior scenario. It would also relieve us of a most dangerous problem; namely, of our knowing Israeli plans but holding them secret as did the British and French at the time of Suez, with all the consequent ugly debate and controversy which continued down to the present day. Our interest, and, in fact, the Israeli interest is to do this job like the sheriff in "High Noon", rather than through tactical surprise and quiet secret understandings between Tel Aviv and Washington.

—*If we regard the transit of oil as the gut issue here, when should oil be brought in and under whose flag?* On this I have no firm judgment but suspect the best auspices would be the most natural situation: a foreign flag backed by the escorting party. But there is some virtue in our taking oil in—preferably not Iranian oil with the U.S. flag flying.

—*What, precisely, is the formula for Aqaba that Israel would accept?* Is it prepared to accept a situation where oil goes through while the issue is taken to the International Court of Justice; trawlers go through with Israeli flag de facto; but, while reserving their legal rights to put Israeli flags through, they do not test that right until the International Court of Justice rules? My inclination would be to use maximum leverage with the Israelis to accept such a deal if Nasser accepts it, demobilizes his forces in Sinai, and accepts the agenda of UN observers; some progress on refugees; development; arms race talks; etc.

VII. USSR.

In the end, whether the outcome is an Arab-Israeli war or a successful transit of the crisis depends a good deal on the USSR. If we move in the way I have indicated, I am moderately optimistic that they will, in the clutch, throw considerable weight on Cairo to accept a pragmatic deal for the following reasons:

—They would not like to see U.S. and other naval powers actually exercised to force the Gulf of Aqaba for non-Israeli ships.

—I believe they honestly fear an Arab-Israeli war because they still believe that the Israelis will win it. If they win it after more than 10 years of pouring Soviet arms into the Middle East, the whole Soviet arms game will be profoundly degraded. It has already been substantially degraded by the outcome in Indonesia. If their military men calculate, like ours, that, at considerable cost in blood, the Israelis could now beat the Arabs armed with Soviet MIG-21s and Soviet tanks, they would do a good deal to avoid that demonstration. On reflection, I suspect this factor has played a big role in their anxiety about the Israelis launching an attack.

—Finally, they have carefully not committed themselves on the question of Aqaba and left it open for them, in the end, to play a kind of Tashkent role.[3]

—Therefore, if we move down this track and assert through the Congress our willingness to back our play on all three 1957 commitments, my hunch is that they will move rather fast to come up with their own kind of formula to avoid the war and try to portray their role as frustrating the designs of American imperialists and Israeli lackeys. If it all ends up with oil going to Eilat, the forces demobilized, UN observers, talk about refugees, development, etc., that would be quite okay with us.

WWR

---

[3] Reference is to the Soviet role in bringing about the Tashkent Communiqué of January 10, 1966, in which India and Pakistan agreed to withdraw their forces to positions held before the 1965 fighting in Kashmir.

145.   Telegram From the Embassy in the United Arab Republic to the Department of State[1]

Cairo, June 4, 1967, 1925Z.

8384. Ref: Cairo 8471.[2]

1. Chargé Nes has just been called separately by Ashraf Ghorbal of Foreign Office and Mustapha Aziz of Presidency and told that Zakariya Mohieddin plans leave for Washington Wednesday June 7.

2. Party will include Mustapha Aziz, perhaps Deputy Prime Minister Fawzi and others. Details of party and travel plans will be given us tomorrow. Chargé has offered all assistance. Ghorbal leaving tomorrow as advance party, with ETA Washington Tuesday.

3. Indications are that Mohieddin will wish discuss totality Palestine problem, resolution of which would permit regulation Tiran Straits issue. More on this later as may be possible following any discussions we may be able have with delegation members prior their departure.

Nolte

---

[1] Source: National Archives and Records Administration, RG 59, Central Files 1967–69, POL ARAB–ISR. Secret; Flash; Nodis. Received at 3:44 p.m. Rostow sent a copy to the President at 5:15 p.m. (Johnson Library, National Security File, Country File, Middle East Crisis, Vol. III)

[2] Nolte reported in telegram 8471 from Cairo, June 4, that the Embassy had informed Riad of the contents of telegram 207861 to Cairo (see footnote 2, Document 134), and that he planned to take up the subject of Mohieddin's visit with Nasser when presenting his credentials on June 5. (National Archives and Records Administration, RG 59, Central Files 1967–69, POL ARAB–ISR) Rusk responded to the latter point in telegram 207994, June 4, which reads in part: "The great value of Mohieddin's visit is opportunity for private discussions. The less said about it the better." (Johnson Library, National Security File, Country File, Middle East Crisis, Anderson Cables)

146. Telegram From the Department of State to the Embassy in the United Kingdom[1]

Washington, June 4, 1967, 9:54 p.m.

208026. Middle East Crisis.

Ambassador Dean called on Under Secretary Rostow this afternoon at Rostow's request.

1. Rostow assured Ambassador British Government notified immediately if we had indication Israeli decision to force Strait alone. Dean stressed UK would not support such unilateral Israeli action. UK recognized that under international law and 1957 arrangements, US/UK position was that Israel justified in striking back if Israeli ship turned back by armed force. UK position, however, was that unescorted probe was invitation to Egyptians to fire. UK support for escorted probe based on judgment that UAR would not fire.

2. Rostow reported clearance obtained today on constituting international naval force. Instructions going out today[2] and Ambassador Harriman would make some special approaches coming week. Entire effort would be coordinated with UK Ambassadors.

3. Some countries had minor problems of wording in maritime declaration. Dean and Rostow agreed that to save time, such countries might make slight alterations in the wording of the declaration and then file separate declarations under common covering letter to the UN. (Further instructions on this are to follow.)

4. Joint naval planning with UK EmbOff starts Tuesday,[3] with London group Wednesday.

Rusk

---

[1] Source: National Archives and Records Administration, RG 59, Central Files 1967–69, POL ARAB–ISR. Secret; Exdis. Drafted by Eugene Rostow's Special Assistant Alan R. Novak, and approved by Rostow.

[2] A memorandum of June 9 from Deane R. Hinton of EUR/RPE to Walsh states that at the time of the outbreak of hostilities, an instruction to the Embassies in a number of countries was awaiting approval by the Secretary. Hinton's memorandum is filed with what he describes as a draft history of the MADEC operation. The attachment is headed: "The Middle East Crisis: Activities of the Task Force Subcommittee on the Maritime Declaration." It includes a brief chronology and 24 attachments. (Ibid., Middle East Crisis Files, E. 5190, Box 14, History of MADEC) Other files on the Maritime Declaration effort are ibid., Box 13.

[3] June 6.

147. Memorandum From the Contingency Work Group on Military Planning to the Middle East Control Group[1]

Washington, June 4, 1967.

SUBJECT

Measures to Test or Force the Tiran Blockade

This paper explores the prospects for unescorted and escorted tests of the UAR blockade of the Strait of Tiran. We face a choice between two basic strategies: (1) a series of tests backed by a naval escort force representing the maritime nations, with the intent to assert free passage by force if necessary; or (2) a test or series of tests sponsored by Israel, with the understanding that if passage is refused Israeli military action (limited or broad-scale) would follow.

During the past week we have also discussed the utility of unescorted tests designed merely to define the limits of the blockade and to build a case for international political or juridical action to relieve it. Under that concept, there is no necessary relationship between the tests and the ultimate decision to organize and use an escort force. This approach seems less relevant now, in view of our greater knowledge concerning the UAR blockade and of the pressures of time.

The Feasibility of Arranging Tests

Under the first choice above, the requirement is two-fold: to assemble test ships of appropriate registries and in sufficient numbers, and to assemble an international naval escort force representing the maritime nations. The neuralgic points of the blockade are (a) oil, (b) Israeli flag vessels, and (c) possibly Israeli-owned vessels.

[Omitted here is discussion of the problems of assembling test ships and an international escort force, possibilities of unescorted passage by U.S. flag or non-U.S. flag tankers and possible consequences, consequences of a test by an unescorted Israeli vessel, the possibility of an escorted probe by a non-Israeli vessel and its possible consequences, and the possibility of an Israeli-sponsored test of the blockade.]

---

[1] Source: Washington National Records Center, OSD Files: FRC 330 72 A 2468, Middle East 381.3. Secret. Sent to Secretary of Defense McNamara with a covering memorandum of June 4 from Hoopes that states the Control Group was to consider it "preliminary" that evening. A stamped notation on the memorandum indicates that McNamara saw it on June 5. A copy of a JCS memorandum for McNamara on "Military Actions—Straits of Tiran," JCSM–310–67, June 2, is attached. It discussed possible military forces that might be used and steps that might be taken in case a decision were made to test the UAR blockade, with the assumption that more time was available than had been assumed in JCSM–301–67, May 27, which had considered only actions that could be taken within approximately 1 week. (See footnote 2, Document 91.)

Conclusions

1. It is important to understand that we face a clear choice between basic, mutually exclusive strategies for testing the blockade. The deliberate attempt to combine them would almost surely produce the worst possible consequences for US interests, as would their intermingling by inadvertence or calculated Israeli action.

2. A US decision to assume responsibility for testing the blockade leads inevitably to the requirement for a naval escort force; and given the probability that the UAR will turn back unescorted tankers (including those of US registry), the organization of a naval escort force will lead almost certainly to its use.

3. The mere organization of such an escort force would be construed as a hostile act by the UAR, and would produce serious political and economic retaliation against US interests throughout the Arab world. On balance, however, these may be manageable if the force is not actually used.

4. The actual use [of] the escort force would produce graver political and economic consequences for US interests (even if the UAR did not resist militarily and the USSR exercised great caution). These would likely include seizure or nationalization of oil companies, closure of the Suez Canal to nations participating in the force, cut-off of oil pipelines to the Mediterranean, and UN action that might either charge the US with "aggression" or place further US actions to run the blockade in violation of the UN. In addition, mob violence against US life and property in the Middle East would be probable.

5. A brief, inconclusive military engagement between the UAR and the escort force would intensify, but not materially alter, the consequences set out in paragraph 4.

6. A serious UAR military effort to prevent escorted passage would project the US into a state of war with the UAR, with no logical or mutually acceptable break-off point. The fact of US belligerency would gravely diminish the possibilities of Soviet restraint in its support of the Arabs, or of joint US-Soviet efforts to limit and terminate hostilities. Such a situation could be quickly escalated and complicated by a major Israeli attack on the Arabs, or a major Arab attack on Israel. Either contingency would be probable if serious fighting between the escort force and the UAR developed in the Strait of Tiran.

7. Under the best possible circumstances (i.e., broad and vigorous adherence to the maritime declaration and a truly international escort force), it might be possible to separate the issue of free passage from the basic Arab-Israeli conflict. But given the present facts (i.e., a fairly narrow, lukewarm support for the declaration and a marked lack of enthu-

siasm for the escort force) such a separation is illusory. Thus if the escort force were used, UAR and Soviet propaganda would succeed in linking the two issues, and in branding the US as the enemy of the Arabs.

8. The strategy involving US-sponsored tests plus an escort force cannot therefore serve US interests in existing circumstances. At best, its pursuit would further polarize Middle East politics, pitting the US and Israel against the USSR and all the Arab states, with the gravest political and economic damage to US and West European interests; at worst, it would embroil the US in a direct war with Nasser and the Arabs, with the serious danger of rapid escalation to military confrontation with the USSR.

9. The alternative basic strategy of an Israeli-sponsored probe would almost surely lead to Arab-Israeli hostilities. An unescorted vessel (either Israeli flag or Israeli owned) would almost certainly be turned back. If it resisted, it would be fired on; Israel would then retaliate, leading to widespread hostilities.

10. A probe sponsored by Israel would have one cardinal advantage. It is that, in the event of hostilities, the US and the USSR would not be directly engaged and would share a mutual interest in limiting the conflict at some point. When this point became manifest, it is reasonable to hope that they would find it possible to cooperate in bringing an end to hostilities and in providing support, both in and outside the UN, for a peaceful settlement. Thus, on the judgment that some bloodletting is an unavoidable precondition to any new political settlement, the alternative basic strategy has the greater merit, in terms of protecting US vital interests and preserving the fabric of world peace.

11. If the US were a belligerent, the chances for limiting and ending hostilities would be infinitely worsened, in part because the UN would be rendered impotent (as in the case of Vietnam) by a fundamental split between the two superpowers.

12. The choice between these two basic strategies for testing the blockade is a cruel one. Pursuit of the first strategy will lead almost inevitably to a total polarization of Middle East politics with the gravest damage to US political and economic interests in that area; and the risks are substantial that it would also lead to war in which the US would be embroiled. Pursuit of the alternative basic strategy will lead almost inevitably to widespread Arab-Israeli hostilities, in which, however, the US could probably avoid direct involvement.

13. The cruelty of the choice impels one to turn to more intensive work on the elements of a third possibility—a compromise political settlement, a course which is beyond the scope of this paper. It is vitally important to recognize that the chances of reaching a political settlement based on less than the maximum demands of Israel and the UAR on the blockade issue (e.g., a settlement based on tacit acceptance by the

UAR of the passage of non-Israeli tankers, and tacit agreement by Israel not to demand more) would be sharply reduced, if not *eliminated*, by a prior resort to either testing strategy. This conclusion points to the critical importance of (a) avoiding actions which would now commit us to the first basic strategy, and of (b) persuading Israel to forego action in the Gulf until all reasonable efforts toward a peaceful effort have failed.

Townsend Hoopes[2]
Chairman

[2] Printed from a copy that bears this typed signature.

---

148.   **Minutes of the Ninth Meeting of the Middle East Control Group**[1]

Washington, June 4, 1967, 11 a.m.

The Control Group Meeting, which began in the morning and continued into the evening, concluded with a meeting with Secretary Rusk, Secretary McNamara, NSC Special Representative Walt Rostow, and Ambassador Thompson. The main element throughout the day was preparation for the visit of the UAR Vice President Mohieddin.

The Group began its discussions with a review of the actions taken since the beginning of the crisis. These included:

1. Presidential messages to the Heads of State of the countries of the area, urging restraint.

2. Continuing efforts in various ways to hold the Israeli "tiger".

3. Structural organization for the crisis, including the establishment of the Task Force and the Control Group. The latter knitted together State, DOD, the White House, CIA and Treasury. Planning had been wide-ranging and in depth.

4. Direct discussions had been held in Washington with UK Minister of State George Thomson and his delegation. There had been a meeting of minds on an assessment of the gravity of the situation. In addition, on an ad referendum working level basis, there had been

---

[1] Source: National Archives and Records Administration, RG 59, Office of the Executive Secretariat, Middle East Crisis Files, 1967, Entry 5190, Box 17, Minutes/Decisions of the Control Group, Folder 1. Secret; Nodis. No drafter or participants are on the source text.

agreement on a course of action involving (a) intensive use of UN facilities in an effort to de-fuse the situation; (b) the preparation of a Maritime Declaration which would express the views and positions of the Maritime Powers on the Gulf of Aqaba and would win maximum international support; (c) bringing into being a multination naval force which, if all political means failed, could provide escorts for passage through the Straits of Tiran.

5. Israeli Foreign Minister Eban had visited Washington and had discussed the crisis with the President, Secretary Rusk, Secretary McNamara, and Members of the Control Group. He explained that the Israeli Cabinet confronted by the alternatives of war or surrender, had chosen the former, only to be restrained by the intervention, under instructions, of Ambassador Barbour, who had presented a "third alternative". A determined effort had been made to dissuade the Israeli Government from resorting to military action. This included an exposition of the "third alternative" of diplomatic activity in the UN and elsewhere, the Maritime Declaration, and the assembly of a Naval Force for possible use in the Red Sea and the Gulf of Aqaba.

6. There had been continuing recourse to the Security Council.

7. There had been extensive diplomatic contacts in Washington and in pertinent capitals around the world.

8. There had been extensive consultations with Congress in respect to the developing situation.

9. Private emissaries had been sent to the area:

a. Charles Yost had been sent to Cairo to help Ambassador Nolte, who had not been able to present his credentials, and to take soundings with members of the UAR Government;

b. Robert Anderson, former Secretary of Treasury, had been in direct contact with President Nasser and had set the stage for the visit of Vice President Zakaria Mohieddin. Nasser had expressed in a letter to the President his willingness to send Mohieddin to Washington or to receive Vice President Humphrey in Cairo.

c. Governor Harriman had been in direct contact with the Shah of Iran.

d. Arrangements had been made for Presidential Counsel Harry McPherson to visit Tel Aviv.

While the original objective of the Control Group had been—starkly stated—to prevent the Israelis from striking the forces closing around them, its objectives had now broadened to include: (1) avoiding either an Israeli-UAR war or a clash between the Maritime Powers and the Arabs, and (2) developing the basic ingredients of an enduring peace in the Middle East.

The immediate tasks before the Group were to complete the staff work for the Mohieddin visit. This was to include the preparation of (1) a viable negotiating position with the UAR; (2) the formulation of assurances acceptable to Israel; and (3) the development of a scenario for use if the negotiations with the UAR should fail. It was noted that the difficulties of these tasks were compounded by (1) the obscurity of UAR objectives, (2) the heavy engagement of Nasser's prestige and the indication that he was striving for a major political victory; (3) the military confrontation of highly mobilized Arab and Israeli forces; and (4) the limited degree of our control over Israel.

As the day wore on, it became evident that Mohieddin would not arrive before the evening of June 7 and talks would not begin before the following day. Furthermore, press tickers from Cairo indicated that the UARG intended to give heavy propaganda treatment to the visit. In view of the manifest dangers that an incident could at any time lead to a clash between the heavily mobilized Arab and Israeli forces, cables were sent to Cairo urging Mohieddin to expedite his arrival, and emphasizing that minimum publicity was desirable. Although the Secretary had informed the Israeli Ambassador of the visit, it was evident that a heavy propaganda play by Cairo would create difficulty for the Israelis. It would also intensify the inherent problem of security. It was agreed that the physical arrangements for the visit, including security, would be delegated to Idar Rimestad, Deputy Under Secretary for Administration, and James Symington, Chief of Protocol. A maximum security effort would be made.

During the course of the day, the Group considered three documents related to the Mohieddin visit: (a) a memorandum to the President; (b) a draft letter to Nasser;[2] and (c) a draft letter to Kosygin. These were extensively revised prior to the early evening discussion with the two Secretaries and Walt Rostow. While there was full agreement that a basic memorandum had to be prepared promptly for the President's use in the Mohieddin talks, there were differences of views about the desirability of sending messages to either Kosygin or Nasser before the talks began. Following a thorough review of the advantages and disadvantages, the Secretary decided that (1) the Memorandum for the President, with certain revisions, should be transmitted to the White House on June 5; (2) he would revise the draft letter to Nasser, with certain "Levantine touches" with the thought that it might constitute a basic talking paper and be presented to Mohieddin when he met the President; (3) the letter to Kosygin should not be sent at this time but a revised letter might be sent after the meeting with Mohieddin.

---

[2] The June 4 draft letter to Nasser is filed with two draft memoranda to the President, both undated. The draft letter bears the handwritten note: "Sec was changing this when time ran out." (Ibid., Central Files 1967–69, POL 15–1 US/JOHNSON)

The draft Memorandum for the President contained the following elements of assessment: (1) time is running out and the Israelis may not stand for more than another week; (2) the rumors of a naval escort plan may be having some effect on Nasser, but the value of the idea as a diplomatic pressure is lessened by the doubts that are being spread by the Soviets and others that we are really serious in considering the naval-escort plan as a genuine alternative; (3) our main effort should be concentrated on Nasser and the Soviets. We should be firm on the issue of the Strait, while indicating the possibilities of a broad and constructive settlement at a later stage for the whole region. We should ascertain what is "under the rug". Do they want war or not? (4) Nasser should be made aware that if he actually uses force to close the Strait of Tiran, and the Israelis have recourse to Article 51, they will be doing so pursuant to the terms of a contract President Eisenhower brought about for the benefit of the Israelis and the Egyptians in 1957; (5) we should not try to negotiate with the Egyptians for the Israelis; (6) rather than agree to the exclusion from the Gulf of Israeli flag ships, the Israelis would fight; (7) in view of the possibility that we may have to face the Evron scenario (putting an Israeli flag ship through the Straits and utilizing armed force under Article 51 if it were attacked) within a few days, it is highly important to make the most strenuous possible diplomatic effort now; (8) the purpose of the proposed letter to Nasser is to get Nasser to stop, look and listen; (9) either an Arab-Israeli war, or the situation that would develop if we, the British, Australians and Dutch forced the Straits, would have great potentialities for hurting our long-term interests in the area, and in the Moslem world; (10) our best option if we can get it within a few days, is to avoid both alternatives without giving Nasser a complete political victory; (11) a maximum political effort is required to restore things as they were in the Gulf, until either the World Court or a political agreement can settle the problem.

Six Days of War, June 5–10, 1967

149. Memorandum for the Record[1]

Washington, November 17, 1968.

SUBJECT

Walt Rostow's Recollections of June 5, 1967

The following is a transcript of a tape recorded talk with Walt Rostow on November 17, 1968:

This is Walt Rostow. I have in front of me Hal Saunders' reconstruction of the log for Monday, June 5, 1967.[2] I shall make some observations on what I remember of that morning. I should preface everything that I am about to say with an acute awareness of the inadequacy of memory, as one looks back on fast-moving events in a single day.

I recall, as the log verifies, that I received about 2:50 a.m. from the Sit Room a report that there were press accounts coming in over the ticker of the opening of hostilities in the Middle East. I told our people to check NMCC and others for official confirmation and then call me back. At 2:35 a.m., I received confirmation and told them I would come in. I dressed and arrived in, I should think, about 3:20 a.m.

I immediately called Secretary Rusk who I believe had already been informed. I do not believe he was yet in his office. One of the questions raised with Secretary Rusk was whether I should inform the President immediately. He suggested that we wait perhaps an hour before informing the President so that we could have a clearer picture of what it was all about and would be in a position to give the President some facts on the situation. Hal Saunders came in very shortly after I did, and he went to work—I believe Art McCafferty also came in early—putting into some kind of order the flow of facts from ticker and intelligence sources of all kinds.

When I called the President at 4:35 a.m.[3] I remember I simply gave him a straight factual report which he took in with very few questions and no comment. If I am not mistaken, he ended up as he often does

---

[1] Source: Johnson Library, National Security File, NSC Histories, Middle East Crisis, Vol. 3. Top Secret; [*codeword not declassified*].

[2] Reference is to a "Chronology: To 5 June 1200 GMT" that Saunders put together summarizing the reports that were received that morning. A version with Saunders' handwritten insertions is ibid. The final typed version is ibid., Country File, Middle East Crisis, Vol. III.

[3] No other record of this conversation has been found.

any factual report by simply saying, "Thank you." I have in front of me a piece of paper from which I first called the President on Monday, June 5.[4] There are some notes at the top, which would suggest that perhaps I called Evron in the morning to see if he knew anything. I don't think there is any record of that call. I have a note saying that we expect the matter to go quickly to the Security Council. I have a UAR statement which probably reflects some Tel Aviv or Jerusalem ticker, saying that the UAR opened an offensive and Israel was containing that offensive. That was the earlier Israel report. But what I have then is reports by Middle East time: 8:00 a.m.—Cairo—Sirens heard. 8:05 a.m.—Israeli army report—tanks were engaged. 8:22 a.m.—Israeli Defense spokesman statement, I can't now make sense out of. At 9:00, Cairo claims it is attacked. I remember having some trouble about what time it was in Cairo. Daylight saving time threw us off and I don't know whether we ever did get it straight as to whether it was 9:00 or 8:00. There was an hour's difference, as I recall.

Then I go down—I have noted a little more fully there were Tass announcements I guess on the Cairo attack. 8:00, and then there is a more full Israeli account at 9:01, indicating that Cairo has been attacked. Then we got something very important and solid. We got indications from intelligence of a whole series of airfields described by the Egyptians as unserviceable. [Editor's note: NSA chronology suggests this was not available until Rostow's second call to the President.][5] That was the first hard military evidence of what the Israelis were up to. It obviously represented a most purposeful and apparently efficient attempt to move against the UAR airbases. At 9:38 Eastern time we get the Jordanians indicating that the airfields and targets there had also been attacked. Well, in any case, what I just ran through is a picture of what the reports were with the President ending up with the hard information of intelligence that the Israeli airforce was all over the place, taking out UAR and Jordanian airfields. That's the nature of the piece of paper I talked to and what we then had by about 4:35 our time, of which as I say you had essentially some press reports out of Cairo and Israel but hard intelligence indicating a systematic and purposeful and effective attack on Arab airfields.

The log says that I reported to the President again at 6:15[6]—with more facts I would assume. According to the log I spoke with the President three more times—at 6:42, 6:49, and 6:55. I am confident that in the course of these calls the President instructed me to bring in the

---

[4] Not found.

[5] All brackets in the source text.

[6] See Document 152.

following men in the morning to discuss the Middle East crisis: Mr. Dean Acheson, Mac Bundy, Clark Clifford, George Ball. I telephoned all of them, but Ball was in Chicago and we did not ask him to return since the President wanted a meeting that morning.

I decided it was important to have an immediate objective assessment of how the war had begun and who had initiated it on the basis of the intelligence and asked Clark Clifford to come in early and make that assessment as Chairman of the President's Intelligence Advisory Board. Clifford came in, I think about 8:30, although I don't see that in the log. I immediately asked him to work with Saunders on the evidence to form a judgment for the President on who had initiated the war (see attachment).[7]

Aside from just assembling the intelligence, my memory focuses on (1) the President's instructions to assemble these men from outside the Government, (2) initiating on my own the request to Clifford to make the assessment as to the initiation of the war, and (3) the word that the "hot line" was up. That came from McCafferty to me and I believe we informed the President. I suspect at either 7:58 or 8:07. Actually, the word we used for the hot line was MOLINK. And so the first word I had from McCafferty was not that the hot line was "up", but that "MOLINK was up."

Then there was the gathering in the Sit Room to deal with the hot line message which had come in from Kosygin.[8] I note, although I wouldn't have remembered it, that the message was in about 8:15 and reply out by about 8:47. None of the outside men had arrived by that time according to the records.

Just as an illustration of how inadequate memory is, when you called it to my attention this morning, I had forgotten that we issued an early press statement[9] and I may have been involved or not. I simply don't remember. Secretary Rusk may have done it with Christian. It does have in it this thought which had been running through our minds even before the war actually broke out that it was time to shoot not sim-

---

[7] No written report by Clifford on this subject has been found. Saunders wrote in a December 19, 1968, Memorandum for the Record "it soon became very clear that the Israelis had launched a pre-emptive strike, pure and simple. However, it must be remembered that, in those early hours, the first thing the Foreign Liaison Officer of the Israeli Defense Ministry told us (0710 GMT) was that Egyptian armored forces had advanced at dawn and that there was a large number of radar tracks of Egyptian jets moving toward the Israeli shoreline and Negev. We had to deal with this Israeli assertion." (Johnson Library, National Security File, NSC Histories, Middle East Crisis, Vol. 3) Saunders' memorandum states that he asked CIA to produce a paper on the question of who had initiated the war; see Document 169.

[8] Document 156.

[9] See Document 152.

ply for a cease-fire, an attempt to stop the war, but for a solid peace in the Middle East. That had been the thought in our minds as we watched this dreadful crisis, as we watched the tenuous chewing-gum-and-string arrangements of 1967 collapse. We found ourselves nevertheless with the Straits of Tiran closed and with a quite unambiguous Presidential commitment from President Eisenhower on Tiran backed up however by a most uncertain UN arrangement which Secretary General could evade. I think that whole experience forced on us a realization of how precarious were the 1957 arrangements. It was before the war itself that we had come to the conclusion that somehow we had to have something more solid in the Middle East if we were ever to have a secure Middle East, so the thought had been in our minds for some weeks.

My next recollection is of the meeting in the Cabinet Room at 11:36 to 12:45, according to the log.[10] We had Secretaries of State and Defense, Mr. Acheson, Mr. Bundy, Mr. Clifford, Tommy Thompson, George Christian, Luke Battle and myself. I frankly do not recall a great deal about that conversation but I believe it was at that time that Mr. Clifford rendered his initial evaluation of how the war started and—to put no fine point on it—his view was that the Israelis had jumped off on minimum provocation in a very purposeful effort to deal with air power and then go after the UAR armies which of course had assembled in the Sinai. It was his judgment at the time as I recall that it was a straight Israeli decision to deal with the crisis by initiating war, although we were all conscious of the provocations at the Straits of Tiran and mobilization in the Sinai.

I might just say parenthetically that President Johnson has never believed that this war was ever anything else than a mistake by the Israelis. A brilliant quick victory he never regarded as an occasion for elation or satisfaction. He so told the Israeli representatives on a number of occasions. However, at the time, I should say that, war having been initiated against our advice, there was a certain relief that things were going well for the Israelis. In part, because it was an intelligence judgment very carefully canvassed in the previous weeks that the Israelis would win briskly. The sense was that they would win pretty briskly even if the Egyptians had started the war. Also behind that satisfaction was not merely a question of our intelligence being right, but it did look as though we would not be put in a position of having to make a choice of engaging ourselves or seeing Israel thrown into the sea or defeated. That would have been a most painful moment and, of course, with the Soviet presence in the Middle East, a moment of great

---

[10] See Document 163.

general danger. So we did indeed know from these airfield accounts right from the beginning that the most essential military act—the neutralization of the Arab air—had probably gone well for the Israelis.

There was an interesting moment, as I remember it. Mr. Acheson looked back on the whole history of Israeli independence and, in effect, said that it was a mistake to ever create the State of Israel. Mr. Clifford, of course, had been deeply involved in the early US recognition of Israel.

I am reasonably sure that there was discussion of the position we should take at the United Nations Security Council at that meeting. I don't remember a great deal about the rest of the day, although the log says that I was very active and I dare say I was. I don't remember anything about the Cabinet Room meeting later in the day.[11]

Sometime during the day we began an organization of Mac Bundy's role—I think it was the first day but I couldn't be confident. As to the reason why the Bundy Committee[12] was set up, I think that the President wanted to make sure that his staff was fully capable of handling two wars at one time. I think that was the basic problem. He wanted a senior and respected man who knew how the White House, State and Defense worked to operate full time on the Middle East affair. He knew that with all the rest of the things going on in the world, including the war in Vietnam, that I probably could not [handle both]. I fully agreed, for what happens in a situation of war, even so minor a war as the short India–Pak engagement, is that the whole network of international ties which operate in this highly interconnected world get reshaped. In this case we had the Arab states breaking relations with us; we had AID relations falling in; we had Americans in danger in different places; we had the whole UN exercise going on; we had oil and Suez and dealings with the British and other interested parties; and it was just a hell-of-a-lot of business of the most particular kind that had to be monitored.

---

[11] The President met in the Cabinet Room from 6:12 to 6:58 p.m. with Vice President Humphrey, Dean Acheson, McGeorge Bundy, Clark Clifford, Secretaries McNamara and Rusk, Richard Helms, Walt Rostow, and George Christian. Battle, who had been meeting with members of Congress on Capitol Hill, joined them at 6:45 p.m. (Johnson Library, President's Daily Diary) No other record of the meeting has been found.

[12] The Special Committee of the National Security Council, with McGeorge Bundy as Executive Secretary, was established on June 7. Saunders, who served as Bundy's principal staff assistant, wrote in a memorandum of July 16, 1968, that the first main job of the Committee was to provide high-level crisis management during the war and immediately afterward and that the Committee's second achievement, although not envisioned at the time of its creation, was to play a leadership role in establishing the postwar U.S. position. (Ibid., National Security File, Special Committee of the National Security Council, Introduction to the Files of the Special Committee of the National Security Council)

Now the truth was, of course, that we had, I think, two interdepartmental committees centered at State, one at the Under Secretary level and one at the Assistant Secretary level. They were working quite well. When Mac undertook his responsibility, he recognized that we were pretty well staffed up and organized, as indeed we had a duty to be since we had been wrestling with the Middle East crisis short of war for some weeks. Nevertheless, I am sure the President's instinctive judgment was correct that one full-time senior staff man over here to manage this was the course of wisdom. In any case, it worked awfully well. Hal Saunders was assigned to Mac. I was kept fully informed. Mac operated with a great economy of effort, working well and collegially with the interdepartmental committees at State which did the basic staff work and he then handled its presentation to the President. For an improvised effort providing for the bringing in of a new Senior man, I can't imagine anything working more smoothly. I really didn't have any problems with it. It was a great pleasure and it was good to have Mac with us again.

I regret that in that fast-moving day that I don't remember more. It was a day of action and I note that I sent the President at the end of the day a summary based on an Israel Defense Ministry assessment of Arab losses in Mid-East air battles—that was at 9:05.[13] I seem to remember (I would have to check it in my own telephone log) that sometime during the end of the day I called Eppie Evron [Israeli Minister] with whom I had been in close touch on the various matters—a man of diplomatic integrity with whom I had been able to talk most frankly about Middle East problems. I spoke to him and in line with previous conversations told him that, if I were an Israeli official, I would begin to think about peace in the Middle East and about the settlement of the refugee problem and other fundamental problems. To this day, Eppie has always resented it a little in an amiable way that I did not tell him that we had solid information that the Israeli air operations had been successful. He had had a hard lonely weary day about how the war was going and he's always teased me a little that I could have saved him some hours of anxiety if I had shared our intelligence with him.

I don't know when I knocked off in the evening, but it was a tolerably long and memorable day of which I now realize how little one actually remembers.

Harold H. Saunders

---

[13] Rostow forwarded press reports and a map with a covering memorandum that reads: "Mr. President: Herewith the account, with a map, of the first day's turkey shoot." (Ibid., National Security File, NSC Histories, Middle East Crisis, Vol. 3)

150.   Editorial Note

At 5:09 a.m. on June 5, 1967, Secretary of State Dean Rusk telephoned President Johnson. He read a draft message to Soviet Foreign
Minister Andrei A. Gromyko, saying that he thought it was better to
send a message of this sort without waiting until the question of responsibility for the war was clarified. The President agreed. (See Document
157.) Johnson asked Rusk whether it seemed to him "reasonably sure
that these tanks kicked it?" A reference to an Israeli report indicates that
a UAR armored force had initiated the fighting. Noting that the fighting
occurred initially over Egypt, Rusk said it was "a little hard to sort out",
but they had intelligence that five Egyptian airfields in the Sinai were
not operational. He added that he would put more weight on the Israeli
claim that there had been a large number of Egyptian aircraft headed
for Israel from the sea, but he thought it was too early to say. He continued, "My instincts tell me that the Israelis probably kicked this off,
but I just don't know yet. And I don't think we ought to make a preliminary judgment on that because it's just hard to say." Johnson asked
if the Israelis were saying the Egyptians "kicked it off." Rusk replied
that each side was claiming publicly that the other started it but that no
direct message had been received from Eshkol or Eban. He thought the
Israeli claim of a tank advance looked "just a little thin on the surface"
but he thought they would soon have more information. He stated that
the Department had asked U.S. representative on the NATO Council
Harlan Cleveland to keep a group of permanent members available for
consultation, and he noted that the Security Council would meet and
would probably call on both sides for an immediate cease-fire. He
repeated, "My guess is the Israelis kicked this off." He suggested that
they might want to arrange a meeting of the Congressional leadership
to bring them up to date on the situation. Johnson agreed, and the conversation concluded. (Johnson Library, Recordings and Transcripts,
Recording of a telephone conversation between Johnson and Rusk, June
5, 1967, 5:09 a.m., Tape F67.11, Side B, PNO 1) According to the Johnson
Library, the dictabelt, with a June 7 note stating that it might have been
made the previous day, was found with post-Presidential material. The
date and time were taken from the President's Daily Diary. (Ibid.)

151. President's Daily Brief[1]

Washington, June 5, 1967.

Arab States–Israel

Hostilities began early this morning. Both sides report heavy fighting in the air and between armored forces along the Israeli border with Egypt. Israeli planes raided airfields in Cairo and other areas beginning at about 8:00 AM local time (2:00 AM Washington time).

Cairo has just been informed that at least five of its airfields in Sinai and the Canal area have suddenly become "unserviceable." Israel's war plans had put high priority on quick action against the Egyptian Air Force because of the threat to its own more vulnerable airfields and vital centers.

Reports are still fragmentary, but the signs point to this as an Israeli initiative. Over the weekend it became apparent that Israeli leaders were becoming increasingly convinced that time was running against them. The new Israeli cabinet was meeting late yesterday with Ambassador Harmel present, and reconvened early today.

Cairo radio is calling on Egypt's Arab allies to attack Israel. [2 *lines of source text not declassified*]

2. Libya

The big US Wheelus base is becoming more and more exposed to nationalist pressures as the Arab war fever sweeps over this desert kingdom. Cairo is going all out to intensify the pressures, and responsible Libyans are worried; they see no way they can convincingly refute the propaganda that the base is being used to support the Israelis.

The Libyan foreign minister has been in Cairo this weekend, and Wheelus surely must have been discussed during his talks with Nasir.

3. Soviet Union

[1 *paragraph (7 lines of source text) not declassified*]

[1 *paragraph (5-1/2 lines of source text) not declassified*]

[Omitted here is a section on an unrelated subject.]

---

[1] Source: Johnson Library, National Security File, NSC Histories, Middle East Crisis, Vol. 6, Appendix A. Top Secret; [*codeword not declassified*]. This information, which has been excerpted from a Presidential Daily Brief ("PDB"), was improperly declassified and released. The declassification and release of this information in no way impacts or controls the declassification status of the remainder of this PDB, other PDBs, or the PDB as a series.

LATE ITEMS

Libya

The US Embassy in Benghazi flashed word at 4:30 AM EDT that it was being attacked by a large mob. It is burning its papers.

Syria

Damascus radio announces that Syrian planes are bombing Israeli cities and that "we have joined the battle."

---

152.   Editorial Note

At 6:15 a.m. on June 5, 1967, Walt Rostow telephoned President Johnson and read to him a draft Presidential statement Rusk sent to the White House, expressing distress at the outbreak of fighting in the Middle East, noting that each side had accused the other of aggression, stating that the facts were not clear, and calling on all parties to support the UN Security Council in bringing about an immediate cease-fire. Rostow said he had read the statement to McNamara, who approved. The President agreed that the statement was all right. Rostow said that the evidence on who had started the fighting was not definitive, but that there was an interesting report from Cairo of indications of unusual activities in the UAR forces before the first Israeli strike at 9 a.m. Cairo time, including a report that a large number of pilots in uniform had been seen at the Cairo airport at 4:30 a.m. Rostow commented that this was "not much but it's something, the only evidence that this is a UAR put-up job." He added that McNamara was inclined to feel the same way because of the reports, and because he thought a UAR public announcement of the plan to send UAR Vice President Mohieddin to visit the United States would be a "good cover." Rostow reported that Foreign Minister Eban said the Israelis had been attacked and he then gave orders to counter-attack. Rostow said that according to Eban, the Israelis were drafting a message to Johnson that would state Israel had no intention of taking advantage of the situation to enlarge its territory and hoped that peace could be restored within its present boundaries and that the conflict could be localized; in this regard, the message would ask U.S. help in restraining any Soviet initiative.

Rostow returned to the subject of the press statement. The President told him to send it to George Christian, and he would talk to Christian about when to release it. He suggested that McNamara and

Rusk go to Capitol Hill and brief the leadership there rather than having them come to the White House. He also suggested "we might ask some of our good friends that might be helpful to come in from the outside and give us some help here." He told Rostow he thought that "just for public appearance's sake" they should ask former Secretary of State Dean Acheson. He wanted Rostow to ask Rusk and McNamara what they thought of this idea "just on your own without [it] coming from me." In addition to Acheson, Johnson suggested asking former Under Secretary of State George Ball, Chairman of the President's Foreign Intelligence Advisory Board Clark Clifford, and former Assistant to the President for National Security Affairs McGeorge Bundy. He definitely wanted Bundy to come. He wanted Rostow to call Bundy and tell him the President would like to talk to him about this and other matters and "I wish he'd come down here and be prepared to stay as long as he can." (Johnson Library, Recordings and Transcripts, Recording of a telephone conversation between Johnson and Rusk, June 5, 1967, 5:09 a.m. Tape F67.11, Side B, PNO 1) This conversation was on the dictabelt with the earlier Rusk conversation. (See Document 150.) The date and time were taken from the President's Daily Diary.

The press statement, with minor changes and an additional paragraph stating that the President would meet with Rusk, McNamara, Walt Rostow, and George Christian at 8:30 a.m. and that Rusk and McNamara would brief Senate and House leaders, was issued by Christian shortly after 7 a.m. For text, see Department of State *Bulletin*, June 26, 1967, page 949. The report from Cairo to which Rostow referred was transmitted in telegram 8504 from Cairo, June 5. (National Archives and Records Administration, RG 59, Central Files 1967–69, POL 27 ARAB–ISR) The report of Ambassador Barbour's conversation with Eban is in telegram 3928 from Tel Aviv, June 5; ibid.

153. Telegram From the Department of State to the Embassy in Jordan[1]

Washington, June 5, 1967, 6:22 a.m.

208031. Ref: Amman 4055.[2]

You may inform King Hussein there are no U.S. aircraft carriers in or anywhere near area cited reftel and no U.S. aircraft have entered area of present hostilities or any country involved therein.[3]

Rusk

---

[1] Source: National Archives and Records Administration, RG 59, Central Files 1967–69, POL ARAB–ISR. Confidential; Flash. Drafted by Atherton and approved by Davies. Repeated Flash to USUN, and to Rabat, Tunis, London, Moscow, Cairo, Paris, Algiers, Beirut, Damascus, Tripoli, Tel Aviv, Khartoum, Baghdad, Kuwait, Jidda, Jerusalem, CINCSTRIKE, CINCEUR, and COMSIXTHFLT.

[2] Telegram 4055 from Amman, June 5, reported that King Hussein had called all chiefs of mission to meet with him at 0730Z. He told them, "In view of the Israeli aggression against the UAR, Jordan is now at war. Our forces have been put under UAR command." He stated that within the last hour, Jordanian radar had picked up the arrival of 16 aircraft at Israeli airfield Ramat David; 8 had taken off from an aircraft carrier 20 miles west of Tel Aviv and 8 from an aircraft carrier 80 miles west of Tel Aviv. He stated that the Jordanians had not been able to identify the aircraft and did not know if they had participated in the fighting. (Ibid.)

[3] Telegram 050944Z from COMSIXTHFLT to Amman, June 5, stated that during the current Middle East situation, no Sixth Fleet aircraft carriers had been closer than 400 miles to Israel and no aircraft from Sixth Fleet carriers had flown closer than 300 miles to Israel or Sinai. (Ibid.) Telegram 208038 to Amman, June 5, stated that further checks had indicated no British or French carriers in the area cited and suggested that Jordanian radar might have picked up returning Israeli bombers. (Ibid.)

154. Memorandum of Telephone Conversation Between Secretary of State Rusk and the British Ambassador (Dean)[1]

Washington, June 5, 1967, 7:08 a.m.

Telephone Call From British Ambassador Dean

D. has a message from George Brown asking what steps Sec. proposes to take. Sec. said at that moment there will be a strenuous effort in the Security Council—Sec. just had a message that a cease-fire had been agreed to in Jerusalem for 12:00 noon. Sec. said this seems to cancel out a lot of other things we have been working on. D. said B. thought it was a good idea to have an appeal in the name of the SYG to cease hostilities—Sec. said he thought an SC resolution on that could be passed quite quickly. Sec. said we have been in touch with Moscow telling them we were astonished—we thought we had commitments on both sides not to start anything and that we all should get behind the Security Council about a cease-fire. We have no idea who started it— this is still murky and we cannot yet make a judgment.

Sec. called D. back as soon as he hung up. Sec. said he wanted to be sure that George Brown understands we had no inkling of this from either side and that there is nothing behind the scenes that he doesn't know about.

---

[1] Source: National Archives and Records Administration, RG 59, Rusk Files: Lot 72 D 192. No classification marking. Transcribed by Jane M. Rothe.

---

155. Editorial Note

At 7:57 a.m. on June 5, 1967, Secretary of Defense Robert McNamara telephoned President Johnson. He said:

"Mr. President, the Moscow hot line is operating and allegedly Kosygin is at the other end and wants to know if you are in the room in which the receiving apparatus is located. Now, we have a receiving station over here in the Pentagon and you also have a hook-up over in the Situation Room in the White House. My inclination is to say that you— to reply that you can be in the room if he wishes you there within a few minutes. Here is what has come in:

'Dear Mr. President, having received information concerning military action between Israel and UAR, the Soviet Government is convinced the responsibility of all the great powers is to attempt to end the military conflict immediately.' Then the question, 'Are you in the room?'"

Johnson said he could be there in 10 minutes. Then he asked McNamara, "And what, what do you think they'll want to do then?" McNamara paused, then replied, "I don't know. I don't know. I, from this, I think they would want you to indicate that you agree the responsibility of all the great powers is—" Johnson broke in, "We've done that in our message to them, haven't we?" He was referring to Rusk's message to Gromyko (see Document 157), which McNamara had not seen. Johnson then asked about procedures. They agreed that McNamara and Rusk would be at the White House in 20 minutes. (Johnson Library, Recordings and Transcripts, Recording of a telephone conversation between Johnson and McNamara, Tape F67.11, Side B, PNO 3) This conversation was on the dictabelt with the earlier Rusk and Rostow conversations; see Documents 150 and 152. The date and time were taken from the President's Daily Diary. (Johnson Library)

The message (Document 156) was the first substantive message sent on the "hot line," established August 30, 1963, to provide a channel for rapid communication between U.S. and Soviet leaders. Between June 5 and June 10, there were a total of 20 hot line messages. The messages were filed in a notebook kept in the President's desk. (Johnson Library, National Security File, Head of State Correspondence, USSR, Washington–Moscow "Hot Line" Exchange, 6/5–10/67; copies are ibid., NSC Histories, Middle East Crisis, Vol. 7, Appendix G)

None of the outgoing messages include drafting information, and no records were made of the meetings at which they were drafted. According to a memorandum of conversation between McGeorge Bundy and Nathaniel Davis on November 7, 1968, recording Bundy's recollections of the meetings, they were "pretty frenetic, with drafts, redrafts, and more redrafts." Bundy said the President watched the drafts with great care, and Rusk did a great deal of the drafting, especially of the earlier messages. He said there were "no real debates in the hot line meetings in the sense of choosing up sides with one group in favor of this language and another group in favor of that." (Ibid., NSC Histories, Middle East Crisis, 1967, Vol. 7, Appendix G) Some drafts of outgoing messages and variant translations of incoming messages are ibid., Rostow Files, President–Kosygin Correspondence.

156.   Message From Premier Kosygin to President Johnson[1]

Moscow, June 5, 1967, 7:47 a.m.

Dear Mr. President,

Having received information concerning the military clashes between Israel and the United Arab Republic, the Soviet Government is convinced that the duty of all great powers is to secure the immediate cessation of the military conflict.

The Soviet Government has acted and will act in this direction. We hope that the Government of the United States will also act in the same manner and will exert appropriate influence on the Government of Israel particularly since you have all opportunities of doing so. This is required in the highest interest of peace.

Respectfully,

A. Kosygin

---

[1] Source: Johnson Library, National Security File, Head of State Correspondence, USSR, Washington–Moscow "Hot-Line" Exchange, 6/5–10/67. No classification marking. The message is labeled "Translation," with a typed notation that a sight translation was made at 8:05 a.m.; the message was received by the President at 8:15 a.m.; a rough translation was made at 8:30 a.m.; and a final, official translation was provided at 10:08 a.m. There is no indication of the transmission time or time of receipt, but a typed notation on a copy of the message in Russian states that it was transmitted by Soviet Molink at 7:47 a.m. and received by U.S. Molink at 7:59 a.m. According to an English translation attached to the Russian copy of the message, the complete message begins: "The Chairman of the Council of Ministers, Kosygin, wishes to know whether President Johnson is standing by the machine. I would like to convey to President Johnson the following information." (Ibid.)

157.   Message From the White House to Premier Kosygin[1]

Washington, June 5, 1967, 8:15 a.m.

Dear Mr. Kosygin,

Preliminary to President's arrival we are repeating message dispatched earlier from Secretary Rusk for delivery to Foreign Minister Gromyko.[2]

"We are astonished and dismayed by preliminary reports of heavy fighting between Israeli and Egyptian forces. As you know, we have been making the maximum effort to prevent this situation. We were expecting a very high level Egyptian Delegation on Wednesday and we had assurances from the Israelis that they would not initiate hostilities pending further diplomatic efforts. We feel it is very important that the United Nations Security Council succeed in bringing this fighting to an end as quickly as possible and are ready to cooperate with all members of the Council to that end."

---

[1] Source: Johnson Library, National Security File, Head of State Correspondence, USSR, Washington–Moscow "Hot-Line" Exchange, 6/5–10/67. Secret. A typed notation on the source text states it was transmitted by U.S. Molink at 8:15 a.m., and received by Soviet Molink at 8:33 a.m. It is addressed "To Chairman Kosygin, From The White House." A copy addressed "To Comrade Kosygin, Chairman Council of Ministers, USSR, From President of the United States, Lyndon B. Johnson" is ibid., Rostow Files, President–Kosygin Correspondence. According to Llewellyn E. Thompson, the U.S. telegraph operators apparently had asked the Moscow operators the proper way to address Kosygin and were told, "Comrade Kosygin." Ambassador Dobrynin, who had been at the Moscow end of the line, told Thompson afterward that he had been quite startled, and that the Russians wondered if the President was making a joke, or making fun of them in some way. Dobrynin, however, told Thompson he guessed what had happened. (Memorandum of conversation between Thompson and Nathaniel Davis; ibid., NSC Histories, Middle East Crisis, Vol. 7, Appendix G)

[2] The message was sent in telegram 208030 to Moscow, June 5 at 5:25 a.m. (National Archives and Records Administration, RG 59, Central Files 1967–69, POL 27 ARAB–ISR) Chargé John C. Guthrie reported in telegram 5349 from Moscow, received at 9:34 a.m. and passed to the White House at 9:55 a.m., that he had delivered the message to Gromyko, who said the Soviet Government was convinced that the great powers should do everything to end the fighting, expressed certainty that the United States could exert influence on Israel, and stated that the Soviet Union had done and would do everything possible to facilitate the end of the fighting. (Ibid.)

158. Telegram From the Embassy in Israel to the Department of State[1]

Tel Aviv, June 5, 1967, 1205Z.

3935. 1. Following message from Prime Minister to the President has just been handed to me for delivery:

"Dear Mr. President: After weeks in which our peril has grown day by day, we are now engaged in repelling the aggression which Nasser has been building up against us. Israel's existence and integrity have been endangered. The provocative troop concentrations in Sinai, now amounting to five infantry and two armored divisions: the placing of more that 900 tanks against our southern frontier; the massing of 400 tanks opposite Elath with the object of sundering the southern Negev from Israel; the illegal blockade in the Straits of Tiran; the insolent defiance of the international and maritime community; the policy of strangling encirclement of which the first stage was the intimidation of Jordan and the most recent—the placing there of Iraqi troops and Egyptian commando regiments, the imminent introduction of MIG 21 aircraft under Iraqi command in Mafraq; Nasser's announcement of 'total war against Israel' and of his basic aim to annihilate Israel; the order of the day by the Egyptian Commander General Murtagi calling on his troops in Sinai to wage a war of destruction against Israel; the acts of sabotage and terrorism from Syria and Gaza; the recent air encroachments culminating in this morning's engagements and the bombardment by Egypt of Kisufim, Nahal Oz and Tsur Maon in Israel territory—all of this amounts to an extraordinary catalogue of aggression, abhorred and condemned by world opinion and in your great country and amongst all peace loving nations.

As you know, Mr. President, nothing effective had been done or attempted by the UN against a ruthless design to destroy the state of Israel which embodies the memories, sacrifices and hopes of an ancient

---

[1] Source: National Archives and Records Administration, RG 59, Central Files 1967–69, POL 27 ARAB–ISR. Secret; Flash; Nodis. Received at 8:44 a.m. Walt Rostow sent a copy to the President at 10:40 a.m. with a brief memorandum stating that Eshkol "builds his case mainly on the general environment, but refers to bombardment of three Israel towns as the trigger." (Johnson Library, National Security File, NSC Histories, Middle East Crisis, Vol. III) At 11:10 a.m. Rostow sent Johnson telegram 3937 from Tel Aviv, June 5, that reported a meeting among General Amit, Barbour, and Special Counsel to the President Harry C. McPherson, Jr. Rostow's brief covering memorandum commented that Amit's argument was consistent with Eshkol's: that there had been artillery fire on three Israeli villages and UAR air incursions, and then the Israelis had "punched all the buttons." Rostow added, "At least that's his story." (Ibid.) For McPherson's report of his visit to Israel, see Document 263.

people, which in this generation lost 6 million of its people brutally murdered in a tragedy without parallel in history.

Mr. President, I am grateful for the friendship expressed in your letters; for your appreciation of our steadfastness and calm; for your policy of protecting the territorial integrity of Israel and other nations; for your undertaking to provide effective American support to preserve the peace and freedom of Israel and the Middle East; and for your undertaking to pursue vigorous measures to keep the Straits of Tiran and the Gulf of Aqaba open as an international waterway to ships of all nations.

These are impressive commitments. Your letter mentions the obstacles which have so far made action difficult. We rely on the courage and determination of our soldiers and citizens. Indeed maximum self-reliance is the central aim of our national revival. My information is that our defense is reaping success. But our trials are not over and we are confident that our small nation can count on the fealty and resolution of its greatest friend.

We seek nothing but peaceful life within our territory, and the exercise of our legitimate maritime rights.

I hope that everything will be done by the United States to prevent the Soviet Union from exploiting and enlarging the conflict. The hour of danger can also be an hour of opportunity. It is possible to create conditions favorable to the promotion of peace and the strengthening of forces of freedom in the area.

At this critical moment I should welcome the closest consultation between our governments at all levels.

Israel appeals, Mr. President, to your friendship, your fidelity and your leadership."

Barbour

159. Message From President Johnson to Premier Kosygin[1]

Washington, June 5, 1967, 8:57 a.m.

Dear Mr. Kosygin:

I welcome your message. We feel that it is the duty of all great states to secure a speedy end to the military conflict, as indicated in Secretary Rusk's earlier message to Foreign Minister Gromyko this morning. We are strongly supporting action to this end in the United Nations Security Council which meets within the hour and trust you will do the same. I have already made a personal appeal to all the governments in the area concerned and you may be assured we will exercise all our influence to bring hostilities to an end. We are pleased to learn from your message that you are doing the same.

Respectfully,

Lyndon B. Johnson

---

[1] Source: Johnson Library, National Security File, Head of State Correspondence, USSR, Washington–Moscow "Hot-Line" Exchange, 6/5–10/67. Secret. A typed notation on the source text indicates it was approved by the President at 8:47 a.m., transmitted by U.S. Molink at 8:57 a.m., and received by Soviet Molink at 8:59 a.m. The message is addressed "To Chairman Kosygin. From President Lyndon B. Johnson." A copy is addressed "Personal from the President to Chairman Kosygin." (Ibid., Rostow Files, President–Kosygin Correspondence) President Johnson met with Rusk, McNamara, Walt Rostow, and George Christian from 8:17 to 9:25 a.m. in the White House Situation Room. (Ibid., President's Daily Diary) There is no record of the meeting. A draft in Rusk's handwriting with Rostow's handwritten revisions is ibid., National Security File, Rostow Files, President–Kosygin Correspondence.

160.   Telegram From the Department of State to the Embassy in Jordan[1]

Washington, June 5, 1967, 9:49 a.m.

208049. Israeli Representative here asks us to convey earnest desire of his government not do any harm to Jordan. They hope that hostilities between the two countries can be avoided or kept to a minimum.[2]

Rusk

---

[1] Source: National Archives and Records Administration, RG 59, Central Files 1967–69, POL ARAB–ISR. Secret; Flash; Nodis. Drafted and approved by Eugene Rostow and cleared by Battle. Repeated Flash to Tel Aviv and Priority to London, Rome, Brussels, Paris, and The Hague.

[2] Telegram 523 from USUN, June 5, reported that UN Under Secretary Ralph J. Bunche had informed Goldberg of a report by UNTSO Chief of Staff Lieutenant General Odd Bull that he had conveyed an Israeli message to King Hussein that no action would be taken against Jordan unless Jordan started it, in which case Israel would hit back hard. (Ibid., Office of the Executive Secretariat, Middle East Crisis Files, 1967, Entry 5190, Arab-Israeli Crisis, Box 6, Chron, USUN) Telegram 1106 from Amman, August 26, reports that King Hussein told Burns he received two messages from the Israelis on June 5, the first through General Bull that morning, after the Jordanian Air Force had already taken off against Israel, and the second through the U.S. Embassy that evening. (Ibid., RG 59, Central Files 1967–69, POL 15–1 JORDAN)

---

161.   Telegram From the Department of State to the Embassy in Israel[1]

Washington, June 5, 1967, 5:07 p.m.

208222. 1. Under Secretary Rostow called in Israeli Chargé Evron morning June 5. Told him we had had urgent and quite constructive exchanges with Soviets in recent hours. Soviets, while casting no blame on Israel, had urged USG use strongest good offices with Israel to achieve cease-fire. Soviets said they would move in same direction. We told Soviets we knew nothing in advance of hostilities that have broken out, that we would move rapidly as possible to urge cease-fire on all

---

[1] Source: National Archives and Records Administration, RG 59, Central Files 1967–69, POL 27 ARAB–ISR. Secret; Immediate; Exdis. Drafted by Wolle, cleared by Davies and Grey, and approved by Eugene Rostow. Repeated Priority to Amman, Beirut, Cairo, Damascus, London, Paris, Moscow, USUN, Khartoum, Baghdad, Jidda, Kuwait, Algiers, Tunis, Rabat, and Tripoli.

parties in interest of restoring peace. Evron asked if Soviets in these exchanges had commented on their position re Strait of Tiran. Rostow replied they had not.

2. Rostow asked Evron cable GOI soonest urging rapid cease-fire. Evron undertook do so.

3. Queried how hostilities originated, Evron said he had seen Israeli military statements, report of Eban–Barbour conversation, and statement by MinDef Dayan saying UAR armor had moved to cut off southern Negev. He understood radios Damascus and Amman claiming everything is finished and Haifa in flames. Over past 2 or 3 days he had seen Israeli military reports showing further buildup UAR armor in central part of southern border. "That is how it started" said Evron.

4. Rostow noted that Eban told Barbour GOI has no intention taking advantage of situation to enlarge Israeli borders. Evron commented there is no question of this and commented there had been no desire by GOI to change territorial status Sharm el-Sheikh area, where sole issue is free passage.

5. Rostow said would appreciate Evron informing him in greatest possible detail how events of morning had started. USG had great interest in this aspect. Evron undertook do so. He said Israel in position tell how it started because it had received first blow.

6. Evron said DG Israeli Foreign Ministry called in Soviet Ambassador June 5 to tell him what happened. Ambassador took usual line but meeting had not been stormy.

7. Evron said Ambassador Harman due back in Washington afternoon June 5.

Rusk

162.   Circular Telegram From the Department of State to All
        Posts[1]

Washington, June 5, 1967, 4:35 p.m.

208191. 1. Undersecretary Rostow asked Chiefs of Mission of fol-
lowing Arab states call at 10:30 a.m. today: UAR, Syria, Lebanon,
Jordan, Iraq, Kuwait, Saudi Arabia, Sudan, Libya, Tunisia, Morocco,
Algeria, Yemen.

2 Rostow noted that this was a deplorable occasion. Stated he
wished inform Ambassadors of USG position toward events which we
regretted. The outbreak of hostilities represented the failure of diplomacy. USG had been active with all governments directly concerned,
especially the UAR and Israel, using all of our influence to promote
restraint and to prevent the firing of first shot. We had looked forward
to visit of Vice Pres Mohieddin to Washington. We regret that he has
now asked to postpone this visit but are gratified that he has not cancelled it. We welcome him at anytime.

3. Rostow then read full text President's June 5 statement re Middle
East crisis.[2] Rostow continued that this morning a resolution would be
presented in the Security Council[3] containing these three elements: 1)
call upon on governments for cease-fire; 2) call upon all governments to
cooperate with United Nations; and 3) request UNSYG to keep Council
promptly and fully informed.

4. Rostow also asked that all Arab governments give full protection
to US diplomatic establishments and citizens in their countries. We had
received disturbing reports from some cities of riots. We hoped that all
governments would take adequate and effective measures protect
American lives and property.

5. UAR Ambassador Kamel, as dean of diplomatic representatives
present, responded by agreeing that this was a deplorable and sad situation. Kamel then read from message from UAR Foreign Office accusing Israel of having fired first shot and trying deceive world opinion.
Kamel continued that Israel attacks on third country shipping in Suez
Canal indicated Israel's desire drag third parties into conflict. Kamel

---

[1] Source: National Archives and Records Administration, RG 59, Central Files
1967–69, POL 27 ARAB–ISR. Confidential; Immediate. Drafted by Bergus, cleared by
Battle and Assistant Secretary of State for African Affairs Joseph Palmer II, and approved
by Eugene Rostow.

[2] See Document 152.

[3] The UN Security Council met in emergency session on the morning of June 5, but
no resolution was introduced.

said that Arabs had stated they would not start hostilities. Arabs had kept their word. Arabs had also felt that whatever differences had existed, normal channel for their solution was U.N.; hence they had participated in the Security Council's deliberations. Arabs felt that Israelis starting hostilities while matter was before Security Council was dangerous action because it was an affront to the United Nations Charter. Kamel noted Arabs had appealed to USG time after time to use its influence to restrain Israel. Israel had now begun shooting. The Arabs would defend themselves. Kamel said the Israelis have proved they did not respect the UN Charter or the effort of the Security Council and had destroyed diplomatic efforts that USG and Arabs were making. Kamel asked rhetorically whether USG believed that imminent arrival UAR Vice Pres was a sign of hostility or a signal that UAR wished intensify diplomatic efforts.

6. Kamel also upbraided leading US newspapers as well as Senators and Congressmen for their constant repetition of theme that "time was working against Israel." Such behavior could only be interpreted as either encouragement or endorsement of Israeli attack.

7. Kamel referred to visits to US of Lebanese and Iraqi FonMins and visit of UNSYG to Cairo. There had been no time to reap the fruit of any of these efforts.

8. Kamel stated Arab diplomats were unable to respond to USG appeal for cease-fire as they un-instructed. However, Arabs had been attacked and they were defending themselves.

9. As to protection of US citizens and property in Arab countries, Kamel said Arab governments would do their utmost to respect and protect Americans, not only because of requirements of international law but because the Arabs are a hospitable and dignified race. He admitted that some mistakes could take place but all ambassadors present would immediately appeal to their governments to redouble their efforts.

10. In response Rostow said that we had tried over last weeks to put train back on track. Arab states knew USG's good intentions. US wanted to be friends to all the people in the Near East and this would remain our desire. We supported the territorial integrity and political independence of all the states in the area. This policy had redounded to benefit Egypt in 1956 and Lebanon in 1958. Thus we pursued an even-handed doctrine.

11. Mr. Rostow stated he had heard with interest UAR Ambassador's charge that Israel had begun hostilities and we would like to study any documentation on this point which Arab states may wish to bring to our attention. This was an important, if not decisive, subject in the context of the rule of law and supremacy of the United

Nations. The most important thing before us now was a cease-fire. As President Johnson had said, we wished to see "end to fighting and a new beginning of programs for peace and development of the area." We were aware of difficulties such problems as Aqaba. The best of lawyers could disagree on such problems. Our efforts to resolve these problems by peaceful means had failed but they must and would be resumed.

12. Kamel warned that Israel was doing its utmost to bring US in on its side. He urged US not to become a third party. All Arabs would be watching US action, direct and indirect, open or behind scenes in this regard. Kamel stated other "friendly powers" would also be watching,

13. Rostow stated that we had pursued even-handed policy in dispute based on two main elements: 1) the international character of the Gulf of Aqaba and 2) our opposition to aggression. USG was not involved in deplorable events but had only tried to prevent them.

14. Kamel urged, view postponement Mohieddin visit, that President Johnson receive Arab ambassadors to clarify USG policy for them.

15. Kuwaiti Ambassador Al-Ghoussein raised Palestine problem. Said he hoped USG would give this serious thought in hope that permanent solution might now be achieved. Rostow replied that more permanent and lasting solution was desire of all of us.

Rusk

163. Memorandum Prepared by the Assistant Secretary of State for Near Eastern and South Asian Affairs (Battle)[1]

Washington, June 5, 1967.

ACTION ITEMS RESULTING FROM MEETING AT WHITE HOUSE
JUNE 5, 1967

At the meeting with the President this morning, he expressed the desire for the following steps to be taken:

1. He wishes to have an assessment of various Embassies in key countries with respect to the current positions of governments to which they are accredited concerning the current Middle East crisis. He would like to know the best estimate of the likely position these countries will take on, among other things, the Maritime Declaration if we decide to move forward with it.

2. He would like to be sure that USIA is given guidance on the proper handling of its output and that we be looking carefully at the matter of what we say to the press at this point. He does not believe there should be anything more than his statement on the record but endorsed the idea of Secretary Rusk having a backgrounder the latter part of this afternoon. He wanted to be sure that news programs in the States were monitored carefully and that we tried to correct misstatements contained within them. He mentioned particularly the tendency to link Vietnam to the Middle East crisis implying in various ways that we had to choose between these two problems and would have to limit our activity in one place or the other to meet the needs of both.

3. He wishes to see us endorse what I am told is a call by the Pope to make Jerusalem an open city.

---

[1] Source: National Archives and Records Administration, RG 59, Office of the Executive Secretariat, Middle East Crisis Files, 1967, Entry 5190, Box 16, State Memos. Secret. Rusk's initials appear on the memorandum indicating that he read it. Marginal notations indicate the persons to whom action on the various items was assigned. The meeting was held in the Cabinet Room from 11:36 a.m. to 12:45 p.m. Those present were the President, Acheson, Battle, Rusk, Thompson, Bundy, Clifford, McNamara, Walt Rostow, and George Christian. (Johnson Library, President's Daily Diary) No other record of the meeting has been found. Bundy recalled later that the meeting was "mainly concerned with the awful shape we would be in if the Israelis were losing. We didn't really know anything about the situation on the ground. When, in the course of that day, it became apparent that the Israeli Air Force had won, the entire atmosphere of the problem changed. It was in a way reassuring when it became clear that the fighting was the Israelis' idea and that the idea was working. That was a lot better than if it had been the other way around." (Memorandum of conversation, November 7, 1968; cited in Document 155.) See also Document 149.

4. The President wants to be sure we have looked into the oil problems related to the Middle East. It was agreed that we need a "Mr. Oil" in the U.S. Government. The fact that Mr. Walter Levy has been available to us is known and appreciated, but the consensus of the meeting appeared to be that "Mr. Oil" should come from within and should be available full time and indefinitely.

5. We must look into the question of what we do if the Israelis ask us for spare parts or resupply of arms during coming days.[2]

I suggest that S/S assign action responsibility for the various items listed above. Perhaps the Secretary would like to see a copy of this list of action items, and he should be reminded that he has agreed to have some kind of backgrounder this afternoon.

At the conclusion of the meeting, the possibility of a further meeting tonight was mentioned although neither time nor the list of those to attend was decided upon.

RRD

---

[2] A June 5 memorandum from Walt Rostow to the President states that the point he had wished to make that morning was: "if we are pressed by Israel for spare parts, etc., we should go hard to the Russians on their equivalent supply to the Arabs." (Johnson Library, National Security File, NSC Histories, Middle East Crisis, Vol. III)

---

164. Editorial Note

At the Department of State press briefing at noon on June 5, 1967, a reporter asked Department spokesman Robert J. McCloskey if he would reaffirm that the U.S. position was neutral. McCloskey replied: "Indeed, I would: I would be more than happy to. We have tried to steer an even-handed course through this. Our position is neutral in thought, word, and deed." The reporter asked, "Do you feel we can continue to maintain a neutral position, no matter what happens in the Middle East?" McCloskey replied, "That will be our effort." (Memorandum from Joseph Califano to the President, June 5; Johnson Library, Appointment File, June 1967, Middle East Crisis)

Special Assistant to the President Joseph Califano called Secretary Rusk at 4:25 p.m. to tell him McCloskey's statement was "killing us with the Jews in this country" and to ask if Rusk could "swamp McCloskey with a statement of his own." Rusk replied that he might be able to say something at his background press briefing at 5 p.m., but that what was meant was that the United States was not a belligerent and its citizens in the area were entitled to the privileges and immunities of citizens of a neutral country. It did not mean the United States did not have a deep concern for the situation and was not working hard in the Security Council to find solutions. (Notes of telephone call from Califano, June 5; National Archives and Records Administration, RG 59, Rusk Files: Lot 72 D 192, Telephone Calls) Attorney General Ramsey Clark and Califano called Rusk at 4:45 p.m. to discuss the matter further. Clark expressed concern that the Neutrality Act might compel the President to issue a neutrality proclamation, which would be "unthinkable." They agreed that Rusk should emphasize that the thrust of U.S. policy was to restore peace in the area and to bring about a cease-fire. (Notes of telephone call from Clark and Califano, June 5; ibid.; Memorandum from Califano to the President, cited above) In a statement released to the press later that day, Rusk referred to President Johnson's May 23 statement reaffirming the U.S. commitment to the support of the independence and territorial integrity of all the nations of the Near East. He stated that the United States was not a belligerent in the current fighting but that this did not mean indifference; the United States was making a maximum effort in the Security Council to bring about a cease-fire. In response to a question, he stated that the U.S. Government had not made any determination as to who had initiated the violence. (Department of State *Bulletin*, June 26, 1967, pages 949–950)

---

165. Minutes of the Tenth Meeting of the Middle East Control Group[1]

Washington, June 5, 1967, 5 p.m.

Decisions

I. Policy on Arms Shipments and Economic Aid

It was agreed:

1. *Arms Shipments*

a. The subject of arms shipments should be kept under constant review by the Control Group.

---

[1] Source: National Archives and Records Administration, RG 59, Office of the Executive Secretariat, Middle East Crisis Files, 1967, Entry 5190, Box 17, Minutes/Decisions of the Control Group, Folder 1. Secret; Nodis. No drafter nor participants are listed in the minutes. A memorandum of the meeting by Hoopes is in Washington National Records Center, RG 330, ISA Files: FRC 76–140, A/I/S, 2–12-6, 1967 Crisis Special File.

b. For the time-being, end items which have left the depots should be permitted to proceed.

c. The possible supply of A4Es and a Hawk battery to Israel will remain under review.

d. Press guidance should be formulated indicating that (1) arms shipments are being carefully reviewed and (2) end items which have left the depots are being permitted to proceed.[2]

2. *Arms Negotiations*

a. Negotiations of arms agreements with Morocco, Libya, Saudi Arabia and Iran should be delayed for at least the next 48 hours.

b. Henry Kuss would be instructed not to sign new agreements with NE countries without specific authorization.

3. *Food Assistance*

a. PL–480 food shipments should not be halted.

b. Practical delivery problems to the immediate area of the conflict will probably foreclose shipments until peace is restored.

4. *Economic Aid*

a . Shipments of end items for on-going projects should continue.

b. No new project agreements should be concluded until the legal ramifications of the conflict are clarified and a policy decision to proceed has been made. Instructions to this effect should be sent to pertinent posts.

II. Instructions to US Carriers

It was agreed:

1. The question of issuing instructions to US carriers operating into the Near East is to be carefully staffed-out and a report submitted to the Control Group.

2. The FAA should be requested to permit the five chartered Flying Tiger flights to proceed with military end items for Israel. In view of the dangers to direct flights into Israel, the material should be off-loaded at an agreed trans-shipment point; such as Rome.

---

[2] At its June 6 meeting, the Control Group adopted the following guidelines for arms shipments to Near East countries with which the United States had diplomatic relations: arms shipments under government-to-government agreements, grant or sale, that had left the depots would not be impeded; existing Munitions Control licenses would be reviewed; all new government-to-government requests and all new requests to Munitions Control would be subject to careful review; and the Israeli request for 143 used half-track personnel carriers, 25 A4Es, and a Hawk battery would remain under review. No new licenses were to be issued and shipments under approved licenses were to be blocked to countries that had broken relations with the United States. (Minutes of eleventh Control Group meeting; National Archives and Records Administration, RG 59, Office of the Executive Secretariat, Middle East Crisis Files, 1967, Entry 5190, Box 17, Minutes/Decisions of the Control Group, Folder 1)

III. Evacuation Plans

It was agreed:

1. Existing instructions to posts should be carefully reviewed and up-dated as necessary.

2. The Task Force should review the evacuation problem in each Near East Country and submit specific recommendations to the Control Group in respect to each.

IV. UN Situation and Outlook

Having received a report on the situation and outlook in the UN,

It was agreed:

The Task Force should submit tomorrow preliminary proposals for a ceasefire and peace settlement. The assistance of Julius Holmes should be sought.

V. Maritime Declaration

It was agreed:

1. Consultations should continue with appropriate governments about the problem addressed by the Maritime Declaration.

2. A current assessment of the number of governments prepared to endorse a Maritime Declaration under the changed conditions which now prevail should be submitted to the Control Group.[3]

VI. Evacuation of UNEF and UNRWA from Gaza

While noting the request of the Brazilian Embassy for assistance in evacuating the Brazilian UNEF contingent, it was agreed that the responsibility for this unit rests with the UN. The matter is to be referred to the Secretary General by IO.

VII. Miscellaneous

It was agreed:

1. The Task Force assisted by CIA should submit to the Control Group an assessment of Israeli military and political objectives, noting that they may be extensive.

2. An assessment of the Wheelus Field situation is to be prepared by ISA and submitted to the Control Group.

VIII. Contingency Planning for Viet-Nam Fuel Requirements

Mr. Vance informed the Control Group that contingency contacts for fuel supplies for Viet-Nam will be signed in a few days. In view of the difficulty in obtaining storage facilities in Taiwan and Japan, additional tankers will have to be reserved under charter.

---

[3] At its June 6 meeting the Control Group decided to suspend operations pertaining to the Maritime Declaration. (Ibid.)

166.   Memorandum From the President's Special Assistant
        (Rostow) to President Johnson[1]

Washington, June 5, 1967, 5:45 p.m.

Mr. President:

Our first thought is that the key to ending the war is how well the Israelis do—or don't do—on the ground. Up to a point this is correct; but it is not wholly correct because what the Israelis are after is not some abstract military victory, but a settlement which, if possible, insures that this will not happen again in another 10 years. Therefore, our behind-the-scenes work with the Russians and others should consist not merely in negotiating a cease-fire; because a cease-fire will not answer the fundamental questions in the minds of the Israelis until they have acquired so much real estate and destroyed so many Egyptian planes and tanks that they are absolutely sure of their bargaining position.

Therefore, we should begin in New York or elsewhere, talking with the Russians and, if possible, with the Egyptians and others about the terms of a settlement:

—Eilat open to oil;
—observers on both sides of the line;
—a Soviet commitment to work with us to damp down the arms race;
—a turn in the road on refugees;
—a Middle East development bank that would bring the Iranians and Turks into the diplomacy of the area; etc.

So long as the war is roughly moving in Israeli's favor, I believe we can shorten it by getting at the substance of a settlement at the earliest possible time.

Walt

---

[1] Source: Johnson Library, National Security File, Country File, Middle East Crisis, Vol. III. Secret. A handwritten notation on the memorandum indicates it was received at 5:50 p.m.; a handwritten "L" indicates it was seen by the President.

167.   Memorandum of Telephone Conversation Between the Representative to the United Nations (Goldberg) and Secretary of State Rusk[1]

June 5, 1967, 8 p.m.

TELEPHONE CALL FROM AMB GOLDBERG

G said he had seen Fedorenko. (Sec said he would have others with him listen.) G said they came close to our formulation. G said they were meeting in 20 minutes. He read the draft resolution, indicating the bracketed portions were what Goldberg would add:

"The Security Council, gravely concerned at the outbreak of hostilities and with the menacing situation in the area, having [considered the report][2] and heard the statement of the Secretary General on the developments in the area (1) calls upon the governments concerned to take the necessary measures for an immediate cease-fire and prompt withdrawal, without prejudice to the respective rights, claims or position of anyone, of their armed personnel behind the armistice lines [and to take other appropriate measures to insure disengagement of forces and to reduce tension in the area]; (2) requests the Secretary General to keep the Council promptly and currently informed about the situation."

G said he had told Fedorenko that if we were going to have withdrawal, we should have it. Sec suggested saying "avoid use of violence in the area." Sec asked what about unconditional cease-fire? G thinks we could get "unconditional". He didn't know how our Israeli friends would like that. Sec said we wanted to be sure we had a case. G said we got "prompt withdrawal" not "immediate withdrawal". The Israelis have a frigid attitude toward any declaration supporting withdrawal. Sec asked about the Straits problem and what the Egyptians could do. G said this doesn't decide the Straits question; their prior formulations did. G said "prompt withdrawal" was a plus. Sec said there were 2,300 UNEF still on the ground. G said he didn't know how much longer we could stand against a unanimous resolution. He said Israelis were out to get Nasser. G said he had been very frank. Sec said if Rafael[3] got rough, let him know the US has its own position and its own responsi-

---

[1] Source: National Archives and Records Administration, RG 59, Rusk Files: Lot 72 D 192, Telephone Calls. No classification marking. The notes of the conversation were prepared in the Secretary's office. Rusk was in Washington; Goldberg was in New York.

[2] These and following brackets are in the source text.

[3] Israeli Representative at the United Nations Gideon Rafael. For his recollections of these events, see *Destination Peace: Three Decades of Israeli Foreign Policy: A Personal Memoir* (New York: Stein and Day, 1981).

bilities and we didn't know what was going to happen this morning. G said politically the price for settlement was that the Gulf be opened. Sec said resolution wouldn't settle the matter. It provides a base for a beginning. Sec said to see what he could do along these lines.

(Katzenbach, Sisco, GRostow, McCloskey present.)

168. Telegram From the Department of State to the Embassy in the United Kingdom[1]

Washington, June 5, 1967, 11:09 p.m.

208406. Ref: State 202732.[2] For the Chargé—You should transmit following message dated June 5, from the President to the Prime Minister:

Dear Harold:

I appreciate your comments[3] on the unfortunate developments in the Near East. We had feared that someone might feel compelled to strike. We had no advance indication that a decision had been taken.[4] We believed, in fact, we had at least a clean week for diplomacy.

---

[1] Source: National Archives and Records Administration, RG 59, Central Files 1967–69, POL 27 ARAB–ISR. Secret; Immediate. The telegram indicates the text was received from the White House. It was approved for transmission by Walsh; the message conveyed in the telegram was apparently drafted by Walt Rostow.

[2] The reference is in error; telegram 202732 to London, May 26, transmitted the text of Prime Minister Wilson's May 25 message to the President (Document 62).

[3] A message from Prime Minister Wilson to President Johnson, delivered to Rostow during the 11:30 Cabinet Room meeting, noted that in their last talk on June 2, "you expressed your sombre belief that war between Israel and the Arabs could not be avoided, despite the efforts we had been making and discussing together earlier that day." Wilson urged, "What we need is a clear demand from the Council for a cease-fire: after which a fresh attempt to thrash out a longer term settlement might be made." Wilson thought that since it was unlikely that the Security Council would be able to agree, members would need to plan for other possible contingencies, underlining the importance of their meeting the previous week. He added, "I am indeed glad that you and I were able to go over the ground so exhaustively so that, in this situation of confusion and uncertainty, we at least are clear in our minds about each other's attitude." (Johnson Library, National Security File, Head of State Correspondence File, UK, Vol. 6, PM Wilson Correspondence)

[4] In an earlier draft the two preceding sentences read: "We had feared that the Israelis might feel compelled to strike, but we had had no advance indication from them that they had actually taken a decision to do so in the face of what they judged to be further Arab provocations." Walt Rostow sent the revised draft to the President for "one more look", noting that he had changed the first paragraph "so that we did not put flatly into the record a judgment that Israel had kicked this off from a standing start." Johnson approved the revised draft. (Johnson Library, National Security File, NSC Histories, Middle East Crisis, Vol. 3)

Arthur Goldberg has had a difficult time in the Security Council. Like you, we had hoped for a quick cease-fire resolution. But we have had to deal with a determined effort to have the Council call for a withdrawal of forces in terms which would legitimize Nasser's action at the Strait of Tiran a subject on which we have both taken unequivocal positions.

We have done everything we could to get an even-handed Security Council pronouncement. We shall work with your people in New York to encourage helpful UN action. If the Soviets, and the French, are more forthcoming than they have been, both of us will want to build on that development to work toward a satisfactory settlement.

Meanwhile, I hope we can keep in closest touch as the military situation develops and put the best minds available to both of us to work on the contingencies that may arise and the constructive possibilities that may unfold.

I think you know the deep satisfaction I derived from our discussions.

Sincerely,

Lyndon B. Johnson

Rusk

---

169. Memorandum Prepared in the Central Intelligence Agency's Office of Current Intelligence[1]

Washington, June 5, 1967.

SUBJECT

The Arab-Israeli War: Who Fired the First Shot

1. An analysis of presently available information suggests that Israel fired the first shots today. The Israelis, however, claim they were responding to a movement by Egyptian air and armored forces

---

[1] Source: Johnson Library, National Security File, Country File, Middle East Crisis, Situation Reports. Top Secret; [codeword not declassified]. The memorandum was not prepared on letterhead and bears no drafting information, but a copy bears the handwritten notation "CIA/OCI memo." (Ibid., NSC Histories, Middle East Crisis, Vol. 3) See footnote 7, Document 149.

"toward" Israel which they interpreted as an attack. Cairo says flatly that Israel attacked Egypt.

2. The Egyptian army's foreign liaison officer informed the US Defense Attaché in Cairo that Israel started raiding the Suez Canal Zone and El-Arish Airfield in northeastern Sinai at 9 a.m. Cairo time (2 a.m. EDT). An announcement on the Israeli army radio service at 9:05 Cairo time (2:05 EDT) said the Israeli army was clashing with an Egyptian armored force "moving toward Israel." An Israeli army spokesman later announced that the Egyptians had "opened an air and land attack." He said Egyptian armored forces moved at dawn "toward" southern Israel and that Israeli forces "went out to meet them." He also said that Egyptian jet aircraft were seen on radar "coming toward the country's shores," and that a similar air movement was occurring along the Sinai border. Air clashes developed, he added, when Israeli planes flew to meet them.

3. Israeli Foreign Minister Eban told Ambassador Barbour that Egyptian ground forces began the fighting by shelling Israeli border villages. An official Israeli report passed to the US Embassy, however, said Egypt's 4th armored division plus a mobile task force had teamed up "with the apparent intention" of striking across southern Israel toward Jordan. The report said Israel armored forces had moved to engage the Egyptian armor, and that Israel had attacked Egyptian airfields.

4. [9 lines of source text not declassified]

170.   Telegram From the Department of State to the Embassy in
        Jordan[1]

Washington, June 6, 1967, 2:53 a.m.

208420. Ref: Amman 4084.[2]

For Tel Aviv.

You should immediately impart information Amman's 4080 to
highest available level Israeli Government urging that Israel agree
immediately take steps move toward cease fire with Jordan imparting
information either through UNTSO or USG channel. You should urge
strongly slackening of attacks against Jerusalem while efforts to bring
about cease fire proceed. Information paras one and two Amman's 4084
may be used. Immediate offer to accept Pope's appeal that Jerusalem be
considered open city by both sides might provide basis for mutual cease
fire Jerusalem and environs. We urging this on Jordan.[3]

For Amman.

Inform King Hussein actions being taken and urge similar actions
by Jordan. Our understanding has been Israel willing respond to
restraint by Jordan. We have asked Israelis to slacken off and urge
Jordan to take all possible steps make this possible. In strongest terms
urge acceptance open city appeal. You should urge Hussein publicly
rebut canard re aircraft carriers.[4]

Rusk

---

[1] Source: National Archives and Records Administration, RG 59, Central Files 1967–69,
POL 27 ARAB–ISR. Secret; Exdis; Flash. Drafted by Davies; cleared in substance by Houghton,
and approved for transmission by Robert D. Yoder of the Operations Center. Also sent Flash to
Tel Aviv and repeated Flash to Cairo, Beirut, Damascus, Jerusalem, Baghdad, Kuwait, Jidda,
and USUN.

[2] Telegram 4080 from Amman, June 6, reported that King Hussein had advised the
Embassy that unless the Israelis stopped their attack on Jordan immediately, Jordan and his
regime would be finished. He said Jordan had no offensive capability and its army was in the
process of destruction, and there was fighting in Jerusalem, endangering the Holy Places. He
asked the U.S. Government to arrange an immediate cease-fire. (Ibid.) Telegram 4081 from
Amman, June 6, reported that the King had not said "cease-fire" but rather "I must have immediate end to the violent attacks." (Ibid.) Telegram 4084 from Amman, June 6, reported that the
King could not afford to accept a unilateral cease-fire; he wanted a decrease in punitive destructive actions. He wanted to reduce his own military effort but could not do so unless the Israelis
responded. (Ibid.)

[3] Barbour reported in telegram 3953 from Tel Aviv, June 6, that he had passed to the highest level Israeli authorities the U.S. position as instructed in telegram 208420. (Ibid.)

[4] At 7:40 a.m., Radio Cairo began broadcasting the charge that U.S. aircraft had participated in Israeli attacks and air defense and that King Hussein had given Nasser evidence of this.
(Telegram 8565 from Cairo, June 6; ibid.) Telegram 4086 from Amman, June 6, reported that after
hearing the broadcast, the Embassy had contacted King Hussein, who said he had made no such
statement. The Embassy had been informed that the report was given to Nasser by the UAR
Commander of the Jordanian Army, Lieutenant General Abdul Munim Riyadh. (Ibid.)

171.   Telegram From the Department of State to the Mission to
the United Nations[1]

Washington, June 6, 1967, 4:06 a.m.

208426. 1. Cairo radio has made false charge US aircraft provided fighter cover over Israel during raids by Israeli aircraft on UAR June 5, and played role against Jordanian forces.[2] Charges are absolutely false. No US aircraft carriers have been in or near area of hostilities nor have US aircraft.[3]

2. You should categorically deny charge at highest level and issue public denial. Both State and Defense Departments have already issued denials.[4]

Rusk

---

[1] Source: National Archives and Records Administration, RG 59, Central Files 1967–69, POL 27 ARAB–ISR. Unclassified; Flash. Drafted by Houghton, and approved by Davies. Also sent Flash to Damascus, Rabat, Khartoum, Tunis, Baghdad, London, Kuwait, Tripoli, Jidda, Algiers, Paris, Beirut, Moscow, Amman, Jerusalem, and Cairo.

[2] See footnote 4, Document 170, and Document 153 and footnotes 2 and 3 thereto.

[3] Telegram 208427 to USUN, June 6, states that at 3:45 a.m. the Department had denied the charges and protested vigorously to Ambassador Kamel, requesting immediate action to terminate the broadcasts. (National Archives and Records Administration, RG 59, Central Files 1967–69, POL 27 ARAB–ISR) Nolte had already telephoned the Foreign Minister to give him a categorical denial that U.S. planes or ships were involved in any way in the fighting, and Political Counselor Richard B. Parker had given a categorical denial to Abdul Aziz in Mohieddin's office. (Telegrams 8567 and 8569 from Cairo, both dated June 6; both ibid.)

[4] A press release issued by the Department of Defense on June 5 stated that reports that Sixth Fleet aircraft had flown to Israeli airfields or had participated in the conflict were erroneous; all Sixth Fleet aircraft had been and remained several hundred miles from the area of conflict. (Telegram 208283 to Amman, June 5; ibid.) Secretary Rusk stated at the White House at 9:05 a.m. on June 6 that the charges were "utterly and wholly false." He also stated, "We know that they and some of their friends know where some of our carriers are. We can only conclude that this was a malicious charge, known to be false, and, therefore, obviously was invented for some purpose not fully disclosed." (Circular telegram 208457, June 6; ibid.; Department of State *Bulletin,* June 26, 1967, pp. 950–951)

172. President's Daily Brief[1]

Washington, June 6, 1967.

1. Arab States–Israel

Cairo may be prepared to launch a campaign urging strikes against US interests in the Arab world. Both Egyptian and Syrian domestic broadcasts this morning called on the "Arab masses" to destroy all US and "imperialist" interests in the "Arab homeland." Last night Cairo radio claimed it had proof of US and British participation in the "aggression."

Demonstrations have now taken place against US embassies and installations all over the Arab world.

Arab oil-producing countries, meeting in Baghdad, say they will stop selling oil to any country which takes part in or supports Israel in the fighting. Baghdad radio said this morning that the pumping of Iraqi oil has been stopped "because of US and UK attitudes."

In the fighting, Israel has gained an early and perhaps overwhelming victory in the air, but the progress of the war on the ground is unclear. If Israeli claims regarding damage to Arab combat aircraft are valid, they have destroyed the entire Jordanian inventory of 21, two thirds of the Syrian inventory of 69, and 250 of some 430 Egyptian planes.

Arab counterclaims of 158 Israeli planes destroyed seem grossly exaggerated, but actual losses to the Israeli force of about 270 aircraft are not known.

Firm information on ground action remains sparse. The Israelis claim they have captured the "outer positions" of Kuntilla in southeastern Sinai and reached the outskirts of al-Arish in northern Sinai.

In Jordan, King Husayn said this morning that Israel is pushing ahead in a "punitive fashion." He ended with a plea that the US intercede.

---

[1] Source: Johnson Library, National Security File, NSC Histories, Middle East Crisis, Vol. 6, Appendix A. Top Secret; [*codeword not declassified*]. Regarding the release of this PDB, see footnote 1, Document 151.

173.   Message From Premier Kosygin to President Johnson[1]

Moscow, June 6, 1967, 5:34 a.m.

Dear Mr. President,

Military activities in the Near East continue, moreover their scope is spreading.

The Soviet Government is convinced that a decisive demand for an immediate cease-fire and the withdrawal of troops behind the armistice line would be in the interests of re-establishing peace. We express the hope that the Government of the United States will support the stated demand in the Security Council. We are supporting it.

Everything possible should be done so that positive decision be taken today on this matter by the Security Council.

Respectfully,

A. Kosygin

---

[1] Source: Johnson Library, National Security File, Head of State Correspondence, USSR, Washington–Moscow "Hot-Line" Exchange, 6/5–10/67. No classification marking. The source text is labeled "Translation," with a typed notation indicating a sight translation was made at 5:50 a.m.; the message was received by the President at 5:50 a.m.; a rough translation was made at 5:54 a.m.; and a final, official translation was provided at 6:23 a.m. A typed notation on a copy of the message in Russian states that it was transmitted by Soviet Molink at 5:34 a.m. and received by U.S. Molink at 5:43 a.m. (Ibid.)

174. Telegram From the Department of State to the Embassy in Israel[1]

Washington, June 6, 1967, 8:55 a.m.

208438. Amman's 4095.[2] You should inform GOI of Jordanian desire for immediate cease-fire and urge GOI that it would be in their interest to make necessary arrangements immediately and directly rather than through UN. This would split Jordan off from other Arab states. It may be preferable that cease-fire remain secret temporarily if King is to maintain control.[3]

Rusk

---

[1] Source: National Archives and Records Administration, RG 59, Central Files 1967–69, POL 27 ARAB–ISR. Secret; Flash; Exdis. Drafted by Under Secretary of State Katzenbach and approved for transmission by Deputy Executive Secretary Herbert B. Thompson. Repeated Flash to Amman.

[2] Telegram 4095 from Amman, June 6, reported that King Hussein had asked the British, French, U.S., and Soviet Ambassadors to arrange a cease-fire, either acting unilaterally or through the United Nations. He said UAR Commander of the Jordanian Army General Riyadh, (Lieutenant General Munim Riyadh), told him he had three alternatives: cease-fire, military evacuation of the West Bank, or continued fighting with loss of the West Bank. When Burns returned to the Embassy, the Prime Minister called to say without an immediate cease-fire, they would be unable to maintain law and order in Jordan. (Ibid.)

[3] Telegram 3967 from Tel Aviv, June 6, reported that Barbour had passed the message to the Prime Minister and had urged Israeli acceptance, arguing the need to end the bloodshed. Barbour commented that because of Jordan's initiation of hostilities in Jerusalem and attacks on civilian areas, it was probably too late to arouse any Israeli interest in preserving King Hussein's regime. (Ibid.)

175.   **Message From President Johnson to Premier Kosygin[1]**

Washington, June 6, 1967, 10:21 a.m.

Mr. Kosygin,

We continue to believe that the fighting in the Near East should be stopped as soon as possible. We were disappointed that the UN Security Council lost a full day yesterday in its effort to call for a prompt cease-fire. I understand that our representatives in the Security Council will be discussing this matter further this morning. The matter is urgent.

I was puzzled, Mr. Chairman, by what has been said by the Soviet Press and Radio since our exchange of messages yesterday morning. It does not help to charge the United States as a participant in aggression, especially when our only role has been to press for restraint at every step of the way.

I know you are not responsible for Cairo. But you should know that we were astounded that Cairo, just a few hours ago, alleged that U.S. carrier aircraft had participated in attacks on Egypt. This wholly false and obviously invented charge has led to attacks on our representatives in various Arab localities in violation of the most elemental rights of legation. Since you know where our carriers are,[2] I hope you can put Cairo right on this matter and help us eliminate that kind of needless inflammation.

We have expressed to your government our views on the Strait of Tiran in my letter to you of May 28 and Secretary of State Rusk's letter to Foreign Minister Gromyko of the same date.[3]

In this personal exchange I should like to emphasize one point which goes beyond general principles about international rights of passage through narrow waters. President Eisenhower, in 1957, was faced with the problem of obtaining the withdrawal of Israeli forces from Sinai. In pressing for a withdrawal which was earnestly desired by Egypt, President Eisenhower committed the United States to international pas-

---

[1] Source: Johnson Library, National Security File, Head of State Correspondence, USSR, Washington–Moscow "Hot-Line" Exchange, 6/5–10/67. Secret. A typed notation on the source text indicates it was approved by the President at 10:03 a.m.; it was transmitted by US Molink at 10:21 a.m. and it was received by Soviet Molink at 10:43 a.m. The President met with Vice President Humphrey, Rusk, McNamara, Katzenbach, Bundy, Walt Rostow, Clark Clifford, and Llewellyn Thompson from 6:40 to 8:54 a.m. in the White House Situation Room. (Ibid., President's Daily Diary)

[2] Telegram 61037Z from COMSIXTHFLT to CINCUSNAVEUR stated that Soviet ships had been shadowing the U.S. carriers in the Mediterranean constantly since June 2 and could confirm that the U.S. carriers had remained at least 200 miles from Egypt, Syria, and Israel. (National Archives and Records Administration, RG 59, Office of the Executive Secretariat, Middle East Crisis Files, 1967, Entry 5190)

[3] Documents 88 and 90.

sage of the strait. President Nasser's declaration of May 22 that he would close the strait runs squarely into a commitment we undertook while supporting Egypt, quite apart from our interests as a maritime nation.

In conclusion, Mr. Chairman, I suggest that we both do our best to obtain prompt action by the Security Council. The Resolution, submitted by Ambassador Goldberg to Ambassador Fedorenko last night,[4] meets the points raised in your communication to me, as well as the realities discussed above. We earnestly hope you can give it your support.

For your convenience, the key paragraph in this Resolution is the following:

"Calls upon the Governments concerned to take the necessary measures for an immediate cease-fire and prompt withdrawal, without prejudice to the respective rights, claims or position of anyone, of their armed personnel behind the Armistice Lines, and to take other appropriate measures to ensure disengagement of forces, to refrain from acts of force regardless of their nature, and to reduce tension in the area."

Respectfully,

Lyndon B. Johnson

---

[4] Goldberg reported his 9 p.m. meeting with Fedorenko in telegram 5632 from USUN, June 6. (National Archives and Records Administration, RG 59, Central Files 1967–69, POL 27 ARAB–ISR/UN)

---

176. Memorandum From the President's Special Assistant (Rostow) to President Johnson[1]

Washington, June 6, 1967, 11 a.m.

Mr. President:

Arthur Goldberg called this morning to tell me he had received a telephone call from Jerusalem from Chief Justice Agranat. (They entered the Chicago bar the same year.) The message is via Goldberg to you from Prime Minister Eshkol. There are two points.

---

[1] Source: Johnson Library, National Security File, NSC Histories, Middle East Crisis, Vol. 3. No classification marking. A handwritten notation on the memorandum indicates that is was received at noon, and a handwritten "L" indicates the President saw it.

1. Eshkol "hopes you understand" the action taken by Israel; that it resulted from a judgment that their security situation had so deteriorated that their national existence was imperiled.

2. Eshkol strongly hopes that we will take no action that would limit Israeli action in achieving freedom of passage through the Gulf of Aqaba. They understand your difficulties in achieving this result; and are prepared to handle the matter themselves.

I shall, of course, make this message available to Secretaries Rusk and McNamara. We should be back with a recommendation about the second point later in the day.

Walt

---

177. Telegram From the Department of State to the Embassy in Lebanon[1]

Washington, June 7, 1967, 10:40 p.m.

209151. Following based on uncleared memcons[2] FYI Noforn and subject revision.

1. Secretary and Under Secretary Rostow separately received Foreign Minister Hakim of Lebanon morning June 6. Following points made in addition to those made with Pachachi (State 206672):[3]

2. Secretary and Mr. Rostow made it clear that Egyptian reports involving US aircraft in fighting were completely unfounded. They said they were deeply disappointed that diplomacy had failed and hostilities had broken out and that they were working desperately for cease fire. Hakim said Israel would have to withdraw to positions it occupied prior to present hostilities for cease fire to hold. Mr. Rostow said this might be arranged if UN presence returned to Sharm el Sheikh. Mr.

---

[1] Source: National Archives and Records Administration, RG 59, Central Files 1967–69, POL 27 ARAB–ISR. Secret; Exdis. Drafted by David L. Gamon (NEA/ARN), cleared by Davies and Houghton, and approved by Eugene Rostow. Repeated to Baghdad, Jidda, Dhahran, Tel Aviv, London, Paris, and USUN. According to Rusk's Appointment Book, the meeting took place at 11 a.m. on June 6. (Johnson Library)

[2] Memoranda of these conversations are in the National Archives and Records Administration, RG 59, Central Files 1967–69, POL 27 ARAB–ISR.

[3] See footnote 2, Document 132.

Hakim believed Nasser could not give up his right to exercise sovereignty over Strait of Tiran, although way in which he exercised this might be negotiable. As practical matter, oil tankers represented only difficulty and, Hakim claimed, other routes could be used at relatively little increase in cost to Israel.

3. Foreign Minister said Arab-American friendship might be one of first victims of "Israeli aggression". The Arabs were convinced that only in event of Israeli military success would the US be non-belligerent, but that the US would intervene on the side of Israel if the Arabs were to gain the upper hand. The Arabs were united in their anger and humiliation and determined some day to bring an end to Israel as an aggressive, militaristic state. The Israelis might win a victory now, Hakim said, but it was time they started thinking about their future in the Arab world, which would depend ultimately on their reaching a modus vivendi with the Arabs. With the help of Soviet arms and their own growing population and economic power, the Arabs would ultimately redress past wrongs.

4. Secretary and Mr. Rostow stressed their determination achieve cease fire, but that USG could not alter its position re international character of Strait.

Rusk

---

178.   Telegram From the Embassy in the United Arab Republic to the Department of State[1]

Cairo, June 6, 1967, 1640Z.

8618 1. Called at 6:30 this evening to FonMin for meeting with El Feki. He announced "withdrawal of recognition" by UARG of USG. No time limit put on exodus, continuation of administrative section under friendly power permitted. Nes and Bartos will pursue details with Chief of Protocol later this evening.

---

[1] Source: National Archives and Records Administration, RG 59, Central Files 1967–69, POL 17 US–UAR. Confidential; Flash. Passed to the White House, DOD, CIA, USIA, NSA, COMAC, and CINCSTRIKE at 11 p.m.

2. Basis of withdrawal is US air support for Israel in current hostilities, not only initially, but "replacing Israeli losses as they occur" according to Cairo Radio.[2]

3. Thus endeth my meteoric mission to Cairo.

4. Request designation of protecting power immediately.

Nolte

---

[2] Battle met with Ambassador Kamel at 2:30 p.m. on June 6 and stated in the "strongest terms" that there was no truth to the UAR charges. He expressed regret that the UAR Government had chosen to break relations on such a charge and stated that the United States would treat the UAR and its diplomatic representation on a reciprocal basis. (Telegram 208613 to Cairo, June 6; ibid., POL 17 US–UAR) Algeria, Syria, Iraq, Sudan, and Yemen also broke relations with the United States on June 6. Documentation is ibid., POL 17 US–ALG and equivalent files.

---

179.   Memorandum From Nathaniel Davis of the National Security Council Staff to the President's Special Assistant (Rostow)[1]

Washington, June 6, 1967.

SUBJECT

The Situation in New York—Tuesday, June 6, 1:15 p.m.

Ambassador Goldberg met with friendly Security Council members this morning and then with Fedorenko. He found Fedorenko wanted a resolution which called for an immediate cease-fire and withdrawal behind the Armistice line—but *without* our language: "without prejudice to respective rights, claims or the position of anyone," and without our language about refraining from acts of force regardless of their nature (which the Russians interpret as an attempt to undo the blockade of the Straits of Tiran).

Fedorenko has now gone back to Moscow for further instructions and the next Goldberg–Fedorenko meeting is scheduled for 3:00 or 3:30.

---

[1] Source: Johnson Library, National Security File, NSC Histories, Middle East Crisis, Vol. 3. Confidential. Rostow sent this memorandum to the President at 4 p.m. with a covering memorandum commenting: "If the Israelis go fast enough, and the Soviets get worried enough, a simple cease-fire might be the best answer. This would mean that we could use the de facto situation on the ground to try to negotiate not a return to armistice lines but a definitive peace in the Middle East." A copy was sent to Saunders.

Tabor hopes to be in a position to reconvene the Security Council by 4:30, but there is no assurance of that. (The Ticker has a story it will not be before 6: 00 p.m.)

Gideon Rafael, the Israeli Representative, has made clear he takes exception to some of our resolution language, and his Government will maintain a "frigid attitude" toward it. What Israel wants is a simple cease-fire. (This was our original position yesterday—and obviously in Israeli interest in light of their gains.)

Fedorenko saw Seydoux, the French Representative, after talking with Goldberg. Foreign Minister Eban of Israel is expected in New York this afternoon.

The continuing delay in convening the Security Council is very much in Israel's interest so long as Israeli forces continue their spectacular military success. We shall undoubtedly be accused of stalling. In point of fact we are not, and the Russians are contributing to the delay more than we are. The Russians suffer a genuine disadvantage in having slower and more distant communications than we do. They have shown signs of trying to adjust their position to the changing situation on the ground in the Mid-East, but their adjustments have not caught up with the deteriorating position of their allies—as of the moment at least. The result is that the hours go by. The delay serves Israel, damages the Soviet position and still further discredits the United Nations.

ND

180.　Editorial Note

The President held his weekly luncheon meeting from 1:25 to 3 p.m. on June 6, 1967, with Secretary Rusk, Secretary McNamara, George Christian, and Walt Rostow. (Johnson Library, President's Daily Diary) No record of the discussion has been found. The agenda prepared by Rostow for the meeting listed the Middle East as the first topic of discussion, with "Jordan," "Oil," and "Forward planning and strategy" as subtopics. Rostow's handwritten notes on his copy of the agenda indicate that they discussed the creation of the NSC Special Committee, which was announced on June 7. The words "Cuba missile crisis" are followed by the names "Mac," "Clark," and "Dean." This is followed by a list of names, led by "DR, chair," and "MB[undy], ex sec." The words

"Oil Dictator" appear next to the name "Arthur Dean," with "Gene Black" written underneath. Below are the words "Canal" and "oil." The words "UN observer" appear with the word "carriers" underneath. Battle's and McCloskey's names appear with the note, "Tighten rein." The words "think out" are attached to "Forward planning and strategy." Notes on an attached page include the words "Arthur Dean—oil—Gene Black?" and the name "Levy" (oil expert Walter Levy). The notations "UAR" and "Algeria" suggest that the news that both countries had broken relations was received at the meeting. (Ibid., National Security File, Rostow Files, Meetings with the President, January–June 1967)

Iraq, Kuwait, and Algeria announced the suspension of oil deliveries to the United States and United Kingdom on June 6. A Conference of Oil Ministers from Kuwait, Saudi Arabia, Libya, Algeria, the UAR, Syria, Lebanon, and representatives from Bahrain, Qatar, and Abu Dhabi declared in a June 5 communiqué that Arab oil should be denied to countries committing aggression or participating in aggression against any Arab state, including any armed attack by any country in support of Israel, and that the direct or indirect involvement of any country in armed aggression against the Arab states would make the assets of its companies and nationals inside the territories of the Arab countries subject to the laws of war. The text of the communiqué is in airgram A–804 from Baghdad, June 6. (National Archives and Records Administration, RG 59, Central Files 1967–69, POL 27 ARAB–ISR) For related documentation, see the compilation on the 1967 oil embargo in *Foreign Relations, 1964–1968*, volume XXXIV, Documents 228–268.

181. Memorandum From Nathaniel Davis of the National Security Council Staff to the President's Special Assistant (Rostow)[1]

Washington, June 6, 1967.

SUBJECT

The Situation in New York, Tuesday, June 6 at 5:15 p.m.

Goldberg and Fedorenko met a few minutes ago. Goldberg pressed our understanding that our resolution would provide for free passage of the Straits of Tiran. Fedorenko demurred—particularly if this understanding were to be explicit. Goldberg then proposed a cease-fire and "steps toward withdrawal." Fedorenko didn't like that.

Fedorenko then suggested returning to Tabor's original resolution. This called for an immediate cease-fire and cooperation with the UN to put the cease-fire into effect. Fedorenko objected to the UN machinery aspect.

Goldberg finally suggested a resolution which calls upon the governments concerned, as a first step, to take forthwith all measures for an immediate cease-fire and for a cessation of all military activities in the area.[2] (This last reference to all military activities could apply to the Straits.)

Fedorenko and Goldberg agreed to a quick referral of this language to their governments.

Goldberg and Fedorenko are scheduled to meet again within the next fifteen minutes to confirm their agreement if possible.[3] The Soviet attitude has shifted further in light of military action on the ground, and they are now pressing hard for UN action as soon as possible to stop the fighting.

If we and the Soviets can agree on language, Hans Tabor, the President of the Security Council, must then consult other members whose noses are somewhat out of joint because of the long delay and the focus of the discussions between the Big Two. The Security Council is scheduled to meet at 6:30 p.m. (It will probably convene at least half an hour late.)

ND

---

[1] Source: Johnson Library, National Security File, Country File, Middle East Crisis, Vol. IV. Confidential.

[2] Transmitted in telegram 5638 from USUN, June 7. (National Archives and Records Administration, RG 59, Central Files 1967–69, POL 27 ARAB–ISR/UN)

[3] New York has just called, confirming agreement. [Footnote in the source text. Goldberg reported on his three June 6 meetings with Fedorenko in telegram 5644 from USUN, June 7. (Ibid.)]

182. Message From Premier Kosygin to President Johnson[1]

Moscow, June 6, 1967, 6:07 p.m.

Dear Mr. President,

We have considered your proposals. We have issued the necessary instructions to the Soviet Representative in the Security Council. We express the hope that you will also issue corresponding instructions to your representative about the adoption today of resolutions concerning the immediate cessation of military actions with the withdrawal of troops behind the armistice line.

Respectfully,

A. Kosygin

---

[1] Source: Johnson Library, National Security File, Head of State Correspondence, USSR, Washington–Moscow "Hot-Line" Exchange, 6/5–10/67. No classification marking. The source text is labeled "Translation," with a typed notation indicating a sight translation was made at 6:12 p.m.; the message was received by the President at 6:15 p.m.; a rough translation was made at 6:17 p.m.; and a final, official translation was provided at 6:38 p.m. A typed notation on a copy of the message in Russian states that it was transmitted by Soviet Molink at 6:07 p.m. and received by U.S. Molink at 6:10 p.m. (Ibid.)

183. Message From President Johnson to Premier Kosygin[1]

Washington, June 6, 1967, 8:23 p.m.

Mr. Kosygin:

Our two Ambassadors in the Security Council have been in close consultation throughout the day. We understand that our Ambassadors agreed to a very short resolution calling for a cease-fire as a first step. We authorized our representative to agree on behalf of the United States Government. The Security Council has just adopted this resolution unanimously.[2] We shall do our best to assist the Security Council's further efforts to restore peace in the Near East on a lasting basis.

I trust we can work together in the days ahead to help solve the problems before us in the Near East and elsewhere.

Respectfully,

Lyndon B. Johnson

---

[1] Source: Johnson Library, National Security File, Head of State Correspondence, USSR, Washington–Moscow "Hot-Line" Exchange, 6/5–10/67. Secret. A typed notation on the message indicates it was approved by the President at 7:45 p.m., it was transmitted by US Molink at 8:23 p.m., and it was received by Soviet Molink at 8:28 p.m. The President met in the Situation Room from 6:29 to 7:15 p.m. with Rusk, McNamara, Thompson, Katzenbach, Bundy, and Walt Rostow. (Johnson Library, President's Daily Diary) Thompson recalled later that during the 8 hours that had elapsed since Johnson's message that morning (Document 175), Fedorenko had agreed to a simple cease-fire, that is, according to Thompson, "to a resolution Kosygin now wanted to get away from." Thompson recalled some discussion in the Situation Room whether they should take advantage of Fedorenko's agreement to a simple cease-fire or stick to the terms of Johnson's earlier message. He thought they would have been prepared to accept the earlier formulation, but everyone agreed they should "take advantage of what had happened in New York." See Document 245.

[2] Resolution 233 (1967); the text is printed in Department of State Bulletin, June 26, 1967, pp. 947–948. The key negotiations at USUN on June 5 and 6 leading to the adoption of the resolution are summarized in telegram 5740 from USUN, June 15. (National Archives and Records Administration, RG 59, Central Files 1967–69, POL 27 ARAB–ISR/UN)

184.   Telegram From the Department of State to the Embassy in France[1]

Washington, June 6, 1967, 9:34 p.m.

208743. Ref: Paris 19726[2] and 19871.[3]

1. Begin FYI. For variety of reasons we prefer hold up on previously-authorized sale of remaining 143 half-tracks to Israel at this sensitive time. While sale unlikely to alter military arms balance in current hostilities there could be political risks in associating US with transaction of "visible" military hardware at this moment. We intend however to keep issue under review. End FYI.

2. You should find pretext which not related to Middle East crisis to delay acting on Israeli request.

Rusk

---

[1] Source: National Archives and Records Administration, RG 59, Central Files 1967–69, DEF 19–8 US–ISR. Secret; Priority; Limdis. Drafted by Political-Military Adviser Colonel Edgar J. Fredericks (NEA/RA); cleared in substance by Davies, Director for Operations Joseph J. Wolf (G/PM), and Director of Foreign Military Rights Affairs Philip E. Barringer (DOD/ISA), and in draft by Atherton; and approved for transmission by Sober.

[2] Telegram 19726 from Paris, June 2, reported that U.S. military authorities had asked the Embassy about the previously approved sale to Israel of 200 half-track personnel carriers, 57 of which had been sold and delivered and the remaining 143 of which were in French military depots and were yet to be sold. Unless it was otherwise instructed, the Embassy planned to inform the U.S. military that the vehicles should be sold. (Ibid.)

[3] Telegram 19871 from Paris, June 5, stated that the Israeli purchasing mission was pressing hard for the sale of the personnel carriers and that in view of the outbreak of hostilities, the Embassy was advising U.S. military authorities not to complete the sale pending instructions from Washington. (Ibid.)

---

185.   Telegram From the Department of State to the Embassy in Israel[1]

Washington, June 6, 1967, 9:41 p.m.

208748. For the Ambassador from the Secretary.

1. I believe that the GOI must look to its own interest in the Arab world. The presence of Jordan and the King has been a stabilizing influ-

---

[1] Source: National Archives and Records Administration, RG 59, Central Files 1967–69, POL 27 ARAB–ISR. Secret; Flash; Nodis. Drafted by Battle and approved by Rusk.

ence which I do not believe the Israelis should lightly see go down the drain.

2. I hope you will find a way to suggest most forcefully to the Israelis that they arrange in the aftermath of the Security Council resolution an immediate cease-fire at least de facto with Jordan.[2] I leave to you the nature of the approach and caution you that we do not want to get in a position of trying to direct Israeli tactics, particularly military ones. In the light of unfounded charges of the last couple of days, any such implication would be dangerous indeed. I do, however, think you may be able carefully to handle this as a matter in interest to the Israelis (to say nothing of our own).

Rusk

---

[2] Telegram 4112 from Amman, June 6, received at 9:40 p.m., reported that Jordanian Prime Minister Juma had telephoned to request U.S. good offices in advising the Israelis that the Jordanian Government desired an immediate cease-fire. (Ibid.) Telegram 208784 to Tel Aviv and Amman, June 6, instructed the Embassy in Tel Aviv to convey this information to the Israeli Government and instructed the Embassy in Amman to inform the Prime Minister and express the hope that the Jordanian Government could notify the United Nations officially at an early date of its acceptance of a cease-fire. (Ibid.)

---

186.   President's Daily Brief[1]

Washington, June 7, 1967.

1. Arab States–Israel (As of 5:30 AM EDT)

At this point, the shooting continues despite the UN ceasefire resolution. Early this morning Israeli planes were hammering Jordanian positions outside Jerusalem. There also was some firing in the city last night.

The Israelis appear to hold substantial portions of the Sinai Peninsula, and Cairo is ordering the Egyptian force at Sharm ash-Shaykh on the Straits of Tiran to withdraw. In fact, there are strong indications that the Egyptians may be withdrawing most, if not all, of their forces from the Sinai.

---

[1] Source: Johnson Library, National Security File, NSC Histories, Middle East Crisis, Vol. 6, Appendix A. Top Secret; [*codeword not declassified*]. Regarding the release of this PDB, see footnote 1, Document 151.

Although the Soviets are airlifting in some spare parts for Egyptian tanks and aircraft, there are no indications of any major Soviet military moves.

[6 *lines of source text not declassified*]

In last night's Security Council meeting, Fedorenko demanded withdrawal of forces after a ceasefire, but this performance seems intended to put the best face possible on the retreat. [6 *lines of source text not declassified*]

The US Embassy in Cairo was not set on fire as reported in this morning's *Washington Post*.

---

187.   Telegram From the Department of State to the Embassy in Jordan[1]

Washington, June 7, 1967, 7:46 a.m.

208800. 1. FYI. In response our urgings they cease fire Israelis have answered to effect JAA still fighting all along the line. Most importantly, shelling of Jerusalem from Mar Ilias has not stopped, and heavy fighting going on Nablus–Toubas area. Israelis believe either King or Government no longer in control or are deliberately following tactic of deception. Latter conclusion Israelis believe supported by fact Hussein still apparently talking about secret rather than open cease-fire.[2] End FYI. You should inform Hussein we strongly urging Israelis cease-fire

---

[1]   Source: National Archives and Records Administration, RG 59, Central Files 1967–69, POL 27 ARAB–ISR. Secret; Flash. Drafted and approved by Deputy Assistant Secretary for Near Eastern and South Asian Affairs Stuart W. Rockwell and cleared by Rusk. Repeated Flash to Tel Aviv.

[2]   Barbour reported this Israeli response in telegram 3976 from Tel Aviv, June 7. He reported that Eshkol's views on Jordan were along the same lines as Rusk's and that Eshkol would lay Rusk's position before the Cabinet when it met that day, but that Israeli information did not jibe with that reflected in recent telegrams from Amman. He commented that if the Jordanians were serious in wanting a cease-fire and if the King and the government were able to make the cease-fire stick, the most effective thing they could do would be to stop shelling Jerusalem, which was especially important to the Israelis and where damage had been great. (Ibid.) Telegram 4119 from Amman, June 7, reported that the Jordanian Foreign Minster had told the British, French, and Soviet Ambassadors that although Jordan had ordered its army to cease firing as of 2400Z, the Israeli army was continuing to attack Jordanian locations on the West Bank; he appealed to the four powers to exert every influence with Israel to end the attacks. (Ibid.) Telegram 4121 from Amman, June 7, reported a similar appeal from King Hussein. (Ibid.)

but they state JAA still fighting, and that shelling of Jerusalem from Mar Ilias continuing. If true we urge JAA cease fire totally and especially that attacks on Jerusalem be stopped in order reinforce our efforts, which being undermined by continuing JAA firing.

2. If Jordan has not formally notified SC of its acceptance cease-fire you should urge it to do so.

3. *For Tel Aviv:* Inform GOI of action we taking in Amman and reiterate our concern for cessation of hostilities with Jordan.

Rusk

---

188. **Message From Premier Kosygin to President Johnson**[1]

Moscow, June 7, 1967, 8:18 a.m.

Dear Mr. President,

According to available information, Israel is ignoring the Resolution of the Security Council, summoning all governments concerned to take as a first step all measures towards an immediate cease-fire and cessation of all military actions in this area.

Such a situation calls for the Security Council to use its authority to guarantee the implementation of its own decision.

In this connection, we have proposed an immediate reconvening of the Security Council to take effective measures for an immediate cessation of military actions and the re-establishment of peace.

Respectfully,

A. Kosygin

---

[1] Source: Johnson Library, National Security File, Head of State Correspondence, USSR, Washington–Moscow "Hot-Line" Exchange, 6/5–10/67. No classification marking. The message is labeled "Translation," with a typed notation indicating a sight translation was made at 8:29 a.m.; the message was received by the President at 8:34 a.m.; a rough translation was made at 8:36 a.m.; and a final official translation was provided at 9:20 a.m. A typed notation on a copy of the message in Russian states it was transmitted by Soviet Molink at 8:18 a.m. and received by U.S. Molink at 8:23 a.m. (Ibid.)

189.   Memorandum From the President's Special Assistant
(Rostow) to President Johnson[1]

Washington, June 7, 1967, 9:50 a.m.

Mr. President:

Herewith some thoughts as of this morning.

I. *The Israeli Situation and Bargaining Position.* It looks as though, with the assistance of Arab delay in implementing the Security Council resolution, the Israelis will end up controlling the west bank of the Jordan river, the whole Jerusalem area, and the whole of the Sinai Peninsula, including the east bank of the Suez Canal. They will also have in their hands the administrative control of perhaps two-thirds of the Arab refugees, depending on how many flee the west bank. Depending a bit— but not much—on whether and how fast the Soviet Union is prepared to replace Arab aircraft and tank losses, the Israelis for the moment are in a position to dominate militarily the region, including a capacity, if necessary, to move across the Suez Canal to the west bank.

II. *The Arab Situation.* The Arabs initially decided to turn down the Security Council cease-fire resolution. It is unclear exactly what they have in mind. It is possible that they may accept it shortly and are merely trying to appear for the moment not excessively eager or hasty. But it is also possible that they may be trying to maintain Arab unity on the Baghdad pledge of the oil-producing powers; that is, to deny pro-Israel western nations mid-East oil. Having lost in the field, Nasser may be trying to preserve something of his position and leadership by using the leverage of oil, pressure on other Western economic interests, and possibly the use of the Suez Canal.

III. *The Central Issue.* The struggle now moving from the battlefield to economic pressure and politics is probably this: whether the settlement of this war shall be on the basis of armistice arrangements, which leave the Arabs in the posture of hostilities towards Israel, keeping alive the Israel issue in Arab political life as a unifying force, and affording the Soviet Union a handle on the Arab world; or whether a settlement emerges in which Israel is accepted as a Middle Eastern state with rights of passage through the Suez Canal, etc.

IV. *U.S. Objective.* The U.S. objective is evidently to try to move from the present situation to as stable and definitive a peace as is possible.

---

[1] Source: Johnson Library, National Security File, Country File, Middle East Crisis, Vol. IV. Secret. A handwritten "L" on the memorandum indicates the President saw it. Copies were sent to Rusk, McNamara, McGeorge Bundy, and Clark Clifford.

This will require Israeli concessions—as well as important moves by others—on the refugee issue. It also involves:

—A transition from the present Arab radical mood towards that of Arab moderates.
—Probably a larger Middle Eastern role for Turkey and Iran.
—Regional arms control arrangements, optimally to be worked out within the region itself.
—The beginnings, at least, of systematic regional cooperation in economic development, including, perhaps, a regional plan for development of water resources.
—The emergence of a spirit of regional pride and self-reliance to supplant the sense of defeat and humiliation engendered in the Arab world in the wake of the failure of Nasser, his strategy, and his ideological rhetoric.

V. *First Tactical Moves.* It is obvious that if the result we wish to achieve is to be brought about, by definition it requires the U.S. to be in a position of quietly stimulating and encouraging the Middle Eastern forces which might wish to move in this direction but not appearing to dominate or dictate the solution. In an only slightly lesser degree, this is also true for the United Nations. The UN role should be to set a framework within which these things become possible but not to become excessively involved in detail. U.S.-USSR understandings, quietly achieved, could play an important role in this outcome; but, as during these days, it is clear that the outcome in our interest is directly contrary to Soviet strategy over the past years; they have suffered a setback of the first order of magnitude; and they will only react in ways consistent with our interests if the political forces on the spot, as well as the military situation, leave them no other realistic alternative.

In the light of this assessment, here are some initial possible tactical moves:

—Quiet discussions with the Israelis about the concept of a definitive Middle Eastern settlement along the lines in paragraph III, above.
—Quiet approaches to, say, President Sunay,[2] the Shah, the King of Morocco, President Bourguiba,[3] suggesting this approach.
—Quiet beginnings of discussions with moderate Arabs along these lines, as opportunity offers. In this connection, men like Eugene Black, Robert Anderson, Raymond Hare, Kermit Roosevelt might be helpful.
—Encouragement of arrangements which tend to split the Arab world, e.g., a Jordan-Israeli cease-fire; the revival of U.S. diplomatic relations with one or another Arab state to break the solidity of the bloc; efforts to break one or another Arab oil-producing state out of the Baghdad understanding; etc.

---

[2] Turkish President Cevdet Sunay.
[3] Tunisian President Habib Bourguiba.

—A willingness to broaden the mandate of Jack Valenti's mission to the whole field of water in the Middle East—or the assignment of, say, Eugene Black to some such enterprise as a supplement to Jack's present mission.

At the heart of this approach, however, is a broad and imaginative movement by Israel on the question of refugees. The Johnson plan is a good initial base; but they, we, and others ought to get at this fast. They will—and should—make acceptance of these arrangements contingent on a general peace settlement; but they should move quickly, from their present position of strength and political unity in Israel, to an explicit willingness to play their part in a refugee settlement.

Walt

---

190.   **Memorandum From the President's Special Assistant (Califano) to President Johnson**[1]

Washington, June 7, 1967, 10:15 a.m.

Abe Fortas called and asked me to pass along two points to you:

1. He thought you should refrain from getting into the "neutrality" issue any more, particularly through an argument on the Neutrality Act. He believes we have taken care of that issue with the American-Jewish community and he has deep reservations about the applicability of the Neutrality Act to this situation.

2. He believes that once there is a cease fire, the United States should not try and draw up blueprints for restructuring the Middle East. His view is that we should let the Israelis and Arabs negotiate this out, and save ourselves until the last half of the ninth inning in the negotiations.

With respect to the second point, Abe believes the post-cease fire situation is going to be the trickiest from the viewpoint of domestic

---

[1] Source: Johnson Library, National Security File, Name File, Califano Memos. No classification marking. The President looked at the memorandum in Califano's office around 10:45 a.m. and told Califano to talk to Bundy about it "confidentially." (Johnson Library, President's Daily Diary)

politics as well as international politics. He indicated that he would like to talk to you at some point about this, but he does not want to bother you.

---

191.   Telegram From the Embassy in Jordan to the Department of State[1]

Amman, June 7, 1967, 1408Z.

4125. Ref: Deptel 208001.[2]

1. Hussein, as we reported twenty-four hours ago, is prepared to have open cease fire.

2. For past several hours Radio Amman has been announcing GOJ acceptance of cease fire. Israelis monitor these broadcasts and thus have no basis to assume GOJ still desires secret cease fire.

3. GOJ formally notified Security Council of its acceptance of cease fire early this morning through El-Farra.

4. Israeli suggestion that King deliberately following tactic of deception hardly supportable. Israeli military intelligence well aware Jordanian losses. IDF briefings to DATT Tel Aviv have covered losses in detail.[3]

5. There is possibility King and government not in communication with all JAA units. However, should Israelis be sincerely prepared for cease fire we assume that, particularly in Jerusalem area, way could be found to use receptive government radios to announce cease fire at set time.

6. I recognize IDF goal may well be total destruction of Jordanian army. I consider that JAA destruction, if achieved, would have disastrous effects on this regime and on area stability as whole. I am gravely concerned about resultant effects on public order and on safety large American community still in Kingdom.

---

[1]   Source: National Archives and Records Administration, RG 59, Central Files 1967–69, POL 27 ARAB–ISR. Secret; Flash. Repeated to the White House and Tel Aviv. Received at 10:57 a.m. Passed to DOD, CIA, USIA, NSA, COMAC, and CINCSTRIKE, and USUN at 11:15 a.m.

[2]   Reference is apparently to Document 187.

[3]   A number of telegrams reporting such briefings are in the National Archives and Records Administration, RG 59, Central Files 1967–69, POL 27 ARAB–ISR.

7. For all these considerations I consider it imperative we spare no effort to arrange this cease fire. Jordanians willing follow any formula we may suggest to achieve this. I respectfully urge that President telephone PriMin Eshkol to bring cease fire into effect soonest.[4]

Burns

---

[4] Howard Wriggins of the NSC staff sent copies of this telegram and telegram 4127 from Amman to Walt Rostow at 3:40 p.m., with a brief memorandum recommending that the President send an urgent message to Eshkol. Attached were a draft memorandum from Rostow to the President and a draft Presidential message to Eshkol. Rostow apparently did not forward the proposal or the telegram. (Johnson Library, National Security File, NSC Histories, Middle East Crisis, Vol. IV) Telegram 4127 from Amman, June 7, reported that Chief of Staff Khammash had advised the Embassy that Jordanian units in the Jerusalem area were cut off and subject to heavy bombardment, that the Jordanian army was trying to evacuate the West Bank, and that withdrawing columns were being strafed and bombarded. Khammash urged immediate Israeli compliance with the cease-fire and stated that the Jordanian military position was hopeless. The record copy is in the National Archives and Records Administration, RG 59, Central Files 1967–69, POL 27 ARAB–ISR.

---

192. Telegram From the Commander of the Sixth Fleet (Martin) to the Joint Chiefs of Staff[1]

June 7, 1967, 1503Z.

71503Z. A. COMSIXTHFLT 070626Z Jun 67.[2]

1. This applies ref A.

2. Prior to 052015Z Jun 67 SIXTHFLT aircraft were engaged in normal training operations in the Sea of Crete and south of the western end of Crete. No air operations were authorized east of lat 30E or within 100 miles of the Egyptian coast. These restrictions provided a minimum approach distance for aircraft to the coasts of Israel and Syria of no less that 240 miles and to the coast of Egypt from Alexandria west of no less than 100 miles. At 052015Z Jun 67 the operating area for SIXTHFLT units was expanded to include all of the

---

[1] Source: Joint Chiefs of Staff Files, 898/392. Secret; Flash. The telegram does not indicate the time of receipt. Repeated to CNO, CINCUSNAVEUR, USCINCEUR, CINC-USAFE, DIA, and DIRNSA. Filed as an attachment to the Report of the JCS Fact Finding Team: USS *Liberty* Incident, 8 June 1967. (See footnote 2, Document 337.)

[2] Telegram 70626Z from COMSIXTHFLT to JCS stated that there had been no direct or indirect communications between COMSIXTHFLT and any Israeli source either military or non-military and none reported by any COMSIXTHFLT subordinate command. (Joint Chiefs of Staff Files, 898/392)

eastern Med except that no operations, either surface or air, were permitted within 1 [100] miles of Israel, Syria, or Egypt or within 25 miles of Cyprus.

3. On 5 May [June] both carriers were operating in positions which were in excess of 400 miles from Israel or Sinai. Flight operations on *America* were conducted from 0915Z until 1235Z and on *Saratoga* from 0828Z until 1313Z. Flight operations were conducted for training purposes and were routine in all aspects. On 6 Jun limited UR operations were conducted during the day for routing purposes. No night operations were conducted by either carrier.

4. All SIXTHFLT CVA pilots who participated in air operations on 5 and 6 Jun have been queried concerning their track lines and any voice communications either transmitted or received. At no time were the airspace restrictions set forth in para 1. above violated, i.e., on 5 Jun no SIXTHFLT CVA aircraft approached the Israel or Sinai coastline closer that 240 miles and on 6 Jun no SIXTHFLT CVA aircraft approached the Israel, Syria or Egypt coastlines closer than 100 miles. Tracks flown were actually farther from Israel/Syria/Egypt than the above limiting figures. During these flights no SIXTHFLT pilot either transmitted or received any radio transmissions from stations either in or under the control of any country in the Mideast engaged in the current conflict, either directly or indirectly by relay. In short, on 5 and 6 Jun no SIXTHFLT aircraft overflew Israel, Syria, or Egypt and no communications were established by SIXTHFLT pilots with any radio stations controlled or utilized by any of these countries.

5. No flight operations are scheduled for 7 Jun for either *Saratoga* or *America*. The limitations set forth in para 2 above continue in effect.

193.   Message From President Johnson to Premier Kosygin[1]

Washington, June 7, 1967, 11:18 a.m.

Mr. Chairman:

We are instructing our Ambassador at the United Nations to agree to an immediate meeting of the Security Council when one is suggested by your Ambassador.

Our Ambassador reports that the Security Council was informed last evening by Foreign Minister Eban that Israel would accept a cease-fire, while noting that he did not know of the reaction of the Arab side. He also reported that the Arab Ambassadors were silent on this point. At the time of this message, we ourselves are not clear as to their attitude, with the possible exception of Jordan.

We are taking steps to see that the resolution of the Security Council is implemented by all concerned. We are prepared to work with all others to establish a lasting peace in the region.

The wholly false reports and invented charges that United States aircraft participated in attacks on Egypt have resulted in mob action against American embassies and consulates and a break in Diplomatic Relations by seven Arab countries with the United States. This despicable act on their part and failure to give adequate protection to American officials and private citizens in Arab countries will lead to a very serious deterioration in the situation. I repeat the hope that you will be able to counsel moderation where it is needed.

Respectfully,

Lyndon B. Johnson

---

[1] Source: Johnson Library, National Security File, Head of State Correspondence, USSR, Washington–Moscow "Hot-Line" Exchange, 6/5–10/67. No classification marking. A typed notation on the source text indicates it was approved by the President at 11 a.m.; it was transmitted by US Molink at 11:18 a.m.; and it was received by Soviet Molink at 11:25 a.m. The message was drafted by Rusk and apparently revised by the President, Walt Rostow, and Bundy. A draft marked "Sect. Rusk, 10:10 a.m., draft," along with a copy of the message as sent, which was similar but somewhat revised, is ibid., Country File, USSR, Hollybush, Vol. III. The President met with Walt Rostow and Bundy for a part of the time between 10:25 and 10:45 a.m. discussing "the wording of some communication." (Ibid., President's Daily Diary)

194. Memorandum for the Record[1]

Washington, June 7, 1967, 12:05–1 p.m.

SUBJECT

National Security Council Meeting, Wednesday, June 7, 1967

The following is a record from my notes made during the meeting, but, because of the fast moving events in the Middle East, not transcribed until today.

Secretary Rusk opened the discussion of the situation in the Middle East by reporting that Nasser had suffered a "stunning loss." He had miscalculated the military situation and Soviet support. There was widespread disillusionment with Nasser in the Middle East.[2] The Soviets seemed to have been guilty of encouraging him. The Arabs in the UN felt that the USSR had let them down. Israel was riding high and its demands will be substantial. Israel will probably demand a peace treaty with the Arabs with the following objectives:

a. Clear resolution of the state of belligerence.

b. Getting rid of the UN truce supervisory machinery. Israel will accept no arrangements that derogate its sovereignty.

c. At the beginning it seemed that Israel was not seeking territorial acquisition, but Ambassador Barbour feels they will want Sharm el-Sheikh and straightened out borders.[3]

---

[1] Source: Johnson Library, National Security File, NSC Meetings File, Vol. 4. Secret. Dated January 7, 1969. The meeting took place in the Cabinet Room. The time and place of the meeting are from the President's Daily Diary. (Ibid.) A list of those present is ibid., National Security File, NSC Meetings File, Vol. 4. A handwritten memorandum, June 7, that Rostow apparently gave to the President during the meeting, conveys a message from Moyers that Eban had told Feinberg he was going to take the position of no withdrawal without a definitive peace, and he would be seeing Goldberg to ask for U.S. support. Feinberg thought this was the way for the President to retrieve his position after the McCloskey statement. (Ibid., Appointment File, June 1967, Middle East Crisis) Rostow evidently received this message in a telephone call from Moyers at 12:28 p.m.; he left the NSC meeting to return Moyers' call. (Ibid., President's Daily Diary)

[2] At 9 a.m. that morning, Rostow sent the President reports from the London press that Nasser's position was threatened by the developments in the war, with a brief covering memorandum that commented, "If Nasser goes, we indeed do have a new ball game." (Ibid., NSC Histories, Middle East Crisis)

[3] Barbour estimated in telegram 3988 from Tel Aviv, June 7, that the Israelis would insist on final peace treaties with their neighbors with firm, accepted frontiers and would not accept any international supervisory organizations. He thought they would not want to absorb the West Bank but would want to hold on to the areas of the Sinai, including Sharm el-Sheikh, from which they withdrew under pressure in 1957, and that they would expect other adjustments to widen the narrow belt between Jordan and the sea and to improve their strategic position toward Syria. (National Archives and Records Administration, RG 59, Central Files 1967–69, POL 27 ARAB–ISR)

Looking ahead, the Secretary spoke of the importance to us of removing belligerent rights, resuming international guarantees, and regional economic and social developments to absorb intra-Arab and Arab-Israeli quarrels. If we do not make ourselves "attorneys for Israel," we cannot recoup our losses. We do have something to bargain with in that Israel must be grateful to the US and Israel requires continuing US support.

The Secretary reviewed the question of "who did what?" He said we had a primary obligation to ourselves to maintain peace. What we would have done had we been in Prime Minister Eshkol's shoes is another question. Eban had laid bare Israeli thinking and we understood it. In any case, the situation on June 8 appeared "more manageable than five days or three days ago." The air battle had been significant.

Mr. Helms said that the Russians had badly miscalculated, even more so than in the Cuban missile crisis.

Mr. Katzenbach said that arrangements for evacuation of Americans were in progress everywhere except in Jordan. We still were holding off in Kuwait and Saudi Arabia.

Mr. Gaud reported that we had had aid programs in six of the fourteen Arab countries (plus Israel)—Sudan, Jordan, Tunisia, the UAR, Morocco, Israel—and a pipeline of one sort or another to twelve. He had stopped obligations to all of these countries. He had frozen everything for those countries who have broken diplomatic relations. In addition there are US contributions to the world food program, UNRWA and voluntary agencies which we had not stopped. The pipeline of unliquidated obligations added up to about $130 million. The President asked Mr. Rostow to pull all of this information together and to see how it sorted itself out.

With regard to our aid through international or private agencies, Secretary Rusk said it would be serious to pull out of the FAO. On the other hand, with American personnel coming out of countries like the UAR, voluntary agency programs might have to give for the time being.

The discussion turned to the question of military equipment. The Vice President said the Congress was watching the flow of arms shipments very carefully. Mr. E.V. Rostow noted Soviet shipments to the Arabs.

The President said "he was not sure we were out of our troubles." He could not visualize the USSR saying it had miscalculated, and then walking away. Our objective should be to "develop as few heroes and as few heels as we can." It is important for everybody to know we are not for aggression. We are sorry this has taken place. We are in as good a position as we could be given the complexities of the situation. We thought we had a commitment from those governments, but it went up in smoke very quickly. The President said that by the time we get through with all the festering problems we are going to wish the war had not happened.

Ambassador Thompson said he could figure out no explanation for the Soviet misjudgment. The Russians should have known the Arabs' capability. He felt the end of belligerence should be relatively easy to handle with the USSR. Barring a direct threat to Cairo, he felt the Soviets would probably stay out of war.

Secretary Rusk felt that, in Moscow, those advising caution may be strengthened.

General Wheeler reported briefly on the air war, noting that the Israelis had caught a large portion of the UAR air force on the ground. He also pointed out that the striking nature of the Israeli success reflected great superiority in maintenance, leadership, training and discipline rather than numerical superiority.

The President then went on to read a statement later released to the press (attached),[4] establishing a Special Committee of the National Security Council to deal with the Middle East crisis, with McGeorge Bundy to serve as Executive Secretary and as a special consultant to the President and with Secretary Rusk as chairman.

Secretary Fowler discussed briefly the effect of hostilities on the money markets of the world. In sum, he felt there was nothing to indicate any massive movement of funds. He said we were not interfering.

At the President's request for comment, Mr. Bundy said the following about his new assignment. He would be in familiar company and would do his best. He needed the help of people who had been working in the crisis and would require the support of a small staff. He knew his job was primarily to take the best possible advantage of work already going on.

Secretary Rusk concluded by suggesting that there be a meeting of the new committee at 6:30 p.m.

H.H.S.

---

[4] For text, see *Public Papers of the Presidents of the United States: Lyndon B. Johnson, 1967,* Book I, p. 599. The President stated that the members of the Special Committee, in addition to Rusk and Bundy, would be Fowler, McNamara, Wheeler, Helms, Clifford, and Walt Rostow. He stated that he would meet with the Committee as necessary, as would Vice President Humphrey and Goldberg.

195.   Memorandum From the President's Special Assistant
        (Rostow) to President Johnson[1]

Washington, June 7, 1967, 3:55 p.m.

Mr. President:

Herewith a plea from Mrs. Krim.[2]

When I talked to Abe Feinberg and gave him your points, his response was much the same: he couldn't be more loyal, but the average U.S. Zionist doesn't understand.

One thing to consider is letting it be known how intensively you worked on the Russians. Without going into any details whatsoever—and never mentioning the hot line—I suggested the importance of your role in the outcome to: Max Frankel, Joe Kraft, and Joe Alsop today.

Lord knows what they'll say tomorrow!!

Walt

---

[1] Source: Johnson Library, National Security File, NSC Histories, Middle East Crisis, Vol. 3. No classification marking. A handwritten notation on the memorandum indicates it was received at 4:07 p.m., and seen by the President.

[2] An unsigned summary of a message from Mathilde Krim, June 7, is attached. It states that there was still resentment in the Jewish community over the McCloskey statement; there were reports of anti-American feelings in Israel because Israelis felt they had won the war not with the United States but in spite of it; and there was danger that a rally the next day in Lafayette Square would be an anti-Johnson, rather than a pro-Israel demonstration. Mathilde and Arthur Krim recommended a Presidential statement saying that the United States would not resume relations with Nasser's government and calling for a peace conference to establish a peace based on recognition of Israel by the Arab nations as a member of the community of nations in the Middle East. A similar message from Mathilde Krim had been sent to the President in a 1:25 p.m. memorandum from Marvin Watson. (Ibid., Appointment File, June 1967, Middle East Crisis) The President read portions of it to Rusk during a 2:42 p.m. telephone conversation. (Ibid., President's Daily Diary) Arthur and Mathilde Krim were friends of the President and leading Democratic Party activists.

196. Telegram From the Department of State to the Embassy in Israel[1]

Washington, June 7, 1967, 5:42 p.m.

208985. You should make strongest presentation of dangerous situation so graphically portrayed in Amman's 4128[2] to highest available level GOI. You should stress influx refugees to East Bank and rapid disintegration Jordan security forces now constitute real threat to regime and to large American and foreign community in Jordan. We are taking action with Eban[3] but you should make most vigorous plea for Israeli acceptance cease-fire offer and immediate public notice this action.[4]

Rusk

---

[1] Source: National Archives and Records Administration, RG 59, Central Files 1967–69, POL 27 ARAB–ISR. Secret; Flash. Drafted and approved by Davies. Repeated to Amman, Moscow, London, Paris, Jerusalem, USUN, CINCSTRIKE, COMSIXTHFLT, CINCEUR, and DIA.

[2] Telegram 4128 from Amman, June 7, reported that Prime Minister Juma had told an Embassy officer that the Jordanian army on the West Bank was retreating on foot and under fire. Juma charged that there had been continuous, massive Israeli violations of the cease-fire for the preceding 18 hours. He said the Jordanians were convinced the Israelis had agreed to the cease-fire to entrap the Jordanian army, and the U.S. failure to stop the attack raised serious doubts as to U.S. intentions. He said that 150 Israeli tanks were moving through northern Israel toward the Jordan border, apparently en route to Syria, and if they crossed the border, Jordan would have no choice but to resist. He declared that unless Israeli attacks ceased immediately there was "no hope for the Jordan regime or for any further American influence in the country," and he pleaded that the President take immediate action. Burns commented that if the United States could not stop the Israeli military action, the 1,200 Americans in Amman and on the West Bank could be subject to mob violence, and the regime would probably be unable to protect them. (Ibid.)

[3] Goldberg reported in telegram 5650 from USUN, June 7, that he had contacted Eban in the late afternoon and urged him to ensure an immediate cease-fire. Eban said he understood that orders to this effect had been given shortly after 4 p.m. Eastern time but that he would contact Tel Aviv to be certain they were being carried out. (Ibid.) Goldberg called Rusk at 8:05 p.m. and said Rafael had just stated the Israelis were sending a letter to the Secretary-General announcing that a cease-fire with Jordan was in effect. (Notes of telephone conversation, June 7; ibid., Rusk Files: Lot 72 D 192, Telephone Calls)

[4] Barbour reported in telegram 4003 from Tel Aviv, June 8, that he had made the representations requested in telegram 208985, even though word of the cease-fire made them out of date. (Ibid., Central Files 1967–69, POL 27 ARAB–ISR)

197. Notes of a Meeting of the Special Committee of the National Security Council[1]

Washington, June 7, 1967, 6:30 p.m.

[THOSE PRESENT]

President	Sisco
McNamara	Battle
Fowler	Clifford
Rusk	W.W. Rostow
Katzenbach	McG. Bundy
Wheeler	Saunders
Helms	

Katz: Jordanian problem

VOA team

McGB's Other reasons.

Wh. Iraqi brigade. One reason Israelis fired up is to get at Iraqi & Egypt. troops.
150 Israeli tanks (brigade) crossed & heading toward Damascus.
Egyptian commandos
Iraqi troops
Eilat cutoff
Get at Syrians

Pr: Want to take most competent people in & outside small working group to det. what probs are & what needs be done. Perhaps some help in solving probs of Viet. Russian Am. trouble—trade out. But enough probs ahead.

Want regular meetings initially—decisions to this meeting—ahead of anything else. Not anything else more important.
McGB. Sparkplug. When he speaks, he speaks for me.

McGB: Ongoing work.

---

[1] Source: Johnson Library, National Security File, NSC Special Committee Files, Minutes and Notes. No classification marking. The meeting was held from 6:32 to 7:55 p.m.; the President left the meeting from 7:03 to 7:32 p.m. Rusk arrived 10 minutes late because he had been on Capitol Hill. (Johnson Library, President's Daily Diary) The notes are Saunders' handwritten notes of the meeting. The only formal records of the Special Committee meetings are memoranda for the record summarizing the committee's decisions, drafted by Saunders and based on his notes. Very brief notes of the meetings by Helms are in Central Intelligence Agency Files, DCI Files: Job 80–B01285A, Box 11, Folder 12, DCI (Helms) Miscellaneous Notes of Meetings, 1 Jan 1966–31 Dec 1968.

Special requirements just down road.[2]

1. Continuing intelligence assessment of—not just tanks—but of attitudes in ME to what's going on. DCI (ways of asking questions: what are people now likely to think.) Keep on top of pol. thinking without getting in way of day to day business.
2. Keeping depts. in touch in economic relationship.

—Solomon: oil coord.
—Deming: money link
—Walter Levy
—Bator.

3. Information coordination: pressures to say I'll be in touch with Depts.

    Marks
    Christian
    B—
    Not deal with day-to-day fires.

1 [4]. How we & USSR relate to one another. Short-run picture not appetizing.

DR: Congr.: Get on Israeli bandwagon. Isr. success.

Resupply problem. We sympathetic to Israel's needs. Israel will be in with bills, we ought to meet.

Leading questions:

1. West Bank
2. Seize & operate Canal.

Divided opinion on how deal with those that have broken [relations].

—Withdraw charge before we resume.

Relieved that we didn't have to get military involved.

No criticism except on "neutrality"—Javits.

No blank check—Jav., R. Kenn.

Sym: give our airmen in Viet some freedom.

Pr.: What will bill be?

Wh. 800 op tanks left.

Damascus: Phase III. Balance has changed.

Sources of supply.

Fr.—acft
Br.—art

---

[2] "This is more operational than I had judged from first talk." is written in the margin next to the three points below.

US—tanks
Switz.

DR: Morse: close: force prev. resupply Arabs.

Pr: [Illegible.] Viet. Sovs?

Pr: Sovs. Rebuild.

Helms: Sovs have taken awful prestige blow. These come pretty hard.

a. Sovs going to come back hard.
b. Leadership could be affected.
c. It didn't read sit. in Viet. any better than ME.
—No rocket rattling (1956, 8)
—Does this strengthen moderates or Hawks?
CPs in ME dead.
Arab reaction in UN.

Missile crisis—Test Ban Peacemaker.[3]

DR: We can't make Isr. accept puny settlement.

Arms: Sov. arms limitation bureaucracy.

NY: Linking withdrawal to peace settlement.

Isr: GAA: badly when face Arabs together. Remember 1949.[4]

Refugees & pol. desolation.

Paradox: now they have 700,000 refugees.

Strong group.

Mtg, late in day.

Wkdays at 6:30, always stop before. Sit. room.
Sats at 11:00. (Not commit to this Saturday yet)

DR: Policy questions urgent:

1. Do we coop. with multilat. agencies, WFP, WHO, FAO, UNWRA.[5]
—surly view.
McGB: prepare good just.
2. Gin up supplementary emergency problems.

McN—Egypt on the ropes.

Fowler—Econ. rehab. prog. for Egypt. Can't do it for Nasser.

WWR: Regional development bank. Unleash Gene Black. Break Nasser.

---

[3] "Cld they retrieve by delivering in Viet or NE." is written next to these points.

[4] The words "Hussein. [Illegible.] Viable? Alternatives" appear in the margin.

[5] "$14 m. cash. $8 m. kind." is written in the margin next to this point.

—Special reg. fund in World Bank.
—Mil. Coup?

Katz: Med. aid.

—Appropr. Hard to get fr. Congr.
—UNWRA.
—Pressure to cut UNWRA.

UN: How to handle tactical problem.

[illegible]: What about UAR?—Pres. of Sec. Council & SYG to go out.

Arms: Our 155's that shelled.[6]

Pr.: Not going to be blackmailed.

Stop arms to Arabs; resupply Isr.

Cliff.: Good case on past shipments. Defy anyone make good case.

---

[6] "Where we have control we have acted." is written next to the points on arms. Bundy's June 8 memorandum for the record recording decisions at the June 7 meeting includes only one point, which reads as follows: "After discussing the importance of keeping close watch on our shipments of military equipment to Arab countries, it was agreed that we must be able to demonstrate that we have acted to halt shipments over which we still have control. We can do nothing about those shipments now on the high seas (many of which have already passed to the recipients' title) and should prepare a good brief explaining our allowing them to proceed." (Johnson Library, National Security File, NSC Special Committee Files, Minutes and Notes)

---

198.   Memorandum From Larry Levinson and Ben Wattenberg of the White House Staff to President Johnson[1]

Washington, June 7, 1967, 7:45 p.m.

We talked to David Brody of the Anti-Defamation League of the B'nai B'rith, and he reported this reaction from the Jewish community in America:

Monday there was sharp disillusion and dismay at the McCloskey statement concerning "neutrality in word, thought, and deed." The row-back by Secretary Rusk did not fully catch up with the original

---

[1] Source: Johnson Library, Appointment File, June 1967, Middle East Crisis. Confidential. A handwritten "L" on the memorandum indicates the President saw it. The President called Levinson at 8:40 p.m. and said he had received the memorandum and was disappointed in some of his Israeli friends and their reactions to what was being done during the crisis. (Johnson Library, President's Daily Diary)

statement—certainly not among the Jewish rank-and-file (who hissed at a Union meeting in New York Monday when the "neutrality" statement was announced). The Jewish *leadership* understands that the statement was *not your policy*, but they feel that it did indicate to them a real feeling in the State Department—that Israel was just another country on the map and that there was little concern for the humanity of the situation there.

On the other hand, they are pleased so far with the American position in the U.N. regarding the cease-fire, and the fact that no withdrawal was stipulated, and, of course, they are highly pleased with the military turn of events.

The major concern today among Jewish leaders now is this: *that Israel, apparently having won the war, may be forced to lose the peace—again (as in 1956)*. They were concerned that the U.N. would attempt to sell Israel down the river—and that *only the U.S. could prevent that*. Today, that is what American Jews are looking to the President for: assurances of a real, guaranteed, meaningful peace in the Middle East, and that Israel not be forced to a roll-back as they were by the Dulles–Eisenhower position in 1956.

(Brody feels that Israel will not withdraw from some parts of the newly occupied territory no matter who demands what.)

There will be a mass meeting of American Jews tomorrow at 2:00 p.m. in Lafayette Park. Brody thought it would clear the air and help your position with the Jewish community if you *sent a message to the gathering*. Brody believes that if you do send a message it ought to stress the "peace, justice and equity" theme of your Tuesday statement, ought *not* to mention "territorial integrity," ought to dramatize your personal understanding and depth of feeling for the humanity involved and your desire to see a lasting and permanent peace in the Middle East.

Events are moving very rapidly—but as of this hour, from a domestic political point of view, it seems to us that this would be a highly desirable action. It would neutralize the "neutrality" statement and could lead to a great domestic political bonus—and not only from Jews. Generally speaking, it would seem that the Mid-East crisis can turn around a lot of anti-Viet Nam anti-Johnson feeling, particularly if you use it as an opportunity to your advantage.

199.   Telegram From the Joint Chiefs of Staff to the Commander
in Chief, European Command (Lemnitzer)[1]

Washington, June 8, 1967, 0110Z.

7347. Subj: USS *Liberty* (U).

Refs: a. JCS 7337/072230Z Jun 67;[2] b. COMSIXTHFLT 071503Z Jun
67 (Notal).[3]

1. (U) Cancel ref a.

2. (TS) Reg *Liberty* comply new op areas defined last sentence para
2 ref b, until further notice, i.e., not closer than 100 NM to Israel, Syria,
Egypt and 25 NM to Cyprus.[4]

---

[1] Source: Johnson Library, National Security File, NSC Histories, Middle East Crisis,
Vol. 7, Appendix H. Top Secret; Immediate. Repeated Immediate to CNO, CINCLANT,
CINCLANTFLT, CINCUSNAVEUR, COMSIXTHFLT, CTF 64, USS *LIBERTY*, HQ-
NSAEUR, NSAEUR OFF GERMANY, DIRNSA, DIRNAVSECGRU, ADIRNAVSECGRU,
DIRNAVSECGRULANT, DIRNAVSECGRUEUR.

[2] JCS telegram 7337 to USCINCEUR, 072230Z Jun 67, modified the instructions in
JCS 6724 (Document 118) to provide that the *Liberty* should approach no closer than 20
NM to the UAR and 15 NM to Israel. (Johnson Library, National Security File, NSC
Histories, Middle East Crisis, Vol. 7, Appendix H)

[3] Document 192.

[4] The U.S.S. *Liberty* did not receive this message. See Document 217.

---

200.   Circular Telegram From the Department of State to Certain
Posts[1]

Washington, June 7, 1967, 9:41 p.m.

209138. 1. Chief of Mission should approach FonOff soonest and
state he under high level instruction make following points:

a. USG regrets fact host government has chosen break diplomatic
relations with US.

b. History will record fact that basis for breaking relations is utterly false allegation that USG participated as belligerent in hostilities on

---

[1] Source: National Archives and Records Administration, RG 59, Central Files
1967–69, POL 17 US–ARAB. Confidential; Immediate.   Drafted by Bergus and Rusk,
cleared by Palmer and Davies, and approved by Rusk.   Sent to Algiers, Baghdad,
Damascus, Khartoum, Nouakchott, and Beirut and repeated to Bujumbura, Conakry,
Bamako, Rabat, Mogadiscio, Dar es Salaam, and Tripoli.

side of Israel. We wish make it of record that USG did not initiate break. We wish also to record our readiness to see relations fully restored when host government and we agree that a basis exists for normalizing relations.

c. We need to know in some detail what host government has in mind about arrangements now to be contemplated. These might range from a limitation to a mutual recall of ambassadors all the way to a complete withdrawal of all official personnel on both sides.

d. In this connection Ambassador may wish to point out that discussion of post-break diplomatic representation is going on between Washington and Cairo in dignified and responsible manner and on basis reciprocity. Egyptians have accepted the maintenance of a number of diplomatic officers and supporting administrative personnel as part of embassy of mutually agreed third power. Egyptians have also agreed re maintenance of our consulates in Alexandria and Port Said. From expressions received from Egyptian FonOff officials, it is clear UAR wishes to avoid total rupture of all means of official communication between our two governments. Despite current status US-UAR relations, there is mutual interest in both governments in retaining contact on basis dignity and reciprocity.

Rusk

---

201. **Telegram From the Department of State to the Embassy in Israel**[1]

Washington, June 8, 1967, 3:38 a.m.

209172. 1. Embassy Amman has just reported Israeli armored battalion crossed Mundesseh Bridge (opposite Wadi Shuaib) at 0530 Zulu June eight. Israelis also reportedly shelling Jordanian position at Ramtha in recent hours. King and Prime Minister frantically demanding why GOI violating cease-fire in this fashion.[2]

---

[1] Source: National Archives and Records Administration, RG 59, Central Files 1967–69, POL 27 ARAB–ISR. Secret; Flash. Drafted and approved by Brewer of the NEA Task Force. Repeated Flash to Amman and USUN.

[2] Burns reported this in telegram 4134 from Amman, also sent as Critic 1 from Amman, both dated June 8. (Ibid.)

2. Request you immediately contact highest available Israeli official to convey foregoing and stress we believe cease-fire must be entirely observed lest Jordanian regime disintegrate immediately which we assume not an Israeli objective. We had understood Israel had accepted cease-fire and that it was effective on June seven at 2000GMT June 7. Continued firing would clearly call in question Israel representative's June seven letter to UNSC President in foregoing sense.

3. Report results Flash, repeated to Amman.[3]

Rusk

---

[3] Barbour reported in telegram 4002 from Tel Aviv, June 8, that on the basis of Amman's telegram 4134, he had urged the Foreign Office to check with the Israeli command, which replied the report was not correct; there was no Israeli force on the East Bank, the Israelis had no intention of putting forces there or advancing from their West Bank positions, and no Israeli shelling was going on. (Ibid.)

---

202. President's Daily Brief[1]

Washington, June 8, 1967.

Arab States–Israel (As of 5:00 AM EDT)

The UN's ceasefire order is being disregarded. Egypt has officially announced it will not comply, and Nasir has personally so informed most other Arab governments. The Israelis may have broken their ceasefire agreement with Jordan.

Early this morning the Jordanian prime minister told our embassy that Israeli tanks were moving into northwestern Jordan. The ultimate aim of such a movement might be to attack Syria. The embassy also says fighting on the Israeli-Jordanian front picked up during the night. [3 lines of source text not declassified]

On the Sinai Peninsula, the Israelis have apparently accomplished most of their military objectives. Yesterday the Israelis approached the Suez Canal so rapidly that they probably cut off the major portion of the retreating Egyptians.

---

[1] Source: Johnson Library, National Security File, NSC Histories, Middle East Crisis, Vol. 6, Appendix A. Top Secret; [codeword not declassified]. Regarding the release of this PDB, see footnote 1, Document 151.

Embassy Cairo believes that public realization of the Arab defeat has generated strong feeling against Nasir, and foreign diplomats in Cairo consider the Egyptians are in a state of panic over the military debacle. [*3 lines of source text not declassified*] Senior Iraqi officials in New York are said to believe Nasir is desperate and might do almost anything to maintain his position.

Mobs in Dhahran, Saudi Arabia, have damaged US installations, and our consulate in Aleppo has been attacked and burned. As the extent of the defeat sinks into the Arab countries, danger to US citizens still there may increase. Refugees from the fighting in Jordan's West Bank are already streaming into Amman, where they could cause disorder directed at Americans.

LATE ITEM

Arab States–Israel (As of 5:30 AM EDT)

The Israelis have just announced (according to the press) that Egyptian armored forces have counterattacked "in force" in an effort to fight their way out of the Sinai Peninsula. This could refer to Egyptian troops trapped in the rapid Israeli advance.

---

203.   Telegram From the Department of State to the Embassy in Israel[1]

Washington, June 8, 1967, 6:31 a.m.

209182. Ref: Jerusalem 1053.[2]

UNTSO report reftel deeply disturbing. You should urgently approach Fonoff at highest level to express deep concern this new indication military action by GOI. If reported bombardment correct, we would assume it prelude to military action against Syrian positions on

---

[1]   Source: National Archives and Records Administration, RG 59, Central Files 1967–69, POL 27 ARAB–ISR. Secret; Flash. Drafted and approved by Brewer and cleared by Katzenbach. Repeated Priority to Amman, Athens, Beirut, Damascus, Jerusalem, London, USUN, and CINCSTRIKE.

[2]   Telegram 1053 from Jerusalem, June 8, reported that at 1000 local time, UNTSO stated that the Israelis had just launched an intensive air and artillery bombardment of Syrian positions opposite the central demilitarized zone, as an apparent prelude to a large-scale attack in an effort to seize the heights overlooking the border kibbutzim. (Ibid.)

Syrian soil. Such a development, following on heels Israeli acceptance SC cease-fire resolution would cast doubts on Israeli intentions and create gravest problems for USG representatives in Arab countries. You should stress we must at all costs have complete cessation Israeli military action except in cases where clearly some replying fire is necessary in self-defense.[3]

Rusk

---

[3] Barbour replied in telegram 4007 from Tel Aviv, June 8, that he was raising the matter and expressing concern in accordance with telegram 209182, but he noted that Syrian shelling of the kibbutzim and settlements below the Syrian heights had been continuous and incessant, with continuous threat to their populations. He commented that he would not be surprised if an Israeli attack took place or had already done so. (Ibid.)

---

204.   Editorial Note

On June 8, 1967, at 8:03 a.m. Eastern Daylight Time (1203Z; 2:03 p.m. local time), the U.S.S. *Liberty* was attacked and hit by unidentified jet fighters, which made six strafing runs. Twenty minutes later the ship was attacked by three torpedo boats. One torpedo hit the starboard side. At the time, the *Liberty* was heading northwest in international waters, a little more than 13 nautical miles from the Sinai coast, approximately 25 miles northwest of El Arish. (Proceedings, U.S. Navy Court of Inquiry; Naval Historical Center, Operational Archives Branch, Immediate Office Files of the Chief of Naval Operations, 1969 Files, Box 110, Liberty Incident, 8 June 1967, Court of Inquiry; Chronology of Events, Naval Security Group File on U.S.S. *Liberty*; Naval Security Group Files, Box 702, CNSG Pre-76 Inactive Files 168, NAVSECGRU File on U.S.S. *Liberty*) At 1235Z, a message from the U.S.S. *Saratoga* to the Commander in Chief, U.S. Naval Forces, Europe, repeated to the Commander, Sixth Fleet, relayed a message from the *Liberty*: "I am under attack. My posit 31.23N 33.25E. I have been hit. Request immed assistance." (Telegram 081235Z from U.S.S. *Saratoga* to CINCUSNAVEUR, June 8 Naval Historical Center, Operational Archives Branch, U.S.S. *Liberty* Incident, Message File, Vol. II)

At 1250Z, the Commander, Sixth Fleet, ordered the U.S.S. *America* to launch four armed A4s, with fighter cover and tankers, which were to proceed to 31–23N 33–25E to defend the *Liberty*, and the *Saratoga* to launch four armed A1s with the same mission. (Telegram 081250Z from COMSIXTHFLT to USS *Saratoga* and USS *America*, June 8; ibid.) At 1316Z the Commander, Task Force 60, reiterated the order to the *America* and the *Saratoga*, adding, "Defense of USS *Liberty* means exactly that. Destroy or drive off any attackers who are clearly making attacks on *Liberty*. Remain over international waters. Defend yourself if attacked." (Telegram 081316Z from CTF 60 to USS *America* and USS *Saratoga*, June 8; ibid.) At 9:11 a.m. (1311Z), the Commander in Chief, European Command, notified the National Military Command Center by telephone that the *Liberty* was under attack, had been hit by a torpedo, and was listing to starboard. (See Document 219.)

Information concerning the U.S.S *Liberty* and its mission is in William D. Gerhard and Henry W. Millington, *Attack on a Sigint Collector, the U.S.S. Liberty* (National Security Agency/Central Security Service, 1981), in National Security Agency, Center for Cryptologic History Historical Collection, Series VIII, Crisis Files, Box 16. Files of message traffic pertaining to the *Liberty* are in the Naval Historical Center, Operational Archives Branch, U.S.S. Liberty Incident, Message File; ibid., Immediate Office Files of the Chief of Naval Operations, 1969 Files, Box 113; National Security Agency, Center for Cryptologic History Historical Collection, Series VIII, Crisis Files, Box 16; ibid., NSA Archives, Accession No. 45981, U.S.S. *Liberty* Correspondence and Messages, 1965–1968; and Naval Security Group Files, Box 896, U.S.S. *Liberty* Pre-76 Inactive Files, Box 1, USS *Liberty* 5750/4, Chronological Message File.

205. Memorandum From the President's Special Assistant (Rostow) to President Johnson[1]

Washington, June 8, 1967, 9:50 a.m.

Mr. President:

We have a flash report from the Joint Reconnaissance Center indicating that a U.S. ELINT (electronics intelligence) ship, the *Liberty*, has been torpedoed in the Mediterranean. The ship is located 60–100 miles north of Egypt.[2]

Reconnaissance aircraft are out from the 6th fleet.

We have no knowledge of the submarine or surface vessel which committed this act.

We shall keep you informed.

Walt

---

[1] Source: Johnson Library, National Security File, NSC Histories, Middle East Crisis, Vol. 3. No classification marking. A handwritten "L" on the memorandum indicates the President saw it. Rostow telephoned the President at 9:49 a.m. This memorandum apparently confirmed information Rostow had given him in that telephone conversation. At 10 a.m., Johnson telephoned Secretary McNamara. (Johnson Library, President's Daily Diary) No record has been found of either of these conversations.

[2] At 10:15 a.m., National Security Agency Director General Marshall S. Carter telephoned Naval Security Group Director Captain Cook to request that he telephone Secretary McNamara with information about the *Liberty* and the number of personnel aboard. At 10:30 a.m., Deputy Naval Security Group Director Captain Thomas briefed McNamara by telephone about the *Liberty*, its mission, its location, and the personnel aboard. McNamara asked whether the Joint Chiefs of Staff had directed the ship's withdrawal to 100 miles from shore. Thomas could not confirm this. (Chronology of Events, Naval Security Group File on U.S.S *Liberty*, Naval Security Group Files, Box 702, CNSG Pre-76 Inactive Files 168, NAVSECGRU File on USS *Liberty*)

206.   Telegram From the Commander of the Sixth Fleet (Martin)
        to the U.S.S. *America* and U.S.S. *Saratoga*[1]

June 8, 1967, 1339Z.

081339Z. USS *Liberty* Incident.

1. IAW CINCUSNAVEUR inst P03611#SB forces attacking *Liberty* are declared hostile.

2. You are authorized to use force including destruction as necessary to control the situation. Do not use more force than required, do not pursue any unit towards land for reprisal purposes. Purpose of counterattack is to protect *Liberty* only.[2]

3. Brief all pilots contents this msg.

4. In addition brief pilots that Egyptian territorial limit only 12 miles and *Liberty* right on edge. Do not fly between *Liberty* and shoreline except as required to carry out provisions para 2 above. Brief fighter cover that any attacks on attack aircraft, *Liberty* or they themselves is hostile act and para two above applies.

---

[1] Source: Naval Security Group Files, Box 896, USS *Liberty* Pre-76 Inactive Files, Box 1, U.S.S. *Liberty*, 5750/4, Chronological Message File. Confidential; Flash. The message was repeated at 1349Z from COMSIXTHFLT to CNO, CINCUSNAVEUR, and CTF 60. Received in the Navy Department at 1402Z. A handwritten note on the telegram states that the message was cancelled by COMSIXTHFLT 081609Z. Prior to that, however, telegram 081440Z from COMSIXTHFLT to the *America* and the *Saratoga* directed: "Recall all strikes." (Naval Historical Center, Operational Archives Branch, U.S.S. *Liberty* Incident, Message File) Telegram 081645Z from COMSIXTHFLT to USCINCEUR reported that all aircraft from the *America* and the *Saratoga* had been recalled and were accounted for. (Ibid.)

[2] JCS telegram 7354 to UNCINCEUR, 081416Z Jun 67, reads as follows: "You are authorized to use whatever force required to defend USS *Liberty* from further attacks." (Johnson Library, National Security File, NSC Histories, Middle East Crisis, Vol. 7, Appendix H) JCS telegram 7369 to USCINCEUR, 081529Z Jun 67, confirmed a telephone conversation from Vice Chief of Naval Operations Admiral Horacio Rivero to Deputy Commander in Chief, U.S. European Command General David A. Burchinal USAF, cancelling this authorization. (Ibid.)

207. Telegram From the Commander of the Sixth Fleet (Martin) to the Commander in Chief, European Command (Lemnitzer)[1]

June 8, 1967, 1320Z.

081320Z. SITREP 06001. Attack on *Liberty*.

SITREP One.

1. At 081252Z USS *Liberty* reported under attack at posit 31.23N 33.25E, was hit by torpedo and was listing badly. Attack forces hereby declared hostile by COMSIXTHFLT IAW CINCUSNAVEURINST P03120.5B. *Liberty* message authenticated.

2. Have directed TF 60 to proceed toward scene. Task Force 60 present posit 34.22N 24.28E.

3. Have directed *America* to launch four armed A4's and *Saratoga* to launch four armed A1's with fighter cover to defend USS *Liberty*. Pilots directed to remain clear of land. Tankers also will launch, will relieve on station.[2]

4. ETA first ACFT on scene one hour and 30 mins after launch. Estimate launch at 1345Z.

[1] Source: National Security Agency, Center for Cryptologic History Historical Collection, Series VIII, Crisis Files, Box 16. Unclassified; Flash. Repeated to AIG 998, JCS, CNO, CTF 60, and CTG 60.2. Received at the National Military Command Center at 10:13 a.m.

[2] See Document 219.

208. Memorandum From the President's Special Assistant (Rostow) to President Johnson[1]

Washington, June 8, 1967, 10:10 a.m.

Mr. President:

It looks as though Kosygin may have contemplated on June 6 sending additional aircraft to Egypt—but he is obviously reluctant and trying to use a cease-fire to avoid that move.[2]

Walt

---

[1] Source: Johnson Library, National Security File, Country File, Middle East Crisis. Top Secret; [codeword not declassified].

[2] Rostow's memorandum forwarded [text not declassified] report that [text not declassified] was working on sending aircraft as [text not declassified] had requested. [text not declassified] the Soviet Union would support the Security Council proposal for a cease-fire. [text not declassified] the Soviets were keeping a close watch on the movements of the U.S. and British forces and [text not declassified] U.S. and British aircraft had not taken part in the hostilities.

---

209. Message From Premier Kosygin to President Johnson[1]

Moscow, June 8, 1967, 9:48 a.m.

Dear Mr. President,

Two days have passed since the Security Council's Resolution concerning the cessation of military actions in the Near East. Facts show that Israel, after the Security Council's appeal, seized considerable territory of the Arab States—United Arab Republic and Jordan—ignoring the Security Council's Resolution. A situation has developed which, in connection with these Israeli actions, demands not simply a cease-fire, but also a withdrawal of Israeli troops behind the armistice line. Israel's

---

[1] Source: Johnson Library, National Security File, Head of State Correspondence, USSR, Washington–Moscow "Hot-Line" Exchange, 6/5–10/67. No classification marking. The message is labeled "Translation," with a typed notation indicating a sight translation was made at 10:28 a.m.; the message was received by the President at 10:31 a.m.; a rough translation was made at 10:34 a.m.; and a final, official translation was provided at 12:35 p.m. A typed notation on a copy of the message in Russian states that it was transmitted by Soviet Molink at 9:48 a.m. and received by U.S. Molink at 10:15 a.m. (Ibid.)

actions have placed the Arab States in such a situation that they cannot but conduct a lawful defensive war against the aggressor, who has challenged the Security Council and all peace-loving states. Until complete withdrawal of Israeli troops from the territory of the Arab States, in the situation that has developed, re-establishment of peace in the Near East cannot be ensured.

We have instructed the Soviet Representative in the UN to place this question before the Security Council for the adoption of an appropriate resolution.

We would like to express that hope, Mr. President, that you personally and your government will take a position which will respond to the interests of cessation of war in the Near East, and to the interests of peace in the Near East, as you have already stated.

Respectfully,

A. Kosygin

210. Memorandum of Telephone Conversations[1]

Washington, June 8, 1967, 10:15 a.m. and 11 a.m.

SUBJECT

USS *Liberty*

PARTICIPANTS

Mr. Yuri N. Tcherniakov, Soviet Chargé d'Affaires a.i.
Mr. Foy D. Kohler, Deputy Under Secretary

Mr. Kohler informed the Chargé that he had an urgent message for the Soviet Government. An American ship, the USS *Liberty*, was torpedoed a few hours ago off Port Said. We are not sure of the exact location where the incident took place. It is an auxilliary ship. We are sending eight aircraft from the Carrier *Saratoga* to investigate. We wanted the Soviet Government to know that this was the purpose and the only purpose of those aircraft approaching in that direction. The Chargé said he assumed these would be military aircraft since they came from the

---

[1] Source: National Archives and Records Administration, RG 59, Central Files 1967–69, POL 27 ARAB–ISR. Secret. Drafted by Kohler's Special Assistant Stephen Low and approved in S/S on June 9.

Saratoga, and he repeated his understanding that their purpose was solely to investigate.

Mr. Kohler called the Chargé again at 11:00 a.m. to inform him that we have just received the information that it was the Israelis who attacked the vessel. He emphasized, however, that this did not change the import of the message he had given the Chargé earlier to the effect that our planes are going to the scene of the incident in connection with the vessel and not for any other purpose.[2]

---

[2] Telegram 209218 to Moscow, June 8, sent at 11:36 a.m., informed the Embassy that the U.S.S. *Liberty*, an "auxiliary ship," had been torpedoed about 14 miles north of the UAR coast, that the *Saratoga* had been instructed to dispatch eight aircraft to the scene, and that the Soviet Chargé had been informed. It instructed the Embassy to inform the Ministry of Foreign Affairs that the Israelis had acknowledged hitting the ship in error and had apologized, the Soviet Chargé had been informed, and as of 11:25 a.m., the planes had been recalled to the carrier. (Ibid.)

---

211.   Telegram From the Defense Attaché Office in Israel to the White House[1]

Tel Aviv, June 8, 1967, 1414Z.

0825. ALUSNA called to FLO to receive report.[2] Israeli aircraft and MTB's erroneously attacked U.S. ship at 081200Z position 3125Z 33–33E. May be navy ship. IDF helicopters in rescue operations. No other info. Israelis send abject apologies and request info of other US ships near war zone coasts.

---

[1] Source: National Security Agency, Center for Cryptologic History Historical Collection, Series VIII, Box 16d, DIA (USDAO, Tel Aviv) re *Liberty*. Confidential; Flash. Sent also to OSD, CNO, the Department of State, COMSIXTHFLT, CINCSTRIKE, CINC-NAVEUR, and JCS. Repeated to DIA, USUN, CINCEUR–USEUCOM, CTG 60, USAFE, and CINCUSAFEUR. The message was received at the National Military Command Center at 10:45 a.m.; see Document 219. An unsigned note on White House stationery, June 8, 11 a.m., states that the Defense Attaché in Tel Aviv "has informed us that the attack on the USS *Liberty* was a mistaken action of Israeli boats." (Johnson Library, National Security File, NSC Histories, Middle East Crisis, Vol. 3)

[2] Telegram 900 from USDAO Tel Aviv, June 15, which provided a chronology of events surrounding the *Liberty* incident as observed and recorded by U.S. Naval Attaché Commander Ernest C. Castle, USN, states that Castle received the report from Assistant IDF Spokesman Lieutenant Colonel Michael Bloch. (Ibid., NSC Special Committee Files, *Liberty*)

212.   Message From President Johnson to Premier Kosygin[1]

Washington, June 8, 1967, 11:17 a.m.

Dear Mr. Kosygin,

We have just learned that USS *Liberty*, an auxilliary ship, has apparently been torpedoed by Israel forces in error off Port Said. We have instructed our carrier, *Saratoga*, now in the Mediterranean to dispatch aircraft to the scene to investigate. We wish you to know that investigation is the sole purpose of this flight of aircraft, and hope that you will take appropriate steps to see that proper parties are informed.

We have passed this message to Chernyakov but feel that you should know of this development urgently.

Respectfully,

Lyndon B. Johnson

---

[1] Source: Johnson Library, National Security File, Head of State Correspondence, USSR, Washington–Moscow "Hot-Line" Exchange, 6/5–10/67. No classification marking. A typed notation on the message indicates it was approved by the President at 11 a.m.; transmitted by U.S. Molink at 11:17 a.m.; and received by Soviet Molink at 11:24 a.m. The message was apparently drafted by either Bundy or Walt Rostow in consultation with the President. Bundy telephoned Johnson at 10:20 a.m. and the President returned a call from Walt Rostow at 10:24 a.m. Johnson telephoned Rostow at 11 a.m., and Bundy called him immediately afterward. The President apparently approved the message in one of these conversations. (Johnson Library, President's Daily Diary)

213. Message From President Johnson to Premier Kosygin[1]

Washington, June 8, 1967, 12:01 p.m.

Dear Mr. Kosygin,

In the light of our understanding of yesterday, we went to all the parties concerned and strongly urged immediate compliance with the cease-fire resolution which had been unanimously agreed in the Council.

The representative of Israel agreed to comply as soon as the other parties also agreed. Of the Arab States, only Jordan agreed to comply; and we are informed that an effective cease-fire is being achieved on that front.

Although we are trying, we doubt that the United States alone can effectively persuade both sides to cease fire.

I instructed Ambassador Goldberg last night to present a resolution today. This resolution calls on all parties in the strongest terms to cease fire immediately.

I am glad to have had your message and have instructed our Ambassador in New York to maintain close contact with the Ambassador of the Soviet Union and trust you will want to do likewise.

Respectfully,

Lyndon B. Johnson

---

[1] Source: Johnson Library, National Security File, NSC Histories, Middle East Crisis, May 12–June 19, 1967, Vol. 7. No classification marking. A typed notation on the message indicates it was approved by the President at 11:35 a.m.; transmitted by U.S. Molink at 12:01 p.m.; and received by Soviet Molink at 12:05 p.m. According to the President's Daily Diary, he met with McNamara, Rusk, Clifford, Katzenbach, Thompson, Bundy, and Walt Rostow, from 11:06 to 11:45 a.m. in the White House Situation Room. (Ibid.)

214.   Memorandum of Telephone Conversation Between
        Secretary of State Rusk and the Assistant Secretary of State
        for Economic Affairs (Solomon)[1]

Washington, June 8, 1967, 12:24 p.m.

TELEPHONE CALL TO MR. SOLOMON

Sec asked for a summary of the present oil situation. S asked if he had gotten his memo with letter to sign. Sec had signed letter[2] but what is the practical situation. S said nothing from Iraq or Syria for anybody; Libya so far ports closed but govt has privately told people that waiting tankers should not go away, feel maybe they can open them shortly; Saudi Arabia, no oil to UK and US destinations but our companies can supply American forces in Southeast Asia; Kuwait, no shipments to UK-US destinations; Iran ok; Algeria, situation confused, most goes to France and it is flowing, no real problem for us there. S said Aramco itself had to close its refinery in Saudi Arabia and its loading facilities there for finished products because of labor troubles, and also the crude oil pipeline to Bahrein. Sec asked about supply to Western Europe. S said normally 9-1/2 million flows to Europe; now 1.3 from Iraq and 1.7 from Libya is out; Saudi 2.3, but that may not be meaningful; Kuwait 2.3, Algeria .7. Sec asked if situation should be characterized as serious, critical, disastrous. S said the most serious immediate impact is the closing of the Suez Canal; if oil producing govts do not escalate, we calculate that short fall will be somewhere for Europe and Japan only 5–15%, but so far the major oil producing govts are not extending the US-UK destination ban to US-UK flags, owners or companies.[3]

---

[1] Source: National Archives and Records Administration, RG 59, Rusk Files: Lot 72 D 192. No classification marking. Prepared by Carolyn J. Proctor.

[2] A letter of June 8 from Rusk to Secretary of the Interior Stewart L. Udall stated that Algeria, Kuwait, and Bahrein had prohibited the export of petroleum to the United States and the United Kingdom; Iraq had ordered the Iraq Petroleum Company to cease operations; Aramco's Trans Arabian Pipeline had been closed, as had the Suez Canal; and Libya had ordered foreign oil companies to cease operations. Rusk stated that these developments created an oil supply emergency adversely affecting the capability of the United States and its allies to meet their security responsibilities. He called for the initiation of emergency procedures. For text of the letter, see Foreign Relations, 1964–1968, vol. XXXIV, Document 235.

[3] A paper titled "The Middle Eastern Oil Problem" that Solomon sent to Bundy on June 9 stated that the flow of Arab oil was about 40 percent of normal. Saudi Arabia, Libya, and Iraq were exporting no oil, Kuwait and Algeria were embargoing oil to the United States and Britain, Abadan was closed by a strike of Iraqi tanker pilots, and Bahrain was operating at reduced capacity. It stated that the flow might increase over the weekend, leaving a relatively limited shortfall of 1.5 million barrels/day, combined with a serious tanker problem as long as the Suez Canal remained closed, but if the Arab producers tried to use oil denials to pressure the United States into dislodging the Israelis from the West Bank, a major supply crisis could extend for a considerable time. (Johnson Library, National Security File, NSC Special Committee Files, Economic)

215.   Telegram From the Department of State to the Embassy in Israel[1]

Washington, June 8, 1967, 2 p.m.

209253. 1. Secretary called in Israeli Ambassador Harman noon June 8. Said he had just spoken with President[2] and was instructed express in very strong terms USG dismay at today's attack on US naval vessel by Israeli naval unit. Said 4 are dead, 53 are injured at latest report. Ship badly listing. Requested Harman convey at once to Prime Minister our real dismay at this very serious matter. Said we consider it amazing that GOI motor torpedo commander could be unable to identify a U.S. naval vessel. We want GOI to issue very explicit instructions in this regard to Israeli naval commanders for we cannot accept attacks on our vessels on high seas.[3]

2. Secretary said we appreciate speed with which GOI informed us this action had been done by one of its craft. This speed of notification in itself may have avoided very serious consequences in many respects.

3. Harman promised inform his government immediately. Noted he had no information yet from GOI on this occurrence but had learned of it within the hour during call on Assistant Secretary Battle to whom he had expressed his great sorrow.

Rusk

---

[1]   Source: National Archives and Records Administration, RG 59, Central Files 1967–69, POL 27 ARAB–ISR. Secret; Flash. Drafted by Wolle; cleared by Rusk's Special Assistant Harry W. Schlaudeman, and approved by Battle. Repeated Flash to CINC-STRIKE, Amman, Beirut, Cairo, USUN, Moscow, USCINCEUR, and CINCUSNAVEUR.

[2]   The President met from 11:06 to 11:45 a.m. with Rusk, McNamara, Clifford, Katzenbach, Thompson, Bundy, and Rostow in the Situation Room. (Johnson Library, President's Daily Diary)

[3]   In a telephone conversation with Goldberg, Rusk told him that the next time he saw Eban, he should "hit him hard on this attack; if Israeli torpedo boats are attacking international shipping in international waters that is very dangerous business; if they were to hit a Soviet vessel that is extremely explosive." (Notes of telephone conversation prepared by Carolyn J. Proctor, June 8, 12:51 p.m.; National Archives and Records Administration, RG 59, Rusk Files: Lot 72 D 192, Telephone Calls)

216. Message From Premier Kosygin to President Johnson[1]

Moscow, June 8, 1967, 12:20 p.m.

Dear Mr. President,

Your telegram concerning the incident with the American Liberty Type Ship torpedoed near Port Said has been received by us and immediately transmitted for information to President Nasser.[2]

Respectfully,

A. Kosygin

---

[1] Source: Johnson Library, National Security File, Head of State Correspondence, USSR, Washington–Moscow "Hot-Line" Exchange, 6/5–10/67. No classification marking. The message is labeled "Translation." A typed notation indicates a sight translation was made at 12:25 p.m.; the message was received by the President at 12:30 p.m.; a rough translation was made at 12:34 p.m.; and a final, official translation was provided at 1:15 p.m. A typed notation on a copy of the message in Russian states it was transmitted by Soviet Molink at 12:20 p.m. and received by U.S. Molink at 12:23 p.m. (Ibid.) Rostow forwarded the message to the President in a 12:45 p.m. memorandum, commenting that this exchange of messages was "one reason the link was created: to avoid misinterpretation of military moves and incidents during an intense crisis." (Ibid., Memos to the President, Walt Rostow, Vol. 30) For Ambassador Thompson's comments, see Document 245.

[2] Kohler telephoned Chernyakov at 12:45 p.m. to tell him of the exchange of hot line messages and to thank him for his cooperation. He also noted that Kosygin had described the vessel as a "Liberty-type ship," but that in fact, U.S.S Liberty was the name of the ship. (National Archives and Records Administration, RG 59, Central Files 1967–69, POL 27 ARAB–ISR)

217. **Telegram From the Commander in Chief, Naval Forces, Europe (McCain), to the Commander in Chief, European Command (Lemnitzer)[1]**

June 8, 1967, 1903Z.

081903Z. Movements and position of *Liberty*.

A. JCS CFWP JA3 sends DTG 011545Z Jun 67[2]
B. CINCUSNAVEUR 061357Z Jun 67[3]
C. COMSIXTHFLT 071503Z Jun 67 PASEP[4]
D. JCS 7347 DTG 080110Z Jun 67[5]
E. CINCUSNAVEUR 080455Z Jun 67 PASEP
F. USCINCEUR ECJC/JRC 09045 DTG 080625Z Jun 67 PASEP
G. COMSIXTHFLT 080917Z Jun 67
H. USS *Liberty* 021330Z Jun 67

1. By Ref A JCS directed *Liberty* to proceed to posit 32–00N 33–00E.

2. By Ref B CINCUSNAVEUR passed OPCON to COMSIXTHFLT. Movements of *Liberty* were still guided by Ref A.

3. At 072350Z CINCUSNAVEUR duty officer received phone call from Major Breedlove, JRC Washington, directing that USS *Liberty* comply with new COMSIXTHFLT OP area restrictions delineated in last sentence paragraph two of Ref C and not to proceed closer than 100 miles to Israel, Syria or UAR. This was verbal directive with no DTG of message available. Necessary messages were then prepared.

4. At 080140Z and prior to release of any messages, the USCINCEUR duty officer, Lt Col Wagner, was called and advised of JRC phone call. In view of no written directive at this time, he was requested to obtain DTG of message from JCS because a previous JCS directive was being modified.

5. At 080325Z USCINCEUR duty officer, Lt Col Russell, was contacted to see what results had been achieved on previous phone call. He called JRC Washington and obtained Reference D, which modified Reference A. (i.e. JCS 011545Z) This was read to CINCUSNAVEUR duty officer.

---

[1] Source: Johnson Library, National Security File, Country File, Middle East Crisis, Vol. V. Secret. The telegram does not indicate precedence, but another copy shows that it was sent Immediate. (National Security Agency Archives, Accession No. 45981, U.S.S. *Liberty* Correspondence and Messages, 1965–1968) Repeated to CNO, COMSIXTHFLT, CINCLANTFLT, and JCS.

[2] Document 118.

[3] References B, E, F, G, and H are tabs 30, 48, 49, 53, and 23 to the "Report of the JCS Fact Finding Team," cited in footnote 2, Document 337.

[4] Document 192.

[5] Document 199.

6. At 080410Z CINCUSNAVEUR established teletype conference with COMSIXTHFLT duty officer, CDR Slusser, and relayed Reference D, and told him "take FORAC[6] official message follows."

7. At 080455Z CINCUSNAVEUR sent immediate message to COM-SIXTHFLT directing him to take Ref D FORAC.

8. At 080914Z CINCUSNAVEUR received USCINCEUR msg, Reference F, directing CINCUSNAVEUR to take Ref D FORAC.

9. At 080917Z COMSIXTHFLT sent a message, Ref G, directing *Liberty* to comply with Ref D and remain 100 miles from coasts UAR, Israel, Lebanon, and Syria. *Liberty* was also info addee on Ref D, sent at 080110Z which directed her to remain 100 miles from belligerent coasts.

10. Am directing COMSIXTHFLT to investigate reason for non-receipt or non-compliance by *Liberty* to respond to two messages, Refs D and G directing her to proceed 100 miles from coast.[7]

11. *Liberty*'s movement report Ref H (of Jun second) indicated she would arrive at position directed in Ref A (posit 32–00N 33-00E) at 080300Z.

---

[6] A handwritten note in the margin reads: "FORAC means: For action."

[7] The *Liberty* did not receive these messages. The reasons for the communications failure are discussed extensively in the "Report of the JCS Fact Finding Team," cited in footnote 2, Document 337. See also *Review of Department of Defense Worldwide Communications, Phase 1: Report of the Armed Services Investigating Subcommittee of the Committee on Armed Services, House of Representatives, Ninety-second Congress, First Session, May 10, 1971* (Washington, 1971), and Chronology of Events, Naval Security Group File on U.S.S. *Liberty* in Naval Security Group Files, Box 702, CNSG Pre-76 Inactive Files 168, NAVSECGRU File or USS *Liberty.*

---

218.   Telegram From the U.S.S. *Liberty* to the Chief of Naval Operations (McDonald)[1]

June 8, 1967, 1715Z.

081715Z. Situation following air attack.

1. At 081205Z while ship on course 283 deg speed 05 knots position 31 deg 35.5 min north 33 deg 29 min east ship attacked by unidentified

---

[1] Source: Naval Security Group Records, Box 896, USS *Liberty* Pre-76 Inactive Files, Box 1, U.S.S. *Liberty*, 5750/4, Chronological Message File. Unclassified; Immediate. Repeated to CINCUSNAVEUR, CINCEUR, JCS (JRC), CINCLANTFLT, COMSIXTHFLT, and COMSERVLANT. Received at 1916Z.

jet fighters, believed to be Israeli. Approximately six strafing runs made on ship. Approximately 081225Z three torpedo boats one identified as Israeli approached ship on stbd qtr at high speed. Hull number of one boat was 206–17. Approximately 081227Z took torpedo under fire with 50 caliber machine guns have range of 2000 yards. Torpedo boat launched torpedo and straffing attack. One torpedo passed approx 25 yards astern approximately one minute later ship sustained torpedo hit stbd side. Ship is 10 deg stbd list water tight boundaries established and holding after attack torpedo boat cleared to east about five miles. Clearing area at 10 knots.

2. Photos of aircraft and boats taken. After attack completed two Israeli helicopters orbited ship at about 081255Z range 500 yards. Israeli insignia clearly visible. Photos taken. Several projectiles have been recovered from topside areas. Number dead is estimated at 10, number seriously wounded at 15. Total wounded 75, number missing currently undetermined.

3. Ship unable to carry out mission, will submit personnel casreps as soon as possible separately.

4. Extensive superficial damage topside. Lower deck spaces forward destroyed.

5. Comm capabilities limited. Will provide film and projectiles recovered as directed. Ship will require drydock and extensive refitting.

---

219.   Memorandum for the Record[1]

Washington, June 8, 1967, 3:30 p.m.

SUBJECT

The USS *Liberty* (AGTR–5) Struck by Torpedo

1. At 080911 EDT June, USCINCEUR notified the NMCC by phone that the USS *Liberty* was under attack, had been hit by a torpedo and was listing to starboard. The ship was operating in the Mediterranean Sea approximately 60–70 miles east-northeast of Port Said.

---

[1] Source: Johnson Library, National Security File, NSC Special Committee Files, *Liberty*. Top Secret. Prepared in the National Military Command Center.

2. The oral report of the incident was confirmed by a COMSIXTH-FLT message reporting the USS *Liberty* had been hit by a torpedo on the starboard side at 080830 EDT. Three unidentified gunboats were reported to be approaching the vessel with the USS *Liberty* listing badly.

3. At 081013 EDT a message from COMSIXTHFLT[2] stated the attack forces were declared hostile. COMSIXTHFLT also reported the following actions: the USS *America* had been directed to launch four armed A–4s and the USS *Saratoga* to launch four A–1s with fighter cover to defend *Liberty*. The pilots were directed to remain clear of land. In addition, TF–60 was directed to proceed toward the scene. Air refueling tankers were also ordered to launch, the first aircraft were on the scene at approximately 0945 EDT.[3]

4. At 081045 EDT, a message was received from the USDAO in Tel Aviv[4] stating that Israeli aircraft and motor torpedo boats had erroneously attacked a vessel in the Mediterranean Sea at 080800 EDT, which was thought to be a US Navy ship. Israeli helicopters were conducting rescue operations. The Israeli government sent abject apologies and requested information on other US ships near the war zone.

5. Late information discloses ten US killed and 75 wounded of whom 15 are in serious condition.

6. Two destroyers from TF–60 have been directed to proceed at full speed to the USS *Liberty*, now underway north on a northwesterly course at 8 knots. The rendezvous is estimated for 0001 EDT 9 June.

7. *Liberty* declined the aid offered by the Israeli helicopters; the status of evacuation of wounded is unknown at this time, however, helicopter evacuation is not feasible.

8. A late report reveals that *Liberty* was subject to six aircraft strafing passes in addition to the attacks of the gunboats cited in paragraph 2, above.

Charles M. Gettys
Brigadier General, USA
Deputy Director for
Operations (NMCC)

---

[2] Document 207.

[3] The Commander of the Sixth Fleet estimated that the aircraft would be launched at 1345Z, or 0945 EDT, and would arrive on the scene 1 hour and 30 minutes later (see Document 207).

[4] Document 211.

220.   Message From President Johnson to Premier Kosygin[1]

Washington, June 8, 1967, 3:58 p.m.

Dear Mr. Kosygin,

I deeply appreciate your transmitting the message to President Nasser. We lost 10 men, 16 critically wounded, and 65 wounded, as a result of Israeli attack, for which they have apologized.

Respectfully,

Lyndon B. Johnson

---

[1] Source: Johnson Library, National Security File, Head of State Correspondence, USSR, Washington–Moscow "Hot-Line" Exchange, 6/5–10/67. No classification marking. A typed notation on the message indicates it was approved by the President at 3:36 p.m.; transmitted by U.S. Molink at 3:58 p.m.; and received by Soviet Molink at 4 p.m.

---

221.   Memorandum From the President's Special Consultant (Bundy) to the Special Committee of the National Security Council[1]

Washington, June 8, 1967.

SUBJECT

Minutes of NSC Special Committee 6:30 p.m., Thursday, June 8, 1967

The President expressed in the strongest terms his view that too many officers talking with foreign diplomats about US policy are going beyond what the President or the Secretary of State has seen or approved. He ordered that all diplomatic contacts involving policy questions be carried out only by the Secretary or by another officer specifically delegated by him in specific cases, and that there should be discussion of major policy positions only after the President himself has approved them.

The President also stated that providing press guidance on policy questions is the direct responsibility of the President or the Cabinet officer

---

[1] Source: Johnson Library, National Security File, NSC Special Committee Files, Special Committee Meetings. Secret. No drafter is indicated on the memorandum, which was prepared June 9. Present for the entire meeting were Rusk, McNamara, Fowler, Katzenbach, Wheeler, Helms, Clifford, Eugene Rostow, Battle, Walt Rostow, Bundy, and Saunders. The President attended from 7:10 to 7:45 p.m. (Ibid., President's Daily Diary)

concerned. He instructed the Cabinet level members of the Committee to handle such press discussions themselves, except as they may specifically authorize senior officers of their departments on particular topics. He expects the Information Subcommittee of the NSC Special Committee to provide routine guidance. But he insists that each Cabinet officer put a stop to the present situation in which other officers discuss their own personal ideas as if they were the position of the U.S. Government.

The President has asked me to emphasize that this guidance is intended to apply to all members of the Government, including the Special Committee.[2]

McGeorge Bundy

---

[2] Bundy had suggested that the President might want to make these points at the meeting in a memorandum that he sent to the President at 5:25 p.m. (Ibid.)

---

222. Memorandum by Harold Saunders of the National Security Council Staff[1]

Washington, June 8, 1967.

NSC SPECIAL COMMITTEE: SUSPENSE

Actions and Policy Questions Pending from
Meeting of Thursday, 8 June

Actions

1. *Visit by King Hassan of Morocco.*[2] Committee agreed we should tell him politely not to come. The President agreed. *Action:* Mr. Battle (a) to

---

[1] Source: Johnson Library, National Security File, NSC Special Committee Files, Suspense. Secret. Saunders sent this memorandum to Bundy on June 8 with a note saying that he would give him each morning, in addition to the minutes, a checklist like this of pending items that he would want to consider for the evening's agenda. The memorandum was based on Saunders' notes of the meeting. Neither Saunders' nor Helms' notes of the meeting indicate any discussion of the attack that day on the *Liberty*.

[2] Telegram 5439 from Rabat, June 8, reported that King Hassan had asked the Ambassador to inform President Johnson that Nasser and other Arab leaders wanted to send Hassan to Washington to discuss the next steps in the Arab–Israel crisis and to determine whether the United States and the Soviet Union were serious about seeking a "real solution" to the Arab-Israeli problem. The King had not decided whether to accept this mission and did not want to do so unless he would be able to report back something of substantive importance. (Ibid., NSC Histories, Middle East Crisis, Vol. 3)

send an interim reply to Ambassador Tasca tonight and (b) to draft a substantive reply for consideration tomorrow.

2. *Report on aid going to the Middle East.* The President asked for a report on all aid, including Ex-Im and IBRD, flowing to the area. *Action:* Report already requested, due tomorrow.

3. *Arms moving to the Middle East.*

a. *Preventing Arab resupply.* The Committee discussed how to preclude Soviet use of the cease-fire to re-equip Arab air forces to make a first strike next time and yet to handle Israeli requests for replacement equipment. *Action:* Mr. Battle to draft a telegram to Paris, London and Moscow to surface issues that must be resolved (a) to get a grip on resupply over the next 30 days and (b) to lay the basis for a longer run attack on Middle East arms limitation.

b. *Handling Israeli requests.* Secretary McNamara reported Ambassador Harman's request for 48 A–4 aircraft. The Committee agreed that we should ask the Israelis for precise figures on their losses and remaining inventory. *Action:* Defense to ask Harman.

c. *US sales and grants to Arab countries.* The Committee discussed how to avoid the political repercussions that arms shipments to Arab countries would trigger. *Action:* The Committee will hear a report tomorrow.

Hal

---

223. Circular Telegram to All Posts[1]

Washington, June 8, 1967, 9:53 p.m.

209525. Subject: Middle East Sitrep as of June 7 [8].

1. Day marked by heavy fighting in Sinai, where by-passed Egyptian units attempted to fight way back to west side of Suez Canal. During course of day, Israelis claim to have closed off all possibility escape of Egyptian units except on foot. Also stated they intend stop few miles short of Canal in order avoid getting entangled in Canal's

---

[1] Source: National Archives and Records Administration, RG 59, Central Files 1967–69, POL 27 ARAB–ISR. Secret; Priority. Drafted by Lambrakis, cleared by Officer in Charge of UN Political Affairs Betty-Jane Jones and William D. Wolle (NEA/IAI), and approved by Davies.

problems. By end of day UAR Government notified SYG Thant it accepts cease-fire provided Israel does too. (Israel has already signified it would.) We have unconfirmed report from some Washington Embassy sources that Canal has been open today to shipping of various nations, though not US or UK.

2. Artillery and air bombardment of Syrian positions on heights overlooking Israeli border settlements commenced today. Syrians have been pounding Israeli settlements steadily since June 5, having reportedly leveled some of them, although settlers protected by shelters. Action expected to continue through night into tomorrow. Syrians have so far refused accept cease-fire.

3. Jordanian front fairly quiet. Israelis have not penetrated in any force east of Jordan River and have stated intention keep to West Bank. They may have bombed Mafraq airfield to prevent its further use by Iraqi planes. Jordan Government puts number of refugees streaming out of West Bank to outskirts Amman at 20–30,000.

4. U.S. Navy technical research vessel *Liberty* attacked by Israeli torpedo boats and aircraft today. Israelis immediately apologized for error to Embassy Tel Aviv. Secretary called in Israeli Ambassador Washington to protest in very strong terms, while also expressing appreciation for quick Israeli notification. Latest count dead at 10, with 50 or 60 injured. Crippled ship limping away under Sixth Fleet air escort.

5. In surprise propaganda coup, Israeli radio reportedly has been broadcasting what it describes as taped radiophone conversation between Nasser and Hussein June 6 which clearly indicates they fabricated story that US and UK aircraft assisting Israelis.

6. Tunisians have informed us they do not intend to break relations. Nor will they send any military assistance to Nasser if war does not drag on much longer. Sudan has interpreted its break of diplomatic relations not to include consular, commercial, economic, or cultural relations.

7. At UN this afternoon, US and Soviet resolutions introduced. US resolution calls for cease-fire to be put into effect by all parties, after which discussions to begin promptly among the parties concerned, using third party or UN assistance if they wish, looking toward establishment of viable arrangements on withdrawal of armed personnel, renunciation of force regardless of its nature, maintenance of vital international rights, and establishment of stable and durable peace in ME.[2] Soviet resolution seeks to condemn Israel as aggressor and

---

[2] UN document S/7952; the text of the resolution as subsequently revised is printed in Department of State *Bulletin*, June 26, 1967, pp. 948–949.

demands Israeli withdrawal behind Armistice Lines.[3] Security Council recessed for day without vote on either resolution.

Rusk

---

[3] UN document S/7951.

---

224.   Memorandum From Peter Jessup of the National Security
        Council Staff to the President's Special Assistant (Rostow)[1]

Washington, June 8, 1967.

SUBJECT

Why the USS *Liberty* Was Where It Was

Attachment 1 shows the JRC forecast for June with the approved mission of the USS *Liberty*.[2]

This was changed by a routine submission on 2 June. These are normally noted by Jessup for the White House, McAfee for State, and Chapin for CIA. Being proposed by DOD, it is assumed this had full Pentagon approval, in this case Vance.

Routine changes without specific indications as to number of nautical miles off shore are merely noted and entered in the book.

It is assumed that such a ship will operate under the discretion of COMSIXTH FLEET and USCINCEUR.

It would seem to have been unnecessary at the time to submit this particular track change to the principals at the date submitted.

Let me make myself clear. There is no doubt in my mind that JRC is in the clear, having submitted this change in plans in good faith and on a timely basis.

Whether the actual nautical distance of the USS *Liberty* from the UAR coast on 8 June was unwise in view of the hostilities or whether this should be gauged as an accident of war is for others to judge.

[Omitted here is a paragraph unrelated to the *Liberty*.]

PJ

---

[1] Source: Johnson Library, National Security File, NSC Special Committee Files, *Liberty*. Top Secret. Also sent to Bundy and Bromley Smith.

[2] Not attached.

225. Memorandum From Secretary of Defense McNamara to the President's Special Consultant (Bundy)[1]

Washington, June 8, 1967.

You have asked what action we are taking to control deliveries of military equipment to Middle Eastern states.[2] The following rules are in effect:

1. No additional matériel can be released for delivery to any Middle Eastern state under either a military assistance program or a Defense Department controlled sale, without the approval of a representative of the Secretary of State and the Secretary of Defense.

2. Military equipment, previously released for shipment to Arab states which have broken relations with us, is being repossessed to the extent that it remains under our control. Today we are tracing a shipment of 134 radios to Iraq, the only remaining shipment in this category.

Both the Arab states and Israel have purchased directly from manufacturers substantial quantities of ammunition, military vehicles, and military spare parts. The manufacturers apply to the Munitions Control Board for licenses to export such equipment. A number of such licenses are outstanding. The Department of State's policy concerning exports of such arms is as follows:

a. Licenses issued for shipments to Arab states which have broken diplomatic relations with the United States have been suspended. United States Customs is refusing clearance of munitions destined for those countries. (This action has gone as far as unloading shipments to Iraq from a Dutch vessel in New York on June 7.)

b. No new munitions licenses are being approved for shipments to Israel or any Arab nation at war with Israel.

c. Existing approved licenses for munitions shipments to Israel and Arab countries which have not broken relations with the United States have not been suspended.

---

[1] Source: Johnson Library, National Security File, Special Committee, Military Aid. No classification marking.

[2] A June 8 memorandum from McNamara to the Secretaries of the Army, Navy, and Air Force and to the Assistant Secretaries of Defense for Installations and Logistics and for International Security Affairs directed the immediate suspension of all matériel shipments, whether grant aid or military sales, from depots, manufacturers' facilities, or other sources, to Morocco, Tunisia, Libya, Saudi Arabia, Israel, Lebanon, Jordan, and Kuwait. Matériel already shipped was to be delivered. It directed that new sales agreements and related commitments should not be signed but that on-going negotiations should not be broken off. All supply actions of either a grant or sales character to Algeria, Mauritania, the UAR, Sudan, Yemen, Iraq, and Syria were to be suspended. (Ibid., Minutes, Control Group Meetings)

We anticipate Israel will request assistance in procuring substantial quantities of ammunition, spare parts, and replacement equipment. Any such requests for items under U.S. control will be personally reviewed by Messrs. Vance and Katzenbach, and their recommendations will be submitted for approval to the National Security Council Subcommittee of which you are Executive Secretary.

Robert S. McNamara

---

226. **Memorandum From the Deputy Assistant Secretary of Defense for International Security Affairs (Hoopes) to Secretary of Defense McNamara**[1]

I–23560/67   Washington, June 8, 1967.

SUBJECT

Fundamental Problems Relating to an Armistice/Political Settlement in the Near East

While the political and military situations remain highly fluid, making comment upon them necessarily speculative, I believe we can now see the outlines of several central problems and opportunities. What follows here is a distillation of current thinking in ISA, and of certain views expressed in recent discussions of the Interdepartmental Control Group. My purpose is to provide you with an interim assessment, in terms of three or four factors that will, I believe, underlie the wide range of problems and papers you are likely to be addressing.

Whether the Middle East is on the verge of a fresh start (based upon Arab acceptance of Israeli legitimacy) turns vitally on (1) whether Nasser survives politically and (2) whether the Soviets attempt resuscitation of Nasser personally or a successor regime. The destruction of Nasser as an effective Pan-Arabist is fundamental to our hopes for gaining a reasonably quick settlement and for thus avoiding a protracted political impasse with all its dangers of further military action, polarization of the US behind Israel, or both. With Nasser removed (or discredited to the point where the Soviets deny him support), the Middle

---

[1] Source: Washington National Records Center, OSD Files: FRC 330 72 A 2468, Middle East, 092. Secret. A notation on the memorandum indicates it was seen by the Secretary of Defense on June 9.

East would probably be relieved, for some years, of the intense and effective extremism that has been constantly stimulated by the Nasser charisma and the UAR political propaganda apparatus. With those removed or seriously discredited, reasonable dealings with individual Arab states on the basis of practical mutual interest would be far more likely for Israel, and also for the US.

Assistant Secretary Battle's best assessment at the moment is that Nasser has less than a 50–50 chance of political survival. He thinks the nature of the succession depends on whether the group around him holds together. If it does, the successor will come from one of the top military leaders; if the Army splits, the successor regime will be faction-ridden and much weaker. A period of political chaos and impotence might follow. Battle estimates that the Soviets will probably not be willing to recapitalize Nasser on the scale required for his genuine resurrection; but he thinks they might encourage any UAR regime to oppose Israeli claims through lower scale assistance, while seeking a new Arab instrument through which to work. The most likely new instrument is Iraq, which has rather interestingly kept its political and military forces intact and relatively uncommitted during the current fighting.

ISA believes it is quite clear that the Israelis will hold fast to all of the territory gained during their remarkable military victory and will yield this up only in exchange for a political settlement which is far more substantial and basic than the armistice agreements under which they have been living since 1948. At a minimum, their demands will be assured access to the Gulf of Aqaba and the Suez Canal and an absolute guarantee of established frontiers. This last requirement clearly implies peace treaties (as opposed to an armistice) either guaranteed by the four major powers or resting on continued Israeli military dominance.

If Nasser is politically destroyed, it is possible that an agreement embodying most of Israel's demands can be achieved in a reasonably short time. However, it seems more likely that any UAR regime (with or without Nasser) will try hard to drag out negotiations and especially to refuse the signing of an actual peace treaty. If there is no prompt settlement, we thus face either further Israeli military action against the UAR designed to assure the destruction of any intransigent regime, or a protracted period of inconclusive political maneuver during which the Israeli armed forces hold their ground. In either case, but particularly in the latter, Israeli stamina will depend importantly on large infusions of economic aid and military resupply; the US will be under great pressure, generated by our real interest in creating the preconditions for a fresh start in the Middle East and by our domestic political situation—to provide this.

Our principal hope of avoiding this kind of situation lies in achieving Soviet cooperation. We would want them to press the UAR into a basic settlement embodying most of Israel's demands (or at least to avoid the kind of salvage operation that would encourage intransigence). The likelihood, however, is that the Soviets will not cooperate. They will probably continue to espouse the Arab cause in an effort further to polarize the political situation, putting the US behind Israel and the USSR behind the Arab world. The way to keep them from such a spoiling operation lies (1) in persuading them of the real dangers to world peace of a continuing military conflict, (2) clear indications that other Arab countries are not enthusiastic about being rearmed by the USSR, and (3) quick political settlements between Israel and other Arab states (e.g., Jordan, Lebanon, Saudi Arabia). Realization of the latter two courses are by no means out of the question. Soviet prestige is being severely damaged by the UAR debacle and the more moderate countries may find it prudent to acknowledge a new relationship with Israel. The US could be a vital influence in either case, pointing out the benefits of a new stability on the one hand, and working to moderate Israeli demands on the other.

With respect to the outcome in Jordan, there is great doubt as to Hussein's ability to survive politically. If he should be forced to flee (which seems at the moment less likely than it did yesterday; there is apparently an effective Israeli-Jordanian cease-fire), this could mean the end of Jordan as a national entity. If Hussein departs, Deputy Under Secretary Kohler believes it quite possible that Saudi Arabia and Iraq would move in to carve up the Jordanian territory east of the Jordan River. If this happened, it would mean a drastic realignment of national boundaries in the Middle East and would greatly strengthen an Israeli claim to retention of the territory on the West Bank (which has now been gained by military means).

The Soviets are continuing military resupply to the UAR. We might usefully test the Soviet attitude on Arab support generally by probing them on the matter of continued arms aid, for it would be in the US interest to achieve an arms limitation agreement with respect to the Middle East (with UK and France also participating). This is true, in my judgment, because neither Nasser nor any likely successor regime could long resist a settlement with Israel if it did not have assurances of substantial economic and military aid from outside. Thus a Soviet agreement to arms restraint would be a signal that they were liquidating their UAR investment. The UAR would then have to settle essentially on Israeli terms in order to remove Israeli troops from the Sinai, etc. If, on the other hand, the Soviets continue to supply arms to the UAR (and perhaps also to Syria and Iraq), it will be difficult for the United States to avoid becoming a major military supplier of Israel and more closely identified with Israeli goals.

If there is a protracted period of uncertainty following the heavy fighting (characterized by far-reaching Israeli demands and Arab refusal to meet them), serious breakdown of social organization could occur in parts of the Middle East (especially in the remnant of Jordan and perhaps also in the UAR). This would be aggravated if the oil-producing countries felt compelled to withhold oil (their principal source of revenue) for political reasons. The situation might require a new effort, by the US or an international body, to organize relief services—food, medicines, the handling of prisoners and refugees, etc. Several alternative approaches are being considered by the State Department. While such an enterprise would be essentially humanitarian, it could be a powerful means of restoring US influence and good standing among the Arabs. On that reasoning, an organization with the US clearly in the lead would be desirable.

Townsend Hoopes

---

227. Telegram From the Mission to the United Nations to the Department of State[1]

New York, June 9, 1967, 2256Z.

5675. Goldberg talk with Eban.

In conversation with Eban June 8, Goldberg stressed that at present moment, when Israel enjoying mil victories, it very important to work for genuine political settlement. Eban said Israel not seeking territorial aggrandizement and had no "colonial" aspirations.

Eban made no specific commitments and was seldom specific on details. Implied Israel really seeking peace treaty with Jordan. While not mentioning status of Jerusalem per se, Eban stressed Israel would make every effort to assure all religious groups concerning holy places. Similarly, Israel had no designs on UAR terr; merely seeking adequate security arrangements to protect Israeli terr. Re Sharm el Sheikh, however, Eban suggested Israel might want some sort of international controls on strait. At no point did Eban refer to Syria or Syrian frontier.

---

[1] Source: National Archives and Records Administration, RG 59, Central Files 1967–69, POL 27 ARAB–ISR. Secret: Priority; Exdis. Received at 7:49 p.m and passed to the White House at 8:05 p.m.

Goldberg strongly emphasized it necessary for American as well as world public opinion that Israel should not emerge from current situation as power with designs to infringe on territorial integrity of other countries.

Eban said Israelis had hoped to avoid any mil activity in areas where refugees congregated (presumably Gaza), but forced by mil action of other side to change battle plan to include these areas.

Goldberg urged Eban to contact Bundy on how peace might best be brought about and rancor and humiliation felt by Arabs overcome. Eban welcomed suggestion. Rafael later told Goldberg Eban had been in touch with Bundy June 8 and would meet with him on his next trip to US.

Goldberg

---

228. Telegram From the Embassy in the United Arab Republic to the Department of State[1]

Cairo, June 9, 1967, 0443Z.

8711. 1. Emboff met Salah Nasir at 0330 local 9 June at latter's request. Salah Nasir said that he wished convey his personal thinking to USG at critical time for Egypt. He stated this action undertaken entirely on his own initiative and emphasized that if it became known to those elements in Egypt which oppose him because of his basically pro-Western attitude, the result could be his ouster as head of intelligence.

2. In essence, he assesses balance of "influence on Nasir" as between Western oriented and Soviet oriented elements in UAR Government to be dangerously even and judges his own position to be precarious. The pro-Soviet extreme leftist elements are gathering strength from the present situation in which Egypt's plight, as it becomes increasingly evident, will have been so successfully portrayed—by Egypt itself—as the result of U.S. connivance with and direct support of Israel. He feels it imperative therefore that the U.S. take an initiative in UN and elsewhere which is, in his words, "pro-

---

[1] Source: National Archives and Records Administration, RG 59, Central Files 1967–69, POL 27 ARAB–ISR. Secret; Flash; Handled as Exdis. Received at 1:58 a.m.

Arab". He understands that there are limits to the extent of U.S. pro-Arabism or pro-UARism, but feels that it is of vital importance that the Soviets be prevented from assuming the role of defender of the Arab position in negotiations or proceedings in UN forum which will follow present cease-fire. If the Soviets are successful in so doing, it may well be impossible for him and likeminded others to arrest and modify the forces in Egypt working toward Sovietization.

3. *Comment:* It is, of course, extremely difficult to judge what proportion of this presentation is correctly attributable to the concern expressed and what to the objective of obtaining support of Arab position versus Israel. To what extent is the spectre of Sovietization a ploy? To what extent is Salah Nasir concerned to protect himself and to what extent is he concerned for Egypt? Emboff judges that while all these considerations are present in some degree, there is in fact—in Salah Nasir's view—a very precarious balance of forces within Egypt, which, if not tipped toward the West by U.S. action, will probably fall in the opposite direction within a fairly short time.[2]

4. Footnote: Our leased line, which has been out for past two days with total lack of cooperation from UAR control, is now working perfectly on the send side result Emboff statement he had no communication with Washington.

Nolte

---

[2] In telegram 8727 from Cairo, June 9, Nolte transmitted his suggestions on steps that might be taken toward establishing a "pro-Arab" position to tip the balance described in telegram 8711. (Ibid.)

---

229.   Telegram From the Embassy in Israel to the Department of State[1]

Tel Aviv, June 9, 1967, 0810Z.

4024. 1. Prime Minister Eshkol asks that the following message be transmitted to the President:

---

[1]   Source: National Archives and Records Administration, RG 59, Central Files 1967–69, POL 27 ARAB–ISR. Limited Official Use; Immediate. Received at 5:14 a.m. Passed to the White House, DOD, CIA, USIA, NSA, COMAC for POLAD, CINCSTRIKE, and USUN at 5:35 a.m.

2. "Dear Mr. President: I was deeply grieved by the tragic loss of life on the U.S. Naval ship *Liberty*. Please accept my deep condolences and convey my sympathy to all the bereaved families.[2]

3. May all bloodshed come to an end and may our God grant us peace evermore. Sincerely, Levi Eshkol."

Barbour

---

[2] Telegram 4028 from Tel Aviv, June 9, reported that Eshkol had asked the Embassy to inform the U.S. Government that the Israeli Government was "willing to make retribution to the families of the victims of the *Liberty* naval incident" and inquired whether such retribution would be acceptable. (Ibid.) Letters of condolence from Eban and Harman to President Johnson and Secretary Rusk, June 8, are in the Johnson Library, National Security File, NSC Histories, Middle East Crisis, Vol. 3, and the National Archives and Records Administration, RG 59, Central Files 1967–69, POL 27 ARAB–ISR.

---

230.   President's Daily Brief[1]

Washington, June 9, 1967.

1. Arab States–Israel

The ceasefire was observed on all fronts during the night. Further Israeli action is still possible against Iraqi forces in Jordan, however, since Baghdad has yet to accept the ceasefire.

The Israeli commander in Sinai reported that his forces were camping on the banks of the Suez Canal and the Red Sea.

Tel Aviv is beginning to discuss the terms it hopes to achieve in a permanent settlement with the Arab states. These include the establishment of an autonomous province of Jordan on the West Bank in which all Arab refugees could hopefully be settled.

The Israelis also intend to insist on the demilitarization of the Gaza strip and the Sinai border, guaranteed access to the Gulf of Aqaba, and an as yet undefined "new status" for a unified Jerusalem. The latter would guarantee people of all religions access to the holy places.

As for the Arab side, attention is now turning to what can be salvaged in post-ceasefire negotiations. Nasir, after earlier proposing an

---

[1] Source: Johnson Library, National Security File, NSC Histories, Middle East Crisis, Vol. 6, Appendix A. Top Secret; [*codeword not declassified*]. Regarding the release of this PDB, see footnote 1, Document 151.

Arab summit as a means of preserving Arab unity, is now proposing the publication of a ten-point joint resolution to be signed by all Arab chiefs of state. The proposed statement trots out all of Nasir's propaganda attacks on the US and other "colonialist forces supporting Israel." On balance, it looks like a rather feeble effort to save face.

Signs are growing that Egypt's defeat has badly damaged Nasir's prestige in the Arab world. He will have trouble getting many other chiefs of state to adhere to his "joint resolution."

2. Arab States

Arab resentment against the West continues to threaten US facilities. Libya appears to be a particularly dangerous spot at the moment.

3. Soviet Union

The Soviets are finding it hard to conceal their shock over the rapid Egyptian military collapse. A Soviet [*2-1/2 lines of source text not declassified*] could not understand "how our intelligence could have been so wrong." He asked despairingly, "How could we have gotten into such a mess?" Comments from other Soviets, while more restrained, reflect a similar state of mind.

[Omitted here are sections on unrelated subjects.]

LATE ITEM

Arab States–Israel

Israeli spokesmen told the press this morning that Egyptian troops had launched an attack on Israeli troops near the Canal, thus violating the ceasefire.

231. Telegram From the Embassy in Israel to the Department of State[1]

Tel Aviv, June 9, 1967, 1505Z.

4039. Ref: Tel Aviv 4026.[2]

1. It is difficult to obtain information on how fighting along Syrian border is going. Best we can get is statement by Argov as of 1630 local time that it was "necessary to weed out the people who had been shelling our settlements for the last two years. This effort is now under way and is proceeding satisfactorily. However, Haon is still being constantly hammered by Syrian artillery fire."

2. The operation may indeed by progressing "satisfactorily" but it is obviously taking longer than had been anticipated and Syrians are still able to fight. DATT estimates IDF AF making maximum air support effort.

Barbour

---

[1] Source: National Archives and Records Administration, RG 59, Central Files 1967–69, POL 27 ARAB–ISR. Secret; Immediate; Exdis. The date-time group on the telegram, 071505Z, is in error. Received on June 9 at 11:47 a.m. and passed to the White House at 12:10 p.m.

[2] Telegram 4026 from Tel Aviv, June 9, sent at 1014Z, reported that the Syrians had shelled Israeli settlements near the border and that Israeli forces were taking action to silence the guns, which they expected to complete in an hour or so. (Ibid.)

---

232. Memorandum From the President's Special Assistant (Rostow) to President Johnson[1]

Washington, June 9, 1967, 12:55 p.m.

Mr. President:

After reading the UPI 080A ticker,[2] Evron asked to come in. He said that he and Harman were as deeply troubled as you must be and as I

---

[1] Source: Johnson Library, National Security File, Country File, Middle East Crisis, Vol. V. Confidential. A copy was sent to McGeorge Bundy. A handwritten notation on the memorandum states that it was received at 1:30 p.m., and a handwritten "L" indicates the President saw it.

[2] Presumably the ticker described in telegram 209662 to Tel Aviv, June 9, which states that a UPI ticker was reporting that Eshkol had made a series of highly disparaging remarks on the U.S. Government attitude before the outbreak of the war. (National Archives and Records Administration, RG 59, Central Files 1967–69, POL 27 ARAB–ISR)

clearly was, by what he called "this nonsense." He said that there were three ways in which it might be turned to some advantage:

—as further evidence to the Arabs and Moscow that there was no collusion between the U.S. and Israel; and
—as the occasion for the Israeli Embassy and Government to work even harder on the Jewish community here to explain that President Johnson's policy has been correct and fundamentally helpful to Israel. He said that Finance Minister Sapir has been working on the West coast to this end.

Following your instructions, I was passive and simply reiterated your concern—which I had expressed yesterday—that there was great danger in Israel overplaying its hand, talking too much, and permitting the emotions of victory in the field to prevent them from doing what was wise for their own long-term interests.

He said that he had persuaded Eban to go back and go to work on planning the future settlement, including refugees, rather than stay in New York and enjoy the glory of the television cameras.

Walt

233.   Telegram From the Defense Attaché Office in Israel to the White House[1]

Tel Aviv, June 9, 1967, 1520Z.

0845. At 09/1300Z the IDF Assistant Army Spokesman Lt Col Michael Bloch telephoned to ALUSNA following seven points as "Further information on yesterday's incident with the American ship."

1. Ship was sighted and recognized as a naval ship 13 miles from coast.
2. Presence in a fighting area is against international custom.
3. The area is not a common passage for ships.
4. Egypt had declared the area closed to neutrals.
5. *Liberty* resembles the Egyptian supply ship *El Quseir.*

---

[1] Source: Naval Security Group Files, Box 896, USS *Liberty* Pre-76 Inactive Files, Box 1, U.S.S. *Liberty*, 5750/4, Chronological Message File. Secret; Immediate; Priority. Sent also to OSD, CNO, DEPT STATE, COMSIXTHFLT, CINCSTRIKE, CINCNAVEUR, and JCS. Repeated to DIA, USUN, CINCEUR–USEUCOM, CTG SIX ZERO PT TWO, USAFE, CINCUSAREUR, and CTG SIX ZERO. Received at the Department of the Navy at 1925Z.

6. Ship was not flying flag when sighted. She moved at "high speed" westward toward enemy coast.

7. IDF Navy had earlier reports of bombardment of El-Arish from sea.

Comment: 1. At first Col Bloch merely read off seven points. ALUSNA pressed him for a label for the statement asking if this were an official explanation of incident. Col Bloch could not supply a preamble on his own and ALUSNA requested he consult with some authority who could. Bloch called back in two minutes with the above quoted heading.

2. While *El Quseir* bears a highly superficial resemblance to *Liberty*, ALUSNA can not understand how trained professional naval officers could be so inept to carry out yesterday's attack. Certainly IDF Navy must be well drilled in identification of Egyptian ships. *El Quseir* is less than half the size; is many years older, and lacks the elaborate antenna array and hull markings of *Liberty*.

3. ALUSNA evaluates yesterday's erroneous attack resulted from trigger happy eagerness to glean some portion of the great victory being shared by IDF Army and Air Force and in which Navy was not sharing.

---

234.   Memorandum for the Record[1]

Washington, June 9, 1967, 3:26 p.m.

SUBJECT

Attack on USS *Liberty* (AGTR-5)

1. This memorandum updates and supplements memoranda, same subject, of 1530 EDT 8 June and 0600 EDT 9 June 1967.[2]

2. USS *Liberty* had been directed by JCS to proceed to 32–00N; 33–00E, a point 39 nautical miles north of the UAR coast. She was authorized to conduct operations south of 32–00N and between 33 and 34E, approaching no closer than 12-1/2 nautical miles of the UAR coast and 6-1/2 nautical miles from the Israeli coast. At 1950 EDT 7 June

---

[1] Source: Johnson Library, National Security File, Country File, Middle East Crisis, Vol. IV. Top Secret; Trine. Prepared in the National Military Command Center. A hand-written note on the memorandum indicates a copy was sent to Clifford.

[2] Document 219; the June 9 memorandum was not found.

CINCUSNAVEUR was notified by telephone by JRC to modify these instructions and to ensure that *Liberty* would operate no closer than 100 nautical miles to Israel, Syria and Egypt. This was confirmed by message dispatched at 072110 EDT. CINCUSNAVEUR passed this information to COMSIXTHFLT at 080010 EDT by teletype conference and by immediate message at 080055 EDT. At 080517 EDT, COMSIXTHFLT directed *Liberty* to operate within a 25 nautical mile radius of 33–40N, 32–30E until further notice, and to approach no closer than 100 nautical miles to the coasts of the UAR and Israel and 25 nautical miles to the coast of Cyprus.

3. At 080250 EDT, *Liberty* reported she was being orbited by two jet aircraft while at 31–27N, 34–00E,[3] a point 14 nautical miles from the coast and 22 nautical miles northeast of El Arish.

4. *Liberty* reported being under attack by jet fighters at 080805 EDT at position 31–35.5N, 33–29.0E, a point 25 nautical miles northeast of nearest land, and 3 nautical miles outside the 100 fathom (600-foot) curve. She was subjected to about six strafing passes and at 080825. EDT three torpedo boats approached the ship at high speed. The torpedo boats attacked and at 080828 EDT, *Liberty* suffered a torpedo hit on the starboard side and took a 10° list.

5. At 08050 EDT, COMSIXTHFLT ordered USS *America* to launch four armed A–4s and USS *Saratoga* to launch four armed A–1s and for *America* to provide fighter cover. However, before reaching *Liberty*, the aircraft were recalled following COMSIXTHFLT's receipt of the Israeli acknowledgment of the attack.[4] At this time, *Liberty* reported she had departed the area and was underway on a northwesterly course at 8 knots. At the same time, two destroyers were dispatched at best possible speed to rendezvous with the damaged ship.

6. USS *Massey* and USS *Davis* joined *Liberty* in position 33–01N, 31–59E at 090025 EDT, and transferred medical personnel to assist *Liberty*'s doctor. At this time *America* was 138 nautical miles from *Liberty* and estimated a closure speed of 30 knots.

7. Casualties from the attack were 10 killed, 90 wounded, and 22 missing, reported believed to be trapped in flooded compartments near the torpedo hit. However, an intercept of the Israeli pilots transmissions indicates they sighted men jumping into the water from the vessel they had attacked.[5] The Captain of *Liberty* was wounded and the ship's Executive Officer was killed.

---

[3] A June 10 memorandum for the record by Rear Admiral Raymond A. Moore, USN, Deputy Director for Operations at the National Military Command Center, states that the correct position had been established as 31–23N, 33–25E. (National Security Agency, Center for Cryptologic History Historical Collection, Series VIII, Crisis Files, Box 16a, NMCC re *Liberty*)

[4] See Document 284.

[5] See Documents 284, 285, and 319.

8. *Liberty* reported carrying out her emergency destruction bill, which includes the destruction of tapes, technical publications and specialized equipment.

9. The helicopter transfer of wounded and dead to *America* is proceeding and a fleet tug will join the formation this afternoon to escort *Liberty* to Souda Bay, Crete. Arrival is estimated at 1800 EDT 10 June.

10. Additional information on this incident will be provided as received.

Raymond A. Moore
Rear Admiral, USN
Deputy Director for
Operations (NMCC)

---

235.   **Memorandum From the President's Special Consultant (Bundy) to President Johnson**[1]

Washington, June 9, 1967, 6:15 p.m.

SUBJECT

The 6:30 Meeting

The main business at the Special Committee meeting tonight will be the tough immediate tactical question of arms and economic shipments to crisis areas. There is a clear division of opinion on the strategy—most of the professionals in the government would keep existing commitments (except arms) to Arab countries that have not broken relations. Clark Clifford takes a harder view. David Ginsburg, somewhat to my surprise, thinks there is merit in distinguishing between the good and bad Arabs. The detailed facts and figures are quite complex and you may wish to stay out of the meeting and let us give you a clear-cut paper for consideration tonight. Alternatively, you may want to come in between quarter of 7 and 7 and let me summarize the situation after we have had a whack at it. I have asked Francis Bator to come because he has such a good quick grasp of economic facts, and the Secretary of State is bringing his usual group, which is a bit too big for comfort but

[1] Source: Johnson Library, National Security File, NSC Special Committee Files, Special Committee Meetings. No classification marking.

apparently necessary while we are trying to sort out relations with that bureaucracy.

The other items which are up for discussion are listed in the attached agenda[2] and I think that they can all be handled without your help unless you choose to come.

My conversations with the Secretary make me doubtful that his back grounder[3] will meet the need you feel before the weekend. But I am more and more persuaded that the only real answer will be a serious public statement.[4] But I think we can and should wait until the actual situation is somewhat clearer. I also think we need time to prepare such a statement. If I had to guess, I think it ought to be from your own mouth and that it should be a calm historic review with basic guidelines and not specific commitments toward the future, and I would hope you might consider doing it about Wednesday of next week unless the situation changes.

[1.] The materials that various subcommittees are gathering can be drawn on for your speech on fairly short notice when you are ready. In essence what it would do is define and describe exactly what we have done since the middle of May—a most creditable record.

2. Report our own view of what has in fact happened and pin a rose or two on Nasser as a liar and others who have slandered the U.S.

3. Make clear that we have now seen a historical event which necessarily changes the landscape.

4. Project a positive picture of our hope for a strong and secure Israel in a prosperous and stable Middle East.

5. Emphasize that this task is in the first instance a task for the nations in the area. This is good LBJ doctrine and good Israeli doctrine, and therefore a good doctrine to get out in public.

6. Warn of the dangers of a new arms race and express our readiness to join with all in arrangements which will avoid the terrible waste of the arms race of the last ten years. (We are assembling detailed facts and figures on all the Soviets have wasted and all that these races have cost all concerned.) This comment should not be surfaced now but

---

[2] Attached but not printed.

[3] The text of a background press briefing given by Rusk at 5:05 p.m. is in the Johnson Library, National Security File, Appointment File, June 1967 Middle East Crisis.

[4] That morning Bundy sent the President a page of possible background comments with a note saying they were "some first thoughts on the way we should react now to all the noises about who did and who did not help Israel." (Note from Bundy to the President, June 9, 10:30 a.m.; ibid., NSC Special Committee Files, U.S. Position—Discussion)

should come after we have begun diplomatic efforts—perhaps tomorrow—with the Soviet Union directly.

7. Make clear the U.S. view that this time there must be a peace and not simply a set of fragmentary armistice agreements.

8. Put us on record in favor of a real attack on the refugee problem—again by the parties concerned.

9. The general effect of such a speech in my judgment should be to show mastery of the factual situation, clarity in the purpose of the U.S. sympathy for the legitimate goals of Israel in a radically new situation, discriminating sympathy for good Arabs as against bad Arabs, and a clear sense of what the role of the U.S. is and is not in this area.

McG. B[5]

---

[5] Printed from a copy that bears these typed initials.

---

236. Notes of a Meeting of the Special Committee of the National Security Council[1]

Washington, June 9, 1967, 6:30 p.m.

THOSE PRESENT

Rusk
McNamara
Wheeler
Katzenbach
E.V. Rostow
Helms
Kitchen

---

[1] Source: Johnson Library, National Security File, NSC Special Committee Files, Minutes and Notes. No classification marking. The President, Vice President, and Senator Joseph S. Clark of Pennsylvania were present from 6:53 to 6:59 p.m. The President returned to the meeting at 7:12 p.m. Except for a brief absence from 7:34 to 7:38 p.m., he was present until 7:53 p.m. (Ibid., President's Daily Diary) The notes are Saunders' handwritten notes of the meeting. A June 9 memorandum for the record by Bundy, headed "Minutes of NSC Special Committee," records three decisions by the committee. It states that the committee approved telling King Hassan "that now is not the time for a visit to Washington", approved acceding to a request by King Faisal that no U.S. naval vessels visit Saudi Arabian ports in the immediate future, and agreed that Helms' rejection of an offer [text not declassified] was the right response but that the matter might be reconsidered. (Ibid., National Security File, NSC Special Committee Files, Minutes and Notes)

Battle
Clifford
W.W. Rostow
McGB
Bator
Saunders
VP in at 6:50

DR: Not proceed now on basis that Nasser is out.[2] Khalifa—Wayne Hays—Lodge—Battle

Battle: to phone Lodge; to see Hays

DR: Telegram to Hassan: Cleared.[3]

Helms: [1 line of source text not declassified] Put if off for several days.

USS Liberty

DR: Senate For. Relats: Put in a bill for damages to USS Liberty. Senators outraged.

McGB: Respond to offer.

Battle: Israel make offer of damages public. Then we'll take posture of responding and figure out bill.

Clifford: My concern is that we're not tough enough. Handle as if Arabs or USSR had done it. Manner egregious. Inconceivable that it was accident. 3 strafing passes, 3 torpedo boats.

Set forth facts.

Punish Israelis responsible.[4]

DR: Do what is normal.

1) Reparation.
2) Punish.
3) No repetition.

Battle: action.

"This incomprehensible attack."

DR: US Naval vessels not visit Saudi ports. Approved.

---

[2] Nasser announced his resignation in a radio and television address on June 9 but withdrew it the following day after massive demonstrations in Cairo. Battle told Rusk in a telephone conversation at 4:58 p.m. on June 9 that he did not think Nasser was "out of the scene" yet. (National Archives and Records Administration, RG 59, Rusk Files: Lot 72 D 192, Telephone Calls) For text of Nasser's June 9 speech, see American Foreign Policy: Current Documents, 1967, pp. 520–523.

[3] In telegram 209982 to Rabat, June 9, Rusk instructed Ambassador Tasca to tell the King that Rusk and the President appreciated his offer and attached great importance to his advice but doubted that a visit at that time could achieve much of a substantive nature. (National Archives and Records Administration, RG 59, Office of the Executive Secretatiat, Middle East Crisis Files, 1967, Entry 5190, Box 17, Middle East Crisis Material)

[4] Saunders' marginal notation next to Clifford's remarks reads: "President subscribed 100%."

Sen. Clark: You have once-in-lifetime to pull out of this situation a disarmament agreement that goes pretty far.

Negotiation: Israelis diminish. Russians back in business[5]

ENDC

McGB: We have a subcommittee. Pres. said full steam ahead. Agenda today: arms shipments. Sovs promising resupply.[6]

McGB proposal: Interim order: We will do everything we can to stop everything to contiguous countries (Leb & Jor) and to those that have broken relations. Look at rest on Monday.

McGB: Stop talking about "the Arab world." Help them come apart. Say this in appropriate committees. We're going to start sorting these people out a bit.[7]

Economic Problems:

Bator:

1. How to stop AID, Ex-Im, CCC. To countries that have broken relations.
2. Magnitudes.
3. How to locate.[8]

Central point. We have legal auth. to stop everything that is not on the high seas. By Monday, be in position to stop.

Alg. $100,000[9]
UAR $85,000   } on high seas.
Saud $1,000,000

Title II & III
II—int'l agencies
III—US agencies, easier to stop.
7 ships 9,600 tons—CRS
2
8 ships to Alg.

DR: Not consistent with dignity of US.

DR: *Backgrounder.* Steer questions to participants. US–USSR.[10]

---

[5] A marginal notation next to Clark's comments reads, "6:50–6:56."

[6] A page inserted at this point, between the 2 pages of Saunders' notes, contains the following note in an unknown hand: "Pres. view that it is not appropriate to treat all the Arab countries [alike?]".

[7] A marginal notation at this point reads: "Pres. out. 7:30."

[8] A marginal notation next to Bator's comments reads: "Pres back." A note boxed off next to this line reads: "Israel: leaves stuff in pipeline. Not putting anything in."

[9] A boxed note next to the figures reads: "McGB formula: Moving as fast to stop as banks being open permit."

[10] A marginal notation at this point reads: "Pres. left at 7:50 p.m."

Message to Eshkol:

Turk amb—Syrians had come to him.

Call Harman again.

DR: Message from LBJ to Eshkol to be read in UNSC by Amb. Goldberg.[11]

---

[11] This comment by Rusk appears at the top of the second page of Saunders' notes. In a box just below it is:

Pres: "I had a firm commitment from Eshkol & he blew it.

"Now he says he did it all himself.

"That old coot isn't going to pay any attention to any imperialist pressures."

A suggested draft letter from the President to Eshkol stressing the importance of immediate compliance with the latest Security Council resolution, which Goldberg had suggested, is in the Johnson Library, National Security File, Country File, Middle East Crisis, Vol. V.

---

237. Memorandum From the President's Special Consultant (Bundy) to the Special Committee of the National Security Council[1]

Washington, June 9, 1967.

I. Interim Policy on Military and Economic Pipelines to the Middle East

1. Military

No materials that we can still control will be allowed to get to any country which has broken relations with us, or to Lebanon or Jordan, until further notice. Materials already authorized for delivery to other Middle Eastern countries are not to be interrupted at this time.

2. Economic Assistance

The same rules will apply as for military goods except that economic assistance shipments to Jordan and Lebanon will not be interrupted for the present.

3. PL 480 Shipments

Foods shipped under Title II and Title III will not be interrupted at all. It is understood that there are no shipments under Title I or Title IV to any countries that have broken relations with us.

---

[1] Source: Johnson Library, National Security File, Special Committee No. 1, 6/7/67–6/30/67. Secret.

4. The Departments of State and Defense will be ready to offer further recommendations, if necessary, for consideration by the Special Committee on Monday together with a simple and more general public statement for public use when necessary.

II. Members of the Special Committee may wish to take note of the President's judgment that in the current situation it is wise not to treat all the Arab countries as if they were identical in behavior or policy.

III. It was agreed that the Department of State will take the strong and firm line which is appropriate in requesting adequate explanation, restitution, and disciplinary action by Israel for the destruction of lives and property on USS *Liberty*.

McGeorge Bundy

---

238.   **Telegram From the Department of State to the Embassy in Israel**[1]

Washington, June 9, 1967, 7:31 p.m.

209890. Amman's 4180.[2]

Dept deeply concerned over reported Israeli attempts encourage West Bank residents to flee to East Bank of Jordan. Marked increase in refugee population on East Bank will exacerbate already dangerous internal security situation existing in that area. It will also complicate our efforts to find a solution of the overall refugee problem which is now being seriously addressed. You should convey our concern ASAP

---

[1] Source: National Archives and Records Administration, Central Files 1967–69, POL 27 ARAB–ISR. Secret; Immediate. Drafted by Marshall W. Wiley (NEA/ARN); cleared by Wolle, Houghton, and Grey; and approved by Davies. Repeated Immediate to USUN, Amman, and Jerusalem.

[2] Telegram 4180 from Amman, June 9, reported that the Jordanian Foreign Minister had appealed to the four big power ambassadors in Amman to use their influence with the Israelis to let the West Bank population stay where it was and "not send them out of the West Bank to be refugees." The British Ambassador said the Foreign Minister had told him the Israelis were going around Palestinian villages with loud-speaker trucks offering safe conduct through the lines for villagers who wanted to leave. (Ibid.)

to appropriate level of GOI and urge them desist from any such encouragement for above reasons.[3]

Rusk

---

[3] Telegram 4057 from Tel Aviv, June 10, reported that the Embassy had taken this up with Argov, who stated that the Israeli Government was not encouraging West Bank residents to leave areas under Israeli control but was telling them they could stay or leave as they wished. (Ibid.)

---

239. Telegram From the Department of State to the Embassy in Israel[1]

Washington, June 9, 1967, 9:32 p.m.

209964. For Ambassador from Secretary.

Please see Eban as soon as possible and tell him, as a personal message from me, that the position of Israel at the UN is deteriorating rapidly because of a general impression that Israel is not throwing itself fully behind the effort of the Security Council to obtain a cease fire. As far as the US is concerned, he knows that we are fully in support of the Security Council resolutions. We consider it very important that Israel demonstrate by actions on the ground that its announcement about the orders it has issued means what it says. If the cease fire on the Syrian front is not effective immediately, there is likely to be broad support in the Security Council for condemnation of Israel. Finally, please tell Eban that I have spent the morning with the Senate Foreign Relations Committee and that there is very strong feeling here about the incomprehensible attack on the USS *Liberty*. We shall be in touch with his government by means of a note on this subject later.[2]

Rusk

---

[1] Source: Johnson Library, National Security File, Country File, Middle East Crisis, Vol. V. Confidential; Immediate; Nodis. Drafted by Rusk and Sisco and approved by Rusk. Repeated to USUN.

[2] For text of the note that Eugene Rostow gave to Harman on June 10, see Document 256.

240.   Memorandum From the Acting Chairman of the Central
        Intelligence Agency's Board of National Estimates (Smith) to
        Director of Central Intelligence Helms[1]

Washington, June 9, 1967.

CURRENT SOVIET ATTITUDES AND INTENTIONS IN THE
MIDDLE EAST

Note: It should be emphasized that this memorandum deals primarily with the immediate and short-term Soviet reactions to the current situation. Further, at the moment of writing, it is still quite unclear who is in control in Cairo, and the outcome of this situation will obviously affect Soviet policies.

1. We do not believe that the Soviets planned or initiated the Middle Eastern crisis. The Israeli-Arab war and, more specifically, the defeat of the UAR in that war, were developments which the USSR did not desire, initially did not foresee and, later, could not forestall. But it is clear that the Soviets were actively involved in the crisis from mid-May on.

2. Soviet propaganda support of the Arabs became strident and specifically accused Israel of planning to attack Syria. More important, the Soviets privately warned the Egyptians (and probably the Syrians as well) that they had learned Israel was preparing some sort of military action against Syria sometime between 17 and 21 May. The Soviets also advised both the Egyptians and Syrians to remain calm and not to provoke Israel militarily, but the effect of Moscow's private and public statements was to heighten Arab fears and passions, already greatly aroused by Israeli acts and statements and by Syrian cries of alarm. The Soviets probably expected to benefit from heightening of tensions. They probably estimated during the early stages of the crisis that a resort to violence by either side could, and probably would, be avoided.

3. We believe that Nasser's decision to blockade the Gulf of Aqaba (announced on 23 May) was made without Soviet counsel and that the Soviets received little or no advance warning of it. The evidence on this matter is fairly skimpy. A variety of Soviet sources have informed us that Moscow had no foreknowledge of the move; the Soviets displayed some uncertainty as to how best to handle the issue; and they carefully avoided any subsequent sanctioning of Nasser's move to close the Gulf

---

[1] Source: Johnson Library, National Security File, Country File, Middle East Crisis, Situation Reports. Top Secret; [*codeword not declassified*]. A handwritten "L" on the memorandum indicates the President saw it.

(though they did say that the entrance to the Gulf was in Egyptian territorial waters, as they had 10 years before). But our belief that the Soviets did not approve the Gulf closure rests partly on our judgment that the Soviets were well aware that this one move could provoke an Arab-Israel war.

4. Clearly they miscalculated the course of events. Nasser moved faster and further than they anticipated. The Israelis did go to war and inflicted on the Arabs a defeat far more rapid and complete than the USSR could have expected.

5. Soviet policy since the outbreak of the war has rested essentially, we think, on several considerations: the USSR's concern to avoid direct involvement in the war and to escape the risk of a direct confrontation with the US; its desire to preserve as many of the gains of the prewar crisis (both Soviet and Arab) as possible through diplomatic and propaganda means; its devout wish to avoid the stigma which would attach to Moscow if the Arabs suffered a complete defeat and the Soviets did little or nothing to prevent it; and, presumably, its hope that—through it all—they could preserve a viable relationship with their principal client in the Middle East, Nasser.

6. On the whole, the Soviets have behaved within the kind of guidelines suggested by the considerations listed above. They have maintained their propaganda attack against Israel; they have continued publicly to support the Arab cause; and after hostilities broke out they quickly made first contact with the US to proclaim their interest in peace and, implicitly, to reassure President Johnson that they plan no confrontation with the US over this issue.

7. Fedorenko's agreement in the UN to a ceasefire without the conditions demanded by the Arabs presumably reflected Soviet fear that, unless the fighting was soon halted, the Arabs would suffer a disastrous defeat. But this same action cost the USSR something within the Arab world. The partial Soviet abandonment of the Arabs at the UN will have to many the appearance of at least a partial sell-out.

8. Moscow has probably decided that its task now is to pick up as many pieces in the Middle East as it can, and has probably already estimated that its chances to recoup from recent setbacks are fairly good, especially over the long term. The Soviets still have impressive advantages in the area, the principal ones being the high tide of anti-US and anti-Israeli feeling, and the Arab belief that the USSR is the only major power likely to provide support for them in the foreseeable future. The Soviets probably believe that the US has suffered more severe and lasting political losses in the Arab world than they have.

9. The Soviets are probably hurting enough to take a new look at their attitudes and policies toward the Middle East. But they are proba-

bly not hurting enough to abandon their normal caution in international affairs to seek compensation for their losses by lashing out against the US elsewhere in the world. There are no places where dramatic Soviet gains could be scored without risking a confrontation with the US or, at the very least, substantial damage to existing Soviet policies.

10. We do not foresee a period of active Soviet cooperation with the US in the Middle East. Soviet willingness to act in at least partial concert with the US on the question of an immediate and unconditional ceasefire was born of the needs of the moment and did not, we think, reflect long-term considerations (other than the standard Soviet desire to avoid direct confrontation with the US). Basic US and Soviet goals in the Middle East—including, for example, the USSR's wish to increase its presence in the area and the US desire to prevent this—have not been altered by the current crisis.

---

241.   Telegram From the Mission to the United Nations to the Department of State[1]

New York, June 10, 1967, 0435Z.

5678. SC Mid-East Crisis. Ref: USUN 5672[2] and 5660, 5664,[3] 5655.[4]

Fol covers origin and conclusions two SC mtgs June 9:

1. When Mellbin (Denmark) consulted with Pedersen at 7 a.m. re Syrian request for urgent meeting of SC June 9, Mellbin gave fol info: Rafael (Israel) had phoned Danes first at 5 a.m. and gave them essen-

---

[1] Source: National Archives and Records Administration, RG 59, Central Files 1967–69, POL 27 ARAB–ISR/UN. Confidential; Priority. Received at 1:56 a.m. Passed to the White House, DOD, CIA, USIA, NSA, COMAC for POLAD, and CINCSTRIKE.

[2] Telegram 5672 from USUN, June 9. (Ibid.)

[3] Telegram 5660 from USUN, June 8, transmitted text of a U.S. draft resolution introduced that afternoon. It called for scrupulous compliance with the cease-fire by Israel and Jordan; immediate compliance with the Council's demands for a cease-fire by the other parties concerned; and discussions among the parties concerned, using such third party or UN assistance as they might wish, looking toward the establishment of viable arrangements encompassing the withdrawal and disengagement of armed personnel, the renunciation of force, the maintenance of vital international rights, and the establishment of a stable and durable peace in the Middle East. (Ibid.) Telegram 5664 from USUN, also June 8, transmitted amendments to the U.S. draft resolution. (Ibid.)

[4] Telegram 5655 from USUN, June 9. (Ibid.)

tially same info contained Tel Aviv 4026.[5] Sometime after 6 a.m. Tomeh (Syria) phoned Danes to request urgent SC meeting since Syria under attack from Israel on ground and in air. Danes consulted SC members and meeting arranged for 10 a.m.

2. Given necessity prompt SC action reaffirm cease-fire and demand compliance of all parties, we considered various tactical possibilities including having Pres table short new draft res, updating longer substantive US draft already on table (USUN 5660, 5664), or offering amendment to Canadian draft (USUN 5655) which also before SC but with priority status. Demark decided it willing put forward text on behalf SC Pres (USUN 5672). When meeting time came Syrians told us they had text calling for cease-fire. We agreed to it with change in op para to refer both to Syria and Israel instead of just Israel. USSR then tried to get preambular para referring to fighting going on in Syria in vicinity Adl. We rejected this in meeting of USSR, Denmark, Syria and ourselves. (*Comment:* Sov intent apparently was to embarrass us for not being prepared at this point to embrace explicit mention of armistice lines.) Finally, after this drafting had cost two hours, Sovs agreed to text as proposed by Syrians, which unanimously adopted after statements by Syria and Israel.[6] (See unclassified summary for SC meeting and USUN 5672 for text of res.)

3. SC reconvened after 7 p.m. in order hear latest SYG info on compliance with cease-fire. After lengthy discussion, in which Syrians cited news reports of Israeli advances and Sovs repeatedly stressed Israeli "aggression," SYG suggested that parties cooperate to permit UNTSO establish facts. Suggestion by Goldberg and motions by Fedorenko (USSR), Caradon (UK), and Tine (France), led to formulation by SC Pres of proposal requesting Israel to make govt house available to Gen Bull and UNTSO, calling upon both parties to permit freedom of movement to Gen Bull and UNTSO observers, and requesting SYG to report info he receives from observers to SC, which adjourned until 10:30 a.m. tomorrow morning, June 10.

4. Sovs submitted ltr after mtg requesting inscription new item entitled (approximately) "on cessation of hostilities by Israel and on the withdrawal of Israeli troops from Arab states". After conversation with Amb Pedersen, Amb Tabor took up with UNSec question of whether to inscribe item "ltr from permrep of the Sov Union," which would be preferable, or "ltr from permrep of Sov Union on cessation of hostilities by Israel and on withdrawal of Israeli troops from Arab states," which Sovs likely to press for. In anticipation this item, Sov continued explor-

---

[5] See footnote 2, Document 231.

[6] Security Council Resolution 235 (1967); the text is printed in *American Foreign Policy: Current Documents, 1967*, pp. 517–518.

ing with other dels, including Japanese and French, possibility of sim-ple withdrawal res. Shevchenko, to whom Sov permrep refers as his commissar, admitted to Plihon (France), however, that problem more complex than could be comprehended by simple withdrawal res.

5. Sov line appeared to harden during day with considerable emphasis placed by Sovs on communiqué of Moscow mtg key sentence of which read as fol: "If GOI does not stop aggression and withdraw its troops behind truce line, socialist states which signed this statement will do everything necessary to help the peoples of Arab countries to administer resolute rebuff to aggressor, to protect their lawful rights, and to extinguish hotbed of war in ME and restore peace in that area." Rafael (Israel) remarked to Pedersen Sovs had taken disturbing line and seemed to want to put statements on record prior to some unspecified action.

Comment: Issue of simple withdrawal as opposed to withdrawal as part of over-all settlement will be main and somewhat tricky problem as soon as cease-fire firms up.

Goldberg

242. Telegram From the Embassy in Israel to the Department of State[1]

Tel Aviv, June 10, 1967, 0550Z.

4045. Ref State's 209964.[2] For the Secretary.

I have just seen Eban (0445 Sat) and have given him your message orally. He asks that I tell you that he and Prime Minister are aware of importance that Israel make its acceptance of cease-fire clear by actions on the ground. They hope to achieve actual cease-fire in next few hours. If Syrians make this impossible, GOI will take steps before Security Council meets today to demonstrate publicly Israel's preparedness to stop where they now are and that it is the Syrians who are defying the Security Council.

[1] Source: National Archives and Records Administration, RG 59, Central Files 1967–69, POL 27 ARAB–ISR. Confidential; Immediate; Nodis. Received at 2:50 a.m.
[2] Document 239.

Eban noted two problems:

1) There is no machinery on the ground to verify actions of parties. He thinking of activating Gen Bull as means solving this one. 2) So far, each time Israelis have stopped firing, Syrians have reopened bombardment of settlements. He thinks Syrian objective is to prove that of all the Arabs, Syria is the only state which had inflicted serious damage on Israel.

Eban emphasized that Israel has no intention of going on to Damascus. It is trying physically to silence the Syrian gun positions but they are well emplaced, almost impervious to air attacks, and have to be taken by ground assault. Israel's forces on the Syrian front are very small. She is many times outnumbered and her whole position and purpose on that front is necessarily defensive.

Eban agreed my strong representation that crux situation is somehow to get fighting stopped or Israel risks prejudicing whole position it has so far achieved on other fronts. I am convinced he, at least, had no illusions this score and that he and Eshkol proposed for Israeli forces to cease all operations at existing positions, provided Syria ceases fire. This is also despite fact that apparently because of terrain and small Israeli forces available (it has been impossible redeploy appreciable forces from south) Israelis have not succeeded in wiping out Syrian gun positions as was intended.

Barbour

243. Message From Premier Kosygin to President Johnson[1]

Moscow, June 10, 1967, 8:48 a.m.

Dear Mr. President:

The events of the last days have forced me to express to you with all frankness our view. As the situation shows, the resolutions of the Security Council are invalid. Israel has completely ignored them. As you can understand, after the many attempts taken in this direction and the resolutions of the Security Council concerning the termination of aggression on the part of Israel in the Near East—these attempts have proved ineffective.

A very crucial moment has now arrived which forces us, if military actions are not stopped in the next few hours, to adopt an independent decision. We are ready to do this. However, these actions may bring us into a clash, which will lead to a grave catastrophe. Obviously in the world there are powers to whom this would be advantageous.

We propose that you demand from Israel that it unconditionally cease military action in the next few hours. On our part, we will do the same. We purpose to warn Israel that, if this is not fulfilled, necessary actions will be taken, including military.

Please give me your views.

A. Kosygin

---

[1] Source: Johnson Library, National Security File, Head of State Correspondence, USSR, Washington–Moscow "Hot-Line" Exchange, 6/5–10/67. No classification marking. The message is labeled "Translation," with a typed notation indicating a sight translation was made at 9 a.m. and it was received by the President at 9:05 a.m. A typed notation on a copy of the message in Russian states it was transmitted by Soviet Molink at 8:48 a.m. and received by U.S. Molink at 8:52 a.m. (Ibid.)

244. Memorandum for the Record[1]

Washington, October 22, 1968.

SUBJECT

Hot Line Meeting June 10, 1967[2]

CIA Director Richard Helms described this meeting in the following manner:

Present were the President, Under Secretary Katzenbach, Secretary McNamara, Mr. Clifford, Mr. McGeorge Bundy, Mr. Walt Rostow, Ambassador Thompson and Helms himself.

Mr. Katzenbach left early in the meeting to call in the Israeli Ambassador to put pressure on Israel to accept a cease fire.

After the English translation of the incoming Soviet message was read, Ambassador Thompson checked the Russian text to be sure that the word "military" was indeed a part of the Russian message in the phrase "take whatever steps are necessary, including military."

The President had his breakfast during the meeting in the Situation Room Conference Room. Then he left for a short period.

While the President was out, Secretary McNamara asked whether we should turn the Sixth Fleet around to sail toward the eastern Mediterranean. Thompson and Helms agreed. Helms pointed out that Soviet submarines monitoring the Fleet's operations would report immediately to Moscow, that the task force had stopped circling and had begun heading eastward.

The President returned and McNamara mentioned this possibility. The President said, "Yes, go ahead and do it." McNamara picked up a secure telephone and gave the order.

[3 lines of source text not declassified]

Recalling the atmosphere of the meeting, Mr. Helms said that conversation during the first couple of hours was in the lowest voices he had ever heard in a meeting of that kind. The atmosphere was tense. As the morning wore on, everyone relaxed a bit as it became clear that the fighting was petering out.

H.H.S.

---

[1] Source: Johnson Library, National Security File, NSC Histories, Middle East Crisis, Vol. 7, Appendix G. Top Secret. Drafted by Saunders.

[2] The President met with his advisers in the White House Situation Room from 8:57 to 11:55 a.m. (Ibid., President's Daily Diary) Helms also recalled the meeting in an oral history interview. (Interview with Helms, April 4, 1969; Johnson Library) For Thompson's comments on the Hot Line exchanges, see Document 245.

245.　　Memorandum of Conversation[1]

Washington, November 4, 1968.

SUBJECT

　The Hot Line Exchanges

PARTICIPANTS

　Ambassador Llewellyn E. Thompson
　Mr. Nathaniel Davis

I called on Ambassador Thompson today at Bethesda Naval Hospital to get his recollections of the hot line exchanges between President Johnson and Premier Kosygin. Ambassador Thompson refreshed his memory by leafing through the hot line texts,[2] and made the following comments:

At the start, the Russians made quite a point that the President be physically present at our end of the hot line before they would start the exchange. They asked more than once when he would be there. (Notice that the first sentence of the Russian text of Kosygin's first message observes that Kosygin would like to know if President Johnson was at the machine.)

President Johnson's first message to Kosygin (Page 6, June 5, 8:47 a.m.)[3] was actually addressed to "Comrade Kosygin." Apparently what had happened was that the American hot line telegraph operators asked the Moscow operators what was the proper way to address Kosygin. They got back the answer "Comrade Kosygin." So the message went. Ambassador Thompson talked with Dobrynin, about this afterward, and Dobrynin—who had been at the Moscow end of the line—said he had been quite startled. The Russians wondered if the President was making a joke, or making fun of them in some way. However, Dobrynin said he guessed how it had happened.

Ambassador Thompson said the first substantive question he remembered was that of cease-fire, or cease-fire *and* withdrawal. On Tuesday morning (Page 10, June 6, 10:02 a.m.)[4] the President suggested that the Soviets support the resolution Ambassador Goldberg gave to

---

[1] Source: Johnson Library, National Security File, NSC Histories, Middle East Crisis, 5/12–1/19/67, Vol. 7, Appendix G. Secret.

[2] In 1968 Davis was a member of the NSC staff. He apparently took a file of the Hot Line exchanges with him when he went to see Thompson. The page numbers in the text are to page numbers in that file.

[3] Document 156.

[4] Document 175.

Fedorenko the night before, calling for cease-fire and a prompt withdrawal behind the armistice lines. Kosygin did not reply for more than eight hours. In the meantime, Fedorenko had agreed to a simple cease-fire in New York. In Ambassador Thompson's words, he had agreed "to a resolution Kosygin now wanted to get away from."

There was some discussion in the Situation Room, according to Ambassador Thompson, whether we should take advantage of what Fedorenko had done—that is the simple cease-fire—or whether we should stick to the message sent in the morning (cease-fire and withdrawal). Everybody agreed we should take advantage of what had happened in New York. There were some calls to Goldberg. The people in the Situation Room were elated—and surprised Fedorenko had done what he had. There was some speculation around the room that Fedorenko would get into trouble. The fact of the matter was that we would probably have been prepared to accept the earlier formulation that included withdrawal. The Russians suffered from a communications problem.

What the President did in his message of Tuesday evening (Page 14, June 6, 7:45 p.m.)[5] was to point out to Kosygin that Goldberg and Fedorenko had agreed to a very short cease-fire resolution, and suggest that both the Soviets and we assist the Security Council's further efforts to restore peace. What we wanted to do in this message, according to Ambassador Thompson, was simply to nail down the cease-fire.

In his message of June 8 (Page 20, June 8, 9:48 a.m.)[6] Kosygin again called for withdrawal.

In his reply (Page 22, June 8, 11:00 a.m.),[7] President Johnson informed Kosygin of the torpedoing of the *Liberty* and the dispatch of our aircraft to the scene. Ambassador Thompson comments that this was a very successful use of the hot line. We were using it in the right way, to prevent a danger of war arising out of misunderstanding. Ambassador Thompson says it made a big impression on the Russians.

The next crisis came with Kosygin's message of Saturday morning (Page 30, June 10, 8:48 a.m.).[8] This message asserted the Russians were ready to act independently if Israeli military actions against Syria were not stopped in the "next few hours." It went on to say that such independent actions "may bring us into a clash, which will lead to a grave catastrophe." The message concluded by saying that Soviet actions "including military" would be taken if Israel did not cease military action.

---

[5] Document 183.
[6] Document 209.
[7] Document 212.
[8] Document 243.

Ambassador Thompson said he personally checked the Russian text to make sure "including military" was actually there. He was impressed how much greater Soviet sensitivity was to the plight of the Syrians than to that of the Egyptians. At the time, the Syrians were the apple of the Russians' eye (although this changed later). Ambassador Thompson voiced a concern in the Situation Room meeting whether the Russians might suspect that our intention was really to knock off the Syrian government.

The main focus of the discussion in the Situation Room was over what was actually happening in Syria. Richard Helms was brought into the meeting to see if he could check the situation on the spot, and verify whether the Israelis were smashing ahead as the Russians said (see Pages 34 and 38). The feeling of those in the Situation Room was that the Israelis were probably doing so. Mr. Helms tried in a number of ways to reach friendly powers with diplomatic missions still open in Damascus, etc.

There was some discussion whether the Soviet message actually meant that the Russians wanted to move into the area with force. There was some back and forth about the tenor of the Soviet message, and the danger that the Russians might be testing us out. If our replies were too polite, we might look as if we were backing down under a threat. Nevertheless, the President—while he could have gone back to the Russians making threats of his own—chose to send the calm and reasoned message he did (Page 32, June 10, 9:30 a.m.).[9]

Kosygin came back with a message saying the Israelis were "conducting an offensive towards Damascus," "and that action cannot be postponed."[10]

There was some discussion whether the Soviets had actually weighed in with the Syrians to get their agreements to a cease-fire or not. A request for confirmation that they had was drafted into President Johnson's message of reply. Fortunately, the televised proceedings at the Security Council in New York soon showed that Israel had informed General Bull that it would accept any cease-fire arrangements General Bull's representative suggested and that Israel regarded the cease-fire as in effect. McGeorge Bundy drafted a paragraph for the President incorporating this information, and tension soon eased—as it became clear that military action on the Syrian front was being concluded.

As a post mortem, according to Ambassador Thompson, there was some discussion among senior U.S. officials whether we might not have been well advised to let the Israelis move on to Damascus. It was clear the Israelis could have done so. Ambassador Thompson says this was strictly post mortem, however, and this possibility was not discussed at the Situation Room meeting.

---

[9] Document 246.

[10] Document 247.

Ambassador Thompson concludes that this crisis shows how important it was for the President to keep his cool. He adds, like Richard Helms (see Harold Saunders; memorandum of October 22)[11] that June 10 was a time of great concern and utmost gravity.

ND

---

[11] Document 244.

---

246. Message From President Johnson to Premier Kosygin[1]

Washington, June 10, 1967, 9:39 a.m.

Dear Mr. Kosygin,

I have your message. You should know that late last night our Secretary of State sent a most urgent message to Israel to say that we considered it very important that Israel demonstrate by actions on the ground that its orders for a cease-fire are effective.[2] We received assurance at 3 A.M. Washington time that Israel fully intended to achieve actual cease-fire on its side.[3]

Consistent with this assurance, Israelis informed the UN Security Council that its authorities were meeting with General Bull of UN to make all arrangements for cease-fire with Syria.

We have no means of reaching Syrian Government and hope that you have been making similar appeals to them.

Our Ambassador Barbour in Israel has now sent us a message, at 7:45 Washington time, today, saying that Israelis tell him they believe the firing has stopped as of this moment.[4]

We continue to watch developments most closely and will keep in touch with you.

Lyndon B. Johnson

---

[1] Source: Johnson Library, National Security File, Head of State Correspondence, USSR, Washington–Moscow "Hot-Line" Exchange, 6/5–10/67. Secret. A typed notation on the message indicates it was approved by the President at 9:30 a.m., and transmitted by U.S. Molink at 9:39 a.m.

[2] Document 239.

[3] Document 242.

[4] Telegram 4054 from Tel Aviv, June 10; not printed. (National Archives and Records Administration, RG 59, Central Files 1967–69, POL 27 ARAB–ISR)

247. Message From Premier Kosygin to President Johnson[1]

Moscow, June 10, 1967, 9:44 a.m.

Dear President Johnson,

I have read your reply to our message and I must tell you that your information concerning the cessation of military actions in Syria on the part of Israel is not borne out. We have constant and uninterrupted communications with Damascus. Israel, employing all types of weapons, aviation and artillery, tanks, is conducting an offensive towards Damascus. Obviously your Embassy in Syria can confirm this if you have representatives there. Military actions are intensifying. It is urgently necessary to avoid further bloodshed. The matter cannot be postponed. I request that you employ all your possibilities for the cessation of military actions and the fulfillment of the resolutions of the Security Council for which we both voted.

Respectfully,

A. Kosygin

---

[1] Source: Johnson Library, National Security File, Head of State Correspondence, USSR, Washington–Moscow "Hot-Line" Exchange, 6/5–10/67. No classification marking. The message is labeled "Translation," with a typed notation indicating that a sight translation was made at 10 a.m., and the message was received by the President at 10:05 a.m. A typed notation on a copy of the message in Russian states it was transmitted by Soviet Molink at 9:44 a.m. and received by U.S. Molink at 9:52 a.m. (Ibid.)

248.   Telegram From the Embassy in Morocco to the Department
of State[1]

Rabat, June 10, 1967, 1315Z.

5462. For President and Secretary.

1. FonMin Laraki asked me remain behind after meeting with four power representatives reported Rabat 5459 (Notal).[2]

2. King wished make special appeal to President regarding support for cease-fire and Israel's return to pre-hostilities positions. King urged USG take very strong position in Security Council this afternoon on both issues. Up until last few hours and Israel's punishing attack on Damascus United States had, in King's view, "bought thirty years to work for peace in NE." Nasser's prestige virtually destroyed. Now, situation wholly reversed. Nasser's gesture of resignation had appealed to hearts of Arab people. Thanks to their unhesitating support of cease-fire and return to armistice lines, Soviet rapidly regaining what prestige they had lost. Israeli military prowess prior their unnecessary attack on Damascus had put the lie to the Arab "progressives" who had been so confident of their Soviet supplied military power. Concomitantly, moderates had been strengthened. Now, in face of Israel's continuing attack, this differentiation between moderates and radicals being obliterated.

3. Laraki concluded that "If you do not act decisively at this point you will be handing the Arab world to the Soviets on a silver platter."

4. *Comment:* At the time I was called to see Laraki Embassy had been working on telegram drawing to USG attention radical change in emotional and diplomatic situation brought about in these last few hours by Israeli invasion of Syria. King's message to President states the situation as we see it accurately and objectively. To the average Arab there is no doubt that we would by this time be militarily involved on Israel's side if she were being attacked by Arabs as she is now attacking them. That we have not yet taken strong public position in favor of withdrawal Israeli forces to armistice lines is being construed as proof that our often stated commitment to territorial integrity of Near East states works in only one direction.

---

[1] Source: National Archives and Records Administration, RG 59, Central Files 1967–69, POL 27 ARAB–ISR. Secret; Flash; Limdis. Repeated Flash to USUN and repeated to Algiers, Tunis, Tripoli, Cairo, Beirut, Damascus, Baghdad, Amman, Kuwait, Jidda, Tel Aviv, and COMAC and CINCSTRIKE for POLADs. Received at 9:58 a.m. Passed to the White House at 9:59 a.m.

[2] Telegram 5459 from Rabat, June 10, reported that Laraki had met with the U.S., British, French, and Soviet Ambassadors and conveyed the King's appeal for their support for a cease-fire and Israeli withdrawal. (Ibid.)

5. I share with King Hassan the hope that US statements this afternoon will leave no room for doubt about US impartiality.[3]

Tasca

[3] Telegram 210120 to Rabat, June 10, stated that the United States had pressed in the United Nations and with the parties concerned for an immediate cease-fire and had made a strong public statement calling on both Syria and Israel to obey the cease-fire resolution. It noted that at the June 9 meeting of the Security Council, Goldberg had reaffirmed the President's May 23 statement supporting the territorial integrity of all states in the area. (Ibid., POL 27 ARAB–ISR/UN) For text of the Goldberg statement under reference, see Department of State *Bulletin*, June 26, 1967, pp. 946–947.

249. Memorandum of Conversation[1]

Washington, June 10, 1967, 10 a.m.

SUBJECT

Israel–Syria Cease Fire

PARTICIPANTS

His Excellency Avraham Harman, Ambassador of Israel
His Excellency Ephraim Evron, Israeli Minister

The Under Secretary
The Under Secretary for Political Affairs
Assistant Secretary Battle
Mr. David L. Gamon, NEA/ARN

The Under Secretary most emphatically told the Ambassador that an effective cease fire along the Israeli-Syrian sector simply had to be reached without delay. The Secretary had sent such a message to Foreign Minister Eban on the night of June 9. The Under Secretary appreciated the difficulties of the situation, but it was extremely important that the shooting be stopped before the diplomatic and political position deteriorated. Ambassador Goldberg reported the frustration and discontent at the United Nations and recommended that President Johnson send a message to President Eshkol. The Soviets, who were trying to recoup their position in the area, were taking advantage of the situation and were busy saber rattling.

[1] Source: National Archives and Records Administration, RG 59, Central Files 1967–69, POL 27–14 ARAB–ISR. Secret; Nodis. Drafted by David L. Gamon (NEA/ARN).

Earlier the Under Secretary said, the Government of Israel had told Ambassador Barbour that the fighting had ceased. The US had passed this on to the Russians. Was this information correct? It had better be or our credibility with the Russians would suffer.

Ambassador Harman said he understood the importance of what the Under Secretary had said. One thing he did want to make clear: there was no invasion of Syria or a move on Damascus and none was intended. The Syrians reluctantly had agreed to a cease fire only after the Israelis had done so. The Syrians then engaged in a wholesale destruction of the Israeli side of the line. Israel had merely been trying to prevent a reoccurrence of this by occupying the high points. General Dayan had now requested a meeting with General Bull to concert on effective steps for a cease fire.

The Under Secretary said that he appreciated the Israeli problem. At the same time an immediate effective cease fire must not be delayed by discussion. The Israelis had been pasting hell out of the other forces. When the firing did not cease, the weight of the assumption was that the Israelis were responsible. Reactions from the Hill indicated that the Congress had had its fill of the failure to stop the fighting.

Ambassador Harman expressed his prayer that the shooting would end. But, he asked, what should be done if the Syrians carried on the fight? The Under Secretary and Mr. Rostow pointed out that it would be extremely important to have the United Nations personnel find out just what was going on. Mr. Evron observed that the Syrians were not allowing UN observers on their side of the line.

250. Memorandum of Conversation[1]

Washington, June 10, 1967.

SUBJECT

Israeli Attack on USS *Liberty*

PARTICIPANTS

Under Secretary Rostow
Ambassador Harman

Ambassador Harman was called in by Under Secretary Rostow[2] who made the following points:

(a) USG wants complete explanation of how Israeli attack on USS *Liberty* occurred. (b) We want complete documentation from GOI re opening of hostilities. (c) USG would appreciate any information either public or private concerning Israeli/Syrian conflict, especially reports from UN observers. Rostow noted reports of UN observers were of critical importance during Korean conflict. Allegations that GOI failed to honor cease-fire agreements having an impact on many governments. These reports linked to politics of problem and would do no harm for GOI to think of White Paper on entire Syrian episode.

In discussion on status of Jerusalem, Harman indicated capture of Jerusalem had been difficult problem for GOI. Israel had deliberately refrained from using air power and as result suffered many casualties. Prime Minister Eshkol called in leaders of various religious communities and told them each group could determine arrangements for safeguarding own holy places.

---

[1] Source: National Archives and Records Administration, RG 59, Central Files 1967–69, POL 27 ARAB–ISR. Secret. Drafted by Grey on July 4 and approved in M on July 4.

[2] This meeting apparently preceded or followed the meeting between Under Secretary Katzenbach and Ambassador Harman; see Document 249. Rostow also met with Harman that afternoon; see Document 257.

251. Diplomatic Note From the Israeli Ambassador (Harman) to Secretary of State Rusk[1]

The Ambassador of Israel presents ____ Honorable the Secretary of State and has th____ he has been requested by the Government ____ expression of deep regret for the tragic acc____ of hostilities in the area, the USS *Liberty* ____ Government of Israel deeply regrets this t____

The Ambassador of Israel has be____ Honorable the Secretary of State that the Government of Israel is ____ pared to make amends for the tragic loss of life and material damage.

The Ambassador of Israel expresses once again in the name of the Government of Israel its deep condolences to the Government of the United States and its sympathy to all the bereaved families.

The Ambassador of Israel avails himself of this opportunity to renew to the Honorable the Secretary of State the expression of his highest consideration.

A.H.

---

[1] Source: National Archives and Records Administration, RG 59, Central Files 1967–69, POL 27 ARAB–ISR. No classification marking. Telegram 210130 to Tel Aviv, June 10, states that Harman had given the note to a Department official that morning. It also states that Congressional and public opinion were incensed over the attack on the USS *Liberty*, and that Eugene Rostow had informed Harman that morning of the great U.S. concern over the incident, "for which we can find no satisfactory explanation." (Ibid.)

252.   Message From President Johnson to Premier Kosygin[1]

Washington, June 10, 1967, 10:58 a.m.

Dear Mr. Kosygin,

I have your last message and you can be assured that we have emphasized our position to Israel by every means. We have just restated our views in the strongest terms to Israelis here and in New York and by message to Tel Aviv.

Could you confirm that you have employed your means with the Syrians for this same purpose.

We are taking further steps to inform ourselves on the present situation in Damascus, through several sources, although we have categorical assurances from Israelis that there is no Israeli advance on Damascus.

You will have seen that President Nasser yesterday repeated his outrageous invention about American and British participation in this conflict. Since you know well that this inflammatory charge is a total lie, peace would be served if your Government could publicly state the facts known to you on this point.

You will have learned of the report just made in the Security Council that Israel has informed General Bull it will accept any arrangements for making cease-fire effective on the ground that General Bull's UN representative suggests.[2] Bull himself replied it would take time to contact Damascus. Meanwhile Israel has announced that it regards cease-fire as in effect now. This seems to make it even more urgent that you use your channels to Damascus to ensure that Syrians also stop their fire so as not to provoke further response.

Respectfully,

Lyndon B. Johnson

---

[1] Source: Johnson Library, National Security File, Head of State Correspondence, USSR, Washington–Moscow "Hot-Line" Exchange, 6/5–10/67. Secret. A typed notation on the message indicates it was approved by the President at 10:50 a.m., and transmitted by U.S. Molink at 10:58 a.m.

[2] According to Thompson, this information came from the televised proceedings of the Security Council meeting; see Document 245.

253. Telegram From the Joint Chiefs of Staff to the Commander-in-Chief European Command (Lemnitzer)[1]

Washington, June 10, 1967, 1522Z.

JCS 7628. Subj: Sixth Fleet Movement (C).

1. (S) Continued lack of Israeli and Syrian response to the cease fire has caused USSR to make a declaration of the possible use of military force against Israeli.

2. (S) The following moves are precautionary only; however necessary, preparatory measures should be taken.

3 (S) Request you direct following movements:

a. TG 60.1 and TG 60.2 steam at moderate speed toward 33°00′ North 33°00′ East. Do not permit fleet elements to operate east of 33°00′ East or south of 33°00′ North unless so directed by JCS.[2]

b. PHIBRON 6 to vicinity off Southern Crete.

4. (S) Do not disclose reason for move to media.

5. (U) Acknowledge receipt.

---

[1] Source: Johnson Library, National Security File, Country File, Middle East Crisis, Vol. VI. Secret; Flash. Drafted by Captain R.L. Kopps (USN), reflecting telephoned instructions from McNamara; see Document 245. Repeated to CINCUSNAVEUR and COMSIXTHFLT.

[2] JCS telegram 7635, June 10, modified paragraph 3a of JCS 7628 to direct TG 60.1 and TG 60.2 to operate in the general area north of 33°00′ North and west of 33°00′ East. It directed that fleet elements, including aircraft, should not be permitted to operate south of 33°00′ North or east of 33°00′ East unless so ordered by the JCS. (Johnson Library, National Security File, NSC Histories, Middle East Crisis, Vol. 7, Appendix H)

---

254. Message From Premier Kosygin to President Johnson[1]

Moscow, June 10, 1967, 11:31 a.m.

Dear Mr. President:

By my instructions, we have just communicated with Damascus. From Damascus we have been informed that military actions are in

---

[1] Source: Johnson Library, National Security File, Head of State Correspondence, USSR, Washington–Moscow "Hot-Line" Exchange, 6/5–10/67. No classification marking. The message is labeled "Translation," with a typed notation indicating a sight translation was made at 11:40 a.m., and the message was received by the President at 11:43 a.m. A typed notation on a copy of the message in Russian states it was transmitted by Soviet Molink at 11:31 a.m. and received by U.S. Molink at 11:34 a.m. (Ibid.)

progress in the vicinity of the city of Kuneitra where Israeli troops continue their offensive operations.

I can assure you that we did everything possible on our part to stop the war against Syria and the UAR. If today all military actions are concluded, it will be necessary to proceed to the next step of evacuating the territory occupied by Israel and the return of troops behind the armistice line.

I consider that we should maintain contact with you on this matter.

Respectfully,

A. Kosygin

---

255.   Message From President Johnson to Premier Kosygin[1]

Washington, June 10, 1967, 11:58 a.m.

Dear Mr. Kosygin:

I have your last message.

It now appears that military action in the Middle East is being concluded. I hope our efforts in the days ahead can be devoted to the achievement of lasting peace throughout the world.

Respectfully,

Lyndon B. Johnson

---

[1] Source: Johnson Library, National Security File, Head of State Correspondence, USSR, Washington–Moscow "Hot-Line" Exchange, 6/5–10/67. Secret. A typed notation on the message indicates it was approved by the President at 11:54 a.m.; transmitted by U.S. Molink at 11:58 a. m.; and received by Soviet Molink at 11:59 a.m.

256.   Diplomatic Note From Secretary of State Rusk to the Israeli
Ambassador (Harman)[1]

Washington, June 10, 1967.

The Secretary of State presents his compliments to His Excellency the Ambassador of Israel and has the honor to refer to the Ambassador's Note of June 10, 1967 concerning the attack by Israeli aircraft and torpedo boats on the United States naval vessel U.S.S. *Liberty*, which was carried out at 1605 and 1625 hours local time,[2] respectively, on June 8, 1967 while the U.S.S. *Liberty* was engaged in peaceful activities in international waters.

At the time of the attack, the U.S.S *Liberty* was flying the American flag and its identification was clearly indicated in large white letters and numerals on its hull. It was broad daylight and the weather conditions were excellent. Experience demonstrates that both the flag and the identification number of the vessel were readily visible from the air. At 1450 hours local time[3] on June 8, 1967, two Israeli aircraft circled the U.S.S. *Liberty* three times, with the evident purpose of identifying the vessel. Accordingly there is every reason to believe that the U.S.S *Liberty* was identified, or at least her nationality determined, by Israeli aircraft approximately one hour before the attack. In these circumstances, the later military attack by Israeli aircraft on the U.S.S. *Liberty* is quite literally incomprehensible. As a minimum, the attack must be condemned as an act of military recklessness reflecting wanton disregard for human life.

The subsequent attack by Israeli torpedo boats, substantially after the vessel was or should have been identified by Israeli military forces, manifests the same reckless disregard for human life. The silhouette and conduct of the U.S.S *Liberty* readily distinguished it from any vessel that could have been considered as hostile. The U.S.S. *Liberty* was peacefully engaged, posed no threat whatsoever to the torpedo boats, and obviously carried no armament affording it a combat capability. It could and should have been scrutinized visually at close range before torpedoes were fired.

---

[1] Source: National Archives and Records Administration, RG 59, Central Files 1967–69, POL 27 ARAB–ISR. No classification marking. A draft, nearly identical to this, with Walt Rostow's handwritten revisions, bears a handwritten notation that it was drafted by Rusk, Katzenbach, and Walt Rostow. (Johnson Library, National Security File, Country File, Middle East Crisis, Vol. V) Telegram 210139 to Tel Aviv, June 10, which transmitted the text of the note, states that Eugene Rostow gave it to Harman that afternoon. (Ibid.)

[2] The times are incorrect; see Document 352.

[3] This time is incorrect, and the sentence understates the number of aircraft that overflew the *Liberty*; see Document 352.

Winslow

1. Does the author have a good title
2. What is the author's thesis?
3. Why should we care about the
4. How does this work connect wi
   difference between primary an
5. What sources does the author
6. What sources does the author
7. Evaluate the paper as a story
   lucid, and economical? Cou
   this paper and understand w
8. After reading the essay, wh
9. Is it reasonable to expect s
   as this?

While the Ambassador of Israel has informed Secretary of State that "the Government of Israel is prepared to make amends for the tragic loss of life and material damage," the Secretary of State wishes to make clear that the United States Government expects the Government of Israel also to take the disciplinary measures which international law requires in the event of wrongful conduct by the military personnel of a State. He wishes also to make clear that the United States Government expects the Government of Israel to issue instructions necessary to ensure that United States personnel and property will not again be endangered by the wrongful actions of Israeli military personnel.

The United States Government expects that the Government of Israel will provide compensation in accordance with international law to the extent that it is possible to compensate for the losses sustained in this tragic event. The Department of State will, in the near future, present to the Government of Israel a full monetary statement of its claim.

---

257.   Telegram From the Department of State to the Embassy in Israel[1]

Washington, June 11, 1967, 4:24 p.m.

210199. Memcon between Amb Harman and Under Secretary Rostow, June 10.

1. Under Secretary Rostow presented Amb Harman text of USG note concerning *Liberty* incident (sent septel).[2] Before reading note Harman noted GOI was appointing committee of inquiry to investigate incident.

2. Harman said he would refrain from commenting on note but expressed hope that any publication of it would follow line that this was a tragic mistake for which GOI accepted full responsibility. Rostow agreed incident tragic mistake but added that circumstances surrounding it very mysterious. Word used in our note was "incomprehensible"

---

[1] Source: National Archives and Records Administration, RG 59, Central Files 1967–69, POL 27 ARAB–ISR. Secret; Priority; Limdis. Drafted and approved by Grey. Also sent to USUN.
[2] See Document 256 and footnote 1 thereto.

and we hope board of inquiry would take appropriate action against responsible parties when investigation concluded.

3. Rostow said USG presenting this case to GOI in same manner in which it would present similar case to any other government.

4. Harman noted three things: GOI did not know location of ship, location was scene of active hostility, and GOI had promptly apologized for this tragic episode.

5. In closing Harman again reiterated GOI desire to handle incident as tragic mistake for which GOI accepted full responsibility.

Rusk

258.   Memorandum From the President's Special Assistant (Rostow) to President Johnson[1]

Washington, June 10, 1967, 5:05 p.m.

Mr. President:

These intercepts[2]—showing some honest ambiguity about the ship after the attack—suggest that there may have been a breakdown of communications on the Israeli side; that is, the tactical base which first received word that the ship was American may not have flashed that information to other air force and naval units.

We shall, of course, analyze this affair further.

Walt

---

[1] Source: Johnson Library, National Security File, Country File, Middle East Crisis, CIA Intelligence Memoranda. Top Secret; Trine.

[2] Attached is a preliminary version of the material discussed in Document 284. Other copies of this material in preliminary and later versions are in the National Security Agency, Center for Cryptologic History, Historical Collection, Series VIII, Crisis Files, Box 16; Naval Security Group Records, NSG Box 896, USS *Liberty*, Pre 76, Box 1, USS *Liberty*, 5750/4, Chronological Message File; and Central Intelligence Agency, DDO/NE Files, Job 68–S–626, Box 1, Folder 5, Israeli Air Including Attack on *Liberty*, and ibid., Folder 8, USS *Liberty* and Other Naval Activity.

259.   Telegram From the Mission to the United Nations to the
        Department of State[1]

New York, June 10, 1967, 1816Z.

5683. Mid-East.

Shortly before Fedorenko (USSR) speech in SC today announcing Sov break in diplomatic relations with Israel and threat of sanctions, Shevchenko (USSR) came over to Pedersen in Council. Said it was by that time obvious to any fair-minded person that Israelis were continuing the conflict in Syria in spite of SC reses and that US must take vigorous measures to stop them. Said that if fighting did not stop situation could go even beyond sanctions into military measures with dangers of Sov-American confrontation undesired by either. Fedorenko then started to speak and conversation broke off.

Fol Fedorenko speech Pedersen showed Shevchenko draft res US had prepared condemning any violations of ceasefire and calling for unequivocal instructions to be sent to military commanders to stop immediately. Told Shevchenko we had approached Israelis vigorously last night and again this morning and that he should have no illusions US policy was determined to bring about immediate ceasefire. Shevchenko looked at res and said it should call on Israel to stop firing. Pedersen replied that Sovs would have to choose between their objectives. One was to bring about an immediate ceasefire. We were prepared to do this and even to propose res to this effect. Another was to point political blame at Israel by naming it specifically. This US was not prepared to do in situation where both sides were still fighting. Pedersen said that in any case Israelis had continued to assure us they were fully committed to a ceasefire, that they had not taken Quentera and were not advancing on Damascus. Key conversation to implement ceasefire was taking place between Gen Bull and Gen Dayan and this was in fact more significant than anything SC might now do. Shevchenko said that if we were not prepared to point res clearly at Israel best thing would be not to have res in SC at all but simply to adjourn subject to call with understanding SYG would continue his efforts to implement the ceasefire. In that case he said US should exert prompt pressures on Israel through diplomatic channels. Pedersen said we were already doing so.

---

[1] Source: National Archives and Records Administration, RG 59, Central Files 1967–69, POL 27 ARAB–ISR. Confidential; Priority; Limdis. Repeated Priority to Moscow and Tel Aviv. Received at 3:41 p.m. Passed to the White House, DOD, CIA, USIA, NSA, COMAC, and CINCSTRIKE at 6:17 p.m.

Subsequently, shortly before end of meeting, Shevchenko approached Pedersen again to discuss exact manner of terminating meeting. In this conversation he reiterated importance of immediate ceasefire. This time he said that issue was critical because while we had our commitments in area USSR also had theirs; if Damascus were taken by Israelis USSR would have to respond. (Impression was a response of some sort of military aid to Syria.)

Pedersen said we regretted that the one day's cooperation between two dels in NY when we first achieved ceasefire res Tuesday had quickly evaporated. Noted it seemed to be easier to consult with USSR in Moscow and Wash than in NY and this made matters difficult. Hoped there might be renewal of cooperation as we approached difficult task of achieving new settlement in ME. Shevchenko said Sov reversion Wednesday to urgent call for SC meeting and deposit of res without consultation with US had been based on rigid instructions from Moscow that they must call "immediate" meeting, coupled with Moscow report that USG had been informed.

Said that as we moved into next phase USSR would stress withdrawal and that it would be difficult to cooperate closely in NY while Israeli forces remained on Arab territory. Pedersen said it might be understandable we would have public differences on this issue but that should not prevent exchange of views privately. Noted simple withdrawal was simply not realistic policy in present circumstances and more fundamental issues needed to be dealt with. Commented, for example, that if USSR had expressed itself in favor of freedom of navigation in straits at outset this conflict would probably never have come about. Shevchenko replied there was not much to be gained from going back to what might have been done before. Also said Sov del recognized some other elements might have to be looked at in connection with withdrawal, but said US res had too many.

In separate conversation Fochine (Sov national in Secretariat) also expressed concern about danger of Sov-American confrontation in ME. Said he regarded situation as more dangerous than Cuban missiles crisis because we could both be drawn into situation by people over whose activities we did not have full control. Referred to the sanctions, with use of term blockade. Also referred to possibility military flights over Turkey and Iran by way of discounting them but said Sov military measures were not excluded.

On settlement of crisis Fochine said he thought there would have to be improvement of UN observation machinery in the area. Said he had been studying this in Secretariat. When Pedersen said this was sort of thing US had always supported but we wondered whether Moscow would favor such move, Fochine said he thought they would.

Comment: Most significant aspect of above conversations seemed to be Shevchenko's second conversation focusing on Sov concern re Israeli capture of Damascus. Shevchenko's manner was one of concern to end the conflict and avoid a Sov-American confrontation rather than one of pressure or threat. It was in utterly marked contrast to Fedorenko's nasty demeanor against US in SC and of Fedorenko's refusal to talk to Goldberg during morning on grounds he could not leave Sov seat in Council.

Goldberg

260.   **Telegram From the Embassy in Israel to the Department of State[1]**

Tel Aviv, June 10, 1967, 2145Z.

4063. Ref: State 210085 and 210034.[2]

1. I conveyed substance UNSEC's statement to Harman to Bitan for Eban and Eshkol immediately upon receipt. Eshkol at Syrian front but Eban and Dayan for whom message equally important were in Tel Aviv and were informed at once.

2. Report of conversation had already been received from Harman and I had impression there no misunderstanding of possible consequences if seriousness of situation in relation to Sovs disregarded. I had been preaching criticality Sov factor since 0645 hours this morning when I saw Eban.

3. However, by time I received reftel 210034, Israelis had already concluded necessity obtain effective ceasefire whatever the military position on the ground, had called in Bull and had given him free hand to get in touch with Syrians to ascertain their position and to make any

---

[1] Source: National Archives and Records Administration, RG 59, Central Files 1967–69, POL 27 ARAB–ISR. Secret; Flash; Exdis. Received at 6:15 p.m. An advance copy was received at 6:10 p.m. and passed to the White House at 6:13 p.m.

[2] Telegram 210034 to Tel Aviv, June 10, summarized the conversation between Katzenbach and Harman recorded in Document 249 and instructed the Embassy to convey this to the highest level and emphasize the seriousness of the situation. (National Archives and Records Administration, RG 59, Central Files 1967–69, POL 27–14 ARAB–ISR) Telegram 210085 to Tel Aviv, June 10, reiterated the instructions. (Ibid., POL 27 ARAB–ISR)

physical arrangements to assure implementation he wished. Israelis and SYG had notified Security Council.

4. Although Sov breaking of diplomatic relations does not seem to me to have caused as much concern in GOI as it perhaps should have (this probably minimum card Sovs had to play sometime to satisfy Arab resentment against them), deteriorating Security Council situation, clear signal of US anxieties, and essentially of extricating themselves from over extension in Syria, which being compounded on political scene by Syrian charges of Israeli advance on Damascus, convinced Israelis implementation ceasefire under any available machinery of top priority.

5. It seems clear that, driven by military necessity of achieving viable military posture for protection border settlements, Israelis played for time in political maneuvers in Security Council to hair raising proximity to brink but also evident tonight that they think they have gotten away with it. There is generally relaxed atmosphere in official circles and every indication intention to hold to ceasefire.

Barbour

---

261. Telegram From the Department of State to the Embassy in Jordan[1]

Washington, June 10, 1967, 7:31 p.m.

210141. Amman's 4190.[2] Please convey to King Hussein at earliest opportunity the following:

---

[1] Source: National Archives and Records Administration, RG 59, Central Files 1967–69, POL 27 ARAB–ISR. Secret; Immediate; Exdis. Drafted by Sisco, cleared by Eugene Rostow and Battle, and approved by Walsh. Also sent to London and repeated to USUN.

[2] Telegram 4190 from Amman, June 10, reported that the previous evening, after Nasser reiterated the charges of U.S. involvement on behalf of Israel, King Hussein urged that this issue should be cleared up and suggested a U.S. invitation to the United Nations to investigate. He said he was willing to take the initiative himself but thought a U.S. initiative would be preferable. He cited the following points for investigation: (a) Jordanian radar readings indicating aircraft flying into Israel from stationary objects in the Mediterranean for 3–4 days preceding the hostilities, (b) reports from Jordanian officers that British Hawker-Hunter aircraft were used in Israeli attacks, (c) Jordanian, UAR, and Syrian reports that British Canberras were used in Israeli attacks, and (d) UAR General Abdul Munim Riyadh was convinced that something more than the Israeli Air Force was involved. (Ibid.)

1) We fully appreciate need to clear up once and for all charges US and UK actively involved in support Israel in hostilities. We have already issued categoric denial, including specific statements by Secretary, Ambassador Goldberg and Defense Dept. British also denied charges.

2) In SC on June 6 Ambassador Goldberg said (unnecessary words omitted): "US prepared, first, to cooperate in immediate impartial investigation by UN of these charges, to offer all facilities to UN in that investigation; second, as part of or in addition such investigation, US prepared invite UN personnel aboard our aircraft carriers in Mediterranean today, tomorrow, or at convenience of UN, to serve as impartial observers of activities of our planes in area and verify past activities our plans from our official records and from log each ship carries. These observers will, in addition, be free interview air crews these carriers without inhibition, to determine their activities during days in question. Their presence as observers on these carriers will be welcomed throughout period this crisis and so long these ships in eastern waters of Mediterranean."[3]

We have now transmitted to UN same offer in official communication for circulation to all Members.[4] This places us in position to take formal initiative at any time. In light this fact any Jordanian initiative would be superfluous. Moreover, it seems to us Jordanians upon reflection would realize not in their own interest take any such initiative which bound antagonize other Middle Eastern states.

3) We are continuing watch problem carefully with view to seeing how play of UAR charges evolves worldwide. UN so far has shown virtually no interest in formal follow-up. We know USSR considers charges have no foundation and has said so to Middle Eastern ambassadors privately, but it obviously will not say so publicly. In this connection Goldberg on June 10 noted that Soviets have been shadowing our fleet in Mediterranean and are in position to disprove charges of involvement by US aircraft. He also remarked that Soviet Ambassador to UN has made no comment on these charges.[5]

4) We will keep in continuous review whether to take further steps including submission specific proposal in light developments.

5) Begin FYI. We will forward comments on Hawker-Hunters and Canberras in septel. End FYI.

6) *For London:* Embassy should urgently review contents of Amman's 4190 with appropriate UK officials and seek their comment on Jordanian impression that Canberras and Hawker-Hunters were

---

[3] For text of the statement under reference, see Department of State *Bulletin,* June 26, 1967, pp. 934–936.

[4] UN document S/7963; printed ibid., July 3, 1967, p. 11.

[5] The text of a statement made by Goldberg on June 10 is ibid., pp. 3–5.

active in area. You should specifically try confirm our impression these aircraft obsolete and no longer in use by any British forces in Middle East.

Rusk

---

262.   Editorial Note

Stephen Green alleges in *Taking Sides: America's Relations with a Militant Israel* (New York: William Morrow and Company, Inc., 1984), pages 204–209, that U.S. Air Force RF–4C photo reconnaissance planes and pilots from the Thirty-eighth Tactical Reconnaissance Squadron (TRS), stationed in Germany, and photo reconnaissance technicians and equipment from the Seventeenth TRS, stationed in England, were sent to Israel on June 4, 1967, and that they flew and provided support for photo reconnaissance missions in support of Israeli forces throughout the war. Green's source for the story claimed to have been a participant in the operation.

No documentation supporting Green's allegations was found in the course of the research for this volume. An investigation in 1996–1997 by two historians of the Office of Air Force History uncovered no evidence supporting Green's account and no evidence that U.S. Air Force members of the Thirty-eighth TRS, Seventeenth TRS, or other units were in Israel during the 1967 war. (Research and Findings on Statements in the Book *Taking Sides*; Office of Air Force History) Richard B. Parker concludes in "USAF in the Sinai in the 1967 War: Fact or Fiction?" *Journal of Palestine Studies*, XXVII, No. 1 (Autumn 1997), pages 67–75, that the story was fabricated by Green's source.

Postwar Diplomacy, June 11–September 30, 1967

263.   Memorandum From the President's Special Counsel (McPherson) to President Johnson[1]

Washington, June 11, 1967, 9:10 a.m.

The solid part of what I understand about the Middle East situation has already been communicated by Wally Barbour; I was with him during most of his meetings with Israeli officials. What follows are additional impressions.

I don't need to remind you that I was almost completely in the dark about the events that led up to the outbreak of war. Saigon newspapers leave a good deal to be desired in world news reporting. I arrived in Tel Aviv at 3 a.m. last Monday, was awakened by Wally at 8, and began my education half an hour later to the sound of air raid sirens.

In four days I met Eshkol once, for about an hour (this was Thursday noon), Eban briefly but rhetorically, the Israeli intelligence chief, and the Army J–2. I talked with Moshe Bitan, head of the Foreign Office American section, two or three times a day. I went to the Negev with a Joint Staff colonel, and got to the Gaza border before we ran out of road and into objections from the Israeli military that the town of Gaza had not yet fallen and that we ought to get the hell out of there. I went north to Haifa, Nazareth, and within a few miles of Tiberias near the Syrian border. They would not let me into Jerusalem before they took the Old City, and when they did take it, it was too late for me to go.

1) Eshkol sends you his best wishes.

2) Bitan told us on the first day that they didn't want our troops or planes; they would do the job themselves; they just wanted us to keep the Russians off their backs, and they wanted "two or three days to finish the job." On the last day, he said they still wanted Sky-Hawks very much.

3) There is no doubt in my mind about how the war started. After their intelligence chief first talked about "responding to Egyptian

---

[1] Source: Johnson Library, President's Appointment File, June 1967. No classification marking. A handwritten "L" on the memorandum indicates the President saw it. McPherson had just returned from a 4-day visit to Israel, following a 2-week trip to Vietnam. Also see Harry McPherson, *A Political Education* (Boston: Little, Brown and Company, 1972), pp. 413–417.

attacks"—this was Monday noon—it became clear after questioning that such attacks, if any, could only have been a provoked artillery exchange. More likely there was no such exchange, but a simple preventive assault on the ground in Sinai and by air in Sinai and Cairo. You know their intelligence about Egyptian armored concentration in Sinai; they claimed to have evidence that an Egyptian assault was "imminent", within a few hours, north of Eilat and into Jordan—thus cutting off the Gulf of Aqaba from northern Israel. My feeling is that it was not so imminent, but that the Israelis simply decided to hit first before the tactical situation got worse.

4) By noon the war was essentially won. We sat outside Eshkol's office about that time. As the sirens went on again, and when we asked the intelligence chief whether we should go to a shelter, he looked at his watch and said "It won't be necessary."

5) On the Gaza border on Tuesday, at a point where one of the earliest thrusts was made, we saw exhausted truck drivers lying about in the shade, sleeping and talking. When I mentioned the fatigue on their faces, my Israeli colonel said "They've earned the right to sleep. They've been driving down here since Sunday afternoon. The place looked like Detroit Sunday night." The "response" began Monday morning.

6) The spirit of the army, and indeed of all the people, has to be experienced to be believed. After the doubts, confusions, and ambiguities of Vietnam, it was deeply moving to see people whose commitment is total and unquestioning. I was told that 8-year-olds went to the telegraph office Monday morning to deliver telegrams, as the regular force of messengers had gone off to military duty. In the Negev one hot afternoon, I saw two good-looking girls in uniform riding in the back of a half-ton jeep, one with a purple spangled bathing cap on her head, the other with an orange turban. They were headed for the front, driven by two burly sergeants. (Incidentally, Israel at war destroys the prototype of the pale, scrawny Jew; the soldiers I saw were tough, muscular, and sunburned. There is also an extraordinary combination of discipline and democracy among officers and enlisted men; the latter rarely salute and frequently argue, but there is no doubt about who will prevail.)

7) The temper of the country, from high officials to people in the street, is not belligerent, but it is determined, and egos are a bit inflated—understandably. Israel has done a colossal job. There was never any doubt of the outcome, because "there was simply no alternative." And what has been done has been done not only for Israel, "but for the U.S.—we got you out of a difficult situation in the Middle East" (Bitan and the military).

8) Some Israelis, chiefly the military, would like to retain most of the territory they have taken. Eshkol, Eban and Bitan do not talk in such

broad terms. I had the distinct impression that they had not thought very clearly, or very long, about what next. Beating the Arabs and keeping the Russians from complicating things had pre-occupied them. Nevertheless every Israeli I talked to said in effect that no government could survive that gave up the Old City or control of Sharm-el-Sheikh, at the straits of Tiran. Regaining the Old City is an event of unimaginable significance to the Israelis. Even the non-religious intellectuals feel this way.

9) Though this could change at any moment, and may be only last week's opinion, my feeling is that

a) they do not want the Sinai, though they do want it "de-militarized"—no longer used as an Egyptian staging area.

b) they do not want to annex the West Bank of the Jordan, as this would involve taking in great numbers of Arabs whose loyalties are unpredictable.

c) they could conceive a "protected state"—neither Jordanian nor Israeli—in the West Bank lands, managed by international authorities. Eshkol said this.

d) they will remain in Sharm-el-Sheikh, and they could imagine a group of maritime nations authorizing Israel to serve as its agent in keeping the Gulf of Aqaba open to shipping; and conceivably joining with Israel in doing the police work. This also from Eshkol.

e) they must either retain the Old City, or *absolute* and *guaranteed* access to it.

f) they would like to straighten a few borders, particularly to cut off some of the Jordanian salients that threaten their access to Jerusalem; and also to widen Israel at its narrowest point, north of Tel Aviv at Natanya. (I am for this; Barbour's house is about five miles south of Natanya, and Tuesday morning I awoke to the sound of bombs hitting Natanya and of shelling over the hills at Herzliyya, about six miles away toward Jordan.)

10) There are constant references and comparisons to 1956. The Israelis do not intend to repeat the same scenario—to withdraw within their boundaries with only paper guarantees that fall apart at the touch of Arab hands. We would have to push them back by military force, in my opinion, to accomplish a repeat of 1956; the cut-off of aid would not do it. While they are contemptuous of the UN's performance, they did not write it off as a forum or means of resolving the main issues. They were far more affirmative, however, about a major-power settlement.

11) What they want far more than territory, of course, is a peace treaty that recognizes the State of Israel.

12) They seem to hate Nasser, but not the Egyptians; to hate all the Syrians; and to feel a kind of enraged contempt for Hussein—"that stupid little king who gave control of his country to Nasser." Nobody really has any ideas about how to bring about a reduction in hatred between themselves and the Arabs.

13) I have no such ideas, either; after listening to Arab radio, with a driver-translator, for four days, I don't think "multilateral aid schemes" will do the trick with the Syrians or the Egyptians. The others are not so intransigent and aid may work. I do think we, the British, and the French should turn every screw in an effort to use this occasion for bringing about Arab recognition of Israel.

Harry C. McPherson, Jr.[2]

---

[2] Printed from a copy that bears this typed signature.

---

264. **Memorandum From the Executive Secretary of the National Security Council (Smith) to President Johnson**[1]

Washington, June 11, 1967, 5:30 p.m.

Mr. President:

Mac Bundy called from New York[2] to ask that the following report be sent to you upon your return here:

1. Bundy will see Ambassador Goldberg this evening from 8 to 9:30 to review the problems we face in the UN this week.

2. Bundy talked by phone today with Secretary Rusk, Secretary McNamara, Ambassador Goldberg and both Rostows.

3. A first priority action is to persuade the Israeli Government to make the most moderate public statement of their position that they can. Secretary Rusk will talk to Ambassador Harman about this.

4. Bundy believes the line we should hold to for the next few days is "let's have peace." He says now is not the time for new policy statements. He opposes those officers in the State Department who want to underline the territorial integrity clause of the May 23 statement. Old boundaries cannot be restored.

5. Bundy believes we should promptly resume conversations with the Soviets by having Ambassador Thompson talk fully but quietly with Dobrynin who is expected in Washington this week.

---

[1] Source: Johnson Library, National Security File, Country File, Middle East Crisis, Vol. V. Confidential. A handwritten "L" on the memorandum indicates the President saw it.

[2] Notes of Bundy's telephone conversation with Rusk are in the National Archives and Records Administration, RG 59, Rusk Files: Lot 72 D 192, Telephone Calls.

6. Bundy will be in Washington in mid-afternoon tomorrow. The Situation Room knows how to reach him at any time.

Bromley Smith

---

265. Telegram From the Department of State to the Embassy in Israel[1]

Washington, June 11, 1967, 6:52 p.m.

210212. 1. We consider it of utmost importance, both politically and psychologically, that urgent and unambiguous effort be made reassure West Bank inhabitants they have nothing to fear by remaining where they are or, for those who have already fled, returning to their homes. Continued mass exodus to East Bank will not only pose added threat to existence Hussein regime but contains seeds of new refugee problem which will greatly complicate settlement of situation created by last week's hostilities. During SC debate June 10, Ambassador Goldberg said following:

"We are concerned for example at the moment about the safety and welfare of the people in Jordan and we express the conviction and the hope and the trust that they will be treated in all humanitarian ways— that they will stay in their houses, have adequate measures for safety and welfare—and we will use our influence and we are using our influence in that direction."

2. Dept considering issuance statement to focus attention on position outlined by Goldberg in SC. What is most needed, however, is public assertion along these lines by GOI, making unequivocally clear that GOI wants West Bank residents to remain and welcomes return of evacuees who have left. To be effective, such statement should outline specific measures being taken to safeguard property, continue civil administration, preserve law and order, maintain public services and restore normal conditions of life as rapidly as possible. Invitation to voluntary international welfare agencies to participate in these efforts would, in our view, be essential factor in generating confidence in Israeli intentions.

---

[1] Source: National Archives and Records Administration, RG 59, Central Files 1967–69, POL 27 ARAB–ISR. Confidential; Immediate. Drafted by Atherton, cleared in draft by Davies and Houghton and in substance by Elizabeth Brown, and approved by Eugene Rostow. Repeated Priority to Amman, Beirut, USUN, and Jerusalem.

3. You should raise foregoing urgently with GOI at highest level, emphasizing need for quick action and maximum publicity to get message across.[2]

Rusk

---

[2] Barbour reported in telegram 4078 from Tel Aviv, June 12, that he had made strong representations on this. He reported that the Israeli estimate was that not more than 30,000 had actually left the West Bank and that Israeli policy was not to have West Bank inhabitants depart. (Ibid.)

---

266. **Telegram From the Department of State to the Embassy in Israel**[1]

Washington, June 16, 1967, 10:05 p.m.

212139. Subject: Rostow–Harman Memcom June 12.

1. Amb Harman opened the conversation by reviewing Israeli intelligence estimates on Arab rearming. He passed on the following list: June 6—Algeria loaded a ship bound for Cairo with tanks. June 8—A ship loaded with 70 tanks, 37 artillery pieces and other military equipment was supposed to leave the Soviet Union for the UAR. June 9—GOI believed that UAR had only 50 planes left. However, on that day, 27 MIG–17's and 2 or 3 MIG–21s arrived in UAR from Algeria. June 10—Iraq promised to send a battalion of Centurion tanks to Jordan and the Saudi and UAR Governments discussed arrangements to allow for the transit of MIG–17's from Yemen to the Arab-Israeli front. June 10—3 Iraqi infantry brigades and 1 armored brigade moved into Jordan. 15 Soviet An–12's arrived in Cairo and since the 10th approximately 35 An–12's had landed at Cairo. The Israelis believe that these transport planes could be carrying MIG–21's. June 11—The 120th UAR brigade left Yemen for the UAR and a tank unit was in the process of leaving. Also on the 11th the UAR was in the process of signing a new military supply contract with the Soviet Union and the Iraqis were also asking for new military equipment from the Soviets.

---

[1] Source: National Archives and Records Administration, RG 59, Central Files 1967–69, POL 27 ARAB–ISR. Secret; Exdis. Drafted by Grey and approved by Eugene Rostow. Repeated to Moscow, Paris, USUN, and London.

2. Mr. Rostow noted that the Algerian Government was taking a hard line in the present situation and that this could involve serious problems for Morocco, Libya and Tunisia.

3. Mr. Rostow remarked that pressure was mounting for a unilateral Israeli withdrawal and that there was some indication that the Arab world might be considering using oil as a weapon to force Israeli withdrawal. There was a possibility that there would be serious trouble in the UN if the Soviets deleted the word "aggression" in their proposed Security Council resolution.

4. Rostow stressed that in the days that lie ahead GOI posture on territorial acquisitions would be of crucial importance. USG takes at face value GOI statements that it has no territorial ambitions and that it is prepared to withdraw to its frontiers if a condition of peace could be arranged. Such a position would not of course exclude appropriate security arrangements, and the problem of Jerusalem required separate study as a matter of international concern. Amb Harman said that USG could take Eban's speech in the Security Council[2] as being GOI's position at that time. Since then, however, other events had taken place. The Jordanian situation was a nasty one and it raised a question of basic security for the GOI. Rostow said USG does not want any misunderstandings between it and the GOI on the question of occupied territory. USG was doing its level best with the Saudis, Kuwaitis and Iranians to introduce some stability into the Middle East situation. However, inflamed Arab passions threatened the stability of moderate Arab regimes.

5. Harman then turned to the *Liberty* incident and passed Under Secretary Rostow the Israeli reply to our note on the subject.[3] Harman stressed the fact that GOI reaction to the incident was one of shock. He was, however, greatly agitated by press reports on the incident, particularly the Periscope item in this week's *Newsweek* which referred to "high officials" as source for an indication that the attack was deliberate. Harman stressed the fact that GOI was making a prompt investigation of the incident. He asked Mr. Rostow if there was any truth in the *Newsweek* allegation that some US officials are not convinced that this incident had been nothing more than a tragic accident. Under Secretary Rostow replied that he had never heard any US official make such a statement. He did regard the episode as "literally incomprehensible." So far as he knew, the *Newsweek* article was not correct. He promised Harman that he would look into the possibility of appropriate press guidance on the subject.

Rusk

---

[2] The text of Eban's June 6 speech before the Security Council is printed in *Israel's Foreign Relations: Selected Documents, 1947–1974*, Vol. II, pp. 784–792.

[3] Document 267.

267.   Diplomatic Note From the Israeli Ambassador (Harman) to
         Secretary of State Rusk[1]

Washington, June 12, 1967.

The Ambassador of Israel presents his compliments to the Honorable the Secretary of State and has the honor to refer to the Secretary of State's Note of June 10, 1967,[2] concerning the attack by Israeli aircraft and torpedo boats on the United States naval vessel U.S.S. *Liberty*.

The Government of Israel feels that the statement that "there is every reason to believe that the U.S.S. *Liberty* was identified, or at least her nationality determined, by Israeli aircraft approximately one hour before the attack" is unfounded.

Nor can the Government of Israel accept the statement that "the attack must be condemned as an act of military recklessness reflecting wanton disregard for human life."

The Government of Israel is of the view that the drawing of such conclusions before a full investigation has been made is unwarranted.

The Government of Israel has already announced the establishment by the Chief-of-Staff of the Israel Defense Forces of a Commission of Enquiry to make a full investigation of all the facts and circumstances. The Government of Israel will make available to the Government of the United States the findings of this investigation, and, for its part, would hope that the Government of the United States will make available to the Government of Israel the findings of its own investigation.

The Government of Israel recalls that as soon as this tragic error occurred it immediately informed the Government of the United States of what had taken place. The Government of Israel immediately assumed responsibility for this error and conveyed its apologies and deep regret for what had occurred and for the grievous loss of life.

Subsequently, as mentioned in the Secretary of State's Note of June 10, 1967, the Government of Israel took the initiative to offer to make amends for the tragic loss of life and material damage. Further, all assistance was offered by the personnel of the Israel Defense Forces to

---

[1] Source: National Archives and Records Administration, RG 59, Central Files 1967–69, POL 27 ARAB–ISR. No classification marking. An attached action slip indicates that it was handled as Exdis. Harman gave the note to Eugene Rostow on June 12; see Document 266.

[2] Document 256.

the U.S.S. *Liberty*, but these personnel were informed by the U.S.S. *Liberty* that such help was not needed. The area around the U.S.S. *Liberty* was immediately searched by Israel Defense Forces personnel, by plane and boat, and subsequently search efforts were renewed.

The Government of Israel has standard instructions of the most stringent nature to all its military personnel that the personnel and property of the United States as of all countries not involved in hostilities, shall not be endangered. These instructions have been renewed.

The Government of Israel regrets that it was not given prior information by the Government of the United States of the presence of a United States vessel in an area which the United Arab Republic had warned neutral vessels to avoid, as it was an area of hostilities. The area was in fact being used by the United Arab Republic for purposes of hostilities against Israel. It would be appreciated if the Government of Israel could be given timely information of the approach by United States vessels to shores where the Israel Defense Forces are in authority.

The Government of Israel renews its offer to make amends and has instructed the Ambassador of Israel to reiterate its profound regret for the consequences of what was admittedly a tragic error.

The Ambassador of Israel avails himself of this opportunity to renew to the Honorable the Secretary of State the assurances of his highest regard.

A.H.

268.   Informal Memorandum From W. Howard Wriggins of the
        National Security Council Staff to the President's Special
        Assistant (Rostow)[1]

Washington, June 12, 1967, 6 p.m.

Walt—

SUBJECT

Today's Thoughts on Arab-Israel Problem

1. Time Perspective

In the euphoria from Israel's remarkable performance, I said last
week, "It's a new ball game." After Nasser's political performance on
Friday, and noting the positions taken by the Arabs since then, I suspect
that if it is a new ball game, it will have many all-too-familiar plays.

While the Israelis occupy substantial parts of neighboring Arab
states, Syria and Egypt can sit it out for some time yet. True, the economic pressures on Egypt will mount as the costs of mobilization continue and the canal tolls remain stopped. While food supplies now in
hand will last three or four weeks, their new harvest will be starting
now and requisitioning of supplies is feasible. If the Soviets are willing
to provide substantial help, Cairo could hold out longer. Much will
depend on whether Nasser can retain his army. My guess is he will be
able to hold out for months rather than weeks.

Jordan, of course, is a different case. Hussein can hardly ignore the
presence of Israeli forces, and the refugee flow they have provoked. On
the other hand, can he settle with the Israelis unless the Israelis are prepared to make a substantially generous offer? There is, I believe, much
wisdom in the attached telegram from Findley Burns. (Amman 4229)[2]

---

[1] Source: Johnson Library, National Security File, Country File, Middle East Crisis,
Vol. V. No classification marking. Wriggins sent a copy to Bundy.

[2] The attached copy of telegram 4229 from Amman, June 11, bears the following
handwritten note in an unidentified hand: "Walt, This is a *wise* telegram from Amman."
The telegram transmitted Burns' recommendations for U.S. policy in the Middle East. It
argued that Israeli magnanimity with the Arabs would be Israel's best means of obtaining real gains and that if there was to be any likelihood of a lasting peace, "Israel must not
further humiliate the Arabs." It declared, "It appears to us that what Israel should want
most are rights: rights of access to the international waterways, to the Holy City, and the
right to have a logical defensible border with her neighbors. If she aims at any semblance
of peace with the Arabs, she should not expect, with but a few small exceptions, territorial changes." It urged immediate U.S. public statements expressing concern at the exodus
of evacuees from the West Bank and calling on Israel to keep them in place and urging
Israeli withdrawal from territories captured in the recent fighting. (National Archives and
Records Administration, RG 59, Central Files 1967–69, POL 27 ARAB–ISR)

However, I fear that unless we weigh in in Tel Aviv, Dayan, rather than Eshkol, will call the tune. I understand the President's reluctance to get his hand in the machinery. But if he doesn't, privately or publicly, I believe we are in for a long and stormy stalemate during which the Russians will more than make up for what they have temporarily lost. And it will be at our expense.

2. Components of a Settlement

I suppose by now the outlines of a possible settlement are fairly clear:

(1) formal Arab recognition of Israel's existence;
(2) safety from Syria's direct threat from the heights (a de-militarized zone on the Syrian heights might do it);
(3) internationalization of the Old City and sharing of tourist earnings;
(4) guarantee of free passage for all ships through Sharm el-Sheik and Suez;
(5) a bold Israeli initiative on Arab refugees. With their new strength they can afford to be more generous than during their frightened past. This might include: (a) free private choice for up to 10–15 percent of the "old" refugees; (b) substantial Israeli and international financing of their resettlement in Israel; (c) training and resettlement arrangements, internationally financed with the cooperation of the oil rich states, for resettlement elsewhere of other refugees; (d) if Israel holds on to Gaza, these refugees, after careful vetting, might also be settled in Israel;
(6) Israel withdraws from Sinai, the West Bank and Syria, leaving (a) an international presence at Sharm el-Sheik; (b) a de-militarized zone on the Syrian heights; (c) an adjustment of frontiers with Jordan to broaden the wedge into Jerusalem, etc.

3. Operational Question

It is unlikely that a settlement reached under international auspices will have the viability of an agreement reached by the Arabs negotiating directly with Israel. On the other hand, this is precisely what the Arabs are the least likely to want to do. How can we encourage a direct negotiation between the two when our own leverage has been so materially reduced by these events? Perhaps we can use the impending Soviet initiative at the UN to promote some form of Arab-Israeli dialogue?

Howard

269. Notes of a Meeting of the Special Committee of the National Security Council[1]

Washington, June 12, 1967, 6:30 p.m.

THOSE PRESENT

Fowler
McNamara
Katzenbach
Vance
Wheeler
Helms
Llewelyn Thompson, U.S. Ambassador to Moscow
Eugene Rostow
Sisco
Clifford
W.W. Rostow
McG. Bundy
Harold Saunders

The President joined the meeting about 7:35 p.m.
George Christian came in at 7:40 p.m.

1. Israeli reply on Liberty.

Consensus: reaction sour. "Terrible note."

—Release our note? Can't decide until facts known.

—Consensus: Publishing exchange wouldn't do any good. Release summary, if needed. Get Israelis to recall it.

—Dept. to provide draft summary statement on the facts to date.

2. Sisco's summary of UN situation.[2]

USSR going to pull out all stops to develop UNGA as a propaganda forum.

—Add to agenda of special GA now in session, or
—New special session.

---

[1] Source: Johnson Library, National Security File, NSC Special Committee Files, Minutes and Notes. No classification marking. The meeting was held in the Cabinet Room of the White House. The notes are Saunders' handwritten notes of the meeting. Special Assistant to the Deputy Assistant Secretary of State for Politico-Military Affairs Raymond L. Garthoff and Assistant Secretary of Defense for International Security Affairs-Designate Paul Warnke were also present. The meeting ended at 8:52 p.m. (Ibid., President's Daily Diary) Rostow's agenda for the meeting is ibid., National Security File, Country File, Middle East Crisis, Vol. V. See also Document 270.

[2] A paper entitled "Developments at the United Nations Over the Next Week or Two," drafted by Sisco on June 12, is in the Johnson Library, National Security File, NSC Special Committee Files, Special Committee Meetings.

We can't prevent.

—Tradition of not opposing.
—General doubt on who fired first shot. USSR cld. get majority.

—UNGA much less manageable for us.

—One alternative: USSR will probably try to get simple condemnation of Israel. Last time: 1951 when we got Chicoms condemned.

—Other possibility: drop "aggression" in favor of "withdrawal behind ADL, Gulf open, return to GAA's." We'd be in small minority.

McGB: More turnaround time? To sort ourselves out.

EVR:

23 May—the three problems
5 June—move to new beginning
UNSC resolution—not attempt withdrawal until condition of peace, end of belligerence.

McGB: This may get us through this week, but we still don't know our position.

Sisco: Does slow down UNSC.

Katz: We need a position that goes beyond UNSC. Political problems in Israel.

Fowler: Have we mentioned requirement for general acceptance of state of Israel?

McGB: We've backgrounded but have never made major policy point.

Sisco: UNGA has a corridor function. Might call FM's.

WWR: How Hussein thinks he can settle his problems? USSR trying to keep Arabs together, prevent [sentence not completed].

3. Telegram to Eban.[3]

Should we pin them down formally at all?

—Shouldn't we find out elements of thinking in GOI. (Clifford).
—EVR: part of process of approaching Russians. Is timetable overtaken if Gromyko coming to NY.
—Danger of freezing positions.

McGB:

(1) Reservations.
(2) Meanwhile asking Barbour.

---

[3] A draft telegram to Tel Aviv with a message from Rusk to Eban, with a covering note of June 12, is ibid.

President: "Purpose can be accomplished in another way without setting their feet in concrete."[4]

Send this telegram to Barbour; ask him to do the job.

4. *Arms*[5]

(a) Pr: Dane?[6]

British: not optimistic, wldn't join. Doubt UN registry wld have much effect.

Pres: Check with USSR. Why don't we both agree? Dane.
    —Went back to Eshkol's statement that Israel stood alone. Noted USSR wld. soon get fed up with Israel's braggadocio.
    —Israelis are mobilizing sentiment against our protest.

(b) Immediate shipments

—General
—MIG airplanes
—CIA: pace routine but not enough to change military knowledge.

If move on Dane, follow-up note to USSR.

5. *Relief:*[7]

Let's hold up
President wished USG didn't have to do it.

6. *Regional Planning.*

—Fowler: reviewed history of development banks in ME
—We will proceed that way.

7. *Contingency public statement on aid policy.*

Hold over.

---

[4] A marginal note at this point indicates that the President came in at 7:35 p.m.

[5] A June 12 memorandum from the Control Group to Rusk and Bundy on the subject "Restraints on Arms Shipments to Israel and the Arab States" recommended "that the US promptly raise with the Soviet Government our conviction that the two countries should seek an understanding on the problem of arms supply to the Arab States and Israel. Such a bilateral approach would supplement other efforts now underway to raise this issue with the Soviets as well as with others in the UN." (Johnson Library, National Security File, NSC Special Committee Files, Special Committee Meetings)

[6] A reference to Danish representative at the United Nations Hans R. Tabor, who was President of the Security Council in June.

[7] A June 12 memorandum from the Control Group to Rusk and Bundy on the subject "Emergency Relief in the Middle East" is in the Johnson Library, National Security File, NSC Special Committee Files, Special Committee Meetings.

8. Tourist ban

    —Israel: pressure to let people go.

9. One other diplomatic move:

    find out what King Hussein wants.
    —Israelis (Jews) are really bitter toward him.
    Pres. agreed.
    Pr. When do we have to stand up and be counted in UN?
    "Real question is whether 'territorial integrity' of all states"

10. President returned to our position: How do we get out of this predicament.

    McN: We're in a heck of a jam on territorial integrity.[8]
    McGB: Eshkol on a spot.
    Fowler

    1. For Isr on belligerence.
    2. Isr has to give territory.

    Clifford: We have to face up to our past statements.
    Pr: Summarize as black a picture as we can of Sov. shipments. Tell Israelis, "It wasn't Dayan that kept Kosygin out."

---

[8] A note written at the side of the page here reads: "Meeker: What has been our position on troop withdrawal in past situations following cease-fire?"

---

270. Memorandum for the Record[1]

Washington, June 12, 1967.

SUBJECT

    Minutes of NSC Special Committee, 6:30 p.m. Monday, 12 June in the Cabinet Room

    1. After reviewing the Israeli Government's reply to our note protesting its attack on the U.S.S. *Liberty*, the Committee decided (a) to clear up our own preliminary understanding of the facts surrounding

---

[1] Source: Johnson Library, National Security File, NSC Special Committee Files, Special Committee Meetings. Secret. Also see Document 269.

the attack and (b) to suggest unofficially to the Israelis that they take back their note and rewrite it in a more moderate vein.

2. The Committee agreed it is important to learn as much as we can about Israeli and Jordanian intentions. However, members felt strong reservations about approaching either government formally now for fear of solidifying unreasonable demands. The President approved informal soundings in both capitals.

3. The President instructed the Acting Secretary of State to pursue a proposal for having the President of the UN Security Council call on all Middle East arms suppliers to register future arms shipments with the UN.

4. The President indicated a strong desire not to have the USG out in front on emergency relief operations. The Committee decided to hold off a US decision for a couple of days.

5. The Committee agreed that we should encourage George Woods to take the lead in longer term Middle East regional development planning.

McGeorge Bundy[2]

---

[2] Printed from a copy that bears this typed signature.

---

271.   Telegram From the Department of State to the Embassy in Luxembourg[1]

Washington, June 12, 1967, 9:34 p.m.

210494/Tosec 15. Ref: Paris 20111 and 20112 repeated Tosec.[2]

1. Last Saturday Under Secretary Rostow asked Ambassador Lucet if we might possibly have the views of the French Government on two questions, by June 12 if at all possible.[3] We understand that Ambassador

---

[1] Source National Archives and Records Administration, RG 59, Central Files 1967–69, POL 27 ARAB–ISR. Secret; Priority; Exdis. Drafted by George M. Bennsky (NEA/UAR) and Country Director for France and Benelux Robert Anderson, cleared by Burgus and Davies, and approved by Leddy. Sent to Luxembourg for Secretary Rusk, who was there to attend a ministerial meeting of the NATO Council June 13–14. Repeated to London, Paris, Moscow, USUN, and DOD.

[2] Telegrams 20111 and 20112 from Paris, June 12; not printed. (Ibid.)

[3] Rostow's June 10 conversation with Lucet is summarized in telegram 210147 to Paris, June 10. (Ibid.)

Lucet discussed these questions with you at Danish reception on Saturday. The first question concerned a GOF initiative with Cairo regarding the reopening of the Suez Canal. The second question asked for GOF views on the substance and procedure on the problem of arms levels and arms limitations in the Middle East.

2. In call on Assistant Secretary Leddy June 12 Lucet made following points from instructions he had just received from Paris:

A. Re Suez Canal, French Government had spoken to UARG immediately following closure Canal. Egyptians said they closed Canal protect it from sabotage and hostile actions and that this was in interest of all who used the waterway. On basis this response, France then decided not make formal written protest but its Ambassador Cairo recalled provisions Constantinople Convention[4] and Egyptian declaration to UN of April 24, 1957.[5] In light this background French Government does not believe it should take further initiatives at this time. To do so would only result UAR opening whole range of issues such as Israeli withdrawal behind armistice lines in return for reopening Canal.

B. Re arms control in Middle East, French Government agreed desirability of arms agreement for Middle East must be part overall political settlement in area and expected arms question would be eventually discussed in this context. As for immediate problem, French did not see how controls could be developed without consulting the Soviets who would argue that Arab position not same as Israelis since Arabs were victims of aggression and therefore had right to be resupplied.

C. As for proposal to consider use of UN and notification SYG re arms shipments to area, French Government thought this would be vetoed immediately by Soviets.

3. Leddy questioned Ambassador Lucet regarding the status of French arms supplies to Israel. The Ambassador said he had nothing on this from Paris but thought arms shipments had stopped on commencement hostilities but that some spares were now being shipped. He said he would check further with Quai d'Orsay.

4. Ambassador Lucet said for time being French Government was not able say more re questions raised by Rostow June 10.

Katzenbach

---

[4] The Constantinople Convention, signed at Constantinople on October 29, 1888, by Great Britain, France, Germany, Austria-Hungary, Italy, Russia, Spain, Turkey, and the Netherlands, provided that the Suez Canal should always be open to every vessel, without distinction of flag. For text, see Department of State *Bulletin*, October 22, 1956, pp. 617–619.

[5] The declaration that Egypt sent to the UN Secretary-General on April 24, 1957, stated that the Egyptian Government would continue to respect, observe, and implement the terms and spirit of the Constantinople Convention. For text, see UN document A/3576, S/3818; also printed in Department of State *Bulletin*, May 13, 1957, pp. 776–778.

272.   Telegram From the Department of State to the Embassy in Israel[1]

Washington, June 12, 1967, 10:32 p.m.

210497. 1. We are attempting to work out best USG positions during coming days on issues we will have to face in UNSC and on other problems on which we are being questioned by Congress and the press—some of which can be deferred but others not. Such questions include UN resolutions re withdrawal to armistice lines, present posture on our repeated statements about territorial integrity of all ME nations, regional arms control, military/economic aid, etc. Arriving at realistic and equitable USG views hinge in considerable measure upon our determination of ultimate GOI objectives, particularly about territorial questions, refugees, status of Jerusalem, Sharm al Sheikh, and Suez Canal.

2. Your 3988[2] and 4065[3] have been particularly helpful in our efforts to face up to these questions. It will be of great importance to us to obtain your continuing assessment of minimum/maximum GOI objectives.

3. We would also like you to discuss GOI objectives with the highest Israeli officials you think appropriate to attempt to gain confirmation of GOI positions at this stage of post hostilities, realizing that there are soft and hard liners in Tel Aviv and that we will have to factor out initial GOI bargaining positions in the process. For this purpose it seems advisable to us not to seek a "final" GOI position on any of the key issues, which might tend to freeze maximum demands, but rather for you to engage in a continuing series of discussions with high GOI officials.

4. We are sending message to you by septel[4] which you may draw upon for background purposes. It was originally drafted as direct message from Secretary to Foreign Minister but we have decided pursue more informal approach for time being.

Katzenbach

---

[1] Source: National Archives and Records Administration, RG 59, Central Files 1967–69, POL 27–14 ARAB–ISR. Secret; Priority; Nodis. No drafter appears on the telegram; cleared by Battle, Eugene Rostow, and Walt Rostow; and approved by Katzenbach. Also sent to Luxembourg as Tosec 19 for Rusk.

[2] See footnote 3, Document 194.

[3] Barbour reported in telegram 4065 from Tel Aviv, June 11, that all signs indicated Israel's major expectation as a result of her military success was the direct negotiation of a political settlement with her neighbors. He concluded: "As the most powerful state in the Middle East, Israel feels entitled to demand peace treaties with its neighbors and it seems likely now that GOI will insist on trying this approach." (National Archives and Records Administration, RG 59, Central Files 1967–69, POL 27 ARAB–ISR)

[4] Document 273.

273.   Telegram From the Department of State to the Embassy in Israel[1]

Washington, June 12, 1967, 10:37 p.m.

210499. For Ambassador Barbour.

You should draw upon following message for background purposes:[2] With the main cease fire arrangements finally in effect, we wish to turn to next steps both within and outside the United Nations. In preparation for these efforts, we need urgently to know your government's policies for the future, most particularly about territorial questions, refugees, the status of Jerusalem, Sharm al Sheikh, and the Suez Canal.

We are facing a violent and determined effort in the Security Council to require Israeli troop withdrawals to previous boundary lines. In broad terms, our posture has been and is that defined by the Resolution we tabled at Security Council.[3] It will now be necessary to give more concrete and specific meaning to what lies behind that Resolution. It is indispensable that we move forward in that process on the basis of a firm understanding of your government's position. We have noted your recent statement to Ambassador Goldberg in New York,[4] as well as Prime Minister Eshkol's statement in his letter to President Johnson of June 5[5] in which he said that "We seek nothing but peaceful life within our territory, and the exercise of our legitimate maritime rights."

In general, we have been proceeding in reliance on Ambassador Harman's repeated statements to us that your government has no territorial ambitions, but that it did not intend to withdraw its forces from the positions they now occupy except "to a condition of peace." If peace can be achieved, he has told us, the Government of Israel is prepared to participate in a constructive approach to the problem of refugees, and other long-standing difficulties.

---

[1] Source: National Archives and Records Administration, RG 59, Central Files 1967–69, POL 27–14 ARAB–ISR. Secret; Nodis. Drafted by Eugene Rostow on June 11, cleared by Kohler and Battle, and approved by Katzenbach. Rostow had earlier initialed Rusk's approval. Repeated to Luxembourg as Tosec 20 for Rusk.

[2] The sentence originally instructed Barbour to convey the quoted message to Eban from the Secretary at the earliest opportunity. Telegram 210498 to Luxembourg (Tosec 21), June 12, states that the President preferred an informal approach "in fear Israelis would present maximum demands and get feet in concrete." (Ibid.) The text of the draft telegram cited in footnote 3, Document 269, is the same as the message in telegram 210499.

[3] See Document 223.

[4] See Document 227.

[5] See Document 158.

In the light of what has happened during last few momentous days, and the difficult political atmosphere at the U.N., I should appreciate a statement of your government's policy in as much detail as present circumstances permit. We do not want any misunderstandings between us to complicate the difficult task we all face in seeking arrangements to assure a just and durable peace in the Near East.

As far as the attitude of the US is concerned, our principal points of departure are (a) President Johnson's reaffirmation on May 23 of long-standing American policy that "the United States is firmly committed to the support of the political independence and territorial integrity of all the nations of the area"; (b) the necessity to establish a regime of peace in the Near East in which neither side claims the right to infringe upon the rights of the other in the name of a state of belligerency; (c) the vital interest of the United States in its own relations with the Arab and Muslim world, a relationship in which Israel itself has an important stake; (d) the overriding necessity through magnanimous and imaginative policies to lay the foundation for a genuine reconciliation among the peoples of the Near East, even though it may require time. On the last point we know that you are at least as aware as we of the vital interest of Israel in its relations with its Arab neighbors who will number some 100 million people in the next quarter century.

We would be glad to have your views as soon as possible because of the developing situation in the Security Council.

Katzenbach

---

274. Memorandum Prepared in the Central Intelligence Agency[1]

Washington, June 12, 1967.

NASIR'S SITUATION AND POSITION AMONG THE ARAB LEADERS

1. The wide-scale and largely spontaneous demands in Egypt that Nasir continue in office have demonstrated that no early replacement of

---

[1] Source: Johnson Library, National Security File, NSC Special Committee Files, Intelligence Reports, June 20–21, 1967. Top Secret; [codeword not declassified]. The memorandum is one of a series: "Special Assessments on the Middle East Situation."

Nasir is likely. Nasir probably counted on getting a favorable reaction to his resignation, though he many have been prepared to step down if sentiment ran against him. While he is unlikely to be thrown out of office, there is some question as to the extent of his power. He may be forced to take advice from top associates, and the wholesale changes in the military command are probably designed at least in part to head off unrest among the officers over the debacle.

2. It would be the sheerest speculation to estimate Nasir's chances for survival over the long term until some clear idea of the dimensions of a peace settlement can be formed. At most, we can say that he probably will not be able to convert this debacle into a smashing victory as he did in 1956. As the extent of Egypt's humiliation becomes known, resentment against him is likely to grow. It is unlikely that any group seeking to oust Nasir would try to do so at a time when it would appear to be capitalizing on Israeli successes, for it would be highly vulnerable to charges of being "agents of imperialism." In the long run, disillusion over Nasir's performance will probably manifest itself in greater discontent within Egypt than he has hitherto faced and in time this might lead to a coup. But, for some time, the immediate traumatic effects of the defeat impel the Egyptians to stick with Nasir and seek other scapegoats.

3. In trying to assess the chance of a move against Nasir, it should be noted that we have had relatively little information in the past on political attitudes in the officer corps and, given the reduction of our diplomatic staff, are unlikely to get more.

4. The state of Nasir's relations with his fellow Arabs varies. His prestige has suffered greatly with the Arab governments. Yet, as demonstrations in dozens of cities testify, he still enjoys wide public popularity. A very large number of people accept the story that Israel could only have crushed Egypt with the assistance of the US and UK. Nasir has succeeded in associating many others with him in defeat, and this tends to mute expressions of discontent. He is trying to reassert leadership through the mechanism of the summit meeting of Arab chiefs of state. But it is an indication of his weakened position that he feels it necessary to have another leader associated with him in calling for such a meeting.

5. Even in defeat, Nasir is unwilling to drop all old quarrels; he remains on bad terms with King Faysal of Saudi Arabia. The Egyptian leader failed to mention Saudi Arabia among those states which "adopted honorable attitudes" in the crisis, though the latter sent troops to Jordan and stopped oil shipments to the US and UK and has so far refrained from encouraging the Yemeni royalists to harass the Egyptians in Yemen, though it apparently has renewed some arms shipments.

6. Jordan's Husayn has a good public image as a loyal colleague of Nasir who fought bravely and whose defeat was no worse than Egypt's. Moreover, he apparently feels secure enough vis-à-vis Nasir to reject a suggestion from the latter on a joint statement condemning alleged US and UK military actions. The other monarchies have made gestures of support—stopping oil shipments, sending small numbers of troops. The monarchs generally, as well as Tunisia's Bourguiba, are pleased that Nasir has been defeated. They share the general Arab shame and bitterness at Israel, however, for having inflicted such a defeat. While all the Arab conservatives would feel obliged publicly to associate themselves with Nasir's moves against Israel, they would probably be far more reluctant to follow Nasir's lead in adopting measures against Western powers, e.g., nationalizing oil, which would seriously harm their interests.

7. Of the revolutionary states, Algeria is disgusted at the humiliating collapse of the UAR Army. Boumedienne has been reported as "out of his mind" with rage at Nasir; the Algerian premier has not, to our knowledge, answered Nasir's plea for him to call an Arab summit conference. The Algerians are suspicious of Nasir's abilities and probably are unwilling to help restore Nasir's prestige among the Arabs. Boumedienne's current trip to Moscow may indicate an intention to upstage Nasir. Syria, berated last week by Cairo and Amman for failing to join vigorously in the fight, has regained some stature and sympathy in Cairo as a result of its 9 and 10 June fighting with the Israelis. We know little of the present situation in Damascus; the leadership is probably badly shaken. There was serious infighting among regime leaders prior to hostilities, and changes at the top are likely. The attitudes of such an altered regime to Nasir are not predictable at this time.

8. In the past year, Iraq had evolved a position of balance between Cairo and other Middle Eastern capitals. It participated in a joint political leadership with Egypt, but sought better relations with Iran and Turkey. Radical sentiment has risen in the present situation; a number of pro-Nasir politicians have been released from detention. Despite the UAR's defeat, it is likely to have a fair amount of influence in Baghdad in coming months, although Iraqi moderation is likely to reassert itself in time.

9. Until armistice arrangements have been worked out, the Arabs will feel considerable pressure to stay together. The emotions wrought by the conflict will encourage this sense of solidarity. However, a number of the Arab states—particularly the oil exporters—realize that their interests are not served by taking anti-Western positions. Hence the disposition of these states to follow Nasir's lead will be limited. In sum,

there will probably be a large measure of solidarity in opposing Israel and rather less in supporting Nasir.

---

275. Telegram From the Embassy in Morocco to the Department of State[1]

Rabat, June 13, 1967, 0946Z.

5492. 1. FonMin Laraki told me last night Nasser and Boumedienne pressing hard for immediate Arab summit in Khartoum. Apparently, most if not all Arab governments, including Tunisia, have agreed. King sent message yesterday to Nasser GOM does not believe summit should be held before meeting of Foreign Ministers in Kuwait to prepare necessary groundwork. Laraki said King feels summit under circumstances would serve Nasser's purposes and assist Boumedienne in his dramatic efforts to replace Nasser as leader of the Arab nations. GOM feels summit now likely be dominated by extremists who would steamroll disastrous series of resolutions which can only exacerbate situation and will not contribute to an effective Arab position in settling present crisis.

2. *Comment:* King considers urgent need for Arab moderates to prevent extremists from retaining control Arab policy. However, position seriously affected by existence of many factors hostile to moderates in present situation, including deep humiliation of the Arabs, Israeli post cease fire thrust into Syria, seizure of sacred sanctuaries of Islam by Israelis in Old City of Jerusalem, substantially uncontested statements of Israeli leaders on intention to follow military hostilities by territorial annexation and deep-seated belief among most Arabs that US and UK indirectly and directly responsible for Israeli military prowess and success against Arabs.

3. In my view, it is highly essential that we consider ways and means of discreetly supporting the moderates. Embassy has already listed leading priorities in this respect. It now becomes urgent that we push ahead on these in every way possible.

Tasca

---

[1] Source: National Archives and Records Administration, RG 59, Central Files 1967–69, POL 7 SUDAN. Secret; Immediate; Limdis. Received at 6:08 a.m. Passed to the White House, DOD, CIA, USIA, NSA, COMAC, and CINCSTRIKE at 7:15 a.m.

276. Telegram From the Defense Attaché Office in Israel to the Defense Intelligence Agency[1]

Tel Aviv, June 13, 1967, 0835Z.

0884. Ref DIAAP–5 7657 June 67.[2]

1. Have queried our primary source who says impossible at this time to go back to the secondary. Secondary source is not, in fact, a witting supplier of info but rather a knowledgeable person whose conversations occasionally reveal useful info. To ask direct questions would put him on guard and dry up the source.

2. Primary source states from context of original conversation he believes strong probability the reference transmissions took place prior to 080600Z.

3. Further information received from Embassy officer who spoke to young IDF Navy officer. The Navy officer claims he was aboard one of attacking MTBs. MTB saw a ship under air attack with smoke issuing from sides. Thought they saw guns on bow. They joined in attack and after torpedo launch at about one mile close to short distance at which time they saw US flag which had been obscured by smoke. Officer says CO of his MTB extremely remorseful and concerned.

4. From data available here ALUSNA reconstructs probable but not certain series of events.

A. IDF aircraft reported ship and identified her as US.
B. IDF AF HQ may or may not have broadcast info to all units, but probably uniformed aircraft returning from strike in Egypt with unused rounds attacked *Liberty.*
C. MTB's saw aircraft attack and presumed *Liberty* to be Egyptian ship. Therefore they eagerly raced into action without waiting to identify our ship.

5. Coordinated with Embassy.

---

[1] Source: National Security Agency Files, Center for Cryptologic History Historical Collection, Series VIII, Box 16d, DIA (USDAO, Tel Aviv) re *Liberty.* Secret; Immediate; Noforn. Repeated to COMSIXTHFLT and CINCUSNAVEUR. Received at the National Military Command Center at 1411Z.

[2] Not found; it apparently requested additional information concerning telegram 0854 from USDAO Tel Aviv, June 10, which reported that an Israel Aircraft Industries official had told a U.S. Air Force representative that on the morning of June 8, he had heard transmissions on Israeli Air Force air-to-ground control frequencies of an aircraft that had sighted a ship and had identified it as having a U.S. flag. (Ibid.)

277. Telegram From the Embassy in Israel to the Department of State[1]

Tel Aviv, June 13, 1967, 1730Z.

4118. Ref: State 210497 and 210499.[2]

1. I saw FonMin Eban in Jerusalem this noon at my request in effort elicit Israeli thinking on questions urgently facing us now that cease fire is in operation. In accordance with State's 210499 I said we now desire to turn to next steps within and outside United Nations and that we urgently need to know GOI's policies for the future. I emphasized the pressures we face in the Security Council to require Israeli troops to withdraw to previous lines. Noting that our posture is that defined by the Security Council resolutions we have tabled, I stressed importance of obtaining as much Israeli precision as to its thinking as possible at earliest moment. As to United States points of departure I mentioned President's reaffirmation on May 23 of our commitment to support the political independence and territorial integrity of all nations in the area, the necessity to establish a regime of peace eliminating claims by either side of the right to infringe on the rights of others because of belligerency, U.S. vital interests in relation to the Arab world, and the overriding necessity that through magnanimous and imaginative policies, the foundations laid for a genuine reconciliation among peoples of the area.

2. Eban apologized that there must of necessity be a lack of precision in Israel's thinking as to detailed polices because of the dramatic, rapid changes which had taken place and had raised opportunities which were inconceivable before and for which Israel unprepared. He repeated what he had said in the Security Council that this hour of danger is also an hour of opportunity and it is essential to move forward to peace and not backward to belligerence. He added that since the earlier exchanges between the United States and Israel, particularly between the President and the Prime Minister just prior to the outbreak of hostilities, the situation had in fact been disrupted. It is impossible now to reconstruct but we must build anew. In the circumstances the point of reference cannot really be the pre-June 4th situation.

3. What Israel wants is quite simple: (a) security and (b) peace. Neither of these has been enjoyed before. Involved in the achievement of these goals are problems in the juridical, demographic and territorial fields. Israel has not yet had an opportunity to study each in detail. He

---

[1] Source: National Archives and Records Administration, RG 59, Central Files 1967–69, POL 27–14 ARAB–ISR. Secret; Priority; Nodis. Received at 3:16 p.m.

[2] Documents 272 and 273.

reiterated that the disruption is so complete that they cannot rebuild but must erect a new edifice. He noted with satisfaction that the U.S. resolution tabled in the Security Council is forward looking in line with this concept.

4. Eban said an intermediate status between war and peace is no longer feasible. What must be done is work out a blueprint for new Arab-Israel relations. This in itself has some negative and some positive implications. The adoption of the backward looking resolution tabled by the Soviets[3] in calling for withdrawal to previous lines is inconceivable. Hopefully it will be resisted with the help of world opinion but if not Israel will resist it alone. Eban again appealed that we not waste the present opportunity and try to return Israel to the straight jacket of 1957. The national will in Israel is resolute and unanimous in rejecting such a concept.

5. Eban said that as he sees the situation at present there are two questions: (a) how to build and (b) what ideas exist as to the shape in which the area should be rebuilt. As to how to build, Israel feels strongly that there should be direct discussions between Israel and its neighbors to achieve viable arrangements for peace. A solution should not be imposed by outside powers. In direct dialogue Israel and Egypt, for example, should together determine frontiers, attitudes toward each other, etc. If Egypt should suggest another forum for the discussion, it should be told it has the wrong address and it should approach Israel. To my comment suggesting some skepticism as to whether Egypt and the others would in fact seek a peaceful solution or might not merely sulk in their tents behind the cease fire arrangement, Eban expressed confidence that Egypt would be under sufficient indigenous pressure to eliminate the present situation and all that had preceded it to seek negotiations. As to ideas about the shape of the new structure in the Middle East, Eban said that the Israeli Government is engaged in urgent consultations to work out specific ideas on each of the problems involved. He could not as yet indicate the outcome of these discussions but suggested that in formulating some of the questions involved he might give some clues as to present thinking. Questions relating to Egypt are, how can Egypt and Israel live together? How can an absence of belligerence

---

[3] Reference is to a Soviet draft resolution introduced on June 8 that condemned Israel's "aggressive activities" and violation of the Security Council's resolutions of June 6 and 7 and demanded that Israel immediately halt its military activities against neighboring Arab states and withdraw its troops behind the Armistice Lines. A revised version submitted on June 13 condemned Israeli "aggressive activities" and continued occupation of UAR, Jordanian, and Syrian territory and demanded immediate withdrawal of Israeli troops behind the Armistice Lines. (UN document S/7951 and Rev. 1 and 2) The text of the revised resolution of June 13 is in Department of State *Bulletin*, July 3, 1967, p. 12. On June 14 the Security Council voted on the operative paragraphs of the resolution; both paragraphs failed to receive a majority.

in two waterways be assured? How can Sinai be prevented from becoming another springboard for attack and perhaps most difficult of all, what about Gaza? As to Syria, how can Israel ensure that it is not perpetually under Syrian guns, or in a position where Syria can cut off its water system. Most complex of all, he said, is Jordan and/or the Palestinian West Bank. He asked whether it is intelligent to endeavor to reproduce the unity between the West Bank and Jordan or some sort of separate relationship between the West Bank and Israel and Jordan. How can religious interests in Jerusalem be assured and also the sanctity and unity of the Israeli Holy Places? He indicated clearly Israel completely rules out the possibility of re-dividing the city of Jerusalem now that is has become united.

6. Eban then turned to tactical considerations. He recognized the requirement for speed particularly under the pressures created by United Nations procedures repeating again that it is tactically most desirable for the parties directly involved to get together and that he hoped very shortly for more specific ideas on the problems concerned. He urged that in the meantime a holding operation of at least short duration be undertaken and that the world not be intimidated by the Soviets. He again said it would be most tragic if the Soviet doctrine reflected in the Soviet Security Council resolution were accepted. Israel will hasten the crystalization of its ideas to permit more constructive consultation with U.S. One problem he describes as almost solved, Jerusalem is in fact united but the problems of international and spiritual interest there remain. On these he thought it wise not to be specific too quickly.

7. Finally, Eban concluded by summarizing Israel's position as wanting peace and direct negotiations and recognized that details require early but intensive study. He urged we not be too fatalistic as to timing. We must gain some time but also must act rapidly.

8. As a postscript, Eban said he may go again to United Nations but before doing so he wants to formulate Israel's ideas. He would not envisage putting specific proposals through the United Nations but recognizes that there are certain problems in which the international community's interests are greater than others.

For example, what international or naval guarantees could be obtained for the straits? The United Nations presence had not helped on that point in the past but some other guarantees might be sought. Also Israel's policy toward the various religions in Jerusalem was of great interest internationally and probably should be the subject of a quick Israeli declaration.

Barbour

278. Memorandum From the President's Special Assistant (Rostow) to President Johnson[1]

Washington, June 13, 1967, 3:55 p.m.

Mr. President:

Minister Evron asked to see me today to pick up a copy of the talk I gave in Middlebury.

In fact, he raised two matters:

1. *The Israeli negotiating position.* He said that a month ago there was no serious crisis in the Middle East; 10 days ago they felt they were being throttled; now there is temporary euphoria and relief at the military victory; but they have not had time to think through their position. The job for Israel is, having won the war, now to try to win the peace. He asked if we had any advice? I said he knew our formal positions, notably the President's statement of May 23 and everything else down to the resolution inscribed at the UN Security Council. We are clearly for both territorial integrity in the Middle East and for peace. Our powers to make peace, however, are extremely limited. A major attempt to retrieve the Soviet-radical Arab positions is under way, including apparently a meeting of the General Assembly. A great deal hinges on what kind of a position they take and especially whether it is one that will draw to it the majority in the UN General Assembly and, in the end, moderate Arabs. As the President had made clear in his press conference this morning, we were committed to certain principles in this situation but did not have a program.

He said that he understood this and, without instructions, he would only say this: It is important that the Arabs find out in the political offensive that the Russians cannot deliver any more effectively than they could deliver militarily. If this political counteroffensive fails, he feels that the Arabs may be willing then to talk. I said, once again, that what happened in the General Assembly and happened with the moderate Arabs depended upon the positions put forward by Israel.

2. He then turned to the *notes concerning the Liberty.* He said that he found no difficulty with our finding the issue "incomprehensible." He was disturbed by the use of the word "wanton"; and he would have

---

[1] Source: Johnson Library, National Security File, Country File, Middle East Crisis, Vol. V. Confidential. Copies were sent to Bundy and Katzenbach. Rostow sent the memorandum and Document 279 to the President at 4:55 p.m. A handwritten "L" on Rostow's covering memorandum indicates the President saw it.

wished that we had recognized how promptly the Israeli government had informed us of the error. He said Golda Meir had been with Rabin when he was informed; that considerable soldier "almost fainted" at the news of the attack. He was greatly disturbed by the *Newsweek* item in Periscope. Without in any way going around his Ambassador or the State Department, it was his personal suggestion that both notes might be amended or dropped and the "tone of the exchange lowered." He repeated that he saw nothing wrong at all in our asking how it could have happened; who did it; and our requesting that the Israeli government do something about it. The implication of purposeful action, however, he felt was most unfortunate.

He said that although final confirmation had not come to Washington, it was his understanding that those involved in the attack were about to be severely punished.

I explained to him that there was a good deal of strong Congressional feeling about the matter. In addition, the President and the military were understandably concerned. The language of the note was precise. We found the incident literally "incomprehensible." He said the Court of Inquiry was working as fast as it could. Perhaps when we had conducted our investigation, we could close out the incident with some kind of joint statement.

I noted and said I would pass along his thoughts.

Walt

---

279.   **Memorandum From Director of Central Intelligence Helms to President Johnson**

Washington, June 13, 1967.

[Source: Johnson Library, National Security File, Country File. Middle East Crisis, Vol. V. Secret. 4 pages of source text not declassified.]

280. Notes of an Informal Meeting of the NSC Special Committee[1]

Washington, June 13, 1967, 6 p.m.

THOSE PRESENT

Katzenbach
McNamara
Vance
W.W. Rostow
McG. Bundy
E.V. Rostow
Battle
Sisco
Saunders

Immediate

1. *UN:* Kosygin or Gromyko.[2]

a. Do we involve President?
b. Do we involve Rusk? (Return for 6:30 mtg.)[3]

2. McGB: Back off for a moment & look at our position.

—Constructive move in Goldberg's resolution.
—Elements of the problem.
—Bargain with Nasser.[4]

WWR:

—Get Israeli position.
—Dialogue with Arabs.

McGB: UNGA won't produce a favorable resolution.

WWR: Territorial integrity & non-belligerence.

Sisco:

—Generalization: no 2/3 majority for resolution we could buy.
—Sovs. Trying to bolster hands diplomatically.

---

[1] Source: Johnson Library, National Security File, Special Committee, Minutes and Notes. No classification marking. The meeting took place in Under Secretary Katzenbach's office. The notes are Saunders' handwritten notes of the meeting. See also Document 281.

[2] A June 13 letter from Foreign Minister Gromyko to Secretary-General Thant requested convening an emergency special session of the General Assembly "to consider the question of liquidating the consequences of Israel's aggression against the Arab States and the immediate withdrawal of Israel troops behind the Armistice Lines." (UN document A/6717)

[3] The word "Agenda" is written in the margin.

[4] "Lodge got invitation to go to Cairo. Not now. *Lodge is a red flag to Israelis.*" is written in the margin, followed by "Anderson." Apparently a reference to Robert Anderson.

—President shld go to UN & get out.

—Not going to get reasonable settlement next 2–4 months.

Consensus: No settlement 2–4 months.

Katz: Caveat: Important we don't get into Kosygin–LBJ confrontation.[5]

McGB: Here's where we were, are, are going.

Katz: Paper on the problems.

NEA consultants—*call tonight for Thursday*

IO consultants

McGB: Suppose Israeli demands shake down to

(a) Gaza
(b) int'l guar. for Aqaba
(c) Sinai back to UAR, perhaps demilitarized
(d) West Bank—to Jordan, refugees,
(e) more than demilitarized Syrian heights
(f) condition of peace.

Could USG be sympathetic to that position?

Katz: At what point do we want to take substantive positions?[6]

McN: We can't take position of any concreteness now or even next week. Don't see how we can take a *position.* Speech ok.

McGB: Pres. can identify problems—leave parties to propose specific solutions. Pres. can say that UNGA can become propaganda debacle.

WWR: Refugees: criticize both Arabs & Israelis.

Battle:

I—Bromide speech.
II—UN Debacle.
III—Someone else enumerate issues.[7]

McGB: Formulate interests of Arabs

—Self-respect in own national pursuits.

McN:

1. Belligerency: state of mind will continue.
2. Territorial question without US *guarantee.*[8]

McGB: I don't see President asking Senate for guarantees.

McN: I don't think we ought to get him into this.

---

[5] The words "Agenda?" and "Draft speech to UN." are written in the margin.

[6] "*Consensus:* President should make speech." is written in the margin.

[7] The comments "McGB: that's safer." and "LDB: doubts we'll know." are written in the margin.

[8] "60 m. U.S." and "2.5 m." are written in the margin.

McGB: A deep policy question. *How firm is the US commitment to Israel.* Had the feeling Monday that we would not—in the end—have put troops in. Debate over this, especially if Israel had been attacked. US constitutional processes—none of these commitments ever backed by Congress.

McN: Territories. Israelis won't ever depend on guarantees. Eban given lesson in US constitutional processes, and he won't ever forget it.

McGB: US President will have to be residual military supplier.

EVR: Oil to neutralize Europe on arms.

LDB: Will be give in our position on territorial integrity. Question is *when.*

President's statement.

Sisco: Here's where we'll give.

(1) Sharm el-Sheikh.
(2) Gaza—nobody wants it.
(3) West Bank.

WWR: Arms control internal to region.

McN: *Don't get far out on elements of solution.* Shld Pres. lead toward a solution?

McGB: No. Pres. by stating problems leads toward solution.

Nasser Options

CIA: *Estimate:* Can Israel hold what it's won? What is cost to them? to us? How long can the [sentence incomplete]. Don't ask Israelis.

LDB:

1. Is military still loyal?
2. Can he cope with econ. problem?
3. Are Russians willing to stake him?[9]

Possibility of living with impossible. "I want him to fall."

Succession:

1. If army in control, turn over to cohorts
2. Unknown Col. Nasser
3. Totally to left (Ali Sabri) or pro-Western elements (unlikely)

Cld N. execute a diplomatic revolution & come to terms with Israel?

LDB: No.

WWR: Need good sophisticated estimate on economics. If he needed $5–600 million & USSR wldn't, shyster.

---

[9] The words "Food, Suez, Tourism, Cotton, Seed Crop, Oil" are listed in the margin.

McGB: Thinks he cld make shift. Wldn't we want to check one more time?[10]

LDB: Don't get on policy again we can't sustain.

CIA: The future of Nasser.[11]

—Econ.

Jobs to be done

1. Political paper on problems & assessments.
2. Draft speech.

Political team—Luke Battle: responsibility

(1) EOB paper
    —binocular view.
    —Dick Ullman.
(2) Battle[12]

Deadline:

Speech: Goldberg–Sisco draft. EVR draft.[13]

Who's the audience?

—US Jews
—UN
—Most Am. people.

Nuclear: Kohler to look.

NPT: guarantees for non-nuclears.

---

[10] The words "'Israel had the courage of our convictions.'—Reston." are written in the margin.

[11] The words "Spanish Amb" and "Canadian Amb—Starnes" are written in the margin. John Kenneth Starnes was the Canadian Ambassador to the United Arab Republic.

[12] The names Eilts, Tasca, and Barbour are written in the margin.

[13] The words "By Wed. night" are written in the right-hand margin. The words "Dream world vs. real world." are written in the left-hand margin.

281. Memorandum for the Record[1]

Washington, June 13, 1967, 6 p.m.

SUBJECT

Minutes of Informal Meeting, 6:00 p.m., 13 June, Mr. Katzenbach's office

1. The group discussed whether the President should speak to the coming UN General Assembly and agreed on the following preparatory actions:

a. Mr. Katzenbach to cable Secretary Rusk laying out the considerations so the Secretary could mull them over and be prepared to discuss them at the 14 June Special Committee meeting.

b. Messrs. Sisco and E.V. Rostow to prepare separate drafts of a UN speech in time for the President's Wednesday night reading.

c. Mr. Battle to assume responsibility for producing a paper covering the whole range of political and territorial problems to settle issues and making some judgment on their acceptability. Mr. Bundy to have a couple of non-government experts produce independent papers along the same lines. Although these papers must necessarily be tentative at this stage, they are necessary as yardsticks for judging the content of the UN speech.

d. Messrs. Battle and Sisco to call a joint meeting of the NEA and IO consultants for 15 June.

2. The group requested two studies:

a. An SNIE on Nasser's prospects for survival, including both economic and political vulnerabilities.

b. A paper answering the questions: How long can Israel hold the territory it has won? What are the costs?

3. The group noted the importance of getting a better picture of the nuclear problem and tentatively agreed to ask Mr. Kohler to take a look at this.

McG B

---

[1] Source: Johnson Library, National Security File, NSC Special Committee Files, Special Committee Meetings. Secret. See also Document 280.

282.   Telegram From the Department of State to the Embassy in
        Saudi Arabia[1]

Washington, June 13, 1967, 9:54 p.m.

210875. 1. FYI. Following oil meeting Kuwait June 11, both Aramco
and Gulf have separately brought to Dept's attention producing countries' appeal that USG take strong position to keep Israelis from gaining
any territory in the present situation.[2] Company reps were told Dept
would give full consideration producing countries' views. Company
reps indicated they would inform host governments of their approaches to us.

2. Dept believes direct USG response to host governments as result
this approach through oil companies would be inappropriate. However,
if you believe would be useful you may give host governments following oral comments re USG position without in any way indicating statement prompted by oil companies' approach. End FYI.

3. In connection problems growing out of recent Arab-Israel hostilities, you may call attention addressee governments to long-standing
USG support for territorial integrity and political independence of all
states of the Near East. This position was re-stated by President Johnson
today.[3] The USG desires the maintenance of friendly ties with all the
countries of the region. In our view it is of the first importance for all to
take steps now to assure that there is an end to the periodic hostilities
and the state of belligerency which have marked Near Eastern history
in the last two decades. The USG is fully prepared to join the other
states to work for lasting arrangements which will serve permanently to
reduce tensions in this region.

4. *For Dhahran.* Please inform Brougham of foregoing.

---

[1] Source: National Archives and Records Administration, Central Files 1967–69, POL
27 ARAB–ISR. Secret. Drafted by Brewer on June 12; cleared by Battle, Solomon, and
Director of the Office of Fuels and Energy John G. Oliver; and approved by Eugene
Rostow. Also sent to Kuwait and repeated to Dhahran and London.

[2] Concerning these approaches, see *Foreign Relations, 1964–1968,* vol. XXXIV, Document 240.

[3] At President Johnson's June 13 news conference, a reporter referred to his May 23
statement reaffirming the U.S. commitment to the territorial and political integrity of
every nation in the Middle East (see Document 49) and asked how he was going to honor
that commitment. He replied: "That is our policy. It will continue to be our policy. How it
will be effectuated will be determined by the events of the days ahead. It will depend a
good deal upon the nations themselves, what they have to say and what their views are,
what their proposals are after they have expressed them." (*Public Papers of the Presidents of
the United States: Lyndon B. Johnson, 1967,* Book I, p. 612)

5. *For Kuwait.* Gulf representative Law reports that Lee will shortly inform GOK of companies' approach to us. Your discretionary use of foregoing applies after Lee has informed Kuwaitis.

6. In addition foregoing, addressees may, of course, draw on President Johnson's comment at his press conference June 13.

Katzenbach

283.　Memorandum From the President's Special Assistant (Rostow) to President Johnson[1]

Washington, June 13, 1967.

SUBJECT

King Faisal's Reply to Your Letter[2]

Faisal reiterates his desire to continue your close personal relationship and urges us to be even-handed in picking up the pieces of the Mid-East war. He has no doubt that the Israelis committed aggression and asks you to help make sure that they don't gain territorially.

I pass this on only because it is typical of the strong pressures we are getting from our Arab friends to say that our support for the territorial integrity of all the states in the area means pulling the Israelis back behind the 1949 Armistice lines and not forcing a peace settlement. Mac Bundy has seen, and we will have recommendations for you soon.

Walt

---

[1] Source: Johnson Library, National Security File, Country File, Middle East Crisis, Vol. V. Secret. A handwritten "L" on the memorandum indicates the President saw it.

[2] For text of the President's June 8 letter to King Faisal, see *Foreign Relations, 1964–1968*, vol. XXI, Document 290. The King's reply was transmitted in telegram 5272 from Jidda, June 12, a copy of which is attached to the source text.

? Why yes? Why no?

hesis?

th existing secondary literature? (Spell out the
d secondary sources)

consult?

make the most use of?

Is the essay engaging? Is the writing correct,
d any person of reasonable intelligence approach
hat the author is getting at?

at additional information would you like to know?
udents in HIS325 to produce a research paper such

**284.   Intelligence Memorandum Prepared in the Central
Intelligence Agency[1]**

SC No. 01415/67   Washington, June 13, 1967.

THE ISRAELI ATTACK ON THE USS *LIBERTY*

The US Naval technical research ship *Liberty* was attacked by Israeli
aircraft and torpedo boats off the Sinai Peninsula on 8 June. The following account of the circumstances of the attack has been compiled
from all available sources.

1. The *Liberty* reported at 9:50 a.m. (2:50 a.m. Washington time) on 8
June that it had been orbited by two delta-wing jet fighters, presumably
Israeli Mirages. At 3:05 p.m. (8:05 a.m.) the *Liberty* was strafed by unidentified jet aircraft. The *Liberty* apparently was not able to establish communications with other units of the US Sixth Fleet during the air attack, and
the first information available to the US commanders was after the subsequent attack by unidentified torpedo boats, which occurred at 3:25 p.m.

2. At 4:11 p.m. (9:11 a.m.) the US Commander in Chief, Europe, notified the National Military Command Center in Washington that the *Liberty*
was under attack and was listing to starboard after being struck by a torpedo. The Commander of the US Sixth Fleet declared the attacking units
hostile and sent attack aircraft from the carriers *America* and *Saratoga* to
protect the *Liberty*. A good part of the ship's communications equipment
was destroyed by the crew during the attack but emergency communications were soon established with the *Saratoga* and with the naval communications station in Greece. Because of the tenseness of the situation and
the communications delays, the initial reports from the *Liberty* were
sketchy and somewhat confusing.

Specifics of the Attack

3. According to these reports, however, the sequence of events took
place as follows. The ship was attacked at 3:05 p.m. (8:05 a.m.) by

---

[1] Source: Johnson Library, National Security File, Country File, Middle East Crisis, CIA
Intelligence Memoranda. Top Secret; Trine; No Foreign Dissem. Prepared in the Central
Intelligence Agency's Directorate of Intelligence. A covering memorandum from Helms to
the President states that it was the "special study" he had requested the previous evening.
Helms' notes of the June 12 meeting of the NSC Special Committee indicate that the
President requested a "special study on strafing & torpedoing of USS *Liberty*—pilot conver-
sations, etc.—everything we can get—NSA, etc." (Central Intelligence Agency Files, DCI
Files: Job 80–B01285A, Box 11, Folder 12, DCI (Helms) Miscellaneous Notes of Meetings, 1
Jan 1966–31 Dec 1968) Rostow sent a preliminary version of this report to the President at
12:45 p.m. on June 13 with a covering memorandum calling it "CIA's first cut at the problem"
and noting, "They do not find evidence of U.S. identification before the attack." (Ibid.)

unidentified jet fighters, believed to be Israeli, at position 31–35N, 33–29E. Six strafing runs were made by the jets. Twenty minutes later three torpedo boats closed at high speed and two of them launched torpedoes after first circling the *Liberty*. One torpedo passed astern, and the other struck the starboard side of the ship in the spaces occupied by the SIGINT collectors. One of the boats was later identified as Israeli and the hull number of one unit was noted as 206–T. Some 50 minutes later two Israeli helicopters arrived on the scene.

Israeli Identification of the Ship

4. None of the communications of the attacking aircraft and torpedo boats is available, but the intercepted conversations between the helicopter pilots and the control tower at Hatzor (near Tel Aviv) leave little doubt that the Israelis failed to identify the *Liberty* as a US ship before or during the attack. Control told (helicopter) 815 at 3:31 p.m. (8:31 a.m.) that "there is a warship there which we attacked. The men jumped into the water from it. You will try to rescue them." Although there were other references to a search for the men in the water and although US units later searched the area, no survivors were recovered from the sea, nor were there any indications that any of the 22 missing personnel from the *Liberty* had been lost overboard.

5. A subsequent message from the control tower to the helicopter identified the ship as Egyptian and told the pilot to return home. Although the *Liberty* is some 200 feet longer than the Egyptian transport *El Quesir,* it could easily be mistaken for the latter vessel by an overzealous pilot. Both ships have similar hulls and arrangements of masts and stack.

6. The weather was clear in the area of attack, the *Liberty*'s hull number (GTR 5) was prominently displayed, and an American flag was flying. The helicopter pilot was then urgently requested to identify the survivors as Egyptian or English speaking (this being the first indication that the Israelis suspected they may have attacked a neutral ship). The helicopter pilot reported seeing an American flag on the *Liberty*. In another intercept between an unidentified Israeli controller and the helicopter number 815, the pilot reported that number GTR 5 was written on the ship's side. The controller told the pilot the number had no significance.

7. Thus it was not until 4:12 p.m. (9:12 a.m.) that the Israelis became convinced that the *Liberty* was American. This was about 44 minutes after the last attack on the ship and the attack had apparently been called off, not because the ship had been identified, but because it seemed to be sinking. (The US Defense Attaché in Tel Aviv reports that Israeli helicopters and the three torpedo boats searched the area until 6:04 p.m. (11:04 a.m.).) The Israeli offer of assistance was declined

because of the sensitive mission of the ship. According to US Navy reports, the ship was saved only through the efforts of her crew.

Damage and Personnel Losses

8. The ship suffered heavy material and personnel casualties. A hole estimated to be 39 feet wide at the bottom and 24 feet wide at the top near the waterline was opened by a torpedo. The ship is flooded below the second deck between frames 52 and 78 (36-inch frame spacing). The crew carried out emergency destruction of classified communications and radar equipment, but the ship's engineering plant is intact. Several flash fires and cannon holes throughout the superstructure caused some minor damage and the ship's motor whale boat and virtually all of its life rafts were lost. Personnel casualties include 10 killed, 90 wounded, and 22 missing, most of whom were probably trapped in the flooded compartments. The wounded and the dead have been removed from the ship and some additional crew members put aboard. The ship is expected to arrive in Malta on 14 June for dry docking and hull repairs. Security precautions are being taken to protect the classified intercept equipment in the flooded spaces. The US Navy has convened a board of inquiry to look into the incident.

The Ship and Its Orders

9. The USS *Liberty* is a converted Victory class merchant ship utilized as a SIGINT collector. The unit had moved from its normal station off West Africa to provide additional SIGINT coverage of the Middle East crisis. Official US statements, however, have described the *Liberty* as an electronics research ship which had been diverted to the crisis area to act as a radio relay station for US embassies.

10. The *Liberty* sailed from Rota, Spain, on 2 June under orders to patrol no closer than 12.5 miles of the UAR coast and 6.5 miles of the Israeli coast. A modification of orders issued by the Commander of the US Sixth Fleet at 12:17 p.m. (5:17 a.m.) on 8 June had not been received aboard the *Liberty*, according to the ship's commanding officer, before the Israeli attack. This change, together with messages from other commands which ordered the *Liberty* to approach no closer than 100 miles of the coasts of the UAR and Israel and 25 miles of the coast of Cyprus, was delayed in transmission in part because of a misunderstanding of responsibilities for delivery.

11. At annex is a listing of events in chronological order.

Annex

CHRONOLOGY OF EVENTS

(Stated times are local; Washington times in parentheses)

2 June 1967	*Liberty* departed Rota, Spain en route to position 32–00N, 33–00E, to remain 12.5 miles from Egyptian coast and 6.5 miles from Israeli coast.
8 June 2:50 a.m. (7 June 7:50 p.m.)	CINCUSNAVEUR Duty Officer received phone instructions from Joint Reconnaissance Center directing *Liberty* to comply with COMSIXTH-FLEET 100-mile operating area restriction.
8 June 9:50 a.m. (2:50 a.m.)	*Liberty* was orbited by two unidentified delta wing single engine jet fighters, presumably Israeli Mirages.
8 June 12:17 p.m. (5:17 a.m.)	COMSIXTHFLEET orders *Liberty* at least 100 miles away from coast of UAR and Israel and 25 miles from Cyprus. This message apparently not received by *Liberty* prior to Israeli attack.
8 June 3:05 p.m. (8:05 a.m.)	*Liberty* attacked by unidentified jet fighters which made six strafing runs. Ship at position 31–35.5N 33–29.0E (25 miles northeast of nearest land).
8 June 3:25 p.m. (8:25 a.m.)	Three torpedo boats, one identified as Israeli, approach ship. One boat bore number 206–T.
8 June 3:27 p.m. (8:27 a.m.)	*Liberty* fires at torpedo boat at range of 2,000 yards.
8 June 3:28 p.m. (8:28 a.m.)	Ship hit by torpedo. Torpedo boats cleared to east about five miles.
8 June 3:30 p.m. (8:30 a.m.)	COMSIXTHFLEET reports *Liberty* hit by torpedo at position 31–23N, 33–25E. Three unidentified gunboats approaching.
8 June 3:31 p.m. (8:31 a.m.)	Hatzor air control (near Tel Aviv) told helicopters (two) to try to rescue men who had jumped into the water from "warship which we attacked."
8 June 3:34 p.m. (8:34 a.m.)	Israeli helicopter identified ship as "definitely Egyptian." Helicopters ordered back to base.
8 June 3:39 p.m. (8:39 a.m.)	Hatzor control told helicopter to rescue men.

8 June 3:50 p.m. (8:50 a.m.)	COMSIXTHFLEET orders carriers to provide air cover for *Liberty*.
8 June 3:52 p.m. (8:52 a.m.)	*Liberty* reported under attack to COMSIXTH-FLEET.
8 June 3:55 p.m. (8:55 a.m.)	*Liberty* reported hit by torpedo starboard side (National Security Agency (NSA) follow-up to Critic, probably a delayed report).
8 June 3:55 p.m. (8:55 a.m.)	Two Israeli helicopters orbited ship at range of 500 yards. Israeli torpedo boats offered assistance which was refused.
8 June 3:59 p.m. (8:59 a.m.)	*Liberty* still under air attack (NSA follow-up to Critic).
8 June 3:59 p.m. (8:59 a.m.)	Hatzor control told helicopter to clarify the nationality of the first man he brings up.
8 June 4:02 p.m. (9:02 a.m.)	Helicopter reports (to Haztor) a big ship and three small ships about a mile from the helicopter. (This places the torpedo boats about eight miles from *Liberty*.)
8 June 4:07 p.m. (9:07 a.m.)	Hatzor told helicopters if men were Egyptians to take them to El Arish; if they spoke English and were not Egyptians, to take them to Lydda.
8 June 4:10 p.m. (9:10 a.m.)	Haztor told helicopter again to clarify nationality. (It appears from the obvious importance of this question that the Israelis suspected they may have hit an American or British and not an Egyptian ship.)
8 June 4:10 p.m. (9:10 a.m.)	Hull number of *Liberty* seen by Israeli helicopter pilot who did not recognize significance.
8 June 4:12 p.m. (9:12 a.m.)	Hatzor asked helicopter, "Did it clearly signal an American flag?" and later requested helicopter to make another pass and check again whether it was really an American flag.
8 June 4:16 p.m. (9:16 a.m.)	Hatzor orders helicopters to return to El Arish.
8 June 5:14 p.m. (10:14 a.m.)	Tel Aviv reports Israeli aircraft and patrol boats attacked ship at 3:00 p.m. (8:00 a.m.) at position 31–25N, 33–33E. Suspecting a U.S. ship, Israel rendering assistance and expresses deep regret.

8 June 6:04 p.m. (11:04 a.m.)	The US Defense Attaché in Tel Aviv reports that Israeli helicopters and the three torpedo boats searched the area until 6:04 p.m. (11:04 a.m.). The Israeli offer of assistance was declined because of the sensitive mission of the ship.

COMSIXTHFLEET then recalled the aircraft launched from the carriers *America* and *Saratoga* and sent two destroyers to assist *Liberty*. *Liberty* proceeding north-west at eight knots.

There was no further contact between *Liberty* and Israeli forces. Two Soviet ships have trailed the *Liberty*, which proceeds under escort to Malta.

---

285.   Memorandum From the Director of the Bureau of Intelligence and Research (Hughes) to Acting Secretary of State Katzenbach[1]

Washington, June 13, 1967.

SUBJECT

INR Comments on the USS *Liberty* Incident, June 8

According to a radio report from the USS *Liberty*, two unidentified delta-wing jet fighters orbited the ship at 0650Z on June 8 at an estimated altitude of 5000 feet and at a distance of two miles. A subsequent sitrep from the *Liberty* establishes the following chronology for the air and surface attacks: 1) at 1205Z, the ship was attacked by unidentified jet fighters, believed to be Israeli, which made six strafing runs on the ship; 2) at 1225Z, three torpedo boats, one identified as Israeli (hull number 206–17) approached the ship from the starboard quarter at high speed; 3) at 1227Z, the attacking boats launched a torpedo and strafing attack, 4) one torpedo struck the *Liberty* at approximately 1228Z; 5) at 1255Z Israeli helicopters orbited the ship at a range of 500 yards. At 0650Z, the *Liberty*'s position was 31 degrees 27 minutes N, 34 degrees 0 minutes E, at 1203Z, the ship's position was 31 degrees 35 minutes N, 33 degrees 29 minutes E. These positions are, respectively, 15 and 23 nautical miles due north of the point on the UAR coast approximately

---

[1] Source: NSA Archives, PCG, ACC 33824, USS *Liberty* Incident. Top Secret; Trine.

midway between the towns of al-'Arish and al-Shu'ts. Al-Shu'ts is located within the UAR adjacent to the Gaza strip (see attached map).[2]

No traffic has appeared pertaining to Israeli military communications in this zone before and during the air and sea attacks on June 8. (We are checking further.) Our first intercept is logged at 1231Z, presumably three minutes after the torpedo attack; this message is the first in a series of commucations believed to have been conducted between Israeli ground radar-control stations and helicopters. The 1231Z messsage refers to "a warship that we attacked," and directs the helicopters to attempt to rescue vessel crew members reportedly in the water. At 1234Z, the ground control station reported that the ship had been identified as Egyptian. (We do not know the basis of this identification.) At 1256Z, the helicopter pilots were ordered to report the nationality of any crew members rescued. At 1302Z, an Israeli ground station, responding to an unaudited message, asked: "did it clearly signal an American flag?" and requested a further check.

In a separate report from USDAO Tel Aviv, a reliable American source was told by a senior Israel Aircraft Industries (IAI) official that on the morning of June 8 he heard IDF transmissions at air-to-ground frequencies. An aircraft reported sighting a ship, was ordered to investigate, and reported back that the ship had a US flag. The aircraft was ordered to recheck and made a second and possibly a third pass, confirming at least for a second time that the flag was US.

The following conclusions appear warranted by the foregoing information: 1) we cannot determine with certainty that the jets that orbited the *Liberty* at 0650Z on June 8 were Israeli. From the ship's location at that hour, however, it would appear probable that the aircraft were Israeli rather that Egyptian, since Israel exercised effective control of adjacent air space on June 8. 2) In the absence of time references, we cannot establish from the USDAO report whether the messages audited by the IAI official pertain to the 0650Z overflight, an unreported pre-attack overflight, the attack period or the post-attack period. From the context of these messages, however, they do not appear to be the helicopter-ground control communications available to us as COMINT. 3) In six strafing runs, it appears remarkable that none of the aircraft pilots identified the vessel as American (or at least non-UAR). 4) The torpedo boat attack was made approximately 20 minutes after the air attack. The surface attack could have been called off in that time had proper air identification been made. 4) *Liberty* crew members were able to identify and record the hull number of one of the small, fast moving torpedo boats during the two minutes that elapsed between their attack run and the launching of the first torpedo, but the Israeli boat commanders apparently failed to identify the much larger and more easily identifiable *Liberty* (11,000 tons, 455 feet long, large identification numbers on hull). 6) The *Liberty* sustained the air attack at

---

[2] Not reproduced.

1205Z and the surface attack at 1225Z. According to COMINT (intercepted by a US Air Force Station), Israeli ground control stations in contact with the helicopters did not ascertain the *Liberty*'s identity until 1302Z, some 58 minutes after the initial encounter. This time lapse, taken in conjuction with the numerous intervening messages indicating doubt on the part of ground control officers as to the nationality of the ship, points to an extraordinary lack of concern on the part of the attackers as to whether the target was hostile. Indeed, the intercepted air-ground dialogue occurring between 1231Z and 1302Z suggests that Israeli ground controllers may have begun to be apprehensive about the possibility of a mistake. The receipt of unaudited messages either from the attacking aircraft or torpedo boats could have raised this question among Israeli ground controllers and led to the rather extensive dialogue that we have intercepted concerning the identification of "rescued crew members". For example, in one instance a ground control station orders at 1307Z: "If they speak Arabic and are Egyptians, take them to al-Arish. If they speak English and are not Egyptians, take them to Lydda [near Tel Aviv]."[3]

---

[3] Brackets in the source text.

---

286. Telegram From the Department of State to the Embassy in Israel[1]

Washington, June 16, 1967, 11 a.m.

211672. At his request, Ambassador Harman called on Undersecretary Rostow on June 14.

1. Ambassador Harman reported that the Israeli Board of Enquiry investigating the attack on the U.S.S. *Liberty* would finish its hearings on Friday afternoon. Its findings would be made shortly thereafter, and would be given us when ready. The Ambassador asked when our Board would complete its own study of the matter. Rostow replied that he did not know but would find out. He assured the Ambassador that the findings of our Board would be made available to GOI when they were prepared. (After consultation with Secretary McNamara, Rostow informed Harman that the U.S. enquiry into the matter would be finished within a few days, and the findings completed shortly thereafter.)

---

[1] Source: National Archives and Records Administration, RG 59, Central Files 1967–69, POL 27 ARAB–ISR. Secret; NATUS. Drafted and approved by Eugene Rostow. Also sent to USUN and repeated to London, Paris, Moscow, Tehran, Kuwait, Jidda, Rabat, Tunis, and Rawalpindi.

2. Harman then informed Rostow that GOI now wished urgently to request a prompt decision with respect to the additional Hawk battery and the 48 Skyhawks discussed at an earlier point with Secretary Vance.[2] GOI, like our government, was watching the pattern of Soviet arms shipments to U.A.R., Algeria and Iraq. Thus far GOI tended to agree with our assessment that the Soviet Union was doing no more than rebuilding the inventory of the U.A.R. and other states for political reasons. The level of supplies was rising rapidly, however, and was a matter of concern. For this reason, GOI regarded the requests as "vital."[3]

3. In the course of a brief review of the problems of political negotiation during the next period, inside and outside the U.N., Harman added nothing new to the estimates as to GOI's ultimate positions he had given in earlier talks, except to stress the possibility of political change in the Israeli Cabinet in the near future. Rostow said that his own view of the situation in prospect required him to put increasing stress on the advice he had offered Harman in recent conversations,[4] namely, that there was considerable anxiety, which propaganda was exploiting, about the possibility that Israel would propose large and permanent territorial changes in the old frontiers, and adopt views about Jerusalem that might not take international interests in the city fully into account. In Rostow's view, an early GOI statement of a moderate position on these problems would help clear the atmosphere, and perhaps reduce resistance to the idea of peace arrangements, GOI's primary goal in the next period.

4. Harman stressed again GOI tactics of delay in the UNGA, to give the government a chance to recover its breath and think through its posture.

Rusk

---

[2] Harman asked Vance on June 17 about the Israeli request for immediate delivery of 48 A–4 aircraft. Vance told him it would be impossible to meet the request without withdrawing aircraft from U.S. forces in Southeast Asia, and that they felt this could not be done. The earliest possible delivery date would be for the four A–4s previously promised for December 1967. (Memorandum for the record by Vance, June 17; Washington National Records Center, OSD Files: FRC 330 72 A 2468, Israel 452)

[3] During a call on Battle on June 14, Harman stated that he was puzzled because in the past 7–10 days, Israeli Embassy officers and attachés had not been getting responses from the Departments of Defense and State on new requests for routine military items; their inquiries were being met with "rather indefinite expressions that matters like this were being looked into at higher levels." Battle said he would try to get a clear answer on this for the Ambassador. (Memorandum of conversation; National Archives and Records Administration, RG 59, Central Files 1967–69, DEF 19–8 US–ISR)

[4] Rostow had made this point in a conversation with Harman on June 13. (Telegram 210999 to Tel Aviv, June 14; ibid., POL 27 ARAB–ISR)

287.   Notes of a Meeting of the NSC Special Committee[1]

Washington, June 14, 1967, 6:30 p.m.

THOSE PRESENT

Vice President
McNamara
Fowler
Katzenbach
Vance
Wheeler
Helms
Clifford
W.W. Rostow
McG. Bundy
E.V. Rostow
Amb. Thompson
Battle
Sisco
Harry McPherson
Harold Saunders

Secretary Rusk and Amb. Goldberg came in about 7:00 p.m.
George Christian came in at 7:30 p.m.
President came in at 7:38 p.m.

1. Restatement US arms supply policy[2]

para 1. no problem
para 2. approved (Jordan. F–104's not a problem until fall.)
para 3. approved
    para 4. Policy[3] guidance—We are reviewing, but review against this policy.[4]

Israel

48 A–4: we don't have; we can't accelerate.

---

[1] Source: Johnson Library, National Security File, NSC Special Committee Files, Minutes and Notes. No classification marking. The meeting was held in the Cabinet Room at the White House. The notes are Saunders' handwritten notes of the meeting. The President's Daily Diary indicates that the meeting ended at 8:25 p.m. It lists NSC staff member Roger Morris and John Devine among those present, in addition to those listed here. (Johnson Library) See also Document 288. Bundy sent an agenda to the President earlier that day, with attached outlines of a possible statement to the United Nations, headed "Another Possible Outline," "Rostow Draft Summary," and "Sisco Draft Summary." (Johnson Library, National Security File, NSC Special Committee Files, Special Committee #1) A notation on another copy of "Another Possible Outline" indicates it was drafted by Bundy. (Ibid., Special Committee Meetings)

[2] See the attachment to Document 288.

[3] The word "Press?" is inserted above the word "Policy".

[4] "Press guidance" is written in the left margin.

250 M–60 tanks

Hawks batteries

McN. wld be unwilling to overrule services.[5]

Must avoid any position that looks as if we are reneging on any agreement.

[Get redraft of earlier order that reflects these points.][6]

Should we unhook from 1949 agreements?

(Sisco: Art. 12 of GAA calls for renegotiation)

Katz: Unhook but don't say those aren't g [sentence not completed].

Circulate full text of Ambassador Goldberg's statement of 13 June.[7]

Rusk:
1. Nothing in lines jeopardize Israel if they are *peace* lines.
2. Self-determination: West Bank.

—Israel's keeping territory wld create a revanchism for the rest of the 20th c.

3. Israel must be accepted.

—McN. doesn't think recognition alone enough.

Goldberg:

1. Israelis willing to create internat'l religious enclaves in Jerusalem.
2. Syria creates greatest USSR concern.

WWR: Use Syrian heights to bargain on arms race.

Thompson: USSR would accept Israel, open Aqaba, Jerusalem—but on territory they wouldn't.

Consensus:

If Kosygin comes, you shld go.
If not, far from clear.

Tents for Jordan:[8]

---

[5] The section headed "Israel" is written to the right of paragraph 4 under section headed "Restatement US arms supply policy."

[6] Brackets in the handwritten source text.

[7] "Morris doing" is written in the left margin. Reference is to Goldberg's first June 13 statement; for text, see Department of State *Bulletin,* July 3, 1967, pp. 5–9.

[8] A June 14 memorandum from Bundy to the Special Committee on the subject "Tents for Jordan," states that the Jordanian Government had requested 5,000–10,000 tents and noted steps that other countries were taking to provide emergency relief. Bundy recommended sending the tents. He stated, "We badly need a few gestures toward our moderate Arab friends to balance the increasingly effective Nasser charges that we have sided completely with Israel. This is a one-shot arrangement. It is not likely to get us dug in on any long-term program of refugee relief. Leonard Marks informs me he can make effective use of a gesture of this kind on The Voice of America." (Johnson Library, National Security File, NSC Special Committee Files, Special Committee Meetings)

—Through UNRWA[9]

Water drops:

If Red Cross agrees, we wld go ahead.

Katz: Tourist ban.

Pres: Not now.[10]

---

[9] "Working for refugees and residents on both sides." is written to the right of these words. The words "President approved." are written below. "Tell USIA," with a telephone number, is written next to those words.

[10] "SA, Kuw, Mor, Tun, Leb?, Israel" are listed next to the last two lines.

---

288. Memorandum for the Record[1]

Washington, June 14, 1967, 6:30 p.m.

SUBJECT

Minutes, NSC Special Committee, 6:30 p.m., 14 June in the Cabinet Room

1. The Committee approved the "Restatement of Current U.S. Arms Supply Policy to the Middle East" (attached) with the two following changes:

(a) At the end of paragraph 4 add: "Any further approvals or shipments will require the prior approval of the Secretaries of State and Defense."
(b) In the footnote on page two, amend line 5 to read: ". . . this policy, *if unmodified over the next several months, would* block shipment of the Israeli arms package approved. . ."

In discussing this item, the Committee (a) noted the importance of not appearing to renege on recent commitments, and (b) agreed specifically that we should not for the moment consider Israel's new requests for A–4 aircraft, M–60 tanks and Hawk missiles.

2. The President approved immediate shipment of 5500 tents to Jordan.

3. The President approved on a contingency basis going ahead with emergency water drops for stragglers in Sinai if the Interna-

---

[1] Source: Johnson Library, National Security File, Special Committee, Special Committee Meetings. Secret. Drafted on June 15; also see Document 287.

tional Red Cross accepts our offer of help and the Israeli government approves.[2]

4. The President rejected a proposal to raise the ban on tourist travel to the crisis area.

McGeorge Bundy[3]

Attachment

Washington, June 14, 1967.

SUBJECT

Restatement of Current US Arms Supply Policy to the Middle East

The Control Group wishes to restate the present arms supply policy, in order to assure its full understanding by all concerned.

1. All shipments of military equipment to those states which have broken diplomatic relations with us have been suspended as of June 8. With respect to government-to-government agreements (grant aid and credit sales under the Military Assistance Program), this has involved stopping shipments at depots, manufacturers' facilities, and other sources; it has also involved efforts to repossess shipments at the port or enroute, to the extent such shipments are still within US control. With respect to direct commercial sales, this has involved the immediate suspension of outstanding munitions export licenses and the stopping at US ports of all shipments under such licenses.

2. Jordan and Lebanon are being treated in the same manner as countries which have broken relations with us.[4]

3. Munitions export licenses issued, prior to June 8, to states in the area which have not broken relations with us remain in effect. Under this arrangement, the following magnitudes of equipment would continue to be deliverable: Israel $38 million; Saudi Arabia $57 million; Kuwait $17,000; and Morocco $16,000.

4. No new munitions export licenses are being approved and no further shipments under the Military Assistance Program (both grant

---

[2] Telegram 210998 to Geneva, June 14, instructed the U.S. mission to approach the International Committee of the Red Cross to ask if the ICRC wanted such assistance. (National Archives and Records Administration, RG 59, Central Files 1967–69, POL 27 ARAB–ISR)

[3] Printed from a copy that bears this typewritten signature.

[4] This policy suspends munitions export licenses covering $238,000 in arms for Lebanon; there are no outstanding export licenses for Jordan. It does, however, stop all scheduled grant aid shipments to Jordan under MAP (about $1.5 million per year in spare parts) and suspends the sales contract for 12 F–104 aircraft under which initial deliveries to Jordan are scheduled for August 1967. [Footnote in the source text.]

aid and credit sales) are being approved even for those countries which have not broken relations. Current credit sales negotiations are continuing, but US negotiators are instructed not to consummate any new sale.[5] Any further approvals or shipments will require the prior approval of the Secretaries of State and Defense.

---

[5] The value of pending requests for munitions export licenses blocked by this action is: Israel $1.2 million; Jordan $59,000; Kuwait $125,000; Lebanon $47,000; Saudi Arabia $3.2 million; Syria $463,000; and Iraq $390,000. In addition, this policy, if unmodified over the next several months, would block shipment of the Israeli arms package approved by the President on May 23 (100 APC for cash, $14 million of Hawk and tank spares for credit), and the 1966 agreement to sell 48 A–4 aircraft to Israel. [Footnote in the source text.]

---

289.   Telegram From the Defense Attaché Office in Israel to the White House[1]

Tel Aviv, June 15, 1967, 1130Z.

0892. Ref DAO Tel Aviv 0886 Jun 67.[2] Subject *Liberty* Incident.

1. Commodore Shlomo Erell, Commander in Chief IDF Navy, asked ALUSNA to call upon him early evening 14 June. Commodore presented apologies and expressions of regret in regard *Liberty* incident to the U.S. Navy on behalf of Israeli Navy and said he was preparing letter to CNO USN. He said incident was great mistake: that IDF Navy personnel involved felt "terrible" and that the incident in fact spoiled all feeling of victory of IDF Navy in recent hostilities.

2. Erell stated he did not want to comment on elements of incident until the Israeli court of inquiry had rendered findings. When asked if those findings would be transmitted to the United States the commodore said he presumed they would be.

3. As in every case when Israeli officer mentions the incident Commodore Erell remarked on how close *Liberty* was to shore line. ALUSNA replied that *Liberty* was in international waters.

---

[1] Source: Johnson Library, National Security File, NSC Special Committee Files, *Liberty*. Confidential. Also sent to OSD, CNO, Department of State, COMSIXTHFLT, CINCSTRIKE, CINCUSNAVEUR, JCS, DIA, USUN, CINCEUR/USEUCOM, CTG 60.2, USAFE, CINCUSAREUR, and CTG 60.

[2] Telegram 0886 from USDAO Tel Aviv reported that Bloch informed Castle on June 13 that General Rabin had appointed an official court of inquiry in the *Liberty* incident. (National Archives and Records Administration, Rg 59, Central Files 1967–69, POL 27 ARAB–ISR)

3. Israeli Government thinking as to specific parameters of a settlement has not yet crystalized. However as of this time they believe certain goals to be obtainable. Tactically the majority of authoritative circles seem confident that pressures created by the impact of their defeat in the neighboring countries will be sufficient to persuade the Arab regimes to seek direct peace negotiations. In such negotiations the Israelis would be guided by a determination that Jerusalem shall not be redivided, that the West Bank and Gaza should not be annexed to Israel for the reason that they contain so many Arabs that annexation would alter the complexion of Israel into that of a binational state, that free access to the Straits of Tiran and the Suez Canal should be guaranteed by the absence of a right on the part of Egypt to invoke a state of belligerency to deny Israeli access, and that insofar as Syria is concerned provision must be made to prevent the border settlements there from continuing to live under the threat of Syrian bombardment.

4. Despite the majority adherence at present to the foregoing as attainable objectives, the last few days have indicated that some skepticism is arising in certain quarters close to the seat of power here as to whether this is a realistic assessment. I detect considerable skepticism as to whether the tactic of achieving bilateral negotiations by merely standing pat will work and a growing belief if direct negotiations are feasible that they will have to be under some international umbrella. Similarly there seem to be those who now estimate that to maintain Israeli sympathy among nations having particular religious interests in Jerusalem and especially the Vatican, it will be necessary to envisage some sort of international regime to control or supervise and thus protect the religious interests generally in the city, although presumably such international arrangement would be within the context of an agreement whereby the political entity of Jerusalem would be maintained under Israeli administration. The same individuals are inclined to doubt the government's exploration of some autonomous status for the West Bank will also turn out to be practicable and tend to assume that after taking account of necessary minor frontier rectification to provide additional Israeli security, the West Bank will probably be returned to Jordan. Further, and perhaps more crucial in views of the power relationships involved, I am beginning to hear important voices question whether physical Israeli possession of the heights in Syria, which is now regarded as an essential security requirement, will ultimately become feasible. If not, an international regime of some sort guaranteeing the demilitarization of that area may finally result. In this connection it may be noted that I am now reliably informed, although second hand, that the cabinet decision to clear the Syrian heights militarily was a last minute, on balance rever-

sal of a decision that, regretfully as the Israelis might feel, Israel would have to accept the cease fire without embarking on that expedition. A communication from 14 Kibbutzim on the frontier that unless the action was undertaken they would resettle elsewhere seems to have tipped the scales. The importance of this episode is the indication that the Israeli Government was aware of the Soviet factor in relation to Syria and is presumably still conscious of it.

5. There is of course an enormous difference between the government's position which the Israelis are now trying to implement and these latter more sober estimates of realistic possibilities. Consequently if things work out in this more limited achievement the psychological let down will be of major proportions. In all probability the United States will have to exercise considerable persuasion with the Israelis to achieve a solution salvaging maximum U.S. interests in the whole area before the course of forthcoming diplomatic maneuvering is run. To minimize the impact here I believe it desirable that so long as the Israelis wish to pursue their tactic of bilateral negotiation and to the extent we do so without taking an unacceptable risk of confrontation with the Soviets, it would be to our interest to avoid specific U.S. initiatives. I would anticipate that as things proceed the Israelis will discover that some, at least, of their stated objectives are not attainable and may then come to us for assistance in a more realistic frame of mind.

Barbour

291.   Memorandum of Conversation[1]

Washington, June 15, 1967, 5:10 p.m.

SUBJECT

Middle East

PARTICIPANTS

The Secretary
Ambassador Battle, Assistant Secretary for NEA
Thomas M. Judd, UK Desk Officer

Sir Patrick Dean, British Ambassador

Ambassador Dean said he would like to have an exchange of views on the Middle East situation. Stressing that he was speaking without instructions, he expressed serious concern regarding developments. He noted that Britain was short of tankers and badly needed to get oil from Libya. He thought Kosygin was up to no good in coming to New York. The Soviets were trying to make matters more difficult for the Western position in the area.

The Secretary said we had received confirmation that Kosygin, Gromyko and the other Soviet leaders were coming to New York. We had a press report to the effect that de Gaulle would be willing to go to New York to attend a summit meeting and another from London saying Wilson was willing to come if Kosygin was also coming. During the recent NATO Ministerial Meeting, the Secretary said, all the discussion was to the effect that NATO members should not provide any of the 62 votes necessary to call a special session of the General Assembly. This position had dissolved when the rumor spread that Kosygin was coming. Many think it would be wonderful if the President and Kosygin could sit down to talk things out. They had forgotten that at the last such meeting we were presented with an ultimatum on Berlin.

Ambassador Dean inquired concerning the Secretary's views as to what could be done to bring about a settlement in the Middle East. The Secretary replied that we were not trying to draw up a clear blueprint. We wished to keep our position flexible in case the countries in the area could come up with any answers themselves. A solution would have to provide for:

(1) recognition of the existence of the state of Israel;
(2) doing away with the "rights of belligerency";

---

[1] Source: National Archives and Records Administration, RG 59, Central Files 1967–69, POL 27 ARAB–ISR. Confidential. Drafted by Judd and approved in S on June 27. The meeting was held in the Secretary's office.

(3) some settlement on the waterways;

(4) progress on refugees; and

(5) progress on arms limitation.

There remained the problem of the old city of Jerusalem. This was going to be tough.

Ambassador Dean asked what type of negotiations we favored. Ambassador Battle replied that our interests would be better served by individual rather than collective negotiations. These would be difficult to arrange. A mediator was needed to go around to the various countries. The Secretary noted that Israel had said it would not accept a mediator.

The Secretary asked if Ambassador Dean had seen a report that the French had said they would not recognize any territorial changes not agreed to by all parties concerned. Ambassador Dean replied that he had not and asked what the French were up to. Ambassador Battle said they seemed to be making a clear effort to play both sides.

---

292.   Telegram From the Mission to the United Nations to the Department of State[1]

New York, June 15, 1967, 2113Z.

5736. Number two man in UAR mission, Amb Hilmy, who is former general, phoned Buffum today to relate fol message. Since there are no diplomatic relations between our govts and since UAR would still like to be able to exchange views with US, he has been detailed to serve as a channel for this purpose. Hilmy indicated he is available to transmit messages or otherwise exchange views at any time. He asked that this info be kept confidential. Buffum said he would transmit this message to Washington and was sure US would welcome fact that official channel remains open despite rupture of relations.

---

[1] Source: National Archives and Records Administration, RG 59, Central Files 1967–69, POL UAR–US. Confidential; Exdis. Received at 6:19 p.m. Rostow sent a copy to the President at 7:40 a.m. on June 16 with a covering memorandum commenting: "Herewith UAR begins to toss an anchor to windward and tries to open a dialogue with us." (Johnson Library, National Security File, Country File, Middle East Crisis, Vol. VI)

Somewhat earlier and quite separately, Mohamed Riad[2] asked MisOff discreetly to inform Amb Battle or Bergus that he is available if either wish to pass info to him in absence of Amb Kamel. He characterized UAR officers remaining Washington as purely "caretakers." Without departing from UAR line, Riad has deliberately conveyed impression he wishes do whatever he can to work for improvement of relations between US and UAR.[3]

Goldberg

---

[2] An alternate member of the UAR delegation to the United Nations.

[3] Telegram 212159 to USUN, June 16, commented, "We know from experience that it is habitual for Egyptians in time of crisis to offer themselves as communications channel. They instinctively believe that maintenance of channels of communication more important than substance of what two countries may have to say to each other." It expressed a preference for Mohamed Riad as a communications channel, should future circumstances warrant. (National Archives and Records Administration, RG 59, Central Files 1967–69, POL UAR–US)

---

293.   Memorandum for the Special Committee[1]

Washington, June 15, 1967.

SUBJECT

Status of Efforts To Curb the Flow of Arms to the Arab States and Israel

1. The Secretary raised the question of avoiding a spiral of arms deliveries to the area at the NATO Ministerial Meeting.[2] In addition, we have raised the question with the British and French Governments; the British have stated a readiness to cooperate in curbing arms supply if, and only if, there were effective multilateral

---

[1] Source: Johnson Library, National Security File, Special Committee, Special Committee Meetings. Secret. No drafting information appears on the memorandum. It is apparently the status report prepared in the Department of State cited on Walt Rostow's agenda for the meeting. (Ibid., Country File, Middle East Crisis, Vol. VI)

[2] Rusk attended the Ministerial Meeting of the North Atlantic Council in Luxembourg June 12–14. Telegram 477 from Luxembourg, June 14, summarizes his statement on the Middle East situation at the June 13 meeting. (National Archives and Records Administration, RG 59, Central Files 1967–69, NATO 3 LUX (LU)) Documentation on his discussions at the meeting is ibid.; also ibid., Conference Files, 1966–1972, Entry 3051B, CF 186–194.

arrangements which were binding also on the Soviet Union.[3] The French were completely noncommittal, professing that the problem need not be addressed until the dust settled, and did not even offer to support a position of restraint contingent upon agreement of the other major arms suppliers.[4] The British have now shifted to a case-by-case consideration; the French have indicated that they will probably resume shipments; the Italians are presently holding to an embargo; and of course the Soviet Union is carrying forward a substantial program—at least for the short run—of supply of military equipment to the Arab States.

2. We instructed USUN to seek to introduce into the Security Council discussion through a neutral third party an appeal for notification to the Secretary General "in advance on a continuing basis of any arms shipment to any of the States that have engaged in the recent hostilities or have asserted a position of belligerency with respect to those hostilities."[5] However, such an appeal has not been made in the Security Council. There may be an opportunity to have this matter raised, and perhaps to float a recommendatory resolution, in the forthcoming General Assembly session.

3. On June 14, Ambassador Thompson expressed to Soviet Chargé Chernyakov our concern that arms shipments to the Near East could lead to a renewed spiral in the arms race. He noted that the problem had both short and long term dimensions. Chernyakov acknowledged concern over this problem, but noted the pressures on the Soviet Union from the Arabs and the need to demonstrate Soviet support.

4. We recommend consideration be given to the position we should take on this subject with Premier Kosygin.

---

[3] Counselor of the British Embassy John E. Killick conveyed the British reply to Deputy Assistant Secretary of State for Politico-Military Affairs Jeffery C. Kitchen. (Memorandum of conversation, June 13; ibid., Central Files 1967–69, DEF 12 NEAR E)

[4] Telegram 20111 from Paris, June 12, reported French views on this. (Ibid., POL 27 ARAB–ISR)

[5] Telegram 210839 to USUN, June 13, conveyed these instructions. (Ibid., DEF 12 NEAR E)

294. Notes of a Meeting of the NSC Special Committee[1]

Washington, June 15, 1967, 6:30 p.m.

THOSE PRESENT

Rusk
McNamara
Fowler
Goldberg
Wheeler
Helms
W.W. Rostow
Clifford
McG. Bundy
Vance
Thompson
Battle
Harry McPherson
H. Saunders

The President and George Christian came in about 7:30 p.m.

1. Fowler's report on market.

2. Kosygin: arriving NY late tomorrow after talk with de Gaulle.

3. France—arms—Algeria.

4. Reply to *Liberty* note? McGB to check action with Katzenbach.

5. Arms control.

—Thompson's conversation with Chernyakov is sufficient for the record.

—Subject should be in any speech to UNGA & *good talking paper for LBJ–Kosygin.*

—Goldberg: *neutral parties not eager to press arms registration.* Shall we advance proposal ourselves? Do we table a proposal? *Do we offer a resolution in our speech?*

—Tied in with UN presentation.

6. Vance: water drop? Planes being prepared.

EVR–Harman–Dayan & UAR Red Cross—they to look over area in Israeli helicopters.

—Reply to Vatican.

—Press guidance OK.

---

[1] Source: Johnson Library, National Security File, NSC Special Committee Files, Minutes and Notes. No classification marking. The meeting was held in the Cabinet room at the White House. The notes are Saunders' handwritten notes of the meeting. The meeting ended at 8:15 p.m. (Ibid., President's Daily Diary)

7. *Wheelus*: McN: "marginally desirable."

—Response telegram: approved with change.[2]

8. *Attend UN*: Two separate questions.

a. President's own decision.
b. Whether we tell UK.

9. Arab Foreign Ministers: add strong para.

10. Jidda. Solomon to talk to Aramco on jet fuel to Vietnam.

11. Should President appear in UNGA?[3]

Alternative: Speak on national TV hookup before.
Let Kosygin have his show.
DR: "I have some preference for your going." In & out.
AG: Problem: will Arabs *walk out*? They have done this on other problems. (USSR wld be against walkout)
Fowler & Christian: Walking out a plus.

Pr: Instinct

(a) this is Kosygin's show
(b) see any heads of state come
(c) no hurry to gallop up there
(d) don't show too much eagerness
(e) any hope of achieving anything?

Thompson & Clifford: Exceedingly important to see K. Use UN speech as excuse, if need be.

Wld. meeting set us back? China spotlight.

Thompson: Key Soviet question: Can they do business?

DR: Ultimatum? Kennedy–Khrushchev.

---

[2] The note "If King wants us out, we have no choice—McN. agrees." is written in the margin. Documentation on U.S. relations with Libya is in *Foreign Relations, 1964–1968*, vol. XXIV, Documents 40 ff.

[3] The Fifth Emergency Special Session of the UN General Assembly met June 17–July 5 and July 12–21.

295.　Memorandum for the Record[1]

Washington, June 15, 1967, 6:30 p.m.

SUBJECT

Minutes, NSC Special Committee
6:30 p.m., Thursday, 15 June, Cabinet Room

1. In response to the Libyan Government's request that we withdraw from Wheelus Base, the Committee approved instructing Ambassador Newsom to reply that, in accordance with our position in 1964, we are prepared to resume discussions leading to withdrawal—no timetable to be specified. The consensus was that if King Idris wants us to leave, we have no choice.

2. The Committee noted progress made in readying equipment for a water drop to Egyptian stragglers in the Sinai Desert and agreed that we should make public our offer to the International Committee of the Red Cross to make planes available. The Committee also agreed to expedite our reply to a plea from the Vatican on this subject.

3. The Committee revised and approved messages instructing approaches to the Foreign Ministers of Morocco, Saudi Arabia, Jordan and Lebanon before the proposed meeting of Arab Foreign Ministers.[2] A separate response to King Hussein's request for assurance of future arms supplies was also approved, explaining our hope to avoid another arms race.[3]

4. The Committee instructed Assistant Secretary Solomon to discuss with Aramco officials their interpretation of Saudi Arabian oil export limitations to include jet fuel for Vietnam. The consensus was that we should not acquiesce.

McG. B.

---

[1]　Source: Johnson Library, National Security File, NSC Special Committee Files, Minutes and Notes. Secret.

[2]　See Document 296. Telegrams 211605 to Beirut, 211610 to Rabat, and 211611 to Jidda, all dated June 14, are similar but not identical. (National Archives and Records Administration, RG 59, Central Files 1967–69, POL 27 ARAB–ISR)

[3]　Telegram 211613 to Amman, June 15, stated that the United States hoped to avoid a new arms race in the Middle East and therefore was not approving any export licenses or any further shipments under the Military Assistance Program to any of the participants in the conflict "at this time." It also instructed the Embassy to assure King Hussein of U.S. concern with Jordan's security and to tell him there had been no U.S. decision in principle against supplying arms to Jordan. (Ibid., DEF 19–8 US–JORDAN)

296.   Telegram From the Department of State to the Embassy in Jordan[1]

Washington, June 15, 1967, 10:32 p.m.

211615. For Ambassador at opening of business June 16.

1. Prior to Foreign Minister Touqan's departure for Arab Foreign Minister's meeting in Kuwait, you should convey to him following USG position on current crisis:

2. We are urgently studying problems growing out of recent Arab-Israel hostilities in an effort to defuse situation. In this connection you may assure him that we stand by our support of the political independence and territorial integrity of all states in the Near East in accordance with the reaffirmation on June 13 by President Johnson (press conference) of his May 23 statement (copies of both should be provided). In our view, it is of prime importance for all states to take steps now to assure that there is an end to the periodic hostilities and the state of belligerency which have marked Near Eastern history in the last two decades. The USG is fully prepared to work both in the UN and directly with other states for lasting arrangements which will serve permanently to reduce tensions in this region. The UN resolution submitted to the Security Council by the USG on June 8 was designed to accomplish that end.

3. We have been and are concerned with conditions on the West Bank. To alleviate the situation, we have vigorously intervened with the Israelis for them to encourage West Bank residents to remain there and resume normal life. We have been somewhat encouraged by these efforts and will continue them. We approve of UNRWA's continuing its operations on the West Bank and we are supporting other measures to assist people in Jordan who have suffered from the hostilities.

4. We realize that GOJ has raised in past days a number of important questions which we have not answered. We can only assure GOJ that we have Jordan's interest very much in mind and will be in touch with the GOJ as soon as we have sorted things out. In the meantime, we hope that the GOJ can continue to exercise, as far as circumstances permit, a moderate influence on Arab counsels, as without moderation on all sides, there is little hope for reducing present tension.

---

[1] Source: National Archives and Records Administration, RG 59, Central Files 1967–69, POL 27 ARAB–ISR. Confidential; Immediate. Drafted by Houghton, cleared by Davies and the NSC Special Committee, and approved by Battle.

5. We are deeply chagrined that some Arab countries have broken relations on the basis of outrageous charges and would be gravely disturbed if there were further action based on the same falsehoods.

Rusk

297. **Draft Briefing by Director of Central Intelligence Helms for the President's Foreign Intelligence Advisory Board**[1]

Washington, June 14, 1967.

MIDDLE EAST COLLECTION CAPABILITIES

I want to discuss with you first our various facilities for intelligence collection in the Middle East, and how they performed during the latest crisis.

I. By and large, we had the right assets, and enough of them, in place and operating when the crisis began. We were able to reinforce them adequately as the crisis developed. They provided timely advance warning, and furnished the basis for an excellent estimate of the probable outcome.

A. Once the shooting started, however, for a variety of reasons I will come to in a minute, we were less than well informed on the tactical progress of the fighting.

[heading not declassified]

II. [9 lines of source text not declassified]
[Omitted here is detailed discussion.]

---

[1] Source: Central Intelligence Agency, DCI Executive Registry Files: Job 80–R01580, Box 10, Folder 210, President's Foreign Intelligence Advisory Board. Top Secret; [codeword not declassified]. Nine annexes are filed with this draft briefing, including a chronology of the crisis, a chronology of the Arab-Israeli Task Force established May 23; and copies of other memoranda entitled: "Overall Arab-Israeli Military Capabilities," May 23; "Israeli Intelligence Estimate of the Israeli-Arab Crisis," May 25; Office of National Estimates memorandum "The Middle Eastern Crisis," May 26; "Military Capabilities of Israel—and the Arab States," May 26 (Document 76); "The Current Focus of the Near East Crisis," June 3; [text not declassified]. The package is filed with a letter from J. Patrick Coyne of the President's Foreign Intelligence Board indicating that he and General Taylor had reviewed it. The briefing was prepared for a PFIAB meeting on June 15–16. No minutes of the meeting have been found.

V. [*10 lines of source text not declassified*]
[Omitted here is detailed discussion.]

Overhead Reconnaissance:

VI. Intensive overhead reconnaissance would have produced a substantial amount of tactical situation intelligence, but political considerations precluded the use of most of our capabilities.
[Omitted here is detailed discussion.]

C. Overhead reconnaissance therefore provided no intelligence during the actual fighting phase, but we did have two satellites—a KH–4 and KH–7—in orbit during the developing period from May 16 to May 30.

1. Each satellite was limited to six or eight passes over the Middle East, but we made the fullest possible use of them.
2. The KH–4 was already up when Nasir began moving his troops forward and closed the Gulf of Aqaba, but we fed in some requirements which were covered in the second basket. The KH–7 was tasked for Middle East targets before it was launched.
3. Photography from the KH–7 on May 29, for instance, revealed no evidence of the 5,000-man force which was supposed to be defending Sharm-Ash-Shaykh. It did find MIG–15s on two previously unoccupied airfields in southern Syria.

[Omitted here is detailed discussion.]

XII. The Mediterranean Bureau of the Foreign Broadcast Information Service bears the blame for disturbing Washington sleep when the fighting started at 2:05 our time Monday morning. Their flash, based on monitoring the Israeli Radio, was 20 minutes ahead of the news agencies and 50 minutes ahead of the first official reporting on the outbreak of hostilities.

[Omitted here is detailed discussion.]

XIII. To summarize, then, we had adequate facilities in place to spot the crisis, and watch it as it developed. If we were somewhat short on the actual play-by-play, once the fighting actually started, it was the result of political decision or mischance, rather than any shortcoming in foresight or planning. I have emphasized the limits on our capabilities because that is the most useful element in seeking benefit from a postmortem. Next I would like to tell you briefly the positive reporting we were able to accomplish with those capabilities.

POSTMORTEM: REPORTING ON THE MIDDLE EAST CRISIS

I. Matching the performance of the intelligence collectors, at the other end of the process the intelligence community displayed a high degree of good analysis, sound evaluation, and timely warning in its finished intelligence production on the Arab-Israeli crisis.

A. It is a bit difficult to pick the starting point for any one particular crisis in a feud which has persisted for 20 years, but a good case can be made that this one began to take shape last November.

B. On November 5, 1966, we reported in the Central Intelligence Bulletin that Tel Aviv probably considered that they had exhausted peaceful methods, channels, and remedies for stopping raids into Israel by Palestinian terrorists.

1. The obvious conclusion was that the Israelis would once again try military reprisals, and we began watching for Israeli deployments or spot mobilizations.

2. Eight days later, the Israelis struck at suspected Arab terrorist bases in Jordan.

C. As we analyzed the effects of this raid, we concluded that:

(*One*) It had badly shaken the stability of the Jordanian regime, the principal moderate on Israel's borders, and might impel the Jordanians to closer cooperation with the Egyptians in military matters;

(*Two*) The Tel Aviv government had probably picked Jordan because the military commanders considered the Syrian border terrain less suitable for sharp, limited reprisal; and

(*Three*) The raid would not deter the terrorists, trained, supported, and directed by the Syrians. The Israelis would therefore soon feel constrained to strike directly at Syria again despite the difficult terrain.

D. In our current intelligence reporting, accordingly, we kept close watch over the ensuing months on both the terrorist raids, and the Israeli reaction.

1. The Central Intelligence Bulletins of January 7 and January 10 reported renewed firing across the Syrian-Israeli border.

2. A finished intelligence report on January 17 called the situation there "explosive."

3. The actual "explosion" was delayed for some weeks by meetings of the Israeli-Syrian Mixed Armistice Commission, but the Central Intelligence Bulletin during this period periodically reported, quite correctly, that the meetings were making no progress on basic issues, and that the Israelis were probably preparing substantial retaliation for the next suitable Syrian provocation.

E. On April 7 the Israelis turned a border shelling incident into an aerial dogfight, and inflicted a sharp defeat on the Syrian Air Force, shooting down six MIG–21s without losing a single Israeli plane.

1. [8 lines of source text not declassified]

2. I should also note at this point one of the soft spots in our record. Our reporting concluded that neither side would soon seek another major engagement. In retrospect, it was a sound judgment in the light of the facts, but it did not make sufficient allowance for Nasir's overreaction to the next Israeli warning against terrorism.

II. On May 10, our daily reporting noted that there had been 14 terrorist incidents in Israel since the air battle on April 7, and that while there had been no fatalities, pressure was mounting in Israel for another reprisal raid.

A. On May 12, Prime Minister Eshkol warned publicly that "if there is no other way," Israel would have to use "appropriate means" to punish the Syrians for terrorist acts.

1. Four days later, the Israeli military intelligence chief implied to the U.S. Defense Attaché that Israel might launch air strikes against Syria if there were fatalities from terrorism.

B. [*4-1/2 lines of source text not declassified*]

C. On May 14 and 15, Nasir placed the Egyptian armed forces on "full alert," and began moving ground forces into Sinai with much fanfare.

D. [*7 lines of source text not declassified*]

III. The result of all this, in effect, was to put the intelligence community on full alert too. The Arab-Israeli situation was a daily item in the Central Intelligence Bulletin [*less than 1 line of source text not declassified*] from May 15 onward, and on May 18 we began issuing additional situation reports twice a day for the White House.

A. We disagreed with the Arab evaluation of Moscow's support, and noted [*1 line of source text not declassified*] that we expected the Soviets to tread warily, but [*less than 1 line of source text not declassified*] that the Syrians seemed to be doubletalking themselves, and possibly the Egyptians, into believing that the Soviets would come to their aid in the event of an Israeli attack.

1. [*6 lines of source text not declassified*]

IV. Early on May 23, Cairo time, Nasir—who by this time had accomplished the complete withdrawal of the United Nations Emergency Force—announced that he was again closing the Gulf of Aqaba to Israeli-flag shipping and to other ships carrying strategic material to Eilat.

A. Early on that same day, Washington time, we noted [*less than 1 line of source text not declassified*] that the Israelis would consider this a justifiable cause for war.

1. I told two Congressional subcommittees that same morning and a White House lunch conference that war could now come at any time "by accident, incident, or miscalculation."

2. I brought to that same White House lunch a CIA memorandum, concurred in by Secretary McNamara and General Wheeler and later passed along to Ambassador Goldberg, which stated that we believed the Israelis would be able to defeat any combination of Arabs, and that Israeli planning was still based on a short war.

B. At this point—May 23—we put a 24-hour Arab-Israeli Task Force to work in our CIA Operations Center, to focus all available intelligence and expertise on the responsibilities for current reporting.

C. I have with me a chronology of the many memoranda produced by the Task Force, examples of some of these papers, and a compilation of our regular reporting on the situation over the past two months in the Central Intelligence Bulletin [1 *line of source text not declassified*].

1. It is a sizable stack, however, and if I may, I will just gist for you some of the more interesting examples:

—[7-1/2 *lines of source text not declassified*]

—On May 26, the Office of National Estimates surveyed the situation, speculated on what had prompted Nasir to run the risk of major hostilities with Israel, and concluded: "We are inclined to believe that unless the U.S. and other major powers take whatever steps are necessary to re-open the Strait of Tiran, the Israelis will feel compelled to go to war. . . . If the Israelis attacked the U.A.R. and waged a successful campaign, . . . we do not believe that the Soviets would intervene in the conflict with their own combat forces . . . They would probably count upon the political intervention of great powers, including themselves, to stop the fighting before Nasir had suffered too much damage."

—Also on May 26, CIA in collaboration with DIA produced a memorandum entitled "Military Capabilities of Israel and the Arab States," which opened with the following summary: "Israel could almost certainly attain air superiority over the Sinai Peninsula in 24 hours after taking the initiative, or in two or three days if the U.A.R. struck first. In the latter case, Israel might lose up to half of its air force. We estimate that armored striking forces could breach the U.A.R.'s double defense line in the Sinai within several days. Re-grouping and re-supplying would be required before the Israelis could initiate further attacks aimed at driving to the Suez Canal. Israel could contain any attacks by Syria or Jordan during this period."

(I might note that in early drafts, our analysts more specifically stipulated "two to three days" to break the Egyptian Sinai defenses, and a total of "seven to nine days" to the Suez Canal if the Israelis had to pause to re-group, but they had to be a bit less specific to get through the coordination process.)

—Finally, let me read you the summary of a CIA Memorandum circulated to the White House, the NSC-level, and the intelligence community on the morning of Saturday, June 3, two days before the fighting began: "Reporting during the past few days has focused on two primary aspects of the Near East crisis. One is the rapidly growing belief in Israel that time is running out, and that if Israel is not to suffer an ultimately fatal defeat, it must very soon either strike or obtain absolutely iron-clad security assurances from the West. The second aspect is the rise of a euphoric, bandwagon spirit among the Arab States, leading even moderate Arabs to believe that the time may in fact have come when the Arabs can close in on Israel with some hope of success. There are in addition a number of reports indicating that anti-U.S. actions are being planned, to be put in motion if the United States moves to frustrate what the Arabs now tend to see as a 'victory.'"

---

298.   Memorandum for the Record[1]

Washington, June 15, 1967.

SUBJECT

Briefing of the President's Foreign Intelligence Advisory Board on Vietnam and the Middle East[2]

[Omitted here is the portion of the briefing concerning Vietnam.]

6. *Middle East.* Messrs. Parmenter, Eisenbeiss and [*name not declassified*] briefed on the Middle East situation. All members were present except Dr. Land. The briefers discussed in detail the current political attitudes and maneuvering among the Arabs, the position of several of their leaders, various factors affecting resumption of oil shipments, etc. Mr. Clifford and other members seemed particularly concerned that we have no reliable information on the exact status of the Suez Canal. The Chairman asked with a note of surprise why we had not conducted aerial reconnaissance, to which the reply was that this is perfectly feasible technically but there has been no political approval for overflights.[3]

7. [*6-1/2 lines of source text not declassified*]

---

[1] Source: Central Intelligence Agency, DDI Files: Job 80–R01447R, PFIAB Correspondence, 1967–1968. Secret. Prepared in the Central Intelligence Agency. Copies were sent to the Director of Central Intelligence, Deputy Director of Central Intelligence, Directorate of Intelligence, Directorate for Plans, Directorate of Science and Technology, and the Special Assistant for Vietnamese Affairs.

[2] The President's Foreign Intelligence Advisory Board met June 15–16. Also see Document 297.

[3] A photographic interpretation report of satellite photography of the Middle East, "KH–4 Mission 1042–1, 17–22 June 1967, Middle East Edition," is printed in *Corona: America's First Satellite Program* (Central Intelligence Agency: Washington, D.C., 1995), pp. 289–297.

8. The members were particularly interested in the details of the information passed by the Soviets to the Arabs before the outbreak of hostilities. Dr. Baker and Mr. Pace inquired at some length as to why the vaunted Soviet intelligence apparatus proved to be so inadequate. Mr. Parmenter and [*name not declassified*] explained that there is no indication that Soviet intelligence was bad but that it is evident that what they passed to the Arabs was not accurate and was probably not a reliable gauge of what they must have known.

Thomas A. Parrott[4]

AD/DCI/NIPE

---

[4] Printed from a copy that indicates Parrott signed the original.

---

299.   **Memorandum From the Chairman of the Central Intelligence Agency's Board of National Estimates (Kent) to Director of Central Intelligence Helms**[1]

Washington, June 15, 1967.

NASSER'S PROSPECTS FOR SURVIVAL

1. The loud demands in Egypt that Nasser continue in office, even though they may have been partly engineered by the leadership, had the intended effect of at least momentarily strengthening Nasser's popularity. The immediate traumatic effects of the staggering defeat impel the Egyptians to stick with Nasser and seek other scapegoats. The widely believed allegation of US and UK military involvement may offset the criticism which otherwise would have been directed at Nasser for the defeat. In the UAR, moreover, there is no obvious alternative to Nasser, nor do we have any reliable indications of plotting among the top ranks to replace him. We conclude that he is not likely to be replaced at least within the next month or so.

2. Nonetheless, the military debacle has undoubtedly raised serious doubts about Nasser's leadership in important segments of the population and even diminished his authority among key figures of

---

[1] Source: Johnson Library, National Security File, Country File, Middle East Crisis, Vol. VI. Secret. Prepared in the Office of National Estimates of the Central Intelligence Agency.

the regime. Despite the grant of extensive personal powers from the rubber stamp parliament, he may be forced to depend much more than in the past on the consensus of his top associates. The resignations of Abdul Hakim Amer and other senior officers indicate disagreements and conflicts within the officer corps and raise questions about the capability of the armed forces to provide Nasser the kind of support on which his authority has depended in the past. The wholesale changes in the military command are probably designed at least in part to head off unrest among the officers over Egypt's defeat. We know little of the political attitudes in the officer corps, however, and are unable to judge the extent of such unrest.

3. Over the longer term Nasser's chances for survival appear more questionable. He probably will not be able to convert this debacle into a positive political victory as he did in 1956. As the extent of Egypt's humiliation becomes known, resentment against him is likely to grow. We expect that at a minimum disillusionment over Nasser's performance will probably manifest itself in greater discontent within Egypt than he has hitherto faced. If this unrest becomes particularly strong within the military establishment it might in time even lead to a coup. Nasser is undoubtedly well aware of these dangers. For one thing he will seek to reequip the armed forces and will hope that this will help ensure their loyalty. He is also likely to seek to disarm his opposition by adopting a tough stance in the political and diplomatic arenas in an effort to identify his enemies with Israel and the West.

4. Nasser's longer range future will depend in some degree on how the problems raised by the present situation are sorted out. Unless he can appear to score political and diplomatic successes against Israel and the West, his standing inside Egypt will weaken further. In seeking any settlement there are clear limits to his freedom of maneuver. Any move by Nasser to come to terms with the Israelis, for example, would run counter to his efforts to recoup his stature among Arab nationalists generally, and would thus tend to weaken him within Egypt. It would also risk touching off a radical reaction within the Egyptian military, particularly as Nasser's control may have been weakened by the recent personnel changes.

5. In the months ahead, the prevailing mood in the Arab world is likely to be one of extreme frustration. Arab solidarity will be severely strained under the pressures of self-interest of individual Arab states, recriminations over failures, and bickering over future tactics. Certain longstanding Arab controversies, suppressed during the crisis with Israel, will be resumed. These trends would of course add to Nasser's difficulties in maintaining his leadership at home.

Economic Aspects of the Situation

6. The Egyptian economy has for some time been laboring under a severe hard currency crisis. Inability to service the foreign debt of over $2 billion[2] has made it almost impossible for the UAR to borrow further sums abroad. The UAR's gold and foreign exchange reserves dwindled to $138 million in March 1967, as Cairo continued to sell gold to meet part of its obligations. Defaults on payments due to the International Monetary Fund have dimmed hopes for assistance from that source. These problems have been aggravated by the UAR's relatively poor cotton crop this year, with exports some $50 million less than normal.

7. While to the best of our information the war itself has done little damage to the country's agriculture and industry, it has worsened Egypt's hard currency problems. The UAR is currently suffering a loss of about $30 million per month—about half of its normal hard currency earnings. Closure of the Suez Canal deprives Egypt of about one-third of its hard currency earnings. When the Canal will be reopened is more a matter of political decision than of physical obstruction. The Israelis have captured UAR oil fields in Sinai which have been providing oil worth $5 million a month in hard currency. Fields remaining under Egyptian control, including the new El Morgan field, meet only about 75 percent of the UAR's domestic oil needs. The UAR has also lost tourist receipts amounting to about $5 million a month.

8. These losses from the war are in addition to the approximately $25 million per month deficit Egypt has been incurring on its hard currency account over the past year. This shortage has been temporarily alleviated by grants of foreign exchange from Communist China ($10 million) and Kuwait ($28 million). Such sums should ease the impact of foreign exchange losses for at least a month. The UAR probably will receive some additional loans and grants in the weeks ahead from both Arab and Communist countries. Meanwhile, the UAR must face the problem of making some provision for its hard currency debt funding of almost $250 million due in 1967.

9. The war itself has not seriously affected the UAR's food situation which was already tight. Soviet deliveries against a pledge of 400,000 tons of wheat will begin arriving this month, and Communist China has pledged 150,000 tons. In addition, Egypt's current wheat crop of 1.6 million tons is now being harvested. The domestic crop, plus scheduled imports, are probably enough to meet the UAR's grain needs until December. The USSR could cover Egypt's food needs for some time,

---

[2] Including $1.2 billion in hard currency obligations to the Free World. [Footnote in the source text.]

especially in view of its bumper crop in 1966, but the Soviets would be reluctant to assume a long-term obligation in this respect.

10. By and large the Communist countries are not in a position to provide the kind and quantity of goods the UAR now gets from the West. The UAR still relies on the West for the supply of machinery and spare parts for most of the old established industries and most of its requirement for sophisticated electrical equipment, chemicals, and fertilizers, all of which must be paid for in hard currency. Since industry accounts for almost a third of GNP, an import curtailment from the West would have severe and fairly immediate impact on the modern sector of the economy.

11. If the Canal remains closed, if Israel retains control of Sinai, and if Egypt receives no substantial financial aid, economic difficulties will become considerably more onerous as time progresses. These will be largely manifest in the cities, where unemployment, shortages, and inflation will probably cause some unrest. While these troubles in themselves would not be likely to cause insurmountable problems of political control, they could add substantially to any pressures within the regime for a change of leadership.

The Soviet Role

12. It is clear from the above that Nasser's ability to cope with his various economic, military, and diplomatic problems depends heavily on the attitude of the USSR. We have no doubt that Moscow is now bent on restoring its influence in the Middle East. But it is by no means clear how far the USSR is prepared to go, particularly in terms of financial and military aid, to bolster Nasser's personal leadership. It is likely that Moscow is still reviewing the situation and is not yet prepared to make major and long-range commitments. While we believe that the USSR will decide to give Nasser substantial support, it may be that Moscow will view his demands for diplomatic backing and particularly for military and economic aid as excessive. The Soviets would thus have an incentive to move Cairo back toward normalization at least of its economic relations with the West. This would give difficulties for Nasser at present, but he might in time judge that he could move in this way and still survive politically.

For the Board of National Estimates:

Sherman Kent

300. Telegram From the Embassy in Jordan to the Department of State[1]

Amman, June 16, 1967, 1326Z.

4370. For the Secretary.

1. If there is to be hope of lasting peace in the Middle East, obviously both the Arabs and Israelis must be brought to want it and to be reasonable regarding the terms of the settlement.

2. It seems to us from Amman that if this is to be accomplished on the Arab side the moderate Arab states must be helped into as strong a position as possible to carry the day against the radical Arabs. If the moderates cannot carry the day, they will feel forced to adopt the stand of the radicals.

3. Thus far our statements have not had the result of strengthening moderate Arab forces.

4. We suggest that the following, if done immediately, would strengthen the moderate hand and counterbalance Soviet support of the radical's position of revanchism.

5. USG to announce at the highest level, hopefully by the President: (A) USG has been and continues to be neutral in the Arab-Israel dispute. (B) USG calls upon all parties concerned to work out through the UN a just, equitable and lasting peace. (C) Pending the conclusion of a permanent settlement, USG proposes that Israeli forces withdraw to the previous armistice lines under a formula which will insure the security and integrity of all parties concerned.

6. One such formula, which would best be proposed by a party other than US, might be demilitarization under UN supervision of Arab territory presently under Israeli occupation.

7. Of the three portions of the statement proposed in para 5 above, the most imperative and urgent is sub-section C. In our opinion, we should make the statement even in the absence of precise formula for implementation.

Burns

---

[1] Source: National Archives and Records Administration, RG 59, Central Files 1967–69, POL 27 ARAB–ISR. Secret; Immediate; Limdis. Repeated to Rabat, Tunis, USUN, Beirut, Jerusalem, Tripoli, Tel Aviv, Khartoum, Kuwait, and Jidda. Received at 10:28 a.m. and passed to the White House, DOD, CIA, USIA, NSA, COMAC, and CINCSTRIKE at 11:45 a.m.

301. Memorandum of Conversation[1]

Washington, June 16, 1967, 3:05–3:55 p.m.

SUBJECT

Middle East Crisis

PARTICIPANTS

Soviet Ambassador Anatoliy F. Dobrynin

The Secretary
Llewellyn E. Thompson, American Ambassador

The Secretary remarked that we thought we had had a commitment from Israel not to initiate hostilities. The Egyptian Ambassador had told us upon instructions that they would not begin them.

We were wholly uninformed of any Israeli attack. When Dobrynin asked if we had not known about it on the eve of the attack, the Secretary said we had no advance information whatever. He himself had been called about 2:30 in the morning. We had thought we had about another 10 days before Israel would make a judgment on what it would do about the closing of the Strait of Tiran. Asking that the Soviets not pass this on to any other Government, the Secretary said that Robert Anderson had had a long personal talk with Nasser. Although no serious problem had been solved, Nasser had decided to send his Deputy Prime Minister here, and we had thought this would be a very important conversation. The Secretary said that on the Strait of Tiran there was involved not only our general attitude on the innocent passage of international straits, but also the commitment by President Eisenhower in 1957 about the Strait of Tiran, which was in the interest of Egypt. Although Egypt had not formally underwritten this commitment, they were well aware of it. Nasser had told Anderson that the Egyptians had been surprised both with the speed with which U Thant acted on their request on UNEF and also on his action in withdrawing all of UNEF although it had only been asked to withdraw from certain areas. Sharm al Shaikh had not been included in the areas from which withdrawal was requested, and if U Thant had not acted so precipitously and had at least referred the matter to the Security Council in order to gain time the whole issue of the Strait might not have arisen.

---

[1] Source: Johnson Library, National Security File, Country File, USSR, Dobrynin–Thompson Conversations, Vol. II. Secret; Exdis. The memorandum is part 2 of 3. Walt Rostow sent all three parts to the President on June 19, with a note stating that he had already been informed of the conversation but might like to see the full record. The time of the meeting is from Rusk's Appointment Book. (Ibid.)

When the Secretary inquired about the atmosphere in Moscow, Dobrynin replied that everyone had lots of work.

The Secretary said he thought he should inform the Ambassador of the strong negative public reaction in this country to the statements that Fedorenko had made in the Security Council debates in New York and particularly to the polemical nature and tone of his remarks. The State Department and the White House had received some 200,000 letters, many of which referred to this aspect. When Dobrynin inquired whether any of this had been on TV, the Secretary replied that almost all of the proceedings had been televised including one session at half past four in the morning.

Dobrynin said that the manner of speaking depended very much on the speaker. While Fedorenko, of course, had his instructions and knew the general line, none of his speeches were written in Moscow.

The Secretary said that the problem was complicated because the big powers could not command or control the small powers in the area. When Dobrynin said they could be influenced, the Secretary replied that we could not command the Israeli, and he doubted whether the Soviets could command Nasser. The Secretary thought that we would have to return to the Security Council at some point.

Dobrynin said that it had made a very bad impression in Moscow that the fighting had continued after the Security Council resolution. While the Soviets had been talking with us on the "Hot Line," they had been directly in touch with their Ambassador in Damascus.

The Secretary said he had sent a strong message to Eban in the middle of the night saying that the fighting simply had to stop. A problem for us had been that the UN observers had been restricted on both sides, as had our military attachés, and it had been difficult for us to get any information.

Dobrynin asked why we opposed Israeli withdrawal. The Secretary asked "withdrawal to what"? Dobrynin replied "to the armistice lines." The Secretary asked whether it was expected that this be done while the Arab States were still in a state of belligerency. The Arabs would not recognize existence of Israel and when we talked to the Egyptians about the Strait of Tiran they rested their case on still being in a state of war. He thought that withdrawal standing alone did not solve anything. He said it was difficult for us to say to the Arabs that we supported territorial integrity if they won't recognize the existence of Israel. The Arabs take part but not all of our position. Over the years we had in fact acted more often on behalf of the Arabs than Israel, and he mentioned Libya, Lebanon, Jordan, and the events of 1956. He concluded that there must be some recognition of the fact of Israeli statehood.

Dobrynin said that the Soviets would like for all of these countries to have better relations. They had no interest in the continuation of tension in this area.

The Secretary said we hoped there could be some limitation on the arms race in this part of the world. As he had often said, it was only the Soviet Union and the United States who were really interested in applying arms reduction to themselves. We were not the principal arms supplier to that part of the world. We thought it would be constructive to have some understanding on this problem.

Dobrynin said that in the present situation it was, of course, difficult because of recent events.

The Secretary referred briefly to the Israeli attack on our ship, the *Liberty*.

---

302.   Telegram From President Johnson to Prime Minister Wilson[1]

Washington, June 16, 1967, 1959Z.

CAP 67542.

Your messages of the last two days[2] have been helpful, as always.

None of us can predict what situations may arise in the days ahead, but my present thinking is this.

First, at the moment I doubt that anything useful can come from my personal participation in the General Assembly.

Second, from the beginning of this crisis I have not looked with favor on a four-power meeting outside the U.N. Security Council. It is something of an illusion that the four powers have the capacity to design and impose successfully a peace plan on the Near East. The states of the area have made it abundantly clear that they are not sub-

---

[1] Source: Johnson Library, National Security File, NSC Histories, Middle East Crisis, Vol. 3. Secret; Nodis. The text was sent to the Embassy in London in telegram 212063, June 16. (National Archives and Records Administration, RG 59, Central Files 1967–69, POL 27 ARAB–ISR)

[2] Messages of June 15 and 16 from Prime Minister Wilson to President Johnson conveyed Wilson's thoughts on the forthcoming Special Session of the UN General Assembly and expressed interest whether Johnson planned to attend. (Johnson Library, National Security File, Head of State Correspondence File, UK, Vol. 6)

ject to effective control from outside. What the major powers can do is to try to create a climate in which the nations of the area themselves might gradually settle their affairs on a peaceful basis. But I am not confident that a four-power session is the best way to do this.

Moreover, I should think both of us would wish to avoid the possibility of having the four of us split or otherwise be strained in such a session.

I hope we can keep in close contact in the days ahead as the situation evolves, and we might wish to counsel together shortly after the smoke clears to assess the situation and see what is required to move things forward towards our common objective of stable peace in the area.

---

303. **Telegram From the Department of State to the Embassy in Israel**[1]

Washington, June 16, 1967, 10:30 p.m.

212156. Following based on uncleared memcon. Noforn, FYI and subject revision upon review.

1. Ambassador Harman at his request called on Secretary June 16. Said FonMin Eban would arrive over weekend for UNGA session with four Parliamentarians accompanying: Mrs. Meir, Shimon Peres of RAFI, Hazan of Mapai and Rimalt of Liberal Party. Asked if Eban inscribed to speak early, Harman said did not know. Secretary said he saw advantage in Eban's speaking soon after Kosygin, both for effect of small country contrast with great power and for sake of getting Israel's case before Assembly early as possible. Asked when USG rep would speak, Secretary said we had reserved first place but had not yet decided whether to use this position.

2. Harman, speaking from typed notes, proceeded to outline current GOI thinking on Arab-Israel issues along lines of Eban's June 13

---

[1] Source: National Archives and Records Administration, RG 59, Central Files 1967–69, POL 27 ARAB–ISR. Secret; Priority; Exdis. Drafted by Wolle, cleared by Atherton, and approved by Carroll Brown (S/S). Repeated Priority to USUN, Jerusalem, Kuwait, Jidda, Beirut, Amman, and London.

presentation to Barbour (Notal).[2] He prefaced this by expression appreciation for USG stand in Security Council and for fact that President in June 14 remarks[3] linked USG position on territorial integrity to question of achieving real settlement. When speaking of West Bank, Harman stressed entire Jordan episode "gave Israel a great trauma," insisting Jordan's rapid assumption of war footing and offensive hostile actions had come as real shock.

3. Secretary said USG position still evolving but some preliminary comments were possible. Said that whatever the dominant mood of moment, it most important that wisdom prevail in terms of long-term need of Israel to live at peace with its neighbors. This was overriding necessity. Also, it important that Israel, if it believes winning time is important (as Harman had just outlined) should also give time for some calming of high emotions pervading Arab lands due to recent events. Secretary said he understood Knesset might be thinking of imminent action to take over old Jerusalem. Such action would signal to other side that time is not an available commodity. It would create impression world would be presented with one fait accompli after another. Said GOI should appreciate there is very strong international interest in Jerusalem, as expressed in early UN resolutions. It should not underestimate sensitivity of this problem. Secretary strongly urged that no action be taken that would be viewed as fait accompli.

4. Harman responded with reference to 1949 USG posture of support in UN for Swedish concept of safeguarding rights in and access to Holy Places without administration as corpus separatum. Secretary said point he wanted to make was that there has existed from the beginning very strong international interest in status Jerusalem. In his view this should be recognized by some form of discussions, not treated unilaterally without possibility of such discussion.

5. When Harman spoke of depth of feeling on Jerusalem among Israelis, Secretary again stressed that he was urging caution on subject. Said that feelings of the moment are not necessarily best basis for re-establishing peace after a bitter fight. Other countries in other circumstances, after bitter wars in which deep feelings aroused, had been able make peace based on reconciliation. Responding to Secretary's direct question as to whether he expected Knesset to act on Jerusalem this

---

[2] See Document 277.

[3] Reference is apparently to the President's remarks at his June 13 news conference; see footnote 3, Document 282.

weekend, Harman said he did not know. Secretary concluded that action would be very unfortunate.[4]

6. Secretary stated we agree with GOI objective of achieving a real peace, with Israel thereafter accepted by all as fully sovereign state with all perquisites going with it. But attaining direct negotiations with Arabs would be difficult and he thought would take some time. He hoped GOI not underestimating difficulty of achieving this.

7. Harman said that for Soviets to be able bludgeon resolution through UNGA would put premium on extremism in Middle East. If this drive blunted, would be very significant, for Arabs might come to realize they are on verge of having to face a new reality, i.e., recognition of Israel. This realization might not now have to dawn first in Egypt, as GOI had previously thought, but might begin elsewhere and spread. Secretary noted that Arab moderates are in difficulty just as are Arab extremists, and that surely Soviets would be making major drive to recoup losses and press for their brand of extremism in as many Arab countries as possible. Receptivity of Arabs and others to this Soviet drive would in part be governed by Israel's attitude, conduct and posture in days and weeks ahead.

8. Harman said flatly that if Soviet resolution goes through, Israel will have to stay where it is. It would not settle for 1957-type arrangement. Israel now feels it has earned a real peace. Harman said recent crisis and hostilities had been frightening experience that "could easily have gone the other way." Secretary said "that is why we advised you not to do it."

9. Secretary said we would study GOI thinking as outlined by Eban and Harman and be in touch later.

Rusk

---

[4] Telegram 212218 to Tel Aviv, June 17, instructed the Embassy to make urgent representations along the line taken by Rusk with Harman, urging the Israeli Government to refrain from action on the status of Jerusalem that would be viewed as a fait accompli on the eve of the Special Session. (National Archives and Records Administration, RG 59, Central Files 1967–69, POL 27 ARAB–ISR) Barbour replied in telegram 4189 from Tel Aviv, June 18, that Rusk's views had been passed urgently to Eshkol. (Ibid.)

304.   Telegram From the Department of State to the Embassy in
        Jordan[1]

Washington, June 16, 1967, 10:03 p.m.

212138. Amman 4355.[2] Deliver to action officers opening of business June 17.

1. If Hussein asks you for categorical assurances that there is no distinction between our policy on arms delivery to Israel and to Jordan you may reply that we have suspended the signing of any sales arrangements or related new commitments concerning arms deliveries to Israel and the Arab states. We have no grant program of arms or military equipment to Israel. We are now undertaking a thorough study of the overall arms supply problem in the Middle East and no final decisions have yet been reached.

2. Department believes instructions contained State's 211613 should be reassuring to Hussein.

3. FYI. We have made a distinction between the two countries as far as commercial shipments where export licenses have already been issued are concerned. We are also continuing negotiations, up to but not including signature, of new agreements with Israel under the conditions described Defense 7852. For example, immediately after outbreak hostilities we shipped moderate quantities of ammunition, gas masks and other sundry items to Israel. You should know also that some [$]38 million of licensed matériel on Munitions List for Israel still in pipeline has not been embargoed. Largest single item is 20 million tank parts. While nothing is in similar category for Jordan, some 56 million is in pipeline for Saudi Arabia, including 50 million for Hawks. We point this out to you so that you recognize that foregoing presentation is intentionally carefully worded. End FYI.

Rusk

---

[1]   Source: National Archives and Records Administration, RG 59, Central Files 1967–69, DEF 12–5 ISR. Secret; Immediate; Exdis. Drafted by Marshall W. Wiley (NEA/ARN) and Houghton; cleared by Hoopes, Director for Operations in the Office of Politico-Military Affairs Joseph J. Wolf, Atherton, and Davies; and approved by Eugene Rostow.

[2]   Burns stated in telegram 4355 from Amman, June 16, that he planned to meet with King Hussein on June 17 to convey the contents of telegram 211613 but anticipated that Hussein would press him for assurances that the United States was making no distinction between Jordan and Israel in military assistance matters. (Ibid., DEF 19–8 US–JORDAN) He noted that SecDef telegram 7852, June 15, appeared to place Israel in a slightly more favored category. Telegram 211613 is summarized in footnote 3, Document 295. SecDef telegram 7852 has not been found.

305.   Paper Submitted by the Control Group to the Special
        Committee of the National Security Council[1]

Washington, undated.

THE NUCLEAR FACTOR IN THE NEAR EASTERN SITUATION

1. The most significant feature of the role of nuclear capabilities during the Arab-Israeli hostilities was the absence of direct impact. In contrast to the situation in 1956, the Soviet Union made no indirect nuclear threats, and did not engage in "ballistic blackmail." Instead, the "Hot Line" was used to reinforce the coincident desire of the USSR and the US to avoid any direct involvement of the nuclear powers in the conflict.

2. The recent belligerents themselves do not, of course, have nuclear weapons, and no allegations to the contrary have so far entered the exchange of charges and allegations. In the short run, it is not likely that the nuclear factor will affect the confrontation or the contest over a settlement.

3. Over the longer run, in the absence of a significant political settlement, it is likely that the recent hostilities and continuing conflict heighten the pressures for one or both sides to acquire unclear capabilities. Despite its recent successes, Israel may conclude that in the last analysis it must rely only on its own military power to defend its vital interests. Especially if Israel is eventually compelled to settle for something much less than it feels it should gain from its victory, concern over the future may well impel the Israelis to proceed with a nuclear weapons program. In the words of Tom Lehrer's ditty, "The Lord is our Shepherd, it says in the Psalm, but just to be sure—we gotta have the Bomb."

4. The Arabs are, of course, highly suspicious of Israeli nuclear intentions, and may be influenced by their suspicions whether these are well-founded or not. If, however, the Israelis in fact take the nuclear road, this would be bound at some point to become known and to

---

[1] Source: National Archives and Records Administration, RG 59, Central Files 1967–69, POL 27–14 ARAB–ISR. Secret; Exdis. The paper, unsigned and undated, was sent to McGeorge Bundy on June 19 by Executive Secretary of the Control Group John J. Walsh with a covering memorandum transmitting two papers submitted by the Control Group to the Special Committee. The second paper, headed "The Arms Supply Question and the UN," undated, is not printed. Both papers were revised and approved for transmission to the Special Committee by the Control Group on June 17. (Minutes of 22nd Control Group meeting, June 17, 11 a.m.; ibid., Office of the Executive Secretariat, Middle East Crisis Files, 1967, Entry 5190, Box 17, Minutes/Decisions of the Control Group, Folder 1)

insure a frenzied Arab reaction of some kind. None of the Arab countries have either the general industrial base, or the foundations of nuclear industry in particular, on which to launch a nuclear weapons program of their own during the period while Israel could be acquiring its own nuclear weapons. The Arabs will, therefore, have to look elsewhere. One possible recourse would be to try to build overwhelming conventional superiority of their own, and perhaps also to stress CW, and then to strike Israel before it could build up a nuclear arsenal. However, in view of the recent debacle, this latter course of action could only be a desperate last resort. Perhaps the Arabs would turn to Moscow, and fall even more into line behind Soviet foreign policy positions in order to get whatever hedged Soviet pledges of nuclear support might be forthcoming. The Soviets are not likely to provide nuclear weapons, even under their own custody. Particularly in view of the lack of direct Soviet military support during the recent hostilities, and actual continuing Soviet caution with respect to potential Great Power nuclear confrontation, some Arabs might be tempted at some point to risk their ties with the USSR by turning to the Chinese Communists for nuclear weapons. And the Chinese might feel they could gain influence with the Arabs and others in the Third World, at modest cost, and with real risks only to the Soviet Union, the Western Powers, and the Near Eastern countries themselves.

5. Thus, the need for effective measures to curb nuclear proliferation in the Near East has grown. Moreover, the credibility of the US as a party able to reassure each side that its adversary is not getting nuclear weapons has certainly been impaired by the recent developments. There would appear to be three possibilities to meet the proliferation problem: (a) a firm non-acquisition undertaking, preferably with mandatory IAEA safeguards, by both Israel and the UAR as a provision in a general settlement; (b) a Near Eastern nuclear free zone; or (c) Israeli and Arab adherence to a general non-proliferation treaty. Possibilities for action along the first course should be kept in mind, but it is unlikely that progress in the highly complex tangle of elements already necessarily involved in the settlement would be facilitated by tossing in yet another contentious problem. However, at some point it might prove possible to raise the proposition of mutual safeguarded undertakings not to acquire nuclear weapons in a general compromise package settlement. A nuclear-free zone might be possible, although the question of defining the area to be covered could raise serious problems for the US. On balance, the best solution—if it becomes feasible—would be a non-proliferation treaty. With respect to a non-proliferation treaty, negotiations in Geneva are now going as satisfactorily as can be expected. If and when a non-proliferation treaty is open for signature, it will of course be important to press hard for Israeli and Arab adherence.

6. At least heretofore, the UAR has endorsed a non-proliferation treaty, with safeguards; Israel has been conspicuously silent as to her stand on such a treaty. In general, the difficulties in getting Israeli, and perhaps UAR, acceptance have probably increased. On the other hand, the Arabs may wish to obtain international safeguards on the more advanced nuclear program of their adversary; it is less likely, but possible, that the Israelis might consider that such a treaty would head off possible Arab acquisition of nuclear weapons from the Russians or Chinese. Of course, the final positions of both sides on non-acquisition or general non-proliferation undertakings will be greatly influenced by progress, or lack of progress, toward a viable general settlement. Israel, as the power whose security is most imperiled by non-nuclear military power in the long-run, and as the power with a real nuclear potential, will be most reticent to give up its nuclear option with substantial progress in meeting its long-term security requirements in some other way.

7. The question of peaceful nuclear programs in the Near East should also be borne in mind. We have been examining the possibility of a nuclear de-salting plant in Israel, including conducting a joint survey with the Israelis. If it is decided to proceed with this project, we might want to tie our agreement not only to Israeli acceptance of IAEA or equivalent safeguards on the nuclear energy component of the desalinization project itself, which would of course be necessary, but also to Israeli acceptance of IAEA or equivalent safeguards on all their indigenous nuclear facilities as well. With due regard to economic feasibility and other considerations, including progress on a political settlement, we might also consider making parallel offers of assistance to the UAR at the time we agreed to assist the Israelis, providing there is a government in power with which we could conclude an agreement.

Annex

INDIGENOUS CAPABILITIES TO DEVELOP NUCLEAR WEAPONS

Israel

The Israelis have two nuclear reactors; a US-supplied research reactor at Nahal Sereq of 5 MW capability, and a larger French built reactor at Dimona of 25 MW capacity. The research reactor is under IAEA safeguards, the Dimona reactor is not under IAEA safeguards, but has been inspected by the US. This latter reactor is capable of producing enough plutonium for approximately one nuclear weapon per year, and the plutonium produced in this reactor to date is equivalent to that required for about one weapon.

The spent fuel rods in which the produced plutonium is present are still at Dimona and have not been subjected to chemical separation. The original plans called for the shipment of these fuel rods back to France for reprocessing, but no schedule for their shipment is known. Although there have been reports of an Israeli chemical separation plant, these have not been confirmed, and it is not believed that the Israelis presently have a chemical separation plant completed or in any advanced state of construction. It would probably be eighteen months before such a plant could be built and the plutonium separated for weapons use.

In summary, it is believed that prior to the recent crisis the Israelis had probably not made a decision to develop nuclear weapons, but probably had decided to keep that option open. If they were to make a decision today, it would probably be 18 months or longer before they could have their first weapon, and then they could produce approximately one weapon per year thereafter.

Arab Countries

The capabilities of the Arab countries for development of nuclear weapons are virtually non-existent. The only Arab country with a reactor is the UAR, which has a small 2 MW Soviet-supplied research reactor at Inchass. This UAR reactor has no potential for fissionable materials production to support a weapons program. Any indigenous weapons program in the UAR could not be carried out for many years. Furthermore, it is not believed that the Soviets would supply the UAR with such potential (or with nuclear weapons) directly.

Nuclear Delivery Systems

Both Israel and the Arab countries have aircraft that could be adapted to deliver nuclear weapons. The recent hostilities demonstrated both the effectiveness, but also the vulnerability, of air forces. Attention is, therefore, likely to be placed on missile delivery systems if nuclear weapons are ever acquired.

The UAR has had a much publicized, but quite ineffective, surface-to-surface ballistic missile development program underway for several years. The best product is the 200 n.m. range Conqueror, but even it has been unsuccessful to date. Unless Cairo receives considerable outside help, the prospects for deploying this or any other missile are remote.

Israel has a modest but energetic missile research and development program of its own, but we have no evidence that it has plans to try to produce a ballistic missile system. At the same time, Israel does have a contract with the French firm Dassault for the MD–620, with a range of 250 n.m. Israel may already have contracted for or at least expressed an interest in buying as many as 250 of these missiles.

306. **Memorandum of Telephone Conversation Between Secretary of State Rusk and the President's Special Assistant (Rostow)**[1]

Washington, June 17, 1967, 5:50 p.m.

TELEPHONE CALL FROM W ROSTOW

[Omitted here is discussion of an unrelated matter.]

R said he had had an interesting talk with Bob Anderson. A was seeing the Arabs in town. He saw Shamaz in Beirut and the consensus was among the Fon Mins that they were prepared to recognize the state of Israel. They don't want to say this as a collective group. They are prepared to have Sinai demilitarized, they cannot live with a totally Israeli Jerusalem; they are worried about Jordan. The main appeal was that this statement of the Pres get as much territorial integrity into it as possible. Nasser is in deep trouble and is sending only Fawzi—an errand boy. Libya, Kuwait and Saudi Arabia in trouble. The French and Russians are trying to get hold of US and Brit economic interests. They hate the Russians. Suez is thorny. Their problem is mob rule. He thinks if you can negotiate and put an end to belligerence it is tantamount to recognize Israel as a state. Sec asked if this would be secretly and bilaterally with each one and announced together? R said Anderson said he didn't want to get in our way but R said he was sure the Pres and the SecState wanted him to sit and listen. R said McPherson was with him now and they were pulling together what Bundy and Rostow (Gene) were doing.

---

[1] Source: National Archives and Records Administration, RG 59, Rusk Files: Lot 72 D 192, Telephone Calls. No classification marking. The notes were prepared by Mildred J. Asbjornson, Rusk's secretary.

307.   Telegram From the Defense Attaché Office in Israel to the
        White House[1]

Tel Aviv, June 18, 1967, 1030Z.

0928. Subject: Israeli Court of Inquiry in USS *Liberty* incident.

1. ALUSNA called to FLO evening 17 June. LTC Efrat, Aide to General Rabin, IDF COS stated following:

A. Gen Rabin extends his personal regrets to the CNO USN for the sad mistake of the USS *Liberty* incident.

B. Gen Rabin decided to provide via ALUSNA a synopsis of the findings of IDF Court of Inquiry although those findings have not yet received final review from CO Shimgar, the IDF JAG.

C. After review and translation to English, a full transcript of the findings of the IDF Court of Inquiry will be transmitted to the USG either though AmEmbassy Tel Aviv or Israel Embassy, Washington, D.C.

2. The synopsis of the findings of the IDF Court of Inquiry as taken down verbatim by ALUSNA from Col Efrats oral presentation is as follows:

"A. It is concluded clearly and unimpeachably from the evidence and from comparison of war diaries that the attack on USS *Liberty* was not in malice; there was no criminal negligence and the attack was made by innocent mistake.

B. Attack rose out of a chain of three mistakes, each of which by itself is understandable: First mistake was decisive. Navy and AF HQ had received a number of wrong reports stating El-Arish was being shelled from the sea. This wrong information formed the background and main factor leading to attack on *Liberty*. IDF CNO and assistants were convinced that shelling was being done by unidentified ship or ships which were discovered at the time near the shore off El-Arish. Even the officers who knew of the identification of *Liberty* early the same morning did not connect *Liberty* with the unidentified ships said to be shelling El-Arish. The IDF Navy is not responsible for the mistaken report of shelling and the reasons for the mistaken report are outside scope of the inquiry at hand. The Navy and AF HQs took the reports at face value.

---

[1] Source: Johnson Library, National Security File, NSC Special Committee Files, *Liberty*. Confidential. Also sent to OSD, CNO, Department of State, COMSIXTHFLT, CINCSTRIKE, CINCNAVEUR, JCS, DIA, USUN, CINCEUR/USEUCOM, CTG 60.2, USAFE, CINCUSAREUR, CTG 60, USDAO London, USDAO Paris, and USDAO Moscow. Received at the Department of State at 8:22 a.m.

Second mistake, which when added to first resulted in aircraft attack on *Liberty*, was a mistaken report that *Liberty* was steaming at 30 knots. This mistake has two significances. A. When *Liberty* was identified in morning, her max speed was determined from *Janes Fighting Ships* to be 18 knots. Therefore, even if the unidentified ship were thought to be *Liberty*, the fact that she was reported to be making 30 knots would have denied the identification.

B. In accordance with IDF Navy standing orders, an enemy ship in any waters which is attacking Israeli ships or shelling the Israeli shore may be attacked. If there is info of enemy ships in the area, any ship or ships discovered by radar which are determined to be cruising at a speed above 20 knots may be considered an enemy. Since the speed of the unidentified ship was fixed at 28 to 30 knots, the IDF Navy was entitled to attack without further identification in view of the background of info on the shelling of El-Arish. IDF Naval OPS section had ordered the MTB's who reported *Liberty*'s speed as 30 knots to recheck and only after confirmation of that speed was the info considered reliable and aircraft were sent to attack. The question of possible negligence in establishing the speed at 28–30 knots when in fact *Liberty*'s max speed is 18 knots is discounted by the IDF CNO who testified 'that such estimations require expertise. In an MTB there may be great discrepancies in fixing the speed of a vessel moving in front of it, especially if the estimate was made only over a short interval of time. It is quite feasible that there may be such a mistake even if you measure it twice or more.' As a result of the incident maybe the standing order should be reconsidered but no criminal negligence is found in the MTB's fixing of *Liberty*'s speed.

Third mistake caused execution of the second stage of attack on *Liberty*, this time with torpedoes from MTB's. This was the mistaken identification of *Liberty* as the Egyptian supply ship *El Quesir*. Here I (that is, the officer conducting the inquiry who LTC Efrat identified parenthetically as Col Ram Ron, former Israeli Military Attaché to Washington, D.C.) must state my doubts whether the identification was not done with a certain overeagerness as this happened when serious doubts were already beginning to arise as to the identification as an Egyptian ship. It has been established by the evidence of the C.O. of MTB Div that the doubts which had begun to arise in the pilots as to their accuracy of identification did not get to the C.O. of the MTB Div at that time, but he already knew that the ship was not a destroyer but a supply or merchant ship and this should have caused extra carefulness in identification. On the other hand, I (again Col Ron) must state the extenuating circumstances and difficulties of identification under the following conditions:

(1) Ship was covered with thick smoke. (2) When asked to identify itself, the ship did not do so and behaved suspiciously. (3) It appeared to the DivCom that there was a gun on the fore-castle of the ship and that the ship was firing toward the MTB's. These observations were recorded in the war diary at the time of action.

If we add to these factors that under the circumstances when the ship was completely covered with smoke there was, in fact, apparently a great similarity between it and *El Quesir*. Two officers a CDR and a LT on two different MTB's who had no communications between them both identified the ship at the same time as *El Quesir*. The IDF CNO decided that on the basis of reports on hand that this identification was feasible. Therefore I (again Col Ron) have come to the conclusion that there was certainly no criminal or serious negligence in this case. Finally I (Col Ron) have to add that a grave additional mistake not less decisive than the three above mistakes made by IDF was made by the *Liberty* itself. On this question, I (Col Ron) have the evidence of the IDF CNO and JAG which complement each other and from which it is clear that the American ship acted with lack of care by endangering itself to a grave extent by approaching excessively close to the shore in an area which was a scene of war and this at a time when it was well known that this area is not one where ships generally pass, this without advising the Israeli authorities of its presence and without identifying itself elaborately. Furthermore, it appears that the ship made an effort to hide its identity first by flying a small flag which was difficult to identify from a distance; secondly by beginning to escape when discovered by our forces and when it was aware of the fact that it had been discovered, thirdly by failing to identify itself immediately by its own initiative by flashing light and by refusing to do so even when asked by the MTB's. From all this I (Col Ron) conclude that the ship *Liberty* tried to hide its presence in the area and its identity both before it was discovered and even after having been attacked by the AF and later by the Navy and thus contributed a decisive contribution toward its identification as an enemy ship."

Comments: 1. All above is dictated by LTC Efrat who was translating from a document written in Hebrew.

2. LTC Efrat paused at one point in his reading to point out the GOI had received a statement from USG saying that *Liberty* had been identified six hours prior to the attack rather than one hour as stated in an earlier USG communication.

3. LTC Efrat probably noted ALUSNA's appearance of surprise and incredulity as he read off some of the above points. When he finished his reading he asked what ALUSNA thought of the findings "off the record." ALUSNA pretended he had not heard the question and

thanked the Colonel for his time. The burden of diplomacy bore heavily on ALUSNA whose evaluations are:

A. The IDF Navy standing order to attack any ship moving at more than 20 knots is incomprehensible.

B. Two of the IDF justifications for their action are mutually contradictory. First they say that since the speed of the unidentified was as high as 30 knots they could not have thought it was *Liberty*. Then they say the ship was feasibly identified as *El Quesir*. *El Quesir* has max speed of 14 knots, four less than *Liberty*. If the "30 knot ship couldn't have been *Liberty*" it follows it also couldn't have been *El Quesir*.

C. That a professional Naval officer of the rank of commander could look at *Liberty* and think her a 30 knot ship is difficult to accept.

D. The smoke which covered *Liberty* and made here difficult to identify was probably a result of the IDF AF attacks.

4. While walking to their cars, LTC Efrat mentioned that Gen Rabin has never been so angry as when he read the current *Newsweek* magazine comment on the *Liberty* incident. ALUSNA remarked that he took no notice of news media reporting on the incident.

5. ALUSNA was called to FLO earlier in the day to receive a copy of IDF CNO letter of regret and condolence to CNO USN. ALUSNA was informed that the Israeli Military Attaché in Washington, D.C. will deliver the original to Adm McDonald.

6. Coordinated with Embassy.

---

308.   Editorial Note

In an address before the Department of State Foreign Policy Conference for Educators on June 19, 1967, President Johnson declared that recent events had proved the wisdom of five principles of peace in the Middle East. The first and greatest principle, he stated, was that "every nation in the area has a fundamental right to live, and to have this right respected by its neighbors." Second was "another basic requirement for settlement: justice for the refugees." Third was that "maritime rights must be respected." Fourth, the conflict had demonstrated "the danger of the Middle Eastern arms race of the last 12 years." As an initial step to deal with this problem, he proposed that the

United Nations immediately call upon all of its members to report all shipments of military arms into the area. Fifth, he declared, the crisis underlines the "importance of respect for political independence and territorial integrity of all the states of the area." He reaffirmed that principle but added that it could be effective "only on the basis of peace between the parties." What the nations of the region needed, he stated, was "recognized boundaries and other arrangements that will give them security against terror, destruction, and war." Furthermore, he declared, there "must be adequate recognition of the special interest of three great religions in the holy places of Jerusalem." He offered the assurance that the U.S. Government would "do its part for peace in every forum, at every level, at every hour" but he declared that the main responsibility for the peace of the region depended on the peoples and leaders of the region. The text is in *Public Papers of the Presidents of the United States: Lyndon B. Johnson, 1967,* Book I, pages 630–634.

Drafts of the speech are in the Johnson Library, Statements of Lyndon B. Johnson, June 15–June 23, 1967. Harry McPherson sent a draft to the President at 11 p.m. on June 17 with a covering memorandum stating that it blended "Gene Rostow's travelogue of world problems, and Mac Bundy's compression of today's final Middle East draft." A June 18 draft bears a note that it was cleared with Rusk.

309. Memorandum of Conversation[1]

Washington, June 20, 1967, 1 p.m.

SUBJECT

Meeting of the President and Chairman Kosygin, the Middle East & Vietnam

PARTICIPANTS

Yuri N. Tcherniakov, Counselor, USSR Embassy
Eugene V. Rostow, Under Secretary for Political Affairs

Part I—Middle East

1. Counselor Tcherniakov apologized for shifting the lunch to which he had invited Rostow some time ago from the Embassy to a restaurant. He explained that the Embassy staff had been sent to New York, and hoped that it would help facilitate a meeting between the President and Chairman Kosygin. Rostow replied that the President did indeed wish to see Chairman Kosygin. As Tcherniakov knew, an invitation had been issued before we had been officially informed that the Chairman was coming. Tcherniakov said that that fact was appreciated, but, he said, there were difficulties, since the main purpose of the Chairman's trip was his appearance at the U.N., and there were complications with respect "to allies and others." Rostow said we understood these problems so far as Chairman Kosygin was concerned. There were complications also for the President. We thought it natural for the Chairman, when in a country, to call on the head of its government. However, the question of discussing the possibility of a visit was in the hands of the Secretary, who was doubtless in touch with Foreign Minister Gromyko on the subject. Tcherniakov said that was the case, and the men were being assisted by the Dobrynin–Thompson "task force." He hoped they succeeded in solving the problem. Rostow said we hoped so too.

2. Tcherniakov asked how Chairman Kosygin's speech[2] was received in the State Department. Rostow replied that we thought it was "not too bad." In reply to a question, Rostow remarked that we thought two points in the speech were of particular importance: (1) Kosygin's assertion that Israel had the right to live; and (2) his comment that the

---

[1] Source: National Archives and Records Administration, RG 59, Central Files 1967–69, POL 27 ARAB–ISR. Secret; Exdis. Drafted by Rostow. The meeting was held at the Madison Hotel.

[2] Kosygin addressed the UN General Assembly on June 19. An excerpt of his speech is printed in *American Foreign Policy: Current Documents, 1967*, pp. 534–537.

leading powers had to find a common vocabulary. Tcherniakov agreed that these two statements were the important aspects of the speech, adding that he hoped we understood that propaganda efforts had to be diminished "gradually."

On the first point—Israel's right to live—Tcherniakov said that there never was any question of the Soviet position on this issue, which they viewed as fundamental. There had been a good deal of discussion about how much emphasis it should receive in the Kosygin speech, but all had agreed that the statement had to be made. Rostow remarked that we were accustomed to reading Soviet speeches with care. The important fact was that the theme had been stated. Tcherniakov said the Arab doctrine of a right to destroy Israel was "nonsense," and the source of a great deal of the "tragedy" in the area.

He hoped we would use our influence with Israel not to be too hard in their victory, referring to Arab pride, and confusion of thought at this point. He thought time was needed for the dust to settle.

Rostow said that as Tcherniakov could see from the President's statement, we did not think, in view of what had happened during the last ten years, that it was practical or realistic to expect the Israelis to withdraw until there were assurances they would return to a condition of peace. Surprisingly, Tcherniakov said he fully agreed. Rostow said there were natural anxieties everywhere that the Israelis had large territorial ambitions. We could not speak for the Israeli Government, but our impression so far was that Israel did not want great territorial changes, but peace and security. There were marginal problems, of course—the Syrian heights, Sharm al-Sheikh, the Gaza strip, and, most difficult of all, Jerusalem. Tcherniakov said that naturally something would have to be done about border security and international interests in Jerusalem.

Rostow said that we had been interested during the last few days by a flow of reports at various levels about a growing interest among the Palestinian Arabs in an arrangement of reconciliation with the Israelis, involving either the West Bank of the Jordan or even the whole of Jordan. We had no governmental position on the question, but, on preliminary consideration, we found the idea important. If the Palestinians could reach an accommodation, through a federation or otherwise, it could eliminate the refugee question, make it easier to solve the question of Jerusalem, and relieve the other Arab states of the incubus of their supposed obligation to wipe out Israel. Such a plan could also simplify problems of border security.

Tcherniakov said, speaking personally, that he was most interested in the possibility. He was not aware that the idea had come forward in recent days. The Soviet Government had supported a proposal of that kind in 1947 or 1948, when the Palestine problem was acute. He asked whether he could call the possibility to the Foreign Minister's attention. Rostow replied that of course he could, stressing, however, that it was not a United States Government position.

Rostow put emphasis on the issue of arms limitation. We thought a resumption of hostilities in the face of the cease fire was unthinkable. Tcherniakov dismissed the possibility.

On the second point in Kosygin's speech—the need of the leading powers to achieve a common vocabulary, Rostow said we were in full agreement. Tcherniakov would have noticed the President's care to avoid making the propaganda war worse. The President's speech stressed our interest in "narrowing differences" with the Soviet Union. The Chairman would find us ready to cooperate in the effort. Tcherniakov referred to the spirit of Tashkent, and the need for us together to work out an approach that could bring peace to the Middle East. He stressed that the Soviet Union had tried to prevent hostilities, as we did, but that there were forces in the situation which couldn't be controlled. Rostow said we had been puzzled by the rumors of an Israeli mobilization against Syria, which seemed to persist even after the Secretary General had denied them. Rostow said that we had been at pains to make our position clear to the Soviet Union throughout the crisis. We had noted that they had never publicly supported the Egyptian claim with regard to the Gulf of Aqaba. From the point of view of the two countries' national interests, and in the light of what Tcherniakov had said, he thought it should not be difficult for the Soviet Union to accept the approach indicated by the President's five principles.

Rostow asked Tcherniakov if they thought Nasser could survive. He replied that in their estimate it was possible. Nasser lacked a sense of reality, but perhaps recent events would help in that regard.

[Omitted here is Part II—Vietnam.]

310.   Memorandum From the Executive Secretary of the NSC
        Special Committee (Bundy) to the Members of the
        Committee[1]

Washington, June 20, 1967.

Three decisions taken by the President[2] are worth reporting for the information of all members of the committee.

1. The President approved an end to restrictions on normal travel by U.S. citizens to Morocco, Tunisia, Kuwait, Israel, Saudi Arabia and Lebanon (subject to check with the Lebanese Government).[3]

2. The President approved resumption of normal relations in all fields of economic, technical and food assistance to all nations in the Middle East area who have not broken relations with the United States. (Among those who have taken diplomatic action in this direction, only the Lebanon is not considered to have broken relations.) It is expected that the usual procedures of Presidential approval with respect to specific economic actions will be followed. No decisions have been made on military shipments.

3. The President directed that Mr. Leonard Marks should be asked to prepare a comprehensive plan for U.S. action to increase the voice of reason on medium-wave radio in the Arab-speaking world—as against the voice of Cairo. Mr. Marks has been asked to draw as required on the appropriate departments and agencies.

McGeorge Bundy

---

[1] Source: Johnson Library, National Security File, NSC Special Committee Files, Minutes and Notes. Secret.

[2] The President met with Katzenbach, McNamara, Helms, Bundy, Walt Rostow, and George Christian at lunch on June 20. (Ibid., President's Daily Diary) Rostow's notes on a copy of the agenda for the meeting indicate that he made the decisions at that time. (Ibid., Files of Walt Rostow, Meetings with the President, Jan.–June 1967) No other record of the meeting has been found.

[3] On June 21 the Department of State announced the lifting of the travel ban to Israel, Kuwait, Morocco, Tunisia, and Saudi Arabia. (Circular telegram 215088, June 23; National Archives and Records Administration, RG 59, Central Files 1967–69, POL 27 ARAB–ISR)

311. Memorandum From the Executive Secretary of the NSC Special Committee (Bundy) to President Johnson[1]

Washington, June 21, 1967, 3:55 p.m.

SUBJECT

Special Committee Meeting at 6:30 today, Cabinet Room

The items of Middle East business for today are as follows. There is no urgent need of decision, and while I think it would be a help to us to get your preliminary reaction to some of the choices, none of these matters is so urgent as to require decision—or even your presence if you are too busy.

1. Emergency relief policy

Michelmore, the Commissioner General of the UN Relief and Works Agency, has reported to the UN that he has an immediate need for a lot more money. He hasn't said how much, but magnitude is not the real problem. We have about $5 million of AID contingency money that could move in this direction if need be, and this would certainly be a reasonable start.

The real problem is to make sure that we do not get sucked in to one more large-scale dole with no prospect of solution in the Middle East. If we get back into the business of paying most of the UNRWA bill, we create an almost automatic dampener to incentives for settlement by either Israel or the Arabs. I have therefore asked State to give intensive study to the question of ways and means of tying any possible new emergency relief to conditions or processes that would somehow constitute a pressure for "justice for the refugees." Nick Katzenbach will lead a discussion of these possibilities this evening.

2. Selective military shipments to our friends in the area

The noises from places as far apart as Morocco and Lebanon suggest that we should be coming to a decision on limited arms shipments to moderate Arabs. From your point of view, this will be a good thing to have done before we have to climb into bed with the Israelis again. From another point of view, the longer we can wait, the better. From still another standpoint, there may be a special virtue in cautious military hand-holding with really decent Arabs (like the strong Lebanese general who seems to have kept the Lebanon out of the war).

---

[1] Source: Johnson Library, National Security File, NSC Special Committee Files, Minutes and Notes. No classification marking. A handwritten "L" on the memorandum indicates the President saw it.

3. The Egyptians and the French

We will be talking a little about the astonishing Egyptian démarche in Paris[2] and about de Gaulle's outrageous statement.[3] My own instinct is to let the Egyptian position ripen before we get too excited about it, since our wheat remains the ace of trumps. At the same time, it might be helpful to begin to let the word get around unofficially of the regret which we and the Israelis share that de Gaulle's violently one-sided statement has damaged his usefulness as a mediator.

4. The special problem of Jordan

We have always been Hussein's best friend and hand-holder and there is a tactical question now whether there will be important things to say to him pretty soon. If there were any sign of a magnanimous peace between him and the Israelis, we should encourage it. One way of moving quietly in this direction with no obvious initiative on our side would be to encourage Hussein in the thought he has expressed that he might wish to come to the United Nations. If he did that his speech would be quite likely to make a favorable impression on the American public (especially if Macomber talked to him beforehand), and it would be natural for you to receive him in Washington as the head of Government and give him some good advice. Since this last one engages you directly, it is obvious that nothing will be done until you have had a chance to consider the case and give orders.

McG. B.

---

[2] Reference is to a document given to Ambassador Bohlen by Winston Guest, who said he had received it from a friend with excellent Arab contacts. It stated that the Egyptian authorities were ready to make great political concessions if serious economic aid, especially U.S. wheat, could be offered to them very rapidly. Telegram 20454 from Paris, June 21, transmitted the text of the document, which had reportedly been given to the French Government on June 20 by the Egyptian Embassy. Rostow forwarded a copy of telegram 20454 to the President on June 21, with a note saying that according to Clark Clifford, the source was extremely knowledgeable in Arab affairs. (Ibid., Country File, Middle East Crisis, Vol. VII) A June 21 memorandum from INR Deputy Director George C. Denney, Jr., to Acting Secretary Katzenbach recommended that he regard the document with skepticism. (Ibid.)

[3] A statement issued by the French Government on June 21 suggested that the war in Vietnam had contributed to the hostilities in the Middle East and stated that "France condemns the opening of hostilities by Israel." The text is printed in *American Foreign Policy: Current Documents, 1967*, pp. 542–543.

312. Memorandum of Conversation[1]

New York, June 21, 1967, 5:30 p.m.

SUBJECT

US-UAR Relations

PARTICIPANTS

UAR

Dr. Mahmoud Fawzi, Asst. to UAR President for Foreign Affairs
Mr. Hassan Sabri al-Khouli Adviser to the UAR President
Mr. Mohammed Riad, UAR Foreign Ministry

US

Ambassador Harriman
Donald C. Bergus, NEA/UAR

Mr. Harriman said that he was calling on Dr. Fawzi informally and in a personal capacity. The US Government was unhappy about the grave situation in the Near East and the false and unnecessary charges made by the UAR. The important thing was to ascertain whether our two Governments had any common objectives which they could support. He referred to President Johnson's statement that all Near East countries had to recognize each other's right to exist and our support of the territorial integrity and political independence of all. We wished to move in that direction. If Dr. Fawzi had anything to say, Mr. Harriman would listen. Mr. Harriman said he had not come to argue but to see if there were a possibility for useful discussions among men of good will. He referred to the Secretary's high personal regard for Dr. Fawzi and his willingness to meet with him if this would be useful.

Dr. Fawzi said he appreciated this initiative. Ambassador Harriman was a good American; he tried to be a good Egyptian. This was a sufficient denominator. Neither had the right to feel peevish or to keep each other in a corner.

What we had to deal with was the outburst of June 5. Ambassador Harriman would appreciate the difficulty of asking people to give under threats of duress. Any gains secured by force and violence should not be allowed. He was not ready to talk about a broad settlement until we could agree on this preliminary.

Ambassador Harriman said it was in the U.S. interest to find a durable peace. This was a situation where both sides could be com-

---

[1] Source: National Archives and Records Administration, RG 59, Central Files 1967–69, POL UAR–US. Secret; Exdis. Drafted by Bergus and approved by Harriman on June 30. The meeting took place at the Waldorf Towers during the Fifth Emergency Special Session of the United Nations General Assembly.

pletely rigid. Suggestions had been made for some intermediary. He did not know who would be agreeable to the UAR. General de Gaulle had been mentioned but he, perhaps, was too much in the international limelight. Dr. Fawzi said the UAR had given no expression to this matter "in public." It was keeping an open mind and exploring all means to get out of this situation. He considered that a mediator had to be carefully selected. He reacted against "volunteers."

Ambassador Harriman wondered whether under present circumstances Dr. Fawzi would like to talk to Secretary Rusk. Dr. Fawzi thought that he and the Secretary could talk freely together, might talk usefully, but that "we might not be able to see matters crystallize through our first talk." He reciprocated Secretary Rusk's personal regard.

Dr. Fawzi continued that the UAR was open-minded regarding the method of resolving the present difficulty but would not cede on the basic principle. "We might at one stage find a good way to differentiate between form and substance," he commented. Ambassador Harriman said that we had taken a position on the Gulf of Aqaba as a result of the 1957 discussions. We were also committed to support the territorial integrity and political independence of every country in the area. The U.S. had no commitment on any other aspect of the substance of the dispute. Ambassador Harriman said that the cease-fire gave us time.

Dr. Fawzi said that we must not overestimate the amount of time we had. Important matters such as the Suez Canal, interests in Arab oil including Egyptian oil, were at stake. The longer the delay the less chance there was for a renewal of serenity. Mr. Harriman said time also worked for the other side. Once people got used to roaming around newly-acquired territory, the harder it was to get them to move away. The Suez Canal was a two-way street. The UAR needed the tolls. We were not much involved, but the UAR's friend India was very much involved. Dr. Fawzi admitted that the UAR needed every pound it earned from the Canal and felt sorry for the Indians. The UAR kept the Canal open to commerce on one sole condition, that it not be attacked.

Dr. Fawzi reiterated an interest in seeing Secretary Rusk. He planned to be in the United States for another week or ten days. He wanted to say that it remained the basic policy of the UAR to have good relations with the United States. He had told the British the same thing. The UAR also prized its good relations with the USSR with whom it had many ties. Dr. Fawzi appeared to indicate a preference that his meeting with the Secretary take place after a possible Johnson–Kosygin meeting, but said he was at the Secretary's disposal any time.

313. Notes of Meeting of the Special Committee of the National Security Council[1]

Washington, June 21, 1967, 6:30 p.m.

THOSE PRESENT

Katzenbach, Acting Secretary of State
McNamara
Wheeler
Helms
Clifford
W.W. Rostow
McG. Bundy
Vance
E.V. Rostow
Battle
Harry McPherson
Harold Saunders
[*name not declassified*], CIA

The President came in at 6:50 p.m.
George Christian came in at 6:55 p.m.

1. Informal discussion:

UAR trying to buy food for cash. Russian wheat problem. Katzenbach sees no objection. Cargill—$10 m.—UAR has asked to buy.[2]

2. Emergency relief:

—Swedish appeal in UN.

—What can we do now to avoid permanent commitment to status quo.

—Responsibility to those holding political authority.

EVR: Work through UNWRA.

---

[1] Source: Johnson Library, National Security File, NSC Special Committee Files, Minutes and Notes. No classification marking. The meeting was held in the Cabinet Room at the White House. Notes are the handwritten notes of Harold H. Saunders. The President joined the meeting from 6:50 p.m. until 7:06 p.m. (Ibid., President's Daily Diary) Bundy's memorandum for the record, June 21, states: "1. The President agreed to see King Hussein if he comes to the United Nations. 2. The President agreed that we should let it be known quietly that we do not consider General de Gaulle an acceptable mediator of a Mid-East solution." (Ibid., National Security File, NSC Special Committee Files, Minutes and Notes)

[2] The following appears at this point in Saunders' notes in a box, apparently added later in the discussion: "President said: 'I'm going to be easily raped by anyone who wants to pay cash. I've been giving it away for so long. . . .'"

—WWR: Regional increment 60%.
—McNamara: We shouldn't put up 70%. Put it on regional basis.
—McGB summary:

   —Less than 70%
   —Regional response
   —Not get out in front

—Battle: decrease share
—Refer back to Dept. for a framework in which our contribution would be well down.

   —Outside vs. regional contribution
   —US vs. US [*USSR?*] non-regional
   —Short-term nature of commitment

Plus soundings on the Hill.
McGB: Signal Israelis?[3]

3. *Military:*

Go over paper[4] at next meeting
McN: Against Libya.[5]

4. *Egyptians & French:*

—Not something we need to rush in on.
—Get it around that de Gaulle not going to be our mediator.

5. *Jordan:*

—Hussein. LBJ wld. see.
—On Am. TV.

General policy guideline:

Moderate the moderates.

---

[3] In a statement released on June 27, the President announced that the United States would join with other nations in a special effort to provide emergency assistance in the Middle East and announced the establishment of a reserve of $5 million from contingency funds for this purpose. He stated that he had directed U.S. participation in the appropriate UN emergency programs of food and medical relief and that the U.S. Government was offering $100,000 for use by the International Red Cross to assist victims of the conflict. (*Public Papers of the Presidents of the United States: Lyndon B. Johnson, 1967*, Book I, p. 660)

[4] Not further identified.

[5] Helms' notes of the meeting say on this point: "DOD opposed to arms shipments for Libya—OK on Morocco and Jordan." (Central Intelligence Agency Files, DCI Files: Job 80–B1285A, Box 11, Folder 12, DCI (Helms) Miscellaneous Notes of Meetings, 1 Jan 1966–31 Dec 1968)

314. Telegram From the Mission to the United Nations to the Department of State[1]

New York, June 22, 1967, 0455Z.

5845/Secto 13. Following uncleared memcon FYI Noforn and subject to revision.

Secretary and Ambassador Goldberg received Israeli FonMin Eban along with Rafael and Harman 7:15 p.m. June 21. Hour's conversation revolved around two main topics: (A) Situation in Near East and Israeli view re settlement and (B) present parliamentary situation in UNGA. This telegram covers topic (A).[2]

Secretary referred to sentiment UNGA re need for reaffirmation principle of withdrawal before meaningful discussions on bases for settlement could take place. He believed there were two separable questions as regards form and substance. If we could be clear on substance we could then be more flexible on modalities.

Eban stated Israeli inter-ministerial committee had come to some tentative conclusions which he would like to discuss with Secretary but not others.

Egypt–Israel. Israelis wanted peace treaty on basis present international frontiers. This would involve Israeli maritime passage through Straits Tiran and Suez Canal and air passage over straits. In context non-belligerency this would mean Israel would be treated like everyone else. In same context Israel envisaged demilitarization of Sinai, which was natural barrier between two countries. From Egypt, Israel wanted only security, no territory. Israelis felt Egypt might be attracted to this concept.

Important thing that there must be treaty which committed Egyptians. Israeli unwilling accept another understanding on basis of assumptions. This had been major fault of 1957 arrangements which had committed much of world but not Egypt.

Israel–Syria. Israelis would like peace treaty on the basis of the international frontiers with some understanding that Syrian hills overlooking Israeli territory would be demilitarized. Israelis would also like assurances that Syria would not use returned territory for purpose of

---

[1] Source: National Archives and Records Administration, RG 59, Central Files 1967–69, POL 27 ARAB–ISR. Secret; Exdis. Repeated to Tel Aviv. Received at 3:27 a.m. Passed to the White House at 3:44 a.m. Secretary Rusk was in New York June 19–June 23 to attend the Special Session of the UN General Assembly.

[2] Telegram 5844 from USUN, June 22, reported the discussion of topic B. (Ibid., POL 27 ARAB–ISR/UN)

diversion of Jordan waters away from Israel. Eban noted that Syrians unable divert these waters now because Israeli held essential territory. Eban concluded that Israel was offering both Egypt and Syria complete withdrawal to international frontiers. These terms not ungenerous.

Gaza. Eban noted that Egypt had never claimed Gaza, had not accepted responsibility for occupying it, or for the refugees. The natural thing was for Gaza to be in Israel. Israelis would make every effort on behalf of Gaza population which totaled over 350,000 people. This plus Israel's present Arab population would bring total Arabs in Israel to about 700,000. Israelis wondered whether some could not be settled elsewhere, e.g. northern part of Sinai, "Central Palestine" or West Bank of Jordan. Israelis would like to maintain status of UNRWA as source of assistance to these people.

West Bank of Jordan. Eban said Israeli thinking "less crystalized" re West Bank. They were still working on basis two tendencies, two conceptions in GOI. One tendency assumed that the Hashemite Kingdom of Jordan would continue and that an agreed settlement on the basis of the demarcation line should be worked out. Another idea was that there should be some kind of association between the West Bank and Israel on the basis of autonomy and economic union. The difficulty with this latter approach, said Eban, was that it would push Hussein back across the Jordan River. Moreover, there were no international constitutional precedents for such an arrangement.

The Secretary interposed by wondering whether there were not precedents on the basis of letting the people concerned decide. Eban replied that GOI was trying to take soundings on the intelligence level. There were some "serious" Arab leaders on West Bank who felt that their relationship with East Jordan had been artificial and had provided them no security. Others had Hashemite loyalties.

Secretary inquired if there were no significant Egyptian military presence in Sinai what would be situation in the Negev? Eban pointed out that until UNEF removed there had been the slenderest military presence possible in the south of Israel.

Secretary commented that it was helpful to have these preliminary thoughts. He was not clear as to whether doctrine of innocent maritime passage through Straits of Tiran also applied to air passage. Eban felt that doctrine would apply, in light of relevant international conventions re air transit, except in times of war. Secretary asked whether economic arrangements between Israel and West Bank might not be conduit to bring Trans-Jordan into similar arrangement. He realized Israelis were angry at Hussein but advised that they should not sell him short. Eban admitted that Israelis' first reaction had been to write Hussein off but they now heard that Hussein was being properly contrite.

Secretary said he wanted to raise two points:

1. Refugees. We continued to get bad information on the refugee situation. Apparently several thousand Arabs per day continue to leave Israel. It would be great tragedy if the refugee problem was re-created. Our information does not agree with Israelis' statements on this matter. Eban said he had spoken with the military governor of Jerusalem (who happened to be his brother-in-law) on this point. The Secretary suggested that Israel be less rigorous in its process of screening of people who left the West Bank during the hostilities and now wish to return. He felt that Israel could take some chances in this respect and that world opinion would press Israel very hard on the refugee question.

2. Jerusalem. Secretary hoped that Israel would be very careful with regard to Jerusalem as it involved actual or latent passions of an enormous number of people. The matter was very delicate and could be a source of strong anti-Israel feeling in the United States. Eban replied that Israel was trying to put the Christian holy places under Christian control and the Moslem holy places under Moslem control. Eban admitted that Israel had a job to do in projecting publicly its intentions regarding access to holy places.

Eban referred to reports of Soviet replacement of military aircraft to Egypt. He agreed that full replacement might take a year. At the same time Israel's own aircraft inventories were low. Israel had lost 42 planes in hostilities. This had led to GOI request for expedited implementation of present contract to supply Skyhawks to Israel. Secretary replied that this was being considered in Washington at the present time. He did not know whether Soviets intended to replenish fully Arab inventories or to make a more modest gesture. Secretary said that he would try to find out from Gromyko if there was any Soviet interest in some arms limitation. Secretary noted that this was issue affecting whole area and that we were under heavy pressure for arms from friendly Arab countries.

Rusk

315. Telegram From the Mission to the United Nations to the Department of State[1]

New York, June 22, 1967, 0455Z.

5841/Secto 9. Eyes Only for President and Acting Secretary.

Before we sat down to dinner tonight Gromyko and I drew aside for a few minutes of private talk about the Middle East. I asked him what the Central Committee meant by accusing the US of being in a plot with Israel. He said they found it very hard to believe the US did not have advance information about the beginning of hostilities and we could have made more of an effort to stop them. I told him categorically that this was not the truth, that we had what we considered to be commitments from both sides that hostilities would not begin, that we had no advance information about the fighting and that our first message to the Chairman expressing our astonishment and dismay represented the exact truth.[2] I told him that Israel was not a satellite of the United States and that I assumed that Egypt was not a satellite of Moscow; otherwise Moscow would bear a heavy responsibility for such acts of folly as the closing of the Strait of Tiran and the whipping up of a holy war psychology against Israel.

We then turned to the immediate problem before the Assembly and it is clear that the central issue will be the relation between the withdrawal of troops and other elements in a general settlement. Gromyko reaffirmed the commitment of the USSR to the existence of Israel as a state and recalled that both they and we had voted for the creation of Israel twenty years ago. He seemed to show flexibility on international maritime rights although he commented perhaps these matters should be dealt with in special arrangements similar to the Montreux Convention on the Bosporus. For lack of time we did not get into other elements of a permanent solution, but it is quite clear that they will press for the priority of withdrawal over against the settlement of other issues. I drew the distinction between procedure and substance and said that I thought if there could be broad agreement on substance, modalities could be found to deal with questions of procedure. I also told him I did not think that Israel had any particular interest in trying to retain Egyptian or Syrian territory. (This was based on an earlier conversation I had had with Eban.)

---

[1] Source: National Archives and Records Administration, RG 59, Central Files 1967–69, POL 27 ARAB–ISR/UN. Secret; Immediate; Nodis. Received at 2:18 a.m. A typed and slightly paraphrased version was sent to the President by Arthur McCafferty at 7:15 a.m.

[2] Document 157.

I talked to him briefly about non-proliferation which we continued at dinner and got the impression that they were reasonably satisfied with the draft text worked out in Geneva which omits article three. He emphasized the importance of controls and said there should be an international system which did not discriminate in favor of members of a particular NATO family. I told him this was not an issue of principle between the USSR and the US but that the obstacle was his friend General de Gaulle. I asked him if Kosygin had discussed NPT with de Gaulle and was told the subject had not come up. He seemed to be more optimistic about the Indian attitude than we.

In a later private exchange Gromyko indicated he would probably stay on for about a week following the departure of Kosygin. This probably means that he will stay around to do his best to get their kind of resolution from the General Assembly. I definitely got the impression that they were prepared to drop the condemnation feature if a simple unadorned demand for withdrawal could get the necessary number of votes.

Remainder of conversation being reported septel.[3]

Goldberg

---

[3] Telegram 5848 from USUN, June 22, reported Rusk's dinner conversation with Gromyko. (National Archives and Records Administration, RG 59, Central Files 1967–69, ORG 7 S)

---

316. Telegram From the Embassy in Morocco to the Department of State[1]

Rabat, June 21, 1967, 1148Z.

5635. 1. FonMin Laraki told me June 20 that FonMin meeting in Kuwait dealt with two basic resolutions. One was presented by the Moroccans at the outset and represented view of moderates. This provided for dealing with Arab-Israeli problem through diplomatic channels, stressing importance of immediate withdrawal of Israelis to 1948 armistice lines. The other resolution strongly supported by UAR, Algeria, and Syria provided for an all-out boycott, nationalization and

---

[1] Source: National Archives and Records Administration, RG 59, Central Files 1967–69, POL 27 ARAB–ISR. Secret. Repeated to Algiers, Tunis, COMAC for POLAD, CINCUSNAVEUR, USCINCEUR for POLAD, USUN, Amman, Beirut, Jidda, Kuwait, London, Moscow, Paris, Tel Aviv, and Tripoli. Received at 5:36 a.m. on June 22.

elimination of all economic ties with imperialists (US and UK) as well as their ejection from "bases" such as Morocco and Libya. Morocco led moderates (I am happy report Libya supported Morocco) and was successful in having its resolution approved. I suspect diplomatic channels meant transfer FonMin meeting to New York and effort in UN to obtain withdrawal of Israelis.

2. Laraki told me he had hard time as "extremists" made all the arguments familiar from Radio Cairo, Algiers, and Istiqlal here and sought to pin down definition of US as an aggressor country as much as were the Israelis.

In his view, it will be impossible continue hold the line against the "extremists" if the US does not come out unequivocally for a withdrawal of Israeli forces. No Arab nation could accept principle of continued Israeli military occupation of Arab lands. In his view, it might be possible to combine the withdrawal with a UN guarantee of the political independence and territorial integrity of all the countries concerned. This is an interesting idea which would have the effect of internationalizing the tripartite declaration of 1950 and is worth exploring.

3. In any event, I must stress again the continued Israeli occupation of Arab lands including Jerusalem puts the moderates in an impossible position and gravely compromises our position with the Arab world as long as we do not state our position unequivocally on this subject in some appropriate forum, reconciling our interests in Israel at the same time.

Tasca

---

317. Intelligence Memorandum Prepared in the Central Intelligence Agency[1]

SC 08384–67   Washington, June 21, 1967.

SUBJECT

The Israeli Statement on the Attack on the USS *Liberty*

1. The preliminary report of the special Court of Inquiry convened by the Government of Israel has concluded that the "attack on the USS

---

[1] Source: Central Intelligence Agency Files: Job 85–01007R, Box 5, Folder 50. Top Secret; Trine. Prepared in the Central Intelligence Agency's Directorate of Intelligence.

Liberty was not in malice; there was no criminal negligence and the attack was made by innocent mistake." The report, however, has been turned over to the military judge advocate who has ordered a preliminary judicial inquiry by an officer empowered to convene court martial.

2. According to the Israeli findings a chain of three regrettable mistakes led to the attack by Israeli jets and torpedo boats upon the USS *Liberty* on 8 June 1967.

First Mistake

3. The first mistake was decisive and set the scenario for the subsequent errors. On the basis of erroneous reports, the Israel Defense Force (IDF) was convinced that Israeli positions near El Arish were being shelled by an unidentified vessel off the coast. However, "even the officers who knew of the identification of *Liberty* early the same morning did not connect *Liberty* with the unidentified ships said to be shelling El Arish."

4. (CIA has no evidence of these erroneous reports, but the information is plausible in light of the very speedy Israeli advance and the heat of battle in the El Arish area. The UAR Navy is not known to have shelled Israeli shore positions on 8 June. The above admission that Israelis had identified the *Liberty*—presumably following the overflight by jets at 9:50 AM (2:50 PM EDT)—is the first indication that the Israelis knew the *Liberty* was in the area prior to the attack.)

Second Mistake

5. The three Israeli torpedo boats patrolling near the *Liberty* reported that the unidentified vessel was steaming at 28–30 knots. A check of *Liberty*'s maximum speed in *Jane's* led IDF headquarters to believe that the unidentified (radar) target was a high speed combatant and not the *Liberty*. Considering the erroneous information on the shelling of Israeli coastal positions, the IDF asked the torpedo boats to verify the unidentified vessel's speed and then ordered an air attack.

6. (It is most bizarre that a qualified naval commander would twice compute *Liberty*'s speed to be 30 knots or that the IDF would authorize an attack solely on the basis of an unidentified high speed contact. There is not a ship of *Liberty*'s general appearance capable of such a speed and few have deck guns capable of shelling coastal installations. If the authorization to attack was made solely on radar tracking, the attacking aircraft would normally make a preliminary identification pass over the ship.)

Third Mistake

7. The Israeli torpedo boats then joined the fray. They claimed they mistook the *Liberty* for the Egyptian transport *El Quesir* and attacked

with torpedoes after the jets had broken off. This attack is laid to the overeagerness of the torpedo boat skippers as the jet pilots were already having their doubts as to the ship's identity. The Israelis further state that the *Liberty* refused to answer a challenge sent by flashing light prior to the attack by the torpedo boats and the ship was firing toward the Israeli torpedo boats.

8. (CIA concurs that the torpedo attack was made by overeager Israeli commanders. There have been no US Navy reports of the visual challenge—probably issued in the heat of battle—but if such a challenge were received it would have been answered.)

9. A partial explanation for some of this unprofessional military performance is found in a report from Tel Aviv that at least one of the officers aboard the torpedo boats was a reservist recalled to service during the mobilization. In light of the demonstrated Israeli military capabilities, however, it is difficult [to] attribute all of the contributing errors to inept personnel.

> (Sources: USDAO Tel Aviv 0928/1 Jun 67, 18 Jun, Confidential USDAO Tel Aviv 0933, Jun 67, Secret No Foreign DissemCIA Intelligence Memorandum, "The Israeli Attack on the USS *Liberty*," SC No. 01415/67, Top Secret Trine

General Comments

10. The findings of the Israeli Court of Inquiry generally are consonant with the conclusions made in the CIA Intelligence Memorandum. It is now known, however, that the IDF Headquarters had identified the *Liberty*, probably more than four hours before the attack. The Israelis presumably thought the vessel they were attacking not to be the *Liberty*, for it is also clear that when the initial attack took place the ground controllers and the pilots believed the ship to be a belligerent. In addition, the Israelis have admitted that the jets were ordered to attack the unidentified vessel and, therefore, the *Liberty* was not taken under fire by overzealous pilots, acting on their own. We do not know if they had been advised of the presence of the *Liberty* in these waters.

11. Two rather incongruous statements in the findings of the Court of Inquiry only detract from their explanation. The Israelis offer as a reason for the air attack a standing IDF order authorizing an attack upon any ship steaming at a speed above 20 knots if Israeli ships or shore positions in the area are being shelled. To say the least, it is questionable military policy to authorize an attack upon an unidentified ship based solely upon a radar track of over 20 knots and erroneous reports that Israeli positions were being shelled. The Israeli statement that the *Liberty* could not be identified because it was covered with smoke also

is a piece of self-serving over rationalization. Clearly the smoke was the result of the Israeli attacks.

12. In light of the findings of the Israeli Court of Inquiry, we conclude that our previous statement that "the Israelis did not identify the *Liberty* as a US ship until some 44 minutes after the second attack" is in error. The *Liberty* had been identified prior to the attacks, but the Israelis were apparently not aware that they were attacking the *Liberty*. The attack was not made in malice toward the US and was by mistake, but the failure of the IDF Headquarters and the attacking aircraft to identify the *Liberty* and the subsequent attack by the torpedo boats were both incongruous and indicative of gross negligence.[2]

---

[2] A DIA memorandum of June 13 to the Chairman of the Joint Chiefs of Staff states: "There is no available information which would conclusively show that the Israelis made a premeditated attack on a ship known to be American. In fact the best interpretation we can make of the available facts is that Israeli command and control in this instance was defective." A June 28 addendum to the memorandum states that further information had clarified the sequence of events but failed to show that the attack had been premeditated and did not alter the interpretation of the incident in the prior memorandum.

---

318.   Notes of Telephone Conversation Between Secretary of State Rusk and Robert B. Anderson[1]

New York, June 22, 1967, 10:30 a.m.

TELEPHONE CALL FROM MR. ROBERT B. ANDERSON (NYC)

A called to report on his morning meeting with Iraqi For. Min. Pachachi and Lebanon FM Hakim. A said it was incomprehensible to him how much animosity they hold for our representatives; this was not meant personally, but P had told him that when he got down to see the Sec and Pres he was told to see Gene Rostow and he said he might just as well have been talking to a representative of the Israeli Govt; they would not discuss this subject or have any faith in resolutions offered by a US Amb or anyone of this faith. A had discussed at some length with them that they must face the realities of life. A said their

---

[1] Source: National Archives and Records Administration, RG 59, Rusk Files: Lot 72 D 192, Telephone Calls. No classification marking. The notes were prepared by Carolyn J. Proctor. Rusk was at the U.S. Mission to the United Nations.

principal point was they must have withdrawal from the territory; they said US has been silent on this. A said he was not speaking for his govt but suggested a declaration by General Assembly or Security Council along the line of the right of all states to live being recognized; if the state of belligerency was declared ended by all parties, then we could see where we are; P said he would be willing to explore that but he could not be commited until he saw the language; he said if A cared to show them something they would discuss it with their colleagues. A said he was not part of the US Govt, but he would not be happy to have them merely explore it—he would expect them to try to sell it; he indicated that if the language could be agreed on, perhaps something could be worked out. P had said we had no idea of the image we had in his country; P said we must believe that US gave them some encouragement, intelligence; when A had explained why he believed this was not so, P had said he had to believe him but we could never get our people to believe it. P said they need some liaison with the Dept; he realized the Sec was busy; A had suggested Battle whom P had not heard of; P had said he had been told ERostow was running Near East affairs. A said P mentioned a Goldberg speech in the early '60s in which he said he was a Zionist. A said their one great thesis was restoration of territory; they were agreeably interested in their ability to look at, examine and if the language was properly phrased consider a meeting of their colleagues to consider such a declaration. Sec said it was just possible something could be worked out on that line. Sec thanked A.

---

319.   Telegram From the Director of the National Security Agency (Carter) to the White House[1]

Washington, June 22, 1967, 1454Z.

SIGINT Readiness Bravo "Crayon" Report Nr. 2149.

Aftermath of Israeli Attack on USS Liberty, 8 June 1967.

1. General

The following activity is based on Israeli plain language VHF/UHF voice communications intercepted on 8 June 1967 between 1229Z and 1328Z. This activity deals solely with the aftermath of the attack by

---

[1] Source: National Security Agency, NSA Archives, Accession No. 45981, U.S.S. Liberty Correspondence and Messages, 1965–1968. Secret; Savin.

Israeli jet aircraft and torpedo boats on the USS *Liberty* (GTR5). There are no COMINT reflections of the actual attack itself.

2. Summary

At 1230Z, two Israeli helicopters 810 and 815, were dispatched by Hatsor to the area of the incident to check for survivors of an unidentified "warship." Approximately at 1234Z, the air controller at Hatsor clarified the identity of the ship to the two Israeli helicopters by informing them that it had been identified as Egyptian. At 1239Z, Hatsor told the helicopters that it was an Egyptian cargo ship.

At 1307Z, Hatsor told helicopter 815 to take any survivors that spoke Egyptian to El Arish ((31–08N 34–54E)), but if they spoke English to take them to Lod ((31–58N 34–54E)).

At 1312Z, the Israeli helicopter 815 apparently informed Hatsor on a different frequency that it had sighted an American flag on the ship. Hatsor then asked the helicopter to make another pass to check "if this is really an American flag."

The helicopters and the MTBs were communicating on a UHF frequency whereas the helicopters and the air controller at Hatsor were using VHF throughout. At 1310Z, helicopter 815 informed the MTB using callword "Pagoda" that the ship was not in danger. The same helicopter then reported that G.T.R.–5 was written on the ship and inquired if this meant anything. The MTB replied in the negative.

Throughout this intercept, the USS *Liberty* is referred to as the "big one" while the three Israeli motor torpedo boats are referred to as the "small ones." The helicopters used call signs 810 and 815. The air controller at Hatsor Air Base used call word "Tribune." The MTBs used callwords "Thorn," "Pagoda," and "Crisis." The callword "Jewel" is not identified, but may be Haifa.

3. Details

Time	To	From	Text
	—	—	I understand the course from Ashdod ((31–55N 34–39E)) is 215.
	—	—	Negative ((the course is)) 250.
	—	—	Roger
	815	(Tribune)	To what altitude are you climbing?
	(Tribune)	(815)	I'm now at 500 feet.
	(815)	(Tribune)	
1230Z	—	—	Five by.

(815)	(Tribune)	Pay attention: there was a warship there which we attacked (((1 WD G)), the men jumped from it ((the ship)) into the water, you will try to rescue them.
(Tribune)	(815)	Roger, I understand it was hit and unable to fire.
(815)	(Tribune)	No fire was seen from her and those ([*less than 1 line of source text not declassified*] onboard) did not fire; heavy smoke is rising from her.
(Tribune)	(815)	Roger.
(Tribune)	(815)	([*less than 1 line of source text not declassified*] crossing the) coast now at a course of 250.
(815)	(Tribune)	Roger, over. What location ((are you))?
(Tribune)	(815)	Over Ashdod.
(815)	(Tribune)	Roger, what's your altitude?
(Tribune)	(815)	500 feet.
(815)	(Tribune)	Are you able to climb to an altitude of ((1,000 feet))?
(Tribune)	(815)	Roger, I'm climbing.

1232Z

(Tribune)	(815)	Altitude 1 ((1,000)), course 250.
815	(Tribune)	Roger.
(815)	(Tribune)	Are you at sea now?
(Tribune)	(815)	About 3 or 4 miles.
(815)	(Tribune)	Roger.
(815)	(Tribune)	Visual ((radar)) contact with you.
(Tribune)	(815)	Roger.
(Tribune)	(815)	((Calling)) ((repeats)).
(815)	(Tribune)	At the moment she ((*Liberty*)) is straight ahead at a distance of about 50 miles.
(Tribune)	(815)	Roger.
Tribune	810	((Calling)).
815	(815)	Five by, 810 is calling you.

	815	Tribune	((Calling)).
	(Tribune)	(815)	Five by.
	(815)	(Tribune)	Pay attention: the ship is now identified as Egyptian, you can return home now.
	(Tribune)	(815)	Roger.
1235Z			
	810	(815)	Establish communications with you also.
	815	(Tribune)	Did you receive?
	(Tribune)	(815)	Affirmative, receive, I'm returning.
	(815)	(Tribune)	Roger.
	(Tribune)	(810)	((Calling)).
	(Tribune)	815	((Calling)).
	(Tribune)	810	Am I to return also?
	(810)	(Tribune)	I'll let you know shortly.
	(Tribune)	(810)	Roger.
1236Z			
	Tribune	810	((Calling)).
	(810)	(Tribune)	Roger, I'll let you know shortly.
	(Tribune)	(810)	OK.
	(Tribune)	(8)10	((Calling)) ((rpts)).
	810	(Tribune)	You remain meanwhile in communications with me.
	(Tribune)	(810)	Roger, what am I to look for?
	(Tribune)	815	((Calling)).
	810	(Tribune)	Where are you?
	(Tribune)	(810)	I'm close to Ashdod.
	(810)	(815)	Roger, I'm also close to Ashdod, on the seaward side.
1238Z			
	Tribune	(810)	Did you receive?
	(810)	(Tribune)	What did 815 request?
	810	(815)	What's your altitude?
	(815)	(810)	Altitude 500 feet, near Ashdod.
	810	(815)	Roger, we're at altitude 1200 feet over Ashdod.
	(815)	(810)	Roger.

810	Tribune	((Calling)).
(Tribune)	(810)	Five by.
(810)	(Tribune)	Pay attention: you will continue meanwhile on a course of 250 from Ashdod. The both of you ((1–2 WD G)) will head toward the ship.
815	(Tribune)	((Calling)).
(Tribune)	(815)	Five by.
(815)	(Tribune)	Roger, you will continue ((at a course)) of 250 from Ashdod. The both of you will head for the ship, for the time being the both of you will be at altitude 1 ((1000 feet)).
810	(Tribune)	Do you see us?
(Tribune)	(810)	Affirmative, affirmative.
(810)	(Tribune)	Where are you?
(810)	(Tribune)	Where are you now?
(Tribune)	(810)	Ashdod, altitude 1 ((1000)).
(Tribune)	(810)	Did you receive?
810	Tribune	((Calling)).
(Tribune)	(810)	Five by.
(Tribune)	(810)	Altitude is 1 ((1000)), at Ashdod.
(810)	(Tribune)	Roger.
(Tribune)	(810)	Going to course 250 together with 815.
(810)	(Tribune)	Are the two of you together?
(Tribune)	(810)	Affirmative, we're together.
(810)	(Tribune)	Roger.
(810)	(Tribune)	Pay attention: you ([*less than 1 line of source text not declassified*] nonetheless) are heading for the ship.
(810)	(Tribune)	You will try to take the men from the water.
(Tribune)	(810)	Roger, okay.
(810)	(Tribune)	For your information: the ship is apparently ([*less than 1 line of source text not declassified*] burning).

	(810)	(Tribune)	((1 WD G)) it is an Egyptian cargo ship.
	(Tribune)	(810)	Roger.
	(810)	(Tribune)	Visual ((radar)) contact with both of you.
	(Tribune)	(810)	Roger.
1240Z			
	(810)	(Tribune)	I understand that you ((1–2 WD G)) both of you?
	(Tribune)	(810)	Affirmative.
	(810)	(Tribune)	Roger.
1241Z			
	810	Tribune	((Calling)).
	(Tribune)	(810)	Five by.
	(810)	(Tribune)	Take the men to El Arish.
	(Tribune)	(810)	Roger, okay.
	(815)	(810)	Did you receive?
	(810)	(815)	I received, affirmative.
1242Z			
	(810)	(815)	How much fuel do you have?
	(815)	(810)	Two and a half tanks.
	(810)	(815)	I have 1,700 ((liters)).
	(815)	(810)	This isn't good.
	(810)	(815)	((1 WD G)) to El Arish.
	(815)	(810)	Roger.
	(810)	(Tribune)	The ship is located now straight ahead at a range of 50 miles.
	(Tribune)	(810)	Roger.
	—	—	Are you first in line?
	—	—	Affirmative.
	—	—	Roger.
	Tribune	815	((2 WD G)) from the coast of El Arish.
1248Z			
	Tribune	810	((Calling)) ((repeats)).
1250Z			
	(Tribune)	810	About how many men are there?

815	Tribune	((Calling)).
Tribune	810	How many men are there?
815	Tribune	Turn right to ((course)) 260.
(Tribune)	(815)	Repeat.
(815)	(Tribune)	Turn right to course 260.
(Tribune)	(815)	((Course)), they want to know how many men are there?
(815)	(Tribune)	At the present time, it still isn't known, the distance to you is now 33 miles.
(Tribune)	(815)	Roger.
(Tribune)	(815)	What is the distance from it ((the *Liberty*)) to El Arish?
(815)	(Tribune)	The distance is approximately 30 miles.
(Tribune)	(815)	Roger.
Tribune	810	((Calling)).
(810)	(Tribune)	Five by.
(Tribune)	(810)	It's noteworthy that it ((1 WD G)).
(810)	(Tribune)	Roger.
Tribune	815	((Calling)).
(815)	(Tribune)	Five by.
(Tribune)	(815)	What is the distance?
(815)	(Tribune)	The distance is now 23 miles.
(Tribune)	(815)	Roger.
815	(Tribune)	Pay attention: call on 86 or on 186 Pagoda.

((Tr Note: 186 and 86 refer to a UHF frequency.))

(Tribune)	(815)	Roger.
(Tribune)	(815)	I'm going over to 186.
(815)	(Tribune)	Roger.
(Tribune)	810	I'm also ((going over to 186)).
(815)	Tribune	Is someone calling ((me)) Tribune?
(Tribune)	(815)	Affirmative, I don't have contact with Pagoda.
(815)	(Tribune)	Roger, clear, the ship is now at a distance of 19 miles.

(Tribune)	(815)	Roger, is Pagoda located near ((the *Liberty*))?
(815)	(Tribune)	Apparently it's located near it ((the ship)).
(Tribune)	(815)	Roger.

1257Z

815	(Tribune)	If you are able, try to call her ((Pagoda)) on 86.
(Tribune)	(815)	I tried.
(Tribune)	(815)	I didn't (C val get anything) ((make contact)).
(815)	(Tribune)	Roger.
Tribune	815	((Calling)).
815	Tribune	Do you have visual contact? Straight ahead, a distance of 18 miles.
Tribune	815	I have visual contact with ((1 WD G)) smoke or it could be ((1–2 WD G)).
815	Tribune	Roger, is there much smoke rising from it?
Tribune	815	Roger.
Tribune	815	I don't have contact with Pagoda.
815	Tribune	Roger.
810	815	((Calling)).
815	810	Five by.
810	815	Do you have contact with Pagoda?
815	810	Negative.
810	815	Roger, I don't either.
815	Tribune	((Calling)).
Tribune	815	Five by.
815	Tribune	When you begin bringing up the men, clarify by the first man that you bring up, what nationality he is.

1259Z

815	Tribune	And report to me immediately, it's important to know.

Tribune	815	Roger.
815	Tribune	What is your altitude now?
Tribune	815	Altitude is 1 ((1000 feet)).
815	Tribune	Roger.
Tribune	815	I have ((visual)) contact with a vessel straight ahead ((at a distance of)) 12 ((miles)) a little from the right, smoke isn't rising; QT the north it isn't smoking.
815	Tribune	The distance is now 13 miles.
Tribune	815	Roger.
815	Tribune	Do you see the ship?
Tribune	815	I see the ship, a little to the right of the smoke. The smoke the smoke isn't rising.
815	Tribune	Roger, it's possible that ((the smoke)) is from one of ours.
Tribune	815	Roger.
Tribune	815	It's worth clarifying.
815	Tribune	Roger.
Tribune	815	Roger, what I see ([*less than 1 line of source text not declassified*] now) is ours, this is clear.
815	Tribune	Roger.
815	Tribune	10 miles is the distance now.
Tribune	815	Roger, I understand at 12 o'clock ((1 WD G)).
815	Tribune	Affirmative, a little on the right side.
Tribune	815	Roger.

1301Z

815	Tribune	The distance is now 9 miles.

1302Z

Tribune	815	I'm going over to 86.
815	Tribune	Roger, I request to receive a report, tell me the nationality.
Tribune	815	((Calling)).
815	Tribune	Go ahead.

Tribune	815	Roger, there is a large ship, smoke isn't rising. At the present time smoke is a little to the right on its left side ((XG)) I see a small vessel.
Tribune	815	Three small vessels.

1303Z

815	(Tribune)	Are you calling me?
Tribune	815	Five by.
815	Tribune	Did you call me?
Tribune	815	Affirmative.
815	Tribune	Roger, what's the matter?
Tribune	815	There is a large vessel, near it are 3 small vessels, could this be it, at a distance of a mile from me?
815	Tribune	Roger, clear.
815	Tribune	Roger, apparently the small vessels are ours.
Tribune	815	Roger.
815	810	((Calling)).
810	815	Five by.
815	810	What's the matter?
810	815	Don't you see it yet?
815	810	I'm behind you, I still don't see the ship ((1 WD G)) on the right side of us.
810	815	Roger, exactly in front of me, there are the small vessels.
815	810	What's with them, what's going on?
810	815	It appears that they are ours.
815	810	On our right side?
810	815	Yes.
815	Tribune	All 3 of them are ours.
(Tribune)	(815)	Roger, the small ones, right?
815	Tribune	Affirmative.
Tribune	815	Roger. I'm heading for the big one ((*Liberty*)).
815	Tribune	Are you going for the big one?
(Tribune)	(815)	Affirmative.

1304Z

815	Thorn	Roger, wait.
—	—	Five by.
—	—	Roger, transmit.
—	—	Yes.
—	—	With you.

((Tr Note: Last 4 transmissions are one way communication—all 4 are from same source—other terminal is on different frequency.))

185 (*sic*)	Thorn	We search around and didn't find anyone.

((Tr Note: It is believed that Thorn made an error and wanted to call 815. The callsign 185 however has been used by an Israeli jet aircraft (either a Mirage or a Mystere). It is of course possible that Thorn had previously been in contact with 185, but if this was the case there are no COMINT reflections of this activity.))

(Thorn)	(815)	Roger.
(815)	(Thorn)	The big one ((*Liberty*)) is not ours.
185 (*sic*)	Thorn	How do you read me?

((Tr Note: Again Thorn says 185 vice 815.))

(Thorn)	815	((Calls)).
815	Thorn	We searched around and didn't find anyone.
Thorn	(815)	Roger.
—	Tribune	We hear you excellently.
Pagoda	810	((Calls)).
810	Pagoda	Transmit.
(Pagoda)	(810)	What are you saying?
(810)	(Pagoda)	Send your report.
(Pagoda)	810	What has to be done here?
Pagoda	810	((Calls)).
(810)	(Pagoda)	Search to see if there are men in the water.

1306Z

(Pagoda)	(810)	Roger.
—	(Tribune)	I understand and for the big one ((*Liberty*)).

(Tribune)	(Pagoda)	Don't speak on the channel now ((rpts)).
—	(Pagoda)	Five by, it appears to me that I found the men.
—	Pagoda	Affirmative?
—	(Pagoda)	Roger, that's clear.
—	(Pagoda)	Roger.
—	(Pagoda)	Negative, it's not men, it's boats, it's not men.
Tribune	810	((Calling)).
810	Tribune	Go ahead.
815	810	((Calling)).
810	815	Five by.
815	810	What's going on?
810	815	I don't know anything ((1 WD G)) ((about them)) I'll try to contact them on 186.

((Tr Note: 815 is trying to get in touch with the 3 small ships on 186 frequency.))

815	810	Are the small ones ours?
815	Tribune	((Calling)).
Tribune	815	Five by.
815	Tribune	Pay attention: if any of them are speaking, and if they are speaking Arabic ((Egyptian)), you take them to el Arish ((31–08N 33–45E)). If they are speaking English, not Egyptian, you take them to Lod (31–58N 34–54E). Is this clear?
Tribune 815		Roger.
815	Tribune	Do you see the men?
815	Tribune	To whom does the big one ((ship)) belong?`

1307Z

815	810	((Calling)) ((repeats)).
810	815	Five by.
815	810	Don't leave the vicinity. If you do leave, report ((to me)).

810	815	I'm not monitoring this channel. I'm speaking on 186 with Thorn. This is the small ones ((*sic*)).
815	810	Roger, what should be done?
810	815	Search for survivors ([*less than 1 line of source text not declassified*] whether you find them or not).
Pagoda	815	((Calls)).
815	Pagoda	Transmit.

1308Z

(815)	(810)	Roger.
810	Tribune	Are you able to go up a little higher in order to see the situation better?
(Tribune)	(810)	Roger.
810	Tribune	((Calling)). ((Repeats)).
815	Tribune	((Calling)).
815	Tribune	Are you over whatever you located?

((Tr Note: It should be noted here that helicopters 810 and 815 are now answering control on another frequency.))

815	Tribune	Roger, the first matter to clarify is to find out what their nationality is.
(815)	(Tribune)	Report to me immediately.

1310Z

(815)	(Tribune)	Roger this is clear.
815	Tribune	Roger, you watch out for the masts there.
815	Tribune	((Calling)).
(Pagoda)	(815)	I understand that the ship is not in danger.
(815)	Pagoda	I am not sure that it ((the *Liberty*)) is not in danger. Are you suggesting the seriousness of it ((the situation)), by ((saying)) this? ((Tr Note: As heard.))

(Pagoda)	(815)	Negative, G.T.R.–5 is written (on it).

((Tr Note: Letters G.T.R. sent in English.))

(815)	(Pagoda)	Roger ((stops)).
(Pagoda)	(815)	Does this mean something?
(815)	(Pagoda)	Negative, it doesn't mean anything.
(Pagoda)	(815)	From behind it ((*Liberty*)) several uninflated boats were seen.
(815)	(Pagoda)	Roger.
815	Tribune	You take 810 with you and return home, ([*less than 1 line of source text not declassified*] bearing) 070, distance of 6 miles.
(815)	(Tribune)	Five by.

1312Z

815	Tribune	Roger, this is clear, did you clearly identify an American flag?
815	Tribune	Thanks, remain meanwhile over the area.
810	815	((Calling)).
815	Tribune	We request that you make another pass and check once more if this is really an American flag.
(Tribune)	(815)	Roger.

((Tr Note: Do not hear from 815 until 1327Z.))

—	(Tribune)	Five by.
(815)	(Tribune)	Roger, this is clear, what kind of flag is it?
(815)	(Tribune)	Roger, this is clear.
(815)	(Tribune)	Five by, remain meanwhile in waiting, and we'll report to you immediately.
(815)	(Tribune)	Is this clear?
(815)	(Tribune)	Take 810, and return home.

(815)	(Tribune)	((Course)) 065, distance of 65 miles.
(815)	(Tribune)	Roger, this is clear.
(815)	(Tribune)	Roger, I received, I will notify you immediately as to what to do.
(815)	(Tribune)	Roger.

1316Z

—	(Tribune)	Pay attention.
815	Tribune	Roger, this is clear. According to the instruction, whoever has the most fuel.

1317Z

(815)	(Tribune)	Roger, I'm checking on it.
815	Tribune	Pay attention: whoever has the most fuel between you will return home, the one with the least will go to El Arish.
815	Tribune	Not at the present time. Apparently the one who is going to El Arish will return later.
(815)	(Tribune)	Which one of you is going home?
(815)	(Tribune)	Who is going home?
(815)	(Tribune)	OK.

[time illegible]

815	Tribune	Roger, this is known. I received the notice and it's known that these orders came from above.

1321Z

—	—	Go over to 170 on the way home.
810	Tribune	He says over to 170 on the way home.
(Tribune)	(810)	Roger.

1327Z

Jewel	815	((Calls)) ((Rpts)).

((Tr Note: 815 calls Jewel until 1328Z.))

((End of radio telephone conversation.))

Comment: This activity had been reported in a condensed version by USA–556 in its 2/J15.[*less than 1 line of source text not declassified*]/R23–67, 082015Z, and follow-ups.

---

320.   **Editorial Note**

President Johnson and Soviet Premier Kosygin met June 23 and 25, 1967, in Glassboro, New Jersey. The situation in the Middle East was a major subject of discussion. During their meeting from 11:15 a.m. to 1:30 p.m. on June 23, Kosygin urged Israeli withdrawal to the prewar armistice lines. According to a memorandum of conversation prepared by interpreter William D. Krimer, Kosygin said that if this were not done, "hostilities were certain to break out again; the Arabs were an explosive people and no other solution to this problem was possible." He told Johnson that UAR Deputy Prime Minister Fawzi had told Secretary Rusk the previous day that if the International Court of Justice were to decide that the Gulf of Aqaba should remain open, the United Arab Republic would abide by that decision. Kosygin said that he thought this communication offered hope for a solution to the Middle East problem. He reiterated that if the problem were not solved, "they would be sure to resume the fight sooner or later. If they had weapons, they would use them. If they did not have them, they would fight with their bare hands or buy weapons and surely someone would be found to sell them these weapons." Johnson said he hoped they could prevail on both sides to agree first that they would talk to each other. He stated that the problem of security had to be dealt with as well as troop withdrawal. He said that if the United States and Soviet Union refrained from furnishing arms to Middle East countries, at most they could fight with their hands, and he expressed the hope that another armed conflict could be avoided. (Johnson Library, National Security File, Country File, Addendum, USSR, Glassboro Memoranda of Conversation) In describing the conversation later, Johnson said after Kosygin's comments about fighting "with their bare hands, if necessary," that he "leaned forward and said very slowly and quietly, let us understand one another. I hope there will be no war. If there is a war, I hope it will not be a big war. If they fight, I hope they fight with fists and not with guns. I hope you and we will keep out of this matter because, if we do get into it, it will be a 'most serious' matter." (Record of debriefing by the President; ibid., Files of Walt W. Rostow, Hollybush) For records of all meetings between Johnson and Kosygin at Glassboro, as well as related material, see *Foreign Relations*, 1964–1968, volume XIV, Documents 217 ff. A position paper and talking points on the Middle East, prepared in the Department of State, are in the Johnson Library, National Security File, Country File, USSR, Hollybush, 6/67 (I), President's Meeting with Chairman Kosygin.

No record of the meeting between Rusk and Fawzi to which Kosygin referred has been found, but see Document 321.

---

321.   Memorandum of Conversation[1]

Glassboro, New Jersey, June 23, 1967.

SUBJECT

Middle East

PARTICIPANTS

Secretary Dean Rusk
Foreign Minister Gromyko

Secretary Rusk opened by reporting that Foreign Minister Fawzi (UAR) had spoken at some length to him the previous evening about the desirability of limiting arms shipments to the Middle East. The Secretary emphasized this was a private conversation and he might not be speaking for his government. Nevertheless, it was interesting. He went on to point out that arms shipments become circular and cumulative. Arms competition exists in the area not only between Israel and Arab states but as between various Arab states.

Gromyko said that the UK had also raised this question.

Secretary Rusk pointed out he had raised the question of smaller arms race at the opening of Geneva conference. He asked if there is some way we can act? He asked Gromyko if he had any sense of what

---

[1] Source: National Archives and Records Administration, RG 59, Central Files 1967–69, POL 7 US. Secret; Exdis. Drafted by Walt Rostow and approved on July 5. Secretary Rusk and Foreign Minister Gromyko were in Glassboro with President Johnson and Soviet Premier Kosygin for their summit meeting, held at "Hollybush," the residence of the president of Glassboro State College. This meeting was held while Johnson and Kosygin had the meeting described in Document 320.

de Gaulle's attitude towards an agreement to limit the arms flow to the Middle East might be? Gromyko said he didn't know.

Secretary Rusk said that Fawzi had underlined that the other needs of the region were so great that it was wrong to divert resources to military purposes.

Gromyko said the arms issue should not be tied to other matters, and he added a disparaging remark about those interested in the use of military force. He went on to say we should give the matter further thought. We know the UK position, we don't know the French position. He recalled Anthony Eden raised the question in 1956, concluding however, that the arms limitation should not be tied as a string to other Middle Eastern issues.

Secretary Rusk said we could be flexible in the matter of procedures.

Gromyko then asked: When the Secretary talked of the Middle East, did he refer merely to Israel and the Arab states or did he include other countries of the region?

Secretary Rusk replied that the problem lay between Israel and the Arab states on the one hand, and as between certain Arab nations on the other. He said we both agree on the necessity of keeping nuclear weapons out of the whole area, to which Gromyko assented with a nod.

Gromyko said that until the Middle Eastern issues before the General Assembly are solved, none of the other area problems can be handled. He said he didn't know what would happen.

Secretary Rusk said some countries of the area believe regional ideas might take some of the heat out of Arab-Israeli confrontation. Fawzi had mentioned, for example, regional work in economic and social development.

Gromyko then probed further Secretary Rusk's conversation with Fawzi.

Secretary Rusk said it was very limited. They talked about the Strait of Tiran; and Fawzi thought, perhaps an answer could be found on an informal basis. It would be hard to settle it on a formal basis.

Gromyko said the distinction was artificial. It was the substance that matters.

Secretary Rusk said they also talked about arms limitation. Beyond these two matters, he was frankly discouraged by Fawzi's attitude.

Gromyko asked if Fawzi was specifically speaking for his government.

Secretary Rusk responded negatively; they had spoken on a personal basis, since there are no relations between the UAR and the US. He could not say that Fawzi's view on arms flows to the Middle East was Nasser's view. But Fawzi is an experienced and careful diplomat.

He doubted that his views were wholly personal; but he just doesn't know exactly how official his statements were.

Gromyko asked: What other points were raised?

Secretary Rusk said the principal difficulty was that the UAR couldn't move to resolve any issues if it appeared that their resolution was related to military action or issues were settled because of military action. Frankly, he got the impression that making peace would not be easy. Going back to armistice lines was no solution. An armistice is inherently temporary. The Arabs claimed the rights of belligerence; that is, a state of war with Israel. That also meant Israel could take the view a state of war existed. The task was to eliminate belligerence and establish permanent frontiers. The Israeli remember that Nasser closed the Strait of Tiran by exercising his rights of belligerence: that is, a state of war with Israel.

Gromyko said the question of degree is very important here. When territory is occupied the situation is very different. If we tried to deal with this question on the basis of everything or nothing, it would be difficult or impossible to solve, so far as he could judge.

Secretary Rusk said that the Chairman's statement before the UN had emphasized that the Soviet Union regards Israel as a state. The question is: how do those who accept that view demonstrate that it is the case?

Gromyko said that the US and the USSR stand responsible for the creation of Israel as a state. Without the US and the USSR it would not have been created. He seemed to remember it had been created in the UN by only one vote. It would not have been possible unless the Soviet Union and the US had agreed. The Soviet Union had established diplomatic relations with Israel, which is the highest form of recognition. Those relations had been broken in 1956 and again in 1967 when there was a second round of aggression; but he stood by the Chairman's statement.

Secretary Rusk said: How can we establish that with sufficient clarity so that the Middle Eastern states will not constantly whip up propaganda urging the extinction of Israel?

Gromyko said you can't stop propaganda. We can't settle that. Let us be practical. Let us start with the Strait of Tiran, as Fawzi indicated.

Secretary Rusk said he could get no answer from Fawzi on Suez. On the Strait of Tiran, Fawzi would like the US and the Soviet Union to go to Israel and say the Strait of Tiran was open de facto. But the credibility of US in Israel is low on that point. That is what we told Israel 10 years ago.

Gromyko urged avoiding artificial problems.

Secretary Rusk asked if the Security Council might not assume responsibility on this question.

Gromyko said that Tiran is not simply a case of territorial waters. It is a complex case. Such cases have been dealt with through international conventions.

Secretary Rusk asked if Gromyko had seen Fawzi before or after he had seen him (between 7:30 and 9:00 p.m., June 22). Gromyko said: Before.

Secretary Rusk said Fawzi was cautious generally with him except on the question of Tiran and the arms flow to the Middle East.

Gromyko said: But he gave the answer. It would be very good to create a situation with withdrawal. Without withdrawal the situation was very dangerous.

Secretary Rusk asked if withdrawal comes about and a state of war persists, what would happen to Israel's relations with Syria and the UAR in the future?

Gromyko pointed out that Japan and the Soviet Union had ended the war and then taken 10 years to sign a peace treaty.

Secretary Rusk asked how was this done.

Gromyko said Prime Minister Hatayama had made a declaration that a state of war had ended.

Secretary Rusk said that perhaps it could be done through similar but unilateral if not joint, declarations.

Gromyko said that we should not be unrealistic. We should look for factual situations. Try to create an absence of tension by withdrawal. This was very important. Although you may not like the word, we would say that the situation should be approached dialectically.

Secretary Rusk said that some of the Latin Americans fancy themselves as lawyers. They take the view that if the UAR considers itself in a state of war with Israel, Israel cannot commit aggression against the UAR.

Gromyko said that the situation is dangerous to everyone in the Middle East, including Israel. They appear to show no concern for the future.

Secretary Rusk said that a concern for the future is precisely the issue with respect to belligerence.

Gromyko said the Arabs want peace.

Secretary Rusk said we must find a way to register that as a fact.

Gromyko said Israel is behaving as if it is more powerful than the US and Soviet Union put together.

Secretary Rusk said he thought there were forces of moderation in Israel as well.

Gromyko said the answer lay in withdrawal.

Secretary Rusk said the question was: withdrawal to state of peace or withdrawal to state of war? The issue was one of the status of relations among the states of the area rather than territory.

Gromyko said the shooting itself has stopped. Military action has stopped. But occupation is a continuation of war. It is still an application of force. This must be eliminated first. He said: you overlook—and please don't overlook—that withdrawal will create an atmosphere more favorable for consideration of other matters. Taking the view that everything must be settled or nothing, is unrealistic and dangerous.

Secretary Rusk said there will be great difficulties so long as Israel believes the Arabs feel free to pursue a policy of destroying Israel.

Gromyko said that thinking and doing are different. Some Arabs want to live in peace. It would be good if there were no propaganda; but, at the same time, if there are no attacks, the atmosphere for solution of other problems will improve. You can't solve all problems at once. Take, for example, nuclear question. We couldn't solve it all at once, so we stopped atmospheric texts. We proceeded realistically. Then we went forward to non-proliferation which, again, is only a partial step. If we are successful, who knows, perhaps we will take a further step. We haven't exhausted all the possibilities. In many fields of international life, including Middle East, we must make progress by being realistic. We must not be controlled by moods. We must rise above our sympathies.

Secretary Rusk said we have mentioned questions such as refugees, arms flows to the Middle East, regional and economic and social development. Of course they cannot all be determined at once. But no partial measure will work if one side wants to leave open the possibility of shooting.

Gromyko said what matters most is that there is no shooting.

Secretary Rusk referred again to Nasser's posture on Tiran.

Gromyko said: Let us look not to the past but to the future. Think it over. It would be good if we could get withdrawal. Israel itself would gain. You and we must accomplish this.

Secretary Rusk said we will be in touch.

322.   Memorandum of Conversation[1]

Washington, June 23, 1967, noon.

SUBJECT

Middle East Crisis

PARTICIPANTS

Eugene V. Rostow, Under Secretary for Political Affairs
J. Harold Shullaw, Country Director for BMI
Robert T. Grey, Staff Assistant, M

Sir Patrick Dean, British Ambassador
Alan B. Urwick, First Secretary, British Embassy

The Under Secretary said that he had a feeling the best chance for a Middle East settlement is in the next few weeks. This is a case where time isn't necessarily working in favor of a settlement.

The Under Secretary said that there are several recent developments which we find encouraging. The Turkish Foreign Minister told Secretary Rusk in New York that he had been approached by a number of Arabs who displayed a conciliatory mood and a willingness to move in a positive direction. Also encouraging is the moderate position being taken by Israel. The Israeli objective is peace and their territorial claims are minimal, much less than we would have anticipated. For example, they are interested in demilitarization along the Syrian border rather than occupation. The Under Secretary said that we have also had various reports that the Palestinian Arabs are willing to consider living with the Jews on the basis of an autonomous status within Israel. If the Palestinians and King Hussein can work out a solution on their own it would convert the refugee problem into an economic development matter. This would also make the problem of Jerusalem easier.

Mr. Urwick said that the UK Government has received similar reports on current attitudes among the Palestinian Arabs. He indicated some doubt whether King Hussein could afford to get out in front on this question. The Under Secretary referred to King Hussein's forthcoming visit to the US and said that the President would see him if the timing could be worked out.

The Under Secretary said that we do not know what the real status of Nasser is at the present time, whether he is in or out. Certainly Soviet efforts are being strongly directed toward saving him. We have an inter-

---

[1]   Source: National Archives and Records Administration, RG 59, Central Files 1967–69, POL 27 ARAB–ISR. Secret. The memorandum is part 1 of 4. Drafted by Shullaw and approved in M June 28. The meeting was held in Rostow's office.

esting report that the UAR is buying for cash $10 million of wheat in the US. The Under Secretary added that we are interposing no obstacles to the transaction.

In reply to the Under Secretary's question the Ambassador said Kosygin had taken a very tough line in his talk yesterday in New York with Foreign Secretary Brown. In effect, Kosygin had demanded an Israeli withdrawal from Arab territory before there could be a discussion of anything else. Sir Patrick said that his Embassy was supplying the Department with a copy of the Foreign Secretary's report on the conversation with Kosygin (copy attached).[2]

The Ambassador expressed the opinion that it should be possible for the US and the UK to get together on a suitable resolution in the GA. Sir Patrick said that an effort should be made with the African states to encourage them to adopt a more constructive attitude, particularly in view of the possible effect on French speaking African states of General de Gaulle's denunciation of Israel.

---

[2] Attached but not printed.

---

323.   Editorial Note

During the June 25, 1967, meetings at Glassboro between President Johnson and Premier Kosygin, they discussed the Middle East briefly at a luncheon and more extensively in a private meeting that afternoon. During their luncheon conversation, Kosygin repeated his position that there could be no peaceful settlement in the Middle East unless Israeli forces were withdrawn from captured Arab territory. Johnson asked Kosygin whether he did not agree with the proposals he had made in his June 19 speech concerning the recognition of Israel's right to exist, the right of free passage through international waterways like the Strait of Tiran and the Suez Canal, and the need to do something for the refugees of this and previous wars. Kosygin said that in his view, after troop withdrawal to the original armistice lines, all other questions could be resolved. Johnson repeated that it was not enough to say "remove the troops"; the Israelis had not followed U.S. advice to refrain from taking military action, and without some arrangements to assure Israel's security, they would not follow U.S. advice to withdraw their troops. He noted that there were alarming reports of new arms shipments to the Arab countries since the cease-fire. So far the United States had refused requests to supply new weapons. The solution of the Middle East had to be found in something that would be acceptable to both sides. (Memorandum of conversation, June 25, 1:30–2:45 p.m.; Johnson Library, National Security File, Country File, Addendum, USSR, Glassboro Memoranda of Conversation)

The discussion in their private meeting after lunch followed along the same lines, with Kosygin arguing that Israeli withdrawal had to precede any other steps toward a settlement and Johnson maintaining that it was not realistic to expect withdrawal without dealing with other problems. Johnson took the position that the Security Council would be better able to deal with the many problems involved, while Kosygin urged a General Assembly resolution on withdrawal, to be followed by Security Council consideration of other questions. (Memorandum of conversation, June 25, 1:30–6:30 p.m.; ibid.) For the complete records of the meetings, see Foreign Relations, 1964–1968, volume XIV, Documents 217 ff.

---

324.   Memorandum From the President's Special Assistant (Rostow) to President Johnson[1]

Washington, June 26, 1967, 2:45 p.m.

Mr. President:

Here is the report proposed for public release of the Navy Court of Inquiry on the USS Liberty.[2]

It has been cleared by Sect. McNamara, Deputy Sect. Vance and Under Sect. Katzenbach.

---

[1] Source: Johnson Library, National Security File, Country File, Middle East, Middle East Crisis, Vol. VII. Secret. A handwritten notation on the memorandum indicates it was received at 3:30 p.m.

[2] A copy of the "Summary of Proceedings" of the U.S. Navy Court of Inquiry, released by the Office of the Secretary of Defense on June 28, is attached. A copy is also in the Washington National Records Center, RG 330, OSD Files: FRC 72 A 2468, Middle East 385.3. The Court of Inquiry, convened by Admiral John S. McCain, Jr., USN, Commander in Chief of U.S. Naval Forces in Europe, conducted classified hearings in London and aboard the Liberty in Malta June 11–17. Rear Admiral I.C. Kidd, USN, who was attached to McCain's headquarters, was president of the court. The Proceedings of the U.S. Navy Court of Inquiry, with covering letters of June 18 from Kidd and McCain are in the Naval Historical Center, Operational Archives Branch, Immediate Office Files of the Chief of Naval Operations, 1969 Files. Box 110, Liberty Incident, 8 June 1967, Court of Inquiry.

Cy proposes to release it at 4 p.m. on Wednesday.[3]

They have considered whether to make it available to the Israelis beforehand. The Israelis have asked for 24 hours lead time. Cy is inclined to feel that 12 hours would be sufficient; but he does recommend that we make it available beforehand since:

—the judgment—not flatly stated in the Report—is that the attack was an accident; and
—they made available to us the report of their court of inquiry.

You will note (page 15) that the report refers to a failure in our communications which delayed a JCS message to move the *Liberty* farther away from the coast.

As stated on page 2: "It was not the responsibility of the Court to rule on the culpability of the attackers, and no evidence was heard from the attacking nation." Cy tells me that, in fact, the members of the court, on the evidence available to them, believe the attack resulted from a failure within the Israeli communications system and not from premeditation. But in his view, on the evidence we have, we should not so state.

Walt

O.K. for public release 4 p.m. Wednesday[4]

O.K. for release to Israelis 24 hours before/12 hours before[5]

See me

---

[3] June 28

[4] This option is checked.

[5] The 12-hour option is checked. A note in Rostow's handwriting states that Vance was informed on June 27 at 10:45 a.m. Katzenbach met with Harman on June 28 and gave him the report. (National Archives and Records Administration, RG 59, Central Files 1967–69, DEF 12 US)

325. Memorandum From the President's Special Consultant (Bundy) to President Johnson[1]

Washington, June 26, 1967.

SUBJECT

Bundy's Return to Ford, and Related Subjects

1. It's time for me to raise this question and give you a recommendation on it, because I think the worst of the immediate crisis is behind us, and also because I'll be meeting my Board of Trustees this Wednesday evening and they'll need to know when and how much to expect me back. (They have been very good about these three weeks, but they're beginning to get nervous.)

2. As I see it, there has been a real need for an extra pair of White House hands these last few weeks, but I think the need for such full-time service will come to an end in another week or two. Already the pressure of special Middle East business is falling back from the level of late May and early June, and already—and properly—much of the day-to-day business is back in the direct channel from State to Walt Rostow, where it belongs. The crisis will continue, but not at the pace of the month since the Straits were closed.

3. There remains one major job which I think I can help to do—and that is to prepare a general policy paper for you and Dean to adopt or reject or modify and then give to about three people here and in State for general guidance until further notice. I suggest this because I think the old mold of Middle Eastern policy is broken forever, and I think we need new guidance. Even if you don't want to adopt a new position formally (still less publicly) I think a written paper that had some informal standing would be helpful. Anyway I think it's part of my job to give you that choice, and I hope to have the paper for you by the middle of next week.

4. Beyond that I am quite willing to be a part-time visitor over the next months if you and Dean want me, and I can always keep track of the cables by calling on Arthur in New York. But before you agree to that, you'll want to know how to arrange the work after I leave.

5. Aside from the usual things a staff man does in a crisis, I think any special usefulness I may have had in the last weeks derives from two special aspects of the situation, and I think you will want me to speak frankly about them, because when I go back to New York—or to

---

[1] Source: Johnson Library, National Security File, Office of the President File, McGeorge Bundy. No classification marking.

a part-time basis—I think you'll want arrangements of some sort to deal with them.

(1) Our Middle East policy almost always requires a special balancing weight against the normal bias of Arab-minded State Department regulars. Presidents usually put a value on the rights and hopes of Israel which is greater than the normal reactions of the State machinery. This is not centrally a matter of the Abe Feinbergs or even the Arthur Krims. It is a matter of the considered choice of Presidents, on wider grounds of national sympathy and interest. Unfortunately the Department has learned to mistrust this White House attitude (for reasons that go back to Truman's recognition of Israel and have had occasional justification in the work of heavy-handed agents of the Jewish community like Mike Feldman) so that they often weight their advice to emphasize the considerations against any pro-Israel course. That makes a White House counter still more necessary. This is a job which Walt is too kind and busy a man to handle, and yet it is hard for any junior officer over here to deal with it, because Dean Rusk himself has always been mildly responsive to the standard Departmental bias. Dean's capacity to weigh other points, *when* they have some standing with the President, is excellent. Thus on your five-point speech to the Educators, he was a first-rate critic of my drafting, and eliminated much that was not wise, but he would not have been the man to turn a Departmental draft into a position that was right for you.

So one conclusion I reach is that you'll need a Middle East watcher here when I leave. I nominate McPherson, and I'll suggest ways and means further on.

(2) [*15-1/2 lines of source text restricted on privacy grounds*]

So I conclude that you need a different arrangement in the State Department. I think the right way is to give the day-to-day job back to Luke Battle, with direct accountability to Dean and Nick, *both* of whom should be fully informed and empowered to give policy advice to you. (I put Nick into it in this way because he has a more *active* policy mind than Dean, because he is a man with a full sense of the President's view, and finally because Nick is damned good at top-level Congressional work with liberals, which is critically important in this case.)

Let me say about Battle that I am really much impressed by his work on this crisis. It has been balanced and skillful at every stage I have seen. I know there has been criticism of him on the Hill, but I believe that he'll do better there with some encouragement—and anyway I think our position there is now pretty solid, thanks to what you yourself have done and said.

6. This new arrangement can be set up, if you want, by reassigning both my present responsibilities and Gene Rostow's, at the same time

(about two weeks from now)—Rostow's back to Battle, and mine to McPherson—both within the regular framework of White House and State Department business. I think you should discharge the Special Committee (though you can keep it on standby if you want). But I would empower Harry to deal with this one in the same way that Francis Bator deals with Europe, and of course you'd want him to keep the closest touch with Walt, as I have been doing, since Walt is the man who handles your in-and-out box on foreign affairs, and there should be only one. Then if you want to continue my appointment on a part-time basis as a consultant, you'd have insurance against any sudden flare-up that might lead to criticism because we had let up too soon on our special arrangements.

7. I want you to know that I have found these last weeks absolutely fascinating, and that I take it as a great honor to have been asked back for this period. If I think it is time to get back to Ford, it is not just because of my obligation there; it is also because in the long pull you'll get better results from a more regular arrangement. This one is going to go on for a long, long time.

nbassy in Israel to the Department of

Tel Aviv, June 27, 1967, 1150Z.

ιy very well be that what has happened
ˑe had considerably less effect on ultimate
tentions than what happens in coming
ˑif Israel is able to achieve durable peace
. for, and indeed any rationale for, going
l.

subject with Israelis since crisis began. In
ficials during this period they have not
ιs been no press speculation on subject.
on in winning war and coping with post-
ˑly that any basic decisions in this regard
have been taken in past several weeks.

3. Still, subject must be on minds of many responsible Israelis. Israel
has come through a harrowing experience in which its national existence was in jeopardy. It did so by dint of its own efforts, a fact of which
Israelis are proud and from which they draw lesson that they must continue to rely increasingly on themselves. If peace proves impossible and
only another nebulous state of armistice results, making another clash
possible, then prudent assumption would seem to be Arabs next time
may be better. Israelis, who have technical capability to build bomb,
would, it may be argued, be foolish not to produce extra-conventional
weapons against enemies whose total conventional military capabilities
conceivably could outstrip Israel's within another decade. If powerful
nation such as Soviet Union is rearming Arabs this could reinforce
Israeli conviction it irrational to eschew nuclear weapons production.
(In this connection we doubt Israelis give credence to stories Chinese
providing nuclear weapons to UAR. If they did they would very likely
have mentioned it to us.)

---

[1] Source: National Archives and Records Administration, RG 59, Central Files
1967–69, DEF 12 ISR. Secret; Limdis. Repeated to US Mission Geneva, and USUN.
Received at 9:03 a.m.

[2] Telegram 215923 to Tel Aviv, June 24, expressed concern that in the aftermath of
the recent hostilities, the Israeli Government might be impelled toward reassessing its
policy toward acquisition of nuclear weapons and ballistic missiles and requested the
Embassy's estimate of the impact of recent events on Israeli nuclear and missile policy.
(Ibid.)

4. We have seen in recent weeks increase of popularity of Dayan, who has been associated with those favoring the nuclear weapons development. If his star continues to rise, and that of his associates Peres and Ben-Gurion (who made the decisions to build Dimona), then, if outlook for Israeli security appears still uncertain, it would seem fair surmise that Israel might be led closer to nuclear route and development of necessary vehicles for nuclear weapons.

5. In this latter connection if French arms embargo continues and delivery of Dassault missile is precluded, quite possible effect would be to stimulate Israeli missile production.

6. All of foregoing necessarily speculative comment dwells on darker side of picture. In spite of this I do not believe that there is any compelling reason at present time for change in GOI policy of abstinence from nuclear weapons and missile production. (This is not to say Israel will not keep its nuclear technology at sufficiently high level to permit it to have option of producing nuclear weapons if changed circumstances seem make this imperative.) Financial considerations will be an inhibiting factor. For military and occupied area demands will be great for some time to come. And in spite of scare it got Israel has won great military victory that will give it time to make its decisions rationally and deliberately. Much, perhaps everything in this regard as in so much else, will depend on degree Arab readiness to come to terms.

Barbour

---

327.   Telegram From the Mission to the United Nations to the Department of State[1]

New York, June 27, 1967, 1630Z.

5935/Secto 27. Following are main points of an hour's conversation which I had with Dr. Fawzi of Egypt this morning.

1. I asked him about Cairo's attitude toward "longer run" relations between Egypt and the US. I told him that those relations had been

---

[1] Source: National Archives and Records Administration, RG 59, Central Files 1967–69, POL 27 ARAB–ISR. Secret; Exdis. Received at 12:43.

deeply injured by the false charge that US aircraft had taken part in attacks on Egypt. I asked him whether the Egyptian Government now contemplated informing other Arab governments privately that their earlier information on this matter was incorrect. I emphasized the importance of this point because it had been the basis on which a number of them had broken relations with the US even though some were relatively remote from the Israeli question itself. Fawzi was vague, said it would take time and rather indicated that relations would depend on our attitude on present issues. I emphasized that maintenance of diplomatic relations was not seen by us as conditional in character and that the structure of diplomacy exists for the discussion of disagreements and cannot be conditioned upon agreement.

2. Reverting to our earlier conversation[2] I said we had not found much interest on the part of the Soviet Union in arms limitations in the area. He said that this is probably a question of time, that he hoped something could be done about it to cut down the diversion of resources to arms away from urgent economic and social problems. He said that perhaps President DeGaulle could take this up on his initiative as an idea of his own.

3. I then referred to his earlier comment about the Strait of Tiran. Fawzi told me that in addition to the US he had discussed the opening of the Strait with the USSR, France, Britain, India and Yugoslavia. I said that opening the Strait could not be as private and secret as he had suggested at his last meeting because ships cannot move in secret and that any arrangement on the Strait would have to be public. I recalled that the original request by Egypt for a removal of a portion of UNEF did not include removal of the UN contingent from Sharm al-Sheikh. Did he anticipate that a UN force would return to Sharm al-Sheik? He said not UNEF but possibly a contingent of UNTSO whose functions would have to be enlarged to cover this point. He said UNEF was dead but that "maybe" UNTSO could do something about this. He confirmed that their original request for a removal of a portion of UNEF had not included Sharm al-Sheik.

4. Fawzi pressed hard for a simple resolution on withdrawal with UN observation of withdrawal. He made no point of condemnation or of reparations. I pressed him equally hard on the necessity for returning to peace and not to a state of war. I told him of Gromyko's remark that Japan and the Soviet Union had eliminated the state of belligerence even though they still do not have a peace treaty. He said formal action of this sort would be extremely difficult and would set the situation back because of Arab public opinion. I

---

[2] See Documents 320 and 321.

reminded him that Egypt could mold Arab public opinion and that the Arabs would probably follow an Egyptian initiative to stabilize peace in the area.

5. He then said if there were a withdrawal resolution the General Assembly could go into all of these other questions in a subsequent resolution. But when he used language on various points which might be in such a second resolution it was quite clear that they have not come very far on recognizing the existence of a state of Israel and the removal of the state of belligerence.

6. He called attention to increasing Egyptian newspaper discussion of new approaches and said that this could not have happened even a few weeks ago. What conclusion he wanted me to draw from that he did not say.

7. My impression is that the Egyptians realize that the General Assembly will insist upon doing more than calling for a withdrawal. He was trying to separate these other issues from withdrawal as such. This represents perhaps some movement but not enough. I made no commitments whatever but simply told him that I would discuss the views he expressed with Ambassador Goldberg and our delegation. At the end he told me that he was seeing Gromyko at 3:30 this afternoon prior to my meeting with Gromyko tonight.

Rusk

328.   Memorandum of Conversation[1]

New York, June 27, 1967, 7 p.m.

SUBJECT

Middle East

PARTICIPANTS

U.S.	U.S.S.R.
The Secretary	Foreign Minister Gromyko
Ambassador Goldberg	Deputy Foreign Minister Soldatov
Governor Harriman	Ambassador Dobrynin
Mr. Adrian Fisher, Deputy	Ambassador Fedorenko
Director, ACDA	Mr. Yuri Vorontsov, Counselor, Soviet
Mr. Malcolm Toon, Country	Embassy, Washington
Director, SOV	Mr. Victor Sukhodrev, Counselor,
Mr. Alexander Akalovsky,	Ministry of Foreign Affairs
First Secretary,	
Amembassy Moscow	

After lengthy discussion of the nonproliferation question, the conversation turned to the Middle East.

Ambassador Goldberg opened the conversation on the subject by stressing that the U.S. wanted to seek common ground. As things stood today, it appeared that no resolution proposed thus far would carry. He stressed that the U.S. was prepared to work hard to find common ground, noting that as in the Security Council common ground in the General Assembly usually emerged once the U.S. and the USSR had found it.

The Secretary suggested that it might be more profitable now to discuss the substance of peace in the Middle East. He thought that a few very short statements could describe that substance. Both the U.S. and USSR agree that it is in their interest to have peace in the Middle East and not to be drawn into an adversary role or hostile posture vis-à-vis each other. Both the U.S. and USSR also agree that Israel has the right to exist. The U.S. and USSR agree that no state of war should exist between Israel and its neighbors. They agree that the refugee problem must be solved. They agree that priority should be given to economic and social development in the area rather than to projects which could be conducive to war. Both the USSR and the U.S. agree that their influence in the area is not unlimited and that they are faced with a very compli-

---

[1] Source: National Archives and Records Administration, RG 59, Central Files 1967–69, POL 27 ARAB–ISR. Secret; Exdis. Drafted by Akalovsky and approved in S/S on June 29. The memorandum is part II of II. The meeting took place at the Soviet Mission to the United Nations in New York.

cated situation. Finally, they agree that there should be freedom of maritime passage to international waters. The Secretary wondered if these statements, to which Mr. Gromyko did not object, might not constitute a basis for peace.

Mr. Gromyko commented that the Secretary had avoided the main question, namely withdrawal of Israeli troops and liberation of occupied Arab territories. Whatever one's motivations, the problem could not be resolved without withdrawal. No one could of course dispute the desirability of peace but what kind of peace could there be if territories remained occupied. In talking about settlement or peace, the Secretary surely realized that a peace treaty would be impossible under present circumstances. As to the question of arms deliveries, this matter was up to the countries concerned to decide at the proper time. In any event, it hadn't been arms but rather Israeli policy that had started the war. Noting that the Secretary had referred with interest to his conversation with UAR Foreign Minister Fawzi,[2] Gromyko said that the question of Aqaba and the Straits of Tiran—which had been raised by the Secretary in more general terms now—should be considered in the light of that conversation. One should not underestimate Fawzi's remarks, and he believed that there was a basis for accommodation here. Mr. Gromyko then criticized Ambassador Goldberg for being overly pessimistic about the situation in the General Assembly. One must not look at things this way and must make every effort to reach an understanding, something the USSR certainly wants. For some reason withdrawal does not suit the U.S. and the USSR and others cannot understand why. If the U.S. were more objective, it would agree that the main problem is withdrawal and that without withdrawal neither the U.S. nor the USSR can be certain about what tomorrow will bring; in fact it could bring precisely what the U.S. and USSR wish to avoid.

The Secretary pointed out that the suggested formulations for withdrawal called for withdrawal to the armistice line rather than to national territory; in other words, withdrawal would continue the state of suspended war. It would be an improvement if one talked about withdrawal to national territory. In this connection, in talking about armistice lines the Arabs put aside the point that Israel was to have access to Suez, and they evidently do not have that in mind when they talk about armistice. The U.S. believed that it was very important that the third struggle in the area be the last one. While there may be contentions or claims, there must be no state of belligerency. It was impossible to ask Israel to act as if there were peace when Egypt exercised the

---

[2] See Document 327.

rights of belligerency. The Secretary said he often heard that withdrawal was a precondition—precondition to what?

Mr. Gromyko said it was precondition to peace; in fact, withdrawal in itself was peace.

Ambassador Goldberg said that peace could perhaps be built on the following formula: prompt disengagement, withdrawal, and termination of belligerency. One could not have withdrawal in the middle of a war; this had been tried before but had not worked. In the past there had been withdrawals and war started again. He wondered if Mr. Gromyko disagreed with this formula.

Mr. Gromyko said that the very fact of the presence of Israeli forces in Arab territory constituted aggression. Even if the guns were silent, war persisted. So from that standpoint Ambassador Goldberg was close to the truth. On the other hand, his statement contained a contradiction inasmuch as he spoke of peace while opposing withdrawal. This contradiction should be eliminated. The U.S. seems to avoid the conclusion that withdrawal, together with what could be done with respect to Aqaba and the Straits of Tiran, would change the atmosphere in the area and create better conditions for solution of other problems. Any solution of those problems was impossible in the present situation. Moreover, the present situation was fraught with dangers for tomorrow.

Ambassador Goldberg commented that his formula took care of Aqaba since it called for termination of belligerency, which had been the basis for UAR action on Aqaba. Mr. Gromyko said that others might have a different interpretation.

Mr. Gromyko continued that progress seemed to be hindered by an accumulation of suspicions, sympathies, and antipathies. Perhaps Ambassador Goldberg's pessimistic assessment was the result of this situation. What the U.S. and USSR should do was to consider the problem from the standpoint of their vital interests and rise above all suspicions and other emotional aspects of the situation. Neither the U.S. nor the USSR wants hostilities between Israel and the Arabs, and no one could dispute that the chances for peace would improve if there were withdrawal. It would be dangerous to approach the situation with pessimism and resignation. One should not underestimate the possibilities for common understanding, which could be achieved if we wanted peace; the Soviet Union definitely wants peace and wants to work for it.

Ambassador Goldberg wondered why Mr. Gromyko disliked his formula. He noted that he had derived it from Mr. Kosygin's statement that all nations must have the right to live; nations could not live except in peace, and this was the common ground between us. He pointed out that in expressing his pessimism about the present situation in the UN he did not mean that the U.S. and USSR should not seek common ground. On the contrary, he was eager to seek such ground.

Mr. Gromyko said that as far as Israel's right to existence was concerned, Mr. Kosygin's statement was sufficiently clear and he did not believe that even the Israelis had any doubts on this score. As to Israeli/Arab relations, the best way towards a settlement would be withdrawal and then everything else would fall into place.

Noting that he was in no position to speak for Israel and that he did not expect Mr. Gromyko to speak for the Syrians, the Secretary wondered if Syria would refrain from resuming the artillery positions and from shelling the low land on the Israeli side if Israel were to withdraw from the hills it now occupies. The Secretary noted in this connection that as far as he knew there was no serious territorial problem between Israel and Syria and that the main problem was the fact that the Syrians had been shelling Israeli territory.

Mr. Gromyko said he also did not know of any territorial claims; moreover, the Soviet Union knew that the Syrians had no aggressive intentions. Perhaps some leaders in Israel did not like the fact that the hills in question were higher than their own heads, but that was their problem. As to the specific question posed by the Secretary, he was not in a position to speak for the Syrians and the question should be asked of them directly.

When the Secretary pointed out that this was not merely a question of risk but rather of experience on the part of the Israelis, Mr. Gromyko said that it was not the hills that were at fault but rather those who had started the war. He reiterated, however, that the question should be addressed to the Syrians directly.

Pointing out that he was not raising the question of responsibility or blame, the Secretary said that in his view the closing of the Straits of Tiran was a unique act of war. Nasser had based this action on the state of belligerency; his action was therefore a belligerent act.

Mr. Gromyko said the question now was how to approach a peaceful settlement. In his view, withdrawal was the best approach and it was hard to conceive what else could be done. In advocating this approach the USSR did not proceed from any selfish interests—all it wanted was restoration and maintenance of peace. While it was true that many Soviet ships had been using Suez and now had to take the more expensive route around the Cape, the USSR was not the only one in such a position. He wanted to reiterate that all the USSR was interested in was peace and to express the view that if the U.S. shared this objective peace could be ensured.

The Secretary expressed the hope that both sides would continue working during the next several days in order to find common ground.

He also hoped that the Soviet side would not discourage flexibility on the part of the Arabs; he counseled Mr. Gromyko not to be more Arab than the Arabs themselves.

Mr. Gromyko said the Secretary had no reason to be concerned in this respect. On his part, he hoped that the U.S. would be flexible and would not raise rigid conditions which would create obstacles in the way toward agreement.

The meeting ended at 10:15 p.m.

---

329.   Memorandum From Acting Secretary of State Katzenbach to President Johnson[1]

Washington, June 27, 1967.

SUBJECT

Suggested Talking Points for Meeting with King Hussein[2]

We attach suggested talking points[3] for your visit with King Hussein, now scheduled for Wednesday. After Bill Macomber's[4] talk with the King, we recommend that you see him alone, at least for a brief period. It will be easier for the King to talk about reality without any witnesses but yourself, and especially without Arab witnesses.

---

[1] Source: Johnson Library, National Security File, Country File, Jordan, Visit of King Hussein, 6/28/67. Secret. No drafting information appears on the memorandum.

[2] Bundy and Rostow both sent memoranda to the President on June 27 with recommendations for his June 28 meeting with King Hussein. Rostow suggested telling the King that Johnson could not get the Israelis out of the West Bank unless Hussein was prepared to take serious steps in return, that Hussein should not rely on anyone else to solve this problem for him but that if he was willing to seek a solution, others could help as intermediaries, with economic resources, and with persuasion of the other party. (Ibid.) Bundy seconded Rostow's recommendations, commenting, "our main purpose must be to let him down as gently as we can from his present conviction that you must pull his chestnuts out of the fire for him." He advised the President to "stay within the State talking points and not press the King toward bargaining with the Israelis (along the lines of the State covering memo)—unless he gives you an opening." (Ibid., Country File, Jordan, Visit of King Hussein, 6/28/67)

[3] Attached but not printed.

[4] Assistant Secretary of State for Congressional Relations and former Ambassador to Jordan William B. Macomber, Jr.

The talks with King Hussein could be crucial to the process of achieving a peaceful settlement in the Middle East. The King is approaching a fork in the road. It should not be impossible for him to choose the right course. If he does so, that fact would be a real beginning, breaking up the hitherto rigid Arab line against peace. If he is convinced that such a peaceful solution is impossible, the tide could run in the wrong direction from our point of view.

The Soviets are already consolidating Nasser in Egypt. Nasser is in touch with us, but we doubt that he will have an acceptable deal to offer. Therefore the Jordanian problem remains the most hopeful opening for us.

There is a difference of view between those who counsel moving ahead with Jordan now, and those who advise waiting for the dust to settle. We recommend taking advantage of the King's presence to open the possibility of prompt action on his part with Israel, directly or through an intermediary—perhaps the Shah, perhaps an American. Our stake in the possible success of these negotiations, difficult as they will be, makes it advisable to consider an American intermediary if the King requests one. A delay, which the Israelis favor, could result in freezing the situation on the West Bank into a pattern of Israeli control which it would be nearly impossible to change later.

The problems between Israel and Jordan—the West Bank and Jerusalem—are more difficult than any of the other issues between Israel and her neighbors, except for the overriding and fundamental problem of obtaining Arab recognition for Israel's right to exist. But there are also greater opportunities, because a Jordan–Israel solution would hold out the hope of transforming the refugee problem, and that of Jerusalem, which are at the heart of the conflict.

Our talks with Israeli representatives in New York and here persuade us that the Israelis are willing to make a pretty favorable deal with King Hussein, provided he accepts the idea of peace. You should not, we think, sponsor or propose any particular bargain, or be drawn into the details of any possible plan. But we do recommend that you be prepared to advise and encourage King Hussein to explore the possibility of negotiations with the Israelis, directly or through an intermediary. (You should know that the King has negotiated secretly with the Israelis in the past, e.g., meeting Eban on the Riviera. This information is of the greatest sensitivity.)

The basic territorial problem dividing Israel and Jordan is the West Bank area. The West Bank was part of the Palestine Mandate given up by the British in 1947. It came under Jordanian control as a result of the hostilities in 1948, and the subsequent declaration of Palestinian notables of their wish to adhere to Trans-Jordan. We have never recognized

Jordanian sovereignty over the West Bank; instead we have recognized the area as being under Jordanian control pursuant to the General Armistice Agreement. We have taken an even more reserved position about Jordanian control in the Old City of Jerusalem and about the whole position in Jerusalem. Our Ambassador to Jordan, for example, does not show the flag while driving in the Old City. A memorandum on the history and legal position of the area is included as a Background Paper in your book.

The Israelis tell us they have not yet finally made up their minds on the position they will take with regard to the West Bank generally, and Jerusalem in particular. So far, we have advised them not to take unilateral actions, nor to present the world with a fait accompli.

The Israelis point out that they have a national security interest in keeping the West Bank out of unfriendly or aggressive hands; that they tried to prevent King Hussein from entering the war and sought a cease fire even after he had taken offensive action; and that their occupation of the West Bank was unanticipated and is unwanted. They were particularly aggrieved by his attack in Jerusalem, where they took heavy casualties because they refrained from the use of air power. On the other hand, they say, these events occurred, a new situation has emerged, and they are still not clear what policy King Hussein represents today. They stress that the City of Jerusalem cannot be divided again, and that the Holy Places must be accessible to all.

There is a good deal of talk in Israel and among Palestinian Arabs about the possibility of an autonomous Arab State on the West Bank, federated with Israel, and of comparable status for the Gaza Strip. Both Dayan and Ben Gurion have suggested such an approach. Some Palestinians are reported to be interested in the possibility. There are rumors of possible meetings of Arab notables. There is always a possibility that such meetings could be stage-managed by the Israelis to come up with a statement or even a declaration calling for a separation of the West Bank from Jordan. Such a procedure would follow that of Jordan in annexing the West Bank in the first place.

There would be political danger if Israel tried to set up a semi-autonomous Arab State on the West Bank by unilateral action. Such a step would make general Arab-Israeli peace more difficult to imagine, and would create a new Arab grievance.

We do not see any possibility that King Hussein could negotiate with Israel, and then accept a state of peace with Israel, unless he retained political control over the West Bank area, subject at most to minor boundary rectifications, and an international solution for Jerusalem.

But it is possible that over time an economic link could develop between Israel and *Jordan as a whole*. This would leave the two states of Israel and Jordan politically independent but with open cooperative economic relationships. A development of this kind should make it easier to solve the issue of Jerusalem, which could become a focus of economic exchange, rather than a salient on a nervous frontier. It could transform the refugee problem into a problem of regional economic development. And by providing an economic opportunity for the refugees, it would begin to relieve the other Middle Eastern states of the burden of the idea that somehow, some day, Arab loyalty requires them to help liberate Palestine and restore the refugees to their rightful property.

We therefore conclude that at this stage the optimum plan should include these elements: (1) economic links between Israel and *the whole* of Jordan, (2) the West Bank under the sovereignty of Jordan, subject, however, (3) to boundary adjustments and (4) a special agreement about Jerusalem, and (5) an end to the state of war, demilitarization of the West Bank, and normal relations. We gather from a conversation between Evron and Walt Rostow[5] that Israel is thinking along similar lines.

We should have no illusion: the odds are against Hussein accepting this sort of package at an early date. But it is worthwhile encouraging him to explore the possibilities.

The Israelis would probably accept some such approach in the near future. They might even accept a less ambitious solution that left the West Bank in Jordanian hands, except for an agreement on Jerusalem.

If the present situation continues very long, however, King Hussein should understand that his risks with regard to the West Bank probably increase. At the moment, he could probably get political control of most of the West Bank, in exchange for a favorable long-term economic arrangement, and a new status, perhaps condominium, in Jerusalem. Later on, such a deal might well become more difficult.

Nicholas deB Katzenbach

---

[5] Evron stated in a June 24 conversation with Rostow that there was increasing thought in Israel about an economic link to Jordan that would leave the two states politically independent but with open cooperative economic relationships. Rostow reported the conversation to the President in CAP 67579, June 24. (Johnson Library, National Security File, Memos to the President, Walt Rostow, Vol. 32)

330.   **Memorandum From the President's Special Consultant (Bundy) to President Johnson**[1]

Washington, June 27, 1967.

SUBJECT

Military Aid Policy in the Middle East

After fighting broke out, we stopped all aid shipments to countries that broke relations with us. For those that did not break, we let the pipeline flow beyond the depot but blocked new approvals. Now in order to get back into business with the moderates, State and Defense recommend a number of selective exceptions to that "no-new-approvals" policy.

The attached paper[2] describes the specific shipments they would like to turn loose. They include no heavy combat equipment and no lethal items, except for a few important for defense or internal security. In cost, they add up to about $170 million from past programs, but would involve no financing not already authorized or contemplated before the fighting.

That sounds like a lot, but $145 million is for two sales programs in Saudi Arabia for improving mobility (vehicles, no tanks or arms, training, construction of maintenance facilities), weapons maintenance and repair and for purchase of one C–130. The next largest is the sale to Israel of $16 million in spare parts for tanks and defensive Hawk missiles. The rest are dribs and drabs of spares and support equipment to Morocco, Libya, Lebanon and Jordan (see page 2 bottom).[3]

The one new program to be negotiated would be the $14 million in credit you approved for Morocco's King Hassan in February. Though this might include APC's and transport aircraft, the lead time on those items ranges from 18 to 36 months.

The most controversial item on the list is the sale of 100 APC's to Israel, but you've been over that many times.

In Libya, we are still hoping to spin out our talks on Wheelus and would go ahead with one C–47 aircraft and a variety of spares, commo and automotive equipment. We would hold the 10 F–5 aircraft we've agreed to sell until we see how the base talks go. Bob McNamara won-

---

[1] Source: Johnson Library, National Security File, Country File, Jordan, Visit of King Hussein, 6/28/67. Secret. Sent through Walt Rostow.

[2] Attached but not printed.

[3] Reference is to the paragraph added after the options at the end of the memorandum.

ders whether we might leave our domestic flank open to go ahead with anything when the Libyans have just asked us to leave Wheelus, but he does not feel strongly. Nick Katzenbach thinks going ahead would improve our negotiating position.

McNamara also wants to flag the problem of domestic reaction to any relaxation of our ban now such as Senator Church's speech. I don't feel these programs are visible enough or military enough to cause a big ruckus—except for the Israeli APC's if they leak. He doesn't feel strongly about Morocco and Tunisia and recognizes that Saudi Arabia is a case by itself. My own view is that the list is pretty carefully drawn to exclude troublesome items and we have to go ahead with the Arabs if we're going to let Israel buy.

McG. B.

Approve exceptions as described

See me[4]

The *Jordan program* a million or so—not fully priced in its new form[5]—would not include any of the ammo originally programmed, any aircraft or any equipment relating to the F–104 sale[6] (first 4 planes were scheduled for delivery in September). It would include such things as automotive, commo and small arms repair parts, clothing, optical equipment and general spares.

---

[4] Neither option is checked. On June 30 Rostow sent a message to the President at the LBJ Ranch saying that it was important to have his decisions that day on three items that could be funded with FY 67 money. They were: the sale of a C–130 to Saudi Arabia, the $9.9 million weapons maintenance and repair program in Saudi Arabia, and the $14 million credit sale for Morocco. He also noted that all Israeli military aid was suspended until Johnson's decision and added: "Evron asked me about this today, but after their move on Jerusalem you may be in no hurry." A handwritten note by Jim Jones on Rostow's message indicates that Johnson approved the three fiscal year items. (Johnson Library, National Security File, NSC Special Committee Files, Arms Limits)

[5] The words following "Jordan program" to this point are handwritten.

[6] Concerning the sale of 18 F–104s to Jordan, see *Foreign Relations, 1964–1968*, vol. XVIII, Document 283.

331. Memorandum of Conversation[1]

Washington, June 28, 1967, 1:30–3:10 p.m.

SUBJECT

Prospects for solution of the Middle East Crisis

PARTICIPANTS

President Johnson	Secretary McNamara
King Hussein	Mr. Walt Rostow
Mr. Nicholas deB. Katzenbach	Mr. George Christian
Mr. McGeorge Bundy	Ambassador Macomber
Foreign Minister Tuqan	Ambassador Shubeilat
General Khammash	
Ambassador Burns	

King Hussein accompanied by Foreign Minister Tuqan and Chief of Staff Amir Khammash were invited to the White House for a working luncheon with President Johnson on June 28. During the luncheon prospects for solution of the Middle East crisis were discussed. The major participants in the discussion were King Hussein, the President, Mr. McGeorge Bundy and Mr. Nicholas deB. Katzenbach.

The King adhered to the public line he had previously expressed at the UN and emphasized the necessity of his obtaining the return of the West Bank.

The King noted that the Arabs were at a major turning point. They could opt for what amounted to a settlement with Israel, to be followed by concentration on economic development; or the Arabs could opt to make no settlement and to re-arm for another round. Hussein favored the first course.

Hussein said that it is his intention to try to sell this position to the other Arabs, since there could be no real stability in the Middle East unless all the Arabs opt for what amounts to a settlement with Israel. Hussein stated that he had some reason to hope for success with the other Arabs in this regard. He pointed out that he, as the Arab leader who had had nothing to do with bringing about the confrontation, who had fought the hardest, and who had lost the most, was now in a unique position to speak for a moderate course. (He told Ambassador Burns on the plane coming down from New York that he had met in New York with Atassi of Syria. Hussein said Atassi had not disagreed

---

[1] Source: National Archives and Records Administration, RG 59, Central Files 1967–69, POL 27 ARAB–ISR. Secret; Noforn; Nodis. Drafted by Burns. The time is from the President's Daily Diary. (Johnson Library)

with his position that a moderate solution was the only sensible one, though Atassi did observe that the Syrian Government could already be too much prisoners of their own propaganda to make this possible.)

Mr. Katzenbach and Mr. Bundy made the following points to the King:

a) The US believes that a peaceful solution is the only solution and all US efforts would be bent towards that end. We realize that if a peaceful solution is to be a lasting solution it must be a just solution.

b) The realities of the situation appear to exclude the possibility (which has appeal for Hussein) that a peace could be imposed on Israel and the Arabs from some outside higher source.

c) A settlement between the Arabs and Israelis would have to be in essence bilateral, though there were options in terms of modalities to get around some of the current irreconcilabilities of the Arab and Israeli positions. (For example, a mediator in place of direct Arab-Israeli negotiations.)

d) The US has never had the influence with Israel that the Arabs thought we had, and in point of fact we now have less influence with Israel than ever. With this caveat the Arabs could count on us to use all of our influence and efforts to insure that a just settlement were arrived at, if the Arabs have the will for a settlement.

e) Only a settlement could inspire the USG, the Congress and the American people to be willing to render economic aid which the area so desperately needs. We are no longer interested in financing activities which do not lead to, or are not part of, a final solution to the Middle East problem.

f) Our guarantee of territorial integrity applied essentially to final boundaries rather than to current armistice lines.

In reply to questions designed to ascertain what King Hussein would settle for with respect to Jordan in connection with a peaceful settlement, King Hussein replied that he could not answer such questions until he had had an opportunity to consult with all the Arab leaders. It was apparent from the conversation, however, that Jerusalem was likely to present the most serious problem. In reply to Mr. Bundy's question as whether Hussein would accept demilitarization of the West Bank, Hussein replied that if there were a peaceful settlement with Israel the problem would be academic and would largely take care of itself. Mr. Bundy pointed out to King Hussein that until peoples who have been traditional enemies have had the opportunity to live in peace for awhile it probably would be necessary to have a demilitarized area.

In reply to the question on his position on free passage of Tiran and Suez, Hussein said this would give no problem to Jordan but obviously would to other Arab states.

The luncheon conversation ended with the King making a statement along the following lines: "The first thing I must do is to try to convince all the Arab leaders to adopt a moderate solution. Only if this fails could I consider whether it would be feasible to pursue a solution on my own."

After luncheon, while King Hussein was meeting alone with the President,[2] General Khammash spoke along the following line with Mr. Bundy. Said Khammash: We are now reforming our military units. We will need in the near future to re-supply the army with equipment. I am not speaking of offensive equipment; I am speaking of basic, defensive equipment. We must do this for two reasons (a) the morale of the army and (b) the fact that the army is still the key to stability in Jordan. The Soviets have already started to re-supply other Arab states. In such a situation we would have a hard time sitting by and taking no action even in the absence of the two considerations I just mentioned. I recognize that what I have said presents the US with a problem, since I am aware that you do not in fact or in appearance wish to rearm the Arabs for another round. I have a problem, too, which I have just outlined to you. What do we do?

Mr. Bundy replied that he understood General Khammash's problem and that obviously General Khammash understood ours. He said this is a very delicate and ticklish problem. He asked the General to keep in close touch with us, since decisions in this regard could only be arrived at in the light of the situation which comes to pass with each unfolding day.

The President and King Hussein met alone for about twenty minutes. When they returned to the other members of the party, the President said that he and the King had discussed nothing new that had not already been discussed at the lunch.

The President then suggested that the King meet alone with Mr. Bundy and Mr. Katzenbach. This meeting lasted for about forty minutes.

The tone of the meeting was marked by seriousness, moderation, and sympathetic frankness.

No part of this memorandum should be revealed to any foreign national by any addressee. Such disclosure could seriously jeopardize any possibility of a peaceful solution to the present crisis. If it is decided to communicate any part of the above to a foreign government, it will be done in Washington.

---

[2] No record of their private conversation has been found.

332. Memorandum From Nathaniel Davis of the National Security Council Staff to the President's Special Assistant (Rostow)[1]

Washington, June 29, 1967.

SUBJECT

The Situation in New York

As you know, yesterday the Yugoslavs presented their resolution calling for a simple Israeli withdrawal.[2] With our support, Tabor is pressing for co-sponsors to present a milder version of our resolution[3] this afternoon. He is trying to line up Norway, Brazil and Argentina as co-sponsors.

The tactical situation will then narrow down to a fight between the Yugoslav resolution and Tabor's. Neither the Soviets nor we are expected to push the original resolutions to a vote. The Yugoslav resolution is expected to get 50 to 60 favorable votes and 25 to 30 "nay" votes. We shall have to scramble to prevent them from getting a two-thirds majority. Their resolution will be voted on first, perhaps as early as tomorrow, although there may be enough countries asking to explain their votes to result in the voting being pushed off until early next week. It is in our interest to push off the voting slightly in order to have more time to spear down negative votes. We have sent a circular cable throughout the world asking our Missions to make urgent representations in home capitals.[4]

---

[1] Source: Johnson Library, National Security File, Country File, Middle East Crisis, Vol. VII. Confidential. A copy was sent to Bundy.

[2] The Yugoslav representative introduced a draft resolution sponsored by 15 countries on June 28. For text, see UN document A/L.522.

[3] The U.S. draft resolution, submitted on June 20, declared that the General Assembly's objective was a stable and durable peace in the Middle East and called for achieving that objective through negotiated arrangements, with appropriate third-party assistance, based on (a) mutual recognition of the political independence and territorial integrity of all countries in the area, encompassing recognized boundaries and other arrangements, including disengagement and withdrawal of forces, that would give them security against terror, destruction and war; (b) freedom of innocent maritime passage; (c) a just and equitable solution of the refugee problem; (d) registration and limitation of arms shipments into the area; and (e) recognition of the right of all sovereign nations to exist in peace and security. For text, see UN document A/L.520; also printed in Department of State *Bulletin,* July 10, 1967, pp. 51–52.

[4] Circular telegram 218514, June 29, asked the 85 embassies to which it was sent to make an urgent approach at the highest appropriate level on the basis of the recommendations in telegram 5965 from USUN, June 29, which asked recipient embassies to approach the foreign ministries in their respective capitals and urge their support of a projected Western European-Latin American draft resolution and/or opposition to the Yugoslav draft resolution. (Both in National Archives and Records Administration, RG 59, Central Files 1967–69, POL 27 ARAB–ISR/UN)

The Tabor resolution is likely to have 50 to 60 votes for and 35 to 40 "nay" votes. The opposition votes the other side can count on are a good deal firmer than ours. If both resolutions fail of two-thirds, the General Assembly is expected to start looking for a lower common denominator, such as a call to send a high-level mediator. In any case, the effort for settlement will go back to the Security Council.

There is an Arab-sponsored resolution focusing on Jerusalem that is likely to be pushed through to a quick vote. Its thrust is to declare that any Israeli measures to incorporate Jerusalem are regarded as "invalid." Justice Goldberg and Joe Sisco are talking with other delegations about minor changes to soften the "invalid" declaration slightly. They have not yet recommended a position to Washington, but probably will propose that we vote in favor, regardless of the outcome of their efforts. The resolution is likely to pass overwhelmingly in any case.

ND

---

333. Telegram From the Department of State to the Embassy in Israel[1]

Washington, June 30, 1967, 6:13 p.m.

219964. 1. At his request Israeli Ambassador Harman called on Under Secretary Rostow on June 29, to explain GOI action on Jerusalem.[2] Emphasized GOI intention maintain full access to Christian, Jewish and Moslem Holy Places. Said question of ultimate status and regulation of Holy Places is open as it was before and is now in hands of religious confessions involved. Legal action would enable GOI take all measures necessary to assure safety and proper access to Holy

---

[1] Source: National Archives and Records Administration, RG 59, Central Files 1967–69, POL 27 ARAB–ISR. Secret. Drafted by Wolle and Eugene Rostow, cleared by Handley, and approved by Rostow. Repeated to London, Paris, Amman, The Hague, Jerusalem, and USUN.

[2] On June 27 the Knesset approved three bills authorizing extension of Israel's laws, jurisdiction, and public administration over the Old City of Jerusalem and other newer areas in the eastern portion of the city which had been under Jordanian control since the General Armistice Agreement of 1949. On June 28 the Israeli Government took administrative action under the legislation to extend its municipal services and controls over the entire city of Jerusalem.

Places. Said Prime Minister had made clear in statement in Jerusalem to religious community heads that GOI open to suggestions.

2. Rostow said he appreciated Ambassador's statements but stressed that point Secretary and other USG officials have been trying to make is much broader. The USG like the GOI has a strong national interest in achieving a condition of peace in the Middle East. To reach that goal, agreements are indispensable. The problem in Jerusalem is broader than the issue of access to the Holy Places. GOI is in Jerusalem, and in the whole of the West Bank, as the occupying power under the SC cease fire resolutions. Under international law, the occupying power has clear rights and duties. One is to use existing law as the basis of its administration, with minimal change. Dayan's long press conference rested on this premise, which we regard as indispensable. Any unilateral change is highly disturbing factor, no matter what the previous situation. (He noted USG has never given legal recognition to Jordanian sovereignty over West Bank.) It was one thing to take position, as in Dayan's June 25 statement, that Israel would use local West Bank municipal councils to govern. This was fine. But to say that Israel municipal laws apply in occupied territory is entirely different concept. Hence USG had made its two June 28 statements on Jerusalem.[3]

3. Rostow said GOI actions on Jerusalem had knocked entire UNGA situation into cocked hat. Weeks of effort there had vanished in smoke. We are instructing Ambassador Barbour to seek clarification GOI action on Jerusalem. Our plea is that GOI make clear publicly it does not regard any step it has taken as irrevocable and final position. Harman and Minister Evron insisted that GOI steps do not constitute annexation but only municipal fusion. Said word "annexation" does not appear in legislation. Rostow stressed hope GOI would make clear publicly its action does not constitute annexation and does not prejudice future negotiations about status of Jerusalem as a whole.

4. Harman referred to Yugoslav-Indian resolution introduced in UNGA and said it being interpreted in corridors as signal for war. Said para 3. calls on member states to act directly to apply its provisions thus authorizing direct use of force to achieve Israeli withdrawals. GOI considers this very serious. Rostow said he had not heard this interpretation and would discuss matter with Deputy Assistant Secretary Popper and Ambassador Goldberg.

5. Harman said GOI convinced there is much at stake in current UNGA proceedings and believes situation can be held if USG continues strong effort it has been making. He wished confirmation USG would

---

[3] The texts of the statements issued by the White House and the Department of State on June 28 are printed in Department of State *Bulletin,* July 17, 1967, p. 60.

continue focus on main situation. (Implication was we should not get sidetracked onto Jerusalem issue.) Rostow confirmed our continued concentration on main strategy and tactics but repeated conviction that GOI actions on Jerusalem caused sharp setback to possibility success. Noted that Secretary's feeling evening June 28 was this might cause loss thirty votes.

6. Rostow said that King Hussein's talk with President was not totally negative. King is in difficult position and knows it, but nothing should be done to interrupt possibility of his coming around ultimately to more moderate position.

7. Harman referred to continued movements Soviet aircraft into Cairo and Damascus, and movement of MIGs into Baghdad. Rostow assured him we are watching Soviet resupply efforts with utmost care.[4]

---

[4] Printed from an unsigned copy.

---

334. Memorandum From the Joint Chiefs of Staff to Secretary of Defense McNamara[1]

JCSM–374–67   Washington, June 29, 1967.

SUBJECT

US Military Interests in the Near East (U)

1. (S) Reference is made to your memorandum, dated 16 June 1967, on the above subject,[2] which requested the views of the Joint Chiefs of Staff on the military implications of a polarized situation in which the Arab world is supported by the USSR and Israel by the United States.

2. (S) For the purposes of this paper, the Arab world includes the following countries: Syria, Iraq, Lebanon, Jordan, Saudi Arabia, Kuwait, Yemen, Sudan, United Arab Republic, Libya, Tunisia, Algeria, Morocco, Mauritania, Bahrein, the Trucial States, and the Federation of South Arabia.

3. (S) The most significant impact of such a polarization would be the creation of an environment in which further conflict and military hostilities between the Arab world and Israel would be almost certain.

---

[1] Source: Washington National Records Center, OSD Files: FRC 330 72 A 2468, Middle East 092. Secret; Sensitive.

[2] Not printed. (Ibid.)

As a result, the United States would be placed in the position of becoming deeply involved by providing direct political, economic, and military support to Israel or having to abandon its policy toward the continued existence of Israel. In addition, future conflicts in an environment of increasing polarization would increase the danger of direct US-USSR confrontation. The increased USSR influence with the Arab nations would cause a reduction in the political freedom of action the moderate Arab states, such as Lebanon, Morocco, Tunisia, Libya, Saudi Arabia, and Jordan, had enjoyed in the more ambiguous situation prior to the present crisis. This situation would probably eliminate their restraining influence on the radical Arab states and could cause the United States to provide military assistance to Israel in view of the increased threat of a more united Arab world.

4. (S) A polarization of this nature would be most detrimental to US interests in the Middle East. The most significant interests having military implications which would be seriously affected are:

a. Promotion of the Western orientation of nations of the Middle East.
b. Elimination or reduction of Soviet influence in the Middle East.
c. Security of the southern flank of NATO.
d. Retention of access to air and sea routes.
e. Retention of base rights and communications-electronics facilities.
f. Retention of access to Middle East oil.

5. (S) The impact of such a polarization on US military interests in the Arab world includes the following:

a. Loss of US military influence in Arab nations.
b. Increase of Soviet influence in the area through stronger ties with the radical Arab nations and establishment of an influential position in the moderate nations of Lebanon, Jordan, Saudi Arabia, Libya, Morocco, and Tunisia where little or no USSR influence exists.
c. Loss of certain important port facilities, base rights, and non-Defense Communications System (DCS) communications-electronics facilities in the Arab states which, coupled with loss of intelligence collection inputs from defense attaché and clandestine sources, would have a most serious and adverse bearing on the national security interests of the United States.
d. Probable denial of Arab oil and a requirement for alternative oil resources for Southeast Asia and Europe, resulting in increased costs of POL.
e. Extension of the sea LOC to support military operations in Southeast Asia.
f. Loss of supporting facilities for MIDEASTFOR in Arab countries will extend the LOC.
g. Loss of the cooperation of Libya and Morocco and increased Soviet influence in those countries would have an adverse effect on the US strategic position on the southern littoral of the Mediterranean.

6. (S) The impact of such a polarization on Turkey and Iran would also have a direct bearing on US military interests in the area. These might include the following:

a. Execution of contingency operations for east Africa, the Middle East, and South Asia would be severely handicapped if the use of Turkish and/or Iranian bases and the required overflight rights were denied.

b. Probable requests for additional US aid from Turkey and Iran because of the increased threat.

c. Reassessment by Turkey of its role in NATO.

d. Creation of divisive pressures in CENTO based on ethnic and religious orientations and differing reassessments of the threat to their individual interests.

e. Possible loss of communications-electronics facilities in Turkey and Iran coupled with a loss of intelligence collection inputs which would have a further serious and adverse bearing on the national security interests of the United States.

7. (S) The impact of such a polarization on US military interests in other neighboring areas would be as follows:

a. Serious effects on the US worldwide military communications system (DCS) in the event Ethiopia does not permit the continued use of the DCS station at Asmara. Loss of non-DCS communications-electronics capabilities would create a void in the intelligence collection programs. (In this connection, the views[3] of the Department of State with regard to continued use of this station should be noted.)

b. The need for US bases in the Indian Ocean would be significantly increased. Development of US facilities there would need to be accelerated.

c. An increase in requirements for use of South African facilities.

d. An improved posture for expansion of Soviet influence into other African regions.

8. (S) In the event of such a polarization, Israel probably would provide base and overflight rights.

9. (S) Attached[4] are details of the specific problems which would be generated or aggravated by a polarization in the Near East resulting from the current crisis. In view of the serious adverse military implications which would probably result, the Joint Chiefs of Staff consider that the United States should make every effort to prevent such a polarization.

For the Joint Chiefs of Staff:

Earle G. Wheeler
Chairman
Joint Chiefs of Staff

---

[3] Letter from the Under Secretary of State, dated 8 May 1967. [Footnote in the source text. For text of Katzenbach's letter, see *Foreign Relations*, 1964–1968, vol. XXIV, Document 337.]

[4] Appendix A, "U.S. Military Interests in the Near East," is attached but not printed.

335. Telegram From the Mission to the United Nations to the Department of State[1]

New York, June 30, 1967, 0336Z.

5985. Hussein Approach on GA Res.

During dinner which he was hosting for departing Japan Amb Matsui, Goldberg received call from Bundy indicating King Hussein wished consult US urgently on non-aligned res calling for withdrawal Israeli forces. Since he could not leave, Goldberg sent Buffum to Waldorf who was received immediately by King accompanied only by Chief Protocol Rafai.

King said he had been meeting during evening with other Arab leaders. Based on these discussions, he said he was greatly concerned that if non-aligned res fails, this would play into hands of extremists. Conclusion that would be drawn, he argued, would be that UN offers no hope for Arab case and that there would be strong tendency to look outside UN for solution, giving Communists ready-made opportunity to exploit. He said he knew we were working against this res, that its chances of adoption were narrow and hoped we could find way to modify our position so that it would be permitted to pass.

Rafai sought to maintain that since res contained para calling for ultimate SC consideration of other aspects of problem this should help meet our concern about issues related to withdrawal of Israeli forces.

Buffum said he wished to inform King frankly that we were in fact solidly opposed to non-aligned res since it was unrealistic and would not be implemented by Israel. In our view, withdrawal issue, which is important principle that we support, is intimately related to another equally fundamental issue, namely, termination of belligerence. US did not consider it reasonable to expect a state which commanded a militarily superior position in wartime would abandon that position while its opponents continued to say that the war goes on. Pronouncements by certain Arab leaders that Israel has no right to exist and that they are intent on Israel's destruction makes it obviously impossible for Israel to withdraw.

At same time, Buffum said we recognized Arab states can probably not issue formal renunciation of state of belligerency, nor would they be

---

[1] Source: National Archives and Records Administration, RG 59, Central Files 1967–69, POL 27 ARAB–ISR/UN. Secret; Priority; Exdis. Received at 12:17 a.m. Passed to the White House at 1:05 a.m. Rostow sent the text to the President in CAP 67610, June 30, noting that Hussein was trying to reconcile the simple withdrawal resolution with nonbelligerence. (Johnson Library, National Security File, Memos to the President, Walt Rostow, Vol. 32)

likely to sit down in the same room and negotiate with Israelis. Judging from many general debate statements, large number of delegations shared this view. It seemed to us that a practical way to get at the problem would be to have the UN despatch a special emissary to the area and seek to work out agreed arrangements with the states concerned which would result in withdrawal of Israeli forces. Buffum indicated that number of UN dels, according to our information, were developing a third party res which would reflect the foregoing concept.

King did not demur at any of these points. He said that he recognized Israel would not withdraw troops immediately upon adoption of non-aligned res, but he felt that once this principle established private arrangements could be worked out satisfying Israel's security requirements permitting it to withdraw.

Buffum responded that we did not read situation this way; that we considered equitable approach would be to mention both withdrawal and termination of belligerence and let UN rep proceed to work out the details.

Hussein then suggested we submit our ideas as amendments to non-aligned res. Buffum replied that we had already made these same points in previous discussions with some of sponsors, particularly Indians, and they had not been accepted. It was clear to us, he said, that necessary 2/3rds vote to secure adoption of amendments could not be obtained over Arab objections. Accordingly, Buffum suggested, if King considered these points legitimate, most effective way they could be incorporated would be for Jordan to propose them to its Arab colleagues privately. Buffum said Arabs had come to look on our approach as pro-Israel and that Jordan itself obviously in far better position to advance these ideas if it really interested.

Hussein acknowledged this was true and said he would be in touch with his Arab colleagues to see if revision of res could be obtained to meet our views. He asked that we use our influence not to have other texts introduced tomorrow until we had consulted with Jordanian del first. Buffum agreed. King expressed appreciation for consultation.

Late evening, Rafai called Buffum to say first contacts already undertaken with other Arabs and looked promising. He said King was determined to use his newly-won status in Arab world for constructive purposes. He felt, based on first discussions, that revised text would go in which included provision for UN rep and which would make "appropriated references" to UN Charter. Buffum said that exact language would be determining factor and that we attached great importance to equating termination of belligerency with withdrawal of forces. Buffum added that if Jordan desired our affirmative vote it would provide us text before it is tabled and not present us with fait accompli as non-aligned mbrs had done. Rafai said this could be worked out with Jordanian del tomorrow and expressed hope that at least text would be improved substantially enough so that we would no longer have to oppose it, even though we might decide to abstain.

Rafai asked that we not reveal tomorrow morning that we had advance indication what changes were being considered in non-aligned text.

Goldberg

---

336. Telegram From the Department of State to the Embassy in Saudi Arabia[1]

Washington, July 1, 1967, 5:49 p.m.

100. The following is an uncleared memcon FYI only Noforn subject to revision upon review.

1. Saudi Ambassador Sowayel, at his request, called on Secretary June 30[2] to inquire as to our reaction Faisal's suggestions that we support condemnation Israel and troop withdrawal.

2. Noting he had discussed subject with DepFonMin Saqqaf in New York,[3] Secretary described three major issues which interact in NE area: (a) Arab-Israel issue; (b) progressive versus moderate split which Arab-Israel issue tends conceal; and (c) Soviet efforts penetrate area at expense both moderate Arab regimes and West. Secretary noted settled USG policy of support for territorial integrity and political independence conceived with all three in mind. At various times USG had implemented this policy, both in support Egypt and in support Egypt's Arab neighbors against Egypt. We had also condemned both Arab terrorism and Israeli reprisal raids.

---

[1] Source: National Archives and Records Administration, RG 59, Central Files 1967–69, POL 27 ARAB–ISR/UN. Secret. Drafted by Country Director for Saudi Arabia William D. Brewer, cleared by Davies, and approved for transmission by Robert L. Bruce (S/S). Repeated to Dhahran, Beirut, Amman, Tripoli, Tunis, and Rabat.

[2] Rusk met with the Ambassador at 4:40 p.m. on June 30. (Johnson Library, Rusk Appointment Book)

[3] Rusk's meeting with Saqqaf on June 22 was reported in telegram Secto 22 from New York, June 23. (National Archives and Records Administration, RG 59, Conference Files: 1966–1972, Entry 3051B, CF 196)

3. Sowayel noted failure USG publicly give unequivocal support Israeli withdrawal would provide opportunity for socialists and communists to exploit. Russians are already talking in language which mobs understand, but USG has not taken position which gives moderates ammunition vis-à-vis their own public opinion. Terms like "territorial integrity" lack impact on masses. Secretary responded USSR no doubt had short-run advantage because of its ability of being extreme.

4. Noting that, except for Old City, where we had publicly criticized GOI unilateral action, there seemed no serious territorial issues, Secretary said status boundary lines was very important. Did they connote peace or war? Nasser's provocation in closing Gulf of Aqaba was act supreme folly. Egypt could not be at war with Israel without Israel being at war with Egypt. If only this state of belligerency could be removed, could make enormous difference. Secretary commented that Russians had told us they had eliminated their state of war with Japan many years before peace treaty achieved. There ought to be way for Arabs to do this with Israel even though no direct agreements feasible. This would be in Arab interest since it would protect Arabs as well as Israel. This connection, Secretary said that there were those with considerable international legal background who felt that, as long as UAR maintained state of war against Israel, Israel could not "commit aggression" against UAR.

5. Sowayel described current Arab scene as "field of phrasing" between radicals and moderates. Former were showing themselves better at this and moderates had to do something. Even in Saudi Arabia mobs had been a problem in Dhahran. Secretary asked whether mobs were satisfied with extent of Soviet support. Sowayel responded mobs were unsophisticated and did not look behind Soviet slogans. Fact that Israel had had no right to attack was central issue on which masses had to be satisfied before specific problems could be taken up.

6. Secretary observed it difficult condemn only one side for acts of war. Saudi Ambassador admitted Nasser had provided provocation. Secretary noted Soviets themselves now reportedly pulling away from idea of condemnation of Israel by special UNGA.

7. Sowayel again stressed USG must say something publicly on central issue in order support its Arab friends. Statements on Jerusalem had been helpful but general comment necessary. He thought President's five principles very good but this was not moment to try implement them. Noting difficulty USG satisfy masses stirred up by Cairo Radio, Secretary wondered whether moderate regime such as SAG could ask even privately who were their friends.

Sowayel replied Saudis knew who were their friends, to which Secretary suggested this should not be lost sight of when chips are down.

8. In conclusion, Secretary inquired whether Arabs able accept idea of elimination state of war with Israel. Sowayel responded affirmatively but wondered what conditions might be. Stressed again that most important thing from standpoint Arab moderates was evidence of clear and unequivocal USG support for principle Israeli withdrawal.

9. *Comment.* FYI. In subsequent discussion with DeptOff, Sowayel went so far as to suggest it would meet need Arab moderates for USG take strong public stance on withdrawal, while at same time privately assuring GOI that such public position could be disregarded. End FYI.

Rusk

---

337. Memorandum From the Joint Chiefs of Staff to Secretary of Defense McNamara[1]

JCSM–379–67   Washington, July 1, 1967.

SUBJECT

    USS *Liberty* Incident (U)

1. (TS) Immediately following the Israeli air and naval attack on the USS *Liberty* (AGTR–5) during the recent Arab-Israeli war, a Joint Chiefs of Staff ad hoc fact finding team was established to investigate the incident. The team conducted an accelerated investigation and submitted a report based upon the information obtained.[2] The time and facts available to the team limited the comprehensiveness of the report.

---

[1] Source: Washington National Records Center, OSD Files: FRC 330 72 A 2467. Top Secret; Sensitive. A stamped notation on the source text indicates that it was received in the office of the Secretary of Defense at 1431 hours, July 1; another notation, July 17, indicates the Secretary saw it.

[2] The "Report of the JCS Fact Finding Team: USS *Liberty* Incident, 8 June 1967," undated, consisting of an introduction, findings of fact, recommendations, and 6 annexes, one of which includes 77 messages, is attached to the source text as Appendix B. A copy is also in JCS Files, 898/392. The fact-finding team was headed by Major General Joseph R. Russ, USA.

2. (TS) This report contained 17 recommendations and attributes the fact that the USS *Liberty* did not receive time-critical messages to a combination of:

a. Human error.
b. High volume of communications traffic.
c. Lack of appreciation of the sense of urgency regarding USS *Liberty* movement and location.

3. (TS) Most of the recommendations relate to the delay attributed to delivery of time-critical messages to the USS *Liberty*. Had these messages been received, the ship might have cleared the danger area prior to the attack. The study requires further analysis. However, preliminary comments on the report are forwarded as Appendix A hereto.[3]

4. (TS) The Joint Chiefs of Staff have referred the report to the Services and the appropriate Joint Staff agencies and directorates for further study and recommendations. You will be apprised of the status of the follow-up actions.

5. (U) A copy of the report is contained in Appendix B hereto for your information.

For the Joint Chiefs of Staff:

Earle G. Wheeler
Chairman
Joint Chiefs of Staff

---

[3] Appendix A, "Comments by the Joint Chiefs of Staff on Recommendations Made by the Fact Finding Team," is attached but not printed.

338.   Telegram From the Embassy in Israel to the Department of State[1]

Tel Aviv, July 2, 1967, 1130Z.

9. Ref: State 218573[2] and 219964;[3] Tel Aviv 0003.[4]

1. I conveyed position State's 218573 to p.m. Eshkol last evening.

2. As to effect of Knesset's enabling legislation on occupied territory other than Jerusalem, Eshkol categorically assures me there no intention take any steps to extend jurisdiction as authorized those enactments to any of occupied territories. FonOff legal adviser takes some exception to the quote from Oppenheim on grounds that Jordanian and Egyptian sovereignties were never extended West Bank or Gaza but GOI not disposed argue point further. Dayan's remarks at press conference that Israel seeks restore life as much as possible to normal relying to maximum on local Arab authorities still remains policy of GOI those areas.

3. However, as to Jerusalem, GOI adamant. It is attempting to reorganize the municipal council by the inclusion of Arab members and otherwise is prepared to use the maximum number of available Arab civil servants from the former Old City governate, but the only really negotiable issue is the holy places. I emphasized Unsec Rostow's comments to Harman (State's 219964), effect on UNGA situation, and particularly the hope GOI would make public its action does not prejudice future negotiations about status of Jerusalem as a whole. Response is that holy places are negotiable. Further clarification not forthcoming.

Barbour

---

[1]   Source: National Archives and Records Administration, RG 59, Central Files 1967–69, POL 27 ARAB–ISR. Secret; Priority. Repeated to Amman, Beirut, Jerusalem, and USUN. Received at 9:25 a.m. Passed to the White House, DOD, CIA, USIA, NSA, COMAC, and CINCSTRIKE at 10:55 a.m.

[2]   Telegram 218573 to Tel Aviv, June 29, instructed Barbour to register U.S. opposition to any unilateral action by Israel to assert de jure control over occupied territories. (Ibid.)

[3]   Document 333.

[4]   Telegram 3 from Tel Aviv, July 1, reported that before receiving telegrams 218573 and 219964, Barbour had discussed the subject of Jerusalem with the Israeli Minister of Justice and several other officials and had strongly deplored the "precipitate issuance unification ordinance re Jerusalem." (National Archives and Records Administration, RG 59, Central Files 1967–69, POL 27 ARAB–ISR)

339.   Memorandum From the Director of the Bureau of
        Intelligence and Research (Hughes) to Secretary of State
        Rusk[1]

Washington, July 3, 1967.

SUBJECT

The Current Situation in the UAR and its Bearing on UAR Approaches to the US
and France

The Situation in the UAR

General. We believe that Nasser remains in control in Egypt and that
he has not become a figurehead for a real governing group. Nasser's
control, however, is threatened by a variety of conflicting forces and factions within and outside the UARG. He is seeking ways out of his
predicament and apparently hopes to convince France and perhaps the
United States that he deserves bailing out. INR has used all available
sources in this analysis, but reliable information is very scanty. Two of
our primary sources have been the alleged Egyptian note to the French
Government of 20 June[2] and the overtures made by Salah Nasir.[3] These
are separately analyzed and commented upon in Part II of this memorandum.

Military. There appears to be fairly serious disaffection in the military. Figures given by various sources on the number of military officers
dismissed ranges from 200 to 750; the truth probably lies somewhere
between two figures. Many of those dismissed probably have been
ousted not because of "incompetence," but because their loyalty to the

---

[1]   Source: National Archives and Records Administration, RG 59, Central Files
1967–69, POL 15 UAR. Top Secret; Nodis. No drafting information appears on the memorandum.

[2]   See footnote 2, Document 311.

[3]   A message received on June 24 stated that the "director," who was presumed to be
head of UAR intelligence Salah Nasr, was ready to fly to Rome to meet with a presidential emissary for negotiations on the basis of "de facto" recognition of Israel, Israeli withdrawal to the June 4 borders, guarantee of the borders by a UN force, free passage in the
Strait of Tiran, compensation for civilian damages in Arab countries during the war, and
a pledge by the United States and other Western countries for a 30-year plan of economic development for the UAR. The U.S. reply stated that Ambassador to Italy G. Frederick
Reinhardt would be willing to meet in Rome for discussions. (Telegram 215944 to Rome,
June 24; Johnson Library, National Security File, Country File, Middle East Crisis, Vol. VII)
A subsequent message stated that Salah Nasr had persuaded President Nasser to allow
negotiations with the United States to proceed, on condition that they be handled by
Fawzi and Rusk. (Memorandum to Katzenbach and Walt Rostow, July 5; ibid.) Further
documentation concerning these overtures is ibid. and in the National Archives and
Records Administration, RG 59, Central Files 1967–69, POL UAR–US.

regime was suspect; this would explain why some of them are reported to have been put under house arrest. These developments tend to support earlier reports of disaffection among the military; they lend credibility to reports that the military pressured Nasser into his June 9 resignation. The military appears to be the only center of effective opposition to Nasser. There is a report that there has been considerable resistance within the army to purge of these "incompetents."

There are also reports of popular resentment against the military and their performance. This resentment appears to be fed by the stories told by the defeated troops returning from the front.

Civilian Administration. A good source has reported that as of June 20 Cairo was confused and disorganized and that the whole machinery of government was dislocated. Nasser's reorganization of the government on June 19 probably was done to halt this trend by bringing the government machinery more directly under his control. Nasser now appears to be trying to cope simultaneously with disaffection in the army, rising discontent among the public and the administration, momentous foreign and Arab policy problems, and staggering economic ones. To judge from reports, the load is becoming almost too great for him to cope with and he is grasping at straws. Nasser's subordination of the UAR's pressing economic needs to his political objectives has put the UAR economy in a parlous state. His closing of the Suez Canal, his urging the Arab states to break relations with the US and the UK, and his inciting the Arab oil producing states to cut off oil to the US and the UK are designed to force the West and the world community to pressure Israel to give up the gains it has made since June 5. However, it is becoming increasingly clear that these measures are hurting the UAR much more than they are damaging Nasser's intended targets and they are beginning seriously to threaten his regime. The USSR, apparently, is unable and/or unwilling to take up the economic slack. Therefore, Nasser may feel that he may have to make some concessions to the West in order to get the necessary economic aid.

Forces of the Left and the Right. The setback seems to have caused a reaction against socialism in at least some quarters in the UAR. It probably is connected with the feeling that the USSR has let the UAR down. This reaction probably has emanated from middle-class elements and from similar elements in the armed forces. They probably are opposed to 'Ali Sabri and his Arab Socialist Union forces. The coloration of the government formed by Nasser on June 19 appears to show a desire on the part of Nasser to soften criticism from these rightist elements. It probably was designed also to attract support from the US.

On the other hand, there reportedly have been arrests of rightist elements in the administration and in the army, indicating that the ASU, 'Ali Sabri and his associates are still able to act against their rivals. The rightists apparently had been attempting to arouse into action the anti-revolutionary and anti-communist forces in the UAR. The USSR apparently is trying to pressure Nasser into letting it carry the ball for the Arabs in the international arena. The Soviets undoubtedly feel that he bungled the job as he bungled the military confrontation with Israel. The USSR probably is resupplying the UAR with arms more in hope of keeping up their credit with the UAR military than with Nasser. Yet to abdicate to anyone else the political role of championing the Arabs against Israel would be unbearable for Nasser. Furthermore, Nasser seems to feel that the Soviets would not be above selling him out, and he probably suspects that they may have Algeria and Syria in mind as replacements for the UAR. The Egyptian communist leadership appears to believe that it is now in a position to exert more influence on UAR policies. This leadership is reported to be advocating the UAR's maintaining a violent anti-Western line and keeping pressure on the Arab oil-producing countries to deny oil to the West. To this end, it is likely that Soviet propaganda will continue to allege collusion between Israel on the one hand and the West and its regional allies on the other. The Soviet aim, however, would probably not be to provoke renewed Arab-Israeli hostilities.

Nasser is struggling with the burden of having to fight on many different fronts, both internal and external. He probably has become suspicious and distrustful of many of the members of his old guard who, he feels, have failed him. But at the same time he is in extremis, and probably is inclined to let them do what they can to salvage the situation. We do not believe that Nasser as yet has become a figurehead. For one thing, we cannot identify any leader or group of leaders who would be manipulating Nasser and who might have been behind the note to the French Government. (See Part II) Such a group probably would have its nucleus in the armed forces, and there might be leftist as well as rightist groups of this nature. In the absence of better intelligence on conditions in the armed forces, we cannot say to what degree organized anti-Nasser trends exist.

Part II

The Authors of the Documents

These documents appear to fall into two groups: 1) Those that emanate from GID Director Salah Nasir, either explicitly or inferentially. It seems likely, as observed in the commentaries on them, that the "Director" and the "friend" refer to Salah Nasir himself; 2) The document of June 18 that was submitted to the French on June 20 by the UAR Embassy in Paris. It is less clear who the people behind this document are.

Salah Nasir's Orientation

The documents attributable to Salah Nasir show an evolution in his attitude from June 9 to June 27 as follows:

From June 9 through 23 Salah Nasir was afraid for his own position, presumably as a result of the purges and the arrests of "rightists" being carried out in both military and civilian circles in the UAR. The source of a TDCS reporting events as of June 20 claimed that Salah Nasir himself had been dismissed and put under house arrest. While incorrect, the report is indicative of the type of rumors that were circulating and of the general atmosphere of uncertainty.

Salah Nasir's main concern on the policy side was that the US should assume a more pro-Arab position in the UN, etc., to prevent the USSR from monopolizing the role of champion of the Arabs in their dispute with Israel. This could well reflect the concern of Nasser himself, who clearly has been worried over this prospect. Salah Nasir may have been delegated by President Nasser to lay the groundwork for an improvement in US-UAR relations.

On June 24 there was a decided shift in Salah Nasir's line. In the aide-memoire given to Secretary Rusk by Fanfani on that date, and in Salah Nasir's June 25 conversation with [*name not declassified*], Salah Nasir reiterates that he is talking to [*name not declassified*] with Nasser's knowledge, but that Nasser did not know of his approach to the US through the Italians. Salah Nasir now gives the clear impression that he is talking less as a spokesman for Nasser and more on his own initiative. The subject of Salah Nasir's proposals shifts from that of asking for a pro-Arab stance by the US to a presentation of the concessions that Salah was willing to make in order to get a Western pledge of 30-year economic aid to the UAR. On June 25, Salah Nasir admitted that he couldn't go to Rome to meet with a US plenipotentiary if Nasser refused, but said that if Nasser didn't approve the trip, he (Salah) wanted to continue the discussions with [*name not declassified*]—apparently whether Nasser agreed or not. For the first time, Salah Nasir expressed disdain for President Nasser.

On June 26 (in the report [*1 line of source text not declassified*]) there is the first clear indication of a seditious attitude by Salah Nasir. The report states that Salah Nasir, supported by the dismissed Marshal Amir, is determined to take extreme anti-Nasser action in favor of the West. Nasser could be got rid of and the transition carried out by Zakariya Muhi al-Din, Salah Nasir, and their friends behind the scenes. This group, he claimed, had the armed forces and the intelligence services solidly in their hands. On the same day, [*less than 1 line of source text not declassified*] reported that Salah Nasir had said that President Nasser "flinched" at the idea of de facto recognition of Israel presented to him as a necessary step by Salah Nasir. This suggests that the conditions for the negotiations were not dictated by Nasser, but were left to Salah Nasir to draw up. However, Nasser didn't object to pursuing the negotiations. The [*less than 1 line of source text not declassified*] report stated that Salah Nasir, Zakariya Muhi al-Din, and 'Amir wanted to use the proposed negotiations as a first step to unseat Nasser.

The Orientation of the Authors of the Proposal Presented to the French on June 20

This proposal, which is dated June 18, contains the same general elements as those in the note purportedly drafted by an unidentified group of high UAR military and civilian officials on June 18 and presented by the UAR Embassy to the French Ministry of Foreign Affairs on June 20. These common features are 1) Recognition of Israel, 2) Free passage for Israel through the Strait of Tiran, 3) Request for economic aid, and 4) Request that negotiations be conducted with a personal emissary of Presidents Johnson and de Gaulle respectively and not through normal diplomatic channels. However, there are also differences. Salah Nasir's proposals, which include Israeli compensation to Arab civilians, are noticeably less liberal than those contained in the June 18 note submitted to the French. Furthermore, the authors of the June 18 note designate Muhammad Hasanayn Haykal, the influential editor of the Cairo daily *al-Ahram*, as the person to deal with the personal emissary whom it requests de Gaulle to send. Salah Nasir, on the other hand, talking to Brommel on June 23, specifically rejected Haykal as "an opportunist with little influence" and designated himself as negotiator with the Americans. This fact suggests that someone other than Salah Nasir is speaking for the authors of the June 18 note to the French.

Conclusions

It is difficult to avoid the conclusion that both the Paris note and Salah Nasir's proposal go back to a single inspiration. This inspiration probably is President Nasser himself. The Yugoslav correspondent Milenkovic, writing in the Belgrade paper *Borba* (Belgrade tel. 3704, June 23, 1967 LOU), after the formation of the new UAR Government on June 19, noted that there was a realization in Cairo that only through negotiations and "crucial concessions" to Israel on the subjects of navigation and recognition could Israel be induced to give up its territorial gains made at the UAR's expense. There probably was also a realization, both before and after Podgorny's visit of June 22, that the UAR could not get from the USSR the economic aid it desperately needed; this aid could come only from the US or France, and concessions would have to be made to them also.

Nasser, however, appears to have realized that he could not hope to get the required aid in his own name. Therefore, he may have delegated one group to deal with the French, as he had delegated Salah Nasir to deal with the Americans. This hypothesis would explain his long delay in deciding whether to sanction Salah Nasir's trip to Rome to talk with a US representative—Nasser was waiting to see the results of the approach to de Gaulle.

The anti-Nasser sentiments expressed in the case of the approaches to the US and France probably should be received with caution. They may have been designed, along with the effusive promise of pro-Western policy orientation, to "sweeten" the proposals in the eyes of the recipients. The note to the French does not talk of getting rid of Nasser; this idea is expressed only by the source who gave the copy of the note to Guest, and even then (as in the case of Salah Nasir) it is postponed into the future. Furthermore, the note stresses that Haykal, with whom the French representative was to negotiate, is a "confidant of President Nasser." Haykal is not known to have defected from Nasser. Salah Nasir's anti-Nasser attitude may have similarly been designed for its effect on the US. We have only his word that he has a group—including 'Amir and Zakariya Muhi al-Din—behind him. He gives the impression of being mainly concerned with the preservation of his own position. It is clear that he has some kind of a mandate from Nasser to negotiate with the Americans, and he undoubtedly is convinced that his position will be a lot safer if he is able to extract aid from the US.

Any aid extended to the UAR as a result of these approaches to France and the US probably would tend to perpetuate Nasser in power, We do not yet seem to have a clearly-identifiable group of anti-Nasserists who appear capable of taking and continuing the exercise of power. Nasser is an extremely adroit manipulator of men and their ambitions, and as long as he remains at the top it is difficult to believe that he could be a mere figurehead controlled by some group behind the scenes. Nagib learned this to his disadvantage some thirteen years ago. As long as Nasser or any other rulers of the UAR are in a position to play the USSR off against the US, it is unlikely that they would recognize Israel, although they might hold out to the West the prospect that they would do so in return for Western support. Nasser and others in the UAR may now also feel they can make Soviet control of the UAR a main issue in their bargaining for aid from the West. Even if the West supplies the aid, however, the UAR would still have to play ball with the Soviets because it is utterly dependent on them for arms and the High Dam. Hence, any talk of orienting the UAR's policy completely toward the West would seem quite unrealistic.

340. Action Memorandum From the Control Group to Secretary
of State Rusk[1]

Washington, undated.

SUBJECT

UNGA Voting on Jerusalem

It is possible that we will be confronted July 4 or July 5 with the
need to take a quick decision on a General Assembly resolution on
Jerusalem. The elements of the problem are as follows.

1. The Pakistan delegation has introduced a resolution declaring
that measures taken by the Israelis on Jerusalem are invalid and calling
upon Israel to rescind these measures and desist from action which
would alter the status of Jerusalem—the Secretary General to report to
the General Assembly and the Security Council on implementation of
the resolution within a week (text at Tab A).[2] This resolution was submitted after the Yugoslav/Indian resolution[3] and the Latin American
resolution,[4] and would not come up for consideration until action on
these two resolutions had been completed.

2. The Yugoslav/Indian resolution does not mention Jerusalem, but it
calls upon Israel immediately to withdraw all its forces to the pre-June 5
positions, and it requests the Security Council to examine all aspects of the
Middle Eastern situation. Presumably the passage of the Yugoslav/Indian
resolution would denote withdrawal from Jerusalem as well as other conquered territory. However, since the Jerusalem problem is in a sense separable from the Middle Eastern problem as a whole, we should have to
expect that a separate resolution on Jerusalem would be pressed.

---

[1] Source: Johnson Library, National Security File, Special Committee, Minutes of the
Control Group Meetings. Confidential. Under Secretary of State for Political Affairs
Eugene V. Rostow initialed the memorandum, which he sent to Bundy with a handwrit-
ten note of July 4 stating that Rusk and Katzenbach had not yet cleared the idea or the text.
Bundy's handwritten note on the memorandum states that he had cleared it.

[2] The tabs are attached but not printed, The Pakistani draft resolution was introduced initially in the General Assembly on July 1. A revised version with six sponsors was
introduced on July 3; for text, see UN document A/L.527/Rev.1.

[3] The Yugoslav/Indian resolution was initially submitted on June 28; see footnote 2,
Document 332. Revised versions, with 17 sponsors, were introduced on June 30 and July
3. For text of the July 3 version, see UN document A/L.522/Rev.2.

[4] The Latin American resolution was initially submitted on June 30 by the representative of Trinidad and Tobago on behalf of a Latin American group; it was subsequently
revised and sponsored by 20 countries. As revised, it requested Israel to withdraw from
the territories occupied as a result of the recent conflict and requested the parties in conflict to end the state of belligerency, to endeavor to establish conditions of coexistence
based on good neighborliness, and to have recourse in all cases to the procedure for
peaceful settlement indicated in the Charter. For text, see UN document A/L.523/Rev.1.

3. The final paragraph of the Latin American resolution reaffirms "the desirability of establishing an international regime for the city of Jerusalem, to be considered by the General Assembly at its 22nd Session" (fall 1967). If the Latin American resolution were to receive a two-thirds majority, the Assembly would probably not adopt any other language on Jerusalem.

4. As of the evening of July 3, our best estimate is that neither the Yugoslav nor the Latin American resolution will be adopted. In this event, we will have to vote on a Jerusalem text. Looking ahead to this eventuality, our delegation has re-phrased the Pakistan proposal in terms falling squarely within the guidelines of the Presidential and Department statements of June 28 (proposed USUN revision, Tab B).[5] The Turks, who are planning to co-sponsor a resolution on Jerusalem with the Pakistanis, have undertaken to discuss our language with the Jordanian Foreign Minister, and there is reason to believe that some of it might be adopted. Obviously, if an altered text could be presented which stressed non-recognition of unilateral action to change the status of Jerusalem, we should vote for it.

We are also preparing to have language on Jerusalem we could support introduced as amendments if we fail to get a satisfactory compromise text from the consultative process.

5. But if—as is more likely—we ultimately have to vote on the original Pakistan text, or something close to it, we shall need a high level decision.

6. Our position on Jerusalem is that we have never recognized unilateral action by any of the States in the area as governing the international status of Jerusalem.

The background for this conclusion is (a) that the Israelis are in Jerusalem, as they are in other territory taken during the recent hostilities, as the occupying power under the cease-fire resolutions of the Security Council; (b) that the occupying power has the duty under international law to conform its administration as closely as possible to existing local law; (c) that Israeli action to establish a unified municipal administration for the city of Jerusalem cannot be regarded and will not be recognized as a valid annexation, or a permanent change in the legal status of Jerusalem in any other sense; at most, it can be considered an

---

[5] The proposed revision stated that the General Assembly declared it could not recognize any unilateral action as determining the status of Jerusalem, called on the Israeli Government to desist from any formal action purporting to define permanently the status of Jerusalem, and requested the Secretary-General to report on the situation and implementation of the resolution, with no deadline. (Telegram 40 from USUN, July 4; National Archives and Records Administration, RG 59, Central Files 1967–69, POL 27 ARAB–ISR/UN)

interim administrative measure to provide a more convenient and efficient occupation regime for the areas formerly under Jordanian control, using Jordanian police and other officials where possible.

The Government of Israel has now publicly and officially retreated from its original position, and has endorsed our view that their unified administration of Jerusalem is not an annexation.

We have continued to stress our opposition to any unilateral efforts to change the permanent position in Jerusalem or elsewhere, and to insist that such change be accomplished only by internationally effective action, taking full account of international interests.

There are positive aspects of the administrative change in Jerusalem, from our point of view. The position of Jerusalem as an open city is having an influence on the attitudes of thousands of Arab visitors and tourists who are dealing with Israel and the Israelis for the first time. And we have received an important comment from Ambassador Barbour (Tab C)[6] which is being studied in connection with the preparation of a policy recommendation for the functional internationalization of the city.

Against this background, we believe it would not be possible for us, consistently with the position we have already taken, to support a resolution along the lines of the Pakistan text. At most, we should recommend abstention if we fail in our efforts to obtain a Jerusalem text we could support. The language of the Pakistani Resolution not only declares that what the Israelis have done is invalid (whereas we would be inclined to recognize the validity of Israeli action if viewed as no more than administrative action of the occupying power), but also calls on Israel to rescind all the measures taken. Construed literally, this would require sealing up the wall, turning off the water, disconnecting the electricity, and reversing all other steps taken to unify Jerusalem.

Moreover, it is unrealistic to expect any useful report on implementation within one week.

USUN agrees with this recommendation.

---

[6] Barbour commented in telegram 4 from Tel Aviv, July 1, that the "overriding consideration would seem to be free access to and protection of religious sites," and that a secondary factor involved the "legitimacy of Israeli territorial acquisition." Concerning the latter, he thought the crucial point was "whether we have any real alternatives to making the best of a potentially good situation." He argued that the Israeli occupation followed Jordan's attack on Israel, that there was every reason to believe the Israelis would safeguard legitimate international interests, and that the Arab inhabitants would benefit materially. He recommended that "we should contemplate eventual US acquiescence in Israeli exercise of sovereignty over united Jerusalem, with maximum negotiable safeguards for the Holy Places." (Ibid. POL 27 ARAB–ISR)

Recommendation:

1. That we urge USUN to continue its efforts to alter the Pakistan resolution or, in the alternative, to have comparable amendments proposed.

2. That if these efforts fail and it is necessary to vote on the original Pakistan text, the U.S. abstain with an explanation of vote based on the June 28 statements and the considerations noted above.[7]

---

[7] Neither the approve nor disapprove option is checked.

---

341.   Telegram From the President's Special Consultant (Bundy) to President Johnson[1]

Washington, July 4, 1967, 1528Z.

CAP 67658. For the President from McGeorge Bundy.

We have had a relatively quiet holiday weekend so far and I see nothing that requires your decision in the next few days. Here is where things stand right now:

1. The General Assembly will probably vote today on the Yugoslav and Latin American resolutions, unless there is a successful compromise effort. We seem to have the votes to prevent a really bad result, and I think both the Department and the New York people are doing a fine job.

2. There is a tricky specific problem of a separate Pakistani resolution condemning Israel for actions in Jerusalem. We cannot vote for it in its present form, because it assumes that the Israeli measures do affect the international status of Jerusalem whereas our position is that they are merely administrative actions which do not have this effect. Ours is a much more practical way of keeping heat on the Israelis, and it has already produced a considerable withdrawal by Eban. Our record would be badly tangled from a legal point of view

---

[1] Source: Johnson Library, National Security File, NSC Special Committee Files, U.S. Position—Discussion. Secret. Received at the LBJ Ranch at 12:04 p.m. A handwritten note of July 4 by Jim Jones on the telegram indicates that the President approved releasing the $2 million mentioned in paragraph 3, agreed with everything in the message, and wanted to express his gratitude for the job Bundy had done. An attached note indicates that Bundy was notified at 2:20 p.m. July 4.

if we were to vote for the current Pakistani draft. Yet we would like to have a record of approving some such protest if possible. In this situation we are tying to get the Paks to accept a modification which would be consistent with our own position. Then we could vote for the resolution and make a little money with moderate Arabs. The situation is highly tactical and the decision to vote for the resolution or to abstain will have to be made on the basis of the fine print as the hours roll along. I think the Department is in good control of this one, and there is no difference on the objective.

3. We continue to look for little things that can give some encouragement to the more reasonable Arabs. In this connection I plan to approve a $2 million budget support grant to Jordan tomorrow. This action is consistent with the language we all used with Hussein and represents a commitment initially made some months ago after the November raid by Israel. It already has your approval as of that time and I believe its release now is consistent with your general directives to us. Nevertheless I inform you of it so that it can be held up if you wish.

4. We are also reviewing tourist policy, and there will probably be a recommendation for renewal of permission for the Lebanon as soon as we have a chance to check reactions to the General Assembly voting and as soon as the Embassy in Beirut is prepared to share responsibility for making such a recommendation. Newspapers today indicate that Lebanese authorities are admitting our tourists even though their passports are not valid for that country. They want the money. We still do not plan tourist permission for the countries which broke relations.

5. The most interesting contest on the scene at the moment is not the well-publicized skirmishing near Suez, but the battle for Libyan oil. The Libyan Government had decided to renew shipments to the European continent, and the labor organization has called a general strike aimed particularly at shipments to West Germany. The result of the tug-of-war will have a great deal to do with the severity of any oil crisis this summer. It is a situation in which we have almost no influence, and in which the quieter we are the less likely we are to rock the boat. As I review the general problem in this holiday period, I am inclined to think this rule applies to the crisis as a whole and underlies your own success in dealing with it.

6. Finally, I should report that I have had a very good talk with Dean Rusk yesterday about my own future relation to this problem. We are in strong agreement on the right steps and we expect to have a recommendation for you in another couple of days. Our central purpose is to handle this so that you have the necessary machinery

on hand at all times—but not so much of it that it gets in its own way.[2]

---

[2] A July 12 memorandum from Bundy to the Special Committee states that the President had agreed to his request to devote part of his time to the work of the Ford Foundation in New York, that Battle would serve as the Committee's Deputy Executive Secretary, and that McPherson would be a member of the Committee. (Ibid., Country File, Middle East Crisis, Vol. VIII) An August 24 memorandum from Bundy to Rusk states that it was understood from recent conversations between them and the President that the Special Committee would remain available if needed and his appointment as Executive Secretary should lapse, but that he would remain available for consultation, and his appointment as Special Consultant should continue. (Ibid., Country File, Middle East, Vol. I)

---

342. Telegram From the Mission to the United Nations to the Department of State[1]

New York, July 5, 1967, 1717Z.

58. Subject: GA—Middle East.

Dobrynin, at his request, called on Goldberg this morning and asked US to agree to a delay of 48 hours in the GA proceedings in order to allow time to work out some compromise between the defeated Yugoslav and LA draft resolutions.[2] Goldberg expressed doubts that the gap could be bridged since GA had tried to do this unsuccessfully over a number of weeks. Reiterating our general desire to be cooperative Goldberg said that he would give careful consideration to Soviet request and that he needed to consult Washington before giving our reply by the end of the day. Dobrynin stressed that the reason

---

[1] Source: National Archives and Records Administration, RG 59, Central Files 1967–69, POL 27 ARAB–ISR/UN. Secret; Immediate; Limdis. Repeated Immediate to Moscow. Received at 1:55 p.m. Passed to the White House, DOD, CIA, USIA, NSA, COMAC, and CINCSTRIKE at 2:35 p.m. Rostow sent the text to the President at the LBJ Ranch in CAP 67668, noting, "Herewith the Russians ask for forty-eight hours to try to salvage something from their setback. We are going along because it can't effectively be opposed." (Johnson Library, National Security File, Country File, Middle East Crisis, Vol. VII)

[2] Regarding the Yugoslav draft resolution, see footnote 2, Document 332 and footnote 3, Document 340. After Cuban and Albanian amendments (UN documents A/L.525 and A/L.524) to the draft resolution were defeated by overwhelming majorities, the Assembly voted on the unamended draft resolution. It received 53 votes in favor to 46 against (including the United States), with 20 abstentions, and was not adopted, having failed to receive a 2/3 majority. For the Latin American resolution, see footnote 4, Document 340. It received 57 votes in favor (including the United States) to 43 against, with 20 abstentions, and was not adopted, having failed to receive a 2/3 majority.

for the request for delay was also because 48 hours were needed for consultation in Moscow to determine course of action which Soviets might pursue.

In view Goldberg's expressed doubts that substantive gap could be bridged, conversation then focused on other ways to conclude the Assembly in circumstances where GA had taken some action. Two possibilities were discussed: (a) a possible initiative by the Secretary General, which would be taken note of by the GA, to "send a distinguished special representative to the area to make contact with those directly concerned about the situation"; and (b) a simple resolution which would transmit the GA proceedings to the Security Council which would give further consideration to this matter.

Dobrynin said he would report this to Moscow.

Regarding a possible UN emissary, Goldberg said we felt it should be a genuine neutral such as a Swiss.

Comment: Of interest is the fact that the Soviets sent Dobrynin rather than Fedorenko to see Goldberg. It is also the first time during the course of the special GA that we have had a specific indication from the USSR of a desire to try to work out something with us. We noted other Soviet reps in corridors this morning touching base with other dels and we assume they probably taking similar line re delay with them. We, of course, must continue to be on guard that this is just a Soviet ploy to try to recoup something from the diplomatic defeat they have suffered at GA and which will give some difficulty in the parliamentary situation. However, since it was direct bilateral request to us, and since specific need for guidance from Moscow was mentioned, it would seem to me we have no alternative but to go along with request for delay. Confirming Secy–Sisco telecon, we will agree at appropriate time to requested delay.

Following are the two possibilities which Goldberg and Dobrynin discussed:

The first is a possible statement by the Secretary-General which he would make and which would be taken note of by the GA.

"Having heard the debates on this question, and on the basis of broad consultations, I sense that it would be desirable and generally acceptable for the Secretary-General to send a distinguished special representative to the area to make contact with those directly concerned about the situation and report through the SYG to the SC."

Second is possible GA resolution remanding matter to Security Council.

"The General Assembly,
"Taking note of the views expressed and the resolutions considered by the General Assembly at this extraordinary session, recommends:

"1. That the records of the proceedings be remitted to the Security Council for its further consideration of the matter;

"2. That the Security Council as a matter of urgency deal with the situation in the Middle East."

Alternative 1 was a US draft. Alternative 2 was proposed by Goldberg but incorporates some suggestions made by Dobrynin, specifically, para referring to resolution before GA came from him. He also suggested addition of word "further".

Goldberg

---

343.   Memorandum of Conversation[1]

New York, July 5, 1967, 6:30–7:45 p.m.

PARTICIPANTS

Foreign Minister Eban
Ambassador Harman
McGeorge Bundy

I met with Foreign Minister Eban at my suggestion in order to have an informal discussion of the situation as we both saw it after the General Assembly vote, and on the eve of his departure for Israel. (In the course of the conversation it appeared that he had not yet definitely decided when he would return to Israel because of residual uncertainties about maneuvering in the General Assembly.)

After an exchange of gossip about the General Assembly vote (centered mainly on an agreed view of the Soviet and French performances), we turned to the future. I said to the Foreign Minister that I thought there were great lessons for both our countries in the recent experience. I said that while I had not been in Washington in May, I could well believe that he would have found our position disconcerting, in that we could not give assurances of the breadth and precision which Israel wanted at a critical hour. I said that in my judgment the President was absolutely right not to give such assurances, but that the experience must be instructive to both sides as to the limits on the meaning of the

---

[1] Source: Johnson Library, National Security File, Country File, Middle East Crisis, Vol. VII. Confidential. The meeting was held at the Plaza Hotel. Rostow initialed the top of page 1.

executive assurances which have been given to Israel over the years. I said that on our side a major conclusion from this experience was that both of us would have been in really terrible trouble (for Israel obviously a matter of life and death) if our common assessment of the real military balance in the Middle East had not been right. I said that to me this moment of crisis had revealed more clearly than ever what I had slowly learned in 1961–66, namely that there is a very high American interest in insuring effective defensive strength to Israel as against her Middle Eastern neighbors. If and only if Israel can defend herself, we can avoid a truly agonizing choice. I said that I believed that the real policy of the United States for several years had been to accept this responsibility and that the events of May and June 1967 simply made it a more compelling necessity for us, in that our interest in Israel's self-defense was even greater than before the crisis, while her ability to rely on others was less. Eban seemed to accept this proposition, although he indicated that the Israelis have not given up hope of reestablishing military supply channels in Western Europe.

I said that while I had not talked to President Johnson in precisely these terms, I thought I could predict that he would agree to what I had just said, but that he would surely add a most important proviso: namely, that if we were to have continuing and effective understanding on a matter as important as the basic defensive strength of Israel, we would also have to have a parallel degree of understanding on other issues. I named four as examples:

the future of Jerusalem;
the future of the Arabs now under Israel's military control;
the continuing desirability of avoiding Soviet arms supply to Jordan;
and the nuclear problem.

I said that if I knew President Johnson at all, I could predict that he would insist on candid and effective discussion of these issues as well as the military issues and that I did not think any major arms deal could be handled satisfactorily in isolation.

In his response Eban made no comment on nuclear matters, and my guess is that we'll have to poke very hard to get what we need on this question.

On my other 3 examples Eban was more helpful. He said that in the light of the June battles, U.S. arms for Jordan would be a matter of real emotional difficulty, but he agreed that they were certainly preferable to Soviet arms. He also agreed on the importance of framing an effective policy toward Arabs now within the Israeli military lines, and he was quite frank in saying that no such policy yet exists. I think that his own personal judgment is beginning to lean against any solution that would involve an end of Jordanian sovereignty over the West Bank—he spoke of the attractions of such a new Palestinian entity, but he also spoke with feeling of the danger that it would simply become for Israel what Algeria became for France. Eban also dissociated himself firmly from Dayan's reputed remarks about Gaza being a part of Israel, though both he and Harman emphasized their view that it was not part of Egypt either.

On Jerusalem, Eban was quite forthcoming and seemed to agree that it was important to work out agreed arrangements for the Holy Places which might well include some form of sovereignty for representatives of Christians and Moslems over their Holy Places. He seemed to agree that in the case of the Moslem Holy Places the Jordanians might be the appropriate custodians.

Indeed I found Eban more forthcoming on the subject of Jordan than I had expected. He recognizes the economic difficulties of Jordan and the importance of tourism. He and Harman argued that in conditions of peace Jordan could have more tourist revenue than ever, even without administrative jurisdiction over the old city. They both spoke warmly of the possibilities of economic cooperation between Jordan and Israel, including access to the Mediterranean for Amman.

I then said to Eban that of course in the long run the relation of Israel to the UAR was the central question and he agreed. He said they had always hoped that some day there would be ways and means of settlement with Egypt. Eban said that he was going home to think about ways and means of establishing some contact with Nasser (parenthetically we agreed that while the political situation in Cairo is obscure, the record of the last fifteen years would suggest that Nasser was not a man to bet against in any Egyptian political struggles). Eban emphasized as he has before that the Israelis want very little from Egypt except peace and free passage, but both he and Harman quite firmly included the right of passage through Suez as one of their requirements.

Eban also speculated on the possibility that there might be a relatively early solution with the Syrians simply because the Israeli demands there are minimal and the Soviets might press their clients to be the first to achieve Israeli withdrawal.

I used the occasion of Eban's remarks on Egypt to remind him that there is very little the United States can do to help anyone with the UAR. I said that our bargaining in the past with Nasser had always included a heavy element of U.S. economic assistance, and that I could see no prospect whatever of any such assistance in the near future. The Congress and the public would not stand for it, even if, against all our current expectations, there should be a good case in terms of the situation on the ground. I also pressed Eban gently on the question of the

Israeli troops at Suez. If it were a necessary condition for an early open-ing of the Canal, would the Israelis consider a limited withdrawal? He gave me no direct answer but suggested that it might depend on whether the Egyptians would stay where they now are or would plan to follow the Israelis back across the desert.

I also exchanged informal thoughts with Eban on the "modalities" of reaching agreement with the Arabs. I said that we thought there might be virtue in a three-act play, in which the first act would be pri-vate negotiations, the second an Israeli withdrawal, and the third a pub-lic peacemaking on the basis agreed on in the first act. The advantage of such an arrangement would be that it would protect Arab pride. Eban did not seem to find this a difficult proposition. He said that a variant might be to get half way to agreement and then half way to withdraw-al, but that in either case the Israelis would not be taking any unaccept-able risk because if the Arabs did not keep to their private bargains or half-bargains, it would be easy in the current situation for Israeli forces to reoccupy their present positions.

I ended the meeting as I had begun it with renewed emphasis upon the importance of working in parallel on all these issues together. Harman had earlier emphasized the importance of aircraft, and I told him that while we understood the problem, we did not think it needed settlement in the weeks immediately ahead, and that once we had made a decision we would be able if necessary to supply the aircraft rapidly. I repeated my view that the President would certainly not wish to sep-arate this issue from the others and that we should keep in touch on all of them together. Eban referred to the most recent exchange between the President and Eshkol and said he thought his Government fully understood this point.

I then said a few words to Eban about my private feelings, as one citizen, about the quality of Israelis soldiers and orators, and we parted friends.

344. Circular Telegram From the Department of State to All Posts[1]

Washington, July 5, 1967, 8:55 p.m.

1508. Subj: Jerusalem Resolution in UNGA.

1. In view of sensitivity of question of Jerusalem throughout the world, explanation of US abstention on Pakistan resolution in UNGA (which passed GA on July 4 by vote of 99 for, none against, 20 abstaining)[2] may be helpful. You should seek to have our position on this issue thoroughly understood, and you may draw on this cable to extent it is useful in discussion with host government officials and other interested persons.

2. During last three weeks US Government has issued series of statements expressing our views on Jerusalem. On June 19, President said: "There must be adequate recognition of the special interest of the three great religions in the Holy Places of Jerusalem". A White House statement on June 28 said that the President "assumes that before any unilateral action is taken on the status of Jerusalem there will be appropriate consultation with religious leaders and others who are deeply concerned . . . The world must find an answer that is fair and recognized to be fair. That could not be achieved by hasty unilateral action and the President is confident that the wisdom and good judgment of those in control of Jerusalem will prevent any such action." Later on the same day, after an announcement of Israeli action to place Jerusalem under a unitary administration, the Department of State issued a further statement reading as follows:

"The hasty administrative action taken today cannot be regarded as determining the future of the Holy Places or the status of Jerusalem in relation to them.

The United States has never recognized such unilateral actions by any of the States in the area as governing the international status of Jerusalem.

The policy of the United States will be governed by the President's statement of June 19 and the White House statement this morning.

The views of the United States have been made clear repeatedly to representatives of all governments concerned."[3]

---

[1] Source: National Archives and Records Administration, RG 59, Central Files 1967–69, POL 27 ARAB–ISR/UN. Confidential. Drafted by Popper and Eugene Rostow, cleared by Meeker and in substance by Davies, and approved by Rostow. Also sent to the U.S. Missions at Geneva and USUN and repeated to Jerusalem.

[2] General Assembly Resolution 2253 (ES-V), adopted July 4, 1967. Concerning the Pakistani draft resolution, see footnote 2, Document 340.

[3] Concerning the June 28 statements, see footnote 3, Document 333.

3. In line with USG views on Jerusalem, we voted in favor of the Latin American resolution in UNGA on July 4, which would have reaffirmed "the desirability of establishing an international regime for the City of Jerusalem, to be considered by the General Assembly at its 22nd Session (Fall 1967)". Unfortunately, this resolution did not receive a two-third majority and failed of adoption.

4. At this point, GA took up Pakistani resolution on Jerusalem which declared (1) that measures taken by Israel in Jerusalem are invalid; (2) called upon Israel to rescind these measures and desist from action that would alter the status of Jerusalem; and (3) asked Secretary-General to report to GA and SC on implementation of resolution within one week. US sought amendment to Pakistani resolution to bring it into line with USG position on Jerusalem as indicated earlier. Regrettably, our suggested changes were not accepted. Since Pakistani resolution as voted contained elements that were unrealistic and appeared unlikely to produce any constructive results (such as provision for SYG report within seven days), we abstained in voting on this resolution.

5. Although we did not feel we could vote for Pakistani resolution, we also did not oppose and vote against it. We agreed with Pakistani resolution in sense of its expressing Assembly concern over situation that would arise if unilateral measures were taken permanently to alter status of Jerusalem. US abstention on this resolution should be interpreted as indicative of our own concern.

6. US views on question of Jerusalem remain as stated by USG on June 19 and June 28 and again by Ambassador Goldberg in UNGA (wireless file carries text of statement released to press by USUN on July 4).[4] We will continue to stress our opposition to any unilateral efforts to change the permanent position in Jerusalem or elsewhere, and to insist that any such change be accomplished only by internationally effective action, taking full account of international interests. We do not recognize Israeli measures as having effected changes in formal status of Jerusalem.

(a) Israelis are in that city, as they are in other recently occupied territory, as a result of hostilities last month.

(b) Israel may thus be said to be an occupying power with duty under international law to conform its administration as closely as possible to existing local law.

(c) Israeli action to establish a unified municipal administration of Jerusalem cannot be regarded and will not be recognized as a valid annexation, or a permanent change in legal status of Jerusalem in any sense.

---

[4] For text, see Department of State *Bulletin,* July 24, 1967, p. 112.

(d) It should be considered an interim administrative measure to provide a more convenient and efficient occupation regime for area formerly under Jordanian control, using Jordanian police and other officials wherever possible.

(e) Government of Israel has made it clear that it does not claim that its unified administration of Jerusalem is an annexation.

7. In spirit of statements already made by US defining our public position, we intend to work toward equitable settlement of Jerusalem problem developed through consultation among all concerned.

Rusk

---

345.   Telegram From the President's Special Assistant (Rostow) to President Johnson in Texas[1]

Washington, July 6, 1967, 1855Z.

CAP 67678. The Israelis have been pressing us for several days to allow them to buy 6,000 rounds of two types of tank ammunition ($220,000) and a rotary coupler for a radar set ($20,000). They could either draw down the $14 million credit you have already approved or use some other credit arrangements.

You have before you a broader memo from Mac Bundy[2] covering the whole range of possible exceptions to our current suspension to military aid shipments to the Middle East. I can well understand why you might want to consider that for a while longer. However, Secretaries Rusk and Nitze have sent you a memo[3] saying that they believe that Israel does urgently need these three items and recommending your approval of these exceptions. There would be no publicity.

I can add a personal note from my talks with Evron. He exhibited great concern when he learned indirectly that we were suspending military shipments, especially in view of the continuing Soviet shipments to the Arabs. I checked with Bob McNamara and put the Israelis back

---

[1] Source: Johnson Library, National Security File, Memos to the President, Walt W. Rostow, Vol. 33. Secret.

[2] Document 330.

[3] The memorandum from Rusk and Nitze to the President, July 5, is filed with Rostow's draft of this message. (Johnson Library, National Security File, Country File, Middle East Crisis, Vol. VII)

into regular Defense–State channels on a case-by-case basis. They must prove real need. I informed Mac Bundy in New York who approved.

This recommendation is the first result. By approving these three small exceptions now, we can, I believe, hold the line and avoid pressure for a while.[4]

---

[4] Neither the approve nor disapprove option is checked.

---

346. Telegram From the President's Special Assistant (Rostow) to President Johnson in Texas[1]

Washington, July 6, 1967, 2058Z.

CAP 67681. Bob Anderson called to report the following, which I shall be taking up with Mac Bundy and our other Middle Eastern hands.

1. The intelligence available to the oil companies suggests that the future of Jerusalem may be the critical and truly explosive problem in the Middle East. Arabs regard the Syrian Heights as a Syrian problem; the West Bank as a Jordanian problem; Gaza as an Egyptian problem; but the Old City of Jerusalem is capable of stirring the mobs in the streets to the point where the fate of our most moderate friends in the Middle East will be in jeopardy and the basis laid for a later holy war.

2. Specifically, they report:

—Feisal is worried about his own future on this issue;
—The Lebanese Government is similarly worried;
—Anti-Americanism is rising due to our abstaining on the Pakistan resolution on Jerusalem.

3. Bob underlined that no government should rely on private intelligence sources; and we should make up our own mind in this matter. He understands that you made a public statement on the Jerusalem question; but he believes we must do more both to press the Israelis and to clarify our own position.

---

[1] Source: Johnson Library, National Security File, Special Committee, Whirlwind. Secret. Received at the LBJ Ranch at 4:40 p.m. A handwritten note by Jim Jones on the telegram, July 6 at 5:30 p.m., recorded Johnson's instruction: "Be sure Anderson gets w/Bundy immediately & see what steps we should be taking." Another note, July 6, indicates that Jones told Rostow.

4. He also told me that he has come to the conclusion that the European oil problem is going to turn out to be more serious than in 1956–57, due to increased European requirements and the unavailability of Mediterranean oil. (On the latter, however, an item has just come over the ticker saying that Libya will resume shipments to France, Japan, Turkey, Greece, and Italy, that would narrow the major problem down to Britain and Germany.)

---

347.   Memorandum of Conversation[1]

Washington, July 8, 1967, 3 p.m.

SUBJECT

Middle East Discussion in UNGA

PARTICIPANTS

The Secretary   Amb. Anatoliy Dobrynin, USSR
Deputy Under Secretary Kohler

The Secretary received Ambassador Dobrynin at the latter's request and had a conversation lasting roughly two hours and ten minutes.

The principal purpose of the Dobrynin visit and the main subject of conversation was the question of the consultations going on in the UN corridors with respect to a resolution on the Arab-Israeli crisis at this Special Session of the General Assembly.

Ambassador Dobrynin said that the Soviet Delegation had been consulting with other delegations in an effort to find a compromise resolution which could be approved by the General Assembly and which would cover the essential point of withdrawal of Israeli forces and at

---

[1] Source: National Archives and Records Administration, RG 59, Central Files 1967–69, POL 27 ARAB–ISR/UN. Secret; Exdis. Drafted by Kohler and approved in S on July 10. Another memorandum covering the conversation was on the subject of arms limitation in the Middle East. According to this, Rusk raised the subject of the desirability of limiting the supply of arms to Israel and the Arab countries. He said the United States was not trying to freeze the situation as it was June 12 after the Arab arms losses, but thought it would be important if the Soviets, British, and French could agree not to contribute to a renewed arms race in the Middle East. He asked, "What are the Soviet Union's real purposes in the area?" He noted that Moscow was supporting regimes they call "progressive," in Algiers, Egypt, and Syria and asked if Moscow was "out to topple the conservative governments." Dobrynin replied that the Soviets were prepared to sell arms to Jordan and Morocco. (Ibid., POL 27 ARAB–ISR)

the same time cover other aspects and receive general acceptance. It did not seem possible to refer specifically to the term of non-belligerency because of Arab opposition. However, it would seem possible to turn this formula around and to meet the point by language which would perhaps in several paragraphs refer to non-use of force and necessity for a peaceful solution and the like. However, yesterday the Soviet Delegation had learned that the US opposed a compromise resolution and Gromyko had asked him to come to Washington to check with the Secretary very frankly about this.

The Secretary replied that we were not opposed in principle to a joint or compromise resolution. However, we would be opposed to a horse and rabbit stew, if the Ambassador understood that term. Our attitude would depend on what combination of language could be found. He felt that the position of the Arabs made it difficult to find a real compromise; we, for example, felt it important that we be clear on the subject of belligerence. Ambassador Dobrynin interjected that compromise language could refer to the non-use of force. The Secretary resumed, saying that we do not control the situation in the UN. For example, many of the Latin Americans have strong views of their own. As far as we are concerned, if some substantive points could be satisfactorily combined in a resolution, this would be acceptable to us in the General Assembly. If not, we felt it was better to get the matter back to the Security Council. The Secretary repeated that we are not opposed in principle, but he could not discuss detailed language. He knew that various versions had been put forward in consultations in New York, and he was not informed in detail.

Ambassador Dobrynin pressed his version that several points could be covered and that in their efforts to find a compromise the Soviet Delegation had in fact even got some ideas from the Latin Americans.

The Secretary commented that at the beginning of the Session a great effort had been made to separate out simply the question of Israeli withdrawal.

Dobrynin resumed to say the resolution they contemplated might refer to Israeli withdrawal and refer the matter to the Security Council for further detailed examination with specific reference to several points which had arisen during the discussion. The Secretary asked whether the Soviets had examined further the question of the formula that they had found to end their State of War with the Japanese which had arisen in his discussion with Foreign Minister Gromyko in New York. He commented in this connection that the term armistice in itself implies a continuing State of War. Dobrynin said that there could be phrases relating to a State of Peace. He then said they had not gone further in examining their formula with the Japanese.

In reply to a question from the Secretary, the Ambassador confirmed that the Soviets had had a meeting yesterday with the Latin Americans, specifically with the Chairman of the group and with two other Ambassadors. He would not say that there had been agreement at that meeting, but the Soviets considered that the Latin Americans had advanced some reasonable thoughts.

The Secretary said that the main difficulty was that it would be hard to find suitable language if it were obscure on the question of a continuance of a State of War. There was a danger that a formula would be found which some members would say meant an end of belligerency, but this would be denied by the Arabs. He would repeat that we were not opposed to a General Assembly resolution from a doctrinaire point of view, but there must be some substantial meaning in such a resolution. It would be very difficult to have a specific call for action by Israel combined with only vague promises as to what would happen on the other side. The Secretary then inquired of Dobrynin as to who was most active on the Arab side.

Ambassador Dobrynin replied that Foreign Minister Gromyko was seeing UAR Foreign Minister Fawzi today, so he could not comment on UAR views. On the whole, none of the Arabs seem to be very "eager". However, the Soviets felt that it was worthwhile to try to find compromise language. The Secretary interjected that we are prepared also to try. Dobrynin then repeated that Gromyko had been disturbed when he had heard that the US was opposed. The Secretary responded that we are opposed to a resolution which would be basically the Yugoslav-Indian resolution with a minimum amount of cosmetics applied. Dobrynin then said again that the Soviets were seeking a version which without mentioning the word belligerence would still in several sentences cover the point.

The Secretary said in principle we are prepared to look at anything. Basically, we are not only concerned with our interest of the Middle East situation itself, but we have some interest in not having the UN General Assembly come out with a zero.

The Secretary then interpolated that he had had trouble in matching his thoughts with Gromyko as to the position of UAR Foreign Minister Fawzi. Personally he had found Fawzi vague and very hard to get a hold of. It was not clear, for example, whether Fawzi was speaking with any authority; even on the question of free passage through the Strait of Tiran, Fawzi had said maybe something could be arranged secretly and the like, which was obviously impossible.

Ambassador Dobrynin commented that Fawzi was supposedly speaking as Foreign Minister and authorized to speak for the UAR Government. He then went on to refer to his approach to Ambassador

Goldberg about the 48-hour delay and took some pains to explain this was all the Soviets had sought and that the week's delay was strictly the work of the Assembly President Pshwak and not of the Soviet Delegation.

Concluding the conversation on this subject, the Secretary said that he would phone Ambassador Goldberg and make sure that he would be available and ready to discuss with the Soviet Delegation any possibilities of finding suitable compromise language.

348. Telegram From the Mission to the United Nations to the Department of State[1]

New York, July 9, 1967, 2023Z.

134. Department please pass White House.

This morning at 10 a.m. I was called by USUN COMSEC and advised that request had been made by Sov mission for urgent meeting with me by Amb Dobrynin. I asked that USUN COMSEC immediately call and advise Sov mission I would be willing to meet with Amb Dobrynin at his convenience this morning. Call was made and 12 noon at USUN was fixed for time and place of meeting. I met with Amb Dobrynin alone for one hour and ten minutes. He stated to me that his call was aftermath of his meeting with Secy Rusk yesterday and was designed to explore whether there would be common ground between Sovs and US for compromise res to wind up Assembly.

I said that throughout whole Middle East crisis we had been seeking common ground with Sov Union to restore peace and stability to Middle East but that up to now we had been unsuccessful in working out common language to this end. I reminded Amb Dobrynin that at the last meeting between Secy Rusk and FonMin Gromyko at which I was present both Secy and I had referred to language of Kosygin speech to GA where he had spoken in terms of common language but that until

[1] Source: Johnson Library, National Security File, Country File, Middle East, Middle East Crisis, Vol. VII. Secret; Limdis. Repeated to Moscow. Received at the White House at 2353. The telegram was sent to the President on July 10 at 8:30 a.m. with a covering memorandum from Walt Rostow that reads: "Herewith Dobrynin, having sounded out Sec. Rusk on the steadiness of our position, probes Amb. Goldberg in a highly civilized way, looking for one compromise or another on a Middle East resolution." (Ibid.) A handwritten "L" on the telegram indicates the President saw it.

now there had been no effort by Sov del to explore with US possibility of common agreement.

Amb Dobrynin then said that this was their present desire and I said that we welcomed this effort and would be glad to hear any concrete proposal on his part. Amb Dobrynin said he had no concrete language to offer but that in general he wondered whether the ideas he had put forth to the Secy yesterday provided basis for common understanding.

I told him there was nothing I really could add very much to what Secy had said to him yesterday with respect to his general ideas and I thought Secy had made it very clear that US feels it very important that both Sov Union and ourselves be very clear that in order to restore conditions of peace in ME an equal-handed approach addressed both to Israel and Arab nations was required. This, as Secy stated and as the President made clear at Glassboro to Chairman Kosygin, involved on one hand withdrawal of troops by Israel and on other hand termination by Arab States of their state or claim to belligerency.

Amb Dobrynin then inquired whether we were fixed to the word "belligerency". I said we were not attached to the word. We were however dedicated to principle that time had come for permanent peace in ME and not merely the fragile patchwork of fragile armistice agreements within the context of belligerency which had produced three wars in 20 years.

Amb Dobrynin then inquired as to whether I thought there was any possibility in a res such as suggested to the Secy that contemplated Israeli withdrawal and referral to SC for further consideration detailed examination of other points which were involved in ME crisis.

I said this was the approach in Yugo res and that I did not believe this offered any possibility of common ground. I emphasized that in our view this would not bring about peace and indeed realistically it would not bring about Israeli withdrawal. I repeated to him what President had said at Glassboro and what Secy has frequently said that while we were prepared to use our influence with Israel and the Arab countries involved, none of these countries was puppet of US and we could not dictate terms obviously unacceptable. He at this point interjected that Arab States were not puppets of Sov Union and I said I recognized this but that real question was whether Sov Union and US were prepared to take stand in this Assembly which might have impact upon various parties concerned.

Amb Dobrynin then said language had been discussed with LA's presumably emanating from Spanish del about some prohibition against use of force. I in turn replied that this language was taken almost verbatim from Armistice Agreements and that we conceived this approach to be merely reformulation of language in Yugo res calling for observance of General Armistice Agreements. I read to Amb Dobrynin from 1951 SC res which contained fol passage: "Considering that since the Armistice Agreement which has been in existence for nearly two and a half years is of a permanent character, neither party can reasonably assert that it is actively belligerent." I pointed out that if this was true in 1951 in a res which the Sovs had supported, it was obviously true in 1967.

Amb Dobrynin then inquired as to whether I had any language ideas in mind. I said that I did and if the word "belligerency" was stumbling block we were prepared to consider with them another formulation as follows:

"(A) Without delay, withdrawal by Israel of its forces from territories occupied by them;

"(B) Without delay, recognition by Arab States that Israel enjoys the right to maintain an independent national state of its own and to live in peace and security, and renunciation of all claims and acts inconsistent therewith."

I pointed out that para (B) was very close paraphrase from Chairman Kosygin's speech to GA.[2] Dobrynin aptly said, and I did not dispute this, that this was a more refined way of saying that Arab States could not profess state of war against Israel, and he added in this connection that while he did not argue that this was correct interpretation of Chairman's statement, nevertheless it would not be acceptable to Arabs. Again I reminded him in turn that para (A) would not be acceptable to Israel and that we were nevertheless prepared to support this even-handed approach.

Amb Dobrynin then inquired as to whether it is fair summary for him to report to Gromyko that we were in disagreement as the principles which might be formulated in final substantive res to Assembly. I said that based upon our exchange of views and his exchange of views with Secy as well as conversation President had at Glassboro and subsequent conversation between Secy and Gromyko, this was correct assessment unless at this stage Sovs were prepared to move in direction of recognizing that peace would not exist in ME with parties in area professing right to make war against each other.

Dobrynin then asked whether LA res had represented our essential position. I said to him that despite doubt which appeared in his facial expression, LA res had been developed without participation on our part and that from our stand point it was compromise res. US basic

---

[2] An extract from Kosygin's June 19 address before the General Assembly is printed in *American Foreign Policy: Current Documents, 1967*, pp. 534–537.

view was expressed by President in his five points but nevertheless we had supported LA res as at least recognizing interrelationship between elements of withdrawal, belligerency and other problems in the area. In this connection I told him that President, as he had indicated to Kosygin, was still very much interested in pursuing with him regardless of outcome at Assembly question of arms limitation in ME. I reminded him of Kosygin's statement in his speech about this. He made no reply to me on this subject.

Amb Dobrynin then asked me if my assessment was that if we could not agree on substantive res whether, notwithstanding, the Assembly would agree. I then said that despite their intensive lobbying, to which he interjected, "and your own", I did not see that situation had changed the basic position of parties.

Dobrynin inquired as to whether res could be redrafted in terms of principles. I replied that indeed it could provided both principles were incorporated into res. Specifically I said res could declare (1) that no state could continue to maintain forces on territory other than its own or (2) pursue policy of war or other threat or use of force against sovereign existence of another state. This declaration of principles could be then followed by referral of matter to SC to implement. I added however that we could not support declaration which would call upon Israel for withdrawal as specific act and then follow it with mere declaration of principle that state of non-belligerence should exist without calling upon Arab States to implement this principle. Dobrynin then correctly commented that this meant again that our basic positions remained unchanged and I again agreed.

Dobrynin then asked whether we had any ideas about procedural disposition of Assembly's work if it turned out it would be impossible to have substantive res. I asked whether he had and he said he had no language to suggest. I then said we had further considered matter and we did have some ideas about procedural res and handed him copy of fol procedural res:

"The GA,

Taking note of the views expressed and the resolutions considered by the GA in its extraordinary session,

1. Requests the SYG to appoint a UN mediator for the ME;
2. Empowers the mediator to perform the following functions:

(A) To use his good offices with the parties concerned for the restoration and consolidation of peace and security in the ME;
(B) To assure the protection of the Holy places, religious buildings and sites in Jerusalem;
(C) To promote a peaceful adjustment of the future situation in the area;

(D) To assure that the parties fulfill in good faith the obligations assumed by them in accordance with the Charter, and in particular,

(1) That they shall settle their international disputes by peaceful means in such a manner that international peace and security, and justice, are not endangered, and

(2) That they shall refrain in their international relations from the threat or use of force against the territorial integrity or political independence of any state, or in any other manner inconsistent with the purposes of the UN Charter.

3. Requests the mediator to report periodically through the SYG to the SC and members of the UN.

4. Transmits the records of the proceedings of the session to the SC for its further consideration of the matter and request the SC to deal with the situation as a matter of urgency."

After reading res Dobrynin asked me whether we had any further thoughts about who mediator ought to be.

I reminded him of our prior conversation in which Wahlen had been suggested but stated that in conversation I had with SYG[3] he had indicated that Wahlen in his view would not be appropriate. I then said Jarring, the Swedish Amb in Moscow, had been mentioned. Dobrynin asked whether we had suggested him. I said we had not, that I did not exactly remember how his name had entered the discussion but I did recall that SYG indicated high regard for Jarring. Dobrynin then observed that he shared that high regard.

Dobrynin then asked about origins of procedural res. I said we took it largely from general mandate given to Count Bernadotte in 1948. He seemed to note this with some interest but then said that as things now stand he did not believe that mandate was explicit enough. I asked in what respects. He replied it did not refer to withdrawal to which I replied that if it referred to withdrawal it would also have to refer to belligerency and we would then be going around in circles.

He then made very interesting observation that perhaps it would be best for us to consider together procedural res when it would be clear that Assembly could not at resumed session on Wednesday agree upon substantive res. I said that we were quite agreeable to talk with them at any time about either substantive or procedural res to which he replied that by our exchange it would not appear that we could agree upon substantive

---

[3] Goldberg's July 5 conversation with Secretary-General Thant was reported in telegram 59 from USUN, July 5. Thant said he would prefer a resolution rather than a statement such as Goldberg had suggested to Dobrynin in their meeting that morning reported in Document 342. He was consulting with various delegations and would be prepared to act pursuant to an appropriate resolution, which he agreed should avoid substantive elements in order to be feasible. (National Archives and Records Administration, RG 59, Central Files 1967–69, POL 27 ARAB–ISR/UN)

res but that we should reserve further consultations on procedural res if Assembly took no further action on substance. I said this was agreeable and again repeated we would be glad to consult with them at any time. Dobrynin suggested that perhaps in the procedural res the reference back to SC could refer to peaceful ways and means for solution of problems underlying situation, legal, political and humanitarian. This obviously was taken from Yugo res. I said that in procedural res we would be glad to negotiate with him on precise language.

Comment: As always with Dobrynin conversation was very cordial in tone and frank in its appraisal of situation. It is quite apparent however that they will continue their lobbying in attempt to obtain reversal of votes taken last week and it is also quite apparent they understand we will continue to stand on position we have taken. How successful they or we will be will depend upon LA's. If LA's remain firm it is my view they will not press for another vote. If however LA's fall into disarray then we can anticipate another res which will reflect views of so-called Spanish draft as possibly revised by some LA's. It is also apparent that Dobrynin really did not expect us to change our position and that he had reached this conclusion following his conversation with Secy yesterday. In any event exercise was useful one since (1) we gave him alternative draft which did not use word "belligerency" but which as I pointed out is nevertheless unacceptable [*acceptable*], and (2) it would indicate willingness to explore procedural disposition with us in event Assembly takes no further action on substance.

Goldberg

---

349.   Telegram From the Embassy in Israel to the Department of State[1]

Tel Aviv, July 12, 1967, 1200Z.

114. Ref: Amman 0124.[2]

1. We did not gather from our conversation with Safran that he had any strong personal commitment to idea autonomous Palestine state.

---

[1] Source: National Archives and Records Administration, RG 59, Central Files 1967–69, POL 27 ARAB–ISR. Secret; Exdis. The date of transmission is incorrect; the telegram was received on July 11 at 9:31 a.m.
[2] Telegram 124 from Amman, July 7. (Ibid.)

His impression that autonomous state idea had edge over other schemes for disposition West Bank seemed to us reasonable as reflection informed comment, though not necessarily official GOI position.

2. We believe that GOI has not yet made any definitive decision re ultimate disposition West Bank or Gaza; if it had it would be moving much more decisively in many realms than it is. It is waiting—and has been waiting for over a month—for Arabs to decide to talk peace.

3. It will not wait indefinitely. In our contacts with middle level Israelis concerned with West Bank and Gaza we sense a growing feeling of impatience and frustration at being unable, in absence of basic policy decisions, to attack many problems outstanding. We would expect this feeling to become more pervasive as Israelis generally became aware of cost and complications Gaza and West Bank mean for them. Being rational people they will surely seek to minimize them. In one area, refugees, Israeli problem solvers are already at work: Eban told Senators Gore and Bayh Sunday Israel is planning to resettle at least token number of refugees on West Bank. This kind of action, as long as number is limited, can be taken without knowing the ultimate political disposition of West Bank. Others cannot. Steps to integrate Gaza and West Bank economies into Israeli economy would minimize economic costs, including foreign exchange costs.

4. Policy questions posed in para 3 of reftel are not for us to answer. We would observe only that any USG efforts to persuade GOI return of West Bank is "must" are going to be increasingly unavailing the longer Jordan seeks to avoid dealing with Israel on the issues. The more time passes the more faits accomplis Jordan and the Arabs will find themselves facing.

Barbour

350.   Memorandum From the President's Special Consultant (Bundy) to President Johnson[1]

Washington, July 11, 1967.

SUBJECT

Pending Middle Eastern Decisions

I see three issues which are ripe for consideration. They are:

I. The arms registration proposal;
II. Selected military aid approvals;
III. Limited extension of PL 480 Title II aid (voluntary agencies) to some of the radical Arab countries—especially Algeria and the UAR.

In this memorandum I attempt to summarize the issues. More detailed papers are at Tabs I (arms registration); Tab II (military aid shipments); and Tab III (Title II).[2]

I. Arms registration

The gut issue here is that while everybody prefers the notion of arms restraint in principle, nearly everyone opposes public lists that might inhibit his own sales or procurement. Because people need our weapons, we can override these objections if we wish, but only at some costs in terms of political sniping from the Israelis, moderate Arabs, and sellers like the British. Most of the State and Defense people advise against an early unilateral disclosure, and I reluctantly conclude that they are right. The alternative which they propose is essentially as follows (although I have sharpened it up a little):

1. We should press the case for general arms registration on every diplomatic line and at the UN. While we should begin by consultation with our friends, we should not let this consultation delay us and we should aim at creating a diplomatic situation in which Goldberg can make a formal proposal at the UN within the next month.

---

[1] Source: Johnson Library, National Security File, NSC Special Committee Files, Arms Limits. Secret. Sent through Walt Rostow. A handwritten "L" on the memorandum indicates it was seen by the President. Bundy sent a copy to McNamara with a July 11 covering memorandum noting that it might be relevant at the Wednesday luncheon meeting of the President's Tuesday luncheon group scheduled for July 12. Bundy's memorandum to McNamara states that he had tried to make the three recommendations to the President consistent with the discussions Bundy and McNamara had had earlier. (Washington National Records Center, OSD Files: FRC 330 72 A 2468, Middle East 092)

[2] The attachments, which include a July 11 memorandum from the Control Group to the Special Committee on Arms Control for the Middle East and an undated memorandum from the Control Group to the Special Committee on Exceptions to Interim Arms Policy for the Middle East, are not printed.

2. Even before such a proposal is made, we should begin to call attention in quite specific terms to the large-scale Soviet resupply operation. We should not overstate the military meaning of these shipments, because we do not want to paint the Soviets as ten-foot high protectors of the Arabs. It should not be hard to find language which tells the facts without fanfare, and which points the finger of responsibility politely but firmly at those who are in danger of starting up the arms race all over again.

3. At the same time, or a little later, we should let it come out that we ourselves are continuing very much more modest and carefully chosen assistance programs, mainly agreed before June 5—first to moderate Arabs and second to the Israelis. The language of any such backgrounding should be carefully drafted to emphasize the fundamentally restraining purpose of these very limited shipments. We should note that in total they represent only a small fraction of what others have done. (There are some who think we should not minimize our contributions, because that will simply lead to further requests, but I think on balance they are wrong. Especially in the United States and on Capitol Hill we need to have a picture of great restraint and selectivity in our arms shipment policy.)

4. Beginning now it should be our understanding, on all new arms agreements, that the recipient will support the principle of arms registration in the UN. We can get this agreement if we ask for it, even though we must accept the fact that most of those who agree will do so in serene confidence that they will never have to honor their promise because of the continuing refusal of the Soviet Union to play ball.

Some combination of principles like these seems to me to give us the best middle road between the conservatives who find the whole notion of arms registration impractical and even dangerous, and the idealists who would like to see us practice what we preach on a one-way basis. In effect what is proposed is a diplomatic campaign in favor of arms registration and a policy of unilateral interim disclosure which would fall short of giving away specific military "secrets."[3]

Go ahead on this basis

Hold for discussion in Tuesday lunch group

Call a Special Committee meeting

II. Certain limited additional arms shipments

There are two interlocking forces here which lead to a need for a reasonably prompt decision. The first is Israeli pressure for addition-

---

[3] None of the options in this memorandum is checked, and there is no indication of the President's reaction.

al shipments under the agreement you approved on May 23, together with an intense Israeli desire to buy about $300,000 worth of tank ammunition and an $18,000 radar coupler—items which they claim to need urgently in the wake of the June fight. Bob McNamara and I reviewed these items last week and he and I agreed that we should be responsive on the May 23 agreement so as to prove that your decisions stick, and that the tank ammunition and the radar coupler are such small items that it would be a mistake to hold them up for long. We have some very major issues to settle with the Israelis when they come in for new major military agreements, and I have already warned Abba Eban that you are not the sort of man who will wish to separate fundamental questions of Israeli defense from major political issues in which we have a legitimate interest—like Jerusalem and the refugees. But these bargains are of a different scale altogether from tank ammunition, and we believe we can negotiate them more effectively if we can point to a record of meticulous and timely fulfillment on the May 23 agreement. So there is an Israeli package that is ready to move.

On the other hand, we do not want Israeli military supplies to hit the papers ahead of limited actions for the moderate Arabs if we can help it. We already have three such limited actions which you approved at the end of June for fiscal year reasons—a $14 million Moroccan program; a $15 million sale of four C–130s to Saudi Arabia, and a $9.9 million weapons repair and maintenance program also for the Saudis. Now we would like to thicken this package with some further limited actions for Saudi Arabia, Jordan, Lebanon, Morocco and Libya. The items involved are well summarized at Table II. None of them involves heavy combat equipment. The only large items are sales (to the oil-rich Saudis), and there is no USG financing which was not already in prospect before the war. I would emphasize especially the Jordanian item—which would resume shipments of about $2 to $4 million over the next six months under previously approved grant and sales programs. The Jordanians need this small action in order to quiet their military, and we have already received grudging acknowledgment from the Israelis (Eban) that we are a better supplier than the Soviets. This Jordanian list includes nothing that would scare the Israelis in the current balance of power.

I think it is really very clear that on policy grounds both the Israeli package and the moderate Arab packages are highly desirable. The only difficulty is in possible Hill resistance. Bill Macomber has checked leaders of the Foreign Affairs and Foreign Relations Committee in both Houses and says that there is reluctant acceptance of the argument, although without enthusiasm. McNamara thinks we can expect a similar result in the Armed Services Committees. I have checked myself with Russell, who says go ahead, with Symington, who says OK if I say so (but reluctantly on Jordan), and with Fulbright, who says we should do nothing and try for an agreement with the Soviets (I answered that we were trying and would keep trying, but could not let places like Jordan sink or swim while we waited). I conclude that we should go ahead, but that Luke Battle should have one more session with the Symington Mid-East Subcommittee before the actions are final.

Go ahead on this basis

Hold for discussion in Tuesday lunch group

Call a Special Committee meeting

III. PL 480, Title II for Arabs who broke relations

As you know, we allowed Title II aid to continue to all Middle Eastern countries as long as the voluntary organizations could oversee offloading and distribution. Now we face a decision on similar action for FY–68, and at Tab III there is a good summary memorandum drafted for me by Howard Wriggins of Walt's staff. In essence what it amounts to is an authorization for Catholic Relief and CARE for $4.5 million for the first quarter, almost $4 million to go to Algeria and nearly all the rest to UAR. We owe nothing to Boumediene or Nasser but on balance I think the value of the humanitarian shipments outweighs the marginal economic usefulness to demagogues.

Go ahead on this basis

Hold for discussion in Tuesday lunch group

Call a Special Committee meeting

351.   Memorandum From Peter Jessup of the National Security
        Council Staff to Harold H. Saunders of the National
        Security Council Staff[1]

Washington, July 11, 1967.

SUBJECT

Intelligence Collaboration with Israel

REFERENCE

Memo dated July 8, 1967, from Mr. Saunders, subject same as above[2]

As you know, the attachés of various countries in Israel are kept under a very tight rein and shown only what the IDF wants them to see. The Americans get no special favors in this channel. Thus, particularly aggressive U.S. personnel feel frustrated.

There is a certain amount of gamesmanship between what the Israeli attachés are allowed to do here and what ours can do there.

There is also a slight resentment in a tightly disciplined country [1 line of source text not declassified].

In regard to captured Soviet equipment, I am informed that every-thing is on order [1 line of source text not declassified]. The Defense attaché, an eager beaver, is a capable officer, and his implication that there may be roadblocks apparently refers only to a larger project under consideration by the JCS to send a 12-man team for exploitation on the spot of both equipment and experience.

Meanwhile, the current relationship is proceeding with the reports and packaging of items for further study here, and I have no reason to believe that a thorough job will not be done and the benefits will be spread through the community.

I think the matter of the 12-man team should be left to the JCS, and it would be inappropriate of the White House to enter any pleas on its behalf at this time. You know the old saw, the job is being accomplished but a special task force will give it momentum, etc., etc., etc.

Peter Jessup[3]

---

[1] Source: Johnson Library, National Security File, Country File, Middle East Crisis, Vol. VII. Top Secret. Also sent to Bundy and Rostow.

[2] Saunders' memorandum states that he had learned that there was a large mine of intelligence information in the experience and the captured Soviet matériel that the Israelis had acquired during the recent fighting. The Defense Attaché had obtained agree-ment for a senior American team to go to Israel to take advantage of this but was afraid that road blocks would be thrown in its way. (Ibid.)

[3] Printed from a copy that indicates Jessup signed the original.

352.   Diplomatic Note From Secretary of State Rusk to the Israeli Ambassador (Harman)[1]

Washington, June 10, 1967.

The Secretary of State presents his compliments to His Excellency the Ambassador of Israel and has the honor to refer to the Ambassador's Note of June 10, 1967 concerning the attacks by Israeli aircraft and torpedo boats on the United States naval vessel U.S.S. *Liberty*, which were carried out shortly after 1400 and 1430 hours local time, respectively, on June 8, 1967 while the U.S.S. *Liberty* was engaged in peaceful activities in international waters.

At the time of the attack, the U.S.S *Liberty* was flying the American flag, and its identification was clearly indicated in large white letters and numerals on its hull. It was broad daylight and the weather conditions were excellent. Experience demonstrates that both the flag and the identification number of the vessel were readily visible from the air.

Beginning at about 0515 hours local time on June 8, 1967, and at intervals thereafter prior to the first attack, aircraft believed to be Israeli circled the U.S.S. *Liberty* on a number of occasions.

Accordingly, there is every reason to believe that the U.S.S. *Liberty* was or should have been identified, or at least her nationality determined, prior to the attack. In these circumstances, the later military attack by Israeli aircraft on the U.S.S. *Liberty* is quite literally incomprehensible. As a minimum, the attack must be condemned as an act of military irresponsibility reflecting reckless disregard for human life.

The subsequent attack by Israeli torpedo boats, substantially after the vessel was or should have been identified by Israeli military forces, manifests the same reckless disregard for human life. The silhouette and conduct of the U.S.S. *Liberty* readily distinguished it from any ves-

---

[1] Source: National Archives and Records Administration, RG 59, Central Files 1967–69, POL 27 ARAB–ISR. No classification marking. The note, dated June 10, is a revised version of Document 256. It was revised by Katzenbach, Meeker, and Walt Rostow on July 11. Most of the revisions were made to correct incorrect times and incorrect statements in the original note. According to a handwritten note by Wriggins on a copy of the draft revised note, Rostow cleared it and deleted the word "wanton." (Johnson Library, National Security File, Saunders Files, Israel, 6/1/67–10/31/67) The note is filed, together with Document 383, and a covering memorandum of July 20 from Walsh to Walt Rostow stating that they constituted the true, corrected versions of the exchange and that all other copies should be destroyed. Battle gave the revised note to Harman on July 11. In discussing the incident, Battle emphasized the "irate reaction" that the incident produced in Congress and the continuing strong interest of many members of Congress in the outcome of the investigations into its cause. (Airgram A–15 to Tel Aviv, July 14; National Archives and Records Administration, RG 59, Central Files 1967–69, POL 27 ARAB–ISR)

sel that could have been considered as hostile. The U.S.S. *Liberty* was peacefully engaged, posed no threat whatsoever to the torpedo boats, and obviously carried no armament affording it a combat capability. It could and should have been scrutinized visually at close range before torpedoes were fired.

While the Ambassador of Israel has informed the Secretary of State that "the Government of Israel is prepared to make amends for the tragic loss of life and material damage," the Secretary of State wishes to make clear that the United States Government expects the Government of Israel also to take the disciplinary measures which international law requires in the event of wrongful conduct by the military personnel of a State. He wishes also to make clear that the United States Government expects the Government of Israel to issue instructions necessary to ensure that United States personnel and property will not again be endangered by the wrongful actions of Israeli military personnel.

The United States Government expects that the Government of Israel will provide compensation in accordance with international law to the extent that it is possible to compensate for the losses sustained in this tragic event. The Department of State will, in the near future, present to the Government of Israel a full monetary statement of its claim.

---

353.   Editorial Note

On July 12, 1967, at 2:45 p.m., President Johnson met with Secretary Rusk, Secretary McNamara, Walt Rostow, and George Christian at luncheon at the White House. According to notes of the meeting by Deputy White House Press Secretary Tom Johnson, who was also present, there was some discussion concerning the Middle East.

The President said that he was "still concerned about the Middle East situation" and was "more concerned about the Soviet position in the Middle East than Secretary McNamara and Secretary Rusk appeared to be." He said he wanted a "report on what U.S. posture should be concerning the arms shipment situation into the Middle East." Secretary McNamara said he would favor "a unilateral report to the United Nations on U.S. arms shipments to Middle East countries even if the Soviets did not decide to make public their arms shipments into the area."

After some discussion concerning Vietnam, they returned briefly to the subject of the Middle East. Rostow reviewed three proposals by Bundy. According to Johnson's notes, they concerned Soviet arms shipments to the Middle East, arms registration with the United Nations, and an Israeli request for more arms. The President asked that Rostow "confer with Rusk and McNamara and come back to the President with a report on these issues." (Johnson Library, Tom Johnson's Notes of Meetings)

Rostow's agenda for the meeting indicates that Bundy's three proposals were the arms registration proposal, selected military aid approvals, and limited extension of PL 480 Title II aid through voluntary agencies to some of the radical Arab countries, especially Algeria and the UAR. Rostow's handwritten notations on the agenda indicate that there was to be a meeting the next day on the first point, that on the second point they should "wait on Hill," and that on the third point the answer was "no—on Hill." (Ibid., National Security File, Files of Walt W. Rostow)

---

354.   Circular Telegram From the Department of State to Certain Posts[1]

Washington, July 12, 1967, 8:26 p.m.

5731. Subject: U.S. Position on a Near East Settlement.

Department wishes to maintain a dialogue on Near East crisis with host governments of addressees to promote understanding U.S. objectives and enlist support for steps necessary for settlement. The following points should be drawn upon as appropriate in discussions or incorporated in follow-up aide mémoires with host government officials and opinion makers.

1. The U.S. position on the Near East crisis was outlined in the President's statement of June 19 and, we believe, provides the basis for

---

[1] Source: National Archives and Records Administration, RG 59, Central Files 1967–69, POL 27 ARAB–ISR. Confidential. Drafted by Eugene Rostow on July 11; cleared by Deputy Assistant Secretary for African Affairs J. Wayne Fredericks, Davies, and Wriggins; and approved by Rusk. Sent to Amman, Jidda, Kuwait, Beirut, Rabat, Tunis, Tripoli, Tel Aviv, London, Paris, USUN, Tehran, Rawalpindi, Djakarta, New Delhi, Ankara, Tokyo, Belgrade, Moscow, Sofia, Rome, Madrid, Brussels, and Bonn.

a just and equitable settlement between the Arab states and Israel. In that speech, the President clearly called for the withdrawal of Israeli forces as essential element NE settlement. We believe the continued presence of Israeli troops on the territory of neighboring states is an unnatural situation. To create the conditions which will assure earliest withdrawal, all parties must take action to guarantee the future security and integrity of all the states involved. Otherwise another war would be probable.

2. In our view, the root of the problem is the claim of some states that a state of war continues with Israel and that they have right to the status of belligerents under international law with respect to Israel. The claim of belligerent rights works both ways. If Egypt claims belligerent rights, it can hardly deny belligerent rights to Israel. Egypt cannot claim the right to mass overwhelming military forces on Israel's borders, issue threats of liquidation, and then deny Israel the right of counter-measures. In 1951, 1956, and in 1957 the Security Council declared that belligerent rights could not be asserted in the Near East. Surely, the time has now come to see if better ways to resolve differences can be found than those which have led to diversion of needed resources to sterile armaments, to nineteen years of fear and suspicion, and to needless death and destruction.

3. The United States believes firmly that termination of the state of belligerency coupled with withdrawal of troops from occupied areas is the only practical and realistic way to achieve that end and thus to initiate a constructive and agreed solution to other problems of peace in the area: justice for the refugees, the status of Jerusalem, unobstructed passage through international waterways, arms limitations, and peaceful progress for all the peoples of the area. In this way, and, in our opinion, only in this way, can the world achieve a condition in which independence, integrity, and security, which rightfully inhere in every nation in the area, can be fully respected and protected.

4. We are deeply concerned for the full and direct protection of the interests of Islam and the other great religions in Jerusalem. We are pledged to firm action with all interested parties to make certain that the interests of Islam, Judaism, and Christianity are fully respected and protected. The public statements made in Washington reflect our determination.

5. Our delegation abstained in the vote on the Pakistani Resolution about the future of Jerusalem at the General Assembly last week for sound reasons. As Ambassador Goldberg said, the Pakistani Resolution assumed that Israel has annexed Jerusalem. The Resolution asked that the supposed annexation be rescinded. But the Government of Israel had announced that its arrangements for the administration of

Jerusalem as a unified city were not an annexation. Jordanian officials and municipal councillors will participate in the administration of the city during the period of occupation. And Israel is consulting with religious representatives and others about possible plans through which the deep interests of Islam and Christendom in Jerusalem can be permanently protected. The Prime Minister of Israel has said that Israel has no need or interest in the ownership of Christian or Moslem Holy Places. It therefore seemed to us that the Pakistani Resolution was not directed to the situation on the ground. We tried to get agreement on amendments that would have made it possible for us to support the Resolution, but we failed.

6. We are not wedded to any particular words or procedures in order to move toward achievement of a just and durable peace. The essential assurances can be given publicly or privately, through mediators, or through agreements. In the last analysis, a solution cannot be imposed from outside: The basic responsibility for achieving peace lies with the governments and peoples of the area. We, with other members of the United Nations, stand ready to help in any way our friends in the Near East deem helpful.

7. The United States has sought and continues to seek the best possible relations with all the states of the Near East on bases of mutual respect and mutual interests. To the extent we had the capability we have extended our assistance over the years in efforts to resolve disputes and prevent conflict. We have undertaken to seek to protect the territorial integrity and political independence of all states in the area. Our influence has been exerted in behalf of many states in the Near East in recent years—of Egypt in 1956, of Lebanon in 1958, and of other states when subjected to pressures on the part of their neighbors. We have sought through programs of economic assistance to help develop the well-being that gives substance and strength to independence.

8. The U.S. used every resource of diplomacy to prevent the outbreak of hostilities between Israel and her Arab neighbors in the present crisis. The closure of the Strait of Tiran, reversing international understandings through which Israel's agreement to withdraw troops from Sinai in 1957 was obtained, clearly was the major factor in heightening the tensions which led to conflict.

9. It should be clear to all that the U.S. does not and cannot control the actions of any nation of the Middle East. If it had such control, hostilities would not have occurred. Not only did we exert our utmost efforts with all parties to avert hostilities, but also we had no prior knowledge they would occur. The calumnies alleging a U.S. role in the preparation or execution of these hostilities are totally and deliberately false, and are deeply resented by the people of the United States. These

charges have caused damage to our friendly relations with some countries of the Near East, a fact we regret and deplore.

10. In this bitter and tragic conflict, we have neither supported nor opposed any country. Our energies have been engaged in seeking to achieve and protect peace, in the interest of all. We seek a peace in which the just rights of all the nations and peoples of the area will be safeguarded. We seek to strengthen bonds of friendship and understanding with all the peoples of the Middle East.

[Omitted here is a message for the Ambassador in Libya authorizing him to use the above as the basis for a presentation and aide-mémoire to the Prime Minister.]

Rusk

355.   Telegram From the Mission to the United Nations to the Department of State[1]

New York, July 13, 1967, 0059Z.

193. Riad (UAR) buttonholed Sisco in back of GA hall and asked to speak to him very privately and confidentially. He said he was concerned there had been insufficient contact between US and UAR since last discussion between Secty and Fawzi and felt it would be well for two of us to take a current reading on where matters stand at GA.

Said he wished to describe candidly how American position is being portrayed to them in corridors. It was being said that we wanted no res, that this Assembly was an unwanted Assembly called by the Sov Union and that US wanted to deny Sovs any possibility that something constructive would come out of GA. He said we felt that time would be required before any solution could be achieved, and that we wanted nothing to come out of Assembly in meantime. He concluded by saying our policy was being characterized as one designed to topple Arab regimes in ME.

Sisco said we have not been and are not against a GA res as a matter of principle. Principal, though not only, problem had been that in all

---

[1] Source: National Archives and Records Administration, RG 59, Central Files 1967–69, POL 27 ARAB–ISR/UN. Confidential; Limdis. Received at 10:14 p.m. on July 12.

of negots non-aligneds, in their discussions with LAs during this past week's recess had been unwilling to accept as a matter of equity a para in which a call on Israel to withdraw would be balanced by a call to Arab States to renounce belligerency. Sisco pointed out it had not been possible to bridge this gap, and that we had been told by numerous dels that it was because UAR, Syria and Jordan unwilling or felt unable to renounce a state of belligerency. Sisco asked Riad whether this is an accurate assessment of the Egyptian position, whether in fact it could renounce belligerency in a res at this time. Sisco added that if LAs and non-aligneds could not agree on principles to be included in a substantive res, we would be prepared to support a simple procedural res devoid of substance, requesting SYG to designate a world statesman to make contact with the parties and to discuss whole situation. What was Egyptian position on this point?

We have been receiving conflicting info but most delegates have stressed unwillingness of Egypt to consider this kind of a suggestion.

Alternatively if in fact Egypt and other Arab States do not want this kind of a proposal to come out of GA, would a simple referral of records of GA to SC for further consideration be a possibility?

Finally, Sisco rejected view that our policy is to topple Arab regimes and said that our policy remains unchanged: We wish to have friendly relations with all countries in area, and we are prepared to do what we can to help bring about a durable and stable peace, as Pres Johnson indicated in his June 19 statement.

Riad asked whether there was some other form of words which might be agreed to on belligerency question. Sisco said if Riad was referring to the Spanish text, LAs had not accepted this proposal, and we felt it fell far short of mark. In particular, it did not contain kind of balance described above.

Sisco said important thing is what are Egyptian intentions. Are they prepared to renounce belligerency and all that this implies and to agree to it explicitly in a res?

Riad urged that Sisco get together with Fawzi and Riad later this evening to see if language could be worked out. Sisco said that we, of course, are always ready to talk and to consider any suggestions from any dels, including UAR. However, negots on this matter were presently in hands of LAs who were meeting with non-aligneds and that any suggestions which Egyptians might have might better be funneled though that channel.

In response to Riad's query as to whether he should seek responses from Fawzi to questions raised, Sisco said he was not asking Riad to do so but if Fawzi could shed some light on these points it might be helpful, if not in the present tactical situation at least at some future time. Sisco concluded by saying he available to continue to exchange views should Riad have any further thoughts on matter.

Goldberg

---

356.   **Memorandum From W. Howard Wriggins of the National Security Council Staff to the President's Special Assistant (Rostow) and the President's Special Consultant (Bundy)**[1]

Washington, July 12, 1967.

SUBJECT

Conversation with Chris Herter on Jerusalem Resolution[2]

Chris Herter telephoned to express to me the acute concern that he and his other oil colleagues have regarding possible repercussions if for a second time we do not support the Jerusalem resolution.

He reports that the effects in the Arab countries of our abstention on the Pak resolution were devastating. None of the Arabs can understand what to them was a technical position which we took—a position which they see as clearly favoring Israel and giving Israel the benefit of the doubt.

He urged us most earnestly, therefore, this time to consider the political effects throughout the Middle East of a second abstention. No amount of technical discussion on the terms of the resolution would help within the Arab world. He sees this largely as a question of passion and posture, not of specific textual language.

Howard

---

[1] Source: Johnson Library, National Security File, Country File, Middle East Crisis, Vol. VIII. Secret.

[2] A resolution submitted by Pakistan on July 12 deplored the Israeli failure to implement resolution 2253 (ES–V) (see footnote 2, Document 344), reiterated the call to Israel in that resolution to rescind measures already taken and desist from taking any action which would alter the status of Jerusalem, requested the Secretary-General to report to the Security Council and the General Assembly on the situation and on the implementation of the resolution, and requested the Security Council to ensure its implementation. For text of the resolution and a revised version submitted the next day, see UN documents A/L.528 and A/L.528/Rev. 1 and Rev. 2.

357.   Memorandum From the President's Special Assistant (Rostow) to President Johnson[1]

Washington, July 13, 1967, 10:30 a.m.

Mr President:

I have just had a long talk with Mac Bundy on Jerusalem. We have one day to turn around since the UN vote will not come until tomorrow.

1. Ambassador Goldberg feels we should not shift off our position of abstention on the Pakistani resolution. He says we have taken our lumps in the UN General Assembly and the international community on this issue. And, in his judgment, the Jewish community here would be up in arms if we switched. He adds a technical argument; namely, that the language of the present Pakistani resolution calls for the Security Council "to take measures" to enforce the General Assembly resolution. This means at the UN that Article 7 of the United Nations Charter be applied; and this involves sanctions or force. That aspect of the resolution has apparently scared off the Canadians and the UK. It may be modified via UK and Canadian pressure on the Paks in the course of the next 24 hours.

2. On the other hand, both Mac and I feel that the Israeli response to the Secretary General[2] was unsatisfactory. Something more than a deal on the Holy Places with the Vatican is required if we are going to have a stable Middle East.

3. We face, therefore, three choices:

—to go with Arthur Goldberg and abstain again;
—to switch our position to support for the Pak resolution, using the unsatisfactory character of the Israeli response as a justification;
—to stay with abstention and make two statements: one by Amb. Goldberg, the other by the Secretary of State in Washington. The statements would make the following points:

a. The pre-war position in Jerusalem was unsatisfactory;
b. The actions taken by the Israelis and their proposals are also unsatisfactory in terms of your statement of June 19: ". . . there must be adequate recognition of the special interest of three great religions in the Holy Places of Jerusalem."

---

[1] Source: Johnson Library, National Security File, Country File, Middle East Crisis, Vol. VIII. Confidential. A handwritten notation on the memorandum indicates it was received at 11 a.m.; a handwritten "L" indicates the President saw it.

[2] Foreign Minister Eban's reply of July 10 to the Secretary-General is reproduced in the Secretary-General's report of July 10 to the General Assembly and the Security Council. For text of the report, see UN document A/6753 (S/8052).

c. This is not an issue which can be settled by abstract resolutions in the UN or by the use of force. It requires negotiation among all the interested parties. In the meanwhile, we cannot accept as definitive the actions and position thus far taken by the Government of Israel.

4. Mac thinks, and I agree, that to get the proper attention and hardness into our position before our own people, the moderate Arabs, etc., a statement from Washington by the Secretary of State is essential. It is his judgment that Amb. Goldberg cannot really swing it politically.

5. Moreover, this is the one immediate issue on which we could begin to balance our accounts somewhat with the moderate Arabs; and it is a good issue because we believe that this position is right both for the U.S. and, in the long run, for the Israelis themselves.

6. In the course of the next 24 hours, as noted above, the language of the Pak resolution may be diluted; and we may wish to consider voting with it. In the meanwhile, Mac and I recommend the third option.[3]

7. The issue will be discussed in the course of the day by those working on the Middle East; and you may wish to discuss the matter with Secretary Rusk. I will keep you informed.

Walt

---

[3] There is no indication of the President's reaction on the memorandum.

---

358. Telegram From the Mission to the United Nations to the Department of State[1]

New York, July 14, 1967, 0131Z.

203. Mid-East Crisis.

Riad (UAR) met with Sisco again today as follow-up to confidential discussions of yesterday. Riad said he had some comments to make regarding Sisco's queries of yesterday as to whether UAR in position now to renounce belligerency, and that if gap on substantive res unbridgeable whether UAR would believe time propitious for GA to decide upon some high level rep to make contact with parties.

---

[1] Source: National Archives and Records Administration, RG 59, Central Files 1967–69, POL 27 ARAB–ISR/UN. Secret; Priority; Limdis. Received on July 13 at 10:34 p.m.

Riad's response to belligerency point consisted of a reversion to three points which Fawzi made to Secy in his last conversation.[2] Riad recalled that Fawzi had informed Secy that UAR is prepared to acquiesce tacitly to freedom of passage of all ships through strait and that this information had been conveyed to UK, USSR and France as well. Secondly, Riad recalled that Fawzi had stressed that UAR is "determined to return to state of quiet". Riad said he would not wish to relate this terminology to other terminology being discussed in corridors but UAR seriously meant return to state of quiet. Third, Riad recalled that Fawzi and Secy had talked about possibilities of placement of UNEF or UN presence and that he wished to make clear on behalf of Fawzi that Egypt would definitely accept UNEF presence provided it was on both sides of line.

Riad said they unable to mention belligerency in res because of its implications with respect to Suez Canal.

Riad said that before he gave any specific answer to willingness accept third party they wished to see how present discussions on possible substantive compromise works out. He indicated that UAR had informed non-aligneds of its willingness to go along with draft presented by Malacela last night to Latinos. (This is draft contained in Annex B of USUN 198[3] and which we informed LAs this morning was clearly unacceptable to US.)

During course of day there appeared shift in UAR position. About 4 p.m. this afternoon Riad sought out Sisco to inform him that it might be possible for UAR to accept word "belligerency" in res provided it is appropriately modified. In saying this Riad was referring to fol Indian formulation which we have already informed Indians is not acceptable to US.

"Further affirms that the political sovereignty and territorial integrity of member states in the Middle East allow them a rightful freedom from threats or acts of belligerency and consequently urges all states in the Middle East to refrain and desist from threats or acts of war."

Sisco focused principally on advantages to everybody concerned in closing down GA promptly so that principal parties could begin to address themselves realistically to serious questions and arrangements that must be sorted out if durable peace is to be achieved in ME. Sisco said as long as public debate continues it will be difficult for parties to begin discussions, indirect or otherwise, and that in our judgment since gap between two substantive positions has been found unbridgeable it

---

[2] See Document 327.

[3] Telegram 198 from USUN, July 13; not printed. (National Archives and Records Administration, RG 59, Central Files 1967–69, POL 27 ARAB–ISR/UN)

would be well to get matter back to SC for further consideration at some appropriate stage. Sisco stressed too advantages of getting some third party involved so that there can be realistic focus on fundamental elements of settlement. Riad did not disagree with this view but dwelt at some length on some need for "something to come out of GA" and in particular expression by Assembly in favor of withdrawal of Israeli forces.

Conversation then turned to internal situation in UAR. Riad said situation very difficult indeed, particularly from economic view. However he felt progress was being made in "reshaping military" and that he personally felt it was very important for influence of US to return to area at earliest possible moment. He said somewhat emotionally that this was in everybody's interests, including US. Implication of what Riad said was concern over possible expansion of Sov influence in area.

Riad concluded by saying Fawzi felt it important that we keep in touch on regular basis. Sisco agreed and said he readily available at any time.

Goldberg

---

359.   Telegram From the Department of State to the Embassy in Morocco[1]

Washington, July 13, 1967, 10:34 p.m.

6578. From the Secretary.

1. I appreciate your 145,[2] and its analysis. Re Laraki views, GOK FonMin took same line with me July 10 (State 4217).[3] I told him Israeli withdrawal could not be separated from central question of need to end

---

[1] Source: National Archives and Records Administration, RG 59, Central Files 1967–69, POL 27 ARAB–ISR/UN. Secret; Exdis. Drafted by Eugene Rostow and Brewer; cleared by Battle, Deputy Assistant Secretary for African Affairs William C. Trimble, and Kohler; and approved by Rusk.

[2] Telegram 145 from Rabat, July 11, reported a conversation with Foreign Minister Laraki, who told the Ambassador that the Kuwaiti and Jordanian Foreign Ministers, plus the Saudi Arabian equivalent, were leaving for the United States, where they hoped to see the President to state that it was absolutely essential to the Arab moderates that U.S. actions in the General Assembly give them something on which to base continued cooperation with the United States. (Ibid., POL MOR–US)

[3] Not found.

state of belligerency. Because of its reciprocal character, finding some formula which would end state of war would seem as much in interest Arabs as Israel.

2. Our policy has indeed been based on clear realization that world community has little time in which prevent Arab-Israel problem from again lapsing into dangerous immobility. Our conviction that time is short underlies our efforts to produce a solution in which Israel would withdraw and the Arabs—and, of course, Israel—would give up warfare. Whatever the Arabs may think, the former cannot be brought about by USG without some reciprocal concessions on belligerency question. Provided genuine, these could no doubt be formulated in manner which would take account Arab sensibilities.

3. We would like to end this situation now, before myths take over and a new arms race becomes inevitable. However, while Arab moderates might well accept (and even be grateful for) any imposed solution of the problem on which we and the Soviets could agree, the Soviets have made it clear to us that they will not sacrifice their credibility in Arab eyes. We recognize that the Arab moderates are probably the prime Soviet target in this crisis. To a considerable extent, so do the moderates themselves. But so far they seem neither able nor willing to do anything about it. No doubt this is because they fear Arab radicals, notably Syria and Algeria, even more than Israelis or Russians. But it is difficult for us to help those who will not help themselves.

4. I want to assure you, however, that we fully understand the difficulties in which the Arab moderates find themselves. We know we need them for the future and are seeking to get across the message that they need us sufficiently to do something in their own behalf. This would involve neither "recognition" of Israel nor "dealing directly" with Israel. Some recognition of the need to avoid a return to the Arab-Israel status quo, as well as willingness on part one or two Arab states to restore relations with us, and to remove discriminatory oil curbs, would materially help us in our continuing efforts to assist good friends like King Hassan in riding out the storm.

Rusk

360. **Telegram From the Department of State to the Mission to the United Nations**[1]

Washington, July 13, 1967, 11:06 p.m.

6581. Please deliver at once following message from Secretary of State to Foreign Minister Eban reported at Plaza Hotel.

Dear Mr. Minister:

We have today received a most urgent and private message from King Hussein.[2] This message informs us that the King has determined that he is prepared to conclude some sort of arrangement with the Government of Israel. In the meeting in Cairo he apparently informed Nasser of the possibility that he may undertake such an action. The exact steps and the circumstances under which negotiation might be possible are yet to be determined and the timing is, of course, a matter of major importance.

In our opinion this is a major act of courage on the part of King Hussein and offers the first important breakthrough toward peace in the current period following active hostilities. It is an opportunity in our judgment that must not be lost, offering as it does a chance to embark on a course in the Arab world which could lead to an acceptance of Israel by its neighbors and to steps which could well change the whole course of history in the Middle East.

We wish that time were available for us to consider abstractly and unrelated to immediate problems all of the issues that are involved in this offer. But we believe we have tomorrow in the vote in the United Nations on the Pakistan resolution an opportunity to pave the way for positive steps in the days ahead—an opportunity that must not be lost. With the knowledge of King Hussein's willingness to risk a very

---

[1] Source: Johnson Library, National Security File, Country File, Middle East Crisis, Sandstorm/Whirlwind. Top Secret; Flash; Nodis; Sandstorm. The telegram indicates Battle as the drafter and that the text was revised at the White House; cleared by Walt Rostow; and approved by Rusk. Repeated Flash to Tel Aviv. "Sandstorm" is written by hand on the telegram. Telegram 6593 to Tel Aviv and USUN, July 14, stated that all cable traffic relating to telegram 6581 should be designated Nodis; Sandstorm, because the Department wished to give it maximum security. (Ibid.)

[2] Telegram 4941 from Amman, July 13, reported a conversation between King Hussein and Ambassador Burns in which the King stated he was prepared to make a uni-lateral settlement with Israel, and that he had discussed this with Nasser, who had said he would raise no objections if Hussein raised this with the Americans. The King said he would like to know what the Israelis would be likely to do vis-à-vis Jordan if he were pre-pared for a settlement. He said Jordan would have to get back substantially all it lost in the war, including the Jordanian sector of Jerusalem. He also said it was essential that Jordan obtain some arms immediately. (National Archives and Records Administration, Central Files 1967–69, POL 27–14 ARAB–ISR/SANDSTORM)

great deal, certainly including his own security, it is imperative, we think, that your government take a step in connection with the consideration of the future of Jerusalem that would be in harmony with the courage shown by the King and which will facilitate negotiations in the days ahead of us. We urge that you attempt to make the broadest kind of gesture possible with respect to the future of Jerusalem. We urge especially that you make a generous offer with respect to the future of Jerusalem that would in effect explicitly interpret as interim the administrative arrangements recently placed in effect with respect to that city. We would also hope that your country could offer more explicitly to enter into international arrangements for a city which would assure that all religions and all faiths have access to the holy places. The offer might include a willingness to discuss with Jordan directly or otherwise the future of the old city based on the concept of universality, possibly pointing to Jordan as the spokesman for the Arab world in view of its location in relation both to Israel and to Jerusalem itself.

Let me add that as you know our own position on Jerusalem has for some years supported its international character, a position to which we still adhere.

The matter is urgent. The events of tomorrow in the General Assembly may have an important bearing on the greatest opportunity we have yet seen to achieve what you and your country have wanted and have suffered through two wars to achieve. I urge your most careful and urgent consideration of this matter. The more moderate and generous the position of Israel tomorrow, the greater the chance that there can be a good result from Hussein's new readiness.

For Tel Aviv:

To save time and emphasize importance we attached to this message Ambassador should deliver it at once to highest available official with urgent informal suggestion it go at once to Eskhol if Eban has not yet had time to report it.

Rusk

361. Memorandum Prepared in the Central Intelligence Agency[1]

No. 1367/67   Washington, July 13, 1967.

MAIN ISSUES IN A MIDDLE EAST SETTLEMENT

Note

This paper assumes that Arab-Israeli hostilities will not be resumed, at least at any early date. It explores the main issues facing Israel and the Arabs in the post-hostilities phase. It is intended to describe briefly the respective points of view of the adversaries, the considerations which affect their attitudes, and to assess the likelihood of resolving particular issues and the terms on which this might be done; in short, to suggest where there might be some room for compromise, and where not.

I. General Considerations

1. The outlook for settlement between Arabs and Israelis is dim indeed. Their respective positions on almost all questions are poles apart and emotions are running high. Arab policy toward Israel remains adamantly hostile. For many years, no Arab leader—except Bourguiba, who scarcely counts in this context—has considered it politically possible to contemplate the recognition of Israel. The Arab leaders are fully aware of magnitude of their defeat, but they do not draw the conclusion that they must acknowledge it. Hence, anything in the nature of peace negotiations is highly unlikely. The Arabs may feel compelled to sign some form of armistice agreements, but they may for a long time resist even this step if—as is likely—the price is significant concessions to Israel. But the shock of their swift and overwhelming defeat has, for the moment, probably prevented them from making decisions on all but immediate matters, and they are reduced to hoping that international pressures will somehow force the Israelis to withdraw from occupied territory.

2. As for the Israelis, promptly after their dramatic victory, they began talking about direct negotiations leading to Arab recognition of Israel and an overall settlement. Israel's great objectives are to break the pattern of the last two decades, to gain Arab recognition of its right to exist, and assurances against further terrorism and other harassment.

---

[1] Source: Johnson Library, National Security File, Country File, Middle East Crisis, Vol. VIII. Secret. Sent to the President with a covering memorandum of July 14 from Walt Rostow. A handwritten "L" on Rostow's memorandum indicates the President saw it.

There are clearly divided counsels within Israel on the strategy and tactics of achieving these goals. The hardliners, represented by Dayan, have the advantage of being identified by many Israelis as the architects of Israel's victory, and their positions have strong domestic appeal because they emphasize what Israel wants and feels it has won, with little regard to what might have to be conceded in the face of international pressures or opinion. Even if Dayan is forced out of the cabinet, Israel will probably remain largely impervious to external pressures to withdraw from occupied areas for months to come, unless there is unexpectedly quick progress toward a settlement tolerable to Israel. The short-term costs of holding captured territories are not high, around $10 million monthly, and are more than compensated by an extraordinary influx of hard currency since early June.

3. In the longer run, however, Israel faces a painful dilemma. The Israelis may hope that the Arabs (and the Soviets) will draw the "correct" conclusion from the recent war, and that a new order will emerge in the area which will involve acceptance of the Israeli state and assurances for its security. But so far there are few indications that any such new order is emerging, and unless it does, Israel must sooner or later face the problem of how to assure its security. Eventually, Israel is probably prepared to trade much of its captured territory in return for security arrangements. Experience does not incline the Israelis to put faith in guarantees by the great powers and certainly not in the effectiveness of UN arrangements. And while the Arabs may reluctantly enter into some more formal armistice arrangements, the chances remain slight that any significant Arab leader will undertake to associate himself with the kind of binding agreements that Israel wants and feels it must have.

4. Soviet actions will probably help to confirm the Arabs in this attitude. Nothing in the events of last month is likely to have altered the USSR's conviction that Soviet interests in the area are best served by an alignment with radical Arab forces. There have been Arab defeats and Soviet miscalculations, and the principal instruments of Soviet policy—diplomatic, economic, and military—have either been damaged or at least had their efficacy called into question. But the Soviets have maintained their strong presence in the area. They are currently engaged in a noisy campaign to convince both the Arabs and the world at large that their ability and determination to maintain this presence has not been undermined by the outcome of the recent war and that among the great powers the USSR represents the only hope for the Arabs.

5. It is true that the USSR is the only major power the radical Arab states—Egypt, Syria, and Algeria—can depend on for meaningful

support. It is no less true, however, that Moscow's policies in the Middle East can only be served by the maintenance of ties with these states. For their own purposes, the Soviets and the Arabs thus need each other. In practical terms, this probably means that, within certain limits, the Soviets will in the main have to go along with Arab policies. While they would probably encourage an Arab disposition to compromise on issues such as Israeli passage of the Strait of Tiran, the Soviets would probably support Arab refusal to compromise, on most issues. For their part, the Arab states will simply have to recognize the limits on Soviet support, viz. the USSR's determination to avoid direct involvement in active hostilities or to risk seriously a confrontation with the US.

6. No matter what the Israelis offer by way of a new order in Palestine or movement on the refugee question, the Arabs will press for a return to something as close to the status quo ante as they can get. In the process, there will be intense maneuvering, not only between Arabs and Israelis, but also among the Arab states. Husayn and Nasir have neither the same interests at stake nor the same attitudes, and the Syrians are something else again.

In addition, there will be considerable controversy and haggling between the regional adversaries and the great powers. The overall outcome is obscure, but it is possible to isolate and analyze contrasting positions on certain of the main specific issues, and to suggest where chances of accommodation now appear best, and where they do not. The following paragraphs are not an exhaustive analysis, and it should be noted that, except in a few obvious cases, they do not explore the relationship between specific issues, i.e., how bargaining over one question might affect any negotiations over another.

[Omitted here are sections II–VII, which show in tabular form the Israeli position, the Jordanian or Egyptian position, and the possibility of compromise or lack thereof on the issues of Jerusalem, the West Bank, the Gaza Strip, access to Eilat through the Strait of Tiran, the Suez Canal, Sinai, the Syrian highlands, and the refugee problem.]

362. Memorandum From the President's Special Consultant (Bundy) to President Johnson[1]

Washington, July 14, 1967, 11:30 a.m.

SUBJECT

Revised agenda for Special Committee, 12:15, Cabinet Room

Since we drafted our first agenda yesterday, the situation has changed on a number of points and there is really only one matter which needs immediate decision—it is our voting posture in the General Assembly on Jerusalem. The Secretary of State's position has just been stated in a memorandum to you which was sent up to you a little while ago by Walt Rostow, and I attach a copy at Tab A.[2] Unless things change in some unexpected way, I think there will be general support for his recommendation of an abstention with a fairly strong statement in explanation.

Unfortunately the statement itself will pose tough problems. I drafted a possible statement yesterday at the Secretary's request, and he found it a bit strong. I am now trying a softer version for size on people who know how Israel and her friends may react. I am not optimistic at the moment that we can find language which suits the Arabs and does not outrage the Israelis, but I am still trying.

The only other action item for today is one on which a confirmation of your view would be helpful. There are diplomatic grumblings which suggest that one or two of the less violent states which have broken relations (such as the Sudan) might want to re-establish relations if we on our part would re-establish some of the previously existing economic aid programs.[3] While this would not be a good bargain with Egypt or Syria, it would make sense with their more marginal allies, and my hope is that you may authorize the Department to tell its diplomats that states like the Sudan which come back into sensible relations with us will find us back in sensible relations with them.

The most important Middle Eastern item at the moment, of course, is Hussein's feeler, but I do not suggest that it be discussed in the Special Committee. I hold to the view I suggested to you last night, namely that we should undertake to pass communications back and

---

[1] Source: Johnson Library, National Security File, Country File, Middle East Crisis, Vol. VIII. No classification marking. Sent through Walt Rostow.

[2] Rusk's July 13 memorandum to the President, with Rostow's covering memorandum, is not attached but is filed ibid. A draft statement on Jerusalem and a brief agenda for the Special Committee meeting are attached to Bundy's memorandum.

[3] "OK" is written in the margin in an unidentified handwriting.

forth but should not appoint ourselves as umpires. If we are in the main line of communications, we can judge for ourselves when the moment is right to press one side or another for a concession. Meanwhile, we can and should be asking ourselves how much of an economic blessing we could give, or get the World Bank to give, to a real settlement. This may be of great importance to both sides as they look at the detailed future of the Palestinian Arabs on the West Bank.

363.   Memorandum From the President's Deputy Press Secretary (Johnson) to President Johnson[1]

Washington, July 14, 1967, 12:30–12:51 p.m.

Attached is a report of the President's Meeting in the Cabinet Room with *Special National Security Council Panel on the Mideast.*

ATTENDING THE MEETING

The President
Secretary Robert McNamara
Under Secretary Nicholas Katzenbach
Secretary Henry H. Fowler
General Earle Wheeler
Mr. Richard Helms
Mr. Clark Clifford
Under Secretary Eugene Rostow
Mr. Lucius Battle
Mr. Walt Rostow
Mr. Harry McPherson
Mr. McGeorge Bundy
Mr. David H. Popper
Mr. John Devlin
Mr. Tom Johnson
Mr. George Christian

The meeting began at 12:30 p.m. It ended at 12:51 p.m.

McGeorge Bundy outlined the agenda of the meeting:

---

[1] Source: Johnson Library, Tom Johnson's Notes of Meetings, Box 1. Secret; Eyes Only. Drafted July 14 at 6:10 p.m. Brief notes of the meeting by Wriggins are ibid., National Security File, NSC Special Committee Files, #2, July 1–31, 1967. Concerning the topic of Resuming Diplomatic Relations with Selected Arab Countries, they read: "The President agreed that the Department should be flexible on this and proceed where there seemed to be opportunities or interest. The first instance would be the Sudan."

1. Arms Registration Policy being examined.
2. Agreed that discussion of selected military aid agreements would be delayed until after Secretary Rusk talks with the Congress.
3. Position on the U.N. General Assembly vote on Jerusalem.

On the matter of the General Assembly vote on Jerusalem, Secretary Katzenbach said that the State Department recommendation still holds. That is to abstain from voting, issue a clarifying statement which would be put out at the White House or at State.

Bundy said there should be a formal statement issued at *State* in the Secretary's name or by the Secretary himself.

Bundy said a vote on the issue was expected in the U.N.

Bundy circulated a proposed statement of view on the Middle East.[2] There was discussion of the language of the statement. The President said the word "deplore" should be changed to "regret."[3] This was done.

There were several suggestions for other changes by Secretary Fowler, Secretary Katzenbach, and Bundy. Bundy said the statement would not cause a violent explosion among the moderate Arabs or the Israelis.

After much discussion of the precise language of the statement, the President said:

"What I want to say is that we regret their unwillingness *to* budge."

There was laughter.

Bundy said that the Israelis are going to budge according to reports from Eban.

Secretary Fowler proposed: "The U.S. regrets the failure of the Government of Israel to make clear that its actions in recent weeks is only provisional." Bundy objected because of the reaction to this.

Clark Clifford said do not be too specific. He said he preferred to approach this in a general way rather than tying ourselves down to specific language.

McPherson suggested that the line in question be moved up in the text. The President agreed. The President concluded the discussion by stating that McPherson should get together with Rostow and Bundy

---

[2] The proposed statement was the draft statement on Jerusalem attached to Document 362.

[3] In Bundy's draft, the sentence reads: "The United States joins in deploring the administrative actions on Jerusalem which have been taken by the government of Israel in recent weeks."

and determine the exact handling of the situation. Then, send the proposal to the President for approval.[4]

On another area, McGeorge Bundy said that feelers should be stimulated to the weaker hangers-on of the Arabs to the effect that if they will come back into diplomatic relations with us, we will get back into relations with them. He mentioned specifically Sudan.

The panel argued that this was a good idea. The feelers should be that "if you will get back into business with us we will get back into business with you."

Clark Clifford explained that a group of leading New York citizens, including David Rockefeller, Eugene Black, and John McCloy, were joining to form a group called The American Committee for Arab Refugee Relief.

The goal of the group is to raise $10 million. Clifford wanted to know if the President considered the approach a wise one. Clifford said the idea has some psychological value among the American people.

The President asked Secretary Fowler for his opinion. The Secretary said IRS Commissioner Sheldon Cohen should look at it, that there are tax considerations, and he was somewhat skeptical about getting the President tied to a program which gave tax benefits to a group. He said many other similar groups have a way of popping up.

Bundy said the proposal should be kept on a staff level. The President said that Cohen should be put in touch with Clifford directly after the meeting to discuss the matter.

---

[4] Bundy sent the approved statement to Read with a covering memorandum of July 14. (Johnson Library, National Security File, Country File, Middle East Crisis, Vol. VIII) The draft resolution on Jerusalem was adopted by the General Assembly on July 14 as Resolution 2254 (ES–V) by a vote of 100 to 0, with 18 abstentions, including the United States. The statement sent from Bundy to Read was released on July 14 by Rusk. For texts of the statement, the resolution, and a statement made by Goldberg in the General Assembly on July 14, see Department of State *Bulletin*, July 31, 1967, pp. 148–151.

364.   Telegram From the Mission to the United Nations to the
        Department of State[1]

New York, July 14, 1967, 1907Z.

218. Ref: State 6581.[2]

Eban accompanied by Rafael informed Goldberg, accompanied by Sisco and Buffum, of Israel's response to Secretary's message. Eban said Israel's response is positive and he wished us to know that Israel is prepared to enter into discussions with Jordanians at convenient time and place.

Eban said in their judgment Secy's description of situation is more "enthusiastic" than Israeli. In this connection he recalled Hussein has made similar statements to other Western leaders (UK and Italy). Nevertheless he attached considerable importance that Hussein's desire to make contact with Israel has been conveyed to US. Eban said question is whether this is genuine utterance on part of Hussein and whether in fact it will result in contact. Israel reserves its position on what may be true significance of Hussein's private message. Eban said he assumed US would convey to Jordanians Israel's positive reply and its willingness to enter into discussions at appropriate time and place, This was in form of quick oral reply on Israel's part and Eban presumed there would be written reply forthcoming to US.

Eban then turned to question of immediate situation confronting us in GA on Jerusalem res. Since this matter was raised in Secy's message to him, Eban said he wished to convey Prime Minister Eshkol's plea and hope that US would not change its vote on Jerusalem question. Prime Minister feels US in position to play important mediatory role and he fears if we should vote for Pakistan res, Hussein would interpret this as identifying US with his position. Eban said he would hope that we would not abandon position of neutrality we had adopted.

Remainder of discussion devoted to statement Eban expects to make in GA hall on Jerusalem this afternoon. We are expecting text momentarily but statement will say that present situation in ME and all of questions relating to it are provisional until they are ratified by agreement. Eban will say that Israel is willing to examine alternative proposals. He will add specifically that administrative measures taken do not prejudice Israel's intention to work towards solution in keeping with

---

[1] Source: Johnson Library, National Security File, Country File, Middle East Crisis, Sandstorm/Whirlwind. Top Secret; Flash; Nodis; Sandstorm. Repeated Flash to Tel Aviv. Received at 3:44 p.m.

[2] Document 360.

spiritual and universal interests. He will say that Moslem Holy Places should be in hands of traditional Moslem authorities near and far. Goldberg suggested that in place where Eban refers to administrative measures Eban should consider adding phrase "which are not of a constitutional nature" and thereby get closer to saying that what has been done does not constitute annexation. In addition Goldberg suggested where reference is made to spiritual interests that phrase "and other appropriate" be added so as to get at political and territorial aspects that are involved. Goldberg asked Eban whether he could say specifically that administrative measures taken in Jerusalem are interim or provisional. Eban's response was that if he did this in such specific terms, "government in Tel Aviv would become interim."

Goldberg

365.   Memorandum of Conversation[1]

Washington, July 14, 1967, 4 p.m.

SUBJECT

   Jordan

PARTICIPANTS

   Secretary Rusk
   Foreign Minister Ahmed Touqan of Jordan
   Ambassador Shubeilat of Jordan
   Ambassador-designate Sharif Sharaf of Jordan
   Deputy Assistant Secretary Davies, NEA
   Marshall W. Wiley, NEA/ARN

Foreign Minister Touqan referred to the traditional ties between the US and Jordan and to the ideals which were shared by the two countries. He said that Jordan had been criticized at various times for its pro-Western attitudes, and now other people are asking the Jordanians why their traditional friends were not helping them. The Arabs came to the UN with the attitude of "give and take" but there was a limit to how far they could go. Jordan had lost much of its territory but the Jordanians

---

[1] Source: National Archives and Records Administration, RG 59, Central Files 1967–69, POL JORDAN–US. Secret; Noforn. Drafted by Wiley and approved in S on July 20. The time of the meeting is from Rusk's Appointment Book. (Johnson Library)

did not feel that they, the Arabs, had been totally defeated. They admitted they had lost a battle but they did not admit they had lost the war. The Jordanians were not able to forget they were Arabs and they hoped the US had not adopted the theory that Jordan should now be isolated from the rest of the Arabs and pushed into accepting a settlement.

The Secretary said that there were three basic issues now operating in the Middle East.

1) *Israel versus the Arab states.* During his experience at the UN in 1948 he had tried to negotiate a stand-still agreement between the Arabs and Israelis at the end of the British mandate. He was aware of the deep roots of the Palestinian problem and the deep feelings which it engendered. He understood these feelings even though he did not fully share them. The US and the Arabs did have some differences in their attitudes towards Palestine and he hoped that both sides could put these differences to one side and get on with the business of living.

2) *The struggle between the radical and moderate Arab states.* The Secretary said that as he looked back over the history of US actions in the Middle East he was impressed by the extent to which we had supported the principle of territorial integrity and political independence for all nations in that area. We supported the UAR during the Suez crisis and acted to insure Lebanon's independence at a somewhat later date. President Kennedy had sent a squadron of aircraft to support the independence of Saudi Arabia and we had, on several occasions, supported Libya against possible interference from the UAR. We had protested strongly against Arab subversion by infiltration into Israel and had also protested strongly to Israel after the unfortunate raid on Samu last November.

3) *Soviet efforts to penetrate the area.* The Secretary said that the Soviets were attempting to increase their influence in the area by shipping arms to certain Arab states. We had tried on many occasions to encourage the Soviets to tone down the arms race. He had personally talked about this with Gromyko but the Soviets were interested only in discussing nuclear weapons as a subject for limitation. He realized that Jordan was not responsible for the recent situation getting out of control. There were two things that had contributed directly to the development of the hostilities. First, the speed of the removal of the UNEF forces and second, Nasser's closing of the Strait of Tiran. The closing of the Strait of Tiran had been more important than most people in the Arab world realized. It was not only a casus belli for Israel, but it also ran directly counter to commitments we had made in 1957 in order to get Israel out of Sinai. The UAR had not signed these commitments but had been aware of them. Nasser had based his action on the right of belligerency against Israel, but this cuts both ways. The Arabs are not consistent if they complain of Israeli aggression while simultaneously asserting belligerent rights against Israel. By his action in closing the Strait of Tiran Nasser had undercut our position with Israel. If

we now ask the Israelis to withdraw they would say that they did so in 1956 on assurances from the US which had not been carried out in 1967.

The Secretary said that we attached great importance to the ending of the state of belligerency. We had no fixed formula but one useful precedent might be the formula used by the Soviets and Japanese to end the state of belligerence after WW II. They were able to do this without a formal peace treaty. He regretted that Jordan had been caught up in the hostilities since the major participants in the actions leading up to the fighting had been Syria, the UAR and Israel. He said he was not trying to lecture on this but he did wish that Jordan could have avoided the fighting. He had the feeling that apart from Jerusalem, which we all knew would be a "wrestle" the territorial problems involved in the settlement were not too serious. The basic and fundamental problem was the ending of the state of belligerency.

Foreign Minister Touqan said that the arms build up was not limited to the Arab side. On Jerusalem, he said that the US position should be the same as that of Jordan, i.e. unilateral actions by Israel were not acceptable. Jerusalem had a very special status with the Arabs as with all Moslems. It was false to say that Jordan had prohibited the Jews from reaching their Holy Places. The demarcation line which had ended the fighting in 1948 prohibited travel by both Israelis and Jordanians to the territory of the other. The Jordanians had had no desire to prevent adherents of the Jewish religion from reaching their Holy Places and, in fact, had allowed many Jewish tourists to enter Jordan.

The Secretary said we had our reasons for abstaining on the Pakistani resolution. The false UAR charges of complicity with Israel had made us very sensitive. Big powers had their sensitivities as well as little powers. These false charges had made several countries break relations with us. We would also have liked to have had an opportunity to negotiate the language of the Pakistani resolution prior to the vote, but we had not been given the opportunity. The Pakistanis had apparently felt that they had enough votes to carry the resolution so there was no need to negotiate with us. We also had not been happy with the Jordan vote on the Cuban amendment to the draft resolution, although our vote on the Pakistani resolution had not been directly linked to Jordan's vote on the Cuban amendment.

Ambassador-designate Sharaf said that the Cuban amendment condemned Israel and Jordan automatically voted for any resolution condemning Israel. He also said that Jordan unfortunately had to vote first on the Cuban amendment before they had realized that some of the other Arab delegations would not vote for it.

Foreign Minister Touqan said that he had become very angry at the way Ambassador Goldberg had acted during the UNGA session.

Ambassador Goldberg had tried to undermine every measure taken by the Jordanian delegation and had obviously used considerable pressure to reduce the number of votes for the non-aligned resolution. Secretary Rusk pointed out that the US could not tell other countries how to vote. The primary US interest was to find some way to bring about an Israeli withdrawal to a state of peace and not to a continuing state of war.

The Secretary asked the Foreign Minister what it was that the Jordanians had objected to in the Latin American resolution. The Foreign Minister replied that the resolution made Israeli withdrawal subordinate to too many other things. Secretary Rusk said it might still be possible to work out a compromise between the Latin American and the non-alignment resolution which would be acceptable to all.

Ambassador-designate Sharaf said that he wished to make two specific points. 1) The often reiterated US assurances on territorial integrity and political independence had been made without conditions. The Jordanians had been shocked to find that so many conditions were now attached to our commitments. 2) Jordan expected more from the US as a result of our past friendly relationship.

The Secretary said that there was one important difference between today and 1956. Nasser had completely undermined our position vis-à-vis Israel by closing the Strait of Tiran. If we were to ask Israel to withdraw now they would say that they had heard this before and our assurances on free navigation in the Strait had not held up. The Secretary then said that as far as Jordan was concerned if they were looking around the world for a friend in terms of Jordan's independence, safety and well being, they could find such a friend in the US.

Ambassador Shubeilat said it would be impossible for Jordan to negotiate directly with Israel. Secretary Rusk said there was some flexibility on this. Working out the procedures of negotiation may be as difficult as agreeing on the substance. One possibility was the use of a UN representative as an intermediary. There were always other possibilities for unpublicized contacts. Ambassador-designate Sharaf said it was not feasible for Jordan to engage in open unilateral dialogue with Israel as Jordan cannot risk being completely isolated from the Arab world.

The Secretary said it was not necessarily true that Jordan should take the lead in the negotiations. It might be better if President Nasser or one of the other Arab states made the first move. It was difficult for us to talk to the Arabs because the Arabs themselves cannot seem to get together except on their opposition to Israel. It was always the extremist voices that were the loudest and which came to the front when we tried to talk to the Arabs. Secretary Rusk then asked if there would be some advantage for Jordan if the situation on the Syrian-Israeli border could be clarified before Jordan made any diplomatic move.

Ambassador-designate Sharaf then said that a formal peace treaty was not possible and he hoped the US could understand this. It would be difficult for both Jordan and the US if Jordan were pushed in this direction since Jordan was well known in the area as a friend of the US. He said that in the Arab world form was very important as opposed to the US where people adopted a more pragmatic approach. The Secretary agreed that there were many ways to renounce belligerency. A Security Council resolution, for example, might be one possibility. The important thing was that the state of belligerency somehow be renounced.

Ambassador-designate Sharaf pointed out that the General Armistice agreement had neutralized the state of war and that the Israelis had undertaken aggression by violating the Armistice Agreement whether or not a state of non-belligerence had been agreed to by the concerned parties. The Secretary conceded that the accusation of aggression applied more to the UAR than to Jordan. The Secretary asked the Jordanians not to discount US support for the principle of territorial integrity. Although the question of Jerusalem was a difficult one the Jordanians can be assured that we intended to stick to this principle. We were interested, however, in seeing that Israel withdrew to international boundaries and not to armistice lines. We must find a way to end the exercise of the rights of war in the Middle East and to stop the recurrent outbreak of hostilities.

---

366. Telegram From the Embassy in Israel to the Department of State[1]

Tel Aviv, July 14, 1967, 2135Z.

167. State 6581.[2]

1. At his request I called on P.M. Eshkol at his house in Jerusalem this afternoon for what developed into one hour dialogue. He started by indicating considerable agitation over Secretary's message contained in reftel. His concern also corroborated by fact this Sabbath eve and he supposed to be on vacation.

---

[1] Source: Johnson Library, National Security File, Country File, Middle East Crisis, Sandstorm/Whirlwind. Top Secret; Immediate; Nodis; Sandstorm. Repeated to USUN. Received at 7:17 p.m.

[2] Document 360.

2. Eshkol welcomed overture from Hussein. However, he professed inability to understand our apparent surprise at Hussein's step. Recalling various recent statements by King which he interpreted to effect King would attempt achieve Arab summit and failing that would feel free to proceed on his own, Prime Minister said move should not have been unexpected. What disturbed Eshkol was tenor of Secretary's message that Israel should respond with concessions on Jerusalem and specifically indicate a willingness to regard renunciation of city under Israeli control as subject modification. He averred most positively that he had stretched his cabinet like a rubber band on a number of problems which had been considered in last few weeks but that rubber band would break immediately if he authorized Eban to make any statements that measures to reunify city only "interim" and subject further debate. As to GA debate and resolution on Jerusalem he urged that we not support resolution calling for retrogression. His argument was that such U.S. support would be disservice to Hussein who would then be expected to achieve more in negotiation than any Israeli Government could ultimately give. He differentiated Holy Places from fundamental attitude toward Israeli control and sovereignty of city and stressed success he believes he is achieving in realistic discussions with Vatican as to suitable arrangements to safeguard religious interests.

3. I said that despite his apparent optimism that Hussein would come forward and seek discussions with Israel, my feeling was we were less sanguine in this regard which might explain our seeming surprise at King's overture. I noted Hussein's public posture had not been uniformly receptive to idea of settlement and obvious hazards such step entailed, as exemplified by fate of King's grandfather. I also stressed significance King's move as possible opening wedge to peaceful discussions with other Arab states, obviously in all our interests. As to Jerusalem, I made clear our non recognition unilateral renunciation, in fact our non recognition over twenty years of Israel's position on Jerusalem and Hussein's claim to West Bank. I urged in strongest terms that what we need is some sort of helpful gesture on part Israel in response to major courageous initiative King is taking. I said I appreciated that Israel's position on fundamentals of unification of Jerusalem under Israeli aegis apparently could not be reconciled with our position that administrative steps Israel has already taken should be regarded as of interim nature and subject international recognition or modification later. I added what we seemed to need was indication of flexibility as to legitimate international interests in city, particularly the interests of Moslems.

4. After considerable back and forth along above lines, Eshkol appeared somewhat more inclined seek formula of more helpful import. He still adamant on fundamentals, but, focusing on religious interests, said he prepared go limit in establishing practical and legal jurisdiction of various religious persuasions over sites their legitimate concern.

Specifically he quite willing accept Hussein as guardian Moslem interests if in fact King could make such position stick in Moslem world. He referred to Islamic concept of caliphate of which many Arab monarchs had claimed right wear mantle. Finally, he concurred in thought that universality of city could well be most productive approach.

5. I cannot, after this meeting, predict that Eban's response to Secretary will, on basis instructions he will receive from P.M., be as forthcoming as we might like. However, within limits of basic issues as Israelis see them, I hope Eshkol will approve instructions authorizing Eban to direct his reply in as positive a direction as his drafting ingenuity, which is not inconsiderable, will permit.

Barbour

---

367.   Memorandum of Conversation[1]

Washington, July 15, 1967, 11 a.m.–12:03 p.m.

SUBJECT

> Near East Settlement

PARTICIPANTS

> Mr. Abba Eban, Foreign Minister of Israel
> Ambassador Avraham Harman, Ambassador of Israel
> Mr. Emanuel Shimoni, Private Secretary to the Foreign Minister

> The Secretary and Under Secretary
> M—Mr. Rostow
> NEA—Rodger P. Davies, Deputy Assistant Secretary

Mr. Eban began the discussion by expressing hope that the General Assembly would adjourn and consideration of the Near East problem

---

[1] Source: National Archives and Records Administration, RG 59, Central Files 1967–69, POL 27 ARAB–ISR. Top Secret; Nodis. Drafted by Davies. The time of the meeting is from Rusk's Appointment Book. (Johnson Library) Eban met with Eugene Rostow over lunch. Rostow stated that the preceding weeks had demonstrated the need for consultation on a continuing basis on subjects in which both sides had a vital interest and in which the United States could be drawn into "difficult situations" as a result of Israeli actions. Pressed for an example, he cited Israel's actions with respect to Jerusalem. Eban said that Israel had also learned lessons from the preceding weeks; the Israeli Government "now recognized that it had no real alternative to self-reliance militarily." (Memorandum of conversation, July 15; National Archives and Records Administration, RG 59, Central Files 1967–69, POL 27 ARAB–ISR)

revert to the Security Council. He did not think a compromise resolution was possible, noted a mood of general resignation among delegations, and said the Francophone African states were playing with the idea of a resolution returning the problem to the Security Council.

The Secretary thought some formula for bridging the gap between withdrawal and termination of belligerency might be found. The Soviets have kept pushing for this in corridor conversations. He noted that a simple move for adjournment of the General Assembly might win a majority, thus returning the issue to the Council.

Mr. Eban said Israel was anxious to move toward a settlement with the Arabs. Its priorities were Jordan, the UAR, Syria, and then Algeria. Hussein's indication that he was interested in terms for a settlement was an important but not entirely new development. He had been responsive to suggestions that he explore terms when raised by the British and by Sarragat, and the Pope. Israel considers Hussein's approach through the U.S. as important since it was made through a great power and after his visit to Cairo. Israel recognizes that Nasser may only want to get Hussein into trouble by not interposing objection. There is, of course, much vagueness in what Hussein has proposed. Definitive arrangements to untangle himself from his mess are essential. As a matter of fact, the Jordanese have been showing themselves realistic on an ad hoc basis. The Prime Minister has been negotiating through UN agencies on practical matters. Through UNRWA's Assistant Commissioner General Reddaway, the Jordanese have proposed an exchange of wheat which is surplus on one bank for vegetables which are surplus on the other bank of the Jordan. The policy of return of refugees is being negotiated in the same channels. These are, however, indirect contacts. Israel hopes Hussein can be brought to something more substantive in the form of a dialogue. It might be possible for Hussein to appoint one or two people to meet either in the area or in Europe to explore modalities. The increased mixing of Arabs and Israelis in the West Bank may make it feasible to maintain secrecy of meetings in the area.

The Secretary said that assuming bilateral arrangements between Israel and Jordan could be arranged, it would be extremely dangerous to Hussein if these surfaced in advance of arrangements with others. Subversion and, possibly, assassination might result.

Mr. Eban said that in preliminary stages he felt the negotiators need not be conspicuous, but they should be capable of defining issues and the limits of policy and concessions ad referendum to their principals. In the case of Egypt and Syria, Israel had a clear idea of what settlement it would work for. With respect to the West Bank and Jordan, however, the situation was more difficult. There is a plurality of thinking in Israel. Some advocate a Palestinian solution: an autonomous Palestine tying the West Bank to Israel or associated with both Israel and Transjordan. Others doubt this is feasible or desirable and urge a Jordanian solution.

The Secretary said that the Palestinian solution would seem to involve a second-class status for the Arabs and could lead to Palestinian demands to become the 14th Arab state.

Mr. Eban responded to Mr. Rostow's comment that a binational secular state might provide a solution by saying this would be the most dramatic of all. He doubted, however, that the 1.3 million Arabs could be mixed successfully with the 2-1/2 million Israelis. In any event, this would mean an entirely different concept than that of Israel as a state embodying Hebrew concepts. In any event, Israel needs an internal decision on whether to seek a Jordanian or Palestinian solution. If the Jordanian formula is decided on, Israel would require better and more viable boundaries and economic association.

Israel would be willing to compensate for the loss of Jerusalem by economic help and access to the sea.

The Secretary said he felt there were advantages in the U.S. avoiding being used as an intermediary between Israel and Jordan. Mr. Eban agreed and thought Israel would not like the U.S. at Hussein's side with the latter hoping the USG would press his claims.

The Secretary saw real trouble ahead on Jerusalem. There are strong feelings in many places on this issue. The USG had never agreed with either the Israeli or Jordanian positions on Jerusalem, and there had been sharp, adverse reaction to recent Israeli steps in Jerusalem. The question of Jerusalem must be kept open for further discussion and negotiations. The U.S. sought solid international arrangements, and this would not be satisfied by scattered rights over a few holy places.

The Foreign Minister indicated that there were some 40,000 Arabs in the old city and 60–75,000 in the Jerusalem area.

Mr. Eban said Israel was much more conciliatory to international interest as opposed to Jordanian interest. Israel was close to agreeing on a formula with the Vatican by which diplomatic status of the holy places would replace the extraterritorial enclave formula previously sought. The Pope expressed interest in having jurisdiction over his prelates in Jerusalem. Rome clearly was moving away from a dogmatic approach, and a practical solution assuring an international presence was in the offing. The Vatican and Israel did not wish UN control over any part of Jerusalem since UN mechanisms in the Near East implied fragility and had been of a transitory nature. The universal interests of the Church were much more permanent.

The Secretary said this formula was interesting but did not exhaust all possibilities.

Mr. Eban said the question of the Haram ash-Sharif (Dome of the Rock) was more difficult. It was inconceivable that Jordan could return to Jerusalem. Hundreds of people had been killed by Jordanian soldiers when there was no need for the King to move on the city. He must now bear the consequences of his unacceptable action. Nevertheless, Moslem interests would be part and parcel of discussions with the King.

On continued fighting along the Suez Canal, Mr. Eban thought the Egyptians might interpret the presence and movement of Israeli forces as mounting a threat at the cease-fire line. Arrival of UN observers this week-end may calm the situation.[2] It was noted that the Egyptians refused to permit the observers to cross from one bank of the Canal to the other. On Sharm ash-Shaykh, Mr. Eban said there was nothing there in the way of habitation, and the best solution might be to leave the place unoccupied.

There was some prospect of settlement of refugees in the El Arish area. Surveys going back to 1902 indicated some water resources.

Mr. Eban thought that Soviet frustration at tactics which blocked their arms in the UNGA may be causing them to advise the Arabs to revise their positions away from intransigency.

In response to the Secretary's question, Mr. Eban said President De Gaulle's views were in sharp contrast to French public opinion. In the latest polls, Israel rated greater popularity than did the General himself. In his conversation with the General on May 24, Mr. Eban was told Israel had a good case, but a solution of its problem could be obtained only in the context of four-power agreement. The French viewed their Near East policy as part of their global policy. De Gaulle felt then that there was a disequilibrium between U.S. and USSR power and, undoubtedly, Soviet reverses in the Middle East made him feel that the gap now was even greater. De Gaulle sought to restore equilibrium by throwing support to the weaker power. He is not able to understand or to recognize the rebuffs he has received from Kosygin. He has refused to accept evidence that the Soviets will work in a two-power but not a four-power context. Despite General De Gaulle, there had been some resumption of military supplies from France. These are enough to keep Israel's Mirages flying.

---

[2] Secretary-General Thant reported to the Security Council on July 11 that the UAR and Israeli Governments had accepted the stationing of UN military observers in the Suez Canal sector. (UN document S/8053) Both Israel and the UAR complained of cease-fire violations in letters of July 12, 13, 14, and 15 from the UAR and letters of July 14 and 15 from Israel. (UN documents S/8054, S/8061, S/8057, S/8062, S/8059, and S/8060) Telegram 1081 from USDAO Tel Aviv, July 16, reported that a cease-fire had begun at midnight, July 15/16. (National Archives and Records Administration, RG 59, Central Files 1967–69, POL 27 ARAB–ISR) Telegram 149 from Jerusalem, July 17, reported that General Bull had informed Consul General Wilson that he had instructed his two teams of UN military observers at Ismailiya and Qantara to commence cease-fire supervision as of 1600 GMT that day. (Ibid., POL 27–14 ARAB–ISR/UN)

368. Memorandum of Meeting[1]

Washington, July 15, 1967, noon.

SAND STORM
(First Special Meeting)
(12:00, July 15, 1967)

1. Amb. Findley Burns, who had just returned from Amman, assessed the situation currently existing in Jordan, the mood of King Hussein, his desires for military equipment, his intent to reach an agreement with Israel, and his optimum terms for such a settlement.

2. This provided a basis for a general discussion of the Jordanian situation, Hussein's relationship with Nassar, and the outlook for a peaceful settlement. It was noted Nassar had recommended that Hussein endeavor, with US assistance, to reach an agreement with Israel. His two expressed conditions were that there should be no peace treaty and no direct negotiations.

3. It was agreed that the US would have to play a major role if the peace effort were to succeed. A danger exists that Nassar would booby-trap us as the intermediary who sold out Hussein. Therefore, we should be very careful if we become engaged.

4. In this respect (1) we should determine whether there is sufficient flexibility in the Israeli position on Jerusalem to justify us to advise Hussein to negotiate; (2) we should support a GA or SC resolution authorizing U Thant to send a Mediator to the Near East with a broad mandate; and (3) we should operate behind the scenes.

5. Hussein and General Khammash have approached Ambassador Burns with requests for military equipment. Khammash has expressed a need for selected spare parts and non-lethal equipment. This could be encompassed within the approximately $1.8 million in MAP grants earmarked for FY 1968 and the $5.9 million outstanding under the sales program. The Jordanians apparently wish to shift from F–104s to F–5s. They also wish to obtain 18 Hawker Hunters from the British. Khammash apparently has a list of the equipment he desires and wishes to come to Washington to discuss it. The King supports this proposal.

---

[1] Source: National Archives and Records Administration, RG 59, Central Files 1967–69, POL 27–14 ARAB–ISR/SANDSTORM. Secret; Nodis. No drafting information appears on the memorandum. The meeting is also recorded in a July 15 memorandum from Wriggins to Walt Rostow and Bundy, which lists the participants as Ambassador Burns, Katzenbach, Eugene Rostow, and Kohler. (Johnson Library, National Security File, Country File, Middle East Crisis, Vol. VIII)

6. The question of the resumption of military supplies to Jordan should be staffed-out expeditiously with the DOD.

---

369. Memorandum of Conversation[1]

Washington, July 15, 1967.

PARTICIPANTS

Abba Eban, Foreign Minister of Israel
Avraham Harman, Ambassador of Israel
Emanuel Shimoni, Private Secretary to the Foreign Minister
W.W. Rostow

1. Following guidance from Sec. Rusk, I mainly listened; but made strongly the two points he wished to leave with Eban:

—their unsatisfactory posture on Jerusalem and its long-run dangers for Israel;
—the need to accelerate movement back to the West Bank, with respect to both numbers and speed.

2. With respect to the West Bank, he said they were doing a good deal but it was hard for Israel to invest much long-run resources in West Bank development until they knew the long run disposition of the West Bank. There is much debate among the Israelis on this question covering four options:

—Take the West Bank Palestinians into an expanded Israel as citizens.
—Make the West Bank an Israeli protectorate with representation in the Israeli Parliament but essentially the status of Algeria in relation to France before Algeria achieved independence.
—Make the West Bank an autonomous state, with its own parliament, economically linked to Israel, but with no military force.
—Give the West Bank back to Jordan as part of the negotiation but develop very close economic relations between Israel and Jordan.

3. I said that I had no confident feel for the region but thought that the desire of those who live there, as well as the negotiation with Jordan, should weigh heavily with Israel in this matter. He said that the

---

[1] Source: Johnson Library, National Security File, Country File, Middle East Crisis, Vol. VIII. Secret. Drafted on July 17. Sent to the President on July 17 with a brief covering note by Rostow. A handwritten "L" on Rostow's note indicates the President saw it.

people of Israel and its leaders were split in this matter. There is no consensus. One reason the government does not wish to push the question to anything like a firm decision is because their judgment would be affected by Palestinian Arab and Jordan government positions. With respect to the attitudes of the Palestinian Arabs, he said in the immediate wake of Jordan's defeat there was considerable talk of autonomy but, as Hussein found his feet, sentiment was moving back to reincorporation of the West Bank into Jordan. He also noted that those responsible for the Israeli economy were all for a prompt return of the West Bank to Jordan.

4. I questioned him on the political and economic situation in Cairo. He didn't seem to know any more than we did. He said that Nasser was in something like Sukarno's position; but one could not identify a Suharto, if, indeed there was one.

5. With respect to a negotiation with the Jordanians, he believed it should be direct and without intermediaries. The critical question for Israel was: Is Hussein serious?

6. With respect to the situation in the UN, he felt that the problem was to get the issue out of the General Assembly as soon as possible and into the Security Council. Prolonged discussions in the General Assembly were postponing other forms of action with higher constructive potential.

7. Eban asked me to inform Sec. Rusk that the Israeli government would like to send a military mission to the U.S., in great discretion, to discuss additional supplies of aircraft, helicopters, and tanks. He said that it looked as though France would supply sufficient spare parts to maintain their Mirage fleet. I simply took note of this.

WR

370.　　Memorandum of Meeting[1]

Washington, July 16, 1967, noon.

SAND STORM
(Second Special Meeting)
(12:00, July 16, 1967)

The Jordan Scenario paper[2] was reviewed and the following course of action was blocked out:

1. Hussein has informed us of his desire to reach a settlement with Israel. He has staked out a negotiating position of a return to the political lines of June 4, including Jordanian control of the Old City of Jerusalem. He is prepared to accept some border rectification, accompanied by over-flight rights and port facilities in Israel. He wishes us to determine whether this would be in the Israeli ball park. The Israelis, in turn, have informed us that they are ready to talk to the Jordanians although they are uncertain about the seriousness of Hussein.

2. The key to a negotiated settlement is Jerusalem. We need a better assessment of Israel's flexibility on this subject before giving a definitive reply to Hussein. Three immediate steps should be taken in this respect:

a. Ambassador Barbour should be recalled for consultations;

b. We should follow up the separate conversations of the Secretary and Walt Rostow with Eban with another approach, preferably by the Secretary, along the following lines:

We are in a difficult position in advising Hussein. If he goes down the negotiating trail and fails to reach a viable understanding with Israel, the consequences could be grave for Israel and Jordan, and on US-Soviet relations. The key to a settlement is Jerusalem. Without revealing the details of your negotiating position, we would wish to ascertain whether you believe that your position would permit the conclusion of an agreement with Hussein.

c. We should probe the Jerusalem issue carefully with selected leaders of the American Jewish community who may be more flexible on this issue than the Israelis.

---

[1] Source: National Archives and Records Administration, RG 59, Central Files 1967–69, POL 27–14 ARAB–ISR/SANDSTORM. Secret; Nodis. No drafting information appears on the memorandum. The meeting is also recorded in a July 16 memorandum from Wriggins to Walt Rostow and Bundy, which describes it as a meeting of the "inner circle of the Control Group"—Katzenbach, Eugene Rostow, Battle, Kohler, and Wriggins, plus Walsh and Burns. (Johnson Library, National Security File, Middle East Crisis, Vol. VIII)

[2] Not found.

3. Assuming that we are unable to get a definitive reply from the Israelis on July 18, we should transmit an interim reply to Hussein informing him that, while we are not yet in a position to assess the chances of success, the Israelis have authorized us to tell him that they are ready to discuss a settlement. We would also inform him that we would endeavor to provide a more definitive response by the end of the week.

4. There is a Jordanian requirement, particularly of a political and psychological nature, for assurances that military supplies will be available from the West. The Jordanian request for non-lethal arms should be reviewed urgently with the DOD. Until our position is firmly established and approved by the President, General Khammash should not be invited to visit Washington. Consideration should be given to diverting him to London to discuss his desires for Hawker-Hunters.

5. If a political settlement can be brought about, we will have to play a basic role, preferably behind the scenes. The cover could be a UN mediator. If possible, he should have a blanket authorization to see what can be done to bring peace to the area, reporting to the Security Council. Ambassador Jarring would be an acceptable mediator.

6. We should complete our study of alternative settlement proposals for Jerusalem, including an optimum solution from the US viewpoint without consideration to its acceptability by the contending parties. NEA will complete this in time for circulation on July 17.

7. Luke Battle will brief Ambassador Dean on the conversation with Eban and the report of Ambassador Burns.

8. The presence of the Iraqi forces in Jordan is dangerous. Necessary measures should be taken to get them out.

371. Telegram From the Department of State to the Embassy in Turkey[1]

Washington, July 16, 1967, 3:51 p.m.

7611. Ref.: Ankara's 216.[2]

1. We are greatly interested report conversation Turk Ambassador Cairo with El Zyyat. El Zyyat known to Battle and others in Department who consider him reliable, relatively pro-Western. Although somewhat out of power structure in UAR, still possible that he is speaking under instructions.

2. Suggest Turks be asked inform El Zyyat that there have been conversations with U.S. and that American officials wonder whether alternative one is really excluded. U.S. and West in general interested keeping in contact with UAR in hope relations can be reestablished and improved in future with possibility advantages to UAR which such improvement could entail. Difficult or impossible be specific at present, but door continues to be open to friendship in future.[3]

Rusk

---

[1] Source: National Archives and Records Administration, RG 59, Central Files 1967–69, POL 27 ARAB–ISR. Secret; Exdis. Drafted by Battle on July 15, cleared by Davies and Berg, and approved by Katzenbach.

[2] Telegram 216 from Ankara, July 14, reported that Foreign Ministry Secretary General Zeki Kuneralp, at the request of Foreign Minister Caglayangil, had informed the Deputy Chief of Mission in Ankara that on July 10 El Zyyat, a high-ranking UAR Foreign Ministry official, had visited the Turkish Ambassador in Cairo and told him Egypt would have to follow the path followed by Turkey under Ataturk: to give up its empire, retire to Turkey's natural boundaries, and pursue a strong, stable, and dignified national policy. El Zyyat said there were only two ways to do this: one was to be perfectly neutral; the second, and the only feasible course now open to Egypt, was to rely on the Soviets. (Ibid.)

[3] Telegram 290 from Ankara, July 18, reported that the Ambassador saw Kuneralp that day and passed on the substance of telegram 7611 to Ankara. (Ibid., POL 17 US–UAR)

372. Telegram From the Mission to the United Nations to the Department of State[1]

New York, July 17, 1967, 2345Z.

258. Early this afternoon I received a telephone call from the Soviet mission stating that Amb Dobrynin would like to meet with me later this afternoon. We arranged a meeting for 4 p.m. at the US mission. Amb. Dobrynin and I then met for approximately 50 minutes.

Amb. Dobrynin opened the conversation by asking me whether the United States desired a constructive result from the Assembly which might lead to a peaceful composition of differences in the ME. I replied that the answer to this was evident. We had been trying since the very inception of the extraordinary session of the Assembly to concert with the Soviet Union and all others in the effort to bring about a just and lasting peace in the ME. I further said that any rumors he had heard to the contrary were unfounded. I added that if it was the Sov's notion that we desired the Assembly to adjourn without adopting any res, this also was unfounded. As proof of this I pointed out that on Sunday, July 9, I had offered alternative suggestions to him both of a substantive and procedural character looking towards a constructive conclusion of the Assembly.[2] I also pointed out that on July 5 and today I had agreed with Sov requests for additional time to permit further consultation about an appropriate res.

Amb Dobrynin replied that he was glad to get this reassurance about our point of view and that he wld convey this through FonMin Gromyko to his govt. He then said they were puzzled that we had not participated in the discussions that the LA's had been holding with the Sovs during the past several days, and inferred that the Sovs assumed from this that we were disinterested in the outcome.

I told him that this inference was completely without any foundation. I said that in my conversation with him a week ago Sunday, I had specifically stressed that we wld be glad to meet again with the Sov del to explore further the possibilities of either a substantive or procedural res which might be mutually acceptable. I emphasized the fact that we had heard nothing from them during the past week indicating any desire on their part to resume discussions with us. With respect to the mtgs with the LA's, I stated that the Sov del had sought the mtgs with

---

[1] Source: National Archives and Records Administration, RG 59, Central Files 1967–69, POL 27 ARAB–ISR. Secret; Priority; Exdis. Repeated to Moscow, Tel Aviv, and the White House. Received at 8:58 p.m. and passed to the White House at 11:18 p.m.

[2] See Document 348.

the LA's and that we had not been invited either by the Sov Union or the LA's to these discussions. I did not see how we cld invite ourselves to these mtgs, absent an invitation from either of the participants. Amb Dobrynin then observed that the LA's had made several references in the course of their discussions with the Sov del about US positions and that he had no doubt that the LA's conferred with us about these mtgs. I replied that I had no doubt that the LA's did refer to our position which was entirely natural since our position was a matter of public record and acknowledged that the LA's, following their several mtgs with the Sov del, had advised us of the course of the discussions.[3]

I reminded him of my earlier comments to him that the LA's had developed their draft without consultation with us and that we supported it notwithstanding that it did not fully meet our views for reasons which I had explained to the Assembly. I then reaffirmed that I and the members of my del were ready and willing to have additional further talks with FonMin Gromyko himself, and other members of the Sov del about the outcome of the Assembly.

Amb Dobrynin then turned to the LA text of July 14. He made the initial observation that LA text of July 14th was somewhat different from other LA texts which had been circulated. I said I did not know specifically what other texts he had in mind but that it was my understanding that the LA text of July 14 represented the agreed LA view of what a final substantive res shld contain.

Amb Dobrynin then inquired whether we would object to adding the words "without delay" to para 2 of the LA text affirming the principle that the withdrawal of Israeli forces to their original position is expected. I replied that we would have no objection to this if the words "without delay" were likewise added to para 3 which stated that the termination of a state or claims of belligerency by all states in the Middle East is expected. Amb. Dobrynin then observed that this of course was consistent with our established position and I acknowledged that it was.

Amb. Dobrynin then inquired whether we could dispense with the language relating to belligerence in para 3. I answered by saying this was a basic concept and that we could not dispense with the concept although we had demonstrated by my former proposal to him as reported in USUN 134[4] that we agree to different language incorporating the same concept. He then reminded me that he thought our revised

---

[3] Circular telegram 242 from USUN, July 16, reported a meeting between Goldberg and a Latin American negotiating committee concerning discussions between the Latin Americans and the Soviets and conveyed the texts of Latin American and Soviet draft resolutions. (National Archives and Records Administration, RG 59, Central Files 1967–69, POL 27 ARAB–ISR/UN)

[4] Document 348.

language would be most difficult for the Arabs to accept and I in turn reminded him of my own observations about this.

He then asked whether any other word than belligerency could be used and I said perhaps another formulation could be employed with the understanding that the concept would be the same, and I then suggested this formulation in para 3: "Termination of all states of war and any and all claims thereto is expected". He in turn inquired if we could accept words which he said had been suggested by Amb. Ruda of Argentina "Renunciation of the legal capacity to wage acts of war by such states is expected." I told him that this language was not appropriate and could lead to great confusion. In fact, I pointed out that it might be construed as a disarmament measure which would not be acceptable to either of the parties and indeed to the Soviets. I added that we had proposed registration and limitation of arms and had not been supported by the Soviets and certainly not by the Arab states or Israel. Amb. Dobrynin contended that this was not the intention of the language to deal with disarmament. I said that in the English version this was a logical interpretation. Moreover, I said that what had to be understood was the concept that all states of war and any and all claims thereto had to be terminated rather than renunciation of the concept of waging "acts of war".

I reminded Amb. Dobrynin that FM Gromyko had stated to Secy Rusk[5] that the Soviet Union and Japan had on October 19, 1956, entered into an agreement terminating the war and re-establishing peace and friendly good neighbor relations between them,[6] notwithstanding that they did not and have not yet signed a permanent peace treaty. I said that this was the basic concept we had in mind, and read to him the text of the joint declaration signed on that date at Moscow by the Chairman of the Council of Ministers of the USSR and the PM of Japan. He followed the text with considerable interest and I then commented that if both of our countries supported such a development which did not have to be exactly in the same form, this in my view was an essential step in bringing about peace and security in the Middle East.

Amb. Dobrynin then turned to the language of the LA text relating to guaranteeing freedom of transit through international waterways. He then inquired whether instead of "guaranteeing" we could accept the language "settling the question of transit through international waterways". I said this would be unsatisfactory because it would not

---

[5] On June 23; see Document 321.

[6] For text of the Joint Declaration signed by Japan and the Soviet Union on October 19, 1956, which terminated the state of war between them and restored diplomatic relations, see 263 UNTS 99.

expressly acknowledge the principle on which I thought both our govts were in agreement—that the innocent right of passage through international waterways should be guaranteed and protected. I added that if a state of war or belligerency were to be renounced or terminated, then the only problem to settle in the SC would be to guarantee freedom of transit through some appropriate means.

In summing up, Amb Dobrynin inquired whether we regarded the LA text with the change I suggested which was semantic rather than substantive to be the irreducible minimum insofar as we were concerned today. I said that it was, although as I previously pointed out I did not exclude further conversations with the Sov del if they desired further mtgs, and believed them to be fruitful.

I then asked Amb Dobrynin if there was any difference in Sov terminology between a state of war and state of belligerency, and he replied that there was and gave me the foll Russian words to indicate this difference: "state of war—sostoyaniye voyny. State of belligerency—sostoyaniye vrazhdebnosti".

Amb Dobrynin then said that he would communicate my thoughts to his FonMin and I in turn reiterated once again that I wld be glad to meet with the FonMin at any time convenient to him and I wld be glad to call upon him at the Sov mission since Amb Dobrynin now on three occasions had done me the courtesy of calling upon me at the US mission. I also emphasized that our govt was quite prepared to extend any appropriate type of hospitality to FonMin Gromyko and his party during their continued stay here.

Amb Dobrynin said he wld be glad to communicate the substance of our entire talk as well as this hospitable gesture to FonMin Gromyko and to the Sov Government.

Comment: It seems obvious from my conversation with Amb. Dobrynin as reported above that Amb. Dobrynin was conducting a probing operation rather than a genuine negotiation. But this may not be the last word. In the announcement made by Pres Pazhwak, Soviets have until Thurs morning to make further moves and their disposition to wait until the last minute is well known.

Additional comment: I briefed Amb. Rafael on the substance of the above.

Any comment AmEmb Moscow would wish to make on above would be appreciated.

Goldberg

373. Memorandum From the Chairman of the President's Foreign Intelligence Advisory Board (Clifford) to the President's Special Assistant (Rostow)[1]

SC No. 07445/67   Washington, July 18, 1967.

SUBJECT

    The Israeli Attack on the USS *Liberty*

In accordance with your request, I have reviewed all available information on the subject.

Based thereon, I submit the enclosed memorandum which deals with the question of Israeli culpability. In the event additional significant information is received concerning the foregoing, I will submit a supplementary report.

Other questions involving U.S. command and control of the *Liberty* are being investigated by responsible officials in the Executive Branch.

Because of discussions held on this subject within the Special Committee, I am sending copies of this memorandum to the Secretary of State and the Secretary of Defense.

Clark M. Clifford

THE ISRAELI ATTACK ON THE USS *LIBERTY*

The Attack

On the afternoon of June 8 (2:05 p.m., Israeli time), the USS *Liberty* while in international waters in the Eastern Mediterranean suffered an attack by Israeli aircraft and motor torpedo boats. When attacked the *Liberty* was approximately 15.5 nautical miles north of Sinai and was traveling in a westerly direction at a speed of five knots.

The initial attack consisted of five or six strafing runs by jet aircraft and was followed twenty-four minutes later with an attack by three motor torpedo boats.

The attack was executed with complete surprise, remarkable efficiency, devastating accuracy and deeply tragic results.

---

[1] Source: Johnson Library, National Security File, Country File, Middle East Crisis, Intelligence Cables. Top Secret; [*codeword not declassified*]. Rostow forwarded the memorandum to the President on July 18 at 5:40 p.m. with a covering note stating that it was Clifford's "brief but definitive analysis" of the attack on the *Liberty*, and was "based on the study of literally thousands of pages of evidence." A handwritten "L" on Rostow's note indicates the President saw it.

Israel's explanation of the Attack

Israel's explanation of the attack is summarized as follows:

a. The attack was an "innocent mistake—no criminal negligence was involved."

b. Israel's Navy and Air Force had received a number of reports that El Arish was being shelled from the sea. These reports were later determined to be erroneous but, at the time they were received, they were accepted at face value by Israeli Naval and Air Force headquarters.

c. Israeli officers who knew the *Liberty* had been identified earlier the same day did not connect her with the unidentified ships said to be shelling El Arish (and apparently the fact that a U.S. flag vessel was in the area was not communicated to subordinate elements of the Israeli Defense Forces (IDF)).

d. A second "mistaken report"—that the *Liberty* was steaming at thirty knots—was received by the IDF. When the *Liberty* was identified on the morning of June 8, the IDF determined from *Janes Fighting Ships* that the *Liberty*'s maximum speed was eighteen knots. The second "mistaken report" led to the conclusion that the earlier identification of the *Liberty* was erroneous and that the vessel allegedly traveling at thirty knots was an enemy ship.

e. IDF standing orders provided that any ships in the area cruising at speeds above twenty knots may be brought under attack without further identification. Thus the air attack was launched.

f. A third "mistake" resulted in the execution of the second (motor torpedo boat) stage of the attack. This third error of the IDF was its mistaken identification of the *Liberty* as the Egyptian supply ship *El Quesir*.

g. Immediately following the air attack, serious doubts began to arise concerning the true identity of the ship, but these doubts were not communicated to the commanding officer of the motor torpedo boats before he launched the second stage of the attack.

h. Prior to launching the torpedo attack one of the Israeli boats sent an "A-A" signal (meaning "what is your identity?") to the *Liberty*. The *Liberty*, instead of identifying herself, responded with an "A-A" signal. Officers on the Israeli boats interpreted the return signal as an evasion and concluded that the vessel in question was Egyptian, whereupon the torpedoes were launched.

i. The *Liberty* acted with lack of care by approaching excessively close to shore in an area which was a scene of war, without advising the Israeli authorities of its presence and without identifying itself elaborately. The *Liberty* tried to hide its presence and its identity both before it was discovered and after having been attacked.

Our Findings of Fact

Based upon a thorough review of all information on the incident which has become available thus far, I wish to submit the following findings of fact:

a. At all times prior to, during, and following the attack, the *Liberty* was in international waters where she had every right to be. As a noncombatant neutral vessel she maintained the impartial attitude of neutrality at all times prior to the attack.

b. Prior to the attack no inquiry was made by the Israeli Government as to whether there were U.S. flag vessels in the general area of the Eastern Mediterranean adjoining Israel and the United Arab Republic.

c. The weather was clear and calm in the area at the time of attack and throughout the preceding hours of June [8]. Visibility was excellent.

d. At all times prior to the attack the *Liberty* was flying her normal size American flag (five feet by eight feet) at the masthead. The flag was shot down during the air attack and was replaced by a second American flag (seven feet by thirteen feet) five minutes prior to the attack by motor torpedo boats. The *Liberty* did not endeavor to hide her identity or her presence in international waters at any time prior to or during the attack.

e. The *Liberty's* U.S. Navy distinguishing letters and number were printed clearly on her bow. The *Liberty's* number was painted clearly in English on her stern. (Egyptian naval ships such as the *El Quesir*, with which the *Liberty* was allegedly confused, carry their names in Arabic script.)

f. The ship's configuration and her standard markings were clearly sufficient for reconnaissance aircraft and waterborne vessels to identify her correctly as the noncombatant ship *Liberty*.

g. At the time she was attacked, the *Liberty* was making only five knots. Her maximum capability is eighteen knots, a fact which had been ascertained by IDF personnel when she was identified on the morning of June 8.

h. Prior to the torpedo attack the *Liberty* neither received nor dispatched an "A-A" signal. The Israeli claim that the *Liberty* transmitted an "A-A" signal prior to the torpedo attack is demonstrably false. The *Liberty's* signal light capability was totally destroyed in the air attack which occurred some twenty minutes before the torpedo boats appeared on the scene. Intermittently prior to the attack *Liberty* personnel observed a flashing light coming from the center boat. The first intelligible signal received by the *Liberty* was an offer of help following the torpedo attack.

i. The *Liberty* was reconnoitered by aircraft of unidentified nationality on three separate occasions prior to the attack—5 hours and 13 minutes before the attack, 3 hours and 7 minutes before the attack, and 2 hours and 37 minutes before the attack. Personnel on the *Liberty*, who observed and in some instances photographed the reconnaissance aircraft, were unable to identify them fully. Positive evidence concerning their nationality is still lacking, however, there are several grounds for assuming they were Israeli: (1) when the aircraft orbited the *Liberty* on three separate occasions the Arab-Israeli war was in its fourth day, the Egyptian Air Force had been substantially destroyed, and the Israeli Air Force was in effective control of the air space in the area; (2) [*less than 1 line of source text not declassified*] Tel Aviv, received information from a reliable and sensitive Israeli source reporting that he had listened to IDF air-to-ground transmissions on the morning of June 8 indicating Israeli aircraft sighting of a vessel flying the U.S. flag; (3) in the course of advancing its explanation for the attack, the Israeli Government acknowledged that the *Liberty* had been identified by IDF officers early on the morning of June 8.

j. COMINT reports that shortly after the torpedo attack, the Israelis began to have doubts as to the identity of the vessel and efforts were intensified to verify its identification. Ten minutes after the torpedo attack an Israeli ground controller still believed it to be Egyptian. Identification attempts continued, and forty-five minutes after the torpedo attack, helicopters were checking the masts, flag and bow number of the *Liberty*. By this time, there appears to have been no question in Israeli minds as to what had happened. The weight of the evidence is that the Israeli attacking force originally believed their target was Egyptian.

Conclusions

Based upon a thorough review of all information on the incident which has become available thus far, I wish to submit the following conclusions:

a. The information thus far available does not reflect that the Israeli high command made a premeditated attack on a ship known to be American.

b. The evidence at hand does not support the theory that the highest echelons of the Israeli Government were aware of the *Liberty*'s true identity or of the fact that an attack on her was taking place. To disprove such a theory would necessitate a degree of access to Israeli personnel and information which in all likelihood can never be achieved.

c. That the *Liberty* could have been mistaken for the Egyptian supply ship *El Quesir* is unbelievable. *El Quesir* has one-fourth the displacement of the *Liberty*, roughly half the beam, is 180 feet shorter, and is very differently configured. The *Liberty*'s unusual antenna array and hull markings should have been visible to low-flying aircraft and torpedo boats. In the heat of battle the *Liberty* was able to identify one of the attacking torpedo boats as Israeli and to ascertain its hull number. In the same circumstances, trained Israeli naval personnel should have been able easily to see and identify the larger hull markings on the *Liberty*.

d. The best interpretation from available facts is that there were gross and inexcusable failures in the command and control of subordinate Israeli naval and air elements. One element of the Israeli air force knew the location and identification of the *Liberty* around 9:00 a.m. and did not launch an attack. Yet, hours later, apparently a different IDF element made the decision to attack the same vessel that earlier flights had identified and refrained from attacking.

e. There is no justification for the failure of the IDF—with the otherwise outstanding efficiency which it demonstrated in the course of the war—to ensure prompt alerting of all appropriate elements of the IDF of the fact that a U.S. ship was in the area. There was ample time to accomplish such alerting because the *Liberty* had been identified as a U.S. flag vessel five hours before the attack took place.

f. The unprovoked attack on the *Liberty* constitutes a flagrant act of gross negligence for which the Israeli Government should be held completely responsible, and the Israeli military personnel involved should be punished.

---

374.   **Paper Prepared by the President's Special Consultant (Bundy)[1]**

Washington, July 18, 1967.

THE U.S. AND A JORDAN–ISRAEL SETTLEMENT

King Hussein has told us that he wants to negotiate a settlement with Israel. His opening terms are a return to June 4 with Jewish access

---

[1] Source: Johnson Library, National Security File, NSC Special Committee Files, Settlement. Secret.

to the Wailing Wall and Jordanian access to the Mediterranean. This is obviously an opening position.

The Israelis have told us that their response is positive and that they are ready to meet with Hussein at a convenient time and place.

We are consulting Ambassador Burns (now in Washington) and Ambassador Barbour (who arrives this evening). In the next day or so we must give Burns instructions on what to say to Hussein when he goes back to Amman. This situation confronts us with both short-run tactical and long-run strategic questions. On the tactics, there is considerable agreement that we need to proceed cautiously and that we should not urge an immediate top-level direct negotiation between Hussein and the Israelis. Both sides need ways and means to communicate back and forth from their opening positions, which are very far apart. Hussein needs an adviser or advisers he can trust. Whatever our eventual position, we should not now be the obvious middleman in the first discussions.

The tactical decisions should await our discussions with Barbour and perhaps should go no further than the initial guidance to Burns on his reply to Hussein. Under Secretary Katzenbach has been on top of this problem and will be presenting matured recommendations to the Secretary and the President over the next day or so.

But he joins me in feeling that the really urgent question before the President and Secretary at the moment is not technical but strategic. It is whether and to what extent the United States is prepared to use its own influence with Israel and Jordan to increase the prospect of a serious settlement between them. Nobody can be certain that such a settlement is possible even if we use all our influence. But it is reasonably certain that it will not come about if we do not. We are the people with the carrot in the form of economic support for an Israel–Jordan partnership. We are also the people with the stick, in that we are the one really big friend of both of these countries, and our weapons, for example, are at present essential to both.

There are many issues between Jordan and Israel—the termination of hostilities, the degree of mutual recognition, the level of economic interconnection, the division of tourist revenues, the degree of common concern for Palestinian Arabs. But the two crucial political issues are those of control of the Old City of Jerusalem and sovereignty over the West Bank of the Jordan. The more King Hussein can get on these two issues, the more likely he can be an enduring force for peace as Israel's eastern neighbor. The less he gets on these two questions, the more risky his future and the less the likelihood of an agreement which can survive.

I think there is substantial agreement within the Executive Branch that Israel's own long-run interests would be served by a truly generous settlement with Hussein. I think there is also agreement that if we use our full influence, we can greatly affect the readiness of the government of Israel to move in this direction. But what is not clear is whether we are ready to apply our full influence in this direction, in the light of the depth and strength of the feelings of the people of Israel and of their supporters in the United States. With the best will in the world, our relations to both Hussein and Israel will tend to involve us more and more in their negotiations. If we mean to use our influence at the clutch, this involvement is desirable simply because it keeps us in touch with the state of play. But if we mean to stand aside on the substantive issues—if we are unwilling to press either side to make concessions it does not now contemplate, then it is of critical importance that our people be restrained and careful.[2]

This memorandum betrays my own beliefs in favor of a strong U.S. role—not now but later. But it is not designed to produce an answer so much as to start a discussion from which top-level guidance can emerge.

McG. B.

---

[2] In a July 17 memorandum to the President, Bundy stated that he thought they would soon face the question of whether to use U.S. influence to promote a settlement between Israel and Jordan, especially whether Israeli access to U.S. weapons should be linked to a settlement with Jordan. He concluded: "If we take a passive role, I doubt if there will be a settlement between Israel and Jordan. Indeed there may not be a settlement in the works no matter what we do. But the worst course of all would be for us to embark on a course which requires pressure on Israel if in fact at the moment of truth we are likely to conclude that it is unwise to apply such pressure." (Ibid., U.S. Position—Discussion)

375. Notes of Meeting[1]

Washington, July 18, 1967, 6:06–7:30 p.m.

NOTES OF THE PRESIDENT'S MEETING WITH

Secretary Rusk
Secretary McNamara
Walt Rostow
McGeorge Bundy
George Christian

The President asked Secretary Rusk and Mr. Rostow if an agreement had been made on the Unger announcement.[2] They replied affirmatively. The President gave the announcement to George Christian for release to the press on Wednesday.

McGeorge Bundy presented a document to the group on "U.S. and Jordan–Israel Settlement."[3] The document was discussed.

Secretary Rusk said he did not know if the U.S. wanted to be a secret mediator. He suggested somebody else, Sweden or Switzerland, would be more appropriate in getting the parties to a "meeting of the minds."

The President said he would be receptive to finding somebody to put it together before "we can't put it together again." The President said he thinks the U.S. should do it. The President said if you can get somebody to front for you that is well and good.

McGeorge Bundy said he agreed with the President. He emphasized the urgent need to "get at it with the Israelis."

The President said he felt we were going to be in a war out there before we know it. Secretary Rusk said he agreed with that.

The President said, "The clock is ticking. There is no question but what the Arabs have no confidence in us. We can't sit and let these things go."

The President said the question before the group is who is the best person to undertake the task as a mediator with the U.S. behind him.

The President said that DeGaulle is saying to the Arabs to confiscate all of the holdings in their area and that they (France) will come in

---

[1] Source: Johnson Library, Tom Johnson's Notes of Meetings, Box 1. The document bears no classification marking but is marked Literally Eyes Only. The meeting took place in the Cabinet Room at the White House.

[2] Leonard Unger's appointment as Ambassador to Thailand was announced on July 19.

[3] Document 374.

and help. The President said that report came to him from Robert Anderson on Monday night.

The President said it did not appear the Arabs were willing to sit down and talk. McGeorge Bundy said that King Hussein *is* prepared to do that, and that his position is unique in that regard.

The President wanted to know who the nominee of the group was to undertake this role as mediator. Bundy recommended the U.S. because "Israel will not listen to anybody else except us." The President asked about Prime Minister Pearson of Canada and Prime Minister Wilson of Great Britain. The President said he wished that we could find something for Wilson to do. Walt Rostow said that Oliver Franks could do it.

The President said that he agreed that we must act quickly. The issue now is who will coordinate all of this. Bundy said that the group would meet together and come back with a scenario for the President on how to proceed. The President asked Secretary McNamara and Secretary Rusk to "watch this very carefully."

On the matter of armed shipments to the Middle East countries, Secretary Rusk [said] that there was going to be a very tough time on this issue with the Congress.

The President said, "We must tell them (the Congress) that we will be out of business in that area if we don't make a sale." The $6 million of economic aid was approved. The $1.8 million in non-lethal aid was approved.

[Omitted here is discussion of unrelated subjects.]

376.　Memorandum of Conversation[1]

Washington, July 18, 1967, 8:20 p.m.

Minister Evron is back from Israel and asked to see me briefly today.

---

[1] Source: Johnson Library, National Security File, Country File, Middle East Crisis, Vol. VIII. Confidential. Rostow sent the memorandum to the President with a covering memorandum of July 18. A handwritten "L" on the memorandum indicates the President saw it.

1. His formal message to the U.S. Government is that the Israeli government is carefully examining all the alternatives for a Jordan settlement. It has not made up its mind. It will have a definitive position in about two weeks. He said that they are all conscious that this is an historic matter which will affect the shape of Israel and the Middle East for a long period and requires detailed study, including economic and demographic estimates.

2. He reported vividly the impact on him of being in Israel. He said it is impossible to understand at this distance the extent to which Israeli emotions and political life have been changed by the war. First, the extraordinary physical facts of the victory. He says, for example, that well over 700 tanks were destroyed or abandoned in the Sinai and incredible tonnages of ammunition were found in the fortresses on the Syrian Heights.

But, above all, the fact of Israeli access to and control of Jerusalem. He said he found himself getting caught up in this fever. He is now convinced that just as it will take the Arabs some time to come to grips with reality, it will also take the Israelis some time to recover from euphoria and grip the difficult real problems that lie ahead. (The latter remark he said was one that would not be approved by his government but was, in his judgment, a fact.)

3. Israeli politics is in complete ferment with men taking positions not so much on traditional party alignments as on an age basis. The war is bringing to the front a new younger lot of people. The results and new directions in politics cannot be predicted.

4. I confined my response to two substantive comments:

—So far as Jerusalem is concerned, Israeli euphoria is no better guide as to what will be wise for the long pull than Arab humiliation and despair;

—The Israelis have a duty to come to grips with the Hussein offer promptly, whatever the rhythm of their staff work.

Walt

377.   Telegram From the Mission to the United Nations to the Department of State[1]

New York, July 20, 1967, 0449Z.

290. Middle East.

1. I met for over an hour this afternoon with Gromyko and Dobrynin at Sov mission "for tea". Meeting held at Gromyko's request in response to my suggestion he have dinner with me tomorrow. Sisco, Buffum and Pederson also present. Only other person present was Soviet interpreter.

2. I opened conversation pursuant to my telecon with Secty by conveying fol points to Gromyko:

(A) Foster return from Geneva was to consult with technical experts and should not be taken as any lessening of interest in our part re nonproliferation agreement.

(B) We wanted to continue to enlist their cooperation in the search for a peaceful solution on Vietnam.

(C) We hoped there could be cooperation and parallel policies in Middle East. We noted USSR had expressed itself in favor of national existence of all ME states and of peaceful solution. We thought our policies coincided in many respects and hoped USSR would use its influence in interests of peace.

3. Gromyko replied:

(A) Non-proliferation was now matter of control and of control system. USSR favored IAEA system.

(B) He did not want to reiterate details of what Kosygin had said about Vietnam. USSR regretted US policy there and had pointed out to US the way out more than once.

(C) On ME we had each expressed our points of view. If US wants peace there then our policies coincide. USSR is for peace. There was no question on Sov side about existence of Israel. We both shared

---

[1]   Source: National Archives and Records Administration, RG 59, Central Files 1967–69, POL 27 ARAB–ISR/UN. Secret; Priority; Exdis. Repeated to Moscow and the White House. Received on July 20 at 2:12 a.m. The telegram contains handwritten corrections based on a cabled correction. (Ibid.) Rostow forwarded a copy of telegram 290 to the President on July 20 with a covering note commenting that the essence of Goldberg's report was that "the Soviets would like to find an agreed formula on the Middle East but they cannot bring around the extreme Arabs." He added that Goldberg particularly wanted the President to read the cable. (Johnson Library, National Security File, Memos to the President, Walt Rostow)

responsibility for its creation. In Arab world there were extreme tendencies, essence of which was inclined not to recognize Israel as a state. Sov Union was not sympathetic to this, which was no secret to US.

US and USSR faced fol situation. There had been discussion in broad forum. Both had agreed on existence such a state and that other views were unjustified. Was it possible we could not settle prevailing situation and then preserve future peace?

Gromyko said he would not use strong words, though they were appropriate to Israel. What was way out? No doubt US can influence Israel, and on withdrawal of troops. USSR had its own influence on certain extreme tendencies. USSR does try to influence these extreme tendencies. He had noticed that in course of GA US had not tried to find way out but had created obstacles on way to normalizing situation in ME and created difficulties on possibility of USSR influencing extremist tendencies in Arab world. For example, he said that if we want to secure peace in region we must find in relation to belligerence a form of expression that would accomplish what you want and at same time temper and if possible put end to extremist tendencies in Arab world. On other hand such formula should be presented in form acceptable to other side. This was question of form, not of principle.

If we want peace and not war, and if we agree on principle, can't we find an expression. Belligerence had become almost a cabalistic formula. Could we not find a formula possible even identical in meaning. Why not a new form with same ideas expressed in way acceptable to other side (Arab states). It was difficult to say right now revolve 180 degrees, not only difficult but impossible. USSR understands them on this. Why not combine withdrawal (nothing is possible without withdrawal) with a formula leading to peace on basis of respect of sovereignty of states in ME—in its broad and deep sense— as expressed in Charter, with or without mentioning Charter. It should be deep enough to express what we believe. Form must be flexible enough to be acceptable to both sides. Too many suspicions had been raised on both sides. Maybe questions of form were causing a high wall to be raised.

4. I replied that I had not intended to burden him about non-proliferation but just to convey a message, and said we persevered in effort to reach an agreed solution. Had also mentioned Vietnam not to re-open discussions but to convey Secty's emphasis on desirability of concerting our effort for peaceful solution. I said he knew our position which had been fully explained by President at Glassboro. We understood each other's positions and obligations, and expressed hope our great countries could find way to peaceful solution.

On ME I said I did not conceive there were wide differences in principle between us based upon Kosygin's statement to GA[2] and what he had just said. US was devoted to peaceful solution in ME. Instability created great dangers in area and for world peace. We were prepared to use our influence wherever it was applicable in avoiding extremism and for moderation. There were no puppets in ME on either side. We were prepared nevertheless to use our influence and welcomed what Gromyko said about Sov's use of influence against extremist points of view. There were problems on both sides, which was not unnatural in aftermath of war. Ever since our meetings here we had used our influence in direction of moderation and against extremism.

To be specific, when Amb Dobrynin had approached Secty and me over week ago first question he had asked was whether we were interested in peace. We had replied definitely yes. There was nothing good to come from lack of peace, and much good from an honorable, just, and peaceful solution. I did not disagree that it was not easy to turn around 180 degrees. His assessment of Arab problems in this regard was true of Israelis as well. This did not mean that we should not try. Our view was that it was important for us both to take position on principles we both could stand on and to agree upon a common expression of them in an appropriately worded res. We did not conceive that proper statements of such principles would necessarily be agreed right now to by either the Arab states or Israelis. We still thought they should be stated by us in the GA or SC and widely supported and that we could build on them for a peaceful solution. Gromyko had stated problems were those of form, not of principle. Between US and USSR I believed that was so, although not true of contending parties. We should continue to try, to make an effort to lead toward an acceptable formula under which we could each use our influence on both sides.

The word "belligerence" seemed to have become a red flag, or perhaps to FonMin of USSR we should just say flag. Recognizing this we had tried another formula. Week ago Sun,[3] without consulting Israelis, we had sought another way, which I had suggested to Ambassador Dobrynin. This included a para on withdrawal of forces to previous positions. Other principle would be statement of recognition by Arab states of Israel's right to maintain independent national state of its own and live in peace, and renunciation of all claims and acts inconsistent therewith. (Then read text exactly as previously given Dobrynin.)[4] I

---

[2] July 9.

[3] See Document 348.

[4] Telegram 289 from USUN, July 20 (erroneously dated July 21), reported discussions concerning this proposed draft resolution. (National Archives and Records Administration, RG 59, Central Files 1967–69, POL 27 ARAB–ISR/UN)

observed that we used word "recognize" not in its diplomatic sense but in sense of "acknowledge". Noted Indians, to whom we had not given the text, had told us Sovs had shown him text. He suggested there might be problem with "recognition". If so we were prepared to modify it.

I observed these paras would be an affirmation of principles. GA could only recommend, and issue would be remitted to SC to work out how to effectuate them. I thought this was a statement that USSR could accept. Most of language in second para came from the Kosygin statement. We still believed this formula contained nothing inconsistent with Sov or US positions or with UN Charter. US had gone considerable distance with this formulation. It included withdrawal in terms desired by USSR. It eliminated word "belligerence", and in our view we could proceed in SC to sort problem out in all its elements.

I said we did not believe it was in interests of either of us to resume sad warlike situation which had prevailed in area all these years. We thought this formula was an appropriate framework, because we thought we did not disagree on principles. To find a framework acceptable to both sides of the conflict, however, would be very difficult, understandably. We had hoped that at least we and USSR could get together and concert actively for overall peace in cooperation. We were still at loss as to why this formula not accepted by USSR. We understood difficulties of Arabs, and of Israel, but not for Sovs.

5. Gromyko replied that maybe we (USSR) had understood word "recognition" wrong. Said if it were just USSR it would be easier for us to talk. It was necessary for him to take into account events and moods there (Arab world). Formula should be definite enough to include peaceful existence and exclude repetition of military events there. On other side it should be flexible enough for Arab countries to accept from point of view of form, so that it would not be in sharp contradiction with mood of area. He was talking about form. For USSR it is certain we want peace there. Can we not have enough ingenuity to find a formula that would coincide with your goals, our goals, peaceful coexistence for all states there. What concrete language would you suggest? Perhaps a short res like LA text. We should avoid cabalistic word "belligerence", but find a formulation that goes in same direction.

Gromyko said wording of formula I had given to Dobrynin was still too harsh. It mentioned Arab states and Israel. Maybe there could be formula meaning same but not mentioning either. This was test of ingenuity, search for flexible formula. On content he had nothing different in mind.

6. I replied we were indeed flexible and suggested para on withdrawal delete word "Israel" and substitute "by the parties to the conflict" and that the para on national existence delete reference both to

Arab States and Israel and instead refer to "acknowledgment by all member states in area that each enjoys right to maintain etc."

7. Gromyko replied that from Arab point of view second para might still give some difficulties, though we all agreed with it, and even common sense and also Charter supported it. Suppose we said: "that sovereign rights must be respected by all states in accordance with Charter of UN". Sovereignty conveyed same idea in different form. Perhaps we could refer to sovereign rights, or to territorial integrity. Asked whether withdrawal to June 5 positions acceptable.

8. I replied that many claims had been made in name of sovereignty, for example blocking of Gulf of Aqaba, and that this language was not precise enough. Either tomorrow or later in SC we must have a solution. Perhaps fresh approach was needed, as Gromyko has said. That was why we had suggested this language. I said that if they could confirm that Aqaba was not involved we would not fuss about June 5 date. Gromyko replied that it was not involved. He then asked whether we did not have a still more flexible formula that all could accept.

I said I thought effort to get a res that all would accept was very difficult. We should aim for the one that both sides involved would not vote for, but that we jointly could support. Said there are also times when flexibility was exhausted. We did have one other suggestion, which I had put to Amb Dobrynin Monday, and which avoided word "belligerence", which was that "termination of all states of war and any and all claims thereto is expected". We could also add words "without delay" in both paras. I said we had undertaken study of Russian formulas about termination of belligerence, and that to best of our knowledge Sovs used same word for state of war and state of belligerence, noting translation Dobrynin had given us seemed to have no legal background.

9. Gromyko confirmed that there was no difference in Russian between state of war and state of belligerence. There was problem term had acquired among Arabs. I pointed out this was not a problem in Russian text but only in English and French versions, which could be met by change such as we had suggested. "Belligerence" was one of the states of war that would be terminated under this formula. I stated that with these proposals I had exhausted my flexibility and asked for some indication of flexibility on his side.

10. Gromyko said he needed some time to think the matter over. He would need to do some consultations. I said I did not think we could get agreement from parties now, but I did not see how they could take exception to such principles. Buffum added that perhaps it would be easier for them if principles were adopted by UN, to which they could later conform; we had some indications from moderate Arabs this might be so.

11. Gromyko then commented that words "without delay" fitted well in first para (on withdrawal) but not so well in second para, which dealt with complex policy questions while first one dealt with an act. He did not raise question of a different approach, but of acceptability, not a question of a change at expense of anyone's interests.

12. I replied we felt there must be equality of principles. We could drop "without delay" from both paras or add it to both. (Gromyko clearly was only going through motions on this point.) I then noted that LA res might be more helpful in this regard. Words "is expected" were, according to our info, strong words in Russian, and could be used in both paras. Then made point I was discussing these two paras in context putting them in LA text.

13. Gromyko then said he wondered if we couldn't get word "states" out without changing meaning. A UN member was a state. I interjected we could say that each member of the UN in the area enjoyed the right to a national state of its own. He then said he would think whole matter over. He did not see clear possibilities, but he would like time to think and study. He as FonMin could take decision for his govt but Arabs have definite instructions here. (I inferred he was saying his instructions were he could agree to anything Arabs would agree to.) He did not know how often they received them; perhaps this depended on urgency of situation. In any case consultations were required, and it would be difficult to conclude them by tomorrow. If he saw possibilities in these texts and needed another day or so he wondered whether we would be agreeable.

14. I said that we wanted to complete the GA, but that if USSR was seriously consulting about possibilities along such lines as I indicated we would be willing for GA to go over until Friday. Gromyko said he thought that would be enough time. Suggested US should consult own position as well. I repeated we had exhausted our flexibility. Hoped we could reach agreement soon either in GA or SC. Gromyko said it would be better in GA so we would not clash in SC.

15. In closing Pedersen pointed out Indians were already circulating procedural text[5] to recess GA among other states for sponsorship. This had been discussed with us and we understood with them. Gromyko said they had told Indians they had no objections to their going ahead to prepare such text, for use if no substantive agreement possible, but without Sov commitment at this point. I told him we had substantially same position.

---

[5] See footnote 4 above.

16. Afterward pursuant to press inquiries we agreed with Dobrynin that we would confirm meeting had taken place and that questions relating to GA were discussed.

Comment: I think it is unlikely Sovs will be able to move far enough away from radical Arabs (especially Algeria and Syria) to accept either of positions I gave him, though he seemed to be considering the first one. On other hand Gromyko was clearly interested in getting something more out of GA than Indian procedural res. Inasmuch as his emphasis was on persuading Arabs to accept something, and inasmuch as all our info indicates they have no intention of doing so, probability, though not certainty, is still return to procedural res Friday.

Goldberg

---

378. Telegram From the Department of State to the Mission at Geneva[1]

Washington, July 19, 1967, 7:45 p.m.

9613. For Ambassador Tubby from Battle.

1. Your 4333.[2] Hafez, Siddiqui, and Chamberlain[3] known to us. We met with them in Washington last summer. While Hafez's influence with Nasser not known, we are aware that Hafez has easy access to Nasser.

---

[1] Source: National Archives and Records Administration, RG 59, Central Files 1967–69, POL UAR–US. Top Secret; Immediate; Nodis; Whirlwind. Drafted by Bergus, cleared by Eugene Rostow and Battle, and approved by Katzenbach.

[2] Reference is to telegram 232 from Geneva, July 19, for Battle from Representative to the European Office of the United Nations Roger W. Tubby. It reported that Elwy Hafez, who identified himself as a member of the UAR National Council and a close friend of Nasser, had called on Tubby. Hafez said that Nasser had told him 6 days earlier that he wanted to reestablish good relations with the United States and would receive anyone close to President Johnson on a secret basis or would send Vice President Mohieddin to Geneva or elsewhere for talks. He said that Nasser was "through with Russians," that he wanted above all else to develop his country, and that he realized the United States could do more than anyone else. He said Nasser told him he wanted the United States to be the sole intermediary between the UAR and Israel; he would not recognize Israel or deal directly with it, but he would agree to "live and let live" if Israel would return to the 1956 borders. (Ibid.)

[3] Donald Chamberlain, Vice President of American Locomotives, Inc., and Wahid Siddiqui, a Pakistani representative of that company in Geneva, accompanied Hafez in his call on Tubby.

2. Would appreciate your delivering following message to Hafez:

Despite very serious problems in US-UAR relations, USG remains prepared for discussions with duly accredited representatives of GUAR. Former Treasury Secretary Robert Anderson, who is known to Nasser and who enjoys full confidence of President Johnson, would be prepared to meet with Vice President Muhieddin on secret basis perhaps in Geneva at time to be mutually agreed. Mr. Anderson is proceeding to London July 27 where plans remain five days. He could go to Geneva during that period. If GUAR desires such a meeting further details can be arranged through US Mission Geneva.[4]

3. Please use slug designator Nodis/Whirl Wind for all communications on this subject.

Rusk

---

[4] Tubby reported in telegram 247 from Geneva, July 20, that he had delivered the message to Hafez, who was returning to Cairo that day. Hafez thought arrangements could be made for Mohieddin to meet with Anderson on a secret basis, preferably in Geneva. (National Archives and Records Administration, RG 59, Central Files 1967–69, POL UAR–US) Telegram 10370 to Geneva, July 20, states that Anderson was willing to go to Geneva and would prefer a meeting on July 30. (Ibid.)

---

379.   Telegram From the Mission to the United Nations to the Department of State[1]

New York, July 21, 1967, 0123Z.

304. UAR Attitudes.

Riad (UAR) informed Sisco and Pedersen at lunch today that Cairo pleased that we have decided to increase our staff from seven to fourteen and that Don Bergus is going since he is known and well liked.[2] Riad said they had not made any decisions regarding the size of their group but that if and when they make decision they would want to send someone to Wash who was well known to Luke Battle. He underscored that US still had many friends in Egypt and trusted there could be an improvement in relations. He stressed too that there was really no need for an intermediary; that the best way for Egyptians and

---

[1] Source: National Archives and Records Administration, RG 59, Central Files 1967–69, POL 17 US–UAR. Confidential; Priority; Exdis. Received on July 20 at 10:28 p.m.

[2] Bergus became principal officer of the U.S. Interests Section of the Spanish Embassy in Cairo in August.

Americans to communicate was directly and in particular in Cairo now that Don Bergus is going.

Turning to GA, he informed us that Gromyko had met with Fawzi this morning and had put to them two formulations "which had been discussed by Gromyko and Goldberg" on previous evening. Riad said that fact that discussion had taken place had enhanced US position in Arab eyes and that UAR at least no longer believed the rumors spread in corridors that US wanted no result whatsoever from GA. Riad implied his del favorable to language (which he did not describe other than to refer to "is expected" formula) which Gromyko had discussed with them this morning but that the decision rested in Cairo. Moreover, he said UAR having great difficulties with the Syrians and Algerians. Also said there would be a question as to who would put forward proposal if there were one.

Riad said UAR had maintained open contact with Americans here on direct instructions of Fawzi, who had resisted criticism from other Arabs in doing so. He said UAR and US both needed each other, perhaps in different degrees, but it was necessary to both. He said we should keep in close touch as matters develop in Cairo and elsewhere. There was no need for any broker between US and UAR; this would only complicate matters and require payment of "broker's fees". He said Bergus would be kept fully informed of views and currents in Cairo.

Riad described Sudan role within Arab group since outbreak of conflict as being a moderating one, saying our impression that Sudan was among extremists was not correct. Described new Iraqi Govt as a strong one, with a leadership which was more closely identified with UAR and a leader who was a nationalist and progressive but not a leftist. Said new govt was more objectionable as previous one to Syrians and effort would be made to pacify Kurdish problem. He assented to our description of Algerians and Syrians as being the most extreme among Arabs.

In spite of some top-level speeches in the past which Riad admitted had caused trouble in US, Riad maintained UAR had over past years generally exercised moderating influence among Arabs and with Syrians in particular in Israeli problem. Said they had specifically told Syrians El Fatah-type activities were not good themselves nor good for general Arab cause when Arab world was not sufficiently strong.

Riad reflected real concern that Israelis might cross Suez Canal and even take Port Said. Thought presence Israeli mil boats at canal was evidence of this possible intention as well as of desire to be on canal itself. He volunteered that in spite of new equipment UAR air force was no match for Israelis. Said they had even heard Israelis might try to open canal and offer to put some of revenues in banks for UAR as they were doing on some of Sinai oil wells.

Goldberg

---

380.   **Telegram From the Mission to the United Nations to the Department of State**[1]

New York, July 21, 1967, 0124Z.

305. USUN 290.[2] Mid-East Crisis.

Dobrynin (USSR) telephoned me this noon to say he wanted to check with me about the wording of the formulas I had discussed with Gromyko yesterday. We met at UN shortly after lunch.

Dobrynin showed me two texts. One "called for" Israeli withdrawal in one para and said renunciation of claims and acts inconsistent with existence of independent national states was "expected" in other. Second version used similar formulas on substance but used terminology "is expected" in both paras. Both versions used words "without delay" in each para.

After looking over text I told Dobrynin I had not used expression "calls upon" in conversation yesterday and further noted that he had used it only in para one and that this created imbalance between the two. He said his purpose was to clarify with me exactly where our position stood.

I then went over with him conversation of yesterday based on his notes (which were accurate) and my own. As a result the two versions attached at end of this tel were completed as accurately reflecting yesterday's intention. (Final drafting reflected two subsequent telecons as well.) Dobrynin confirmed by telephone that Gromyko agreed these texts, and not ones Dobrynin had explored with me earlier, represented

---

[1] Source: National Archives and Records Administration, RG 59, Central Files 1967–69, POL 27 ARAB–ISR/UN. Secret; Immediate; Exdis. Repeated Immediate to the White House and Moscow. Received on July 20 at 10:25 p.m. Passed to the White House at 11:10 p.m. Rostow sent a copy to the President on July 21 at 9:35 a.m. (Johnson Library, National Security File, Country File, Middle East Crisis)

[2] Document 377.

what we had talked about. Version I is the text in which Dobrynin appeared to have greatest interest.

Dobrynin also told me Gromyko had been in touch with Fawzi (UAR) about these new formulas and that Fawzi thought he might need more time to consult his govt. Dobrynin therefore wondered if we would consent to two or three days more time. I told him we were suspicious that constant requests for delay were simply a bargaining tactic. Also that we had heard of possible efforts to bring Jerusalem into SC and wondered whether this request for a further delay was not simply effort to complicate issue with that of Jerusalem again. Dobrynin said USSR knew of no intention to have early SC meeting on Jerusalem, which he reconfirmed after talking to Gromyko. I told him we nevertheless had indication some Arabs were thinking of this. I told Dobrynin it was our view that session must be completed tomorrow afternoon as agreed or at latest on Saturday morning. Dobrynin said he would inform Gromyko of this reaction.

In separate conversation Riad (UAR) told Sisco and Pedersen UAR del had sent to Cairo today two variant formulas given them by USSR, indicating one of them used "is expected" phrases in both paras and that second para was based on "independent national state" concept. Riad implied Fawzi thought text had some merit but Cairo would take decision. He also foresaw difficulty with Algerians and Syrians. We are uncertain exactly what texts he referring to, as conversation preceded agreement between Dobrynin and me as to what proper texts were.

In separate conversation Sov Couns Shevchenko told a Belgian Sovs could see no reason not to accept res calling for withdrawal of Israeli forces and recognition Israeli right to exist, both "without delay". When queried whether Sovs would be prepared to break with Arabs in agreeing such res, Shevchenko reportedly made fuzzy reply, main point of which seemed to be they would not necessarily be breaking with all Arabs.

Nevertheless our assessment is proposals will be unacceptable to Arabs, that Sovs will not be willing to break with Arabs, and that we are most likely to end GA shortly with procedural res along lines being discussed by Finland, Sweden and Austria.

Fol are the two texts:

Version I

The GA,

Having examined the grave situation in the ME,

Considering that the crisis in the ME merits the attention of all member states and indeed requires the full participation of all members to achieve a just and lasting peace,

1. Declares that peace and final solutions to this problem can be achieved within the framework of the Charter of the UN;
2. Affirms the principle under the UN Charter of:

A. Without delay withdrawal by the parties to the conflict of their forces from territories occupied by them in keeping with the inadmissibility of the conquest of territory by war;
B. Without delay acknowledgment by all member states of the UN in the area that each enjoys the right to maintain an independent national state of its own and to live in peace and security, and renunciation of all claims and acts inconsistent therewith;

3. Requests the SC to continue examining the situation in the ME with a sense of urgency, working directly with the parties and utilizing a UN presence in order to achieve an appropriate and just solution of all aspects of the problem, in particular bringing to an end the long-deferred one of the refugees and guaranteeing freedom of transit through international waterways.

Version II

The GA,

Having examined the grave situation in the ME,

Considering that the crisis in the ME merits the attention of all member states and indeed requires the full participation of all members to achieve a just and lasting peace,

1. Declares that peace and final solutions to this problem can be achieved within the framework of the Charter of the UN;
2. Affirms the principle that conquest of territory by war is inadmissible under the UN Charter, and consequently that the withdrawal by the parties to the conflict to the positions they occupied before June 5, 1967 is expected;
3. Affirms likewise the principle that acknowledgment by all member states in the area that each of them enjoys the right to maintain an independent national state of its own and to live in peace and security and renunciation of all claims and acts inconsistent therewith are expected;
4. Requests the SC to continue examining the situation in the ME with a sense of urgency, working directly with the parties and utilizing a UN presence in order to achieve an appropriate and just solution of all aspects of the problem, in particular bringing to an end the long-deferred one of the refugees and guaranteeing freedom of transit through international waterways.

Goldberg

381. Telegram From the Department of State to the Embassy in Israel[1]

Washington, July 21, 1967, 7:48 p.m.

11414. 1. Ambassador Harman called on Assistant Secretary Battle afternoon July 20. Referred to current state of suspension in USG handling of routine GOI military requests for ammunition, spare parts, etc. Said Eban intended raise this with Secretary July 15 but had not gotten around to it, though he had mentioned it to Walt Rostow. GOI hopes suspension can be unscrambled soon as possible. It would hope these "routine" supplies could be viewed as normal replacement items and considered apart from question of new equipment requests. Battle replied he was well aware of GOI view. Noted that matter complicated for us by Congressional attitudes on worldwide arms sales. Told Harman we would try to unscramble this soon as possible.

2. Harman then raised what he termed procedural request stating GOI wishes to send "couple of military people" to Washington for secret discussions on area military situation and related subjects. He noted there are at least two recent precedents (Rabin visit of 1963[2] and Weizman visit of 1965[3]). Harman stressed that on those occasions publicity had successfully been avoided or played down, and said GOI would do likewise in this instance if we wish. Asked by Battle for names of people GOI had in mind to send, Harman replied they would be similar people to those involved in earlier visits and that names could be given once visit agreed in principle. Re timing, Harman said GOI thinks it very important have this fairly soon. Battle said he would discuss proposal with Defense and let Harman have reaction soon as possible.

3. Harman said he wished underline point made by Eban at July 15 lunch that GOI would take very negative view of any U.S. arms supply to Jordan at this stage. Said GOI wants to make sure there is no misunderstanding in Washington as to its position. Battle responded that he wanted make sure GOI in considering this question has given thought to alternatives for Jordan. There is definite Russian offer of arms to Jordan. Consequences of no U.S. sale must be weighed very carefully.

---

[1] Source: National Archives and Records Administration, RG 59, Central Files 1967–69, POL 27–14 ARAB–ISR/SANDSTORM. Secret; Nodis; Sandstorm. Drafted by Wolle and approved by Battle.

[2] Reference is to U.S.-Israeli talks November 12–13, 1963; see *Foreign Relations, 1961–1963*, vol. XVIII, Documents 359 and 360.

[3] Reference is to U.S.-Israeli talks October 12–13, 1965; see ibid., 1964–1968, vol. XVIII, Document 246, footnote 2.

Harman reacted with general comment that GOI believes it will not know until some time has passed just what it is dealing with in Jordan. He added that GOI ready to talk with King Hussein or his people, preferably with King himself, at any time. There is strong feeling in Israel that it must deal direct with King or otherwise signals might be misread. Asked by Battle if that meant GOI rules out UN or other negotiator, Harman simply repeated that it is feeling of GOI that it must find "a direct route" to assess the situation.

4. Harman mentioned he expects return Israel for short period in week or so.

Rusk

---

382.   **Memorandum From Secretary of State Rusk to President Johnson**[1]

Washington, July 20, 1967.

Hussein has asked us to intervene to achieve a possible settlement with Israel and to discover their terms of settlement and their willingness to negotiate. He says he has Nasser's blessing (which we would have little confidence in) as long as he does not engage in direct negotiations or conclude a peace treaty. He clearly would like us to lean on the Israelis to secure an agreement with which he can survive.

The Israeli Government is prepared to discuss a settlement with the Jordanians and has suggested we convey to Hussein their willingness to engage in private talks with Hussein or with his representative. Our estimate of their position, which is not yet formal, is that there could be agreement on various elements of a viable settlement except with respect to Jerusalem where the two sides are very far apart indeed on an issue which both regard as crucial. The Israelis do not wish to deal

---

[1] Source: Johnson Library, National Security File, Country File, Middle East Crisis, Sandstorm/Whirlwind. Secret; Nodis; Sandstorm. Rostow sent the memorandum to the President at 6:20 p.m. with a covering memorandum of July 20 noting that the Rusk proposal was "designed to protect the U.S., while still permitting us to follow the negotiation closely; insert ideas; and throw our diplomatic weight at the right moment." A handwritten "L" on the Rostow memorandum indicates the President saw it. A handwritten note of July 21 by Saunders on a copy of the Rostow memorandum states that the President had approved and asked that McNamara be briefed. It continues: "He was a little jumpy about the American lawyer but said OK." (Ibid., Saunders Files, Jordan, 4/1/66–10/31/67)

through an intermediary, and clearly do not wish the intermediary to be the U.S.

While the prospects for settlement are not particularly good, every-one—the U.S., Jordan and Israel—has such enormous stake in success, that it may be possible to achieve. While time might moderate positions, Hussein's present political status is such that we cannot risk delay in starting the process.

We do not believe we can achieve a satisfactory foreign mediator or that the U.S. should presently play this role. Despite danger to Hussein from his Arab colleagues, we believe direct negotiation is the most feasible and productive course and one which would permit the U.S. to use our influence at appropriate stages to promote agreement without direct U.S. involvement in the total process.

We therefore propose that we respond to Hussein's request along the following lines:

1. The Israelis tell us they are prepared to discuss a settlement on a confidential basis. They wish direct discussions and suggest two on each side.

2. We do not know the Israeli terms for a settlement and doubt that they have been formulated as yet.

3. We are inclined to believe that the possibility exists of working out a settlement of most of the issues and problems that would be involved. Jerusalem, however, will be very difficult and we do not know if there is any flexibility in the Israeli position except in respect to the direct administration of the Holy Places by religious authorities.

4. We do not know if an overall settlement will prove feasible, but we believe it would be worth the try. In any event, we are confident that the Israelis would protect the secrecy of their contacts with Hussein and the Jordan Government.

5. Hussein should keep in mind, however, that we do not trust Nasser, Boumediene and Atassi who are aware of Jordan's intentions and we doubt that Hussein should trust them.

6. Finally, Hussein would be asked how he contemplates staffing-out the negotiations. If he expresses uncertainty, as we expect, the suggestion would be made that private legal counsel would help. If he desired, we would assist him in finding a competent and discreet American firm. While this would marginally increase our involvement, it would lessen the imbalance of negotiating talent that would otherwise exist and permit us to make appropriate inputs at the staffing level throughout the negotiating process.

You will note that Paragraph 6 involves the use of a private American. This seems to us constructive since it provides a method for us to be involved in the process which is controllable and which allows us both a private and public role. The American lawyer will not be acting as an American official, but would be a person in whom we had great confidence.

I have discussed this approach with Mac Bundy, who agrees with it.

Dean Rusk

---

383.   Diplomatic Note From the Israeli Ambassador (Harman) to Secretary of State Rusk[1]

Washington, June 12, 1967.

The Ambassador of Israel presents his compliments to the Honorable the Secretary of State and has the honor to refer to the Secretary of State's note of June 10, 1967 concerning the attack by Israeli aircraft and torpedo boats on the United States naval vessel, the U.S.S. *Liberty.*

The Government of Israel has instituted a full investigation into this accident and has already announced the establishment by the Chief-of-Staff of the Israel Defense Forces of an Enquiry to make a full investigation of all the facts and circumstances. The Government of Israel will make available to the Government of the United States the findings of this investigation, and, for its part, hopes that the Government of the United States will make available to the Government of Israel the findings of its own investigation.

Pending the results of its investigation the Government of Israel feels it is premature to draw conclusions.

The Government of Israel recalls that as soon as it became aware of the tragic error which had occurred it immediately informed the Government of the United States of what had taken place. The Government of Israel immediately assumed responsibility for this error

---

[1] Source: National Archives and Records Administration, RG 59, Central Files 1967–69, POL 27 ARAB–ISR. No classification marking. The note is a revised version of Document 267. The note is filed, together with Document 352, and a covering memorandum of July 20 from Walsh to Walt Rostow stating that they constituted the true, corrected versions of the exchange and that all other copies should be destroyed.

and conveyed its apologies and deep regret for what had occurred and for the grievous loss of life.

Subsequently, as mentioned in the Secretary of State's Note of June 10, 1967 the Government of Israel took the initiative to offer to make amends for the tragic loss of life and material damage. Further, all assistance was offered by the personnel of the Israel Defense Forces to the U.S.S. *Liberty*. The area around the U.S.S. *Liberty* was immediately searched by Israel Defense Forces personnel, by plane and boat, and subsequently search efforts were renewed.

The Government of Israel has standard instructions of the most stringent nature to all its military personnel that the personnel and property of the United States, as of all other countries not involved in hostilities, shall not be endangered. These instructions have been renewed.

The Government of Israel notes that the incident occurred in an area which the United Arab Republic had warned neutral vessels to avoid, as it was an area of hostilities. It would be appreciated if the Government of Israel could be given timely information of the approach of United States vessels to shores where the Israel Defense Forces are in authority.

The Government of Israel renews its readiness to make amends and has instructed the Ambassador of Israel to reiterate its profound regret for the consequences of what was admittedly a tragic error.

The Ambassador of Israel avails himself of this opportunity to renew to the Honorable the Secretary of State the assurances of his highest regard.

A.H.

---

384.   Telegram From the Mission to the United Nations to the Department of State[1]

New York, July 22, 1967, 0207Z.

314. Re: Middle East.

Dobrynin (USSR) came to see me this morning to talk about status substantive text. Said USSR was prepared to vote for res we had worked

---

[1] Source: National Archives and Records Administration, RG 59, Central Files 1967–69, POL 27 ARAB–ISR/UN. Secret; Priority; Exdis. Also sent to the White House and repeated Priority to Moscow.

out. On other hand some Arabs would probably vote against it and rest would abstain. He wondered in circumstances what our assessment would be of prospects and desirability of going ahead and what Israeli attitude was. I told him I thought Israel would probably also vote no.

Said I could not give him assessment of voting prospects without consultations with my staff and suggested we talk again at 2:30. I agreed with him that prospects of active opposition to reses by parties directly concerned raised questions which needed to be examined.

In course conversation we checked text of res as it had been circulated to Arabs and Sov bloc by Sovs. In process discovered that Sovs had introduced reference to June 5 date in Version I.[2] I told Dobrynin this was not acceptable and that it had not been included in that version as given to him yesterday by US and as reported to Wash.

I told Dobrynin we had just received word from Indians that substantive res was "off" and that they wanted to talk again about procedural res. Dobrynin said Indians were not acting on their request but indicated Sovs still thought text of yesterday was satisfactory.

It was obvious from this conversation that Sovs wanted to disengage from substantive text and to revert to procedural ending of GA. About noon time Dobrynin telephoned back to say Gromyko would like to see me at 2:15 to talk about the procedural res.

When I called on Gromyko, latter opened conversation by saying they had discussed text with Arabs. Latter had referred to US rigidity. Some of them were definitely negative about res. Further Arab meeting was still going on and he had not heard final results, so Arab attitude was at least inconclusive. Arab attitude created more difficulties. He said there was of course the "Scandinavian" res,[3] which he then produced.

I said that if there were no substantive conclusions of GA it would be my view that US and USSR should continue to put our heads together in SC and work cooperatively for peaceful conditions in area, recognizing difficulties involved.

Gromyko said he took note of what I had said. Sov position had been fully outlined, notably in Kosygin statement. USSR would see

---

[2] Telegram 343 from USUN, July 26, transmitted the texts of the two versions of Soviet-U.S. compromise language in the form "in which we believe Sovs gave them to Arabs." In Version I, Section 2.A. reads: "Without delay withdrawal by the parties to the conflict of their forces to the positions they occupied before June 5, 1967, in keeping with the inadmissibility of the conquest of territory by war". In Version II, Section 2 reads: "Affirms the principle that conquest of territory by war is inadmissible under the U.N. Charter, and consequently that the withdrawal by the parties to the conflict of their forces to the positions they occupied before June 5, 1967, is expected".

[3] For text of a draft resolution introduced on July 21 by Austria, Finland, and Sweden, and revised later that day, see UN documents A/L.529 and A/L.529/Rev. 1.

what position US would take in next stage "or stages". Said reference of issue to SC was acceptable to USSR provided GA continued to be in session. Said USSR had nothing definite in mind at this point. It had nothing against referral to SC and besides there was no other place for it to go. Whenever any member requested SC meeting, of course, USSR would not be opposed. He noted Arabs did not like first para of Scandinavian res, which dealt with SC, but USSR did like it and agreed to text as it stood. Reiterated that there was no other place to go.

I said we agreed to text with one understanding. Previous version had included with respect to reconvening of GA by Pres that this should be done after appropriate consultations. We understood USSR had objected to that. We did not insist on these words but we did insist on consultations. These should be with perm members of SC, sponsors of reses which had been put before GA, and with the parties concerned. We also had no objection if he wanted to speak to heads of groups as well. These consultations were not a veto but were necessary as a minimum for timing, convenience and appropriateness. I told Gromyko I had said to Jakobson (Finland) that we would agree to removal of words if we were agreed in private on such consultations and if Pres would say he would convene GA after appropriate consultations. I noted that was process in SC and that it should be followed in GA, and that we had had difficult experiences during this session where Pres had done things without consultations. I observed that not being a member of a group we were sometimes not consulted by GA Pres and that unlike USSR, which was member of a group, US was only non-aligned member of UN. Gromyko smiled and asked when we had become non-aligned, last night?

Gromyko said recognized this as following normal processes and that USSR would neither encourage nor discourage GA Pres.

Gromyko then said he would make a brief statement after adoption of procedural res, which he agreed should go forward today. Said some of Arabs also might make statements.

In closing I alluded to his comment Arabs were still in session and said I would be willing to bet 100 to 1 that they would be opposed to substantive text. Gromyko asked where I found the one.

Goldberg

385.   Memorandum From the President's Special Consultant
        (Bundy) to President Johnson[1]

Washington, July 21, 1967.

SUBJECT

The Middle East as we Approach the Weekend

1. I foresee no major action issue before Monday[2] so this memo is for information—and a little advance notice for things that may come up for decision next week.

Walt passed me your message of approval on our plan to reply to Hussein.[3] I will ask Nick to have another look at the question of the lawyer, but I think our second thoughts will be the same as our first— that the advantage of having a lawyer we can talk to outweighs the risk of guilt by association.

The Israelis are now telling us that they are not ready for serious talks (though they can handle opening feelers), and it looks as if it would take a little time to get this thing going in any event.

2. Arthur Goldberg tells me that the most recent effort to get an agreed resolution on substance has run up against an Arab stone wall. It was a good game to play out, and I think he handled it extremely well in the face of Israeli worries which were both foolish and foolishly expressed. He is talking this afternoon with the Russians about a pro-cedural resolution, and it is conceivable that the General Assembly may wind up today—although its capacity for continued existence should not be underrated. (He has just called to say he and Gromyko agreed on a procedural resolution and the General Assembly will wind up today.)[4]

---

[1] Source: Johnson Library, National Security File, NSC Special Committee Files, U.S. Position—Discussion. No classification marking. Sent through and initialed by Walt Rostow. A handwritten notation on the memorandum indicates it was received at 4:45 p.m., and the President saw it.

[2] July 24.

[3] See footnote 1, Document 382.

[4] On the evening of July 21, the General Assembly adopted the draft resolution intro-duced by Austria, Finland, and Sweden, by a vote of 63 to 26 with 27 abstentions, with the United States voting in favor. Resolution 2256 (ES–V) asked the Secretary-General to for-ward to the Security Council the records of the fifth emergency special session to facilitate the Council's resumption of its consideration of the Middle East situation, and decided to adjourn the fifth emergency special session temporarily and to authorize the President of the General Assembly to reconvene it as and when necessary. The text is printed in the Department of State *Bulletin*, August 14, 1967, p. 218. Rusk commented to Goldberg in a telephone conversation the next day that it was an extraordinary result that the United States and the Soviet Union voted together against the Arabs, with Israel abstaining. Goldberg thought they were "off stride in the Kremlin", and Rusk thought "we came out of this very well". (Notes of telephone conversation July 22, 9:43 a.m.; National Archives and Records Administration, RG 59, Rusk Files: Lot 72 D 192, Telephone Calls)

3. As you may remember, we have a tentative plan (as we told the oil men, Nickerson and Rambin) to make a new statement after the General Assembly. If you agree, I think the best time for such a statement would be early next week, perhaps in the context of a press conference if you plan to have one. The State Department and I will be drafting over the weekend and we will hope to have a fresh draft for you on Monday.

4. With the end of the Assembly, we shall also wish to look again at the arms registration proposal. As you may remember, the first step in that scenario will probably be a letter to the Secretary General. The Department is slowly making progress toward acceptance of your decision for a plan which could include a unilateral U.S. decision to register shipments if others will not play ball. We all feel strongly that no move should be made until the General Assembly is out of our hair, and there are other diplomatic subtleties in the draft scenario, but it does look as if we will have such a scenario for your consideration early next week.

One element in this problem that you can judge better than the rest of us is whether an arms registration initiative limited to the Middle East would help or hurt in the arms sale row on the Hill. Some think that it might simply lead Reuss or McCarthy to try to extend the principle worldwide. Others think it would show us moving in a useful direction on a specific problem. Dean Rusk holds the latter view, but he and I agree that your judgment is best on this question, and you do not have to decide it until you see the full scenario and the opening shot to the Secretary General next week.

5. The next really tough issue *may* be arms for Israel. Wally Barbour reports that their losses are more serious than they are telling us on other channels, and there are some intelligence reports which suggest that Nasser or the Syrians may be tempted into some act of folly like a sudden air attack some time in the next weeks. We think the odds are against such an action, and still more strongly against any real Arab victory, but we all remember the lessons of May and June, and if the Israelis really come in hard for early airplanes, we would be right up against the hard set of bargaining questions which I have mentioned before.

The immediate problem is to get a clear fix on the situation (as well as our own available supplies). The Israelis still seem less concerned than some of our own people. Rusk and McNamara will be concerting a recommendation to you on this in the next few days. It may take the form of a proposal that we let the Israelis send a top air officer over here some time after Bob's military assistance testimony.

As a matter of information, I might add that the Israelis are now telling us that they could not support any U.S. arms shipment to Jordan in the current mood of their country. If and when we send the Israelis some stuff, we shall at a minimum have to move them off this new hard line.

Finally, I should report that there are a number of other signs of hardening Israeli positions up and down the line. Their intemperate reaction to Goldberg's skillful round with Gromyko, their edginess about the Jordanian negotiations, their increasing interest in solutions that would not return the West Bank to Jordan, and the evidence of political jockeying among their leaders (each tougher than the other) make me think that the time is coming for American words and actions which will have at least a constructive effect in knocking you off the top of the Israeli polls. The trick will be to achieve that result without any parallel impact at home.

---

386.   Telegram From the Department of State to the Embassy in Jordan[1]

Washington, July 21, 1967, 7:10 p.m.

11347. For Ambassador Burns.

A. We have developed following position in response to Hussein's request that we help him achieve a possible settlement with Israel and to discover their terms of settlement and their willingness to negotiate. Our position is based on our knowledge that the Israeli Government is prepared to discuss a settlement with the Jordanians. The Israelis have suggested that we convey to Hussein their willingness to engage in private talks with him or with his representatives. Our informal estimate of their position is that there could be agreement on various elements of a viable settlement except with respect to Jerusalem, where the two sides are very far apart on an issue which both regard as crucial. The Israelis do not wish to deal through an intermediary and even if they did, do not wish the intermediary to be the United States.

B. While the prospects for a settlement are not promising, our belief is that everyone—the US, Jordan and Israel—has such enormous stake

---

[1] Source: National Archives and Records Administration, RG 59, Central Files 1967–69, POL 27–14 ARAB–ISR/SANDSTORM. Secret; Priority; Nodis; Sandstorm. Drafted by Houghton, cleared by Battle and Walt Rostow, and approved by Katzenbach. Repeated to London for the Ambassador.

in success that it might just be possible to achieve one. We realize that time might moderate positions, but Hussein's present political status is such that we believe he should not risk delay in starting the process.

C. We do not believe that we can find a satisfactory foreign mediator, or that the US should presently play this role. Despite the danger to Hussein from his Arab colleagues, we believe that direct negotiations between Jordan and Israel is the most feasible and productive course and one which would permit the US to use our influence at appropriate stages to promote agreement without direct US involvement in total process.

D. With the above in mind, you should therefore respond to Hussein's request along the following lines:

1. The Israelis inform us that they are prepared to discuss a settlement on a confidential basis. They want direct discussions and suggest that there be two representatives on both sides.

2. We do not know the Israeli terms for a settlement and doubt that they have been formulated as yet.

3. We are inclined to believe that the possibility exists of working out a settlement of most of the issues and problems which would be involved. Jerusalem, however, as the King is aware, will be very difficult and we do not know if there is any flexibility in the Israeli position except in respect to the direct administration of the holy places by religious authorities.

4. We do not know if an over-all settlement will prove feasible, but we believe it would be worth the try. In any event, we are confident that the Israelis would protect the secrecy of their contacts with the King and his Government.

5. Hussein should keep very much in mind, however, in making his final decision that we do not trust Nasser, Boumediene and Atassi, who are aware of the King's intentions. We doubt if the King should trust them either.

6. In view of the foregoing, we believe that at least in the preliminary meetings with the Israelis, the King should consider whether he should become directly engaged. He should review carefully the possibility of using a special Jordanian representative who should obviously be selected most carefully.

7. We believe that you should raise with Hussein how he contemplates staffing out the negotiations. He is undoubtedly aware that Israeli negotiators will be well prepared and will be supported by highly competent staff. If he expresses some uncertainty on this score, you might suggest that he consider obtaining private legal counsel. If he desired, we would assist him in finding a competent and discreet

American firm to provide staff support. FYI. While this would to some extent increase our own involvement, it would lessen the imbalance of negotiating talent that would otherwise exist and permit us to make a contribution at the staffing level through the negotiating process. The American lawyer would not be acting as an American official, but would be a person in whom we had great confidence. End FYI.

Rusk

---

387. Letter From Secretary of State Rusk to Secretary of Defense McNamara[1]

Washington, July 22, 1967.

Dear Bob:

The Israelis, as you know, have asked to send a high-level military team to Washington to discuss their security concerns and their needs, as they see them, for additional military equipment.

I believe we are all agreed that a decision on providing new arms to Israel must be looked at most carefully in the context of the over-all situation in the Middle East and of Congressional views on the shipment of arms to areas of conflict. At the same time, there are several factors which make protracted inaction worrisome, including the Soviet resupply of the radical Arab states and the vociferous militancy of the Algerians and Syrians. Even assuming that the Soviets do not want their clients to become involved in a new round with the Israelis, I do not believe we can completely rule out the possibility of an early military strike against Israel by one or a combination of radical Arab states. A related possibility is that the Algerians and Syrians may attempt to carry out their threat to launch guerrilla attacks against Israel.

For these reasons I think it behooves us to adopt an understanding posture vis-à-vis the Israelis and to listen soon to their views in this matter. I would therefore like to recommend to the President that he authorize us to receive the military team which the Israelis want to send to

---

[1] Source: Washington National Records Center, OSD Files: FRC 330 72A 2468, Israel 400. Secret; Exclusive Distribution. Received in the Office of the Secretary of Defense on July 24 at 9:29 a.m.

Washington. I hope you will concur in this recommendation, which is set forth in the enclosed memorandum to the President.[2]

Whatever the final decision may be in this respect, it would be most useful to have an early estimate by the Joint Chiefs of the radical Arabs' ability to launch and Israel's capacity to withstand a surprise attack in the immediate future. I suggest that the estimate cover the guerrilla warfare contingency as well. If you agree, I would appreciate your asking the Joint Chiefs to undertake this study on an urgent basis.[3]

Sincerely yours,

Dean

---

[2] The draft memorandum is attached but not printed. Katzenbach sent a slightly revised memorandum to the President on August 8. (Johnson Library, National Security File, Country File, Middle East Crisis, Vol. IX)

[3] Nitze replied on July 29 agreeing with the recommendation and suggesting that the Israeli team should be invited to come to Washington in early September. He had requested a USIB assessment of the Arab threat to Israel and USIB and JCS analyses of Israel's ability to withstand such a threat, and he recommended that they should not receive the Israeli military spokesmen until they had those assessments and had time to reflect on them. (National Archives and Records Administration, RG 59, Central Files 1967–69, DEF 19–8 US–ISR)

---

388. Memorandum From the President's Special Assistant (Rostow) to President Johnson[1]

Washington, July 24, 1967.

SUBJECT

Your Talk with Ambassador Barbour at 12:30 p.m. today[2]

We thought you ought to see Wally Barbour in order to get first hand his picture of how much negotiating room the Israelis may have. He came back feeling that they are prepared to make reasonable arrangements on the West Bank—in the context of an overall settlement—but show very little give on Jerusalem.

It is important for him to take away (a) your feeling that the Israelis will have to show some imagination and give on Jerusalem and (b) a

---

[1] Source: Johnson Library, National Security File, Country File, Middle East Crisis, Vol. VIII. Secret.

[2] No record of the conversation has been found.

sense of just how deeply you see us getting involved in the Jordan–Israel talks. You may want to begin by asking him how he sees these negotiations working out.

As you know, Wally did an outstanding job during the June crisis, so you may want to give him a pat on the back.

W.W. Rostow[3]

---

[3] Printed from a copy that bears this typed signature.

---

389.   Memorandum of Conversation[1]

Washington, July 24, 1967, 12:30 p.m.

SUBJECT

Middle East

PARTICIPANTS

The Secretary	Amb. Anatoliy Dobrynin, USSR
Deputy Under Secretary Kohler	

Ambassador Dobrynin called on the Secretary at 12:30 p.m. in response to the latter's invitation. The meeting lasted through luncheon and broke up at 2:20 p.m.

Ambassador Dobrynin opened by reading from handwritten notes the following oral statement which Soviet Foreign Minister Gromyko had asked him to make to the Secretary:

"We have reviewed the results of the last period of work of the United Nations General Assembly. Our statements at the Assembly set forth the position of the Soviet Union. If the American press tries to interpret that the position as it was expressed in the statements of the Soviet representatives at the General Assembly, at the final meeting in particular, was too rigid, then we must disagree with such an assertion. One cannot deny the fact that Israel unleashed the war, that she was the first to launch an attack and that she has subscribed to this at the General Assembly. This is the main thing.

---

[1] Source: National Archives and Records Administration, RG 59, Central Files 1967–69, POL 27 ARAB–ISR. Confidential; Limdis. Drafted by Kohler and approved by Walsh.

"Defending the Arabs and insisting on the necessity to adopt recommendations on an immediate withdrawal of the Israely (sic) troops we, the Soviet Union, were trying to make the situation easier in certain sense for the Americans too, that is to work out such wordings of the recommendations which would be mutually acceptable, though possibly being not completely to the liking both of Israel and of the ultra extremist circles in the Arab countries which cannot reconcile to the very fact of Israel's existence.

"This is what we proceeded from in our latest talks with Amb. Goldberg and other U.S. representatives in New York.

"We noticed that the latest wordings which were suggested from the American side were somewhat different in form from all the previous ones on respective questions and we gave the American side understand this.

"We hope that this would be taken note of. But we also have noted that the U.S. Government if it indeed does not want a resumption of the war in the Middle East and does not push development of events in that direction should have displayed greater flexibility.

"Under these circumstances it would be also easier for the Soviet Union to take steps in the direction of finding of mutually acceptable solutions corresponding to the lawful interests of the Arab States as well as to all countries of the Middle East.

"You, Mr. Secretary, know the position of the Soviet Union toward Israel as a state. Thus, what was said on our side during the last two meetings with Amb. Goldberg and other American representatives in New York with regard to the need of more flexible approach on the American side as well as what was said by the American side concerning Soviet-American relations and the link of the entire problem with the relations between the USSR and the US, all this still holds its significance.

"Noting the importance of the question of Israeli troops withdrawal we must emphasize it once again that if the American side are prepared to keep consultations going as a continuation of the latest talks then we shall be also ready for this to find formulas—fully acceptable to both sides—of the recommendations of the General Assembly which has not completed its work yet. It would facilitate the settlement of question concerning the liquidation of the results [of] Israeli actions; and in our opinion the US must have no interest in resumption of the war in the Middle East if the US Government is indeed guided by long range fundamental interests but not by the present day interests and does not follow conjuncture demands by Israel which are being dictated rather by spirits of military success today than by the care for tomorrow."

The Secretary said that he appreciated Mr. Gromyko's statement and would probably have an oral statement in response which Foy Kohler would transmit to the Ambassador before his prospective departure for Moscow on leave. Meanwhile, he commented that in his view both the United States and the Soviet Union have an interest in not having military solutions in the Middle East. We must face the fact that both of us have some "crazy people" to deal with in this area. We had been hopeful but not optimistic on the formula of a resolution worked out between Ambassador Dobrynin and Ambassador Arthur Goldberg in New York last week. We had thought the moderate Arab representatives might accept the formula, but we knew they were intimidated by Cairo, Algiers, and Damascus. He had even thought it possible in the light of his conversation with UAR Foreign Minister Fawzi in New York that the Egyptians might be reasonable. However, they were apparently impressed by the more extreme positions of Algiers and Damascus. The dynamics of the situation among the Arabs were that the most extreme position tended to become the common position. If there could have been a secret vote of the Arabs he felt that many would have accepted the agreed formula. Dobrynin interjected, "Yes, 8 or 9".

The Secretary continued that the United States has no interest whatsoever in inflammation of the situation on the Middle East or in maintaining Israel in the territorial positions it occupies. However, it was clear that Israel would be difficult and that the question of Jerusalem in particular would be a severe issue.

Ambassador Dobrynin asked why the United States had abstained on the Pakistani resolution on Jerusalem. This was hard to understand in view of the statements on the subject issued by the White House and the Department. The Secretary replied that we had tried to negotiate with the Pakistanis to get reasonable language to which we could agree but they had refused to talk with us since they had the votes required for passage. Dobrynin commented that nobody knew about our attempts to negotiate with the Pakistanis so that the result was that the whole Assembly had been very surprised by our abstention.

The Secretary resumed, saying that we were now looking ahead and felt it was important soon to take some first steps. We were considering what this might be. We had no Government positions yet but speaking personally he thought it possible that if UN observers were placed at Sharm-el-Sheikh, it was then possible that Israel might withdraw well back into the Sinai Peninsula, perhaps half way. Dobrynin asked why not the whole way. The Secretary responded that Israel was not likely to be persuaded to go that far. He repeated that what we needed in the near future was some demonstration of movement. Sharm-el-Sheikh was a simple and uncomplicated problem. The Suez

Canal would be much more complicated. In any case, he felt that the atmosphere might be improved in the Middle East by some such step as partial Israel withdrawal in the Sinai Peninsula. Dobrynin asked from what point the Israelis might withdraw. In response, the Secretary repeated that he was speaking personally and unofficially simply in order to illustrate his point. He then referred to a map and speculated that if Sharm-el-Sheikh were taken care of the Israelis might pull back to a point about half way up the Peninsula.

The Secretary then said that Syria was another point where something might be done. For example, if it could be agreed that for some distance on both sides of the Syrian-Israeli border there would only be police forces. Dobrynin interjected that he hesitated to use the term but would the Secretary mean a "demilitarized zone"? The Secretary replied that he had in mind essentially that, i.e., a zone in which there would be no heavy equipment and guns. He reiterated that he was only thinking aloud and searching for some practical steps, that there had been no consultation and that these were not U.S. Government positions or proposals. However, he felt that he would like to keep in touch with the Soviets as to what could be done. On the whole, he said he was optimistic except on two points: First, how to get the Arabs to accept non-belligerence and, second, Jerusalem. Ambassador Dobrynin asked why Jerusalem was so difficult. The Secretary responded by recalling that the United States has never recognized rights of any one to control Jerusalem, but commented that there were some very strong feelings involved and that there would be great difficulties with Israel on this point. Ambassador Dobrynin wondered why the Secretary had not mentioned Jordan. The Secretary said that in the case of Jordan the principal problem would be that of Jerusalem.

He wanted to mention another thing; he felt that when public discussion focused on Israel this tended to conceal another basic problem, that is the fear which other Arab Governments feel of the so-called progressive Arab States—Egypt, Algeria, and Syria. It would be useful if these three could give assurances that they had no hostile intentions against the moderate Arab States. Ambassador Dobrynin professed some surprise that these States should need assurances. He commented that it would be very difficult for the Soviets to talk to the Egyptians in such terms. The Secretary resumed, recalling that U.S. relations with the UAR have been good sometimes in the past and with the other Arab States as well, but at other times difficult. He cited the instance when U.S. planes had been sent to Saudi Arabia when that country felt threatened. He commented that the Arabs seemed able to unite only against Israel. When one talked to an individual Arab alone he might seem reasonable, but if another were present, he became crazy. He then remarked that the Soviets had probably learned this in connection with their own consultations with the Arabs and cited as an example of what he meant the Saudi Arabian representative Barodi, who in public made very violent speeches. Dobrynin replied that the Soviets had not even tried to consult with Barodi. The Secretary then repeated he felt a number of Arabs would have accepted the UN resolution had it not been for the extreme positions of Algeria and Syria. He had the impression that even Fawzi would have accepted the compromise language.

Ambassador Dobrynin then noted that the head of the Department's Egyptian Desk was going to Cairo. The Secretary confirmed this and said that this move was in accordance with our stay-behind agreement with the Egyptians.

Later at luncheon Ambassador Dobrynin returned to the subject asking how the United States intended to proceed with respect to the Arabs. He commented it was evident from Soviet contacts with the Arabs in New York that the latter harbor some very hard feelings towards the United States. The Secretary responded that he felt some of the Arab States would be quite willing to make peace with Israel. However, they were all afraid of Radio Cairo which was able to stir up their people and bring them out into the streets. We had once felt that Nasser would exercise a moderating even restraining influence in the Arab world but this time had apparently gone. Ambassador Dobrynin observed that there had been some "ultra-extremists" pressures on Nasser (by implication which he had resisted). Then had come the Israel surprise attack. The Secretary said it was very important that Soviet Chairman Kosygin believe the assurances which President Johnson had given him at Glassboro. He must understand that there had been no double dealing. The United States had made every effort to restrain Israel and we had felt that we had an assurance that they would not move while we tried to find a solution for the question of passage through the Strait of Tiran. We had simply been unable to control them and had had no advance information whatsoever about their move. He himself had been awakened at 2:30 in the morning to receive this information.

390. Telegram From the Department of State to the Embassy in Jordan[1]

Washington, July 25, 1967, 0139Z.

12561. For the Ambassador. Ref: State's 11347,[2] 11928,[3] and 11929.[4]

We are repeating to you an exchange of cables with London which we trust will resolve any misunderstandings which may have existed between Washington and London about the nature of your instructions to convey the Israeli reply to Hussein's inquiry about their willingness to negotiate and their terms for a settlement.[5]

You should now proceed to carry out instructions in reftels, substituting following text for Para D(3) of reftel 11347.

"We have not yet been able to develop a detailed or firm assessment of the prospects of successfully negotiating a settlement with Israel. From what we now know we are inclined to believe that there are influential elements in Israeli Cabinet who attach importance to the presence of a moderate and peaceful neighbor on Israel's eastern flank. This would argue in favor of Israel's being reasonable on many of the problems of interest to Jordan, including basic economic issues. However, as the King is undoubtedly aware, the problem of Jerusalem will be very difficult for all concerned. The King knows of the attitude of the United States about Jerusalem over the past twenty years and our

---

[1] Source: National Archives and Records Administration, RG 59, Central Files 1967–69, POL 27–14 ARAB–ISR/SANDSTORM. Secret; Immediate; Nodis; Sandstorm. Drafted by Eugene Rostow on July 24; cleared by Katzenbach, Kohler, Battle, and Bundy; and approved by Rusk. Repeated to London.

[2] Document 386.

[3] Telegram 11928 to Amman, July 24, states the British Chargé had confirmed that the British and U.S. positions were basically the same; both wished to stress that the King had to make his own decision on the question of direct talks with the Israelis. (National Archives and Records Administration, RG 59, Central Files 1967–69, POL 27–14 ARAB–ISR/SANDSTORM)

[4] Telegram 11929 to Amman, July 24, provided instructions concerning King Hussein's request for resumption of U.S. arms shipments. It states that the U.S. Government hoped to resume an arms supply relationship with Jordan, and a Defense Department representative had been sent to London to discuss the subject with General Khammash, but the situation in Congress on the general question of military assistance precluded immediate action. On the subject of economic aid, Burns was authorized to tell the King that the $6 million budget support payment which would fall due during the summer would be released on time and that the other aid projects discussed between the two governments before the outbreak of hostilities were under active review. (Ibid.)

[5] Telegrams 12559 and 12560 to London, July 25, which transmitted messages from Rusk to Foreign Secretary Brown and Ambassador Bruce, were repeated to Amman. Both messages stated that the proposed reply to King Hussein was an interim reply, to be supplemented as more information about the Israeli position became available. (Ibid.)

differences both with Israel and Jordan on that subject. There seems to be some readiness in Israel to accept protection of the Holy Places by the respective religious authorities. We would not be candid with the King, however, if we led him to believe that we see any easy solution for Jerusalem as between Israel and Jordan."[6]

Rusk

_____

[6] Burns reported in telegram 502 from Amman, July 25, that he had seen King Hussein that evening and carried out the instructions in telegrams 12561, 11928, 11929, and 11347. The King's reaction was one of deep disappointment. (National Archives and Records Administration, RG 59, Central Files 1967–69, POL 27–14 ARAB–ISR/SANDSTORM)

---

391.   Editorial Note

President Johnson held his regular weekly luncheon meeting on July 25, 1967, with Secretary Rusk, Secretary McNamara, Walt Rostow, and George Christian. Tom Johnson's notes of the meeting state that there was a discussion of the Middle East and that the President told Rostow "to tell Bundy to channel future requests by leading Jewish leaders to Bundy and not to the President. The President said he was seeing too many." Rusk said that Israel "has won a battle and not a war." Rostow discussed conversations he had had with David Ginsburg and Abe Feinberg. The President said "many of the Jewish leaders want us to *make* the Arabs sit down and talk with the Israelis." He commented, "We know no mediator who is going to set himself up" to handle this situation. (Johnson Library, Tom Johnson's Notes of Meetings)

A July 26 memorandum from Bundy to the President states that he had been "well filled in" by David Ginsburg the day before and he thought Ginsburg and Feinberg had a clear signal on two points:

"(1) that they should make their contacts with me and not bother you for a while, and

"(2) what Israel most needs now is not to have our whole overseas arms program knocked apart by the Congress. David assured me they understood this point and would do everything they could with Symington and their other friends."

Bundy continued:

"I think in fact your visit with them was helpful simply because it reassured them that you will always listen. That wise man, Wally

Barbour, made a good comment the other day: that since the Israelis and their friends cannot possibly help using every channel they have got, we have to accept that fact and make use of it ourselves. This is what you did yesterday and I think they understand that enough is enough for a while." (Johnson Library, National Security File, NSC Special Committee Files, Special Committee #2, July 1–31, 1967)

No other record has been found of the conversation to which Bundy referred.

---

392.   Memorandum of Conversation[1]

Washington, July 27, 1967.

SUBJECT

Middle East

PARTICIPANTS

Amb. Anatoliy Dobrynin, USSR
Deputy Under Secretary Kohler

I had lunch with the Soviet Ambassador today at his invitation and talked with him from approximately 12:30 to 2:20.

The Ambassador inquired if I had brought the response to Foreign Minister Gromyko's oral statement which the Secretary had promised in his conversation with Dobrynin on July 24. I told him that I had and read to him and then left with him a copy of the following oral statement:[2]

"We welcome Foreign Minister Gromyko's message of July 24, indicating that the USSR is willing to continue bilateral discussions on the Middle East situation.

"Though the United States had reservations regarding the utility of the emergency General Assembly session, it sought earnestly to reach

---

[1]   Source: National Archives and Records Administration, RG 59, Central Files 1967–69, POL 27 ARAB–ISR/UN. Secret; Limdis. Drafted by Kohler. The memorandum is part II of IV.

[2]   The text of the oral statement was cleared by the President. (Memorandum from Walt Rostow to the President, July 26 at 7:30 p.m., with Johnson's handwritten "L. OK"; Johnson Library, National Security File, Country File, USSR, Dobrynin/Kohler Conversations, Vol. I)

agreement with the Soviet Union and with others on a general resolution which would contribute to a stable and durable peace in the Middle East. The position taken by Ambassador Goldberg with Foreign Minister Gromyko and members of your delegation was intended to bring about a productive result; our objective was to find words which would provide a solid base for constructive solutions to Middle East problems without offense to any party.

"We were pleased that it was possible to reach common ground with you in New York on a draft text which envisaged the withdrawal of Israeli troops and at the same time recognized the right of Israel and all other states in the area to maintain an independent national existence and to live in peace and security. We hope you agree that Ambassador Goldberg cooperated fully, and in a spirit of accommodation, with you and with others in working out language which would be broadly acceptable. In our view, the principles stated in that resolution are basic and inseparable elements in building of a lasting peace in the Middle East.

"Assuming as we do that you would not wish to encourage intransigence among the Arabs, it is possible to envisage further conversations which may help stabilize and improve the situation in the area. Our purpose, like your own, is to curb irresponsible extremism with respect to the Middle East dispute from whatever quarter it may arise.

"We consider that as permanent members of the Security Council with special responsibilities it would be useful and desirable in the spirit of Article 33 of the UN Charter for the USSR and the US to carry forward their discussions looking toward a stabilization of the situation in the Middle East. In particular, the conditions for settlement would naturally be improved if the US and the USSR, together with other Governments with interests in the area, could find ways and means to bring about restraint in the arms race in the Middle East. This is a matter we would like to discuss further with you.

"I will be glad to have your thoughts on how further discussion on Middle East questions can be pursued with your government.

"In the meantime, we hope both our governments can exercise their influence on the parties concerned to help maintain the cease-fire proclaimed by the UN and, in particular, to urge cooperation with the efforts being made by the Chief of Staff of UNTSO to this end. We would be deeply concerned about a resumption of hostilities in the Middle East and will do everything we can to move the situation promptly toward a peaceful settlement."

After listening to and then reviewing this statement, the Ambassador asked whether this meant we would envisage action in the Security Council. I replied that we would be quite prepared to have the

Security Council adopt the resolution which had been discussed between him and Ambassador Goldberg during the Special General Assembly. He commented that the Arab position would probably remain the same and that the Arabs would still probably not accept the resolution. I responded that we were open-minded as to tactics, provided that the basic principles embodied in the resolution were preserved. Speaking personally, it seemed to me that if we consulted we might well agree that it would be better to let a little time pass and allow Arab passions to cool before acting. From the US point of view, we were certainly not interested in a repeat of the acrimonious debates and the impasse characterizing the last special session of the General Assembly.

He probed a bit on the question of arms restraint. In reply I referred to the President's proposal that arms deliveries to the region might be registered to the UN. However, I continued that we were open-minded as to methods and tactics but did feel that the principal supplying powers should agree to restrain their supply of arms to the end that there be a reasonable balance, so that no one in the area would be tempted to resume hostilities. I said that at present the principal unsettling factor was the Soviet resupply of arms to their friends. He interjected that this resupply was at a level much less than what the Arabs had lost to the Israelis. I said I was willing to accept this statement but that the Soviet resupply was real enough to begin causing some alarm and to develop pressures for arms deliveries not only to the Israelis but to the moderate Arabs. In this connection, I reminded him of the Secretary's statements at his recent press conference.[3]

He then inquired about the reference to supporting the efforts of General Bull, referring to the differences between the Israelis' claim that the cease-fire line ran through the middle of the Suez Canal and the Egyptians' claim that the Suez Canal was theirs. I replied that as long as the Suez Canal was closed, this was certainly a hypothetical question. We are not talking about a legal settlement of the boundaries between Israel and Egypt; these could only be determined at a later stage and in another context. As far as we were concerned, the Sinai Peninsula was still within UAR sovereignty, but we recognize that they would have some difficulty in exercising this sovereignty at the present time. Consequently, our present interest was limited to the question of establishing an effective cease-fire line wherever that might be and having that line accepted by Israel and the UAR.

In reply to his inquiry, I told him that we had purposely left the question of venue for further discussion vague. As far as we were con-

---

[3] Rusk commented on this at a news conference on July 19; for the transcript see Department of State *Bulletin*, August 7, 1967, pp. 159–167.

cerned, this could take place in Moscow or Washington or New York. However, we had realized that they might have more of a problem than we had in this respect, so we had left the decision to them. The Ambassador expressed his appreciation, indicating that he was not at all sure what Moscow would prefer. In this connection, he referred to his own hopes to go on leave (though adding that he has not yet received specific approval). He also said that while there had been some rumors that Fedorenko would be replaced, there had to his knowledge been no decision on it.

In conclusion, the Ambassador expressed appreciation for the message, saying that he now fully understood it and that he would report to Moscow.

---

393. Telegram From the Embassy in Jordan to the Department of State[1]

Amman, July 28, 1967, 1512Z.

554. Ref: Amman 547.[2]

1. I saw King late on the afternoon of July 27 at my request. I told him that I had returned to see him in order to continue the conversation we had on July 25 (Amman 519).[3]

2. I said that I felt his question regarding the US guarantee of territorial integrity and my reply required further discussion and clarification. I pointed out that our guarantee was really premised on a situation involving an unprovoked attack against a Middle Eastern state designed to alter the territorial limits of that state. The recent Arab-

---

[1] Source: National Archives and Records Administration, RG 59, Central Files 1967–69, POL 27–14 ARAB–ISR/SANDSTORM. Secret; Immediate; Nodis; Sandstorm. Received at 2:32 p.m.

[2] Telegram 547 from Amman, July 27, reported that Burns had seen King Hussein that day. (Ibid.)

[3] Telegram 519 from Amman, July 26, elaborated on the report in telegram 502 (see footnote 6, Document 390) of Burns' July 25 conversation with King Hussein. It states that the King asked Burns whether the U.S. guarantee of territorial integrity applied in the current situation. Burns said that he had no choice but to indicate that the United States could not undertake unilaterally to guarantee a return to the pre-June 5 lines. Hussein expressed deep disappointment. (National Archives and Records Administration, RG 59, Central Files 1967–69, POL 27–14 ARAB–ISR/SANDSTORM)

Israeli war did not, in our opinion, as the King was aware, originate without provocation. Furthermore, on the matter of major concern to the King—namely, Jerusalem—we had never recognized either Jordanian or Israeli sovereignty over the city, so that our territorial guarantee for Jerusalem related, technically at least, to a corpus separatum. I said I had understood his question to mean: Would we guarantee him the return of the West Bank by unilateral use of US force if necessary. The answer to that is "no". If his question meant would we support him unilaterally or collectively to reach a just and lasting settlement with Israel, the answer is definitely "yes". I said I had received in that morning's pouch from Washington a memorandum of a conversation which took place July 14 between Secretary Rusk, Jordanian FonMin Touqan, and Jordanian Amb-designate to Washington Sharif Abdul Hamid Sharaf.[4] Sharif Abdul Hamid had asked Secretary Rusk the meaning of the US territorial guarantee in the light of present circumstances. I said there could be no more authoritative reply to his and Sharif Abdul Hamid's question than that given by Secretary Rusk. I then gave the King to read the Secretary's reply in this connection.

3. I told the King that his statement to me on July 25 to the effect that it was now apparent America had made its agonizing choice and had chosen Israel disturbed me greatly because it simply was not correct. I said that we had an enormous stake—motivated by the most compelling of all incentives, self-interest—to preclude an East-West confrontation from developing in the Middle East. For this reason we desired to retain our position in the Arab world, and we wanted peace.

4. I then told the King I was such an unsubtle being I was going to have to ask him to tell me exactly why the instructions from Washington I had read him on July 25 represented such a deep disappointment to him.

5. The King replied that when he was at the White House last month, during private conversations with the President, Mr. Bundy, and Mr. Katzenbach, he had gained the impression that if he were prepared for a settlement with Israel, the US was prepared to lend him the strongest possible support. The subsequent indications of our support had struck him as being on a descending curve.

6. When FonMin Touqan returned to Amman, he reported to the King on the discussions he had had with American officials. From this briefing, said the King, he detected what he considered to be a weakening in American support for Jordan.

7. The instructions I had read him on July 25 appeared to him to be a yet further retreat from the degree of support he had concluded from

---

[4] See Document 365.

his talks at the White House he might expect. On arms, for example, he said, he appreciated our Congressional problem, but the net result for him, no matter how valid our reasons, was that we were not going to be able to move as fast in that direction as the King desired and felt necessary.

8. I said that he should have no doubt about US support and that what the President, Mr. Bundy, and Mr. Katzenbach told him at the White House still very much obtained. The King said he appreciated my returning to see him and what I had said to him was reassuring. In sorting out his own thoughts during the past 48 hours he, too, had figured that the US would support him to the extent that the overall situation permitted. He only hoped our support would not prove to be too little too late.

9. Hussein said that, taking all considerations into account, he had concluded his own position was too weak to try to undertake bilateral negotiations with the Israelis at this moment. For one thing, he said, he agreed with US that Boumediene and Atassi, and Nasser probably, could try to pull the rug out from under him during the course of his trying to negotiate a bilateral settlement with Israel or just afterward. Nasser, he suspects, wants to see how far Jordan can get in reaching an accord with Israel as an indicator of how Nasser should go about doing the same thing, but Hussein doubts that Nasser could resist the temptation somewhere along the line to try to overthrow him.

10. Secondly, said the King, his security situation is too weak for the risks that would be involved in pursuing a settlement course at this moment. The Syrians, he reminded me, retain intact the greater part of their military establishment, whereas Jordan has lost a tremendous amount of equipment and has an air force consisting of one Hawker-Hunter. He noted, too, that until he could do something about replenishing some of his equipment losses he was in a difficult position vis-à-vis Jordanians and others in justifying the withdrawal of the 15,000 Iraqi troops.

11. A third reason, said the King, was that the Jerusalem problem at the moment looked insoluble and that before he undertook the risks of bilateral negotiation with Israel, he would have to have some indication that the Israelis have more flexibility on Jerusalem than would now appear to be the case. The risks to the regime of bilateral negotiations with Israel are so great, he said, that it would be folly to undertake them unless there was at least a chance of his being able to bring back a settlement that would be accepted. He said he guessed his position was similar to that of former President Eisenhower who was reluctant to attend summit meetings with the Russians unless there were some prospect of success. The King then quoted an Arab proverb to the effect

that everyone acclaims the rainmaker who makes rain but that rainmakers who try but fail to bring rain are quickly disposed of.

12. I asked him how long he thought he could hold his position on the East Bank without forward motion in some direction. He replied "three or four months, assuming all the breaks do not go against me. Who knows, Nasser may crack before then and be forced to reach a settlement with the Israelis, in which case the danger of my doing so would be immeasurably reduced." (*Comment:* By the "breaks" the King has specifically in mind two things: (a) that refugees would start moving from east to west, and (b) that we would furnish him with a certain amount of military equipment.)

13. The King said that during the next three-to-four month period he was much more concerned about the West Bank than the East Bank. He said that the euphoria that had appeared in the immediate wake of hostilities had vanished and that friction was developing between the Arabs and the Israelis. He said that if the Israelis react to this friction by repressive policies, this would have two results: (a) it would convince the Arabs that the Israelis are not serious about a settlement and of living in peace with the Arabs, and (b) it would transmit great agitation to the East Bank. He said that the indications were now that the East Bank would support him on a settlement, but this support would disappear quickly if the Israelis follow a repressive policy on the West Bank, fail to facilitate the return of refugees to the West Bank, or let the West Bank fall into worse economic straits. "Please tell the Israelis," said the King, "that if they want peace, they must be patient and exercise self-restraint." I reminded the King that the GOJ, too, must use self-restraint and not take actions which have the result of exacerbating Arab-Israeli relations on the West Bank.

14. I asked the King if he thought Nasser might resume hostilities in the foreseeable future against the Israelis in Sinai. The King said that Nasser was in no position to undertake major hostilities against the Israelis, though he retained, of course, the capacity to stage minor clashes along the Suez Canal. Nor did Hussein think that the Syrians would undertake major hostilities against Israel.

15. Hussein said that he expected to leave Amman this weekend for Tehran, there to meet with the Shah and the President of Turkey. He said he hoped that somehow a grouping could be worked out to include Turkey, Iran, Pakistan, Iraq and Jordan. This would put him in a stronger position vis-à-vis the Arab radicals in trying to reach a settlement with Israel.

16. Hussein also intends to try to visit the moderate Arab states, and prior to Aug 10 in the event an Arab summit is held. Hussein said he felt that the Arab moderates could be on the verge of a break-through

if they could only band together. Nasser's fangs had been loosened and now was the time to move. If he were successful in this endeavor, this, too, would strengthen his position vis-à-vis the Arab radicals.

17. Hussein said he was still expecting to meet with President Aref in Amman although he did not know exactly when Aref would come. The question of the removal of Iraqi forces from Jordan had, at Aref's request, been postponed until Hussein and Aref meet.

18. I asked the King was he by any chance toying with the idea of some sort of confederation with Iraq. The King replied that his head was full of ideas of every conceivable description, but before he was prepared to formulate any particular idea he would have to do a lot of probing first. The King noted that Iraq was the only Arab state to provide him with any substantial assistance (other than monetary) during the past two months. Hussein said that if some sort of arrangement could be worked out with Iraq, then perhaps the Saudis might be interested in joining.

19. I concluded the interview by saying to the King that I wished to revert to the subject of Jerusalem and want to put to him a purely hypothetical question which I assured him was of my own devising. The question was this—"Supposing Jerusalem were made an international city, incorporating the major parts of the Jordanian and Israeli sectors, though omitting the suburban areas . . ." the King had already started to shake his head. I said, "permit me to finish sir . . . and the United Nations headquarters were transferred to this international city of Jerusalem?" The King took a long time answering and finally said "I guess in that case we would all have to accept it, wouldn't we?"

20. I asked the King that in the event Jerusalem might be internationalized along the line I had hypothetically posed, would he still want the West Bank back. He answered in the affirmative. He said he would never be forgiven by the Arabs if the West Bank were left to Israeli control, either direct or through a puppet state. He said that the Palestinians have caused him a great deal of trouble in his lifetime, but they would cause him, and indeed all of us, even more trouble if they were not rejoined to Jordan.

21. Comment follows by separate telegram.

22. Please repeat this telegram to London and Tel Aviv.

Burns

394.   Memorandum of Conversation[1]

Washington, July 28, 1967.

SUBJECT

The Situation in Egypt

PARTICIPANTS

His Excellency The Marquis de Merry Del Val, Spanish Ambassador
NEA—Ambassador Lucius D. Battle
EUR/SPP—George W. Landau
NEA/UAR—H. Eugene Bovis

The Spanish Ambassador said that he had received two letters, the contents of which he wished to convey to Ambassador Battle. The first letter concerned the difference of views between the US and Spain on the present Middle East situation. The Spanish Ambassador in Cairo, Angel Sagaz, thought the Spanish saw the issues more clearly than the US. He feared that the US was alienating the Arabs and opening the door wider to increased Russian influence.

The second letter reported the views of various groups in Cairo with which Ambassador Sagaz had come in contact. The first set of views were those of El-Zyyat. As a result of events in the UN, Mr. Zyyat apparently has arrived at the conclusion that the US is now the foremost political power as well as the foremost military and economic power in the world. Ambassador Angel Sagaz viewed Mr. Zyyat's remarks as an admission that the USSR was unable to retrieve the situation for the Arabs.

Ambassador Sagaz reported the views of two groups that thought that there should be a dialogue between the US and Egypt. The first group said that the dialogue must begin now and that it must be through Nasser, since he is the only leader capable of putting the brake on the Russian advance in the Arab World. The other group believed that a US-Egyptian dialogue was possible only after the disappearance of Nasser. This group thought that a coup d'état was not far away and that it was likely to be bloody.

Ambassador Sagaz also reported an interview with Dr. Drubi, the Syrian Ambassador to the UAR. The Syrian Ambassador felt there was only one solution to the present crisis, and that was a resumption of open war by whatever means the Arabs could muster, including gueril-

---

[1] Source: National Archives and Records Administration, RG 59, Central Files 1967–69, POL ARAB–ISR. Confidential. Drafted by Bovis on August 3 and approved by Battle.

la activity. Dr. Drubi said the boycott, the cessation of oil shipments and the closing of the Canal had not been sufficient to bring the West around. In any event, Saudi Arabia and Libya were not willing to go along any longer. Nasser had told Dr. Drubi that the Egyptians had lost 20,000 troops during the hostilities. Ambassador Sagaz said this had been a revelation, since the previous figure on Egyptian dead had been given as 5,000.

Ambassador Battle thanked Ambassador Merry Del Val for conveying to us Ambassador Sagaz' analysis. He thought our analyses did not differ substantially. We were aware that the Soviets were making increased inroads in the Near East. The question was now how far the USSR was willing to go in backing up the UAR militarily, economically, and politically. Mr. Battle said that while we were concerned about the Soviet maneuvers, there was little we could do in the UAR at the moment. After all, it was the Egyptians who had broken relations and it was up to them to make the first move for a resumption of relations. Nevertheless, we were willing to talk to Egyptians any time and any place. There have already been numerous meetings in private channels. There were three prerequisites for the resumption of relations:

1. Compensation for the damage to American property in Egypt.
2. Retraction of the "big lie".
3. A quiet period in which statements about the US and President Johnson were restrained.

Mr. Battle said that in the meantime Spain and other European countries could help by maintaining a Western presence in Egypt.

395. Telegram From the Department of State to the Embassy in the United Kingdom[1]

Washington, August 1, 1967, 0030Z.

14537. Subject: Middle East.

1. UK Amb Dean called on Under Secretary Rostow and Assistant Secretary Battle morning of July 29 to raise questions put by Fonmin Brown about next steps in ME, particularly reopening of Suez Canal.[2] Although anxious to conceal UK concern, UK is suffering from Canal closure. UK would like to work for substantive res in SC covering withdrawal and an end to belligerency relying on Dobrynin drafts as a basis. Language on freedom of innocent passage would have to be strengthened and all concerned accept that end to belligerency entailed reopening of Canal. Brown saw advantage in trying to build on considerable area of agreement reached between US and USSR at GA. He feels allowing matters to drift could freeze position making matters worse. He suggests preliminary approaches in capitals including some in the ME and with leading SC members such as India. UK objective would be to get substantive res along these lines through the SC by the end of August. Would the US see any objections to UK pursuing this matter of Security Council Resolution with the Russians and to draft Brown letter to U Thant suggesting he pay personal visit to area, perhaps leading to appointment of SYG rep? UK might also pursue Soviet hints that UNEF be reconstituted and used to open Strait of Tiran.

2. Rostow stated he had discussed matter with Secretary Rusk who shared Brown's view that matters not be allowed to drift. The US had no objection to the UK talking to the Russians; indeed, encouraged it. Stressed coordination between US and UK important to keep actions on the same track. On substance of resolution Rostow stressed US attached great importance to preventing any erosion whatever of substance of draft agreed between US and USSR. In our view, Soviet would probably seek weakening of agreed formula which we would regard as disastrous. Dean said HMG fully agreed it was indispensable to stick firmly to position we had held together throughout UNGA, as noted in talking points he had given Rostow previous evening. Rostow added that it

---

[1] Source: National Archives and Records Administration, RG 59, Central Files 1967–69, POL 27 ARAB–ISR/UN. Secret. Drafted by Eugene Rostow's Special Assistant Alan R. Novak on July 29, cleared by Battle and Popper and by telephone by Sisco, and approved by Eugene Rostow. Also sent to Moscow and USUN and repeated to Copenhagen, Monrovia, New Delhi, Oslo, Paris, and Tel Aviv.

[2] A paper entitled "Middle East," July 28, set forth Brown's questions. (Ibid., POL UK–US)

might be difficult to obtain appropriate SC res in August. Soviets do not seem interested in immediate SC action now; the three top Soviet reps were all on vacation during August. Rostow suggested raising question with French, SC Chairman during August. He agreed UK approach to Indians could be useful. Battle suggested that UK also talk to other important users of Canal such as Norwegians, Danes and Liberians as well as Indians and French. They are countries who should carry load on this matter. After all, UAR now in flagrant violation of international obligations.

3. US had doubts about reconstitution of UNEF in view of recent history. Perhaps agreement to demilitarize Sinai could be obtained at an early stage in exchange for troop withdrawals if rights of passage in Canal and Aqaba for all vessels could be assured through UAR acceptance of SC resolution embracing renunciation of belligerence by Arabs.

4. We would take up draft letter to SYG with USUN. We liked idea of UN rep in area but our present thinking we prefer a mediator cloaked with authority of SYG rather than SYG himself. In a phone call after visit, Rostow added suggestion that letter request SYG to consult with US, USSR and France about possibility of his sending representative to the area as mediator.

5. Amb Dean stated that Sir Lesley Glass, DCM UKUN, would come to Washington on Tuesday (8/1) to discuss possible action on res in SC.

6. *Comment:* As indicated above, we share UK view that matters should not be allowed to drift. However, we must proceed carefully in preparing any next round in the Security Council and coordinate closely since Soviet objective still remains to get a withdrawal resolution out of UN while paying a minimum price for it. As Rostow made clear in above conversation, we attach great importance to preventing any erosion on substance of draft agreed between US and USSR. UK was very wobbly throughout entire Special General Assembly; in fact, we had to keep at Caradon constantly in order to avoid an erosion in our position. While we could not disagree that they should talk to Soviets, we would be very concerned indeed if such talks led to reopening of resolution agreed to between US and USSR. This point will be reaffirmed to UK representatives Tuesday, who are coming into Dept for follow up conversation. Coalition we put together at UN will take constant nurturing and consultations in order to maintain necessary solid front in any SC round. While we have no objections in principle to UK going to capitals in support of early opening of Suez Canal, important there be prior clearcut understanding through fullest possible consultations between us to assure that approaches made in capitals are directed toward mutually shared objectives. In particular, we think it unrealistic to contem-

plate early opening of Canal except in circumstances where all vessels including Israeli, go through.

7. We already have indications through further informal consultations with UKRep here that UK has in mind weakening of US-Soviet agreed draft by moving principal operative paragraph into preamble.

8. Full prior consultations with Israelis would be essential on above moves. UK has in mind to assure them we do not intend erode position and so that there be full understanding re any next round in SC.

Rusk

---

396. Telegram From the Department of State to the Embassy in Israel[1]

Washington, July 29, 1967, 1847Z.

14236. For Ambassador from Secretary.

Following is for your guidance in discussions with GOI following your consultations Washington. We will take same line with Israelis here, as well as in New York and elsewhere:

1. USG commitment to and support of Israel's statehood remains firm as ever. We believe our role in recent Security Council and General Assembly sessions clearly attests to our steadfastness in this regard.

2. Public mood in US is one of widespread sympathy for Israel's cause in recent war and admiration for Israel's demonstrated courage and determination.

3. Underlying this mood is strong "pro-peace" sentiment coupled with sense of uneasiness that somehow, despite setback suffered by Soviets and their friends in area, Arabs will come back for second round.

---

[1] Source: National Archives and Records Administration, RG 59, Central Files 1967–69, POL 27 ARAB–ISR. Secret; Immediate; Exdis. Drafted by Atherton; cleared by Battle, Barbour, Sisco, and Walt Rostow; and approved by Rusk. The President approved the draft cable on July 29. Rostow sent it to him on July 28 with a covering memorandum noting that it stated U.S. policy for Israeli consumption and for internal guidance. He concluded, "Barbour participated in the drafting of the cable and he and I think it is consistent with your own thinking, though perhaps less pungently phrased than you would do it. Since a cable that is used for external and internal distribution has fairly wide distribution, this is probably just as well." (Johnson Library, National Security File, Country File, Middle East Crisis)

4. It is of utmost importance to maintain momentum towards a political settlement. The longer the present situation remains frozen, the greater will become the danger that Israel's military victory will not produce commensurate political results.

5. We are convinced that achievement such results justifies some risk and large measure of flexibility on part of GOI. United States has from own experience in recent wars learned long range benefits of being magnanimous in victory. We think Israel will similarly benefit if it take similar approach. American people would not understand effort turn military victory into territorial gains. We appreciate the assurances of GOI in this respect, recognizing, of course, the need for security arrangements and the peculiarly difficult problems of Jerusalem. What is important is to emphasize continuously that the objectives are peace and security, not territorial gains.

6. This is consistent with our own basic commitment to seek Arab renunciation of state of belligerency, to assure freedom of navigation, and to uphold territorial integrity of all states of area. Within this framework there are number of issues on which USG and American public will be closely watching Israel's actions for evidence that GOI seeks truly magnanimous and stable peace which will not contain seeds of future conflict. Two areas in which Israeli policies over the years have occasionally troubled this country are Jerusalem and refugees. Should Israel now appear inflexible on these issues to point of jeopardizing constructive political settlement, there could be gradual erosion of broadly based sympathy and support which Israel now enjoys in US.

7. We fully recognize that achievement of a settlement does not depend on Israel alone. Recent Arab intransigence at UN does not reflect any serious facing up to realities of situation. Should settlement efforts fail, however, it is imperative that Israel have demonstrated its willingness to make every reasonable effort avoid that outcome. Dangers in such a failure are obvious, including inter alia further consolidation Soviet position in area, inability of US to recoup losses it has suffered, further decline of moderates in area and ultimately renewed threat of further hostilities. Israel and USG must make every effort to avoid this path.

8. One hope we now see for breaking out of vicious cycle lies in settlement with Jordan. It is essential, however, to recognize dangers this involves for Hussein, for Western position in Jordan and for Israel itself. We realize Israel disillusioned by Hussein's role in recent war. Whatever one's views of Hussein, however, we see no alternative which would not be infinitely worse. It is difficult envisage how moderate regime could survive in Jordan in absence settlement which respected the principle of Jordan's territorial integrity. Disappearance of moderate

Jordanian regime would open vast new area for Soviet influence with correspondingly increased threat to Lebanon and Arabian Peninsula–Red Sea Basin–Persian Gulf bastion.

9. While Arab military defeat was blow to Soviets, it could backfire against Israel and the West unless a blow is now struck for peace. It is for this reason that we urge Israel to be flexible, patient, discreet and generous, particularly with respect to refugee problem and question of arrangements for Jerusalem which will take more than pro forma account of Jordanian and international interests in that city. Only such an approach will assure continued broad US and international solidarity with Israel as it pursues legitimate goal of stable national existence in difficult and dangerous days ahead. As Prime Minister Eshkol wrote to President Johnson on first day of war, "the hour of danger can also be an hour of opportunity." We urge Israel to rise to challenge of this opportunity for peace, as it did to challenge of war.

Rusk

---

397. Telegram From the Department of State to the Embassy in Jordan[1]

Washington, July 30, 1967, 1638Z.

14287. 1. In the forthcoming Foreign Ministers' Conference on August 1,[2] the moderate states should be a majority of the Arab states attending. We would hope that they would take a strong stand in favor of a constructive and moderate position towards a resolution of the Middle East crisis. To this end, you should deliver as soon as possible the following message from the Secretary to the Foreign Minister of your country (in case of SAG, to Deputy Foreign Minister).

---

[1] Source: National Archives and Records Administration, RG 59, Central Files 1967–69, POL 7 SUDAN. Confidential. Drafted by Houghton on July 28; cleared in draft by former Ambassador to Iraq Robert C. Strong, Ambassador to Libya David D. Newsom, and Country Director for North Africa John F. Root, and by Eugene Rostow and Battle; and approved by Rusk. Also sent to Beirut, Jidda, Kuwait, Tripoli, Tunis, and Rabat. The handwritten revisions on the telegram noted below appear to be Rusk's.

[2] A meeting of foreign ministers of Arab States was held in Khartoum August 1–5 in preparation for an Arab summit conference.

2. Excellency:

"Now that the Special Session of the UN General Assembly is behind us, I thought I should share with you some of my thoughts regarding the future. I am particularly anxious to discuss these thoughts with you on the eve of the Arab Foreign Ministers' Conference which should have an important influence on the evolution of Arab policy and the course of our relations in the days and weeks ahead, as well as on the future well-being of the entire Near East. I shall be frank and hope you will receive my frankness as coming from one who wants peace and who is sincerely and deeply interested in the welfare of (host country) and of the Arab world as a whole.

3. "In these critical days the Arabs should have a constructive position if it is to elicit world support and meet their diverse problems. I think that you would agree that the meetings at the United Nations over the past weeks confirm the validity of this point. If the coming meeting, in which moderate representatives will be more numerous, can reach realistic common ground, the position of the Arab world will be much improved.

4. "Arab self-interest would at the moment seem to require that all the Arab states devote their energies to the development of both their physical and human resources in order to realize the full potential of a great heritage. It seems to me such a development can only occur under conditions of peace. To have such an atmosphere I believe two steps are indicated:[3] First, the Arabs need to find a way to stop the interference of some Arab states in the affairs of other Arab states. We on our side have committed ourselves to the territorial integrity of all states of the Near East. Might not the Arab states make the same commitment to each other and thus avoid wasteful, divisive activities?

5. "Secondly, if the Arabs are to devote their energies to badly needed development, some arrangements for peace throughout the area[4] are essential. I am fully aware of the deep-rooted impediments[5] to such arrangements, but to me their achievement is the only realistic way. The Arabs need time and the return of territory. The Israelis need security and acceptance[6] of their state's existence in the area, as it has already been recognized by the United Nations and the bulk of its members, including the US and the USSR. The objectives of both sides received wide acceptance in the United Nations by both the Western and the

---

[3] The original text "required" was changed to "indicated".

[4] The original text "peaceful coexistence with Israel" was changed to "peace throughout the area".

[5] The original text "historical and emotional impediments" was changed to "deep-rooted impediments".

[6] The original text "recognition" was changed to "acceptance".

Soviet world. The concept of a return to the overall situation existing before June 5, 1967 does not enjoy wide international support. I believe it in the Arab self-interest to take a moderate and constructive approach to this difficult problem. If the Arabs do so, they can count on the full support of the United States, whose interest lies in correction of the present unnatural situation through withdrawal by Israel from the positions it occupied during the conflict. This brings me to my last point.

6. "I am naturally concerned with the state of US-Arab relations and am most appreciative of the mature and rational stance your country has taken on this problem. My concern is not only for US interests, but is for Arab interests as well. If our Arab friends are weak, we ourselves are also weakened. Boycott on trade and the sale of oil, for example, will hurt the Arabs both economically and politically and will provide further opportunities for the Communists to exploit. The United States can do a great deal to bring about an equitable settlement and to further Arab area development. My country is willing to help, but it is difficult[7] as long as the Arabs take measures against us. I hope at the Foreign Ministers' Conference the positive advantages of good relations with the United States can be very carefully studied.

7. "The US values its relations and long friendship with (host country). This friendship requires that we make together an earnest search for understanding. This is essential if we are to overcome the problems that confront us.

8. "Excellency, I hope this frank exposition of my views may be helpful in your own further consideration of these issues. I realize naturally that we do not look at all problems in the same light. I am sure, however, that you and your colleagues, in your deliberations of these difficult and complicated problems, will make sure that the course you take is truly in the long-term self-interests of the Arab world. In your endeavors you have my sincerest best wishes. With warm regards, Sincerely,"

9. We would hope that the Foreign Minister would consider the message as confidential. You should also confidentially inform the Minister that the Secretary has written in similar vein to the Foreign Ministers of those Arab States which have maintained relations with us.

Rusk

---

[7] The original text "cannot" was changed to "it is difficult".

398. Memorandum of Conversation[1]

Washington, July 30, 1967.

Mr. Ephraim Evron, Minister, Embassy of Israel, called me yesterday [July 30] and asked if he could drop by at my home on his way back from the airport where he was leaving his wife at 10:00 p.m. I agreed.

His points were these.

1. He was approached the other day by U.S. officials and urged to use Israeli influence on the Hill in support of our military aid program, notably the maintenance of the revolving fund. The argument was acceptable to Israel and conformed to its interest as well as to the interest of the U.S.; namely, that military assistance was required in the Middle East to balance Soviet arms shipments to radical Arab countries and thus to support not only Israel but also moderate states. The Israel Embassy was acting on this request. But they were now disturbed to find some U.S. officials (unnamed) were pressing the argument on the Hill in the simple form that Israel needed the military aid bill. This was apparently reported by certain of Israel's friends on the Hill. He observed that, given the low level of U.S. military aid to Israel, the argument in that form did not make much sense and that it would be better and more effective if the lobbying were done by representatives of the Israel Embassy.[2]

2. He then went on to discuss the situation with Jordan. He said Israel had problems with Hussein who no longer was regarded as a reliably moderate figure after joining with the radical Arabs for the second time in an attack on Israel—the first being 1956. They were "dismayed" by the refusal of Hussein to collaborate in the return of refugees to the

---

[1] Source: Johnson Library, National Security File, Country File, Middle East Crisis, Vol. VIII. Confidential; Sensitive; Very Limited Distribution. Drafted by Rostow on July 31. A handwritten notation on the memorandum indicates that copies were sent to Bundy and Saunders. A copy was sent to the Department of State with a covering memorandum of July 31 from Rostow to Benjamin Read.

[2] Saunders commented in a July 31 memorandum to Bundy that the main Congressional threat to the military aid program as it related to Israel was the Church amendment to eliminate the revolving fund for military credit sales. He noted that Israel would by no means be the only country affected by the amendment and commented that Evron made a fair point in saying that they should not be trying to save the whole program by arguing Israel's case alone. (Johnson Library, National Security File, NSC Special Committee Files, Military Aid) The amendment to the foreign assistance authorization bill (S. 1872) proposed by Senator Frank Church would have terminated as of December 31, 1967, the special Defense Department military assistance credit account used to guarantee loans by the Export-Import Bank for arms purchases by underdeveloped countries. On August 9 the Senate Foreign Relations Committee adopted the amendment and reported out S. 1872.

West Bank by failing to distribute a questionnaire with an Israeli government heading. They were also disturbed by the Jordanian radio stirring up hostile attitudes towards Israel among the West Bank and Gaza refugees and inhabitants. He went on to repeat a theme he had earlier stated—that it was going to take time for the Arabs to explore their options and come to a sensible position; and this was also true for Israel, although his government would not thank him for saying so. He said that there might well be anti-Israeli incidents in the West Bank area, which would make those who thought of holding the West Bank less interested in that outcome. The economic costs of holding the West Bank would also work in that direction. But time would be needed.[3]

At the present time the criterion of security was overriding in Israeli government discussions—security in the literal short-run sense. From that perspective, holding the West Bank was quite attractive, although, in the long run, it might well be judged less attractive.

3. Evron then told me he had put into the Israel government, when he was home, a proposal to initiate soon some action on the refugees, starting in Gaza. The proposal would be for the Israelis to pay an indemnity to Arab refugees if they moved out and settled in other countries. The West Bank could take some but not many. Others could go to Iran, Western Europe, etc. About 100,000 would be left in Gaza.

4. I confined myself to observing that we were now in an interval of re-thinking. We did not know where Israel government thoughts were tending. Nor did we know what the outcome would be of Hussein's talks with the Shah or the meeting of Arab Foreign Ministers in Khartoum. We did not know what Nasser's position was or Nasser's thoughts on when and how to proceed towards a settlement. Time would evidently be required; but there was danger for all if there was no forward movement in the direction of a settlement in the weeks ahead. Degenerative forces were at work as well as forces making for increased realism and moderation.

His only response was to probe as to whether we had any information on Nasser's thoughts or willingness to move towards a settlement. I said: No.

Walt

---

[3] Evron told Battle in a luncheon conversation on July 31 that the Israelis were convinced that "time is on their side and that the longer the Suez Canal is closed and the greater the economic problem in the UAR, the better chance that Nasser will be the first Arab country to come to peace terms with them." (Memorandum of conversation, July 31; National Archives and Records Administration, RG 59, Central Files 1967–69, POL 27 ARAB–ISR)

399. Memorandum From the President's Special Consultant (Bundy) to President Johnson[1]

Washington, July 31, 1967.

SUBJECT

The Middle East at the End of July

Walt tells me that this subject is on the agenda for lunch tomorrow[2] and there are some aspects of it which are better for talk than for paper, but this preliminary assessment may be helpful to you overnight:

1. The Israeli position appears to be hardening as the Arabs still resist all direct negotiations. The Israelis have great confidence in their short-run political and military superiority. I think the evidence grows that they plan to keep not only all of Jerusalem but the Gaza Strip and the West Bank, too.

2. Unless the Arabs make a drastic change in their bargaining position, we have no practical way of opposing this Israeli position. We can insist on the principle of "withdrawal from danger" but as a practical matter the Israelis will continue to confront the Arabs—and us—with small accomplished facts (today they put in their currency in much of the occupied territory), and we will find it unwise to take any practical action in reply. When the Israelis come to us for major military supplies, we shall need to have serious talks, but I begin to think that our bargaining power even on this issue is not overwhelming. I think we can trade hard on such matters as nuclear policy and perhaps even get them to back off from the French missiles they have had on order, but as long as the Arabs are adamant, I doubt if we can or should make the Israeli view of Jerusalem or the West Bank into a federal case. We can't tell the Israelis to give things away to people who won't even bargain with them. We may well be heading toward a de facto settlement on the present cease-fire lines, and we do not want to play King Canute if that is the flow of the tide in the Middle East. We want it to be Nasser's fault, not ours, if the Israelis decide to stay where they are. I think the

---

[1] Source: Johnson Library, National Security File, NSC Special Committee Files, U.S. Position—Discussion. Secret. Sent through Walt Rostow.

[2] The President met at luncheon on August 1 with Rusk, Nitze, Walt Rostow, Bundy, and George Christian. No record of the meeting has been found. The agenda for Middle East discussion includes the question of naming a new coordinator on Israeli and UAR desalting plants, progress on the military aid fight, what to say to King Hussein concerning his planned trip to Moscow, and the difficulties "of getting a statement that can help the moderate Arabs without arousing the Israelis and their friends." (Ibid., Files of Minutes and Notes) For documentation on U.S. policy concerning possible cooperative desalting projects, see *Foreign Relations, 1964–1968*, vol. XXXIV, Documents 130 ff.

Secretary may have a slightly different view—and you may want us to go around the alternatives a little tomorrow.

3. The Arab Foreign Ministers meet tomorrow in Khartoum. I think the odds on an eventual Arab summit are a little less than even; the odds on friction between the Arab right and left are pretty good. I see no current opportunity for us to take any important initiative with any of the Arabs—moderate or radical. We should wait until they come to us.

In sum, I think the current short-run position should be one of quiet watchful waiting. The most we might want to do this week is to get out a low-key statement which would offer some encouragement to responsible Arabs and yet not affront the Israelis. I have a new scheme for such a statement, namely, that it might be made in an exchange of letters with some outstanding American who is favorably known to the Arab world. Such a man might ask you if we still love the reasonable Arabs and you would then have an excuse to tell him that we do, without too much repetition of other points which they don't like. I hope to have a draft of such an exchange tomorrow. I also hope to have a further report on arms registration, which still takes lots of time in the Department. (It really is complex, though you don't believe it!)

As Hussein draws back from negotiation, a lot of us find ourselves looking once again at Nasser. Egypt remains the key country on the Arab side, and sooner or later Nasser is likely to put out stronger feelers toward us—he still hasn't come near solving his economic problems. I have commissioned a major intelligence estimate of just where Egypt now stands—especially in relation to the Soviets. I don't think a full Soviet "takeover" is imminent, nor do I think the Egyptians are going to re-open the war tomorrow, but these are the two dangers which we need to be alert for, even if the odds are small.

I think the sum of it all is that the situation remains tense but not immediately explosive. The worst thing that happened to it today was the drafting of David Ginsburg for other duties,[3] but I had to tell him that as a citizen I was delighted. I also told him that he could have this office, because my own needs are already much more modest than the generous space I now occupy. He reminded me that the office was not mine to sublet, so I report its availability to you.

---

[3] On July 31 President Johnson announced Ginsburg's appointment as Executive Director of the National Advisory Commission on Civil Disorders. (*Public Papers of the Presidents of the United States: Lyndon B. Johnson, 1967*, Book II, p. 726)

400. Telegram From the Department of State to the Embassy in the Soviet Union[1]

Washington, August 1, 1967, 1638Z.

14613. Subject: Middle East Bilateral Talks with Soviets. For Ambassador Thompson.

1. We have sent you separately Memcon between Secretary, Kohler and Dobrynin containing Gromyko oral message to the Secretary,[2] and Memcon containing oral message which Kohler handed to Dobrynin on July 27,[3] for him to take back with him to Moscow.

2. You will note Soviets have in effect suggested continuation of bilateral talks which took place in New York and have indicated desire to "find formulas—fully acceptable to both sides—of the recommendations of the General Assembly which has not completed its work yet." In our reply we have indicated willingness to participate in further consultation on a number of Middle Eastern problems. It seems apparent from language quoted above and Dobrynin's inquiry of Kohler regarding further SC action that Soviets are probing to determine whether there is any give in language of resolution agreed to by the US and USSR in closing days of UNGA. We wish to avoid renegotiating that resolution since it is hard to see how its language could be changed without risk of unraveling all that has been accomplished by our firm stand at UNGA.

3. Subject to foregoing, we see every advantage in pursuing broad consultations with the Soviets on Middle East problems both from the standpoint of trying to work out a peaceful settlement and from the standpoint of bilateral relations. Present situation in Middle East is so disturbing and ceasefire so precarious that it is desirable to carry forward exploration of possible approaches to peace settlement with Soviets and others. At the same time, in the short term, there are certain procedural difficulties in the way of progress through UN organs, particularly on basis Soviets desire.

4. Following points will help to give you additional flavor of our thinking:

(a) You will note that we have invited Soviet views as to when and how discussion should be pursued. Discussion of modalities would

[1] Source: National Archives and Records Administration, RG 59, Central Files 1967–69, POL 27 ARAB–ISR/UN. Secret; Exdis. Drafted by Sisco and Popper on July 31; cleared in draft by Stoessel (EUR), Kohler, and Battle; and approved by Eugene Rostow. Repeated to USUN.

[2] Document 389.

[3] Document 392.

gain us a little time which would be useful from procedural standpoint in New York. Situation there indicates that barring unforeseen developments a Security Council meeting is unlikely much before middle August, if by then.

(b) You will note that while Sovs suggest discussions which in effect would carry on those we held in the final stages of the emergency General Assembly, our response is pitched in much more general terms. Sovs have obvious interest in trying to whittle away at agreement they reached with us on terms of GA Res on troop withdrawal and belligerency. We have very strong interest in not going beyond terms of agreed Soviet-American draft, which is rock-bottom formula from our standpoint. We do not contemplate any compromise of fundamental linkage between troop withdrawal and end of belligerency.

(c) Correspondingly, we would resist any Soviet effort to resume the emergency GA session, even though we recognize that door for resumption was left open in final procedural resolution which led to "temporary adjournment" of session. Further discussion of ME problem in GA all too likely to lead to erosion of strength we helped to mobilize against Soviet and non-aligned proposals which represented Arab views.

(d) Our reply indicates that we have a special interest in subject of arms limitation in ME. We would be encouraged by any sign that Soviets willing to exercise restraint in arms supply.

(e) We will also want to impress on Soviets need for them to exert their influence on Arab extremists against any resumption of hostilities and in favor of serious consideration of reasonable settlements. Ending claims of belligerency should enable all parties with interest in Middle East to establish normal political relationships and resume normal economic activities, including free maritime passage in international waterways.

(f) One procedural proposal we would regard as useful to permit further cooling off in area and to explore prospects for agreement, would be appointment of a mediator under UN auspices to explore possibilities with parties directly concerned. We tried unsuccessfully to float such an idea during emergency GA, but Arabs would only accept it if mediator's terms of reference were focused on troop withdrawals. We would be interested in anything you might pick up with respect to Soviet attitude regarding a mediator.

Rusk

401.   Telegram From the Department of State to the Mission at
         Geneva[1]

Washington, August 1, 1967, 1901Z.

14643. Ref: Geneva 350.[2]

Please inform Siddiqui as follows:

1. US continues believe that communication between US and UAR through various channels may be helpful toward removing those obstacles which have clouded relations between two countries. It is impossible, however, at present time send personal representative of President to Cairo. If there are envoys of President Nasser available in Europe from time to time, US will endeavor provide suitable representative for discussions.

2. Mr. Anderson will be returning Europe in few weeks and there are other Americans, who could serve as channel, available from time to time if President Nasser wishes utilize them.

3. The US continues to note statements repeating outrageous and erroneous charges with respect to the US and its actions during the recent hostilities. These statements known to be false cannot be considered helpful in the direction of improving the climate between the UAR and the US.[3]

Rusk

---

[1] Source: National Archives and Records Administration, RG 59, Central Files 1967–69, POL UAR–US. Top Secret; Immediate; Nodis; Whirlwind. Drafted by Battle on July 31; cleared by Eugene Rostow, Kohler, and Saunders; and approved by Katzenbach. Saunders sent a draft of this telegram to Walt Rostow with an August 1 memorandum recommending clearance and stating that Bundy agreed; a handwritten "OK" appears on the memorandum. (Johnson Library, National Security File, Country File, Middle East Crisis, Sandstorm/Whirlwind)

[2] Telegram 350 from Geneva, July 31, reported that Siddiqui had informed Tubby of a message from Hafez saying that Nasser agreed to meeting with the President's representative at any time but preferred it to be in Cairo. (National Archives and Records Administration, RG 59, Central Files 1967–69, POL UAR–US) A message for Siddiqui transmitted in telegram 12837 to Geneva, July 25, stated that Anderson could not visit Cairo at that time but was frequently in Europe and would be available at a later date if desired. (Ibid.) This replied to telegram 296 from Geneva, July 25, which reported that Siddiqui had shown Tubby a message from Hafez in Cairo that Nasser said Mohieddin could not leave Cairo at that time but would welcome Anderson in Cairo. Siddiqui said he would accompany Anderson to Cairo and felt sure he could arrange a meeting with Nasser. (Ibid.) Telegram 12837 to Geneva relayed to Tubby that the Department was reluctant to have Anderson make a trip that appeared to be at U.S. initiative and wondered whether the fact that Siddiqui was not sure he could arrange a meeting with Nasser meant that Siddiqui and Hafez were acting on their own initiative. (Ibid.)

[3] Telegram 366 from Geneva, August 2, reported that Tubby had given this message to Siddiqui. (Ibid.)

402. Telegram From the Department of State to the Consulate General at Jerusalem[1]

Washington, August 1, 1967, 2236Z.

14759. Ref: Jerusalem 250.[2]

State 13222 was addressed to Jerusalem but apparently not transmitted due communication error. Following is text, slightly modified in Para 1 d., to correct inaccuracy in original version:

1. In process of considering possible solutions to Jerusalem problem that might be acceptable to all parties, we have attempted to identify assumptions upon which any workable plan must be based. They are:

a. Our overriding objective is to achieve peaceful settlement between Israel and Jordan and settlement of Jerusalem problem should be within this context.

b. Israel will agree to no settlement which involves return of Old Jerusalem to exclusive Jordanian rule.

c. Jordan will agree to no settlement which fails to take into account Jordanian interests in Old City.

d. Jerusalem should not again become Middle Eastern Berlin, divided by barbed wire, no-man's-land and virtually complete ban on movement from one part of city to another. The only theme the Israelis state about Jerusalem is that it must be a unified city under single administration, which now includes Jordanian personnel previously employed by Old City government. They propose that Holy Places be placed by agreement with religious authorities under religious "sovereignty" and be given diplomatic status.

e. There should be guarantee, satisfactory to the three religious communities with special interests in Jerusalem, that Holy Places will be safeguarded and members of three faiths will have access to them.

2. We would appreciate comments of all addressees as to soundness and completeness these assumptions. Tehran, Rawalpindi, Djakarta, Kuala Lumpur, requested comment as to whether approach based on these hypotheses is likely satisfy local Muslim interests con-

---

[1] Source: National Archives and Records Administration, RG 59, Central Files 1967–69, POL 27 ARAB–ISR. Secret; Exdis. Drafted and approved by Atherton and cleared by Grey. Repeated to Amman, Tel Aviv, USUN, Beirut, Jidda, Tunis, Tripoli, Rabat, Kuwait, Rome, Rawalpindi, Tehran, Kuala Lumpur, Djakarta, and London.

[2] Dated July 31. (Ibid.)

cerning Jerusalem. Rome comments requested re probable Vatican reaction.

Rusk

---

403.   Memorandum for the Record[1]

Washington, August 1, 1967.

SUBJECT

Israel

I had a telephone conversation with McGeorge Bundy today at approximately 1900. He had seen Evron at 1700. Evron admitted that his acceptance on Friday[2] of Bundy's promise to provide approximately $300,000 worth of tank spares, etc. in exchange for friendly lobbying against the Church amendment had been made with the understanding that this dollar figure represented the extent of Israel's urgent military requirements. On checking with his Military Attaché, he had learned that this was quite wrong; the fact is that pending Israeli requests for export licenses (for purely cash transactions through commercial channels) aggregate about $7.2 million. This is of course exclusive of other requested items (APCs, Hawk and tank spares, Hawk battery, etc.).

Bundy told me that he has subsequently reached an agreement with Evron which had the President's endorsement. The agreement is that the US will accept and act upon Israeli purchases (cash and credit) amounting to $3 million of military equipment during the first 15 days of August or until the arrival of the Israeli military team.

I told Bundy that we had recommended to Nitze a more deliberate pace with regard to the team's arrival: namely, a meeting in early September which would give US officials time to digest the JCS paper (due 25 August) and the DIA paper (due at an earlier date). Bundy

---

[1] Source: Washington National Records Center, ISA Files: FRC 330 76–140, A/I/S, 2–12–6, 1967 Crisis Special File. Secret. Drafted by Townsend Hoopes. Copies were sent to Nitze, Assistant Secretary of Defense for International Security Affairs Paul C. Warnke, and Colonel Amos A. Jordan, Jr., Regional Director for Near East and South Asia in Warnke's Office.

[2] July 28.

expressed the view that this would cause political problems, and that he did not quite see the need for "diddling with small things" while we were at the same time refusing to provide Israel with requested military equipment.

I checked with Nitze who had signed out the letter to Rusk on Saturday. Nitze said however that he had done so on the assumption that the situation involved neither political nor military urgency. He said that, if the White House considers that we faced a political problem, DoD was willing to be flexible. I then called Bundy again who said that he would like to make an agreement with Evron for the US to receive the Israeli team some time during the week of 21 August. He said he would confirm this with Rusk and would represent this date as being acceptable to Nitze and DoD. I concurred in this.

TWH
Principal Deputy

---

404.   Memorandum of Conversation[1]

Washington, August 2, 1967.

SUBJECT

    Talks with Egyptians

PARTICIPANTS

    Mr. Walter McDonald, Pan American Oil Company
    Lucius D. Battle, Assistant Secretary, NEA

1. I had a lengthy lunch today with Mr. Walter McDonald of Standard Oil of Indiana of which Pan American Oil is a subsidiary. I have known Mr. McDonald for about three years. During the time that

---

[1] Source: National Archives and Records Administration, RG 59, Central Files 1967–69, POL UAR/US. Top Secret; Nodis. Drafted by Battle on August 3. Rusk's initials with a line drawn through them appear on the memorandum indicating that he read it; and a note on the memorandum states that Battle had reported the conversation briefly at the staff meeting the previous day. Saunders sent a copy to Bundy with an attached note stating that Battle regarded this "as more serious than other feelers, but still doesn't think it comes from Nasser." Since Battle "doesn't think we can offer much" he was not eager to talk, but Eugene Rostow had sent a memorandum to Rusk recommending an expression of willingness to talk in Geneva. (Johnson Library, National Security File, NSC Special Committee Files, Whirlwind)

I was in Cairo, he was a frequent visitor in connection with the oil finds of Pan American. He is on excellent terms with senior officials in the UAR Government. Mr. McDonald has just returned from the UAR and has seen a number of the top officials of the Government. He informs me that these officials and a number of private individuals with whom he talked convey the following impressions:

(a) Nasser has had it. The UAR is, however, better off with him for a few months than without him. If he goes now, there will be chaos and serious inroads by the communists. He must stay until some real plan exists for a governmental structure without him.

(b) The pro-Western elements in the country all believe that there must be a clear sign that the West will still deal with the UAR. This signal must come very soon or the absence of an alternative will drive the UAR completely into communist hands as the pro-Western elements will give up any hope of restraining the situation.

(c) There is general despondency throughout the country, particularly over the economic situation which is acutely serious.

(d) The desire of the USSR for an air base in Yemen and a naval base either in the UAR or in the Red Sea area is widely discussed.

2. Mr. McDonald said that he had been asked by Vice President Mohieddin, Mahmud Younis, and Aziz Sidki (former Ministry of the Treasury) to convey the following to me and through me to the U.S. Government.

(a) Either Zakaria Mohieddin or a senior representative of the UAR would like to come to the U.S. in the very near future. If Mohieddin comes, he would have to be received by the President or the Vice President. While he would not expect any aid, he could not go back to Cairo empty handed politically. The object of his trip would be to give evidence of an alternative relationship with the West to the only relationship apparent now; i.e., Russia.

(b) If the Israelis will withdraw 25 miles from the Suez Canal, the UAR will begin work immediately on clearing the Canal. While the UAR will not agree to Israeli shipping transiting the Suez Canal, it will publicly agree to the Straits of Tiran being open to Israeli shipping.

(c) The Israelis might be able to accept such an arrangement as a concession to world commerce with the possibility that the Suez might in time be open to them even though not initially.

(d) Time is of the essence if the remaining pro-Western elements in the country are not to give up any hope of Western help. While these elements all recognize that Nasser is a major stumbling block, they prefer to have him in office temporarily to having the alternatives available. While no one will suggest that a plot is underway against Nasser, almost all pro-

Western elements refer to the need for a leader who reflects the changing times. While Nasser served his purpose as a revolutionary leader, that need is finished and he will ultimately have to be replaced.

(e) Most of the pro-Western or non-aligned elements are aware of the fact that the U.S. cannot grant government aid directly. They hope for an IMF agreement, rollover of credits, private business activity, etc. sufficient to keep them going until ties with the U.S. can be reestablished.

(f) Somewhat inconsistent with the view that the Russians are waiting to take over is the fact that they appear to have told the Government of the UAR that the Russians can give only token food assistance.

(g) The message regarding the visit of Mohieddin or another senior representative is a serious message, the reply to which is to be passed through the Pan American representative in Cairo as soon as possible.

---

405.   Telegram From the Department of State to the Embassy in Israel[1]

Washington, August 4, 1967, 0001Z.

15897. 1. During Evron call August 2, Under Secretary Rostow reported that Ambassador Burns, on basis his recent talks with King Hussein, thought Hussein still wanted settlement and was attempting strengthen his position as preparatory step.

2. Rostow said our own soundings indicated there was strong feeling about Jerusalem in Moslem world. If formula on Jerusalem could be found which would permit Jordanian-Israeli deal, this could be of crucial importance. It should not be beyond the wit of man to find such formula. Rostow recalled Eban's statement to Secretary that Israeli stand on Jerusalem represented "negotiating position" and that key consideration for Israel was preservation "unified administration." This was not excluded by Hussein.[2] (Evron interjected to say "you mean uni-

---

[1]   Source: National Archives and Records Administration, RG 59, Central Files 1967–69, POL 27 ARAB–ISR/SANDSTORM.   Secret; Nodis; Sandstorm.   Drafted by Atherton, cleared by Battle, and approved by Rostow. Repeated to Amman and London.

[2]   Burns commented in telegram 668 from Amman, August 4, that he hoped all the caveats of Hussein's position on Jerusalem, as contained in telegram 554 from Amman (Document 393), had been spelled out to Evron. (National Archives and Records Administration, RG 59, Central Files 1967–69, POL 27 ARAB–ISR/SANDSTORM)

fied Israeli administration.") Rostow said we would continue to explore Jerusalem question and Israel must not exclude consideration of alternative arrangements.

3. Evron said GOI less sure than USG that Hussein wanted settlement. Doubts had been raised, for example, by Jordanian position on refugee questionnaire. If Hussein wanted settlement, it was inconsistent to refuse recognize existence of State of Israel by rejecting questionnaire with that heading. Doubts also raised in Israeli minds by recent Radio Amman broadcasts calling for non-cooperation and resistance to Israeli occupation on West Bank.[3]

4. Evron continued that further changes on Jerusalem not now on agenda. Eban had made clear that Israel prepared find role for Hussein as custodian of Moslem Holy Places. In Evron's view, dual sovereignty idea and other such proposals were not negotiable. However, these were matters for Ambassador Barbour to discuss with GOI.

5. Rostow said Eban's position, as he understood it, was that Jerusalem should be last item on the agenda of the negotiation and could be dealt with if other items settled. Rostow said Hussein had reported that he had been in direct touch with Israelis. Having noted earlier in conversation that Israel had lost some confidence in Hussein, Evron commented only "that is another agreement Hussein has broken."[4] He added "but we have no secrets from you. I now understand what McGeorge Bundy meant when he said to Eban you can't keep us out of the room." Rostow commented that this was what he meant when he urged a new relationship of candor between USG and GOI.

6. Re Iraqi troops in Jordan, Rostow said our latest information was that Hussein had requested their removal but was now awaiting Aref visit to discuss question. Evron commented that Hussein was not a free agent so long as foreign troops remained in Jordan. Furthermore, Hussein–Nasser military pact still in force. If Hussein serious about wanting settlement, he should renounce pact with UAR.

Rusk

---

[3] Burns commented in telegram 668 from Amman that the Jordanian Government rejected the refugee questionnaire because the form appeared to it to constitute an affirmation of Israeli sovereignty over the West Bank and it feared use of the questionnaire would lead to a strong reaction and perhaps riots from the refugees. He commented that the Jordanian Government was "clearly ambivalent" about how to handle West Bank resistance, but he thought it was not necessary to hypothesize outside encouragement to explain the continuation of resistance on the West Bank.

[4] Burns pointed out in telegram 668 from Amman that Hussein had told him he had been in contact with the Israelis only when Burns asked him directly.

406.   Memorandum From the President's Special Assistant (Rostow) to President Johnson[1]

Washington, August 3, 1967.

SUBJECT

Israeli Military Visit

As part of his bargain last week to stave off a public outcry against our clampdown on military shipments to Israel, Mac Bundy agreed to try to arrange for the visit here of a top Israeli military officer to explain Israel's current and future military requirements. Secretaries Nitze and Rusk have agreed to the week of 21 August and recommend we go ahead. The purpose of this visit would not be announced, and we would again ask the Israelis to keep this low key.

We have known for some time that we would have to go through another exercise like this. It is impossible to reconcile Israeli requests with our military's view of Israelis actual needs without this sort of confrontation between the experts. Whatever we decide later on political grounds, talks like this are an essential first step.

On another level, this visit along with releasing $3 million worth of equipment now is our payment for the time we've bought with the Jewish community. Mac asked me to tell you that he was grateful to you for approving that $3 million on the phone for his gentlemen's agreement.[2] He felt it was basically a paper transaction selling the same horse twice, since that $3 million will come from the $14 million credit you already approved back on May 23.

Once this visit is over and we have had a chance to digest its results, we'll come to the big decision on what we will and will not bargain about with the Israelis. We may have to do another small interim deal after the visit to buy a little more time for making up our minds, but any major supply agreement would depend on larger political considerations. After he has had a chance to sort out his thoughts and talk around a bit, Mac wants to come in and see you at your convenience toward the end of next week to discuss this. Meanwhile, he wanted you to know that he believes we have to go ahead with this visit. He

---

[1]   Source: Johnson Library, National Security File, Country File, Middle East Crisis, Vol. IX. Secret.

[2]   See Document 403. A memorandum of August 10 from McNamara to the Secretaries of the Military Departments approved the release to Israel of $3 million in minor items of military equipment as an exception to his June 8 memorandum (see footnote 2, Document 225). (Washington National Records Center, OASD/ISA Files: FRC 330 71 A 4919)

assumes you have no objection since we have contained this pressure for about as long as possible now.[3]

Walt

---

[3] A note on the memorandum in Johnson's handwriting reads: "I seriously doubt wisdom of this visit now. Let's get for[eign] aid further along—ask Mc call me—L." An attached memorandum of August 4 from Rostow to the President reported that Bundy was convinced that if the visit did not take place, pressures would grow to expand military aid to Israel in the wake of Soviet military aid to the Arabs. An attached memorandum of August 11 from Bundy to Rostow states that the President had never approved the visit, now planned for September 11, but "the painful fact is that I told Evron we could plan for it." Bundy stated that he saw no way they could avoid discussion of military questions with the Israelis and concluded: "I think we have a bargain and I sure hope that the President will let us keep it. Otherwise, I'll have to move to Cairo."

---

407.   Telegram From the Department of State to the Embassy in Turkey[1]

Washington, August 4, 1967, 2208Z.

16257. Ref: Ankara's 460.[2]

1. Suggest you thank Kuneralp for his initiative. USG appreciates close and helpful relation with Turkish Government throughout ME crisis and believes Turkish influence will be constructive force in helping to bring situation to a sound and peaceful resolution. You may pass the following comments to him for transmittal to El Zyyat. For the sake of clarity, you may transmit these thoughts as an unofficial memorandum.[3] Such a paper should be transmitted by the Turkish Government

---

[1] Source: National Archives and Records Administration, RG 59, Central Files 1967–69, POL 17 US–UAR. Secret; Exdis. Drafted by Eugene Rostow and Battle, cleared by Sisco, and approved by Rusk.

[2] Telegram 460 from Ankara, August 4, reported that Secretary General of the Turkish Foreign Office Kuneralp had told the Chargé that Turkish Ambassador Gunver in Cairo had reported that El Zyyat had expressed pleasure that the United States wanted to keep the door open for friendship in the future. He referred to Fawzi's contacts with Rusk in New York and said Rusk had never given Fawzi a clear indication of U.S. views. (Ibid.)

[3] Telegram 613 from Ankara, August 9, reported that the Ambassador had given the unofficial memorandum to Kuneralp, who said they would transmit it to the UAR in the manner requested. (Ibid.) Telegram 249 from Cairo, August 14, reported that Foreign Office Counselor Riad indicated on August 12 that he was fully aware of the contents of telegram 16257 to Ankara. Bergus commented that this confirmed his view that "Zyyat approaches typical Egyptian feeler made in time of stress with full knowledge GUAR." (Ibid.)

as their own summary of USG views not as a direct communication of the USG.

2. Before any constructive steps can be taken to bring about an improvement in UAR-US relations, there are several things that need to be cleared away. The US did not break relations with the UAR. This action was taken by the UAR. We regret that decision. We believe diplomatic relations are particularly necessary during periods of strain. UAR took this step on the ground that the US had engaged in an attack upon the UAR and other countries with which the US had friendly relations. These charges were untrue. We believe they were known by the UAR to be untrue. Either the original charges or variants thereon continue to be made, including those stated by President Nasser in his recent speech. In addition, personal attacks on President Johnson are not in keeping with a desire for better relations.

3. It is difficult to see how a nation that wishes friendly relations with another can make such charges and continue to make them knowing that they are false, can slander President Johnson, and at the same time profess through various channels to wish an improvement in relations. If the UAR really wishes to rebuild its relations with the US, it could begin by ceasing to make charges it knows to be erroneous and by ceasing to attack President Johnson. This would be only a beginning but would be a good beginning. At some stage thereafter it would become necessary for the UAR to request resumption of diplomatic relations if it wishes their reestablishment.

4. The degree to which US-UAR bilateral relations can be improved is heavily dependent on constructive and responsible steps by the UAR, in its own interests, to deal (a) with the realities of relations between the nations of the Middle East which were engaged in the recent Arab-Israeli hostilities and (b) with problems of UAR relations with other states of the area heightened by the conflict in Yemen.

5. Regarding the Arabs and Israel, the fundamental principle of non-belligerence is at the heart of the present crisis. The US strongly favors withdrawal of Israeli forces to permanent national boundaries for Israel at the earliest possible time. What is required to achieve this is Arab acknowledgment that the state of war is over. The UAR can be influential in bringing this about. It is only in the above context that US weight can be brought to bear effectively on Israeli withdrawal.

6. Regarding the Yemen conflict and its outgrowths, we note with hope the report from Khartoum that initiative has been taken to return to the idea of the Jidda agreement. Deterioration in our relations prior to the recent Arab-Israel conflict stemmed largely from differences over the course followed by UAR in Yemen, in South Arabia and toward other Arab countries.

7. The US seeks good relations with all Arab countries and has played an active role in development programs designed to improve stability and promote economic growth. We continue to seek a means toward these ends. There is a basic desire for friendship with the Egyptian people and a strong hope in the USG to join with the UAR in efforts to make that friendship viable and lasting despite damage which recent events and charges have done to our bilateral relations. The USG respects the right of each state to organize and conduct its internal affairs as it chooses. Steps along foregoing lines might permit UAR and US to move in a direction helpful to both.

Rusk

---

408.   Telegram From the U.S. Interests Section of the Spanish Embassy in the United Arab Republic to the Department of State[1]

Cairo, August 7, 1967, 0946Z.

186. I had two hour conversation with FonOff Counselor Mohamed Riad evening Aug 5. Wide-ranging, many topics covered but main thrust was what lay ahead in current ME crisis. I said I had received fragmentary report from USUN to effect Indians and others were working toward some kind of SC resolution embodying quasi-consensus reached between Goldberg and Dobrynin/Gromyko in closing days July ESSGA.

I said that if at UN there could be legislative act clearly affirming Israel's right to exist adopted as result understanding between world's two greatest powers and accepted by Arabs, this would open new vistas for just and honorable settlement. Otherwise picture very gloomy indeed. In absence some such development, present situation could well harden.

Arabs, I continued, seemed presently bemused by concept of "pressure". In Arab view, US "pressure" had facilitated Israel military victory, stymied UN action favorable to Arabs, and continued be exercised for purpose humiliating and dismembering Arab world. This erroneous

---

[1] Source: National Archives and Records Administration, RG 59, Central Files 1967–69, POL 27 ARAB–ISR/UN. Secret. Received at 1534Z.

concept seemed to be guiding present exercises in Khartoum. Evidently Arabs felt they had only to develop sufficient "counter pressure" through oil, Suez Canal, etc. force US and West to "pressure" Israel return to June 4 situation. This unrealistic to extreme. GUAR had learned during April–May US-UAR crisis over Yemen that one country's "pressure" on another, even in situation of almost total dependency YAR on UAR, could not be applied preemptorily. So long as Israel could plead her very existence at stake, Arabs would be foolish count on Arab "pressure" on West to generate decisive "pressure" on Israel. Much more likely probability was interminable stalemate and increasing risk situation would again blow up in our faces.

I concluded by saying that even with acceptable UN action soonest, complications of present crisis made it likely that comprehensive sorting out would take considerable time. Therefore need for early start imperative.

Riad seized on final point to convey at some length that UAR would be much more interested in conceding Israel's existence if some quick and tangible development would follow. Could, for example, UAR be put in position say to its own people and to other "more radical" Arabs that acknowledgment Israel's existence would in fact begin process Israel withdrawal? Would "ironclad" arrangement re Aqaba make it possible for Israel forego claims to use of Suez Canal for time being? (I pointed out US position re Israel rights Suez Canal went back to 1951.) Would Israel really accept meaningful UN presence on its side as well as Arab side of frontiers?

GUAR and other Arabs were genuinely concerned, concluded Riad, lest any gesture made to acknowledge Israel's existence would only be read by US and Israel as sign of Arab weakness. He asked if I were sure USG did not aim at overthrow of Arab "nationalist" regimes. He cited stream of pointed questions re UAR internal stability which had been posed to him and other UAR reps by Americans in New York. I said USG interested in peaceful stable NE, not personalities.

Finally he said I should know our meeting was taking place with full knowledge and consent GUAR authorities who hoped this contact would flourish in full frankness. He indirectly but clearly cautioned me against discussing these matters with Spanish or other diplomats or "others of US."

I said we had covered a lot of very high ground and raised a lot of difficult questions. He should understand my comments had been largely personal. Under present US set-up in Cairo I could not take hourly pulse of USG and was operating very much out of my hat. Would report highlights our conversation, await USG reaction, and in any case, stay in close touch.

Bergus

409.   Telegram From the Embassy in Israel to the Department of
        State[1]

Tel Aviv, August 7, 1967, 1030Z.

391. Subject: August 4 Discussion with Foreign Minister Eban.

Ref: Tel Aviv 385.[2]

1. Since August 4 luncheon discussion with Foreign Minister Eban,
Ambassador Harman and Moshe Bitan offered opportunity carry out
my instructions (State 14236)[3] in relation several subjects, I am reporting them together in a single wire.

2. UN matters.

A. Conversation commenced with my remark that we still could
not understand why GOI became so jittery in latter stages of UN
Emergency Assembly meeting when it appeared that US and USSR
were finally getting together on text which contained essentials of our
position with which Israel agreed. Eban instantly produced from his
pocket copies of US text of June 20 and subsequent US-USSR draft (indicating, I suppose, he had either expected to bring up subject himself or
anticipated my approach). He contended that latter text was erosion in
that it did not talk about negotiated political settlement and first place
went to troop withdrawal, leaving second emphasis only on permanent
settlement and security. Eban said that term "negotiation" was omitted
in latter text as though it were an "impolite word." Eban and I agreed
that there was little chance that Arabs would have accepted US-USSR
text anyway, but when I stressed that this was chance for US to get
together with Soviets, he claimed that Soviets had not been persuaded
to accept US objectives but were merely attempting to erode US position. Eban went on to comment that in UN context symbols too were
important and US-USSR draft omitted terminology about ending "state
of belligerency." He advised that in future discussions with Soviets we
should talk about policies and not drafts. I agreed on basis of ideal
desirability but pointed out that discussions in UN context naturally
center around drafts.

B. Later in conversation Ambassador Harman raised point that
Arabs had also insisted on removal of word "peace" from late version of

---

[1]   Source: National Archives and Records Administration, RG 59, Central Files
1967–69, POL 27 ARAB–ISR. Secret; Priority; Exdis. Received on August 9 at 0759Z.

[2]   Telegram 385 from Tel Aviv, August 4 (ibid.), reported briefly that Barbour had carried out the instructions in Document 396.

[3]   Document 396.

draft resolution indicating that they still were not willing to face up to end of state of belligerency with Israel. I indicated that Secrurity Council was much wound up in its own particular procedures and that meanings of words took on different significance there and stressed again that if we looked broadly at our relations with Soviets since end of World War II, contrast was impressive. Our interests coincide now more than ever before, I pointed out, citing Chinese Communist problem and general significance of Soviets becoming "have" nation. To be sure there was not yet real meeting of minds but we do talk together more now and seem to be making progress towards actions in our mutual interest. I referred also to pre-Six-Day War Israeli statements that peace would only come to Middle East if US and Soviet Union could get together. Eban admitted that he had agreed to "harmonization" of great powers as requirement for peace but added that he had always meant by it that USSR should accept US policies. He remarked that in fact Soviet Union had not closed the "hole" when it should have during the last five or six years if it had genuine interest in settling world problems. When he referred to current Nuclear [Non-]Proliferation Treaty negotiations, I interjected that Israel's signature would help too. After acknowledging this remark with short laugh, Eban continued that if Soviets had been afraid of Communist China, they would have made settlement in Vietnam. I told him we were not becoming starry eyed but gratifying change had occurred. Eban advised "don't leave well fortified positions and go into no-man's land at this point." In GOI opinion, he stated, US position in UNSC should be based on restatement of President Johnson's five points and original June 20 draft resolution. He pointed out in that draft freedom of maritime passage was treated as something absolutely required so that no question could be raised later regarding Canal, I asked him pointedly whether this meant that GOI had no apprehensions about taking up freedom of transit in Security Council. Eban said in his opinion our original draft was so worded that this right would not have been vulnerable to Soviet veto. He mentioned that perhaps he should make a statement of Israeli attitude on essential points for UN consideration but I cautioned him against making any public statements about alleged changes in our position. Eban praised Ambassador Goldberg's handling of Emergency Session which he said showed great skill but reiterated importance which Israelis see in symbolism involved in retaining reference to "belligerence." He warned again that Soviet objective to get Israel out of occupied territory remained unchanged to which I replied that Soviets would not have gone so far with us if they had still thought they could get Israel out unconditionally, which was object of original position they had abandoned.

C. Eban recommended that we try to persuade Soviets to concert with us in limiting arms supply to which Harman remarked we have tried this often. Eban agreed that US had tried it often and Soviets had always declined. If we bring it up again, it would show whether Soviets have an international interest in peace in this area rather than desire achieve local advantage. I pointed out that we could not go that far yet with Soviets but our common interests were growing broader.

D. Regarding UN tactics Eban said GOI felt it would be helpful not to resume public discussions until September. He reported that he had found in talking with Seydoux that nobody was enthusiastic including Arabs and Soviets who, to French distress, were "more interested in a duet than a quartet." When I remarked that Geroge Brown did not appear so happy about waiting, Eban replied that UK thinks Canal closure weighs more heavily on it than anyone else but GOI believes best way to be diplomatically effective in immediate future is in traditional channels. I told him we agreed it would probably be best not to resume discussion until sometime around end of August.

E. Concerning Jerusalem Eban remarked that as we may have noticed there has been some domestic political difficulty here but GOI will accept someone coming over to look around on behalf of SYG provided he is well balanced in his outlook.

3. Movement Towards Settlement.

A. Eban expressed opinion that present tactical situation might be more important now than examining broad area objectives. He believed what we need most is "obdurate patience." He recalled that outcome of UN Emergency meeting shut door on unconditional withdrawal and that Arabs now must realize that they cannot get what they want without coming to Israelis directly. Choice, Eban added, was between "cease fire or peace." He cautioned strongly against becoming jumpy, nervous and running around excitedly in Washington. Some people, he added, appeared patient but others claimed things were getting worse thus demonstrating loss of nerve. He quoted one LA delegate as saying that free world is so unaccustomed to victory that when they get it, they just run around trying to give it away.

B. I told Eban that there could be two trends of thinking in regard to tactics. On the one hand it could be argued that time favors Israel and US in efforts towards achieving settlement; on the other, time may not necessarily be on our side. Perhaps Israel has too good nerves after nineteen years of conditioning. They reason that due largely to GOI restraint early in crisis (something for which I said I claimed a little credit, thus enabling Eban to say he had had something to do with it too), it was made clear to world that Israel was ringed around with enemies who were harassing it. Hence, when one last Egyptian incitement occurred and Israel pushed all buttons, in world estimation it was victim of aggression and gave good account of itself militarily. Now, however, this "victim" is sitting on territory of its neighbors in improved security situation. Under these conditions its status as "victim" will to an extent tend to be forgotten and will be replaced by image of Israel as "top dog." Any apparent reluctance to move toward reasonable solutions now will react against Israel. I pointed out that refugee problem including early return of those on East Bank is very important in this. Ideally, I added it is possible to see advantages of just sitting until Arabs forced to talk but with world made up of human beings this may not be best course.

C. Eban stated he agreed that victim concept is fading internationally as illustrated by vacillating UN and disappearing French and Canadian support. Yet, he emphasized, GOI must have nerve to let time pass and refuse to make known its peace terms. Eban did admit, however, that much research was now going on as to possible conditions of settlement, including matters such as economic, demographic, and political factors in Israel–Palestine equation. He said that GOI was conducting exercises as though they were real negotiations with Arabs. I interjected that danger is if present situation is crystallized with Israel as only real power in area, it will take on all attributes of former so-called imperalism and all its troubles. Eban responded by statement that I was authorized to say GOI was not just sitting but that "a certain solidity is now required." He said that very fact I felt so strongly on this matter showed problem is arising. Yet, he commented, Arabs are just now coming up against realities which they would not have done before July [June] 4. He expressed hope that after another few weeks or months more progress could be expected from them. I told him few weeks or months might be all right but not to let it go too far. Eban countered with view that changes required in Arab outlook are so fundamental that more time might be needed for them to make necessary adjustment. Harman said he admitted need for movement towards peace but that quick movement could bring us to conclusion short of full change which [garble] would be self-defeating. In his opinion things are moving in right direction as result of Assembly [garble]. He referred to possible Yemen settlement and withdrawal of Egyptian troops now there. I told Harman that I personally accepted much of what he said but to be realistic, vis-à-vis Soviets US had lost a lot. I observed that now it was clear we were not looking for love and esteem of Arabs, perhaps relationship based on mutual interests such as oil could be re-established on more realistic basis, but present situation certainly was not favorable. Eban interjected that it would have been much worse for our relations with Arabs if Israel had not helped us out on June 5. I told him with some vehemence not to press me on what might have happened if Israel had not won victory. As result, I said, now we have to wrestle with peace problems. Returning to charge on refugees I pointed out that image made great difference, and right now question arose whether Israel did not appear to be more interested in holding real estate than in solving basic problems. Bitan interjected that Israel's preference for sticking to essentials over images was like ours in Vietnam. I said it seems to me that action on refugees would show whether Israeli image was like ours in Vietnam. I said it seemed to me that action on refugees would show whether Israeli image was becoming that of an obstinate victor or remained that of victim of aggression. As to refugees going to East Bank, their motives were multiple which was all more reason to show everyone there were no road blocks to returning them. Eban remarked that Jordanian willingness to meet for discussion on problems of returning refugees showed they accepted necessity of coming to agreement. I told Eban that frankly Israeli requirements regarding meetings, forms and so on did not add to Israel's credit in face of great humanitarian problem. Eban commented that he had been attracted by idea of making some refugees "non-refugees" and that he had talked to Horowitz about it who thought that they might get some outside assistance for such move. Then I recalled lunch I gave for Nixon on June 22 when Allon and other ministers appeared enthusiastic to get started on refugee problem. I said that although I might be speaking out of turn, if GOI could find projects which would really move towards solution, I felt sure we could find ways of helping. Harman added that limited specific project on refugees brought to West Bank would set wheels in motion but would "cost x millions of dollars" for equipment and other essentials. I repeated that we would be sympathetic to project involving final solution to human problem. Eban observed that maybe transition time between cease fire and peace could be used to move forward on refugee problem but important thing was not to become impatient. Certain processes could only occur with "time plus firmness," especially on part of those who set high value on Soviet behavior. He admitted that progress was less apparent on Arab side but claimed that something was happening there too and reiterated GOI position that it had no favorites and would talk to anyone.

4. Arms Supplies.

A. Eban brought up question of arms supplies from US stating that he found our attitude puzzling in view of Soviet rearmament of Arabs. Although this admittedly was more dangerous now politically than militarily, it would serve discourage Arabs from making moves for peaceful settlement with Israel. I remarked that some in Washington do not rule out possibility of suicide air attack on Israeli cities even now. Eban observed that such an attempt would merely strengthen Israel's point. In any event, he claimed, in one European country where embargo on arms for Israel was publicly announced GOI could now get what it needed to maintain equipment, which it had, although admittedly not obtain more planes. In US, however, nothing was moving. Using contents State 15900,[4] I told him about decision supply up to $3 million worth of spares, possible Weizman trip and fact that we had not said "no" to request for planes. Ambassador Harman stated US position has amounted to "suspension of routine supplies" as well as refusal provide new items of equipment and that he had raised matter first about six weeks ago with Mr. Battle who said he thought it could be unscrambled. Weeks went by and still, according to Ambassador, no progress was made and even at meeting to which I had referred, all we did was talk about an amount, we did not raise the suspension. Harman said he could find no rhyme or reason in our reluctance to supply arms in view of our close relations. I responded that outlook appeared favorable judging from tenor of reftel.

B. Eban commented that he had impression some minds in Washington were attached to idea of withholding arms as form of pressure on Israel. If so, he stated firmly, there should be no misunderstanding. GOI feels present situation is its fundamental chance for peace and security and that Israelis would lose by giving anything away before proper time. Here, he added, it was problem of Arabs and not of Soviets. I reminded him that we could not agree that sitting on occupied territory would be enough and concluded with admonition "don't start digging in."

Barbour

---

[4] Telegram 15900 to Tel Aviv, August 4, conveyed information concerning an August 2 conversation between Eugene Rostow and Evron. (National Archives and Records Administration, RG 59, Central Files 1967–69, POL 27 ARAB–ISR)

---

410.   Telegram From the Department of State to the Embassy in Yugoslavia[1]

Washington, August 9, 1967, 0103Z.

17945. Please deliver following message to appropriate level Foreign Office for conveyance to President Tito. Make presentation orally but leave copy for convenience Foreign Office:

"The President appreciates the willingness of President Tito at this time to take responsibility for trying to contribute to a peaceful solu-

---

[1] Source: National Archives and Records Administration, RG 59, Central Files 1967–69, POL 27 ARAB–ISR. Secret; Immediate; Exdis. Drafted by Eugene Rostow; cleared by Battle, Sisco, Harriman, Stoessel, Meeker, and Walt Rostow; and approved by Katzenbach. Repeated Priority to London, Tel Aviv, Moscow, and USUN.

tion of the crisis, and wishes him success in his mission to the Middle East.[2] He wishes to assure President Tito that within the context of his statement of principle on June 19, we will use our best efforts to cooperate in every effort to find a just and lasting solution of the Middle East crisis.

The United States agrees with President Tito that a Middle Eastern settlement now should be realistic and long-term. The world cannot accept an indefinite continuation of the risks of the precarious armistice regime which exploded on June 5th. The United States agrees also that the settlement should not humiliate the Arab states, or require them to give up any rights or interests they may legitimately claim. President Tito may be assured that in approaching the problem of a settlement the United States will take fully into account the rights and interests of the Arab states, along with those of Israel and of other nations with interests in the Middle East.

The United States has long standing ties of friendship and interest in the Middle East. It wishes to have friendly and cooperative relations with all the nations of the region. Its concern for these fundamental factors in the situation, and its respect for the true long-term interests of the Arab states, led the United States from the outbreak of hostilities on June 5th to adopt the policy of seeking not another armistice, but a solution of peace.

In our view, the dispute over Israel's right to exist is the root of the trouble in the Middle East. The United States agrees with President Tito's comment that most of the countries represented at the United Nations accepted the legitimacy of the existence of Israel in the course of the recent session of the Assembly. This fact, as he rightly remarked, should now have its impact on the Arabs themselves.

While the United States agrees that the Arab States should not be humiliated, the United States does not feel that it can be regarded as unreasonable for one member of the United Nations to acknowledge the existence of another, or to state that it is not engaged in a war to destroy that state, or that it is not free to resume hostilities against that state at will. The continuance of the dream of destroying Israel has

---

[2] Ambassador C. Burke Elbrick met with Tito at Brioni on July 29 and delivered a message from President Johnson, which stated that the U.S. position on the Middle East was based on the five principles Johnson had announced on June 19 and centered on the conviction that each nation of that area must accept the right of its neighbors to peaceful and secure existence. It also expressed the hope that the United States and Yugoslavia could work together in the interests of a just and durable settlement in the Middle East. (Telegram 13567 to Belgrade, July 27; ibid.) Tito discussed the Middle East situation with Elbrick and told him that he expected to visit the UAR, Syria, and Iraq after the middle of August and would do everything possible to work toward a peaceful solution. (Telegram 292 from Belgrade, July 30; ibid.)

become a burden to world peace, and a threat to the interests of the Arab states as well. The Arab states can hardly claim rights of belligerency for themselves, and object if Israel exercises the same claims reciprocally.

The United States hopes that the Government of Yugoslavia agrees that the time has come for every member of the United Nations in the area to acknowledge that each enjoys the right to maintain an independent national state of its own, and to live in peace and security, and that all claims and acts inconsistent with this should be renounced.

There has been some misunderstanding of what the United States means by belligerent rights. In the view of the American Government, an abandonment of claims of belligerency would not require the United Arab Republic, for example, to extend recognition to Israel or to establish diplomatic relations with it, normal and desirable as both our governments regard this to be. It would, however, among other things, assure the right of all nations to use the Strait of Tiran and the Suez Canal, and eliminate any claim of a right to threaten or to use armed force on the part of one Middle Eastern state against another.

There are many ways in which a movement towards peace can begin. In view of the United States, one simple first step would be for the United Arab Republic to accept the Draft Resolution upon which the Soviet Union and the United States reached agreement during the final days of the General Assembly. This Resolution would have broad support in the Security Council. It could become the basis for a general settlement which deals constructively with all the other elements of the problem mentioned by President Johnson in his speech of June 19: the tragedy of the refugees, the protection of international rights in Jerusalem, and the withdrawal of Israeli forces to agreed and secure national boundaries.

In this process, there can be no substitute for the responsibility of the states of the region. Others can help. But these problems cannot be solved unless they take responsibility for dealing with them directly and realistically.

The Yugoslav delegation to the United Nations has discussed with American representatives the possible appointment by the Secretary General of a prominent individual who could undertake the important process of mediation between the parties, within the framework of the principles mentioned above. The United States hopes President Tito will explore this possibility in the course of his trip since the United States believes the appointment of a mediator could be a constructive next step towards a durable and stable peace in the Near East.

The United States notes the concern of President Tito about any attempt on the part of Israel to extend the territories it now occupies. In this connection, the United States considers it essential that the ceasefire be respected by both sides and that every member of the United Nations support General Bull's efforts to this end until such time as conditions of peace are established that permit a permanent withdrawal.

The United States Government is giving careful study to President Tito's thought that the great powers of the Security Council undertake direct responsibility for guaranteeing the agreements reached by way of settlement, including a possible guarantee of Israel against future attack.

President Tito's suggestion is worthy of most serious consideration. In the first instance, however, it would be necessary to consult the parties directly concerned, and, subsequently, other parties in interest. The United States Government knows that President Tito appreciates that for any security arrangements and guarantees to be effective, they must not only reflect undertakings by both Israel and the Arabs, but must be in the context of durable and stable peace in lieu of the state of war which has existed in the past.

The United States Government is not in accord with a statement about arms shipments made by President Tito in his talk with Ambassador Elbrick; the United States Government does regard Soviet arms deliveries in the Middle East with concern. These arms deliveries since 1955 have been on an excessive and provocative scale. While it is true, as President Tito remarked, 'arms do not fight by themselves,' there are many Arab leaders who say they wish to resume hostilities in one form or another. Therefore, the risk remains. The United States considers an effective practical agreement on arms limitation in the area as an important aspect of any plan for durable peace in the region.

The United States notes with approval and agreement President Tito's determination to make every effort to help the Arab countries economically. The United States deplores the state of affairs whereby economic gains labored for by Arab leaders are being dissipated. With the state of belligerency removed and a permanent peace estabished, the United States would foresee economic progress quickly resuming in those countries. Since the end of the second World War, successive United States administrations have pledged their support for economic progress and for the political independence and territorial integrity of all states in the Middle East. This position has not changed. The United States will do its part in any such effort.

The United States Government wishes to emphasize the importance it attaches to mutual understanding between the United States and Yugoslavia, and its appreciation for President Tito's initiative in behalf of peace."[3]

Rusk

---

[3] Telegram 421 from Belgrade, August 9, reported that the message had been delivered to Acting Foreign Minister Dimitrij Vosnjak that morning. (Ibid.)

---

411. Telegram From the Department of State to the Embassy in Israel[1]

Washington, August 9, 1967, 0134Z.

17947. On reviewing the first talks between King Hussein and Ambassador Burns, we are sending this message to supplement State 14236[2] as guidance for you during the next stage of the negotiations between Israel and Jordan.

1. While we are not at this point pressing King Hussein to move forward into a negotiating position, our posture vis-à-vis GOI is not symmetrical. We wish GOI to be under no doubt that we regard successful negotiations between Israel and Jordan as greatly in their interest and in ours. Peaceful arrangements between Israel and Jordan could have positive and far-reaching effects on the entire situation in the Middle East. Tactically, such a step could stimulate others in the same direction. Strategically, it would give the parties and others a chance which is not now really available to make progress on the refugee problem and on Jerusalem, and to help lift the curse of the Palestine issue from the soul of the Arab world. Although we know the chances of success are not

---

[1] Source: National Archives and Records Administration, RG 59, Central Files 1967–69, POL 27–14 ARAB–ISR/SANDSTORM. Secret; Priority; Nodis; Sandstorm. Drafted by Eugene Rostow on July 31; cleared by Battle, Walt Rostow, Kohler, and Katzenbach; and approved by Rusk. Repeated Priority to London and Amman. The telegram includes handwritten revisions, apparently in Rusk's handwriting. Bundy sent the draft telegram to the President on August 1, with a memorandum stating that Rusk wanted him to see it and that it was designed "to keep the attention of the Israelis on the need not to freeze the status quo either in fact or in their bargaining positions." Rostow forwarded it to the President with an August 2 memorandum, concurring in Bundy's recommendation and commenting that he thought "we shall have to find a way not merely to get a reasonable Jerusalem position out of the Israelis but also a way of letting Hussein know such a position exists, before he will put his stack into a negotiation." (Johnson Library, National Security File, Country File, Middle East Crisis, Vol IX)

[2] Document 396.

great, the opportunity is so important and so transitory that we believe we should try to persuade the Israelis to see their own true interest here.[3]

The political advantages of an understanding between Israel and Jordan are highlighted by considering the probable consequences of not having such an accord: the possible partition of Jordan; a radical, highly armed state on Israel's Eastern frontier; a status for Jerusalem which would permanently affront large parts of the Muslim world; and continued agitation to liberate the Palestinians throughout the Middle East.

We are aware of the revival of interest among some Israelis, Jordanian West Bankers, and Saudis in the idea of a semi-autonomous Palestinian state on the West Bank, possibly with Gaza. On the whole we rate its chances for success as less than that of a Jordanian-Israeli agreement. We prefer trying latter course first in any event.

2. We do not agree with the view often expressed here by representatives of GOI that time and immobility will produce results favorable to peace. The influence of the Soviet Union in the Middle East is far greater today than in 1956–57, both through Egypt and more directly. Weak countries like Libya and Jordan could succumb, thus imperiling several other governments. The level of arms in the Middle East is an autonomous threat to peace.

To counter Soviet efforts, to strengthen Arab moderates, and in simple interest of peace itself we therefore seek a succession of steps towards peace at this time, small or large, agreed or unilateral. We believe that such a process could favor such chances of progress as there may be in our talks on the Middle East with the Soviet Union.

3. You should stress to GOI that our central commitment is to support the territorial integrity and political independence of all the states of the Middle East. It is as much in the interest of GOI as it is in our interest to maintain the credibility of that support. As applied to Jordan, as King Hussein understands, the issue of territorial integrity raises problems not present in the case of Syria or Egypt. The Jordanian and Israeli boundaries include armistice lines, which have a legal status somewhat different from that of definitive international frontiers. While King Hussein has remarked that the armistice lines "make no sense" and will require revision, it is in our view nonetheless highly probable that no peace settlement between Israel and Jordan would be accepted by the world community unless it gives Jordan some special position in

---

[3] In the original draft, the last part of the sentence reads: "we believe we should use our influence in Israel to encourage a favorable outcome." The following paragraph was crossed out: "In this process, if it develops, we shall consult with leaders of the American Jewish community. We believe they may favor a compromise solution between Israel and Jordan, even if it involves concessions on Jerusalem."

the Old City of Jerusalem. We assume that Jordan would receive the bulk of the West Bank, which is equally regarded as "Jordanian territory".

Against this background, it is a matter of high importance that a settlement between Israel and Jordan respect our commitment to support the territorial integrity of all the states of the area. If in the end negotiations between Israel and Jordan fail for any reason, and we face an indefinite continuation of the status quo, it is necessary that both we and GOI be in a position to show that every reasonable effort towards an agreement has been made, and made in good time and good faith.

4. We understand the strength of the Israeli attachment to Jerusalem. Other peoples also have strong feelings with regard to the Holy Places of Jerusalem, equally rooted in history.

Taking the political stakes into account, we cannot conclude at this early point that it will be impossible to find a formula for the Old City and its environs which could satisfy (a) the Israeli interest in an open city under unified administration; (b) the Jordanian and Muslim interest in an acknowledgment of Jordanian sovereignty for a section of the city; and (c) the Christian interest in the status of the Holy Places.

We could probably accept any solution on which GOI and Hussein could agree. We continue to believe that the issue will not be faced realistically except in the context of actual negotiations.

5. Your course therefore should be to advise a realistic preparation by GOI for a beginning of negotiations, bearing in mind that chance of such negotiations depends to major degree on this review. Before negotiations could have any chance of success, GOI must be ready to face issue of Jerusalem with far more flexibility than they have yet displayed. We recognize that they will not at once agree to this view, but we should keep pressing it upon them privately.[4]

Rusk

---

[4] In the original draft, the last two sentences read: "Before such a negotiation can begin with any chance of success, GOI must agree to face issue of Jerusalem with far more flexibility than they have yet displayed. At a later point, we could perhaps assist in the articulation of plans for the Old City, if necessary, to prevent a breakdown of negotiations."

412.   Telegram From the U.S. Interests Section of the Spanish
Embassy in the United Arab Republic to the Department of
State[1]

Cairo, August 10, 1967, 0858Z.

214. US-UAR Relations.

During conversation ninth, Presidency Adviser Al-Khouli stressed
equally with his point on need for Israel withdrawal (septel)[2] view of
Nasser and GUAR that there should be effective "relationship" between
USG and UAR. Khouli specifically differentiated between "relationship" and "diplomatic relations." He recognized all sorts of obstacles on
both sides to resumption of latter and felt this might well take year or
two. But both govts should realize "relationship" was to mutual interest and that it should be maintained at all costs. GUAR wanted concentrate "relationship" through me in Cairo.

Khouli had before him seven page memcon of my August 5 conversation with Mohamed Riad of FonOff. He referred to my comments
on "big lie" as obstacle to US-UAR relations. He said Nasser was personally convinced that he had been subject deceit by President Johnson.

I not only denied this but said President Johnson had every reason
to repose something less than full confidence in President Nasser. I cited
LBJ's very friendly letter to Nasser sent in latter half May.[3] Nasser not
only took his time about answering it but even had told French
Ambassador that he did not intend to answer it. I referred to GUAR's
systematically opposing every measure which USG took during that
critical period to defuse crisis. US proposals re maritime declaration
were greeted with hostility. GUAR instead of showing US any flexibility in its position re Gulf of Aqaba took more intransigent stand each
time we consulted it. GUAR newspapers even published reports that
Straits had been mined. Nasser's letter of June 3 to LBJ which came only
after Anderson visit contained summation of extremely hard position
with only grudging acceptance in final paragraph of proposal for
Muhyieddine visit. In short GUAR had given us nothing work with in
our endeavors persuade Israel see peaceful solution.

---

[1]   Source: National Archives and Records Administration, RG 59, Central Files
1967–69, POL UAR–US. Secret; Exdis.

[2]   Telegram 216 from Cairo, August 10, reported that the main thrust of Presidency
Adviser Hassan Sabri al-Khouli's remarks during his conversation with Bergus the previous day was the urgent need for withdrawal of Israeli forces, while Bergus stated and
restated the "absolutely essential link between withdrawal and recognition Israel's right
to exist." (Ibid., POL 27 ARAB–ISR)

[3]   See Document 34.

I said it might be useful for us to sit down together with a day-by-day chronology on both sides and argue this thing out point by point. He warmly accepted this suggestion. I said I would consult Washington. (*Comment:* Recognize this is handing Dept pretty tall order in requesting that somebody bring together the many highly restricted messages which flew back and forth during crisis period and summarize them in chronological order. At same time feel this device might give Nasser excuse in his own rather complex mind crawl off his present anti-US posture.)

Khouli said that for "technical, diplomatic questions" I should see Mohamed Riad of FonOff. For matters of real importance between our two govts, or for personal problems or for anything else I should see him at any time.[4] He gave me three phone numbers by which I could reach him at any time of day or night.

Khouli said I should resume all my old contacts here. He specifically suggested that I get in touch with Heykal. He indicated that I should resume seeing Muhyieddine and other old friends but that I should do it "gradually".

Khouli said GUAR hoped it would be possible for ex-Ambassador Badeau to visit Cairo during his upcoming visit to NE. Nasser had indicated he would be happy see Badeau.

Khouli said it essential we maintain cultural ties during this difficult period. He had succeeded reversing PriMin's decision call back all UAR students in US on grounds dollar shortage. He had kind words for Cairo American College and AUC.

Khouli said his attitude towards Russians had not changed and their role in touching off crisis by false allegations of imminent Israel invasion of Syria was fully appreciated by Nasser.

Khouli said we should meet at least once weekly. I agreed. I told him I planned return Washington for week's consultation in mid-September. He thought this good idea.

Bergus

---

[4] Telegram 213 from Cairo, August 10, reported that during Bergus' conversation with al-Khouli the previous day, the latter said Nasser had authorized him to say that all "special messages" between the U.S. and UAR Governments should be sent through Bergus. The latter had the trust and confidence of the UAR Government and no other intermediaries were required. He also said that two high-ranking CIA officials were trying to contact Nasser. (Department of State, INR/IL Historical Files, Roger Channel, Cairo) Telegram 20412 to Cairo, August 14, replied that the U.S. Government was unaware of any such initiatives and intended that its views should be conveyed through Bergus. It stated that the CIA had indicated that reports alleging CIA officials were trying to contact Nasser were not true. (Ibid.)

413.   Telegram From the Department of State to the Mission to
        the United Nations[1]

Washington, August 11, 1967, 0104Z.

19237. Subject: Re Kulebiakin Approach.[2]

We are interested in fact Kulebiakin approach seems to indicate Sovs concerned about opening canal and may be willing accept necessity all vessels, including Israeli, going through canal as the price. Whether this is Sov policy or simply a feeler is not yet clear.

However, we do not want to shift from res discussed with Gromyko at end of GA, under which canal opening would be included among much wider objectives. Consequently suggest reply be conveyed to Kulebiakin along following lines:

(1) Dept has noted with interest Kulebiakin indication Sov recognition opening of canal would have to involve freedom of navigation for ships of all states, including Israel. We wonder whether Sovs have any indication UAR views on this point. (We will be especially interested, without showing interest ourselves, in Kulebiakin's reaction to such comment, e.g., whether he backs away, or gives any indication Sovs may in fact be thinking of something less, such as cargoes and not flagships, etc.)

(2) We also note with satisfaction indication Sov interest in continuing consultations with US in interests maintaining peace in area. As Sovs aware our objective remains to establish a permanent peace in ME, not to revert simply to an armistice or absence of war, which has not been a success, and hope Sovs will also work for this objective.

(3) Kulebiakin may not be aware that when Dobrynin returned to Moscow he carried message from Secty to Gromyko[3] stressing we had gone as far as we could go at end of GA in text upon which US and Sov Dels had reached agreement at that time, and urging that Sovs should continue to stand on that policy. We indicated also our willingness to

---

[1] Source: National Archives and Records Administration, RG 59, Central Files 1967–69, POL 27 ARAB–ISR. Confidential; Priority; Exdis. Drafted by Sisco on August 10. Cleared by Battle and James W. Pratt (EUR/SOV), approved by Eugene Rostow, and repeated to Moscow and Tel Aviv.

[2] The approach by fourth-ranking Soviet representative N.P. Kulebyakin to Pedersen was reported in telegram 413 from USUN, August 8, which summarized his main points as the desire to clear the Suez Canal for traffic through a partial Israeli pullback, with Israeli traffic to go through the canal, the desire to have a U.S.-Soviet agreement before the next Security Council session and to ensure it dealt with broad Middle East issues or with the Canal rather than with Jerusalem, and an expression of approval of a resumption of U.S.-UAR diplomatic relations. (Ibid., POL 27 ARAB–ISR/UN)

[3] See Document 392.

continue consultations on ME. USG is awaiting response to that message as next appropriate step in our consultations. (We do not wish to proceed on other levels until that reply received.)

Please report on any observations Kulebiakin makes in response to this reply.[4]

Rusk

---

[4] Pedersen reported in telegram 449 from USUN, August 11, that he met with Kulebyakin that day. He commented that his impression was that the Soviets were thinking about the possibilities of solving specific issues, possibly because of Arab opposition to a broader approach, that they were not thinking of moving ahead on anything unless they had substantial Arab support, and that they were not clear how far they could bring the Arabs along either on a generalized approach or on specific issues. (National Archives and Records Administration, RG 59, Central Files 1967–69, POL 27 ARAB–ISR)

---

414. Special National Intelligence Estimate[1]

SNIE 30–3–67   Washington, August 10, 1967.

THE SHORT-TERM ARAB-ISRAELI MILITARY BALANCE

The Problem

To assess the military capabilities of Israel and the Arab states, and to estimate Arab military intentions toward Israel, particularly over the next few months.

Scope Note

For the purposes of this estimate, we assume that the Arabs will not abandon their claim that a state of belligerency with Israel exists, and further that Israel will continue to occupy Arab territory taken in the war.

---

[1] Source: Central Intelligence Agency Files, Job 79–R01012A, ODDI Registry of NIE and SNIE Files. Secret; Controlled Dissem. According to the cover sheet, the estimate was submitted by the Director of Central Intelligence, and concurred in by the U.S. Intelligence Board on August 10. The Central Intelligence Agency and the intelligence organizations of the Departments of State and Defense and National Security Agency participated in its preparation. The CIA, State, Defense, and NSA representatives on the USIB concurred; the AEC and FBI representatives abstained because the subject was outside their jurisdiction.

Conclusions

A. UAR, Jordanian, and Syrian military forces were badly mauled by Israel in the recent war. Soviet resupplies have restored much materiel to the UAR and Syria, but Israel's margin of superiority is even greater than before. We believe that the Arab states will be unable to launch an effective attack against Israel in the next few months, and indeed for a considerable time thereafter.

B. We believe that Arab leaders are generally aware of these realities and that no Arab state intends to engage Israel military in 1967. A surprise Arab air attack cannot be completely ruled out, but it is unlikely and would probably be anticipated by Israeli intelligence.

C. Arab sabotage and terrorist activities may occur, but a major guerrilla warfare campaign against Israel is unlikely. Even if attempted, it could not pose a serious threat to Israel's security.

Discussion

1. The Israelis inflicted very heavy losses on the Arabs in the June 1967 war. Syria lost most of its 85 fighter aircraft and about 100 of its 425 tanks. The small Jordanian air force was completely destroyed; two-thirds of Jordan's 200 tanks were destroyed or captured. The UAR, with the largest Arab armed force, lost about two-thirds of its 365 fighter aircraft, 55 of its 69 bombers, and about half of its 1,000 tanks. Though UAR pilot losses were probably small, the UAR had only 200 pilots who were combat ready in jet fighters when the war began. Losses among armored vehicle crews were very heavy, as were casualties in ground forces. The Sinai fighting eliminated from the UAR order of battle two of its four infantry divisions, one of its two amored divisions, and 15 of its 23 independent brigades. Less tangible but just as significant was the great damage to morale and leadership in all three armies.[2] Israel holds several thousand commissioned and noncommissioned UAR officer prisoners, including nine generals.

2. Israel emerged from the war with a greatly enhanced military superiority over its Arab neighbors. Its losses were light. Less than a hundred of its 1,100 tanks were destroyed. Of Israel's 256 aircraft, 48 were lost—including 14 of its 46 fighter bombers; 24 of its 450 jet pilots were killed. Even with these losses—and the subsequent resupply of Soviet aircraft to the Arabs—the Israeli air force remains qualitatively much stronger than all the Arab air forces combined. Though lost Israeli

---

[2] Iraq played a minor role in the war. It lost some 19 fighters and one bomber; its infantry was only slightly engaged and suffered few losses. Though Algerian and Saudi units were dispatched to the area, none of them participated in the fighting. [Footnote in the source text.]

aircraft have not been replaced, aircraft spare parts are still being imported from France,[3] and there is no shortage of air-to-air missiles or aircraft gun ammunition. As compared with the Arabs' personnel losses of more than 7,000, the Israelis lost about 700 killed, though this included a high proportion of officers. In addition, the Israeli army now occupies territory which would give it great advantage in the event of a resumption of hostilities. Though Israel has received no large new amounts of foreign military supplies since the war, it captured vast amounts of ground force equipment, a certain amount of which can and will be integrated into its units.

3. Since the war, Syria has received some replacements of its losses; Jordan has received nothing except some obsolescent tanks from Iraq and some radar from the UAR. Neither Syria nor Jordan poses a serious military threat to Israel in the near term, and they are not, either by themselves or in concert with the UAR, likely to do so for some time to come. Of Israel's immediate neighbors, only the UAR has gotten substantial replacements of lost equipment. These include at least 60 percent and perhaps as much as 90 percent of the fighter aircraft, between 20 and 40 percent of the bombers, and about 50 percent of the tanks it lost in the war. Most of the planes were acquired in an emergency airlift from the USSR and Algeria in the three weeks following the end of the war. Since then, resupply has slowed notably; most equipment in being brought in by sea, and at a pace approximately that of prewar days.

4. We do not believe that the Soviet resupply has significantly lessened Israel's military superiority over its Arab neighbors, and it is not likely to do so for some time to come at least.[4] The forces which the various Arab states could bring to bear against Israel are substantially less than those available on 4 June. Unless the Soviets drastically increase the present pace of resupply, it would take about a year substantially to replace UAR and Syrian equipment losses. The forming and training of new units to use these weapons, especially in the UAR, would probably require 18 months or more. (Logistics limit the Iraqis to about the 10,000–15,000 men they presently have in Jordan, and would probably impose a similar limitation on Algeria.) The Arabs' ability to use modern weapons was proved demonstrably inferior to that of the Israelis in the recent war, and this is likely to remain the case for some time.

---

[3] On 2 June 1967, France imposed an embargo in shipments of military items to the Middle East, but the embargo does not apply to spare parts previously contracted for. In addition, there probably has been some evasion of the ban. [Footnote in the source text.]

[4] See SNIE 11–13–67, "Probable Soviet Objectives in Rearming Arab States," dated 20 July 1967, for an assessment of Soviet policy and objectives toward the Arabs. [Footnote in the source text. SNIE 11–13–67 is not printed. (Central Intelligence Agency Files, Job 79–R01012A, ODDI Registry of NIE and SNIE Files)]

Hence, we see no likelihood that the Arab states will acquire the capability to attack present Israeli positions with any degree of success in 1967.

5. As for Arab intentions in respect of military actions against Israel, the views in Arab capitals vary. The most belligerent statements come from Syria and Algeria; those Arab leaders whose forces suffered the greatest losses are least inclined to press for renewed fighting. Jordan has made it clear that it wants no further fighting, and it is trying to get Iraq to withdraw its troops from the East Bank. Cairo appears to be aware of its military weakness vis-à-vis Israel. In fact, it appears to be afraid that the Israelis might renew the attack. The tone of its public statements is one of determination to rebuild for the long haul, not one of encouragement to war. The present deployment of UAR, Syrian, and Jordanian forces is clearly defensive. There is a possibility, though a very slight one, that some Arab leaders might ascribe their loss of the war to the success of Israel's preemptive air strike and draw the conclusion that Arab forces, if they destroyed the Israeli air force in a surprise blow, might win at least a limited victory on the ground. It is far more likely, however, that Arab leaders—especially those in the UAR, whose air force would have to be used—are aware that Israel's aircraft are well protected and that the Israelis would be likely to detect Arab plans for preemption and strike first, or at least retaliate quickly and effectively. In addition, the last two months have demonstrated to the Arabs that there are clear limits on what they can depend on in the way of Soviet support, and this awareness almost certainly works to discourage them from serious thoughts of another round in the near future. In these circumstances, we believe that any major Arab attack on Israel is highly unlikely in 1967, and indeed for a considerable time thereafter.

Guerrilla Warfare

6. Algerian and Syrian leaders, as well as Ahmed Shuqairi, chief of the Palestinian Liberation Organization, have publicly demanded that the war against Israel be converted into a large scale and sustained guerrilla campaign. If attempted, this would, in practice, be less likely to take the form of classical guerrilla operations than of terrorist and sabotage raids. Since the early 1950's, terrorist activities have been carried out in Israel by Palestinians infiltrated from Syria, Jordan or Egypt. These raids have on occasion caused casualties and some physical damage, but they have done little or no harm to Israeli military forces. Instead of weakening the Israeli will to resist, they have strengthened the hand of those Israelis who advocate a hard line against the Arabs.

7. Recent Israeli victories have made the renewal of such terrorist activity more difficult in some ways, easier in others. Arab infiltrators

can no longer operate from bases in the Gaza Strip or the West Bank within close range of targets in Israel. Infiltration of terrorists and saboteurs across the Jordan River, at least in small numbers, could probably be accomplished despite the efforts of Israeli and Jordanian security forces to prevent it. As before, such infiltrators would probably be trained Palestinian terrorists who know the people and the area in which they would operate. (Algerians, or even Syrians, whatever their skills, would probably be much less effective in unfamiliar territory.) Palestinians would probably receive considerable protection and aid from a sympathetic Arab populace. They could be particularly effective in the West Bank and Jerusalem in punitive operations against other Arabs, e.g., those who were collaborating with the Israelis.

8. Nevertheless, we do not believe that the Arabs are capable of mounting irregular operations in such numbers or strength as to have military significance. The present lines between Israel and its Arab neighbors are easier to defend and patrol than before; the infiltration of any significant number of guerrillas into Israeli territory from Lebanon, Syria, and Jordan would be difficult. Infiltration from the UAR is virtually impossible except for isolated commando raids against communications routes in Sinai. The effectiveness of such tactics in Israeli populated areas (in contrast to those inhabited by Arabs) has been and will continue to be very limited. At best, the Arabs can hope to carry out isolated, small-scale harassments.

9. Further, irregular warfare of even small proportions would be likely to evoke Israeli countermeasures which Arab leaders wish to avoid. The Israelis have consistently, vigorously, and sometimes brutally retaliated against raids in the past. Recent victories have enhanced their capabilities to do so, by enabling them to inflict such blows deep within the Arab states themselves. Fear of Israeli retaliation would tend to inhibit occupants of the West Bank from giving support to infiltrators. Finally, a major guerrilla effort would probably be seen, by the UAR and Jordan at least, as damaging to the international support which the Arab cause needs. Given all these factors, we believe that Arab irregular activity will offer no real military threat to Israel over the next several months, and probably over the next several years, though a certain amount of harassment is probable.

415.   Memorandum From the President's Special Consultant
        (Bundy) to President Johnson[1]

Washington, August 11, 1967, 4 p.m.

SUBJECT

The Middle East on August 11

I have spent the enormous amount of time of one morning here catching up on the cables and memoranda and as I leave to take the family to Expo 67, I am impressed by how much better things go when I am out of town. Given the very difficult facts, I think your policy and its execution are in good shape.

Dean Rusk and Arthur Goldberg are coming in tomorrow to talk about our posture in the UN.[2] They do not expect a Security Council before September and their basic recommendation will be that we should stick with the formula that Arthur worked out and discussed with the Russians in full, slightly modified to include the idea of a UN mediator, which both the British and we think well of. My impression is that it is Arthur who wants this meeting with you and that his purpose is to make sure that you and he are in full agreement. The Israelis have never liked the particular formulation that emerged from Arthur's talks with the Russians and are still nervous about any Moscow–Washington accommodation. I think Arthur may be afraid that the Friends of Israel may try an end-run to the White House. My own belief is that his position is very fair and that he is the best possible man to explain it both to the Israelis and to their friends in the US. If his resolution were accepted in the Security Council it would be a major diplomatic victory for you and it would provide an umbrella over the detailed bargaining that would have to follow. I attach a copy of Arthur's current resolution so that you can check it for yourself. In essence, it provides for (1) withdrawal; (2) acknowledgment by all of the right to all to national life; (3) justice for the refugees; and (4) innocent maritime passage. These are four of your five principles and the fifth—moderation in the arms race—belongs in a separate category for purposes of UN negotiation. To give you a preview of what Arthur will tell you tomorrow, I attach a summary

---

[1] Source: Johnson Library, President's Daily Diary. Secret. The memorandum is marked to be sent through Walt Rostow, but Rostow did not initial it. A handwritten "L" on the memorandum indicates that the President saw it.

[2] No other record of this meeting has been found but according to the President's Daily Diary he met with Rusk, Goldberg, and McNamara for lunch on August 12. (Ibid.)

of his most recent talk to Evron.[3] You will see that he is our best lawyer on this subject.

The situation in the Middle East and among the major interested powers moves very slowly—if at all. Each party seems to be waiting for something to turn up, and none is yet taking the lead in serious negotiations. George Brown is jumpy about Suez but he has no solid scheme for getting it open. Nasser is making feelers and is perhaps a shade more reasonable, than in June, but he has such a long experience of seeking something for nothing that there is nothing of substance in his moves so far.

Our most complex problems, as usual, are with our friends the Israelis, but even these are not urgent. I have briefed Walt separately on the small but touchy issue of a visit by General Weizman and I assume he will discuss it with you this afternoon. In essence, the problem is that we simply cannot refuse to talk to the Israelis on these matters, and the fact is that I agreed in principle to a meeting (and even an August meeting) before the matter was first reported to you. So I think I had pretty good reasons for taking this course, but I will leave them to Walt to explain. Obviously, I can always be overruled, but quite aside from my own sentiments, I really don't think we would gain from such a decision. We have real things to strike bargains with the Israelis and the timing of one subordinate visit is not one of them. Those real issues are now being studied in State and Defense and they should be ready for your consideration toward the end of August. In essence, they all come down to one question: How much influence can we really have with the Israelis and how far do we want to use it? I find myself more and more cautious about the limits of what we can or should do, and I am quite sure we all need the time for reflection which the present stalemate gives us.

I will be back here early in the week of August 21, and of course can be reached by the White House operators in the time in between.

---

[3] A copy of telegram 19238 to Tel Aviv, August 11, is attached. It states that Goldberg, Rostow, Sisco, Battle, and others met August 10 with Evron to fill him in on the U.S.-UK talks and to discuss a possible future course in the United Nations on the basis of the tentative draft resolution. The record copy is in the National Archives and Records Administration, RG 59, Central Files 1967–69, POL 27 ARAB–ISR/UN.

Attachment

DRAFT RESOLUTION

The Security Council,

Having further considered the grave situation in the Middle East, bearing in mind the resolutions adopted and proposals considered at the 5th emergency session of the General Assembly and having taken note of the records of that session,

Considering that the crisis in the Middle East merits the attention of all member states and indeed requires the full participation of all members to achieve a just and lasting peace,

1. Declares that peace and final solutions to this problem can be achieved within the framework of the Charter of the United Nations;

2. Affirms the principle under the UN Charter of:

A. Without delay withdrawal by the parties to the conflict of their forces from territories occupied by them in keeping with the inadmissibility of the conquest of territory by war;

B. Without delay acknowledgment by all member states of the United Nations in the area that each enjoys the right to maintain an independent national state of its own and to live in peace and security, and renunciation of all claims and acts inconsistent therewith;

3. Determines to work directly with the parties and utilize a United Nations presence in order to achieve an appropriate and just solution of all aspects of the problem, in particular bringing to an end the long-deferred one of the refugees and guaranteeing freedom of transit through international waterways;

4. Requests accordingly that the Secretary General appoint a personal representative to assist him in seeking implementation of the present resolution in agreement with the parties concerned.

5. Decides to continue examining the situation in the Middle East with a sense of urgency and requests the Secretary General to keep the Security Council advised of the progress and results of the consultations by the Personal Representative with the states concerned.

416. Telegram From the Department of State to the Embassy in Israel[1]

Washington, August 12, 1967, 0051Z.

19842. Subj: Israeli Occupation. Ref: Jerusalem's A–3 of July 14 and A–5 of July 17.[2]

1. Department believes it useful to remind GOI authorities of interest with which world is following their actions as occupying power particularly where large concentrations of Palestinians involved. USG well aware from own extensive experience as occupying power that it is impossible to prevent all friction under conditions of military rule. Dept. also aware that GOI record on this score on balance quite good so far. Nevertheless this is subject requiring constant alertness, as occasional incidents show. Embassy should take early opportunity to approach Foreign Ministry and perhaps IDF contacts in low key citing recent examples of allegedly rough handling given local population by IDF. Examples should be specific but suitably sanitized to avoid compromising source, or indicating too clearly that they were reported by Jerusalem.

2. Destruction of villages near Latrun (Jerusalem's A–5) cannot forever be hidden from public knowledge, as witness mimeographed account put out by Israeli group and Alfred Friendly articles in *Washington Post*. It could be pointed out to Israelis that, whatever may have been IDF's reason for depopulating this area, act itself and manner in which it carried out likely to linger in memories of wide Arab audience much as do few cases of Israeli brutality and destruction of villages during war of 1948–49.

3. Department officers undertaking parallel low-key approaches here in hope the reminder will help prevent recurrence of such acts.

Rusk

---

[1] Source: National Archives and Records Administration, RG 59, Central Files 1967–69, POL 27 ARAB–ISR. Confidential. Drafted by Lambrakis on August 11; cleared by Atherton, Houghton, and Grey; and approved by Davies. Repeated to Jerusalem, Amman, Beirut, and London.

[2] Neither printed. (Ibid., POL 27–9 ARAB–ISR)

417.   Telegram From the Department of State to the Mission to the United Nations[1]

Washington, August 12, 1967, 2118Z.

20152. Re: 18566,[2] 19238.[3]

1. British Ambassador Dean informed Assistant Secretary Sisco that London agreed with draft res discussed here, subject following comments:

a) British believed in para 3 word "ensure" definitely preferable to "guarantee" because it was "stronger" and carried meaning of obligation. Urged we try this out at appropriate time on Israelis and Soviets. Should it prove non-negotiable further consideration would be required.

b) London support based on assumption that resolution also permitted partial settlement approach at some stage in event this proved best way to proceed. This reflects UK continuing concern over Suez.

2. After indicating we would consider British comments Sisco said he wished recall several points. First, draft not fully cleared in USG and discussions continuing here at high level. Second, we still were awaiting response from Soviets as to how further discussions on Middle East should be pursued. Informal contacts in New York between USUN and Russians yesterday gave us impression Soviets awaiting results of Arab summit and not interested in any early UN move. Third, we had prepared draft res as tentative working paper in order be ready for another UN round, but we did not anticipate this was likely before some time in September; much stock-taking remained. Fourth, we were awaiting Israeli reaction which likely to take some time.

3. Ambassador Dean again noted British interest in finding way to get at Suez, which we took to mean that if it proved impossible to proceed on basis draft res British may seek to revive idea of separate move on Canal. Dean again reiterated hope some UN action take place at least some time before opening GA; it clear UK continues feel sooner the better.

---

[1]   Source: National Archives and Records Administration, RG 59, Central Files 1967–69, POL 27 ARAB–ISR/UN. Secret; Exdis. Drafted by Sisco and Brown, cleared by David L. Gamon (NEA/ARN), and approved by Sisco. Repeated to London, Tel Aviv, and Moscow.

[2]   Telegram 18566 to London, August 10 (ibid., POL 27 ARAB–ISR), states that Goldberg that day gave British representatives the text of the draft resolution attached to Document 415 on a restricted and exploratory basis as the tentative U.S. idea for a possible next round in the Security Council and as a way to get at the Suez problem. He stressed that it was only a working paper not yet cleared in the U.S. Government.

[3]   See footnote 3, Document 415.

4. Ambassador Dean said Foreign Secretary Brown extremely pleased with results US-UK consultations and fact we finding ways to cooperate even though there may be differences of view between us on certain aspects of policy. Sisco agreed to convey this message to Secretary.

5. In conversation August 11 with Israeli Minister Evron Sisco got impression Israelis likely to react very negatively to move along lines we have in mind. Evron agreed we probably will face SC initiative in September and anticipatory preparations necessary and desirable. However, Israelis feel time on their side and no early move should be made in SC. Furthermore, if we must move in SC starting point in Israeli view should be US res previously submitted and containing five principles rather than draft based on US-USSR agreed language because they fear erosion if starting point is this language. On basis Evron's remarks Sisco believes Israelis likely suggest language changes to highlight objective of "agreed arrangements" and "direct negotiations," as well as to insist on specific mention of "belligerency."

6. Sisco asked Evron what he meant in his conversation other day with Battle that separate solution of Canal is possible on condition there no violation of rights of two parties stemming from cease-fire. Evron said he meant that provided the Canal was open to all vessels, including Israeli, and parties abided by arrangements made by Bull (which provide for neither side putting military ships on Canal), Israel would be willing consider separate arrangement regarding Suez. Sisco asked what would happen to Israeli troops? Evron said "Of course, they would remain right where they are along Canal, UAR troops would remain where they are, and Israel could not agree to disengagement or withdrawal of Israeli forces." Sisco said such proposal likely to be a non-starter.

Rusk

418.   Memorandum for the Record[1]

Washington, August 15, 1967.

SUBJECT

Discussion with Israeli Minister

Following up Mac Bundy's recent conversations with Israeli Minister Evron, I saw him today to tell him of Mr. Bundy's feeling that the USG should not release more than $3 million in arms aid for Israel at this time. I said we had discussed this in detail before reaching this decision, but that we did not feel we should re-open the question right now while the aid bill is on the floor of the Senate and will be uncertain until the House/Senate conference is over.

When I said I hoped his Government could live with this, he said, "Of course—if we have to." It is not a question of military urgency, but a political problem of undercutting those in Israel who argue that Israel cannot trust the U.S. and should go it alone. There are those who view our aid freeze as a harbinger of a confrontation over post-war settlement such as we had in 1956–57. Evron argues that a small additional release—such as those items on the Munitions Control List which Israel would normally buy through commercial channels—would do the trick. However, he said he wouldn't press us further but asked us to keep an open mind on the idea of making a small additional release as a good will gesture on our own, perhaps between the end of Senate debate and General Weizman's visit.[2]

His argument rests on two points:

(a) Crudely put, there are some in Israel who argue that if there is to be a U.S.-Israeli confrontation, the arms embargo is the issue to have it on. Their case is excellent given Soviet resupply of the Arabs, and Israel's friends could exert a good deal of pressure. They feel Evron should have turned down the $3 million in order to preserve this issue.

---

[1] Source: Johnson Library, National Security File, Files of Harold H. Saunders, Israel, 6/1/67–10/31/67. Secret; Nodis. The memorandum is filed with a covering memorandum of August 17 from Saunders to Battle stating that Bundy "did not want any papers to circulate on the arrangement he made with Evron on the $3 million release" but that Saunders thought Battle should "have the flavor of the attached and then throw this memo away."

[2] An August 9 memorandum from Saunders to Bundy summarizes a conversation between Saunders and Evron in which Evron "professed not to be reopening your gentlemen's agreement on the $3 million release" but indicated that he felt U.S. bureaucrats were interpreting the terms of the U.S. aid suspension too narrowly. Saunders advised Evron against reopening the issue with the President but agreed to pass on his request to Bundy. (Ibid., National Security File, NSC Special Committee Files, Suspense)

He does not want a confrontation on anything and is trying to take the wind out of their sails by offering proof that our hearts are in the right place.

(b) He believes that helping Israel would support—rather than endanger—the military aid bill. He feels that enough Senators support Israel's cause—not only because of the Jewish vote, but out of broad sympathy for the underdog—that we could argue from Israel's case outward to broaden understanding of our purpose in selling arms.

I told him it was the judgment of those responsible for getting the Administration's bill through Congress that now was not the time to rock the boat. While the friends of Israel may have usefully argued their case, we did not feel certain enough of our position to justify going further at this point. On the one hand, there are those in Congress who generally oppose arms supplies anywhere and who are particularly concerned when the U.S. ends up supplying arms to both parties in a war. On the other hand, some of these same people admittedly recognize the legitimacy of Israel's cause. Given the contradictory nature of the arguments and emotions involved, no one could guarantee which sentiment would dominate. Therefore we chose not to throw any new issues into the forum at this time. (Comment: Try as I did with my questions, I could not figure out how another $1 million would break the back of resentment over our military aid suspension.)

Turning to other issues, Evron voiced his Government's increasing disillusionment with King Hussein. He felt the King was trying to bring together an Arab summit meeting mainly to show us that the Arabs could not produce a solution and confront us with responsibility for finding one ourselves. He felt Jordan's recent efforts to stir up resistance on the West Bank fitted this picture of trying to build an eventual case for U.S. intervention to produce a pro-Jordanian settlement. I thought he over-stated the situation considerably and felt that while we did not fully understand Hussein's motives, it was quite reasonable to assume that Hussein would have to have some general Arab support before he came to terms with Israel. I did not feel, as Evron had argued, that Hussein was free to settle with Israel entirely by himself.

I expressed concern that Israel seemed to be digging into its present position more solidly every day. Each new headline painted a darker image. Without even arguing the merits of letting the dust settle, I saw a problem for both of us in the rapidly sharpening image of Israel as the intransigent victor holding onto its spoils. Evron said it was inevitable that Israel (and we) would have a hard time in the coming UNGA. I suggested that there are two ways of dealing with the inevitable. One is to sit on your hands and accept all its consequences; the other is to see whether you can't do something to face it with some dignity instead of just sticking your head in the sand and letting the brickbats fly.

At the end of our conversation he cited an interesting report from Israeli Ambassador Eytan in Paris. Eytan, on the basis of recent conversations with members of the French military who were party to some remarkably free remarks of De Gaulle, made on his recent sea voyage to Canada, reports that De Gaulle's position vis-à-vis Israel is based on two points: (a) At the heart of De Gaulle's American policy is the feeling that America's strength will lead to war. Therefore the U.S. must be weakened. Since Israel and the United States have grown closer, the U.S./Israeli alliance must be weakened in order to undermine the U.S. position in the Middle East. (b) De Gaulle is just plain annoyed with Israel for not having followed his advice in May and June. De Gaulle's idea then was that Israel should test Nasser's blockade by sending a ship of its own into the Gulf of Aqaba.

H.H.S.

---

419.   **Memorandum From Secretary of State Rusk and Secretary of Defense McNamara to President Johnson**[1]

Washington, August 15, 1967.

SUBJECT

Exceptions to the Military Supply Freeze to the Near East

Recommendation:

That you authorize us to obtain Congressional reactions to a relaxation of the current freeze on arms shipments to Israel and the moderate Arab States along the lines outlined below.[2]

Discussion:

Since the outset of hostilities last June we have maintained very tight restrictions on the shipment of military equipment to the Near East and North Africa. This policy was correct at its inception from both a military and political viewpoint. With the passage of time, however, it has become increasingly difficult to justify its rigidity in terms of our

---

[1] Source: National Archives and Records Administration, RG 59, Central Files 1967–69, DEF 19–8 US–NEAR E. Secret; Nodis.

[2] Neither the approve nor disapprove option was checked.

national interest in helping certain countries to meet their legitimate defense needs, and thus contain the spread of Soviet-Nasserite influence. The Soviets have conducted a large-scale rearmament of the radical states and have indicated clear intent to influence both Jordan and Morocco through offers of cheap and extensive arms supplies. This is in sharp contrast to our restraint in the supply of arms. As indicated below, we feel the time for some relaxation is at hand.

—With the exception of the $3.0 million cash sales authorized in early August, sales and deliveries to Israel have been blocked. The Israeli Government can be expected, as a minimum, to press for early release of their remaining requests for items on the Munitions Control List which were pending as of June 5. Since the value of this material is less than $1 million, we would like to be in a position, if Israeli pressures should mount, to authorize the remaining release this month. We would, however, continue for the time being to hold up the $14 million spare parts credit sales program and the 100 APCs authorized by you on May 23. We would contemplate discussing these, as well as subsequent Israeli arms requests, with General Weizman during his proposed visit next month.

—In the case of Jordan, there is a clear military and political requirement for an early resumption of limited arms supply. Jordan is the most vulnerable of the moderate Arab States in terms of internal security and pressure from radical Arab neighbors and is the key to a satisfactory Arab-Israeli political settlement. Failure to obtain some arms from the West would increase the dangers to Hussein's fragile regime and might force him into a supply relationship with the Soviets. This, in turn, could have serious consequences in the highly volatile situation in the area.

We have already told Jordan we intend to resume the suspended program as soon as the situation on the Hill permits, and that we expect to have definite word for them on or about September 1.[3]

—Our inability to proceed with the Arms Sales Program with Morocco agreed with King Hassan last February has been a contributing factor in his decision to purchase tanks from Czechoslovakia and, if continued, may lead him to turn to the Soviets.

—Small sales programs to Lebanon remain blocked even though the equipment involved would strengthen the ability of the Lebanese Armed Forces to carry out their important role in maintaining internal security.

---

[3] Telegram 20137 to Amman, August 12, transmitted the text of a talking paper on this subject prepared for Colonel Amos Jordan for use in August 12–13 talks in London with General Khammash. (National Archives and Records Administration, RG 59, Central Files 1967–69, DEF 12–5 JORDAN) Telegram 853 from Amman, August 14, reported that Burns had read the message to the King and had made every effort to reassure him of continued U.S. support for Jordan. (Ibid.)

—In the case of Libya, our agreement of last May to provide ten F–5s on a cash sales basis remains blocked, as does our ability to ship materials under the small existing grant and sales programs. Yet these are significant elements of our negotiating approach in respect to Wheelus.

—Comparable problems exist in respect to Saudi Arabia where the on-going air defense and transportation communication supply programs have been blocked. These are not only significant to the future security of Saudi Arabia and our relations with the Saudi Arabian Government but are also lucrative contracts totaling about $130 million which we would not wish to lose.

—Our offer to supply $5.2 million in training and material to Tunisia is the cornerstone of the Tunisian armed forces modernization program. President Bourguiba believes that he must possess a deterrent capability in view of the large-scale Soviet arms deliveries to Algeria.

We recognize the delicacy of the Congressional situation in respect to arms supply issues and would wish to consult carefully on the Hill before proceeding with any of these programs. These consultations would not begin until after the Senate and House vote on the Foreign Assistance Authorization Bill.[4] If Congressional reactions are deemed manageable, we would request your authorization to proceed promptly with the limited arms programs summarized above and in greater detail in the enclosed sheets.[5]

Dean Rusk[6]
Robert S. McNamara

---

[4] On August 15 the Senate passed S. 1872, including the Church amendment; see footnote 2, Document 398. The House version of the bill (H.R. 12048), reported out by the House Foreign Affairs Committee on August 11, did not include any equivalent of the Church amendment. It was passed by the House on August 25. The Senate–House Conference on the bill began September 14.

[5] The enclosures are attached but not printed. The recommendation was on the agenda for discussion at the President's August 22 luncheon meeting. (Johnson Library, National Security File, Files of Walt W. Rostow, Tuesday's Luncheon—Suggested Agenda) Unsigned, informal notes of that meeting include the following:

"Middle East Arms. No. Don't do a thing until after the conference.

"Keep Cabot Lodge working on the Hill. Get out there until you have got it organized. I want our position heard. Get our people to defend it. Get 15 key questions and get answers to them—the way Bunker answered three questions about the elections. Keep at it, organize it, and make sure it goes. Pres. said he is just not getting enough help from his Cabinet." (Ibid., Files of Walt W. Rostow, Meetings with the President, July–December 1967)

[6] Printed from a copy that indicates Rusk and McNamara signed the original.

420. Telegram From the Embassy in Israel to the Department of State[1]

Tel Aviv, August 16, 1967, 0945Z.

483. Ref: State's 19238[2] and 18566.[3]

1. Bitan (FonOff) at behest of Eshkol and Eban gave me August 15 substance of instructions which have gone to Evron to respond to remarks re U.S. thinking on further steps in UN as put to Evron in conversation August 10 with Amb. Goldberg, Under Secretary Rostow et al. I had given Bitan for Eshkol and Eban close paraphrase of State's 29238 [19238] reporting that conversation which I considered particularly clear and convincing exposition our views. It was my hope that in thus supplementing Evron's report strength and logic our position might be enhanced with GOI and helpful reply stimulated.

2. Unfortunately, GOI position not helpful. As anticipated, Israeli reaction is definitely negative.

3. Bitan expounded to me Israeli thinking, which, he said is largely reflected in Evron's instructions but, he added, Prime Minister and Eban wanted him to make doubly sure depth of their concern is understood.

4. As he put it, Israelis are prepared to discuss with us at this time, in UN context, principle but not tactics. If principles are agreed, tactics are relatively easy to devise as developments occur. They particularly feel necessity we keep each other informed and Bitan expressed some unhappiness that they had not been told at outset of exchanges with Tito. I protested that both Under Sec. Rostow and I had filled Israelis in on Tito as soon as possible. He did not pursue matter. Continuing, he said that as to principles the U.S. and Israeli positions coincide. Israel

---

[1] Source: National Archives and Records Administration, RG 59, Central Files 1967–69, POL 27 ARAB–ISR. Secret; Priority; Exdis. Repeated to London, Moscow, and USUN. Received at 1042Z. Saunders sent a retyped copy to the President with an August 18 memorandum noting that it was the Israeli answer to Goldberg's discussion of a possible UN resolution. He commented that a notion of impending confrontation was creeping into U.S.-Israeli conversations and added: "Some Israelis remember 1957 when we eventually put the heat on them to withdraw, and they see our military aid suspension as evidence that we may be preparing a similar move this time. The ugliness of the threat in paragraph 12 [paragraph 11 in the original telegram] suggests that they expect the worst." A handwritten note from Rostow on the memorandum recommended that the President read the full text of the telegram. A handwritten "L" on the memorandum indicates the President saw it. (Johnson Library, National Security File, Country File, Middle East Crisis)

[2] See footnote 3, Document 415.

[3] See footnote 2, Document 417.

agrees with the five principles set forth by the President on June 19. However, we seem to be deviating from those principles in our inter-pretation of them. As to withdrawal, President's statement refers to rec-ognized boundaries and Israel security. There no mention of recognized boundaries in draft resolution. In talking to Tito, we referred to possible consideration of international guarantees of Israel's security. No con-sideration should be given to such guarantees as it not in Israeli or U.S. interest to do so. International guarantees were in effect in May 1967 and were violated. To return to that situation is not to progress toward new situation of peace. Israel should be in position to take care of its own defense without UN presence or great power guarantees which would not be useful.

5. Bitan's next point was in regard to Soviets. He said Israelis dis-agree with our apparent assessment that they are prepared to act moder-ately. GOI sees no signs such moderation. They are skeptical that Soviet willingness to proceed with draft resolution agreed with U.S. at end General Assembly reflects any meeting of minds between USSR and U.S. positions. Israel regards Soviets as merely determined to erode U.S. prin-ciples in favor their pro-Arab attitude. GOI urges we not envisage start-ing any further UN consideration from this point but return to original U.S. draft of June 20[4] which conformed to President's five points.

6. Bitan then expatiated on Israeli estimate of more fundamental change he alleged is taking place in U.S. attitude. He referred to Tito's comment that Arabs would be humiliated by being forced to recognize Israel. It is basic to U.S. and Israel policy that Israel is recognized and recognition is accepted. It symptomatic of degree of slippage that has taken place in last 19 years that such acceptance should be questioned at this time. Israel insists that this situation change and is prepared to sit in its present positions for 10 years if necessary to accomplish this end. Recognition is the only choice to avoid another war.

7. Returning to "Goldberg draft resolution,"[5] Bitan said Israel is "asking, begging" that U.S. not start with this resolution but resubmit original U.S. resolution on June 20. Israel abstained on the LA resolution as a matter of tactics in the UN parliamentary situation as it then ex-isted. The LA resolution was a necessary evil and it was important to defeat the Yugo resolution. GOI now believes it should have voted against LA resolution.

8. Turning to specifics of current US-USSR draft, Bitan particularly referred to para two and the phrase relating to the "inadmissibility of conquest of territory by war, etc." He challenged this language. States

---

[4] See footnote 3, Document 332.
[5] See the attachment to Document 415.

aggressed against, like Israel, had in the past held territory conquered by war where it necessary to do so to defend themselves against further aggression. GOI considers it has right to hold such territory which was used as a base for attack on Israel until it is assured such aggression will not occur again. Also, President's statement as to "recognized boundaries" not included in language present resolution nor is there any reference to security against territory destruction and war which likewise part of June 19 declaration. Again Bitan referred to draft's mention of UN presence, a further difference from U.S. draft of June 20. Perpetuating UN in area, he said, is not perpetuating a bridge to Arabs but a wedge between Arabs and Israel. The PCC, he claimed, has shielded the Arabs from the necessity of agreeing to Israel's existence and has perpetuated Arab intransigence. In short, insofar as next steps in UN concerned, Bitan reiterated that if we must discuss tactics rather than principles we should stick to U.S. June 20 resolution. It is in U.S. as well as Israeli interest to do so. Soviets are talking to U.S. as result of GOI's victory. Soviets are in trouble in Egypt, Syria, and elsewhere. Hussein may also in time see it in his interest to talk to Israel.

9. Israel, Bitan summarized, is not in better military position than it has been before, is not asking for guarantees nor for massive armaments, only enough of latter to keep things as is, and will withdraw when it is convinced there will be no further aggression from the territories it occupies and not before.

10. Incidentally as to possible mediator, GOI considers it too early to consider at present. If at outcome of SC or GA, a mediator is appointed, he should be without terms of reference but merely with mandate to do what he can to bring parties together.

11. In conclusion, and with some diffidence, although nonetheless forthrightly, Bitan said he instructed to say on behalf Eshkol and Eban that in their view, if we persist along what they regard as our current line, we could be on collision course. They attempting current discussions with us to "persuade, not to argue," but if necessary, prepared to pull out all the stops available to them to prevent erosion of principles enunciated in President's five points and statement therein that solution on all five indivisible.

12. I remonstrated at this attitude, noting that outcome of Israeli collision with U.S. should not be very attractive to GOI but adding that, in any event, there no intention on U.S. part deviate from principles expressed by President regardless how GOI might interpret course our efforts implementation. I also said I hoped Israelis would not consider it in their interest, despite presently favorable situation they enjoy, to sit in Olympian grandeur and immobility in mountains of Jerusalem in expectation they could dictate settlement in Middle East without taking

into account interplay of interests other powers in world. No power, great or small, can operate in the complete isolation it might regard as optimum to its national concerns in the world today. Israel cannot expect to call tune on Middle East settlement as if its interests were only factor involved in area and problem could be sealed off from wider world influences.

Barbour

---

421. Telegram From the U.S. Interests Section of the Spanish Embassy in the United Arab Republic to the Department of State[1]

Cairo, August 17, 1967, 0901Z.

288. 1. What was to have been very brief call on Presidency Adviser Khouli August 16 turned into another ninety minute marathon covering a lot of ground. Will endeavor reproduce highlights in chronological order.

2. Khouli said my August 12 conversation with Mohamed Riad[2] had not been very "glamorous." It developed that GUAR had been hoping for some give in USG position on Middle East crisis, a hope precipitated perhaps by Tito visit. I then reviewed USG position.

3. Khouli then referred to US press and other indicators of USG hopes for overthrow Nasser regime. Perhaps this was USG desire. Perhaps this is why US was insisting on Israel right use Suez Canal. USG was welcome to try overthrow regime. It would be a gamble. Khouli did not think it would succeed, but he might be wrong. If US thought that successor to Nasser might make for more stable Egypt, it might be wrong. He continued: "People used to say that our power base was the army. If this were ever true, it is not true now. We have no army any more. Our army was defeated. No, our power base is the people."

---

[1] Source: National Archives and Records Administration, RG 59, Central Files 1967–69, POL 27 ARAB–ISR. Secret; Exdis. Received at 1451Z.

[2] Bergus reported his August 12 conversation with Mohamed Riad in telegram 248 from Cairo, August 14. (Ibid.)

4. Khouli then said, "Let's put aside technical questions of diplomatic relations and the like. Let's ask people think of the relations between the American people and the Egyptian people. We have a chance to write a new chapter." He then reiterated deeply felt conviction of all Egyptians that US could order Israel around. He accepted this might not be true but said conviction was political fact which had to be dealt with.

5. I said that wide UAR suspicions of US intentions towards UAR had beclouded our relations for well over a year. I reviewed concern high levels USG at these suspicions and sincere efforts we had made to overcome them. We simply had to face up to this problem. I had not asked to return to Egypt to mastermind a plot against the government. I had come precisely because I believed in the ties between the two countries, despite present difficulties. I said there were enough very open and very serious differences between our two countries. We did not need to invent more. I repeated previous arguments re USG lack control over Israel.

6. He said USG should not underestimate patriotism and resilience of Egyptian people. GUAR economy was in desperate shape. Middle classes who used to better things of life would suffer and they were complaining. But the majority of people who had always been poor anyway were not.

7. He said he now thought there would be an Arab summit. He felt Hussein's peregrinations would lead to this. If everyone came except Faisal then Faisal would be isolated. He said Faisal did not want UAR withdrawal from Yemen but UAR humiliation. "But enough of this Arab stuff," he said. "I'm not going to talk about the US and the Arab world. I'm talking about the US and Egypt. We think the Suez Canal issue is not an Israeli issue, but an American issue."

8. I recalled that USG had labored patiently for five long months in 1956–57 create rather shaky modus vivendi which had worked for ten years. During those ten years Israel had used Gulf Aqaba (with no harm whatsoever to UAR national interests) and had muted its Suez Canal claims. Who, I asked had upset these arrangements? Khouli did not deny responsibility. Said that if Muhyieddine visit to Washington had come off, latter would have offered "moratorium" on Aqaba issue and pullback of UAR troops from Sinai including Sharm Al-Shaykh.

9. I then said I too had respect for Egyptian people and thought some might be underestimating their pragmatism and practicality. I did not see how occasional appearance, in conditions of peace, of Israel flag at Suez would be spark setting off mass uprisings. Seemed to me that Egyptians, more than any other Arabs I knew, would be

relieved know that twenty year burden of Arab–Israel hostility, burden which in great part they had carried, was now off them and that Egypt could now turn its attention to better things. I recognized that Suez transit was not an easy issue for Egypt but it was up to us both continue our discussion in search of any conceivable glimmer of light. He agreed.

Bergus

---

422.   Special National Intelligence Estimate[1]

SNIE 36.1–67   Washington, August 17, 1967.

THE SITUATION AND PROSPECTS IN EGYPT

The Problem

To assess the situation in Egypt and the domestic and foreign factors affecting Egyptian policy, and to estimate probable developments over the next 6 to 12 months.

Conclusions

A. Shock waves from the UAR's humiliating defeat are still spreading, but no drastic political changes have occurred. The top command of the armed forces has been ousted, some senior commanders are reportedly on trial for treason, and there is discontent among many younger officers at their elders' incompetence. Nasser has, however, been confirmed in office and apparently still enjoys the support of his long time associates.

B. The war has placed additional strains on an already troubled economy. Food supplies are assured until early in 1968, but an adequate supply thereafter will require some expenditure of scarce foreign

---

[1] Source: Central Intelligence Agency Files, Job 79–R01012A, ODDI Registry of NIE and SNIE Files. Secret; Controlled Dissem. Submitted by the Director of Central Intelligence and concurred in by the U.S. Intelligence Board on August 17. The Central Intelligence Agency and the intelligence organizations of the Departments of State and Defense and National Security Agency participated in its preparation. The CIA, State, Defense, and NSA representatives on the USIB concurred; the AEC and FBI representatives abstained, because the subject was outside their jurisdiction. The title on the first page is "The Situation and Prospects in the UAR"; the title used is from the cover sheet.

exchange. The loss of foreign earnings will begin to have severe internal effects about the end of 1967. There is unemployment in the cities, and this will probably get worse. A stringent austerity program has been adopted entailing higher taxes, stricter rationing, and reduced availability of consumers goods; pressures for relaxation of these controls could lead to some inflation. Such circumstances are likely to cause some discontent in the cities, but are unlikely to erupt into unmanageable problems of public order.

C. Most Egyptians are probably not ready to envisage the UAR without Nasser. Yet economic and political stresses, as well as the difficulties of making progress on a resolution of the Israeli problem, may erode Nasser's popular appeal and perhaps encourage the growth of opposition, or even weaken the prospects of his remaining in office. All things considered, however, we believe the chances are better than even that he will remain the dominant influence in the regime for at least the period of this estimate.

D. The UAR is more than ever dependent on the USSR for military and economic aid and for political support. This gives Moscow a substantial degree of influence, which is partially offset by Egyptian suspicion of foreign advice and a certain resentment of Soviet attitudes. There are increased numbers of Soviet military advisors, though we do not know how far their functions go beyond the technical level. In its political organization, the UAR may develop a sort of regimentation resembling Soviet and East European models. In part at Moscow's urging, Cairo seems to be following a relatively moderate policy toward Israel.

E. Nasser probably believes that the closure of the Canal acts as a lever on the big powers to force Israel to make concessions. Accordingly, the present confrontation along the Canal is likely to persist—perhaps beyond the period of this estimate—despite the economic loss to Egypt and pressures for resolution from both Communist and non-Communist countries.

F. In essence, the Egyptians are attempting to regain a degree of flexibility in their foreign policy. They must, in the interest of security, demand and accept Soviet military resupply, but in so doing they will seek to avoid Soviet domination. Nasser is attempting to restore his position in the Arab world, while keeping open the option of making some concessions to Israel. In his dealings with the US, he will remain distrustful and to some degree inhibited by his dependence on the USSR; yet he will not foreclose some improvement in American-UAR relations. Because of these conflicting objectives and the narrowness of the available options, it will probably be some time before he feels able to undertake any very firm policy initiatives.

Discussion

I. Introduction

1. The shock waves from Egypt's defeat are still spreading, and the country's prospects, both domestic and foreign, are clouded by a number of uncertainties. Many of these uncertainties are inherent in the situation itself; a number of difficult dilemmas have still to be resolved, and longstanding relationships within the regime have almost certainly been strained and unsettled by the traumatic experiences of this summer. Additional uncertainties arise from the fact that the policies of foreign powers—especially the USSR—will inevitably affect Egypt's outlook, and these external factors are still far from clarified. Finally, some uncertainties arise from the paucity of our information concerning the state of affairs in the UAR.

2. In the weeks immediately prior to the fighting, Nasser was riding high in the Middle East. The efforts of the US and other Western Powers to lift the blockade of Eilat had gotten nowhere. Other Arab states were rallying to the UAR's side. Jordan had signed a defense pact; Kuwait had sent troops to Egypt; an Iraqi force was on the way to Jordan. There was mass enthusiasm within Egypt for the confrontation with Israel. Then, within four days, the Egyptian air force was destroyed, the Egyptian army shattered and routed, and the entire Sinai Peninsula in Israeli hands. Today, the Israelis sit on the east bank of the Suez Canal and have a voice in deciding its future.

3. Despite the profound humiliation and shock of defeat, the war has apparently brought no drastic political changes within Egypt. Nasser has been confirmed in office and apparently continues to rely on the same group of senior officials, including two close collaborators of many years standing, Zakariya Muhi al-Din and Ali Sabri. No new blood has been introduced, nor has Nasser recalled any of the half dozen former members of the revolutionary command council who had been edged out of the inner circle in the past decade. Only one of Nasser's inner circle of advisors, Field Marshal Abd al-Hakim Amir, formerly chief of the armed forces and the senior Vice President, has resigned.

4. Beyond this, our information on the political situation in the UAR is very limited. We do not know whether senior officials have a controlling influence on Nasser's major decisions or circumscribe his authority. Nor do we know in any detail the thrust of their advice. In a general way, Sabri is more doctrinaire and more disposed to work with the USSR, while Muhi al-Din is more comfortable dealing with Westerners and Western concepts. Nonetheless, both of them support Nasser's Arab socialism at home and his foreign policies of anti-impe-

rialism and Arab nationalism, though they differ in their opinion as to how far and how fast socialization should go, and the extent to which compromise with socialist doctrine and "anti-imperialism" is required by economic and political realities. Both have over the years displayed consistent loyalty to Nasser and neither has shown signs of aspiring to displace him. In the postwar government, Muhi al-Din and others like him have a more prominent role.

5. In the military establishment, the changes have been more far-reaching. Not only has Abd al-Hakim Amir departed, but the War Minister and most of the top command of the armed forces have been ousted. The air force chiefs and a number of other high-ranking officers are reported to be on trial for treason, and several hundred officers further down in the military establishment may have been retired. There is severe criticism of those officers with upper and middle class backgrounds for spending more time feathering their own nests than attending to their military duties. Many of the officers who came into the military establishment during the 15 years of the Nasser regime are reported to be unhappy with the wartime performance of their elders. The morale of the armed forces has been impaired, and discipline may be more difficult to maintain.

[Omitted here are Sections II–IV on the economic situation, the domestic outlook, and foreign policy.]

---

423.   Telegram From the Department of State to the Embassy in Israel[1]

Washington, August 19, 1967, 0108Z.

23795. Subject: US-Israeli Talks on Proposed ME Resolution.

1. Goldberg, Rostow, Battle and Popper had long talk late August 17 with Israeli Chargé Evron, Israeli UN Ambassador Rafael and Cahana of Israeli UN Mission to continue talks begun Aug. 10 on tentative US-UK draft resolution.

---

[1] Source: National Archives and Records Administration, RG 59, Central Files 1967–69, POL 27 ARAB–ISR/UN. Secret; Immediate; Exdis. Drafted by Popper, cleared by Battle, and approved by Eugene Rostow. Also sent Immediate to London, Moscow, and USUN.

2. Tone was much milder than in Barbour Tel Aviv report on the Israeli instructions (Tel Aviv 483).[2] Essentially Israeli position was that we must not compromise on principles contained in President's June 19 speech; that Russians had been seriously weakened by Middle East developments; that basic Israeli posture was and should be to sit tight on present positions until the Arabs would directly negotiate with them a general settlement which would give both sides peace and security; and that latest Soviet-American and US-UK draft resolutions seemed to Israelis to depart from President's principles and thus to open way to third party activity which would weaken the Israeli position.

3. Goldberg and Rostow warned against underestimating Soviet potentialities for consolidating their influence in Arab world at expense of Israel; denied new draft resolution departed from our principles; refused to accept view that direct Arab-Israel negotiation was the only road to peace; and emphasized the need for close and candid Israeli-US consultation in handling tactical problems at the UN.

4. It was agreed to continue discussion, focusing on specific terminology, during week beginning August 28. Full report follows septel.[3]

Rusk

---

[2] Document 420. Barbour commented in telegram 526 from Tel Aviv, August 21, that the tone of the conversation in Washington was milder but that the substance was largely identical. He noted that Bitan had talked to him "from extensive notes which he said closely reflected Eshkol and Eban's comments." (National Archives and Records Administration, RG 59, Central Files 1967–69, POL 27 ARAB–ISR)

[3] Telegram 23821 to Tel Aviv, August 19, states that Goldberg began the discussion by stating that Barbour's report of his conversation with Bitan indicated Israeli misconceptions concerning their discussions. U.S. thoughts concerning tactics in the United Nations had been put forward only to the British and the Israelis. The terms used in the Israeli response were "not appropriate and hardly acceptable. We were seeking a decent peace settlement, probing for ways to reach it, and we expected frank and sympathetic response from them." He stated that the President's statement of June 19 remained the basis of U.S. policy, and U.S. relations with Israel would continue to be based on full and frank consultation. When Rafael stated that the Israeli assessment was that it was best to sit tight and do nothing in the United Nations, Rostow "disagreed profoundly", stating that the best way to a settlement was to use the draft resolution as a means of facilitating agreement, otherwise "we would be faced with greater pressures to accept less palatable solutions." (Ibid., POL 27 ARAB–ISR/UN)

424.   Draft Memorandum From the Assistant Secretary of State for Near Eastern and South Asian Affairs (Battle) to the Under Secretary of State (Katzenbach)[1]

Washington, August 18, 1967.

SUBJECT

> The *"Liberty"*—Handling of Israeli Inquiry
> Report and Release of Diplomatic Correspondence

On August 15, 1967, Israeli Minister Evron handed Under Secretary Rostow a copy of the report of the Judge who presided over the Israeli military inquiry into the attack on the *Liberty.* (Tab A.)[2] Minster Evron in delivering the report requested that it be treated on a restricted and confidential basis. He did indicate that "we could, if we wished, show it to interested members of Congress and others".

We have considered the practical aspects of dealing with the Israeli report. Several factors are involved, including the fact that the Israelis made the report available through several channels. (DOD received it via the Defense Attaché in Tel Aviv.) It seems unrealistic to assume that the report or elements thereof will not begin to leak at some stage.

Further, the deep interest of the families of U.S. personnel killed or injured in the incident has been reflected in the keen Congressional questioning we have been exposed to on the hill as well as in Congressional letters received requesting information. We must anticipate that once there is an intimation that the Israeli report had been received in the Executive Branch it will be exceedingly difficult to withhold it from members of Congress.

A related problem has existed with reference to the diplomatic notes exchanged with the Government of Israel concerning the *Liberty*

---

[1] Source: Washington National Records Center, OSD Files: FRC 330 72 A 2468, Middle East, 385.3. Confidential. Drafted by Wehmeyer; cleared by Macomber, Deputy Legal Adviser Murray J. Belman, Assistant Secretary for Public Affairs Dixon Donnelley, and Eugene Rostow. The draft, which is a copy sent to the Department of Defense for clearance, is filed with an August 22 letter from Nitze to Representative George H. Mahon of Texas, sending him on a confidential basis a copy of the report of the judge who presided over the preliminary Israeli inquiry into the attack on the *Liberty.* Also attached are a note to Nitze stating that Defense clearance on Battle's memorandum was requested, an August 21 memorandum from Nitze's military assistant, Commander C.A.H. Trost, USN, to Warnke saying that Nitze had no objection to the proposal but wanted Warnke to look at it, and an August 21 memorandum from Warnke to Nitze questioning recommendation (6) but otherwise approving the proposal. A handwritten comment by Hoopes on Warnke's memorandum suggested deleting recommendation (7) but otherwise concurred.

[2] The tabs are ibid. A copy of the decision of the examining judge in the Israeli Defense Forces preliminary inquiry, issued July 21, is attached to an August 15 memorandum from Rostow to Walsh that states Evon had given it to him the previous day.

(Tab B). As you know, we have been under considerable pressure to make available the text of the U.S. note to confirm our oral assurances that the Department was diligent in pursuing the matter with the Israeli Government. On July 28, Bill Macomber sent Chairman Fulbright a classified report on the incident (Tab C), which included a brief narrative description of the notes exchanged between the two Governments.

It seems likely that the decision will be considered a "whitewash" by the press, public, and Congressional officials.[3]

While there are numerous details which invite comment, the following appear to be those most likely to receive critical attention:

(1) The *Liberty* was seen and reported at approximately 0600 hours by an Israeli patrol aircraft with a naval observer abroad, reportedly 70 miles westward of Tel Aviv. At 10:55 "the Naval Liaison Officer at Air Force HQ reported to Navy HQ that the ship about which he had reported earlier in the morning was an electromagnetic audio-surveillance ship of the U.S. Navy, named *Liberty,* whose marking was GTR–5." (Report, para. 11.)

(2) The *Liberty* was displayed on the "Combat Information Centre Table" at Navy HQ for a time, first as an unidentified target (red), later as "a neutral ship" (green). At about 1100 hours (i.e. shortly after it had been identified and presumably marked in green), the Acting Chief of Naval Operations "ordered its erasure from the table, since he had no information as to its location at the time of the report." (Report, para. 12.)

(3) The report emphasizes that the attack on the *Liberty* was pressed in response to reports from the Southern Command in the Sinai that between 1100 and 1200 hours El-Arish "was being shelled from the sea." "Reports about the shelling continued to reach G.H.Q./ Operations, and pressure was exerted on the Naval representative, on the lines that 'the coast has been shelled for hours, and you—the Navy—are not reacting.'" (Report, para. 5.)

No explanation is offered as to why neither the Navy nor the Air Force were able to assure the Southern Command on the basis of the air reconnaissance which had been going on in the area since 0410 hours, that no military vessels capable of carrying out a significant "shelling from the sea" had entered the area. In short, both the Air Force and Navy reacted to the reports of shelling as if they had no information regarding potential enemy targets just off the coast in the El Arish area.

---

[3] Assistant Secretary Hughes sent a copy of the decision to NSA Director Carter on August 22. In a handwritten note of August 26, NSA Deputy Director Louis W. Tordella commented, "A nice whitewash for a group of ignorant, stupid and inept xxx." (National Security Agency, Center for Cryptologic History Historical Collection, Series VII, Crisis Files, Box 16)

(4) Efforts to "identify" the *Liberty* immediately prior to attack by Israeli aircraft and torpedo boats were apparently cursory at best.

(a) *Aircraft.* "According to their statements [the crew's],[4] they were looking for a flag, but found none; likewise no other identification mark was observed." "On the assumption that they were facing an enemy target, an order was given to the aircraft to attack." (Report, para. 7.)

The report elsewhere indicates that the torpedo boat commander apparently reported that "the target . . . was moving at a speed of 28 knots" (Report, para. 6), "towards Port Said" (Report, para. 23).

(b) It is clear therefore that even in the eyes of the Israeli military forces the vessel was not considered in a menacing posture immediately prior to the attack. "During the last run, a low-flying aircraft observed the marking 'GTR–5' on the hull of the ship." This was apparently about 1400 hours. No explanation is offered as to why this observation was possible after the attack when the *Liberty* was afire and smoking but not visible at the time of the pre-attack identification runs over the ship.

(c) *Torpedo boats.* Upon receipt of the information about the markings, so observed by the pilot, an order was transmitted to the torpedo boat division not to attack the ship, "since its identification might not be correct." (Report, para. 8) The Division Commander was ordered to approach the ship in order to establish visual contact and to identify it but the effort was apparently confined to exchanges of signals which the Israeli commander considered unsatisfactory. "Meanwhile the Division Commander . . . came to the conclusion that he was confronting an Egyptian supply ship by the name of *El-Kasir.*" At 1436, the Division Commander authorized the Division to attack with torpedoes "only at a later stage, when one of the torpedo boats approached the ship from the other side were the markings GTR–5 noticed on the hull . . . ." (Report, para. 8.)

The Israeli Judge construed his task as a narrow, technical function, specifically "to decide whether any offense has been committed by any military personnel involved in this incident." (Report, para. 16.) He concluded that "there is no sufficient amount of prima facie evidence, justifying committing anyone for trial." (Report, para. 26.)

At such time as the report becomes public, Congress, the press and the public will want to know what we have said to the Israeli Government after receiving the report. We believe that the report warrants a strong reiteration of the position originally set forth in our note of June 10 and an indication that whatever limitations the Judge may have considered he was under from the standpoint of Israeli military regulations, the report clearly reflects a failure on the part of the Israeli

---

[4] Brackets in the source text.

military establishment to exercise normal precautions before launching an attack. We cannot, therefore, accept the report as exonerating the Israeli Government from our expectation that Israel will take the disciplinary measures which international law requires in the event of wrongful conduct by the military personnel of a state. Neither had the U.S. received any assurance that Israel has issued instructions to ensure that U.S. personnel will not again be endangered by the wrongful actions of Israeli military personnel.

Recommendation:

That you call in Minister Evron and inform him

1) We have reviewed the report and consider that it confirms that the negligence on the part of the Israeli military establishment was even greater than we were aware at the time of our June 10 note;

2) The United States accordingly reiterates the position expressed in the June 10 note that the attack must be condemned as an act of military irresponsibility reflecting reckless disregard for human life;

3) The United States cannot accept the report as exonerating the Israeli Government from taking the disciplinary measures which international law requires in the event of wrongful conduct by the military personnel of a state. The entire incident cannot be construed in any light other than as one involving such wrongful conduct;

4) The United States further expects to receive some specific assurance that the Government of Israel has issued instructions necessary to ensure that United States personnel will not again be endangered by the wrongful actions of Israeli military personnel;

5) The USG is now actively engaged in the process of obtaining information necessary to determine the amount of compensation which it will claim for the personal injury and death [and] damage to property suffered in this regrettable incident, and it intends to inform the GOI of the amount of compensation claimed as soon as the amount has been determined;[5]

---

[5] On May 27, 1968, the Israeli Government paid $3,323,500, the amount of compensation claimed by the U.S. Government on behalf of the families of the 34 men killed in the attack on the *Liberty.* (Department of State *Bulletin,* June 17, 1968, p. 799) On April 28, 1969, the Israeli Government paid $3,566,457, representing payment in full of 164 claims totaling $3,452,275 on behalf of members of the crew of the *Liberty* who were injured in the attack, and claims for expenses incurred by the U.S. Government in providing medical treatment for the injured and in reimbursing crew members for personal property lost or damaged in the attack. (Ibid., June 2, 1969, p. 473) Documentation on the negotiations concerning these claims is in the National Archives and Records Administration, RG 59, Central Files 1967–69, PS 8–4 US–ISR. On December 17, 1980, the Department of State announced that the U.S. Government had accepted an Israeli proposal to pay $6 million as final settlement of the U.S. claim for compensation for damage to the *Liberty.* (Department of State *Bulletin,* February 1981, p. 55)

6) We believe there is a real possibility that the report or portions thereof will leak out either here or in Israel and that in any event it will be exceedingly difficult to withhold the report in the event of Congressional requests which are likely;

7) We believe the Government of Israel should give urgent consideration to whether it would not be beneficial from its standpoint to take the initiative in releasing the document at an early date;

8) We feel obliged to release the exchange of correspondence between the two Governments concerning the incident, which we plan to accomplish in a routine, low-key manner.[6]

---

[6] The draft memorandum does not indicate whether the document was approved or disapproved, but see Document 433.

---

425.   Telegram From the Embassy in Israel to the Department of State[1]

Tel Aviv, August 21, 1967, 0900Z.

524. Ref: State 23385.[2]

1. We share Dept's concern at recent spate statements by Israeli political leaders indicating hardening of positions in [garble] permanently expanded Israel. (See also our A–109 and A–113.)[3] If Arabs continue unready to talk peace and Israeli political scene continues as hotly competitive as it has been—at this juncture both contingencies seem likely—then Israeli opinion, stimulated by politicians staking out ever more advanced frontiers in the occupied territories, must perforce be increasingly conditioned to accept [as] permanent many aspects of the present territorial situation.

---

[1] Source: National Archives and Records Administration, RG 59, Central Files 1967–69, POL 27 ARAB–ISR. Confidential. Repeated to Amman, Beirut, Jerusalem, London, and USUN.

[2] Telegram 23385 to Tel Aviv, August 18, states that the Department had noted with increasing concern recent statements by Israeli public figures about long-term Israeli policy on the West Bank and other occupied areas and was concerned that they might indicate increasing Israeli determination to occupy permanently the territories currently under military occupation. (Ibid.)

[3] Airgram A–109 from Tel Aviv, August 15, reported a discussion with several Knesset members concerning the occupied territories and refugees. (Ibid., POL 28 ARAB) A–113 from Tel Aviv, August 16, reported a talk by Minister of Labor Yigal Allon concerning the West Bank and refugees. (Ibid., POL 1 ISR)

2. It should be emphasized however that matters have not come to this bleak point yet. Eban told a press conference August 14 (our 479)[4] by way of disassociating the GOI from Dayan's territorial claims that the GOI had no "public view on territorial specifics of problem." We continue believe that in spite of what Dayan, Allon and others say GOI if it could make peace now with one or more of its neighbors, achieving its security desiderata, would be willing to restore substantial Arab territory it now holds (Jerusalem and probably Gaza Strip being most important exceptions).

3. I doubt whether any formal approach to GOI at this time would be productive. It would probably draw simple retort that such statements do not reflect GOI policy and GOI cannot limit freedom speech. My staff and I have left no doubt in minds our Israeli interlocutors our view permanent Israeli possession of occupied territories would foreclose indefinitely any chances of Arab-Israel peace.

4. Low key Dept. approach to Israeli Embassy in similar vein pegged to recent statements would I think be helpful in indicating we do not discount these statements as empty political rhetoric but recognize they could eventually have undesirable consequences.

Barbour

---

[4] Telegram 479 from Tel Aviv, August 15. (Ibid., POL 15–1 ISR)

---

426. Circular Telegram From the Department of State to Certain Posts[1]

Washington, August 24, 1967, 0132Z.

26123. 1. Following message should be conveyed to your Foreign Minister before his departure for Khartoum.[2] At your discretion you may leave with him aide-mémoire embodying these points.

---

[1] Source: National Archives and Records Administration, RG 59, Central Files 1967–69, POL 7 SUDAN. Confidential; Priority. Drafted by Eugene Rostow, Sterner, Davies, and James E. Akins of the Office of Fuels and Energy and approved by Eugene Rostow. Sent to Amman, Beirut, Jidda, and Kuwait and repeated to Cairo, USUN, London, Paris, Tel Aviv, and Jerusalem.

[2] Foreign Ministers of 13 Arab states met in Khartoum August 27–28 in preparation for a summit conference of the leaders of those states in Khartoum August 29–September 1.

2. We have welcomed opportunities to exchange thoughts with you on how to bring about a just and durable peace in the Near East. The views as conveyed by our ambassadors have contributed greatly to the evolution of our own thinking. As Secretary Rusk's letter to you last month[3] made clear, the United States is willing to support any reasonable proposal that will lead to a peaceful solution consistent with the five general principles set forth by President Johnson in his statement of June 19.

3. We believe there has been an improvement in the general atmosphere insofar as a disposition is concerned to work realistically toward a resolution of the crisis. Your statesmanship at the last Khartoum Conference, and at subsequent meetings, has helped materially to bring about this change in atmosphere. We fully appreciate the difficulties of maintaining a moderate and responsible course in present circumstances. For this reason, it has been encouraging to see a greater willingness on the part of the moderate Arab states to assert leadership in Arab councils. If this momentum can be maintained at the forthcoming Foreign Ministers' and Chiefs of State conferences at Khartoum, I feel sure the road to peace will be appreciably shortened.

4. We have as yet had no report of his conversations.[4]

5. In our view the coming meetings at Khartoum will be critical in determining whether movement toward a settlement can be achieved. As time goes by it will become more difficult to bring about those changes that will be necessary to reach a mutual accommodation. If matters are allowed merely to drift, they might well drift toward a consolidation of the present unsatisfactory and insecure status quo. I know your government does not see this to be in its interests.

6. We do not underestimate the difficulties of finding a way out of the present impasse, but we do believe there are a number of ways, fully ensuring Arab rights and interests, in which the movement toward peace could be started. One step could be for all the states of the area to accept positions expressed in the Draft Resolution upon which the

---

[3] Document 397.

[4] The majority of paragraph 4 was crossed out on the telegram. Circular telegram 26320, August 24, transmitted a revised paragraph 4 that reads: "Shortly before President Tito left on his recent trip to several Arab states we took the opportunity to have a full exchange of views with him on Near East problems. President Tito informed us of his view that the political settlement of the crisis must be fair to the Arab States. He also told us that he believed the General Assembly proved that most countries of the world now agreed that Israel's right to exist had to be accepted. We told him that we agreed entirely with both of these views. We stressed that in approaching the problem of a settlement, the United States would take fully and sympathetically into account the rights and interests of the Arab States, as well as those of Israel and of other nations with interests in the Near East and North Africa. We have as yet had no report of his conversations." (National Archives and Records Administration, RG 59, Central Files 1967–69, POL 7 SUDAN)

United States and the Soviet Union reached agreement during the final days of the General Assembly. Another might be for the Arab states to assert, on their own initiative, a policy of non-belligerence and acceptance of agreed international boundaries in the area. I am impressed by the reasoning of some Arab statesmen that an end of belligerence would in no way mean a surrender of Arab principles.

7. Two concepts all too prevalent in Arab thinking should be corrected. The first is that the United States can determine Israeli actions or the actions of any other Near Eastern state. The second is that oil can be cut off without permanent damage to the Arab states. While there can be no denying that the consuming state would be hurt by a total boycott, there are alternate sources which would be developed rapidly if necessary, and once the Arab countries decided to resume production the consumers would continue looking to their new sources as more reliable and more secure. As for the Suez Canal, the new supertankers now under construction can transport oil from the Persian Gulf to Europe via the Cape for considerably less than Suez tolls.

8. As you know, the United States has been reluctant to advance specific formulas concerning a settlement to the present crisis believing that these will be most effective if they stem from the states directly concerned. That is why we are hopeful that at the Khartoum meetings the full range of possibilities can be explored in a constructive atmosphere. We are confident a start can be made if a sufficient number of states determine not to be deterred from this purpose. It may be a long time before all the issues which lie at the heart of the Arab-Israel problem can be fully and justly resolved. In the meantime there is no reason for the Arab states to place unnatural obstacles in the path of their own progress and growth. The vital tasks of social and political development, the exploration for mutually advantageous cooperative arrangements among the Arab states, and above all economic development must proceed. None of these tasks can be effectively pursued under the present unstable conditions in which even Arab states far from Israel's borders are exposed to the constant danger of being drawn into crises over which they have little control. It is obvious, we believe, that the creation of peaceful and stable conditions is very much in the interest of the Arab states themselves.

9. We value greatly our continuing exchange of views on these all-important matters. We hope it will be possible to meet with you at an early date after your return as we will be most interested in your views on the results of the Khartoum meetings. (*End of Message*.)[5]

---

[5] Telegram 26856 to Tunis, Tripoli, and Rabat, August 25, transmitted identical messages to the Tunisian, Libyan, and Moroccan Foreign Ministers. (Ibid.)

10. In delivering the above message, please stress that our purpose is to exchange views and if possible to concert our diplomatic influence in the days and weeks ahead. Follow up the first talks as far as you can with respect to the themes in the letter, and in other recent policy telegrams. We should like to elicit the views of the government to which you are accredited on the Soviet-American resolution. From here, that document seems the simplest and most promising starting point, both in the area (Suez Canal) and in the United Nations.

Rusk

---

427.   Memorandum From the Joint Chiefs of Staff to Secretary of Defense McNamara[1]

JCSM 474–67   Washington, August 25, 1967.

SUBJECT

Analysis of Israel's Military Capability (U)

1. (S) Reference is made to a memorandum by the Deputy Secretary of Defense, dated 29 July 1967, subject as above,[2] which requested the views of the Joint Chiefs of Staff on the following two points:

a. Whether Israel can defend itself in the near future against both the conventional and guerrilla threats it faces with its present military equipment; and
b. If additional equipment is necessary, the types and amounts of such further equipment.

2. (S) By JCSM–55–67, dated 2 February 1967, subject: "Military Equipment for Israel (U),"[3] the Joint Chiefs of Staff reported their assessment that Israeli military forces were capable of defending themselves against any individual or collective Arab attack. As reported in SNIEs 11–13–67[4] and 30–3–67,[5] the Arabs suffered heavy losses in per-

---

[1] Source: Washington National Records Center, OSD Files: FRC 330 72 A 2468, Israel, 400. Secret.
[2] See footnote 3, Document 387.
[3] For text, see *Foreign Relations, 1964–1968*, vol. XVIII, Document 387.
[4] See footnote 4, Document 414.
[5] Document 414.

sonnel and equipment during the recent Arab-Israeli conflict. The Soviets have already replaced much of the equipment and may replace most of the equipment losses within the next year. The Arab capability for reorganization and training of personnel is difficult to predict, but a minimum of 18 months probably would be required to restore the defeated Arab ground forces to a fighting force capable of conducting a campaign against Israel.

3. (S) The possibility exists that the United Arab Republic and/or Syria, with support from Iraq and Algeria, might launch a surprise air or ground attack on Israel. However, it is doubtful that a preemptive air strike by Arab forces would be successful. The Israelis have an excellent intelligence organization and would be likely to detect Arab plans for preemption and strike first or at least retaliate quickly and effectively. Additionally, Israeli aircraft are well camouflaged and dispersed in revetments.

4. (S) Though there have been public statements by Arab leaders suggesting guerrilla-type actions against Israel, it is doubted that the Arabs are capable of planning, organizing, and executing an effective guerrilla campaign against Israel. The present lines dividing the Arab countries from Israel are much easier to defend than the prehostility boundaries, and Israel is fully capable of countering and coping with any guerrilla effort which might be mounted by the Arabs.

5. (S) In consideration of the foregoing, the Joint Chiefs of Staff conclude that Israel has the military capability to defend itself in the near future against both conventional and guerrilla threats with its present military equipment and that additional equipment is not needed for this purpose.

6. (U) Additional information on current Arab-Israeli capabilities and pre/posthostilities personnel and equipment inventories is contained in Appendices A and B hereto.[6]

For the Joint Chiefs of Staff:

Harold K. Johnson
Acting Chairman
Joint Chiefs of Staff

---

[6] Appendix A, "Discussion," and Appendix B, "Selected Armaments and Forces, Middle East Countries," both undated, are attached but not printed.

428.   Telegram From the Department of State to the Embassy in
        Jordan[1]

Washington, August 26, 1967, 0153Z.

27525. Subj: Middle East—US-USSR Resolution. Ref: State 26123.[2]

1. With respect to reftel, some further clarification is desirable re
discussions with Arabs of US-USSR draft resolution (para 10 reftel).
Such discussions should not be in terms specific wording of res. We
would prefer that there not be widespread discussion of such details at
this time. Rather we had in mind obtaining clearer indication of Arab
attitude toward a resolution embodying general concept of US-USSR
draft and seeking encourage Arab acceptance such approach.

2. One problem in attempting discuss US-USSR text with other
govts, particularly Arabs, is fact we not certain which text or texts Sovs
gave Arabs, or whether they gave Arabs partial or full text. Essence of
US-USSR res explained by Goldberg in July 27 speech reported Deptel
14091.[3]

3. Agreed res included para which, in speaking of solution all
aspects Middle East problem, specifically referred to "guaranteeing
freedom of transit through international waterways." In discussions
with Soviets Goldberg made clear this essential part of res, but here
again we do not know whether Sovs showed this para to Arabs. We also
made clear our agreement on draft res was based on our understanding
that it to be interpreted to mean: 1) Israeli withdrawal had to be based
on end to all claims of rights of belligerency, which includes inter alia
rights of passage in both Strait of Tiran/Gulf of Aqaba and Suez Canal,
and 2) withdrawal to state of peace necessarily implies agreement on
boundaries.

Rusk

---

[1] Source: National Archives and Records Administration, RG 59, Central Files
1967–69, POL 7 SUDAN. Secret; Priority; NATUS; Limdis. Drafted by Betty-Jane Jones in
the Office of United Nations Political Affairs on August 25, cleared by Popper and Davies,
and approved by Eugene Rostow. Also sent Priority to Beirut, Jidda, and Kuwait and
repeated to Cairo, USUN, London, Paris, Tel Aviv, and Jerusalem.

[2] Document 426.

[3] For text of Goldberg's speech before the International Platform Association at
Washington, D.C., on July 27, see Department of State *Bulletin*, August 28, 1967, pp.
262–265.

429. Telegram From the Department of State to the U.S. Interests Section of the Spanish Embassy in the United Arab Republic[1]

Washington, August 26, 1967, 0204Z.

27535. Ref: Cairo's 316[2] and 333.[3]

1. In your next conversation with Muhammad Riad or Khouly you may pass along following comments on Fonmin Riad's remarks reported reftel and in your 247[4] as appropriate.

2. We appreciate hearing Riad's views and are pleased that he has been frank with us. We would like be equally frank in return. First of all, with regard to his apparent belief that US has applied double standard in its respective attitudes toward Egypt and Israel, we do not believe it useful for us to trade recriminations. Neither we nor Israelis provoked last June's crisis, which we did our diplomatic best to avert. Nor do we now have any plan for imposing a solution. We hope however that parties concerned can take positive and constructive steps to repair the damage which has been done. In this connection we note with interest Riad's reported view that a negotiated solution is called for. We agree.

We have no desire and no capacity to impose a solution against the will of the parties. We shall of course do everything possible to facilitate negotiations should the parties wish us to do so.

Our position is that one possible first step toward such a solution is Egyptian acceptance of draft resolution on which we and the Soviets agreed. President Tito told us that as result of Special Session of General Assembly it evident in his view that most countries of the world now clearly support the right of Israel to peaceful existence, and that this fact should have a constructive impact on Arab thought. The premise of our approach therefore is not the Israeli position, as Riad charges, but a position we have upheld for many years—a position with which the

---

[1] Source: National Archives and Records Administration, RG 59, Central Files 1967–69, POL 27 ARAB–ISR. Secret; Limdis. Drafted by Parker and Eugene Rostow on August 25; cleared by Davies, Battle, and Popper; and approved by Rostow.

[2] Telegram 316 from Cairo, August 21, transmitted the text of an oral message from Foreign Minister Riad that Mohamed Riad had given Bergus the previous day. (Ibid.)

[3] Telegram 333 from Cairo, August 23, commented that the message transmitted in telegram 316 contained little new in terms of substance. (Ibid.)

[4] Telegram 247 from Cairo, August 14, conveyed the text of an oral message on Yemen and South Arabia that Riad had given Bergus on August 12. (Ibid., POL 27 YEMEN)

Soviet Union, Yugoslavia, India, France and most other countries now agree. To support this position is not to depart from objectivity or to seek impose a settlement along Israeli lines.

3. UAR should note that the word "waterways" is in the Draft Resolution agreed between the US and the USSR. The end of all claims of belligerent rights necessarily opens the Suez Canal to all flags under the Convention of 1888. We are aware of political problems this creates for UAR, but the essence of a negotiated solution such as Riad mentioned is a willingness to examine the modalities as well as principles of a settlement. We have no detailed proposals however and do not intend to put any forward at this time.

4. We have not yet heard from Tito, and cannot comment on his proposals until we do, but proposals summarized in para. 11 of your 316[5] would not end the state of war which has prevailed in the region for twenty years. It is that condition itself, and all that flows from it, that constitutes a burden to world peace.

5. USG of course fully agrees on need to solve problems of refugees, Jerusalem, security, and other issues. And it places particular stress on importance of arms limitation agreements.

6. We are pleased to note Riad's assurances contained in your 247 regarding UAR intentions in Yemen and South Arabia. We continue hope these two vexing problems can be settled peacefully without further loss of life or destruction of economic and social life.

7. We welcome reports of an agreement on Yemen between the UAR and Saudi Arabia. Resolution of this long-standing problem to permit the Yemenis to determine their own future would contribute substantially to easing area tensions.

Rusk

---

[5] Paragraph 11 of telegram 316 stated that Tito had a "pragmatic platform" which he would be conveying to Johnson and that its main points were withdrawal, restoration of UNEF, and a four-power guarantee of the lines, preferably through the Security Council.

430. Telegram From the Embassy in Israel to the Department of State[1]

Tel Aviv, August 28, 1967, 1520Z.

613. Subject: US-Israeli Middle East Discussions. Ref: State's 23821.[2]

1. At end of meeting arranged for discussion different subject (refugees return) reported separately,[3] FonMin Eban, who is vacationing in neighborhood Tel Aviv, told me this morning he would like to make some general observations as to Israel's views on broader problems, including particularly the situation in regard to the United Nations which has been subject of various discussions the last being that reported reftel.

2. By way of general observation Eban commented that he feels it important that the onus for initiative towards a Middle East solution remain with the other side. He believes this position to be the effect of the rejection by the United Nations in the last General Assembly of various resolutions which would have provided for Israeli withdrawal under particular circumstances. Unless there is a fundamental change among the Arabs toward Israel he sees no reason to expect Israel to do something. As to the pace of movement in the current situation, Eban recognizes that there has been some movement on the part of the Soviets but he believes there has also been considerable exaggeration as to the extent thereof. In public the Soviets continue to take line that the only course is unconditional Israeli withdrawal. Furthermore the Soviets do not appear to be tied to the US-USSR resolution which arose from tactical considerations. Additionally, Eban doubts the extent to which the Soviets may be helping the Arabs towards realism. Eban finds even less movement among the Arabs themselves, except for statements by Bourguiba and the possibility that Hussein may do something after the summit meeting, Eban concludes that this situation confirms the wisdom of the Arabs having to continue to confront a wall. If in fact something is growing he thinks it important we not pluck it before it has reached maturity.

---

[1] Source: National Archives and Records Administration, RG 59, Central Files 1967–69, POL 27 ARAB–ISR. Secret; Exdis. Repeated to London, Moscow, and USUN.

[2] See footnote 3, Document 423.

[3] Telegram 604 from Tel Aviv, August 28, reported that Eban had given Barbour details of an Israeli decision to remove an August 31 deadline for refugees to return to the West Bank from the East Bank. (National Archives and Records Administration, RG 59, Central Files 1967–69, REF ARAB) Eugene Rostow had urged extension of the deadline with Evron on August 25, and Barbour had made a similar approach to Argov on August 26. (Telegram 27794 to Tel Aviv, August 26, and telegram 594 from Tel Aviv, August 27; ibid.)

3. Eban went on that the purpose and objective to which we must continue to be dedicated is recognition by the Arabs of Israel's right to coexist with them in peace. It is not in his view time to seek agreed UN text or in fact texts covering specific language of possible settlement. In this connection Eban's concrete views may be summarized under three headings:

(A) We must still wait for time to exert pressure on the Arabs which will result in their coming to Israel.

(B) As to the so-called US-USSR draft resolution, Israeli criticism of the text centers primarily on the problem of agreed national boundaries. Such national boundaries are essential conditions of peace and therein lies a crucial distinction. Boundaries cannot be based on any concept of a continuance of belligerency. In this regard Eban mentioned Bitan's conversation with me (Tel Aviv's 483).[4] He said that Bitan's presentation was from notes dictated by him (Eban) and that he confirms what Bitan had said about the strength of Israeli feeling. He urged complete candor between the US and Israel which he said is a duty of friendship. It is one thing for the US to interpret the President's policy statements. Eban's apprehension is that unless the clear language in that statement is closely adhered to others will take advantage to interpret alternative language to their own ends. Reiterating, he said the core of the problem is agreed boundaries, peace and security resulting from negotiations.

(C) Apparently the operative section of the proposed resolution is the appointment of an emissary. Israel has as yet no firm position on the desirability of such an appointment. In any event, Eban is convinced that it is tactically unwise to tie the hands of any such emissary by specifying particular positions which both parties oppose. He should be left entirely free. Otherwise he will become the advocate of each side to the other.

4. Eban added that he is also concerned as to where we stand on the "working paper," that is the draft of a possible resolution. It was his understanding that the draft had been circulated only to the British and Israel but he now is informed by a message today from Washington that it is also being distributed among some Arabs. He very much hopes the US will adhere to its own position as indicated in the President's policy declaration of June 19 and as set forth by US speeches in the special General Assembly which he considers as apt at this time as they were then.

5. Finally, Eban said he believed next step contemplated was for further US-Israeli talks and when Argov, who was also present, said

---

[4] Document 420.

they just received a telegram that such talks were scheduled for Thursday the 31st in New York, the Foreign Minister indicated he will set forth his views as outlined above in somewhat more detail for Israeli presentation on that occasion.[5]

6. I urged Eban to make a particular effort to be forthcoming and forward looking despite GOI's essentially negative attitude towards timing. I reiterated my previous comment to the effect that Israel cannot enjoy splendid isolation and that it essential we both concentrate on ways to contribute to progress towards settlement.

Barbour

---

[5] The text of an aide-mémoire that Rafael gave to Goldberg on August 31 was transmitted in telegram 644 from USUN, September 1. (National Archives and Records Administration, RG 59, Central Files 1967–69, POL 27 ARAB–ISR/UN) Additional text was transmitted in telegram 745 from Tel Aviv, September 8, in which Barbour reported that Bitan had given him the full text the previous day with the explanation that, through error, part of it had not been transmitted to New York. (Ibid.) The full text of the aide-mémoire, marked "New York, 30 August 1967, with addendum dated 6 September 1967, 7 September 1967," is filed with a September 27 covering memorandum from Saunders to Walt Rostow noting that Eban had given it to Goldberg the preceding week. (Johnson Library, National Security File, Country File, Israel, Vol. VII) The aide-mémoire states that in May and June, the "external factors" on which Israel had been urged to rely for its security had proved "fragile or illusory" and that Israel could not be required or expected to yield its current security advantages for anything less than a stable peace settlement.

---

431.   Memorandum of Conversation[1]

Washington, August 29, 1967.

Minister Evron came in, at his request, to make two points on direct instruction from Foreign Minister Eban.

---

[1] Source: Johnson Library, National Security File, Country File, Middle East Crisis, Vol. IX. Secret. Rostow sent the memorandum to the President at 4:45 p.m. A handwritten "L" on the covering note indicates the President saw it. Copies were also sent to McPherson, Saunders, and the Department of State.

1. The Macomber letter to Senator Fulbright of August 15, 1967[2]

Eban respects the candor of our response to question 2 relating to commitments in the Middle East.[3] He notes, however, the narrowness of our interpretation of our commitment to Israel. In the light of that statement he observes that Israel cannot be assured beforehand of help from the U.S. in case of attack. In his judgment, it follows that:

—the U.S. should continue its support for Israel in its search for a secure peace settlement as the only realistic and safe alternative to the present situation; and
—the U.S. should accept a responsibility for insuring a flow of necessary arms to Israel.

Evron also noted that the narrowness of this statement of the U.S. commitment to Israel could prove "pernicious"; that is, it might encourage the Arabs and the Soviet Union to engage in future aggression against Israel.

2. The UN Resolution

The heart of the Israeli objection to the joint U.S.-Soviet resolution is its implication that Israel must return to the territories occupied on June 4. Even in exchange for a peace treaty Israel is not prepared for a simple return to the June 4 boundaries. What Israel will seek by agreement with the Arabs are "secure" boundaries, in addition to maintaining the unity of the city of Jerusalem. When I noted that we had not accepted the June 4 date in the UN resolution, Evron said the resolution still contained the language: "withdrawal from all occupied territories." He said that the Israeli Government was quite content with the carefully designed language used by the President with respect to boundaries, most recently in his communication with Tito; but it was essential that the U.S. position in the UN not clash with the President's formula of "secure and agreed borders."

---

[2] The August 15 letter from Assistant Secretary of State for Congressional Relations William B. Macomber to Senator Fulbright set forth the Department's replies to questions concerning U.S. commitments to foreign powers. For text of the letter and its attachments, see *U.S. Commitments to Foreign Powers*, Hearings Before the Senate Committee on Foreign Relations, Ninetieth Congress, First Session (Washington: 1967), pp. 49–71.

[3] Question 2 asked whether the United States had a commitment to come to the military or economic aid of Israel or any of the Arab States in the event of an attack. The letter replied: "President Johnson and his three predecessors have stated the United States interest and concern in supporting the political independence and territorial integrity of the countries of the Near East. This is a statement of policy and not a commitment to take particular actions in particular circumstances. Unrest and conflict in the Middle East have been of serious concern to the United States for a long time. The use of armed force in the Middle East can have especially serious consequences for international peace extending far beyond that area. We have bent our efforts to avoid a renewal of conflict there. Thus, we have stated our position in an effort to use our influence in the cause of peace."

3. Egypt

In the course of a general conversation on events in the Middle East over the last month, Evron noted that their information about the political situation in Cairo was not very good. It was his feeling, however, that three forces were at work, all pushing Egypt towards a more moderate position:

—the economic situation;
—a growing feeling among Egyptians that they were becoming excessively tied to Moscow and losing their independence; and
—a deep struggle for power which Nasser could not or would not control—evidenced by open polemics in the Cairo press usually tightly controlled.

WR

---

432.   Memorandum of Conversation[1]

Washington, August 30, 1967, 7:15 p.m.

SUBJECT

Call of Yugoslav Foreign Minister Nikezic on the President

PARTICIPANTS

President of the United States
Foreign Minister Marko Nikezic of Yugoslavia
The Honorable Bogdan Crnobrnja, Ambassador of Yugoslavia
Walt W. Rostow, Special Assistant to the President
Ambassador C. Burke Elbrick, U.S. Ambassador to Yugoslavia
Lucius D. Battle, Assistant Secretary of NEA

The President received the Foreign Minister of Yugoslavia at approximately 7:15 p.m. for a conversation that lasted just under one hour.

The President greeted the Foreign Minister warmly, expressing gratitude for his visit to the United States. The President indicated his pleasure at President Tito's interest in the Middle East and at his willingness to involve himself with these problems of concern to both countries.

---

[1] Source: Department of State, NEA Files: Lot 71 D 287, Middle East Crisis (3). Secret; Exdis. Drafted by Battle. Filed with a covering memorandum of August 31 from Battle to Walsh.

The Foreign Minister expressed satisfaction on the part of President Tito with the message from the President and joined with President Johnson in stressing the value of good relations between the United States and Yugoslavia.

The Foreign Minister then presented to the President the message from President Tito[2] which President Johnson read and commented on as he studied the message.

With respect to the reference in the message referring to Israeli aggression, the President stated that it was difficult to be certain who really committed the aggression. There had been extreme provocation in the movement of troops and the manner in which Arab actions had inflamed the situation. The Russians had made a great mistake in stirring up the situation—an act that was difficult for us to understand. The United States considered that the problem had to be dealt with at its root, and the causes of the difficulties that had led to war must be removed. It was not adequate to take an aspirin to deal with a major illness. Causes must be faced. A call for withdrawal alone was no answer.

The President took exception to the statement in President Tito's message with respect to the possible "disassociation" of the United States from the occupation policy of Israel. The President noted that it was impossible to disassociate oneself from something one had not been associated with. He then reviewed the very serious efforts he had made to prevent hostilities, recalling his own conversations with Foreign Minister Eban in which he had urged that the Government of Israel exercise restraint in this situation. Similarly, the United States had urged restraint on the Egyptians in the hope that neither side would engage in hostilities.

The President referred to the reference in the communication from President Tito that indicated that the Arab countries consider the attitudes of the United States as "one sided". He agreed that some Arab countries did in fact feel this way. This attitude is unfortunate and does not reflect United States attitudes. The United States has great, in fact vital, interests in the Arab world. We seek a solution to the basic issues. In each talk the President has had with Arab leaders or Ambassadors, he has reaffirmed United States interest in the Arab world and a deep hope that a road to peace can be found.

---

[2] Tito's August 24 message proposed: withdrawal of all troops from the territories they had occupied since June 4, under the control of UN observers; guarantee of the security and borders of all states in the region by the Security Council or the four great powers, pending the definitive solution of questions under dispute, with the possible stationing of UN forces on both sides of the borders; free passage for all ships through the Strait of Tiran pending a decision by the International Court of Justice; navigation in the Suez Canal as before June 5; and steps by the Security Council, with the direct participation of the parties concerned, for the resolution of other questions under dispute, including the problem of Palestinian refugees and the question of passage of Israeli ships through the Suez Canal. (Johnson Library, Special Head of State Correspondence File, Yugoslavia—President Correspondence)

The United States is in a difficult position with respect to arms races in various parts of the world. In the case of Jordan we had sold planes and arms with a guarantee that they would be used for defensive purposes only and not directed at Israel. It is difficult to explain to the American people a circumstance in which we have sold arms to both sides of a conflict.

The Foreign Minister then commented that the Yugoslavs had heard from the Egyptians that they considered that the United States had obtained promises that Israel would not engage in war and that the Egyptians had because of this refrained from opening hostilities.

The President replied that we had in fact urged restraint on both sides and had believed that each side would refrain from initiating hostilities. It is difficult, however, to place fault in view of the barrage of propaganda threatening the very existence of Israel in a very tense situation.

In commenting on the message from President Tito, the President noted with respect to the statement concerning passage through the Suez Canal that there must be an understanding that international waterways are open to all and noted that the Israelis would not accept opening the Canal and excluding themselves.

The President noted the statement in the letter that statesmen of the Arab countries cannot accept the Soviet-American resolution. He then indicated that the Israelis would not accept this resolution either.

The President also commented on the paragraph stating that the present situation in the Near East is untenable and extremely dangerous to peace in that region and in the world. The President expressed his strong agreement with this concern. Each day is more dangerous, particularly in view of the continued actions of the Russians in replacing military equipment including aircraft and tanks. Such action does not contribute to a solution to the problem. We understand the need for a solution that does not humiliate the Arabs, and we seek no such solution.

The President then completed reading the text of the message, commenting that the United Nations forces had disappeared pretty quickly when they were particularly needed in the period before the recent war.

The President then stated he would, with his advisers, study the message from President Tito, giving it careful consideration. Some aspects were, he thought, manageable and constructive. Others would not be acceptable. The exchange had been useful and the fact that President Tito prepared the letter and sent the Foreign Minister to see President Johnson was most encouraging.

The Foreign Minister then asked if he might add a few words. President Tito's trip had, the Foreign Minister thought, been constructive and useful and Arab leaders had found it so. President Tito had not asked these leaders to endorse his proposals. They were, however, very close to the views expressed by the Arab leaders. The Foreign Minister acknowledged that his government connected withdrawal with the other issues in the area and expressed the opinion that progressive steps must be found which could lead to de facto (if not de jure) recognition.

President Nasser is probably closest of all the Arab leaders to a realistic approach to the situation. If he attempts to be moderate, he does so at great risk as he is under pressure from all quarters, particularly from the left. Everyone is trying to be a "better Arab than Nasser is."

President Tito believes we must not make the situation more difficult for President Nasser than it already is. He has problems that are real and difficult to overcome, particularly in light of what his people have been told in the past. President Nasser is, in President Tito's opinion, the only hope for peace and real and permanent guarantees with perhaps a de facto recognition of Israel that exists in the Arab world today.

President Johnson said that he had had some hope of improving relations before the war with President Nasser. President Johnson had hoped to approach the area in its entirety with a humanitarian plan based on need of food and water by all. He had considered sending the Vice President to the area. All of these plans had been set back by the war.

The President then referred again to President Tito's message saying that while we cannot accept the formula, there were some basic things that were acceptable. Everyone must deal with realities. The Israelis cannot be asked to put down guns and then have their throats cut. Withdrawal, therefore, alone was no answer. There must be answers for maritime rights, for Jerusalem, and for the refugees. There must be an answer to a permanent peaceful existence for Israel. It would take all the pressures, powers, and wisdom of all concerned to work out answers to these problems, but we must try to find them.

The Foreign Minister replied that three months had passed since the war and that the world must attempt to deal with the issues. He admitted the connection between these problems and withdrawal. He reaffirmed, however, the need to work with those who could try for a solution. If those who existed today were removed from office (regardless of whether from the left or the right), those who came after would find the same dilemmas in the situation and the world would be no nearer a solution.

The President thanked the Foreign Minister for his visit and expressed again his pleasure that President Tito was taking an active part in finding solutions to the Middle East. He reaffirmed warmly a desire for friendship between Yugoslavia and the United States.

433.   Telegram From the Department of State to the Embassy in
         Israel[1]

Washington, August 31, 1967, 2107Z.

30382. Subj: U.S.S. *Liberty*.

1. Under Secretary called in Chargé Evron August 30 to comment on
Israeli examining judge's report.[2] Explained it has already been given on
confidential basis to a few Congressional committees. Also, quite a few
people in the USG had handled it, as it was received through more than
one channel from GOI. At least its existence, and perhaps some of its substance, can be expected to leak out. It may then become necessary for US
to publish the exchange of notes. We shall inform GOI in advance if that
eventuality arises and will do any publishing in low-key. We have no
desire to exacerbate the issue. If this procedure causes major problems for
GOI now is the time to speak out. Some leakage has occurred already in
this week's *Newsweek* magazine.

2. Evron said he would refer matter back to his government. He speculated it might be possible for his government to acquiesce in such publication of the notes, in which case it could be done jointly. He wished to
express GOI's deep appreciation of restrained manner in which entire
affair was handled by USG.

3. On substance of report, Under Secretary said he personally had
been very surprised with the ending. Report was obviously candid since
any such confusion could not possibly have been invented. Examining
judge laid out point after point confirming negligence on part of various
Israeli officials in affair, yet ended up finding no deviation from normal
conduct. Surely, Under Secretary said, one cannot believe such conduct
was consistent with normal Israeli practice and did not involve culpable
negligence on part of officials involved.

4. Evron was subdued in manner and said there was little he could
add. He had raised matter with GOI when in Israel in July and had spoken personally with COS Rabin. Rabin had stressed that investigation
being entrusted to impartial military judge, and COS would have to
abide by judge's findings. Affair had obviously been very damaging for
GOI, Evron continued, and everything will be done to avoid repetition
of such incident if ever similar circumstances arose, which he devoutly
hoped they would not.

---

[1] Source: National Archives and Records Administration, RG 59, Central Files
1967–69, POL 27 ARAB–ISR. Secret; Exdis. Drafted by Lambrakis on August 30; cleared
by Bahti, Wehmeyer, and Davies; and approved by Katzenbach.
[2] See Document 424, and footnote 2 thereto.

5. Under Secretary reiterated his surprise at judge's findings though he assured Evron he did not intend publicly to express these personal conclusions. If GOI should ever decide to publish the report, he added, we would appreciate identification of *Liberty* as US communications ship, in keeping with manner in which it identified in our own public utterances.

6. Evron agreed this manner of identification should present no problem but thought GOI would not publish report at all.

Rusk

---

434. Telegram From the U.S. Interests Section of the Spanish Embassy in the United Arab Republic to the Department of State[1]

Cairo, September 11, 1967, 0741Z.

502. 1. Two and one-half hour session with Presidency Adviser Khouli September 9. It hard after these talkathons separate gold from dross but will try best.

2. I drew on very helpful State 34112[2] and related telegrams to state US–UAR differences re Middle East settlement revolved around two vital points: 1) belligerence, and 2) commitment. Neither Tito nor Khartoum,[3] commendable as both were in many respects, had satisfactorily addressed themselves to these.

---

[1] Source: National Archives and Records Administration, RG 59, Central Files 1967–69, POL UAR–US. Secret; Limdis.

[2] Telegram 34112 to Cairo, September 8, authorized Bergus to express U.S. pleasure with the constructive attitude reportedly taken by Nasser at the recent Arab Summit meeting in Khartoum but to point out that a settlement would require the Arabs to renounce belligerency in a manner sufficiently convincing to the Israelis. (Ibid., POL 27 ARAB–ISR)

[3] The Conference of Arab Heads of State met in Khartoum August 29–September 1. Resolution 3 adopted by the Conference states that the participants had agreed to unite their political efforts on the international and diplomatic level "to eliminate the effects of the aggression and to ensure the withdrawal of the aggressive Israeli forces from the Arab lands which have been occupied since the 5 June aggression." This was to be done "within the framework of the main principles to which the Arab states adhere, namely: no peace with Israel, no recognition of Israel, no negotiations with it, and adherence to the rights of the Palestinian people in their country." For texts of the resolutions, see *American Foreign Policy: Current Documents, 1967*, pp. 590–591.

3. Khouli went back to argument re importance US–UAR "relationship." He again distinguished between "relationship" and "relations." He said Nasser had at Khartoum encouraged Arab states having relations with U.S. to intensify such relations for total Arab cause. As for UAR, it would for time being prefer deal with me, who was known rather than "some strange ambassador we don't know." He felt US–UAR relationship more important than Arab-Israel conflict, although FonMin would probably not agree with him. He said Nasser realized that only U.S., because of its "control" Israel, could establish durable peace in NE ("not Podgorny or Kosygin"), that only U.S. had scientific and technological know-how help NE become a happy and prosperous area. Nasser had meant what he said when he had referred to U.S. as most powerful nation on earth.

4. UAR felt that foreign policy changes it had made in Khartoum context would make it easier for US–UAR relationship to develop. Khouli referred to "recent internal changes" in GUAR.[4] He said there more in offing, which would also improve atmosphere in this regard. But at present, continued Khouli, situation clouded by Arab belief that U.S. had become partial. He, for one, was perfectly willing agree that concept Arab belligerency against Israel was unrealistic and outmoded. Ways could be found blaze a new trail, but why did U.S. keep insisting on hitting Egypt in the face with Suez Canal as most important issue in this connection? Why did we not think about establishing precedent of non-belligerency first on such issues as demilitarization of Sinai in context arrangements for Israel withdrawal and then moving on to Suez issue? USG should not underestimate Egyptian hatred and fear of Israel, recently exacerbated by Israeli shelling of civilians in Canal Zone. Whole thrust of this part of argument was that USG could make belligerency issue much more palatable to Arabs if it could demonstrate a little impartiality. I cited forceful démarches we had made to Israelis re return of West Bankers. This seemed impress him.

---

[4] On August 25 UAR authorities arrested former Vice President and Deputy Supreme Commander of the Armed Forces Field Marshal Amer on the charge that he was preparing a coup. At least 50 other persons, including Saleh Nasr, the head of the General Intelligence Department, were also arrested. Bergus commented in telegram 442 from Cairo, September 5, that the episode had the appearance of a personal power struggle. He wrote, "Feeling around town is that Nasser has won this one. There is less certainty that there won't be a next one." (National Archives and Records Administration, RG 59, Central Files 1967–69, POL 23–9 UAR) An Intelligence Note of September 13 from Deputy Director of the Bureau of Intelligence and Research George C. Denney, Jr., to Rusk states that there was no evidence that Amer was conspiring to overthrow Nasser. (Ibid., POL 29 UAR)

5. On issue of commitment, Khouli was surprisingly relaxed and frank. He said President Johnson had been right when in pre-hostilities correspondence with Nasser, LBJ had in effect stated that UAR had broken "gentleman's agreement" re Aqaba. Khouli admitted that such "gentleman's agreement" had existed. He recounted Nasser's desire in early June reestablish "gentleman's agreement" by sending Zakariyah to Washington. He looked forward opportunity joint review of chronology May–June events as soon as U.S. was ready. He recognized need for meaningful Arab commitments but felt, too, that this would be fairly simple problem if only Arab confidence in U.S. impartiality could be reestablished.

6. Other bits and pieces:

A. Memcons my conversations with Mohamed Riad being restricted to FonMin personally and Presidency.

B. Nasser has been in Alexandria, in better health than he has been in months, "He swam two hours straight on Friday."

C. GUAR would like see return U.S. dependents as indication USG desires normalize relations. If, say, by October 15, I can tell him U.S. in principle favors return dependents, he will take care of such matters as necessary GUAR assurances and quashing of Ministry Interior expulsion order.

D. He would like see TWA resume flights to Cairo and I could count on him for any necessary support this connection.

E. My travel plans to U.S. well-known to Presidency and he thought I should stay as long as necessary make GUAR viewpoint known to powers that be. I cautioned him this was routine consultation.

F. He sees Nasser again 12th. He will get in touch with me 13th if anything further I should take to Washington.

Bergus

435.   Telegram From the Embassy in the Soviet Union to the
Department of State[1]

Moscow, September 12, 1967, 1403Z.

1033. 1. In course my conversation with Gromyko today, I raised
Middle East situation, expressing hope US and USSR could reach
understanding on problem. This connection, I recalled US-Soviet draft
resolution of last July, and wondered if Arabs still opposed to it.

2. Gromyko recalled Kosygin had said to President, and he himself to Secretary and Goldberg, that US position too one-sided
although they had transmitted it to the Arabs. Soviets had given
Goldberg list of considerations which should be taken into account in
seeking solution. He said that the Soviet Govt would like very much
to find a solution, and attaches great importance to this matter. Soviet
Govt believes neither US nor USSR interested in tensions in Middle
East; this, of course, based on assumption Soviet reading US position
accurate. Gromyko continued that any solution must be sought on
realistic basis. Israel claims not realistic and pull rug from under
search for solution. It must be realized that 100 million Arabs must be
allowed to live. As to Israel's existence, Soviet position well known
and should not raise doubts in anybody's mind. Yet, Israeli ultimata
did not help. Gromyko maintained that key to solution was in US
hands. If withdrawal Israeli troops can be secured, solution can be
found. He said he would be glad hear US views on problem in New
York and elsewhere; USSR prepared not only to listen but also to take
certain steps to facilitate solution.

3. I said we did not think July draft resolution was pro-Israel, stressing that withdrawal must be connected with recognition Israel's right to
exist. On other hand, I noted we regarded Yugoslav proposal as being
one-sided and unrealistic in that it separates the two problems. I said I
was sure Secretary would want discuss this matter with him and noted
solution should be sought on urgent basis since situation might deteriorate.

Thompson

---

[1] Source: National Archives and Records Administration, RG 59, Central Files
1967–69, POL 27 ARAB–ISR. Secret; Limdis. Repeated to USUN and Tel Aviv. Received
at 2150Z.

436.   Memorandum From the President's Special Assistant (Rostow) to President Johnson[1]

Washington, September 12, 1967.

SUBJECT

General Weizman's Presentation[2]

General Weizman today wound up two mornings of formal talks in the Pentagon on Israel's aircraft requirements for the next five years. The first reaction of all who attended was that, while details of any such presentation are debatable, his requests and tone were both modest.

The attached table[3] shows how Weizman sees the Israeli air force developing 1968–73. His request from us boils down to: (1) complete on schedule (beginning in December) delivery of the 48 Skyhawks contracted for in March 1966; (2) sell an additional 27 Skyhawks; (3) sell 50 F–4 Phantoms. In short, he wants 77 more US planes from us roughly by the end of 1968.

He rests his argument on these main points:

1. Airpower will continue to be the decisive factor in Israeli strategy. Israel with its small population has mustered about all it can manage in ground forces.

2. If there is another war, Israel will face a tougher enemy: There will be greater Arab cooperation, and Israel won't be able to count on the luxury of fighting one enemy at a time. Arab airfields will be better defended, more numerous and more widely dispersed and hardened. The Arab air forces on Israel's borders alone will number around 900 combat aircraft by 1970, against a planned Israeli force of 350.

3. Israel still believes that it must maintain a force that will *deter* aggression. Weizman feels that one cause of the June war was that Israel's force was so close to the margin of visible superiority that it lost its credibility as a deterrent and allowed Nasser to miscalculate his chances.

---

[1]   Source: Johnson Library, National Security File, Country File, Israel, Vol. VII. Top Secret.

[2]   Saunders' notes of General Weizman's presentation on September 11, with a covering memorandum of that date to Rostow, are ibid. A joint State–Defense message of September 15 to Tel Aviv is in the National Archives and Records Administration, RG 59, Central Files 1967–69, DEF 7 ISR. A transcript of the proceedings is ibid., NEA/IAI Files: Lot 70 D 304.

[3]   Attached but not printed.

4. If there is a next time, Israel will have to be prepared to absorb a first strike, since the Arabs are now painfully aware of the advantages of this strategy.

We told Weizman he could expect no answers while he was here, and staff work will now begin grinding out a recommendation for you. But I wanted you to have immediately the flavor of Weizman's presentation.

Walt

---

437.   Memorandum of Conversation[1]

Washington, September 12, 1967.

SUBJECT

Evron on the Arms Deal

While riding back from our second session with General Weizman, Evron informally suggested we consider handling the arms deal (if any) as follows.

There are two possible approaches. One would be to exact conditions for aircraft. The other would be to meet Israel's arms request without formal conditions but simultaneously to say through some informal channel that we were doing this at some political cost and would therefore expect something from them in return. They fully expect this, but the *way* we do it will be important.

Evron feels we'll get more out of the Israelis by taking the second tack. He feels that the President understands that the way to deal with Israelis is to treat them as close friends and to expect them to respond in kind, rather than treating them like bazaar hagglers.

This strikes once again at the heart of our relationship with Israel. The Israelis have always tried to get close to us and to build the kind of relationship we have with the British. We have—at least at the professional level of our government—kept them at arms length, and they have been deeply hurt. Evron and I have discussed this aspect of our relationship before, and it's no surprise that he sees here a chance for a new start.

---

[1] Source: Johnson Library, National Security File, Country File, Israel, Vol. VII. Secret. Drafted by Saunders.

Comment. Taking Evron's tack would be a noble experiment as well as a calculated risk. I recall saying when we were debating our military aid package for Israel before the war that the argument had nothing to do with dollars or numbers of APCs—that the real argument was over what kind of relationship we should have with Israel. In my mind, there is no question, so I'm tempted to take the risk Evron suggests. This is not to rule out a pretty blunt dialogue on what we expect of the Israelis. But as Evron suggests, the real leverage we have is not a specific number of aircraft but our total relationship. In a situation such as we face today nothing short [apparent omission] is big enough for the kind of stakes we're talking about, but I'm not sure we're in a position to bargain with it. In any case, Evron's idea warrants serious consideration since our decision on tactics will set the tone of our relationship with Israel for some time.

Hal

438.   Notes of a National Security Council Meeting[1]

Washington, September 13, 1967, 12:32 p.m.

SUBJECT

National Security Council Meeting in the Cabinet Room
Wednesday, September 13, 1967

ATTENDING WERE

The Vice President, Secretary McNamara, Under Secretary Katzenbach, General J.P. McConnell, Leonard Marks, Ambassador Goldberg, Under Secretary Paul Nitze, CIA Director Dick Helms, Secretary Henry Fowler, Joe Sisco, Bromley Smith, Walt Rostow and George Christian

The President opened the meeting calling on Under Secretary Katzenbach.

Katzenbach pointed out that Secretary Rusk will be going to the United Nations for the usual meetings of Foreign Ministers. He said these are very helpful and useful to have these bilateral discussions, although it is very wearing on Mr. Rusk. Katzenbach said that the

---

[1] Source: Johnson Library, Meeting Notes File, NSC Meetings. Secret. Prepared by Assistant to the President Jim R. Jones. The President joined the meeting at 12:32 p.m. and departed at 12:58 p.m.; the notes record only that part of the meeting. Notes of the entire meeting by Bromley Smith are ibid., National Security File, NSC Files, NSC Meetings, Vol. V, Tab 57; and by Nathaniel Davis are ibid., Agency File, United Nations, Vol. VIII.

Africans are better than they used to be. They held together well, and they are more realistic than they used to be. Katzenbach said the President's announcement of the U.N. Delegation with new and different people is very helpful politically both to the United Nations and to this Administration domestically. Katzenbach said that Joe Sisco briefed the NATO people on the Middle East and this was helpful, but he is not sure that they will stay considering the pressure the NATO countries are under. On Vietnam, Katzenbach said Goldberg has been having discussions with the U.N. delegates.

The President said he appreciated what Katzenbach said about the United Nations delegation. The President then called on Goldberg for discussion of the major issues facing the United Nations General Assembly.

Goldberg said there are about 100 items on the General Assembly agenda, many of these are repetitious. The principal issues listed by Goldberg were Middle East, Vietnam, non-proliferation, Chinese representation, oceanography and African problems.

Goldberg began with the Middle East saying that there are some signs of moderation in the Arab camp, and some signs of hardening in the Israeli camp. He said this presents a problem for us. Israel has serious internal problems and it is difficult for any Israeli spokesman to be "sweetly reasonable." Goldberg pointed out that Israel takes the President's statement of June 19 and uses those portions it likes and omits those portions it does not like. On the withdrawal issue, they have referred to the President's statement on June 19. Goldberg said he believes the United States has a sound policy. We don't charge the Israelis with aggression. Goldberg said it will be more difficult in the next session to hold the line against a resolution in line with our desire for peace in the Middle East. He said he believes Israel feels now that they would have been better to support the Latin proposal we supported which also included a withdrawal provision. They were with us tactically in getting the Latin Resolution voted, but they now say that was merely a tactical support, Goldberg said. Goldberg said the minimum conditions for a sensible peace in the Middle East is a commitment by the Arab states that they are not in a state of war with Israel. If the Arab states do this (and Goldberg pointed out that the Khartoum Conference did not say this) we may have to part with the Israelis on formulation. . . . Goldberg said the Israelis have not faced up to the demographic problem. . . . [2]

[Omitted here is discussion of other subjects.]

---

[2] Davis' notes state, "In conclusion, Goldberg noted that the other side had badly misplayed its cards in the special General Assembly and we could, perhaps still count on the stupidity of our adversaries. The President laughed and said that in other cases as well this sometimes proved an asset indeed."

439. Memorandum From Harold Saunders of the National Security Council Staff to the President's Special Assistant (Rostow)[1]

Washington, September 13, 1967.

SUBJECT

Weizman's Position on Missiles

As you know, we have been after the Israelis and the Egyptians since about 1964 to persuade them not to introduce more sophisticated weapons into the Middle East arms race.

We decided before General Weizman came that we ought to use his visit as an occasion for continuing this dialogue. We had Wally Barbour warn him that we wanted to hear his views on this subject, and Weizman presumably cleared his position with Eshkol before coming.

In sum, his answer to our probing was that Israel is merely keeping itself in a position to go into missiles, if it has to, to counter a similar Arab move. But Weizman insisted that "nothing is imminent."

We tried to find out whether there was any specific Israeli contract with France for the delivery or serial production of the missiles France has been developing for Israel. He answered that Israel's contract with France is "quite flexible" and repeated that nothing was imminent.

Weizman does not see the surface-to-surface missile as a militarily important weapon. He made quite clear that aircraft would rank ahead of missiles on any Israeli priority list. Missiles, in his view, would only have value as "deterrence in kind." If Nasser acquired this kind of weapon, it might be essential for Israel to have a similar weapon simply to frighten Nasser from using his.

Despite more of an exchange on this subject than we were able to have with Weizman in 1965, his statement was obviously guarded. Our discussion was a significant one, but I would not regard it as the last word on the subject. I simply want you to be up to date on this aspect of our arms relationship, since some people in State are strongly inclined to make a prohibition against missiles a condition for our selling aircraft.

Hal

---

[1] Source: Johnson Library, National Security File, Country File, Israel, Vol. VII. Secret.

440.   Letter From President Johnson to President Tito[1]

Washington, September 15, 1967.

Dear Mr. President:

I was glad to receive your letter of August 24[2] reporting on your visit to Arab capitals. I particularly appreciated your thoughtfulness in sending Foreign Secretary Nikezic to deliver the letter personally. This gave us a welcome opportunity to talk with him about this most serious problem, to the solution of which you have devoted such tireless effort. Our representatives will be continuing to exchange views, particularly in New York, during the coming period, and Foreign Secretary Nikezic and Secretary Rusk will themselves have further opportunity to meet during the General Assembly session. However, I would like to make some observations myself concerning your report and the problem with which it is concerned.

It appears to us that the key to the situation is that both sides agree on principles and conduct which provide conditions for a durable peace. It is in this light that we have studied your proposals. The relationship of withdrawal and the cessation of the state of belligerency is obviously fundamental. Withdrawal without accompanying actions by those concerned which ended the state of belligerency and acknowledged Israel's right to exist in peace and security would only reestablish the situation which existed prior to the recent war. What is now needed is acceptance by the parties that each nation in the area is entitled to live within accepted, recognized and secure state boundaries—a principle to which we all subscribed in signing the UN Charter.

We believe a useful expression of this principle is embodied in the US-USSR draft resolution, and that the Yugoslav proposal falls considerably short of it. Here there is both equivalence and a simultaneity of action. We do not claim that withdrawal should come last any more than we believe it can come first. It must come together with an actual

---

[1] Source: Johnson Library, Special Head of State Correspondence File, Yugoslavia—President Correspondence. No classification marking. Telegram 38996, September 18, which transmitted the text of the letter to Belgrade indicates that it was drafted by Arthur R. Day (UNP). (National Archives and Records Administration, RG 59, Central Files 1967–69, POL 27 ARAB–ISR) Telegram 917 from Belgrade, September 20, indicates that the Chargé delivered the letter that day. Tito stated that he had visited the Middle East in the hope of convincing the Arabs of the necessity of seeking a political solution. He thought he had succeeded, although it was "no easy task" to convince Arab leaders on this point. He further stated that he had told the Arab leaders that Israel was a reality from which one must proceed. (Ibid.)

[2] See footnote 2, Document 432.

end to belligerency. There must be real and effective progress in both respects at the same time so that fulfillment of the objectives of both sides may be guaranteed.

You note that the Arabs feel the US interprets the draft resolution to imply a change of frontiers to their detriment. We have no preconceptions on frontiers as such. What we believe to be important is that the frontiers be secure. For this the single most vital condition is that they be acceptable to both sides.

It is a source of regret to us that the Arabs appear to misunderstand our proposal and misread our motives. It would be a real contribution to the cause of ultimate peace in the area if you, with your close contacts in the Arab capitals, could help dispel such misunderstandings.

The second point of your approach is a guarantee by the Security Council or the four great powers. We have given careful study to this proposal. We inevitably come back to the central point which is that the essential element is agreement by the parties themselves. The device of having the Security Council declare no belligerency has been tried before and has not been effective. Guarantees could serve as auxiliary insurance as necessary. In themselves they cannot meet the need for an acknowledgment of Israel's right to exist, and for renunciation by the Arab States and by Israel of any claims of belligerent rights. We do agree with you, however, that the Arabs would not need for this purpose to recognize Israel formally.

In your third and fourth points you deal with the waterways. As you propose, the Strait of Tiran should be open to all shipping. So, in our judgment, should the Suez Canal, as required by the 1888 Convention[3] and the Security Council resolution of 1951.[4] We see no point in remitting either of these questions to litigation instead of permanently resolving the issues involved by international agreement. To postpone dealing with them and with the refugees until after other aspects of the problem have been settled risks permitting these two critical problems to be perpetuated indefinitely.

You report in your letter that as a result of your trip you are further convinced that the Arab countries must have adequate defense capabilities. We believe both the Arabs and the Israelis should have the capacity to defend themselves but that arms should not be maintained at such a level as to be a source of tension and danger. It is our firm conviction that it would be in the interests of all countries in the area and would

---

[3] The Constantinople Convention of 1888; see footnotes 4 and 5, Document 271.

[4] A Security Council resolution of September 1, 1951 (UN document S/2322), called upon Egypt to terminate restrictions on the passage of international commercial shipping and goods through the Suez Canal. For text, see *Foreign Relations,* 1951, vol. V, pp. 848–849.

advance the cause of lasting peace if the flow of arms to all those countries involved in the recent hostilities were to be restricted; we hope that the suppliers of arms to the region will exercise due restraint in this regard.

In the weeks and months ahead, which will be so critical for the future of the Middle East, the United States will continue to work for solutions designed to advance the long-run interests of all people of the area, Arabs and Israelis alike. I would again recall to you the statement I made on June 19 which reflects the policy of my government and which I am firmly convinced is in the interests of peace.

In conclusion, let me again express my appreciation for this frank contact with you concerning your discussions with Arab leaders.

Sincerely,

Lyndon B. Johnson

441.   Memorandum From the Under Secretary of State for Political Affairs (Rostow) to Secretary of State Rusk[1]

Washington, September 18, 1967.

SUBJECT

Reflections on my talks about Middle Eastern Problems in Europe between September 10–16, 1967

This memorandum is an attempt to see the forest through a TWA window en route home.

Except in England, discussion of the Middle Eastern crisis as we are accustomed to see it—as a prolonged "Cuban missile crisis" with the Soviet Union, not primarily an Arab-Israeli affair—provoked interest and surprise, but not resistance or dissent. All were agreed that Europe failed to meet its responsibilities, and to protect its own interests during

---

[1] Source: National Archives and Records Administration, RG 59, Central Files 1967–69, POL 27 ARAB–ISR. Secret. Copies were sent to Katzenbach, Kohler, Harriman, Assistant Secretary for African Affairs Joseph Palmer II, Assistant Secretary for European Affairs John M. Leddy, Battle, Hughes, Sisco, Meeker, Chairman of the Policy Planning Council Henry D. Owen, Julius C. Holmes, who was heading a special State–Defense Study Group on the region, Walt Rostow, Goldberg, and pouched to London, Tel Aviv, Cairo, Amman, and Paris NATUS.

the crisis, and that the lessons of this mistake, on our part and theirs, should be taken into account now in devising more effective methods of political consultation and crisis management, ad hoc and through the Harmel exercise report. The cream of the jest was Schuetz' question to me last night: "Why didn't you press us to act?"

In general, most people agreed that the political situation with regard to the Middle East is moving, and moving on the whole in the right direction. But they also agreed that there are risks. There is no sign yet of action. It will take a number of steps to minimize the risks, and maximize the opportunities, both in the field and in the UN.

The Soviets seem to have decelerated. They are not so conspicuous as they were in Egypt and Algeria. Manifestly, Nasser is not following their suggestions slavishly (i.e., the Canal, the opening to the West, Alexandria). On the other hand, the Soviets seem to be disengaging from their tentative agreement with us at the end of the Assembly. Arms shipments continue, with their implicit menace, accentuated by Heikal's threat that war is inevitable unless a miracle occurs. And there are reports of Soviet advisers, arms offers in the Yemen, etc.

For the moment, like nearly every other player on the stage, the Soviets are saying, "It's your move", in the context of the tentative hypothesis that we both want a relaxation of Middle Eastern tensions. Like the others, too, they seem to have forgotten that we tabled a Resolution in the Security Council—a Resolution still on the agenda, and still unvoted.

The British are talking less about the Canal, but they are still pressing for quick action, and hinting that if we fail to obtain either the US–USSR Resolution or its equivalent in their Security Council, they, like other middle powers, may change their position in quest of a deal.

It is a cliché of the newspapers, and accepted wisdom, that the Israeli position is "hardening". We examined the subject with the British experts at some length, and then with Ambassador Barbour. All agreed that the Israeli position was still officially exactly what is was when they first laid it out to us. They agree that political currents in Israel are equivocal, but on the whole tended more towards "hangover" than "euphoria". Ambassador Barbour explicitly agrees with Evron's evaluation, stated in his (carefully planned) lunch with me,[2] that the question of Jerusalem is negotiable, as the final item of a politically important settlement with Jordan.

Everyone who professed to have an opinion about the trend in Egypt had roughly the same opinion: (a) that Nasser was still in charge, and was not yet quite a complete Soviet prisoner; (b) that on the whole

---

[2] Rostow's luncheon meeting with Evron on August 22 was reported in telegram 25406 from Tel Aviv, August 23. (Ibid., POL 27–14 ARAB–ISR/SANDSTORM)

the signs from Khartoum are pretty good—they surely could have been worse with regard to the West, and to relations among the Arabs—although there was less agreement about their implications for a peaceful settlement between Israel and the Arabs. (It may be, some thought, that the purpose of Khartoum was to separate us and the British from the Israelis, or in any event to separate the British from us and the Israelis); and (c) that Egypt has not yet made a single clear step.

It is hard to tell whether the Egyptian position is "hardening", since Egypt has never taken an official position. We don't even know whether Egypt would support the Tito draft. But so far the Egyptian posture is largely atmosphere, without a clearly defined statement of terms or of procedures for reaching them. We are told that Egypt prefers a "political" solution, although it warns that war is "inevitable" unless we obtain Israeli troop withdrawal. But the substance and the scenario for such a result are unstated. Here again, their question is, what do *we* propose?

There is an aspect of the Egyptian position we might be able to use as an opener with them: they say it would be humiliating for them to negotiate with Israel and that they will not do so. We might ask them in reply how they imagine reaching a political settlement without negotiating, at least through third parties. They negotiated, after all, in 1948 and 1956.

Assuming that the cease fire holds, there are two possible roads forward: (a) more United Nations debates and votes or (b) negotiations, bilateral or multilateral, secret or public, in New York or elsewhere. The two procedures are not necessarily alternatives. The goal of the United Nations after all, is peace, not the production of Resolutions. Thus far, at least, the sessions of the Security Council and the General Assembly have had the effect of preventing, not encouraging the process of negotiation.

I believe all our weight from now on should be to promote negotiation, and to direct UN votes and debates to that end.

II

Now let me turn to the more specific issues discussed at one or another capital during my trip.

1. *Defensive Steps.*

(a) My interlocutors agreed that all of us should keep talking with Tito, in order to move him as rapidly as possible and as far as possible from his five points, and towards our five principles, in which the Yugoslavs profess to believe. Some people think we shall face another Yugoslav Resolution in the Assembly; others think Tito will not sponsor a Resolution unless he is sure it can win, and probably not unless it has our support in advance. All agree there is a risk, however, that he will sponsor a bad resolution, and that there is some risk of erosion in the Security Council or the Assembly, where the yearning for a settlement is strong, and frustration, boredom, impatience and worse are increasingly evident. The British carefully articulated that risk as to themselves. The sense of frustration is likely to be translated into pressure on the Israelis to do something they won't do, and we won't want to ask them to do since it is so hard to get a concession from the UAR.

There are some positive potentialities as well as risks in Tito's activities. He does have influence in Egypt. He might be able to accomplish something.

In any event, the people I met (a) affirmatively wanted not to shut the door in Tito's face; (b) hoped an orchestrated dialogue with Tito would move him to a position of utility, or of less disutility, thus hopefully preventing a rough round in the UN. I said in this connection that we hadn't yet altogether made up our minds on how to handle Tito; but that I should be inclined to recommend the effort, on prudential grounds. But I added that we all ought to remember that it might be harder to hold off a more "moderate", plausible but still unsatisfactory Tito Resolution than one which is visibly unfair and unrealistic.

2. Jerusalem.

The two Jerusalem Resolutions have been passed. The Secretary General has sent Thalman[3] out to Palestine. A report has been filed.[4] Most people agreed that a piecemeal approach, dealing separately at this point with the Jerusalem problem in isolation, made no sense and could do no particular good. On the other hand, I heard no strong voices of resistance to another Resolution. All hoped we could get by without one, and in any event persuade the Pakistanis and the Jordanians to put up a text that could be understood—a text consistent with our own position—if there has to be a Jerusalem Resolution.

We shall face pressure at home to vote "with the Arabs for once" if a Jerusalem Resolution does come up. The Europeans are not very staunch on this subject, although they are sympathetic, and some of the Dutch at least are knowledgeable.

I recommend that we pursue low-level talks about possible texts with the Pakistanis, as a precaution. It ought to be possible to get a text we might approve tactically, for purposes of such a Resolution.

---

[3] Ambassador Ernesto A. Thalmann of Switzerland was named by the Secretary-General as his Personal Representative to obtain information on the situation in Jerusalem as a basis for the report requested by General Assembly Resolution 2254 (ES–V) of July 14, 1967.

[4] For text of the Secretary-General's report of September 12 on the situation in Jerusalem, see UN document S/8146 (A/6793).

3. Initiatives

  A. The United Nations.

There was general—though not universal—agreement that the West should move forward soon in the Security Council to obtain the best possible Resolution calling for the appointment of a Special Representative to talk to the parties.

Everyone thought that on the whole we should probe the Soviets well before the Assembly to ascertain whether they would go back on our understanding about the Draft Resolution. Even the appearance of a Soviet-American front should nudge the process forward.

If that draft fades, what do we do? The Israelis, of course, would prefer doing nothing in New York, until they reach Hussein and Nasser. The British urge Security Council action as soon as possible, preferably on the basis of the US–USSR draft, otherwise on any basis that might open the Canal.

I pointed out the risks of such a course. The Egyptians are openly ignoring their international obligations under the Treaty.[5] No one is saying a word on the subject. If now we make a deal, offering Nasser a reward for his sins, we prepare the way badly for serious negotiations later. We know that no partial, Suez-only Resolution will work; if we waste time and effort on such a non-starter, we simply postpone the day of movement on the one problem that could begin troop withdrawals: a declaration of non-belligerency. I raised the only-half facetious thought of a leak to the press to the effect that we were talking to the Soviets about moving the cease-fire line five miles West of the Canal if the UAR continues to ignore its obligations under the Convention. Such a story could help bring talk back to the real world—and indeed, action along these lines would be the quickest way to open the Canal!

  B. Direct Negotiations.

This subject was discussed only in London, with the British, with David Bruce, and with Ambassador Barbour, whom I met there Saturday[6] morning.

Clearly, the British put a higher priority on getting Nasser started than on Hussein. They are probing Nasser's recent trial balloon about opening a dialogue with them.

There was very little talk about what concrete suggestions could or should be made to stir Nasser into action, either by us, by the British or by the Yugoslavs. I told the British simply that we were thinking about how to answer Cairo's request for "modalities", but hadn't yet decided

---

[5] The Constantinople Convention of 1888; see footnotes 4 and 5, Document 271.

[6] September 16.

what to say, and with what degree of formality. We want to avoid "creeping recognition".

Problems in connection with the possibility of negotiation between Israel and Jordan are discussed in a separate memorandum.

And I shall shortly circulate a rough sketch of a memorandum or talking points we might use in responding to the requests of the Soviets, the Saudis, the Egyptians, and others, as to what we think might be done now.

---

442. Telegram From the Mission to the United Nations to the Department of State[1]

New York, September 23, 1967, 1711Z.

950. Re: Israeli Views on Middle East.

In dinner conversation with me Sept 19 Eban outlined current Israeli policy flowing from internal debate during summer and recent series of cabinet meetings. Essential points he made are set out below.[2] Rafael and Harman present on Israeli side, and Sisco, Buffum and Pedersen on US side.

Eban said most important thing was that they had decided to take current stands on position of security principle rather than on territorial basis and to keep their options open for future negotiations. Implications that their position had hardened since last June was not true, he said. However, if Israel were compelled to state its specific policy publicly at this time they would have to be stated in a maximalist position. Israel's general position was that in the absence of a situation of peace Israel would have to maintain its positions on basis of considerations of national security but in a peace agreement with Arabs they could be in a flexible negotiating position.

---

[1] Source: National Archives and Records Administration, RG 59, Central Files 1967–69, POL 27 ARAB–ISR. Secret; Priority; Exdis. Repeated Priority to Tel Aviv. A retyped copy of this telegram was sent to the President with a covering note from Walt Rostow commenting that it was "a pretty full portrait of Israel's frame of mind at the moment." (Johnson Library, National Security File, Country File, Israel, Vol. VII)

[2] Telegram 949 from USUN, September 23, reported that Eban also said that Israel was uncertain about the prospects for a settlement with King Hussein, since what had emerged from the conference at Khartoum was a call for a common policy which seemed to have tied the King's hands. (National Archives and Records Administration, RG 59, Central Files 1967–69, POL 27 ARAB–ISR/SANDSTORM)

With respect to Egypt, Eban said their idea was that border would follow the international frontier. There would be an international presence in Straits of Tiran to assure freedom of navigation, possibly of major maritime powers in Gulf or something on the shore. There would be a demilitarization of the Sinai. Suez Canal would be open to ships of all nations on basis of "declaratory" assurances (i.e., without some external presence). Demilitarization of Sinai would be assured by some sort of international presence, possibly an enlarged UNTSO type of operation, and possibly including UAR and Israeli troops. Idea of demilitarization of Sinai was difficult to achieve if UAR stayed in Gaza Strip.

Gaza territory was also security problem for Israel. Israel would like have the territory without the population but did not see how that could come about. He intimated there may even be an exchange of territory along the international frontier in favor of Egypt in return for Gaza Strip going to Israel. He thought Egypt might even be glad to be rid of Gaza Strip. Another possibility apparently under consideration was some form of international authority of Gaza Strip. (Eban noted this had been discussed in 1956 with US and that he had memcon with Dulles in his files about it.)[3]

On Syria, he said it was hard to contemplate an early peace agreement as long as Syrian Govt retained its present complexion. There had been a discussion of a demilitarization arrangement on Syrian Heights similar to idea re Sinai. Conclusion, however, which he shared, was that this would not be safe and that some territorial adjustments would have to be made.

Re Jerusalem, the Holy Moslem quarter would create perpetual emotional religious problems as long as it under Israeli control. GOI therefore had in mind arrangement which would put it under Moslem control and sovereignty. Rest of city was now united, and Arab inhabitants were free to travel throughout Israel. There could be some arrangement which would insure free Jordanian access to and participation in economic life of city.

West Bank presented particularly difficult problems. Incorporation of West Bank into Israel, with its large Arab population, would completely transform Israel's national existence and reason for being. An Israeli demographic expert had estimated that at present rate of population growth this would produce an Arab majority in Israel within 15 years. In any case it would cause a total reshaping of Israeli politics, as

---

[3] Eban and Dulles discussed Gaza a number of times during the months after the Suez crisis; for records of those conversations, see *Foreign Relations, 1955–1957*, volumes XVI and XVII.

Arab votes were sought, and thus produce alterations in structure of Israel that they did not desire. Neither could Arabs be incorporated into Israel without granting them Israeli citizenship. This would not be permitted by international community nor would it be acceptable to Israeli people themselves.

Eban said they had also given thought to establishment of separate, autonomous Palestinian state on West Bank. This also has serious drawbacks. Days of autonomous dependent regions had really passed. Creation of Palestinian state might simply increase irredentist desires. There would be yet another Arab state on Arab scene. In a year or two it would ask for UN membership, and it would be admitted. Such prospects did not look attractive. On the other hand, now that Israelis for first time had opportunity to visit areas of historic significance to them, it would be difficult for their citizens to understand govt simply turning the area back. Sort of thinking they were therefore thinking of would include two elements: (a) demilitarization of West Bank, with a UN inspection system; and (b) some form of economic, customs or travel arrangements which would permit access to and larger cooperation with the area. He referred to possibility of a free port on Mediterranean for Jordan as a move in same direction. I believe he also had in mind some border adjustments for security purposes, as he referred to Israeli security psychosis resulting from fact entire population was in range of Arab guns but he was not precise about what they might be.

Re refugee problem, Eban made clear Israel was deliberately opening up travel from Gaza to the West Bank in hopes it would relieve population pressures in Gaza. He also said Israel was issuing a few small pilot projects for economic resettlement for a few refugees in order to demonstrate feasibility of doing this within reasonable length of time. He implied Israel would welcome external international help for a much larger effort.

Re General Assembly, Eban thought there would be a substantial Arab effort to obtain political backing for their position requiring Israeli withdrawal without compensating actions on their side. If this failed, possibilities of direct settlement would be enhanced. He thought objective in Assembly should be to insure that no such decision were taken. He said specifically that appointment of a UN rep without any precise terms of reference would be acceptable, but indicated GOI does not want to play this card yet.

In explaining Israel's insistence of a settlement directly committing parties in the area, Eban expounded Israel's considered assessment of events leading up to current outbreak of fighting. One of their basic conclusions from this was that external restraints, including both the UN and direct support that could be expected in the interests of its security by Israel from various countries including France and US and from maritime powers with respect to maritime rights, were weaker than both they and UAR had calculated. In future, therefore, security guarantees had to come from the area and to a much lesser extent from external forces.

Their appreciation of sequence of events was:

(A) In middle of May Nasser's objective was to apply pressures on Israel to prevent Israel from retaliating against Syrian Al Fatah raids. He had been spurred on to this by Sov Union which wanted to protect Syria and which gave UAR false intelligence about Israeli troop concentrations on Syrian border. Nasser's intention was to hold a corridor to Israel so that his troops were in direct confrontation with Israel. Israel knew as a fact that he was prepared to have UNEF stay in Straits of Tiran, Gaza, and Quintella.

(B) Nasser expected that UN and other external pressures, particularly US, would prevent him from going further. When UN proved unexpectedly weak, both in SC and in saying UNEF would have to be pulled out entirely, he changed his objective to restoration of the pre-1956 status, i.e. including blockade of the Gulf. He again expected international pressures to restrain him at that point. Inability of maritime powers to agree on an effective course of action and general weakness of resistance to his moves then caused him to make the next decision.

(C) From about 29th May, UAR objective changed to one of open [illegible]— against Israel. He began to create the alliances with Jordan and to obtain the support of Iraq and countries as far away as Algeria for a final assault. Eban described UAR policy from this point on as moving forward in a drunken fashion. Messages to troop commanders indicated clear offensive indications, and UAR began to reconnoiter by air Israel's key industrial and other facilities suitable for aerial attack. (He implied that Israel had a great deal of firm intelligence on this period both from captured documents and from intercepted telephone conversations at the time.)

Amb Harman expressed considerable sensitivity about arms supplies from US, saying he had been able to obtain the delivery of only about $700 thousand of equipment out of the $3 million total which they had already paid, and that there were considerable uncertainties about future plane sales. He said they would need 79 planes but not for delivery before end of 1968. He stressed importance to their logistics of "nuts and bolts" and said military value of captured Sov equipment had been considerably exaggerated in the press.

I conveyed to FonMin substance of message Sisco had brought us with him about need for Israel to express itself and act with magnanimity and not be too rigid about method of negotiating a settlement.[4] I also urged them to continue to exercise leniency about return of refugees from Jordan to West Bank. Eban said they had decided to allow return to be extended but with a larger degree of control in Israeli hands. They would allow hardship cases and relatives to continue to return.[5]

Goldberg

---

[4] The Sisco message has not been found. A draft telegram to Barbour instructing him to see Eban before his departure for New York to express concern at "indications Israeli objectives may be shifting from original position seeking peace with no territorial gains toward one of territorial expansion" was sent to President Johnson for clearance on September 15. His reaction was that they should not send the telegram but "let Goldberg do it." (Johnson Library, National Security File, Country File, Israel, Vol. VII)

[5] Rusk expressed the hope that the Israelis would resume permitting the refugees to return to the West Bank without political conditions in a letter to Eban transmitted in telegram 31492 to Tel Aviv, September 2. (National Archives and Records Administration, RG 59, Central Files 1967–69, REF ARAB) Eban replied in a letter transmitted in telegram 37827 from Tel Aviv, September 15. (Ibid.)

---

443.   Memorandum of Conversation[1]

Washington, September 20, 1967, 1 p.m.

SUBJECT

The Middle East

PARTICIPANTS

Mr. Yuri N. Tcherniakov, Minister Counselor, Union of Soviet Socialist Republics
Mr. Eugene V. Rostow, Under Secretary for Political Affairs

Under Secretary Rostow lunched with Counselor Y. N. Tcherniakov at the latter's invitation on September 20, 1967, at the Residence of the Soviet Ambassador.

The conversation concerned several topics, and is reported in separate memoranda of conversation.

After preliminary amenities, Mr. Tcherniakov asked what prospects we saw for a peaceful solution in the Middle East. Rostow answered

---

[1] Source: Johnson Library, National Security File, Country File, USSR, Vol. XVI. Secret; Exdis. Drafted by Rostow. Walt Rostow sent the memorandum to the President on September 22 along with the memorandum of the portion of the conversation concerning Vietnam.

that we thought the strongest base for going forward was a Security Council resolution based on the principles and ideas on which we had agreed at the end of the General Assembly. This had been the tenor of our recent talks with Tito and the Arabs, and with other governments. Mr. Tcherniakov said this was also the view of his government.

(At this point Mr. Tcherniakov switched the conversation to Vietnam. He led the way back to the Middle East at a later point.)

Mr. Tcherniakov enquired broadly about Israeli views on a settlement. Rostow commented that while we could not speak or negotiate for Israel, it was our impression that their official position on these matters had not changed in either direction—that the Israelis would make great sacrifices for a condition of peace. Both men agreed that at this point the parties were in a state of negotiating from a distance—making signals in their speeches and actions, and naturally quite strong ones. So far as Egypt was concerned, we did not think the problems of settlement should present serious difficulties, once the principle of the resolution on which we had agreed in July was accepted. There was the Gaza Strip of course, but that had never been Egyptian territory. Security arrangements would certainly be necessary. Nodding, Tcherniakov asked whether we thought a solution for Syria would be difficult. Rostow said we had originally thought not, but that the Israelis had been shocked by the fortifications they found on the Golan Hills. We were not clear whether demilitarization would be enough. Both men agreed that the armistice lines between Jordan and Israel would present serious problems.

Tcherniakov hoped that we would use our influence with Israel to obtain concessions in the process of peace-making. He said he was glad that both our governments were agreed that the starting point was to link troop withdrawals with an end of the claims of belligerency.

Rostow said he hoped we could begin on that general footing in the Security Council, and soon. The world was beginning to think that nothing could be accomplished through the U.N. It would be electrified if we sponsored a resolution together in the Security Council. Tcherniakov said that some period in the Assembly might be necessary, but he agreed that the nations had had a sufficient opportunity to express themselves on the Middle East in the General Assembly. "They have talked enough," he said.

Tcherniakov referred to the Gromyko–Goldberg agreement between the two governments at least four times, and concluded, referring back to the conversation about Vietnam, that if we succeeded in acting together in one place, it could help elsewhere. None of these local quarrels in small distant countries, he said, were worth a confrontation between the United States and the Soviet Union, but such episodes kept recurring.

(Rostow decided not to press for greater clarification about whether the language of the July draft[2] could be negotiated further. Instead, he sought reiteration of the basic point—that the agreement was still alive—and notice that we might have some drafting changes to suggest.)

---

[2] See Documents 380 and 384.

---

444. Information Memorandum From the Assistant Secretary of State for Near Eastern and South Asian Affairs (Battle) to Secretary of State Rusk[1]

Washington, September 21, 1967.

SUBJECT

Ambassador Pachachi's Conversation with Mr. Robert Anderson

Mr. Robert Anderson called me to report that Ambassador Pachachi of Iraq had called on him Thursday[2] for a full review of the Middle Eastern situation. During the special session of the General Assembly, Mr. Pachachi was the spokesman for a group of moderate Arabs with Mr. Anderson and others.

Mr. Pachachi, basing his comments on a meeting of his group (although UAR and others are not yet in New York), said that there was general concern because the Arabs did not believe they knew the position of the United States. The United States has not been explicit, they felt, in describing that position. There is some concern that this stems from U.S. support of the Israeli desire that nothing happen for a time since the Israelis are convinced that time is on their side. The moderate Arabs hope that our position is not also one of inaction as they consider that there must be an early settlement to the difficulties. If there is not an early settlement, U.S.-Arab relations will suffer considerably.

The moderate Arabs do not consider that their dialogue with the U.S. is adequate. They believe that there should be more contact with Ambassador Goldberg (which I urged during the last Assembly and urged today). Representatives of the group would like to meet with me,

---

[1] Source: National Archives and Records Administration, RG 59, Central Files 1967–69, POL 27–14 ARAB–ISR. Secret. Copies were sent to Katzenbach, Rostow, Kohler, Sisco, and USUN. Rusk's initials on the memorandum indicates he read it.

[2] September 21.

and I have agreed to get together with them the early part of next week in New York.

Ambassador Pachachi was asked how far the Arabs were prepared to go at this time. He replied that they were willing to accept "almost complete rights of passage" in the waterways. There is no problem on Aqaba, and the Suez Canal could be opened to all but Israeli flagships. When Mr. Anderson expressed doubt that the Israelis would accept such an arrangement, Mr. Pachachi replied that, while he could not speak for Nasser, it was even possible that the Canal could be opened to Israeli flagships if necessary to obtain a settlement.

The Arabs are willing to guarantee all borders, but they must have retreat from occupied territories.

Withdrawal from Sinai could be coupled with a demilitarization arrangement.

They would accept demilitarization of the Syrian Heights under United Nations direction.

They will accept a unified Jerusalem provided there is some kind of administration by the Arabs (presumably the Jordanians) over the old Arab quarter.

Mr. Pachachi remarked that the Russians will "go as far as the Arabs want them to go provided the United States will join." The Eastern Bloc is, according to Pachachi, largely pro-Israel in attitude and the Russians cannot ignore this feeling on the part of satellite countries.

The Arabs are willing to accept a declaration of the end of a state of belligerency in some form.

They cannot accept direct negotiations alone with the Israelis. They will accept, if necessary, negotiations with a third party in the room. They would prefer to have the Arabs in one room, the Israelis in a second room, and a representative of the third country in a room between the two. They admit, however, that there is some precedent for them to sit at the same table provided a third party is present.

Comment: The foregoing is the most forthcoming offer yet reported. As I told Mr. Anderson, it is possible that Pachachi will be more open with him than he would be with a Government official. I would suspect that Pachachi's position with Mr. Anderson will not be fully reflected in an official talk, but I will try to find out during the next few days. If the Arabs are willing to make a deal along the foregoing lines, this is very encouraging.

445. Memorandum From the President's Special Assistant (Rostow) to President Johnson[1]

Washington, September 22, 1967.

SUBJECT

Comment on Evron's Talk with Harry McPherson[2]

On Evron's first point—suspicion in the Jewish community about our position before June 5—I should think these straightforward comments would suffice: (1) There was no question at any point before or during the war that we would have let Israel be seriously hurt or destroyed. (2) We made a serious effort to prevent the war. (3) Israel in the end did not ask us for help; it is to Israel's advantage and ours that it handled this problem entirely on its own. (4) These statements fairly represent thinking at the policy-making levels of our government and far outweigh all the later talk at professional levels about what our commitment to Israel was or wasn't.

On Evron's second point—that we are holding Israel at arms length until she changes her position toward the Arabs—I think we can make a categorical denial, but this would be worth discussing with Secretary McNamara. We have clamped down hard on all military shipments to the Middle East since the war. But we have repeatedly and, I think, quite honestly told the Israelis privately that since early July our aid freeze had been for one purpose only—not rocking the boat during the extremely touchy Congressional debate over military sales. We've reviewed the freeze several times (chronology attached)[3] but each time accepted Secretary McNamara's judgment that we shouldn't move until the military aid bill was safe, though we did let $3 million go to Israel to tide them over if they'd help on the Hill.

It is admittedly true that we do not want to make decisions on any new major military sales to Israel until we've worked out a comprehensive arms policy for the whole area. The Senior Interdepartmental Group has already requested a recommendation for you by 1 November. But I feel that is a separate issue beyond the freeze on past programs because you could not approve any recommendation that

---

[1] Source: Johnson Library, National Security File, Country File, Israel, Vol. VII. Secret.

[2] A memorandum of September 20 from McPherson to the President reporting on a conversation that day with Evron is attached. A notation in President Johnson's handwriting on McPherson's memorandum reads: "Walt. Give me your reaction & comment. L."

[3] The attached chronology, undated, begins with the NSC Special Committee decisions of June 8 and 14 on the suspension of all military shipments to the Middle East and continues with points at which aspects of this issue were considered.

reneged on past promises to Israel. However, others may not agree with me, and if I'm wrong Evron may have a point.

Two things have irked the Israelis: (1) that our freeze applies to all items with a military application—even those which they want to buy commercially for cash like the Piper Cubs Evron mentioned to Harry; and (2) that no one in the USG will promise that the freeze will end when the aid bill passes.

As I see it, the way to dampen Israeli suspicions would be to do now some combination of the following: (1) quietly to lift the freeze on items to be bought for cash from commercial suppliers (probably less than $20 million); and (2) to say secretly but officially that we will lift the suspension on other items from past deals in which USG money is involved as soon as (a) the aid authorization bill becomes law or (b) the aid appropriation is passed. Even (1) by itself would help. At the same time I would relax the suspension on a few comparable items for a couple of friendly Arab states.

This action would in no way pre-empt the basic policy study of our longer-term Mid-East arms policy. That would continue to concentrate on future arms transfers. This decision would affect only a limited number of long-approved transactions now frozen. Nor would this action undercut our line with the Congress that we continue to act with the utmost restraint.

You wouldn't want to do this without talking again with Bob McNamara. If you are concerned enough about mounting Israeli feeling, I would suggest putting this subject on our next Tuesday lunch agenda. I had planned to re-open the question at the first Tuesday lunch after the Congressional conference on the aid bill ended. But now that is going to hang over until early October, and the appropriations process will reach into November. We held the Israelis off with the $3 million in early August on the assumption that we might be able to raise the freeze some time in early September (although we made no promises). Now that the pressure is mounting, it might be worth taking another reading.

Walt

Put it on the Tuesday agenda[4]

See me

P.S. I think Evron's mention of the "hold-up" on licenses for the $3 million we have released is unfair. Actually, the Israelis themselves in making up their own list put on some items with a long lead time and

---

[4] This option is checked.

have since asked to shift to some that are more immediately available. Whatever delay that may have caused is their fault since Defense accepted their list just as they wrote it.

---

446.   Memorandum of Conversation[1]

New York, September 25, 1967, 12:15 p.m.

SUBJECT

Middle East

PARTICIPANTS

UK Side
Foreign Secretary George Brown
Lord Caradon, UK Permanent Representative to the UN
Sir Patrick Dean, British Ambassador
P.T. Hayman, Assistant Under Secretary, Foreign Office
Sir Harold Beeley, Deputy Leader UK Disarmament Delegation, Geneva
Donald Murray, Counselor, Foreign Office
T.F. Brenchley, Foreign Office
D.J.D. Maitland, Principal Private Secretary to Foreign Secretary

US Side
The Secretary
Ambassador Arthur Goldberg
Ambassador Llewellyn Thompson
Lucius D. Battle, Assistant Secretary, NEA
Joseph J. Sisco, Assistant Secretary, IO
J. Harold Shullaw, Country Director, BMI

Foreign Secretary Brown said that he got the impression from talking with Gromyko last week that the Soviet Government wants to see some movement on a Middle East settlement but does not want to get out in front. Ambassador Thompson said the Soviet interest in the Suez Canal was substantial, that approximately 1400 Soviet ships used it in a year. Foreign Secretary Brown, in response to a question from Assistant Secretary Battle, said that the resumption of oil shipments following the

---

[1] Source: National Archives and Records Administration, RG 59, Central Files 1967–69, POL 27 ARAB–ISR. Secret; Exdis. Drafted by United Kingdom Country Director J. Harold Shullaw, and approved in S on October 3. The memorandum is part 3 of 3. The meeting took place in the Secretary's suite at the Waldorf Astoria Hotel in New York, where Rusk was attending the 22nd Session of the UN General Assembly.

Khartoum Conference would not have much effect on the British balance of payments. The Canal closure is costing about £ 200 million per annum in foreign exchange. The Foreign Secretary emphasized the importance of some progress on the Canal question by at least securing the opening of the southern end to release the trapped ships. This action, he said, would not necessarily involve the question of Israeli access to the Canal and for that reason should be easier.

The Foreign Secretary said that he had been impressed by the Yugoslav Foreign Minister who appeared to have some authority and to be willing to consider amending the original Tito proposals on a Middle East settlement. The Yugoslav Foreign Minister had pointedly remarked that Tito's proposals had been formulated before the Khartoum Conference. Foreign Secretary Brown thought it might be possible to amend the Yugoslav proposals in the direction of the balanced formulation of the earlier Goldberg–Dobrynin draft.

Sir Harold Beeley said that a solution in the Middle East had to be based on both Israeli withdrawal and acceptance by the Arabs of Israel and an end to belligerency. The Foreign Secretary strongly supported the idea of a UN representative going out to the area to assist in finding solutions. He emphasized that this representative should not be referred to as a mediator. Sir Harold Beeley said the Soviets would not accept the appointment of a UN representative unless the appointment of such a representative were coupled with specific proposals for a Middle East settlement. Lord Caradon agreed with this view.

The Foreign Secretary asked Mr. Battle how he read the situation in the UAR. Mr. Battle replied that he thought Nasser's days were numbered, perhaps six months to a year. Economic problems facing the UAR are tremendous. Foreign Secretary Brown said the question was who would succeed Nasser. A moderate regime might wish to turn to the West in an effort to obtain help in bailing itself out of its economic difficulties. On the other hand if a Leftist regime were to succeed Nasser it might be followed by a Soviet decision to increase arms supplies to the UAR. Foreign Secretary Brown said there is a danger that the Arabs may have learned the value of a preemptive air strike from Israeli actions in the June war.

The Foreign Secretary said that he realized the importance before proceeding in the UN of being certain there was enough agreement on the terms of a solution with the Soviets so that they did not torpedo it. He said, however, that he did not believe we had to be assured in advance of agreement on exact details of a settlement. Mr. Sisco pointed out that the Arab emphasis is still on withdrawal in the first instance and that the Khartoum Conference had rejected recognition of Israel and an end to belligerency.

447.   Letter From President Johnson to King Faisal[1]

Washington, September 25, 1967.

Your Majesty:

In view of my continuing close concern with the difficult situation in the Near East, I particularly welcomed your thoughtful letter of September 6[2] and have carefully considered Your Majesty's views. Our warm personal relationship permits us to speak as friends, and I would like to reply in the same spirit of frankness and constructive concern which characterized Your Majesty's own message.

I agree that the recent Khartoum conference marked notable progress for the forces of Arab moderation. Your Majesty's own statesmanlike role at these meetings was a major contribution to this result.

I am especially encouraged by the decision to liquidate the long-standing Yemen problem. It will, I hope, mark the beginning of a return to stability in Southwest Arabia in which both your country and mine are so deeply interested. I congratulate Your Majesty warmly on this happy result of your long efforts, as well as on the progress already discernible in implementing the decision.

The decision to lift the oil embargo was also welcome. This action has removed a complicating factor in relations between the Arab countries and the West which was not of our making. American public opinion has reacted favorably to this evidence of Arab desire to return to business as usual.

The Khartoum decisions regarding an Arab–Israel settlement are more difficult for us to evaluate. The final communiqué states what the Arabs will not do but, except by indirection, is silent on what the Arabs

---

[1] Source: Johnson Library, National Security File, Special Head of State Correspondence File, Saudi Arabia. No classification marking. Walt Rostow sent a draft of the letter to the President with a covering memorandum of September 19 stating that the Arab leaders at Khartoum had commissioned Faisal to write to him, and the draft letter was thus "our response to Khartoum." He commented that at Khartoum the Arabs had taken "a first short step toward realism and, while it isn't enough, we don't want to throw such cold water on it that we discourage further efforts or cause our friends to give up all hope of sympathy from us." (Ibid., Memos to the President, Walt W. Rostow, Vol. 43) A copy of the draft was sent to Bundy with a September 21 memorandum from Saunders that states the President had written Rostow a note asking him to be sure Rusk and Bundy were "on board on this one." Bundy's handwritten revisions appear on that copy of the draft. (Ibid., NSC Special Committee Files, Saudi Arabia) Telegram 45719 to Jidda, September 28, transmitted the text to Jidda for delivery. (National Archives and Records Administration, RG 59, Central Files 1967–69, POL 7 SUDAN) Telegram 1356 from Jidda, October 5, reported that Ambassador Eilts had presented the letter that day. (Ibid., POL 27 ARAB–ISR)

[2] For text of the King's letter, see *Foreign Relations, 1964–1968*, vol. XXI, Document 301.

may be willing to do. The Arab decision to turn away from a military solution is most welcome. But the absence of any statement on the key issue of belligerency leaves a major obstacle to settlement unresolved.

Frankly, we do not see how one party can continue to invoke rights of belligerency while attempting to impose on the other obligations of a state of peace. An Israeli withdrawal, unaccompanied by appropriate assurances from the Arabs, would seem to us prejudicial to Israel's territorial integrity, in which we are as interested as we are in the integrity of each Arab state. Return to the unstable armistice existing before June 4, 1967, can hardly be in anyone's interest, since this very instability led to such grave consequences.

I believe what is needed is a more permanent settlement to which all governments in the area would in some manner be committed. Only this result will assure peace and progress for the region in which both the Arabs and Israelis must live together.

The draft resolution tentatively agreed upon by the United States and the Soviet Union during the Emergency Session of the General Assembly, linking troop withdrawal to an end of belligerency and renunciation of attendant rights or claims by all the parties, could in our view be a useful basis for such a settlement. The United States Government has, however, no fixed position as to exactly how a settlement may be achieved. In this connection, when I spoke on June 19 of the need to recognize rights of national life, I of course meant the acceptance by each state of its neighbor's right to exist free from any menace of belligerency. I was not prejudging the question of formal recognition.

The United States Government played a central role in bringing about Israeli withdrawal in 1957, but at that time no such mutually accepted basis for coexistence was established. Those arrangements accordingly did not endure. I do not think it possible to travel the same road again. In our view, those who inhabit the area must themselves take the primary responsibility for finding a mutually acceptable basis on which coexistence is tolerable. This naturally applies to both sides, and we are, of course, ready to help when it is clear what concrete steps are envisaged.

I cannot stress too strongly to Your Majesty that our principles— which I outlined publicly on June 19—are designed to be both even-handed and beneficial to all parties concerned. We oppose threats or use of force by both Arabs and Israelis. On the basis of those principles, we favor Israeli withdrawal and an end to military or paramilitary actions by either side. Above all, we see a vision of the better life which peace would bring to all the people of the Middle East.

Our position is not based on transient considerations, such as the attitude towards us of certain Arab states, but rather on an assessment of what we believe is required to prevent yet another round of warfare at some later date. We naturally hope that those Arab states that have broken relations with us will soon manifest an attitude towards us that will permit relations to return to normal. It is hard to have understanding without contact, and restoration of our relations with these Arab countries would be helpful. But we believe that realism and willingness to compromise by the parties directly concerned are the basic ingredients needed to end the present Arab-Israel impasse.

In closing, I should emphasize to Your Majesty that I continue to value highly our close and friendly relations with you and your government. We will try at the coming session of the United Nations to help find some way to resolve the current difficulties. Meanwhile, I welcome our continuing personal exchanges as a means of strengthening our mutual understanding of the great difficulties which still lie ahead.

All best personal regards,

Sincerely,

Lyndon B. Johnson

---

448.   Memorandum of Conversation[1]

New York, September 25, 1967.

SUBJECT

Middle East

PARTICIPANTS

Adan M. Pachachi, Minister of Foreign Affairs, Iraq
Lucius D. Battle, Asst. Secretary of State for NEA

I received Mr. Pachachi on September 25 in my room at the Waldorf. He remained for approximately one hour and twenty minutes. The meeting grew out of Mr. Pachachi's conversations with former Secretary of the Treasury Robert Anderson.

After a brief exchange of pleasantries, Mr. Pachachi launched vigorously into a discussion of the Middle East. He said that the cur-

---

[1] Source: National Archives and Records Administration, RG 59, Central Files 1967–69, POL 27 ARAB–ISR. Secret; Exdis. Drafted by Battle on September 26. Copies were sent to Walt Rostow, Sisco, Goldberg, Eugene Rostow, and Davies.

rent session of the United Nations must not let an opportunity go by to solve the Middle East problem. Action through either the General Assembly or the Security Council during this session was imperative. The Arabs had accepted a moderate course at the Khartoum meeting and this must be built upon and as soon as possible or moderate leadership would give way to more radical influences. The United States had been very general in its pronouncements and it is imperative that we define carefully and precisely what we mean by the principles we have enunciated. The Israelis, in Mr. Pachachi's opinion, want no action at the present session and he feared the United States was supporting them in this course. Moreover, he detected in Ambassador Goldberg's statements an erosion of the US position which he found alarming.

I replied that the Middle East presented problems for the world and that a dangerous situation continued to exist there. Clearly we hoped for as early a solution as possible and we felt that the United Nations General Assembly offered one opportunity to come to grips with difficult problems. However, many levels of conversation and discussion were necessary and every forum should be utilized to the fullest extent. While speed of solution was important, it was equally imperative that we have a just and lasting solution as the world could not afford to risk a war every ten years or so.

I said that the United States position had been stated in the President's speech of June 19 and that there had been no change in our position. We still sought a lasting and just peace and to us an obvious starting point was for both sides to agree that the war was over and the state of belligerency ended.

We had refrained from defining what we would find acceptable in terms of a solution. What was acceptable to us was a solution the parties themselves could agree upon. We had no magic formula and had offered no overall plan. The general principles we had stated remained our position and we were reluctant to attempt to define a solution the parties themselves might reject. In this connection I pointed out that contrary to some opinion we had neither the right nor the power to dictate a solution.

Mr. Pachachi then spoke at great length on the need for the United States to define its views either privately or publicly. Private discussions should come first and reflect what the parties would agree to which could then be stated publicly.

I asked Mr. Pachachi whether a UN Representative could usefully, by exploring the issues in detail with the parties, give a sense of direction which might lead to peace. Mr. Pachachi said that a mediator was impossible unless the outlines of peace had already been agreed to in a UN context. To send a mediator first put the Arabs in a position of negotiating with Israeli troops on their soil. This was an impossible situation and the Arabs could not be expected to negotiate while occupied by foreign troops.

We returned to the possibility of finding a formula to end the state of belligerency. I told Mr. Pachachi that it was difficult indeed for us to encourage the Israelis or anyone else to believe the Arabs wanted a political settlement when statements continued to emanate from Arab countries indicating the war would go on.

I tried to draw Mr. Pachachi out on specific issues such as the Suez Canal, the Straits of Tiran, and refugees without much success. He returned each time to the need for the United States to say what it wished to see happen after which there could be discussion leading to General Assembly or Security Council action. He reaffirmed Arab unwillingness to negotiate directly or to recognize Israel.

Mr. Pachachi urged that the United States keep in touch with the Arabs and do all possible to prevent increasingly hostile attitudes from developing in the Arab world toward the United States. I told him that we were willing always to talk. Ambassador Goldberg with whom he had had a friendly relationship for some time was always willing to see him, Ambassador Meyer would be here for several weeks, and I was available in Washington and occasionally in New York if conversations with me would be helpful. Mr. Pachachi said he would try to see Ambassador Goldberg and also keep in touch with Ambassador Meyer.

Comment:

I found very little latitude in Mr. Pachachi's discourse. None of the moderation evident in his talks with Mr. Anderson was repeated to me. He adamantly insisted that it was up to the United States to do something but gave little evidence of desire on the part of the Arabs to do anything except continue a dialogue. The conversation was friendly although fairly firm on both sides.

449. Telegram From the Mission to the United Nations to the Department of State[1]

New York, September 26, 1967, 0250Z.

989/Secto 3. Following based on uncleared memcon, and subject to change on review, Noforn and FYI:

FonMin Eban accompanied by Ambassadors Harman and Rafael called on the Secretary September 25. Ambassador Goldberg, Sisco and Battle were present.

In reviewing current situation General Assembly, Eban said it too early to assess situation. Vietnam involves loss of life, and Middle East therefore secondary issue at moment. In preliminary conversation other delegations, Israel noted no major changes in basic convictions, although some tactical change evident. Secretary reaffirmed US position rests on President Johnson's June 19 speech.

Secretary asked whether Israeli public opinion so frozen that it would be difficult for Israel to make peace. Eban replied that press more chauvinistic than actual public opinion. When opinion of Israeli people assessed, it is always more rational and responsible than press would lead one to believe.

Eban then assessed prospects for peace with UAR and Jordan respectively. He stressed there were no territorial issues with UAR, it was principally question of peace and natural results of peace, such as right to navigate international waters. Problem of Jordan more difficult, involving territory and history. Eban noted there were several points of view on this question in Israel.

First, there is group that sees security in terms of territory.

Second, this view balanced by those concerned over future character of Israeli state. Arab majority in Israel. At present only 3 or 4 members of Cabinet of 21 would vote for annexation in Eban's opinion. There has been, however, no need to vote since positions to be taken on these issues are not before Cabinet as long as there are no negotiations with Arabs. Economic Ministers are all against.

Third was possibility making deal with new Palestinian state which would be 14th Arab state. West Bank leaders have given evidence of desiring to discuss their future. Mayor of Hebron, for example, has evidenced interest perhaps because he sees an opportunity to exert leader-

---

[1] Source: National Archives and Records Administration, RG 59, Central Files 1967–69, POL 27 ARAB–ISR. Secret; Immediate; Exdis. Repeated Priority to Tel Aviv. Received at 1808Z.

ship in a sovereign new state. Gleam of sovereignty among leaders in West Bank similar to attitudes evident in communities in Cyprus. This only an incipient movement, but some "state personality" could emerge on West Bank.

Fourth, which had broad support, was to make best possible deal with Hussein. Hussein must recognize that he can make better deal sooner than later. If Hussein said he was ready to negotiate tomorrow, majority of Israeli people would support such move. However, Jordan cannot get back to June 4 situation. Emphasis in Jordanian settlement, however, would not be on territory but on security. Possibility exists for a free port, economic integration of Jordan. Eban also mentioned possibility of a demilitarization of West Bank with some kind of Israeli military presence.

Later in conversation, Eban made point that Iran and others had suggested more pressure be put on UAR to negotiate in first instance than on Jordan. Secretary acknowledged issue with UAR less difficult than with Jordan: availability of Voice of Arabs radio to support Egyptian decision to negotiate is of importance. Eban indicated Israel has passed message to UAR but not sure UAR understands clearly relationship between end of belligerency and territorial problems. Eban gave impression that Israel has tried to and will try again to make it clear to Egyptians that they could get substantial part of territory back in return for what Eban called a "juridical definition of relations between Israel and Egyptians". Peace was issue with UAR, not primarily territorial problem. Israel must have relationship on a "contractual basis", which includes recognition of Israeli sovereignty and "total nonbelligerency".

In response Ambassador Goldberg's question whether some form armistice agreement precluded basis from which peace can be fashioned, Eban replied armistice cannot be intermediate step between war and peace. Eban made clear he was less concerned over "form or semantics" of peace, but more in substance of it.

Secretary asked Eban assess current attitudes British and French. Eban replied he had conversation with Couve in which latter gave evidence great despair. At beginning and end of any discussion with French is an opinion re US, that US is inordinately powerful and therefore under French reasoning ready "to make war". French believe whatever happens in area must be within framework of Israeli recognition. Eban believes French may be moving away from position in last GA toward more reasonable position. He attributed this to two reasons: (a) adverse public opinion reaction in France; and (b) French pragmatism. Eban said French finding ways to continue delivery spare parts through commercial channels to Israel. Delivery planes less certain but French do not find it easy not to honor contracts. Eban opined French will probably be less active in UN, an instrument they never looked upon with favor. Present French representative to UN has leeway and does not share obsession re US.

In discussing UK attitudes, Eban stated Britain concerned with problem of Suez Canal and have probably exaggerated its economic importance to UK. Eban recognized Suez was a political issue in UK. He said UK fundamentally with US but wished to appear publicly more congenial to Arabs than is US. UK recognizes impossibility return June 4 and supports privately, though not publicly as yet, recent US statement on ME in GA. Eban said support of US is more than tactical problem and some delegations see substantive differences between US and UK. Expressed concern UK posture weakens solidarity and influences other Europeans. Eban referred to documents captured which indicated one reason UAR permitted situation get out of hand before war is conviction there was lack of coordination between Western powers. Expressed hope UK would make policy decision to support US, which would permit better tactical coordination.

In response to Secretary's inquiry as to whether Israel expected initiatives at UN, Eban responded there would be some from extremist delegations which would not be troublesome. We should watch Latin Americans carefully, he said, and we could expect a UN move along lines of Tito proposal. Secretary also noted he and Amb. Goldberg would be talking to the Soviets on three separate occasions this week and there would be opportunity to ascertain their current position. Eban said Tito proposal so far below minimal acceptance level, he would not expect too much trouble dealing with it.

In discussing Suez Canal, Eban indicated FonMin Brown had possible separate solution in mind. Eban said Israeli requirements regarding Canal are equality and no discrimination. If UN ran the Canal, this would be a form of internationalization. Eban suggested to Brown that UK ascertain whether UAR would accept this position which would be a major shift for UAR. At same time Eban made it clear no proposal relating to Canal would be acceptable unless it included freedom of passage for Israeli ships from outset.

With respect current flareups along Canal, Eban stated Bull had not been able to define accepted movements of respective parties. Such definition imperative when two countries are as close together physically as UAR and Israel. Any moves in Canal area in such circumstances became troublesome and dangerous.

Secretary asked whether Israel would object to steps UK might take to clear Suez Canal. Eban replied that Israel did not close Canal and would not wish to get in position being responsible for difficulties caused Western friends. Any plan reopen, however, must include use by Israeli ships, and mutuality between Egypt and Israel. Eban also said UK would not need to get Israeli approval to get its ships out of Canal. Eban has indicated to Brown Israel's belief that UK should reduce its reliance on Suez rather than retain past mystique regarding it.

Eban discussed current arms shipments of Russians to area stating they have apparently slowed down resupply and were being more selective, apparently based on desire not give aggressive capacity to UAR. Harman mentioned however, Russians have stepped up SU–7 deliveries. Israel believes UAR has more than twice number fighter bombers than pre-war, which suggests Arabs and Russians have drawn strategic conclusions from war. These conclusions similar to those drawn in Heikal article and is reflected in comments made Khartoum. In connection arms shipments Harman expressed hope US could act release pending shipments to Israel. Eban hoped US arms supply of Israel would be "pragmatic, normal, and commercial". Secretary explained current Congressional difficulties, and said we could not know what US could do until Congressional action on aid bill is final.

In this connection Secretary Rusk asked whether Israel had dealings with Cuba, to which Eban replied negative. Secretary called attention paragraph in OAS resolution regarding action by "other friendly countries." Suggested Israel let Latin American countries know directly that it had noted this paragraph and already fully complied.

Regarding strategy at UN, both Secretary and Goldberg indicated we had made no final determination and will discuss this matter over days ahead. Eban indicated that Middle East item would probably not be considered before mid-October. Eban agreed with Secretary's observation that Soviets would probably not be leading pack in the regular session.

Rusk

450.   Memorandum of Conversations[1]

New York, September 26, 1967.

SUBJECT

Middle East Crisis: US-UAR Relations

PARTICIPANTS

Mr. Mohamed Riad, Counselor, UAR Foreign Ministry

Mr. Hassan Sabri al-Khouli, Personal Representative of the President of the UAR

Donald C. Bergus, Principal Officer, U.S. Interests Section, Cairo

I lunched for two hours with Mohamed Riad at the Waldorf. He was eager to know the results of my consultation in the Department. I reviewed various conversations and said it all boiled down to the conclusion that the United States Government hesitated to play a more active role in seeking a resolution of the crisis as long as the Arabs were unprepared to face up to the problem of belligerency. He was keenly disappointed at this.

The conversation continued but we kept coming back to this point. He said that the US attitude made it hard for those in Egypt who were doing their best to improve US–UAR relations and cited his efforts on behalf of the American University, Cairo American College, etc. I said that the future of these institutions and other cultural relations would be meaningful only if they were jointly recognized as worthwhile. He agreed.

He was not responsive to questions as to how far the Arabs intended to push the Tito proposals. He waffled as to current Arab and Russian attitudes toward the Dobrynin–Goldberg resolution. He did say that as a result of his recent visit with his boss to Moscow he could assure me that the Soviets were not interested in continuing the present situation. They had made it clear that they would like a settlement. The conversation ended on a friendly but rather mournful note. Mohamed was sure that his government would be very disappointed.

I then repaired to USUN where I reported the foregoing to Ambassador Meyer and Mr. Thatcher. Ambassador Meyer asked me to accompany him to the General Assembly. In the Delegates' Lounge we encountered several members of the UAR Delegation including Ismail Fahmy and Hassan Sabri al-Khouli. Ambassador Meyer talked with Ismail Fahmy. I had a fairly lengthy private discussion with Hassan Sabri.

---

[1] Source: National Archives and Records Administration, RG 59, Central Files 1967–69, POL 27 ARAB–ISR. Confidential. Drafted by Bergus.

Hassan Sabri said that Mohamed Riad had briefed him about our luncheon conversation. He would not pretend to be pleased but neither was he particularly disappointed. He recognized that it would be a long time before the Middle East crisis was resolved. He said that the Israelis could occupy Sinai for months, years, even decades. He felt that over the long run world public opinion would turn against Israel as it continued to expel people, blow up Arab houses, etc.

Hassan Sabri returned to his theme that US–UAR relations were more important than the Arab–Israel problem. He said he wanted normalization as quickly as possible. He said he had full authority from President Nasser to work for normalization and that I should not hesitate to raise any problem with him in this regard. He said that Nasser's victory over the forces headed by Field Marshal Amer would facilitate the improvement of relations. He said that relations among peoples overshadowed political crises. He cited in this connection the lasting impact that Ambassador and Mrs. Battle had made on the Egyptians. He said the UAR wanted the return of dependents, resumption of TWA flights, and as much cultural exchange as possible. For the first time since the crisis, he spoke favorably about a resumption of diplomatic relations. He came as close as an Egyptian can to requesting assistance in arranging a meeting between the UAR Foreign Minister and Secretary Rusk.

I said that in Washington I had had a couple of meetings with an Israeli friend. The Israeli position was that while they would insist on recognition of Israel's rights as a full-fledged member of the Near East, they had no desire to humiliate Egypt. They would not accept a settlement which did not include their right to use the Suez Canal. They felt that in direct conversations with the Egyptians, modalities could be worked out whereby this could be done without threatening the existence of the Cairo regime. The Israelis had no fear about their capability for defending themselves from their Arab neighbors. At the same time, they were tired of war and wanted something better. Hassan Sabri asked regarding the source. When I said it was the Minister-Counselor, he said, "Why not the Ambassador?" I said the Ambassador had a slipped disk. Hassan Sabri said that improved US–UAR relations were essential to creating confidence between Israel and the UAR.

451.   Telegram From the Department of State to the Embassy in
        Israel[1]

Washington, September 29, 1967, 1952Z.

46190. 1. Ambassador Harman and Minister Evron called on
Assistant Secretary Battle September 28 for tour d'horizon. In reply to
query, Battle repeated assurances given Israelis in New York that
Secretary's meeting with Jordanian Foreign Minister[2] took routine
course and produced no surprises. Could not explain basis for reportedly optimistic statement made by Jordanian to press following meeting.
(2) Battle referred to indirect report of unknown reliability through third
Embassy sources in Cairo to effect high Foreign Ministry official now
regretted that US-USSR draft resolution had not been adopted by Arabs
in the first place. Battle offered up his own estimate that Soviets have not
entirely moved away from that draft but wish to avoid taking lead at
present in UNGA and are concentrating on rebuilding their position
with Arabs. They may eventually move back to where they were at end
of special GA but no evidence yet. Harman agreed Soviet tactic seems to
be give full public backing to Arabs and not get out in front. He recalled
GOI feeling that US-USSR draft open to varying interpretations.

3. Touching on outcome of Khartoum, Harman stressed GOI need
to get "nothing less than contractual relationships" with Arab states. He
asked for US assessment, in light recent Heikal articles. Battle said original nebulous reports of growing moderateness after Khartoum have so
far not been borne out by any concrete Arab steps. Would appear that
pledges of financial support made Nasser at Khartoum have helped
him to put off facing realities again. Heikal articles and other recent talk
on Arab side of continuing the war are extremely disturbing.

4. Moving on to question of announced establishment Israeli settlements on West Bank and Syrian border,[3] Battle said he wished to stress
two points. First is need to avoid airing differences of opinion between

---

[1] Source: National Archives and Records Administration, RG 59, Central Files
1967–69, POL 27 ARAB–ISR. Confidential. Drafted by Lambrakis, cleared by Atherton,
and approved by Battle. Repeated to Amman, Beirut, Jerusalem, Jidda, London, Moscow,
Paris, and USUN.

[2] Rusk met with Jordanian Foreign Minister Muhammad Adib Al-'Ameri on
September 26 in New York. A memorandum of the conversation is ibid., POL JOR-
DAN–US.

[3] Press reports that Eshkol had announced plans for establishment of Israeli settlements in the occupied territories near Baniyas in the Golan Heights, at Etzion between
Bethleham and Hebron, and at Beit Haarava on the northwest shore of the Dead Sea are
summarized in telegram 43163 to Rio de Janeiro for Eugene Rostow, September 25. (Ibid.,
POL 27 ARAB–ISR)

us in public press. On other hand, in all honesty it is extremely important GOI actions during this period not provide ammunition for those
at UN who would interpret GOI position as hardening in direction of
territorial acquisition rather than negotiated settlement. Battle himself
is telling all inquirers that GOI has assured USG all options remain open
for negotiation. Question had come up only last night at a reception
when two Congressmen separately expressed concern to Battle about
the Israeli settlements. Evron interjected that it is not only reports from
Israel of contemplated GOI actions which can cause such alarm among
Congressmen but also reports in US press, such as Hedrick Smith article in *NY Times,* which allege official USG unhappiness at GOI measures. Battle admitted these part and parcel of same thing, but reiterated
that concern in Congress and elsewhere among American people can be
stirred up by raw facts alone, even if USG kept silent on subject. In fact,
he confided, Department already being criticized in some press circles
for reacting in overly cautious manner to Israel's announcement.[4] Also,
many delegations in UN ready to pounce on story and dramatize it.
Harman and Evron agreed there is much truth in this.

5. Harman adverted briefly to *NY Times* story that morning alleging
serious US discussions are underway with Soviets on area arms limitation. He thought he saw implication in article that Soviets had not provided Arabs much new equipment, thus Israel needed none. Battle said
he thought that story fell wide of the truth in many respects. He
expressed reservations about possibilities for even a tacit agreement
with Soviets on area arms limitation in near future. Harman and Evron
concurred.

Katzenbach

---

[4] Telegram 44390 to Rio de Janeiro, September 27, recorded an exchange at the
Department press briefing that day between Department spokesman McCloskey and *New
York Times* reporter Hedrick Smith, who asked about the reports of plans for Israeli settlements in the occupied territories. McCloskey replied that the U.S. position on territorial
matters in the area remained as stated by the President on June 19. He stated that if the
plans to establish permanent Israeli settlements had been accurately reported, they would
be "inconsistent with the Israeli position as we understand it—that they regard occupied
territories and all other issues arising out of the fighting in June to be matters for negotiation." He replied to a further question that the United States had not been informed officially of any change in that policy but was attempting through diplomatic channels to
clarify the Israeli position. (Ibid.)

452.   Telegram From the Department of State to the Embassy in
        Jordan[1]

Washington, September 29, 1967, 2039Z.

46230. Ref: Amman's 1256.[2]

1. Believe it would be useful on eve King Hussein's visit to Moscow
for you to give King our understanding current Israeli position on negotiations and our general reaction to Arab position taken at Khartoum.

2. We have recently been reassured in categoric terms by Israelis
that their position on settlement with Jordan remains flexible including
point of negotiating some status for King Hussein in Jerusalem. They
also noted they had no recent indication of further Jordanian interest in
exploring settlement although King had reason to know that it was possible to establish contacts with utmost discretion. They questioned
whether in view of King's public commitments to common policy
evolved at Khartoum he had changed his approach and was no longer
interested in an early agreement with Israel. Israelis, of course, adhere
to basic position that any agreement must lead to genuine state of
peace.

3. Aware of the considerable political and personal risks involved,
we cannot in full conscience tell King what we think he should do with
regard establishing contacts with Israelis. We do, however, wish to
share our feeling there is real danger that Israel's position on the ground
may become even more entrenched and public pressure within Israel

---

[1] Source: Johnson Library, National Security File, Country File, Middle East Crisis,
Miscellaneous Material. Top Secret; Priority; Nodis; Sandstorm. Drafted by Davies,
cleared by Katzenbach and Saunders, and approved by Battle. Repeated to USUN as
Tosec 52. A September 29 memorandum from Saunders to Walt Rostow, attached to the
source text, states that Saunders had made revisions, which he had cleared with Davies.
A handwritten note by Rostow indicating his approval of the revised telegram is on
Saunders' memorandum.

[2] Telegram 1256 from Amman, September 4, reported that on the previous day, Burns
had relayed to King Hussein a proposal from Eban for a direct meeting. The King replied
that he did not think the time was ripe; the Israeli attitude on refugees, as well as indications of the Israeli attitude concerning a settlement, made direct negotiations appear
unprofitable for the time being. (National Archives and Records Administration, RG 59,
Central Files 1967–69, POL 27–14 ARAB–ISR/SANDSTORM) The proposal under reference has not been found, but in a message that Evron conveyed to Eugene Rostow on
August 25, Eban recalled that in a recent talk between him and Rusk, the latter had
expressed willingness to consider ways in which a secret meeting between Israeli and
Jordanian representatives could be arranged; Eban thought the time was approaching
when such a step would be useful and requested U.S. views on how it could be accomplished. Rostow said he would take this up with Rusk at once. (Ibid.)

move GOI from position of maximum flexibility if some hope for movement toward settlement not maintained. Therefore, time not necessarily on Jordan's side.

4. In imparting above, you should avoid any implication that USG is advising him to proceed and make clear that decision is King's alone and that we will continue to try to be helpful no matter which way it goes.[3]

5. We are repeating to you President's message to King Faisal.[4] You should draw on this without identifying source to provide King with our views on results of Khartoum meeting.

Katzenbach

---

[3] Burns reported in telegram 1692 from Amman, October 2, that he had met with the King on October 1 to convey the points in telegram 46230. He reported that the King had not commented directly concerning this, but that he had referred to a conversation that Jordanian Minister of National Economy Hatem Zu'bi had had with Eugene Rostow in Rio de Janeiro, in which, according to Zu'bi, Rostow had made a statement that the King interpreted as pressure for direct negotiations. Burns assured him that this was not the case. (Ibid.)

[4] Document 447.

UN Security Council Resolution 242, October 3–November 22, 1967

453.   Memorandum of Conversation[1]

Washington, October 3, 1967, 6:10–9:30 p.m.

NOTES OF THE PRESIDENT'S MEETING WITH

Secretary Rusk
Secretary McNamara
Mr. Rostow
CIA Director Helms
George Christian

The President called on Secretary Rusk to review the discussions at the United Nations.

Secretary Rusk: While at the United Nations I had sessions with the editorial boards of *Newsweek*, McGraw-Hill, and the *Wall Street Journal*. Those meetings were most profitable.

On the Middle East question, Gromyko had no taste for going through the General Assembly again. The provisional draft is still the basis for talks.

There is considerable movement on the Arab side but not enough. Egypt is not close to settling the Suez problem. The Arabs want our views on territory. I told them it was not for the United States to come up with a blueprint made in Washington. I referred them to our five points.

In my opinion we are going to have to wrestle with Israel.

The President told about the New York State poll which shows strong Jewish support.

Secretary Rusk: We still have a good deal of time to work out a formula on the Middle East. It is my feeling that we should put it in the Security Council rather than in the General Assembly. We do not have enough votes to go to Israel and say that this proposal is something that you should accept.

The Turkish Ambassador said something which was very disturbing. He said Moscow sent a message to Egypt that the Arabs should

---

[1] Source: Johnson Library, Tom Johnson's Notes of Meetings, October 3, 1967. Top Secret; Eyes Only. Drafted by Tom Johnson. Filed with a covering memorandum from Johnson to the President. The meeting was held in the Cabinet Room at the White House.

take a very modest stand. And if Israel does not respond to this position, the Soviets say they will give aid to the Arabs going far beyond economic aid.

Some of the members—India for example—said that we should be a mediator. For the moment we are working on the basis of the President's five points.

[Omitted here is discussion of unrelated matters.]

---

454.   Telegram From the Mission to the United Nations to the Department of State[1]

New York, October 3, 1967, 2240Z.

1174/Secto 44. Following is uncleared memcon.

Secretary met with FonMin Riad (UAR) at latter's request for about one and a half hours to review Middle Eastern situation. Sisco only other person present.

Conversation opened by both Secy and Riad confirming desire for better relations. Riad said there had been mistakes made in past by everybody, by UAR, US, and others. He was not attempting to exonerate UAR, for main responsibility for past mistakes rests with it. Stressed a strong desire to work towards better relations between UAR and US and recounted some of his efforts in past to this end.

Secy said we have over years supported principle of political independence and territorial integrity for all in area. He recalled our action at time of Suez, support of the government during the Lebanese crisis, support of certain countries who sometimes felt themselves under pressure from UAR, and affirmative vote last year in SC censuring Israel. We made major efforts in all capitals during pre-June 5 period in order to avoid hostilities. When we invited Vice Pres Mohieddin to visit US, we thought we had commitment from Israel they would not resort to hostilities. Should Riad or anyone in UAR Govt be under impression we acted in bad faith, this would be a fundamental misunderstanding of

---

[1] Source: National Archives and Records Administration, RG 59, Central Files 1967–69, POL 27 ARAB–ISR/UN. Secret; Priority; Exdis. Received on October 4 at 0144Z. Another copy of the telegram indicates that the memorandum of conversation was cleared in S on October 19. (Ibid., POL UAR–US)

our position. There was no deception on our part and we were aston-ished at events as were a good many others.

Moreover, Secy expressed regret that after beginning of hostilities it was not possible to achieve a cease-fire promptly; this would have pre-vented many headaches for a number of us. Crucial problem ahead, said Secy, is how conditions of peace get established in ME.

Secy said when Nasser announced closing of Gulf, we knew Israel regarded this as a casus belli. This action by Nasser also cut our throats by undermining our credibility with Israel. If we were today to ask Israel to withdraw on basis of an informal indication that everything would be all right, they would laugh in our face. This approach was tired in 1957 and failed. Secy said it is important to bear this back-ground in mind to understand why we attach fundamental importance to question of renunciation of belligerency, ending the state of war, and bringing about a state of durable peace in area. Too often, Secy said, Arabs have been too late in seeing, determining, and acting on basis their own national interests.

As he did on Saturday with Goldberg,[2] Riad told of confusion in Cairo during early period of hostilities. He told of Soviet reports of an Israeli build-up along Syrian border, he lamented that generals exag-gerated military information given to Nasser, and recalled Hussein's report that hundreds of airplanes were involved, and their belief these must be American. He confirmed their air force was out of action in first two and a half hours of hostilities. He expressed UAR disappointment at failure of US to come out categorically against Israeli aggression as in 1956.

Raid described Israel as still drunk over its recent military victory. He confirmed UAR trying to build up its armed forces. He stressed UAR has no territorial claims, and that principal problem between it and Israel is refugees. He admitted their past propaganda has been a mistake. He said recognition of Israel's right to exist not being chal-lenged by UAR. He said UAR has signed the Armistice Agreement,[3] the Lausanne Protocol,[4] and asked for implementation of UN partition

---

[2] Telegram 1127 from USUN, October 2, reported the meeting on Saturday, September 30, between Goldberg and Riad. (Ibid., POL 7 UAR)

[3] See footnote 4, Document 53.

[4] The Lausanne Protocol, signed separately at Lausanne on May 12, 1949, by Arab representatives and Israeli representatives with the United Nations Conciliation Commission for Palestine, provided that an attached map showing the 1947 UN partition plan for Palestine would be taken as a basis for discussion during negotiations then underway at Lausanne. The text is printed in the Commission's third progress report, UN document A/927; also printed in *Yearbook of the United Nations, 1948–49,* p. 198; also see *Foreign Relations,* 1949, vol. VI, pp. 998–999.

plan.[5] All these things implicitly mean recognition of Israel. Serious problem is that of borders. In his judgment Articles I and II of the Armistice Agreement are key features of peace.

Riad also seemed to imply, though he was not explicit, that giving expression to non-belligerency should not be a problem. However, no UAR Govt could accept Israeli vessels going through Suez Canal. This is not a practical question but one of prestige for both UAR and Israel. He said Israel is presently destroying installations along canal.

Riad said UAR could accept certain principles, provided other side also accepted them. He then went on to link, in perhaps a more direct way than in conversation with Goldberg, solution of refugee problem with opening Suez Canal to Israeli flag ships. He said Israel must respect the resolutions of the UN on refugees. (We assume he meant para 11 of Res 194,[6] though he did not mention it specifically.) Riad said we cannot surrender. If we were to give in on Suez, it would become an Egyptian national objective to remove "this surrender". A solution of this kind, if imposed upon us, would be temporary and not permanent.

Riad felt time was not in favor of peace. There was need for prompt peaceful settlement. He has pointed out to other Arabs that if Arabs had won war there would still have to be a peaceful settlement. In such circumstances, maximum Arab objective would have been implementation of UN partition plan.

Secy said we need a handle in order to move towards a peaceful settlement. Secy agreed on importance of refugee problem and regretted that solution had been frustrated because of political factors. He had always thought that if refugees could be given a private opportunity for choice, results would be acceptable to all. Trouble has been that if such an opportunity was given to refugees, Shukairy would indicate to them their throats would be cut unless all voted for return to Palestine. Riad interjected if it came to that UAR could remove Shukairy. UAR policy has never been to place any impediment on any Palestine refugees if they should want to leave.

---

[5] The UN partition plan was set forth in Resolution 181 (II), adopted by the General Assembly on November 29, 1947. The text is printed in *Yearbook of the United Nations, 1947–48*, pp. 247–256, and in *A Decade of American Foreign Policy: Basic Documents, 1941–1949*, pp. 695–709.

[6] Resolution 194 (II), adopted by the General Assembly on December 11, 1948. The text is printed in *Yearbook of the United Nations, 1948–49*, pp. 174–176, and in *A Decade of American Foreign Policy: Basic Documents, 1941–49*, pp. 719–720. Paragraph 11 stated that refugees wishing to return to their homes and live at peace with their neighbors should be permitted to do so at the earliest practicable date and that the compensation should be paid for the property of those choosing not to return and for loss of or damage to property.

Secy agreed time was not on side of peace. He said some in Israel realize basic problem is how Israeli people are to live in peace with 200 million Arabs in area. Riad should not conclude from Israeli press that Israel is not in position to make necessary decisions which would facilitate peace. Our present consultations with other dels are intended to ascertain what is possible in terms of peace. Five principles stated by President Johnson on June 19 remain our basic point of departure. We have no interest in supporting Israeli territorial expansion, but we cannot write a blueprint or impose on Israel a settlement. Our objective is to help find a way to peace with understanding of parties. Riad expressed doubt understanding could be built in circumstances where Israel is occupying UAR territory. He expressed regret US seemed to be on sidelines. Secy said we were doing more than that. Riad said if we can get understanding on principles involved, UAR could concern itself with a UN rep.

Turning to Soviet policy, both Secy and Riad agreed that it is neither in UAR nor US interest for a confrontation to take place in ME between major powers. Riad expressed concern regarding our view that two parties must work out understanding. He insisted it is too late for that, US is involved. If US remains on sideline, it would result in a settlement imposed on UAR. Riad then ticked off principles he believes essential: withdrawal of Israeli forces; freedom of passage; no territorial gains from use of force; and respect for UN resolutions on refugees. He said SC should endorse these principles, and practical implementation could take place subsequently with assistance of a UN rep. Secy said when US announces support for certain principles, this has practical consequences, and we are asked what we are going to do about them. If resolution is passed by SC which does not ask parties to take specific acts, there will be no peace in area. Riad said again if there is no understanding and a solution is imposed on UAR "this govt or some other UAR Govt" would sign surrender, people would be told this, and elimination of "surrender" would become an objective of UAR policy. Secy agreed surrender is not path to peace. Riad said any Israeli territorial gains means surrender, though not a change from a state of war to a state of peace.

Secy said he wished to raise a procedural point. From time to time he has received reports that attempts have been made by this or that Egyptian to make contact with US, and that we had made it difficult to achieve this contact. We are not clear as to who such Egyptians are, and whether they are authentic representatives. Could Riad give us any guidance on this matter since US does not want to get involved in an internal UAR matter. Riad said he did not know why US and UAR should discuss matters in any mysterious way, there is no need for third parties between us, and that he hoped that discussions and contacts made could be continued. Secy made clear that for our part Don Bergus in Cairo is a most official contact for US, that Amb. Goldberg available, and that if there was need he himself could come back to New York at some future date. Riad was vague about his future plans, saying he would probably stay in New York to see whether something can come out of SC. He stressed that contacts should be continued and a SC resolution would be a starting point towards peace.

Secy emphasized there must be great precision and clear understanding regarding any UN resolution. US–USSR resolution was a constructive approach, but both Arabs and Israelis objected to it. Secy said we have had enough resolutions which mean different things to different people. It may take some time to assure that there is full understanding of what any resolution means. We need "something" to move toward peace, but we do not see that "something" in detail.

Secy asked whether Riad believed that concept of a "holy war" is primarily in propaganda field or whether this is a policy question. Riad did not answer question directly, but said "holy war" approach achieves nothing, that UAR propaganda had been a mistake, and that UAR is presently suffering as a result. Nasser tried to face up to public opinion problem at Khartoum, and this is why a number of Arabs said he had been very courageous. Riad agreed that Nasser is probably still only Arab who can lead public opinion in area. Riad said Cairo Radio has been changing its approach in recent days.

Meeting concluded on note that both sides would maintain contact.

Rusk

---

455.   Memorandum From the President's Special Assistant (Rostow) to President Johnson[1]

Washington, October 3, 1967.

SUBJECT

Your Talk with Arab Ambassadors—Wednesday, October 4

As background for your meeting with the Arab Ambassadors at Ernie Goldstein's[2] lunch, the following describes the tactical situation

---

[1] Source: Johnson Library, President's Appointment File, October 4, 1967. Secret; Nodis. A handwritten "L" on the memorandum indicates the President saw it.

[2] Special Assistant to the President E. Ernest Goldstein.

which will be uppermost in their minds. I'm also attaching talking points and sketches of each Ambassador and his problems.[3]

I. *The situation*, in a nutshell, is that the key Arabs have just about agreed to the US–USSR draft resolution linking Israeli withdrawal with the end of belligerency. Now the focus is shifting to defining what practical steps would be needed to carry out such a resolution. Neither we nor the Israelis want to settle for mere words. As we begin to spell out possible follow-up steps, this comes as a new shock to the Arabs, who see it as further evidence of our backing Israeli demands. In detail:

A. *The Arabs* decided at Khartoum to try regaining their lost territories by political rather than by military means, and they turned Nasser and Hussein loose to see what they could get. As a group, they showed no real change of heart about Israel and not much realism about the kinds of concessions they might have to make to get a settlement.

Nasser and Hussein decided Saturday[4] to accept the substance of the draft US–USSR resolution, but they still aren't thinking seriously about steps to implement such a resolution. Hussein is in Moscow with Nasser's proxy to persuade the USSR to approach us on reviving a slightly revised version of the July resolution. Ayub, also in Moscow, will back Hussein.

B. *The USSR.* Foreign Minister Gromyko confirmed to Secretary Rusk that our joint July draft resolution is still the basis of their position, but he felt we were interpreting it differently on (1) the type of follow-up we expected from the Arabs and (2) Suez Canal passage for Israeli ships. Gromyko left the impression that he could support any solution Nasser would accept. He agreed that the trick is to find a formula for ending belligerency that the Arabs won't find humiliating.

C. *The British.* Wilson is hard pressed to get the Suez Canal open. Caradon has suggested aiming for a Security Council meeting next week, just to show movement.[5] But both Eban and Goldberg urged him to slow down until there is a wider consensus on the wording and meaning of a resolution. Meanwhile, the British are moving to resume relations with the UAR.

D. *The Israelis* are generally satisfied with our cautious strategy in New York, though they've repeated their serious reservations about the US-Soviet draft. They recognize that the Arabs at Khartoum faced up to the reality of their defeat and believe that letting more time pass is the

---

[3] None of the attachments is printed.

[4] September 30.

[5] Telegram 1124 from USUN, September 30, reported that Caradon had suggested this to Goldberg that day. (National Archives and Records Administration, RG 59, Central Files 1967–69, POL 27 ARAB–ISR/UN)

only way to force them to face up to the further steps they must take to reach a real settlement. They object strongly to the US-Soviet draft resolution because they believe the Soviets and Arabs would read it as requiring withdrawal to 4 June borders. This would not give them latitude to negotiate the "reasonable and secure boundaries" you spoke of on June 19.

II. *Our position* is still evolving. In New York, Secretary Rusk and Arthur Goldberg have been saying that the US-Soviet draft is a good starting point. We've also been pointing out, however, that any such resolution is only half of the equation. It's no good unless everyone agrees in advance how he will follow up. These are the questions we will be answering for ourselves in the next days:

A. *Do we stick with the US-Soviet draft ourselves?* Ambassador Goldberg on August 12 explained this draft to you and discussed Israeli objections.[6] The fact that Nasser and Hussein want the Russians to try a slightly revised version on us (to justify reversing the earlier Arab rejection) may give us a chance to take account of some of Israel's concerns. We don't want to get stuck forcing Israel back to 4 June borders as a matter of principle, but we will probably have to work from the July draft.

B. *Where should we focus the UN discussion—in the General Assembly or the Security Council?* The Arabs may push for a Security Council resolution so they won't be forced to vote on it. The bleakest interpretation of their motives is that they would then feel free to ignore it. The best is that Nasser and Hussein want to avoid voting so they can make a private deal free from Arab scrutiny. We're still undecided, but Goldberg told Caradon we favor going to the Security Council only if there is prior agreement among the parties involved on what it means. Eban agrees.

C. *Whose side does time serve? Should we push?* Right now, we're waiting for the Arabs to play out their negotiations with the Russians and to come to us. This squares with Eban's approach. However, we don't think time is on our side. Time will make it harder for any Israeli government to give up the security which present borders provide. Time works against us in the Arab world because the longer Israel sits on occupied territory, the harder it will be to convince friendlier Arabs that we're not reneging on our commitment to territorial integrity. Therefore, we've hinted to the Jordanians that they ought to get serious about working out a deal with the Israelis that could carry out any UN resolution.

---

[6] No other record of this conversation has been found.

III. *What's on the Arab Ambassadors' minds* boils down to one big question: Will we make good on our pledge to support the *territorial integrity* of all states in the Middle East?

Our best answer is that we stand by that pledge, but the only way to make good on it is to have a genuine peace. The tough question is whether we'd force Israel back to 4 June borders if the Arabs accepted terms that amounted to an honest peace settlement. Secretary Rusk told the Yugoslav Foreign Minister: "The US had no problem with frontiers as they existed before the outbreak of hostilities. If we are talking about national frontiers—in a state of peace—then we will work toward restoring them."[7] But we all know that could lead to a tangle with the Israelis.

Jerusalem is an equally important but separate issue. Our basic position is that we won't go along with unilateral changes and the people on the ground are best able to work out practical arrangements. Beyond that, these principles make sense:

—No one wants Jerusalem divided by barbed wire again.
—All religions must have access.
—It's logical for Jordan to resume a role as custodian of the Islamic Holy Places.
—It's also logical that Jordan should continue to share the economic gains from tourists in Jerusalem.

IV. *Our purpose at lunch.* The most important thing you can accomplish is to give these Ambassadors the feeling that you haven't closed your mind to them and that you honestly feel our position serves their long-term interest in peace.

Walt

---

[7] Rusk met with Foreign Minister Nikezic on August 30. According to telegram 30825 to Belgrade, September 1, which summarizes the conversation, Rusk said the key to a settlement was to end the state of war and belligerence and that if a way could be found to deal with this, other things would fall into place; the difference between pre-June 5 positions and secure national boundaries was an important difference. (National Archives and Records Administration, RG 59, Central Files 1967–69, POL 27 ARAB–ISR)

456.   Memorandum of Conversation[1]

Washington, October 4, 1967, 1 p.m.

OCCASION

Luncheon Hosted by Mr. Goldstein in the Fish Room at The White House, 1:00 p.m., 4 October 1967

PARTICIPANTS

Ambassador Abdul-Hamid Sharaf, Jordan
Ambassador Talat Al-Ghoussein, Kuwait
Ambassador Ibrahim Hussein El-Ahdab, Lebanon
Ambassador Ibrahim Al-Sowayel, Saudi Arabia
Ambassador Rachid Driss, Tunisia
Ambassador Fathi Abidia, Libya
Ambassador James W. Symington
Mr. Walt W. Rostow
Mr. E. Ernest Goldstein
Assistant Secretary of State Lucius D. Battle
Mr. Harold H. Saunders
The Vice President came in part way through the luncheon
The President joined the group at the end of the meal for twenty minutes

Before the President came in, there was a general conversation with the Vice President and Mr. Rostow striking generally the following themes:

[Omitted here is discussion concerning the possibilities of technology, communications, and regional cooperation.]

When the President entered, he explained—because he had just come from a session with Secretary Fowler—his problems with the Congress over budget cutting. This introductory part of the discussion ended when the Ambassador of Kuwait responded by thanking the President for giving the Ambassadors an opportunity to meet with him. The Ambassador concluded by suggesting to the President that now is a time of great opportunity in the Middle East for the US to make an important move for peace. In the ensuing discussion, the President made generally the following points:

---

[1] Source: Johnson Library, National Security File, Saunders Files, Middle East, 9/1/67–10/31/67. Confidential; Exdis. This copy of the memorandum is filed with a copy of an October 5 memorandum from Saunders to Battle enclosing the original for Battle's approval. According to the President's Daily Diary, the President arrived early in the luncheon, accompanied by Vice President Humphrey, Secretary Rusk, and Secretary McNamara. After introductions were made, the President, Rusk, and McNamara departed, while the Vice President remained and joined the group for lunch. The President returned after lunch.

1. He felt he understood the problems and positions of the Arab countries and welcomed hearing the Ambassadors' ideas and suggestions. He said he continues to be deeply immersed in the problem of achieving peace in the Middle East and pledged the continuing concern of Secretary Rusk, Ambassador Goldberg, Mr. Battle and other U.S. officials in the search for peace.

2. In response to Ambassador al-Ghoussein's point, the President described our difficulty in arranging a peace settlement:

—He cited the advice he had received from an older man early in his career: "You can tell a man to go to hell, but making him go there is different thing entirely." He said he had tried in May to persuade President Nasser not to go to war, but that didn't work. He had pleaded with Foreign Minister Eban not to go to war, but that didn't work. Now making Israel pull back is easier said than done.

—He had found in situations like this again and again that one party to a dispute urging a third party to become involved always assumed that the third party had influence over the second party that the third party did not have over the first party itself. For instance, the President said Senator A asks him to use influence with Senator B that Senator A knows the President doesn't have over Senator A himself. The same is true in the Arab-Israeli dispute.

—There is some similarity to a marriage. Once it gets into trouble, a third party may be useful in salvaging it but that third party risks the worst kind of abuse for meddling.

3. In response to the Ambassador of Jordan, he said he continued to support strongly the territorial integrity of all states in the area. However, he repeatedly linked this with the other four principles stated on 19 June. By way of analogy, he noted that he was having iced tea with the Ambassadors but that he did not consider this his whole lunch but would have a hamburger and some ice cream later on. Similarly he could not talk about the territorial integrity without returning to the other four principles of peace which he had stated over and over again. He implied further that he could not make the Israelis withdraw no matter how much he believed in territorial integrity.

4. He did not see how a settlement could be reached if the parties to the dispute could not "reason together." He said he had spent most of his life trying to get people to reason together and find areas of agreement, but so far he had not succeeded in this case.

5. He reiterated our desire for peace. Alluding to charges by some Arab governments that we had attacked them on 5 June, he recalled the Russians saying to him at one point that one problem in Vietnam is that no one believes us when we say we will withdraw and we have no long range intention of staying. The President said it is absolutely true that we have no such intention but the problem was making people believe that. Similarly, in the Middle East, he had found it difficult to convince

people that we are sincere in our desire for peace and have no other motives.

6. The President concluded by quoting a story about Charles Lamb who, on reading a distasteful story, threw the book on the floor and said of its author, "I hate that man." His wife retorted, "How do you know? You don't even know him." Lamb replied, "If I knew him, I'd like him." The President said his purpose in wanting to visit with the Ambassadors was for everyone to get to know each other a little better in the hope that "when we know each other, we will like each other."

In the course of the conversation, the Ambassador of Lebanon picked up one of the President's analogies. The President had said he couldn't tell his daughters whom to marry and when. In fact, he said with a smile, he couldn't even pick the preacher for the wedding. The Lebanese Ambassador said that the West had been the preacher at an earlier marriage in the Middle East and that what the Arab countries were asking for was for the preacher to return as a counselor now that the marriage was in trouble.

The Jordanian Ambassador made the most articulate—and most moving—Arab presentation. He began by saying that the problem, of course, had its roots but he did not want to argue history. His main concern was that the Government of the United States over the years had solemnly reiterated its support for territorial integrity to all the states in the area. The Arab governments feel they have a right to expect the Government of the United States to honor that pledge. They have been deeply hurt that we have not. He pointed out that half of Jordan is occupied and that, while the Government of Jordan is willing to discuss the elements of peace, it is impossible for it to negotiate while its territory is occupied. All this was said in the most moderate and inoffensive way possible and it was in response that the President responded that we continue to support strongly the principle of territorial integrity but that the problem of putting that support in practice was a difficult one which we had not yet solved.

Harold H. Saunders[2]

---

[2] Printed from a copy that bears this typed signature.

**457.   Memorandum From Harold H. Saunders of the National
Security Council Staff to the President's Special Assistant
(Rostow)[1]**

Washington, October 4, 1967.

SUBJECT

Your Talk with Ambassador Harman This Afternoon[2]

Ambassador Harman got a rocket from Eshkol a couple of days ago about our military aid freeze. He has since seen Luke Battle and asked to see Nick Katzenbach.[3] He has also seen Senator Symington and maybe some others on the Hill. Unfortunately, this is building up to a major political storm which we could have headed off.

You should be aware of how Katzenbach and Nitze authorized Battle to handle Harman yesterday. They've all had calls from Symington similar to yours.[4]

Luke told Harman that there are all kinds of people against our sending any arms to the Middle East—those who don't want war, those who don't want a fuel and arms race, and those who don't like either Arabs or Israelis. One reason for the continuing freeze has been the feeling that we could not move on Israel alone and that Israel's friends would oppose our moving anything to any Arabs.

Then Luke went down the list of things being held up for the Arabs and asked whether the Israelis have any objection to our moving them. Harman said that, except for Jordan, he didn't think they would, but he would let Luke know if he was wrong.

---

[1] Source: Johnson Library, National Security File, Country File, Israel, Vol. VII. Secret.

[2] No record of this conversation has been found.

[3] Harman's conversation with Battle on this subject on October 3 is recorded in telegram 49692 to Tel Aviv, October 6. (National Archives and Records Administration, RG 59, Central Files 1967–69, DEF 12–5 ISR) His conversation with Katzenbach on this subject on October 6 is recorded in telegram 51187 to Tel Aviv, October 9. (Ibid.)

[4] A memorandum of October 3 from Walt Rostow to the President states that Senator Stuart Symington had called him that day. Symington said there was great "anxiety, vexation and deep bitterness" in the Israeli Government over U.S. military aid policy; the Israelis were convinced that the United States was holding things up to put pressure on them. Rostow commented that the situation was "political dynamite." He said Symington intended to take the floor of the Senate soon to insist on resumption of military aid to Israel and that Symington said there would be no opposition to military aid to the moderate Arabs. Rostow concluded that Symington said he could, if necessary, easily get a special bill passed supporting military aid to Israel in the face of the continuing shipments of Soviet arms. Rostow sent copies of the memorandum to Rusk and McNamara. (Johnson Library, National Security File, Country File, Israel, Vol. XII)

Luke feels likewise that Senator Symington does not object to moving with the moderate Arabs. Therefore, it looks as if we have established a point that we can move some things to both Arab and Israelis without upsetting some of our main problem people on the Hill.

Unfortunately, there is enough evidence around town that (a) Congress is not a problem and (b) some people in the Executive Branch are thinking of keeping the freeze on until the Israelis change their position toward the Arabs to create suspicion in Jerusalem which we have been unable to breach with all of our assurances.

I think the best you can do with Harman is to say about what you did to Evron last week:[5]

1. It has been the judgment of the men responsible for getting this legislation through Congress that having a big headline to the effect that we were resuming military assistance to the Middle East would do great damage to the aid bill. We have reviewed this a couple of times at their request and as recently as last week that was still our judgment.

2. We are willing to pursue the matter along the lines he and Luke discussed because we have no ulterior motive in maintaining the freeze.

3. We are sorry that our solemn assurances have been thrown aside so lightly in Jerusalem.

Hal[6]

---

[5] No record of this conversation has been found.

[6] Printed from a copy that indicates Saunders signed the original.

---

458. Telegram From the Department of State to the Embassy in Israel[1]

Washington, October 7, 1967, 0118Z.

50528. Following are highlights of conversation during call by Israeli Ambassador Harman on Under Secretary Rostow October 4:

1. *Middle East Settlement.* Harman described recent "movement" on Arab side as tactical, designed present moderate face but without real substance. Essential goal remained agreement between parties which

---

[1] Source: National Archives and Records Administration, RG 59, Central Files 1967–69, POL 27 ARAB–ISR. Secret. Drafted by Atherton on October 5; cleared by Grey and Battle, and in draft by Arthur R. Day (UNP); and approved by Eugene Rostow. Repeated to USUN, Amman, Jerusalem, and London.

Harman said Israel considered central to President's five points of June 19. Rostow said problem remained of finding route to settlement and emphasized importance of UN as backdrop for this effort. It was still our thinking that we should seek resolution linking withdrawal and non-belligerency and calling for UN mediator. It was essential to have someone talk seriously to both sides in order to get parties focusing on realities. We have been doing what we could in this direction and felt there were some signs that Arabs becoming more realistic. In response Harman's expression of concern at UK pressure to "rush into Security Council," Rostow said we had been discussing tactics with British and believed U.S. and UK were working together closely, and that reports of differences in approach were exaggerated.

Harman warned against dangers of seeking UN resolution at any cost, arguing that resolution subject to different interpretations would be worse than no resolution at all. Israel prepared accept UN mediator, although it not particularly enamoured of this idea, but thought USG agreed he should have no mandate other than to seek achieve agreement between parties. Difficulty with resolution linking withdrawal and non-belligerency was that "withdrawal" required precise action by Israel while "non-belligerency" was imprecise term which left open question of what was required of Arabs. UAR Foreign Minister Riad's discussion of General Armistice Agreements in his UN address, which Harman described as "amazing performance," underscored pitfalls in seeking "form of words" as substitute for direct agreement between parties. Such attempts to gloss over basic issues weakened UN. Despite its image of opposition to UN role, Israel in seeking true peace in spirit of Article 33 of Charter was in fact contributing to strengthening UN. (Without pursuing point, Harman wondered if totally new UN resolution could not be devised referring simply to Article 33.)

2. *Israeli Settlements in Occupied Territory.* Responding to Rostow's query, Harman said two areas involved: (a) Baniyas, in DZ on Israeli side of international border; this was vital from security point of view, inter alia because it commanded Baniyas tributary of Jordan River; (b) Etzion area between Jerusalem and Hebron on West Bank; this was also strategic location. Harman emphasized that Israel described these projects as "strongpoints," not "settlements"; they were being manned by Nahal units—military formations within Army which also engage in some agricultural work. Rostow asked whether these "strongpoints" could be evacuated if settlement reached. Harman replied he could not make prediction in this respect but would hope any settlement would not leave borders sealed, so that there could be Jews in Jordan as there were Arabs in Israel.

3. *Refugees.* In response Rostow question whether there had been progress on refugee problem, Harman said GOJ not interested in progress but only in scoring propaganda points. Hussein's handling of West Bank situation as well as refugee return question did not contribute to resolution of problems. This connection Harman cited specifically Amman radio and other incitement for school strike on West Bank and GOJ criticism of Israeli action to excise anti-Israeli material from text books.

Rostow noted that Israeli position on refugee return was raising question in Arab minds whether Israel really wanted political settlement. It would help clear atmosphere in this respect if Israel offered take back all refugees who have left West Bank. It was important recognize that Khartoum Conference had changed matters; other Arabs now had stake—in form of financial subsidy—in seeking settlement. In response Harman's comment that Israel does not agree with this interpretation of Khartoum and considers Hussein more inflexible than before, Rostow said our private contacts with Jordanians did not support Israeli interpretation.

Without responding directly to Rostow's point re refugee return, Harman said with census occupied areas now completed, Israel may soon have something to say on overall refugee problem in context of peace settlement. Rostow stated we were ready to discuss refugee problem at any time with Israelis.

4. *Arms Supply.* Harman referred to his talk previous day with Battle re difficulties for Israel's security situation arising from suspension of arms deliveries (septel).[2] Rostow described serious difficulties with Congress on whole arms supply question, which had made it impossible so far to respond to Israeli requests and reinforced what Ambassador Battle had told him the day before, i.e., that the delays in arms supply decisions were caused by political realities here, and not by any other factor.

Rusk

---

[2] See footnote 3, Document 457.

459.   Memorandum From Secretary of State Rusk to President
Johnson[1]

Washington, October 6, 1967.

SUBJECT

Robert Anderson's conversation with Foreign Minister Eban Wednesday,
October 4, 1967

Foreign Minister Eban had a conversation with Robert Anderson yesterday in New York. Eban had asked several times to see Anderson, who checked with Gene Rostow and me before he accepted the invitation.

Their talk is summarized in the enclosed memorandum.[2]

In essence, Mr. Eban asked for Mr. Anderson's advice about how to initiate private, secret, and indirect contacts between Israel and some of the Arab states of the Middle East. The implication is that Israel would like Anderson to act as a mediator. Mr. Eban must have had Egypt in mind, because of Mr. Anderson's long connection with that country, and perhaps other countries in the Middle East as well.

Our advice is that we should encourage the possibility of Bob Anderson's undertaking to continue his talks with Eban, and undertaking also to act as a go-between on a private, secret, and informal basis. In this connection, you should also know that in Rio, the Egyptians approached Anderson about a possible visit to Nasser. His response was that he would discuss the matter with the government, but that he could not consider going without a direct invitation from Nasser.

This could be the break in the Middle Eastern impasse we have been seeking for a long time. It could be a crucial development—to start a real exchange going on real questions, while we continue to work away on Resolutions in the United Nations.

There are risks of course in our undertaking even this limited responsibility for having an American act in this capacity. But I believe

---

[1] Source: Johnson Library, National Security File, Country File, Israel, Vol. VII. Top Secret; Nodis. Walt Rostow forwarded the memorandum to the President at 7:35 p.m. with a covering memorandum briefly summarizing it and commenting, "My inclination is that we go ahead."

[2] The memorandum, headed "Sandstorm," a report of an October 4 telephone conversation between Robert Anderson and Eugene Rostow, is attached to the source text but not printed. A copy is filed with a memorandum from Eugene Rostow to the President stating that he had told Walt Rostow about Anderson's telephone call and that Rostow wanted a copy of the memorandum of conversation to show the President. It also states that McNamara, Katzenbach, Kohler, Battle, and Sisco all agreed "we should go ahead on this line." (National Archives and Records Administration, RG 59, Central Files 1967–69, POL 27–14 ARAB–ISR/SANDSTORM)

the risks of refusing to participate, and allowing the situation to drift, are definitely greater.

If you agree, we shall discuss possible procedures for initiating these talks with Mr. Anderson before he sees Mr. Eban again.[3]

Dean Rusk

---

[3] Neither the approve nor disapprove option is checked. An attached typed note, dated October 6 at 9:05 p.m., contains the President's reaction: "Find out through Harry or somebody else how Evron, Eban, and Israel would look upon this."

---

460. Telegram From the Mission to the United Nations to the Department of State[1]

New York, October 10, 1967, 0235Z.

1303. Subj: Results of Goldberg–Caradon October 6 Meeting re ME. Ref: USUN's 1302.[2]

1. Para 3 below contains text of "draft summary of agreed US-UK proposals resulting from Goldberg–Caradon talks on Middle East, October 6, 1967".[3] When advising Pedersen Oct. 9 of Caradon's agreement to text and referendum, Hope (UK) stated Caradon had two reservations:

(A) He remains of view that, in any effort agreement on SC res, it best not to go beyond principles set down in US-Soviet draft of July or US-UK Washington working paper, without seeking to get agreement on specifics of those principles;
(B) Caradon is not satisfied with language in para 6 of text stating "withdrawal must be understood to mean withdrawal from occupied territories of UAR, Jordan and Syria . . .". Hope said Caradon realizes this language is not meant to include Jerusalem and Gaza and would have preferred language such as "withdrawal from all occupied territories" (one of possible formulations which [emerged] during USUN-UKUN staff consultations of Oct. 7 and 9).

---

[1] Source: National Archives and Records Administration, RG 59, Central Files 1967–69, POL 27 ARAB–ISR/UN. Secret; Priority; Exdis.

[2] Telegram 1302 from USUN, October 10. (Ibid.)

[3] Telegram 1278 from USUN, October 9, transmitted the text of an earlier version of this document, which it called "our version of 'agreed minute' of Goldberg–Caradon talks on Middle East, October 6, 1967." (Ibid.)

2. While Caradon has these reservations, we are convinced UK del as whole fully understands problems which would be involved in going ahead with effort to formulate principles for SC res such as those in US-USSR draft without agreement on their specifics.

3. Text of "draft summary" agreed to ad referendum to capitals as follows:

"1. It is preferable to deal with ME item in the SC rather than in the GA, and as soon as agreement is reached on a common course of action.

2. Before we go to the SC the US, UK, USSR and France should have a uniform understanding of the meaning of the principles to be laid down by the SC and of the specific actions they envisage in accordance with these principles.

3. The US is prepared to pursue further conversations with the USSR to ascertain whether it stands on the correct text of version one of the US–Sov draft of July[4] and whether it concurs in agreed interpretation of the text, or if not what conditions or reservations it has. This discussion would be open-ended on both parts so that if changes in the text were asked for by them, changes could also be asked for by the US without being subject by them to accusations of hardening its position.

4. An agreed text of version one of the US-Sov draft of late July, with the addition of a UN ref and adjusted to fit the SC (such as the UK-US Washington working paper), is an appropriate basis for discussions as to SC action. In addition to consultations with the USSR, Israel and the Arab states would have to be consulted to determine the acceptability of the proposed course of action, and their suggestions be given consideration.

5. It must be understood, both among the permanent members and among the parties, that para 2B of the US-Sov draft envisages in implementation affirmative actions to acknowledge Israel's right to live in peace and security and to terminate belligerence, details of which would have to be worked out along the lines of para 9 below, but that such termination would mean, inter alia, that both Tiran

---

[4] Concerning the two versions of the U.S.-Soviet draft resolution, see Document 380 and footnote 2, Document 384. Telegram 1226 from USUN, October 5, reported that USUN had received the text of the U.S.-USSR resolution in the form it had been given to the Arabs by the USSR. The telegram states: "As we had previously speculated, USSR gave out version I and only para 2 thereof, without including preamble, op para I or op para 3. In para 2A they gave out words 'to the positions they occupied before June 5, 1967' instead of words 'from territories now occupied by them.'" It also reported that C.P. Hope of the British delegation had told Pedersen that the Soviets had indeed given the Arabs the wrong version, but that they now had the full text. (National Archives and Records Administration, RG 59, Central Files 1967–69, POL 27 ARAB–ISR)

Strait and Suez Canal would be open to ships of all states, including Israel.

6. Para 2A of that text referring to withdrawal must similarly be understood to mean withdrawal from occupied territories of the UAR, Jordan and Syria, details of which would have to be worked out along the lines of para 9 below, taking into account the peace and security problems mentioned in para 2B. (In discussing this with the USSR, the US would elucidate that demilitarized zones, possibly with UN supervision, and other possible arrangements and agreements are envisaged, and that it is anticipated that the armistice lines would be replaced by international boundaries.)

7. Desirable as it would be, it is not likely that the parties in the Middle East will commit themselves to specifics in advance of SC action; however, they must have the same understanding of the SC resolution as do the big four.

8. In addition to the private understanding by the parties of the meaning of the resolution, they would be expected to signify their commitment to it by publicly 'accepting' it after its adoption and agreeing to cooperate with the UN representative in its implementation.

9. The implementation of the principles in the resolution, and the details thereof, would be worked out between the parties with the assistance of a UN representative.

10. It is not at all certain that such an approach will be successful; if not, there should be a diligently pursued attempt to produce a resolution laying down more generalized Charter principles and an even-handed mandate for the dispatch of a UN representative to consult with the parties concerned, with a view to assisting in establishing a just and durable peace in the Middle East (or even simply such a mandate)."

Goldberg

461.   Telegram From the Embassy in the Soviet Union to the
Department of State[1]

Moscow, October 9, 1967, 1445Z.

1388. For Secretary. Subject: UN Resolution on Near East.

1. Gromyko called me to Foreign Office today and referred to his conversation with you in New York on Middle East.[2] He said he had then told you that if you agreed it would be well for us both to work toward one of the American forms of the resolution worked out during the Special Assembly. At that time the Arabs were opposed. He said that he did not say that all Arab doubts had disappeared, but now all Arab countries took a more realistic position. This however was on the basis that there would not be any one-sided interpretation. He was proposing that the resolution be adopted as it is. You had pointed out that it was difficult to adopt a resolution without knowing whether or not it would be acceptable to the Arab countries. Before adopting a resolution, the Soviets and ourselves could ascertain the Arab position. He thought that if necessary the resolution could receive some kind of public Arab approval. The Soviets were ready to try to get the Arabs to say that after the resolution was adopted, they would say they would carry it out. You had asked about determination of belligerency and had pointed out that the Arabs might make statements maintaining a state of belligerency and nothing would have been changed. Gromyko said that he had countered by asking how this was possible as the resolution itself provided for recognition of the independence and national existence of all states in the area. He thought this covered the problem since the Arabs would say they would carry out the resolution. You had indicated that you would study the problem and that an answer would be made either to Washington or Moscow. So far there had been no reply. The problem was rather tense and charged with uncertainties. He thought that neither the US nor the Soviet Union was interested in resumption of military activities in that area. The Soviet Union was prepared to work with the Arab countries to try to convince them that perhaps even before the adoption of the resolution they would agree to carry it out if Israel did so. In this connection he mentioned specif-

---

[1]   Source: National Archives and Records Administration, RG 59, Central Files 1967–69, POL 27 ARAB–ISR/UN. Secret; Limdis. Received at 1838Z.

[2]   Reference is apparently to a September 27 conversation between Rusk and Gromyko, at which they discussed a number of subjects, including the Middle East. Telegram 1055 (Secto 16) from USUN, September 28, in which Rusk reported the conversation, is printed in *Foreign Relations, 1964–1968*, vol. XIV, Document 247.

ically the UAR and Jordan and said perhaps other Arab countries might be persuaded.

2. I said I would of course inform you promptly of his remarks but I wished to point out it was necessary to get agreement of both sides. The Israelis would surely ask us if this meant that the Suez Canal would be open to their ships.

3. Gromyko replied that this would be discussed on the basis of the resolution as would also the question of refugees. He indicated however if this had to be dealt with specifically by an interpretation in advance, there would be no progress.

Thompson

---

462. Memorandum From the President's Special Assistant (Rostow) to President Johnson[1]

Washington, October 9, 1967.

SUBJECT

Letter from King Hussein[2]

Attached is a long letter from King Hussein (key passages marked) reporting his view of the Middle East situation following the Khartoum Conference and recent trips to Cairo and Moscow. He hopes to visit the U.S. toward the end of the month.

It's a strong but dignified letter and lays out Arab reasoning clearly. He expresses deep hurt at what he considers our basic pro-Israeli position. Insofar as we are trying to make the Arabs face up to the existence of Israel, he's not just giving way to polemics. In much the same language as his Ambassador used with you at lunch last Wednesday,[3] he laments the double standard we apply to Arabs and Israelis and says, humbly and sadly, he doesn't find it worthy of a great leader or a

---

[1] Source: Johnson Library, National Security File, Special Head of State Correspondence File, Jordan, 8/1/67–7/31/68. Secret.

[2] The text of the October 7 letter was transmitted in telegram 1777 from Amman, October 8. (National Archives and Records Administration, RG 59, Central Files 1967–69, POL 27 ARAB–ISR) A retyped copy is attached but not printed.

[3] October 4; see Document 456.

great nation to discriminate this way. He told Ambassador Burns he had written because he felt "so personally let down by the USG in recent weeks."[4]

He feels the Arabs at Khartoum reached a reasonable and responsible position. He says even Israeli passage through the Canal is negotiable if linked to redressing the wrongs inflicted on the Arab people of Palestine since 1948. Now he says it's up to the great powers to act, since they were responsible for creating Israel in the first place.

He put two questions to Burns: (1) Will we support a resolution moving UN debate from the General Assembly to the Security Council? He fears that Assembly debate would cause some Arabs to take positions that would tie his hands. (2) Will we support a slightly revised version of the July US-Soviet draft resolution? He says the Soviets will but told him our position had hardened. What he refers to is Arthur Goldberg's effort to work out a more precise understanding of what specific steps would follow such a resolution.

Nick Katzenbach already had his staff working on these questions before this letter came in. We will have an answer for you as soon as possible. But I want you to be aware that this potentially opens a new round of negotiations in New York on the resolution which we felt represents progress if properly interpreted but which the Israelis have objected to vigorously.[5]

Walt

---

[4] The quoted language is from telegram 1797 from Amman, October 9, which reported a conversation with the King that afternoon. (National Archives and Records Administration, RG 59, Central Files 1967–69, POL 27 ARAB–ISR)

[5] The following comment in President Johnson's handwriting appears on the memorandum: "Ask Mc Bundy to read & comment. Could we see him soon? L." Another handwritten note in Rostow's hand states that the message was telephoned to Saunders on October 11.

463. Memorandum From the President's Special Assistant (Rostow) to President Johnson[1]

Washington, October 9, 1967.

SUBJECT

Your Talk with Abe Feinberg—7:30 p.m. Today[2]

First, he probably wants to discuss our Mid-East aid freeze. After getting a rocket from Eshkol last week, Harman did the rounds, including getting Senator Symington steamed up. As a result, Secretary McNamara took another look at the problem and is considering a formula for moving ahead that he will probably wish to discuss at our Wednesday lunch.

The Israelis have two concerns: (a) Our freeze is beginning to hurt their production lines. (b) More important, they are deeply suspicious—despite our contrary assurances—that our freezing past aid means we're going to use it as leverage to force them to terms with the Arabs. They well remember 1956–57 when we froze their assets here and then forced them back to the armistice lines.

As I understood our discussions, Secretary McNamara's sole reason for wanting to continue the freeze has been to avoid upsetting his ticklish negotiations on military credit sales in Congress.[3] Anything you can say to reassure Abe and quiet Jerusalem's suspicions will take the heat off you.

You may want to warn him that we want to go ahead with a few things for moderate Arabs (except Jordan) when we release military shipments for Israel. You believe this is in our national interest—as well as Israel's—and hope Israel's friends will agree that this makes sense.

Second, Abe may want to support General Weizman's request for 77 new jet aircraft. Harman told me he hopes you can give Eban an answer on 24 October. Our staffs are working full time on this, but big

---

[1] Source: Johnson Library, National Security File, Saunders File, Middle East, 9/1/67–10/31/67. Secret.

[2] No record of the meeting has been found.

[3] Rostow elaborated on this in a note to the President at 6:50 p.m. that day. It states that McNamara was "most seriously worried about further Soviet penetration of the Middle East via arms" and therefore wanted full Israeli cooperation in going forward when Secretary Rusk thought the time was appropriate with the sale of arms to Israel and moderate Arab countries, including Jordan. Rostow concluded that McNamara wanted Johnson to explain to Feinberg why he needed support for alteration of the Church amendment and support for selling arms to moderate Arabs when this appeared to be in the interest of peace and stability in the area. (Johnson Library, National Security File, Country File, Israel, Vol. VII)

questions are involved—such as Israel's nuclear intentions—and we may not want to answer so quickly. While you'll want to sound sympathetic, I don't think you'll want to hem yourself in by promising not to bargain with these planes or raising hopes for an answer on the 24th.

Third, he may want to encourage you to stick to your June 19th principles throughout the UN negotiating season. We know (he probably doesn't) that Hussein, Nasser and the Soviets will soon be trying out on us a revised version of the US-Soviet draft resolutions worked out in July. Since we will be renegotiating language which the Israelis didn't like to begin with, you may want to pre-empt by assuring him we won't do anything we don't honestly believe serves the interest of achieving a permanent peace.

W.W. Rostow[4]

---

[4] Printed from a copy that bears this typed signature.

---

464. Memorandum From the President's Special Counsel (McPherson) to the President's Special Assistant (Rostow)[1]

Washington, October 10, 1967.

The attached notes[2] were dictated by Abba Eban, with the understanding that Eppie would give them to me.

When he delivered them today, Eppie said that the one thing the notes do not convey very well is Anderson's sense of disappointment over the "chill" Eban put on the intermediary idea. Eppie says the Israelis did not intend at any time in the first or second meeting with Anderson to ask him to be an intermediary. Eban did not even report

---

[1] Source: Johnson Library, National Security File, Memos to the President, Walt W. Rostow, Vol. 45. No classification marking. Rostow sent this memorandum and the attachment to the President with an October 10 memorandum noting that the proposed Anderson mission was out and adding, "I suspect Eban *did* raise it with Anderson, very cautiously; checked with Jerusalem; and was turned down." He commented further: "I do fear the Israelis will overplay their hand; but, then, I don't live in the Middle East." (Ibid.)

[2] The attachment, headed "Notes of a meeting between Foreign Minister Abba Eban and Mr. Robert Anderson in New York, Monday, October 10, 1967," is not printed. A memorandum of an October 10 conversation between Battle and Anderson contains Anderson's summary of his meeting with Eban. (National Archives and Records Administration, RG 59, Central Files 1967–69, POL 27–14 ARAB–ISR)

his first conversation with Anderson to Jerusalem, and my call to Eppie was the first indication the Israelis had that we were seriously interested in the matter.

I asked Eppie in all candor whether Jerusalem had in fact suggested intervening between the first and second meetings and he said absolutely not.

The Israeli policy line—for waiting, for looking to direct negotiations, against talking with Nasser, whom they believe is weak and indeed tottering—is as you described it to me on the telephone.

Harry C. McPherson, Jr.[3]

---

[3] Printed from a copy that bears this typed signature.

---

465. Memorandum From the President's Special Assistant (Rostow) to President Johnson[1]

Washington, October 10, 1967.

SUBJECT

King Faisal's Reaction to Your Letter[2]

Since you've now seen King Hussein's somewhat bitter letter,[3] you will also want to be aware of King Faisal's testy reaction to your recent letter. Both reflect Arab feeling that we have let them down and are taking a pro-Israeli line by not pressing Israel to withdraw as we did in 1957. Ambassador Eilts reports that he had about as difficult a session with Faisal as he's ever had when he presented your letter.[4]

Faisal is sensitive about our intimating that the Arabs didn't go far enough at Khartoum. He feels we don't understand the risks Arab leaders are taking by any show of moderation toward Israel.

---

[1] Source: Johnson Library, National Security File, Country File, Saudi Arabia, Vol. II. Secret. A handwritten "L" on the memorandum indicates the President saw it.

[2] For President Johnson's September 25 letter to King Faisal, see Document 447.

[3] See Document 462.

[4] Eilts said this in telegram 1357 from Jidda, October 5, commenting on the meeting with Faisal the previous day at which he presented the President's letter. (National Archives and Records Administration, RG 59, Central Files 1967–69, POL 27 ARAB–ISR)

He, like Hussein, clearly sees Israel as the aggressor. He's no longer willing to admit that Arab provocation played a role in bringing on the June war.

Significantly, he says he'd be willing to end the "state of belligerency" provided Israel recognized such Arab rights as the refugees' right to go home. He, like Hussein, feels we're asking them to give up their hole card—ending the state of war—in return for Israeli troop withdrawal but not for settlement of *their* main long-term grievances. (This same theme creeps into Hussein's report that Nasser now links opening the Canal with a refugee settlement.)

At the root of Faisal's reaction are 20 years of frustration beginning with the UN resolution creating Israel, which he believes came about only as a result of US pressure. He was at the UN himself in 1948 and speaks from deep personal conviction. Ever since, with the exception of 1956–57, he believes we have leaned toward Israel. He just doesn't believe—no matter how many times we say it—that we can't influence Israel.

Jerusalem is his most sensitive spot. As guardian of Islam's holy places, he believes he has a special obligation. Our abstention on the Jerusalem resolutions in July hit him especially hard—as it did most Moslems.

Eilts did his best to calm Faisal, but he was clearly upset. He may relax a little when he has time to reflect.

Walt

---

466.   **Telegram From the Department of State to the U.S. Interests Section of the Spanish Embassy in the United Arab Republic**[1]

Washington, October 12, 1967, 1902Z.

52853. 1. Battle met with UAR Fonmin Riad at latter's suite in Waldorf Oct. 10. Conversation relaxed and friendly but somewhat inconclusive. Following items of particular interest.

---

[1]   Source: National Archives and Records Administration, RG 59, Central Files 1967–69, POL 27 ARAB–ISR. Secret; Limdis. Drafted by Parker on October 11 and approved by Battle. Repeated to USUN, London, Tel Aviv, Amman, Jidda, Beirut, Tripoli, Rabat, Tunis, and Ankara.

2. Riad said UAR had broken relations with US because of confusion of first day's fighting compounded by false information supplied by Air Force commanders, Syrians, and Jordanians. UAR civilian leadership had been misled by military who unwilling admit scandalous state of unpreparedness which responsible for crushing defeat UAR Air Force on June 5. To cover their own disgrace military had alleged presence US planes and pilots as excuse. Details his remarks this regard will be reported separately.[2] They as close as we likely to come to getting apology from UAR.

3. Riad said UAR drawn into confrontation with Israel by chain of circumstances starting when Kosygin or Brezhnev told Anwar Sadat in Moscow that the Israelis were concentrating troops and would attack Syria on a specific day. This was not idle speculation at military attaché level but appeared to be solid and well-based information. A similar report was given by Soviets to Jordanians. Egyptians had no alternative but to take it seriously and therefore move troops into Sinai. Army Commander in Sinai found UNEF between his forces and Israelis in central sector. He therefore asked for withdrawal UNEF from that sector, but there had been no thought of asking for withdrawal UNEF from Gaza or Sharm ash-Shaykh. U Thant had given all or nothing reply, however, and Egyptians had found themselves in difficult position. One thing led to another and they found themselves at Sharm ash-Shaykh. Once there, as reaction to constant needling from Saudis and Jordanians on subject, they closed Straits, not thinking passage through them very important to Israelis. Then they realized that Straits were used for oil tankers. "I forgot Israel's oil pipeline." Everything connected with Sinai operation and closure Straits had been done without prior planning and without study. Army had not been ready. Its troops were not trained and did not know how to use their equipment. Equipment itself was not ready. Troops had been placed in Sinai like toy soldiers in a shop window.

4. Battle said all our efforts had been toward preventing outbreak of war. He had been very glad Zakaria Muhi al-Din was coming to Washington and had been immersed in plans for visit. He had hoped

---

[2] An October 10 memorandum of conversation contains the details of Riad's remarks on this subject. He said there was great confusion on the day of the attack, and "the wrong information had been given even to the President." The military command had "deliberately misled Nasser in order to cover up its own errors." On June 4 and 5 the air force generals were quarreling with each other; furthermore, the radar and anti-aircraft facilities were shut down the morning of June 5 because Amer and Air Force Commander Sidqi Mahmoud were scheduled to depart for Sinai at 9 a.m. When the Israelis came over, "there was not a single UAR fighter in the air." The air force generals, unwilling to admit their unpreparedness, had invented the story that the Israelis had twice as many planes as they actually had and therefore must have had outside help. (Ibid.)

once we began talking something could be worked out. We too had been in difficult position. Basis for Israeli withdrawal in 1957 was USG assurances regarding freedom navigation in Straits of Tiran. Egyptians had pulled rug out from under us. This was past history, however, and we had to look at future, which was not going to be easy. All of us had obligation to find a more permanent solution to problem. Middle East must be allowed develop peacefully and could not face prospect of war every ten years. A permanent solution was imperative. We did not know the answer but we knew it was imperative.

5. Riad said UAR was facing aggression and must remove traces. Main problem, Palestine, continued to exist. If not solved it will always be a case of future troubles. He had been working on this problem for 20 years already and another 20 years were as nothing in terms of time. Israelis after defeating Arabs were not ready compromise. Why should they?

6. Riad said settlement meant (an Israeli) state with borders. Question was where borders were. Quarrel was not about existence of Israel but about its borders. It had been a mistake for the Arabs to talk of Israel's destruction. They should have concentrated on refugees and partition, because Arabs even if they defeated Israeli army would not be able to destroy Israeli people. Arabs were prepared for a settlement. Shukairy himself had endorsed the principle of settlement when he signed the Lausanne protocol and when he called for an implementation of the partition resolution at the UN after 1948. It was difficult to discuss a settlement, however, while Israeli forces were on UAR territory. We must remove them. It will be difficult but we must do it.

7. Battle commented that hostilities offered no solution. There was, however, more flexibility in the Israeli position than Arabs seemed to think. Israelis want to find contractual basis for their existence. While we want Israelis to withdraw it very awkward for us to press them on this issue until participants can come to terms on belligerency. Such an agreement would be beginning. At least it would create the basis for a settlement. Suez, Tiran and the refugees were all tied to belligerency.

8. Riad asked if we thought a single word would change things. German/Soviet non-aggression pact did not prevent aggression. No word or a piece of paper would create peace. Starting point was not non-belligerency. Arabs had found word "belligerency" in book on international law and used it as a basis for political stand. UAR could not expect USG to create miracles or to force any country to do something against its will. But UAR did expect USG to make correct analysis of situation and to have clear stand on question of refugees and aggression. It was not question of dictionary definitions but question of US attitude. If US had position on Canal, it should state it. Maybe

Egyptians would accept, maybe they wouldn't. Point was USG should make its attitude clear. For Egyptians' part they had to make clear determination to get Israelis to withdraw. "There is war today; there is firing on our cities and soldiers. Security Council does nothing. We do not expect it to, but must control our nerves and do our best to solve situation. Resolution in UN is not a solution. It is a start, but no UAR government can grant passage through Suez to Israeli ships and survive."

9. At this point Battle asked whether Egyptians were talking about Israeli flag shipping only or whether they meant Israel cargo and Israel-owned ships as well. Riad obviously had given no thought to this question and seemed puzzled by it.

10. Riad said he had told Goldberg UAR accepted five points of President Johnson. If something could be done about refugees then there would be no problem between Israel and UAR.

11. Battle said it was heartbreaking to see what was happening to the Canal. Super tankers were making it obsolete. Denial of the Canal, however, was not hurting the world but was hurting Egypt. Riad said UAR not trying to hurt anyone. Closure of Canal was a political measure. Riad said UAR had no territorial designs on anyone. Just let Israelis withdraw and they could have peace.

12. Battle said this appeared to be a welcome change in the UAR attitude. Riad said previous Arab propaganda had been in error. It was in UAR's interest to settle Palestine problem.

13. Riad said we needed to restore and normalize relations. There were many things to settle, he was not talking in terms protocol. (Implication was restoration relations must await some progress on settlement crisis.) UAR knew US could not give orders to Israel and should not be angry if we did not do so. At same time US should not be angry at UAR if it stood up for its rights. Battle said that with regard to relations we had a problem in the formal sense of the word. We were ready to have that problem removed, but we had not sought the break in relations. Initiative up to UAR. UAR had its problems of dignity and we had our own dignity. There would have to be compensation for property and something had to be done about Big Lie. We did not want to be legalistic or difficult but in some way history had to be corrected. We had no fixed ideas on this score and wanted to be fair. We also wanted a fair, just and permanent solution to Middle East crisis. We should not have to face a nightmare there every ten years.

14. In closing, Riad said he had hoped to return to Cairo in mid-October but did not know now when he would be going. Battle said he would be at Riad's service if the latter wished to see him or others in Washington at any time.

Rusk

467.   Memorandum From the President's Special Assistant
        (Rostow) to President Johnson[1]

Washington, October 12, 1967.

SUBJECT

US and Soviet Positions on Mid-East Resolution

We have had a series of talks with the Soviets this week on where we go in the UN.[2] Arthur Goldberg—and apparently Dobrynin—thinks we've hit a dead-end. Since Secretary Rusk wants to discuss this with you soon, here is a preview of the argument.

A more detailed rundown of issues and positions is attached, but the key question is whether we make any concessions in order to revive the US-Soviet draft resolution of July.

The problem is that, despite our July agreement on the wording of that resolution, we and the Soviets were interpreting it differently. They want a loose resolution calling for Israeli withdrawal which states Arab obligations loosely enough that they can be disregarded.

Arthur told Dobrynin Tuesday[3] that we are prepared to go ahead with the July draft subject to consultations by both us and the Soviets with the principal parties and provided we have a clear understanding on what the resolution means and what would be required in the way of affirmative acts by the parties. He said it must be clear that the resolution means that (a) Arabs renounce belligerency and that (b) if belligerency ends, the Canal would be open.

The question we haven't solved yet is whether there's a half-way position between Arthur's hard line and moving to our fall-back position of a general resolution using language from the UN Charter and appointing a UN representative to see what he can work out.

---

[1] Source: Johnson Library, National Security File, Agency File, United Nations, Vol. 8. Secret. A handwritten "L" on the memorandum indicates the President saw it.

[2] Telegram 51942 to USUN, October 11, recorded an October 10 conversation between Goldberg and Dobrynin. It states that the principal impressions to emerge from the conversation were that the Soviets wanted to negotiate down from the tentatively agreed U.S.-USSR draft and that they wished to avoid a specific interpretation of the resolution which would require affirmative acts by the Arabs to recognize Israel and renounce belligerency. Goldberg said the United States had been flexible but was not interested in negotiating down from the U.S.-USSR draft. Both sides would want to consult the parties concerned, and therefore talks should be on an ad referendum basis, but the negotiations had to be open-ended both ways; if one side could suggest changes, the other side must be free to do the same. (National Archives and Records Administration, RG 59, Central Files 1967–69, POL 27 ARAB–ISR/UN) Under Secretary Rostow and Soviet Minister Tcherniakov also discussed the Middle East at lunch and again later in the afternoon on October 11. (Memoranda of conversation, October 11; ibid., POL 27 ARAB–ISR)

[3] October 10.

Most of us feel we ought to try to salvage something from our July understanding with the Soviets, although we recognize that any dilution of our July position would bring us into a head-on clash with Israel.[4] Also, we have to consider that the Israelis say we've already gone too far in committing ourselves in essence to withdrawal to 4 June boundaries. Only the Israelis are content to see time run on.

I will be having breakfast with Secretary Rusk and Arthur tomorrow, and we will try to report to you later in the morning.

Walt

Attachment

ISSUES AND POSITIONS ON A MID-EAST RESOLUTION

I. Should we press urgently for a UN resolution?

A. *Most of us* believe, as Secretary Rusk said this morning, that "time is not working for a peaceful settlement."[5] We don't want to miss a chance for settlement while positions are still fluid. Even the Arabs are in a hurry because they know that the longer Israel sits on the West Bank the harder it will be to dislodge her. The USSR wants to look as if it's helping the Arabs. The UK is the itchiest of all since the Canal's continued closure is costing Wilson—and Britain—a great deal.

B. Only *Israel* is in no hurry. Eban feels the Arabs won't face up to reality—and the necessity to accept and deal with Israel—until they realize no one else will solve their problems for them. Eban feels they'd be readier to negotiate if the UN failed to provide an answer.[6]

II. Is the US-USSR draft resolution acceptable?

A. The *Arabs and the Soviets* now want to change the language to be tougher on the Israelis. For instance, they'd like to call for withdrawal to lines of June 4th rather than to negotiated final boundaries.

B. Goldberg told Dobrynin we considered the July draft acceptable provided we could agree in advance on interpretation. He said this is as

---

[4] A comment in Bundy's handwriting next to this sentence on his copy of the memorandum reads: "Nothing in it." (Johnson Library, National Security File, NSC Special Committee Files, UN Resolutions)

[5] Rusk made this comment at his October 12 news conference. (Department of State *Bulletin*, October 30, 1967, p. 561)

[6] A comment in Bundy's handwriting next to Section I on his copy of the memorandum reads: "U.S. need not be in a hurry. Agree with Eban." (Johnson Library, National Security File, NSC Special Committee Files, UN Resolutions)

far as we could go. (The Israelis objected strongly to that.) If the USSR was going to allow the Arabs to change the language, we should be allowed to reconsider too.[7]

III. How much do we have to nail down before we go to the Security Council?

A. Despite our desire to move ahead, we can't see passing any resolution which can be interpreted later to suit each party's policy. Ambassador Goldberg told Dobrynin that the major powers must agree before passing a resolution on what it means. The main Mid-East belligerents must share this understanding, including the fact that ending belligerency means opening the Suez Canal to Israeli shipping.[8]

B. The *Arabs and Soviets* now want to avoid specific interpretation. They argue that we're trying to write a peace treaty before we'll let a resolution go through the Security Council. They're probably trying to get away with a resolution they can cite as calling for Israeli withdrawal while they get away with as little response as possible. But they do have a point when they say, "Why would we give up our hole card—ending belligerency and opening the Canal—before we're sure the Israelis will come to terms on issues that are basic to us, like refugees?"[9]

IV. How can we be sure both parties accept the UN principles when passed?

A. *We and the British* currently agree that the necessary follow-up to pre-agreed interpretation would be some affirmative act by the Arabs to show that they were really renouncing belligerency. Among other things, Goldberg would require pre-agreement that Tiran and the Suez Canal would both be opened to Israeli shipping. Gene Rostow has indicated to the Soviets that we would consider a two-step process by which there was general acceptance of the principles of withdrawal and the end of belligerency as guidance for negotiation but no actual withdrawal until negotiations ended.

B. *The USSR and the Arabs* believe the question of opening the Canal should be left to a later stage of the negotiations along with the refugees and that we should not try to pin these points down before passing the resolution. Nasser sees the end of belligerency as his ace in the hole and neither he nor Faisal understands why the Arabs should give this up

---

[7] A comment in Bundy's handwriting next to paragraph II.B. on his copy of the memorandum reads: "Goldberg is no longer the ideal negotiator." (Ibid.)

[8] A comment in Bundy's handwriting next to paragraph III.A. on his copy of the memorandum reads: "This won't happen." (Ibid.)

[9] A comment in Bundy's handwriting next to this paragraph on his copy of the memorandum reads: "Nonsense—refugees and Canal were not [illegible—tied?] till Nasser tied them." (Ibid.)

before they get satisfaction on some of their basic aims like a refugee settlement.[10]

V. Should we shoot for direct negotiation or settle for a mediator?

A. *Israel* publicly rejects mediation and maintains that the only believable sign that the Arabs are terminating the state of belligerency will be their willingness to sit down and talk with the Israelis. Privately Eban would be willing to accept a UN mediator without a specific mandate but believes there's no point in going to this "fall back" position until we've ascertained whether the US and USSR can come to terms or not. *The Arabs*, of course, refuse to negotiate directly with Israel.[11]

B. The *US-UK* believe a UN mediator will be necessary in any case to work out the details of carrying out a resolution. But we also recognize that, if we fail to reach a common interpretation of a resolution with the USSR, we may have to settle for a very general resolution quoting more general principles from the UN Charter and throw the matter to a UN representative.[12]

---

[10] A comment in Bundy's handwriting next to paragraph IV.B. on his copy of the memorandum reads: "Nonsense." (Ibid.)

[11] A comment in Bundy's handwriting next to paragraph V.A. on his copy of the memorandum reads: "U.S. and USSR cannot come to terms." (Ibid.)

[12] A comment in Bundy's handwriting next to paragraph V.B. on his copy of the memorandum reads: "Correct." (Ibid.)

---

468. Memorandum From the President's Special Assistant (Rostow) to President Johnson[1]

Washington, October 12, 1967.

SUBJECT

Secretary McNamara's Agreement with Eban (as per my barber-shop conversation)[2]

Bob feels he worked out the following procedure with Eban:[3]

1. We will proceed immediately on the items which Israel now has on order and which have been held up by our military aid freeze. At the

---

[1] Source: Johnson Library, National Security File, Country File, Israel, Vol. VII. Secret.

[2] The words in parentheses were added in Rostow's handwriting.

[3] A memorandum of McNamara's October 12 conversation with Eban is in the National Archives and Records Administration, RG 59, Central Files 1967–69, POL ISR–US.

same time, we will proceed with parallel shipments to moderate Arab states (excluding Jordan).

2. We will deliver the Skyhawks from the 1966 contract[4] on schedule, beginning in December. This requires a decision before the weekend to arrange shipping.

3. Secretary McNamara will write Eban a letter explaining the above and expressing his (McNamara's) understanding that Israel does not object.[5] (This will have to be delicately worded.)

In addition Bob made a hard pitch to the Israelis to get to work on the aid bill conferees.

This is for your information. I will send you the formal recommendation from Secretaries Rusk and McNamara (they did not want to sign until after today's meeting) spelling out the equipment we would be moving. They will presumably want to consult on the Hill once they have your tentative OK to this course of action.

McNamara warned Eban that, while we are not moving shipments to Jordan now, we may well in about a month.

Walt

This sounds all right
I'll hold my decision till I have the formal paper[6]

I still think you should have a word directly with Bob & check also with Sect. Rusk. W[7]

---

[4] For information concerning the 1966 agreement to send Skyhawks to Israel, see *Foreign Relations, 1964–1968*, vol. XVIII, Document 283.

[5] McNamara's October 12 letter to Eban states that the United States was able to release the existing backlog of spare parts, components, and other items and would be able to proceed on schedule with the shipment of the 48 A–4H aircraft on order together with the requisite support matériel. It notes that the ability to respond to Congressional inquiries was crucial to U.S. efforts to preserve the legislative authority to make future credit sales and continues: "In response to such inquiries we plan to state that we have reviewed with officials of your Government our intention to resume some arms shipments in discharge of existing commitments to the moderate Arab states. We will also state our understanding that your Government does not regard as contrary to its interests the resumption of such arms shipments to moderate Arab states that were not participants in the recent hostilities." (National Archives and Records Administration, RG 59, Central Files 1967–69, DEF 12–5 ISR)

[6] This option is checked.

[7] This postscript appears in Rostow's handwriting.

469.   Intelligence Memorandum Prepared in the Central Intelligence Agency's Directorate of Intelligence[1]

No. 1392/67   Washington, October 12, 1967.

NASIR'S CURRENT STATUS WITHIN EGYPT

Summary

Nasir's hold on Egypt has been weakened considerably as a result of the Arab-Israeli war, but it appears that he will remain as Egypt's leader at least for the immediate future. Following the Sinai debacle and the arrest and subsequent death of the former military chief, Abdul Hakim Amer, Nasir's stock with the military has dropped. Nasir still has the support of the masses but some civilians—both in and out of the government—reportedly would not be unhappy to see him go. Nasir himself is said to be depressed over recent events, and this together with health problems reportedly caused him to contemplate at least a temporary semiretirement. No likely successor appears willing to assume the responsibility of attempting to work out a settlement with Israel and this circumstance will act to support Nasir's tenure.

1. Recent reporting from Egypt indicates that Nasir's once undisputed hold on Egypt has been seriously undermined and that he may be on the way out as the effective leader of that country.

2. Since the end of hostilities with Israel, factors have been at work in Egypt which appear to have eroded Nasir's position and to have paved the way for his eventual departure from the center of the Egyptian power structure. Until the Arab-Israeli war, Nasir could almost unreservedly count on the allegiance of the military. In the wake of the debacle in the Sinai, however, much of this loyalty has been lost.

3. Originally Nasir himself publicly accepted the blame for Egypt's defeat, but this was soon shifted onto the military, reportedly causing no small amount of bitterness among those officers forced to take the rap for a situation which many probably viewed as Nasir's doing. The subsequent wholesale cashiering of large numbers of military officers alienated those directly involved. Still other elements of the military, already unhappy with the corruption and inefficiency prevalent among

---

[1] Source: Johnson Library, National Security File, Country File, UAR, Vol. VI. Secret; No Foreign Dissem/Background Use Only; No Dissem Abroad/Controlled Dissem. Prepared by the Office of Current Intelligence and coordinated with the Office of National Estimates and the Clandestine Services. Copies were sent to Bromley Smith, Walt Rostow, Saunders, and the White House Situation Room.

the officer corps, are reportedly dissatisfied because the postwar shake-ups did not go far enough.

4. The arrest of former deputy supreme commander of the armed forces Abdul Hakim Amer probably embittered the large bloc of Amer supporters in the military, which Nasir had previously counted on as the mainstay of his own military support. Amer's subsequent suicide deepened the resentment of this group which, in all likelihood, blamed Nasir for his death. Amer's death and the ensuing purges of those working with him have probably eliminated the immediate threat of a military move against Nasir, but the possibility of a sudden coup attempt by some relatively unknown junior officer remains.

5. Nasir still appears to hold the allegiance of the masses, but there are reports that some civilian elements—middle and upper class—would not be unhappy to see him go. For some time there have been indications that certain Western-oriented business and intellectual groups have been unhappy with Nasir's policies. Recently, even some medium-grade government officials have reportedly expressed the opinion that Nasir must be replaced. A number of reports allege that contending factions are vying for dominance in the government, but there is no comprehensive picture of the situation.

6. There seems little doubt, however, that some form of maneuvering for predominance is in progress. This factional maneuvering appears to be a further indication that Nasir's control over the situation has weakened. The falling out among some members of the ruling clique is the most vivid illustration of the current disarray in the Egyptian leadership. The arrest of Salah Nasir (one of the clique) and other members of General Intelligence may have undermined President Nasir's control of one of the country's primary security mechanisms and thus contributed to the loosening of his hold on the country.

7. Nasir himself, according to a number of recent reports, has indicated a desire to step down, at least temporarily. His depression over the military defeat and the death of Amer, his long-time friend, seems to be genuine. [4-1/2 *lines of source text not declassified*] He also is said to think and even talk from time to time of retiring altogether.

8. Many details of the state of affairs in Egypt remain obscure, but there does appear to be a distinct possibility that Nasir's days as Egypt's functioning head are numbered. Although a military move against him appears unlikely at present, the political and physical pressures facing Nasir may in time produce a situation in which he feels forced to step down. It has been reported a number of times, however, that he is reluctant to do so until he is able to work out at least an Israeli withdrawal from Egyptian territory. Furthermore, it is unlikely that any of his prospective replacements would be willing to assume responsi-

bility for working out a settlement with Israel. At present Deputy Prime Minister Zacharia Mohieddin appears to be the front runner among possible successors. The potential of Ali Sabry, the alleged leader of a left-wing faction said to be vying for predominance, to stage a take-over at this time is doubtful.

9. In light of these considerations, Nasir probably will continue as Egypt's leader, at least until the question of Sinai is resolved. Nasir's prestige and influence, nonetheless, are likely to continue to decline.

---

470.   Telegram From the Embassy in Israel to the Department of State[1]

Tel Aviv, October 13, 1967, 0755Z.

1145. Subject: Surface to Surface Missiles. Ref: Tel Aviv 971.[2]

1. After pondering our questions PM provided his reaction in form of following points which, in view of approaching Yom Kippur holiday, he asked Bitan to pass to me.

A. GOI is engaged in a missile research and development program in conjunction with France.

B. This program is not expected to be completed for at least another two to three years.

C. As to evaluation of UAR missile program there may be different views. As an example, within past month UAR has rebuilt its air force with some 250–300 planes. They have 25 COMAR rocket-carrying boats which are capable of shelling Israel's coastal towns. It is in fact not possible to determine when and how UAR will achieve a ground-to-ground rocket capability.

---

[1] Source: National Archives and Records Administration, RG 59, Central Files 1967–69, DEF 12–5 ISR. Secret; Priority; Exdis. Repeated to London, Paris, Rio de Janeiro, and USUN. Received at 0829Z.

[2] Telegram 971 from Tel Aviv, September 28, states that the Chargé was trying to arrange an early approach to Eshkol to obtain his reactions to the points raised in telegram 44235 to Tel Aviv, September 26. (Both ibid.) Telegram 44235 to Tel Aviv states that information obtained during the Weizman talks was fragmentary. Despite some U.S. intelligence indicating that MD–620 development might have reached the stage where a decision on production would seem to be required in the very near future, Weizman said an Israeli decision was "definitely not" imminent and the thinking about missile deployment was "not very serious." The telegram requested that Barbour approach Eshkol and ask him to confirm U.S. understanding of several points.

2. Prime Minister would not be drawn out on more specific answers to our questions. In his opinion it is premature to get into that much detail.

3. Bitan commented that there is "no reason for anxiety" on our part as regards Israeli-French missile program. He indicated that progress had been so slow that whenever PM asked for report from his experts, reply was invariably that program would not be completed for "two to three more years."

4. When I pressed for additional info on domestic missile development activity I was referred again to point 1–A above. (This may carry inference that GOI is making contribution to joint effort in ways other than financial.)

5. FYI. Although Prime Minister was relaxed when I was discussing our request with him personally, Bitan did remark subsequently that PM believes we are carrying our inquiries in this field too far. Although this is not new feeling, it is at present strong, according to Bitan, due to PM's irritation over US suspension of arms shipments since Six-Day War. End FYI.

Dale

---

471. Memorandum From the President's Special Assistant (Rostow) to President Johnson[1]

Washington, October 13, 1967, 10:15 a.m.

Mr. President:

At breakfast this morning, Sect. Rusk and Arthur Goldberg agreed that we should shift off our present position on to a draft like the attached.[2] This draft, while stating certain broad principles would,

---

[1] Source: Johnson Library, National Security File, Agency File, United Nations, Vol. 7. Secret. The handwritten notation "For 11 a.m. meeting" appears at the top of the page. The President met from 11:05 to 11:32 a.m. on October 13 with Bundy, Rusk, Goldberg, Rostow, Battle, Sisco, and Pedersen to discuss a possible draft resolution on the Middle East. (Ibid., President's Daily Diary) No record of the meeting has been found.

[2] In addition to the attached draft resolution, an unsigned, undated memorandum from Rusk to the President is also attached. It recommended that he authorize Goldberg to initiate consultations with the United Kingdom and with other delegations on the basis of the draft resolution.

operationally, take the issue of negotiations out of the hands of the U.S. and USSR and put it in the hands of a mediator. There is quiet agreement that the mediator would be Ambassador Jarring, now Swedish Ambassador to Moscow.

The reasons are the following:

1. The Soviet Union has been trying to achieve an interpretation of our earlier Joint Resolution which would lean heavily favorable to the Arabs, unfavorable to Israel; that is, it would lean heavily on troop withdrawals and will have everything else fuzzy.

2. Arthur, on the other hand, has been trying to get everything so clear beforehand that in fact it would pretty nearly constitute a settlement.

3. In the face of this situation, Sect. Rusk and Arthur want to put in the attached new resolution which calls for no act at the beginning; reiterates your 5 points; contains basic language incorporating Arab as well as Israeli principles; but throws the work into the hands of a mediator.

4. The resolution would be introduced not by the U.S. but by some other party; perhaps the Finns and Swedes would float it, or the British.

5. Arthur would have the task of talking with the Russians about this and explaining that this resolution, in effect, is a way of doing what they have urged; namely, to have a resolution which each party could, for the time being, interpret in his own way until they became gripped of a negotiating process via an intermediary.

6. Your 5 principles are put into this draft because Riad, the Egyptian, has said that they "have no objection" to your 5 principles. We think the Israelis will buy this; and it may be that the Arabs will also, because they have been saying that the U.S. position has been hardening;" but we shall see.

My own feeling is that if we were to pursue the US/USSR resolution on Arthur's track of making it explicit, this could only be done if the US/USSR were, in fact, the mediators in this crisis, getting into all details, and especially into the sequence of negotiation of the various issues in the Middle East. It may be the part of wisdom to get the U.S. and USSR out of that position, working on the flanks of a mediator, if we can get a consensus on this procedure.

With respect to detail, it is unlikely that the "arms race" phrase will survive; and the paragraph on the second page beginning with "affirming" may be either modified, or go.

Walt

Attachment

The Security Council.

Having further considered the grave situation in the Middle East,

Affirming that the Security Council has an obligation to bring about a just and durable peace in which every state in the area can be assured security,

Bearing in mind the resolutions adopted and proposals considered by the Fifth Emergency Special Session of the General Assembly, and the resolutions adopted and actions taken by the Security Council in considering this matter.

Considering that the Charter calls upon all member states to practice tolerance and live together in peace with one another as good neighbors;

Recalling the Charter requirement that a member state act in accordance with the following principles:

1. That the Organization is based on the principle of the sovereign equality of all its members;
2. That member states shall settle their international disputes by peaceful means in such a manner that international peace and security and justice are not endangered;
3. That they shall refrain in their international relations from the threat or use of force against the territorial integrity or political independence of any states or in any other manner inconsistent with the purpose of the Charter;

Declaring that these principles require for their full implementation a context of peace, based on the recognized right of national life for all states, justice for refugees, free and innocent maritime passage, limits on a wasteful and destructive arms race, and political independence and territorial integrity for all,

Affirming, in light of the foregoing, that none of the states in the area should maintain forces on the territory of another state against its will or persist in refusing to withdraw them, or claim the right to assert or pursue a state of belligerency against another state or persist in refusing to recognize its sovereign existence and right to live in security.

1. *Requests* the Secretary General to designate a special representative to work with the parties concerned with a view to assisting them in the implementation of this resolution and establishing a just and lasting peace in the Middle East.

2. *Requests* the Secretary General to keep the Security Council advised of the progress and results of the efforts of the representative.

472. Memorandum From Secretary of State Rusk to President Johnson[1]

Washington, October 13, 1967.

SUBJECT

Exceptions to the Military Supply Freeze for the Middle East

Recommendation:

That you authorize us, subject to satisfactory consultation with key members of the Congress, to proceed with a selective relaxation of the current freeze on arms shipments to Israel and the moderate Arab states along the lines outlined below.[2]

Discussion:

It has become increasingly difficult to maintain the very tight restrictions on the shipment of military equipment to the Near East and North Africa, which we imposed during the June hostilities. Great pressure is being put on us by Israel as well as the Arab states which maintain—and want to continue to maintain—friendly relations with us, to ease the freeze so they can meet their legitimate defense needs. The Soviets have slowed down in the pace of their rearmament of the radical Arab states, including the UAR, but are continuing their arms shipments to them. The Soviets are also undoubtedly interested in a possible breakthrough by arms sales on easy terms to some of the moderate Arab states which have hitherto resisted buying arms from them. Our arms freeze has served a useful purpose, but with the passage of time, we feel a need now for some relaxation.

—The Israeli Ambassador has made a very sharp plea for our lifting the suspension on shipments to *Israel.* The $3 million exception which you authorized in August helped for a brief period. Now Israel's arms maintenance facilities and defense-support industries are severely hampered by lack of parts and other supplies needed from the United States. The Israelis fear that a continued U.S. suspension could encourage the French not to go ahead with delivery of fifty Mirage V aircraft

---

[1] Source: National Archives and Records Administration, RG 59, Central Files 1967–69, DEF 12–5 ISR. Secret. A handwritten note on the memorandum by Deputy Executive Secretary John P. Walsh reads: "Approved by Secy Rusk, Secy McNamara, & the President, 10/13/67. JPW." An October 16 memorandum from Saunders to Rostow with an attached copy of the memorandum indicates that the President approved it at the 11 a.m. meeting on October 13. (Johnson Library, National Security File, Country File, Middle East, Vol. I)

[2] Neither the approve nor disapprove option is checked.

scheduled to begin in November, as well as other equipment. Sharp concern over the effects of our arms freeze to Israel has also been voiced to us by a number of Senators and Representatives, as well as in correspondence from the public. We believe the time has now come to confirm to the Israelis that we will go ahead with the previously agreed delivery schedule on our 48 A4H aircraft, for which agreements were signed in 1966, beginning with delivery of the first four in December. We should also now approve pending Israeli requests for the delivery of a variety of spare parts, components, and miscellaneous supplies (involving no major combat end-items); these items may total in the neighborhood of $30 million, mostly in cash sales but some on credit previously extended. We would, however, continue to defer for the time being on the new $14 million spare parts credit sales program and the 100 APC's authorized by you in May, as well as the recent Israeli request for further deliveries of new aircraft which we are now studying.

—As we relax our freeze to Israel, we should also take steps to protect our important interests in the *moderate Arab world*. Our failure to meet insistent demands to carry out agreements previously concluded for the supply of military equipment would be particularly dangerous if word gets out on our deliveries to Israel. We have in mind nothing that we have not already agreed to, and nothing involving any further new USG credit at least until Congressional uncertainties on this score are resolved.

—For the countries in the vicinity of Israel, we recommend going ahead with: (a) deliveries of communications gear and some air navigation equipment to *Lebanon* (totaling under $4 million in cash sales); and (b) with the existing air defense and transportation-communications supply programs in *Saudi Arabia* (contracts totaling about $130 million over a number of years, which we would not wish to lose), plus cash sales of pistols for the Saudi police and miscellaneous spares and support equipment (involving no major end-items) for the military. The equipment involved for these two countries does not have a high political "visibility" from the outside but its supply would be an important confirmation to the Lebanese and especially to the Saudi government that we want to continue our good relationship with them.

—*Jordan* is a special case. We remain intensely interested in having Jordan retain its general pro-West orientation. But its active participation in the fighting against Israel, together with King Hussein's seeming interest in keeping open an option to get Soviet arms, involves policy and Congressional problems for us. We will recommend no action on the arms freeze to Jordan at least until the results of Hussein's recent visit to Moscow, become clearer.

—For the North African countries also affected by our arms freeze, we see a need to proceed with previously agreed programs in *Morocco, Tunisia,* and *Libya.* The Moroccans and Tunisians believe they must have a deterrent capability in view of the large-scale Soviet arms deliveries to Algeria. For the Libyans, our making good on our supply commitment is a vital factor in the negotiations over Wheelus. These countries are following a relatively moderate policy with respect to a possible political accommodation with Israel. The key items involved are six F–5's to Morocco remaining under a 1965 agreement (combination of grant and sale) and the cash sale of ten F–5's to Libya under a contract, signed on May 1, 1967. We would begin an F–86 training program for Tunisia, anticipating the delivery at a later stage of twelve aircraft under a MAP program agreed to in April 1967.

In recent discussions initiated by Ambassador Harman on Israel's requests, our officials have indicated to him what we were thinking of as necessary exceptions on our arms freeze to the Arabs, as outlined above.

Ambassador Harman stressed that his primary concern is in lifting the suspension for Israel; expressed particular concern over arms shipments to Jordan—which he pointed out were not being considered at this particular moment; and said he would convey to us any comments the Israeli Government might have. It is our belief the Israelis will not seek to cause any trouble for the Administration if you approve the exceptions for the Arabs which we recommend.

We recognize the continued delicacy of the Congressional situation on the arms supply issue. We had hoped, as you know, to defer relaxation of our arms freeze until the foreign aid legislation was enacted. In view of the unexpected delays on the Hill, however, we believe we should not wait any longer. We therefore wish to explain our situation to Congressional leaders and then proceed promptly with the limited program summarized above and outlined in some greater detail in the enclosed sheets.[3]

Dean Rusk[4]
Robert S. McNamara

---

[3] Separate pages with recommendations for Israel, Lebanon, Saudi Arabia, Morocco, and Libya follow. All include options to check approval or disapproval; none is checked.

[4] Printed from a copy that indicates Rusk signed the original.

473.   Memorandum of Conversation[1]

Washington, October 13, 1967.

Minister Evron asked to see me today. The only time available was lunch, so we dined together at my office.

1. He said he had prepared to come in a state of agitation and crisis because of the discussions yesterday with Sec. McNamara; but, just before lunch they had received Sec. McNamara's letter to Minister Eban,[2] which eased the situation they thought they faced yesterday. It had been immediately forwarded to Jerusalem and they would await a response.

2. He described the "shock" of their discussion yesterday with Sec. McNamara in which they had understood him to be requesting formal Israeli support now for the shipment of military spare parts to Jordan. He said this was politically impossible and explained why.

3. I explained at length Sec. McNamara's position, underlining that he was not insensitive to Israel's political problems but was laying before Minister Eban a situation and a fact which Israel could not ignore or evade:

—The Russians had given Hussein a most attractive offer for military equipment on the basis of a "single supplier";
—The U.S. could not accept sole responsibility for dealing with this problem when it arose.

He said he now understood the problem and the proposal made by Sec. McNamara.

I took the occasion of lunch to make as strongly as I could the point that it would be impossible for the U.S. to have an Israel policy without a Middle East policy; and a Middle East policy without having a global policy including a policy of seeing our commitments through in Southeast Asia. I underlined that I had heard nothing more dangerous in recent months than the doctrine that we could somehow look after Israel's arms requirements while living with the Church amendment and all it implied.

---

[1] Source: Johnson Library, National Security File, Country File, Israel, Vol. VII. Secret. Rostow sent this memorandum to the President that afternoon with a covering memorandum stating, "Herewith an account of my lunch today with Minister Evron. Harry [presumably McPherson] tells me that after lunch Evron feels a bit easier." A handwritten "L" on the covering memorandum indicates the President saw it.

[2] See footnote 5, Document 468.

Evron agreed that this was correct and then went on to say the following: If we are to work together, as we must, on issues like Middle East arms supply, we ought to try to work out a more lucid common strategy for the whole region. He did not mean we would always agree in detail. Israel did some things with which we disagreed and vice versa. He underlined the beginnings of Israel's uneasiness as starting with the Goldberg–Gromyko draft resolution, which they saw and on which they were "permitted to comment only at virtually the 12th hour." He suggested that we use the occasion of Eban's presence in the country for the frankest possible talks so that our tactical problems could be handled within the framework of a fairly lucid common strategic approach to the Middle East and Middle East settlement.

I took the occasion to get out Eban's aide mémoire of 30 August 1967[3]—emphasizing that this was a personal view, not that of the President or the Secretary of State—and emphasized my judgment that it was a most dangerous illusion for Israel to believe that it in fact could rely for its security on its own without reference to "external factors." The recent Middle East crisis required not merely Israeli feats of arms but a U.S. policy that kept the Soviet Union from engaging in the Middle East and which kept a working majority in the UN General Assembly. An Israel surrounded by hostile Soviet-dominated Arab states would be no answer to its problems no matter what the U.S. arms supply might be; nor would an Israel which had lost its support in the world community.

He noted these comments with some sympathy.

He concluded by saying that he was sure that in the week ahead the friends of Israel in the U.S. would make a maximum effort to get the Church amendment removed.

WR

---

[3] See footnote 5, Document 430.

474.   Telegram From the Mission to the United Nations to the
        Department of State[1]

New York, October 17, 1967, 0101Z.

1478. Re ME res—SC.

Amb Goldberg met with Riad to discuss SC situation. Sisco also present for US and Mohammed Riad for UAR.

Amb. Goldberg filled in Riad generally on his discussion with Dobrynin pointing out that differences over interpretation of US-USSR draft have been encountered. Soviets do not agree that under para 2 of res renunciation of belligerency means opening of Suez Canal for all vessels, including Israeli. Moreover, it was not our view that refugee question was linked to opening of Canal. Riad indicated he was prepared to discuss a draft res and how to proceed in the SC or alternatively, to discuss the various problems relating to a settlement one by one. He once again reiterated his principal interest is what general policy of US is since UAR is looking for better relations with US and stability, and UN operation is secondary. He said he willing to discuss settlement problems by going back to beginning, or be prepared to consider a new approach at UN.

Amb. Goldberg indicated that Dobrynin conversation had not clarified what Sovs had in fact distributed to various dels at end of ESSGA. Net result of Dobrynin conversation was to underscore differences between us as to meaning of US-USSR res and what affirmative acts would be required by parties in connection with such res. Goldberg said our policy is clear as stated by the Pres on June 19th. We welcome friendly relations with all countries in area, and seek a durable peace. We believe SC could be helpful in making a start towards peace in area. We have listened with great care to Riad's observations in previous conversations and have noted in particular that UAR has said categorically it politically impossible to take certain steps in connection with a SC res. For example, Riad has said no UAR Govt could now agree that Israeli flag ships could tranist Canal. In view of the difficulties which Riad has previously indicated, perhaps best way to proceed would be for the SC to develop broad guidelines. Such an approach would not exact from either of the parties any affirmative acts at the time of the adoption of the SC res. Such SC res might call upon the SYG to appoint a rep whose task would be to assist parties in effectuating purposes of

---

[1] Source: National Archives and Records Administration, RG 59, Central Files 1967–69, POL 27 ARAB–ISR/UN. Secret; Exdis. Repeated to Tel Aviv and Amman. Received at 0206Z.

guidelines. Such approach would also avoid need for common interpretation by sponsors, and call upon the parties would be limited to a call to cooperate with SYG's rep. Throughout Goldberg stressed need for balance in any SC res. If a UN res could help make a start, US would be prepared to use its influence to help achieve a permanent solution. Our objective is to help establish honorable conditions of peaceful coexistence. Goldberg then indicated very generally to Riad kind of charter principles that might be included as part of a broad mandate for a UN rep. In recounting principles to Riad, latter noted avoidance of mention of refugees. Goldberg pointed out that we could not accept linking of refugees with opening of Canal. Riad stressed one principle—the political independence and territorial integrity for all in area.

Riad focused on desirability of achieving a final settlement, viewing SC operation as a beginning point, and expressing belief that various problems relating to a settlement would take time to work out. He did not seem to preclude territorial adjustments as part of a settlement. He then focused on quest of who "should put something down on paper" in form of a res so that UAR, SC members, and Israelis could make a judgment based on a specific text. In response to Amb Goldberg's query, Riad said that non-permanent members are scheduled to meet on ME and they might be asked to put something down on paper. Amb. Goldberg said we have no objections to having non-perms see what they could develop.

Since Caradon this morning seemed to doubt our view of UAR unwillingness to interpret renunciation of belligerency to mean opening of Suez and had suggested that explicit language regarding free and innocent passage thru international waterways should be added to para 2–B of US-USSR draft, we tried this out on Riad. As expected, Riad did not think such language would be helpful.

Conversation concluded with both Goldberg and Riad stating that any UN rep appointed should be agreeable to principal parties. In response to Goldberg's inquiry, Riad agreed that US and UAR should discuss directly with each other any text developed by non-perms.

Comment: Amb Goldberg will meet with Danes, Canadians and two LA members of SC early Tues AM before non-perm member mtg scheduled later in morning. We will be giving them our views re kind res which might be constructive next step for SC, and ascertain whether they willing to take initiative.

Goldberg

475.   Memorandum From the President's Special Assistant (Rostow) to President Johnson[1]

Washington, October 17, 1967.

SUBJECT

Nasty Situation on Israel–Jordan Border and Your Talk with Eban Next Tuesday

Terrorist incidents on the Israeli occupied West Bank have increased in the last couple of weeks. Sunday,[2] the Israelis asked us urgently to pass a message to King Hussein requesting a meeting of Jordanian and Israeli commanders to coordinate efforts to stop infiltration across the Jordan River.[3]

Hussein came back and asked that the Israelis clarify what they thought such a meeting would achieve since Jordan was already making a maximum effort to stop infiltrators. His prime minister persuaded him that he shouldn't allow this sort of contact because the Israelis would exploit it. At the same time, he told us that the Israelis could have all the contact they wanted and at higher levels if we could just get a UN resolution passed for Jordan to operate under.[4]

The Israelis consider Hussein's answer evasive and claim they know he's allowing the terrorists to operate openly in Jordan. They've answered that they have nothing more to say to Hussein. Publicly they've indicated they may have no choice but to strike at the roots of terrorism.

This sounds ominously like the noises that preceded Israel's raid on Jordan last November and last May's mobilization. We've asked Arthur Goldberg to tell Eban they'd be making a terrible mistake to strike at anyone now.[5]

---

[1] Source: Johnson Library, National Security File, Country File, Israel, Vol. VII. Secret. A handwritten notation on the memorandum indicates it was received at 6 p.m.

[2] October 15.

[3] Telegram 1158 from Tel Aviv, October 15, reported that Bitan had asked an Embassy officer for U.S. assistance to convey a message in the Prime Minister's name to Amman suggesting that the Jordanians designate a senior military commander to meet as soon as possible with a senior Israeli commander to discuss ways in which Israel and Jordan could coordinate their efforts to prevent Fatah crossings of the Jordan River. Bitan pointed to incidents that morning and the previous day and said he did not have to dwell on the dangers of "escalation, et cetera." He expressed the hope that something could be done "before nightfall." (National Archives and Records Administration, RG 59, Central Files 1967–69, POL 27 ARAB–ISR)

[4] Telegram 1893 from Jordan, October 16, reported the King's reply. (Ibid.)

[5] Telegram 55494 to USUN, October 17, conveyed instructions to Goldberg. (Ibid., POL 27 ARAB–ISR/UN) Telegram 1567 from USUN, October 20, reported that in a conversation with Rafael, Goldberg had urged against Israeli retaliatory action against Jordan. (Ibid., POL 27 ARAB–ISR) Telegram 54810 to Tel Aviv, October 16, records a similar conversation between Davies and the Israeli Counselor. (Ibid.)

I pass this along because (a) it could lead to new fighting (20% likelihood) and (b) it sets the backdrop for your talk with Eban next Tuesday.[6]

We think Israel is pursuing a policy that's more likely to lead to another explosion than to a peace settlement. While we appreciate their desire to let time make the Arabs more realistic, once the UN gets a mediator in the field they are going to have to show some give in their position or kill all chances for a settlement.

You will have more formal advice from Secretary Rusk before you see Eban. But the tentative judgment is that you'll want to consider being pretty stern with him. Unless we are fairly tough, he'll go home thinking we buy their line. The attached[7] is to give you a picture of what a tough line might look like since you might like to mull over the line you want to take.

Walt

---

[6] October 24.

[7] The attachment, dated October 17, headed "Possible Line With Eban," is not printed.

---

476. Memorandum From Harold H. Saunders of the National Security Council Staff to the President's Special Assistant (Rostow)[1]

Washington, October 17, 1967.

SUBJECT

Defining our Position on "Territorial Integrity" in the Mid-East

I have spent some days in discussions of what our commitment to territorial integrity in the Middle East means today. We still are not agreed.

This is not just an academic exercise because the answer will eventually determine how hard we lean on Israel if and when a territorial settlement is negotiated. We need a tentative view soon because Eban sees the President 24 October. As Evron told you, now while Eban is here is the time to understand each other, disagreements and all. If we

---

[1] Source: Johnson Library, National Security File, Country File, Israel, Vol. VII. Secret.

say nothing about how our commitment relates to the West Bank, Eban will go away thinking it's not important to us.

In the slightly longer term, we will need to know where we stand because any UN representative will need US muscle behind him. If we're serious, it may be the time to begin showing Eban a little of this muscle while he's here.

The policy question is: Do we think the pre-war map of the Middle East is about right and will we work to restore it? Or do we accept the seeming Israeli argument that it would be better to have the West Bank than to rely again on an unreliable King Hussein?

The tactical questions are: Will we lean on Israel and, if so, should we lay the groundwork with Eban to avoid later misunderstanding? Or do we want to avoid facing this issue until the situation is riper and we have to?

There is a wide gap within our ranks over how we should interpret our past commitment in the wake of the June war. Since the argument is neither open nor sharp, there's some value in trying to sort out what's behind the contending positions.

Secretary Rusk has told several foreign ministers now that we had no trouble with pre-June boundaries and would work to restore them if we could do so in the context of permanent peace. Without ascribing the following arguments to the Secretary, those who take a similar position have these considerations in mind:

a. This position is the logical extension of the President's re-commitment to territorial integrity on 19 June and his statement that "certainly there must be withdrawal."

b. It also reflects the strong feeling, which the Secretary expressed movingly last week in speaking of Vietnam, that it is important to preserve the credibility of the "pledged word" of the US. Though the Senate has not formally committed us to defend territorial integrity in the Middle East per se, we cannot dismiss lightly the word of four Presidents backed by Congressional support of the related Truman Doctrine, Eisenhower Doctrine and CENTO.

c. It reflects some sympathy for the Arab case. Our Arab friends and oil executives argue persuasively that we can't let them down by breaking our word.

d. We seem to be signed onto the principle that the conquest of territory by war is "inadmissible." Many people argue that this is unrealistic because Israel's pre-June boundaries were themselves determined in battle. But though we shied away from this in the 19 June principles, we accepted it in the US-Soviet draft resolution, and a lot of people feel strongly about it.

e. It is hard to dispute that, for 17 years, our commitment referred to 1949 Armistice lines. The Tripartite Declaration (1950) specifically referred to them, and in 1956 we pressed Israel back behind them.

Others are more cautious about going that far. They feel, for one reason or another, that the drastically changed post-June situation requires some redefinition of past positions. Their position stems from these considerations:

a. Anyone who fully appreciates Israel's position knows how hard—maybe impossible—it will be to force Israel back to 4 June lines, especially in Jerusalem. We got a foretaste of their position in their sharp reaction to the US-Soviet draft resolution in July. The professional levels of our government frankly doubt that the President will be willing in an election year to exert the kind of pressure on Israel that would be necessary to restore armistice lines, even as permanent boundaries.

b. The President himself feeds this view when he tells all his Arab visitors that he *can't* influence Israel to do what it doesn't want to do.

c. The 19 June statement itself says territorial integrity can only be defined "on the basis of peace between the parties." That is read almost everywhere as qualification of our earlier commitment. In essence, it says we'll settle for whatever the parties can negotiate. As the President's last letter to Tito said, "We have no preconceptions on frontiers as such."

d. In all fairness, this is more than weaseling in the face of Israeli intransigence. It's belated recognition that our pledges to oppose aggression are sometimes not intended to cover provoked aggression. We've always told the Saudis this about our commitment to their territorial integrity. But we never got around to qualifying our general pledge similarly. One of the main differences between 1956 and 1967 is that we honestly feel that the Arabs asked for what they got by pulling the rug out from under our 1957 peace settlement.

e. Some may instinctively feel that the Israelis are right in saying that the Arabs will only get serious about working out a settlement when they realize no one else will do it for them. If we are ready to act on the basis of past commitment to territorial integrity, the Arabs will go on expecting us to pull their chestnuts out of the fire. Therefore, we're better off redefining our commitment in terms of the 19 June principles and dragging our feet.

So *here we are:* The Secretary of State intimating that we are honor-bound to go back to 4 June lines if only we can establish conditions of peace. The Secretary of Defense saying we have to stick by Jordan in Israel's interest as well as our own. Israel disagreeing violently. The President saying, at least for effect, that we can't get back to June 4 lines.

Ambassador Goldberg opposing any further public effort to define our position because it will just get us in further trouble with everyone. The professionals remembering sadly that Israel is Israel, believing the President and trying to build a position that bridges these two contradictory positions.

IRG/NEA has been working steadily on these issues, as well as on the related problems of Jerusalem and where we go with Jordan. Secretary Rusk will have his own meetings on them later this week. But since both you and the President will be seeing Eban next week, I want to let you begin mulling these questions over well in advance.

Hal

---

477. Memorandum of Conversation[1]

Washington, October 18, 1967.

At my request Ambassador Harman joined me this morning to discuss the resumption of arms deliveries to Israel and the associated Israeli support of the resumption of arms deliveries to certain of the Arab nations. After a long conversation during which I expressed our need for their support of our deliveries to moderate Arab states and our understanding that they could not be expected to announce that support publicly, I suggested that we act as though there had been no letter from us to them and hence no reply required in writing from them to us.[2] I emphasized that when queried on this subject by Members of Congress, we would say that we had discussed with representatives of

---

[1] Source: Johnson Library, National Security File, Country File, Israel, Vol. VII. Secret; Sensitive. Rostow forwarded the memorandum to the President with a brief covering memorandum. A handwritten "L" on the memorandum indicates the President saw it.

[2] Concerning McNamara's October 12 letter to Eban, see footnote 5, Document 468. An October 16 memorandum from Rostow to the President states that the Israelis had been pressing Goldberg, and Goldberg had been pressing McNamara to change two sentences in his letter to read: "In response to such inquiries we plan to state that we have advised officials of your Government of our intention to resume some arms shipments in discharge of existing commitments to the moderate Arab states. We will also state our conviction that such action is not contrary to Israel's interests." The Israelis proposed to reply stating their appreciation for the resumption of shipments and for the consultation and would merely "note" the above paragraph. (Johnson Library, National Security File, Country File, Israel, Vol. VII)

Israel the resumption of deliveries to the Arab countries and that Israel recognized the necessity for our taking the actions we did. Harman agreed to my proposal and stated that while even in private he might find it impossible to state categorically that Israel supported our action, he would find a way of indicating, perhaps by silence, that they did not oppose it.

Harman asked, as he did yesterday, whether they could be assured of further consultations on U.S. arms deliveries to Arab countries. I said the future would have to take care of itself and our action would depend upon the circumstances existing at the time, including the support we had had from the Israeli Government between now and then.

Harman also asked whether we would agree now to accept in the future orders from Israel for spare parts, ammunition, and similar kinds of military equipment and supplies. I stated, as I had yesterday, that we would examine lists of whatever they wished to buy and promptly give our answer with respect to each item on the list.

Robert S. McNamara[3]

---

[3] Printed from a copy that bears this typed signature.

---

478.   Telegram From the Mission to the United Nations to the Department of State[1]

New York, October 18, 1967, 2215Z.

1521. Dept pass Cairo. Middle East.

Following further preliminary consultations between Hope (UK) and Pedersen, Caradon (UK) called on Goldberg for further ME discussion this morning. Discussion was most fruitful one we have had in two weeks, and we believe we have gotten over, for moment at least, main difficulties between two delegations.

Caradon said SC Pres was calling on him today following meeting of non-perm members, and he understood he had called on us last night. Goldberg said this was correct and we had authorized him to report to SC members we were not in agreement with USSR but did not

---

[1] Source: National Archives and Records Administration, RG 59, Central Files 1967–69, POL 27 ARAB–ISR/UN. Secret; Exdis. Repeated to London and Tel Aviv. Received at 2323Z.

wish to discuss details, that we concurred in effort on non-perm members to seek new approach, and that we thought consultation with parties was important.

Caradon said he thought it was very important US and UK not speak with different voices to non-perm members. Caradon said he planned to make similar points, i.e. approval of non-perm members efforts, importance of consultations with parties, desirability of producing an early draft, and interest in general and balanced statement of principles followed by appointment of special rep. Goldberg said this was quite satisfactory.

Caradon said he wished to raise important question on content of res. UK had always assumed res must include provision for withdrawal. In recent conversations with him Goldberg had used different formulations of possible language covering this point. Caradon said he had raised questions about our formulations but now he understood Goldberg had talked to FonMin Riad (UAR)[2] in framework which did not refer to withdrawal at all. He had been very worried about this yesterday, as we knew.

Goldberg replied that on this matter we thought it was very important not to be more Catholic than the Pope. Every effort to produce agreement in past had floundered over relationship between wording of withdrawal and of non-belligerence. It was now our impression that Arabs were stressing more strongly terminology referring to territorial integrity and political independence. We had previously conveyed this reaction to him after conversation with Riad, and subsequent info, including conversation with Rifai (Jordan), tended to confirm this. Goldberg said we could of course not be sure until people began to look at actual texts. Caradon said he would be extremely surprised if this proved to be correct but indicated he had no objection to possibility being explored.

Goldberg then told Caradon that in light of our various conversations we had in fact gone ahead to complete a new draft. This was not to be a US draft, and if it began to appear in such fashion we would disown it. Told Caradon we had given this text (USUN 1504)[3] in both short and long form to LAs, Canada, and Denmark yesterday morning for their guidance in meetings of non-perm members.

Goldberg observed that consensus in that group had been that best approach was to start with shorter version, i.e. without para containing language on withdrawal and non-belligerence and then see what developed.

[2] See Document 474.

[3] Telegram 1504 from USUN, October 18. (National Archives and Records Administration, RG 59, Central Files 1967–69, POL 27 ARAB–ISR/UN)

Caradon expressed appreciation for receipt of texts, said he would respect our confidence, and reiterated agreement to continuing on course outlined.

Comment: There is still difference of assessment of chances of progress along lines we have outlined. There also continues to be difference of opinion between US and UK which could re-appear at subsequent stage, on proper balance of wording between withdrawal and non-belligerence. However for moment we are operating in coordinated tactical fashion.

Goldberg

---

479. Action Memorandum From the Assistant Secretary of State for Near Eastern and South Asian Affairs (Battle) to Secretary of State Rusk[1]

Washington, October 18, 1967.

SUBJECT

Mr. Robert Anderson's Talk with Foreign Minister Riad of the UAR

Mr. Robert Anderson called me today. He wanted to report on a conversation he had with Foreign Minister Riad of the UAR preceding a dinner Mr. Anderson gave for a group of Arabs last night.

Mr. Riad came early saying that he had just met with a group of Arab representatives including, among others, the Moroccans, Kuwaitis, Lebanese, Libyans, and Saudis. The group had been astonished to learn through Moroccan channels that Secretary Rusk had informed the Foreign Minister of Morocco that the U.S. had a contract to provide Skyhawks to the Israelis and intended to honor this contract in the near future.[2]

Mr. Riad said that the opinion of the group which he met was that if the U.S. gave military assistance to Israel while it occupied Arab ter-

---

[1] Source: National Archives and Records Administration, RG 59, Central Files 1967–69, POL UAR–US. Secret; Exdis; Eyes Only. Drafted by Battle.

[2] A handwritten note in the margin reads as follows: "Sir: The memcon (at clip) does *not* bear out this flat Moroccan assertion." The memorandum of Rusk's conversation on October 16 with Moroccan Foreign Minister Laraki is not attached to the source text. (Ibid. POL 7 MOR)

ritory, the result would be "fatal" in terms of U.S. relations with Arab countries. Mr. Riad remarked that while the UAR was getting equipment from Russia, it was not as good as Skyhawks and was not in the quantity widely reported. Moreover, the Egyptians have no one to operate such equipment effectively. Mr. Anderson said that Riad was more vehement than he had ever seen him and that later Pachachi of Iraq had called Mr. Anderson making similar statements in the same tone.

Mr. Riad also told Mr. Anderson that Secretary Rusk had asked several people who spoke for the UAR. Riad wanted Secretary Rusk to know that Riad had greater authority to speak now for President Nasser than he had had before the war. There would have been no Yemen settlement except for Riad's advice. He had shaped President Nasser's policy on Yemen as well as on other subjects and could say that he represented President Nasser totally and completely.

Mr. Riad said that he had had a message yesterday from President Nasser asking when Robert Anderson would be visiting Cairo. Nasser considers these talks essential and to be conducted as soon possible. Mr. Anderson will be in Iraq in connection with a sulfur project from October 27 to October 29. He could go to Cairo before or after the pending trip to Iraq.

I told Mr. Anderson that I had hoped to hear from Mr. Eban before a decision was made as to the wisdom of Mr. Anderson's going to Cairo. It would be impossible for us to know were we stood on the Israeli side of the equation until after we talked with Eban the first of next week. Since this did not give Mr. Anderson much time, I could understand his need to make a decision quickly. If he had to decide now, I would recommend that he agree to go.

Do you approve the foregoing?[3]

---

[3] Rusk initialed his approval.

480. Letter From Premier Kosygin to President Johnson[1]

Moscow, October 20, 1967.

Dear Mr. President,

The Soviet Government feels concerned over the fact that so far there has been no progress in the matter of a political settlement in the Near East.

Although as a result of the known resolutions of the Security Council which were supported by our two states, it was possible to halt military actions in the Near East, the occupation of the Arab territories seized by Israel in the course of the aggression, still continues. Israeli leaders are putting forward more and more openly plans for the annexation of these territories, or at least parts of them, and are even undertaking practical steps for their colonization.

Information is available about concentrations of Israeli forces in positions which can hardly be viewed otherwise than staging areas for the organization of new military actions against Syria and Jordan. The government of Lebanon shows concern over the threats directed at it as well. There is a growing evidence of increasing arms supplies to Israel from abroad.

In such an atmosphere of growing tension during the recent period one cannot exclude serious complications in the Near East, the possibility that the armed incidents provoked by Israel which continuously occur along the Suez canal and along the Israeli-Jordanian and Israeli-Syrian frontiers, will turn into a broad military confrontation.

All states, with the exception of the aggressor, stated during the Emergency Session of the UN General Assembly that the use of force should not result in any benefits and advantages, and that Israel should withdraw her forces from the seized Arab territories. You also spoke in the same sense during the meeting last June.

In continuing to behave in such a provocative and defiant manner the leaders of Israel seem to rely, first of all, on aid and support from the USA.

---

[1] Source: Johnson Library, National Security File, Head of State Correspondence File, USSR, Kosygin Correspondence, Vol. I. No classification marking. The copy printed here is headed "Translation." Two copies of a slightly different translation headed "Unofficial translation" are ibid. Dobrynin called Rusk at 3:30 p.m. on October 21 and told him he had just received the letter and that Kosygin wanted him to deliver it in person. (Notes of telephone conversation, prepared by Mildred Asbjornson; National Archives and Records Administration, RG 59, Rusk Files: Lot 72 D 192, Telephone Calls) Dobrynin called on the President from 7:30 to 8:03 p.m. that evening and evidently delivered the letter at that time. (Johnson Library, President's Daily Diary) No record of the conversation has been found.

As is apparent from contacts between Soviet representatives and responsible officials of your government, and from the whole course of events during the present session of the General Assembly of the UN, Israel's expansionist ambitions find on the American side a benevolent attitude.

After the opening of the present session we were greatly surprised to learn that the American side not only has not moved forward in the search of a political settlement in the Near East but has shown a somewhat different attitude even toward her own proposals which had been proposed by her during the Emergency Session of the UN General Assembly.

One gains the impression that the American side is actually trying to abandon her own proposals, judging by the statements made by her representatives in New York. Under the pretext of an interpretation of these proposals, substantially new and additional conditions are being put forward in the spirit of the aggressive demands made by Israel. Attempts have also been made to steer the negotiations along a twisting and swampy path with many stops and retreats.

Meanwhile it should be made completely clear that: if the question of speedy withdrawal of Israeli forces is not solved then there can be no peace in that area. The unstable, explosive situation will continue and will introduce complications into international relations as a whole.

Where would lead the reliance of the leaders of Israel on US assistance? Some will help one side, others the other side. And thus, link by link, the chain of events will follow. Is this the way to strengthen peace in the Near East? Will this be of benefit to states?

The Soviet Government proceeds from the position that it is necessary to eliminate without delay the after-effects of aggression and, at the same time, to prevent the breakout of a new military conflict in this area in the near or more distant future.

The Soviet Government firmly believes that now there exists an objective opportunity to put an end to further dangerous protraction of the political settlement in the Near East. This can and must be done by means of a speedy adoption, let us say, in the Security Council of a resolution which was discussed at the end of the Emergency Session of the UN General Assembly and which provides for the withdrawal of troops without delay from the occupied territories to the positions as of June 5, 1967, at the same time recognizing the principle of independent national existence of all states in that area and their right to live in peace and security. Each side would be bound to observe such a Security Council resolution.

Of course, in addition to those mentioned there is a number of other questions awaiting a solution. There is the question of free navigation.

We are convinced that these questions, too, should be solved in the interest of all countries on the basis of the aforementioned resolution, if adopted by the Security Council.

References to the effect that the Arab states are allegedly not agreeable to recognize Israel's right to independent national existence are groundless. You are also undoubtedly aware that the Arab states, at any rate, those immediately concerned, have adopted a sound and realistic position.

The time has come to take resolute steps to put an end to the present dangerous situation in the Near East. One must not allow the political settlement be wrecked because Israel would like to realize her extreme claims behind which hides an unrestrained drive towards expansion. It appears that the Israeli leaders are little concerned with how this state will live tomorrow, without thinking of the consequences their political short-sightedness may bring about.

We are convinced that the overwhelming majority of states, perhaps all of them, will support every positive step in the direction of a settlement. And hardly anybody could come out against the decision of the Security Council which reflects the interests of states and is dictated by the desire to relieve tension and to bring lasting peace to the Near East.

In the positive results of such efforts nations would see not only a contribution to the strengthening of peace in that area but also a ray of hope in the cause of solving other problems facing mankind and, not in the least, by our countries.

I hope, Mr. President, to receive your early reply. One would like to believe that this reply will help to remove from the agenda a problem which has become a source of friction and conflicts.

Respectfully,

A. Kosygin

481. Telegram From the Mission to the United Nations to the Department of State[1]

New York, October 24, 1967, 0151Z.

1676. 1. Amb. Goldberg, accompanied by Sisco and Pedersen, had a long and friendly two and one-half hour conversation October 21 on ME with Kuznetsov, Fedorenko, Mendelevich, and Shevchenko. Principal points which emerged are:

A. Kuznetsov continues to maintain that both versions I and II contain June 5 dates:[2] Goldberg said this was totally unnecessary argument as it could be resolved on basis documents. Requested Soviets check their own files to find handwritten copy of version I handed to Dobrynin at time and later confirmed as correct by Dobrynin to Goldberg and which did not contain that date.[3]

B. Goldberg said in response to question US supported version I (without date) subject to common interpretation at time, and on ad referendum basis subject to consultation with principal parties concerned.

C. Kuznetsov maintained Sov support for version I (with date), but without common interpretation subject Arab approval and "as basis" for current action. He also avoided confirming Sov support for version II (we also avoided this). Kuznetsov said, if any other res submitted, paras 2A and B of USUSSR text should be included.

D. With above underbrush having been gone over Amb. Goldberg and Kuznetsov agreed we would await efforts of non-perm members to see what they develop. Goldberg having Kuznetsov to dinner Wednesday.

---

[1] Source: National Archives and Records Administration, RG 59, Central Files 1967–69, POL ARAB–ISR/UN. Secret; Priority; Exdis. Repeated to Moscow Priority and to Tel Aviv and Amman. Received at 0338Z.

[2] In a meeting with Rusk on October 19, Dobrynin gave him two pieces of paper, both dated July 20, headed "1st version" and "2nd version." The first consists of paragraph 2 of the first version of the U.S.-Soviet draft resolution, as transmitted in Document 380, except that in sub-paragraph 2.a, the words "to the positions they occupied before June 5, 1967" are substituted for the words "from territories occupied by them." The second consists of paragraphs 2 and 3 of the second version of the draft resolution as transmitted in Document 20. The two pieces of paper are attached to a memorandum of October 20 from Read to Rusk, which also forwarded a copy of Version I as transmitted in Document 380 and states that the first version text Dobrynin had given Rusk the previous day was clearly an altered form of the July version. (National Archives and Records Administration, RG 59, Central Files 1967–69, POL 27–14 ARAB–ISR) No record of Rusk's October 19 meeting with Dobrynin has been found.

[3] See Document 380.

2. Ambassador Goldberg said he had requested meeting Kuznetsov for two reasons: To discuss two versions of US-USSR ESSGA text; and review where we are and where we wish to go on Middle Eastern question at UN. Goldberg said it important in our bilateral relationships to avoid misunderstandings and recriminations. We attach considerable importance, as we know Sovs do, to privacy and confidential nature of our discussions. He realized we both operating under pressure in last days of ESSGA, but whatever difference there may be regarding interpretations, there should be no disagreement about documents or drafts on which common ground achieved. We understand Dobrynin gave Secretary on Oct. 19 two versions, both containing June 5 date, and Fedorenko gave these texts to SC Pres. (Tsuruoka) with indication that USSR did not consider these confidential documents. If this is case, we would like to know since we have refused to reveal to SC Pres such private information.

3. We note that version I left with the Secretary and with SC Pres contained June 5 date. This is not what was agreed to between US in July: There was no date in version I. Two versions were written out by hand by Amb. Pedersen at meeting with Dobrynin and handed to him. We suggest therefore that Sovs check own files to find hand-written texts Goldberg gave Dobrynin, and later confirmed telephonically as correct by Amb. Dobrynin after checking with Gromyko. Goldberg made clear we not charging bad faith, but expressed hope matter could be clarified since he did not believe it was dignified for US to reveal documentation and charge that texts given out are falsified.

4. Goldberg said he also wished to raise question on ground rules of discussions between us. When each of us had reviewed texts, does this mean they become non-confidential and public in character? For example, SC Pres asked us for these documents, but we refused to give them to him. As Kuznetsov knows, we and they have had confidential discussions within context of US-USSR relations, and for our part, we do not recognize competence of SC to cross-examine us on them.

5. Kuznetsov, speaking slowly and deliberately through an interpreter, noted with satisfaction opportunity for exchange of views on this important problem. He considered it absolutely right that our meetings and others of this character should be carried out in business-like and frank manner. Sov experience in negotiations shows results can be obtained only when discussions are frank and business-like, and where no side seeks to outflank other and play with arguments. Regarding Middle Eastern question, USSR, its government, and its delegation have been trying and will, by all necessary steps, continue to take measures in order to achieve solution corresponding to interests of parties concerned and directed toward consideration of peace in Middle East and

lessening of tensions elsewhere. Sov ready to unite with other states, fully understanding importance of US role, to seek solution of ME question. This, in large measure, will depend upon extent to which there is mutual understanding and a mutual approach between US and USSR. During three or four days he has been in New York, Kuznetsov has tried to understand atmosphere and mood of delegations. He wished to share his impressions with Amb. Goldberg. He has had meetings with Arabs, primarily with UAR, which have provided him with belief UAR approach is now characterized by more understanding and realism than at end of ESSGA. He has same impressions from his conversations with Jordanians and Iraqis and believes this would be a positive factor which should be considered when attention is given to best way to settle ME problem. His impression, objectively and candidly, is that there is a more favorable possibility for a solution acceptable to all parties concerned and for preparation and adoption of an SC or GA res.

6. Kuznetsov continued he had second impression. While Arabs were taking more realistic approach, other side moving toward more unacceptable requirements leading away from a peaceful solution.

7. Kuznetsov said he would be as open and frank as Amb. Goldberg had been regarding two versions discussed at end of session. Sovs also have certain documents and info from which they derive certain impressions. He was aware that some called it an American draft, others an LA draft, and others a Sov-American draft. He confirmed their acceptance of US-USSR [draft] had been subject to Arab agreement. Draft (Kuznetsov at times used word "draft" in singular and other times in plural) contained balanced provisions. He said first version contained provision for withdrawal of Israeli forces to positions occupied before June 5 and a second provision called for discontinuance of the state of war, and a provision for settlement of questions by peaceful means in accordance with international law, including freedom of shipping, and solution of refugee problem. Unfortunately, that draft did not command support, and he need not dwell on reasons. He said now Arab states are more interested in a solution, agree to support this draft, taking it as a basis for a solution and for resolution to be adopted by SC or GA. If now other side, and above all US, remains at same point as it was at end of ESSGA, it would not be difficult to reach agreement on that text and make a contribution to a solution.

8. From what Amb. Goldberg had said, Kuznetsov understands US has problem with June 5 date. Without going into details, Sovs have two versions and both mention June 5 date. US did not deny fact that in one version date is included. Sovs had to think why US attached so much importance to date, what lay behind this: maybe US seeking to go back on its position. If both of us proceeded from fact that Israeli forces should

be withdrawn to positions occupied before June 5, then there is no problem. Dropping date Kuznetsov argued could only create opinion that US favors solution not requiring full liberation of Arab territories and leaving certain territories under Israeli occupation so that withdrawal would be incomplete. This position would not contribute to settlement in spirit necessary for ME solution. It would be dangerous step. ME situation would not be conducive to lessening of tensions, good neighborliness, establishment of peace. In passing, he would point out that all resolutions put to vote at ESSGA stated definitely that Israelis should withdraw troops to positions they occupied before the aggression.

9. Amb. Goldberg said at outset Kuznetsov expressed common Sov-American view. We agree our efforts should be used in and out of UN to help bring parties to an understanding leading to durable peace. Both of us have expressed this as a common conviction and goal. It serves neither US nor USSR national interests to have lack of stability in area. US hoped to do everything it could to achieve a peaceful solution in concert with Sovs. But unfortunately, as famous jurist once said, "Concrete cases cannot be decided without general propositions." Nevertheless there ought not be any difference on what we agreed to ad referendum regarding drafts. Amb. Goldberg repeated he was not charging bad faith or that USSR did not stand by its agreements, but he believed it was important to know what we agreed: he could say flatly and categorically that Soviet first version, which included date, was not what was agreed. He urged again that Sovs check their own files for hand-written text handed to Dobrynin which would show no date in version I. In looking at paras 2(A) and (B) of versions I and II, which Sovs had given us (both containing date), Goldberg pointed out these documents were also incomplete since full document contained preambular material in addition to an important para 3 calling for the "guarantee" of Suez Canal and making reference to refugee problem. Goldberg then read following para from USUN's 314, rptd Moscow, dated July 22,[4] referring to conversation with Dobrynin: "In course conversation we checked text of res as it had been circulated to Arabs and Sov Bloc by Sovs. In process discovered that Sovs had introduced reference to June 5 date in version I. I told Dobrynin this was not acceptable and that it had not been included in that version as given to him yesterday by US and as reported to Washington."

10. Goldberg also reviewed in detail discussions between Gromyko and himself to highlight joint character of Sov and US participation in development of draft res and contributions each made. He informed Kuznetsov that Gromyko himself suggested some of ideas in draft and

---

[4] Document 384.

that "there were two parents to language," though admittedly, he did not know who father was and mother was. Goldberg recalled first meeting with Dobrynin in early July. Dobrynin said USSR could accept basic concept of LA res but asked whether other words could be used for belligerency. Nothing more happened until US meetings with FonMin Gromyko. At that time, US made clear that we were firm in concepts, though flexible re language, and wording and ideas contained in 2(B) were discussed between Goldberg and Gromyko. At one point, Gromyko had asked whether the word "guarantee" could be replaced by word "consider" in para 3. Amb. Goldberg rejected this suggestion on ground that renunciation of belligerency in para 2(B) opened waterways as matter of principle and that under para 3 of draft res, SC role formula, came primarily from LA-Soviet talks and was largely LA formulation. Second version, unlike first, contained date, but did not have such strong words as "without delay" as contained in version I. Finally, Amb. Goldberg said at no time during those conversations was there ever asserted by Sovs a linkage between opening of Suez Canal and solution of refugee question. This was new factor Sovs had subsequently introduced.

11. Goldberg recalled that discussion with Sovs also focused on how and what "affirmative acts" would be required by parties. We had asked what renunciation of belligerency and recognition of Israel would encompass. In one of our conversations Gromyko had referred to a document which had been signed by Japanese and Sovs in which state of war was renounced. In later conversation with Dobrynin, Goldberg discussed such a document as an example of a possible declaration and affirmative act by parties that could be taken in connection with renunciation of belligerency.

12. Amb. Goldberg then reviewed last conversation he had with Dobrynin in October at which time latter confirmed negotiations between us in future were ad referendum, subject to Sov check with Arabs, and US consultation with principal parties concerned. In this same conversation with Dobrynin, Goldberg had indicated that what he had said constituted US reply to Gromyko's questions.

13. Question was, Goldberg said, how we make progress. US had met with UAR FonMin and Jordanian Dep FonMin, on several occasions. Riad had asked whether we objected to non-perm SC members making an effort to develop SC res; our response had been that we had no objection on understanding, of course, that we would be fully consulted by them. On timing, we said we were ready to go ahead in SC promptly, provided there was an understanding on a constructive course of action. In these conversations we had stressed need for precision in SC res and had asked whether non-belligerency would include opening Suez; Riad's response had been no UAR Govt could last if it

took this step. He had indicated, however, that UAR would be willing to consider res which included principles based on June 19 statement of President and which called for appointment of a UN rep. Our impression from these discussions was that UAR willing to consider general statement of principles in SC res for mandate of UN rep. We had impression from Riad that it would be less difficult for them if they were not called upon by SC res to do specific things. We stood ready to approach SC res from point of view of appointment of a UN rep with broad guidelines. Such statement of principles would not require interpretation or acceptance by parties other than expression their willingness to cooperate with UN rep. We were now waiting to see what emerged from non-perm members discussions.

14. Kuznetsov, referring to history and drafts of July 19 and 20, stated USSR had carefully examined that question and wished to assure the US it was not Sov intention to distort or display what was agreed to in wrong light. He said we have all the records, and what we have given you are genuine versions. Sovs agree, of course, that drafts include preambular and other points. On basis question of June 5 date, Kuznetsov repeated USSR continues to support version I (with date) and asserted that draft remained good basis for a consequent solution and is position to which USSR adheres. He asked whether US supporting that draft and if not, what was US position. Sovs did not feel they had answer to this question.

15. Amb. Goldberg responded very precisely: US supports proper formulation of version I, with common interpretation discussed with Sovs and on understanding it is ad referendum in relationship to parties. US could not support version I in a vacuum.

16. Kuznetsov asked if US supported any version that contains a date and asked again if US refused to support it. Goldberg replied no, US supported proper version of I on agreed basis; there was never a date.

17. Fedorenko then asked about version II. Amb. Goldberg said this academic since Kuznetsov has just said that the Sovs support version I with a date. Amb. Goldberg asked for Sov position on version II. Kuznetsov smiled and said he had asked first. Fedorenko interjected that version II was US draft. Amb. Goldberg responded that it was not and that it was largely LA draft.

18. Kuznetsov said Sovs could now see from discussion that US is taking steps to depart from draft agreed to on July 20. US wants to hamper carrying out a constructive solution and Sovs still adhere to position that drafts of July 19 and 20 are and can be good basis for a solution; if other side (meaning US) retreats from that position then we have to consider what can be done now. USSR also aware non-perms trying to pre-

pare something and would welcome any steps and measures towards a solution which would be acceptable to all parties. If another draft res is developed, formulation contained in July 19–20 draft should be included.

19. Amb. Goldberg replied that we did not want to get into polemical argument. However, we do not accept concept that we have retreated from anything; there were common understandings as to meaning. We agree that we should now await results of Sov efforts.

20. Kuznetsov again returned to question of date and asked why US against date. Amb. Goldberg replied this has long history. Date being used to roll everything back to conditions existing before war. If you revert to pre-June 5 situation, you return to unstable conditions of armistice agreements; Canal and Straits can be closed at whim of UAR; armies confront one another on frontiers; and there are no demilitarized zones.

21. Kuznetsov said that date refers only to territory occupied and not to other problems. He asked if US favored Israel retaining territory. Amb. Goldberg said US not in favor of territorial aggrandizement or restoration of old conditions. Question where forces would withdraw would have to be cleared up in discussions among parties. Kuznetsov said if no date included in res, other side may not withdraw from all Arab territories. This would aggravate situation and become permanent source of discord. Amb. Goldberg asked whether Kuznetsov agreed withdrawal should take place in context of peace. Kuznetsov did not respond directly but said Sovs support July 19–20 draft. He said there should be withdrawal of Israeli troops to pre-June 5 positions and other problems should be considered in accordance with this res.

22. Amb. Goldberg asked Kuznetsov for his interpretation of para 2(B)—what did it mean and what did it require the parties to do. Text called for acknowledgments and renunciations, which were positive actions. What did Sovs conceive these meant? Kuznetsov refused to interpret it. Amb. Goldberg said it is important we know what US and USSR understand is meaning of such para. For example, FonMin Gromyko had made clear even though word "belligerency" was not mentioned, para 2(B) did in fact mean renunciation of belligerency. Kuznetsov said question of interpretation was a new problem and a complication. Amb. Goldberg said all he was asking was confirmation of understanding achieved.

23. Meeting concluded in expectation we would continue conversation at Wednesday[5] dinner meeting, if not sooner.

Goldberg

---

[5] October 25.

482. Memorandum of Conversation[1]

Washington, October 23, 1967, 11 a.m.

PARTICIPANTS

>Abba Eban, Israeli Minister of Foreign Affairs
>Avraham Harman, Ambassador of Israel
>Ephraim Evron, Minister of Israel
>W. W. Rostow
>Harold H. Saunders

Mr. Eban began by alluding to the sinking of the Israeli destroyer over the weekend.[2] In his view, it raised the questions of both Egyptian motivation and Egyptian technological proficiency. He said the Israeli Government found itself asking some of the same questions which had been faced after 23 May: What is the extent of Soviet involvement? Do the Egyptians feel they are operating under the cover of Soviet protection?

Eban said the Israelis had felt the Egyptians were pursuing a "conservative policy" on the cease-fire. However, there could be no question that the sinking was a "classic act of war." Israel would prefer to deal with this incident as a matter between them and the Egyptians.

Mr. Rostow reminded Mr. Eban that this was not the first Egyptian-Israeli military engagement since the cease-fire and that there had even been a previous naval engagement. Mr. Rostow said that our intelligence suggests that the Israeli destroyer was within ten miles of the Egyptian coast. Mr. Eban said his information was that it was more like 13.5 or 14 miles away. Mr. Evron, who had been called out to the phone momentarily, returned with the word that the Soviet Deputy Defense Minister had just arrived in Cairo. Mr. Rostow concluded this part of the conversation by saying he hoped that the Foreign Minister's discussion with the President would range more widely than the weekend's naval engagement.

Moving on to Soviet intentions, policy and position, Mr. Rostow said we had some intelligence reports which suggest that the Soviets have urged the Arabs to try for a political settlement but have said the Arabs could count on some unidentified Soviet support if the Israelis made a political settlement impossible.

---

[1] Source: Johnson Library, National Security File, Country File, Israel, Vol. XII. Secret. Drafted by Saunders. The meeting was held in Rostow's office at the White House. Rostow sent the memorandum to the President on October 24 with a brief covering memorandum. A handwritten "L" indicates the President saw it.

[2] The Israeli destroyer *Eilat* was sunk on October 21 off the Sinai coast by UAR missile-equipped patrol craft.

Mr. Eban characterized Soviet policy as follows: The USSR is not looking for peace, although it is not looking for war either. It uses the Middle East as an arena for pursuing its global interests, many of which relate to the U.S. Its objectives are to make the Arab-Socialist countries more Socialist, to draw other Arabs away from their Western ties and to divide the Western allies.

Speaking on the Soviet position in the Middle East, he felt that the Soviets have lost ground in the last few months. They did not come through on their commitments in June. The Arabs are now more interested in the U.S. (and the UK) than before because they see the West as essential to their own development and to their ability to arrive at a settlement with Israel. The total result has been a weakening of the Soviet position, despite all the superficial difficulties that the West suffers. Mr. Rostow agreed in general except for the weakening of the British pound. Mr. Eban said that even the British Foreign Minister tended to down-play this. Mr. Rostow agreed that in general we had been drifting in a positive direction.

With that, the conversation shifted to the question of who gains from the passage of time. Mr. Rostow agreed that some time had been on the side of a basic settlement but that our Government differs with the Israelis in feeling that the continued passage of time is not in a linear sense on the side of permanent peace. Mr. Eban felt that time "in the sense of weeks and months—not in the sense of years—is on the side of a realistic settlement."

Mr. Eban, commenting on how time's passing had affected Egyptian attitudes, said he believed that Egyptian Foreign Minister Riad now understands the need for a stable peace structure, is prepared to distinguish between Gaza and Egyptian territory and feels that the range of problems between Israel and the UAR is relatively limited and boils down to the question of an Israeli flag through the Suez Canal. One question he said the Israelis are not quite sure of is whether the UAR could conceive of a bilateral settlement with Israel or whether it would have to link its settlement with others this time.

Mr. Eban said he hoped we could soon move from the "tactical to the strategic plane." He saw the discussions in New York as a "watershed to be got over without prejudice or damage to future positions." He felt that if the Arabs could see that no one else would make a settlement for them, they would be face to face with a sharp picture of their alternatives: (1) to accept the present situation with a vague vision of one day being able to eliminate Israel; or (2) to settle down and find out what terms are available to them. If they chose the second course, the UAR "has reason to know" that they could get back Egyptian territory under the right circumstances.

Mr. Rostow felt that the Arabs at Khartoum had moved broadly in the direction of political settlement and were mainly struggling for modalities. Mr. Eban said he was certain that what we and the Israelis meant by "political settlement" was somewhat different from what the Arabs meant.

Speaking of settlement terms, Mr. Eban said that, while the Israelis were not unanimous on the way the map should look after a settlement, they were unanimous on two points:

1. Juridically, this settlement must move from the impermanent arrangements of the past twenty years to a permanent basis.
2. Since they hoped to draw the map "with finality" this time, they must be sure that it is drawn to "maximize territorial security."

"We can not go back to June 5 lines in peace or war," Eban said. Israel has not decided how different the new lines should be. That will depend on how arrangements on the West Bank work out. Israelis are sure, however, that they can not tolerate a "divided jurisdiction" in Jerusalem, although they can go a long way toward accommodating non-Jewish interests there. Israel would hope to eliminate Egyptian influence in Gaza.

When Mr. Rostow said our Government feels there is a great difference between "minor and major modifications" in the lines, Mr. Eban came back with, "What your Government may consider minor may seem major to us." He spoke of the Syrian Heights and Gaza as "major."

On the West Bank, he said that Israel still had not decided what the proper relationship between "security and demography" should be. They had not decided whether to deal with the Palestinian Arabs "from within or from without." If Hussein presented himself for a settlement, Israel would have to decide. The nature of the settlement will depend on whether there is a context of negotiation and peace. The longer Hussein stays away, the greater will be the pressure in Israel to explore with the leaders of the West Bank the possibility of a separate Palestinian existence. He cited the example of Cypriot leaders who have given up their interest in enosis now that they have tasted independence. He said the same forces operate on the West Bank, but before West Bank leaders aspire to an independent existence, they insist on knowing whether Israel feels Hussein will be coming back or not.

Mr. Rostow asked whether the dialogue with Hussein had continued. Mr. Eban said the main discussion had been over whether and when to meet. Israel would like to discuss such things as the benefit of long-term economic relationships but found this impossible until the two sides could talk.

When Mr. Rostow asked how the Israelis view the situation in Cairo, Mr. Eban described it as the characteristic Middle Eastern one of "stable instability." However, whereas he had thought earlier in the summer that Jordan's position was worse, now he felt that the UAR is suffering more heavily than Jordan, both politically and economically.

Mr. Eban said we should not forget that things are not standing still in Israel There are numerous "wildcat committees" studying the "integrity of the homeland." He mentioned a convention beginning tomorrow and consisting of a good portion of the Weizmann Institute and Hebrew University. These groups are suggesting to the Israeli Government that it should not discard lightly the possibility of retaining all of Palestine and working out some dignified relationship with the West Bank Arabs. Taking the long view, they felt this would be more to Israel's advantage than any agreement calculated to improve the short-term atmosphere. When he was asked whether this would not mean that some time is working against the Israeli Government, he concluded by saying that, despite these pressures, if Hussein were to present himself for a settlement today, the Government of Israel would probably decide to give the West Bank back.

The discussion turned to King Hussein's intentions. Ambassador Harman interjected that Hussein's posture had been one of "active belligerency." When Mr. Rostow asked him how Israel viewed Hussein's position on infiltration, Harman said that either Hussein knows what is going on and does not stop it, or he can not. He says Israel has evidence that infiltrators have "wandered around openly in Jordan and have received help from Jordanian soldiers." Mr. Evron said that even the Jordanian Director of Military Intelligence had been involved. In the same vein, Ambassador Harman said that King Hussein must know what his representative in New York is doing.

Mr. Eban said that "Hussein no longer evokes the same feeling from Israelis" as he did before the war. Israelis blamed the Jordanians for three serious developments: (1) It was Jordanian gibes that provoked the Egyptians to move into Sharm-el-Sheik; (2) it was the defense pact of 30 May that "made the war inexorable", (3) it was Jordan's actions on June 5 that killed all faith in him.

There is in Israel what Mr. Eban described as "casualty psychology." The Israelis, having suffered, are not about to let their sacrifices be in vain. Mr. Rostow cautioned against Israel's letting itself be lured by the false short-run stability that hard-headedness might bring. Too hard a policy might in the long run make Israel's objective of achieving peace impossible. Mr. Rostow asked, for instance, why Israeli forces were on Tiran Island.[3] Mr. Eban answered that "nature abhors a vacuum." The Egyptians had been on Tiran Island as far back as 1950 and Israel had a memorandum from the USG conveying Cairo's assurance that this would not prejudice Israeli freedom of passage through the Straits.[4] More important, however, Mr. Eban said that if the Israelis moved out, the Saudis would probably move in. It is central to Israel's position that it can not leave its right to free passage on such a "fragile lease." Arrangements for free passage there must be "concrete."

Mr. Rostow spoke of his anxiety about the Israeli feeling—conveyed in the aide-mémoire given to Ambassador Goldberg[5]—that they had learned in June the importance of being self-sufficient. Mr. Rostow said he felt it was dangerous to ignore that the US had held back the USSR and continued responsible for maintaining a Middle East policy that would limit the Soviet position. He said bluntly that, although he does not know whether the Secretary of State or President would agree with his view, he objected to an Israeli position which said that whether we give arms to moderate Arabs or not is our business, not theirs. Our recent discussions on ending the military aid freeze left him "troubled" because of the seeming failure to recognize Israel's interest in our maintaining a position with the Arabs.

Mr. Eban said that his only concern in the recent discussions over our military aid freeze was that his government not be put in a position of endorsing American military shipments to governments like that of Saudi Arabia which we might consider moderate but which had just called for the destruction of Israel.

On the broader point, Mr. Eban noted the "harsh facts" Israel faced in May and June. He acknowledged "fully and gratefully" the US ability to "neutralize the USSR." But Israel found that, on questions involving Israel and the Arab states, the US operated under certain inhibitions, both domestic and international. He felt he was only

---

[3] The Saudi Government had complained to the Embassy in Jidda on August 19 that an Israeli detachment had occupied Tiran Island, an island in the Red Sea at the entrance to the Gulf of Aqaba. (Telegram 675 from Jidda, August 20; National Archives and Records Administration, RG 59, Central Files 1967–69, POL 27 ARAB–ISR) Documentation concerning discussions with the Israelis and the Saudis concerning Tiran Island is ibid., POL 32–6 TIRAN and POL 27 ARAB–ISR.

[4] For information concerning the Egyptian aide-mémoire of January 30, 1950, containing the Egyptian assurances, see Foreign Relations, 1950, vol. V, p. 711. Evron told Saunders on November 2 that the U.S. Ambassador had passed the aide-mémoire to the Israeli Government. (Memorandum for the record by Saunders, November 2; Johnson Library, National Security File, Saunders Files, Israel)

[5] For information concerning Eban's August 30 aide-mémoire, see footnote 5, Document 430.

expressing a US interest in Israel's ability to defend itself so the US would not have to answer the question of what to do if Israel were overrun.

Mr. Rostow asked about plans for the refugees. Mr. Eban said that his government hoped to have a "blueprint" in November and hoped to consult with us on it. He said Israel had found out that the numbers of refugees were not so great as had originally been imagined. Also, resettlement was not just an agricultural matter because many of the refugees envisioned themselves as moving into an industrial job. Nevertheless, he said the problem is so vast that it would require an international and regional solution in which Israel would participate. He felt it would be essential to involve a consortium of interested countries to supplement UNWRA. He noted the irony that this year's UNWRA report had for the time "confessed" that many of the refugees had already been integrated into Arab economies.

Mr. Rostow suggested that the refugee problem offered a focus for regional cooperation. He mentioned that the financial arrangements made at Khartoum were a start on regional Arab economic cooperation and said he felt it was important to link this somehow to the refugees as a stepping stone to more permanent regional development cooperation.

In concluding, Mr. Eban stressed the importance of our making a decision on Israel's aircraft requests soon because the production line for the peculiar configuration of Skyhawk Israel is interested in closes down early in November.

H.S.

483.   Notes of Meeting[1]

Washington, October 23, 1967, 1:05–3:40 p.m.

NOTES OF THE PRESIDENT'S MEETING WITH

Secretary Rusk
Secretary McNamara
Walt Rostow
George Christian
General Wheeler

[Omitted here is a brief discussion of demonstrations against the Vietnam war.]

The Israeli response to the sinking of a ship was discussed.

Secretary Rusk: The Israelis have not consulted us. I think if they want our support they ought to consult us. I do not know what they have in mind. They are waiting awfully late for a response.[2]

Mr. Rostow: I would not ask Eban. Our intelligence shows that the ship was 10 miles off shore. CIA feels they will retaliate against the Egyptians' fleet. CIA says Egypt wanted to show its power.

Mr Helms: This ship was doing the same thing the *Liberty* was. It is strange that the Israelis didn't do anything about the attacks. There were no planes or ships. We will try to find out where they intend to retaliate.

Secretary Rusk: They will equate this with the Gulf of Tonkin. But our vessels were 50 miles from shore and there was no cease fire in the Gulf of Tonkin. I think we should leave this matter to the U.N. and recommend prudence and hope for a long-term settlement.

The President: Do you have a final draft of the letter to Kosygin?[3]

Secretary Rusk: This is a message dated Friday.[4] Dobrynin received it Saturday.

Mr. Rostow: We knew about the ship before we knew about this letter.

---

[1] Source: Johnson Library, Tom Johnson's Notes of Meetings, October 23, 1967, 1:05 p.m. Top Secret; Eyes Only. Sent to the President with a covering memorandum from Johnson of October 25. Director of Central Intelligence Richard Helms was also present. (Ibid., Daily Diary)

[2] Barbour reported in telegram 1285 from Tel Aviv, October 23, that he raised the subject with Bitan that day and expressed the hope that the Israelis would not feel constrained to embark on a course of retaliation, the outcome of which was unpredictable. Bitan said the Israeli Government had taken no decision to retaliate. (National Archives and Records Administration, RG 59, Central Files 1967–69, POL 27 ARAB–ISR)

[3] See Document 484.

[4] October 20; see Document 480.

The President read and suggested changes in the proposed Kosygin letter.

[Omitted here is the text of the draft letter.]

The President: I want Goldberg to make sure that we have documented evidence of all of the statements made in this message.

[Omitted here are comments by Helms concerning Vietnam.]

Mr. Rostow: Should the President see Abba Eban?

The President: I wish all of you would try to keep so many of these visiting dignitaries off me.

Secretary Rusk: Abba Eban's own position is one of moderation. I am inclined to tell him that the last time you were over here we advised you not to get into a fight. Now you're in a fight. We're not anxious to come over there and fight the Soviets for you.

[Omitted here is discussion concerning Vietnam.]

---

484.   Letter From President Johnson to Premier Kosygin[1]

Washington, October 23, 1967.

Dear Mr. Chairman:

I fully share the concern expressed in your letter of October 20 about the continued tense atmosphere in the Near East and the lack of

---

[1] Source: National Archives and Records Administration, RG 59, Central Files 1967–69, POL 27–14 ARAB–ISR. Secret; Nodis. Filed with a memorandum of an October 24 conversation between Dobrynin and Kohler at which Kohler handed the letter to Dobrynin. The memorandum of conversation includes the text in translation of an oral message in Russian that Dobrynin gave Kohler. It reads as follows: "The Soviet Government believes it would be beneficial now to have a confidential [Note: also carrying the sense of authoritative] exchange of views concerning a political settlement in the Near East. We proceed from the assumption that such a confidential exchange of views would better assist the task of settlement. In this we see purpose in possible consultations between representatives of our two states. The aim of our approach is to find a path leading to the settlement of the Near East crisis through common efforts on the basis of respect and due regard for the lawful rights and interest of all states of this region. Of course, such a course of action can only be successful in circumstances of appropriate mutuality of efforts undertaken." Brackets in the original quote.

Drafts of the letter to Kosygin, along with related materials, are in the Johnson Library, National Security File, Head of State Correspondence File, USSR, Kosygin Correspondence, Vol. I.

progress toward a political settlement in that area. I cannot, however, subscribe to your assessment of the causes or to your inaccurate description of United States policy.

The explosive nature of the situation was dramatically underscored by the news of the sinking of an Israeli destroyer in the eastern Mediterranean by an Egyptian patrol boat equipped with surface-to-surface missiles. This act of war was the most serious of a series of threats and counter-threats, acts of terrorism, and hostile deployments of armed forces during recent weeks. The situation calls for the best efforts of both of us and of others to secure strict observance of the existing cease-fire and to exercise restraint in the provision of arms to the countries in the Near Eastern area.

Unlike the Soviet Union, the United States has for many years followed a policy of restraint in the arms field, a policy which has been even more restrained since the hostilities of last June. However, the continued flow of massive quantities of Soviet arms to certain States in the area has created a situation very difficult for others to ignore. While we have sought and will continue to seek to limit the arms race, the continued flow of Soviet arms will necessarily bring about some response by various countries in and out of the region. We may well have to resume shipments of arms ourselves to some of the Arab countries as well as to Israel. In these circumstances I would again propose that the Soviet Government agree with us that arms supplies to the Near Eastern countries should be registered with the United Nations. I would be glad if we could go on from there toward an agreement on an effective arms limitation program which would diminish the dangers and permit the countries of the Near Eastern area to use their limited resources for their much needed economic development. I assure you that we are prepared to undertake immediately serious discussions towards this end.

As for political settlement, my Government has been doing its part for peace in every forum, at every level and at every hour, both before and since the outbreak of hostilities. We have consistently upheld the principles which I stated publicly and repeated to you at Glassboro:

First, the recognized right of national life;
Second, justice for the refugees;
Third, innocent maritime passage;
Fourth, limits on the wasteful and destructive arms race; and
Fifth, political independence and territorial integrity for all.

We were guided by these principles when our representatives in New York worked out jointly with your representatives, toward the close of the Emergency Special Session of the General Assembly, alternative drafts of a resolution which would bring about force withdrawals, an end to the state of belligerency between Israel and its Arab neighbors and establishment of a stable basis for peace in the Near East. We were prepared to have either of those drafts presented and adopted by the Emergency General Assembly, but, as you know, this was not possible because of objections from certain Arab countries.[2] We have attached no new conditions or new interpretations, nor have we weakened our adherence to any understandings with your government or other governments. On the other hand, we have been surprised that your representatives in New York have been circulating to delegations at the current General Assembly drafts, the texts of which do not conform to those agreed in the Emergency Session. I believe it is desirable that our representatives in New York continue their consultations to try to clear up any misunderstandings. We should ascertain whether we do not in fact agree on underlying policies.[3]

I believe that the opportunity is before us to move forward. Recently representatives of some of the Arab States have stated to our representatives that an acceptable resolution of the Security Council can be formulated on the basis of the five principles of peace set forth in my statement on June 19. This could be implemented by a special United Nations representative working with the parties on the basis of such a framework. My representatives in turn have made it clear that this would be an acceptable way to make progress toward peace in the area.

The same Arab representatives have said that the best way to achieve the objective of securing an acceptable Security Council resolution would be for the non-permanent members of the Council to proceed promptly to draft a resolution along these lines. My representatives assured the Arab states concerned that we would of course cooperate wholeheartedly in their effort.[4] We have confirmed that position both to the President of the Security Council and to Deputy Foreign Minister Kuznetsov in New York.

---

[2] In the text of the draft letter included in Document 483, this sentence and the following sentence read: "We were prepared to have either of those drafts presented to and adopted by the Emergency General Assembly when, because of objections from certain Arab countries the Soviet side withdrew its support. We would still be prepared to go ahead with those drafts which we considered joint ones and not, as you state in your letter, the United States 'own proposals.'"

[3] In the text of the draft letter cited above, this sentence reads: "We should ascertain whether we do not in fact agree on underlying policies and determine whether we can achieve agreement promptly on a Security Council resolution which would help move the parties toward peace."

[4] In the text of the draft letter cited above, this sentence reads: "My representatives assured the Arab states concerned that while we continue to adhere to our understanding of the provisional agreement we reached with your government in July, we should of course also cooperate wholeheartedly in their effort."

Mr. Chairman, I stated to you at Glassboro that the first and greatest principle of peace is that every nation in the area has the fundamental right to live free from claims and acts of war and belligerency and to have this right respected by its neighbors. I welcome your statement of belief in this principle. Equally, there need be no doubt of the United States position that troops must be withdrawn. But there must also be, as I made clear in my statement of June 19 and again directly to you at Glassboro, recognized rights of national life, guarantees of the freedom of innocent maritime passage in international waterways, limitation of the arms race, a solution to the refugee problem and respect for the political independence and territorial integrity of all states in the area.

Mr. Chairman, in a context of peace, no state is justified in either refusing to withdraw its forces from the territory of another state or claiming the right to assert or pursue a state of belligerence against another state.

On this common basis, which we believe is acceptable to the great majority of the world community at the United Nations, there should be no difficulty in fashioning a resolution which will promote negotiations through the good offices of the United Nations in order to bring about a just and durable peace in which every state in the area can be assured security.

Sincerely,

Lyndon B. Johnson

---

485.   Telegram From the Mission to the United Nations to the
          Department of State[1]

New York, October 24, 1967, 0223Z.

1671. Dept pass Cairo. Re: Middle East.

1. At his request, Rifai (Jordan) called on Goldberg Oct 23 to review current situation regarding consultations on possible SC res on ME. Rifai said some non-perms have formulated group of principles as basis

---

[1] Source: National Archives and Records Administration, RG 59, Central Files 1967–69, POL 27 ARAB–ISR. Secret. Repeated to Brasilia, Rio de Janeiro, Buenos Aires, Ottawa, Copenhagen, New Delhi, Tokyo, London, Moscow, Paris, Amman, Beirut, Tel Aviv, Jerusalem, Lagos, and Addis Ababa and passed to Cairo.

for res. As Arabs pressed for time "before we come again to GA", Rifai had called to discover US views.

2. Goldberg reaffirmed basic US postulate that ME question should not be settled between US and USSR, but rather principally by parties themselves. Goldberg said US certainly supports non-perms taking initiative and that, in reply to their question, he had told UAR FonMin and SC pres this. US not [*now*] awaiting results of non-perm effort.

3. Rifai said consultations have moved past stage of US-USSR discussions, because Arabs now in direct contact with US which "shortens distance and brings us closer to positive results". Rifai then referred to several initiatives for res of which he aware: (1) US-USSR draft of July; (2) a res linking withdrawal and non-belligerency and sending UN rep to area (with other matters such as free navigation and refugees to be taken up subsequently); and (3) current Indian draft which incorporates "larger group of principals". Rifai identified (2) as a text shown Jordanians by Caradon (UK) and asked if US had ever seen this text. Goldberg said we had seen no such text and that Caradon had told us he had no text. Rifai said Caradon text was balanced and he (Rifai) did not know why it had not further materialized. (Pedersen subsequently raised question of this text with Hope (UK), indicating Rifai had asked Goldberg about this text and we were in embarrassing position of having to say we had not seen it. Hope said he sure UK had not shown Jordanians any such text; that Rifai must be talking about correct (as opposed to unilaterally modified by USSR) US-USSR text of July. Hope agreed check matter with Caradon and let us know.)

4. Re Indian text, Rifai said he thought it "could in a way be considered as general and as specific at same time". He said it contains larger group of principles enunciated by various dels, including those contained in Goldberg's General debate speech, and should provide some sort of basis for further SC considerations.

5. Goldberg said we had heard of Indian text but since Indians have not given it to us, we don't know exactly what it entails and therefore cannot comment on it.[2]

6. Rifai further pursed question of grouped principles. Goldberg said his guidelines remained President's June 19 statement. Rifai noted President's statement included "withdrawal of troops" and that with-

---

[2] Telegram 1702 from USUN, October 25, reported that Goldberg had asked Indian representative G. Parthasarathi on October 24 about the Indian draft. Parthasarathi told him there was no such thing as an Indian draft, but "only a working paper which is being discussed in a group of six non-perm members." The telegram commented, "We are convinced and he did not deny that he has put forward Indian draft for discussion with non-perms only after full consultations with Arabs and Sovs and without any attempt to get our views." (Ibid., POL 27 ARAB–ISR/UN)

drawal "primary" among principles for GOJ. Goldberg said withdrawal obviously tied into Charter principle of territorial integrity and that territorial integrity and non-belligerence were parallel concepts tied into the principle of renunciation of force. Rifai said Jordanians would like withdrawal to be "given prominence", adding he "doubted" it could be covered by territorial integrity. (He said this however in such a way as to indicate that, while Jordanians would not be happy about it, withdrawal might be covered by concept of territorial integrity. Also notable that Rifai at no point mentioned June 5 date, but did refer to need for recognized boundaries.)

7. Rifai said he thought Indians and non-perms should conclude their discussions on a possible text today or early tomorrow with some positive results. Goldberg reiterated our support for the non-perm effort and our feeling that they ought to get on with the job rather than dealing with collateral questions, particularly in light of events in area over weekend. Rifai agreed as to seriousness of weekend developments which he said might lead to a series of events which could get out of control. Rifai and Goldberg agreed this new factor increased urgency of early moves for res in SC and toward ME settlement.

Goldberg

---

486.   Telegram From the Department of State to the Embassy in Jordan[1]

Washington, October 24, 1967, 1759Z.

58791. 1. Will be known shortly that we are going to proceed in releasing selectively certain items under outstanding arms agreements suspended for over four months, for shipment to Israel and selected Arab states but not including Jordan.[2] We are keenly aware difficulties which this action presents for our relations with Jordan and to you in answering queries concerning it. We believe frankness here is in order.

---

[1] Source: National Archives and Records Administration, RG 59, Central Files 1967–69, DEF 12–5 ISR. Secret; Immediate; Exdis. Drafted by Houghton; cleared by Macomber, Schwartz (DOD), and Katzenbach; and approved by Battle.

[2] Telegram 58793 to Beirut and other missions, October 24, set forth U.S. military supply policy for the Middle East. (Ibid., DEF 19–8 US–NEAR E)

2. Problem lies in large body Congressional opinion that GOJ attacked Israel in face (a) legal conditions U.S. provided military equipment for defensive purposes only and (b) Israel appeal (which well known here) to Jordan for mutual restraint. Although we think we understand reasons for Hussein's Moscow visit, it did not help our public or Congressional problem. Our previous discussions with Khammash were based on belief that Congressional situation would improve as AID bill progressed. Unfortunately, opposite has happened and situation has become aggravated as Congressional debate continued. Such is depth of feeling that to proceed at this juncture could seriously endanger Administration's military assistance program.

3. These are facts of problem but we leave to your discretion which of these you use in approach GOJ and whom you approach. In your approach, you should emphasize that question of resumption of military shipments to Jordan remains open. We are continuing to keep matter under very close review. We expect arms supply question will be discussed during King's visit here in November.

Katzenbach

---

487.   Memorandum From the President's Special Assistant
         (Rostow) to President Johnson[1]

Washington, October 24, 1967.

SUBJECT

Your Talk with Eban—5:30 p.m. Today

Our original plan was to tell Eban frankly that we've been disturbed by Israeli actions that make Israel look as if it is being so hard-nosed that it doesn't care whether it kills chances for a peace settlement or not. While we had no intention of lowering the boom and provoking a sharp reaction, we did not want Eban to go away feeling that our silence amounted to a blank check.

---

[1] Source: Johnson Library, National Security File, Special Head of State Correspondence File, Israel, 7/1/67–2/28/68. Secret. A handwritten "L" on the memorandum indicates the President saw it.

With Secretary Rusk yesterday, Eban turned aside discussion of thorny issues and talked out the clock. He made just about the same pitch to Secretary Rusk as he had to me.[2] While Eban did most of the talking, the Secretary did manage to put across the following: We understand Israel's desire to maintain a common front, but this depends on our knowing where that front is. Israel has gone its own way, consulting us little. The Secretary also made clear that our support for secure permanent frontiers doesn't mean we support territorial changes. (Memcon at Tab A of the attached.)[3]

Nick Katzenbach this morning was able to take the offensive. He argued against too great Israeli rigidity on the mechanics of negotiation. He pressed Israel's obligation to assure Hussein that Israel wanted to live in peace with Jordan, since some of Israel's acts since the war left doubt in Jordanian minds. He pointed out that Israel's position on boundaries creates the impression that Israel feels free to keep everything it has conquered. He reminded Eban of Arab interests in Jerusalem. (Memcon at Tab B of the attached.)[4]

The one surprise in this morning's meeting was a message for you from Eshkol (Tab C of the attached).[5] This is designed to undergird Eban's presentation with a formal statement of Israel's position, which boils down to this: (1) Israel needs arms to take care of itself; (2) Israel hopes we can convince the Sovs that they must not continue to fan the flames of tension; (3) Israel wants the kind of security it believes only direct negotiations with the Arabs will provide. The best tack until you've had a chance to study the message is probably just to say you've read it. You might want to say we're studying the arms requests urgently.

Nick's memo to you is attached.[6] He suggests you say you're familiar with Eban's earlier talks and see no need to go over the same grounds and then make these points:

1. Nobody knows better than we how hard it is to make peace. We also know it takes a lot of restraint to avoid escalation.

---

[2] For Eban's conversation with Rostow, see Document 482.

[3] The attachment, not printed, is a draft of telegram 58735 to Tel Aviv, October 24. (National Archives and Records Administration, RG 59, Central Files 1967–69, POL 27 ARAB–ISR)

[4] The attachment, not printed, is a draft of telegram 58955 to Tel Aviv, October 24. (Ibid.)

[5] The message from Eshkol was transmitted in an October 23 note from Harman to Rusk, sent to the President with an undated memorandum from Katzenbach stating that it had been handed to him that morning by Eban. (Johnson Library, National Security File, Special Head of State Correspondence File, Israel, 7/1/67–2/28/68)

[6] Dated October 24; attached but not printed.

2. But, as you said on 19 June, we can't afford to lose this real opportunity to build a permanent peace. Hard as it is, we *have to* find the way to peace this time.

This is where Nick's recommendation stops. If you feel you can go a step further, I'd recommend adding this: We don't kid ourselves about what the Arabs are trying to do (make Israel withdraw without paying the price of a permanent settlement). But we're frankly afraid Israel will take such a hard position that it will kill chances for a settlement. We don't believe time is indefinitely on the side of Israel or of peace.

We'd hate to see the discussion get bogged down in a debate over the merits of Israeli retaliation for the sinking of their destroyer,[7] but we do want to make a clear record of urging restraint as Nick did this morning. We do not know whether the shelling along the Suez Canal today will satisfy the Israelis or not. But we feel strongly that any systematic retaliation will only make peace negotiations harder.

Walt

---

[7] Israeli forces shelled Egyptian refineries and installations at Suez on October 24. A memorandum Rostow sent to the President at 5 p.m. on October 24 informed him of this and commented, "This gives you a chance not only to lean on Eban on the necessity of their struggling for peace, but letting it be known quietly that that was your message to him: there is no future for Israel or the Middle East in this kind of mutual violation of the cease-fire." (Johnson Library, National Security File, Country File, Israel, Vol. VII)

488.   Memorandum of Conversation[1]

Washington, October 24, 1967, 5:44–6:32 p.m.

SUBJECT

The Middle East

PARTICIPANTS

The President of the United States
Walt W. Rostow, Special Assistant to the President
George Christian, Press Secretary to the President
Lucius D. Battle, Assistant Secretary for NEA

Foreign Minister Abba Eban of Israel
His Excellency Avraham Harman, Ambassador of Israel
Mr. Ephraim Evron, Israeli Minister

President Johnson received Foreign Minister Eban at the latter's request for a meeting lasting approximately one hour. After an exchange of pleasantries, the President stated that he had been informed of Mr. Eban's discussions with Secretary Rusk, Under Secretary Katzenbach, etc. and that it was unnecessary to review the items taken up in those meetings.

Mr. Eban said that he brought the President warm greetings from Prime Minister Eshkol as well as a letter from him. The President acknowledged that he had received the letter and would study it immediately and reply in due course.

Mr. Eban said that Mr. Eshkol might visit the United States in early 1968 and that he hoped, if circumstances brought him here, he would be able to renew his acquaintance with President Johnson.

Mr. Eban then dealt at some length with the current situation in the Middle East. He remarked that the events of yesterday and today had underlined the essential need to move away from armistice arrangements and cease-fire arrangements and to move to a condition of peace. Of the alternatives available to the Arabs, the most attractive by far is peace; and it is the only alternative not tried. The Israelis cannot go on with a jerry-built structure. What is needed both politically and juridically is peace with mutual recognition of countries' rights. Peace is needed in a legal sense, not an emotional sense. Frontiers, permanent

---

[1] Source: National Archives and Records Administration, RG 59, Central Files 1967–69, POL 27 ARAB–ISR. Secret; Exdis. Drafted by Battle on October 25 and approved by the White House on October 27. The meeting took place in the Cabinet Room at the White House. The time and location of the meeting are from the Johnson Library, President's Daily Diary. Copies were sent to Rusk, Katzenbach, Leddy, Battle, and the Embassy in Tel Aviv. George Christian's notes of the meeting are ibid., Meeting Notes File.

and agreed to, must be accepted by both sides. The ideas of the Israelis are very close to those stated in President Johnson's June 19 speech. Three points are particularly attractive to the Israelis. The first is the recognition in that speech that we cannot go back to the June 4 situation. The second point is the recognition that there must be a durable peace, and the third is the need to supersede fragile armistice lines with something more permanent. That really is all there is to the basic problem.

It is essential, Mr. Eban continued, that in the next weeks the Russians and the Arabs not use their voting strength in the United Nations to prevent a forward-looking policy. There can be no withdrawal without peace. The Israelis accepted that arrangement in 1957. To do so twice in one decade would be ridiculous. National suicide is not an international obligation.

The Government of Israel hopes that the United Nations will say it wants the Israelis and the Arabs to work out their differences with United Nations help. If we are able to "knock down some things" in New York in the next weeks, Mr. Eban believed that the Israelis could become very active beginning in January in an effort to bring about a solution. There was, he felt, a chance of forward motion with the UAR and Jordan. There was not much chance with Syria. Even the Russians admit that the Syrians are unpredictable and irresponsible. The problem for the UAR should not be great. Gaza is the only territorial issue, and the Egyptians have never claimed that it was their territory. Each Arab state would get a good deal if it moved forward now. Moreover, the Israelis are willing to work with anyone who can bring the two sides together. They consider that direct negotiations are important, but they are not rigid about techniques. The important thing is that they not move from the cease-fire lines to "a wilderness of anarchy". The United States and the Israelis are close together on principles, but there may be more difficulty on details.

Regarding arms supply, the Minister said that he had been surprised at Russian speed in replenishing Arab losses, particularly in planes. The United States must remember that the difference for Israel between survival and extinction in the last war had been 100–150 planes. The Israelis are happy to have had the understanding with regard to the 48 planes reconfirmed. General Weizman has reviewed Israeli needs for the future. They are not excessive and represent an emphasis in quality rather than quantity. The total force would consist of 250 planes which would require delivery of 77 by the end of 1968. Secretary McNamara has agreed to talk with Mr. Eban a week or so before he leaves the United States.

Mr. Eban continued that it was not Israeli policy to sit and wait for Arab action. Israel will be active and try to accelerate progress. The Israelis are "not entirely without contact" with the UAR and Jordan.

With respect to Jordan, the Israelis were deeply disappointed in the King. They had hoped he would avoid war with Israel even though pressed by Nasser. Nevertheless, the King is there. If he wants peace, the Israelis would be willing to reach an understanding with him which would make Jordan better off economically and politically. They hope the King can be made to understand this and be encouraged to move towards peace. Also, the Israelis hope that he understands "he can't get a good deal without talking". Some Arabs on the West Bank are telling the Israelis that they wish Israel would forget Hussein. They point out that the population of the West Bank is greater than many states in the United Nations. The Israelis have not encouraged this, however, because they have not given up hope that there can be a peace arrangement with the King of Jordan.

Mr. Eban expressed his appreciation for the great help the United States has been to the Israelis. He said, however, that the Israelis were glad they had relied on themselves and had not expected others to shed blood in their behalf.

President Johnson repeated that he saw no point in reviewing the matters discussed in conversations with Secretary Rusk, Secretary McNamara, Under Secretary Katzenbach, etc. He had nothing to add on the matters discussed.

United States objectives and Israeli objectives are much the same in general. We share the feeling of need to fashion a peace structure for the Middle East and will do all possible to help bring it about. It can be best done, however, by those in the area, and we look to them to move in that direction.

The President said he had little to add to his June 19 statement and the other statements we have made with respect to principles guiding the United States. He said he would be less than candid if he failed to say he regretted that the advice he had given in his last meeting with the Foreign Minister[2] had been ignored. While there may seem to be a victory now for the Israelis, in the long term he was not sure anyone had gained. It had been a difficult moment, and the President must say that the most awesome decisions he had taken since he came into office resulted from the Hot Line talks with Kosygin in matters relating to the crisis. The President said he thought at the time that Israeli action was unwise. He still thought so. While he could understand Israeli reluctance not to counsel with the United States, he regretted that we had not been consulted on some actions the Israelis have taken even though the fact that we were not consulted meant we had no commitment thereto. The United States has a strong conviction of its responsibility in the

---

[2] See Document 77.

Middle East and a strong tie to the Israeli people. There are many dangers ahead—many more than some people realize even within the Executive Branch of the Government. The aid cut cannot be brushed aside. Neither can the growing desire to "come home" whether it be from Saigon, Berlin, or elsewhere. The voices of isolation are increasing in intensity and effectiveness. The problems of arms sales are increasingly difficult ones for us, and to suggest any sale is to appear to be joining the Mafia. However, we had commitments, and the President will do everything possible to live up to those commitments. The Israelis should understand the difference between a Presidential commitment and Congressional action on that commitment.

With respect to the Middle East, the President said the Israelis should not forget what we had said about territorial integrity and boundaries. We could not countenance aggression.

The Russians think we have great influence with the Israelis which is perhaps not the case, and the Israelis consider that we have great influence with the Russians which is no more true than the first statement.

With respect to arms sales in the area, the President said he was more concerned than anyone in his Administration about the arms build-up in the area which is a difficult and dangerous development. He was worried about the ultimate situation. It is essential in considering the attitudes of the countries in the area not to overlook the humiliation the Arabs suffered and their own need to recoup their loss of prestige. The United States must try to maintain its position throughout the area to keep the USSR from putting its tentacles on other nations. We shall do all possible to pursue vigorously a peace structure for the area. The President wished to caution the Israelis that the further they get from June 5 the further they are from peace.

With respect to the specific items raised, the United States will do what it can in the arms field. The Israelis must recognize the extreme difficulty we faced in proceeding with sales given the current atmosphere. As to acceleration of the delivery date of the planes, we would have to work that out with technicians, and anything that we did would have to be consistent with our own needs and our own schedules. We will try to live up to earlier understandings unless Congressional action limits our ability to do so. Arms sales are a more serious problem than when the President last met with Mr. Eban. The President had hoped to get a Congressional endorsement of programs which had not been forthcoming. Nevertheless, we would do the best we could within the limits of our own situation. It is essential that we maintain the maximum influence that we can throughout the area. Our policy there will be a just one. The President said he looked forward to seeing Mr. Eshkol and would study the letter from the Prime Minister with interest.

In conclusion Mr. Eban said that he believed that the United States had considerable influence with the Russians. He believed that the Glassboro meeting had kept the Russians from being more unreasonable during this period than they might have been. He pointed out that the Israelis did take the President's counsel. The meeting with the President was May 26. Without that meeting, there might have been action the following day. The situation did, however, reach a state where the military authorities refused to be responsible if a prolonged stalemate occurred. That had led to the June 5 war.

---

489.   Telegram From the Mission to the United Nations to the Department of State[1]

New York, October 26, 1967, 0142Z.

1742. Middle East.

1. Goldberg reviewed current situation with Eban and Rafael morning Oct 25. Eban began by expressing great pleasure at his reception in Wash and gratification US stood by five principles announced by Pres July [June] 19. Sisco, Buffum and Pedersen also present.

2. Without mentioning precise source of info, Goldberg said USSR told us directly they understood Israel deploying forces for attack on Jordan and Syria. We had indicated US had no such info. Eban said it is significant such reports coming directly from Sov Union but added mil attachés in Israel cld provide answer to this.

3. Conversation then turned to negots on SC res. Goldberg said today and tomorrow can prove critical in determining whether successful outcome is possible. Tabor is trying his best and seems reliable.[2] However LAs and Indians are not under control and we are trying to steer the LAs toward the Danes. One complicating factor is info that Russians are now proving more Arab than the Arabs. Moreover, Jordan

---

[1]   Source: National Archives and Records Administration RG 59, Central Files 1967–69, POL 27 ARAB–ISR/UN. Secret; Priority; Limdis. Repeated to Tel Aviv Priority, and to Jerusalem, Amman, London, Copenhagen, Ottawa, Moscow, and Paris.

[2]   Telegram 1708 from USUN, October 25, reported a conversation on October 24 between Goldberg and Danish representative Tabor and conveyed the text of Tabor's draft resolution. (Ibid.)

is proving tougher than UAR. Under circumstances we have foll basic choices:

A) Sit by quietly and let LAs and Indians proceed; this wld not produce good res. Difficulty is that we cannot make LAs understand importance assuring that withdrawal clause wld be described "in context of peace", which is the great protective phrase for Israel.

B) Permit Tabor continue his efforts and hope he can achieve reasonable draft.

C) Another possibility might be for US to take initiative and put in res. while keeping language on recognition of Israel's right to exist as contained in earlier drafts, reasonable formulation on withdrawal in our view could be reference, in context of peace, to withdrawal from all territories occupied by it. We believe such formula would not prejudice Israel's position and would not exclude boundary adjustments. Our policy on this matter has not changed.

4. Eban said he would like to see what happened with the Danish effort. He had talked to Tabor this a.m. and felt he had properly inspired him with the need to have a draft that both sides could accept. While Goldberg said he did not want an immediate answer to the question about Israeli reaction to a possible US move along lines described, in para 3C, Eban commented that Israel would want to be absolutely sure that no action taken would prejudice her position on withdrawal, which was simply and clearly that they will not withdraw from all the territories they had occupied. He said that it was particularly important to Israel that the US should not support a proposition that prejudiced her position. He claimed that pressure by UN to get Israel back behind the June 5 lines would strengthen the hands of those in GOI who want to create fait accompli by annexation.

5. It was left that Eban and Goldberg would consider matter further in light of progress made by Tabor.

6. Later in morning Rafael informed Sisco that if SC res was passed which unacceptable to Israel on territorial-withdrawal point, he under instructions from cabinet to announce Israeli unwillingness to cooperate with UN rep.

Goldberg

490. Telegram From the Mission to the United Nations to the Department of State[1]

New York, October 26, 1967, 1816Z.

1754. Dept pass to White House and Moscow (Immediate).

At dinner given for Kuznetsov by Amb. Goldberg following significant points emerged. Sisco, Buffum and Pedersen also present on US side; Fedorenko and Shevchenko for USSR. Dobrynin bowed out during course of day giving as reason pressing business with State Dept. Conversation was friendly, business-like, avoided entirely past differences over text and interpretation, and focused exclusively on where we go from here.

1. Kuznetsov stressed Sov concern over situation in the area, as reflected in incidents of the last few days, and Sov desire to cooperate with US in SC action that will move matter towards peaceful resolution. In discussing dangers current situation he said Sov Govt seriously concerned Israelis are planning to take further military action against Arabs, and in particular that they might make attack across Suez Canal. (Interesting that his concern related to UAR while in July it related to Syria.)

2. Goldberg pointed out that US even before hostilities broke out and at all times since has been using its influence to counsel restraint on part of all concerned. Goldberg said that it would be helpful in this connection if Sovs in their public declarations were as even-handed as US had been in calling upon all parties to discontinue all military activities. Goldberg made specific reference to SC meeting of last few days. In this meeting US said that violation of cease fire could not be countenanced by any of parties. On other hand Sov statements in SC would seem to ignore military activities on part of UAR which undoubtedly contributed to tension in the area. It was helpful for Sovs to vote for the res but in addition to voting for res it is necessary for both USSR and US to use their respective influences publicly and privately in interest of maintaining peaceful conditions. Kuznetsov did not reply to this presentation although he implied acceptance of validity of our argument by emphasizing that USSR had voted for a res which encompassed violations by both sides.

3. Kuznetsov then inquired as to what our thoughts were about facilitating progress at UN towards a resolution on ME problem. In

---

[1] Source: Johnson Library, National Security File, Agency File, United Nations, Vol. 7. Secret; Immediate; Nodis. Walt Rostow forwarded this telegram to the President with an October 27 covering memorandum.

response to Kuznetsov inquiry Goldberg stated that there was no point in reviewing or renewing past differences as to Sov and US discussions at ESSGA. Goldberg said that Sovs knew our position on this matter but that the important consideration now was how to proceed at present juncture in pursuit of what should be common objective, namely just, durable and permanent peace in the Middle East. Goldberg emphasized that problem was not merely getting words into UN res but rather obtaining cooperation of parties without which such peace could not be maintained. Kuznetsov agreed and then renewed his inquiry as to what our views were now as to how we should proceed at UN. Amb Goldberg then made principal pitch in favor of US and USSR getting together promptly on basis of Danish text, which he felt was even-handed and consistent with US and USSR common views expressed last July and would achieve objective which we assumed we and Sovs share in common, to get both sides to cooperate in efforts of UN rep to achieve a peaceful settlement.

4. Kuznetsov in turn said that he believed that US and USSR could use Indian draft as basis for discussion and possible SC action. He also almost by way of passing added that US-USSR draft of ESSGA (and this time he described it in terms of version one) could be discussed but touched on this only lightly and concentrated on Indian draft. Kuznetsov referring to recent high level exchange between us, saying that whatever differences of view there were, their letter and our response were mutual indications that we both wished to work together in trying to achieve a constructive result in SC. He made no real pitch to retain June 5 date mentioning possibility of reference to Israeli withdrawal "from territories it had occupied." In response to Goldberg statement that UAR had not recently talked about date to us, Kuznetsov replied that UAR had "mentioned" date to them. Our impression is that while Sovs and Arabs will seek its inclusion, Sovs would agree to its exclusion. We also believe UAR would not make this breaking point, although Jordan feels much more strongly.

5. Goldberg's response was affirmative and positive but explicit that Danish draft rather than Indian should be basis for joint discussion on ground that it most closely approximated President's five points and also past joint conversations. Kuznetsov did not preclude consideration of Danish draft, though expressed what is unusual for Kuznetsov, a strong personal dislike for Tabor, whom he said he distrusted because he had on several occasions misrepresented his position to other dels, particularly Arabs, in last few days.

6. Goldberg expressed complete willingness to continue discussions with Sovs and suggested that these might resume Thursday

morning[2] to discuss all drafts. Kuznetsov while agreeing that discussions should go on expressed preference to see first if non-permanent members would come up with draft on Thursday. Kuznetsov however expressly reserved option of US and USSR getting together on basis of whatever texts had been thrown into non-permanent group hopper. Goldberg said he was sure and Kuznetsov agreed that whatever text or texts which emerged from non-permanent meeting, agreement of US and USSR would be necessary and that any text to be helpful should have as a minimum acquiescence of parties. While Kuznetsov did not demur, our impression is that Sovs hope that Indians will drag LAs along on their draft and set stage for final negotiation on basis of text most favorable to them and to Arabs. In this connection Kuznetsov confirmed that Indian text had been cleared by Arabs. Our impression also is that if Indians and LAs disagree on text Sovs will be prepared to discuss with US seriously Danish text.

7. Kuznetsov said his instructions were to work closely with us to achieve constructive solution in interest of peace in ME. Said these instructions had just recently been renewed. Goldberg said our instructions were to make every effort consistent with American position as stated by President on June 19 and expressed at Glassboro to agree with Sovs on basic policy and to achieve agreement promptly on SC res which could help move parties toward peace.

8. Goldberg stressed problems which existed in Arab group and necessity paying attention principally to states directly concerned, notably UAR and Jordan. Kuznetsov agreed.

9. We found the meeting a very satisfactory one, and importance attached by Kuznetsov to exchange at high levels came through loud and clear.

10. Confirming Secretary–Sisco telcon,[3] we will make clear to Eban this morning serious consequences we feel could ensue and adverse effect on Israeli position here if further military action is taken by them in further retaliation over *Elath* sinking.

Goldberg

---

[2] October 26.

[3] The conversation took place at 9:25 a.m. on October 26. (Notes of telephone conversation prepared by Mildred Asbjornson; National Archives and Records Administration, RG 59, Rusk Files: Lot 72 D 192, Telephone Calls)

491.   Telegram From the Mission to the United Nations to the Department of State[1]

New York, October 26, 1967, 1740Z.

1753. Goldberg first raised two points with Eban in conversation Oct 26 at which Rafael and Sisco also present.

First, he felt there was a lesson to be learned from the recent occurrences in area with respect to Israeli reporting methods to UN. UAR officer fully reported to UN rep in area his interpretation of events and these reproduced fully in Bull report,[2] thereby tending to give them some indirect UN authenticity by virtue its reproduction in SC document. On other hand, Israeli case had to await actual statements by Rafael in Council. Goldberg therefore had to spend a considerable part of afternoon making sure res also referred to "statements" made in SC, otherwise SC cease-fire res would have dealt only with Suez incident. Eban agreed two things should be corrected: Israel would have to exercise greater care as to what was said by its reps in area promptly after such incidents, and Israel would have to report fully its statements to UNTSO reps so they become part of UN documentation before SC.

Second, and much more important point which Goldberg wished to make is that we feel strongly that no further military action should be taken by Israel in retaliation for *Elath* sinking. He under instructions to convey this to Eban in very strong terms and wished Eban to convey this to Prime Min. We now at critical stage at UN on ME discussions. While we have surmounted in last 48 hours diplomatic difficulties which have ensued as a result of military action in area, he wished Eban and Prime Min to know very confidentially that Sovs through Kuznetsov expressed great concern last night to us that Israel is planning to take further military action against Arabs in Suez Canal area. We responded to Sovs that we have no such info, that we have and are urging restraint and the Sovs should do same on Arabs.

Eban's response was assuring and he said he understood need that no further military action be undertaken by Israel. He wld report

---

[1] Source: National Archives and Records Administration, RG 59, Central Files 1967–69, POL 27 ARAB–ISR/UN. Secret; Immediate; Exdis. Repeated Immediate to Tel Aviv.

[2] The Secretary-General transmitted reports from UNTSO Chief of Staff General Bull to the Security Council on October 24. (UN documents S/7930/Add.48-49)

Goldberg's strong démarche promptly and confidentially to Eshkol. He said that when cabinet cmte considered matter of Israeli counter action, propositions calling for Israeli forces to cross Canal or Israeli planes to take action were turned down. Decision was that whatever military action would be taken in the circumstances would come from Israeli side of Canal. He recalled that in July Israel had received message from Sovs, through Swedes, that if Israelis crossed Canal Sovs would no longer consider this merely an Arab-Israeli matter. Israel therefore viewed with seriousness info given Amb. Goldberg re Sov concern. If Sovs really believe this it would be serious, or if they are building up an alibi for possible Sov action, it would be serious. Eban said he would convey message to Eshkol, and both he and Rafael urged Dept instruct Barbour to tell this directly to Prime Min for his ears alone. (Eban and Rafael obviously both want help.) Goldberg once again reiterated that we expressed to Sovs greatest necessity for exercising restraint and avoiding provocation.

Conversation then turned to current status of matters re SC and Goldberg and Eban both agreed it was important for LAs to hold line and to try to get Danes put forward their draft. Goldberg told Eban we did not enter into any negotiations in our discussions with Kuznetsov last night, but made him understand that if non-perm effort fails we likely be discussing matter further with Sov Union. Eban did not show nervousness re US-USSR talks which evident in late stages of ESSGA. Goldberg then checked following fall-back preambular language with Eban in event we need it in negotiations:

"Affirming, in light of the foregoing, that these Charter provisions require for their just implementation a context of peace in which the sovereign existence, political independence, and territorial integrity of all states in the area should be respected and Israel should not, in derogation of this principle, persist in refusing to withdraw its forces, nor should any Arab state in derogation of this principle claim the right to assert or pursue a state of belligerency against Israel or persist in refusing to recognize its sovereign existence and right to live within secure national frontiers."

Eban found it acceptable, saying if this formulation adopted Israel as well as Arabs could adapt their positions to it. Eban said it was important that either party be able to take refuge in its own interpretations. He assumed Arabs would interpret language to mean withdrawal to pre-June 5 positions, whereas Israel could say language embraces concept of agreement on effective frontiers. In this connection, he felt it important US say in connection with its vote that language was not incompatible with June 19 statement of Pres. Eban stressed there are two critical points in SC res in their view: (a) the context of peace and that withdrawal could only take place within this context; and (b) that formula on withdrawal be sufficiently flexible that it does not tend to foreclose substance of negotiations. Goldberg assured Eban that we would be in a position to say in connection with our vote that such a formulation was consistent with June 19 statement.

Then discussion focused on our efforts to maintain solidarity of LAs, the Israelis having been active with Brazilians and Argentines both here and in capitals. At their request, we agreed to consider desirability of making further approaches in both capitals, depending on results of Indian-LA consultations today.

In a further comment regarding above language, Eban and Rafael both agreed Jordanians could find some sustenance in it because of emphasis on sovereign existence and call in operative para asking UN rep to cooperate with "member states". This gave assurance to Jordanians, Rafael said, that Israel did not have in mind dealing with Palestinians in West Bank for some separate existence.

Rafael said their impression is that UAR has been shaken as result of military events in Suez area and are looking now for a "life belt". He believes the time is ripe for prompt SC action (this is first time such positive statement made to us) since Arabs believe SC res with acquiescence of both sides will have a tranquilizing effect on the area. He found it significant that Fedorenko yesterday in SC said twice there must be a political solution. Rafael said if SC can act promptly on acceptable basis, we may be reaching a "turning point" and can move towards a solution. Eban then commented on his discussions in Washington. He said impression which emerged in his discussions with Secretary and Katzenbach, and to lesser degree with Pres, perhaps we might have impression Israel is immobile and that Israel believes if we "sit on our behinds" for months and years a satisfactory result can be achieved. This is not the case, Eban said quite categorically. Once UN rep is appointed Israel envisages extremely active period of discussion and negotiation. He expects a very busy November and December. They expect to have full contacts both with UAR and Jordan, and there are variety of ways to do this. He therefore hoped officials in Washington understood Israel's views and plans in this regard. Rafael chimed in that when negotiating stage is reached there would be "completely new landscape", implication being they would take a flexible attitude re settlement.

Eban asked for our views re Jarring and both Goldberg and Sisco indicated our favorable impression of him. Israelis seem to have a similarly good impression. Eban said that a man such as Jarring would not be willing to take on job unless res adopted has at least acquiescence of both sides and offers some hope that both sides intend to cooperate with UN rep's efforts.

Comment: Recommend strongly Barbour be instructed take up matter with Eshkol promptly.[3]

Goldberg

---

[3] Telegram 60511 to Tel Aviv, October 27, instructed Barbour to make the points made to Eban by Goldberg to Eshkol, underlining the gravity of the situation that could emerge from further Israeli retaliatory action. (National Archives and Records Administration, RG 59, Central Files 1967–69, POL 27 ARAB–ISR) Telegram 1328 from Tel Aviv, October 27, reported that Bitan had told Barbour that the Israelis intended no further military retaliation for the sinking of the *Eilat.* (Ibid.) Telegram 1351 from Tel Aviv, October 29, reported that Eshkol had confirmed Bitan's assurances. (Ibid.)

---

492.   Memorandum for the Record[1]

Washington, October 26, 1967, 11:40 a.m.–12:12 p.m.

SUBJECT

    NSC Meeting 11:30 a.m. October 26, 1967, on Economic Elements of a Middle East Peace Settlement

THOSE PRESENT

    The President
    The Vice President
    Secretary of State
    Secretary of the Treasury
    Secretary of Defense
    Secretary of the Interior
    Director of Central Intelligence
    Administrator of Agency for International Development, William Gaud
    Director, U.S. Information Agency, Leonard Marks
    Director, Office of Emergency Planning, Gov. Price Daniel
    Assistant Secretary of State, Lucius D. Battle
    W. W. Rostow
    Bromley Smith
    Harold H. Saunders

Secretary Rusk, at the President's request, opened the meeting with the following presentation of the problem:

For the moment, "politics is queen." We do not expect that economic steps will solve political problems. On the other hand we feel that there could come a stage soon where injection of potentially attrac-

---

[1] Source: Johnson Library, National Security File, NSC Meetings, Vol. 4. Secret. Drafted on October 27. The time of the meeting is from the President's Daily Diary. (Ibid.)

tive economic arrangements could encourage the parties to reach satisfactory political agreements. Therefore, we have pursued *staff work* urgently *in several areas.*

First, and most urgent, is a solution to the *refugee problem.* Some of us believe the situation is more fluid now than it has been for years. If the refugees could be given some private choice on where to settle permanently and some help, it is possible we might dissolve the problem. This might cost as much as $1 billion over ten years. However, the international mood is such that considerable help is likely from other nations, and Congress would probably be reasonably forthcoming on any program that promised a permanent solution in place of the year by year drain on US resources that has characterized the past patchwork arrangement.

The *second* category of studies falls under the heading of *Israel's relations with its immediate neighbors.*

It is possible to paint a fairly attractive picture of *Israeli-Jordanian* economic relations. It is too early to inject this into the negotiating scene, but it is important to hold this picture in reserve. Such arrangements would not necessarily involve heavy US resources. Meanwhile, we have a problem of how much aid to give to Jordan pending a political settlement.

If *the UAR* comes to terms with Israel, we may want to review the West's interests there and perhaps even reconsider some surplus food sales at some stage. However, until there is movement toward a political settlement, we should stay out of the aid business.

Third, there has been some setback to our *water and fertilizer* planning as a result of the war. It will probably not be possible to move ahead until there is a political settlement. The Secretary had discussed with several Arab foreign ministers the possibility of setting up a Middle East water authority as a way of proceeding toward indirect relations with Israel, but he had not received much encouragement. He suspected we would go ahead with the Israeli desalting plant as soon as it was politically feasible. This would cost $80–$100 million. The World Bank is working on plans for developing the fertilizer resources of the region and we will stay in step with them.

In *conclusion*, we meant to pursue our studies urgently in order to reinforce the political dialogue when the occasion offers. The Secretary wanted the President to have this report of staff work in progress.

The President asked the Secretary to spend a couple of minutes discussing *action in the UN the day before.*

The Secretary misunderstood briefly and launched into a discussion of whether or not we should press for Security Council action on Vietnam, but then returned to explain the developments on the Middle

East in New York since July. He concluded by indicating that the non-permanent representatives of the Security Council are now considering a resolution which would state general principles and then appoint an intermediary to go to the Middle East. He said that the Soviets appear interested in seeing what the non-permanent representatives produce. In the next two or three days, we should know whether such a resolution will succeed. He noted, by way of background, that Israel's position has deteriorated since mid-summer.

At the President's request, *Secretary Udall reviewed possibilities for water development in the area.* The Secretary said he had come to the subject initially with one big concern—that we would have to do the first big desalting plant here in the U.S. Now, however, the Los Angeles plant is underway and he felt we were free to move ahead elsewhere.

"As a resource man," he would prefer not to talk about desalting separately but to talk about the total water picture. He felt we could increase the run-off of the Jordan River by 20% with weather modification. He felt that water must be keyed in with the refugee problem and hoped that in moving ahead on the Israeli plant we could extract some concessions from Israel that would tie the plant into greater Arab use of the Jordan River water. He felt that nothing could be a stronger force for peace than linking vital public utilities—canals, power grids, etc.—across national boundaries. We must think on a regional basis and, insofar as possible, "make" local governments plan together.

The President asked about the *status of the Baker resolution.*[2] Secretary Udall said the Foreign Relations Committee had held hearings, largely as a courtesy to the Senator. The purpose of Administration witnesses was to show that we are on top of the subject. The flaw in the Strauss plan,[3] as the Secretary sees it, is that there is at least a four to five year lead time before any desalting plants could begin to produce. Therefore, the *Strauss Plan* is not an "overnight panacea." We will have to start whatever we do with the water already present in the Jordan River system.

The President asked how much money the Strauss Plan would cost.

Secretary Udall said that the Plan envisioned three large desalting plants, which would produce so much power that the region could not

---

[2] S. Res. 155, introduced August 14 by Senator Howard H. Baker, Jr., of Tennessee and 52 cosponsors, called for the construction of nuclear desalting plants to alleviate the chronic shortage of fresh water in the Middle East.

[3] Reference is to a proposal by former Atomic Energy Commission Chairman Lewis J. Strauss for the creation of a public corporation to assist in the construction of nuclear desalting plants in the Middle East. For a memorandum Strauss sent to former President Eisenhower on June 23 setting forth his proposal, see *Foreign Relations, 1964–1968*, vol. XXXIV, Document 166.

use it now. He said we might do something like this in thirty to forty years, but the best thing to start with was the Israeli plant which is already on the books. The Strauss Plan would cost something like $1 billion.

The President asked whether there was any *disagreement within the Administration on the Strauss Plan.*

Secretary Udall said he thought not. However, he thought that the State Department's letter to the Senate Foreign Relations Committee was a bit pessimistic and made the Administration look more negative than necessary,

At the President's request, Mr. Gaud commented on water development. He pointed out that AID had some question about the economic feasibility of the *Israeli desalting plant.* Moreover, as far as he could see, this looks like an Israeli and not a regional project. One virtue of a larger desalting plant would be that Israel would not have to take any water out of the Jordan Valley, but the "pick and shovel question" was that AID had no money in its budget for the Israeli plant.

Secretary Udall said he assumed that if a desalting plant were to become part of a political settlement, we would want to handle this outside of normal AID programs. He felt that tactically this was a better way to work with the Congress anyway.

The President asked whether there is any merit in the Republican position that water will solve the Middle East political problems.

Secretary Udall said, "That's the panacea approach." Secretary Rusk said he thought not. Mr. Gaud said he felt that the Republican position was "too simplistic."

[Omitted here is brief discussion concerning Vietnam and foreign aid legislation.]

The meeting adjourned.

Harold H. Saunders

493.   Memorandum to President Johnson[1]

Washington, October 27, 1967, 3:40 p.m.

Mr. President:

As a result of your conversation with Bob Anderson,[2] Secretary Rusk is requesting your authorization to give Anderson the following answer for Nasser if Nasser asks about restoring relations with us: We're willing, provided (1) they take the initiative; (2) they agree in principle to compensate us for properties damaged in June; (3) they retract their false charges of our participation in the June war; and (4) they agree to respect the normal rights of legation.[3]

I think this is a fair position for us to take. We obviously don't want to rush headlong into Nasser's arms. On the other hand, we still have an interest in giving him a window to the West. We could maintain a minimal relationship by just having a Chargé in Cairo for the time being.

Anderson leaves New York at 10:00 a.m. tomorrow.

The President indicated to WWR that he did not, repeat not, wish Mr. Anderson to be regarded or used as an informal intermediary between the U.S. Government and the UAR.[4]

---

[1] Source: Johnson Library, National Security File, Country File, Middle East Crisis, Sandstorm/Whirlwind. Confidential. A handwritten note on the memorandum indicates it was received at 3:42 p.m. The memorandum is not signed, but an October 27 memorandum from Saunders to Bundy indicates that it was from Walt Rostow. (Ibid., Saunders Files, Middle East, 9/1/67–10/31/67)

[2] The President met with Anderson on October 25 and talked to him by telephone on the morning of October 27. (Ibid., President's Daily Diary)

[3] A memorandum of October 27 from Rusk to the President with these recommendations is attached.

[4] Rostow told Rusk in a telephone call at 7:05 p.m. on October 27 that the President thought it was inappropriate to approach Cairo through a private citizen on the question of recognition. When Rusk replied that the idea was to say nothing unless Nasser raised the matter, Rostow said the President was uneasy about a "Texas businessman handling this." (Notes of telephone conversation prepared in Rusk's office; National Archives and Records Administration, RG 59, Rusk Files: Lot 72 D 192, Telephone Calls)

494.   **Memorandum From the President's Special Counsel (McPherson) to President Johnson**[1]

Washington, October 31, 1967, 4:30 p.m.

For the President

I had lunch with Eppie Evron today. These points emerged:

—Eshkol was "trying to strengthen his position at home" with his tough speech to the Knesset yesterday.[2] The *Times* report made it sound tougher than it was, but it nevertheless took an adamant line on the West Bank and Gaza.

—What the Israelis mean is, until Hussein talks with us about the West Bank, we're sitting still. If Hussein or his representatives will talk with us, our position will automatically change.

—Though they differ on many other points, Eban and Dayan are pretty much together on this.

—They are both willing to give up the West Bank to Jordan *if* it is demilitarized.

—The Israeli press reported that Eban was "quite satisfied" with his talk with you. Eppie believes we should now leak the story of the Sixth Fleet turning toward the Eastern Mediterranean when the *Elath* was sunk. An unaccredited story in the *Post* or *Times* would be helpful both with the Israelis and with American Jews.[3]

—Fulbright, through Carl Marcy, let it be known that he is "burned up" about Israeli efforts to eliminate the Church amendment to the foreign aid bill.

—As to Eshkol's trip here, Eppie and Abe Harmon tried to dissuade him from coming this summer and fall, but he persisted. He now wants to arrive immediately after the General Assembly adjourns; he is thinking about Dec. 21.[4] Eppie wonders if a dinner here could be arranged, with a guest list supplied in part by Feinberg, Krim, and Ginsburg.

---

[1] Source: Johnson Library, National Security File, Country File, Israel, Vol. VII. No classification marking. McPherson forwarded the memorandum to Walt Rostow on November 1.

[2] Excerpts of Eshkol's October 30 statement in the Knesset are printed in *American Foreign Policy: Current Documents, 1967*, pp. 603–605.

[3] A note in the margin in President Johnson's handwriting reads: "No, no, no! This starts trouble with Russia." No further documentation concerning a move by the Sixth Fleet at the time of the *Eilat* sinking has been found.

[4] A note in the margin in President Johnson's handwriting reads: "Not Xmas week. I'll be in Texas."

—He hopes some practical step forward can be arranged for the Eshkol visit, such as a desalination offer that would include "such other states as desire to join with us."

—Eppie himself has pretty much had it here. The stresses on policy between the Israeli embassy and Jerusalem have been severe. (He said he and Abe would have written a "very different" speech for Eshkol yesterday. The one real benefit of Eshkol's visit here, he said, would be to "expose the Prime Minister to the world of Washington—to let him see and feel reality as Washington sees it. They have a very insular view—a very narrow, parochial view of the world in Jerusalem. A conversation with the President should open his eyes.")

At any rate, Eppie will leave next summer, after he helps Gen. Rabin get started as Ambassador. He has been offered the American desk in the Israeli foreign office, but will probably decline it and leave the government for a while. Between now and next summer, he plans to speak to Jewish groups most weekends, helping you wherever he can.

Harry

---

495.   Memorandum From the President's Special Assistant (Rostow) to President Johnson[1]

Washington, October 31, 1967.

SUBJECT

Robert Anderson's Report from Cairo (Text attached)[2]

Bob Anderson saw Kaissouni (Nasser's top economics minister), Mohieddin (most frequently mentioned now as Nasser's likely successor) and Nasser himself. He has another meeting with Nasser on Thursday.[3] These main points emerge:

---

[1] Source: Johnson Library, National Security File, Country File, Middle East Crisis, Sandstorm/Whirlwind. Secret. A handwritten "L" on the memorandum indicates the President saw it.

[2] Telegram [*text not declassified*] to the White House, October 31, attached but not printed, transmitted the text of a message from Anderson. (National Archives and Records Administration, RG 59, Central Files 1967–69, POL UAR–US)

[3] November 2.

—They believe the US is entirely aligned with Israel. They cite our close coordination with Israel in the UN and our resumption of military shipments as evidence. They believe Israel will do whatever we say. They admit charges of our involvement in the June war were mistaken.

—They want a political peace but the terms have to be acceptable to the Arab people, not just to the leaders. The alternative is long and continuous warfare.

—No Arab leader would survive direct negotiations with Israel. No Arab government would settle until all agree.

—They would prefer the great powers to impose a settlement.

—They could accept only these terms: (1) the restoration of all territory that had been taken by the Israelis, (2) the settlement of the refugee question, and (3) the auspices of some international body which would obviate the necessity of direct negotiations between the Israelis and the Arabs. A single mediator at the table would not be adequate cover. Nasser could not allow Israeli annexation of the Gaza Strip. He would allow an Israeli flag vessel through the Canal if the refugee problem were settled, although he couldn't guarantee that some radical wouldn't shoot at it. He thought demilitarization of some territory possible.

—They think it important to restore diplomatic relations with us "as soon as things are a little better." They were "prepared to go more than halfway."

In conclusion, Bob judges that Nasser is still master of the political situation and that there is little committee rule. Nasser appears in good health.

Walt

496. Memorandum From Nathaniel Davis of the National Security Council Staff to the President's Special Assistant (Rostow)[1]

Washington, November 1, 1967.

SUBJECT

The Situation in New York November 1

On the resolutions there has been some modification of both the Indian and the Canadian-Danish drafts. On the key issue of withdrawal the Indian draft has dropped the date and adopted the formula of the Latin American draft of last July[2] (which we supported):

"withdraw from all territories occupied by it as a result of the recent conflict."

The new Canadian-Danish draft[3] is really a modification of language worked out by Dick Pedersen. What it tries to do is to adopt as much verbiage as possible from the Indian draft without giving up anything essential. The key withdrawal language reads:

"None of the states in the area should retain forces on the territory of another state against its will or persist in refusing to withdraw them."

Ambassador Goldberg is having a working lunch with the Danes, Canadians and Japanese to try to figure out where we go from here. The alternatives seem to be further efforts by the non-permanent members or US-Soviet talks. The feeling in New York is that the danger of the Indians getting nine votes in the Security Council for their draft is receding. As a result of our vigorous efforts to push the Argentines and Brazilians back on to the reservation, at this point they could probably muster about eight votes. However, the Argentine continues to argue for points in the Indian draft and is pretty shaky.

We are making some headway with our argument that a UN representative can make real progress only with some degree of cooperation from both sides.

According to New York, Bergus may not be too far off in his guess that the Indian draft might get a healthy GA majority. The main thing

---

[1] Source: Johnson Library, National Security File, Agency File, United Nations, Vol. VII. Confidential.

[2] See footnote 4, Document 340.

[3] Telegram 1873 from USUN, November 1, transmitted the text of the revised Canadian-Danish draft. (National Archives and Records Administration, RG 59, Central Files 1967–69, POL 27 ARAB–ISR/UN)

standing in the way of this is the considerable realization in New York that one more GA resolution-to-be-ignored might not be helpful. There is also less than total enthusiasm for a repetition of last summer's acrimonious and fruitless GA debate.

The non-permanent members of the Security Council meet again at 3:00 p.m.

ND

---

497. Telegram From the Mission to the United Nations to the Department of State[1]

New York, November 4, 1967, 0342Z.

1969. Dept pass to Cairo Priority.

Goldberg accompanied by Sisco and Pedersen had long session November 1 with FonMin Riad, accompanied by El Kony and Mohamed Riad. There were two principal questions discussed.

1. Resumption of UAR-US relations. Riad said UAR wants to normalize relations with US. There had been statements by Secretary and Goldberg that US wants better relations with UAR, but Riad had not seen any specific signs of this. He wanted to know when and how to get into specifics, and just how this can be achieved. In response, Goldberg reiterated June 19th statement in which President said US wants good relations with all states in area. Goldberg expressed disappointment that Nasser had not been as explicit as Hussein in making clear publicly that US has not been involved militarily in recent conflict. Goldberg said US prepared to talk about how and when better relations with US can be achieved and invited Riad to take initiative to request such discussion in Washington. Goldberg said we did not break off relations, and if Riad wished to discuss resumption this a bilateral matter which should be raised in Washington.

2. Second part of discussion related to peaceful settlement and what steps SC might take to this end. Riad, describing basic problem as one of Israeli aggression, asked whether US intended to take a clear stand re

---

[1] Source: National Archives and Records Administration, RG 59, Central Files 1967–69, POL UAR–US. Secret; Priority; Exdis.

Israeli withdrawal. He had asked this question and had gotten no answer from US. He was under instructions to do something about this and improvement of relations, and he would have to go back to Cairo reporting failure. In discussing this second aspect, Riad reinterpreted what he had told Goldberg in one of our past conversations regarding UAR willingness to accept five principles contained in June 19th statement as basis for settlement and possible SC res. He said UAR could accept five points (he later pointed out impracticality of arms limitation point) provided territorial integrity principle meant withdrawal of all Israeli forces from UAR, Jordan and Syria to pre-June 5 position. Riad complained that we are giving economic and military support to Israel while its aggression continues, latest evidence being Skyhawks. As to our attitude on withdrawal, US has said to him we are against territorial gains. He said this is very vague and we do not know what exact stand of US is regarding withdrawal. He continued that he has been here 41 days and he is tired of merry-go-round of discussions. He said it is essential that we be clear as to what SC is trying to do, and critical question is whether US is for or against territorial gains. For its part, UAR's prime objective is not SC res that gets 9 votes, it is not looking for political gains, it wants something practical done. UAR wants to talk about this in detail specifically. From all of discussions he does not know with whom he can do business. He said we need to talk about details of the solution as well as specifics of res.

Goldberg, after pointing out ways in which Egyptian press had been misinterpreting Goldberg/Riad discussions and telling Riad we are not revealing to press substance of our conversations, detailed our views regarding a settlement. He said we do not believe that forces should be stationed on UAR territory, that UAR territorial integrity and political independence should be respected, and that a stable and durable peace should be achieved. We are prepared to use our influence to this end and for a solution of the basic problems of area. Riad had raised question of what we meant by the context of peace, and we meant all of these things, including recognition of existence of Israel, renunciation of belligerency, and freedom of passage of international waterways as stated by President on June 19. He then read to Riad certain parts of June 19 statement relating to need for secure boundaries and asked Riad whether he agreed with this, to which Riad responded affirmatively.

Goldberg also spent a good deal of time reviewing our proposals designed to help bring under control arms race in area, and stressing need for an agreement among all of suppliers. He underscored we cannot do this unilaterally, that Soviets had poured back a substantial amount of arms into area. Goldberg said we attach importance to maintenance of balance of arms in area in light of fact it has not been possible to achieve an arms limitation agreement. Goldberg countered Riad's contention that Skyhawks were a new dimension, since UAR was getting planes of comparable capacity from Soviets.

As to present activities in UN, Goldberg agreed with Riad that present efforts of non-perms have been extended and drawn out. Goldberg told Riad we are prepared to discuss with him specific language of a res which would not prejudice either side's position. Our approach is to find an SC res which will assure that both sides will cooperate with UN rep on basis of mandate which would not prejudice either side's position. As to withdrawal, we have made it clear that we favor withdrawal in context of peace. We believe an appropriate res can be drawn up which meets situation, and we are ready to talk about it specifically with UAR. Riad readily agreed to talk specifics and meeting concluded with the understanding that we would get together with them in the next day or so.

Goldberg

---

498.   Memorandum of Conversation[1]

Washington, November 2, 1967.

PARTICIPANTS

W.W. Rostow
Ephraim Evron, Minister of Israeli Embassy
Harold H. Saunders

Israeli Minister Evron came in this afternoon mainly to deliver a copy of Foreign Minister Eban's letter to Ambassador Goldberg.[2] After

---

[1] Source: Johnson Library, National Security File, Files of Harold H. Saunders, Israel, 11/1/67–2/29/68. Secret.

[2] Eban declared in his November 1 letter to Goldberg that for Israel to move away from the cease-fire lines except to stable agreed and secure frontiers, embodied in a peace settlement, would be so irrational and unjust that Israel would be willing to incur any consequence rather than to agree to such a course. He urged that the United States make known its opposition to any resolution calling for restoration of the June 4 situation. Some non-permanent members, he declared, were engaged in prejudicial formulations on the issues of withdrawal, permanent frontiers, and peace, which would have the effect of creating a conflict between Israel and the Security Council. If necessary, he declared, Israel would not recoil from such a conflict, but he urged the United States to use the full weight of its influence to prevent such a situation. Telegram 1910 from USUN, misdated October 2 but received on November 1, transmitted the text of the letter. (National Archives and Records Administration, RG 59, Central Files 1967–69, POL 27 ARAB–ISR/UN)

indicating that he had read it, Mr. Rostow described the Arabs' need for some cover and dignity before they could negotiate. Evron made two points:

1. Israel does not want a resolution which in effect defines and negotiates positions before actual negotiations begin. Any resolution referring to withdrawal will give the USSR and the Arabs a whip to use on Israel, and they will conveniently forget other balancing points in the resolution as they have in the past.

2. The Arabs—particularly Nasser and Hussein—are still grasping for a third-party solution. But the Egyptians seem to realize their own economic weakness, and the passage of time will work in the interests of further realism in Cairo. The US has a chance to inject realism into the thinking of Hussein, who may have his head in the clouds after his numerous summit talks.

Mr. Rostow concluded by saying, "You just want everybody to go home without a resolution or mediator, run out of money and then come to you." Evron just smiled.

Comment: It appeared that the Israelis' motive in writing and presenting this letter was to stiffen our spines against a repeat of our "sudden" bilateral agreement with the USSR in July, which they regarded as a dangerous erosion of our position.

H.S.

499.   Memorandum of Conversation[1]

Washington, November 3, 1967, 1–3:15 p.m.

SUBJECT

Middle East

PARTICIPANTS

U.S.	USSR
The Secretary	V.V. Kuznetsov, First Deputy
Foy D. Kohler, Deputy	Foreign Minister
Undersecretary	Anatoliy F. Dobrynin,
John M. Leddy, Assistant	Soviet Ambassador
Secretary for EUR	Yuri N. Chernyakov,
Malcolm Toon, Country	Minister-Counselor,
Director, SOV	Soviet Embassy
	Igor D. Bubnov, Counselor,
	Soviet Embassy

The Secretary said that he understood the non-permanent members of the Security Council were still engaged in trying to work out a resolution. If they should not succeed he assumed that our two delegations may have to meet over the week-end to ascertain if they could be of some help.

Kuznetsov said he would like to sum up his impressions from discussions in New York of the Middle East problem. It is clear that the Arab countries, and especially those most directly concerned with the problem such as the UAR, have adopted a more constructive realistic position. They now are ready to agree to substantial forward steps in the spirit of resolutions already adopted or agreed to by our two delegations. This is encouraging; we should recall, for example that the position of the UAR differs considerably now from the position taken during the emergency session. Kuznetsov went on to say that six non-permanent members (India, Brazil, Argentina, Nigeria, Mali, Ethiopia) have worked out a draft resolution which has come to be known as the Indian draft. Kuznetsov had held the impression, perhaps naively, that this resolution had some chance of acceptance. He had met with the U.S. delegation and had discovered that the delegation was not prepared to cooperate and in fact was not even willing to support resolu-

---

[1] Source: National Archives and Records Administration, RG 59, Central Files 1967–69, POL 27 ARAB–ISR. Secret; Nodis. Drafted by Toon on November 3. Approved in S on November 8. The memorandum is part I of IV. The time is from Rusk's Appointment Book, which indicates that the conversation took place during luncheon at the Department of State. (Johnson Library)

tions that it had helped draft at the end of the emergency session. Kuznetsov felt that so long as the U.S. delegation took this attitude the prospects for agreement were not bright. He doubted that India, Argentina and Denmark, which had been assigned tasks of working out still another resolution, could succeed unless there should be a change in the position of the U.S. delegation.

The Secretary suggested that there might be a possibility of merging the Danish and Indian drafts, but Kuznetsov said this was impossible since the Danish draft makes no reference to the June 5 date. It was his view and that of a good many other delegations at the UN that the Danish draft would simply amount to rewarding Israeli for aggression. Kuznetsov said the crucial question for his government was to ascertain why the United States had retreated from the position it apparently held early this summer when it supported the Latin American resolution and the two draft resolutions prepared and agreed to by the U.S. and Soviet delegations.

The Secretary said that the basic problem was not whether Moscow and Washington can agree on the elements of a settlement but rather whether a resolution can be worked out which would be acceptable to the countries directly concerned. In the Secretary's view there are two alternative roads we can follow: the first is to settle all problems in the area; the second is to work out general principles for the settlement of these problems. The Secretary pointed out that he did not wish to engage in negotiations on the Middle East problem since these should properly take place in New York. He did, however, wish to make a few general observations. Reverting to his point that there are two approaches we can follow, he pointed out that some delegations tend to apply one approach to the problems of particular interest to them and the other approach to problems of direct concern to the other side. For example, both the Arabs and Israelis seek a formula which would be precise on what they seek but imprecise on what the other side seeks. A resolution drawn along these lines would cause real trouble; a formula for example that would be precise on withdrawal but imprecise on the use of the Suez Canal was simply unacceptable.

Kuznetsov again asked why the United States is not prepared to support the draft resolutions worked out at the end of the emergency session which, in his view, were in accord with the principles stated by the Secretary.

The Secretary said that he did not wish to discuss in detail the controversy over the draft resolutions which was well known to both sides. The important thing was to ensure that we have agreed understandings of any draft resolution that may be developed. This had not been the case with the earlier draft resolutions. The Arabs, for example, had subsequently taken the position that the clause "freedom of international waterways" did not apply to the Suez Canal. In any case, the Secretary felt that we should now focus on how we should proceed from here.

Kuznetsov again said that he could not understand why we were not prepared now to support the draft resolutions worked out earlier. Does the problem concern only the date? He would remind the Secretary that both drafts contained the June 4 date; the only difference between the two was that one draft was expressed in precise terms and the other reflected general principles. There was considerable suspicion at the UN as to the motive for omitting a date relating to withdrawal. Kuznetsov himself wondered about this. He had noted the recent speech by the Israeli Prime Minister and had also noted that there had been no statement by any U.S. official publicly disagreeing with that speech. If this should mean that the United States now favors awarding Israeli aggression with territorial gains the situation is indeed dangerous. It was understandable, therefore, that Kuznetsov should seek a straight answer to the question: Does the United States favor withdrawal of Israeli forces to the positions held before June 5?

Dobrynin interjected at this point that there is a feeling among the Arab delegation that the entire question should be aired publicly in the General Assembly. The Soviet delegation would be reluctant to see this happen since this would give rise to a polemical atmosphere which would not facilitate agreement. Thus it is vital to clarify the question raised by Mr. Kuznetsov if we are to have a clear understanding between our two governments.

The Secretary said that the U.S. position from a national point of view was clear; we had no interest in nor did we favor territorial changes in the area. He would point out that if the Arabs had cooperated in bringing about an early cease fire the question of territorial gains would never have arisen since Jordan and Syria would not have become involved. The fundamental question, however, in the Secretary's view is how is peace to be secured in the area. Peace cannot be ensured if we are to be precise only on withdrawal and imprecise on such vital questions as belligerency, the right of Israel to exist as a state, freedom of navigation, etc. A formula which suffered from this weakness would leave open the possibility of a request for immediate sanctions against one party's failure to abide by precise conditions but would not provide for any enforcement measures in the event the other party should choose to ignore imprecise conditions. The Secretary felt strongly that either we move with precision on all points or we move on the basis of general principles.

Kuznetsov agreed that any formula for settlement should incorporate the basic peace measures cited by the Secretary as well as provision for withdrawal. The two draft resolutions worked out by the U.S. and Soviet delegations incorporated both elements. If the United States should agree to support either of these draft resolutions a solution can be found. It was Kuznetsov's impression that both drafts were acceptable to the United States, and this impression was reenforced by the following passage contained in the President's letter to Kosygin of October 23:

"We were guided by these principles when our representatives in New York worked out jointly with your representatives, toward the close of the Emergency Special Session of the General Assembly, alternative drafts of a resolution which would bring about force withdrawals, an end to the state of belligerency between Israel and its Arab neighbors and establishment of a stable basis for peace in the Near East. We were prepared to have either of those drafts presented and adopted by the Emergency General Assembly, but, as you know, this was not possible because of objections from certain Arab countries."[2]

The Secretary asked Kuznetsov if he were convinced that the two governments had the same understanding of the two draft resolutions.

Kuznetsov said that it was precisely to clarify this point that he sought an answer to the question of whether the United States favors complete withdrawal or not. He would like at this point to cite the following passage from Kosygin's letter to the President of October 21:

"The Soviet Government proceeds from the position that it is necessary to eliminate without delay the after-effects of aggression and, at the same time, to prevent the breakout of a new military conflict in this area in the near or more distant future."[3]

The Secretary observed that it was important that we not be more "Israeli" in our attitude than Israel and that the Soviets not be more "Arab" in their position than the Arabs.

Kuznetsov completely agreed with this.

The Secretary again observed that if the non-permanent members of the Security Council should not be successful in working out a formula our two delegations should resume their discussions. He wished again to stress the distinction between our mutual national views and the positions of the states in the area. For example, we have disagreed with Israel for almost 20 years over the questions of Jerusalem and Jordan; other territorial problems in the area present less difficulties. It would be useless for us to agree to a resolution which would be unacceptable to the states directly concerned.

Kuznetsov said he assumed from the Secretary's remarks with regard to differences between the United States and Israel that Gaza could remain under UAR control. In any case, he felt strongly that if the

---

[2] Document 484.

[3] Document 480.

United States could support the Indian draft a solution could be found. The Arab delegations are now in a bad mood; they fear that the tabling of the new Danish draft, which deviates from previously agreed principles, would mean that all the efforts made and work done so far would go down the drain. It is important to recognize that there is a limit to how far the Arabs can go; they cannot risk humiliation or support any action which would be interpreted as an infringement on or diminution of their national sovereignty. The situation will become more dangerous as time goes on and if the Arabs should feel that the other side does not want peace in the area.

The Secretary said that it was unfortunate that India had worked out a draft which incorporated the essence of the Tito plan.

Kuznetsov said that this was simply not true. The Indian draft was much easier on the Israelis and imposed more obligations on the Arabs than the Latin American draft.

The Secretary said that he had the feeling that the Indians were trying to be more Arab in their outlook than the Arabs themselves, possibly because of their problems with Pakistan. Beyond this the Indians had not bothered to consult with us in the preparation of their draft, and we did not feel that this was a proper way to proceed. In any case, the Secretary would have an opportunity to discuss the problem further with Ambassador Goldberg this afternoon and he would assume that Ambassador Goldberg and Mr. Kuznetsov would be meeting over the week-end.

---

500.   Telegram [*text not declassified*] to the White House[1]

Washington, November 3, 1967, 1516Z.

[*document number not declassified*]. Eyes Only to Secretary of State and White House for the President:

---

[1] Source: Johnson Library, National Security File, Country File, Middle East Crisis, Sandstorm/Whirlwind. Secret. Also sent to the Department of State. Rostow sent the telegram to the President at 2:30 p.m. with a covering memorandum, in which he commented that the Nasser–Anderson conversation was important and interesting. Citing paragraph 25, he noted that Anderson was "wholly correct" in his conversation and in dealing with the press, and he added that he had "talked firmly" to the Chief of the United Press International Washington Bureau, "who promised to try to kill the story." The handwritten note "PS, 11/3/67" on the memorandum indicates the President saw it.

Following is text message dictated (but not read) by Anderson in presence [*less than 1 line of source text not declassified*], and edited and in parts reorganized by latter at specific Anderson request, early evening 2 November. For the Secretary of State attention of the President from Anderson.

1. This will be a somewhat difficult message because of the circumstances under which it is being dictated at the Beirut airport en route between Cairo and Baghdad.

2. I met today with President Nasir at 1230. He advised me that he was leaving later today for a vacation in the desert near Al Almayn, and that this would be the first real vacation he had taken in fifteen years. He was looking forward to swimming, sitting in the sun and having time to think and relax. He opened the conversation by saying, "above all else, try to make clear to your government and your people that we are eager for a political settlement, for a political peace." He stated that this had not been true in the very beginning, after the cessation of hostilities on 9 June, because "we were in a state of confusion, uncertainty and doubt. We did not know, but we feared what the Israelis were going to do." Now, he said, "we know that our interest lies not in war, but in peace."

3. He then said, "Please try to convince your people and your government that any question of direct negotiation, or even of negotiations with a third party mediator present, would be an act of suicide. It would be so for me, and it would be so for any other Arab leader." He further said that even if he attempted this or agreed to it, it would be suicide on the part of any other Arab leader not immediately to denounce it and to demand to resume hostilities against the Israelis. Nasir said, "under these circumstances, let us try to be practical and, if we all want peace, and we do, then let us find a way to settle our differences and live in peace." He said we did not believe that the details of an agreement could be worked out in public, or that anything could be effectively begun by negotiations by a committee or any mediator appointed by the U.N. until some formal action had been taken by the U.N. "as a first step." He then suggested that a resolution be offered to the Security Council which would involve as its basis the five points that President Johnson had made, and which he described as follows:

A. The right of Israel and of all other nations in the area to live;
B. Free movement of "innocent" shipping in the waterways of the Gulf of Aqaba and the Suez;
C. Full withdrawal by the Israelis from the territories which they had occupied at the time of the hostilities;
D. A declaration of non-belligerence between Arab states and Israel; and
E. Finally, settlement of the problem of the refugees.

4. Nasir stated that after the adoption of this type of resolution, which he thought we should accept because it was based on the principles announced by our President, the resolution should direct the Secretary General to appoint one or more persons to consult with the Arab nations involved and with Israelis and, from these negotiations, to draw up "a declaration for detailed implementation, which would then be submitted again for adoption or ratification by the Security Council.

5. At this point, I told him that as I understood it, the Israelis professed they would not be satisfied with any declaration made by third persons, even including the Security Council, and that they wanted some contractual undertaking between them and the Arab countries which would ensure non-belligerence and the other ideas he had referred to. Nasir said that he could not speak for all the other Arab countries, but as for himself, he would be willing to sign such a (Security Council) declaration "after it had been agreed to," or, as an alternative, write a letter or other document to the Secretary General or to the Security Council undertaking to carry out the details and implications contained in the declaration. He felt that the other Arab countries would be willing to do the same thing, but reiterated that "he could not speak for them." It is quite clear that he is willing to undertake contractual obligations, just so long as they are not incorporated into a simple treaty jointly made and signed between the UAR and Israel. This point he made from time to time, referring always to the fact that even such an agreement would be suicide.

6. Nasir then said that the most difficult problems were going to be the Suez Canal and Jerusalem. I said that obviously I could not speak on any of these topics, but could only explore his own thinking. In this connection, I asked if he could agree to let any ship, including the Israelis, transit the Suez Canal if such ships carried not the flag of the country involved, but the U.N. flag. Nasir said, "I do not rule this out but there is still the question of logs, manifests and trouble with the people. On the other hand, if you will settle the refugee problem then I can allow Israeli ships to transit," he said. I told him I was skeptical that the Israelis would ever negotiate for a resettlement in Palestine. At this point, Nasir said, "All right, then, let us settle with them by agreeing to pay them compensation." In order to clarify this point, I stated again that I wanted to be quite sure that he would agree to a mutual settlement of the refugee problem without giving the refugees the alternative choice of resettlement (*comment:* in Palestine) or of taking money instead, and he again said that if resettlement is not possible, we can agree on a mutual compensation. He continually links the free passage of Israeli ships through the Suez Canal with the settlement of the refugee problem.

7. He then brought up the question of territory. Here, Nasir said that the key point is that Israel cannot be allowed to expand, that for every Muslim nation, regardless of whether or not it borders on Israel, the consuming fear is that Israel plans territorial expansion. He said this is one of the basic problems in trying to unite the New and the Old City of Jerusalem. It is regarded by everyone of the Muslim faith as a violation of their religious rights and as Israeli expansion.

8. He then stated this, that again he would speculate that certain territory surrounding the state of Israel might be regarded as essential to their own security. Nasir said that if this is so, let us demilitarize it. Again he said, "I cannot speak for all others, but as for me, I will withdraw permanently all forces 10 miles, 15 miles, or any agreed number of miles from the borders." I asked him what he would think about the complete demilitarization of the Sinai Peninsula. He said, ("This I cannot do, because it is too big and extensive a land for me to say that no military personnel can ever be placed there. I can agree that no military personnel will ever be placed in Sharm al Shaykh, or within 10 or 15 miles of the Israeli borders, if they or their state will agree not to place troops within the same distance." He said again, "I cannot speak for Jordan or Syria, but I believe that the same principles would be agreed to by them."

9. Nasir said that except for territory, most of the Arab nations are leaving other details of the Arab settlement to him. He said, "It is a task I do not want, but one which others have asked that I undertake. It, however, must be expected that each will decide with reference to his own territory, and each of the neighboring states must agree on the final settlement." I told Nasir that obviously I was going fully to communicate his views to my government, and he said, "This is exactly why I am telling you, and I hope we will be getting a response that is favorable from your government. You are going to Iraq. If you get any kind of response, please advise my Ambassador in Iraq, and I will be glad to receive you at any time you want to return." Nasir stated, "Please try to explain to your government that however desperately we want peace, we cannot have it at the price of destroying ourselves or any other Arab leader, when you can be absolutely sure that anybody who succeeds me or any of the other Arab leaders will be much more radical against the Israelis than we are."

10. Nasir said that some of the Arab states, notably Syria and Algeria, had been very vehement with him in stating, "You cannot agree to a resolution or a declaration which includes the right to live for Israel." Nasir said, "I merely pointed out to them that we are no longer talking about Israel's right to live. We are talking about our own right to live." He repeated this two or three times. He also said he believed

the Israelis had in mind his economic destruction, because at present he had no revenue from the Suez Canal or from tourism, and now they had destroyed his refineries. He said, "Therefore, my task is now to build a strong economy within my own country. This is the best way I can retaliate."

11. I asked Nasir if he would give me his own version of the sinking of the Israeli ship *Eilath*. He said he would be glad to. He said this ship had been patrolling in and out of UAR waters for a number of weeks, "just on the border." On or about 11 July, this same ship had attacked and sunk two Egyptian torpedo boats and killed their crews. This, he said, attracted no world attention. "Also, they sank them in our own waters." He said then General Rabin issued a statement saying that the Israelis were looking for the Egyptian navy, but the navy was hiding. He said that in addition to this, an Israeli plane sank another Egyptian torpedo boat in the Suez. As far as the actual sinking of the *Eilath* was concerned, Nasir said, "It was all finished and done with before I even heard about it. I was first informed about 6:30 in the evening. At that time, I was not dealing with what should or should not be done. I was dealing with a fact that had already happened. I am sure that military commanders in other parts of the world do not ring up their presidents and ask them what to do every time there is an invasion of their territory." Nasir ended the conversation by saying, "I want nothing but peace. I want to go as far as humanly possible to achieve it. But I must not be asked to do the impossible. I must not be asked to do something that would be condemned by every other leader and by my own people. I am willing to go as far as the facts of life will allow me, and I hope you will make this clear to and get a favorable response from your government. Surely, they can support the principles of your President, and surely we can find ways to work out the details of implementation. Surely, peace must not depend both on circumstances and procedures, upon the demands of the Israelis, some of which they themselves know are impossible for us." Nasir again asked me to stay in touch with his Ambassador in Iraq and be prepared to return if a response for his government was forthcoming.

12. I asked Nasir whether all of the difficulties concerning Yemen had been finally settled and if his agreement with the Saudis was going to be carried out. Nasir replied, "Our relationships in Yemen have been settled for good. We are going to carry out our agreements. The same goes for all of the other states in the Southern Arabian Peninsula. My concentration is going to be on the development of the UAR."

13. Note that in my talk on the first day I arrived, I told Nasir we were still puzzled as to why he had massed troops in the Sinai and we believed this was why the whole issue had come about. Nasir did not

refer to the Gulf of Aqaba, but said, "Whether you believe it or not, we were in fear of an attack from Israel. We had been informed that the Israelis were massing troops on the Syrian border with the idea of first attacking Syria, there they did not expect to meet great resistance, and then commence their attack on the UAR." I said to him that it was unfortunate the UAR had believed such reports, which were simply not in accordance with the facts. Nasir said that the information had not come to him from sources he would suspect. He added that among other signs "your own State Department called in my Ambassador to the U.S. in April or May and warned him that there were rumors that there might be a conflict between Israel and the UAR." I told him that so far as I knew, I had never heard this report before.

14. Nasir observed that the U.S. must remember that Jerusalem presents a special problem for all three faiths. He commented that "In this country, we are Muslims, but we are not Islamic." I asked Nasir if he would consider permitting both the Old and New City of Jerusalem to come under a single Israeli administration with respect to such things as public utilities, etc., but with each faith to have custody and supervision of its Holy Places. Nasir replied that even if he agreed to this any such solution would leave Israel ultimately confronted with war or resistance so far as anybody could see into the future. He said that nothing he or any other ruler in the world could do would prevent that people will do things in the name of religion that they would not consider doing in the name of politics. On the other hand, he thinks Jerusalem could be zoned so that each faith would have the administration of its own sector. "My country is Muslim, Christian and Jewish, and I expect it always to be so. Each has his own particular interest in how we settle the issue of Jerusalem." We had no further discussion on this subject, because Nasir said this was obviously a matter of such importance that it would have to be the subject of negotiations, and one or more persons should be appointed by the Secretary General pursuant to the Security Council resolution discussed earlier above to manage such negotiations.

15. Concerning the shelling of the Suez refineries, Nasir commented that he recognized it as retaliation for the sinking of the *Eilath*, and that he thought the Israelis had done this because it would hurt the UAR economically. He said, "We could have attacked their refineries, but we decided that this had gone far enough, and we should have peace and not escalation."

16. Nasir's willingness to sign an agreed UN declaration or writing a letter to the UN agreeing to the terms of such a declaration is, of course, conditioned on Israel's willingness to do the same.

17. On conclusion of our meeting, Nasir thanked me for coming and expressed the hope that he would receive a favorable response to the suggestions incorporated in the foregoing.

18. After leaving Nasir, I proceeded to see Zakariyah Muhyi Al Din at his home. Zakariyah began by asking me to brief him on what had taken place between Nasir and me, and I did so. Zakariyah asked whether we had gotten into discussions of details concerning the territories involved, especially the Gaza Strip. I told him Nasir had said other nations must be consulted insofar as their territories were concerned, but that the Gaza Strip had not been mentioned today. Zakariyah said that relinquishing the Gaza Strip could not be decided on by the UAR or the Israelis. The UAR had never annexed Gaza formally because it is territory belonging to the Palestinians, as is some of the territory on the West Bank of the Jordan. I asked that if this is true, who speaks for the Palestinians. Zakariyah smiled and said he did not know. I asked whether it would be Ahmad Shukayri, and Zakariyah again smiled and commented that Shukayri was an appointed, not an elected official, and that there might well be some other political voice who could speak for the Palestinians. He seemed disappointed that the issue had not been discussed by Nasir. I take it as Zakariyah's implication, and only that, that he does not believe the fate of the Gaza Strip should be a determining factor. He is, however, concerned about the people in the Gaza Strip, as to whether or not they could be incorporated into the State of Israel, and perhaps more importantly, as to whether the Israelis would allow them to stay. He said, "The real problem is not the land but the people, and whether after we make peace the natives would be ejected as undesirable." I told him that these were the sorts of things I had gathered from Nasir, and that they would be the subject of discussions by one or more persons who might be appointed by the Secretary General pursuant to the resolution cited above.

19. Zakariyah said that he thought so far as he knew I had clearly outlined Nasir's views. He said, "We want to go as far as we can, because we know that war can only destroy us both, and that peace can allow us to fulfill our obligations as a nation. But please do not ask us to do the impossible, and please try to tell your people that regardless of what others might say, direct negotiations or negotiations with a mediator could not be possible, and even the Israelis know this as well as we. I asked Zakariyah if it were not possible to change public opinion on this subject, and he said, "No. Neither in this country nor in other Arab countries. We might change their opinion on other topics, but not on this."

20. I asked Zakariyah if there were anything he would like to add to the review of Nasir's views. He said, "Yes. First of all, we would like to have a new start in relationships between our two countries. We have been through a period of confusion. We know beyond all doubt that it is not in our interest to have any misunderstandings with the U.S. We

hope that your country feels the same way. We are fearful that your government just does not understand us and that your people do not understand us. We are fearful that they do not know what is possible and what is impossible. Please explain that above everything else, we are nationalists. We are Egyptians and we are not trying to rule the Arab world. You may not believe that Nasir from time to time has felt that he has been put into a corner. He feels he has been personally disliked at high levels of your government." I said that this was not so. Zakariyah went on, "He has great respect for your President and for your people. He knows he has made mistakes, but he thoroughly wants, as we all do, the friendship of the United States and their help in making peace—but within the framework of what is humanly possible. We do not think we can accomplish this. We do not think our public relations are good, and we would like to be able to depend on someone to get our point of view across. I hope that you get a favorable response from your government along the lines of your talks with President Nasir and that we can move to peace. We will be anxiously awaiting the response that is made as the result of our conversations."

21. Zakariyah made the point that prior to the Khartoum meeting, the feeling for continuation of some form of hostilities against Israel was very strong. He said in fact that only on this aspect has there ever been Arab unity. But at Khartoum, Nasir took the initiative in seeing that the UAR must have political peace, correct its own errors and settle its own problems with Yemen and the other states in the Arabian Peninsula.

22. Regarding Jerusalem, Zakariyah made essentially the same points as had Nasir. He noted that this problem was of concern not only to the Arab countries, but also to a great many of the African and other countries where there were high concentrations of the Muslim faith.

23. I was advised that if the UN Secretary General were to appoint an individual or group to draft a resolution along the lines noted above, Zakariyah might well be sent to join Foreign Minister Riyad in the discussions in New York. Like Nasir, Zakariyah thanked me for coming to Cairo and expressed his hopes for a favorable response.

24. I suspect the only way for me to be advised of the response to the foregoing is to return to Beirut. When I return will depend on how far we get in contractual discussions with the Government of Iraq. I can and will, however, interrupt those discussions and come to Beirut to communicate with you [*less than 1 line of source text not declassified*]. We have devised a method so that he can discreetly request me to return here. I assume there is no great hurry about getting back to Nasir, since he told me he was going on vacation. I gather this is to be a short vacation, but Nasir did not specify the number of days. I also suppose he

would want to be in touch if you consider the response a matter of urgency. I will do nothing until I hear further from you. If it is decided for any reason that I should not communicate a response to Nasir, I will return to Beirut after conclusion of the conversations in Iraq and from Beirut proceed home.

25. I was asked by Pace of *The New York Times* and Carruthers of the *Los Angeles Herald* whether I would visit with them. I only spoke to Pace on the telephone and told him that I was discussing commercial fertilizer and land reclamation as I have been doing for some years. I would not give him the names of anybody with whom I had had conversations. I did say that I was acting entirely on my own, discussing commercial matters of long standing and was not in the UAR with any official status.

26. I have dictated this [*less than 1 line of source text not declassified*] in Beirut and will not have time to have it transcribed for reading before I depart for Baghdad. I shall read it and make such corrections as may be necessary on my return to Beirut.

27. One final point from discussion with Zakariyah: While he spoke of making a new start in our relationships, he said that of course at some point, we must renew formal, diplomatic ties. I said only if this were the wish of President Nasir and that they should then instruct their Foreign Minister to be in touch with our Secretary of State. I noted it was they who broke relations, and they who would have to take the necessary steps to discuss their resumption.

---

501. Telegram From the Mission to the United Nations to the Department of State[1]

New York, November 4, 1967, 0513Z.

1973. Amb Goldberg, accompanied by Sisco and Pedersen, called on King Hussein Nov 3. Rifai and Sharaf also present on Jordanian side. Principal development as result of mtg was that King agreed, despite determined effort by Rifai to try to get us to negotiate on basis Indian

---

[1] Source: National Archives and Records Administration, RG 59, Central Files 1967–69, POL 27 ARAB–ISR/UN. Secret; Immediate; Nodis. Repeated Priority to Amman. Received at 0709Z.

text, to receive our specific views on a new draft res. We will meet with King Hussein again on Saturday[2] at 4:30 in order to discuss a specific text. Before doing so, however, we will be meeting with Eban Saturday AM on specific language of a new text we will develop. Also apparent from discussion is that Jordanians here, in good rug dealing fashion, have been pressing beyond the principles expressed to us by King Hussein this evening.

Goldberg opened conversation by explaining our position within broad policy framework previously communicated to Rifai (USUN 1507 of Oct 17).[3] Goldberg read portions of this telegram to King in which he stressed UN rep's function would be to achieve peace which would include agreement on Israeli withdrawal as well as peace arrangements. Other points included: US prepared use its influence to help achieve reasonable settlement; fact that we did not visualize a Jordan limited only to East Bank; our desire to have a Jordan protected in permanent boundaries; the need for some territorial adjustment; and our desire to help even on Jerusalem where we do not have the same views. Goldberg also stressed that "Our purpose is to create context of peace in which Israeli withdrawal will take place and Jordanian territorial integrity and political independence will be protected." While we could not guarantee that everything would be returned to Jordan, and that some territorial adjustment will be required, we would be prepared to use our influence to help Jordan get best deal possible.

This set the stage for Goldberg's subsequent comments re where we go from here at UN. Recalled that we, Riad and Rifai had agreed to give non-perms opportunity and these efforts have now been exhausted. Goldberg affirmed we are ready resume dialogue and wish take advantage of King's presence to carry on dialogue. Informed King that Nasser had indicated to Anderson a willingness to accept SC res based on five points and that he envisaged UN rep who would produce a declaration, based on consultations with both sides, for subsequent ratification by SC. Goldberg indicated that this was only a brief provisional report on this discussion and if this is approach UAR had in mind this offered some hope. It should not be difficult to find right form of words for res in such circumstances, Goldberg said.

Goldberg continued time is running out, time has come for peace. We are ready to help, we do not wish to go back to fragile Armistice Agreements. We are committed to principle of political independence

---

[2] November 4.

[3] Telegram 1507 from USUN, October 17, reported a conversation that day with Deputy Foreign Minister Rifai and Ambassador Sharaf. (National Archives and Records Administration, RG 59, Central Files 1967–69, POL 27 ARAB–ISR/UN)

and territorial integrity and we are ready to reaffirm it bilaterally and publicly in SC res. US believes in territorial integrity, withdrawal, and recognition of secure boundaries. Principle of territorial integrity has two important sub-principles, there must be a withdrawal to recognized and secure frontiers for all countries, not the old armistice lines, and there must be mutuality in adjustments. If Jordan makes an adjustment along the Latrun salient there ought to be some compensatory adjustment for it. We wish to work to this end so that equitable agreement can be achieved. We believe, Goldberg said, that "He who seeks equity must do equity." As to Jerusalem this is a tough one in light of our historical position with which His Majesty is familiar. But even here we are prepared to be helpful. We are willing to use our influence to see what arrangements can be worked out for an appropriate Jordanian role in Jerusalem, and do not accept Israel's contention that Jerusalem is not negotiable. We are anxious to use our influence if given a chance, but we are not able to do so as long as protracted haggling continues on res. We recognize there are genuine security problems and West Bank part of Jordan, for example, should be settled as security matter with compensating adjustments. We attach great importance to principle of freedom of waterways. In our judgment this was the prime cause of 6-Day War. We want to see refugee problem solved and we have been surprised that its solution has been linked to opening of Canal. We stand firm in support of 1951 SC res which linked opening of Canal with ending of belligerency, not with solution of refugee problem. Must be real efforts to settle refugee problem. We also want to see something done on arms limitation since this is a principal source of tension in area.

Goldberg said with some disdain that what has been going on at UN is exercise in rhetoric not in solving basic problems. US wants to engage UN in peace making process at a pragmatic level and we wish to participate in this in important way. While non-perm members have disagreed on specific language they did agree on three important points: appointment of special rep; and SC res should be within framework of Chap 6 and not Chap 7; and that UN rep should have specific mandate. We have some thoughts regarding specific language in SC res. We believe UN should send out a rep to seek "political solutions," to "work with parties" and seek to solve the problems of "withdrawal, boundaries, waterways and refugees" and report back to SC. The notion of instant peace which is embraced in Indian res is nonsense. Time is running out, and there is need to get UN rep out promptly. The objective should be for him to get at fundamental problems and nobody's position should be prejudiced by any SC res adopted in the meantime. We are ready to carry on dialogue with King. He is the chief of state and has the authority to do business. With all due respect to Riad, he is not in same position. We would have no hesitancy to put some of these ideas down on paper if His Majesty wished.

King, very solemnly and systematically and with a good deal of feeling, recounted difficulties facing his country. He opened by saying this is matter which concerns Jordan and US, probably greatest power in world. The problems in area are of interest to world community and of interest to US since finding solutions would help lessen tensions. He wished to speak as frankly as did Amb Goldberg. He has been in close contact with Cairo throughout. Jordanian policy has never been one of extremism and despite 6-Day War it continues its policy of moderation. He intends to continue this policy so long as there is distinction between moderation and giving away the rights of his people. We appreciate friendship of US. There are today many stresses and strains in Arab family due in part by outside pressures. Principal difficulties arise in the failure to solve Palestine problem. This has been at the root of the trouble. Jordan has tried to help refugees, to give them dignity, and its main resource has been its people and their determination. Now Jordan is in ruins again, and 15 years of his own efforts have been involved. His sole interest is Jordan, its people and the Arab world; any attempt to differentiate among these is not in Jordan's or anybody else's interest. The King said he felt deeply that Arabs must communicate with rest of world and present their case as reasonable, the more reasonable the stronger its case would be. He feels that there is now a chance to do something, the opportunity is right, and it is essential there be a just and peaceful solution of the Palestine problem. He sought to counsel his Arab colleagues to meet and tackle their responsibilities. He characterized Khartoum as a "turning point" and believes Arab position has become reasonable. He said we haven't much time, pressures are building up inside and out, and there are still a number in the Arab world who believe that attempt at political solution will not succeed. He saw the self-criticism at Khartoum as a positive factor. He believes Arab people do not understand the Western world since they feel they have been wronged. Regardless of fact that some believe political solution is not possible, the King said we must try very hard to find a just solution. He went on to describe in some detail the human misery of 200 thousand refugees to document his belief that there is not much time left to find a political solution. He maintained that his armed forces are under control, that he has given strict orders, though he admitted that when armed forces are close together there are bound to be incidents.

He described withdrawal as serious problem and key to any solution. Question was where to. To Israel as it was now or where. Jordan could not accept results of war but was not adverse to fair territorial adjustments on both sides. As to Jerusalem, Jordan had been custodian of Holy Places for last 20 years, it is not Jordanian or Arab but a Moslem and a world problem. Jordan is not against rights of any religious group to visit Holy Places. As to arms, King said he would be discussing this matter in Washington. The question of old arms balance has become unrealistic. Had the 6-Day War not occurred balance might have been achieved about "a year and 2 months from the date of the 6-Day." However war has altered this situation and no balance exists or will exist for a long time. Israel has acquired a substantial amount of arms from UAR, from Jordan, and is secure. Soviets have supplied Jordan with some definite "requirements". Unless he meets military needs of his own troops better, Jordan will have to continue keep Arab troops on its territory. His Majesty said he cannot get the Arabs out from his territory unless he can stand on his own two feet. He realized he received US arms on conditions they would not be used against Israel. As member of Arab League he could not back away from this fact when the war came. He had no other way than to face up to situation. While he is not asking for arms, as long as there is not a political solution he will have to find arms and equipment wherever he can, particularly if pressures continue. He wanted the US to understand this.

As to SC, basic difficulty has been what mandate should be given to UN rep, question was what principles was UN rep to discuss. Arabs do not wish to return to GA since this would cause difficulties among them. GA was only a platform. In his discussions with US and Sovs in Moscow he has found misinterpretations on both sides.

Then King described succinctly agreement which he and Nasser reached on October 17 in Cairo. (In view of fact that Jordanians have been pressing very hard in connection with SC res in favor of Indian draft, this description seemed to make both Rifai and Sharaf nervous.)

King said that he had proposed to Nasser that:

1. Arabs would all declare end of state of belligerency;
2. Recognize right of every state in area to live in peace and security;
3. Waterways would be open to vessels of all nations, including Israel.

In turn Israel would be expected to:

1. Declare an end to state of belligerency;
2. Recognize the right of every state in area to live in peace and security;
3. Withdraw its forces "from territories it had occupied";
4. "Cooperate toward finding a permanent solution of refugee problem" (which King described as a part result of state of war and an element of state of belligerency).

King said it was "decided" by himself and Nasser that Jordan and Egypt were ready (1) to "declare" an end of state of belligerence,

(2) "recognize" right of every state in area to live in peace and security and (3) open Suez Canal and other international waterways on condition and understanding Israel would declare its acceptance of end of state of belligerence, as described above.

King said once this was understood there should not be any trouble with SC res. He then stressed firmly that this was limit as far as Jordan was concerned. There was no question of bargaining, that they had gone a very long way. Time was running out, and they wanted a political solution. He stressed need for a UN umbrella and by this he meant a mandate for a UN rep that could get on with job of implementing a solution.

Amb. Goldberg said he found himself in agreement with much of what His Majesty had said. There have been problems here at UN though they have not been of making of Jordanian reps. The problem has been that activities here at UN are not in keeping with principles the King had just enunciated. The effort here had gone far beyond these principles. Goldberg cited question of Canal for example. We were not hearing here that Canal should be opened to all vessels, including Israeli. He pointed out that His Majesty properly had linked opening of Canal with ending of state of belligerency as in case of 1951 SC res.[4] But here the opening of Canal was linked with solution of refugee question. Moreover, in the Indian res there is phraseology which referred to the waterways being opened "in accordance with international law and practice." Word "practice" had been dropped because that would have meant going back to pre-June 5 situation by which the Straits and Canal were closed on the basis of belligerency. Phrase "international law" is still in Indian draft since this would give UAR continuing opportunity to close the Straits on the basis of "sovereign rights". US shares King's impatience and we are prepared to put something down on paper—a fresh approach. Specifically, we believe objective should be: (1) permanent peace; (2) there should be a political solution, not a military one; (3) this political solution should emcompass (a) withdrawal of occupying troops, (b) end of belligerency, (c) political independence and territorial integrity, (d) recognition of every state to live in peace and security in area, (e) solution of refugee problem, and (f) freedom of passage through international waterways. UN rep could work out these problems with parties concerned.

His Majesty stressed that world organization must deal with problem since it played such major role in creation of Israel. He did not feel solution had to be dealt with on piece-meal basis. Since Goldberg had

---

[4] Reference is to the UN Security Council Resolution of September 1, 1951 (UN document S/2322); see Department of State *Bulletin*, September 17, 1951, p. 479.

read to him the press ticker today coming out of Cairo severely criticizing American policy, King said he appreciated misunderstandings that such things caused, but that we must deal with them patiently, particularly as one takes a look at the press all over the world. His impression is that Nasser wants good relations with US though Nasser feels Washington is trying to humiliate him. He said many Arabs feel that US wants to rub their noses in the dust.

His Majesty let Rifai carry the ball regarding discussions re SC res. Rifai first said that he was much surprised to read in *New York Times* that Anderson was on official mission. Rifai was present when Anderson spoke to Riad and that the contents of *New York Times* article had astonished him. He noted that reports mentioned "joint declaration," and he recalled in this connection that this was idea contained in Brazilian text which Arabs did not consider very seriously. He contended that Indian text used the five principles as starting point (with exception of arms limitation). He stressed that first order was to end the military occupation of the territories; once this achieved one could move on to solution of other matters. He stressed that Jordan has gone as far as it could by accepting changes in 6-power draft. This draft was drawn largely from texts which US had previously supported. If LA text were re-introduced in GA unchanged, the Arabs would go with it. Rifai then made effort to try to get US to focus and negotiate on basis Indian text. In process he stressed what he considers to be one basic essential—withdrawal of Israeli forces and need to be absolutely clear on this point. He argued that respect for territorial integrity should come *after* withdrawal. Goldberg rebutted this by saying that Charter of UN does not envisage withdrawal in circumstances of state of war.

Conversation concluded by King responding affirmatively to our suggestion that we put down something on paper which takes into account agreement on principles achieved by Nasser and Hussein in Cairo on Oct. 17.

Goldberg

502.   Telegram From the Mission to the United Nations to the Department of State[1]

New York, November 5, 1967, 0233Z.

1992. Goldberg brought Eban and Rafael (Israel) up to date on consultations of last few days.

1. Kuznetsov–SecState:[2] Very general and non-productive. Kuznetsov was told we were available to meet with him, but no contact as yet.

2. Riad–Goldberg:[3] Riad appeared "insecure". We are not sure how "wired in" he is and did not get too far with him.

3. Hussein–Goldberg:[4] King obviously wants to do business although his advisers may not. Goldberg reported to Eban that King had his Secretary read from minutes of Oct 17 Cairo agreement between King and Nasser, repeating in effect what Goldberg had told Caradon earlier re this meeting. (See USUN 1989.)[5]

Eban had received cable from Israeli Amb in London that King was saying similar things there, but with the addition that Israel should "restore June 4 situation". Eban said this difference was crucial. Furthermore, there was no indication that other Arabs would even "nod

---

[1]   Source: National Archives and Records Administration, RG 59, Central Files 1967–69, POL 27 ARAB–ISR/UN. Secret; Immediate; Exdis. Repeated Immediate to Tel Aviv. Received at 0401Z.

[2]   See Document 499.

[3]   Telegram 1972 from USUN, November 4, reported a meeting on November 3 between Goldberg and Foreign Minster Riad. Sisco, who was also present, told Riad that according to a preliminary report from Anderson, Nasser had suggested three steps: (1) adoption of a Security Council resolution containing the President's five points; (2) appointment by the Secretary-General of one or more individuals to talk to the Arabs and Israelis, after which a declaration would be drawn up; and (3) submission of the declaration to the Security Council for ratification. Riad said he did not have any report in these terms. He was ready to accept the President's five points provided that they were given the "right interpretation"; a reference to territorial integrity and political independence should mean that Israel had no right to territorial gains and must withdraw from territories occupied. (National Archives and Records Administration, RG 59, Central Files 1967–69, POL 27 ARAB–ISR/UN)

[4]   See Document 501.

[5]   Telegram 1989 from USUN, November 5, reported a conversation between Goldberg and Caradon on the morning of November 4. Goldberg told Caradon that U.S. representatives had begun a new effort based on UAR and Jordanian intimations that they preferred dealing directly with the United States rather than through the Russians. He told Caradon of his meeting the previous day with King Hussein and said that the United States planned to develop language to submit to the King. He asked Caradon to refrain over the weekend (November 4–5) from making British views known in order to give the United States a chance to work something out. (National Archives and Records Administration, RG 59, Central Files 1967–69, POL 27 ARAB–ISR/UN)

assent". Eban gathered that King thought only matter to negotiate was question of borders. This was clearly unrealistic.

In response Goldberg pointed out that he was not reporting to Eban something Hussein had *said* but what had been *read* to Goldberg from the minutes, and that what was read bears out Nasser–Anderson consultations.

Goldberg informed Eban that he had told King if King would take leadership for "Arabs" we would give him some of our ideas on res and would be in touch with him. At this point Rifai said that if we were unsuccessful, they would go to GA on LA res, "unchanged".

Goldberg then set out problems of timing, noting that UK had been given definite instructions to vote either for revised Indian or Danish-Canadian text. Furthermore, they had instructions to make their views known and, if necessary, to table their own text. Although unwilling to show us their text even in confidence, in essence it was combination of Danish-Canadian (B) (USUN 1829)[6] and revised Indian (1.) (USUN 1777).[7] Eban noted that was exactly opposite of what UK had told him, and he would ask Wilson about it when he saw him early next week.

Goldberg said that if Caradon's combined res goes to SC, it would get all votes except US. If US blocks SC, the July LA res would be taken to GA.

In effort to avoid both these developments, US wanted to try out some ideas for a res. First version Goldberg read to Eban said in part:

"Considering that the time has come, in the context of respect for and acknowledgment of the sovereign existence, territorial integrity, political independence and right of every state in the area to live in peace and complete security from threats or acts of force, to move from the cease-fire to a state of just and lasting peace:

1. Accordingly requests the SYG:

(A) To designate a special rep to proceed to the Middle East to establish and maintain contacts with all the states concerned with a view to assisting them in working out a political solution to the problems of the withdrawal of all forces from territories occupied by them, the termination of the state or claim of belligerence, the guarantee of freedom of navigation through international waterways in the area, the ensuring of secure and recognized frontiers, the just settlement of the refugee question, the guarantee of territorial inviolability in the area through measures including the establishment of demilitarized zones, and the limitation of the wasteful and destructive arms race in the area."

---

[6] Telegram 1829 from USUN, October 29, conveyed the text of a possible compromise resolution prepared by Pederson and a Canadian representative based on the Danish-Canadian resolution and the modified Indian draft. (Ibid.)

[7] Not found.

Goldberg viewed this as non-prejudicial to both sides since formulation does not settle matter but merely identifies problems of which SYG's rep would assist parties in working out "political solution". Eban rejected this version commenting in particular on phrase "withdrawal of all forces from territories occupied *by them*," and absence of "within a context of peace," and criticizing order of presentation.

Goldberg then gave Eban second US trial version, reported septel (USUN 1988).[8] Surprisingly, Eban and Rafael preferred this version to first version (which would have been more difficult to get Arab agreement on) Eban said he liked it. Was, however, concerned with fact that sequence in "affirms" para illogical and would tend to encourage working first on withdrawal, and subsequently on termination of claims of belligerence, recognition, etc. Pedersen and Sisco explained this was a linked para and modalities of sequence would be one of things to be worked out. Eban reiterated GOI would find res distasteful because (1) no direct negotiations; (2) withdrawal clause was first in sequence; and (3) "political solution" instead of peace "agreement".

Goldberg told Eban he might be able to get British support for this res. Eban was doubtful, implying Caradon was not just recipient of instructions but influenced their tenor to some extent by nature of his reporting.

Goldberg recommended that privately Israel should stay out of things for a while, this is US initiative. Sisco asked Eban what he thought of US sponsorship, noting advantage that US could then supply interpretation. Eban said in some respects it would be a disadvantage since US could work better behind scenes if it were not the sponsor. However, US res would not be viewed in Israel as retreat if approach was that res based on five points of LBJ's June 19 speech. Goldberg concluded that best sponsorship would be SC Pres, on behalf of SC, or as SC consensus.

In response to Eban's request, "mutual acknowledgment and respect for the right of every state in the area, etc.," of "affirms" para was changed to "mutual *recognition* and respect," and, in same para, "secure and recognized borders" was changed to "secure and recognized *boundaries.*"

In subsequent telcons Rafael also sought deletion of words "in achievement of" in the "affirms" para and of "agreed" before solutions. Late in evening also called to say Eban wished him to make clear to us

---

[8] Document 504.

again that Israel would not be considered "subscriber nor co-sponsor" of the text.

Comment: Nature of Eban's comments and attitude was one of acquiescence.[9]

Goldberg

---

[9] Goldberg told Rusk in a telephone conversation at 1:37 p.m. that he had just finished talking to Eban and had a text which he could present to the King. He thought it was "not bad; they moved a little bit." (Notes of telephone conversation prepared in Rusk's office, November 4; National Archives and Records Administration, RG 59, Rusk Files: Lot 72 D 192, Telephone Calls)

---

503. Telegram From the Mission to the United Nations to the Department of State[1]

New York, November 4, 1967, 2345Z.

1985. Goldberg provided Caradon (UK) with US draft resolution (septel)[2] November 4 which we made available earlier in day to King Hussein.[3] Goldberg asked Caradon to communicate it urgently to his govt with a request for full support by UK. Goldberg informed Caradon we were asking AmEmb London to make similar démarche at high level to UK FonOff.

Draft resolution is being considered by Hussein with whom we expect to meet again on Sunday afternoon[4] to receive his reactions. We believe prompt indication of UK support would be very helpful in tactical situation here and as latter part of this tel will indicate, our hope is Caradon will be in position to see King before us on Sunday to indicate his agreement with and support of resolution.

We believe this res has reasonable chance of getting cooperation of both sides with UN rep and should be well received by UK in light fact

---

[1] Source: National Archives and Records Administration, RG 59, Central Files 1967–69, POL 27 ARAB–ISR/UN. Secret; Immediate; Exdis. Repeated to London Immediate. Received on November 5 at 0022Z.

[2] Document 504.

[3] Telegram 1991 from USUN, November 5, reported the meeting with King Hussein on the afternoon of November 4. (National Archives and Records Administration, RG 59, Central Files 1967–69, POL 27 ARAB–ISR/UN)

[4] November 5.

it based on formula expressed by Brown in GA general debate. Formulation used by Brown: "Britain does not accept war as a means of settling disputes, nor that a state should be allowed to extend its frontiers as a result of a war. This means that Israel must withdraw. But equally, Israel's neighbors must recognize its right to exist, and it must enjoy security within its frontiers. What we must work for in this area is a durable peace, the renunciation of all aggressive designs, and an end to policies which are inconsistent with peace."

Goldberg said he had emphasized to Hussein that this text designed to take account of stress King had placed on having principles in operative section of res and on need to refer to Israeli withdrawal from occupied territories. UK has expressed similar view. He said he had not asked for Hussein's reaction, since he considered it unfair to ask for reaction on such short notice.

After reading text, Caradon said he warmly welcomed its general framework and layout, and its use of affirming language in operative section. He also said text Goldberg had given him was very close to text UKUN had itself worked out during past two days. He questioned whether res left adequate role for UN to play. Goldberg pointed out references to demilitarized zones and guarantees re freedom of navigation and solution refugee problem, all of which leave room for UN role. Went on to stress main thrust of res is to have UN express itself on essential points and designate UN representative whose job will be to get parties themselves to move as far as possible toward these points.

Caradon said UKUN would have preferred to include language re inadmissibility of territorial conquest by force. Goldberg said this would raise great problems with Israelis. Went on to stress "withdrawal from occupied territories" in present res would be bitter pill for Israelis to swallow and, thus, he not inclined make pill even more bitter.

Caradon raised point of most effective role UK might play at this point. Said he not sure it was to make text Goldberg had given him into joint US-UK text. Expressed view it might be best for him, assuming London's reaction favorable, to inform Hussein that he (Caradon) had seen text prepared by US and that UK felt it contained essence of points UK supports; he could then urge that Hussein give it sympathetic consideration.

Goldberg indicated this would be most helpful and again expressed hope Caradon would get immediate reaction from London so that UK could speak to Hussein along above lines tomorrow afternoon before Goldberg calls on Hussein.

Goldberg

504.   Telegram From the Mission to the United Nations to the
        Department of State[1]

New York, November 5, 1967, 0057Z.

1988. Dept pass Cairo Immediate. Middle East—New Draft Res.

Fol is US compromise draft res which Goldberg made available to Hussein today. We expect to receive King's reaction Sunday afternoon, when Goldberg will meet with him again. Text has been made available to Israelis, UK, Danes and Canadians. Text not yet made available to LA's and Embassies should refrain from doing so unless advised otherwise.

"The Security Council

Expressing its continuing concern with the grave situation in the ME,

Recalling its Resolution 233 (1967)[2] on the outbreak of fighting which called, as a first step, for an immediate cease-fire and for a cessation of all military activities in the area,

Recalling further GA Resolution 2256 (ES–V),[3]

Emphasizing the urgency of reducing tensions and bringing about a just and lasting peace in which every state in the area can live in security,

Emphasizing further that all member states in their acceptance of the Charter of the UN have undertaken a commitment to act in accordance with Article 2 of the Charter,

1. Affirms that the fulfillment of the above Charter principles requires the achievement of a state of just and lasting peace in the ME embracing withdrawal of armed forces from occupied territory, termination of claims or states of belligerence, and mutual recognition and respect for the right of every state in the area to sovereign existence, territorial integrity, political independence, secure and recognized boundaries, and freedom from the threat or use of force:

2. Affirms further the necessity

A. For guaranteeing freedom of navigation through international waterways in the area;

---

[1] Source: National Archives and Records Administration, RG 59, Central Files 1967–69, POL 27 ARAB–ISR/UN. Secret; Immediate; Exdis. Repeated Immediate to Amman, and to Brasilia, Buenos Aires, Copenhagen, London, Ottawa, Rio de Janeiro, and Tel Aviv. Received at 0133Z.

[2] June 6; see footnote 2, Document 183.

[3] July 21; see footnote 4, Document 385.

B. For achieving a just settlement of the refugee problem;

C. For guaranteeing the territorial inviolability and political independence of every state in the area, through measures including the establishment of demilitarized zones;

D. For achieving a limitation of the wasteful and destructive arms race in the area;

3. Requests the Secretary-General to designate a special representative to proceed to the ME to establish and maintain contacts with the states concerned with a view to assisting them in the working out of solutions in accordance with the purposes of this resolution and in creating a just and lasting peace in the area;

4. Requests the Secretary-General to report to the SC on the progress of the efforts of the special representative as soon as possible."

Goldberg

---

505. Telegram From the Department of State to the Embassy in Israel[1]

Washington, November 5, 1967, 2154Z.

65127. Rostow–Harman Conversation: Part I of III parts.[2]

1. At his request Ambassador Harman called on Under Secretary Rostow, requesting information about the Anderson talks in Cairo and Ambassador Goldberg's talk with King Hussein in New York.

Begin FYI: Rostow's object was to reiterate to Harman the strength of U.S. interest in the success of possible negotiations between Israel and Jordan, and to elicit firm Israeli statements about GOI interest in the negotiations, and their willingness to deal with Hussein, and to negoti-

---

[1] Source: National Archives and Records Administration, RG 59 Central Files 1967–69, POL 27–14 ARAB–ISR. Secret; Priority; Nodis. Drafted by Atherton and approved by Eugene Rostow. Repeated to Amman Priority, and to USUN Immediate.

[2] Part II, Rostow's summary of Anderson's conversation with Nasser, made in response to a query by Harman, was conveyed in telegram 65128 to Tel Aviv, November 5. Rostow said the U.S. reading of the talks was "not discouraging." (Ibid.) Part III, Rostow's brief summary of Rusk's November 3 meeting with Kuznetsov, made in response to a query by Harman, was conveyed in telegram 65129 to Tel Aviv, November 5. Rostow said the meeting had "not been very satisfactory." Kuznetsov had "spoken in threatening tones about risks of renewed hostilities." (Ibid.)

ate about Jerusalem, conveying a general encouraging sense of the situation without entering into negotiation positions or the negotiating process. End FYI.

Rostow started, referring to conversations during Eban visit, by emphasizing vital US interest in success of negotiations between Jordan and Israel, which we thought was equally in interest of GOI. This connection he noted our concern that Israeli doubts about Hussein's policies may be leading Israel to turn its back on negotiations with Jordan. Rostow said we feel negotiations can make major contribution to peace, leading to solution of refugee problem, resolving Jerusalem issue to satisfaction of Christian and Moslem interests, eliminating Palestine problem as curse on Arab world, opening Middle East to Israeli economic cooperation, and ending Arab boycott. Successful negotiations with Jordan would also enable USG fulfill its territorial integrity pledge. We considered that any alternative to Hussein would be worse for both US and Israel and intended to make major effort to convince Hussein that he should enter negotiations.

2. Harman replied that Israel had not given up hope of settlement with Hussein. He recalled recent Eshkol statement offering to meet with King Hussein. What troubled Israel, however, were indications in Jordanian press and elsewhere that present Arab posture purely tactical, designed achieve return to pre-June 5 situation at minimum cost and by political rather than military means. Israel feared that Arabs, having achieved that aim, would return to earlier posture, claiming they retained freedom of action to solve Palestine problem in their way at the right time. He mentioned alleged Hussein statement in Germany that Arab mistake was to stick to original D-Day of August, 1968. In Israeli view, Arabs had made conscious decision to improve their international posture by avoiding talk of "destruction of Israel"; they were willing to pay price of words, which were cheap, to achieve that end. For these reasons, Israel considered it critical that any solution be "in context of peace," that UN language and actions make this clear and that any UN resolution not prejudice final solution, especially with respect to territorial settlements which essential to Israeli security. There was question in Israeli minds whether there had been any real change in Hussein's policy, and this was principal source of current doubts.

3. Rostow said we had made clear our view that there should be movement from General Armistice Agreements to conditions of peace and that this would involve some adjustments of Armistice lines as foreseen in Armistice Agreements. As we had stressed to Foreign Minister Eban, however, we expected thrust of settlement would be toward security and demilitarization arrangements rather than toward major changes in Armistice lines. We recognized that Jerusalem pre-

sented special case. Our position was that it should be open city, that is, a city without walls, with access assured to all. We had told everyone we would not enter into the negotiating process although our good offices would be used in the interest of helping to achieve a settlement compatible with our national interest in peace in the Middle East, and our historic policies towards the separate issues. We took note of Israeli position that Jerusalem should be an open city under unified administration but that the Jordanian interest in Jerusalem could be met through arrangements including "sovereignty". We assumed (and Harman confirmed) that despite public statements to the contrary, the GOI position on Jerusalem was that which Eban, Harman, and Evron had given us several times, i.e., that Jerusalem was negotiable. Taking Israeli position and willingness to negotiate into account, we thought that with good will arrangements should be possible which would be consistent with interests of Jordan and international community.

4. Harman said Israel saw number of positive developments in recent weeks as result US position: (a) UAR was now saying that USG was decisive factor; (b) both Arabs and Soviets were now coming to USG rather than UN; (c) group of ten non-Perms including Bulgaria had agreed that context of SC resolution was chapter 6 of Charter; and, (d) in recent Israeli talk with Mali representative, latter had agreed any resolution must be acceptable to all parties. Important thing now, Harman said, was to resist attempts in New York to devise language prejudicial to direct contractual arrangements. Rostow said our view had been clear that Resolution must not be a substitute for negotiations, or a "solution", but a framework for negotiations. To Rostow's comment that there were many ways of concluding a contract, Harman said direct negotiations were basic principle; Israel interpreted President's June 19 speech as recognition that contractual arrangements necessary. It also important that settlement be in "context of peace;" it must have this positive aspect rather than negative aspect implied by such concepts as non-belligerency. There could be no solution through verbal gimmicks, even if latter went further than Arabs had been willing to go for past twenty years.

5. In response to question, Under Secretary Rostow described November 3 Goldberg–Hussein meeting as satisfactory and said Jordanians apparently agreed. Rostow then summarized for Harman in general terms following portions of Goldberg–Hussein conversation (USUN 1973):[3]

(a) Goldberg remarks on territorial integrity, withdrawal, adjustments in Armistice lines (but omitting reference to principle of mutuality) and Jerusalem;

---

[3] Document 501.

(b) Goldberg assurance that our influence would be available to help assure fair settlement;
(c) Hussein's comments on withdrawal and Jerusalem;
(d) Hussein's description of his October 17 agreement with Nasser;
(e) Rifai's discussion of UN negotiations.

6. Harman said Israel had impression from recent moves by Hussein that, if King did not get what he wanted from present efforts, he would be prepared to go it alone. In response to Rostow's query whether Israel had direct indications to this effect, Harman said this was "more than general impression." It possible that Arabs had concluded they would have to retreat from Khartoum line of no negotiations, no peace and no abandonment of Palestine cause. This underlined importance of resisting pressures generated by threat of renewed hostilities and of giving up nothing in UN. Any ambiguity in language of SC resolution would permit Arabs to hide behind divergent interpretation of that language and would make Arab-Israeli dialogue impossible.

7. Rostow summarized US position as follows: we now see opportunity to move toward conditions of peace. Whether or not Arabs enter settlement with mental reservations and see language of resolution as mask for future aggressive intentions, our goal should be to devise arrangements, for which parties assume responsibility, that create conditions in which peace can be achieved over time. We have never doubted depth of Arab feeling on Palestine question. Common effort of all who seek peace in Middle East should be to transform this environment over next decade or so in such ways that Arab dream of future victorious war will vanish. We do not view Security Council resolution as negotiations but only as providing basis for negotiations. For this reason we have adamantly resisted inclusion of June 4 withdrawal date. We need resolution which GOI, GOJ and UARG can accept as basis for negotiations, and this is focus of our present efforts in New York.

8. In response to Harman's query about when we envisage next round with Soviets, Rostow said this not yet fixed. We do not want to talk to Arabs through Soviets and are therefore talking directly to Arabs as well as others in UN.

Rusk

506.   Telegram From the Department of State to the Embassy in Israel[1]

Washington, November 30, 1968, 0126Z.

280026. Ref: Tel Aviv 6157.[2] Subj: Territorial Assurances to Jordan.

1. The following, FYI, is full text of memorandum of November 6, 1967[3] referred to in Amman 7409:[4]

2. "On instructions from Ambassador Goldberg King Hussein was told the following on the afternoon of November 5 just prior to the King's meeting with Ambassador Goldberg:

3. 'The draft resolution which Ambassador Goldberg has presented is the best language vis-à-vis the Arabs which the United States Government can support. A resolution which the United States Government cannot support will be a meaningless document, since it is going to require US influence on Israel to achieve the objectives of any resolution. Furthermore, the resolution which Ambassador Goldberg has presented is the best the United States can do today. There is no guarantee that the United States could support such a favorable resolution next month or the month after. The Arabs have consistently made the mistake of rejecting resolutions which they later wished they had accepted. By rejecting this resolution they may be making the same mistake again. The United States as a matter of policy does not envisage a Jordan which consists only of the East Bank. The United States is prepared to support a return of the West Bank to Jordan with minor boundary rectifications. However, the US would use its influence to obtain compensation to Jordan for any territory it is required to give up. For example, if Jordan is required to give up the Latrun salient, the USG will use its influence to obtain in compensation access for Jordan to a Mediterranean port in Israel. Finally, although as a matter of policy we do not agree with Jordan's position on Jerusalem, nor do we agree with

---

[1]   Source: National Archives and Records Administration, RG 59, Central Files 1967–69, POL 27–14 ARAB–ISR. Secret; Nodis. Drafted by Atherton, cleared by UNP Deputy Director Arthur R. Day and Jordan Country Director Talcott W. Seelye, and approved by Davies.

[2]   Telegram 6157 from Tel Aviv, November 20, 1968. (Ibid., POL 27 ARAB–ISR)

[3]   No other copy of the memorandum has been found.

[4]   In telegram 7409 from Amman, November 11, 1968, Ambassador Symmes reported a November 9 conversation with King Hussein. Symmes stated that in accordance with the Department's instructions that he could repeat the assurances given Hussein in New York a year earlier, he had read to him verbatim the assurances contained in the memorandum dated November 6, 1967. (National Archives and Records Administration, RG 59, Central Files 1967–69, POL 27–14 ARAB–ISR) For the instructions, see *Foreign Relations, 1964–1968*, vol. XX, Document 312.

the Israeli position on Jerusalem, we are prepared to use our influence to obtain for Jordan a role in Jerusalem. In short, we are prepared to make a maximum effort to obtain for Jordan the best possible deal in terms of settlement with Israel. We can only do this under the United Nations resolution and the present resolution is the maximum that we can support. Therefore, the best advice that the United States can give Jordan at this time is to accept this resolution and to rely on our promises that under it we will help Jordan get the best possible settlement.'

4. The King asked whether this could be viewed as a commitment by the United States. He was told that the exact language as to what this was should be obtained from the Secretary or the President. Whether it was a commitment or a promise should be left for someone else to specify. Later the Jordanians stated that they were prepared to accept this advice, but they pointed out that what they were doing by accepting it was to sacrifice previous Arab insistence on certain resolution language which they felt protected their position in return for a promise from the USG."

Rusk

---

507. **Telegram From the Mission to the United Nations to the Department of State**[1]

New York, November 6, 1967, 0350Z.

1999. Goldberg met with King Hussein again this afternoon (Nov. 5) at King's request. Also present were Abdul Monem Rifai, Said Rifai, Sharaf, and Sisco, Buffum and Pedersen.

King initiated conversation. Said his position was as follows. Jordan was interested in substance not words. This was why he had encouraged US to seize opportunity that might be last one for all of us. Jordan's interest was laying foundation for just and lasting peace. We should not waste more time on details and on words.

Problem was in US hands. He realized US objectives were to exercise its rights in attempting to solve problem which affected all of us. A

---

[1] Source: National Archives and Records Administration, RG 59, Central Files 1967–69, POL 27 ARAB–ISR/UN. Secret; Immediate; Exdis. Repeated to Amman Priority. Received at 0806Z.

just and peaceful settlement was US and his purpose as well. Without US help he could not get very far.

He had been in touch with many other SC members. Right now issue was in US hands and that of SC. He wished US success for best results. We knew in light of his frank exposition to us of his policy and his discussions in Cairo how far he would be able to go. He did not wish to comment on text we had given him (USUN's 1988)[2] but he wished US all success. He hoped that before he went, US efforts would meet with success.

King concluded by saying he looked forward to his visit in Washington.

Goldberg replied that King had correctly summarized situation. He had also been correct in understanding US had not offered res in bargaining context but as best and most appropriate step we could make to facilitate settlement within umbrella of UN. We hoped we could get on with job of restoring peaceful situation in area and being of assistance to Jordan.

Goldberg noted he had in previous conversation made reservations about our policy position on key words (occupied territory). He had since discussed them at appropriate levels and could say they had US approval.

King had appropriately said issue was now in our hands and that of SC. On this he had some important observations. Time was not working in favor of peace.

Before fighting had commenced in June US had put proposal forward in SC that might have prevented the war. This had been rejected by USSR and by Arabs. Rejection of this proposal, which involved only freedom of transit through Gulf, had been a great mistake.

After fighting broke out in early days US in SC had offered [proposal] including withdrawal and opening of Straits of Tiran in discussion with Sovs. They had said we should show it to Arabs. This also had been turned down. Then in GA we had supported proposal (LA text) which we thought had been appropriate to that time. This also had been turned down. Then we had worked out new texts with USSR. These too were turned down.

Goldberg said let us not make same mistake again. What is available today often is not available in future. Events often take over for themselves. Three months from now may not offer same opportunities for progress as today. We knew he was reflective on that himself.

---

[2] Document 504.

Goldberg then referred to request by Kuznetsov to see him and said he would shortly be talking to him.[3] He did not want to break confidences with King and his inquiry was accentuated by his remark that issue was in hands of SC. He wondered what King's attitude would be towards what he should say to Kuznetsov.

King replied that "Prior to my reaching my very clear understanding with Nasser as to how far we could go" he had gone to Moscow. In Moscow he had encouraged Sovs to carry on conversations with US. He believed this should continue and we should feel no compunction about what we discussed with them.

Goldberg expressed appreciation and meeting adjourned.

Comment: While in light of Riad's statement yesterday that he intended to go to SC with Indian text,[4] conversation could have been interpreted as a disengagement by King, our assessment after careful consideration was that it was to be taken exactly as King expressed it, i.e., that he was encouraging us to go ahead with this text but wished to leave himself in situation where it could not be said be had agreed to it (possibly because of complications with other Arabs).

This assessment later confirmed by information conveyed to Caradon by Said Rifai in which he reported that subsequent to this conversation King had talked to Riad and given him very favorable reaction to US text.

Goldberg

---

[3] Telegram 2001 from USUN, November 6, reported that Goldberg spent an unproductive 2 hours with Kuznetsov on the evening of November 5. The Soviets strongly urged acceptance of the 6-power draft resolution as a basis for negotiations. Goldberg refused. He gave the text in Document 504 to Kuznetsov, but the latter refused to accept it as a basis for discussion. (National Archives and Records Administration, RG 59, Central Files 1967–69, POL 27 ARAB–ISR/UN)

[4] Telegram 1987 from USUN, November 5, reported that Foreign Minister Riad had told Goldberg on November 4 that he had decided to go ahead with the "India/Argentine, etc." He requested U.S. support and cooperation. Goldberg told him he could not expect U.S. support of such an effort as a fait accompli. He noted that the United States still had not been officially consulted or given a copy of the text of which Riad spoke, which had been developed in consultation with India, the UAR, and the Soviets. (Ibid.) Telegram 1990 from USUN, November 5, reported on the conversation in more detail. It stated that the meeting was disappointing, and that Riad had backed away from his willingness the previous day to negotiate on the resolution language and in effect insisted on U.S. acceptance of the 6-power resolution without change. (Ibid.)

508.   Telegram From the Department of State to the Mission to the United Nations[1]

Washington, November 8, 1967, 1521Z.

66350. Following based on uncleared Memcon[2] FYI and subject revision:

1. On November 6 the Secretary hosted a working lunch for King Hussein, who was accompanied by the Jordan Ambassador Sharaf and Chief of Royal Cabinet Rifa'i. The Under Secretary, Assistant Secretaries Battle and Sisco and Harrison Symmes, Ambassador-Designate to Jordan also attended.

2. The meeting covered three main subjects—refugees, US Middle East arms policy, and a Security Council resolution on the Arab-Israeli crisis. Discussion on refugees uncovered no new ground. Hussein emphasized that Jordan continued to need relief assistance for the refugees, but that real need was return of refugees to their homes on West Bank. Hussein explained on his own initiative the tie-in between the refugee problem and Israeli transit of the Suez Canal. He said Israeli transit could begin before a complete solution of the refugee problem was reached. What was required was a start towards a solution.

3. In discussing arms problem, Secretary expressed keen disappointment at Soviet refusal to cooperate with us in effort restrain arms race in Middle East. Our decision sell aircraft to Israel directly related to influx Soviet arms as we are concerned with arms balance in area. Hussein replied problem was meaning of word "balance". There was no balance before June 5. Had there not been a war, the Arabs might have reached a balance with Israel within 14 months from last June. Jordan, however, was not only worried about conventional arms, but also about reports Israelis would have atomic weapons in one year. Jordan faced currently with arms requirements which it had not yet been able to satisfy. In interim Jordan compelled retain Iraqi forces its territory for own defense. Jordan had to have arms from some source which definite and continuous.

4. Secretary hoped Hussein could understand our problem re arms supply. Problem was to avoid all-inclusive legislative prohibition against supply of arms. He could not exaggerate effect India–Pakistan situation had in this respect. Many legislators upset that American arms

---

[1] Source: National Archives and Records Administration, RG 59, Central Files 1967–69, POL 27 ARAB–ISR/UN. Secret; Exdis. Drafted by Houghton on November 7, cleared by Symmes and Battle, and approved by Walsh. Also sent to Amman and Tel Aviv.

[2] Not printed. (Ibid., POL JORDAN–US)

being used by both sides conflict. Congressional attitudes persisted and therefore we had to move slowly. Secretary emphasized it would be disastrous if nuclear weapons introduced in Middle East. Our policy absolutely firm. King could leave it to us because we were very serious on this issue, which we regarded as fundamental.

5. Rifa'i indicated Jordan's understanding of problem explained by Secretary. He could not understand, however, why US gave Israel arms and not its ally Jordan. Ambassador Sharaf added that what had shocked Arab world was that decision sell aircraft to Israel made at same time Israel public position towards settlement current crisis hardening. Secretary understood Arab feelings, but other elements had to be considered. We did not believe it in interest US or Arabs for major powers become involved militarily in Middle East.

6. On broader problem UN resolution, Secretary indicated he was not pessimistic and that he hoped we could get started along present lines. Mr. Sisco told Hussein that Ambassador Goldberg and US Delegation very impressed by their talks with His Majesty over the weekend. He emphasized that time was of essence and it important to get a UN representative into the area. Once this done, as Ambassador Goldberg had noted, US could play strong supporting role. Secretary remarked that we are now making some headway. We see shape of possible solution and are prepared use our muscle in supporting a permanent solution that corresponded to sober, reflective judgment of responsible leaders in area.

7. In discussing results of Khartoum Conference, Mr. Sisco commented that there appeared inherent limitations on freedom of action given Hussein. In recent days we had wondered if Arab group en masse had not been making decisions in New York rather than individual countries. The Jordanians confirmed again that Khartoum Conference had decided that other Arabs would go along with what King Hussein and President Nasser could work out. Mr. Sisco emphasized that this was a crucial point. An early resolution in July which seemed acceptable to Jordan and the UAR had been killed by other Arabs. It was therefore important that countries primarily concerned should make up their minds and not worry about group psychology. We hoped therefore Jordan could have dominant voice.

8. Mr. Sisco then stressed that resolution discussed with King over weekend was crucial. If King and Nasser agreed, everything would be all right. King responded that only difficulty had been matter of withdrawal and how it should be defined. Jordan could accept statements with regard to withdrawal, but what was important was meaning of those statements and Jordan needed a commitment as to their meaning. Ambassador Sharaf commented that Jordan would need to know in its

bilateral negotiations with the United States how latter stood with regard to matters such as withdrawal. The Secretary commented that key question of reciprocity did not involve the US. The United States had not closed the Tiran Straits and if Tiran had not been closed, there would have been no June war. The United States would certainly work to support a settlement that had prospects of success, but the United States was not in complete control of all parties. Our answers alone could not settle problem. Neither Arabs nor Israelis would take our answer as final.

9. In summarizing UN situation Mr. Sisco said consultations were continuing. Ambassador Goldberg was discussing draft that was discussed with the King, with other key delegations and in next day or two we should know whether there reasonable chance of success. While Israel not yet signed on, draft provides good starting point. The positive views of Jordan and the UAR would of course be crucial.

Rusk

---

509.   Memorandum for the Record[1]

Washington, November 6, 1967.

SUBJECT

Hussein Visit and Security Council Situation

Messrs. Katzenbach, Battle, Sisco and Walsh met with the Secretary at 4:15 p.m. to discuss the Hussein visit and the situation in New York. It was reported to the Secretary that the USSR, Indians and the UAR were continuing to lobby for the Indian resolution. While we believe we can block this effort, we will have to move aggressively to do so. We will have messages ready this evening to go from the Secretary to the Foreign Ministers of Brazil, Argentina and Ethiopia in an effort to persuade them from supporting the Indian resolution.[2] In addition, the Secretary was informed

---

[1]   Source: National Archives and Records Administration, RG 59, Central Files 1967–69, POL 7 JORDAN. Secret; Exdis.

[2]   The messages were sent in telegrams 65690 to Buenos Aires and Rio de Janeiro and 65691 to Addis Ababa, all dated November 7. (Ibid., POL 27 ARAB–ISR) A message from Rusk to Indian Foreign Minister Indira Gandhi, urging India's support for the U.S. draft resolution was sent in telegram 65734 to New Delhi, November 7. (Ibid.)

that Ambassador Goldberg and the group believe we should have [*less than 1 line of source text not declassified*] urge King Hussein that, if he wants our resolution to pass, he should help head off the Indian resolution. If the King does not enter the fray, the snows will have fallen heavily before any resolution passes. In so doing, [*less than 1 line of source text not declassified*] should be authorized to reaffirm the assurances given the King on November 3[3] and by the Secretary in his private meeting with the King at 12:30 today (see attachment).[4] The Secretary then authorized [*less than 1 line of source text not declassified*] to reaffirm to the King that the Secretary had in fact incorporated into his remarks what Arthur Goldberg had told him on November 4.[5]

The Secretary then summarized his private talk with the King along the following lines. The King, who was in a good mood, did most of the talking, touching on the basic problems in the area, such as refugees. The King's reactions to the US draft resolution were favorable. The Secretary responded in general terms about the situation in the Middle East and in New York, incorporating Goldberg's assurances on November 4 within the framework of his own comments. No details were discussed.

The Secretary was informed that Goldberg was leaning toward the tabling in the Security Council of the draft US resolution and the group could see advantages in such a course of action. This step might be taken as a preemptive move if it became likely that the Indian resolution would be tabled. It would be designed to show the Arabs what we stand for instead of merely what we oppose. It was pointed out that, since Goldberg may have to move fast, it would be desirable to obtain the President's prior approval of such action. Joe Sisco assured the

---

[3] Reference is to Goldberg's November 3 conversation with the King; see Document 501.

[4] The attachment is a copy of a November 6 memorandum from Sisco to Rusk stating that Goldberg wanted Rusk to confirm to King Hussein the essence of what Goldberg had said to the King and summarizing what Goldberg had said. The summary states that the United States did not visualize a Jordan limited only to the East Bank and believed a settlement should involve the return of a substantial part of the West Bank to Jordan. It states that the United States could not guarantee the return of everything to Jordan but was prepared to give political and diplomatic support to a UN representative and that even with respect to Jerusalem, on which the U.S. position had differed from both Jordan and Israel, the United States would be prepared to do what was possible diplomatically to assure an appropriate role for Jordan.

[5] Reference is apparently to Goldberg's November 3 conversation with the King. Their November 4 discussion, summarized in telegram 1991 from USUN, November 5 (see footnote 3, Document 503), was primarily concerned with the U.S. draft resolution, but the telegram states that at one point Goldberg referred to their conversation the previous day:

"Goldberg continued that we had tried to create terms of reference to move in two directions King had emphasized as requisites—specific withdrawal reference and operative provisions for guidance of special rep. Said that apart from res with such text, U.S. would do best it could to achieve these objectives, having regard to what he had told King about our views toward Jordan."

Secretary that the resolution, which is an amalgam of the Indian, Danish and other drafts, had been carefully reviewed with the Israelis and that he and Arthur Goldberg were confident that they would go along with it. The Secretary then authorized the transmission of a memorandum on this subject to Walt Rostow for discussion with the President.

John P. Walsh
Deputy Executive Secretary

---

510.   Memorandum From the President's Special Assistant (Rostow) to President Johnson[1]

Washington, November 6, 1967, 7:15 p.m.

Mr. President:

I have talked with Nick Katzenbach; and he tells me that he and Sect. Rusk wish you to be brought up to date on the following:

1. It looks as though the Soviet Union and Nasser are moving away at this time from a mutually acceptable resolution; and they may put on the table of the Security Council at any time the Indian draft resolution (Tab A).[2]

2. On the face of it, the Indian resolution looks not unreasonable; but it is unacceptable to the Israelis because it gives priority to a call for withdrawal of Israeli forces to the pre-June 5 positions, and it is much less precise on the question of the recognition of Israel and the termination of belligerency.

3. Arthur Goldberg does not wish to get into a tactical position of looking negative and defensive in the face of the Indian resolution, and he may wish to pre-empt the Indian resolution by placing his resolution on the table (Tab B).[3]

4. Secretary Rusk and Nick, therefore, wish your clearance, on a contingency basis, for Arthur to proceed if the tactical situation demands it.

---

[1] Source: Johnson Library, National Security File, Agency File, United Nations, Vol. 7. Secret. A handwritten note on the memorandum indicates it was received at 7:30 p.m.

[2] "Indian Draft Resolution," November 6; not printed.

[3] "Draft U.S. Resolution," undated; not printed.

5. A somewhat fuller explanatory memo to me from the State Department Secretariat is attached (Tab C).[4]

Walt

Clearance to pre-empt, if necessary, granted[5]

No

See me

---

[4] Memorandum from Walsh to Walt Rostow, November 6; not printed.

[5] This option is checked; a handwritten note on the memorandum states that Katzenbach was notified on November 7.

---

511. Memorandum From Nathaniel Davis of the National Security Council Staff to the President's Special Assistant (Rostow)[1]

Washington, November 7, 1967.

SUBJECT

The Situation in New York, November 7—11:00 A.M.

The following table may help explain the tactical situation in New York:

On our Side	Swing Group	Pro-Indian Resolution[2]
U.S.	Ethiopia	USSR
Canada	Argentina	Bulgaria
Denmark	Japan	India
China		Mali
U.K.		France
Brazil		Nigeria

---

[1] Source: Johnson Library, National Security File, Agency File, United Nations, Vol. 7. Secret. A copy was sent to Saunders.

[2] Telegram 2027 from USUN, November 7, transmitted the text of the Indian draft resolution as most recently revised. (National Archives and Records Administration, RG 59, Central Files 1967–69, POL 27 ARAB–ISR/UN) The draft resolution, with additional revisions, was submitted on November 7 by India, Mali, and Nigeria. (Telegram 2034 from USUN, November 7; ibid.) For text, see UN document S/8227.

The last three on our side have varying problems. Last weekend the British—who are hurting economically from the closing of Suez and have their oil interests much on their minds—were in a mood to go along with the Indian resolution. USUN tells me they are now firmer, but there is still a danger of their becoming unstuck. China is acutely unhappy about alienating the Afro-Asians because of the Chirep issue, but USUN says she is with us if she must be. Brazil, like Argentina, is uneasy because the Indian resolution has virtually the same withdrawal language as the Latin Americans' own resolution last summer. Apparently she is also with us in a pinch.

Of the six on the Russian-Arab-Indian side, Nigeria is the least firm. Although Nigeria has agreed to co-sponsor the Indian resolution, they are generally anxious to seek consensus rather than ram the Indian resolution down the throats of the Israelis and ourselves.

The swing countries, Ethiopia, Argentina and Japan, could give the Soviets their nine-vote majority. Ruda, the Argentine representative, has personally been very active in favor of the Indians. Part of the problem is that he is a little out in the front of his government—although his government would obviously prefer to support the Indian resolution (with its similarities to the Latin American draft last summer). The Ethiopians will probably support the Indians if the matter is pressed to a vote. We are not sure about the Japanese. Several countries would like to support *both drafts*. If they did, the Indian draft would get at least nine votes.

One can explain the hardening Soviet and UAR position by the fact that they may well think they have the nine votes. It would put us into quite a box to have to veto. Going for us is the fact that quite a few countries are very anxious to work out some formula that will enable us to come along. Therefore, the pressures to seek an accommodation—even after the Security Council is convened—will be very considerable.

Even now, we are not likely to have things come to a head right away. When the Security Council meets there will be many speeches and much maneuvering—probably lasting several days. We shall have time to put more pressure on home governments if needed.

My personal opinion is that our new draft[3] will not float. It is too explicit in calling for "a state of just and lasting peace in the Middle East

---

[3] The U.S. draft resolution was submitted on November 7. The text is identical to that in Document 504, except that "territories" was substituted for "territory" in the first operational paragraph. (Telegram 2035 from USUN, November 8; National Archives and Records Administration, RG 59, Central Files 1967–69, POL 27 ARAB–ISR/UN) For text, see UN document S/8229.

g and had been encouraged to put down on paper our precise ideas
↑ res. Goldberg speculated Sovs have exercised their influence in sit-
ion, and also Cairo. Rafael reported very confidentially that
znetsov had told Riad on Sunday that, whatever the outcome, UAR
uld go ahead on Indian res. Sisco interjected that we found
znetsov very sensitive Sunday night re any piece of paper with
erican label on it.

Goldberg expressed regret that as a result of Israeli slow and neg-
e reaction, we permitted the Indian res to be submitted first and
ieve priority.[3] Eban was obviously embarrassed and by implica-
↑ indicated this had been a mistake on their part. Rafael later told
:o Eban had bawled him out since he realized there may be two or
:e Council members who will be able to vote for both resolutions
↑ a vote on American res first would have been advantageous.

Rafael confirmed our knowledge that Japanese are consulting
↑rmally on basis of a draft of their own,[4] as a way of avoiding
)arrassment re Indian draft. Israelis have been strongly discour-
↑g Japanese from its submission. While agreeing Japanese should
liscouraged, Pedersen opined that Arabs would not find Japanese
: acceptable.

Goldberg underscored UK problem. We know Caradon has sent
)mpromise text to London, and is anxious to come out as great
↑promiser. In response to Eban's query, Goldberg said he expected
:eat drive over next week to achieve a compromise res. Goldberg
orted to Eban that both Rifai, Riad and Sovs have tried very hard
;et us to negotiate on basis Indian draft, and we have categorical-
efused to use that text as basis. It was agreed that Eban would see
adon promptly in order to keep the UK aboard and to discourage
↑elpful initiatives and changes.

Rafael said American support would be greatest asset for any SC
.. US therefore has enormous leverage since Arabs know that noth-

---

[3] Sisco told Rusk in a November 7 telephone conversation that Katzenbach had
ved White House approval to table the U.S. draft "but in circumstances where Israelis
↓d say go ahead." After the UAR called for a meeting of the Security Council that
↑ing, Goldberg talked to the Israelis, who said the text was acceptable as a final
ed solution but not as a text to table. Goldberg requested the President's approval to
· it. (Notes of telephone conversation with Goldberg and Sisco prepared in Rusk's
e, November 7, 1:45 p.m.; National Archives and Records Administration, RG 59,
< Files: Lot 72 D 192, Telephone Calls) Rostow told Rusk later that the President said
lberg should use his judgment. (Notes of telephone conversation with Walt Rostow,
ember 7, 2:05 p.m.; ibid.) Telegram 2066 from USUN, November 8, reported
lberg's November 7 discussions on this subject with Rafael. (Ibid., Central Files
–69, POL 27 ARAB–ISR/UN)

[4] Telegram 2027 from USUN, November 7, cited in footnote 2, Document 511, also
:mitted the text of an informal Japanese draft.

embracing (*sic*) withdrawal." Rather than take this draf
would probably prefer to accept the Danish-Canadi;
somewhat modified withdrawal formula.[4]

---

[4] Telegram 2027 from USUN, November 7, cited in footnote 2 a
ted the text of the revised Danish-Canadian draft.

---

512. Telegram From the Mission to the United Nat Department of State[1]

New York, Novembe

2071. Goldberg and Eban concerted closely on tacti(
both Indian and US res submitted and SC will convene T
Sisco, Pedersen, and Rafael also present at conversation

Eban, a bit chagrined for having been away in Lo
moving situation unfolded yesterday, reported that h
Brown felt that US draft helped situation and helpe
from embarrassing situation re Indian text. However, (
changes were suggested to Eban in US formulation b
them in London saying that if UK were to open up
require Israelis to seek further changes since res does
cept of direct negotiations. Eban reported that Hussei
a sense of urgency in his London discussions. Eba:
position has hardened in last few days and that Cair(
sigent than position taken here by Riad up to last Frid
ter made a sharp shift in full support of Indian res. Eb
understanding of Hussein–Nasser agreement of Oct 1
Eban found great speculation in London as to where S
ent situation, and what role they have played in chan;
UAR.

Goldberg said he found Riad a troubled man, that
tone has been moderate, but it seemed to change once

---

[1] Source: National Archives and Records Administration, Centr
27 ARAB–ISR/UN. Secret; Immediate; Exdis. Also sent to the White
Immediate to Tel Aviv, and to London. Received at 1835Z.

[2] November 9.

ing can get done diplomatically without US prestige being engaged. Both Eban and Goldberg felt that this point must be made explicitly clear to King. Both Eban and Rafael urged that Pres say to King this evening, that if Hussein wants help he must get behind American res promptly, that he must direct his reps at UN to work within this framework rather than the posture they have adopted of undermining the King's efforts and giving impression to other dels that in effect Jordan is opposed to American text and in favor of Indian res. It was felt that if Pres could indicate that we are trying to get King the UN umbrella he wants in form of UN rep, as a means to starting dialogue, then word exercise going on at UN should come to a halt promptly and US res adopted. Important thing is that King know that US is prepared to help get him the best possible deal in any settlement, provided text is kind US can support.

Finally, it was agreed that Israeli efforts in capitals and at UN would be concentrated on preventing nine votes from being mobilized in favor of Indian text, but they would remain aloof from American draft as the best possible way not to prejudice support for it. Eban said they would do everything to create a "non-bandwagon psychology" for Indian res. It was agreed too that we would bore in with other dels on the idea that Arabs cannot be expected to achieve anything in way of reasonable settlement without having US aboard on a res.

Goldberg

513. Memorandum From Secretary of State Rusk to President Johnson[1]

Washington, undated.

SUBJECT

Present Status of King Hussein's Visit

You will have seen a detailed memorandum of my conversation with King Hussein at lunch yesterday.[2] I met privately with him for a half hour preceding that luncheon and, among other things, referred to his conversations with Ambassador Goldberg in New York.[3] I intended to incorporate the statements made by Ambassador Goldberg to him and by reference to indicate my approval of Ambassador Goldberg's statements.

Following the luncheon, a member of the King's party inquired as to whether I had specifically meant to include a reference to the statements made by Ambassador Goldberg with respect to territorial integrity. I authorized a U.S. official to confirm to the King that I had by reference incorporated Ambassador Goldberg's assurances in my comments.

The net effect of this incorporation is to state that the United States as a matter of policy does not envisage a Jordan which consists only of the East Bank. The United States is prepared to support the return of a substantial part of the West Bank to Jordan with boundary adjustments. However, the United States would use its influence to obtain compensation to Jordan for any territory it is required to give up.

For example, if Jordan is required to give up the Latrun salient, the United States will use its diplomatic and political influence to obtain in compensation access for Jordan to a Mediterranean port in Israel. Finally, although as a matter of policy we do not agree with either Jordan's or Israel's position on Jerusalem, we are prepared to use our diplomatic and political influence to obtain for Jordan a role in

---

[1] Source: Johnson Library, President's Appointment File. Secret; Exdis. The Department of State record copy of this memorandum is dated November 8 and indicates it was drafted by Battle on November 7. An attached note states that Rusk took the memorandum to the President on November 8. (National Archives and Records Administration, RG 59, Central Files 1967–69, POL 7 JORDAN) He presumably took it with him when he attended the President's lunch meeting at 1 p.m. that day. The Middle East situation at the United Nations and plans for the meeting with Hussein were on the agenda. (Johnson Library, National Security File, Rostow Files, Meetings with the President)

[2] See Document 508.

[3] See Document 509 and footnotes 3 and 5 thereto.

Jerusalem. In short, we are prepared to make a maximum diplomatic and political effort to obtain for Jordan the best possible deal in terms of settlement with Israel.

The foregoing was conveyed to the King with a clear statement that we cannot guarantee that everything will be returned to Jordan since, of course, we cannot speak for Israel.

King Hussein's visit has so far gone quite well. During his visit, King Hussein will have made a number of public appearances in addition to meeting with the Senate Foreign Relations Committee and the Foreign Affairs Committee of the House. He appeared on the TV program "Face the Nation" on November 5. He also has delivered an address at Georgetown University and at the National Press Club.

The major theme of the King's public statements is the need for a permanent understanding between Israel and its Arab neighbors. In what he described as the "new and positive approach of the Arabs towards a lasting peace in the Middle East", he has stressed the willingness of the Arab world to consider a political approach to the Arab-Israel question.

Specifically, he has called on Israel to state what it proposes to do with respect to Arab lands it has occupied, Arab refugees it has displaced, and the future of the Old City of Jerusalem. He has stressed the Arab desire for peace and has pointed out that Israel has a choice of either living with the Arabs peacefully or of remaining an isolated outpost in the Arab world.

A separate memorandum is being submitted with respect to the current situation at the United Nations.[4]

Dean Rusk

---

[4] An unsigned, undated memorandum from Rusk to the President with supplementary talking points for his meeting with King Hussein urging that he do everything possible to persuade the Arab delegations, especially the UAR delegation, to accept the U.S. draft resolution, is filed with this memorandum.

514. Memorandum From the President's Special Assistant (Rostow) to President Johnson[1]

Washington, November 8, 1967, 4:15 p.m.

SUBJECT

Talking Points for King Hussein, 5:30 p.m.

Here is the file of background material for your talk with Hussein, including (Tab A)[2] the cable from Arthur Goldberg that Secretary Rusk mentioned at lunch.

In brief, we recommend you make these points:

1. Secretary Rusk and Ambassador Goldberg have told you in detail of their conversations with His Majesty.

2. You wish to reaffirm what they have told him: We are prepared to make a maximum diplomatic and political effort to obtain for Jordan the best possible deal in a settlement with Israel. (The exact language Secretary Rusk used is at Tab B.)[3]

3. Our ability to make good on this reassurance will depend on what kind of arrangement comes out of the UN. We need a resolution that both sides will work with. Anything else would be no more than a hollow tactical victory.

4. We hope His Majesty can persuade his Arab colleagues to accept a workable resolution. (We do not think the Indian draft is workable. We think ours is.)

5. Time is not on the side of peace. What we can do today we may not be able to do 2 or 3 months from now.

If he asks about military aid, you might explain your tough problem in bringing Congress along. You have to say honestly that we can't resume military shipments now, but you hope the situation will improve if there's some movement toward a settlement. Meanwhile, you hope he'll be able to buy what he needs in Western Europe. His turning to Moscow at this stage of the game would just kill chances of progress toward a settlement and make it very hard for us to help.

Walt

---

[1] Source: Johnson Library, President's Appointment File. Secret; Exdis.

[2] A memorandum from Rostow to the President, November 8 at 3:15 p.m., contained a summary of Document 501. Other briefing memoranda from Rostow to the President and talking points prepared in the Department of State for his meeting with King Hussein are in the Johnson Library, President's Appointment File.

[3] Document 513.

515.   Memorandum for the Files[1]

Washington, November 8, 1967, 5:37–6:29 p.m.

SUBJECT

Meeting Between President Johnson, King Hussein and Secretary Rusk on Wednesday, November 8 at 5:30 p.m.

Following the meeting between the President and the King, Secretary Rusk gave me some of the highlights of the discussion.

The meeting was cordial and a few minutes were spent in pleasantries, including the presentation of a cigarette lighter to His Majesty by President Johnson.

Discussions centered on the U.S. resolution currently before the Security Council. The President pressed the King to support the U.S. resolution. He pointed out that the resolution is to be a compromise resolution. The Government of Israel is not happy with the text; the Arabs are not happy with the text. It is difficult to draft a resolution that makes both sides happy, but it is imperative that both sides accept the resolution if it is to be implemented.

King Hussein tried his best to get precision on the clause with respect to withdrawal of Israeli forces. The President replied that it was difficult to be precise in one part and not on the others. There were imprecise statements in the resolution in several respects. The King then said that if it was impossible to be precise as to when or where withdrawal should take place, he hoped that it would be possible to be precise with regard to the question of who was to withdraw. The phraseology of the resolution calling for withdrawal from occupied territories could be interpreted to mean that the Egyptians should withdraw from Gaza and the Jordanians should withdraw from the West Bank. This possibility was evident from the speech by Prime Minister Eshkol in which the Prime Minister had referred to both Gaza and the West Bank as "occupied territory".

The President agreed to talk with Ambassador Goldberg in New York and he and Secretary Rusk told the King that we would be back in touch with him by noon the following day with respect to his suggestion for inclusion of the word "Israeli" before the word withdrawal in the resolution.

---

[1] Source: Johnson Library, National Security File, Country File, Jordan, Vol. IV. Secret. Drafted on November 11. An attached note of November 22 from Saunders to Walt Rostow's secretary, Lois Nivens, instructed her to put a copy in her files, since it was the only record of the President's meeting with King Hussein that would be available in the White House. The meeting took place in the Oval Office. The time and place of the meeting are from the President's Daily Diary. (Ibid.)

The President urged strongly that the Jordanians support the U.S. resolution, and expressed the hope that Jordan would try to get the UAR on board also. The U.S. will use its leverage to bring about a settlement. We have to move one step at a time, however, and the King must understand that we too have problems.

After the King left the President's office he had a brief exchange with Secretary Rusk concerning the provision of arms to Jordan.[2] I heard him say that he hoped for an answer before he departed from the U.S. The Secretary later told me that he had predicated this hope on there being progress made in New York.

Lucius D. Battle

---

[2] The King raised the question of arms with Secretary McNamara at dinner on November 8. According to a memorandum of the conversation, McNamara's reply was "along the lines we want to be as helpful as possible, have some problems at the moment, but would do what we could at a later date." (National Archives and Records Administration, RG 59, Central Files 1967–69, POL 7 JORDAN)

---

516.   Editorial Note

Central Intelligence Agency Information Report B–321/33403–67, November 9, 1967, summarized a report received from an unnamed U.S. citizen who said that on a recent trip to Tel Aviv, some Israeli friends had commented on the attack on the *Liberty*. According to the report, "They said that Dayan personally ordered the attack on the ship and that one of his generals adamantly opposed the action and said, 'This is pure murder.' One of the admirals who was present also disapproved the action, and it was he who ordered it stopped and not Dayan. My friends believe that the attack against the US vessel is also detrimental to any political ambition Dayan may have."

A note dated January 12, 1968, attached to a copy of the report, forwarded it to [*text not declassified*], who commented in a handwritten note: "Thank you. There is only one problem with the story and that is it's not true. Curiously, Dayan and Eshkol are finding themselves natural allies in the more important issues—whatever their personal differences." (Central Intelligence Agency, DO/NE Files: Job 85–01007R, Box 5, Folder 50, Israeli Attack on USS *Liberty* During 1967 Six Day War, Vol. I)

Chief of the Near East Division in the CIA Directorate of Operations Alan D. Wolfe commented on the report in a note of September 20, 1977, to the Deputy Director for Operations forwarding a transcript of a September 19 television interview with Director of Central Intelligence Admiral Stansfield Turner. In the interview, Turner had been asked about a published accusation, based on documents released by the Central Intelligence Agency under the Freedom of Information Act, that Dayan had ordered the attack on the *Liberty*. Wolfe commented that of four documents on this subject released under the Freedom of Information Act in 1977, three were "raw reports which in historical hindsight were garbage, but which appeared worthy of dissemination at the time." (Ibid., Folder 51, Israeli Attack on USS *Liberty* During 1967 Six Day War, Vol. II) The report cited above was one of the three reports to which he referred. The second was an Intelligence Information Cable, TDCS DB–315/02297–67, June 23, 1967, reporting that the general opinion in the Turkish General Staff was that the Israeli attack on the *Liberty* was deliberate. (Ibid.) The third was an Information Report dated July 27, 1967, summarizing a report by an unnamed U.S. citizen that an Israeli acquaintance had told him that Israeli forces knew the ship's identity and what it was doing. The Israeli had said, with reference to the *Liberty* incident, "you've got to remember that in this campaign there is neither time nor room for mistakes." (Ibid.)

In the 1977 note cited above, Wolfe stated that the fourth document was a sanitized version of an intelligence memorandum of June 13, 1967 (Document 284), which concluded that the Israeli aircraft and patrol boats attacking the *Liberty* were unaware of its identity. He noted that a June 21 memorandum (Document 317) re-examined the June 13 conclusions in the light of the Israeli court of inquiry findings and drew a distinction between Israeli Government knowledge of the *Liberty*'s presence in the battle zone and the ignorance of the attacking force. Wolfe concluded, "All rational judgment thus supports the idea of gross stupidity and negligence but not malicious intent." (Central Intelligence Agency, DO/NE Files: Job 85–01007R, Box 5, Folder 51, Israeli Attack on USS *Liberty* During 1967 Six Day War, Vol. II)

517. Telegram From the Mission to the United Nations to the Department of State[1]

New York, November 11, 1967, 1934Z.

2181. Subj: ME—UK Draft Res.

1. Caradon, in call on Goldberg November 11 am, said Brits have felt for past day or two that neither US nor Indian draft res likely to succeed in SC, not so much because of substance as because of circumstances in SC, allegiances and emotions of parties concerned, etc. Thus Brits have thought it best maintain independent position, commit UK to no text and leave way open for UK to come forward with helpful move or compromise.

2. Caradon then gave us copies of UK draft.[2] Said had given text to no one else so far; planned to discuss it with Eban later in day, but not yet pass it to Arabs, though we would let them know he is working on possible compromise res. Said he would like Goldberg's reaction to text but, even more important, advice on how UK best proceed, i.e., is this best time to bring forward such text in effort to reach agreement through some compromise.

3. As preliminary comment, Goldberg said US has no objection such effort by UK in principle. Stressed that acid test we apply to any proposed text is whether it is acceptable enough to both sides so that they would cooperate with UN rep. Goldberg said our preference would be to have no SC res rather than res to which one side objects and therefore refuses cooperate with UN rep.

4. Regarding Caradon's other question, Goldberg noted we have not yet heard reply from King. Though we not optimistic King will succeed in securing favorable reaction from other Arab states to revised US

---

[1] Source: National Archives and Records Administration, RG 59, Central Files 1967–69, POL 27 ARAB–ISR/UN. Secret; Immediate; Exdis. Repeated Priority to London. Received at 2121Z.

[2] The text of the British draft, transmitted in telegram 2178 from USUN, November 11, was largely similar to that of Security Council Resolution 242, adopted November 22 (Document 542), except that (1) the second preambular paragraph reads as follows: "Emphasizing the need to work for a just and lasting peace in which every state in the area can live in security," (2) the opening section of paragraph 1 reads as follows: "Affirms that in fulfillment of the above Charter principles a state of just and lasting peace in the Middle East should be achieved through action in accordance with the following principles:", (3) sub-paragraph 1.ii (1.II) includes the phrase "within secure frontiers" rather than "within secure and recognized boundaries", and (4) paragraph 3 includes the phrase "to promote and assist efforts" rather than "to promote agreement and assist efforts". (National Archives and Records Administration, RG 59, Central Files 1967–69, POL 27 ARAB–ISR/UN)

draft as worked out with King,[3] we believe it essential to await word from King. Moreover, any move by UK before that effort comes to end would only undercut King's efforts. Said we expect reply from King today, probably in pm, and would advise Caradon promptly of reply.

5. Turning to UK text, Goldberg said there are obvious points of difficulty from Israeli point of view. First would be wording of UK text regarding withdrawal. Noted we had pulled Israelis inch by agonizing inch to present wording US res and have been told it is Israeli Cabinet decision not to go any further. Noting Eban has insisted all discussions regarding texts be held only in New York, Goldberg said it our impression Eban staking political future on outcome negotiations regarding SC res and that he more forthcoming regarding withdrawal language than any member of Israeli Cabinet.

6. Second, Goldberg said, there would probably be even stronger reaction to wording of UK text dealing with frontiers (i.e. "right to live in peace within secure frontiers"). Said Eban clearly cannot tolerate language which is not within framework of envisaging established, recognized or agreed frontiers. Language in UK draft could mean return to armistice lines plus demilitarized zones. Noted Israelis had pressed us very hard to use "agreed frontiers" in our res but we had resisted and offered instead "secure and recognized boundaries." Even this accepted reluctantly by Israelis and they will resist strongly going any further, as in UK draft. Pedersen interjected that, in any case, Arabs have not focused on or objected to "secure and recognized boundaries" in US res.

7. Third, Goldberg said Israelis will be most vigorous and unyielding regarding op para 3 of UK draft. Said GOI, while prepared accept language which does not say there should be direct negotiations, will not tolerate language which would leave UN rep latitude to make recommendations to SC for settlement (such as was done by Galo Plaza in Cyprus dispute). Goldberg added this also not his concept of how UN rep should operate. Caradon said UK res does not preclude direct negotiations. Goldberg agreed; but recalled how strongly Israelis had

---

[3] Battle met with King Hussein on November 10 and told him the United States was prepared to make some revisions in paragraph 1 of the U.S. draft resolution, including the change of "withdrawal of armed forces from occupied territories" to "withdrawal of Israeli armed forces from occupied territories", if this would result in a clear signal from the King to the other Arabs and Indians that the new text was acceptable. Rifai, who was also present, immediately proposed more changes. Battle told the King later that day that there was "great disappointment at high levels" at the Jordanian response and that further discussions should take place in New York. (Telegram 67603 to USUN, November 10; ibid., POL 27 ARAB–ISR/UN) That evening Goldberg suggested to the King simply adding the word "Israeli" in connection with withdrawal with no additional revisions. The King indicated that this would be satisfactory to him and that he would present it favorably to the UAR and other Arabs, but he appeared to be pessimistic about the prospects. (Telegram 2172 from USUN, November 11; ibid.)

pressed us to add phrase in our res such as "assisting parties in working out agreed solutions." Possibility of changing op para 3 of UK draft to read "promote and assist efforts to achieve a peaceful and agreed settlement" was raised. Goldberg said he thought Israelis would accept this and perhaps find it preferable to our res.

8. Fourth point to which Israelis might object was raised by Pedersen. He noted op para 1 of UK draft gives impression that it is action in accordance with principles listed there which will bring peace. Israelis will resist this strongly, for they insist upon wording which conveys concept that just and lasting peace includes or encompasses or embraces certain principles, is not the result of specific action under those principles.

9. Caradon said he understood points we had made, that he would present UK text to Eban, and ask him directly what sticking points would be. This is purpose in consulting Eban. After securing Eban's reaction, Caradon said he will then have to decide how to go forward. Repeated belief that some new formulation is necessary in order to provide face-saving device on both sides. Thus, subject to assurance he not interfering with present US efforts, he would want to go forward very promptly. Noted he has authority circulate UK text and seek agreement on it. Also said UK not prepared permit SC failure without some further effort, that UK determined not to let SC just peter out. Also added that something like UK text is essential for UK's own position, since under present instructions UK "could" vote for either Indian or US res. He said that his present thinking is to circulate UK text so that UK then in position it would not have to vote for either or both Indian and US reses.

10. Goldberg told Caradon his effort would interfere with our efforts if he went ahead, even to discuss UK text with Eban, before we receive a definitive reply from King. Caradon said he understood and would anxiously await word from us regarding King's reply.

11. Just before meeting broke up, Pedersen sought clarification of UK instructions, asking whether Caradon's comment UK "could" vote for either or both Indian and US reses meant UK instructed vote for both. Pedersen also asked what effect would be in deciding how to vote on Indian and US drafts, where one of parties officially states that it will refuse to cooperate with UN rep. Caradon said he not saying anything to anyone else about UK ability to vote for either text. Avoided clear answers on both questions. Following meeting, Hope stressed to MisOff that he had pushed Caradon very hard to lay all cards on table with Goldberg; hoped US understood that it absolutely essential Caradon soon proceed with consultations re UK text so that situation thereby created in which UK can avoid voting for Indian draft res.

Goldberg

518.   Memorandum From John Foster and Harold H. Saunders of
        the National Security Council Staff to the President's Special
        Assistant (Rostow)[1]

Washington, November 11, 1967.

SUBJECT

Mid-East Terrorism

Jim Critchfield[2] is right in saying that terrorism increased markedly a week ago. However, it has been quiet again for the last three days.

By and large, there were few incidents during the summer. They
began to increase at the end of September, and since 1 October there
have been 22. The situation was serious enough by late October that the
Israelis asked us to arrange a meeting between the Israeli and Jordanian
military to discuss ways to stop infiltration. Hussein's advisers talked
him out of it, to the Israelis' disgust. The most serious incidents took
place in the few days after 3 November, and on 7 November the Israelis
wrote a note to the UNSC. Those incidents followed a week of relative
quiet, which may have resulted from caution after the previous week's
sinking of the *Elath* and shelling of the Suez refinery.

There are several possible explanations for this pattern:

1. The increase could just be part of the Arabs picking themselves
up after the war and getting back to business, rather than the result of
any particular decision in Damascus. After the war, the Arabs were so
disorganized that they could mount only minor operations, and they
weren't sure what they ought to be attacking. By September, they had
recovered enough and the political situation had solidified enough to
make conditions ripe for terrorism. On top of that, Arabs viewed the
Israeli line as hardening and became increasingly disillusioned with the
continuing stalemate.

2. The increase could be the hard-liners' answer to Khartoum.
Having failed to persuade their brethren to continue the fight, they may
have decided that this was their only recourse.

3. The Soviets may or may not have relaxed restraint. We have no
clear recent evidence either of a strong restraining influence or of incitement. Nat Davis has confirmed his view in talking with State and CIA

---

[1] Source: Johnson Library, National Security File, Name File, Saunders Memos.
Secret. A handwritten note on the memorandum reads: "For 2:00 p.m. meeting." Rostow
sent a copy to Eugene Rostow with a covering memorandum of the same date.

[2] James H. Critchfield, Chief of the Near East and South Asia Division in the
Directorate of Operations, Central Intelligence Agency.

colleagues that the Soviets are unlikely to see their interests served by renewed hostilities at this time. While they no doubt see the risks in renewed terrorism, they have not acted very strongly to enforce restraint and have tended to underestimate the dangers from this sort of thing. Vinogradov in Cairo and the Soviet naval visits don't contribute to restraint.

Our view is that Hussein himself is doing his best to stop the terrorists who move across Jordan from Syria. The Israelis disagree and say that Hussein could not possibly be unaware of Jordanian military complicity. They cite such events as Jordanian artillery joining in one Jordan River fight between Israelis and terrorists, while we think the Jordanians were probably just replying to anti-terrorist shells that landed in Jordan. There is no question, however, that individual Jordanians are becoming involved, so this may be another case of the King not being in complete control. Officials, soldiers, police and people along the infiltration routes are becoming less and less inclined to interfere with the terrorists.

The Israelis have assured us that they won't retaliate in present circumstances but the British military attaché thinks a raid is imminent. What the Israelis do will depend partly on whether they think Hussein is being cooperative in reaching a political settlement and on how much they think we're backing him. I shouldn't think they'd do anything while the UNSC is still in session. No Israelis have been killed recently, and this has helped keep the Israeli popular cry for revenge manageable.

Our view is that #2 above is the most likely explanation. This is consistent with all the Khartoum and post-Khartoum evidence, and so far we lack any convincing evidence of a specific Soviet decision or encouragement. The Syrians have never needed encouragement in this field, and the Soviets have never been remarkably successful in restraining them, even when Moscow tried.

Hal
John

519. **Telegram From the Embassy in Lebanon to the Department of State[1]**

Beirut, November 10, 1967, 1256Z.

3905. Reference: Beirut 3901.[2] From Robert Anderson.

1. I just visited with Ambassador Ghaleb.[3] He told me that he had received a message from Nasser "some time ago" saying that the Ambassador would expect a call from me when I had received some "word from my country." I told him that so far as my country was concerned they still thought I was in Iraq where communication was impossible and that I had only advised them this morning that I was back in Beirut and would be here until Sunday when I would return to Baghdad.

2. I told him that Ambassador Metwally in Iraq told me that he would advise me through Ghaleb what the Egyptian attitude was toward the American resolution. I also stated that it seemed to me that the American resolution contained all the points covered in my discussions in Cairo with the possible exception that the representative of the UN instead of being required to go to the Middle East would consult with both sides in a less conspicuous manner, which might be more effective in getting results. He stated that he would either receive a wire from Nasser today or would inquire as to Nasser's attitude. I told him that it was going to be very difficult, if not impossible, for me to return to Cairo not only because I had been away so long, but because I wanted to have the opportunity of visiting with my old friend dating from Finance Ministry days, Japanese Prime Minister Sato, while he was in the States. I said I had been invited to dinner with Sato. I thought that I should cast considerable doubt on any possibility of returning to Cairo

---

[1] Source: National Archives and Records Administration, RG 59, Central Files 1967–69, POL 27–14 ARAB–ISR. Secret; Priority; Nodis. Received on November 11 at 4:17 a.m. Rostow sent a copy of this telegram, along with telegrams 3901 and 3908 from Beirut (see footnotes 2 and 5 below), to the President on November 11 with a memorandum noting that Anderson reported that Nasser wanted to see him again. The memorandum stated: "We shall have a recommendation for you shortly—conscious of your grave reservations in this matter." (Johnson Library, National Security File, Country File, Lebanon)

[2] Telegram 3901 from Beirut, November 10, transmitted a message from Anderson, who had arrived in Beirut from Baghdad the previous evening. He reported that the UAR Ambassador to Iraq had told him on November 6 that he had received a message from Cairo asking that Anderson return to Cairo. Anderson stated that he planned to return to Baghdad no later than November 12, return to Beirut on November 14 or 15, and then return to the United States unless he was advised that he should go to Cairo. (National Archives and Records Administration, RG 59, Central Files 1967–69, POL 27–14 ARAB–ISR)

[3] UAR Ambassador to Lebanon Abdul Hamid Ghaleb.

until I knew more about the Department's attitude. When I told Ghaleb that it was doubtful that I could return to Cairo he asked me if this would be true even though President Nasser considered it very important. I replied by saying that I would not foreclose any matter if Nasser thought it of sufficient importance although perhaps the same thing could be accomplished either by Nasser sending someone to meet me here or by communication through Ghaleb. He stated he would explore this possibility if Nasser thought it sufficiently important.

3. Ghaleb then asked me if I knew about the current happenings at the Security Council and I told him I did not. He spent a long time telling me about the US request for Abba Eban to speak following Mahmoud Riad,[4] and stated that we insisted on "our colleague" speaking second following Riad. He said "Isn't it possible for US to do anything which doesn't appear one-sided, do the Americans have to take the pro-Israeli point of view in everything including procedure?" His telephone rang almost constantly and he told me that he was receiving continuous calls from Lebanese protesting that the Americans were insisting even on procedural matters to accommodate the Israelis. He said that if the Americans did want Abba Eban to speak second, why did we have to propose it? Why not somebody else? Impression from Arab side is that US deliberately antagonizing the Arabs and he said he was worried about the strong reaction, even in Lebanon.

4. I said that since he had raised the question of the Security Council, I was at a loss to understand why UAR had suddenly demanded a meeting of the Security Council. I thought his President had felt, during my conversations with him, that more could be accomplished quietly and behind scenes, and that perhaps an agreed resolution (whether with US label or not) could be taken to the Security Council where the procedure would be more or less pro forma. He stated "I cannot speak officially, but it is my impression that we feared the outbreak of another Israeli attack either against us, Syria or Jordan and that this attack would be less likely if the Security Council were in session". I have no idea as to whether he is expressing a personal judgment, just offering an excuse, or whether he knows more than he is telling me. The rest of the conversation was rather academic in which he said that he thought Israel had initially been established as a cat's paw so that either we, the Soviets, or other major power could use this small country to

---

[4] Reference is to a procedural dispute in the Security Council on November 9 over whether Israel should be heard after the UAR, which had requested the meeting, or later in the proceedings. A U.S. motion to hear both the UAR and Israel as parties to the dispute before the Security Council members spoke failed of adoption by one vote. (Telegram 2138 from USUN, November 10; National Archives and Records Administration, RG 59, Central Files 1967–69, POL 27 ARAB–ISR/UN)

our advantage in the Arab world but that the cat's paw was rapidly becoming the cat and they did not know where it would bite next.

5. He stated that he would call me in Beirut if he heard anything else from Cairo.[5]

Porter

---

[5] Telegram 3908 from Beirut, November 10, reported that Ghaleb had just notified Anderson that Nasser had indicated he was very anxious for discussions with Anderson in Cairo. (Ibid., POL 27–14 ARAB–ISR)

---

520. Telegram From Acting Secretary of State Katzenbach to Secretary of State Rusk in Williamsburg[1]

Washington, November 11, 1967, 2138Z.

CAP 67946. The following is from John Walsh for your information.

Memorandum for the President.

Subject: Robert Anderson Trip to Cairo.

Discussion: Robert Anderson informs us that Nasser is very anxious to have him go back to Cairo for further discussions. Anderson has indicated some reluctance but has been careful to leave his options open. We here had at first felt that it would not be desirable for Anderson to visit Cairo on the ground that the trip might give rise to public speculations on the part of the Egyptians which would give the appearance of division within the U.S. Government.[2]

However, after consultation with Ambassador Goldberg, I agree with him that Anderson should go to Cairo, as quickly as possible. We do not want it said that we did not do everything possible to bring about a settlement, and that we turned down a direct request from Nasser to engage in further talks. Moreover, since King Hussein has

---

[1] Source: National Archives and Records Administration, RG 59, Central Files, 1967–69, TRV ANDERSON, ROBERT B. Secret. A handwritten notation on the telegram indicates it was received at 2245Z. According to Rusk's Appointment Book, the Secretary was in Williamsburg, Virginia, to attend the Gridiron Dinner at the Convention Center. A notation on the telegram indicates Rusk read it.

[2] Telegram 65484 to Beirut, November 7, transmitted a message from Rusk to Anderson stating that it had been concluded that it was best for him not to return to Cairo at that time; his return would cast doubt on statements made in Washington about his private status and could cause confusion in New York. (Ibid., POL 27–14 ARAB–ISR)

asked us to try to bring the UAR on board, a further talk with Nasser in a sense would represent a step to keep faith with Hussein. Since Hussein will be talking with the Arabs in New York until tomorrow night, prompt action is important.

We would ask Anderson while in Cairo to do the following:

1. He would make it plain to Nasser that there is no division within the U.S. Government. We cannot support an unworkable UN resolution.

2. We are continuing to try to work out a UN resolution with which both sides can live. Such a resolution would not in itself produce a Middle Eastern settlement, but it would open the way toward one which would be as fair and as helpful to both sides as possible.

Ambassador Goldberg is preparing talking points on the negotiating problem in New York for Anderson's use. In agreeing to return to Cairo, Anderson would tell the UAR Ambassador with whom he is in contact that we expect his return will not be followed by UAR publicity attacking the U.S. or the President for our attitude on the Middle East.

Recommendation:

That you authorize us to tell Anderson to proceed to Cairo.

Acting Secretary

---

521. Telegram From the Department of State to the Embassy in Lebanon[1]

Washington, November 12, 1967, 0130Z.

68061. For Anderson from Under Secretary.

1. Following are contingency instructions referred to in Flash message you have received.[2]

---

[1] Source: National Archives and Records Administration, RG 59, Central Files 1967–69, POL 27–14 ARAB–ISR. Secret; Immediate; Nodis. Drafted by Popper, cleared by Battle, and approved by Acting Secretary Katzenbach.

[2] Telegram 68058 to Beirut, November 12, for Anderson from Katzenbach, stated that the Department was sending him contingency instructions to be used if a high-level review of the desirability of his prompt return to Cairo resulted in an affirmative decision. (Ibid.)

2. You should tell Ghaleb that US move to hear UAR and Israel prior to members of SC was strictly in accordance with rules and practice of SC for 20 years. US move was to permit both to be heard, with UAR speaking first. That was course of equity. Failure SC to support this position set Arab cause back because it resulted in unusual and inequitable procedure and made Israel aggrieved party. It also created rancorous atmosphere instead of reasonable one. You should tell him that neither UAR nor Jordanian Dels had any objection to Israel speaking in customary position and that Sovs and Indians are to be blamed for producing such a bad result for Arabs. You should say US took initiative because we believe in equity, would have done so likewise if situation had been reversed, and because issue was sprung in SC one minute before meeting had opened, members previously having been informed that first two speakers would be UAR and Israel. (Preferable you get this issue out of way with Ghaleb so you do not have to raise it in Cairo.)

3. We would like you to tell Nasser that US res before SC is a serious proposal which we are convinced contains best prospects for peaceful solution in ME. Indians res on other hand is unworkable, cannot be made workable by tinkering, and would not produce real progress in area even if it had nine votes, which we doubt. You should leave him in no doubt that US would not use its influence in implementation of such a res.

4. You should also tell him that US has continued to give careful consideration to views of Arab Dels in New York as to their problems and concerns. While we have never thought we could produce text completely satisfactory either to Arabs or to Israel, we have endeavored to cover each important element of current situation. Taking into account legitimate Arab concerns and suggestions, Amb Goldberg yesterday told King Hussein that US would be willing to add word "Israeli" before "Armed Forces" in first operative paragraph. USG took this decision with considerable hesitation at strong Arab urging. You should also point out that US had previously made another significant change in text by substituting word "territories" for "territory," which we had also done on basis of concerns and advice of our Arab friends.

5. In addition, Amb Goldberg had been instructed to make in SC a specific statement of diplomatic support which US would extend in interests of a successful outcome under US res. This had followed private statements of which President Nasser must be aware. Specifically, Amb Goldberg stated following: "On behalf of my government, I pledge to SC and to parties concerned that our diplomatic and political influence would be exerted under this draft res in support of

efforts of UN rep to achieve a fair and equitable settlement so that all in area can live in peace, security and tranquillity."[3]

6. Amb. Goldberg also made in SC on behalf of USG following significant statement with respect to method of achieving objectives of res and to positions of those directly concerned:

"How these objectives can be achieved in practice, what modalities, methods, and steps may be can only be worked out in consultations with parties, which special rep would undertake.
"In our view all objectives must be taken fully into account in concept and in practice in achievement of common aim. Furthermore, text of US res does not prejudice positions of those directly concerned."

7. USG feels it has now gone extra mile in meeting Arab concerns, taking into account that objective is not just a res but to set into motion a process of diplomatic action within framework of UN with which States in area would be expected to cooperate. Further efforts of verbalism will only endanger entire project and set back whole process of movement towards honorable peace. Much more significant for Arabs in current context is that this res contains basic principles critical to them, if not in exact words they would wish, while also having two major plus factors which would not follow from texts more perfectly worded from UAR point of view: commitment of US political backing and prospects of Israeli cooperation with reps in spite of its basic view that there should only be direct negotiations.

8. You should, therefore, strongly urge Nasser to instruct Riad to accept res as modified and in concert with Rifai (Jordan) seek to assure its passage in SC.

9. If Nasser objects to fact of US sponsorship you should say US had told Arabs when we first gave text to them that it need not have US sponsorship. We were compelled to move ourselves only when UAR suddenly called SC mtg and India submitted its text; we are not interested in credit but in results.

10. You should not negotiate on texts on grounds you have a message but no authority to discuss language. If Nasser should suggest any further changes you should repeat that your advice is to take res as it would now be modified, noting that it would be tragedy for opportunity now available with full US support to be missed, that same opportunity would not likely be there two months from now, and that we are convinced further verbal efforts will jeopardize everything. FYI Only. Israelis have said in New York that their Cabinet has taken policy decision against inclusion of words "all" or "occupied in the recent conflict"

---

[3] Goldberg said this in a statement before the Security Council on November 9. For text, see the Department of State *Bulletin*, December 18, 1967, pp. 834–836.

as applied to territories, words Nasser would be most likely to request. Our own assessment is that we have reached end of road with Israel on wording of any major importance to UAR. End FYI.

11. For full background on our current thinking, please read USUN's 2305,[4] Amb. Goldberg's Nov 9 statement in SC sent all ME posts, and Secy's circular message to all Ambs (Deptel 67978)[5] before you see Nasser.

12. In summary the guts of the American position in the UN is simply that any solution of problems in the Middle East will have to be worked out in detail by the countries involved with the assistance of a special UN representative and cannot be negotiated in advance in the Security Council. Therefore, any resolution in the SC which attempts to tip the scales in such a way as to make the UN special representative unacceptable to Israel or to key Arab states will have no result whatsoever in terms of any solution of the basic problems. We cannot overemphasize that the USG will not support in the SC or subsequently any resolution with which the parties will not cooperate. You should know that the Israelis do not like the current US resolution and that it represents maximum with which they will cooperate. Our effort is to get a UN representative with whom the parties will talk and if this can be accomplished, we will give our full diplomatic support to his mission. The Indian or similar resolutions are sure non-starters in substantive terms and we will not be associated now or later with their failure to achieve peace.

13. Please report by Flash tel repeated to USUN any observations Nasser has. These will be very helpful and appreciated.

14. You are authorized at your discretion to draw upon the above material in conferring with any Arab official whether or not a further meeting with Nasser is approved.[6]

Rusk

---

[4] The reference is in error; telegram 2305 from USUN is dated November 15. (National Archives and Records Administration, RG 59, Central Files 1967–69, POL 27 ARAB–ISR/UN)

[5] Circular telegram 67978, November 10, transmitted a message from Rusk to all ambassadors instructing them to stress that the key to a political solution in the Middle East lay in the five principles in the President's June 19 statement and the U.S. resolution. It stated that the United States was convinced that the principal parties concerned could cooperate without insuperable difficulties with a Special UN Representative to work out a political solution on the basis of the U.S. resolution, that it had made it clear to the principal parties concerned that U.S. influence would be exerted under that resolution for a fair and equitable settlement, and that the Indian resolution was not workable, since Israel had already publicly rejected it. (Ibid.)

[6] Anderson was not authorized to return to Cairo. Instead, Bergus, acting on instructions from Washington, conveyed the substance of paragraphs 3–8, 12, and 13 in writing to Salah Hassan of the UAR Foreign Office and discussed it with him in detail. Salah Hassan later telephoned Bergus to tell him that the message had been delivered to Acting Foreign Minister Feki. (Telegram 950 from Cairo, November 14; ibid., POL 27 ARAB–ISR) Telegram 68090 to Cairo, November 13, had instructed Bergus to deliver the substance of the message. (Ibid., TRV ANDERSON, ROBERT B.)

522. Telegram From the Mission to the United Nations to the Department of State[1]

New York, November 13, 1967, 0118Z.

2198. Subj: Middle East—Goldberg–Caradon Talk Nov. 12. Ref: USUN 2178.[2]

1. In mid-day talk Nov. 12, Caradon told Goldberg he had seen King Hussein alone previous day. Said King had preferred not to talk about texts of SC reses, but had made it clear he recognizes both US support for and Israeli acquiescence in any res are essential. Caradon commented he found King greatly disturbed and that he (Caradon) was for first time beginning to fear entire situation too much for King. Caradon said King plans leave NY Nov. 12 pm, first for Paris, then London, and return to Amman in about one week.

2. Caradon also reported one-hour meeting with Riad earlier on Nov. 12, saying he had stressed to Riad it would be madness for Arabs to throw away what res offers them and US offer to put its weight behind such res. He said he seeing reps of India and Iraq later in day and would stress same point. Riad's reaction, according to Caradon, was that UAR could not sign blank check for Israel to draw boundaries wherever Israel wants them.

3. Caradon said he had discussed UK draft res with Eban and, thereafter, with Danes and Canadians. After describing Eban's reaction briefly (texts of comments and aide-mémoire Eban has given Caradon sent septel)[3] Caradon said it his feeling UK could go all way or nearly all way to meet Israeli objections.

4. Caradon said it continues to be his feeling that there will be need for new draft res without any of present labels (US or Indian) by middle of week and he plans seek London's approval to consult with Arabs re UK draft res, as revised to take into account Israeli objections. His aim, Caradon said, is to have "winning horse" all saddled and ready to go so that, at appropriate moment, stable door can be opened.

5. Goldberg asked whether Caradon would propose, assuming he gets ok from London to discuss revised UK draft res with Arabs, to have

---

[1] Source: National Archives and Records Administration, RG 59, Central Files 1967–69, POL 27 ARAB–ISR/UN. Secret; Priority; Exdis. Repeated Priority to Amman, and to London and Tel Aviv. Dated November 12 in error; received on November 13 at 0317Z.

[2] See footnote 2, Document 517.

[3] Telegram 2196 from USUN, November 13. (National Archives and Records Administration, RG 59, Central Files 1967–69, POL 27 ARAB–ISR/UN)

further talks with Israelis. Caradon made no commitment, simply commented he would at least consult with us again before moving.

Goldberg

---

523. Information Memorandum From the President's Special Assistant (Rostow) to President Johnson[1]

Washington, November 13, 1967, 8:45 a.m.

Mr. President:

RE: Bob Anderson

1. After you spoke to me last evening I called Nick Katzenbach. He told me the attached cable[2] had been promptly despatched after you spoke to Sec. Rusk—definitely closing out the trip to Cairo.

2. Re contingency instructions: He said he took full responsibility for their despatch:

—the situation in New York justified raising with you again the possibility of Anderson's seeing Nasser;
—the lack of communications to Baghdad, where Anderson was going from Beirut, made it important that the instructions be available in Beirut, should you have agreed the trip would go forward.

Nick still believes the move was correct.

3. In general, he feels the national interest in doing all that is humanly possible to get a resolution—and a UN negotiator in the field—outweighs the common reluctance to use a private contact with Nasser.

Walt

---

[1] Source: Johnson Library, National Security File, Country File, Lebanon. Secret; Sensitive. A handwritten note "PS, 11/13/67" on the memorandum indicates the President saw it.

[2] Telegram 68086 to Beirut, November 12, a copy of which is attached, transmitted a message from Rusk to Anderson stating that after a thorough review of all aspects of the situation, it was decided he should not proceed to Cairo.

524. Memorandum From Nathaniel Davis of the National Security Council Staff to the President's Special Assistant (Rostow)[1]

Washington, November 13, 1967.

SUBJECT

The Situation in New York, November 13—4:00 P.M.

It is increasingly unlikely we can forestall the introduction of the Latin American's resolution. Their present plans are to put it in tomorrow. (Text at Tab A.)[2] The withdrawal clause is identical to the LA resolution in the GA last summer—which we voted for ("Israel to withdraw all its forces from all territories occupied by it as a result of the recent conflict").[3]

It is pretty clear the Israelis won't buy the LA resolution. Its withdrawal phraseology is even worse from their point of view than the Indian one.

We have just talked to Lord Caradon, who has his own compromise resolution (Tab B).[4] The Israelis don't like this resolution either, but it is beginning to look increasingly attractive when compared to the viable alternatives. We are encouraging Lord Caradon—without committing ourselves on the text—to talk with the parties and see if he can get some measure of Israeli cooperation. He will have to make changes in text to accomplish this, as the Israelis strongly oppose his present formulation.

Discussion of the Japanese text (Tab C)[5] does not seem very active at the moment—probably because the Arabs are climbing onto the LA draft (with its history of U.S. support). The Japanese draft is not substantially different in its withdrawal clause from the LA text.

We expect to make one more effort to hold off the Latin Americans. The problem is that their resolution would have nine votes. Its weakness is that Israeli non-cooperation would make it extremely difficult for the UN representative to be useful and effec-

---

[1] Source: Johnson Library, National Security File, Agency File, United Nations, Vol. 7. Secret. A copy was sent to Saunders.

[2] The tabs are attached but not printed. Tab A is telegram 2200 from USUN, November 13. Another copy is in the National Archives and Records Administration, RG 59, Central Files 1967–69, POL 27 ARAB–ISR/UN.

[3] See footnote 4, Document 340.

[4] Telegram 2178 from USUN, November 11; see footnote 2, Document 517.

[5] The relevant portion of telegram 2027 from USUN, November 7; see footnote 2, Document 511.

tive. If the members of the Security Council can be convinced of this, the LA's might be prevailed upon not to press their resolution to a vote and withdraw in favor of a modified British draft.

Both the Indian and U.S. drafts are fading. If the LA's really push their draft, we shall have a difficult decision on how to vote. The prospects are for furious maneuvering between now and Wednesday,[6] when the Security Council next meets. Our efforts will be directed at convincing the parties that Israeli cooperation (and our own) are worth compromising for.

ND

---

[6] November 15.

---

525. **Telegram From the Embassy in Lebanon to the Department of State**[1]

Beirut, November 14, 1967, 1025Z.

3998. Ref: Beirut 3933.[2] For Secretary from Anderson.

1) Following message for Secretary [from] Anderson now in Iraq delivered to me morning November 14 by his business associate John McCrane. I quote verbatim text from Anderson's handwritten notes. This message covers conversation Anderson had November 12 with UAR Amb Metwally.

2) "Message of President Nasser to RBA through Ambassador Metwally.

Para (A)—The Americans did not mention clearly and frankly the question of withdrawal and the Arabs cannot accept a draft of withdrawal that is not detailed (Note: I think he meant explicit rather than detailed) and expressed with frankness. This would be against the principles and Charter of the UN which says that no profit or territorial gains are allowed to be secured by force.

---

[1] Source: National Archives and Records Administration, RG 59, Central Files 1967–69, POL 27–14 ARAB–ISR. Secret; Immediate; Nodis. Received at 7:33 a.m.

[2] Telegram 3933 from Beirut, November 13, reported that Ambassador Porter had sent word to Anderson that he should not go to Cairo. (Ibid.)

Para (B)—The first part of the draft contains many subjects such as peace with justice and this means that all the subjects are connected and the timing for the execution of any subject is not known. The logical consequence to assume is that the withdrawal will not be completed unless all other requirements are executed such as peace with justice.

Para (C)—The statement in the draft concerning *mutual* recognition can be considered a new text not found in any previous draft. This is considered a new request by the US. This is different from US confirmation that *mutual* recognition would not be mentioned.

Para (D)—What is said about borders, for example 'the secured and recognized borders' is a new text. To execute this subject there would have to be *mutual* agreement on both sides and this would require a recognition prohibited by the Khartoum Conference.

Para (E)—The draft concerning refugees is very mild and contains nothing obligatory (Note: I am sure he means obligations by Israel) and takes no note of the UN resolutions on this subject.

Para (F)—The reference to demilitarized areas in the draft is considered an echo of the Israeli spokesmen who have spoken of 'greater Israel' and the disarmament of the Sinai. The latest statement on this subject is that made by the Chairman of the Committee on Foreign Affairs in the Knesset on November 10 when he stated that Israel wanted to disarm Sinai. This would make the UAR very anxious and is one reason not to approve the US draft.

Para (G)—The draft in setting out the mission of the representative of the Secretary General of the UN gives the idea that direct contact is necessary between the Arabs and the Israelis and this has not been in any draft resolution before.

Para (H)—Generally, the US resolution is many steps backward when compared with other drafts offered in the UN or through contacts outside the SC or the GA up to now. It is a step backward from the draft the US and Soviets agreed to and which the UAR, after study, refused.

Para (I)—The offering of this draft cannot be final as it is. The chance is still open in front of the US to prove its desire to reach a just political solution to the Israel–Arab dispute.

Para (J)—Riad has said he is very keen to cooperate with the US representative in New York and has confirmed to Amb Goldberg that even if the SC could not reach any result this will not mean that the contacts between the US and the UAR will be stopped.

Para (K)—He (Nasser) is anxious to see me again and continue our talks.

Para (L)—End of message from President Nasser."[3]

3) Anderson's present plans, unless things go wrong in Iraq, are return Beirut tomorrow November 15, overnight Beirut, depart for US via London morning November 16, arriving NY either November 17 or 18.

4) McCrane reports Anderson feels he is going back on what Nasser will assume is personal commitment, if he does not visit Cairo. Anderson worried about implications and has no appropriate rationale for explaining to Egyptians why he not going. He had originally tried avoid return visit as his previous messages indicated, but now he understandably feels Nasser expects him.

5) He starting to spread thin excuse in Iraq that McCrane brought him news family illness in US where he may have to return quickly.

6) Anderson's concern will not be lessened by *Cairo–NY Times* November 12 article, carried *Herald Tribune,* November 13, which seems to be official UARG leak that Anderson planning revisit Nasser soon.

7) I do not know what if anything Anderson will tell Amb Metwally in Baghdad. Anderson informs me he already has had talk with Metwally in which he (Anderson) bore down hard on damage done by Heikal article and asked Metwally pass on to Nasser his strong feeling that it hurt Arab cause and cause of peace. Metwally reporting this to Nasser. Anderson describes Metwally as fairly strong individual who seems have good connections.

8) According McCrane, Anderson still prepared go to Cairo if Dept wishes, and if he can help. He could leave Beirut for Cairo morning November 16. Our recent experience makes it clear it impossible get messages to Anderson in Baghdad except through courier. Anderson tried send his son Beirut with message night November 12 but flights weathered in. He apologizes to Secretary for delay.

9) McCrane prepared return Baghdad tonight if we wish pass message. Otherwise I will see Anderson in Beirut about 1030 local November 15. Please advise.

Porter

---

[3] Bergus reported in telegram 961 from Cairo, November 15, that Acting Foreign Minister Feki had asked him to call at 5 p.m. that day to hand him a copy of Nasser's message to Anderson as translated by the UAR Foreign Office. Feki said the message had been sent before Bergus had given the substance of Anderson's contingency instructions to the UAR Government. Bergus gave Feki the substance of comments by Goldberg on Nasser's message. (Ibid., POL 27 ARAB–ISR/UN) Goldberg's comments are in telegram 2239 from USUN, November 14. (Ibid., POL 27 ARAB–ISR) The copy of the message given to Bergus, which he sent with a November 24 letter to Battle, is filed with a letter of December 8 from Battle to Bergus. (Department of State, NEA Files: Lot 71 D 79, 1967–1968) For Bergus' delivery of the substance of Anderson's contingency instructions, see footnote 6, Document 521.

526. Memorandum From Nathaniel Davis of the National Security Council Staff to the President's Special Assistant (Rostow)[1]

Washington, November 16, 1967.

SUBJECT

The Situation in New York, November 16, 3:30 P.M.

Lord Caradon has just tabled his resolution (attached).[2] He met with five Arabs this morning and got support from all of them (the "Steering Group" consisting of Morocco, Lebanon, Iraq and Jordan) except the UAR. The UAR asked him to make two changes (marked on your copy) which he refused to do. The UAR is still considering its position.

The Israelis don't like the text—but it is better than the Latin American one (which the Latin Americans have not yet submitted and may hold off on). The real question is whether the Israelis will state their objections but agree to cooperate with the representative, or whether they will announce that they will not cooperate.

If the Israelis go into full opposition we shall have a difficult choice in deciding what to do ourselves—vote in favor, abstain or veto. It is possible that this decision could come as early as tomorrow, but we are not likely to be on the spot today.

Goldberg is seeing Riad at Riad's request right now. The Security Council meets at 4:00 p.m. (probably a half an hour late, so better say 4:30 p.m.) and Caradon is the only one presently listed to speak.

ND

---

[1] Source: Johnson Library, National Security File, Agency File, United Nations, Vol. 9. Secret. A copy was sent to Saunders. Rostow sent this memorandum to the President at 4:50 p.m. with a covering memorandum commenting that it indicated that "we are the closest we have come in New York to movement on the Middle East" and that it posed an issue "which you may have to decide tomorrow—or even, less likely, today."

[2] Not attached. The text of the draft resolution as introduced that day (UN document S/8247) is in telegram 2296 from USUN, November 16. (National Archives and Records Administration, RG 59, Central Files 1967–69, POL 27 ARAB–ISR/UN) Caradon met with Goldberg at 10 a.m. on November 16 and indicated his intention to table the draft resolution. Goldberg told him the U.S. efforts to reach agreement with the UAR on the U.S. draft had apparently broken down, and Caradon could go ahead with U.S. support. (Telegram 2336 from USUN, November 17; ibid.)

527.   Telegram From the Mission to the United Nations to the Department of State[1]

New York, November 17, 1967, 0356Z.

2331. Middle East.

1. Goldberg saw Riad at his request at 3:15 this afternoon. Mohammed Riad, El Kony, and new person whose name we do not know, were present for UAR. Sisco, Buffum, and Pedersen with Goldberg.

2. Riad opened conversation by saying that he had seen Lord Caradon this morning. Understood Caradon was introducing res. Said he had given Caradon his comments. It was still his feeling withdrawal language was not specific enough in UK text, as was case in US text. Problem remained at same point. Question of withdrawal must be specific if we are to avoid problems in future. Are we to have full or vague withdrawal. If it is vague, nothing is being accomplished.

2. Goldberg noted he had stated US policy explicitly yesterday in SC.[2] Asked Riad whether he found anything in that statement of policy that caused him difficulty. Riad said yes, withdrawal statement was difficulty. Goldberg said he regretted Riad had not come to Arab working group meeting yesterday. Lebanese FonMin had referred to Arab understanding there would be border adjustments and wondered why US had not spoken of this. Goldberg replied that he did not feel US had right to say anything that would prejudice Arab or Israeli positions. Riad repeated that vagueness on withdrawal was problem. Said he would make short statement this afternoon to make UAR position clear, how withdrawal must be behind June 5 line. He thought it very important to know, when UN rep comes, on what basis he comes. Principle of no territorial gains must be very clear; withdrawal must be very clear. UAR plans must be based on principle of no territorial gains. It was up to SC to decide on res.

3. Goldberg said that on behalf of USG he had tried hard to produce an acceptable formula. Fahmy had approached MisOff with certain comments yesterday. These comments had not been dissimilar from

---

[1] Source: National Archives and Records Administration, RG 59, Central Files 1967–69, POL 27 ARAB–ISR/UN. Secret; Priority; Nodis. Received at 12:03 a.m.

[2] The text of Goldberg's November 15 statement in the Security Council is printed in Department of State *Bulletin,* December 18, 1967, pp. 836–841.

conversation with Riad on Sunday (Nov. 12).[3] From them both he understood that only difficulties on our text were withdrawal language and possibly word "mutual". Fahmy had asked question what our reaction would be if certain changes proposed. He had replied to Fahmy that we want a workable text and that he did not expect either UAR or Israel to give up its position. We were striving for cooperation with a UN rep to bring peace to area.

4. Goldberg then said that if Riad was saying that his govt would be prepared to cooperate under US text with changes in only those two areas, he also prepared to give it constructive thought. Riad asked what were our ideas. Goldberg said he was talking about our text and he wanted to know if these (withdrawal language and word "mutual") were the sole two areas of UAR concern. Riad said there were no other problems, only these two. Goldberg then said that US of course would not send armies but that we would do our best to work out a peaceful settlement if we could come to an understanding. We had stated our position; UAR had stated its; Israel had stated its. If Riad thought it was worthwhile in this framework he had a personal thought not yet communicated to Washington. If in his view as FonMin he really thought we could come to terms he could advance this thought and if FonMin thought it was worthwhile he would put it to govt. But we could not start from beginning and could not deal with other words. Riad said yes, we should talk without record, without putting forward writing.

5. Goldberg then said we thought withdrawal language, which was what we had worked out with Soviets in summer, might be substituted for present withdrawal language. We would suggest picking up language from version one of that text exactly in words then used in following form: "Withdrawal by the parties to the conflict of their forces from territories occupied by them, in keeping with the inadmissibility of the conquest of territory by war." We said everything else in US res would remain the same.

6. Riad said so it is addition of this principle. My first reaction is that it is the same. Exactly the same as present US text. Goldberg replied that it was just personal thought and perhaps we should forget it. Riad then said it was of course good to add such a phrase and that it was of

---

[3] Telegram 2193 from USUN, November 12, reported on Goldberg's November 12 meeting with Foreign Minister Riad, in which Riad commented on the U.S. draft resolution. He argued that the withdrawal paragraph should refer explicitly to withdrawal to the June 4 line, and he questioned the term "mutual recognition," arguing that it was not clear whether this meant recognition of Israel's right to exist, which the UAR could accept, or diplomatic recognition, which he could not accept. Goldberg assured him that diplomatic recognition was not intended. (National Archives and Records Administration, RG 59, Central Files 1967–69, POL 27 ARAB–ISR/UN)

course an improvement. This was not time for arguments. He thought he would not repeat language to anyone else, not even other Arabs.

7. Goldberg said that for him to put the language to his govt would be a serious step. He did not wish to embark upon it unless Riad was receptive. We could not deal with parts of proposal. It would have to be dealt with as whole thing. Otherwise we should go ahead with discussions in SC. We would not circulate idea as it was a personal one.

8. Riad asked whether we could make any additional changes in US text. Goldberg said no. Riad said that we should keep in contact, and meeting adjourned.

9. Subsequently, Sisco told Mohammed Riad we had been greatly disappointed at Riad's reaction and that we thought there was no point in going further. Riad replied that they had not meant to terminate matter and that they would be giving suggestion very careful consideration. He subsequently came back to ask whether we would agree in these circumstances to deletion of word "mutual". Sisco conveyed back that he would reiterate again that these were personal ideas that would be put to Washington only if Riad found them agreeable. Mohammed Riad said they understood this entirely.

Goldberg

---

528.   Telegram From the Mission to the United Nations to the Department of State[1]

New York, November 18, 1967, 0336Z.

2368. 1. At mtg with Eban Nov. 17 a.m. Goldberg said LAs appear to be running for cover in effort avoid US-UK-Israeli approaches to them in capitals. He said our Ambs have instructions to tell LAs as fols: UK draft res is quite tough on Israel. Nevertheless, if LA refrain from submitting own draft and give their support to UK draft, it is our judgment both Arabs and Israel will give grudging acceptance to UK draft.

---

[1] Source: National Archives and Records Administration, Central Files 1967–69, POL 27 ARAB–ISR/UN. Confidential; Priority; Exdis. Also sent to Tel Aviv. Received at 0629Z.

2. Eban said he has instructions that moment LA draft is submitted, he must issue statement saying Israel cannot comply with or cooperate with UN rep sent under LA res. He said he had advised Ruda (Argentina) yesterday evening that he had recommended to Tel Aviv that Israel cooperate with UN rep sent under UK res. But recommendation conditional upon LAs refraining from submitting their own text.

3. Goldberg advised Eban that Riad had sent three-point reply to Goldberg's approach to Riad on Nov. 16 as fols: (a) UAR appreciates US interest and effort; (b) has given careful consideration to US suggestions; and (c) on careful analysis, UAR has decided US proposals did not go further than previous US text and, thus, SC should proceed.[2] Stressing he was speaking off the record, Eban said he felt it had been a good move for US to make proposals to Riad and for Israel not to object thereto.

4. Eban asked if LAs did not submit their res today whether Sovs would seek to amend UK draft. Goldberg replied this would undoubtedly happen and that, at minimum, it seemed likely effort would be made to insert "the" before "territories." Eban commented this would remove all flexibility from Israeli position.

5. Goldberg read to Eban note that he intended to give to Ruda on behalf of USG before noon requesting: (a) LAs not submit their res today, and (b) they give their support to UK res.[3]

Department may wish to pass to Cairo.

Goldberg

---

[2] Telegram 2346 from USUN, November 17, reported that Mohamed Riad had called Sisco that day to give the UAR reply to Goldberg's proposal. (Ibid.) Goldberg reported the message to Rusk by telephone that morning. He commented that they were "left with the British resolution" and concluded, "We have now gone full circle." (Notes of telephone conversation with Goldberg prepared by Mildred Asbjornson, November 17, 10:22 a.m.; ibid., Rusk Files: Lot 72 D 192, Telephone Calls)

[3] The text was transmitted in telegram 2344 from USUN, November 17. It stated the U.S. judgment that the UK draft had a good chance of getting the acquiescence of both sides and therefore a very good chance of beginning the peace-making process in the Middle East but that submission of the Argentine-Brazilian draft, which was unacceptable to the Israelis, would irreparably undermine the UK effort. (Ibid., Central Files 1967–69, POL 27 ARAB–ISR/UN) Telegram 2360 from USUN, November 17, reported Goldberg's meeting that day with Argentine representative José María Ruda. (Ibid.)

529. Telegram From the Mission to the United Nations to the Department of State[1]

New York, November 18, 1967, 0414Z.

2376. Subj: ME: Caradon–Goldberg Meeting.

1. Following adjournment of SC mtg PM Nov. 17 (until PM Nov. 20), Caradon and Goldberg met to review current tactical situation and prospects for UK res.

2. Caradon said SC Pres had told him he prepared go through night with mtg Nov. 20 if necessary. Caradon said he wanted to make every effort to assure that SC would in fact conclude with vote on UK res Nov. 20. To this end he seeing LAs AM Nov. 18. He said LAs were talking of "marrying texts", but that this clearly impossible for UK and he had given no indication to LAs that such marriage could be performed. He said he surprised LAs had instructions not vote today for UK text.

3. General discussion then developed on reasons contributing to current LA posture and extent to which LAs might or might not be satisfied with cosmetic changes in UK text. Sisco said Bernardes (Brazil) had said LAs committed publicly at home to LA text and that repeated requests for delays in its submission had irritated both govts. Sisco said Bernardes feels cosmetic changes would be sufficient and with them Brazil might be able co-sponsor UK text. If cosmetic changes possible, Bernardes said he prepared tell his govt result represents merger of LA and UK texts which will keep balance and get acquiescence both sides. If necessary, Brazil might then dissassociate itself from Argentina. Hope (UK) said Pinto, who played role in drafting LA text, partly responsible for firm Argentine line. He added that Gobbi, though not Ruda, had suggested cosmetic changes would be sufficient. Goldberg said problem with LAs was in NY, rather than in capitals, and Ruda (Argentina) primarily responsible for unyielding LA position.

4. To Caradon query on what to do to stop LAs, Goldberg replied this very tough problem since LA pride involved. He suggested UK be responsive if LAs really have only cosmetic changes in mind. Caradon said he did not himself think UK could change text to satisfy LAs. Once some changes made other attempts at changes would follow. If UK went back to SC Nov. 20 with new text there would be further delay. Caradon expressed hope he might convince LAs give UK text "clear run" first. Goldberg pointed out this would not be enough since UK

[1] Source: National Archives and Records Administration, RG 59, Central Files 1967–69, POL 27 ARAB–ISR/UN. Confidential; Limdis. Repeated to London, Rio de Janeiro, Brasilia, Buenos Aires, Tokyo, and Addis Ababa. Received at 0608Z.

must have LA votes. Caradon asked if LAs would not vote for UK text; Goldberg replied negatively and that this precisely the problem and reason that LAs must be nailed down. At same time, Goldberg suggested UK make strenuous efforts also with Japan and Ethiopia. Goldberg said he had requested of Tsuruoka that Japan support UK text, but that Tsuruoka had only replied he would meditate on question and decide. (Sisco said we would try to have Dept phone FonMin Miki who currently en route with Sato in US.) On Ethiopia, Pedersen said we had report from UK Amb Addis that Ethiopia instructed vote yes on India, abstain on US, and vote yes on UK text if Indian text fails. Goldberg urged Caradon make special effort with Makonnen since latter tends to waver and USSR would be after him. On France, Goldberg said Berard had said he still without final instructions. Caradon said he thought Nigeria would come along with UK.

5. Sisco conveyed to Caradon report from Rafael (Israel), who had just spoken to Gobbi (Argentina). Gobbi told Rafael Argentina under instructions to reach agreement with UK, that changes only in preamble would be satisfactory, and that LAs had no intention of touching UK language on rep's mandate, withdrawal, navigation, or belligerency. Goldberg said if cosmetics in preamble only point at issue, he thought Israel would not object. It would be far better to have such change in UK text—with possibility that LAs would co-sponsor—than be faced with tabling of LA text. Pedersen urged that UK get LAs signed on and firmly committed to text with cosmetic changes so as to head off any further amendments—particularly addition of "all the" before territories which USSR and friends will push and which will be attractive to LAs because it more like LA text than UK text. Hope asked if letter from FonMin Brown to FonMin Costa Mendez (Argentina) would be helpful. Goldberg said this would be very helpful and Pedersen suggested such letters be sent to both LAs after UK meets with LAs AM Nov 18 and gets them committed to cosmetically modified text.

6. Re Arab attitude toward UK text, Caradon said Pachachi (Iraq) and Benhima (Morocco) had urged him to stick to current text. Goldberg said we have told Ruda that we have hard info that both sides would acquiesce in UK res, but that he has remained unconvinced.

7. Sisco said it clear further delay in SC exclusively Soviet ploy. In reply Caradon query as to USSR motive, Goldberg and Pedersen said Kuznetsov seemed basically bitter and that it may be Sovs desire keep pot boiling in ME, as well as prevent either US or UK (which also would be Western) political success in SC. Caradon asked what USSR would do on vote on UK text. Goldberg said he thought USSR would go along reluctantly by abstaining.

Goldberg

530. Information Memorandum From the Assistant Secretary of State for Near Eastern and South Asian Affairs (Battle) to Secretary of State Rusk[1]

Washington, November 17, 1967.

SUBJECT

Israel's Peace Aims

The attached telegram (USUN 2191—Tab A),[2] reporting the text of a resolution adopted by the Israeli Cabinet November 8, is the latest and presumably most authoritative statement of Israel's peace aims. Its particular significance lies in the explicit exclusion, in a formal GOI policy statement not intended for public consumption, of any settlement not arrived at through "direct negotiations" and formalized by "peace treaties."

Comparison of this Israeli position with earlier Israeli peace settlement objectives shows the evolution of Israel's position since the war. Specifically, the November 8 Israeli Cabinet resolution reflects a marked shift from Israel's earlier emphasis on the need for security from attack and acceptance by its neighbors to a pre-occupation with legalisms and an emphasis on the modalities of achieving such security and acceptance. In addition, freedom of passage for Israeli ships through the Suez Canal, which was not raised by the Israelis as a peace aim until some time after the end of the war, is prominently mentioned ahead of free passage through the Straits of Tiran, which was the immediate casus belli. Furthermore, paragraph 5 of the Israeli Cabinet resolution would appear to defer consideration of even a start toward solution of the refugee problem until after peace treaties are concluded.

The November 8 Israeli Cabinet resolution is in effect a prescription for "instant peace" entirely on Israel's terms. In our judgment it is patently unrealistic and a far cry from the goal recently described to Ambassador Harman by Gene Rostow. As Gene so eloquently put it, that goal as we see it is to devise arrangements binding on and accepted by the parties which, while safeguarding Israel's security, can create

---

[1] Source: National Archives and Records Administration, RG 59, Central Files 1967–69, POL 27–14 ARAB–ISR. Secret; Exclusive Distribution. Drafted by Atherton and Lambrakis on November 16 and cleared by Davies. Copies were sent to Popper, Katzenbach, and Eugene Rostow. A notation on the memorandum indicates Rusk read it.

[2] Telegram 2191 from USUN, November 12, attached but not printed, transmitted the text of a communication of the same date from Eban to Goldberg, transmitting the text of a resolution approved by the Israeli Cabinet on November 8. A copy is also ibid., POL 27 ARAB–ISR/UN.

conditions that will transform the Middle Eastern environment *over time* into one in which true peace eventually becomes possible.

The effect of the latest Israeli formulation is two-fold. First, it will further limit Foreign Minister Eban's flexibility in the UN context. Second, it gives the GOI's most formal stamp of approval—of much greater importance than similar public resolutions of the Israeli parliament—to a legally unassailable rationale for remaining in the occupied territories indefinitely, if the Arabs as seems likely, do not directly and immediately change their deeply ingrained attitudes of the past two decades and enter into negotiation of formal peace treaties. The Israeli Cabinet's position thus lends considerable credence to Joe Alsop's analysis in a recent *Washington Post* article (Tab B).[3]

Israel's increasingly rigid emphasis on the modalities of a peace settlement is paralleled by expanding emphasis on the territorial elements of a settlement. In the papers handed Lord Caradon by Foreign Minister Eban over the weekend of November 11–12, the GOI states inter alia that "Israel would not reconstruct that map [the map of June 4][4] at any time or in any circumstances" and "we are less interested than in July in the non-belligerency concept." It has become clear over the past months that Israel envisages its future boundaries as including not only the entire city of Jerusalem but also a good slice of the Syrian Golan Heights (which lie outside Mandated Palestine) and the entire Gaza Strip (whose half million Arab Palestinian inhabitants can by no means be assumed to prefer a future under Israeli rule). In addition, there are strong emotional and historical pressures for Israeli retention of the West Bank or at least substantial portions thereof, even though the official GOI position remains that border adjustments in that area will be based only on security considerations (which implies that they would be minor). Finally, there are other areas to which firmer claims may be in the process of maturing, such as the El-Arish area of the Sinai (where an Israeli paramilitary settlement is at present reviving the fishing industry).

While the precise nature of Israel's minimum territorial demands remains unclear, probably even to the GOI, there is no doubt that Israel has come a long way from its position in June. On June 8, for example, Foreign Minister Eban told Ambassador Goldberg that Israel was not seeking territorial aggrandizement and had no colonial aspirations.[5] On

---

[3] Tab B, a column by Joseph Alsop from the November 13 *Washington Post*, is attached but not printed.

[4] Brackets in the source text.

[5] See Document 227.

June 13, in a speech to military units in Sinai, Prime Minister Eshkol said Israel had no intention of acquiring new territory as a result of the war.

We must, I think, assume that the Israeli Cabinet resolution of November 8 is not simply a bargaining position. Viewed in the context of growing Israeli territorial appetites, I find that resolution a profoundly disturbing development. If Israel insists on pursuing the "direct negotiations" and "peace treaties" course to the exclusion of all others, then I fear we do indeed face the prospect of permanent Israeli occupation of the Arab territories now held.

There is, it seems to me, a growing gap between what we and the Israelis mean when we speak of territorial "adjustments." Given this fact plus Ambassador Goldberg's statement to Foreign Minister Riad on November 12 ("Israeli preference would be peace treaties arrived at through bilateral negotiations, but we are not asking for this"),[6] the enclosed Israeli Cabinet resolution would appear to put Israel and us on divergent courses.

---

[6] No record of this conversation has been found.

---

531.   **Telegram From the Department of State to the U.S. Interests Section of the Spanish Embassy in the United Arab Republic**[1]

Washington, November 18, 1967, 2003Z.

71775. Ref: Cairo's 982.[2]

You are authorized give Heykal for passage to Nasser categoric affirmative to his inquiry whether USG would give same measure of

---

[1] Source: National Archives and Records Administration, RG 59, Central Files 1967–69, POL 27–14 ARAB–ISR/UN. Secret; Flash; Nodis. Drafted by Walsh; cleared by Goldberg, Battle, Sisco, and Katzenbach; and approved by Rusk. Also sent Flash to USUN.

[2] Telegram 982 from Cairo, November 18, reported that *Al Ahram* editor Mohamed Heikal had told Bergus that morning that the UAR Government had studied with great interest the remarks Bergus had made to Salah Hassan on November 13 (see footnote 6, Document 521), and that Nasser had asked him to ascertain whether the U.S. Government would give the same measure of political and diplomatic support to the UK draft resolution that it had committed itself to do with regard to the U.S. draft resolution. (National Archives and Records Administration, RG 59, Central Files 1967–69, POL 27–14 ARAB–ISR/UN)

political and economic support to UK draft resolution presently before SC that it committed itself to do with regard US draft resolution.

In respect to Cairo's 989,[3] you should make clear to El Feki that absolutely no further change can be made in UK text and that UAR should grasp opportunity in UK text now; furthermore, there can be no assurance of our political support on behalf that resolution at some future time. Now is the moment of decision in respect to UK draft.[4]

Rusk

---

[3] Telegram 989 to Cairo, November 18, reported that in a meeting between Bergus and El Feki, the latter discussed the "need for very minor adjustments" in the language of the UK draft resolution and told Bergus that it was essential that the UAR Government be assured that the U.S. Government would give the same support to the implementation of the UK draft resolution as it had promised to give to the U.S. resolution. (Ibid., POL 27 ARAB–ISR)

[4] Telegram 992 from Cairo, November 19, reported that the substance of telegram 71775 had been delivered to Heikal and the Foreign Office. (Ibid., POL 27 ARAB–ISR/UN)

---

532. Telegram From the Department of State to the Embassy in the United Kingdom[1]

Washington, November 18, 1967, 2155Z.

71787. We wish following message[2] from Secretary delivered to King Hussein, who we understand is presently in either London or Paris, as soon as possible:

"1. We wish His Majesty to know of our appreciation for determined effort he made in New York to obtain successful outcome of negotiations on Middle East resolution. We regret it did not prove possible for agreement to be reached on US resolution. We wish King specifically to know that both in conversation with Riad and in public statement Ambassador Goldberg made in SC, US stated its willingness to make amendments to the US draft discussed with His Majesty. UAR, however, refused to agree to US resolution as so amended.

---

[1] Source: National Archives and Records Administration, RG 59, Central Files, 1967–69, POL 27–14 ARAB–ISR/UN. Secret; Flash; Nodis. Drafted by Walsh; cleared by Goldberg, Sisco, Battle, and Katzenbach; and approved by Rusk. Also sent Flash to Paris and repeated to Amman and USUN.

[2] The message was drafted in New York. Telegram 2384 from USUN, November 18, transmitted the text and requested that it be delivered to King Hussein. (Ibid., POL 27 ARAB–ISR/UN)

2. Since that time and largely as result inconclusive result those efforts, UK has presented another resolution, of which His Majesty no doubt fully informed.

3. We have concluded in circumstances that UK resolution should be adopted without change and that it can be basis for constructive action in area with assistance of a UN representative. US is correspondingly prepared to vote for UK resolution. We would also be prepared to extend our diplomatic and political support to UN representative under that resolution, inasmuch as we consider it to be consistent with President's speech of June 19, which remains our policy.

FYI: Ambassador Goldberg said in SC on November 9 with respect to US resolution:

'On behalf of my Government, I pledge to the SC and to the parties concerned that our diplomatic and political influence would be exerted under this draft resolution in support of the efforts of the UN representative to achieve fair and equitable settlement so that all in the area can live in peace, security and tranquility.'

We are prepared to give similar support to his efforts under UK resolution. End FYI.

4. We do not understand current trend of UAR policy on such matters. It was our impression that UAR blocked efforts to reach agreement on US resolution. It also supported Soviet move in SC Friday[3] to delay vote on UK text and in our opinion has recently been following obstructive policy in SC. These UAR moves do not appear to us to be consistent with Nasser's agreement of October 17 with you.

5. We are, of course, aware that Prime Minister Talhouni has gone to Cairo. We consider this weekend to be a critical one. If UK resolution is not adopted Monday we foresee deterioration of diplomatic situation in New York from one of effort to achieve real action to one of political maneuver and argumentation. We would not see such development as being useful to Jordan or indeed to anyone.

6. Accordingly, USG would appreciate any further efforts His Majesty may be able to exert with Nasser this weekend. We are also conveying information regarding our support of UK resolution directly to Cairo, and urging UAR to cooperate with UN representative on this basis."

Rusk

---

[3] November 17.

533. Telegram From the Mission to the United Nations to the Embassy in Argentina[1]

New York, November 19, 1967, 1827Z.

2402. You will be getting immediately report of meeting held with Caradon (UK) and two LA's Sun AM.[2] In addition to drawing upon it, you should make following points to FonMin. UK also will be weighing in along similar lines.

1. We have firm evidence that while both sides still may try to get changes they will acquiesce in UK text unchanged and cooperate with UN rep. In this connection, as part of supporting evidence, please point out that UAR has had four full days to convey to UK its unwillingness to cooperate with UN rep on basis of its text, and it has not done so. Moreover, based on all info we have both sides will go along with UK res and receive UN rep based on this text.

2. There is no doubt that 9 necessary votes will be available in support of UK text if Argentina and Brazil go along. In fact, there is good chance of unanimous support for UK text. UK, which has been doing the lobbying in capitals for its text, can convey such voting info.

3. Brazilian del here has told us it is recommending to its govt that LA text not be put in, and that Brazil supports UK text even without changes discussed this morning in four power meeting reported septel.[3]

4. You should point out that UAR has announced today resumption of diplomatic relations with UK and it is inconceivable to us that 24 hours later it would announce its non-cooperation with UN rep on basis UK text.

5. Very confidentially you should tell FonMin that Nasser has asked us in last 24 hours whether we are willing to commit our political and diplomatic support to implementation of UK text in same way in which we had made similar commitment to him on US text. We have sent Nasser categoric "yes" answer. LA reps were so told this morning.

---

[1] Source: National Archives and Records Administration, RG 59, Central Files 1967–69, POL 27 ARAB–ISR/UN. Secret; Flash; Exdis. Also sent to Rio de Janeiro and Brasilia and repeated Flash to the Department of State. Received at 1908Z.

[2] Telegram 2407 from USUN, November 19, reported the meeting that morning among Goldberg, Caradon, and Brazilian and Argentine representatives. Caradon urged Brazilian and Argentine support for the U.K. draft resolution but suggested as an alternative Brazilian and Argentine co-sponsorship of a revised resolution containing a few non-substantive changes from the U.K. draft. (Ibid.) Telegram 2403 from USUN, November 19, conveyed the text of the proposed alternative draft. (Ibid.)

[3] See footnote 2 above.

6. Also very confidentially, tell FonMin that we have been in further direct communication with King Hussein and he has told us categorically he approves UK text in present form and wants it adopted immediately.[4]

7. You should also know that contrary to indication Quijano gave Amb that Ruda instructed to consult with US, he categorically denies he has any such instructions or indeed any instructions since Fri. Indeed he has taken great umbrage to fact we referred to your telegram indicating he is supposed to be in touch with us and that Argentina would accept UK withdrawal language. Emb should be aware that Ruda's personal involvement is increasingly interfering with discharge of what we understand to be Argentine policy and that he is sending home biased reports colored by his own personal views.

8. In summary, in concert with UK we continue urge (a) LA's vote for UK text without changes as best and safest course of action, and (b) vote UK text with changes discussed this morning if needed for LA's.[5]

9. Rio should also draw upon pertinent elements above and weigh in immediately with FonMin.[6]

Goldberg

---

[4] Telegram 3994 from London, November 19, reported the delivery to the King of the message transmitted in Document 532 and his reaction. (National Archives and Records Administration, RG 59, Central Files 1967–69, POL 27 ARAB–ISR/UN)

[5] Telegram 1317 from Buenos Aires, November 20, reported that the Foreign Minister had confirmed that Argentina would vote for the British draft resolution. (Ibid.)

[6] Telegram 3398 from Rio de Janeiro, November 20, reported that a Foreign Ministry official had informed the Ambassador that the Foreign Minister would recommend approval of the British draft resolution when he saw the President in the morning. (Ibid.)

534. Letter From Premier Kosygin to President Johnson[1]

Moscow, undated.

Dear Mr. President,

In the letter of October 23[2] you state that the Government of the United States continues to stand for prompt political settlement in the Middle East, attaches no new conditions or new interpretations to alternative draft resolutions which were discussed in accordance with the proposals made by the American side toward the close of the Emergency Special Session of the U.N. General Assembly last July. You particularly emphasize that there need be no doubt of the United States position that Israeli troops must be withdrawn from the territories of other states. We take note of your statements and expect that your representatives will proceed exactly from these statements in the consultations mentioned in your letter. So far, however, in discussing the Middle East problem your representatives have followed the line which only creates additional obstacles for the solution of the question of the withdrawal of the Israeli troops and which is at obvious variance with the contents of your letter.

You mention the question of the fundamentals of policy in this area. However, the latest events show that the crux of the problem is not only in the general principles but in concrete actions by one or another side in a given situation and how in fact these actions correspond to the declared principles. Nor do I think that the consideration of the position of the USSR by the American side in a distorted light can do any good.

Your representative in New York suggested that in order to avoid the waste of time our two states should propose an agreed draft resolution on the political settlement in the Middle East for its consideration in the Security Council. We agree with this suggestion. As enclosure to this letter I am sending to you a draft resolution of the

---

[1] Source: National Archives and Records Administration, RG 59, Central Files 1967–69, POL 27–14 ARAB–ISR/UN. No classification marking but filed as an attachment to a Secret telegram, telegram 71851 to Moscow, November 20, which transmitted the text. The letter is marked "Unofficial translation." Telegram 71851 notes that Dobrynin had given the letter to Rusk that afternoon and that in his preliminary comments, Rusk pointed out that it presented certain problems of content and timing. A copy of the signed original and a translation prepared in the Department of State is filed with a covering memorandum from Read to Rostow, March 13, 1968. (Johnson Library, National Security File, Head of State Correspondence File, USSR, Kosygin Correspondence, Vol. I)

[2] Document 484.

Security Council,[3] which, in our opinion, could be adopted. The draft is based on the proposals to which the U.S. Government agreed toward the close of the Emergency Special Session and which the U.S. Government itself had put forward. In working out the draft we have taken into consideration the views expressed in your letter and particularly your assurance with regard to the invariability of the US position concerning the withdrawal of the Israeli troops.

Now about the general principles, that you especially stress.

The Soviet Union is vitally interested that the Near and Middle East be an area of stable peace. We are strongly opposed to turning this area into an arena of dangerous frictions and conflicts.

The Soviet Union further proceeds from the fact that the Middle East plays and will continue to play a great role in the system of world economics and in the international life. The fruits of national labor, natural resources of the Arab states and peoples, as well as services provided by them in the interests of international communications are of great importance to Europe, Asia and also to North America. We are convinced that proposals and decisions on the Middle East problem should be based first of all upon due respect to this contribution by the Arab states, irrespectively of their internal political systems. One cannot allow the aggressor to gain through his actions a prize in terms of territories which did not belong to him, or in any other form.

To take the route toward which the Israeli extremists, intoxicated by war chauvinism and wave of adventurism are now pushing, would mean to show benevolence for aggression, to defy the basic principles of justice and the U.N. Charter which bears not only our signatures but also that of Israel.

The Soviet Union stands for the acknowledgment of an undeniable right for independent national existence of all states of the Middle East, including Israel.

Political independence and territorial integrity for all the states, prevention and curbing of aggression—whoever launches it—this is the basic provision from which our policy proceeds, and in this area, too.

In this concrete situation the Soviet Government proceeds first of all from the necessity of elimination without delay of the consequences of the Israeli aggression against the Arab countries and of restoration of peace and first of all of the solution of the most acute and basic prob-

---

[3] The attached draft resolution, not here printed, is similar in substance to the Soviet draft resolution introduced in the Security Council on November 20. (UN document S/8253)

lem—the withdrawal of the Israeli troops from the territories of the Arab states occupied by them.

The Soviet Union stands for peaceful and just solution of the problem of the Arab refugees on the basis of due regard to their legitimate rights and interests. The Soviet Government stands for a peaceful passage of ships of all countries through international waterways with due respect to the sovereign rights and territorial integrity of the states through which lands these waterways come.

As for the problem of limitation of the arms race in this area, its solution on the basis of elimination of the consequences of the Israeli aggression, naturally cannot be but welcome. We do not think, however, that the resumption of shipments of American arms to Israel—the country that has committed and is still continuing aggression against the Arab states—will contribute to the awakening of the sense of reality with the Israeli leaders. By her latest brazen war provocations Israel is obviously seeking to complicate the way to settlement, to cross out the work which is being done in the interest of arriving at some common platform. The Soviet Union proceeds and will proceed from the fact that states cannot live by a political calendar written to please Israel.

Our proposal is clear. It is necessary firstly, that the Security Council should adopt without any procrastination a decision on a withdrawal without delay of troops by the parties to the Middle East conflict to the positions they occupied before June 5, 1967, proceeding from the inadmissibility of conquest of territory by war, as well as on acknowledgment without delay of the right of all states in this area for independent national existence in the conditions of peace and security. Secondly, to proceed on the basis of such a decision by the Security Council to practical actions towards its realization.

The Soviet Government expresses its hope that within shortest period of time the parties will come from declaring the principles to their concrete implementation.

Sincerely,

A. Kosygin

[Omitted here is the text of a draft resolution.]

535.   Letter From President Johnson to Premier Kosygin[1]

Washington, November 19, 1967.

Dear Mr. Chairman:

I have studied your message on the Middle East which Ambassador Dobrynin handed to Secretary Rusk this afternoon. I wish to comment immediately upon one point in your message because of its bearing upon the situation in the Security Council tomorrow.

Our delegation at the United Nations has, on instruction from me, tried to find a Security Council resolution with which both sides in the Middle East could cooperate. We attach great importance to this point since both you and we have learned that peace in the Middle East can not be imposed from the outside. We think it most unlikely that there could be a resolution which both sides would approve enthusiastically. But we have felt that it ought to be possible to draft a resolution which both sides could find tolerable. It was this purpose which lay behind the United States draft.

The United Kingdom Delegation has, however, made an additional effort and has combined several elements of various resolutions in an attempt to find a result which would enlist the cooperation of both sides. The UK draft could, we understand, obtain this cooperation. Under the circumstances, therefore, we hope very much that you can support the United Kingdom resolution in order that a UN Representative can begin the peacemaking process promptly. In our view, further delay would be highly undesirable and would prejudice chances for the peaceful solution which you and I desire.

The draft resolution which was appended to your message could not obtain the necessary cooperation of the parties. This present reply does not enter into various points raised in your message. Because of the urgency of time I am sending this immediate response to solicit your support of the United Kingdom draft. It would be our intention to use our influence in the capitals concerned to support the efforts of a United Nations Representative to find a peaceful solution in the Middle East. I am encouraged to believe that your and our views as to the general nature of that peaceful solution are not far apart.

Sincerely yours,[2]

---

[1] Source: Johnson Library, National Security File, Head of State Correspondence File, USSR, Kosygin Correspondence, Vol. I. No classification marking. The text was transmitted in telegram 71850 to Moscow, November 20. (National Archives and Records Administration, RG 59, Central Files 1967–69, POL 27–14 ARAB–ISR/UN)

[2] Printed from an unsigned copy.

536. Telegram From the Department of State to the Mission to the United Nations[1]

Washington, November 20, 1967, 1916Z.

71934. Subj: Middle East: Reaction to Goldberg–Kuznetsov conversation, November 19. Ref: USUN 2408.[2]

1. Based on our impression of tone and content of Soviet démarche here yesterday, plus your report on Kuznetsov conversation, we would speculate that Goldberg's view as set out in para 19 of reftel—i.e., spoiling operation—is probably closer to the mark than alternative hypotheses laid out in paras 20 and 21.[3] We have no doubt that the tabling of the Soviet text will impair the prospects for the UK Res, unhooking one or more of the more doubtful affirmative votes particularly if the UAR feels impelled to backtrack upon presentation of USSR draft.

2. However, we see no alternative to proceeding as planned today and thereafter. Obviously, we would not want to force a vote in which UK Res would fail, but we do not believe, subject to your tactical judgment, that it is possible to bargain usefully with the Soviets over word changes at this juncture. In short, whatever the Soviet motivation turns out to be, we believe you ought to proceed as far as possible along lines already contemplated.

Rusk

---

[1] Source: National Archives and Records Administration, RG 59, Central Files 1967–69, POL 27 ARAB–ISR/UN. Secret; Immediate; Exdis. Drafted and approved by Popper and cleared by Battle and Kohler. Repeated to Moscow.

[2] Telegram 2408 from USUN, November 20, reported a meeting between Goldberg and Kuznetsov on November 19 in which Kuznetsov gave Goldberg a copy of the Soviet draft resolution, which he said he would table the next day. (Ibid., POL 27 ARAB–ISR/UN)

[3] Paragraph 20 stated Buffum's view that although the Soviets might hope to prevent adoption of the UK draft, they might also be prepared to let the Security Council adopt it with the minimal non-substantive changes required to get Latin American cosponsorship. Paragraph 21 stated Pedersen's view that the Soviet text was a platform from which the Soviets would seek to force changes in the UK text and that it might be capable of compelling change in the withdrawal paragraph; for example, the addition of the word "the" before "territories".

537.   Telegram From the Mission to the United Nations to the
         Department of State[1]

New York, November 21, 1967, 1715Z.

2449. Dept pass to Moscow.

Goldberg, accompanied by Sisco, Buffum and Pedersen, had dinner with Kuznetsov Nov 20 who had with him Fedorenko, Mendelevich, Morozov, Shevchenko, and Kulebiakin. With exception of brief discussion at end of dinner, evening primarily social. Only brief reference in support of Sov position on non-use of nuclear weapons was made during evening and remainder focused exclusively on Middle East.

1. Kuznetsov, making very little reference to USSR draft, concentrated on Sov desire for "improvement in UK text." To this end, he suggested that at least word "all" be added to withdrawal para in UK text, if not "withdrawal to positions before June 5." Kuznetsov seemingly ran through his brief in a perfunctory and low key manner, made above suggestions within the context of statement that USSR and US are basically in agreement on general principles, and that USSR wants a peaceful settlement of the ME question. Stressed need for clear terms of reference and contended that question of "balance" in res depended on vantage point from which one looked at res.

2. Amb Goldberg restated our position and said our response has been given to Kosygin in Pres Johnson's letter. This constitutes our mandate and instructions here. Amb Goldberg expressed hope USSR would support UK res and that no further delay in SC action would take place. Amb Goldberg placed particular stress on fact there is now broad consensus in SC, that UK draft should be adopted promptly, and that it constitutes equitable balance, indeed razor edge balance, which has acquiescence of both sides and embraces indications by them of willingness to cooperate with UN rep. As was case in Sun[2] night conversation, Kuznetsov did not challenge this assessment; in fact he said openly there are "a number of good things" in UK draft, but that it could be improved by the addition of word "all", thereby making mandate clearer with respect to withdrawal of Israeli forces. So as not to give encouragement to Kuznetsov, Goldberg said response given to Kosygin was our final and firm position. Kuznetsov gave every sign that he expected this response from us.

---

[1]   Source: National Archives and Records Administration, RG 59, Central Files 1967–69, POL 27 ARAB–ISR/UN. Secret; Immediate; Nodis. Received at 12:38 p.m.

[2]   November 19.

3. Fedorenko told Sisco after dinner, and Shevchenko said same to Pedersen, that USSR expected SC action to be completed at Wed's meeting.

4. *Comment:* Our overall impression from above is that Kuznetsov, while getting a response he expected, is likely to discuss matter further with Arabs, and that whether he puts forward an amendment to withdrawal para will depend in considerable measure on Arab attitude. Fact that press report Kosygin has written to Nasser, if accurate, indicates we not out of woods yet, but we remain vigilant, active, and hopeful that we will be at our home rather than Security Council table for Thanksgiving dinner.

Goldberg

---

538.   Memorandum of Conversation[1]

Washington, November 21, 1967, 10:30 a.m.

PARTICIPANTS

Yaacov Herzog, Director General of the Israeli Prime Minister's Office
Avraham Harman, Ambassador of Israel
Ephraim Evron, Minister of the Israeli Embassy
Walt W. Rostow
Harold H. Saunders

Herzog said he felt we could be on the road to peace in the Middle East provided three conditions were met: (1) that the Arabs be left in no doubt about the strength of Israel's military forces; (2) that the US continue to make clear to the Soviet Union that it will not tolerate further

---

[1]   Source: Johnson Library, National Security File, Saunders Files, Israel, 11/1/67–2/29/68. Secret. Filed with a covering memorandum of November 24 from Saunders to Walt Rostow that summarized a portion of a conversation among Herzog, Davies, Atherton, Evron, and Saunders during lunch. Davies and Saunders pressed Herzog about Israeli attitudes toward a settlement, saying they saw two Israeli policies: one prepared to accept a compromise to get a settlement, and one that appeared designed to scuttle all chances of a settlement by hardening Israel's terms while paving the way for Israeli settlement of the captured territories. Herzog replied that the Israeli Government was deeply divided, and no one would know where the balance lay until the Cabinet had to accept or reject a specific proposal. He said his own guess was that in that moment of truth, desire for a peace settlement would be "overriding" and that those willing to gamble on a reasonable settlement would win over those who would rather bet on the physical security that they felt the current borders provided. Copies of the memorandum of conversation were sent to McGeorge Bundy, Nathaniel Davis, and Roy Atherton.

Soviet penetration in the Middle East; and (3) that the Arabs not be given the false hope of UN or other intervention on their behalf to force a settlement on Israel.

Herzog recalled his discussion with Mr. Rostow last March and noted that the June war may turn out to be the milestone in blunting the latest Soviet thrust into the Middle East. The Egyptians are backing out of Yemen and pose less of a threat in Aden. The Arabs are disillusioned with Soviet commitments. If the US stands firm in New York against the Soviet UN resolution, the Arabs will realize further that only the US has the power and influence to bring about a reasonable settlement.

Mr. Rostow said he did not disagree seriously with specific points Dr. Herzog had made, but said he would prefer a somewhat different formulation. Mr. Rostow said that, while the US obviously has an important role to play in the Middle East, what will really determine the future shape of the Middle East is more in Israel's hands than in ours. The moderates (we define them as those leaders who have rejected nationalist adventures and turned their attention to internal development) have gained ground in the Middle East over the past several years. Whether or not they continue on their course or are consumed in building for another round of Arab-Israeli fighting will depend on Israel's posture in the coming months. If these moderates find that they have no resource but to give in to popular pressures and prepare for another round of fighting, the door will be further opened to Soviet penetration. If, on the other hand, the moderates appear to have a reasonable chance of reaching an accommodation with Israel, the chances of their surviving and prospering increase markedly. This is in Israel's hands, not in ours.

Mr. Rostow went on to cite our experience in dealing with the Soviet Union elsewhere. We had found in the Berlin crisis, in Cuba and in Vietnam, that the way some of these problems get isolated is not by any direct US-USSR confrontation, but in the end by the local forces which build up around the problem area. In Latin America, for instance, Castro has been all but isolated because Latin Americans have turned their attention to bigger regional issues and have found hope in them rather than in going Castro's route.

When the conversation turned to the meaning of the Soviet introduction of its own resolution in the United Nations Security Council, Ambassador Harman suggested that the main Soviet motivation was to spoil the possibility of a settlement process getting under way and to keep the pot simmering in the Middle East. Mr. Rostow countered by saying that, although his mind remained open, two points kept him from accepting that view categorically: (1) If there is no possibility of a settlement, the Soviet Union would have to count on picking up the bill for UAR survival; (2) The USSR would have to assume that there might well be another round of fighting if there is no settlement, because of the rising trend of terrorism and likelihood of Israeli retaliation. Moscow should have learned in May and June that it can not control these forces in the Middle East and shouldn't count on being able to keep the pot just simmering without boiling over. The USSR is traditionally uncomfortable in situations it does not control.

The Israelis concluded the conversation by reiterating the importance of our resisting any Soviet efforts to pass their resolution or using it to dilute the British resolution.[2]

Harold H. Saunders[3]

---

[2] A conversation the afternoon of November 21 between Herzog and Harman and Battle is recorded in part in a memorandum of conversation and in telegram 72855 to Tel Aviv, November 22. Telegram 72855 states Battle raised the subject of recent Israel–Jordan shooting incidents, noting that in the U.S. view, they were disturbing and inherently dangerous, and that the Israeli posture before the world was "placed in jeopardy by such acts as shelling of refugee village and escalating to use of aircraft." He expressed the hope that Israel and Jordan would agree to accept UN military observers along the Jordan–Israel cease-fire line. (National Archives and Records Administration, RG 59, Central Files 1967–69, POL 27 ARAB–ISR) Further documentation related to these incidents and U.S. expressions of concern about them is ibid.

[3] Printed from a copy that bears this typed signature.

---

539.   Letter From Premier Kosygin to President Johnson[1]

Moscow, undated.

Dear Mr. President:

We have received your letter of 19 November and have studied it attentively. I wish to remind you that in your preceding letter of 23 October it was stated in the name of the Government of the United States of America that the position of the United States on the Middle

---

[1] Source: Johnson Library, National Security File, Head of State Correspondence File, USSR, Kosygin Correspondence, Vol. I. No classification marking. The letter is a translation. Dobrynin gave the letter to Kohler at 2:15 p.m. on November 21 and told Kohler that if the U.S. side could reply that day, the Soviet Government could get instructions to Kuznetsov in New York before the next day's session of the Security Council. Kohler referred to the Arab acceptance of the British resolution and "wondered why the Soviets were trying to be more Arab than the Arabs themselves." Dobrynin said he was sure that if the Arabs really did accept the British resolution the Soviets would not vote against it. Rostow sent the letter and Kohler's memorandum of his conversation with Dobrynin to the President on November 21 at 3:55 p.m. (Both ibid.)

East had not undergone change in comparison with that which had been set forth at the end of the extraordinary session of the General Assembly of the United Nations.

If your last reply does not mean a change in your position to the detriment of the victims of aggression—the Arab States—then evidently it is necessary to reach a mutual understanding, above all on two questions:

A. The immediate withdrawal of Israeli forces from the territories of the Arab States seized by them, that is, to the lines which they occupied before 5 June of this year should be in fact ensured.

B. Israel should not make territorial claims on the other side and exploit the situation which has developed as the result of the war unleashed by them in order to take possession of foreign territories and change for its own benefit boundaries which actually existed before the conflict.

Without resolution of these problems there can be no permanent peace in the region of the Middle East in which both our countries should be interested.

It is understood that together with this there should be decided the question of immediate recognition of the rights of all states of this region to independent national existence in conditions of peace and security.

In the presence of such understanding we would not oppose the acceptance of the British Draft if, of course, it is acceptable to the Arabs. We would like to receive from you an urgent reply.

Respectfully,

A. Kosygin

540. Letter From President Johnson to Premier Kosygin[1]

Washington, November 21, 1967.

Dear Mr. Chairman:

Thank you very much for your prompt reply to my letter of November 19. I, too, am responding promptly since the Security Council is scheduled to meet tomorrow afternoon to vote on the United Kingdom draft resolution. It is imperative in the interests of early progress toward peace that a constructive result be achieved at that meeting.

The United States position on the Middle East has been consistent throughout. I explained our policy directly to you at Glassboro and I subsequently set it forth publicly in my statement of June 19. This statement continues to be the policy of the U.S.

Ambassador Goldberg set forth yesterday in the Security Council the United States position on the United Kingdom resolution.[2] This resolution deals, in a balanced way, with essential ingredients for a just and lasting peace in the area, including withdrawal of Israeli armed forces. We consider the United Kingdom draft to be consistent with my statement of June 19 and will vote for it.

Moreover, we have been informed that the key Arab States principally concerned and Israel are willing to receive a United Nations representative on the basis of the United Kingdom draft. I am sure you will agree, Mr. Chairman, that the special representative is entitled not only to cooperation from the parties but to the full support of all the members of the Security Council, permanent and elected, as he undertakes his arduous and difficult peacemaking tasks. We are prepared to extend our diplomatic and political support to the efforts of the United Nations representative under the United Kingdom resolution to achieve a fair

---

[1] Source: Johnson Library, National Security File, Head of State Correspondence File, USSR, Kosygin Correspondence, Vol. I. No classification marking. Walt Rostow sent a draft letter to the President at 5:10 p.m. with a covering memorandum that referred to it as Rusk's draft reply, noted that the basic draft was Goldberg's, and added that Goldberg was "fully aboard." The draft is virtually identical to the letter as sent except that it did not include the second to the last paragraph, which was apparently added by the President. A paper with the text of that paragraph, with a note indicating that it was to be inserted before the last paragraph of the letter and a handwritten note stating that it was sent electronically to Ben Read at 5:40 p.m., is ibid. Kohler gave the reply to Dobrynin at 7 p.m. His memorandum of the conversation with an attached copy of the letter, identical to the one sent, is in Department of State, Kohler Files: Lot 71 D 460, Kohler/Dobrynin Memcons.

[2] The text of Goldberg's statement in the Security Council on November 20 is in Department of State Bulletin, December 18, 1967, pp. 841–842.

and equitable settlement so that all in the area can live in peace, security, and tranquility. I hope that your government will be prepared to do the same.

I am sure that we should not try to negotiate the details of a Middle East settlement in the corridors and meeting halls of the United Nations.[3] What we urgently need is a well-balanced resolution that would permit a United Nations representative to go to the area, listen to those directly concerned, reason with them, and find on the spot fair and equitable agreements with which these nations can live in peace and dignity.

It is my considered view that we must not let pass this opportunity to initiate the peacemaking process. I therefore express the hope that you can join the broad consensus of the Security Council by voting for the United Kingdom resolution tomorrow.

Sincerely,

Lyndon B. Johnson[4]

---

[3] The copy of this paragraph cited in footnote 1 above contains a handwritten revision of this sentence, in which the words "in the corridors and meeting halls of the United Nations" are crossed out and the words "thousands of miles from the scene" are added. The revised language does not appear, however, in the copy of the letter Kohler gave to Dobrynin.

[4] Printed from a copy that bears this typed signature.

---

541.   Editorial Note

On November 22, 1967, the United Nations Security Council unanimously adopted the British draft resolution as Resolution 242 (Document 542). Before the vote the Indian representative made a statement declaring that the sponsors of the three-power draft resolution (see footnote 2, Document 511) understood the British draft to commit the Security Council to the principle of total withdrawal of Israeli forces from all the territories occupied by Israel as a result of the June conflict, and that on the basis of that understanding, they would not press their resolution to a vote. Lord Caradon replied that the British draft resolution was a balanced whole and that to add to it or subtract from it would destroy that balance. All delegations might have their own views and interpretations and understandings, but only the resolution would be binding. The text of Caradon's statement was transmitted in telegram 2497 from USUN, November 23. (National Archives and Records Administration, RG 59, Central Files 1967–69, POL 27 ARAB–ISR/UN) Excerpts from other statements made in the Security Council were transmitted in telegram 2518 from USUN, November 23. (Ibid.) The text of the statement made by Ambassador Goldberg after the vote is in Department of State *Bulletin*, December 18, 1967, pages 842–843.

Telegram 2496 from USUN, November 23, states that the U.S. delegation learned late on November 21 that the Indians planned to make a statement interpreting the British draft resolution to mean withdrawal of all Israeli forces from all Arab territories, to be specified by name, including Sharm El Sheikh, and that U.S. efforts on November 22 were directed primarily at preventing an unchallenged Indian statement of interpretation before the vote which might have upset the balance enough to prevent action. It states that in the early afternoon, the Romanians started passing the word that the Soviets would vote against the resolution unless the Indian interpretation went unchallenged, and that the U.S. delegation was not certain how the Soviets would vote until Soviet representative Kuznetsov finally raised his hand with all the other members in favor of the resolution. (National Archives and Records Administration, RG 59, Central Files 1967–69, POL 27 ARAB–ISR/UN)

---

542.   United Nations Security Council Resolution 242[1]

New York, November 22, 1967.

The Security Council,

Expressing its continuing concern with the grave situation in the Middle East,

Emphasizing the inadmissibility of the acquisition of territory by war and the need to work for a just and lasting peace in which every State in the area can live in security,

---

[1] Source: UN document S/RES/242. The resolution was adopted unanimously by the Security Council.

Emphasizing further that all Member States in their acceptance of the Charter of the United Nations have undertaken a commitment to act in accordance with Article 2 of the Charter,

1. *Affirms* that the fulfillment of Charter principles requires the establishment of a just and lasting peace in the Middle East which should include the application of both the following principles:

(i) Withdrawal of Israeli armed forces from territories occupied in the recent conflict;

(ii) Termination of all claims or states of belligerency and respect for and acknowledgment of the sovereignty, territorial integrity and political independence of every State in the area and their right to live in peace within secure and recognized boundaries free from threats or acts of force;

2. *Affirms further* the necessity

(a) For guaranteeing freedom of navigation through international waterways in the area;

(b) For achieving a just settlement of the refugee problem;

(c) For guaranteeing the territorial inviolability and political independence of every State in the area, through measures including the establishment of demilitarized zones;

3. *Requests* the Secretary-General to designate a Special Representative to proceed to the Middle East to establish and maintain contacts with the States concerned in order to promote agreement and assist efforts to achieve a peaceful and accepted settlement in accordance with the provisions in this resolution;

4. *Requests* the Secretary-General to report to the Security Council on the progress of the efforts of the Special Representative as soon as possible.

Index

References are to document numbers

ISBN 0-16-051513-0

DATE DUE

NOV 1 3	2009	
NOV 3 0 2012		
11-4-2016		